Encyclopedia of Home Cooking

FOR THE
CULINARY PRESS

- *Director*   KATHERINE SAYER
- *Managing Editor*   LINDA TIMKO GONZALEZ
- *Art Director*   MAUREEN MARSH
- *Editor*   DINAH WITCHEL

BANNER PRESS, INC. NEW YORK

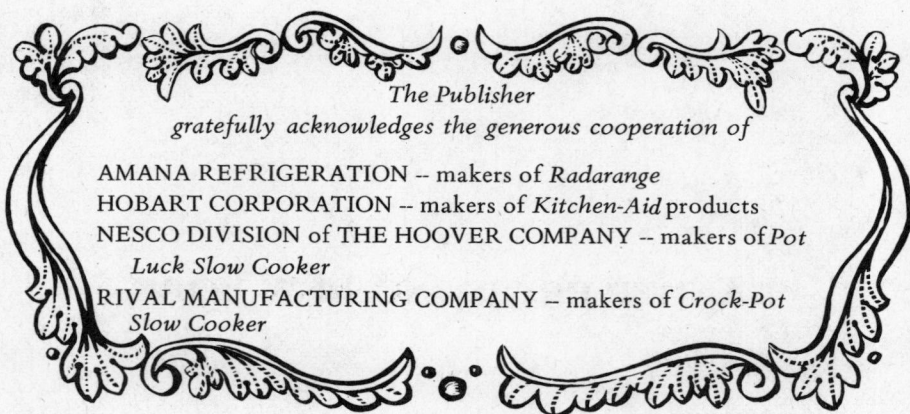

The Publisher
gratefully acknowledges the generous cooperation of

AMANA REFRIGERATION -- makers of *Radarange*
HOBART CORPORATION -- makers of *Kitchen-Aid* products
NESCO DIVISION of THE HOOVER COMPANY -- makers of *Pot Luck Slow Cooker*
RIVAL MANUFACTURING COMPANY — makers of *Crock-Pot Slow Cooker*

Encyclopedia of Home Cooking

The Plan for This Cookbook originated around a luncheon table when it was suggested that the far-flung membership of the Peoples Book Club and the Sears Readers Club probably included some of the best cooks in America. A contest was proposed to test the idea, and the 300,000 members were invited to submit their best recipes. *The Family Home Cookbook* was the result of that contest.

The Culinary Arts Institute was employed to judge the entries, kitchen-test the recipes and develop them into a cookbook. Headed by Miss Melanie De Proft and staffed by college-trained home economists, the Culinary Arts Institute is an organization famed for its creative ability in writing and testing recipes, and conforming them to the high standards of modern home economics.

Response to the contest invitation was enormous. A flood tide of treasured recipes engulfed the Culinary Arts Institute. Recipes came from everywhere—from farms and cities, from yellowed recipe collections that are family legacies, from kitchens in which the traditions of European cookery mingle with what we call native American, even from some Americans outside the continental limits of the U.S.

More than one third of the recipes in this cookbook are prize winners. The others have been created by the Institute to give the book balance and completeness. Many recent trends in the art of preparing cookbooks are represented here. The typography ensures easy reading. Photographs are numerous and have been selected for their visual education in methods of cooking and serving food. Other illustrations have been designed to depict the American historical and geographical scene. Every recipe has been kitchen-tested and all have been written in a style that is intended to instruct as well as inform, to indicate *step-by-step* procedures in

such explicit detail that the most inexperienced and timorous cook is assured of creating a culinary masterpiece on the first attempt.

The Microwave Oven and Slow Cooker portions of this cookbook are not manufacturers' manuals for using your appliance. They are part of an indispensable, all-purpose, creative cookbook which realistically combines the pleasures of the old-fashioned kitchen—the smell of bread baking, the sound of sauces bubbling—with the extraordinary ease and convenience of modern cooking techniques.

Under home cooking conditions, the Culinary Press Kitchen Staff has extensively tested the recipes in *The Family Home Cookbook* for preparation in the microwave oven and the slow cooker. Those recipes which have passed the rigid standards of acceptance have been expanded to include directions for cooking in these appliances. The result is the *Encyclopedia of Home Cooking.*

Criteria for success required dishes to not only taste and look good, but to be comparable to, if not better than, the quality produced using conventional cooking methods. The majority of expanded recipes not only do so, but can be prepared with a fraction of the effort and time without sacrificing fresh ingredients for commercially-prepared, quick-cooking foods. This will help you to economize your food dollars.

Recipes are presented in a form which is unique. The clear, step-by-step directions of the master recipes are retained, with only variations in cooking time, modifications of ingredients and techniques of preparation noted as necessary. Most important, you are given the guidelines for judging when a dish is properly cooked. And, throughout the book, you will find invaluable hints on how to get the best results from your microwave oven or slow cooker.

Contents

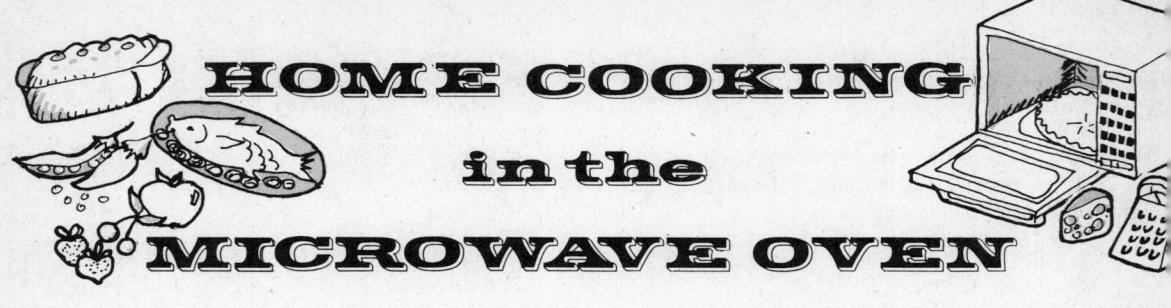

HOME COOKING in the MICROWAVE OVEN

The microwave oven is truly magical: roasts are done in minutes instead of hours; cookies in less than 3 minutes instead of 20. Almost as magical is the discovery that the microwave oven can produce good home cooking, the kind of cooking which captures the flavors, aromas and textures of an old-fashioned kitchen without the old-fashioned hours spent over a hot stove.

This cookbook tells you the secrets. No more being intimidated by recipes which dictate split-second timing. No more hesitation about whether to try a favorite family recipe in the microwave oven.

We tell you:
- How to judge when a dish is done.
- What adjustments, if any, to make in measuring and preparing ingredients.
- What types of recipes are good, better and best—and what types are not suitable at all, and we tell you why.
- About utensils, stirring, standing time, rotating and combinations of ingredients.
- How to take the mystery out of microwave cooking—but leave the magic.

The small investment of effort in learning to master the microwave oven is well rewarded. Not only is the microwave oven fast, but it is:
- Cooler—no heat in the kitchen, no wave of hot air when the oven door is opened, a welcome bonus in summer.
- Safer—utensils don't get hot and chances of burns are minimized.
- Cleaner and neater—spills wipe up easily since there is no heat in the oven to bake them on. Utensils are disposable or easy to clean because no scouring is necessary.

- More efficient—many preparation steps can be consolidated and food can go directly from oven to the table, sometimes it can even be cooked directly on the dinner plate.
- More nutritious—the oven cooks without heat and therefore, vitamins and other nutrients are less likely to be destroyed or diminished in potency.
- More economical—not only does a microwave oven use less energy than a conventional stove, but it is possible for a cook on a tight schedule to prepare meals with fresh ingredients rather than the more expensive commercially-prepared or frozen foods. It's also easier to cook a double batch of bread, stew or casserole to freeze for another meal. And don't forget it can be defrosted quickly in the microwave oven.

All of these advantages are possible because the microwave oven cooks not by heat, but by electromagnetic waves. These microwaves, directed from all sides of the oven to the center, are absorbed by the molecules in food which then generate their own heat. Microwaves are deflected by metal and not absorbed by paper, glass or certain kinds of plastic. That is why metal utensils cannot be used in the oven and why microwave-safe containers do not get hot. (For a more detailed explanation, see manufacturers' booklets.)

One of the differences between cooking with microwaves and conventional cooking with heat is that moisture does not evaporate in the microwave oven. This is a great advantage with vegetables, fish, certain meats and other foods which may have a tendency to dry out in a conventional oven. In some cases, this may mean that the amount of water used to cook a particular dish must be reduced. We tell you in which recipes this is necessary.

Certain foods or types of ingredients, notably sugar and fat, cook faster and generate more heat in the microwave oven than others. That is one reason why meats, for instance, cook so quickly. Also for that reason, greasing a pan is rarely necessary, even with breads and cakes. The thin layer of fat has a tendency to cook the batter with which it is in contact more quickly than the remainder of the batter, cooking the bottom and sides of a cake before the center. Fried eggs cannot be cooked satisfactorily in the microwave oven because the yolk, which contains fat, will cook much more quickly than the white. The result is a hard yolk and a sometimes runny white.

In general, we found the following foods not only faster and easier to prepare, but even better in taste and texture than when cooked using the conventional stove: vegetables, fish, pork, veal, lamb, sauces of all kinds, frostings and fillings for desserts and cakes, custards and ice cream mixtures.

Egg and cheese dishes are also outstanding when cooked in the microwave oven. However, these are quick cooking even on the conventional stove, so there is not a great saving in time, but the results are superior.

Breads, cakes and cookies are not quite as successful as the foods mentioned above primarily because of the lack of color. They do not brown acceptably in the microwave oven. The taste, however, is certainly good and the convenience and speed of cooking considerable. We include some of these recipes and suggest ways of compensating for the lack of color.

Certain cuts of beef, ground beef and the variety meats are also not as successful in the microwave oven. Some flavor seems to be lost and the meats seem somewhat tough. It's also difficult to cook a beef roast that is rare on the inside and sufficiently brown on the outside.

In all chapters, we have omitted microwave directions for recipes which we felt did not measure up to certain standards. Foods cooked in the microwave should look and taste at least as good, if not better, than the same foods cooked with a conventional stove. Among the recipes which did not measure up were those for pastry crusts, broiled hamburgers, broiled steaks and chops, and recipes with combinations of ingredients which cook at different speeds. **Asparagus Parmesan** *(page 286)* for instance, was unsuccessful because the asparagus overcooks by the time the cheese topping is melted.

We have also omitted recipes which call for a combination of cooking in both the microwave and conventional ovens. Cornish hens can be cooked in this two-step fashion. You may want to experiment with some of these foods once you have mastered the microwave method

TOOLS AND TECHNIQUES—Following are some of the tools and techniques used to assure success and maximum convenience in microwave oven cooking.

Proper Selection of Pots and Cooking Utensils— Manufacturers' directions will list utensils which can and cannot be used in microwave ovens. For most of our recipes, we used heatproof glassware or paper products, including paper cups and plates. In some cases, we used ingenuity to design our own cookware, for instance, baking sheets made of cardboard. If you don't already own appropriate utensils, the glass dishes are readily available in department or hardware stores and are not expensive.

The single investment we made in special equipment was a microwave-safe "browning skillet," used in many of the recipes for sautéing onions or mushrooms or lightly browning meat. This is a special, microwave-absorbent pan which can be placed empty in the microwave oven (not possible with other kinds of utentils) and preheated. The surface becomes hot and when food is placed on it, is seared or browned as in a conventional skillet. It's available through most microwave oven dealers.

If you do not use a browning skillet, the food will cook in about the same amount of time, but it will not brown and certain nuances of flavor will be lost.

We specify what type of utensils to use.

Covers—Covering cooking containers helps retain heat and moisture and does not retard cooking because microwaves will pass right through them. Some recipes call for covers, some do not. If a cover is not specified in the microwave oven directions, follow the procedure noted in the master recipe.

Use the glass covers which come with the cooking dishes or cover the dish with plastic wrap. It is usually recommended that plastic wrap be punctured in several places to prevent buildup of steam.

Arranging Food in the Oven—The general rule to remember is that food cooks from the outside of the oven in. Where arrangement of food is critical or differs from the general rule, it is specified in the recipes.

Rotating Dishes—To assure even cooking in the oven, it is important to rotate most dishes during the cooking period. Depending on the length of time the food will take to cook, the container should be turned 180 degrees or halfway around at least once, or 90 degrees several times. We specify in each recipe when and how often to rotate.

Stirring—This is one of the secrets of success in microwave cooking and is crucial for such recipes as sauces, gravies, custards and frostings. It blends flavors, prevents curdling of milk and eggs and promotes a uniquely pleasurable texture in the foods which require stirring. Because there is no heat in the microwave oven or the pan, it is much more convenient and safer to stir frequently than it is on the conventional stove. We specify how often to stir with each recipe that requires it. It is important to follow these directions carefully in order to get successful results.

Standing Time—Many dishes cooked in the microwave call for a "standing time" after cooking to allow the flavor and texture to develop to the proper point. This is an essential part of the microwave process and it is important to follow directions. For instance, when meat is finished cooking in the oven, it will often have a somewhat coarse "bloody" taste and grainy texture. This will disappear during the standing time and the flavor and texture will be exactly right when it is time to serve. Leaving it in the oven a longer time will not improve the texture, but will only succeed in overcooking the meat. We tell you with each chapter exactly what to look for to determine when the food should be taken from the oven and how long to let the dish stand. Usually, the dish must be covered during standing time. Plastic wrap is a satisfactory cover.

OUR TEST CONDITIONS—These recipes were tested with a standard Amana Radarange with three cooking cycles: DEFROST, SLOWCOOK and COOK. We did not use the DEFROST cycle in any recipe. We estimate the SLOWCOOK cycle to be about half the speed of the COOK cycle in our kitchen. We used no special attachments, such as the automatic turntable. All our ingredients were at room temperature and all were purchased at local supermarkets. We used standard cuts of meat and nationally distributed brands of other foods. In other words, we duplicated home conditions. If, because of container or oven size, the amount of food we cooked differs in any way from the master recipe, we specify the adjustment.

We tell you the conditions of our testing because, as any microwave oven user knows, microwave cooking times are easily affected by a number of variables: the type and temperature of the ingredients, the shape and size of individual pieces, the brand of oven and the wattage delivered, and even the size or shape of the container.

At the end of this section we have included a chart showing how to compare settings among different brands of ovens so you will find it easy to make adjustments in cooking time from our recommendations. Most important, however, because we believe cooks like to cook and do not like to be computers or mathematicians, we have designed these recipes so that you will know how to judge for yourself when the food is ready to take out of the oven and are not dependent on a clock. For instance, if a recipe reads

COOK, stirring every 1 min., until sugar is dissolved (about 3 min.)

we are telling you that in our oven set on the COOK cycle, it took about 3 minutes, stirring the mixture every 1 minute, to dissolve the sugar. It may take another cook under other conditions 2½ minutes or 4 minutes, but the goal is for the sugar to dissolve, not for a bell to ring after 3 minutes.

Each chapter in this book which is expanded for microwave cooking contains a brief introduction noting special microwave techniques for that type of food and comments on which recipes were successful and which were not.

HOW TO USE THIS BOOK—First, find the recipe you want to cook. A microwave symbol **12** next to the name of the recipe indicates it is suitable for preparation in the microwave oven. The symbol will contain a number. In the microwave section following the chapter, the same number will appear next to the name of the recipe. Read both recipes and the microwave oven introduction for that chapter.

Follow the master recipe for amounts of ingredients, instructions on preparing ingredients, sequence of preparation and tests for doneness, noting any deviations from these instructions included in the microwave recipe.

The speed of the cooking cycle (COOK or SLOWCOOK) and approximate cooking times are given in the microwave oven recipe.

Also included in the microwave directions are the type and size of utensils, the recommended standing time, if any, and the *OVERALL COOKING TIME*. This figure is the approximate minimum number of minutes it will take to cook the entire recipe and is given in minutes and seconds. For instance, 12 and one-half minutes will be noted as *12:30*. Not included in the *OVERALL COOKING TIME* figure is the time necessary to melt butter or fat since this can vary as much as 2 minutes depending on the temperature of the pan and the type of fat used.

Where it is necessary to cook foods in batches, such as when browning meat balls, the *OVERALL COOKING TIME* includes the combined cooking times for all batches. We do not include an *OVERALL COOKING TIME* if one or more of the ingredients, such as a white sauce, must be prepared using a separate recipe.

If one or more of the ingredients in a master recipe, such as a vegetable or a sauce, has a separate recipe, the page number is given. If this page number is followed by a microwave symbol, the cross-referenced recipe can be cooked in the microwave oven. Simply turn to the page on which the master recipe is given and note the microwave symbol number. Then turn to the microwave section immediately following the chapter to locate the microwave symbol number which will be accompanied by the proper directions.

Microwave symbols which are circled indicate a recipe which produces superlative results.

3 The recipe can be cooked in the microwave oven. Turn to the microwave section following the chapter and look for the number and the name of the recipe.

The recipe referenced is suitable for microwave oven cooking. See master recipe on indicated page number, note microwave symbol number and locate it in the microwave oven section immediately following the end of the chapter.

1 A best recipe. Definitely try it.

WHAT YOU SHOULD KNOW BEFORE USING THE CHARTS—The microwave oven directions in the recipes refer to two cooking cycles:

COOK is a full power cycle using 675 watts.

SLOWCOOK is a half-power cycle using about 355 watts.

The chart of COMPARATIVE SETTINGS BY MODEL lists directions for adjusting dial settings on ovens which have different power ratings or ovens which have only one setting or multiple settings with smaller variances.

Power Output Rating—This is the manufacturer's rating, given in watts, of the maximum power of the microwave-producing magnetron tube. It is the major factor in comparing the cooking times among different ovens.

Comparative Dial Settings—The dial settings listed provide cooking power which most closely approximates the COOK and SLOWCOOK cycles used under test conditions. The SLOWCOOK cycle provides approximately one-half the cooking power of the COOK cycle. If your oven does not have a setting comparable to SLOWCOOK, recipes requiring gentle cooking, such as cream sauces and cakes, may not be successful.

Relative Cooking Time—Here you will find additional suggestions which will help you to adapt the times and settings found in the microwave oven cooking directions to your model microwave oven. The approximate differences in cooking times you can expect when using the equivalent dial settings are indicated. This difference is due to variations in both power output ratings and the amount of power provided by these settings.

Since variations exist even for ovens of the same model, it is always best to test the dishes frequently when first using the recipes. The cooking times given in the recipes are minimum recommended cooking times, so you will not be likely to overcook the foods.

Remember that in all microwave oven cooking, the composition of the food being cooked and the total time it is in the oven, as well as the power output, affect the relative cooking time. Foods having low moisture or high fat or sugar contents will cook faster. Also, if the recipe calls for food to be in the oven more than about 10 minutes, the carry-over of heat generated by the food itself will contribute to reduce the length of cooking time. Therefore, you can expect long-cooking foods, such as roasts, to cook a little more quickly than the relationship specified.

Use the chart of COMPARATIVE SETTINGS BY POWER if your brand and model microwave oven are not listed in the COM-PARATIVE SETTINGS BY MODEL chart.

Consult your manufacturer's handbook to determine which power output rating on the chart corresponds to your oven. Also, determine which of the settings, if any, is equivalent to one-half full power. When COOK is specified in the recipe directions, use your full power setting; use the one-half power setting when SLOWCOOK is specified. Then note the adjustments given under **Relative Cooking Time**.

If your oven does not have variable power settings, recipes requiring the gentle-cooking quality of the SLOWCOOK cycle may not be as successful. These include recipes for cakes, cream sauces and long-cooking stews. However, fish, vegetables and many egg and cheese dishes will be good. You may wish to experiment using the full power cycle. If you do, expect foods to cook twice as fast as the SLOWCOOK times specified in the recipes. Therefore, be sure to test for doneness often. Frequent testing will not affect the cooking process.

COMPARATIVE SETTINGS BY POWER

Power Output Rating—This is the major factor in comparing the cooking settings and times among different brands of ovens. The manufacturer's rating of the maximum power of the microwave-producing magnetron tube is given in watts.

Relative Cooking Time—Indicates the approximate differences in lengths of cooking times. Test foods frequently when first using the recipes. Longer-cooking foods, such as roasts, will cook faster than the relationships specified.

Power Output Rating	Relative Cooking Time (for COOK at full power setting and SLOWCOOK at half-power setting)
450-500	Increase 33%
525-550	Increase 20%
600-625	Increase 10%
650	Increase slightly
675-700	Same

COMPARATIVE SETTINGS BY MODEL

Manufacturer/Model—Note the exact model number for your brand of microwave oven.

Power Output Rating—This is the major factor in comparing the cooking settings and times among different brands of ovens. The manufacturers' rating of the maximum power of the microwave-producing magnetron tube is given in watts.

Settings to Use—For each model, the corres-

ponding dial settings which provide cooking power most nearly approximating the COOK and SLOWCOOK ratings used in the recipes are given. SLOWCOOK is about one-half power of COOK.

Relative Cooking Time—Indicates the approximate differences in lengths of cooking times. Test foods frequently when first using the recipes. Longer-cooking foods, such as roasts, will cook faster than the relationships specified.

Manufacturer/ Model	Rating Output Power	To COOK Use Setting	To SLOWCOOK Use Setting	Relative Cooking Time
AMANA models				
R3, R4D	675	HIGH	DEFROST	COOK: Same
				SLOWCOOK: Increase slightly for long-cooking foods.
RR6	675	COOK	SLOWCOOK	COOK: Same
				SLOWCOOK: Same
RR7, RR9	675	HIGH	MEDIUM	COOK: Same
				SLOWCOOK: Same
GENERAL ELECTRIC models				
JET 89T, 90T	625	HIGH	LOW	COOK: Increase 10%
				SLOWCOOK: Increase 10%
LITTON models				
420	650	Full power	52% full power, just to left of SIMMER	COOK: Increase slightly
				SLOWCOOK: Same
413, 415 969, 989	650	Full power	Just to left of SIMMER	COOK: Increase slightly
				SLOWCOOK: Same
102	600	Full	None	COOK: Increase 10%

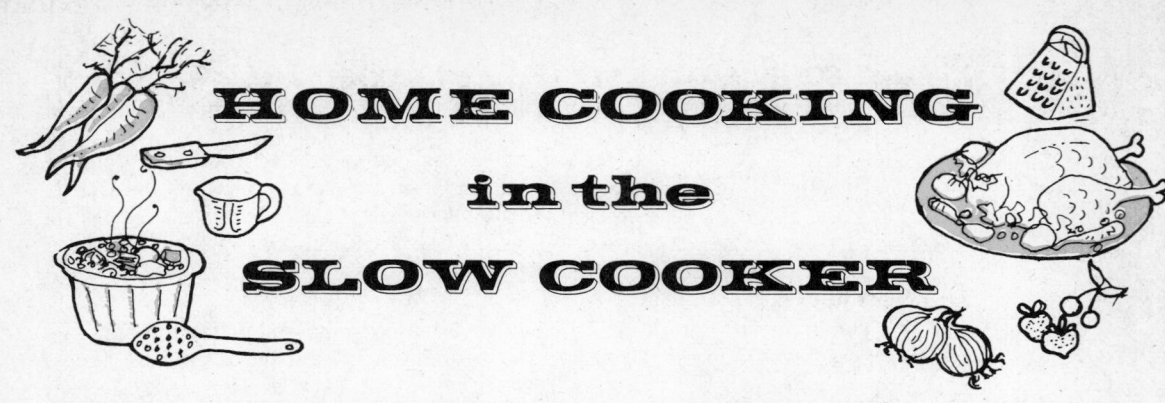

HOME COOKING in the SLOW COOKER

A slow cooker is a small investment in a lot of luxury. In the morning, just plug it in, say a warm goodbye as you go out the door to office or appointments, and come home to a perfectly cooked, ready-to-serve meal with the smells and tastes suggestive of long, loving hours spent in preparation.

The slow cooker is most frequently recommended for stews and casseroles, but it has greater versatility than most people imagine. In this book we pass along the secrets of slow cooking a treasury of recipes from soups through desserts, including breads and cakes.

Don't be wary of trying these recipes. They take advantage of the slow cooker's many assets. No only can this appliance cook unattended, but it can:

• Save money—by consuming less energy than the conventional stove and making possible the use of less expensive cuts of meat.
• Reduce preparation time—because in most cases all the ingredients can be added to the slow cooker at the same time.
• Keep the kitchen cooler—and the cook cooler because its low heat is contained.
• Make serving easier—food can go directly to the table in the pot.
• Reduce clean-up—by cutting down on the number of cooking utensils.

The slow cooker can boast most of these advantages because it uses extremely low wattage to produce a low steady cooking temperature (between 200° F. and 300° F. depending on the setting) which can be maintained for as many hours as are necessary to cook the food. Once the pot has reached the proper temperature, there is little fluctuation because its construc-

tion permits negligible escape of heat. It also promotes cooking from all sides, not just from the bottom.

The slow cooker portions of this book tell you how to make the best use of this type of cooking. We tell you which foods will work and which will not, which are excellent and which are acceptable. We pass along general hints on how to get the most out of your slow cooker so that you will not only get successful results with the recipes included, but will be able to adapt your own favorite family recipes.

Slow cooking produces meats which are extremely tender and flavorful and vegetables which are done but not overcooked. It's obviously an ideal appliance for less expensive cuts of meat such as shoulder or ribs. We consider it less than thrifty to prepare expensive meats such as veal cutlet or beef steaks in this appliance.

The slow cooker also retains liquids and enhances the flavor of spices and herbs. If amounts of liquids or spices need to be reduced, we specify the amounts with each recipe. The most successful recipes cooked in the slow cooker are the stews and soups, with beef, lamb and veal stews the best. Hams and fresh pork roasts are excellent, stewed fruits delicious and the breads and cakes included in the slow cooker sections of these chapters at least as good, if not better, than when cooked in the conventional oven.

Not successful in the slow cooker are noodles and other pastas which tend to get glutinous; milk products and eggs which curdle and lump; and fish which cannot withstand lengthy cooking, even at a low temperature.

In every chapter, we have omitted directions for the slow cooking of recipes which we felt did not measure up to the following standard: Foods cooked in the slow cooker should look and taste at least as good, if not better, than the same foods cooked in the conventional oven. There are a few exceptions to this rule, including the pork chop recipes and some of the casseroles, vegetables and sauces. A few of these dishes are slightly different in flavor and texture from the same dishes prepared using the conventional stove, but the convenience of cooking and preparation is sufficient to offset the difference in flavor.

We show you which recipes are the best by circling the slow cooker symbol which appears next to the name of appropriate recipes. These dishes adapted most easily and produced outstanding results in the slow cooker.

We have tried to eliminate recipes which call for a combination of cooking in the slow cooker and on the conventional stove such as spareribs and roast duck.

In some recipes, however, we found it necessary to sauté onions or finish sauces on top of the stove. Sautéing onions on top of the stove first assures they will finish cooking at the same time as the other ingredients.

We do tell you how to brown or sear meat or other ingredients in the slow cooker. However, browning on the stove does give better color and improve the flavor of some ingredients. We specify in each recipe when this step is necessary; in most cases it is optional.

If you do take the option of browning on the stove and it is not specified in the recipe, use the minimum cooking time given. For example, if the range of cooking time is 4 to 6 hours, use 4 hours.

TOOLS AND TECHNIQUES—Following are some of the tools and techniques used to assure success and maximum convenience when cooking with the slow cooker.

Pot Size—We specify the size pot required for each recipe. If a larger pot is substituted for a smaller one, cooking times must be adjusted downward. If the recipe is doubled and the larger pot is used, cooking times remain the same; if the recipe is cut in half and the smaller pot is used, cooking times remain the same.

The Setting—When to use the HIGH and LOW settings are noted with each recipe. If you wish to change the setting from HIGH to LOW (or their equivalent settings on your slow cooker)

to extend the cooking time, estimate that it will take about twice as long to cook. If changing the setting from LOW to HIGH, reduce the cooking time by about one-half. Some recipes like cakes, breads and rice cannot be changed and directions must be followed exactly.

In all cases, we provide the guidelines which will help you to judge when the food is fully cooked. You are not dependent on the clock.

Preparing Ingredients—All ingredients were prepared according to the directions given in the master recipe, with a few exceptions noted in individual recipes. Cooking time is affected by the size of the pieces of food. If a recipe calls for meat cut into 1½-in. pieces and you put 3-in. pieces into the pot, the meat will cook more slowly.

OUR TEST CONDITIONS—When testing these recipes we simulated home conditions. All ingredients were at room temperature and all were purchased at local supermarkets. We used standard cuts of meat and nationally distributed brands of other foods. We used no items of special equipment or special attachments for our slow cookers, except a 2-qt. baking tin for cakes and breads. A 2-lb. coffee can is a satisfactory substitute for the baking tin, as explained in the introductions to the chapters on breads and cakes.

Recipes were tested using the Rival Crock-Pot in both 3½-qt. and 5-qt. sizes, each with a HIGH and a LOW setting.

While timing is not usually critical in a slow cooker, settings and timings do vary from manufacturer to manufacturer. At the end of this section is a chart showing comparisons among different brands of slow cookers. You will find it easy to make any necessary adjustments in cooking times or settings.

In all cases, our cooking times are minimums. Usually, food will hold much longer in the slow cooker. If the margin of time is less flexible, it is indicated within each recipe group.

HOW TO USE THIS BOOK—First, find the recipe you want to cook. The slow cooker symbol next to the name of the recipe indicates it is suitable for preparation in the slow cooker. The symbol will contain a number. In the slow cooker section following the chapter, the same number will appear next to the name of the recipe. Read both recipes and the slow cooker introduction for that chapter. Follow the master recipe for amounts of ingredients, instructions on preparing ingredients, sequence of preparation and tests for doneness, noting deviations given in the slow cooker recipe.

The brief slow cooker introduction to each chapter also contains suggestions and notes any special techniques necessary and comments on which recipes are the most successful, which are not and why. If the introduction does not contain the size slow cooker to use, it will be given with the individual recipes.

If one or more of the ingredients in a master recipe, such as a sauce, must be cooked separately, it will be cross-referenced to the appropriate page number. If the cross-referenced recipe can be prepared in the slow cooker, the page number will be followed by a slow cooker symbol ◆ . Simply turn to the page on which the master recipe is given and note the slow cooker symbol number. Then turn to the slow cooker section following the chapter to locate the same recipe title and numbered slow cooker symbol accompanied by directions.

Slow cooker symbols which are circled indicate a recipe which produces superlative results.

Manufacturer/Model	Given Size (quarts)	Usable Capacity (quarts)	Equivalent HIGH
CORNING Electromatic Table Range	2½	1-3/4	350°
	4½	3½	350°
DOMINION Crock-A-Dial and Crock-A-Dial II		3	HIGH-COOK
FARBERWARE Pot Pourri	3	2½	300°
	5	4	300°
GRANDINETTI	3½	3	HIGH
	4	3½	HIGH
	5	4	HIGH
HAMILTON BEACH Continental Cooker		3	HIGH-COOK
Crock Watcher		3	HIGH COOK
Simmer On		3	HIGH COOK
NESCO Pot Luck Cooker		4½	250°
OSTER 8-Quart Super Pot	8	7	300°

The recipe can be cooked in the slow cooker. Turn to the slow cooker directions following the chapter and look for the number and name of the recipe.

 The recipe referenced is suitable for slow cooking. See master recipe on indicated page number, not slow cooker symbol number and locate it in the slow cooker section following the end of the chapter.

 A best recipe. Definitely try it.

WHAT YOU SHOULD KNOW BEFORE US-ING THE CHART—The cooker directions in the recipes refer to two settings:

LOW is the lowest setting, about 200°F maximum.

HIGH is the highest setting, about 325°F maximum.

The chart provides instructions for using the slow cooker recipes in the most commonly available brands. Information is arranged in alphabetical order by manufacturer. Find the manufacturer of your slow cooker and the model. Read across the columns for comparative dial settings and additional guidelines

Settings LOW	Relative Cooking Time	Special Comments
240°	Same using ½ recipe as given for 3½-qt. pot.	
240°	Same.	
AUTO-SHIFT	Same.	HIGH will take slightly longer. Use appropriate recipes. Cakes, breads and unconverted rice not successful on LOW.
200°	Reaches maximum temperature quickly. If given cooking time is over 8 hrs., cook only 75% of time. If given cooking time is less than 8 hrs. cook 50%-75% of time.	
200°	See above.	
LOW	Same.	
LOW	If given cooking time is over 5 hrs., add 4 hrs. on LOW or 2 hrs. on HIGH. If given time is less than 5 hrs., add 2 hrs. on LOW or HIGH.	
LOW	Same.	
AUTO-SHIFT	Same for LOW. Add at least 2 hrs. to given time on HIGH.	
AUTO SHIFT	See above.	
LOW COOK	Add at least 2 hrs. to given times on HIGH or LOW.	
200°	If given time is over 8 hrs., cook 75% of time. If given time is less than 8 hrs., cook 50%-75% of time.	
200°	Same.	

PRESTO	Slow Cooker	2-3/4	2	between HI and BROWN
		5	4	
	Create 'n Serve	2-3/4	2	See above.
		5	4	See above.
RELIABLE	Crockery Slow Cooker	5½	5	HIGH
RIVAL	Stoneware Cooker	2	1-3/4	HIGH
	Casserole Cooker/Server	3	2½	HIGH
	Electric Slow Cooker	3½	3	HIGH
	Deluxe Buffet Cooker	3½	3	HIGH
	Deluxe Cooker/Server	4½	4	HIGH
	Deluxe Cooker/Server	4½	4	HIGH
SEARS	Create 'n Serve Pan	2-3/4	2	between HI and BROWN
		5	4	
	Crockery Cooker	4	3½	HI
	Tray Model Crockery Cooker	4	3½	HI
SUNBEAM	Crocker Cooker Fryer		4	between 325°-350°
WARDS	Crockery Slow Cooker	5½	5	HIGH
WEAREVER	Poker Pot		3	HIGH
WEST BEND	Colonial Crock Slo-Cooker		2	—
	Bean Pot		2	—
	Home Maid Slow-Cooker		3½	4
	Lazy Day Slo-Cooker		5	4

HIGH If given time is over 8 hrs., cook 75% of time. If given time is less than 8 hrs., cook 50%-75% of time.

LOW

Similar if recipe doubled. If given time is 6 hrs. on LOW, reduce by 1 hr. If given time is 4-8 hrs. on HIGH, cook 75% or less of time.

LOW

LOW Same using ½ recipe given for 3½-qt. pot.

LOW Same.

LOW Same.

LOW Same.

LOW Same.

Same.

HIGH

If given time is over 8 hrs., cook 75% of time. If given time is less than 8 hrs., cook 50%-75% of time.

MED

MED Same.

Same.
Must always have 1 cup liquid. Use appropriate recipes. Breads, cakes and unconverted rice will not be successful on LOW.

200° is not marked on dial. Set dial just to left of red band.

200° Same.

LOW Similar if recipe doubled. If given time is 6 hrs. on LOW reduce by 1 hr. If given time is 4-8 hrs on HIGH, cook 75% of less of time.

LOW Same for LOW. Reduce given time for HIGH by at least 2 hrs.

H Same for LOW.
Use appropriate recipes. Breads, cakes and unconverted rice will not be successful on LOW.

H Same for LOW.
See above.

3 Same for LOW. Increase time on HIGH by 3-4 hrs.
Temperatures may be too low for successful breads, cakes, and unconverted rice.

2

It's Smart To Be Careful

There's No Substitute for Accuracy

Read recipe carefully.

Assemble all ingredients and utensils.

Select pans of proper kind and size. Measure pans inside, from rim to rim.

Use standard measuring cups and spoons. Use liquid measuring cups (rim above 1-cup line) for liquids. Use nested or dry measuring cups (1-cup line even with top) for dry ingredients.

Check liquid measurements at eye level.

Level dry measurements with straight-edged knife or spatula.

Sift all flour except whole-grain types before measuring. Spoon lightly into measuring cup. Do not jar cup.

Preheat oven 12 to 20 minutes at required temperature. Leave oven door open first 2 minutes.

Beat whole eggs until thick and piled softly when recipe calls for well-beaten eggs.

Beat egg whites as follows: *Frothy*—entire mass forms bubbles; *Rounded peaks*—peaks turn over slightly when beater is slowly lifted upright; *Stiff peaks*—peaks remain standing when beater is slowly lifted upright.

Beat egg yolks until thick and lemon-colored when recipe calls for well-beaten egg yolks.

Place oven rack so top of product will be almost at center of oven. Stagger pans so no pan is directly over another and they do not touch each other or walls of oven. Place single pan so that center of product is near center of oven.

Covering foods to be stored in the refrigerator will depend upon the type of refrigerator used.

For These Recipes—What To Use

AC'CENT—the brand of monosodium glutamate which is available everywhere through retail grocery stores. It is a basic seasoning, produced solely from natural sources, which is popularly used because of its unique property of improving natural food flavors without adding flavor of its own. Ac'cent is the registered trademark of International Minerals & Chemical Corporation.

BAKING POWDER—double-action type.

BREAD CRUMBS—one slice fresh bread equals about 1 cup soft crumbs or cubes. One slice dry or toasted bread equals about ¾ cup dry cubes or ⅓ cup fine, dry crumbs.

BUTTERED CRUMBS—soft or dry bread or cracker crumbs tossed in melted butter or margarine.

Use 1 to 2 tablespoons butter or margarine for 1 cup soft crumbs and 2 to 4 tablespoons butter or margarine for 1 cup dry crumbs.

CHOCOLATE—unsweetened chocolate.

CORNSTARCH—thickening agent. One tablespoon has the thickening power of 2 tablespoons flour.

CREAM—light, table or coffee cream, containing not less than 18% butter fat.

HEAVY or WHIPPING CREAM—containing not less than 36% butter fat.

FLOUR—all-purpose (hard wheat) flour. (In some southern areas where a blend of soft wheat is used, better products may result when minor adjustments are made in recipes. A little less liquid or more flour may be needed.) If cake flour is required, recipe will so state.

GRATED PEEL—whole citrus fruit peel finely grated through colored part only; white is bitter.

CROUTONS—slices or cubes of toasted bread, plain or browned in melted butter.

HERBS and SPICES—ground unless specified.

HERB BOUQUET—a bunch of aromatic herbs (such as a piece of celery with leaves, a sprig of thyme and 3 or 4 sprigs of parsley) tied neatly together and used to flavor soups, stews, braised dishes and sauces. Enclose fine, dry herbs in cheesecloth bag.

JULIENNE STRIPS—vegetables, meat or poultry cut into narrow strips.

LEEK—long bulb with flavor like that of an onion but milder and sweeter. Used mainly in soups. In light soups use white part only.

PEPPERCORNS—the dried berries of the pepper plant; used in pepper grinder or whole.

OIL—salad, cooking. Use olive oil only when recipe states.

ROTARY BEATER—hand-operated (Dover type) beater or electric mixer.

SCALLION—young green or "stick" onion.

SHALLOT—a member of the onion family; the small pear-shaped bulb of the shallot is milder in flavor than onions.

SHORTENING—a hydrogenated vegetable shortening, all-purpose shortening, butter or margarine. Use lard or oil when specified.

SOUR MILK—sweet milk added to 1 tablespoon vinegar or lemon juice in measuring cup up to 1-cup line and stirred well; or use buttermilk.

SUGAR—granulated (beet or cane).

VINEGAR—cider vinegar or use type of vinegar specified in recipe.

(See section introductions for information about specific types of food preparation.)

How To Do It

BASTE—spoon liquid (or use baster) over cooking food to add moisture and flavor.

BLANCH NUTS—the flavor of nuts is best maintained when nuts are allowed to remain in water the shortest possible time during blanching. Therefore, blanch only about ½ cup at a time; repeat as many times as necessary for larger amounts.

Bring to rapid boiling enough water to well cover shelled nuts. Drop in nuts. Turn off heat and allow nuts to remain in the water about 1 min.; drain or remove with fork or slotted spoon. Place between folds of absorbent paper; pat dry. Gently squeeze nuts with fingers to remove skins; or peel. Place on dry absorbent paper. To dry thoroughly, frequently shift nuts to dry spots on paper.

GRATE NUTS—use a rotary-type grater with hand-operating crank. Follow manufacturer's directions. Grated nuts should be fine and light.

GRIND NUTS—put nuts through medium blade of food chopper. Or use electric blender, grinding enough nuts at one time to cover blades. Cover blender container. (Turning motor off and on helps to throw nuts back onto blades.) Grind nuts until particles are still dry enough to remain separate—not oily and compact. Empty container and grind next batch.

TOAST NUTS—place nuts in a shallow baking dish or pie pan and brush lightly with cooking oil. Heat in oven at 350°F until delicately browned. Move and turn nuts occasionally. Or add blanched nuts to a heavy skillet in which butter (about 1 tablespoon per cup of nuts) has been melted; or use oil. Brown lightly over medium heat, constantly turning and moving nuts with a spoon.

SALT NUTS—toast nuts; drain on absorbent paper and sprinkle with salt.

BOIL—cook in liquid in which bubbles rise continually and break on the surface. Boiling temperature of water at sea level is 212°F.

BOILING WATER BATH—set a deep pan on oven rack and place the filled baking dish in pan. Pour boiling water into pan to level of mixture in baking dish. Prevent further boiling by using given oven temperature.

CHILL GELATIN MIXTURES—set dissolved gelatin mixture in refrigerator or in pan of ice and water. If mixture is placed over ice and water, stir frequently; if placed in refrigerator, stir occasionally. Chill gelatin mixtures until slightly thicker than consistency of thick, unbeaten egg white. Then add the remainder of ingredients, such as chopped or whole foods which would sink to the bottom of the mold if the gelatin were not sufficiently thickened. When gelatin mixture is already thick because of ingredients or is not a clear mixture, chill mixture until it begins to gel (gets slightly thicker) before adding chopped or whole foods.

UNMOLD GELATIN—run tip of knife around top edge of mold to loosen. Invert mold onto chilled serving plate. If necessary, wet a clean towel in hot water and wring it almost dry. Wrap hot towel around mold for a few seconds only. If mold does not loosen, repeat.

CLEAN CELERY—trim roots and cut off leaves. Leaves may be used for added flavor in soups and stuffings; leaves may be left on inner stalks when serving as relish. Separate stalks, remove blemishes and wash. Then proceed as directed in recipe.

CLEAN GARLIC—separate into cloves and remove outer (thin, papery) skin.

CLEAN GREEN or RED PEPPERS—rinse and cut into quarters. Remove stem, all white fiber and seeds with spoon or knife; rinse. Prepare as directed in recipe.

CLEAN and SLICE MUSHROOMS—wipe with a clean, damp cloth and cut off tips of stems; slice lengthwise through stems and caps.

CLEAN ONIONS (dry)—cut off root end and a thin slice from stem end; peel and rinse. Prepare as directed in recipe.

CRUSH CRUMBS—place cookies, crackers, zwieback or the like on a long length of heavy waxed paper. Loosely fold paper around material to be crushed, tucking under open ends. With a rolling pin, gently crush to make fine crumbs. Or place crackers or cookies in a plastic bag and crush.

If using electric blender, break 5 or 6 crackers, cookies or the like into blender container. Cover container. Blend on low speed, flicking motor on and off until crumbs are medium fine. Empty container and repeat blending until desired amount of crumbs is obtained.

CINNAMON SUGAR—mix thoroughly ¼ cup sugar and 2 teaspoons cinnamon. Use to sugar doughnuts, cookies or toast.

CUT MARSHMALLOWS or DRIED FRUITS (uncooked)—with scissors dipped frequently in water to avoid stickiness.

DICE—cut into small cubes.

FLAKE FISH—with a fork separate cooked fresh or canned fish into flakes (thin, layer-like pieces). Remove bony tissue from crab meat; salmon bones are edible.

FLUTE EDGE of PASTRY—press index finger on edge of pastry, then pinch pastry with thumb and index finger of other hand. Lift fingers and repeat procedure to flute around entire edge.

FOLD—use flexible spatula and slip it down side of bowl to bottom. Turn bowl quarter turn. Lift spatula through mixture along side of bowl with blade parallel to surface. Turn spatula over to fold lifted mixture across material on surface. Cut down and under; turn bowl and repeat process until material seems blended. With every fourth stroke, bring spatula up through center.

GRATE CHOCOLATE—use a rotary-type grater with hand-operating crank. Follow manufacturer's directions. Grated chocolate should be fine and light. Grated chocolate melts more rapidly.

MELT CHOCOLATE—melt over simmering water to avoid scorching.

MARINATE—allow food to stand in liquid (usually a seasoned oil and acid mixture) to impart additional flavor.

MEASURE BROWN SUGAR—pack firmly into measuring cup so that sugar will hold shape of cup when turned out.

MINCE—cut or chop into small, fine pieces.

POUND MEAT—to increase tenderness in less tender cuts of meat, place meat on flat working surface and repeatedly pound meat on one side with meat hammer; turn meat and repeat process. Meat may also be pounded with the edge of a heavy saucer or plate.

PREPARE DOUBLE-STRENGTH COFFEE BEVER-AGE—prepare coffee in usual manner (method and grind of coffee depending upon type of coffee maker), using 4 measuring tablespoons coffee per standard measuring cup water. Use 6 measuring tablespoonsful for **triple-strength coffee.**

PREPARE QUICK BROTH—dissolve in 1 cup hot water, 1 chicken bouillon cube for **quick chicken broth** or 1 beef bouillon cube or ½ teaspoon concentrated meat extract for **quick meat broth.**

PREPARE QUICK-COOKING RICE—carefully follow directions on package for amount and timing when using packaged precooked rice.

REDUCE LIQUID—continue cooking the liquid until the amount is sufficiently decreased, thus concentrating flavor and sometimes thickening the original liquid. Simmer when wine is used; boil rapidly for other liquids.

RICE—force food through ricer, sieve or food mill.

SIEVE—force through coarse sieve or food mill.

SCALD MILK—heat in top of double boiler over simmering water just until a thin film appears.

SIMMER—cook in a liquid just below boiling point; bubbles form slowly and break below surface.

WHIP CREAM—(for use as topping or filling or as an ingredient in a cake) chill bowl, beater and whipping cream. Pour chilled cream into chilled bowl. Using chilled beater, beat (on high speed if using electric mixer) until soft peaks are formed when beater is slowly lifted upright. If whipped cream is to be incorporated into a frozen or refrigerator dessert or salad, beat only until of medium consistency (piles softly).

The maximum amount of cream that should be whipped at one time is 1½ cups. If recipe calls for more than 1½ cups whip 1 cup at a time. Whipping cream doubles in volume when whipped.

OVEN TEMPERATURES—Use a portable oven thermometer for greater accuracy of oven temperatures.

Very slow................250°F to 275°F
Slow......................300°F to 325°F
Moderate.................350°F to 375°F
Hot.......................400°F to 425°F
Very Hot..................450°F to 475°F
Extremely Hot.............500°F to 525°F

WHEN YOU BROIL—Set temperature control of range at Broil (500°F or higher). Distance from top of food to source of heat determines the intensity of heat upon food.

WHEN YOU DEEP-FRY—About 20 min. before ready to deep-fry, fill a deep saucepan one-half to two-thirds full with hydrogenated vegetable shortening, all-purpose shortening, lard or cooking oil for deep-frying. Heat fat slowly to temperature given in recipe. A deep-frying thermometer is an accurate guide for deep-frying temperatures.

If thermometer is not available, the following bread cube method may be used: A 1-in. cube of bread browns in 60 seconds at 350°F to 375°F.

If using automatic deep-fryer, follow manufacturer's directions for amount of fat and timing.

WHEN USING THE ELECTRIC BLENDER—Cover blender container before starting and stopping motor to avoid splashing. To aid even mixing, frequently scrape down sides of container with a rubber spatula, first stopping motor.

To grind, put in blender container enough food at one time to cover blades. Cover; turn on motor and grind until very fine. Turning motor off and on helps to throw food back on blades. Empty container and grind next batch of food.

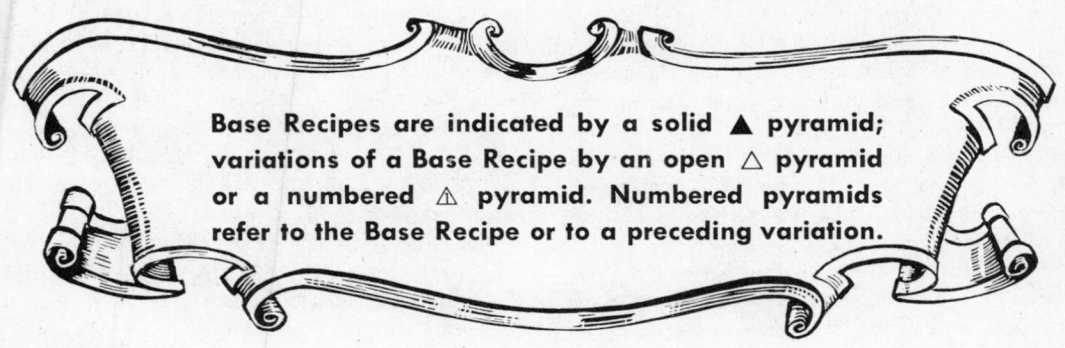

Base Recipes are indicated by a solid ▲ pyramid; variations of a Base Recipe by an open △ pyramid or a numbered ⚠ pyramid. Numbered pyramids refer to the Base Recipe or to a preceding variation.

Hors d'Oeuvres, Canapés and Cocktails

Small, dainty, tempting to the eye and teasing to the palate, appetizers are artful little contrivances for putting company in a company mood. Such at least is their purpose. But they are so delicious and charming in their almost infinite variety that it is sometimes difficult to remember that it is the obligation of hostess and guest alike to maintain a sensible restraint where appetizers are concerned.

Appetizers are found all over the world. In this country they are grouped into three main types: hors d'oeuvres, canapés and cocktails.

PLANNING APPETIZERS—There is no limit to the kinds of meat, poultry, fish, cheese, vegetables and fruits that can be used. Though imagination and ingenuity are the only limiting factors in selecting appetizers, there is one rule that should be followed—*Do not repeat any food in the main part of the meal that has been used in the appetizers.* Remember they are a part of the whole menu; select them to harmonize with the rest of the meal. Choose them for complementary flavors, for contrast in texture and color and variety of shape. Picture the serving dishes, trays and other appointments as you plan the menu.

Avoid a last-minute rush by wise selection (do not include too many appetizers that require last-minute doing), by careful buying and beforehand preparation.

Take cues from assembly-line production techniques for organizing your work. For example, use large sandwich loaves, cut in lengthwise slices, for canapé bases and finger sandwiches; stack several slices together and cut several identical shapes at one time; spread canapé bases all at one time.

HORS D'OEUVRES—Cold or hot, simple or elaborate, hors d'oeuvres are savory tidbits about one bite in size and are eaten with the fingers or from wooden or plastic picks. They are usually passed in the living room or on the terrace to a gathering of people at a cocktail party or before dinner. A Continental custom is to serve the hors d'oeuvres at the table as the first course of a luncheon or dinner. Here the use of a fork is acceptable.

For successful hors d'oeuvres remember and practice the general suggestions and the rule given in PLANNING. The **Taste Teasers** (*page 16*) will give a helpful start. Look also at **Raw Vegetable Relishes** (*page 308*) for the pick-ups. Don't forget about the many dips and dunks and the snacks such as **Nibblers** (*page 21*), nuts and potato chips.

Fill miniature shells made from puff paste or choux paste, or spread waffle squares, thin griddlecakes or crêpes with piquant mixtures—delectable hors d'oeuvres!

Holders for pick-type hors d'oeuvres are available in housewares departments or can be made from a molded cheese (such as Edam), grapefruit, oranges, apples, a small head of red or green cabbage, a melon, eggplant, cucumbers or a cauliflower. If necessary, level base by removing a thin slice from the underside. Put hors d'oeuvres on wooden or plastic picks and insert into the holder.

CANAPÉS—Finger foods too, canapés are small bits of well-seasoned food spread on a thin base such as a slice of fancy-cut toast or bread or a cracker. They should have a fresh appearance and be easy to handle.

Take time to arrange canapés in an attractive design on the serving tray—the effect will be gratifying. Prepare enough to replenish the tray, recreating the original arrangement.

Bases for canapés are the many breads (plain, toasted or deep-fried), crackers and the packaged commercial products such as melba toast and potato chips. Brown bread, nut breads, rye, wheat, white and pumpernickel bread give variety to canapés. The bread slices, never more than ¼ in. thick, can be cut into many shapes—rounds, squares, diamonds, ovals, rectangles or crescents.

Spread canapé bases with any one of the **Seasoned Butters** (*page 25*), then with the filling or spread, and finally top with a garnish. Garnishes should be scaled to the dainty size of canapés and should be as good to eat as they are to behold.

Garnishes for Canapés

Anchovies—Fillets or rolled
Bacon (crisp, cooked)—Crumbled or small pieces
Carrots—Thin notched rounds
Caviar—Black or red
Cheese (sharp)—Grated
Cream cheese—Softened, plain or tinted and forced through pastry bag and No. 27 star decorating tube to form rosettes or border; a No. 2 or 3 decorating tube for designs or borders
Chives—Minced or chopped
Cucumbers—Notched slices, half slices or thin unpared slices
Eggs (hard-cooked)—Rings, slices, sieved egg yolk or egg-white cutouts
Green pepper—Cutouts or narrow strips
Lobster—Small pieces of claw meat
Mint—Sprigs or chopped
Mushrooms (slices)—Cooked in butter
Nuts (plain, toasted or salted)—Chopped, ground or whole
Olives (green or ripe)—Slivered, chopped, rings of pitted olives or pimiento-stuffed olives

Parsley—Sprigs, chopped or minced
Paprika
Pickles—Chopped or slices
Pimiento—Strips or chopped
Radishes—Thin slices
Shrimp (cooked, fresh)—Whole
Tomato—Cutouts
Water cress—Sprigs

Garnishes for the Canapé Tray

Carved vegetable flowers
Fresh flowers
Frosted Grapes (*page 312*)
Kumquats—With peel drawn back in petal shapes
Parsley bouquets
Radish Roses (*page 308*)
Water cress

COCKTAILS—The sea food or fruit (one or more kinds of fruit) cocktail is served as the first course of a meal at the table. Vegetable or fruit juices are served either at the table or in the living room before the meal.

Sea-food cocktails usually are served with peppy sauce that has ketchup, chili sauce, French dressing or mayonnaise as a base.

Fruit cocktails should be tart, though sometimes made with sweetened fruits. Frequently they are sprinkled with rum, kirsch or a liqueur that harmonizes in flavor with the fruit.

Add seasonings such as Worcestershire sauce, tabasco sauce or lemon juice to spark the flavor of vegetable juices.

Float a small scoop of fruit-flavored ice or sherbet on small servings of fruit juice—a refreshing shrub.

All cocktails should be fresh, colorful and appetizing in appearance and tantalizing in flavor. Thoroughly chill all ingredients and the serving dishes. Fruit and sea-food cocktails often are kept cold in beds of crushed ice. Sea-food and fruit cocktails are served in stemmed or footed cocktail glasses while the juices and shrubs are served in small glasses or punch cups. Some juice cocktails are served hot; be sure they are steaming hot and served in cups or glasses that are comfortable for your guests to hold.

Taste Teasers

Select an attractive array of Taste Teasers from these recipes. All are delightful bits of finger food, though some may be easier to serve if they have stems of wooden or plastic picks.

Meat 'n' Cheese Wedges—With a round cutter, cut 2½- to 3-in. rounds from slices of **ham,** canned **luncheon meat, ready-to-serve meat, bologna,** or other **sausage.** Repeat the process with thin slices of **Swiss** or **Cheddar cheese.** Alternately stack the meat and cheese rounds, using five in all. Wrap in waxed paper and chill in refrigerator until time to serve. Cut stacks into small wedges. Insert picks.

Bacon-Wrapped Olives—Wrap **pimiento-** or **almond-stuffed olives** in pieces of **bacon.** Fasten with picks. Put in shallow baking dish. Bake or broil until bacon is done.

Biscuit Bites—Dot toasted bite-size **shredded wheat biscuits** with **peanut butter.** Thread on picks alternately with thin slices of **sweet pickle.**

Pecan Sandwiches—Lightly brush large **pecan halves** with **butter** and spread one layer deep on baking sheet. Toast at 350°F about 20 min., or until delicately browned. Grate **Swiss cheese;** blend in **cream** to spreading consistency. Spread one side of one pecan half with cheese mixture and top with a second half. Press gently together.

Pineapple Delights—Wrap drained **pineapple chunks** each in one third of a slice of **bacon;** secure with a whole **clove** or wooden pick. Arrange in shallow baking dish and bake or broil until bacon is done.

Smoked Cheese Blossoms—Soften **smoked cheese** and mix with chopped **pimiento, sweet pickle** and crisp crumbled **bacon.** Roll into small balls and chill in refrigerator. Or pack mixture into a small pan, chill and cut into squares. Insert picks.

Caviar with Egg—Cut **hard-cooked eggs** into halves lengthwise or cut forming sawtooth edges (see photo, *page 88*). Remove yolks and set aside for use in other food preparation. Fill whites with chilled **caviar,** black or red. Garnish with small piece of **lemon.**

Cheese Popcorn—Sprinkle **salt** and ½ cup (2 oz.) grated sharp **Cheddar** or **Parmesan cheese** over 1 qt. hot buttered **popped corn.**

Dried Beef Tasters—Flavor **cream cheese** with a small amount of **prepared horse-radish.** Roll into small balls. Then roll and press balls in minced **dried beef.** Insert picks.

Olive Teasers—Coat large **stuffed olives** with softened **cream cheese.** Roll in finely chopped **nuts.** Chill in refrigerator; insert picks.

Stuffed Celery Spears—Blend together softened **cream cheese** and **milk.** Mix in few grains **celery salt,** few drops **Worcestershire sauce** and very finely chopped **radish** and **green pepper** or **pimiento** and **parsley.** Stuff cleaned **celery** with the cheese mixture.

Apple Sandwiches—Wash and core but do not pare small **apples.** Cut crosswise into thin slices, forming rings. Dip in **lemon, orange** or **pineapple juice** to prevent darkening. Spread **peanut butter** or a **cheese spread** on one ring; top with a second ring. Cut into thirds.

Fruit and Ham "Kabobs"—Alternate cubes of cooked **ham** or canned **luncheon meat** on picks with seedless **grapes** or cubes of **melon** or **pineapple.**

Stuffed Prunes or Dates—Pit and dry plump soaked **prunes** and pit **dates.** Stuff with a tangy **cheese spread.** If desired, add chopped **nuts,** drained **crushed pineapple** or chopped **maraschino cherries** to cheese.

Bacon-Wrapped Shrimp with Chili Dip

Bacon-Wrapped Shrimp

Prepare
    1 lb. fresh shrimp with shells (see Cooked Shrimp, *page 242*)

Prepare and set aside
    Chili Dip (*page 22*)

Combine in a small saucepan
    ½ cup butter or margarine
    1½ teaspoons chili powder
    1 clove garlic (*page 12*), minced; or crushed in garlic press

Set over low heat, stirring occasionally, until butter or margarine is melted and heated thoroughly. Remove from heat and set aside.

Cut into halves
    8 slices bacon

Wrap one-half slice around each shrimp and secure with a wooden pick.

Set temperature control of range at Broil. Arrange shrimp on broiler rack. Brush with butter sauce. Place rack in broiler with tops of shrimp about 3 in. from source of heat. Broil 5 min., brushing once with sauce. Carefully turn shrimp, brush with sauce, and broil second side (brushing once again with sauce) 5 min., or until bacon is cooked.

Place shrimp appetizers on a warm platter; remove picks if desired. Garnish with
    Lemon wedges and parsley

Serve immediately with the Chili Dip.

About 16 appetizers

Alaskan Nuggets
MRS. GEORGE TEXTER, SEATTLE, WASH.

Set out a deep saucepan or automatic deep-fryer (*page 13*) and heat fat to 375°F.

Set out
    ¼ cup mashed potato

Cut into ½-in. cubes and set aside
    2 oz. sharp Cheddar cheese

Drain, flake (*page 12*) and set aside contents of
    1 7¾-oz. can salmon (about 1 cup, flaked)

Heat in a small skillet over low heat
    1 tablespoon butter or margarine

Add and cook slowly over medium heat until onion is transparent, stirring frequently
    1 tablespoon finely chopped onion
    1 tablespoon finely chopped celery

Mix with the flaked salmon, the mashed potato, the onion and celery
    1 teaspoon Worcestershire sauce

and a mixture of
    ¼ teaspoon salt
    ¼ teaspoon Accent
    ⅛ teaspoon pepper

Use about 2 teaspoons of the salmon mixture and one cheese cube for each nugget. Shape the salmon around the cheese to form a ball about 1 in. in diameter.

Dip the nuggets in
    1 egg, beaten

Coat nuggets by rolling in
    ⅓ cup (1 slice) fine, dry bread crumbs

Deep-fry only as many nuggets at one time as will float uncrowded one-layer deep in fat. Deep-fry 1 min., or until golden brown. Turn once or twice to brown evenly. Drain over fat for a few seconds; remove to absorbent paper.

Insert a wooden pick into each nugget and serve immediately. *About 1½ doz. appetizers*

Celery Whirls

Clean (*page 12*)
> **1 medium-size bunch celery**

Set aside to drain on absorbent paper while preparing one of the cheese stuffers.

For Roquefort or Blue Cheese Stuffer—
Crumble and set aside
> **4 oz. Roquefort or Blue cheese (about 1 cup, crumbled)**

Thoroughly blend together
> **3 oz. (1 pkg.) cream cheese, softened**
> **1 tablespoon mayonnaise**

Add cheese and beat until well mixed. Blend in
> **2 teaspoons lemon juice**
> **1 teaspoon onion juice**
> **¼ teaspoon garlic salt**
> **⅛ teaspoon Accent**
> **Few grains cayenne pepper**

Beat until smooth and mixed thoroughly.

For Cheddar Cheese Stuffer—Grate
> **4 oz. Cheddar cheese (about 1 cup, grated)**

Set aside.

Thoroughly blend together
> **3 oz. (1 pkg.) cream cheese, softened**
> **3 tablespoons milk or cream**

Add grated cheese and beat until well mixed. Blend in a mixture of
> **1½ teaspoons dry mustard**
> **½ teaspoon salt**
> **¼ teaspoon Accent**
> **Few grains pepper**

Stir in
> **1 or 2 drops tabasco sauce**

Mix thoroughly.

To Complete Celery Whirls—Fill the full-length crisp stalks of celery with one of the stuffers. Rearrange filled stalks into natural shape of celery bunch. Wrap bunch tightly in waxed paper, moisture-vapor-proof paper or aluminum foil and place in refrigerator to chill for several hours.

Cut into crosswise slices ¼ to ½ in. thick and serve. *About 20 Celery Whirls*

Deep-Fried Cheese Balls
MRS. ROBERT J. GREEN, WACO, TEXAS

Set out a deep saucepan or automatic deep-fryer (*page 13*) and heat fat to 375°F.

Grate and set aside
> **7 oz. Cheddar cheese (about 1¾ cups, grated)**

Finely crush (*page 12*) and set aside
> **8 crackers (about ⅓ cup crumbs)**

Mix together and set aside
> **1 tablespoon flour**
> **½ teaspoon salt**
> **¼ teaspoon paprika**

Beat until rounded peaks are formed and egg whites do not slide when bowl is partially inverted
> **3 egg whites**

Sprinkle the flour mixture and grated cheese over the egg whites. Quickly and gently fold (*page 12*) together.

Spoon about 1 teaspoon of batter at a time onto the cracker crumbs. Quickly work to form a ball and to coat with the crumbs.

Deep-fry only as many balls at one time as will float uncrowded one layer deep in fat. Deep-fry 3 to 5 min., or until golden brown. Turn occasionally to brown evenly. Drain over fat for a few seconds; remove to absorbent paper.

Serve immediately. *About 2 doz. cheese balls*

Empanadas

MRS. MILTON LEE NASH
GATUN, CANAL ZONE

A zestful version of the familiar turnover, empanadas have been a prized feature of Spanish-American cooking since colonial times.

Set out baking sheets.

For Pastry—Sift together
  4 cups sifted flour
  1 teaspoon salt
  ½ teaspoon sugar
Cut in with pastry blender or two knives until pieces are size of small peas
  1 cup shortening
  ½ cup butter or margarine
Mix in with a fork
  2 egg yolks, slightly beaten
Sprinkle gradually over mixture, a teaspoon at a time
  6 tablespoons iced water
Mix lightly with fork after each addition. Add only enough water to hold pastry together. Work quickly; do not overhandle. Shape into a ball, wrap in waxed paper and place in refrigerator while preparing filling.

For Filling—Set out a large skillet having a tight-fitting cover.

Chop enough vegetables to yield
  ⅓ cup finely chopped green pepper
  ¼ cup finely chopped carrot
  ¼ cup finely chopped celery
  ¼ cup finely chopped green onion
    or scallion
  ¼ cup finely chopped onion
Set aside.

Heat in the skillet over medium heat
  ¼ cup shortening
  1 tablespoon olive oil
Add and cook until browned, breaking into small pieces with a fork or spoon
  1¼ lbs. ground beef
When meat begins to brown add the vegetables and continue to cook, stirring occasionally, until vegetables are tender.

Meanwhile, rinse and dip, one at a time, into boiling water for a few seconds
  2 medium-size ripe tomatoes
Plunge tomatoes into cold water. Peel tomatoes, cut out and discard stem ends. Cut tomatoes into small pieces and mix with
  2 tablespoons capers
and a mixture of
  1 teaspoon flour
  1 teaspoon salt
  ½ teaspoon crushed dried red pepper
  ¼ teaspoon Accent
  ¼ teaspoon pepper
  ⅛ teaspoon cayenne pepper
Add the chopped tomato mixture to skillet, with enough water to cover. Cover skillet. Cook over low heat about 30 min.

Remove from heat and blend in
  2 tablespoons chopped parsley
  2 tablespoons chopped raisins
  2 tablespoons chopped green olives
  1 tablespoon chopped hot red pepper

To Form Empanadas—Remove pastry from refrigerator to a lightly floured surface and shape into 2 balls. Lightly flour rolling pin. Roll one ball at a time from center to edge about ⅛ in. thick. With a knife or spatula, loosen pastry whenever sticking occurs and sprinkle flour underneath. Using a lightly floured cookie cutter or a knife, cut into rounds about 3¼ in. in diameter. Place about 1 tablespoon of the filling onto each round. Moisten edges with cold water, fold pastry over and press edges together with a fork, or flute (*page 12*). Seal tightly. Place empanadas on baking sheets. Prick tops with a fork.

Beat together until blended
  1 egg yolk, slightly beaten
  2 tablespoons milk
Brush top of each pastry with egg-milk mixture.

Bake at 450°F 10 min., or until golden brown.

Serve hot.   *About 3 doz. appetizers*

Note: Empanadas may be made larger and served as a main dish.

Olive-Ham Appetizers and Tomato Cocktail (page 563)

Olive-Ham Appetizers

Set out a baking sheet.

Grind (*page 107*) enough cooked ham to yield
   ¾ cup ground cooked ham
Combine with the ham and mix thoroughly
   ½ cup chopped ripe olives
   1 tablespoon thick sour cream
   1 teaspoon prepared mustard
   1 teaspoon Worcestershire sauce
Set aside.

Set out
   1 tablespoon caraway seeds
Prepare and shape into a ball
   Pastry for 1-Crust Pie (page 442)
Divide dough into 6 equal portions; roll each portion into a 5x3-in. rectangle. Sprinkle about ½ teaspoon of the caraway seeds over each rectangle. Spread ham mixture evenly over each rectangle almost to edges. Starting with long edge of each rectangle, roll up and pinch long edge to seal (do not pinch ends). Place on baking sheet, sealed edges down.

Bake at 450°F 10 to 12 min., or until appetizers are lightly browned.

Slice rolls; serve with **Radish Roses** (*page 308*) and ripe olives threaded with carrot sticks.

About 2½ doz. appetizers

Nippy Sausage Rounds

Baking sheets will be needed.

Drain contents of
   1 4-oz. can Vienna-style sausages
Cut each sausage into 4 crosswise slices and set aside.

Prepare and roll ⅛ in. thick
   Cheese Pastry for 1-Crust Pie (page 443)
Using a lightly floured 2¼-in. cookie cutter, cut pastry into rounds. Put a sausage slice in the center of one half of the pastry rounds. Spread top of each sausage slice with
   Prepared mustard
Moisten edges of sausage-topped pastry rounds with water. Cover with remaining pastry rounds. Using a floured fork, gently press edges to seal.

Place rounds on the baking sheets and bake at 450°F about 10 min., or until lightly browned.

About 2½ doz. appetizers

Note: If desired, spread the top of each sausage slice with **prepared horse-radish** or **chili sauce** instead of mustard.

Veal-on-a-Pick

Grind (*page 107*)
   ¼ lb. veal loaf (about 1 cup ground)
Mix until well blended
   3 oz. (1 pkg.) cream cheese, softened
   1 teaspoon Worcestershire sauce
   ¼ teaspoon paprika
Blend in the ground veal loaf. Shape mixture into ¾-in. balls. Roll each ball in
   Minced parsley
Chill thoroughly before serving. Insert a wooden pick into each ball to serve.

About 1 doz. appetizers

Lollipop Franks

Set out a deep saucepan or automatic deep-fryer (*page 13*) and heat fat to 365°F.

Prepare and set aside to chill
Peppy Cocktail Sauce (*page 29*)
Set aside to drain contents of
1 6-oz. jar cocktail franks
Sift together into a bowl
½ cup sifted flour
4 teaspoons sugar
¾ teaspoon baking powder
¼ teaspoon salt
Mix in
⅓ cup corn meal
Cut in with pastry blender or two knives until pieces are size of small peas
1 tablespoon shortening
Mix together thoroughly
1 egg, slightly beaten
⅓ cup milk
Few drops tabasco sauce
Make a well in center of dry ingredients. Add egg mixture and stir until batter is well mixed. Using a fork, dip each frank into batter, coating evenly.

Deep-fry only as many franks at one time as will float uncrowded one layer deep in fat. Turn franks as they rise to surface and several times during cooking (do not pierce). Fry 2 to 3 min., or until golden brown. Drain over fat a few seconds; remove to absorbent paper.

Insert a wooden pick into one end of each frank. Serve piping hot with Peppy Cocktail Sauce as a dip.   *About 2½ doz. tidbits*

Nibblers

(*See photo on page 566*)
RACHEL SENNER, BUHLER, KANS.

Chili or curry powder adds extra piquancy.

Set out a 15½x10½x1-in. baking dish.

Melt in a small saucepan over low heat
½ cup butter or margarine

Meanwhile, mix together in a large bowl
2¾ cups (2 oz.) crisp oat cereal
2 cups (3 oz.) bite-size shredded rice biscuits
1½ cups (1½ oz.) stick pretzels
¾ cup (about 4 oz.) salted peanuts or mixed nuts
Mix into melted butter
¾ teaspoon Worcestershire sauce
¾ teaspoon salt
¾ teaspoon garlic salt
½ teaspoon Accent
Pour butter mixture over cereal mixture and toss lightly to coat evenly. Spread cereal mixture evenly in baking pan.

Place in 250°F oven for 2 hrs., moving and turning mixture occasionally with a spoon.

Serve in a large bowl. Store in tightly covered jars.   *About 7 cups snacks*

Hawaiian Coconut Chips
MRS. H. W. FINLEY, KNOX CITY, TEXAS

Set out baking sheets.

With an ice pick, force holes through indentations of
1 medium-size fresh coconut
Drain liquid from the coconut. Put the coconut in a baking dish and heat at 350°F for 30 min. Remove from oven and break the shell by tapping sharply with a hammer. Remove meat from the shell and, if desired, pare off brown skin. (The skin imparts a delightful, nutty flavor to coconut chips.) Form chips by pulling the coconut meat across a shredder.

Put the chips in a single layer on each baking sheet. Sprinkle over coconut on each sheet
1 teaspoon salt
Place in a 375°F oven for 8 to 10 min., or until chips are light brown.

Chili Dip

(*See photo on page 17*)

Thoroughly mix together in a small bowl

¾ cup Mayonnaise (*page 319*)
3 tablespoons chopped sweet pickle
1 tablespoon chopped stuffed olives
1 Hard-Cooked Egg (*page 87*), chopped
1½ teaspoons grated onion
1 tablespoon chili powder

Cover and set aside in refrigerator 1 to 2 hrs. to chill and to allow flavors to blend.

About 1 cup dip

Fabulous Cheese Mousse

Lightly oil with salad or cooking oil (not olive oil) a fancy 1-pt. mold. Set aside to drain. Put a small bowl and rotary beater into refrigerator to chill.

Pour into a small cup or custard cup

¼ cup cold water

Sprinkle evenly over cold water

1 tablespoon (1 env.) unflavored gelatin

Let stand 5 min. to soften. Dissolve completely by placing gelatin over very hot water.

Force through a fine sieve

3¾ oz. (3 1¼-oz. pkgs.) Roquefort cheese
2⅔ oz. (2 1⅓-oz. pkgs.) Camembert cheese

Blend in until mixture is smooth

1 egg yolk, slightly beaten
1 tablespoon sherry
1 teaspoon Worcestershire sauce

Stir dissolved gelatin and add to cheese mixture, blending thoroughly.

Beat until rounded peaks are formed

1 egg white

Beat, using chilled bowl and beater, until cream is of medium consistency (piles softly)

½ cup chilled whipping cream

Fold (*page 12*) whipped cream and egg white into the cheese mixture. Turn into the mold. Chill in refrigerator until firm.

Unmold (*page 12*) onto a chilled serving plate.

Garnish with

Stuffed olive slices

Serve with crackers.

One 1-pt. mold

Avocado-Cottage-Cheese Dip

Force through a sieve or food mill and set aside

1 cup (8 oz.) cream-style cottage cheese

Rinse, cut into halves, and remove pit from

1 large ripe avocado

Carefully scoop out fruit, reserving the shells to use as containers for serving the dip. Put avocado into a bowl and mash well with a fork.

Blend in

2 teaspoons lemon juice

Mix in the sieved cottage cheese and

3 tablespoons minced parsley
2 teaspoons grated onion
½ teaspoon salt
½ teaspoon Accent
¼ teaspoon pepper
1 clove garlic (*page 12*), minced; or crushed in a garlic press

Blend until ingredients are thoroughly mixed. Spoon the dip into the avocado shells. Place in refrigerator to chill.

Before serving, sprinkle with

Paprika

Accompany with potato chips or small crackers.

About 2 cups of dip

Fabulous Cheese Mousse

Tuna Sensation

Drain and flake (*page 12*) contents of
1 7-oz. can tuna (about 1 cup, flaked)
Set aside.

Beat until very soft
8 oz. cream cheese
Add and beat until smooth
½ cup thick sour cream
1 tablespoon prepared horse-radish
1 teaspoon Worcestershire sauce
Blend in the flaked tuna and
2 tablespoons minced onion
1 clove garlic (*page 12*), minced; or
crushed in a garlic press
and a mixture of
1 teaspoon crushed chervil
½ teaspoon salt
¼ teaspoon Accent
Few grains pepper
Cover and put into refrigerator for 2 to 3 hrs. to allow flavors to blend. One half hour before serving, remove from refrigerator and let stand at room temperature so that the mixture will be of dipping consistency.

Serve as a dip with crackers or potato chips.
About 1⅔ cups dip

▲ Buffet Cheese Spreads

For a big party, arrange cheese balls on a large serving dish or tray. For a smaller party, one of the three may be served as an appetizer. A variety of crisp crackers should accompany the cheeses.

For Cheese Base—Set out to soften at room temperature
½ lb. Roquefort cheese
8 oz. cream cheese
5 oz. (1 jar) sharp process
cheese spread
Blend the cheeses together until well mixed. Divide the mixture into thirds (about 1 cup each) and combine each third with one of the following cheese spread variations.
3 cheese balls

⚠ Parsley Cheese Spread

MRS. G. R. ENGEMAN
MOUNTAIN LAKE, MINN.

Mix together ½ cup (about 2 oz.) finely chopped **pecans** and ½ cup minced **parsley**. Mix ⅓ of Cheese Base ▲ with one half of the pecans and parsley, 1 tablespoon minced **onion** and ½ teaspoon **Worcestershire sauce**. Shape into a ball and roll in the remaining pecans and parsley. Chill in refrigerator. Let stand at room temperature before serving.

⚠ Nippy Cheese Spread

MRS. R. D. BOWER, BREMERTON, WASH.

Mix together ½ cup (about 2 oz.) finely chopped **pecans** and ½ cup minced **parsley**. Mix ⅓ of Cheese Base ▲ with one half of the pecans and parsley and 1 tablespoon grated **onion**, 2 teaspoons **prepared horse-radish**, 2 teaspoons **prepared mustard**, ½ teaspoon **Worcestershire sauce** and ⅛ teaspoon **salt**. Shape into a ball and roll in the remaining pecans and parsley. Chill in refrigerator. Let stand at room temperature before serving.

⚠ Rosy Cheese Spread

MRS. RAY GARRISON, BOWLING GREEN, KY.

Chop very finely ⅔ cup (about 4 oz.) blanched **almonds** (*page 11*). Mix ⅓ of Cheese Base ▲ with one half of the almonds and 1 tablespoon minced **pimiento**, 1½ teaspoons grated **onion**, 1 teaspoon **lemon juice** and ½ teaspoon **Worcestershire sauce**. Shape into a ball and roll in the remaining almonds. Sprinkle generously with **paprika**. Chill in refrigerator. Let stand at room temperature before serving.

*Assorted
Appetizers*

Canapés

Savory canapés are the prologue to the meal, whetting the appetite. Plan a selection to harmonize with your menu.

Anchovy Canapés—Mix together thoroughly 1 finely chopped **hard-cooked egg**, 1 medium-size peeled, chopped **tomato**, 2 tablespoons flaked **tuna**, 2 tablespoons chopped **green pepper** and a mixture of 2 tablespoons **mayonnaise** and 6 mashed **anchovy fillets**. Spread **Lemon Butter** (*page 25*) on **bread crescents**. Spread anchovy mixture on each crescent. Sprinkle 1 or 2 drops **Worcestershire sauce** on each canapé. Garnish each with a sprig of **parsley**.

Dried Beef 'n' Cheese Squares—Blend together 4½ oz. softened **cream cheese** (1½ 3-oz. pkgs.) and 2 tablespoons **orange marmalade**. Spread part of the cream cheese mixture onto 3 slices white **bread**. Cut each bread slice into quarters. Place a slice of **dried beef** over each canapé. Top each with a small amount of remaining cream cheese. (For a special touch, force cream cheese through a pastry bag and No. 27 star tube.)

Bologna Diamonds—Blend thoroughly ½ cup ground **bologna**, 3 sieved **hard-cooked egg yolks**, 2 tablespoons **mayonnaise** and ⅛ teaspoon **garlic salt** and a few grains **pepper**. Spread small **bread diamonds** with **Mustard Butter** (*page 25*). Top with the bologna mixture. Garnish each with a strip of **pimiento**.

Clam and Cheese Canapés—Drain contents of 1 7-oz. can **minced clams**. Blend together 3 oz. softened **cream cheese**, 2 teaspoons **lemon juice**, few drops **tabasco sauce** and a mixture of ¼ teaspoon **salt**, ¼ teaspoon **Accent** and ⅛ teaspoon **pepper**. Blend in the minced clams. Spread on **toast fingers**. Garnish with sieved **hard-cooked egg yolk**.

Crab Nippies—Drain, remove and discard bony tissue and flake contents of 6- to 7-oz. can **crab meat**. Spoon crab meat onto **buttered toast rounds** and sprinkle **Accent** over tops; cover generously with grated sharp **Cheddar cheese**. Set temperature control of range at Broil. Arrange canapés on broiler rack and place rack in broiler with top of canapés 3 in. from source of heat. Broil 3 to 5 min., or until cheese is bubbly. Serve piping hot.

Anchovy and Egg Canapés—Spread **toast rounds** with **Parsley Butter** (*on this page*). Blend together 3 oz. softened **cream cheese**, ¼ cup **anchovy paste** and 1 teaspoon minced **parsley**. Set aside. Mix together 2 **hard-cooked egg yolks**, 2 tablespoons **mayonnaise**, ¼ teaspoon **dry mustard**, ⅛ teaspoon **salt**, a few grains **pepper** and ⅛ teaspoon **Accent**. Place a thin ring of **hard-cooked egg white** on each toast round. Fill centers with anchovy mixture. Top with a slice of **ripe olive**. Place a small amount of the egg-yolk mixture on each olive.

Shrimp Canapés—Marinate 12 cooked **shrimp** in **Garlic French Dressing** (*page 318*). Meanwhile, finely chop 6 more cooked **shrimp** and blend thoroughly with 2 tablespoons **butter** or **margarine**. Spread the Shrimp Butter onto 12 crisp **crackers**. Place 1 shrimp on each. Top with sieved **hard-cooked egg yolk**.

Cream Cheese Bits—Spread onto crispy **crackers** a mixture of 3 oz. softened **cream cheese**, 1 tablespoon minced fresh **mint leaves**, 1 tablespoon **brandy** and ¼ teaspoon **salt**. Garnish each with a tiny sprig of **parsley**.

Crispy Ham Bites—Mix together until well blended ½ cup ground, cooked **ham**, ¼ cup grated **Cheddar cheese**, ¼ cup **condensed tomato soup**, 1 tablespoon minced **onion**, ¼ teaspoon **prepared horse-radish**, ¼ teaspoon **prepared mustard**, and ⅛ teaspoon **Accent**. Spread mixture on small **bread diamonds**. Set temperature control of range at Broil. Arrange canapés on broiler rack and place rack in broiler with top of canapés 3 in. from source of heat. Broil 3 to 5 min., or until lightly browned. Serve piping hot.

Liver Sausage Rounds—Blend together 3 oz. softened **cream cheese** and ¼ teaspoon **prepared mustard**. Spread mixture on **bread rounds**. Place 1 thin slice of **tomato** on each round and season with **salt** and **pepper**. Place 1 thin slice of **Braunschweiger liver sausage** on top of each tomato slice. Sprinkle minced **parsley** around the edges and place a slice of **stuffed olive** in center.

Pastry Canapés—Prepare ½ recipe **Pastry for 1-Crust Pie** (*page 442*). Roll ⅛ in. thick. Cut into small strips or shapes. Sprinkle with grated sharp **Cheddar cheese** and **Accent**. If desired, sprinkle **poppy** or **caraway seeds** over cheese. Place on baking sheet; bake at 425°F about 10 min., or until lightly browned.

Cheese Pastry Sticks—Prepare ½ recipe **Cheese Pastry for 1-Crust Pie** (*page 443*). Roll ⅛ in. thick. Cut into small strips. If desired, sprinkle **caraway** or **poppy seeds** over pastry. Place on baking sheet; bake at 425°F about 10 min., or until lightly browned.

Seasoned Butters

Butters can be prepared hours ahead of time and refrigerated in a tightly covered container. Before using, cream to a spreading consistency.

FRESH HERB BUTTER—Cream ½ cup **butter** or **margarine** until softened. Gradually cream in 1 teaspoon **lemon** or **lime juice**. Blend 1 tablespoon fresh minced herbs, such as **chives**, **dill**, **parsley** or **mint** into the creamed mixture. *About ½ cup butter*

PERKY BUTTERS—Follow recipe for Fresh Herb Butter; omit fresh herbs. Blend in one of the following:

Anchovy Butter—1 tablespoon **anchovy paste** and ¼ teaspoon **paprika**

Horse-radish Butter—2 tablespoons **prepared horse-radish**

Lemon Butter—Increase the lemon juice to 1½ teaspoons

Mustard Butter—1 tablespoon **prepared mustard**

Parsley Butter—¼ cup minced **parsley**

Pimiento Butter—2 tablespoons minced **pimiento**

Water Cress Butter—4 tablespoons minced **water cress**

Hot Sardine Canapés

MRS. ED JENSEN, SIOUX CITY, IOWA

Set aside to drain the contents of
2 3¼ oz. cans sardines

For Sauce—Melt in top of a double boiler over simmering water
2 tablespoons butter or margarine
Blend in
1 tablespoon flour
Add gradually, stirring constantly until smooth, a mixture of
½ cup milk
⅓ cup mayonnaise
½ teaspoon vinegar
Continue to cook over simmering water until mixture thickens. Remove from heat and stir in
1 tablespoon chopped stuffed olives
1 tablespoon chopped sweet pickle
1 teaspoon chopped onion
2 teaspoons capers
Keep warm over simmering water.

For Canapés—Trim crusts from
6 slices white bread
Toast the bread on one side only.

Spread the untoasted sides with
Butter or margarine
Cut each slice into thirds. Arrange one drained sardine on each piece of bread. Spoon hot sauce over the sardine; sprinkle with
Paprika
Set temperature control of range at Broil.

Arrange canapés on broiler rack and place rack in broiler with top of canapés 3 in. from source of heat; broil about 5 min., or until canapés are slightly browned.

Serve piping hot. *1½ doz. canapés*

Cheese-Asparagus Canapés

Cook
1 pkg. (10 oz.) frozen asparagus spears
Drain if necessary. Set 8 spears aside for use in canapés. (Reserve remaining asparagus for use in other food preparation.)

Grate and set aside
2 oz. Cheddar cheese (½ cup, grated)
Prepare and set aside
Mustard Butter (page 25)
Trim crusts from
4 slices white bread
Toast the bread on one side only. Cut each slice into halves and spread the untoasted sides with the butter. Arrange one drained asparagus spear on each bread slice. If necessary, trim spears to fit. Sprinkle about one tablespoon of the grated cheese over each. Cut into halves and sprinkle with
Paprika
Set temperature control of range at Broil. Arrange canapés on broiler rack and place rack in broiler with top of canapés 3 in. from source of heat; broil 5 min., or until cheese bubbles.

Serve piping hot. *16 canapés*

▲ Summertime Melon Bowl

Set out

1 medium-size ripe cantaloupe or honeydew melon

To cut melon, use narrow, sharp-pointed knife. Mark points in a saw-toothed line at 1-in. intervals around center of melon.

Carefully cut down through marked line to center of melon. Pull halves apart. Remove and discard seedy center. Wrap one half in waxed paper and place in refrigerator for use in other food preparation. With a melon-ball cutter, scoop out balls from remaining half of melon. Wrap shell in waxed paper and place in refrigerator to chill with melon balls.

Prepare and chill in refrigerator

Watermelon balls or chunks, pitted cherries, strawberries, pineapple wedges, or any available fresh fruit

To serve, partially fill melon "bowl" with chipped ice. Impale the chilled fruit on wooden picks. Heap fruit, picks upright, on top of ice. Sprinkle over fruit

2 or 3 tablespoons lime juice

△ Pineapple Bowl

Follow ▲ Recipe; substitute a **fresh pineapple** for the melon. To prepare, cut whole pineapple into halves lengthwise through crown (spiny top). Wrap one of the halves in waxed paper and place in refrigerator, reserving for use in other food preparation. Cut out and discard core from remaining half. With a grapefruit knife or sharp paring knife, remove pineapple from its shell. Cut pineapple into chunks and use with other fresh fruit pieces. Chill fruit in refrigerator. To serve, fill the pineapple shell with the chilled fruits.

Fresh Fruit Cocktail
MRS. VIRGIL L. YOUTZ, CANTON, OHIO

The cooling fragrance of mint leaves tinges the flavor of this perfect-for-warm-weather cocktail of chilled fresh fruits.

For Mint Sirup—Measure into a small saucepan having a tight-fitting cover

1 cup water

½ cup sugar

2 tablespoons chopped fresh mint leaves

4 teaspoons lemon juice

1 teaspoon grated orange peel (page 11)

1 teaspoon grated lemon peel

Put saucepan over medium heat and stir mixture until sugar is dissolved. Bring mixture to boiling. Reduce heat, cover and simmer for 5 min. Uncover; cook 10 min. longer. Remove saucepan from heat and strain the mixture. Set aside to cool.

When sirup is cool, add

1 tablespoon chopped mint leaves

Cover and put into refrigerator for several hours or overnight. Strain before using.

For Preparing Fruit—Set out

2 slices fresh pineapple, cut 1 in. thick

Cut away rind and "eyes" and remove core. Cut the slices into small wedges. (Reserve remaining pineapple for use in other food preparation.)

Rinse, drain and set aside

1 cup fresh blueberries

With a sharp knife, remove peel and white membrane from

1 large orange

Remove sections by cutting on either side of dividing membranes; remove section by section over a bowl to save the juice. Put fruit into refrigerator to chill.

When ready to serve, carefully mix the fruit and strained mint sirup. Serve in chilled sherbet glasses garnished with **mint leaves.**

4 servings

▲ Herring Bits in Sour Cream

Drain and put into a bowl contents of
1 16-oz. jar herring fillets
Mix together and pour over herring
1 cup thick sour cream
3 tablespoons lemon juice
1 large onion (page 12), thinly sliced
1 tablespoon peppercorns
1 teaspoon salt
¼ teaspoon Accent
Carefully turn with fork to coat all pieces
evenly. Let stand in refrigerator at least 2
hrs. before serving.

Serve garnished with
Lemon slices
Paprika

About 3 cups

△ Herring and Apples in Sour Cream

Follow ▲ Recipe. Whip chilled sour cream
until it piles softly before blending in remaining ingredients. Omit peppercorns. Wash,
quarter, core and dice ½ lb. (about 2 small)
apples. Mix into herring mixture; chill.

Pickled Tuna and Sour Cream Appetizer
MRS. ED JENSEN, SIOUX CITY, IOWA

Set out a small saucepan.

Tie together in a spice bag (*page 571*)
2 bay leaves
2 teaspoons whole mixed pickling spices
Measure into the saucepan
⅓ cup wine vinegar
¼ cup water
Add the spice bag and put saucepan over
medium heat. Bring to boiling. Reduce heat
and simmer for 10 min. Remove spice bag and
set liquid aside to cool.

Drain and separate into small chunks contents of
2 7-oz. cans tuna (about 2 cups)
Rinse, cut off ends and slice thinly (discarding
seeds)
1 lemon
Cut into thin slices
2 medium-size onions (page 12)
Gently toss the onion, lemon and tuna chunks
together with the cooled liquid and
½ teaspoon salt
Spread over mixture and gently mix in
1 cup thick sour cream
Chill in refrigerator.

Serve as a dinner appetizer. Arrange chilled
lettuce on small plates. Spoon tuna mixture
onto lettuce and garnish with **parsley.**

About 8 servings

Oysters on the Half Shell

To Open Oysters—Wash thoroughly in cold
water
2 doz. shell oysters
Place flat side up and carefully open by inserting knife between edges of shell opposite
hinges. (If necessary, break off the thin edges
of the shell before inserting tip of knife.) Cut

Oysters on the Half Shell

the muscle from the top shell and remove top shell. Cut the lower part of the same muscle from the deep half of the shell, leaving oysters in the shell. Discard the top shells.

To Serve—Arrange oysters-in-the-shell on individual plates. Garnish with sprigs of **parsley** and **lemon wedges.** Serve with

Peppy Cocktail Sauce (on this page; omit onion juice and add 1 teaspoon chopped parsley and ¼ teaspoon dried tarragon)
Crackers

Clams Casino

4 servings

Shrimp with Peppy Cocktail Sauce

For Shrimp—Prepare

1½ lbs. fresh shrimp with shells (see Cooked Shrimp, page 242)
Chill in refrigerator until ready to serve.

For Peppy Cocktail Sauce—To make about 1 cup sauce, mix thoroughly in a small bowl

1 cup ketchup
1 tablespoon lemon juice
1 teaspoon onion juice
¼ teaspoon Worcestershire sauce
Few drops tabasco sauce
1 tablespoon sugar
1 tablespoon prepared horse-radish
½ teaspoon salt
¼ teaspoon Accent
Chill in refrigerator.

For Completing Cocktail—Arrange in 6 chilled sherbet glasses

Lettuce or curly endive
Arrange about 5 shrimp in each glass. Top each serving with the Peppy Cocktail Sauce.

6 servings

Clams Casino 3

Set out a 15½x10½x1-in. baking dish and fill ¼ in. deep with coarse salt.

Open (see Oysters on the Half Shell, *page 28*)

2 doz. clams
Remove clams from the half shell and drain juice from shells.

Blend together thoroughly

¼ cup butter or margarine
1 teaspoon anchovy paste
Spoon a small amount of the mixture into each shell. Cover with the clams. Sprinkle with

Lemon juice
Spoon over the clams a mixture of

¼ cup finely minced green pepper
¼ cup finely chopped onion
Season with

Salt
Pepper
Accent
Cut into small pieces

3 slices bacon
Top each clam with a few pieces of bacon. Place shells in the pan, pushing them down into the salt to keep shells from tipping.

Bake at 450°F 15 to 20 min., or until bacon is thoroughly cooked.

Serve immediately. *4 to 6 servings*

APPETIZERS in the MICROWAVE OVEN

For heating already-prepared appetizers to serve at a moment's notice the microwave method is invaluable. One of its finest qualities is the ability to heat quickly without drying out the food. Serving and clean-up are simplified when you heat the appetizers on paper plates, waxed paper or even directly on serving trays (be sure they are microwave safe).

The microwave oven recipes included here were quite successful. For the most part, however, hot appetizers involving a combination of ingredients which cook at different speeds were failures. For instance, **Shrimp-in-Bacon**, when cooked in the microwave, produced under-cooked bacon and overdone shrimp. Recipes which required pastry emerged with overcooked fillings, but the pastry still its original color and, therefore, unappetizing in appearance. Make the best use of the microwave oven by preparing these kinds of appetizers in the conventional oven ahead of time and reheating them when it is time to serve.

REMINDERS—Before preparing the recipes we do include here, review the introductory chapter, **Home Cooking in the Microwave Oven**, in the beginning of this book for other general hints and to learn how we have adapted these recipes. We have also provided an easy-to-read chart comparing the settings among different brands of microwave ovens.

Nibblers *(page 21)* 1

Use a 2-qt baking dish.

COOK butter until melted.

Add cereal-pretzel-nut mixture and toss to coat evenly. COOK for 15 min., rotating the baking dish 90 degrees every 4 min.

OVERALL COOKING TIME: 15:00

Cheese-Asparagus Canapés *(page 26)* 2

COOK bread slices on waxed paper until crisp (about 1½ min.).

Prepare asparagus spears (see **Vegetables in the Microwave Oven**).

Arrange assembled canapés in a circle on paper plates or a piece of waxed paper. COOK until cheese bubbles (about 1 min. 15 sec.).

OVERALL COOKING TIME: 3:00

Clams Casino *(page 29)* 3

Use a 2-qt. baking dish. This will hold about 1 doz. clams; reduce amounts of all ingredients by one-half.

COOK bacon until partially done *(page 161)* and crumble or cut into small pieces.

Blend together butter or margarine, anchovy paste, green pepper and onion. Spoon some of the mixture into each shell.

Puncture the outer membrane of each clam to allow trapped air to escape. Cover mixture in shell with a clam and top with more mixture. Sprinkle with lemon juice and seasonings and top with bacon pieces.

Arrange clams in a circle in the baking dish. COOK, rotating every 2 min., until bacon, onions and peppers are cooked (about 6 min.).

OVERALL COOKING TIME: 7:00

APPETIZERS in the SLOW COOKER

The slow cooker is most useful for keeping hot appetizers warm. Most of the recipes in this section are either quick-cooking or demand a combination of ingredients which are unsuitable for slow cookers. We have included two recipes, both of which can be prepared in the slow cooker, if you are going to be away from home until just before guests arrive. The **Hawaiian Coconut Chips** are particularly delicious.

REMINDERS—The recipes in this section call for the use of a 3½-quart slow cooker.

We strongly suggest you review the introductory chapter, **Home Cooking in the Slow Cooker**, in the beginning of this book for other general hints and to learn how we have adapted these recipes. We have also provided an easy-to-read chart comparing the settings among different brands of slow cookers.

Nibblers *(page 21)*

Mix cereals, pretzels and nuts in slow cooker.

Melt butter on top of the stove. Add butter and seasonings to slow cooker. Toss to coat evenly. Cover and cook on LOW for 2½ to 3½ hrs. If convenient, toss every hour. Uncover and cook 30 to 40 min. additional.

Hawaiian Coconut Chips *(page 21)*

Prepare coconut for opening as in Recipe. Let cool (it will harden slightly) and cut into chips.

Place chips in slow cooker, add salt and toss to mix. Cover and cook on HIGH for 3 to 5 hrs. Chips will be cooked and crisp when done, but not uniformly brown. For more even browning, toss every hour.

Soup Lore

Gone is the soup pot of yesteryear—the heavy iron kettle that bubbled on the cook stove the livelong day. The fire-blackened pot has gone, but its legacy remains, and soup—thick or clear and all the varieties in between—is still a national favorite. Soup making is a fine test of a homemaker's skill in striking a harmonious balance of flavors. Much of the satisfaction and special pleasure of making soup come perhaps from the simple fact that nothing is more gratifying than good soup.

ENDLESS VARIETY—Soups, usually served as a first course, are main-dish fare too. Thin, clear soups (such as broths, bouillons and consommés), fruit soups, delicate cream soups, thick hearty soups (such as chowders and bisques), winter hot or summer cold—there is no end to the variety.

REMINDERS—Always add hot, thickened tomatoes to cold milk to avoid curdling.

Thorough blending of fat and flour and cooking with the milk or cream help prevent a film of fat on cream soups. There will be a film of fat if soup is too thin.

Cream soups should be the consistency of a thin sauce. The vegetable used will determine the amount of flour needed to thicken the soup. At least ¼ cup chopped or ⅓ cup sieved vegetable per cup of thin white sauce will give a most satisfactory soup; 2 to 3 tablespoons sieved spinach per cup is a desirable proportion for cream of spinach soup. Add a little hot milk or cream if the soup is too thick or thicken with a flour-water mixture if the soup is too thin.

Instructions for clarifying soups are given in **Consommé** (*page 31*).

The electric blender is the modern soup pot—blending everything and anything into savory soups. Remember—add liquid first, usually ½ to 1 cup, then add the other ingredients.

Cool soups to lukewarm before storing in covered container in refrigerator; keep several days only.

SOUP GARNISHES—Garnishes are to soup as jewels are to the costume—a glamorous accent. They need not be elaborate. The normally stocked refrigerator will usually yield the wherewithal for garnishes that furnish a touch of enticement.

Bacon—Diced and panbroiled, supplies a touch of crispness, color and flavor.

Croutons—Provide texture contrast (see *page 65*).

Grated Cheese—Parmesan is the classic accompaniment for onion soups, but other sharp cheeses enhance flavor of chowders and other soups.

Herbs—Chervil, chives, tarragon, parsley—fresh, minced or chopped—add a flash of color.

Lemon Slices—Notched or cut in fancy shapes and set afloat in clear bouillon or consommé.

Sour Cream—Connoisseur's preference for borsch.

Vegetables—Thin, small raw pieces floating on clear soups give appealing color and flavor.

Whipped Cream—Salted or plain; perfect with cream of tomato soup.

Toasted Almonds—Sliver; garnish cream soups.

▲ Pot-on-the-Fire

The simmering soup pot, Pot-au-Feu, is part of French-American cooking traditions and the savory source of many eating pleasures. It is prepared with varied ingredients. A noble dish in its own right, Pot-au-Feu also yields stock used for other soups and for sauces.

Wipe with a clean, damp cloth

1 soup bone, cracked
3 lbs. lean beef (chuck or plate), cut in 1-in. pieces

Put into a large sauce pot or kettle with

3 qts. cold water
1½ tablespoons salt
2 teaspoons Accent

Cover sauce pot and bring water slowly to boiling. Skim. Cover, reduce heat and simmer about 4 hrs. Skim off foam as necessary.

Then add

5 carrots, washed, pared or scraped, and cut in large pieces
2 turnips, washed, pared and cut in large pieces
4 leeks (white part only), sliced
1 large onion (*page 12*), sliced
Herb bouquet (*page 11*)

Insert

2 whole cloves

in

1 medium-size onion

Add onion to kettle. Cover and bring to boiling. Reduce heat and simmer about 1½ hrs.

Strain the broth through a fine sieve. Set broth aside to cool.

When the broth is cool, put it into the refrigerator to chill. Before using in soup or sauces, remove the hardened layer of fat from the broth. (If broth is to be used immediately, skim fat from the cooled broth and reheat the broth.) The meat and vegetables removed from stock may be served as desired.

About 2½ qts. stock

⚠ Brown Stock

Follow ▲ Recipe. Cut meat from soup bone and brown meat with the beef in ¼ cup **fat** before cooking. Add to kettle with bone and proceed as in ▲ Recipe.

⚠ White Stock

Follow ▲ Recipe; substitute **veal shank** and **breast** for beef. Add one half of a disjointed ready-to-cook **chicken.**

⚠ Consommé

Follow ⚠ Recipe. The stock should be chilled in refrigerator and the hardened fat removed. In a large kettle mix into chilled stock 2 **egg whites**, slightly beaten, crushed **shell** of the eggs and 4 teaspoons cold **water.** Heat slowly to boiling, stirring constantly. Remove from heat and let stand 25 min. Strain through two thicknesses of cheesecloth.

⚠ Bouillon

Follow ⚠ Recipe; substitute **Brown Stock** for White Stock.

▲ Chicken Broth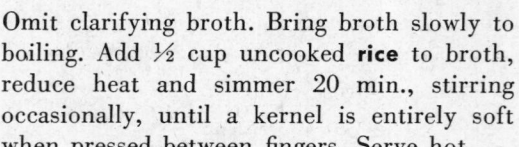

Set out a 4-qt. sauce pot or kettle having a tight-fitting cover.

Clean, rinse and disjoint

1 stewing chicken, 4 to 5 lbs., ready-to-cook weight

(If chicken is frozen, thaw according to directions on package.)

Put chicken into the sauce pot and cover with

2 qts. cold water

Cover sauce pot and bring water slowly to boiling. Skim off foam as necessary.

Add

2 or 3 stalks celery (page 12) with leaves
2 carrots, washed and pared or scraped
1 medium-size onion (page 12)
2 teaspoons salt
1½ teaspoons Accent
2 or 3 peppercorns
1 bay leaf
3 parsley sprigs

Cover and simmer 3 hrs., or until thickest pieces of chicken are tender when pierced with a fork.

Remove chicken for use in other food preparation. Strain liquid through a fine sieve and set aside to cool. When cool, put into refrigerator to chill. Remove the hardened layer of fat from the chilled broth.

To clarify broth, stir into the cold stock

1 egg white, slightly beaten
Crushed shell of the egg
1 tablespoon cold water

Heat slowly to boiling, stirring constantly. Boil gently, stirring constantly, 7 to 10 min. Remove from heat and let stand 25 min. Strain through 2 thicknesses of cheesecloth. Reheat broth and serve very hot. Garnish with **parsley.**   *About 1 qt. Chicken Broth*

⚠ Chicken Broth with Rice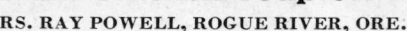

Omit clarifying broth. Bring broth slowly to boiling. Add ½ cup uncooked **rice** to broth, reduce heat and simmer 20 min., stirring occasionally, until a kernel is entirely soft when pressed between fingers. Serve hot.

⚠ Greek Chicken Soup

MRS. RAY POWELL, ROGUE RIVER, ORE.

Prepare ⚠ Recipe. When the rice is almost cooked, beat 1 **egg yolk** until thick and lemon-colored. Beat 1 **egg white** until rounded peaks are formed. Add the beaten yolk to the beaten white, and beat until well blended.

Add and beat in 1 teaspoon **lemon juice.** Add about one cup of the hot broth to the egg mixture, while stirring vigorously. Immediately blend into the hot broth and cook over low heat for 1 min. Serve immediately.

French Onion Soup with Cheese

Originated by a king, French Onion is, in the opinion of many, the king of soups. The inspiration for this noble dish came to Louis XV one night when he returned to his hunting lodge and found only onions, butter and champagne in the royal cupboard. With imperious disregard for tradition and spurred on by the pangs of hunger, Louis simply combined all ingredients and created a new masterpiece.

Set out a heavy 3-qt. saucepan having a cover.

Cut into thin slices

5 medium-size (about 1 lb.) onions (page 12)

Heat in the saucepan over low heat

3 tablespoons butter

Add the onions and cook over medium heat,

occasionally moving and turning with a spoon, until the onions are just golden in color (about 10 min.).

Blend in gradually

1½ qts. Bouillon (*page 31*) or quick meat broth (*page 13*)

Season with

½ teaspoon salt
½ teaspoon Accent
⅛ teaspoon pepper

Bring to boiling. Reduce heat, cover saucepan and simmer about 15 min.

Meanwhile, measure

1 to 2 tablespoons butter

Grate

¼ cup (1 oz.) Gruyère or Cheddar cheese

Set aside.

Set temperature control of range at Broil.

Arrange on broiler rack

6 slices French bread

Place in broiler with top of bread 3 in. from source of heat. Toast one side only. Remove and spread untoasted side of each slice with ½ to 1 teaspoon of the butter. Cut slices into halves if desired. Place slices, buttered side up, on broiler rack.

Sprinkle about 2 teaspoons of the grated cheese onto each slice. Place in broiler with top of bread about 3 in. from source of heat. Toast until cheese is melted.

Pour soup into tureen, hot soup plates or earthenware bowls. Float a toast slice on top of each serving.

Bread may be toasted lightly, floated on top of soup, and grated cheese sprinkled over toast. Serve additional grated cheese in a bowl. Accompany with

Bread sticks

6 servings

French Onion Soup with Cheese

Chilled Cucumber Soup

MRS. MARY HUGHES, PHILADELPHIA, PA.

Wash, pare and finely chop

1 medium-size cucumber

Peel, rinse, trim tops to within 3 in. of white part and finely chop

6 green onions or scallions

Finely chop

¼ cup (1 oz.) walnuts
1 sprig parsley

Mix the vegetables and nuts together.

Blend together thoroughly

1 pt. yogurt
1 cup water
½ teaspoon salt
½ teaspoon Accent

Blend the vegetable mixture into the yogurt mixture. Serve in chilled bowls. If desired garnish with thin **cucumber slices.**

4 servings

Note: To make extra-smooth soup, put water into an electric blender container. Add vegetables, nuts and seasonings. Cover container, turn on motor and blend until thoroughly mixed. Add contents of blender container to the yogurt and mix thoroughly.

Chicken Chowder

ETHELYN S. BEORGEON, OCONTO, WIS.

Set out a 6-qt. sauce pot or kettle having a tight-fitting cover.

Clean, rinse and disjoint
- **1 stewing chicken, 4 to 5 lbs. ready-to-cook weight**

Put chicken into the sauce pot and add
- **3 qts. water**
- **5 teaspoons salt**
- **2 teaspoons Accent**

Cover sauce pot and bring water slowly to boiling. Reduce heat and simmer 3 hrs., or until thickest pieces of chicken are tender when pierced with a fork. Skim off foam as necessary.

Remove chicken with a slotted spoon and set aside to cool slightly. Strain liquid through a fine sieve and set aside to cool. Remove meat from bones, cut into pieces and set aside.

Skim the fat from the cooled broth and return the broth to the sauce pot. Add to the broth
- **4 medium-size carrots, washed, pared or scraped, and diced**
- **2 medium-size potatoes, washed, pared and cubed**
- **3 stalks celery (*page 12*), chopped**
- **2 small onions (*page 12*), chopped**

Cover and bring to boiling over moderate heat. Reduce heat and simmer 20 min.

Meanwhile, remove rind from and dice
- **½ lb. salt pork**

Put the salt pork into a skillet and cook over

medium heat, occasionally moving and turning with a spoon, until lightly browned on all sides. Using a slotted spoon, remove the diced salt pork to absorbent paper.

Add to the sauce pot the chicken meat, the salt pork, and
- **2½ cups (No. 2 can) whole kernel corn**
- **4 oz. (about 1½ cups) uncooked noodles**

Cover and bring soup to boiling; reduce heat and simmer 10 min., or until vegetables and noodles are tender.

Add, stirring constantly
- **1½ quarts milk**
- **½ teaspoon white pepper**

Heat thoroughly.   *About 5 qts. soup*

Clam Chowder

A typical New England clam chowder that is fit for a gourmet.

Set out a heavy 3-qt. saucepan.

For Clam Broth—Rinse well in cold, running water
- **12 large clams**

Put clams into a large, heavy saucepan and pour in
- **3 cups water**

Cook over moderate heat until clam shells open completely. Drain the clams, reserving the broth; set broth aside.

Remove clams from shells. Cut off the hard outside of the clam (comb) and mince the clams. Set aside.

For Clam Chowder—Wash, slice thinly, and wash again, enough leeks to yield
- **¼ cup thinly sliced leek (white part only)**

Combine with
- **¼ cup minced onion (*page 12*)**
- **¼ cup diced celery (*page 12*)**

Heat in the saucepan
- **2 tablespoons butter or margarine**

Add the vegetables and cook over medium heat, occasionally moving and turning with a spoon, 6 to 8 min., or until vegetables are partially tender.

Meanwhile, wash, pare and finely dice enough potato to yield
½ cup finely diced potato
Set aside.

Scald (*page 13*)
1 cup cream
1 cup milk
When vegetables are partially tender, blend in
3 tablespoons flour
Heat until mixture bubbles. Remove from heat. Add gradually, stirring constantly, the scalded milk and cream. Return the saucepan to heat and bring mixture to boiling, stirring constantly. Cook 1 to 2 min. longer.

Remove from heat; gently stir in the clam broth, potato, and
½ teaspoon Worcestershire sauce
½ teaspoon salt
½ teaspoon Accent
⅛ teaspoon thyme
3 drops tabasco sauce
Few grains white pepper
Bring to boiling over moderate heat; reduce heat and cook very slowly 35 to 40 min., stirring frequently. Add the minced clams and cook 5 min. longer. Pour soup into a tureen or individual soup bowls. Sprinkle over top
Finely chopped parsley
Serve with **chowder biscuits** or **crackers**.

4 to 6 servings

Corn Chowder

MRS. HENRY TOWNSEND
ISLAND FALLS, ME.

Set out a 3-qt. saucepan having a tight-fitting cover.

Remove rind from and dice
¼ lb. salt pork
Put salt pork into the saucepan and cook over medium heat, occasionally moving and turning with a spoon, until slightly browned on all sides. Using slotted spoon, remove to absorbent paper.

Add to saucepan and cook over medium heat, occasionally moving and turning with a spoon, until transparent
1 medium-size onion (page 12), chopped
Wash, pare and dice enough potatoes to yield
2 cups (2 to 3 medium-size) diced potatoes
Add to the saucepan the pork, potatoes and
1 cup water
2 teaspoons salt
½ teaspoon Accent
⅛ teaspoon pepper
Cover saucepan, bring mixture to boiling, and cook 15 min., or until potatoes are tender.

Add gradually, stirring constantly
1 qt. milk
Stir in
2 cups (1-lb. can) cream-style corn
Heat thoroughly, stirring occasionally.

If desired, garnish with **parsley**.   *8 servings*

Creamy Tomato Soup, Picture-Puzzle Sandwich (page 74) and milk

Creamy Tomato Soup 4

Always a favorite of the small fry, tomato soup tempts young appetites by giving eye-appeal to the entire lunch.

Put into a 2-qt. saucepan and mix thoroughly

2½ cups (No. 2 can) tomatoes
⅓ cup finely chopped onion
3 to 4 tablespoons sugar
1 teaspoon salt
½ teaspoon Accent
½ bay leaf (optional)

Simmer for 5 min. Remove bay leaf; force mixture through sieve or food mill. Set aside.

Wash the saucepan; melt in it over low heat

2 tablespoons butter

Blend in

3 tablespoons flour
½ teaspoon salt

Increase heat to medium and cook, stirring constantly, until mixture bubbles. Remove from heat and gradually add hot tomato mixture while stirring constantly. Return mixture to heat and bring rapidly to boiling, stirring constantly. Cook 1 to 2 min. longer. Stirring constantly, gradually add the hot tomato mixture to

2 cups cold milk

Return soup to saucepan. Heat rapidly, stirring occasionally; do not boil. Serve hot with **popcorn**. *About 1½ pints soup*

Lobster Bisque 5

Prepare and set aside

5 cups quick chicken broth (page 13)

Melt in a large sauce pot or kettle over low heat

¼ cup butter or margarine

Blend in

¼ cup flour
1 teaspoon salt
½ teaspoon Accent
⅛ teaspoon pepper

Heat until mixture bubbles. Remove from heat. Add gradually, stirring constantly, 2 cups of the broth. Return the sauce pot to heat and bring rapidly to boiling, stirring constantly. Cook 1 to 2 min. longer. Remove from heat; gently stir in the remaining broth.

Add to the sauce pot

½ cup (1 medium-size) minced onion (page 12)
⅓ cup (about 2 medium-size) minced carrots
1 leek, white part only, minced
1 bay leaf

Cover and simmer over low heat about 10 min.

Meanwhile, drain and mince, reserving a few large pieces of lobster for garnish

2¼ cups (three 5-oz. cans, drained) lobster meat

Stir the minced lobster into simmering soup. Cover and simmer about 10 min. longer. Remove from heat and remove the bay leaf.

Place a food mill over a large bowl and pour soup mixture through the food mill, forcing through as much lobster as possible. Return soup to saucepan and reheat.

Beat slightly

2 egg yolks

Quickly stir about 3 tablespoons hot soup into the egg yolks. Immediately return egg-yolk

mixture to soup, stirring vigorously. Cook until well blended, about 5 min., stirring constantly. Do not boil. Add gradually, stirring in

1 cup cream

Add lobster remaining in food mill and reserved large pieces of lobster to soup. Stirring constantly, heat soup thoroughly.

6 servings

▲ Mushroom Soup

Set out a heavy 10-in. skillet and a large sauce pot or kettle having a tight-fitting cover.

Wipe with a clean, damp cloth

1 veal soup bone, cracked

Put soup bone into the sauce pot with

1½ qts. water
1½ teaspoons salt
½ teaspoon Accent
3 or 4 sprigs parsley
2 or 3 peppercorns

Bring water slowly to boiling. Skim off foam. Cover sauce pot and simmer soup about 1 hr., skimming as necessary.

Shortly before end of cooking period, cut off and discard tops, wash, pare or scrape and cut into ¼-in. slices

4 medium-size carrots (about 1 cup, sliced)

Add carrots to sauce pot, cover and simmer 15 to 20 min., or until carrots are tender.

Meanwhile, clean and slice (*page 12*)

1 lb. mushrooms

Heat in the skillet

½ cup butter or margarine

Add mushrooms with

1 small onion (*page 12*), chopped
2 tablespoons chopped parsley
1 teaspoon paprika
½ teaspoon salt

Cook slowly, occasionally moving and turning with a spoon, 5 to 8 min., or until mushrooms are lightly browned and tender; set aside.

Prepare and set aside

Croutons (1½ times recipe, *page 65*)

Remove kettle from heat. Remove and discard bone, peppercorns and parsley sprigs. Blend contents of skillet into soup. Vigorously stir ⅓ cup of the hot soup gradually into

4 egg yolks, slightly beaten

Immediately blend into hot soup. Stirring constantly, cook over low heat 2 to 3 min. (Do not overcook or allow soup to boil.) Remove immediately from heat and cover.

Combine in a bowl

1 cup thick sour cream
1 teaspoon lemon juice

Add gradually, stirring vigorously, about 1 cup hot soup to sour cream mixture. Immediately blend into the remaining hot soup. Heat thoroughly; do not boil. Serve with Croutons.

6 or 7 servings

△ Sweet Cream Mushroom Soup 14

Follow ▲ Recipe; substitute 1 cup **heavy** or **light cream** for the thick sour cream. Omit lemon juice. Add cream directly to the soup.

Oyster Stew 6

Set out a saucepan.

Scald (*page 13*)

2 cups milk
2 cups cream

Meanwhile drain, reserving liquid

1 pt. oysters

Pick over oysters to remove any shell particles.

Heat in the saucepan

¼ cup butter

Add oysters with reserved liquid. Simmer 3 min., or until oysters are plump and edges begin to curl.

Stir oyster mixture into scalded milk with

2 teaspoons salt
¼ teaspoon Accent
⅛ teaspoon pepper

Serve at once with **oyster crackers**.

6 servings

▲ Potato Soup

Every country has its own way with potato soup. In this delicious recipe the addition of sour cream reveals the touch of central Europe.

Set out a heavy 8-in. skillet.

Bring to boiling in a 3-qt. saucepan having a tight-fitting cover

1½ qts. water

Meanwhile, wash, pare and cut into 1-in. cubes

3 large (about 1½ lbs.) potatoes

Add the potatoes to boiling water with

1½ teaspoons salt

½ teaspoon Accent

Cover saucepan and cook 15 min., or until potatoes are tender when pierced with a fork.

Meanwhile, prepare, reserving fat

4 slices Panbroiled Bacon (p. 161)

Crumble cooled bacon; set aside for garnish.

Heat in the skillet

2 tablespoons reserved bacon fat

Add and cook over medium heat, occasionally moving and turning with a spoon, until the onion is transparent

2 tablespoons finely chopped onion

Blend in with the onion and fat

2 tablespoons flour

Heat until mixture bubbles and is lightly browned, stirring constantly. Remove from heat and add gradually, stirring constantly

¼ cup water

Add onion mixture to contents of saucepan and bring rapidly to boiling, stirring constantly; cook 1 to 2 min. longer.

Just before serving, vigorously stir about one cup of the hot soup, adding it gradually, into

1 cup thick sour cream

Immediately blend into hot soup. Heat thoroughly; do not boil. Garnish with crumbled bacon.   *6 servings*

△ Sweet Cream Potato Soup

Follow ▲ Recipe. Substitute **sweet cream** for sour cream, adding it directly to soup.

Split Pea Soup ⑮

Set out a large sauce pot or kettle having a tight-fitting cover.

Wash, pare or scrape and cut into ¼-in. slices

6 medium-size carrots (about 1½ cups, sliced)

Finely chop

1 medium-size (about ½ cup, chopped) onion (*page 12*)

Set vegetables aside.

Wipe with a clean, damp cloth

1 ham bone, cracked

Put bone into sauce pot with

1½ qts. water

Cover sauce pot and bring water slowly to boiling.

Meanwhile, wash thoroughly and sort

1 cup (about ½ lb.) split peas

Set peas aside.

Skim foam off the water in sauce pot. Put the carrots and onion into sauce pot and again bring water to boiling. Add peas gradually so that boiling will not stop. Add

1 teaspoon salt

½ teaspoon Accent

⅛ teaspoon pepper

Cover sauce pot and simmer about 3 hrs.

Meanwhile, prepare and set aside

Croutons (double recipe, *page 65*)

Remove and discard ham bone from kettle.

Vigorously stir about 3 tablespoons hot soup into a mixture of

2 egg yolks, slightly beaten

1 tablespoon sugar

Immediately blend into hot soup. Stirring constantly, cook over low heat 2 to 3 min. (Do not overcook or allow soup to boil.)

Set out about

1 cup milk

Blend into soup enough of the milk for consistency desired. Heat thoroughly, but do not boil. Serve immediately with the Croutons.

About 8 servings

My Own Mutton Soup, Toast Fingers (page 65)

My Own Mutton Soup 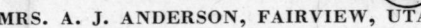 16

MRS. A. J. ANDERSON, FAIRVIEW, UTAH

Set out a 4-qt. sauce pot or kettle having a tight-fitting cover.

Wipe with a clean, damp cloth
  2 lbs. stewing lamb or mutton (half lean meat; half bones)
Put into sauce pot the lamb or mutton and
  2 qts. water
  1 medium-size onion (*page 12*), chopped
  5 teaspoons salt
  1 teaspoon Accent
  ⅛ teaspoon pepper
Cover sauce pot and bring water slowly to boiling. Cover and simmer 2 hrs., or until meat is tender when pierced with a fork. Remove meat and bones with slotted spoon. Strain broth through a fine sieve and set aside to cool.

When cool, put into refrigerator to chill. Remove hardened layer of fat from chilled broth. (If broth is to be used immediately, skim fat from cooled broth and continue with recipe.)

Remove meat from bones. Cut into pieces and put meat into refrigerator until soup is being completed.

Heat the skimmed broth and add
  ½ cup pearl barley
Cover and bring slowly to boiling. Simmer over low heat 1 hr.

Meanwhile, wash, pare and cube
  1 medium-size potato (about 1 cup, cubed)
Wash, pare or scrape, dice and set aside
  2 medium-size carrots
Add to the sauce pot the potato, carrots, meat and
  1 stalk celery (*page 12*), chopped
  2 tablespoons chopped parsley
Cover and simmer 20 min. Meanwhile, rinse and shell enough fresh peas to yield
  ¾ cup shelled peas (about ¾ lb.)
Add peas and cook until peas are tender.

If desired, float **parsley** in the soup for garnish. Accompany with
  Toast Fingers (*page 65*)
  About 2½ qts. soup

Philadelphia Pepper Pot 17
MRS. L. S. HEEBNER, NORRISTOWN, PA.

Set out a large sauce pot or kettle.

Wipe with a clean, damp cloth
- **1 lb. tripe**
- **1 veal knuckle, cracked**

Cut the tripe into small pieces (about ¼-in.) and put knuckle and tripe into the sauce pot.

Add to the sauce pot
- **3 qts. cold water**
- **2 tablespoons salt**
- **1 teaspoon Accent**
- **½ teaspoon peppercorns**
- **½ teaspoon pepper**
- **¼ teaspoon thyme**

Cover sauce pot and bring water slowly to boiling. Skim. Cover and simmer about 4 hrs., or until tripe is tender when pierced with a fork. Skim off foam as necessary.

Remove veal knuckle at end of cooking period.

Strain liquid through fine sieve; discard peppercorns and set tripe aside. Cool stock.

When stock is almost cooled, heat in sauce pot
- **⅓ cup butter**

Add and cook over medium heat, occasionally moving and turning mixture with a spoon, until onion is transparent
- **3 carrots, washed, pared or scraped and chopped**
- **2 stalks celery (page 12), chopped**
- **1 medium-size onion (page 12), sliced**
- **1 green pepper (page 12), chopped**

When onion is transparent, carefully remove vegetables from sauce pot with a slotted spoon, allowing butter or margarine to drain back into sauce pot; set vegetables aside to keep warm.

Skim the fat from the cooled soup stock.

Stir into the sauce pot, blending thoroughly with the butter
- **2 tablespoons flour**

Heat until mixture bubbles. Remove from heat. Add gradually, stirring constantly, one cup of the soup stock. Return to heat and bring mixture rapidly to boiling, stirring constantly. Cook 1 to 2 min. longer. Stir in the remaining soup stock and the vegetables. Cover and simmer about 20 min., or until vegetables are tender.

Meanwhile, remove meat from the veal knuckle. Add to sauce pot the tripe, meat and
- **1½ cups (12-oz. can) tomatoes, cut into pieces**
- **½ cup (about 1 oz.) uncooked noodles**
- **3 tablespoons chopped parsley**

Bring to boiling over moderate heat; reduce heat, cover and simmer about 10 min., or until noodles are tender.   *About 3 qts. soup*

▲ Square-Meal Vegetable-Beef Soup 18

Set out a 6-qt. sauce pot or kettle having a tight-fitting cover.

Wipe with a clean, damp cloth and cut into 1-in. pieces
- **1 lb. lean beef (chuck or plate)**

Coat meat evenly by shaking 2 or 3 pieces at a time in a plastic bag containing a mixture of
- **½ cup flour**
- **1 teaspoon Accent**
- **½ teaspoon salt**
- **⅛ teaspoon pepper**

Heat in the sauce pot
- **2 to 3 tablespoons fat**

Add meat to the sauce pot, and move and turn meat occasionally with a fork or spoon until browned on all sides.

Wipe with a clean, damp cloth
- **1 large soup bone, cracked**

Put into the sauce pot with
- **½ cup (about 1 medium-size) chopped onion (page 12)**
- **2 qts. boiling water**

Cover the sauce pot and over high heat bring water again to boiling. Reduce heat and simmer 2 to 3 hrs., or until meat is almost tender.

Remove soup bone from sauce pot.

Square-Meal Vegetable-Beef Soup

Vegetable Cream Soup and Crackers

Add to the sauce pot

2 cups diced raw potato
1 cup sliced raw carrots
1 cup sliced celery (page 12)
¼ teaspoon Accent

Cover and simmer 30 min. Remove from heat; set aside to cool. Skim fat from cooled soup.

Meanwhile, force through a sieve or food mill

2½ cups (No. 2 can) tomatoes

Stir the sieved tomatoes and their liquid into the skimmed soup with

¼ cup chopped parsley

Reheat soup and serve hot. If desired, float **celery leaves** in the soup for garnish.

10 to 12 servings

⚠ Vegetable-Noodle Soup 19

Follow ▲ Recipe. After vegetables have cooked for 20 min. add ½ cup (about 1 oz.) uncooked **noodles.** Cook 10 min., or until vegetables and noodles are tender. Cool and add tomatoes and parsley as in ▲ Recipe.

⚠ Vegetable-Rice Soup 20

Follow ▲ Recipe. After vegetables have cooked 10 to 15 min. add ⅔ cup uncooked **rice.** Continue cooking 15 to 20 min., stirring occasionally, until vegetables and rice are tender. Cool and add tomatoes and parsley as in ▲ Recipe.

Vegetable Cream Soup
(Blender Method)
PHINA W. NORMAN, PORTLAND, ORE.

(See *page 13* before using electric blender.) Set out a 1½-qt. saucepan having a cover.

Put into a blender container

1 cup water
1 cup cooked peas
½ cup cooked carrot pieces
2 stalks celery with leaves (page 12),
   cut in several pieces
1 medium-size cooked potato, cut in
   pieces
1 beef bouillon cube
1½ teaspoons salt
⅛ teaspoon white pepper
½ teaspoon Accent

Cover and blend until almost smooth.

Add contents of blender container to the saucepan and blend in

1 cup milk

Bring to boiling, stirring constantly. Reduce heat, cover and simmer about 5 min.

Garnish with **parsley.** *About 4 servings*

41

SOUPS in the MICROWAVE OVEN

All of the soups included in this section are very good; truly excellent are the cream soups. The microwave method enhances a rich, smooth texture which is characteristic of cream soups at their best.

Those the microwave oven does not do well are the long-simmering, slow-cooking soups, such as **Chicken Broth**, which cook too quickly to really develop flavor. Therefore, we have omitted them from this section.

Since most of the soups included take a relatively short time to cook, even on the stove, we did not find using the microwave a great time-saver. However, we have included the most successful recipes, should you prefer the microwave method.

REMINDERS—As you know, timing is crucial in microwave cooking.. There will be variations from our recommended times with each cook and each oven. See the chart in the introductory chapter, **Home Cooking in the Microwave Oven**, in the beginning of this book for

measured differences in timing and setting among different brands of ovens. We also recommend that the first time you prepare a recipe, you check frequently to see if the soups are done to your taste and note adjustments in timing as necessary.

As indicated in the recipes, frequent stirring is necessary with most of the soups to insure that they are evenly cooked and heated through.

One recipe, **Corn Chowder**, calls for the use of a browning skillet. This type of container does get hot in a microwave oven, so take the precaution of using a potholder.

If you plan on reheating the soups for a later meal or snack, remember that reheating takes almost as much time in the microwave as it does on top of the stove. Use whichever appliance is most convenient.

Review the introductory chapter, **Home Cooking in the Microwave Oven**, in the beginning of this book for other general hints on using the microwave oven and to learn how we have adapted these recipes.

French Onion Soup with Cheese *(page 32)*

Use a 3-qt. casserole.

Place butter in casserole and COOK until melted.

Add sliced onions and COOK, stirring every 30 sec., until wilted (about 20 min.).

Add the liquid and seasonings and stir. Cover and COOK, stirring and rotating the casserole every 5 min., until flavors are blended (about 20 min.).

After the soup is cooked, prepared the cheese as in Recipe.

The bread can also be prepared in the microwave oven. Arrange bread slices in a circle on waxed paper or a plate. COOK to crisp bread (about 1 min.). Butter bread, top with grated cheese and COOK until cheese melts (about 30 sec.).

Serve as in Recipe.

OVERALL COOKING TIME: 23:30

Clam Chowder *(page 34)*

You will need a baking dish or large pie plate for opening the clams, a small casserole for scalding the milk and cream and 3-qt. casserole for the chowder.

For Clam Broth—Clams open quickly and easily in the microwave oven. Rinse clams and arrange them in a circle or around the sides of the baking dish. Cover the dish with plastic wrap. COOK until clams open (about 3 min.). Drain and reserve the liquid from the clams, adding water now as necessary to complete the broth as in Recipe.

For Clam Chowder—Put milk and cream in a small casserole and COOK until scalded (about 6 min.).

In the large casserole, COOK until melted 3

tablespoons butter(instead of 2). Add the leek, onion and celery and COOK, stirring every 30 sec., until vegetables are partially tender (about 2 min.). Blend in flour and COOK, stirring every 30 sec., until mixture bubbles (about 3 min.).

Add the milk-cream mixture, one-third at a time; stir and COOK 1 min. after each addition. Then stir in the broth, potato and seasoning. SLOWCOOK, stirring every 2 or 3 min., until potatoes are tender (about 10 min.).

Add the clams and SLOWCOOK until heated through (about 1 min.).

Serve as in Recipe.

OVERALL COOKING TIME: 28:00

Corn Chowder *(page 35)*

Use a 3-qt. covered casserole for the soup, a browning skillet for the salt pork and a bowl.

Combine milk and corn in bowl and set aside.

COOK diced salt pork in the browning skillet, moving and turning it every minute, until pork is slightly crisp (about 6 min.). Remove pork to absorbent paper. You may drain and discard some of the fat, if you prefer.

Add chopped onion to remaining pork fat in browning skillet. COOK, stirring every 45 sec., until transparent (1 to 2 min.). Transfer to casserole.

Add diced potatoes, reserved pork, water and seasonings to casserole. Cover and COOK until potatoes are tender (about 9 min.). Add milk-corn mixture. COOK, stirring every minute, until thoroughly heated (about 3 min.).

Serve as in Recipe.

OVERALL COOKING TIME: 20:00

Creamy Tomato Soup *(page 36)* **4**

Set out a 2-qt. casserole and a bowl.

COOK tomato mixture to simmer (about 2 min.). Transfer to bowl. Wash casserole.

COOK butter in casserole until melted. Blend in four and salt; COOK until mixture bubbles (about 1 min.).

Add reserved tomato mixture, one-third at a time; stir thoroughly and COOK 2 min. after each addition.

Add the milk and COOK, stirring every minute, until heated (about 3 min.). Cover and COOK to simmer (about 3 min.). Do not boil.

Serve as in Recipe.
OVERALL COOKING TIME: 15:00

Lobster Bisque *(page 36)* **5**

Use a 3-qt. casserole.

Melt butter. Blend in flour and seasonings (except bay leaf) and COOK, stirring every minute, until mixture bubbles (about 3 min.).

Add half the broth and COOK, stirring every 3 min., until mixture boils (about 6 min.). Add remaining broth and COOK, stirring every minute, until mixture boils (about 10 min.).

Add vegetables and bay leaf and SLOWCOOK until wilted (about 5 min.).

Add lobster and SLOWCOOK to heat (about 5 min.).

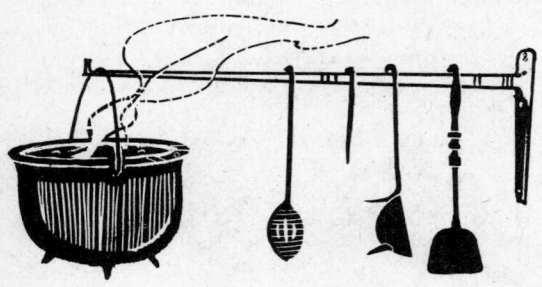

Continue as in Recipe. After adding egg yolk-soup mixture, COOK, stirring every minute, until thoroughly heated (about 3 min.). Do not boil.

Add cream and remaining lobster as in Recipe. COOK, stirring every minute, until soup is thoroughly heated, but not boiling (about 2 min.).

Serve as in Recipe.
OVERALL COOKING TIME: 34:00

Oyster Stew *(page 37)* **6**

Set out a 2-qt. Casserole and a baking dish.

Combine milk and cream in casserole and COOK until milk is scalded (about 6 min.).

Prepare oysters as in Recipe, being sure to puncture the outer membrane of each oyster to allow trapped air to escape.

Add butter to baking dish and melt. Add oysters and reserved liquid and stir. COOK until edges of oysters curl (about 5 min.).

Stir oyster mixture into milk-cream mixture, add seasonings and COOK until heated thoroughly (about 5 min.).

Serve as in Recipe.
OVERALL COOKING TIME: 16:00

Vegetable Cream Soup *(page 41)* **7**
(Blender Method)

Use a 2-qt. casserole.

Transfer vegetable blend to casserole and stir in milk. COOK, stirring every minute, until soup begins to simmer (about 6 min.). Cover and COOK 2 min.

Serve as in Recipe.
OVERALL COOKING TIME: 8:00

SOUPS in the SLOW COOKER

The slow cooker is at its best with the traditionally long-simmering soups, really extracting and blending the flavors. Most of the soups in this section are of that variety. Cream soups and quick-cooking soups do not really take advantage of the slow cooker's assets. However, we do include two soups using milk, the popular **Clam Chowder** and **Corn Chowder,** which emerged from the slow cooker with an excellent flavor.

Using the slow cooker can save time in the preparation of many soups, as steps can often be combined or even omitted.

Some of the recipes call for ingredients to be browned or sauteed before being introduced into the soup. Although not essential when using the slow cooker, we strongly recommend that you do not skip this step. The **French Onion Soup with Cheese**, for instance, has a much richer flavor if the onions are lightly sauteed first. Some of the recipes call for a flour-butter thickening. This step can be done using the slow cooker, if no other appliance is available. Set the cooker on HIGH, melt the butter, stir in the flour as directed. However, it

takes about 30 minutes for the flour to lose its rawness. This process takes only about 5 to 10 minutes in a skillet on the stove and does not seem to us worth the difference in time simply to avoid the use of an extra pot. This is also the case when browning the meat for the **Square-Meal Vegetable-Beef Soup.** While it can be done in the slow cooker in about 20 to 30 minutes, it is quicker and more efficient to brown it on the stove, if possible.

REMINDERS—Use the smaller (3½-quart) pot unless specified otherwise.

If the pot, whether large or small, is full, the slow-cooking times are about the same. If the pot is only half-full (if you are using a 4-quart pot for a 2-quart recipe), then cooking times must be adjusted downward.

Times indicated in the recipes are minimum cooking times; however, soups can be held on the LOW setting for much longer periods without damaging flavor.

See the chart in the introductory chapter, **Home Cooking in the Slow Cooker,** in the beginning of this book for variations in temperature and setting among different brands of slow cookers. We also suggest that you review the entire section for general hints on slow cooking and to learn how we have adapted these recipes.

Pot-on-the-Fire *(page 31)*

This recipe requires a 5-qt. slow cooker; for a smaller pot, halve the recipe but use the same slow-cooking time.

Combine all ingredients in slow cooker. Cover and cook on HIGH for 5 hrs., then on LOW for 2 to 3 hrs. *Or,* cook on LOW only for 10 to 11 hrs.

Complete soup as described.

Brown Stock *(page 31)*

Follow **1** Recipe. Brown the meat as in ⚠ Recipe and add to slow cooker.

White Stock *(page 31)*

Follow **1** Recipe with substitutions as in ⚠ Recipe.

Consommé *(page 31)*

Follow **3** Recipe and complete as in ⚠ Recipe.

Bouillon *(page 31)*

Follow **4** Recipe with substitution as in ⚠ Recipe.

Chicken Broth *(page 32)*

In order to fit all of the ingredients in a 5-qt. slow cooker, a smaller chicken (3 to 4 lbs.) must be used.

Combine disjointed chicken, water and all other ingredients in slow cooker. Cover and cook on HIGH for 5 hrs., then on LOW for 2 to 4 hrs. *Or,* cook on LOW only for 10 to 11 hrs.

Complete broth as in ▲ Recipe.

Chicken Broth with Rice *(page 32)*

Follow **6** Recipe with changes as in ⚠ Recipe, except cook rice separately and add to clarified broth. Heat thoroughly.

Greek Chicken Soup *(page 32)*

Follow **6** Recipe. Cook rice separately and add to hot chicken broth.

Follow ⚠ Recipe for preparing egg and lemon mixture; add to slow cooker, stirring. Cover and cook on HIGH until thoroughly heated. Return to LOW until serving time.

French Onion Soup with Cheese *(page 32)*

For the richest flavor, first sauté the onions in a large skillet as in Recipe.

Transfer to slow cooker and add the bouillon and seasonings. Cover and cook on HIGH for 4 hrs., then on LOW for 1 to 3 hrs. *Or,* cook on LOW only 7 to 9 hrs.

Prepare cheese and bread and serve as directed in Recipe.

Chicken Chowder *(page 34)*

This recipe will fit in a 5-qt. slow cooker if a smaller chicken (3 to 4 lbs.) is used. For a smaller pot, halve the recipe but use the same slow-cooking times.

Combine chicken, water, salt, Accent, carrots, potatoes, celery and onions in slow cooker. Cover and cook on HIGH for 5 hrs., then on LOW 3 to 5 hrs. *Or,* cook on LOW only 11 to 13 hrs.

To complete the soup, remove the chicken and vegetables, strain the broth, skim the fat and prepare the chicken meat as in Recipe.

Cook noodles separately.

Prepare salt pork as in Recipe.

Return the chicken meat, vegetables and salt pork to the pot with the broth. Add corn and cooked noodles. Add milk with pepper gradually, stirring constantly. Cook on HIGH until thoroughly heated (about 20 min.). Return to LOW until serving time.

Clam Chowder *(page 34)*

For Clam Broth— Prepare clam broth according to recipe.

For Clam Chowder— Sauté vegetables as in

Recipe. (To sauté in slow cooker, see **Home Cooking in the Slow Cooker** in the beginning of this book.)

Meanwhile, scald the milk and cream.

Add flour to vegetables as in Recipe.

Combine scalded milk and cream, vegetables, potato, clam broth and seasonings in slow cooker. Stir to blend ingredients.

Add minced clams. Cover and cook on LOW for 5 to 6 hrs.

Serve as in Recipe.

Corn Chowder *(page 35)*

Cook the salt pork separately on the stove as in Recipe.

For richer flavor, onions may also be sautéed on the stove. (See **Home Cooking with the Slow Cooker** in the beginning of this book.)

Combine all ingredients, including milk and corn, in slow cooker. Cover and cook on HIGH for 2½ to 3½ hrs., then cook on LOW for 3 to 4 hrs. *Or,* cook on LOW only for 8 to 9 hrs.

Serve as in Recipe.

Mushroom Soup *(page 37)* 13

Preparation of this soup is greatly simplified using the slow cooker as the mushrooms need not be precooked.

Combine veal bone, water, carrots, mushrooms, butter and seasonings in slow cooker. Cover and cook on HIGH for 3 hrs., then on LOW for 3 to 4 hrs. *Or,* cook on LOW only 8 to 9 hrs.

Remove and discard bone, peppercorns and parsley sprigs.

Prepare egg yolks as in Recipe; stir into soup. Cook a few minutes on LOW to heat through.

Prepare sour cream-lemon juice mixture as in Recipe. Add to slow cooker, stirring constantly, until thoroughly heated. Do not boil.

Prepare croutons and serve as in Recipe.

Sweet Cream Mushroom Soup *(page 37)*

Follow 13 Recipe with changes as in △ Recipe.

Split Pea Soup *(page 38)*

This recipe requires at least a 5-qt. slow cooker. For a smaller pot, halve the recipe but use the same slow-cooking times.

Combine vegetables, ham bone, water and seasonings in slow cooker. Cover and cook on HIGH for 4 hrs., then on LOW for 3 to 4 hrs. *Or,* cook on LOW only for 9 to 10 hrs.

Remove ham bone.

Prepare and add egg yolks as in Recipe. Cook on HIGH to heat through (about 5 min.).

Add milk and cook on HIGH until thoroughly heated (about 20 min.). Reset to LOW until serving time.

Prepare croutons and serve as in Recipe.

My Own Mutton Soup *(page 39)* 16

This recipe requires a 5-qt. slow cooker. For a

smaller pot, halve the recipe but use the same slow-cooking times.

Combine meat, water, onion, potatoes, carrots, celery, peas and seasonings in slow cooker. Cover and cook on HIGH for 4 hrs. *Or,* on LOW for 7 to 8 hrs.

Remove meat and set aside as in Recipe. Strain and skim fat from broth. Return broth to cooker and heat on HIGH. When broth is hot (about 20 min.), add barley and cook on HIGH until barley is soft (about 35 min.).

Serve as in Recipe.

Philadelphia Pepper Pot *(page 40)*

This recipe requires a 5-qt. slow cooker. For a smaller pot, halve the recipe but use the same cooking times. Using the slow cooker for this soup really cuts down on preparation time.

Sauté carrots, celery, onion, green pepper as in Recipe. Prepare flour-butter mixture as in Recipe. Transfer both to slow cooker.

Add tripe, knuckle, water and seasonings and

stir to mix thoroughly. Cover and cook on LOW for 8 to 9 hrs.

Meanwhile, prepare noodles on top of the stove.

Remove veal knuckle; strain and skim the stock, discarding the peppercorns, return to the slow cooker the stock, vegetables, tripe and meat from the veal knuckle.

Add tomatoes, noodles and parsley and cook on HIGH until noodles are thoroughly heated.

Vegetable-Noodle **19** Soup *(page 41)*

Follow **18** Recipe with changes as in ⚠ Recipe, except precook noodles on top of the stove and add to slow cooker with the tomatoes and parsley.

Cook on HIGH until thoroughly heated.

Serve as in Recipe.

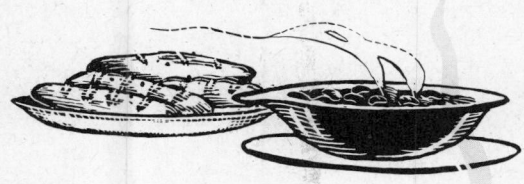

Square-Meal Vegetable-Beef Soup *(page 40)* **18**

This recipe requires a 5-qt. slow cooker. For a smaller pot, halve the recipe but use the same slow-cooking times.

Combine browned beef (see **Home Cooking in the Slow Cooker** in the beginning of this book), soup bone, onion, water, potatoes, carrots, celery and the ¼ teaspoon Accent in slow cooker. Cover and cook on HIGH for 2 hrs., then on LOW for 2 to 4 hrs. *Or,* cook on LOW only for 6 to 8 hrs.

Skim the fat and add tomatoes and parsley as in Recipe. Cook on HIGH until thoroughly heated (about 30 min.).

Serve as in Recipe.

Vegetable-Rice **20** Soup *(page 41)*

Follow **18** Recipe with changes as in ⚠ Recipe, except precook rice on top of the stove and add to soup with tomatoes and parsley.

Cook on HIGH until thoroughly heated.

Serve as in Recipe.

BREADS

Bread and life, home, and hospitality are inextricably associated in the human imagination and experience. Old as history, breadmaking was one of the first culinary arts practiced—and at a time when home itself was little more than a few flat stones arranged round a fire. Now most of the peoples of the earth have breads characteristically their own. In our own country we have no single traditional bread. We have, instead, welcomed the traditions of all the peoples that have come here and made them our own. Made with or without leavening, bread appears in a hundred different, delightful guises—as soft loaves and crusty loaves, holiday breads and coffee cakes, waffles, griddlecakes, popovers, muffins and doughnuts, and in other forms too numerous to mention.

YEAST BREADS

YEAST grows in the presence of a given amount of moisture and sugar at a temperature of about 80°F, producing in the process tiny bubbles of carbon dioxide gas which leaven the bread dough. A dough must be leavened to rise and become light.

Compressed Yeast (*moist cake*)—Grayish tan though may be slightly browned at edges; breaks with a clean edge and crumbles easily between the fingers when fresh; must be kept in refrigerator and used within a week for best results; soften in lukewarm liquid (80°F to 85°F).

Active Dry Yeast—May be kept without refrigeration; to obtain best results use before date on package expires; one package when softened has the leavening power of one cake compressed yeast; soften in warm water (110°F to 115°F) only.

FLOUR—All-purpose flour is used for breadmaking in the home. The moisture content of flour varies with changes in humidity and also from one flour to another. To allow for this difference and to obtain the desired consistency of the dough, indefinite amounts of flour are given in recipes.

A small amount of flour (about 1 cup) is added to the fat-liquid mixture before the softened yeast is added to prevent the yeast from becoming coated with fat. Fat tends to retard the growth of yeast.

LIQUID—Water and milk are the liquids most commonly used in bread doughs. Fluid milk must be scalded before using in breadmaking. Evaporated milk does not need to be scalded because it has been preheated. The liquid must be hot enough to

melt the shortening when added to shortening-sugar-salt mixture. For optimum yeast growth, this mixture, plus a small amount of flour, must be *lukewarm* (80°F) when softened yeast is added.

REFRIGERATOR DOUGHS are richer and sweeter than plain bread dough and can be successfully kept in the refrigerator (45°F to 50°F) three to four days. Place dough in the refrigerator immediately after mixing and kneading or after the first rising period (be sure it does not rise too much). Dough must be punched down occasionally if it rises during refrigeration. The dough is greased and well covered to keep the surface of the dough moist and elastic. When ready to bake, remove dough from refrigerator, shape, allow to rise until light and doubled before baking.

KNEAD DOUGH by folding opposite side over toward you. Using heels of hands, gently push dough away (see photo 1). Give it a one-quarter turn. Repeat process rhythmically until the dough is smooth and elastic, 5 to 8 min., using as little

additional flour as possible. Always turn the dough in the same direction.

RISING—When dough looks double its original size, test by gently pressing two fingers into the dough; if dent remains, dough has doubled and is light (see photo 2). Punch down doubled dough with fist (see photo 3); pull edges in to center and turn dough completely over in bowl. Dough is either allowed to rise again or it is shaped.

SHAPING LOAVES—Form dough into a smooth round ball and with a sharp knife, cut dough into halves. With fingers flatten one half of the dough (see photo 4) and form it into a 9x7x1-in. oblong. The width should be about the same as the length of bread pan (see photo 5). Fold narrow ends to center of oblong, overlapping slightly (see photo 6). Press each end down firmly; shape evenly. Seal dough into shape by pinching center fold and ends. Round top of loaf and place sealed edge down, in prepared pan. Repeat for other half of dough. Cover loaves and let rise until doubled.

A Check-List for Making Sucessful Yeast Breads

(See FOR THESE RECEIPES—WHAT TO USE, HOW TO DO IT and OVEN TEMPERATURES on *pages 10–13*.)

√ **Read again** "It's Smart To Be Careful—There's No Substitute for Accuracy" (*page 10*).

√ **Prepare pan**—grease only bottom of pan or lightly grease baking sheet. If recipe directs, "Set out pan or baking sheet," do not grease. Some rich yeast doughs should be baked in lightly greased pans.

√ **Test** for lukewarm liquid (80°F to 85°F): a drop placed on wrist will feel neither hot nor cold.

√ **Apply baking tests** when minimum baking time is up. Yeast breads are done when they are golden brown and sound hollow when tapped lightly (see photo on *page 48*).

√ **Remove rolls and loaves** from pans as they come from the oven, unless otherwise directed. Set on cooling racks to cool.

√ **Keep tops** of yeast loaves and rolls soft by immediately brushing with butter or margarine as they come from the oven. For a crisp crust, brush loaves and rolls before baking with milk or a mixture of egg yolk and water.

√ **Store bread** when completely cooled—Wrap in moisture-vapor-proof material and store in freezer (it will remain fresh for several weeks) or wrap in waxed paper, aluminum foil or moisture-vapor-proof material and store at room temperature.

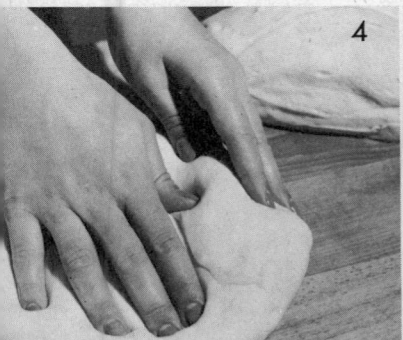
4

5

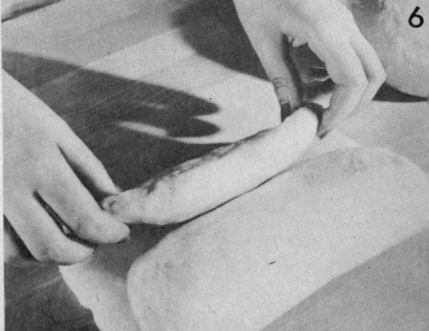
6

▲ Yeast Rolls 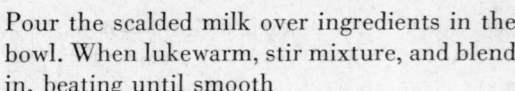 to 5

Scald (*page 13*)
> **2 cups milk**

Meanwhile, soften
> **2 pkgs. active dry yeast**

in
> **½ cup warm water, 110°F to 115°F (Or if using compressed yeast, soften 2 cakes in ½ cup lukewarm water, 80°F to 85°F)**

Let stand 5 to 10 min.

Meanwhile, put into a large bowl
> **½ cup sugar**
> **6 tablespoons shortening**
> **2 teaspoons salt**

Pour the scalded milk over ingredients in the bowl. When lukewarm, stir mixture, and blend in, beating until smooth
> **1 cup sifted flour**

Stir softened yeast and add, mixing well.

Measure
> **5 to 6 cups sifted flour**

Add about one-half the flour to the yeast mixture and beat until very smooth.

Beat in
> **2 eggs, well beaten**

Then beat in enough remaining flour to make a soft dough. Turn dough onto a lightly floured surface and allow it to rest 5 to 10 min. before starting to knead.

1 *Fantans:* Roll dough into rectangle ¼ in. thick. Brush with melted butter or margarine. Cut 1½-in. strips. Stack 7. Cut 1½-in. pieces. Place in muffin-pan wells (bottoms greased).

 Parker House: Roll dough into round ¼ in. thick. Cut with floured 2½-in. cutter. Brush with melted butter and margarine. Make off-center crease. Fold smaller side over and seal.

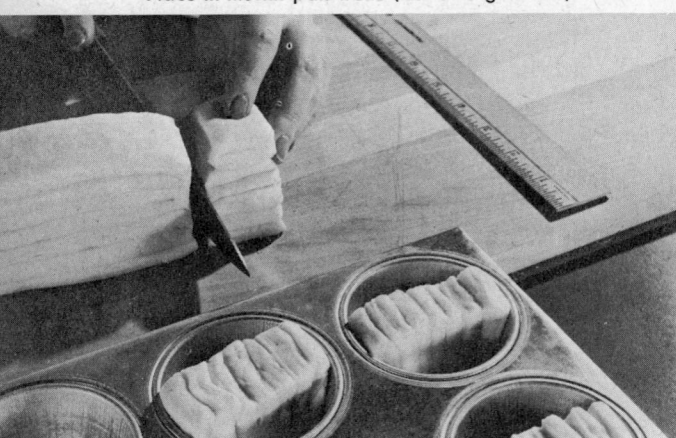

Bowknots: Roll dough into rectangle ¼ in. thick. Cut off strips ½ in. wide, 4 to 5 in. long. With hands, roll and stretch the dough into longer strips. Twist and tie strips into knots.

Crescents: Roll dough into 9-in. rounds, ¼ in. thick. Brush with melted butter or margarine. Cut into 8 wedges. Roll each wedge from the wide end. Seal firmly. Form crescents.

Knead (*page 43*). Form dough into a large ball and place it in a greased, deep bowl just large enough to allow dough to double. Turn dough to bring greased surface to top. Cover with waxed paper and towel and let stand in a warm place (about 80°F) until dough is doubled (about 1 hr.).

Punch down dough with fist; pull edges of dough in to center and turn dough completely over in bowl.* Cover and let rise again until almost doubled (about 45 min.). Again punch down the dough and turn it onto a lightly floured surface. Cover and allow the dough to rest 5 to 10 min.

Follow suggestions for the shaping of rolls (see photos), using amount needed for a single baking. Place rolls about 1 in. apart on greased baking sheets. Brush with

Melted butter or margarine

Cover and let rise again 15 to 25 min. or until dough is light.

Bake at 425°F 15 to 20 min.

4½ to 5 doz. rolls

Note: This dough may be kept 3 days in the refrigerator. Grease top of dough and cover. Punch down dough occasionally. Remove enough for a single baking and return remainder to refrigerator immediately. When ready to use, shape rolls and let stand at room temperature for 1 hr. or until light.

Cloverleaf: With hands, shape dough into rolls 1 in. thick. Cut off bits of dough and form balls about 1 in. in diameter. Place three balls in each muffin-pan well (bottoms greased).

 Butterflies: Roll dough into rectangle ¼ in. thick, 6 in. wide. Brush with melted butter or margarine. Roll, starting with long side. Cut into 2-in. pieces. Press with knife handle.

Clothespins: Roll dough into rectangle ¼ in. thick. Cut strips ½ in. wide, 6 in. long. Roll and stretch into longer strips. Wrap around greased clothespins, edges touching.

Snails: Roll dough into rectangle ¼ in. thick. Cut off strips ½ in. wide and 4 to 5 in. long. With hands, roll and stretch into longer strips. Coil each strip around index finger.

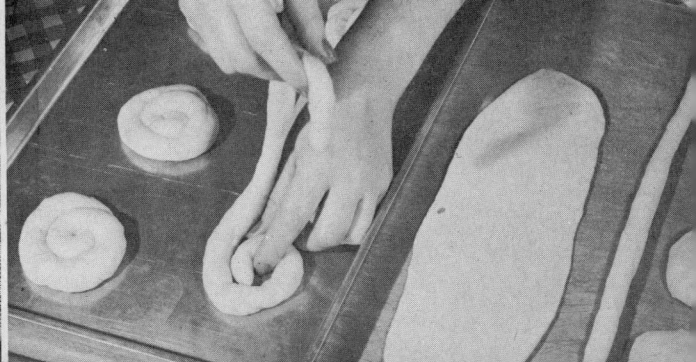

Cinnamon Rolls

⚠ Cinnamon Rolls 4

Follow ▲ Recipe (*page 44*) to shaping process. Use one third of dough and roll into a rectangle ¼ in. thick. Brush with melted **butter** or **margarine**. Sprinkle with a mixture of ⅔ cup **sugar**, 2 teaspoons **cinnamon** and ⅓ cup seedless **raisins**. Beginning with longer side, roll dough; press edges to seal. Cut roll into 1-in. slices; place, cut-side down, in a greased pan or muffin-pan wells. Brush with melted butter or margarine. Bake at 350°F 25 to 30 min.

⚠ Pecan Rolls 5

Follow ▲ Recipe (*page 44*) to shaping process. Lightly grease bottoms of about 24 muffin-pan wells. Cream together ½ cup **butter** or **margarine,** softened, 1 cup firmly packed **brown sugar** and 1½ teaspoons **cinnamon**. Spread one half of the creamed mixture in bottom of wells. Arrange ½ cup (about 2 oz.) **pecan halves** over mixture and set aside.

Use one half of the dough; roll into a rectangle ½ in. thick. Spread remaining one half of creamed mixture on dough and sprinkle with ½ cup (about 2 oz.) chopped **pecans**. Beginning with longer side, roll dough and press

edges to seal. Cut roll into slices ¾ to 1 in. thick and place, cut side down, in muffin pan-wells. Cover and let rise until doubled.

Bake at 350°F 25 to 30 min. Invert pans on cooling racks. Allow to stand a few seconds before lifting off pans. Cool, pecan side up.

⚠ Coffee Braid

Follow ▲ Recipe (*page 44*). Sift ¼ teaspoon **mace** with the first flour addition. Mix 1 teaspoon grated **lemon peel** (*page 11*) and ½ cup seedless **raisins**; mix into batter before last flour addition. After second rising, divide dough into 3 equal portions. Roll each into a strip about 14 in. long. Braid strips together, tucking open ends under. Cover and let rise about 45 min., or until doubled.

Bake at 350°F 35 to 40 min. While warm, spread with frosting made by blending 1 cup **confectioners' sugar**, 2 tablespoons warm **water** and ½ teaspoon **vanilla extract**. Top with candied **cherries, pecan halves** and bits of candied **citron**.

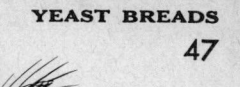

⚠ Apple Kuchen

Follow ▲ Recipe (*page 44*) to shaping process. Pat about one third of the dough, ¾ in. thick, into a greased 9-in. round pan. Brush surface of dough with 1 tablespoon melted **butter** or **margarine**. Wash, pare and thinly slice 2 tart **apples** and arrange in circles starting at center of the dough. Sprinkle apple slices with a mixture of ⅓ cup **sugar**, ½ teaspoon **cinnamon** and 2 tablespoons **currants** or seedless **raisins.** Cover and let rise until doubled.

Bake, covered with greased paper for first 10 min., at 375°F 20 to 30 min.

⚠ Prune-Nut Coffee Cake

MRS. H. G. PUREFOY
WEATHERFORD, TEXAS

Grease bottom of 10-in. tubed pan. Set out ¾ cup chopped **nuts.** Prepare 24 (about ½ lb.) **prunes** (see Stewed Prunes, *page 494*). Prepare ½ ▲ Recipe (*page 44*). Follow ▲ Recipe to shaping process.

Roll dough ¼ in. thick into a rectangle 18x12-in. Cut into 3-in. squares. Shape each square into a ball around a cooked, pitted prune, pinching to seal edges. Dip balls into ½ cup melted **butter** or **margarine.** Then roll balls in a mixture of 1 cup firmly packed **brown sugar** and 1½ teaspoons **cinnamon.** Arrange 8 coated balls in two rows in the pan. Sprinkle layer with one third of the nuts. Top with 8 more balls. Sprinkle with one half of the remaining nuts. Top with the 8 remaining balls and sprinkle with the remaining nuts. Cover and let rise about 45 min., or until doubled.

Bake at 375°F 35 min., or until golden brown. Let stand in pan on a cooling rack 5 min. before removing. Cover with a cooling rack. Invert and transfer to serving plate.

⚠ Hot Cross Buns

Prepare one-half ▲ Recipe (*page 44*). Sift 1 teaspoon **cinnamon** and ¼ teaspoon **allspice** with the first flour addition. Mix together ½ cup (about 3 oz.) coarsely chopped **candied citron** and 1 cup (about 5 oz.) **currants.** Stir in after addition of the egg. Follow ▲ Recipe to shaping process. Form dough into a long roll 2 in. in diameter. Cut crosswise into 1½-in. pieces. Tuck under ends of each piece to make a smooth, round bun. Place buns on baking sheet about 1 in. apart. With lightly greased knife or scissors, cut a deep cross in top of each bun. Brush tops with **butter** or **margarine.** Cover and let rise 15 to 25 min., or until light.

Bake at 425°F 12 to 15 min., or until buns are golden brown.

While buns are baking, blend together ½ cup plus 2 tablespoons sifted **confectioners' sugar,** 2 teaspoons **water** and ¼ teaspoon **vanilla extract.**

Remove buns from baking sheet to cooling rack. Cool buns slightly; using a spoon, drizzle frosting onto cross on each bun.

Hot Cross Buns

▲ White Bread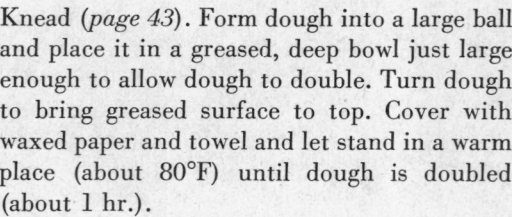

Two 9½x5¼x2¾-in. loaf pans will be needed.

Scald (*page 13*)
> **2 cups milk**

Meanwhile, soften
> **1 pkg. active dry yeast**

in
> **¼ cup warm water, 110°F to 115°F (Or if using compressed yeast, soften 1 cake in ¼ cup lukewarm water, 80°F to 85°F)**

Let yeast stand 5 to 10 min.

Meanwhile, put into a large bowl
> **2 tablespoons sugar**
> **1½ tablespoons shortening**
> **2½ teaspoons salt**

Pour scalded milk over ingredients in bowl. When lukewarm, stir mixture and blend in, beating until smooth
> **1 cup sifted flour**

Stir softened yeast and add, mixing well.

Measure
> **5 to 6 cups sifted flour**

Add about one-half the flour to the yeast mixture and beat until very smooth. Then beat in enough remaining flour to make a soft dough. Turn dough onto a lightly floured surface, and let rest 5 to 10 min.

Knead (*page 43*). Form dough into a large ball and place it in a greased, deep bowl just large enough to allow dough to double. Turn dough to bring greased surface to top. Cover with waxed paper and towel and let stand in a warm place (about 80°F) until dough is doubled (about 1 hr.).

Punch down dough with fist; pull edges of dough in to center and turn dough completely over in bowl. Cover and let rise again until almost doubled (about 45 min.).

Grease bottoms of the loaf pans.

Punch down dough and turn onto a lightly floured surface. Divide into two equal portions and form into smooth balls. Cover and allow to rest 5 to 10 min. Shape into loaves (*page 43*). Place in the greased loaf pans. Cover and let rise until dough is doubled (about 1 hr.).

Bake at 400°F about 50 min., or until loaves are golden brown.

Cool and store as directed (*page 43*).
> *Two 1-lb. loaves bread*

White Bread: Place bread pans on center oven rack so that they do not touch each other.

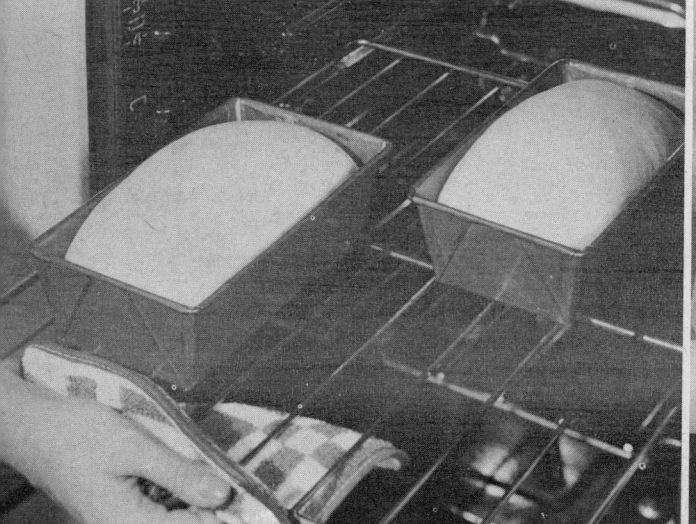

Tap sides or bottom of each loaf of bread. A hollow sound indicates that the bread is done.

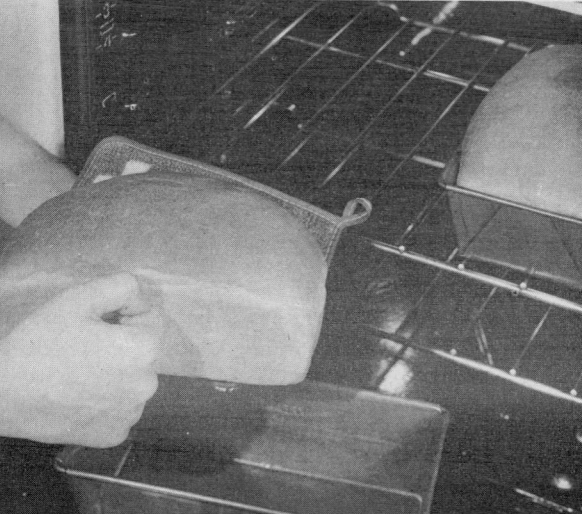

△ **Whole Wheat Bread**

JOYCE GRAHAM, OMAHA, NEBR.

Follow ▲ Recipe. Increase milk to 2¼ cups. Increase yeast to 2 pkgs. active dry yeast or 2 cakes compressed yeast softened in ½ cup water. Substitute ¼ cup **honey** for the sugar. Increase shortening to ¼ cup and salt to 1 tablespoon. Substitute 1 cup **whole wheat flour** for the cup of sifted flour. Decrease the measured sifted flour to 4 cups, and measure 3 cups whole wheat flour. Add the whole wheat flour and ½ cup of the sifted flour to the yeast mixture. Then beat in enough of the remaining sifted flour to make a soft dough. Proceed through remaining steps of ▲ Recipe.

Bake at 350°F about 45 min., or until loaves are golden brown.

Oatmeal Bread—a wonderful lunch-box treat with steaming hot coffee

Oatmeal Bread ③

Two 9½x5¼x2¾-in. loaf pans will be needed.

Soften
>   **2 pkgs. active dry yeast**

in
>   **½ cup warm water, 110°F to 115°F (Or if using compressed yeast, soften 2 cakes in ½ cup lukewarm water, 80°F to 85°F)**

Let stand 5 to 10 min.

Meanwhile, put into a large bowl
>   **1 cup uncooked rolled oats**
>   **⅔ cup molasses**
>   **½ cup shortening**
>   **1 tablespoon salt**

Pour over ingredients in the bowl
>   **1 cup hot double-strength coffee beverage** (*page 13*)
>   **½ cup boiling water**

When lukewarm, stir mixture and blend in, beating until thoroughly mixed
>   **1 cup sifted flour**

Stir the softened yeast and add, mixing well.

Measure
>   **4½ cups sifted flour**

Add about one-half the flour to the yeast mixture and beat until well blended.

Beat in
>   **2 eggs, well beaten**

Beat in enough of the remaining flour to make a soft dough. Turn into a greased bowl. Turn dough to bring greased surface to top. Cover with waxed paper and a towel and put into refrigerator to chill at least two hours.

Grease bottoms of the loaf pans.

Turn dough onto lightly floured surface. Divide into two equal portions and form into smooth balls. Shape into loaves (*page 43*). Place in the greased loaf pans.

Cover and let rise until the dough is doubled (about 2 hrs.).

Bake at 350°F about 1 hr.

Cool and store as directed (*page 43*).

2 loaves bread

My Fruit Bread 8 4

MARTHA J. CHASTAIN, ST. GEORGE, UTAH

Set out two 1-lb. coffee cans.

Scald (*page 13*)
   ½ cup milk
Meanwhile, soften
   1 package active dry yeast
in
   **¼ cup warm water 110°F to 115°F (Or if
   using compressed yeast, soften 1 cake
   in ¼ cup lukewarm water, 80°F to
   85°F)**
Let yeast stand 5 to 10 min.

Meanwhile, put into a large bowl
   ½ cup shortening
   ¼ cup sugar
   ½ teaspoon salt
Pour the scalded milk over ingredients in bowl.
When lukewarm, stir mixture and blend in,
beating until smooth
   1 cup sifted flour
Stir the softened yeast and add, mixing well.

Measure
   2 cups sifted flour
Add to yeast mixture one-half the flour and
   **½ lb. (about 1¼ cups) assorted
   candied fruits, diced**
   ¼ cup uncooked rolled oats
   ¼ cup chopped nuts

Add
   ¼ cup thick, sweetened applesauce
Beat until very smooth. Then beat in enough
of the remaining flour to make a soft dough.

Turn dough onto a lightly floured surface and
let rest 5 to 10 min.

Knead (*page 43*). Form dough into a large ball
and place it in a greased, deep bowl just large
enough to allow dough to double. Turn dough
to bring greased surface to top. Cover with
waxed paper and towel and let stand in warm
place (about 80°F) until dough is doubled
(about 2 hrs.).

Punch down dough with fist; pull edges of
dough in to center and turn dough completely
over in bowl. Cover and let rise again until
almost doubled (about 1 hr.).

Grease bottoms of the coffee cans.

Punch down dough and turn onto a lightly
floured surface. Divide dough into two equal
portions and form into smooth balls. Cover
and allow to rest 5 to 10 min.

Shape into round loaves; place in the cans.
Let rise until doubled (about 1 hr., 20 min.).

Bake at 350°F 55 min., or until well browned.

If desired, frost with **Confectioners' Sugar
Frosting** (*page 399*).   *2 loaves fruit bread*

Sour Cream Kuchen

MRS. JOHN TRAEGER
PORTERVILLE, CALIF.

The contestant modestly described her prize-winning coffee cake as "tasty." We suggest you bake it, taste it, and use your own superlatives.

Set out three 9-in. round layer cake pans.

Scald (*page 13*)
¾ cup milk
Meanwhile, soften
1 pkg. active dry yeast
in
¼ cup warm water 110°F to 115°F (Or if using compressed yeast, soften 1 cake in ¼ cup lukewarm water, 80°F to 85°F)
Let yeast stand 5 to 10 min.

Meanwhile, put into a large bowl
¼ cup sugar
¼ cup butter
1 teaspoon salt
Pour scalded milk over ingredients in bowl. When lukewarm, stir mixture and blend in, beating until smooth
1 cup flour
Stir softened yeast and add, mixing well.

Measure
3 cups sifted flour
Add about one-half the flour to yeast mixture and beat until very smooth.

Beat in
2 eggs, well beaten
Then beat in enough remaining flour to make a soft dough. Form dough into a large ball and place in a greased, deep bowl just large enough to allow dough to double. Turn dough to bring greased surface to top. Cover with waxed paper and a towel and let stand in a warm place (about 80°F) until doubled (about 2 hrs.).

Meanwhile, lightly grease the pans.

When dough has doubled, punch down and turn onto lightly floured surface. Divide into three equal parts and form into smooth balls.

Cover and allow to rest 5 to 10 min. Shape into three rounds. Put dough into prepared pans and pat rounds evenly to fit pans. Cover and let rise again until doubled.

Just before dough is doubled, put into a bowl
2 cups firmly packed light brown sugar
Cut in with a pastry blender or two knives until mixture is crumbly
2 tablespoons butter
Set aside.

Blend together thoroughly
1 cup thick sour cream
1 teaspoon vanilla extract
and a mixture of
2 tablespoons confectioners' sugar
1 tablespoon cornstarch
Reserve one half of mixture.

When dough has doubled, spread dough in the pans with remaining sour-cream mixture and then sprinkle with brown-sugar mixture. Sprinkle with about
1 tablespoon cinnamon
Bake at 400°F 20 min., or until golden brown. Remove kuchens from oven and spread with reserved sour-cream mixture. Return to oven and bake 5 min. longer.

Three 9-in. round kuchens

Swedish Rye Bread

MYRTLE C. WORLEY, GOLD BEACH, ORE.

A baking sheet will be needed.

Soften
    1 pkg. active dry yeast
in
    ¼ cup warm water 110°F to 115°F (Or if using compressed yeast, soften 1 cake in ¼ cup lukewarm water, 80°F to 85°F)
Let yeast stand 5 to 10 min.

Meanwhile, put into a large bowl
    ¼ cup molasses
    ¼ cup firmly packed brown sugar
    1 tablespoon shortening
    1 tablespoon salt
    1 teaspoon anise seed
    ½ teaspoon caraway seed
Pour over ingredients in bowl
    1½ cups very hot water
When lukewarm, stir mixture and blend in, beating until smooth
    1 cup sifted flour
Stir softened yeast and add, mixing well.

Measure
    3 to 3½ cups sifted flour
    2 cups rye flour
Add the rye flour and beat until very smooth. Then beat in enough of the remaining flour to make a soft dough. Turn dough onto a lightly floured surface and let rest 5 to 10 min.

Knead (*page 43*). Form dough into a large ball and place it in a greased, deep bowl just large enough to allow dough to double. Turn dough to bring greased surface to top. Cover with waxed paper and a towel and let stand in a warm place (about 80°F) until dough is doubled (about 1 hr.).

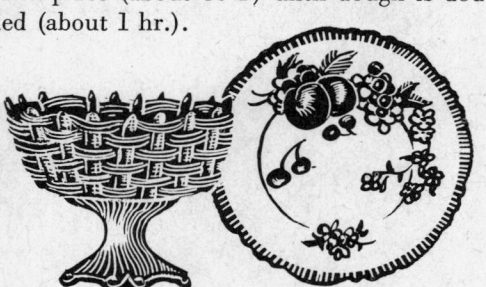

Punch down dough with fist; pull edges of dough in to center and turn dough completely over in bowl. Cover and let rise again until almost doubled (about 45 min.).

Grease the baking sheet.

Punch down dough and turn onto a lightly floured surface. Divide into two equal portions and form into smooth balls. Cover and allow to rest, 5 to 10 min. Place on the greased baking sheet. Cover and let rise until dough is doubled (about 1½ hrs.).

Bake at 400° about 50 min., or until loaves are golden brown.

Cool and store as directed (*page 43*).

2 loaves rye bread

Give us this day our daily bread

Kolachky
(Koláčky)

MRS. A. HENNIGAN, BAYTOWN, TEXAS

Kolachky originated in old Bohemia. There are almost as many ways of making this delicious bread as there are families that bake it.

Two baking sheets will be needed.

Scald (*page 13*)
    1 cup milk
Sift together and set aside
    1 cup flour
    ½ teaspoon mace
Meanwhile, soften
    1 pkg. active dry yeast
in
    ¼ cup water 110°F to 115°F (Or if using compressed yeast, soften 1 cake in ¼ cup lukewarm water, 80°F to 85°F)
Let yeast stand 5 to 10 min.

Meanwhile, put into a large bowl

⅓ cup shortening
⅓ cup sugar
1 teaspoon salt
½ teaspoon grated lemon peel
   (page 11)

Pour scalded milk over ingredients in bowl.

When lukewarm, stir mixture and blend in the dry ingredients, beating until smooth. Stir softened yeast and add, mixing well.

Measure

3 to 3½ cups sifted flour

Add about one-half the flour to the yeast mixture and beat until very smooth.

Beat in

2 eggs, well beaten

Then beat in enough remaining flour to make a soft dough. Turn dough onto a lightly floured surface and let rest 5 to 10 min.

Knead (*page 43*). Form dough into a large ball and place in a greased, deep bowl just large enough to allow dough to double. Turn dough to bring greased surface to top. Cover with waxed paper and towel and let stand in a warm place (about 80°F) until dough is doubled.

Punch down dough with fist; pull edges of dough in to center and turn dough completely over in bowl. Cover and let rise again until almost doubled (about 35 min.).

Grease the baking sheets.

Again punch down dough and turn onto lightly floured surface. Cover and allow dough to rest 5 to 10 min.

Roll dough ½ in. thick. Cut into rounds with a lightly floured 2-in. biscuit cutter. Place about 1½ in. apart on baking sheet. Cover and let rise 10 min.

Make a depression in center of each round and fill with 2 to 3 teaspoons **jam** or with Prune, Apricot or Cherry-Filbert Filling.

Cover the rounds and let rise until doubled (about 40 min.).

Kolachky and Cherry-Almond Coffee Cake

Bake at 400°F 15 min., or until browned.
                                    About 2½ doz. Kolachky

For Prune Filling—Prepare
   Stewed Prunes (one-half recipe,
      page 494)

Chop the pitted prunes and mix well with
   ¼ cup chopped nuts
   ¼ cup sugar
   ¼ teaspoon cinnamon
      Enough to fill about 1 doz. Kolachky

For Apricot Filling—Prepare
   Cooked Apricots (one-half recipe,
      page 494)

Force the apricots through a sieve or food mill. Blend with the apricots
   2 tablespoons sugar
      Enough to fill about 1 doz. Kolachky

For Cherry-Filbert Filling—Set out
   48 canned dark, sweet cherries, pitted
   48 filberts

Insert a filbert in the center of each cherry. Put 4 cherries in each kolachek.
      Enough to fill 1 doz. Kolachky

Note: Kolachky may be served warm or cold. Just before serving, sprinkle with **Vanilla Confectioners' Sugar** (*page 415*).

QUICK BREADS

Quick breads get their name from the relatively short time of preparation as compared with yeast breads. The leavening of quick breads is usually achieved by the use of baking powder or baking soda. Popovers are an exception, requiring steam to leaven them. Quick breads include different types of products—muffins, biscuits, loaves (fruit and nut), popovers, corn bread, dumplings, brown bread, waffles, griddlecakes, some doughnuts and fritters.

One method of classifying quick breads is by the proportion of liquid to flour. *Thin batters* (popovers, timbales, griddlecakes)—usually 1½ to 2 cups liquid to 2 cups flour. *Stiff batters* (muffins,

fruit and nut loaves)—usually 1 cup liquid to 2 cups flour. *Soft doughs* (doughnuts, baking powder biscuits)—usually ¾ cup liquid to 2 cups flour.

Quick breads do not have the keeping quality that richer products do because they are low in ingredients such as shortening, eggs and sugar.

Most quick breads are at their peak in flavor when served fresh from the oven. Many of the loaves that have higher amounts of sugar and shortening along with fruits and nuts are usually cooled before serving. Some loaves slice more easily and improve in flavor if they are served the following day.

An important reminder—never overmix a quick bread batter or dough.

A Check List for Making Successful Quick Breads

(See For These Recipes—What To Use, How To Do It and Oven Temperatures on *pages 10–13*.)

√ **Read** recipe carefully.

√ **Assemble** all ingredients and utensils.

√ **Have all ingredients** at room temperature unless recipe specifies otherwise.

√ **Select pans** of proper kind and size. Measure inside, from rim to rim.

√ **Use standard measuring cups and spoons.** Use liquid measuring cups (rim above 1-cup line) for liquids. Use nested or dry measuring cups (1-cup line even with top) for dry ingredients. Check liquid measurements at eye level. Level dry measurements with straight-edged knife or spatula.

√ **Preheat oven** 12 to 20 min. at required temperature. Leave oven door open first 2 min.

√ **Place oven rack** so top of product will be almost at center of oven. Stagger pans so no pan is directly over another and they do not touch each other or walls of oven. Place single pan so that center of product is as near center of oven as possible.

√ **Prepare pan**—Grease only bottom of pan or lightly grease baking sheet. If recipe directs, "Set out pan or baking sheet," do not grease pan.

√ **Sift all flour** except whole-grain types before measuring. Spoon lightly into measuring cup; do not jar. Level with straight-edged knife or spatula.

√ **Cream shortening** (alone or with flavorings) by stirring, rubbing or beating with spoon or electric mixer until softened. Add sugar in small amounts; cream after each addition until all graininess disappears and mixture is light and fluffy.

√ **Beat whole eggs** until thick and piled softly when recipe calls for well-beaten eggs.

√ **Beat egg whites** as follows: *Frothy*—entire mass forms bubbles; *Rounded peaks*—peaks turn over slightly when beater is slowly lifted upright; *Stiff peaks*—peaks remain standing when beater is slowly lifted upright.

√ **Beat egg yolks** until thick and lemon-colored when recipe calls for well-beaten yolks.

√ **Fill pans** one-half to two-thirds full.

√ **Apply baking tests** when minimum baking time is up. For *coffee cakes* and for *quick loaf breads*, insert a cake tester or wooden pick in center; if it comes out clean, cake or bread is done.

√ **Remove quick loaf breads and coffee cakes** from pans as they come from the oven, unless otherwise directed. Set on cooling racks to cool.

√ **Wrap cooled quick loaf breads** in waxed paper, aluminum foil or moisture-vapor-proof material; store overnight for easier slicing.

▲ Muffins 12

Prepare (*page 54*) 12 2½-in. muffin-pan wells.

Melt and set aside
¼ cup butter or margarine
Sift together into a bowl and set aside
2 cups sifted flour
⅓ cup sugar
1 tablespoon baking powder
½ teaspoon salt
Blend thoroughly
1 egg, well beaten
1 cup milk
Blend in the melted shortening. Make a well in center of dry ingredients and add liquid mixture all at one time. With not more than 25 strokes, quickly and lightly stir until dry ingredients are barely moistened. Batter will be lumpy and break from spoon. (Too much mixing will result in muffin tunnels.)

Cut against side of bowl with spoon to get enough batter at one time to fill each muffin-pan well two-thirds full. Place spoon in well and push batter off with another spoon or spatula. Fill any empty wells half-full with water before placing pans in oven.

Bake at 425°F 20 to 25 min., or until muffins are an even golden brown.

Run spatula around each muffin and lift out. If necessary to keep muffins warm before serving, loosen muffins and tip slightly in wells. Keep in a warm place. Serve warm.

1 doz. Muffins

Blueberry Muffins

⚠ Blueberry Muffins 13

Follow ▲ Recipe. Rinse and drain 1 cup fresh **blueberries**. Fold into batter with final strokes.

⚠ Cranberry Muffins 14

Follow ▲ Recipe. Wash and drain 1 cup **cranberries**; chop coarsely. Mix with 3 tablespoons **sugar**. Mix into sifted dry ingredients.

⚠ Double-Top Muffins

Follow ▲ Recipe; place a cooked, dried **apricot** half in bottom of each greased muffin-pan well. Spoon batter into wells. Top with mixture of ½ cup firmly packed **brown sugar**, ½ cup **butter** or **margarine**, softened, ⅓ cup sifted **flour** and 1 teaspoon **cinnamon**.

Graham Gems 15
MRS. MERLE FISH, FAIRVIEW, KANS.

Prepare (*page 54*) 12 2½-in. muffin-pan wells.

Melt and set aside
5 tablespoons shortening
Sift together into a bowl
1 cup sifted flour
1 teaspoon baking powder
1 teaspoon salt
½ teaspoon baking soda
Mix in
¾ cup graham flour
½ cup firmly packed brown sugar
Set dry ingredients aside.

Blend thoroughly
1 egg, well beaten
1 cup buttermilk or sour milk (*page 11*)
Blend in the melted shortening. Make a well in center of the dry ingredients. Add liquid mixture all at one time. With not more than 25 strokes, quickly and lightly stir until dry ingredients are barely moistened. Batter will be lumpy and break from spoon. (Too much mixing will result in muffin tunnels.)

Cut against side of bowl with spoon to get enough batter at one time to fill each muffin-pan well two-thirds full. Place spoon in well; push batter off with another spoon or spatula. Fill any empty wells half-full with water.

Bake at 400°F 25 min., or until muffins are an even golden brown.

Run spatula around each muffin and lift out. If necessary to keep muffins warm before serving, loosen muffins and tip slightly in wells. Keep in a warm place. *1 doz. muffins*

▲ Prune Bran Muffins 16

Prepare (*page 54*) 12 2½-in. muffin-pan wells.

Melt and set aside
2 tablespoons fat
Sift together into a bowl
1 cup sifted flour
¼ cup sugar
2½ teaspoons baking powder
1 teaspoon cinnamon
½ teaspoon salt
Add, but do not mix in
1 cup bran
½ cup chopped prunes, uncooked (if too dry, soak 15 min. in boiling water)
Set aside.

Blend thoroughly
1 egg, well beaten
1 cup milk
Blend in the melted shortening. Make a well in center of dry ingredients. Add liquid mixture all at one time. With not more than 25 strokes, quickly and lightly stir until dry ingredients are barely moistened. Batter will be lumpy and will break from spoon. (Too much mixing will result in muffin tunnels.)

Cut against side of bowl with spoon to get enough batter at one time to fill each muffin-pan well two-thirds full. Place spoon in well; push batter off with another spoon or spatula. Fill any empty wells half-full with water.

Bake at 425°F 20 to 25 min., or until muffins are an even golden brown.

Run spatula around each muffin and lift out. If necessary to keep muffins warm before serving, loosen muffins and tip slightly in wells. Keep in a warm place. *1 doz. muffins*

△ Sugary Apple Muffins

Follow ▲ Recipe. Substitute ¾ cups finely chopped pared **apples** for prunes. Sprinkle top of each muffin with about ½ teaspoon of a mixture of 2 tablespoons **brown sugar**, ½ teaspoon **cinnamon** and ½ teaspoon **nutmeg**.

Stay-Popped Popovers

Grease thoroughly with cooking oil 6 or 7 heat-resistant glass custard cups; or grease iron popover pans and preheat 15 min. in oven.

Sift together and set aside
 1 cup sifted flour
 ½ teaspoon salt
Beat until thick and piled softly
 2 eggs
Mix in
 1 cup milk
 2 teaspoons melted butter or margarine
Make a well in center of dry ingredients. Pour in liquid mixture. Beat with rotary beater until batter is very smooth. Fill custard cups one-half full of batter.

Bake at 450°F 10 min. Reduce temperature to 350°F and bake 40 min.

Serve immediately.   *6 or 7 large popovers*

Note: If a drier interior is desired, make a slit in the side of each baked popover to allow steam to escape. Return to oven with heat turned off and allow popovers to dry 10 min.

▲ Corn-Bread Squares 17

Prepare (*page 54*) an 8x8x2-in. pan.

Melt and set aside
 5 tablespoons shortening
Sift together into a bowl
 1 cup sifted flour
 ¼ cup sugar
 1 tablespoon baking powder
 ¾ teaspoon salt
Mix in
 1 cup yellow corn meal
Set dry ingredients aside.

Mix until blended
 1 egg, well beaten
 1 cup milk
Blend in the melted shortening.

Make a well in center of dry ingredients. Add liquid mixture all at one time. Beat with a rotary beater until just smooth, being careful not to overmix. Turn the batter into pan and spread to corners.

Bake at 425°F about 20 min., or until bread tests done (*page 54*).

Cut into squares and serve.   *16 servings*

△ Crisp Corn Sticks

Follow ▲ Recipe. Spoon batter into 12 hot, greased corn-stick pan sections, filling each three-fourths full. Bake at 425°F 10 to 15 min.

Stay-Popped Popovers

Crisp Corn Sticks

Golden Spoon Bread

Serve this delicious hot bread with butter and honey, maple sirup or jam for a compliment-attracting breakfast treat.

Thoroughly grease a 2-qt. casserole.

Grate and set aside
   6 oz. sharp Cheddar cheese (1½ cups, grated)
Scald (*page 13*) in double boiler top
   2 cups milk
Beat until thick and lemon-colored
   4 egg yolks
Set aside.

When milk is scalded, add very gradually, stirring constantly
   1 cup yellow corn meal
Stir until mixture thickens and becomes smooth. Remove double boiler top from simmering water. Quickly and thoroughly mix in the beaten egg yolks, grated cheese and
   ¼ cup butter or margarine
   1 teaspoon sugar
   ½ teaspoon salt
Beat until rounded peaks are formed
   4 egg whites
Gently spread beaten egg whites over cornmeal mixture. Carefully fold (*page 12*) together until just blended. Turn mixture into casserole.

Bake at 375°F 35 to 40 min., or until bread tests done (*page 54*).

Serve at once.   *6 to 8 servings*

Ranch Bread

IDA M. PAXTON, THEDFORD, NEBR.

A rich and hearty quick bread that symbolizes the generous and open-hearted hospitality of the Great Plains. Keep it on hand for ready sociability.

Prepare (*page 54*) a 9½x5¼x2¾-in. loaf pan.

Melt and set aside
   ½ cup shortening
Sift together into a large bowl and set aside
   2 cups sifted flour
   1 cup sugar
   2½ teaspoons baking powder
   ½ teaspoon salt
Peel and force through a sieve
   2 to 3 bananas with brown-flecked peel (about 1 cup, sieved)
Set sieved bananas aside.

Beat until thick and piled softly
   2 eggs
Blend in the bananas, melted shortening and
   ¼ cup chopped nuts
   ¼ cup chopped maraschino cherries, drained
   ¼ cup chocolate chips
Make a well in center of dry ingredients and add liquid ingredients all at one time. Stir only to moisten dry ingredients. Turn batter into pan and spread to corners.

Bake at 350°F about 45 min., or until bread tests done (*page 54*).

Cool and store (*page 54*).   *1 loaf Ranch Bread*

Irish Batter Bread 1937

BERTHA L. STICKNEY, HERSEY, MICH.

Prize-winning story of a favorite recipe:

"This recipe was brought to America from Ireland in 1640 and became known to my grandmother in 1829 when she received it, together with a wedding gift, from a Boston cousin. Migrating to Michigan in 1840, by ox-cart, covered wagon and canal boat, she, her husband and six children settled in Owosso. With no grist mill, no wheat, no flour, bread-making became a dreary task. She labored through by pulverizing corn into meal with a mortar and pestle, baking bread in iron bread pans in an open fireplace. For a long time white bread was a delicacy seldom attained.

"Grandmother died in 1910 and among her keepsakes this recipe, yellow from age, the ink faded to a rusty tan, was found in a box, with the Boston cousin's wedding gift—a handsome, purple velvet, beaded pincushion.

"The recipe as it appears here has been somewhat altered to meet modern facilities."

This bread should be stored for 12 to 24 hours before serving.

Grease bottom of a 9½x5¼x2¾-in. loaf pan.

Melt and set aside
  2 tablespoons shortening
Sift together into a large bowl and set aside
  3 cups sifted flour
  ½ cup sugar
  4 teaspoons baking powder
  2 teaspoons cinnamon
  1 teaspoon salt
Mix until blended
  1 egg, well beaten
  1½ cups milk
  3 tablespoons grated orange peel
    (page 11)
Blend in the melted shortening. Make a well in center of dry ingredients and add liquid ingredients all at one time with
  1 cup (about 5 oz.) currants
Stir to moisten dry ingredients. Beat until smooth. Turn dough into pan and let stand at room temperature for 20 min.

Bake at 325°F 1 hr. to 1 hr. 15 min., or until bread tests done (*page 54*).

Cool and store as directed (*page 54*).

1 loaf bread

▲ Date-Nut Bread

Prepare (*page 54*) 9½x5¼x2¾-in. loaf pan.

Melt and set aside
   ⅓ cup shortening
Sift together into a bowl
   2 cups sifted flour
   ¾ cup sugar
   4 teaspoons baking powder
   ¾ teaspoon salt
Mix in
   1 cup whole wheat flour
   1 cup (about 7 oz.) pitted dates, cut
   (*page 12*)
   1 cup (about 4 oz.) chopped nuts
Set dry ingredients aside.

Mix until blended
   1 egg, well beaten
   1 cup milk
   ½ cup molasses
   1½ teaspoons vanilla extract
Blend in the melted shortening.

Make a well in center of dry ingredients and add liquid mixture all at one time. Stir only enough to moisten dry ingredients. Turn batter into pan and spread to corners.

Bake at 350°F about 1 hr., or until bread tests done (*page 54*).

Cool and store as directed (*page 54*).
   1 loaf Date-Nut Bread

△ Fruit-Nut Bread

Follow ▲ Recipe. Substitute for dates, ¼ cup each of **currants**, chopped **candied citron**, **candied cherries** and **candied orange peel.**

Nut Bread

CAROLYN E. ARNOLD, KINGSTON, N. Y.

Prepare (*page 54*) a 9½x5¼x2¾-in. loaf pan.

Melt and set aside
   2 tablespoons shortening
Sift together into a bowl
   3 cups sifted flour
   ¾ cup sugar
   4 teaspoons baking powder
   ¾ teaspoon salt
Mix in
   ¾ cup (about 3 oz.) coarsely
   chopped nuts
Set dry ingredients aside.

Blend thoroughly
   1 egg, well beaten
   1½ cups milk
Blend in the melted shortening.

Make a well in center of dry ingredients and add liquid mixture all at one time. Stir only to moisten dry ingredients. Turn batter into pan and spread to corners.

Bake at 350°F about 1 hr., or until bread tests done (*page 54*).

Cool and store as directed (*page 54*).
   1 loaf Nut Bread

▲ 30-Minute Coffee Cake

A quickie—but a coffee cake that you can depend on to win friends of its own. This handy recipe becomes a holiday treat with the addition of spices and candied fruits.

Prepare (*page 54*) an 8-in. round layer cake pan.

For Streusel Topping—Blend together
   ⅓ cup sugar
   ¼ cup sifted flour
   1 teaspoon cinnamon
Cut in with a pastry blender or two knives until mixture is crumbly
   3 tablespoons butter or margarine
Set aside.

For Coffee Cake—Melt
  2 tablespoons shortening
Set aside.

Sift together
  1 cup sifted flour
  1½ teaspoons baking powder
  ½ teaspoon salt
Blend thoroughly
  1 egg, well beaten
  ½ cup sugar
  ½ cup milk

Mix in the melted shortening. Make a well in center of the dry ingredients and add liquid mixture all at one time. Stir only enough to moisten dry ingredients. Turn batter into pan. Sprinkle topping evenly over batter.

Bake at 375°F 20 to 25 min., or until cake tests done (*page 54*).   *1 coffee cake*

△ Festive Coffee Cake

Follow ▲ Recipe for coffee cake. Substitute for topping a mixture of 3 tablespoons **sugar,** 2 teaspoons **cinnamon,** ¼ cup (1 oz.) chopped **nuts** and ⅓ cup chopped **candied fruit.**

△ Apple Coffee Cake

Follow ▲ Recipe for coffee cake. Omit topping. Wash, quarter, core, pare and slice 2 medium-size **apples.** Mix together 2 teaspoons **cinnamon** and ¼ cup **sugar.** Melt 2 tablespoons **butter** or **margarine.** Lightly brush top of batter with part of the melted butter or margarine. Arrange apple slices on batter, pressing slightly. Sprinkle sugar mixture evenly over apples. Drizzle remaining butter or margarine over topping.

Cherry-Almond Coffee Cake

(*See photo on page 53*)

For Topping—Measure
  1 cup canned, pitted light sweet
    cherries, drained
Reserve ¼ cup of the cherries for garnish.

Mix together
  ⅓ cup firmly packed brown sugar
  2 tablespoons flour
  2 tablespoons melted butter or
    margarine
Mix in ¾ cup of the cherries and
  ⅓ cup whole almonds
Set aside.

For Coffee Cake—Prepare (*page 54*) an 11x7x1½-in. baking pan.

Melt and set aside
  ¼ cup shortening
Sift together into a bowl
  2 cups sifted flour
  3 tablespoons non-fat dry milk solids
  1 tablespoon baking powder
  1 teaspoon salt
Blend together
  2 eggs, well beaten
  1 cup sugar
  ⅓ cup water

Mix in the melted shortening. Make a well in center of dry ingredients and add liquid mixture all at one time. Stir only to moisten dry ingredients. Turn batter into pan. Sprinkle topping evenly over batter.

Bake at 350°F about 35 min., or until cake tests done (*page 54*).

Garnish with the reserved cherries.

About 12 servings

Tender-Rich Biscuits

▲ Tender-Rich Buttermilk Biscuits

Set out a baking sheet.

Sift together into a bowl

2 cups sifted flour
2 teaspoons baking powder
1 teaspoon salt

Cut in with a pastry blender or two knives until mixture resembles coarse corn meal

⅓ cup lard

Make a well in the center of the dry ingredients. Pour in all at one time

¾ cup buttermilk

Stir with a fork until dough follows fork. Gently form dough into a ball and put onto a lightly floured surface. Knead lightly with finger tips 10 to 15 times.

Gently roll out dough ½ in. thick. Cut with a floured cutter or knife, using an even pressure to keep sides of biscuits straight. Place biscuits on baking sheet, close together for soft-sided biscuits, or 1 in. apart for crusty sides.

Lightly brush tops with

Milk

Bake at 450°F 10 to 15 min., or until biscuits are golden brown.

About 2 doz. 1½-in. biscuits

⚠ Tender-Rich Biscuits

Follow ▲ Recipe; substitute ¾ cup **milk** for buttermilk.

⚠ Tender-Rich Drop Biscuits

Follow ▲ Recipe or ⚠ Recipe. Increase buttermilk or milk to 1 cup. Omit kneading, rolling and cutting. Drop by spoonfuls onto baking sheet.

⚠ Tender-Rich Rolled Shortcakes

Follow ▲ Recipe or ⚠ Recipe. Sift 2 tablespoons **sugar** with dry ingredients. Cut dough with floured knife into squares or into rounds with 3-in. cutter. Or cut dough into halves and roll each portion to fit an 8-in. round layer cake pan. Spread one half of the rounds, or one of the large rounds, with melted **butter** or **margarine.** Top with remaining rounds or round. Place on baking sheet or in layer cake pan and bake as in ▲ Recipe.

⚠ Cinnamon Pinwheels

Follow ▲ Recipe or ⚠ Recipe. Grease the baking sheet. Roll dough into rectangle about ¼ in. thick. Brush dough with 2 tablespoons melted **butter** or **margarine.** Sprinkle with a mixture of ¼ cup firmly packed **brown sugar,** ¼ cup (about 1 oz.) finely chopped **nuts** and 1 teaspoon **cinnamon.** Beginning with long side, roll and press edges together to seal. Cut into 1-in. slices. Do not brush tops with milk. Place flat on baking sheet and bake.

⚠ Apple Roll

Follow △ Recipe. Omit the brown sugar mixture. Spread dough with a mixture of 1½ cups (about 2 medium-size) finely chopped **apple,** ½ cup **sugar** and 1 teaspoon **cinnamon.**

⚠ Peanut-Butter Whirlamajigs
ETHEL L. PATTERSON, PATTERSON, ARK.

Follow △ Recipe. Omit the brown sugar mixture. Spread dough with Peanut-Butter Filling.

For Peanut-Butter Filling—Cream together ½ cup **peanut butter** and ¼ cup **butter** or **margarine**. Add gradually, creaming until fluffy after each addition, ½ cup firmly packed **brown sugar**. Blend in 1 **egg**, well beaten. Blend in 8 **graham crackers**, crushed (*page 12*).

All-in-One Biscuit Mix

Sift together into a large mixing bowl
>   **8 cups sifted flour**
>   **¼ cup baking powder**
>   **4 teaspoons salt**

Cut in with pastry blender or two knives until mixture resembles coarse corn meal
>   **2 cups lard, hydrogenated vegetable shortening or all-purpose shortening**

Store mix in tightly covered container in a cool place. (Biscuit mix made with lard should be stored in refrigerator.)

About 12 cups biscuit mix

Note: Before measuring for use in recipe, lighten mix by tossing with fork.

▲ Rolled Baking Powder Biscuits

(*See photo on page 572*)

Set out a baking sheet.

Measure into a mixing bowl
>   **3 cups All-in-One Biscuit Mix**
>   (*on this page*)

Make a well in center of biscuit mix and add all at one time
>   **⅔ cup milk**

Stir with a fork until dough follows fork. Gently form dough into a ball and put on a lightly floured surface. Knead lightly with finger tips 10 to 15 times.

Gently roll out dough about ½-in. thick. Cut with a floured cutter or knife, using an even pressure to keep sides of biscuits straight. Place biscuits on baking sheet. Lightly brush tops with
>   **Milk**

Bake at 450°F 10 to 15 min.

About 18 2-in. biscuits

▲ Drop Biscuits

Follow ▲ Recipe. Increase milk to 1 cup. Omit kneading, rolling and cutting processes. Drop by spoonfuls onto baking sheet.

▲ Scones

Follow ▲ Recipe. Add 2 tablespoons **sugar** to biscuit mix. Decrease milk to ½ cup. Mix 1 **egg**, well beaten, with the milk. Cut biscuits into diamonds, squares or triangles. Sprinkle with **sugar** after brushing with milk.

▲ Orange Tea Biscuits

Follow ▲ Recipe. Dip **loaf sugar** into **orange juice** and press one loaf into top of each biscuit before baking. Sprinkle biscuits with grated **orange peel** (*page 11*).

▲ Cheese Biscuits

Follow ▲ Recipe. Blend ½ cup (2 oz.) grated **Cheddar cheese** into biscuit mix. Or, sprinkle grated **Parmesan cheese** over tops of biscuits before baking.

▲ Chive Biscuits

Follow ▲ Recipe. Add ¼ cup finely chopped **chives** to the biscuit mix.

Deep-Fried Rosettes: Using a wire whisk (or wooden spoon) beat until the batter is smooth.

Heat rosette iron in hot fat for about one minute. Dip iron into batter; batter will adhere to the iron.

Plunge iron coated with batter into hot fat; deep-fry one layer of rosettes at a time, do not crowd.

▲ Deep-Fried Timbale Cases

Set out a deep saucepan or automatic deep-fryer (*page 13*) and heat fat to 365°F.

Sift together into a bowl
> **1 cup sifted flour**
> **2 teaspoons sugar**
> **½ teaspoon salt**

Mix together
> **2 eggs, slightly beaten**
> **1 cup milk**

Make a well in the dry ingredients and add the liquid ingredients all at one time.

Using a wire whisk or wooden spoon, beat batter until very smooth. If necessary, strain batter through a fine sieve to remove any lumps. If necessary, allow batter to stand until it is free from air bubbles.

Heat timbale iron in hot fat about 1 min. and drain well. Dip hot iron into batter so that batter covers about two-thirds to three-fourths of the mold. Immerse in hot fat and fry 1 to 2 min., or until case is golden brown. Drain upside down over fat; remove to absorbent paper. Gently remove case from mold with fork.

Drain hot iron, if necessary, dip it into batter and deep-fry timbale case as before. Repeat procedure for each timbale case.

Fill cases with creamed meat or vegetables.
> *About 3 doz. timbale cases*

△ Deep-Fried Rosettes

Follow ▲ Recipe. Use a rosette iron instead of a timbale iron. When batter on mold has set but not browned, carefully remove rosette from mold with a fork. Repeat procedure for other rosettes.

Deep-fry only one layer of rosettes at a time; do not crowd. Fry until golden brown, turning with a fork to brown evenly (do not pierce). Remove from fat with slotted spoon. Drain over fat before removing to absorbent paper.

Serve rosettes for dessert sprinkled with **Vanilla Confectioners' Sugar** (*page 415*).

Toastee Baskets

Ringlet Shells—To serve four persons, use 12 **bread slices,** about ½ in. thick. Trim off crusts and cut all slices into large squares, rectangles or rounds (making all 12 slices the same shape). Use a biscuit or cookie cutter for cutting the rounds. Set aside four shapes. With a sharp pointed knife or cookie cutter, cut out centers from the 8 remaining shapes to make rings at least ½ in. wide.

Thoroughly brush tops of uncut shapes and both sides of rings with **milk.** Stack 2 rings on each uncut shape. Brush inside and outside with melted **butter** or **margarine.**

Place on a baking sheet and toast at 325°F 12 to 20 min., or until golden brown and crisp.

Croustades—Cut **day-old bread** into slices 1¼ to 2 in. thick. Remove crusts and cut bread into desired shapes—triangles, squares, diamonds; or cut into rounds or fancy shapes with a large biscuit or cookie cutter. If cutter is not deep enough, mark with it and finish cutting with the point of a sharp knife. Following outline of shaped piece, carefully cut out center ¼ to ½ in. from edge, and down to within ¼ to ½ in. of bottom, leaving a neatly cut shell.

Brush outside and inside of shells with melted **butter** or **margarine.**

Place on baking sheet and toast at 325°F 12 to 20 min., or until lightly browned and crisp.

If shells are not used immediately, reheat in oven for a few minutes before filling.

Or deep-fry (*page 13*) unbuttered shells at 375°F until lightly browned. Drain for a few minutes on absorbent paper.

Fill Croustades or Ringlet Shells with creamed eggs, meat, fish, poultry or vegetables.

Shell centers and crusts may be toasted or dried, ground and saved for crumbs. Or centers may be toasted and used as a garnish to top filled Croustades.

Loaf Basket—Neatly trim the crusts from top and sides of a loaf of **unsliced bread.** Using a sharp pointed knife, hollow out center, leaving ¾-in. sides and bottom. Brush inside and out with melted **butter** or **margarine.** For a cover on the basket, cut a ¾-in. slice from length of loaf before making the basket. Brush both sides with melted **butter** or **margarine.** Place on baking sheet with basket.

Toast at 325°F 15 to 25 min., or until golden brown and crisp.

Fill with any creamed mixture and serve.

Toast Cups—Cut crusts from thin slices of **bread.** Lightly brush both sides with melted **butter** or **margarine** and press each slice into a muffin-pan well, corners pointing up.

Toast at 325°F 12 to 20 min., or until crisp and lightly browned.

Toast Points—Trim crusts from **bread slices.** Toast and spread with **butter** or **margarine.** Cut each slice diagonally in half.

Toast Fingers—Trim crusts from **bread slices.** Toast and spread with **butter** or **margarine.** Cut slices into fingers about 1 in. wide.

Croutons—To prepare about 1½ cups Croutons, melt 2 to 3 tablespoons **butter** or **margarine** in a large, heavy skillet over low heat. Meanwhile, if desired, trim crusts from 2 slices **toasted bread.** Cut bread into ¼- to ½-in. cubes. Put cubes into the skillet and toss until all sides are coated and browned.

Plan Well, Pack Well—The Carried Lunch

The carried lunch is a familiar sight in any community in America—the school child bounces along swinging a lunch box, the career girl dashes to the bus with lunch bag tucked under her arm, the laborer swings off to work with his lunch box. And many times the brief case of a business man conceals a lunch.

Let's take a look into those carried lunches. From their depths comes an important meal—not just a snack, but a meal that should provide about one third of the day's nutritional requirements. Each packed lunch should contain: a protein food such as meat, poultry, fish, eggs or cheese provided in a sandwich, soup or main dish; a salad or raw vegetable; a beverage; a dessert; and a surprise.

Such an important meal deserves careful planning. No luncher, no matter how unconcerned he is about food, likes a dull, unattractive lunch every day. How can it be made interesting, attractive and appetizing? *Planning* is the answer.

Start with the working area. Take a look at the kitchen. Pick the most convenient spot for making and packing lunches. Assemble here, in drawers and cabinets, all the necessary utensils, materials and equipment. Keep on hand a good supply of waxed paper, aluminum foil or moisture-vapor-proof material, napkins (colored ones will add a gay note), plastic, paper or wooden forks and spoons, plastic or heavy paper cups and plastic or waxed containers for salads, main-dish foods and desserts. Make use of the equipment and materials that are designed for the packed lunch—such as an individual wedge-shaped plastic container for pie and a vacuum bottle for beverages or soups.

The next step is planning the menu, keeping in mind the luncher himself—his likes and dislikes. It is wise to plan lunches along with other meals. Thus you will be sure they are varied and nutritionally adequate. This also will save time.

Sandwiches are the universally favorite packed-lunch item. The many kinds of bread, the wide assortment of ready-to-serve and cooked meats, sliced cheeses and cheese spreads and the numerous fillings and spreads make possible a variety of sandwiches and good, satisfying eating.

A reminder—Spread the bread with softened butter or margarine to keep the filling from soaking in. (See THE ART OF SANDWICH MAKING, on *pages 74 and 75*.)

Fried chicken is another way to include a protein food (chill thoroughly before packing).

Salads and raw vegetables add texture, flavor and color contrast to the carried lunch. Citrus salads, stuffed tomato shells, cabbage slaws, kidney-bean, meat-vegetable and potato salad pack well. Deviled and hard-cooked eggs travel well too. Or tuck in carrot or celery sticks, radishes, green pepper rings, lettuce leaves or a tomato.

Beverages are best kept cold or hot in a vacuum bottle. Chill the bottle by filling it with ice cubes and cold water; cover and allow to stand while beverage is chilling. Preheat vacuum bottle by filling it with warm water, then boiling water; cover and allow to stand while preparing food. Empty before filling with cold or hot beverage.

Dessert completes the perfect packed lunch, and there are many to choose from. Fresh fruits are always enjoyable, and though apples, oranges and bananas are the usual favorites, other fruits in season, such as cherries, plums and pears, provide a welcome change. Or pack a fruit cup prepared from fresh, frozen, canned or dried fruits. When choosing sweets for the lunch box be careful to include only those that bear up well in packing—cakes with durable frostings, brownies, cookies, cupcakes, gingerbread, turnovers, double-crust pies with fillings that do not ooze. Many puddings, such as rice or tapioca, are suitable for the lunch box if packed in tightly covered containers.

The surprise—be it candy or a stick of gum, olives or pickles, a newspaper clipping or note—lets the lunch carrier know that the lunch was packed with loving thoughtfulness.

Packing the lunch takes planning also. With work organized it takes little time to assemble prepared foods, wash fruits and pat them dry and fill the vacuum bottle. Wrap everything separately and flavors will stay where they belong. Pack neatly and carefully, fasten securely and the lunch is ready for school or work.

Dumplings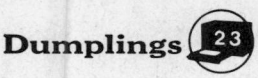

Sift together
- **2 cups sifted flour**
- **4 teaspoons baking powder**
- **1 teaspoon salt**

Cut in with a pastry blender or two knives until pieces are size of rice kernels
- **1 tablespoon shortening**

Quickly stir in with a fork until just blended
- **⅔ cup milk**
- **1 tablespoon chopped parsley**

Drop by tablespoonfuls on top of stew or fricassee. Dumplings should rest on meat and vegetables; if dumplings settle down on the liquid, they may be soggy. If necessary, pour off excess liquid to prevent this. Cover tightly and cook over medium heat 20 min. without removing cover.   *About 6 servings*

Note: ¼ cup chopped **mint** can be substituted for parsley.

Yorkshire Pudding

Pour into an 11x7x1½-in. baking dish and keep hot
- **¼ cup hot drippings from roast beef**

Beat until thick and piled softly
- **2 eggs**

Add to beaten eggs and beat with rotary beater until smooth
- **1 cup milk**
- **1 cup sifted flour**
- **½ teaspoon salt**

Pour into baking dish over hot meat drippings.

Bake at 400°F 30 to 40 min., or until puffed and golden brown.

Cut into squares and serve immediately with **Standing Rib Roast of Beef** (*page 108*).

About 6 servings

Dumplings with Stewed Chicken (page 205)

Potato Pancakes

Heat in a heavy skillet over low heat.
- **Shortening to at least ¼-in. depth**

Mix together and set aside
- **2 tablespoons flour**
- **1½ teaspoons salt**
- **¼ teaspoon baking powder**
- **⅛ teaspoon pepper**

Wash, pare and finely grate
- **6 medium-size (about 2 lbs.) potatoes (about 3 cups, grated)**

Set grated potatoes aside.

Blend the dry ingredients into a mixture of
- **2 eggs, well beaten**
- **1 teaspoon grated onion**

Pat the grated potatoes dry with absorbent paper and add potatoes to egg mixture. Mix thoroughly.

When shortening is hot, but not smoking, begin cooking. Using about 2 tablespoons for each pancake, spoon batter onto skillet, leaving at least 1 in. between cakes. Cook over medium heat until golden brown and crisp on one side. Turn pancakes only once and brown second side.

If desired, serve with hot **Rosy Pink Apple-sauce** (*page 495*).

About 20 medium-size pancakes

Brown Sugar Doughnuts and hot coffee

Brown Sugar Doughnuts

DOROTHY J. MARCUSSEN, RIVERTON, ILL.

The warm sweet smell of fresh doughnuts and the dark fragrance of freshly brewed coffee— a time-tried invitation to comfort and cheer.

Set out a deep saucepan or automatic deep-fryer (*page 13*) and heat fat to 365°F.

Sift together and set aside
> **5 cups sifted flour**
> **2 teaspoons baking powder**
> **2 teaspoons baking soda**
> **2 teaspoons cinnamon**

Beat until thick and piled softly
> **4 eggs**

Add gradually, beating thoroughly after each addition
> **2 cups firmly packed brown sugar**

Blend in dry ingredients alternately with
> **½ cup thick sour cream**

Stir lightly until well blended. Dough will be soft. If dough seems very sticky, measure
> **½ cup sifted flour**

Add enough of the flour to make an easily handled but soft dough. Save remainder for rolling. Chill dough in refrigerator for 1 hr.

Turn dough onto lightly floured surface. Handling very lightly, roll dough ½ in. thick and cut with a lightly floured doughnut cutter.

Deep-fry doughnuts and "holes" in heated fat. Fry only as many doughnuts at one time as will float uncrowded one layer deep in the fat. Turn doughnuts with a fork as they rise to surface and several times during cooking (do not pierce). Fry 2 to 4 min., or until lightly browned. Drain doughnuts and "holes" over fat for a few seconds before removing to absorbent paper.

Serve plain or shake 2 or 3 warm doughnuts at a time in a plastic bag containing
> **½ cup confectioners' sugar**
> *About 2 doz. doughnuts plus "holes"*

Halloween Fried Cakes

MRS. MERLA VOUGHT, BOYNE CITY, MICH.

A deep saucepan or automatic deep-fryer will be needed.

Sift together and set aside
> **4 cups sifted flour**
> **1 tablespoon baking powder**
> **1 teaspoon salt**
> **½ teaspoon baking soda**
> **1 teaspoon pumpkin pie spice**

Cream together until lard is softened
> **2 tablespoons lard**
> **1 teaspoon vanilla extract**

Add gradually, creaming well after each addition
> **1 cup sugar**

Add in thirds, beating thoroughly after each addition
> **2 eggs, well beaten**

Blend in
> **1 cup canned pumpkin**

Measure
> **1 cup buttermilk or sour milk (page 11)**

Stirring until well blended after each addition, alternately add dry ingredients in fourths, liquid in thirds, to pumpkin mixture. Dough will be soft. Chill in refrigerator about 1 hr.

About 20 min. before ready to deep-fry, heat fat to 365°F (*page 13*).

Turn dough onto a floured surface. Handling

very lightly, roll dough ¼ in. thick and cut with a lightly floured 2-in. doughnut cutter.

Deep-fry doughnuts and "holes" in heated fat. Fry only as many at one time as will float uncrowded one layer deep in the fat. Turn doughnuts with a fork or tongs as they rise to surface and several times during cooking (do not pierce). Fry 3 to 4 min., or until lightly browned. Drain doughnuts and "holes" over fat for a few seconds before removing to absorbent paper.

Serve plain or shake 2 or 3 warm doughnuts at a time in a plastic bag in a mixture of

½ cup granulated sugar
1 to 2½ tablespoons cinnamon

4 doz. doughnuts plus "holes"

▲ Old-Fashioned Apple Fritters

Set out a deep saucepan or automatic deep-fryer (*page 13*) and heat fat to 365°F.

Melt and set aside

1 tablespoon shortening

Sift together into a bowl and set aside

1⅓ cups sifted flour
2 tablespoons sugar
1 teaspoon baking powder
½ teaspoon salt

Wash, pare, core and cut into ¼-in. rings

4 firm apples

Or cut apples into ¼ in.-thick lengthwise wedges. Sprinkle over apples

3 to 4 tablespoons lemon juice
2 tablespoons confectioners' sugar

Toss apples lightly. Let stand about 5 min.

Blend thoroughly

2 eggs, well beaten
1 cup milk

Blend in the melted shortening.

Make a well in center of dry ingredients. Add liquid mixture all at one time and mix until batter is smooth.

Drain apple pieces. Using a large fork or slotted spoon, dip apple pieces in batter to coat well, allowing excess batter to drip into bowl before lowering apple pieces into fat. Deep-fry only as many fritters as will float, uncrowded, one layer deep in fat. Turn with a fork as they rise and frequently thereafter (do not pierce). Deep-fry 2 to 3 min., or until golden brown. Drain over fat for a few seconds before removing to absorbent paper.

Serve hot.   *5 or 6 servings*

△ Corn-Gold Fritters

Follow ▲ Recipe. Omit apples and sugar. Decrease milk to ⅔ cup and shortening to 1 teaspoon. Add 1 teaspoon **Worcestershire sauce,** ⅛ teaspoon **pepper** and 1⅓ cups (1 12-oz. can) whole kernel **corn,** well drained. Drop by tablespoonfuls into the heated fat. Serve with **Cheese Sauce** (double recipe, *page 323*).

△ Sweet Banana Fritters

Follow ▲ Recipe. Substitute 4 firm **bananas** having green-tipped peel for apples. Peel and cut into halves lengthwise, then into thirds crosswise. Omit confectioners' sugar before dipping into batter.

▲ Pioneer Griddlecakes 24

Heat a griddle or heavy skillet over low heat.

Melt and set aside to cool
2 tablespoons shortening
Sift together
2 cups sifted flour
1 tablespoon baking powder
1 tablespoon sugar
¾ teaspoon salt
Blend thoroughly
1 egg, well beaten
1½ cups milk
Blend in the melted shortening.

Make a well in center of the dry ingredients. Add the liquid mixture all at one time, stirring only until blended.

Test griddle; it is hot enough for baking when drops of water sprinkled on surface dance in small beads. Lightly grease griddle or skillet if manufacturer so directs. Pour batter from a pitcher or large spoon into small pools about 4 in. in diameter, leaving at least 1 in. between. Turn griddlecakes as they become puffy and full of bubbles. Turn only once.

Serve immediately with **butter** or **margarine, Panbroiled Link Sausages** (*p.161*) or **Panbroiled Bacon** (*p.161*), **brown sugar, honey, maple sirup, jam** or **jelly.**

To keep cakes warm, place between folds of absorbent paper in a moderate oven.

About 24 griddlecakes

⚠ Buttermilk Griddlecakes 25

Follow ▲ Recipe. Substitute 1 teaspoon **baking soda** for baking powder and 2 cups **buttermilk** for milk.

⚠ Blueberry Griddlecakes 26

Follow ▲ Recipe. Add 1 cup rinsed, fresh (or drained, canned) **blueberries.** Serve with topping. Or bake silver-dollar-size griddlecakes; sift **confectioners' sugar** over each. Arrange on plate around **whipped cream** (*page 13*).

Pioneer Griddlecakes and Panbroiled Bacon (page 161)

⚠ Corn Meal Griddlecakes 27

Follow ▲ Recipe or ⚠ Recipe. Reduce flour to 1 cup and mix ¾ cup **corn meal** into the dry ingredients.

▲ Buttermilk Waffles

Heat waffle baker while preparing waffle batter.

Melt and set aside
½ cup butter or margarine
Sift together into a large bowl and set aside
2 cups sifted flour
1 tablespoon sugar
2 teaspoons baking powder
1 teaspoon baking soda
½ teaspoon salt
Beat until thick and lemon-colored
3 egg yolks
Add gradually, blending thoroughly, melted butter or margarine and
2 cups buttermilk
Add liquid mixture all at one time to dry ingredients; mix only until batter is smooth.

Beat until rounded peaks are formed
3 egg whites
Spread the beaten egg whites over the batter and gently fold (*page 12*) together.

Unless temperature is automatically shown on

waffle baker, test heat by dropping a few drops cold water on baker. It is hot enough when drops of water dance in small beads. Pour batter into center of baker. (It is wise to experiment to find the exact amount of batter your baker will hold; use that same measurement in future waffle baking.)

Bake according to manufacturer's directions, or until steaming stops (about 10 min.). Do not raise cover during baking period. Lift cover and loosen waffle with a fork.

Serve immediately with **butter** or **margarine** and warm **maple sirup**. *About 6 waffles*

△ Sweet Milk Waffles

Follow ▲ Recipe. Omit baking soda and increase baking powder to 1 tablespoon. Substitute **milk** for buttermilk.

▲ French Toast
(See photo on page 332)

Set out a heavy skillet.

Beat slightly in a shallow dish or pie pan
   2 eggs
Mix in and set aside
   ⅔ cup milk or cream
   1 tablespoon sugar
   ½ teaspoon salt
Set out
   8 slices bread, white or whole wheat
   (Slightly dry bread produces firmer
   French Toast)
Heat in the skillet over low heat
   2 to 3 tablespoons butter or margarine
Dip bread slices one at a time into egg mixture. Coat each side well and place in hot skillet at once. Brown over moderate heat, turning once with spatula. If necessary, add more fat to keep slices from sticking.

Serve with **butter** or **margarine, maple sirup, honey, jam** or **confectioners' sugar**.

8 slices French Toast

Note: For oven method, place coated bread slices on a well-greased baking sheet. Brown in oven at 450°F about 10 min. for each side.

△ Oahu Toast

Drain contents of 1 No. 1 flat can **pineapple slices**. Follow ▲ Recipe, omit sugar and substitute **pineapple sirup** for milk. If can does not contain enough sirup, add **water**. Lightly brown pineapple slices in 2 to 3 tablespoons **butter** or **margarine**. Serve one-half pineapple slice with each slice of toast.

▲ Orange Sugar Toast

For Orange Sugar—Blend and set aside
   2 tablespoons sugar
   1 tablespoon grated orange peel
   (page 11)
   2 teaspoons orange juice
   ⅛ teaspoon nutmeg

For Toast—Remove crusts from
   4 slices bread
Set temperature control of range at Broil. Place slices on broiler rack; place in broiler about 3 in. from heat source. When brown, remove and spread untoasted sides with
   Butter or margarine
Sprinkle with Orange Sugar and return to broiler rack; broil until sugar is melted.

If desired, cut slices into fancy shapes.
4 slices Orange Sugar Toast

△ Cinnamon Caramel Toast

Follow ▲ Recipe. Substitute a mixture of 2 tablespoons **brown** or **maple sugar** and 1 teaspoon **cinnamon** for Orange Sugar.

△ English Muffin Crisps

Follow ▲ Recipe or △ Recipe. Substitute 2 split **English muffins** for bread. Butter and toast split sides only. Sprinkle with sugar mixture and continue as in ▲ Recipe.

BREADS in the MICROWAVE OVEN

A bonus for microwave oven users is to discover that both yeast breads and quick breads can be cooked by the microwave method. It is also an unexpected pleasure to produce a loaf of bread in 5 minutes!

There will be no questions about the quality of these breads. The flavor is good and the texture is light for all the breads included in this section, even the **Pioneer Griddlecakes**. The **Dumplings** are really excellent.

What does demand some re-education is the appearance of the breads. There is little browning and there is no firm crust, only a very light, crisp film on the surface of the breads. For breads which are colored by their ingredients or covered by a topping, such as **Sour Cream Kuchen**, this characteristic is not as evident. For plain **White Bread** we found one trick which turns the lack of crust into an advantage: make "crustless" sandwiches. They look like the most elegant tea sandwiches and are very impressive in unexpected places like lunch boxes.

Although some of the recipes in the main

text, when baked in the microwave oven, tasted good and had the proper texture, we have eliminated those which we considered unsuccessful due to appearance, such as the **Cherry-Almond Coffee Cake**. For the other recipes, it is relatively easy to get used to the lighter color.

REMINDERS—Do not grease pans or cooking dishes unless otherwise specified. Fat conducts heat more quickly in the microwave oven; even a light coating of grease will make the breads cook unevenly.

Making the Dough—One recipe, **Irish Batter Bread**, required an adjustment in the quantity of baking powder to make it rise evenly. For most of the other recipes, ingredients and preparation of the dough remain exactly as the recipe in the main text directs. Of course, the cooking times change, as is characteristic of microwave cooking. We have arranged all but four of the base recipes in an easy-to-read chart indicating the type of pan to be used, the approximate length of cooking time and clues as to when each bread is done. Be sure to read the information given at the top of the chart before preparing any of these recipes.

For Even Cooking it is very important to rotate the baking pan a full 360 degrees during the cooking cycle. Plan on rotating the pan 90 degrees at least 3 times while baking.

Test for Doneness—How do you know when the bread is done? Since color will not tell you, use your senses of touch and hearing and look for other clues in their appearance. Breads should spring back when pressed gently with a finger. The center of the bread is the last part to cook and will finish cooking while standing. So, test for springiness on the outer perimeter of the loaf. Also, tap the bread and listen for a hollow sound. The bread may pull away slightly from the sides of the pan and you may see crumbs through the glass sides of the baking dish or at the edges of the loaf. The rolls and also the **Sour Cream Kuchen** and **Kolachy** will feel somewhat spongy, but the top will be dry and spring back when touched lightly.

When the Bread is Done, immediately invert it onto a wire rack and remove any waxed paper (do not remove paper cups used for muffins); Let cool . To complete cooking, let the breads which you wish to serve hot stand for at least 5 minutes before you do so. This eliminates the somewhat doughy taste present when the bread is first removed from the oven. If the bread is not to be served immediately, let it cool , wrap it in plastic wrap or aluminum foil to prevent drying and store. Incidentally, all these breads are excellent for freezing. Of course, do not forget to thaw them quickly in the microwave oven.

FOR OTHER TIPS on successfully adapting recipes, see the introductory chapter, **Home Cooking in the Microwave Oven**, in the beginning of this book. This section also includes a chart of comparative settings among different brands of microwave ovens.

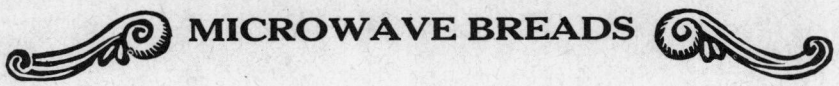
Read the material in the beginning of this section before proceeding.

RECIPE—The recipe title and page on which it appears in the main text are noted in this column. Times given are for the number of rolls or muffins per batch indicated or 1 loaf.

PAN USED—Unless otherwise specified, use one of the following as directed in the chart.

Loaf Pan—Use a 9x5x3-in. (2-qt.) glass loaf pan. Line the bottom only with ungreased waxed paper.

Baking Sheet—There are a number of options here. You may use paper plates or set the dough directly on a sheet of waxed paper placed on the bottom of the oven. For one recipe, we improvised a sheet of cardboard covered with waxed paper. This also made rotation of the bread much easier. For small quantities, use an 11-in. glass baking dish lined with waxed paper.

Muffin—The best results come from using the pleated muffin cups. Place each one in a 6-oz. glass custard cup or a wax-coated paper cup cut down to the appropriate height. Muffin batter can also be placed directly in the cut-off paper cup, if necessary. Cook the muffins while still in the pleated paper cups.

MINUTES TO COOK—Use the COOK setting. (See the Introductory chapter, **Home Cooking in the Microwave Oven**, for a chart of comparative settings among different brands of microwave ovens.) For each recipe, the time given in this column is the OVERALL COOKING TIME. For muffins and rolls, the time depends on the number cooked in each batch. If you vary from the quantities specified for each batch, adjust the length of cooking time accordingly (more time for more volume; less time for less volume).

Rotate the Baking Pan 90 degrees at least 3 times during the cooking period.

Standing Time is an essential part of baking these breads. Allow at least 5 minutes; do not cover.

TEST FOR DONENESS—This column tells you what to look for in a full-cooked bread. These "keys to doneness" are more thoroughly described in the material preceding this chart.

YEAST BREADS

	Recipe	Pan Used	Minutes to COOK	Test for Doneness
1 to **5**	**Yeast Rolls** (page 44) (6 per batch)			
1	**Fantans** (page 44) (6 per batch)	Muffin	5:00	Just springs back; top is dry; spongy; not brown.
2	**Parker House** (page 44) (6 per batch)	Muffin	3:00	See **Fantans**.
3	**Butterflies** (page 45) (6 per batch)	Muffin	3:30	See **Fantans**.
4	**Cinnamon Rolls** (page 46) (6 per batch)	Sheet	7:00	See **Fantans**.
5	**Pecan Rolls** (page 46) (6 per batch)	Muffin	6:00	See **Fantans**.
6	**White Bread** (page 48)	Loaf	5:00	Springy on edges; crumbs on side; hollow sound.
7	**Whole Wheat Bread** (page 49)	Loaf	6:00	See **White Bread**.
8	**My Fruit Bread** (page 50)	Loaf	COOK milk to scald (45 sec.) COOK 10:30	Pulls away from sides of pan; cake-like crumbs.
10	**Swedish Rye Bread** (page 52)	Sheet	5:00	Springy on edges; crumbs on side; hollow sound.
11	**Kolachy** (page 52) (8 per batch)	Sheet	3:00	Springy.

QUICK BREADS

	Recipe	Pan Used	Minutes to COOK	Test for Doneness
12	**Muffins** *(page 55)* *(6 per batch)*	Muffin	4:00	Pulls away from sides of pan; crumbs; slightly springy.
13	**Blueberry Muffins** *(page 55)* *(6 per batch)*	Muffin	4:00	See **Muffins**.
14	**Cranberry Muffins** *(page 55)* *(6 per batch)*	Muffin	4:00	See **Muffins**.
15	**Graham Gems** *(page 56)* *(12 per batch)*	Muffin	7:00	See **Muffins**.
16	**Prune Bran Muffins** *(page 56)* *(6 per batch)*	Muffin	2:30	See **Muffins**.
17	**Corn-Bread Squares** *(page 57)*	8x8x2-in. glass baking dish	4:00	Pulls away from sides of pan; cake-like crumbs.
18	**Ranch Bread** *(page 58)*	Loaf	6:00	See **Corn-Bread Squares**.
20	**Date-Nut Bread** *(page 60)*	Loaf	7:00	See **Corn-Bread Squares**.
21	**Fruit-Nut Bread** *(page 60)*	Loaf	7:00	See **Corn-Bread Squares**.
22	**Nut Bread** *(page 60)*	Loaf	6:00	See **Corn-Bread Squares**.

Sour Cream Kuchen **9**
(page 51)

Use an 8-in. square glass baking dish. Grease the bottom of the dish and cover it with waxed paper.

Prepare only half the recipe since only 1 layer at a time can be cooked in the microwave oven and this should be served warm.

COOK milk until scalded (about 1½ min.).

COOK cake, rotating every 2 min., until it springs back from the touch and is dry on top (about 7½ min.).

Add toppings and SLOWCOOK to heat sour cream (about 2 min.).

Cover and let stand 5 min.
OVERALL COOKING TIME: 11.00

Irish Batter Bread (page 59) **19**

Use a 9x5x3-in. glass loaf pan. Line the bottom only with ungreased waxed paper.

Follow Recipe for preparation of dough except use 2 teaspoons (instead of 4) baking powder.

COOK, rotating every 1½ min., until bread is springy to the touch and has a hollow sound when tapped (about 6½ min.).

Let stand 5 min.
OVERALL COOKING TIME: 6:30

Dumplings (page 69) **23**

Cook dumplings atop the main dish. (Be sure the container is microwave safe.)

COOK until the liquid reaches a full boil. (Time to reach full boil will vary depending upon the type of food and the volume of food.)

Drop dumplings. Cover and COOK until "tight" and a little springy to the touch (about 3 min.). Do not stir.
OVERALL COOKING TIME: 3:00

Pioneer Griddlecakes **24**
(page 72)

Use a browning skillet. The times in this recipe are for a 10-in. skillet which will hold 4 griddlecakes.

COOK batter until bubbles appear on the top and the bottom is set, testing after 1 min. (about 2 min.). Turn and COOK other side until done (about 2 min.). Griddlecakes will not brown.

To keep warm until ready to serve, set aside in a covered dish.

COOK to reheat skillet (about 1 min.) between batches.
OVERALL COOKING TIME: 4:00

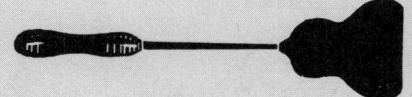

Buttermilk Griddlecakes **25**
(page 72)

Follow ⚠ Recipe for batter.

COOK as in **24** Recipe.
OVERALL COOKING TIME: 4:00

Blueberry Griddlecakes **26**
(page 72)

Follow ⚠ Recipe for batter.

COOK as in **24** Recipe.
OVERALL COOKING TIME: 4:00

Corn Meal Griddlecakes **27**
(page 72)

Follow ⚠ Recipe for batter.

COOK as in **24** Recipe.
OVERALL COOKING TIME: 4:00

BREADS in the SLOW COOKER

There is something about cooking breads in the slow cooker which seems to tease out extra flavor, giving these recipes a very special taste.

All of the ingredients and the preparation of the dough are exactly the same as given in the main text. The only change is in the cooking times. We have, therefore, listed these recipes in the form of a handy chart.

REMINDERS—There are a few generalities about cooking these breads in the slow cooker which you should bear in mind.

All of the recipes in this section were baked in the 3½-quart slow cooker set on HIGH.

The dough is not placed directly in the slow cooker, of course, but in a separate baking container. Best for this is the specially designed slow cooker baking pan, available with cover as an accessory for most slow cookers. We used the 6-inch diameter, 2-quart size which is perfect to accommodate the size of one loaf of bread as specified in the recipes.

If a baking pan is not available for your brand of slow cooker, use a 2-pound coffee can (this will also hold the equivalent of one loaf). Cover coffee cans with aluminum foil, fasten with string and use a toothpick to puncture a few holes in the foil. This will allow steam to escape.

A great deal of steam is given off by the slow cooking method. To absorb the steam and prevent it from falling back onto the bread, line the lid of the slow cooker with crumpled paper towels, holding the towels in place with rubber bands. Also leave the top of the slow cooker slightly ajar. This permits some steam to escape while the paper towels absorb the remainder.

Timing with breads in the slow cooker is not as flexible as with other dishes. They will overcook if you are detained away from home that extra hour.

Test for Doneness—Check the breads for doneness no more than 30 minutes before the end of the recommended cooking times. If you peek sooner or more often, the breads will fall. A toothpick inserted in the bread should come out clean when the bread is done. Also, the bread will pull away slightly from the side of the container, have a slightly brown crust on the top and sides and spring back when pressed lightly on the perimeter of the loaf. The texture of the bread will be slightly heavier than when cooked in a conventional oven.

When done, remove the baking pan from the slow cooker and let the bread cool in the baking pan about 10 minutes on a wire rack. Then turn the loaf out of the baking pan to cool completely on the rack.

For more tips, see the introductory chapter, **Home Cooking in the Slow Cooker**, which includes a chart of comparative settings among different brands of slow cookers. We suggest you review this chapter to also learn how we have adapted these recipes.

SLOW COOKER BREADS

Read the introductory material in the beginning of this section before proceeding. Pay special attention to **REMINDERS**.

When preparing the dough for these recipes, follow exactly the directions given for each recipe in the main text. The page on which you will find these instructions is noted with each recipe.

Place the dough in a specially-designed baking container or coffee can covered with aluminum foil and set it in the slow cooker. Turn the setting to HIGH and begin cooking time.

The test for doneness should be made 30 minutes before the end of the recommended cooking times given in the chart below.

YEAST BREADS

	Recipe	Cooking Time
1	White Bread (page 48)	2 hrs.
2	Whole Wheat Bread (page 49)	3½ hrs.
3	Oatmeal Bread (page 49)	3½ hrs.
4	My Fruit Bread (page 50)	3½ hrs.
5	Swedish Rye Bread (page 52)	2 hrs.

QUICK BREADS

	Recipe	Cooking Time
6	Ranch Bread (page 58)	2½ hrs.
7	Irish Batter Bread (page 59)	3½ hrs.
8	Date-Nut Bread (page 60)	3 hrs.
9	Fruit-Nut Bread (page 60)	3 hrs.
10	Nut Bread (page 60)	2½ hrs.

SANDWICHES and Sandwich Fillings

The Art of Sandwich Making

The Earl of Sandwich had only hunger and speedy service in mind when he called for his meat to be placed between two slices of bread. Little did he know what he started. In exploring his beguiling creation, homemakers have found that practically every food on earth is in some form or other suitable and indeed delectable as a sandwich filling.

VARIETY—Name a time, an occasion, or a meal—there is an appropriate sandwich for each of them.

The sandwich travels with the lunch carrier or picnicker. It accompanies soup or salad for luncheon. A hearty one is a main course for supper. The sandwich bar, where guests create their own, stars at late evening meals. The sandwich dons "fancy clothes" for parties, receptions and teas. It can be toasted or grilled. It can be made with as many slices of bread as desired: one for the open-face, the usual two, three for the club or decker, four or more for the super-stack. Even breakfast has its sandwich—**Eggs Benedict** (*page 89*). The variety in sandwiches is endless.

BREAD—Fresh bread is a must for a good sandwich. Achieve interest and appeal by using different kinds of bread. Bake or buy enriched white, square sandwich, French, Italian, Vienna, potato, pumpernickel, raisin, rye, whole or cracked wheat, nut or fruit bread, hard rolls, frankfurter rolls, or hamburger buns.

Ready-sliced bread is a great help for the sandwich maker. Always use adjacent slices so that sandwiches will be uniform and easy to cut when assembled. For party sandwiches the unsliced loaf is best because it can be cut into lengthwise slices.

To prevent rolled sandwiches from breaking, lightly roll soft bread slices with a rolling pin.

For Picture-Puzzle or Mosaic Sandwiches (*page 36*)—Cut shapes (rabbits, chickens, dogs for children's delights), or small geometric designs (crescents, rounds, diamonds, stars for party fancies) from centers of an equal number of dark and white bread slices. Fit dark bread cutouts into cutouts of white bread and white cutouts into cutouts of dark bread. Bottom slice is a whole piece; if desired use contrasting breads.

FILLINGS AND BUTTERS—Spread softened butter or margarine or seasoned butters evenly to the edges of the bread slice. This keeps the bread moist and the filling from soaking into the bread. Cream cheese and peanut butter also give protection.

Let not the hand that bestows the filling be skimpy. But neither should the filling be *too* generous; use just enough for appetizing, attractive sandwiches. Be sure the filling, either mixture or sliced food, extends to the edges.

In Choosing and Making Fillings Think About:
WHO *is going to eat the sandwich*—school child, afternoon tea guest, man-of-the-house.
WHAT *part of the menu the sandwich will be*—main course, accompaniment, accessory.
WHERE *the sandwich will be eaten*—picnic grounds, living room, kitchen.
WHEN *the sandwich will be eaten*—immediately, later in the day, in two or three weeks.
HOW *the sandwich will be eaten*—with a fork, from the fingers, from the hand.

Crisp lettuce leaves and tomato slices should be added to the sandwiches just before serving or wrapped separately when part of the carried lunch. Fillings that make the bread limp or soggy are not for the traveling sandwich.

Several thin slices of meat, poultry or cheese in a sandwich are better tasting and easier eating than one thick slice.

Fillings that are used in party sandwich loaves are good too in other sandwiches.

The old maxim, "Serve hot foods hot and cold foods cold," also applies to sandwiches. Hot sandwiches should never wait to be eaten. Sandwich makings that have been chilled, such as lettuce, tomatoes and salad fillings (chicken, fish, egg), are best when eaten still cold.

Warning About Sandwiches That Are Prepared a Few Hours Before They Will Be Eaten—Some fillings, such as meat, fish, poultry, eggs, soft cheeses and mayonnaise require special care to prevent growth of food-poisoning bacteria. The addition to sandwich fillings of an acid ingredient such as pickles, lemon juice or green olives helps to retain their keeping qualities. It is safest to eat these sandwiches within four hours after removal from refrigerator or freezer. When using meat leftovers for fillings, subtract the time they have been at room temperature from the safe keeping time— FOUR hours for prepared sandwiches.

Sandwiches made with jelly, peanut butter, hard or semi-hard cheese and raw vegetables usually are safe for summertime packed lunches when the heat might damage more perishable fillings.

PREPARATION—A hardwood cutting board, portable or built into the kitchen counter, is an excellent surface on which to prepare sandwiches. A short, flexible spatula with a blade 1½ inches wide and long enough to reach across a slice of bread is a useful tool. Be sure all knives are sharp.

Begin sandwich preparation by preparing fillings and by softening the spreads.

Be systematic when assembling sandwiches—do one job all at one time. Use tools and equipment, handling the sandwich as little as possible.

Line up adjacent slices of bread in pairs and evenly spread bread to the edges with the softened spread (see FILLINGS AND BUTTERS) at one time.

Spread fillings evenly or place sliced food to edges of one slice of each pair. Spread or place all of one kind of filling before using a second one. If desired, place lettuce leaves, slices of tomato or pickles over filling.

Top filling with matching bread slices and cut into halves, quarters, wedges or other interesting shapes and sizes (see illustrations).

Sandwich loaves, club sandwiches or sandwich stacks are assembled in a similar manner. Use matched slices of bread for each sandwich; spread both sides of inner bread slices with softened butter or margarine or seasoned butters.

WRAPPING—Wrap one whole sandwich or each section, securely and separately, in waxed paper, aluminum foil or in moisture-vapor-proof material. *Never* wrap or cover sandwiches (including those previously wrapped) with a damp cloth; the added moisture will encourage growth of some bacteria.

REFRIGERATION—Store wrapped sandwiches in refrigerator until the last minute. Sandwiches may be kept successfully in the refrigerator at 50°F or below up to 12 hours. Fillings should always be refrigerated until ready to use.

FREEZING—Sandwiches may be kept in the freezer for two or three weeks or held in the freezing compartment of the refrigerator for one week. Sandwich fillings that freeze best include sliced or chopped meat or poultry, fish, American Cheddar or cream cheese or peanut butter.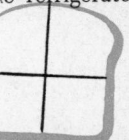

Precautions to Heed When Freezing Sandwiches Do not spread with mayonnaise, salad dressing or jelly—they soak into the bread. Leave out lettuce, tomatoes, parsley and water cress—they lose their crispness. Do not use egg salad or sliced hardcooked eggs—freezing toughens egg white.

To Prepare Sandwiches for Freezing—Wrap each separately in moisture-vapor-proof material; seal and label with description and date. Wrapped sandwiches may be placed together in an appropriate carton for compact storage. Open-face sandwiches should be placed on squares of heavy cardboard covered with moisture-vapor-proof material and then wrapped. Wrap rolled sandwiches and sandwich loaves uncut.

Frozen sandwiches will thaw in 1 to 2 hours depending upon size. Sandwiches packed directly from the freezer into the carried lunch or picnic basket thaw in 3 to 3½ hours, just in time to be eaten. Open-face sandwiches thaw most quickly. Unwrap sandwiches when partially thawed. Sandwiches should be thawed just in time for serving; if not served immediately place in the refrigerator.

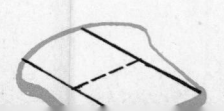

Each recipe on pages 76 and 77 makes enough filling for 4 sandwiches.

▲ Bacon and Liver Filling

The Earl of Sandwich himself would be pleased with these variations of his popular creation.

Prepare, put into a bowl and toss together
- ¾ cup (about 6 oz.) chopped, cooked liver
- 4 slices Panbroiled Bacon (page 161), crumbled

Blend in lightly a mixture of
- 3 tablespoons salad dressing
- 2 teaspoons minced onion
- 1 teaspoon prepared mustard
- ½ teaspoon salt
- ⅛ teaspoon Accent

△ Egg and Liver Filling

Follow ▲ Recipe. Mix in 1 **Hard-Cooked Egg** (*page 87*), finely chopped.

▲ Ham 'n' Cheese Supreme Filling

Prepare, put into a bowl and toss together
- ¾ cup (6 oz.) cream-style cottage cheese
- ⅓ cup (3-oz. can) deviled ham
- ¼ cup (about 1 oz.) salted peanuts without skins, chopped

Blend in lightly a mixture of
- 2 tablespoons salad dressing
- 1 tablespoon prepared horse-radish
- 1 teaspoon chopped chives
- ¼ teaspoon Accent

△ Fruit 'n' Cheese Supreme Filling

Follow ▲ Recipe. Omit ham, horse-radish and chives. Mix in 3 tablespoons **fruit preserves.**

▲ Beef Sandwich Filling

EVELYN N. REED, WHITE RIVER JCT., N.H.

Grind (*page 107*) together
- 4 oz. dried beef
- 3 Hard-Cooked Eggs (page 87)

Blend in, mixing lightly but thoroughly
- 2 tablespoons chopped celery
- 2 tablespoons chopped onion
- ⅓ cup mayonnaise

△ Nippy Beef Sandwich Spread

Follow ▲ Recipe. Blend 1 to 2 teaspoons **prepared horse-radish** with mayonnaise. Spread on thin slices of **rye bread.**

▲ Basic Egg Salad Filling

Gets the vote of the carry-a-lunch crowd.

Prepare, put into a bowl and toss together
- 4 Hard-Cooked Eggs (page 87), finely chopped
- 3 tablespoons chopped sweet pickle

Blend in lightly a mixture of
- 3 tablespoons salad dressing
- ½ teaspoon prepared mustard
- ¼ teaspoon onion salt
- Few grains pepper
- Few shakes Accent

△ Egg Filling Variations

Follow ▲ Recipe. Blend in one of the following: 2 tablespoons finely chopped **water cress;** 2 tablespoons chopped **green pepper;** 1 **frankfurter,** finely chopped; 2 tablespoons chopped **green** or **ripe olives;** ¼ cup finely chopped **celery;** 1 tablespoon drained, chopped **pimiento;** 1 tablespoon chopped **chives;** 1 tablespoon **prepared horse-radish.**

He-Man Cheese Filling

MRS. ROBERT KARLOSKE
PITTSVILLE, WIS.

Blend together thoroughly
- **1 cup (8 oz.) cream-style cottage cheese**
- **¼ cup (1 oz.) crumbled Roquefort cheese**
- **1 tablespoon mayonnaise**

Add, mixing lightly but thoroughly
- **4 slices Panbroiled Bacon (page 161), crumbled**
- **1 tablespoon chopped stuffed olives**

Peanut Butter-Raisin Sandwich Filling

ETTA DEVINE, FARMINGTON, N. MEX.

Blend together.
- **1 cup (8 oz.) peanut butter**
- **¾ cup orange juice**

Blend in, mixing lightly but thoroughly
- **¾ cup (about 4-oz.) ground seedless raisins**
- **1 teaspoon grated orange peel (page 11)**

Waldorf Water Cress Salad Filling

Prepare, put into a bowl and toss together
- **¼ cup chopped water cress**
- **¼ cup finely chopped celery**
- **¼ cup (about 1 oz.) finely chopped walnuts**
- **½ cup (about 1 medium-size) finely chopped, unpared apple**

Blend in lightly a mixture of
- **2 to 3 tablespoons salad dressing**
- **¼ teaspoon salt**

Garden Variety Filling

Prepare, put into a bowl and toss together
- **¾ cup (about 3 medium-size) grated carrot**
- **½ cup (about 2 stalks) finely chopped celery (page 12)**
- **2 tablespoons grated sharp cheese**
- **1 tablespoon finely chopped green pepper**

Blend in lightly a mixture of
- **2 tablespoons salad dressing**
- **1 tablespoon chili sauce**
- **¼ teaspoon salt**
- **¼ teaspoon Accent**
- **Few grains pepper**

▲ Favorite Fish Filling

Prepare, put into a bowl and toss together
- **¾ cup flaked (page 12) salmon or tuna**
- **½ cup finely chopped cabbage**
- **3 tablespoons chopped ripe olives**

Blend in lightly a mixture of
- **3 tablespoons salad dressing**
- **1 tablespoon olive juice**
- **¼ teaspoon Accent**
- **¼ teaspoon paprika**
- **2 or 3 drops tabasco sauce**

⚠ Favorite Sea Food Filling

Follow ▲ Recipe. Substitute ¾ cup chopped, cooked **shrimp** or shredded, cooked **crab meat** (bony tissue removed) for tuna or salmon.

⚠ Fish-Cheese Filling

Follow ▲ Recipe or ⚠. Substitute 2 tablespoons crumbled **Roquefort** or **blue cheese** for olives; increase the salad dressing to ¼ cup and omit the olive juice.

Bacon and Tomato Double-Decker

MRS. R. A. TILMANN, ELKHART, IND.

Set out to soften at room temperature
¼ cup butter or margarine
Blend together
½ cup (4 oz.) peanut butter
8 slices Panbroiled Bacon (page 161), crumbled
Rinse and cut away stem ends from
2 medium-size tomatoes
Cut tomatoes into eight slices and set aside.

Rinse and pat dry
4 crisp lettuce leaves
Set out on a flat working surface
12 slices white or whole wheat bread
Spread each slice with the butter or margarine.

Arrange one lettuce leaf and two tomato slices over the butter on each of four bread slices. Spread buttered sides of four slices with pea-nut-butter-bacon mixture. Stack these on the first slices. Top with remaining bread slices, buttered side down. Cut each sandwich diagonally into four sections.   *4 sandwiches*

Cottage Cheese and Tomato Sandwiches

MARGARET M. SMITH, BOISE, IDAHO

Blend together and chill in refrigerator
¾ cup (6 oz.) cream-style cottage cheese
2 tablespoons chopped water cress
2 tablespoons chopped stuffed olives
Rinse and cut away stem ends from
2 medium-size tomatoes
Cut tomatoes into eight slices and set aside.

Set out on a flat working surface
8 slices white or whole wheat toast, buttered on one side only
Spread buttered sides of four slices of toast with the cottage cheese mixture. Arrange two tomato slices on each. Top with remaining slices, buttered side down.   *4 sandwiches*

Shrimp Sailboats

For Shrimp Filling—(This makes about 2 cups filling.) Set out to soften at room temperature
½ cup butter or margarine
Cream butter thoroughly in a bowl. Blend in
1½ cups (2 5-oz. cans, drained) shrimp, finely chopped
Blend in, mixing thoroughly
¼ cup chili sauce
2 tablespoons lemon juice
4 teaspoons minced onion
½ teaspoon salt
⅛ teaspoon Accent
3 drops tabasco sauce
Chill in refrigerator about 1 hr.

Shortly before serving, prepare "Sailboats." Spoon filling into toasted "boats" and set "sails" in place. Garnish each "boat" with a bit of **water cress** or **parsley.**

For "Sailboats"—Set out
8 3½x2-in. hard rolls
Make a rectangular cut ½ in. from edges of rolls and ½ in. deep in each roll. Carefully remove rectangles and cut each diagonally into halves to form two "sails." Spread the inside of the "sailboats" and "sails" with a mixture of
¼ cup butter or margarine, softened
¾ teaspoon lemon juice
Place the "sailboats" and "sails" in a 350°F oven about 15 to 20 min., or until toasted.
          8 shrimp sailboat rolls

Tuna Club Sandwiches
PAT HART, GRAND FORKS, N.DAK.

Set out to soften at room temperature
¼ cup butter or margarine
Drain and flake (*page 12*) contents of
1 7-oz. can tuna (about 1 cup, flaked)
Blend in, mixing lightly but thoroughly, a mixture of
½ cup mayonnaise
1½ tablespoons lemon juice
1 tablespoon finely chopped onion
1 teaspoon salt
¼ teaspoon curry powder
¼ teaspoon Accent
Place in refrigerator until ready to use.

Rinse and cut away stem ends from
2 medium-size tomatoes
Cut tomatoes into eight slices and set aside.

Rinse, pat dry and set aside
4 crisp lettuce leaves
Set out on a flat working surface
12 slices white bread
Spread each slice with the butter or margarine.

Arrange one lettuce leaf and two tomato slices on each of four bread slices. Spread four bread slices with tuna mixture. Stack these on first slices. Top with remaining bread slices, buttered side down. Cut each sandwich diagonally into four sections.   *4 sandwiches*

Baked Cheese Loaf-Sandwich

IRENE BURI NELSON, KENOSHA, WIS.

Prepare and put into a bowl
1 cup (4 oz.) grated Cheddar cheese
3 tablespoons chopped stuffed olives
2 tablespoons finely chopped onion
Blend in lightly a mixture of
3 tablespoons chili sauce
1 tablespoon prepared horse-radish
¼ teaspoon Worcestershire sauce
¼ teaspoon Accent
Put the mixture in refrigerator to chill until ready to use.

Rinse and cut away stem end from
1 medium-size tomato
Cut tomato into four slices and set aside.

Set out
4 slices cooked ham
Using a sharp knife, cut into halves lengthwise
French or Vienna Bread
Spread cheese mixture on cut sides of each half of bread. Arrange cooked ham slices and tomato slices on bottom half; cover with top half. Wrap loaf in aluminum foil.

Bake at 400°F 20 min., or until the loaf is thoroughly heated.

Cut crosswise into four servings. Serve immediately.   *4 servings*

Baked Bean, Bacon and Brown Bread Sandwiches
MRS. G. N. TIDD, BIGGERS, ARK.

Blend together and set aside
1½ cups (1-lb. can) canned
  baked beans in tomato sauce
¾ cup drained sweet pickle relish
1 tablespoon minced onion
Cut crosswise into halves
4 slices bacon
Set temperature control of range at Broil.

Set out on a flat working surface
8 slices Boston brown bread
Spread bread slices with
¼ cup softened butter or margarine
Spread baked-bean mixture over buttered side of bread slices. Top each sandwich with one-half slice of the bacon.

Arrange sandwiches on broiler rack. Place in broiler with tops about 3 in. from heat source. Broil about 4 min., or until bacon is crisp.

Serve immediately.   *8 sandwiches*

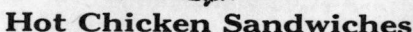

▲ Grilled Tuna or Salmon Salad Sandwiches

Set out a 10-in. skillet or an electric grill.

Drain and flake (*page 12*) contents of
**1 7-oz. can tuna or 1 7½-oz. can
   salmon (1 cup, drained and flaked)**
Set aside.

Grate
**1 oz. process cheese food (about
   ¼ cup, grated)**
Mix cheese and tuna with
**3 to 4 tablespoons salad dressing
1 teaspoon lemon juice
¼ teaspoon salt
¼ teaspoon Accent
⅛ teaspoon paprika**
Set out
**12 slices bread
¼ cup softened butter or margarine**
Spread one side of each slice with some of the butter or margarine. Spread fish mixture on buttered sides of six bread slices. Top with remaining bread slices, buttered side down. Press sandwiches firmly together.

Heat in the skillet
2 to 3 tablespoons butter or margarine
If using electric grill, heat and grease according to manufacturer's directions. Dip each sandwich (coat *both* sides) into a mixture of
**2 eggs, well beaten
1 cup milk
¼ teaspoon Accent**
Allow excess milk mixture to drain over bowl. Dip only as many sandwiches at one time as will lie flat in the skillet. Place sandwiches in skillet and brown over low heat about 5 min. Turn and brown other sides. Add more butter or margarine to skillet as necessary. Cut diagonally and serve immediately.   *6 sandwiches*

△ Grilled Chicken Salad Sandwiches

Follow ▲ Recipe. Substitute 1 cup minced, cooked **chicken** for tuna or salmon.

Hot Chicken Sandwiches

MRS. G. R. ENGEMAN
MOUNTAIN LAKE, MINN.

For Sandwich Spread—Prepare, put into a bowl and toss together
**1½ cups chopped, cooked chicken (see
   Stewed Chicken, page 205)
1 cup (4 oz.) grated Cheddar cheese
⅓ cup chopped celery
¼ cup finely chopped blanched almonds
   (page 11)**
Blend in lightly a mixture of
**½ cup Mayonnaise (page 319)
1 tablespoon chopped onion
1 tablespoon lemon juice
½ teaspoon Accent
¼ teaspoon salt**

For Sandwiches—Split with a sharp knife
6 sandwich buns
Spread the halves with
Butter or margarine, softened
Spoon an equal amount of the spread onto the bottom halves of buns. Top with remaining halves. Wrap separately in aluminum foil.

Place in a 350°F oven for 10 min., or until thoroughly heated.

Serve immediately.   *6 sandwiches*

Grilled Salmon Salad Sandwiches

Taste-Teaser
Tuna Sandwiches

For Tuna Filling—(*This makes about 2 cups filling.*) Mix thoroughly and set aside

   1 cup (7-oz. can, drained) flaked tuna (page 12)
   ¼ cup Panbroiled Bacon (page 161), crumbled
   ¼ cup chopped celery
   2 tablespoons chopped chives
   2 tablespoons chopped green pepper
   3 tablespoons mayonnaise
   ¼ teaspoon Accent
   ⅛ teaspoon pepper

For Sandwiches—Lightly grease an 8-in. square baking dish.

Arrange in two stacks on a flat working surface
   8 slices white or whole wheat bread
With a sharp knife, trim crusts from slices.

Spread one side of each slice with
   Prepared mustard
Spread four slices bread, mustard-side up, with the Tuna Filling. Place in baking dish. Top filling with remaining bread slices, placing them mustard-side down.

Spread lavishly over each sandwich
   Process cheese spread with pimiento
Set aside.

Beat until thick and piled softly
   3 eggs
Add and blend thoroughly
   1½ cups milk
   ¾ teaspoon salt
Pour the egg mixture over the sandwiches.

Bake at 325°F 40 min., or until golden brown.

Serve sandwiches hot, garnished with sprigs of **parsley** and a sprinkling of **paprika**. Accompany with relishes such as **Carrot Curls** and **Radish Fans** (*page 308*).   *4 sandwiches*

Taste-Teaser Tuna Sandwiches

Hot Creamy
Ham Sandwiches   ⑤
MRS. M. L. KERANEN, PELKIE, MICH.

Set out a 13½x8½x2¾-in. baking dish.

Prepare and chop finely
   1 Hard-Cooked Egg (page 87)
Blend together
   1 cup (about 4 oz.) ground cooked ham
   3 tablespoons mayonnaise
   ½ teaspoon Worcestershire sauce
Toast
   6 slices white or whole wheat bread
Spread ham mixture over toast. Arrange toast slices on bottom of the baking dish. Set aside.

Prepare
   1½ cups Medium White Sauce (one and one-half times recipe, page 323; add ¼ teaspoon dry mustard with the seasonings)
Stir in the chopped egg and
   1 tablespoon chopped green pepper
   ½ teaspoon salt
   ¼ teaspoon Accent
Pour sauce over toast slices in baking dish.

Top with
   6 slices (6 oz.) Cheddar cheese
Bake at 350°F about 20 min., or until cheese is melted.

Serve immediately.   *6 servings*

Hot California Sandwiches 6
MAXINE DENTON, OMAHA, NEBR.

For Sandwich Spread—Mix lightly
- ¾ cup (3 oz.) grated **Cheddar Cheese**
- 1 cup (1 medium-size) diced **tomato**
- ¼ cup chopped **onion**
- 2 tablespoons chopped **green pepper**
- 2 tablespoons **vinegar**

and a mixture of
- ½ teaspoon **salt**
- ¼ teaspoon **Accent**
- ¼ teaspoon **chili powder**

Set aside.

For Sandwiches—Set temperature control of range at Broil.

Toast on one side only
- 4 slices **white or whole wheat bread**

Spread the untoasted sides with
- **Butter or margarine**

Spread buttered side of each bread slice with the cheese mixture. Arrange sandwiches on broiler rack. Place in broiler with top of sandwiches 3 in. from heat source. Broil about 2 min., or until cheese is melted.

Serve immediately. *4 sandwiches*

Turkey or Chicken Supreme
MILDRED JAMISON, CHICKASHA, OKLA.

Set a bowl and rotary beater in refrigerator to chill.

Prepare and set aside
- 3 **Hard-Cooked Eggs** (page 87)

For Whipped Cream Dressing—Blend together thoroughly
- 3 tablespoons **mayonnaise**
- 2 tablespoons **chili sauce**
- 1 tablespoon minced **chives**

Using chilled bowl and rotary beater, whip (*page 13*)
- 1 cup chilled **whipping cream**

Gently blend in mayonnaise mixture. Place in refrigerator until ready to use.

Rinse, pat dry and set aside
- 3 large crisp **lettuce leaves**

Rinse and cut away stem ends from
- 2 medium-size **tomatoes**

Cut tomatoes into 6 slices. Season with
- **Salt**
- **Accent**

Set aside.

Set out
- 3 slices cooked **turkey or chicken**
- 3 slices **Swiss cheese**
- 3 slices **white bread**, toasted and buttered on one side only

To make each sandwich, place 1 slice of the toast, buttered side up, on a plate. Top with a lettuce leaf, 1 slice turkey or chicken, 1 slice Swiss cheese and 2 tomato slices. Slice the Hard-Cooked Eggs and top each sandwich with 3 or 4 slices. Spread lightly about ¾ cup of the Whipped Cream Dressing over each.

For an attractive luncheon plate, arrange on each plate with the sandwich
- Whole spiced **apple**
- **Potato chips**

Garnish with **water cress.** *3 sandwiches*

▲ Asparagus Roll-Ups

Trim crusts from
- **Bread slices**

Flatten slightly with a rolling pin. Spread each slice with
- **Mayonnaise or salad dressing**

Lay across each bread slice
- **Asparagus stalk**, cooked, chilled, and cut to length of sandwich

Roll bread around asparagus. Place the sandwiches, overlapping side down, close together on waxed paper, moisture-vapor-proof material or aluminum foil. Wrap; chill thoroughly.

△ Asparagus Miniatures

Follow ▲ Recipe. Cut roll-ups crosswise into ½-in. slices. Chill before serving.

Creamy Anchovy Stars

For Creamy Anchovy Spread—(*This makes 1 cup spread.*) Measure into a small bowl

¾ cup thick sour cream
¼ cup mayonnaise
1 teaspoon anchovy paste
½ teaspoon onion salt

Blend ingredients together thoroughly.

For Sandwiches—Trim crusts from
Bread slices

With a star-shaped cookie cutter, cut stars from the bread. Spread each star with
Butter or margarine

Then spread each star with Creamy Anchovy Spread. Garnish each with a slice of
Ripe olive

Or, lay a rolled **anchovy fillet** in center of each. For variety, stack two or three stars.

Citrus Ribbon Sandwiches

For Lemon-Cream-Cheese Filling—(*This makes about ½ cup filling.*) Blend together thoroughly

1 pkg. (3 oz.) cream cheese, softened
1 tablespoon milk
1 tablespoon lemon juice
1 tablespoon grated lemon peel
   (page 11)
¼ teaspoon salt

This filling may be prepared hours in advance, refrigerated, and softened at room temperature just before preparing sandwiches.

For Orange-Apricot Filling—(*This makes about ½ cup filling.*) Force through a sieve
½ cup apricot preserves

Add to sieved preserves and blend thoroughly
1 tablespoon orange juice
½ teaspoon grated orange peel
   (page 11)

For Sandwiches—Trim crusts from
4 slices bread

Spread each slice with
Butter or margarine

Assorted Party Sandwiches

Spread Lemon-Cream-Cheese Filling over two of the slices. Spread Orange-Apricot Filling over one slice. Stack the filling-spread slices together, filling side up. Top with the remaining bread slice, buttered side down. Press slices together firmly but gently; wrap and chill.

When ready to serve, cut sandwiches into ½-in. slices. If desired, cut each slice into smaller pieces. Or cut diagonally into four triangles or into quarters and then into smaller triangles.

Hawaiian Sandwiches
EVELYN N. REED, WHITE RIVER JCT., N.H.

Soften with a fork
8 oz. cream cheese

Blend in and chill in refrigerator
½ cup (about 2 oz.) chopped walnuts
⅓ cup chopped ripe olives

Drain contents of
1 9-oz. can sliced pineapple (4 slices pineapple)

(Reserve sirup for use in other food preparation.) Cut pineapple slices to make 8 rings.

Cut into 3-in. rounds
8 slices white or whole wheat bread

Place one pineapple slice on top of each bread round. Spread cream cheese mixture over pineapple slices. Garnish with **parsley.**

8 sandwiches

Frosted Sandwich Treats and coffee

Frosted Sandwich Treats

The dark rich flavor of coffee rounds out this luncheon treat of sandwiches five-fillings high.

Set out to soften at room temperature
>   **1 cup butter or margarine**

For Almond-Olive Spread—Blend together
>   **¾ cup (about 4 oz.) toasted, blanched almonds (*page 11*), finely chopped**
>   **½ cup (about 3 oz.) chopped stuffed olives**
>   **2 tablespoons mayonnaise**
>   **1 teaspoon prepared mustard**
>   **⅛ teaspoon Accent**

Place in refrigerator until ready to use.

For Avocado Spread—Blend together
>   **1 cup (about 1 large) sieved avocado**
>   **¼ cup (about 1 oz.) crumbled Roquefort cheese**
>   **1 teaspoon lemon juice**
>   **¼ teaspoon garlic salt**

Place in refrigerator until ready to use.

For Ham-Horse-radish Spread—Blend together
>   **2 cups (about ½ lb.) ground cooked ham**
>   **¼ cup minced parsley**
>   **2 tablespoons thick sour cream**
>   **2 tablespoons prepared horse-radish**

Place in refrigerator until ready to use.

For Cucumber Spread—Beat together until fluffy
>   **8 oz. cream cheese, softened**
>   **⅔ cup (about 1 small) grated cucumber**
>   **1 teaspoon finely chopped chives**
>   **¼ teaspoon Accent**
>   **⅛ teaspoon onion salt**
>   **⅛ teaspoon salt**
>   **⅛ teaspoon pepper**

Place in refrigerator until ready to use.

For Crab-Meat Spread—Blend together
>   **1½ cups (6½-oz. can) drained crab meat (bony tissue removed)**
>   **¼ cup mayonnaise**
>   **2 tablespoons ketchup**
>   **1 tablespoon lemon juice**
>   **½ teaspoon Worcestershire sauce**
>   **¼ teaspoon salt**
>   **¼ teaspoon Accent**
>   **⅛ teaspoon pepper**

Place in refrigerator until ready to use.

For "Frosting"—Beat together until fluffy
>   **8 oz. cream cheese, softened**
>   **3 tablespoons orange juice**
>   **2 drops yellow food coloring**

Cover and set aside.

For Sandwiches—Arrange in several stacks on a flat working surface
>   **42 slices thin-sliced white bread**

With a sharp knife, trim off crusts. Spread each slice with the softened butter or margarine.

Spread 7 bread slices with Crab-Meat Spread, 7 bread slices with the Almond-Olive Spread, 7 bread slices with the Ham-Horse-radish Spread, 7 bread slices with Cucumber Spread and 7 bread slices with Avocado Spread.

Arrange these slices in 7 stacks, 5 different fillings in each stack. Top each stack with one of the 7 remaining bread slices, buttered side down. Cut each stack diagonally into halves. Spread top and one side of each stack with the cream cheese "Frosting."

Garnish each triangle with one of the following which has been impaled on a cocktail pick:

pimiento-stuffed olive, small cooked shrimp, pickled onion or anchovy fillet.

Arrange triangles on serving platter in two pinwheels (see photo). Garnish with **Radish Roses** (*page 308*) and **parsley**.   *14 servings*

Party Sandwich Loaf

Set out to soften at room temperature
   ½ cup butter or margarine

For Chicken-Bacon Filling—Thoroughly blend together
   1 cup finely chopped, cooked chicken (see Stewed Chicken, *page 205*)

   8 slices Panbroiled Bacon (*page 161*), crumbled
   ¼ cup mayonnaise
   1 tablespoon finely chopped pimiento
And a mixture of
   ¼ teaspoon salt
   ¼ teaspoon Accent
   ⅛ teaspoon pepper
Place in refrigerator until ready to use.

For Toasted Pecan Filling—Blend together
   1 pkg. (3 oz.) cream cheese, softened
   1 cup (about 4 oz.) finely chopped, toasted pecans (*page 12*)
   ¾ cup (9-oz. can) well-drained crushed pineapple (reserving sirup for "Frosting")
Place in refrigerator until ready to use.

Party Sandwich Loaf

For Shrimp Salad Filling—Blend together
   1⅓ cups (7-oz. can) finely chopped shrimp
   ¼ cup finely chopped celery
   ¼ cup chili sauce
   1 Hard-Cooked Egg (*page 87*), chopped
   2 tablespoons lemon juice
   ¼ teaspoon salt
   ⅛ teaspoon Accent
   Few grains pepper
Place in refrigerator until ready to use.

For "Frosting"—Beat together until fluffy
   Reserved pineapple sirup (about ¼ cup)
   8 oz. cream cheese, softened
   1 or 2 drops red food coloring
Cover and set aside.

For Sandwich Loaf—Set out on a flat working surface and trim crust from
   1 unsliced loaf sandwich bread
Cut the loaf into four equal lengthwise slices. Slightly flatten each with a rolling pin. Spread one side of each slice with the softened butter. Place 1 bread slice, buttered side up, on a serving platter. Spread evenly with Shrimp Salad Filling. Top with second bread slice and spread evenly with Toasted Pecan Filling. Top with third bread slice and spread evenly with Chicken-Bacon Filling. Top with remaining bread slice, buttered side down. Frost sides and top of loaf with "Frosting."

Garnish top of loaf with
   Pickle relish
   Stuffed olive slices
Garnish with crisp greens or decorate platter with huckleberry leaves.

Place in refrigerator to chill until "Frosting" is firm (1 to 2 hrs.).

Serve loaf cut into slices.   *8 to 10 servings*

SANDWICHES in the MICROWAVE OVEN

The sandwiches included here are ideal for lunch or supper on days when the family is on an erratic schedule. The fillings can be prepared and the sandwiches partly or completely assembled at your convenience, then heated quickly as children, spouse or friends arrive. Because you can heat the sandwiches directly on plates (be sure they are microwave safe) or waxed paper, the serving of these dishes is simplified and you eliminate some of the chore of cleanup.

REMINDERS—A note on toasting bread. Bread will not brown in the microwave oven; it will become sufficiently crisp to hold the fillings.

As you know, the more volume a microwave oven contains, the longer the cooking time. One recipe, **Grilled Tuna or Salmon Salad Sandwiches**, calls for the use of a 10-inch browning skillet which will hold only half of the sandwiches. If you use a smaller or larger browning skillet (less or more volume) you will have to adjust the cooking times accordingly. This will also hold true for **Hot Creamy Ham Sandwiches.**

Review the introductory chapter, **Home Cooking in the Microwave Oven**, in the beginning of this book for other general hints and to learn how we have adapted these recipes.

Baked Cheese Loaf-Sandwich *(page 79)*

Assemble sandwiches as in Recipe, but cut into 4 servings before cooking. Wrap each separately in plastic wrap, NOT aluminum foil. To melt cheese, COOK, rotating every minute (about 3 min.).

OVERALL COOKING TIME: 3:00

Grilled Tuna or Salmon Salad Sandwiches *(page 80)*

Use a 10-in. browning skillet.

COOK butter in browning skillet until it starts to brown.

For coating mixture, combine 4 beaten eggs (instead of 2) with the milk and Accent and assemble sandwiches as in Recipe. Only two sandwiches will fit in the browning skillet at the same time. COOK until slightly brown (about 4 min.), turn sandwiches over and COOK other side until slightly brown (additional 4 min.).

Serve as in Recipe.

OVERALL COOKING TIME: 8:00

Grilled Chicken Salad Sandwiches *(page 80)*

Follow **2** Recipe, substituting chicken as in △ Recipe.

OVERALL COOKING TIME: 8:00

Hot Chicken Sandwiches *(page 80)*

Wrap each sandwich separately in plastic wrap, NOT aluminum foil. Arrange on sheet of waxed paper or plates. COOK until heated (about 2½ min.).

OVERALL COOKING TIME: 2:30

Hot Creamy Ham Sandwiches *(page 81)*

Set out a baking dish. Times given here are for a baking dish which will hold only 4 sandwiches.

COOK all 6 slices of bread until slightly crisp (about 3 min.).

Assemble sandwiches as in Recipe, arrange in baking dish and top with sauce. COOK until cheese melts (about 4 min.).

COOK remaining sandwiches until cheese melts (about 1 to 1½ min.).

OVERALL COOKING TIME: 10:30

Hot California Sandwiches *(page 82)*

Place bread on waxed paper and COOK until crisp (about 2 min.).

Arrange assembled sandwiches on waxed paper and COOK until cheese melts (about 4 min.).

OVERALL COOKING TIME: 6:00

SANDWICHES in the SLOW COOKER

Sandwiches are probably the last item most people would consider for the slow cooker, and in general, most people would be right. However, we have included two recipes which proved successful and which are ideal for days when everyone, including the cook, is on a tight schedule. The sandwiches, after the minimum cooking times we indicate, can be held hot and ready for family or friends to serve themselves.

REMINDERS—Review the introductory chapter, **Home Cooking in the Slow Cooker**, in the beginning of this book for general hints and to learn how we have adapted these recipes.

Baked Cheese Loaf-Sandwich *(page 79)* **1**

Use a 5-qt. slow cooker.

Cut loaf into 4 sandwiches before cooking. Wrap each sandwich in aluminum foil and arrange in slow cooker.

Cook on LOW for 3 to 4 hrs.

Hot Chicken Sandwiches *(page 80)* **2**

Use a 5-qt. slow cooker.

Wrap each assembled sandwich in aluminum foil and arrange in slow cooker.

Cook on LOW for 2 to 4 hrs.

EGG and CHEESE DISHES

What You Should Know About Eggs

The perfection of an egg is one of Nature's miracles. For here is an object lovely in form, filled with nourishment, and possessed of a flavor that is delicious in itself and is an admirable flavor foil for innumerable seasonings and sauces. Few foods match the egg in versatility. Eggs can take us through the day with grace and ease—are equally appealing in the morning, at noon or night.

Grading—Graded eggs in cartons kept in a clean, cold refrigerator by the dealer are safe buys.

Eggs may be graded according to federal, state or private standards. U.S. grades refer to interior quality; sizes refer to weight per dozen.

Grade AA and A eggs are top quality. They have a large amount of thick white and a high, firm yolk. Good for all uses, they are the best choice for poaching, frying or cooking in the shell. Grade B and C eggs have thinner whites and somewhat flatter yolks which may break easily. Offering the same food values as top-grade eggs, these less expensive eggs are a practical buy for scrambling, thickening sauces, making salad dressings and combining with other foods. Quality of eggs should be checked before using by breaking each egg into a small dish.

Most eggs are grouped according to these sizes: extra large, large, medium and small—with a minimum weight per dozen of 27, 24, 21 and 18 ounces respectively. Medium and small eggs are usually more plentiful in summer and early fall and at that time are likely to be a good buy.

Whether the color of the egg shell is brown or white makes no difference in the quality or food value of the egg, though in some localities it does influence price.

Nutrients—Eggs are an important food for children and adults alike because they contain many important nutrients—complete protein, vitamins A and D, the B vitamins, iron and phosphorus.

Storing—As soon as possible after purchasing, put eggs into the refrigerator or store at a cool temperature (large rounded end up). Remove only as many eggs as needed at one time. Washing eggs before storing removes the film or "bloom" which seals the pores of the shell and helps keep out bacteria and odors. If necessary wipe eggs with a damp cloth. Wash eggs just before using.

Food Preparation—The fundamental rule in egg cookery—*Cook eggs with low to moderate, even heat.* This applies to all methods of cooking eggs—and cheese dishes. Too high a heat toughens the protein in eggs and cheese, making eggs leathery and curdled and cheese stringy and separated.

In combining hot mixtures with whole eggs or egg yolks, always *slowly* add the hot mixture (3 or 4 spoonfuls or entire amount) to the beaten egg, stirring or beating constantly.

Separating egg yolks from egg whites is quicker and easier if eggs are about 60°F. Remove eggs from refrigerator about 45 min. before using. Eggs at room temperature, especially egg whites, beat to a larger volume than eggs taken directly from the refrigerator. (For stages of beating eggs see *page 10*.)

Leftover egg whites may be stored in refrigerator; use within 10 days. Uses for egg whites: angel food or white cake, seven-minute frosting, meringue. Store leftover egg yolks in refrigerator; use within 2 or 3 days. Or hard-cook egg yolks; use for salads, sauces, garnish.

▲ Soft-Cooked Eggs

Put into a saucepan and cover completely with cold or warm water

4 eggs

Cover. Bring water rapidly to boiling. Turn off heat. If necessary to prevent further boiling, remove saucepan from source of heat. Let stand covered 2 to 4 min., depending on firmness desired.   *4 servings*

Note: Eggs are a protein food and therefore should never be boiled.

△ Hard-Cooked Eggs

Follow ▲ Recipe. After bringing water to boiling, let eggs stand covered 20 to 22 min. Plunge cooked eggs promptly into running cold water. Immediately crackle shells under water. Roll egg between hands to loosen shell. When cooled, start peeling at large end.

▲ Creamed Eggs

Prepare

6 Hard-Cooked Eggs (*on this page*)

Meanwhile, prepare

2 cups Medium White Sauce (double recipe, page 323)

Slice the eggs crosswise into the sauce. Heat quickly, moving mixture gently to avoid breaking egg slices. Add additional salt and pepper if desired.

Serve on hot, buttered, toasted **bread** or **English muffin halves**, **waffles** or **baking powder biscuits.**   *4 or 5 servings*

⚠ Piquant Creamed Eggs

Follow ▲ Recipe. When sauce is thickened, quickly blend in 2 to 4 tablespoons **ketchup** and 1 teaspoon **prepared mustard** before adding sliced eggs.

⚠ Country Creamed Eggs

Follow ▲ Recipe. Place 2 or 3 slices of **Pan-broiled Bacon** (*page 161*) on each serving of the suggested breads. Spoon creamed eggs over bacon. Garnish as desired.

⚠ Eggs Goldenrod

Follow ▲ Recipe. Cut the eggs into halves lengthwise and remove yolks. Cut egg whites into pieces and add to white sauce. Serve on slices of hot buttered toast; top with sieved or riced egg yolks.

⚠ Creamed Eggs with Mushrooms

Follow ▲ Recipe. Prepare **Medium White Sauce II** (double recipe, *page 323*). Reserve slices from two of the eggs for garnish. Add 1 cup cooked, sliced **mushrooms** to white sauce with the sliced eggs; heat thoroughly. Serve over hot buttered **Toast Points** (*page 65*) in individual serving dishes. Garnish with reserved egg slices.

Creamed Eggs with Mushrooms

▲ Eggs Stuffed with Chicken Liver Paste

MRS. ED JENSEN, SIOUX CITY, IOWA

Prepare
5 Hard-Cooked Eggs (page 87)
Meanwhile, rinse with cold water and drain on absorbent paper
¼ lb. chicken livers
Put livers into a saucepan and add
Hot water to barely cover
Cover saucepan and simmer 10 to 15 min., or until livers are tender when pierced with a fork. Drain and set aside to cool.

Prepare
4 slices Panbroiled Bacon (page 161)
Crumble bacon and set aside.

Force chicken livers through a sieve or food mill and set aside.

Cut each egg into halves lengthwise. Remove egg yolks to a bowl and mash with a fork or press through ricer or sieve into the bowl. Mix into egg yolks the liver, crumbled bacon and a mixture of
**1 tablespoon chopped parsley or
   dried parsley flakes**
1½ teaspoons minced chives
½ teaspoon onion salt
¼ teaspoon tarragon leaves, crushed
¼ teaspoon salt
¼ teaspoon pepper
Few grains cayenne pepper

Stir in, moistening to a thick, paste-like consistency
1½ to 2 tablespoons mayonnaise
Fill egg whites with liver mixture; sprinkle with
Paprika
Chill thoroughly in refrigerator.

To serve, garnish with **water cress** or **parsley.**

5 servings

△ Deviled Eggs

Follow ▲ Recipe; prepare 9 **Hard-Cooked Eggs.** Omit chicken livers and bacon. To cut eggs, use a narrow, sharp-pointed knife. Mark points in a saw-tooth line at ½-in. intervals lengthwise around each egg. Carefully cut down through marked line to yolk of egg; pull halves apart and carefully remove egg yolk. Omit seasoning mixture. Mix with riced or sieved egg yolks 6 tablespoons **thick sour cream,** 3 tablespoons **salad dressing,** ¾ teaspoon grated **onion,** 3 to 6 drops **tabasco sauce,** and a mixture of ½ teaspoon **garlic salt,** ½ teaspoon **celery salt,** ⅛ teaspoon **Accent** and ⅛ teaspoon **white pepper.** Omit mayonnaise.

Deviled Eggs: Mark sawtooth lines with a knife lengthwise around hard-cooked eggs.

Cut through egg white on marked line, gently pull halves apart; carefully remove egg yolk.

▲ Poached Eggs

Grease bottom of a heavy shallow pan or skillet. Add water to 2-in. depth or enough to rise 1 in. above tops of eggs.

Add to water
⅛ to ¼ teaspoon salt
Bring water to boiling and then reduce heat to keep water simmering.

Break separately into a saucer or small dish
4 eggs
Tilting dish toward edge of the pan, quickly slip each egg into water; do not crowd. Cook 3 to 5 min., depending upon firmness desired. Carefully remove eggs with slotted spoon or pancake turner. Hold on paper napkin a few seconds to drain.

Serve plain or on hot, buttered, toasted **bread** or **English muffin halves.** Season with **salt** and **pepper** or **paprika.** Garnish. *4 servings*

⚠ Poached Eggs with Mushroom or Cheese Sauce

Follow ▲ Recipe. Top with **Mushroom Sauce** (*page 323*) or **Cheese Sauce** (*page 323*), allowing about ¼ cup per serving.

⚠ Poached Eggs and Greens

In individual heat-resistant dishes, make nests of finely chopped, hot, well-seasoned **spinach, Swiss chard** or other cooked **greens.**

Grate 2 oz. (½ cup, grated) **Swiss, Parmesan** or **Cheddar cheese.** Sprinkle one half of cheese over greens. Keep hot while proceeding with ▲ Recipe. Place a poached egg in each nest of greens. If desired, top with **Medium White Sauce** (*page 323*), allowing about ¼ cup per serving. Sprinkle remaining cheese; arrange dishes on broiler rack.

Set temperature control of range at Broil and place rack in broiler with tops of eggs about 3 in. from source of heat. Broil about 5 min. or until cheese is melted.

Eggs Benedict

⚠ Eggs Benedict

Cover toasted, buttered **English muffin halves** with thin, round slices of hot **ham.** Proceed with ▲ Recipe. Place a poached egg on each ham round and top with **Hollandaise Sauce** (*page 324*), allowing ¼ cup per serving.

⚠ Savory Poached Eggs

Follow ▲ Recipe; use **meat** or **chicken stock** or **milk** instead of water. If desired, add additional seasoning, such as **marjoram** or **tarragon.** Garnish with crisp **bacon slices** (see Panbroiled Bacon, *page 161*).

⚠ Poached Eggs and Patties

Brown **Codfish Cakes** (*page 231*) or rounds of **hash** in 2 or 3 tablespoons **fat.** Keep hot while proceeding with ▲ Recipe. Top servings with poached eggs and serve with **Mock Hollandaise Sauce** (*page 323*) or **Cheese Sauce** (*page 323*), allowing ¼ cup per serving.

▲ Baked (Shirred) Eggs

Butter 6 individual casseroles or heat-resistant custard cups.

Break one at a time into a saucer or small dish
6 eggs
Slip each egg into a casserole. Sprinkle with
Few grains salt
Few grains pepper
Top each egg with
1 tablespoon cream
¼ teaspoon butter or margarine
Bake at 325°F, uncovered, 12 to 20 min., depending upon firmness desired.

Garnish and serve in casseroles.   *6 servings*

Baked Eggs in Bacon Rings

⚠ Baked Eggs in Bacon Rings

Line individual baking dishes or muffin pan wells with 1 or 2 slices partially-cooked **bacon** (see Panbroiled Bacon, *page 161*). 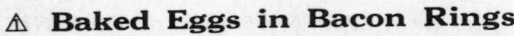 Omit buttering dishes. Proceed with ▲ Recipe.

⚠ Baked Eggs with Cheese

Follow ▲ Recipe. Add ⅛ teaspoon **Worcestershire sauce** with each tablespoon cream. In addition to seasonings, sprinkle each egg with 1 tablespoon grated **Swiss** or **Cheddar cheese** blended with ⅛ teaspoon **dry mustard**.

⚠ Nested Baked Eggs

Prepare 6 **Baked Filled Potatoes** (*page 295*). Stuff potato shells two-thirds full. Slip an egg into each. Season. Top with grated **cheese** if desired. Bake as in ▲ Recipe.

▲ Fried Eggs

Heat in a heavy skillet
1 to 2 tablespoons fat (kind of fat used will affect flavor of eggs)
Break into a saucer one at a time and slip into skillet
2 eggs per serving
Reduce heat and cook slowly about 4 min., or until eggs reach desired stage of firmness. Frequently baste eggs with fat in skillet. Or instead of basting, cover pan; or with spatula turn eggs over once.

Arrange eggs on **toast** (from which crusts have been removed) on a platter and accompany with **Broiled Canadian-Style Bacon** (*page 160*) and **Apple Rings** (*page 161*); garnish with sprigs of **parsley**.

△ Steamed Eggs

Follow ▲ Recipe, using just enough **butter** to cover bottom of skillet. Cook eggs about 1 min., or until edges turn white. Then, for each 2 eggs, add 1 teaspoon **water**. Slightly decrease proportion of water for each additional egg. Cover skillet tightly and let the steam which is formed cook the eggs to desired stage of firmness.

Deep-Fried Eggs with Mushroom-Wine Sauce

These hard-cooked eggs have a new look and new taste. The new look is due to their pancake-batter coating and the new taste to a mushroom-wine sauce.

For Mushroom-Wine Sauce—Set out an 8-in. skillet.

Prepare and set aside
  1 cup quick meat broth (page 13)
Clean and slice
  ½ lb. mushrooms (page 12)
Heat in the skillet over low heat
  6 tablespoons butter
Add the mushrooms to the butter with
  3 tablespoons finely chopped onion
  2 tablespoons finely chopped parsley
Cook slowly, moving and turning with a fork or spoon, until mushrooms are lightly browned and tender and onion is transparent. Remove contents of skillet to a bowl; cover bowl and set aside.

Melt in the skillet
  3 tablespoons butter or margarine
Blend in
  3 tablespoons flour
  ¾ teaspoon salt
  ⅛ teaspoon pepper
Heat until mixture bubbles and is lightly browned. Remove from heat. Gradually add the reserved broth, stirring constantly. Return to heat and bring rapidly to boiling, stirring constantly; cook 1 to 2 min. longer. Remove skillet from heat. Add gradually to sauce, stirring constantly
  ¾ cup dry white wine
Mix the mushrooms and the liquid in bowl with the sauce in skillet; cover and set aside.

For Eggs—Set out a deep saucepan or automatic deep-fryer (*page 13*) and heat fat to 375°F.

Prepare
  10 Hard-Cooked Eggs (page 87)

For Batter—Sift together and set aside
  1⅓ cups sifted flour
  ½ teaspoon salt
Put in a 1-qt. bowl and stir to blend
  2 eggs, slightly beaten
  ¼ cup milk
Add to egg mixture enough of the flour mixture to make a very stiff batter, stirring just until smooth.

Dry the Hard-Cooked Eggs thoroughly with absorbent paper. Cut two eggs into halves and wrap in waxed paper; set aside for garnish. Place remaining eggs in batter, a few at a time, and coat thoroughly. Carefully remove eggs from batter with fork or slotted spoon to the heated fat. Deep-fry eggs 3 to 4 min., or until golden brown. Fry only one layer of eggs at a time; do not crowd. Turn eggs occasionally to brown evenly. Remove eggs with slotted spoon; drain over fat for a few seconds before removing to absorbent paper.

Place the eggs on a warm platter. Garnish the platter with the reserved Hard-Cooked Egg halves and **parsley.** Serve with the Mushroom-Wine Sauce.   *4 servings*

Deep-Fried Eggs with Mushroom-Wine Sauce

▲ French Omelet

Set out an 8- to 10-in. skillet.

Beat together until well blended but not foamy

6 eggs
6 tablespoons water or milk
¾ teaspoon salt
⅛ teaspoon pepper

Heat the skillet until just hot enough to sizzle a drop of water. Heat in skillet

3 tablespoons butter or margarine

Pour egg mixture into skillet and reduce heat. As the edges of omelet begin to thicken, with a spoon or fork draw cooked portions toward center to allow uncooked mixture to flow to bottom of skillet. Shake and tilt skillet as necessary to aid flow of uncooked eggs. Do not stir.

When eggs no longer flow but surface is still moist, the heat may be increased to quickly brown the bottom of omelet. Loosen edges carefully and fold in half. Slide onto a warm serving platter. Garnish.   *4 to 6 servings*

Note: Omelets to which other ingredients are added are often cooked in smaller portions, pancake-fashion, or the larger ones are cut into wedges and served.

▲ Country-Style Omelet 9

Panbroil 6 to 8 slices **bacon** until crisp (see Panbroiled Bacon, *p 161*) . In 2 tablespoons of the **bacon fat**, brown 1 cup cooked, cubed **potatoes.** Coarsely crumble bacon and combine with browned potatoes. Proceed with ▲ Recipe, pouring egg mixture over bacon and potatoes in skillet. If necessary, add more fat. Stir slightly to allow egg mixture to settle under potatoes and bacon.

▲ Cheese Omelet * 10

Follow ▲ Recipe, adding to egg mixture 1 teaspoon **Worcestershire sauce,** 3 tablespoons minced **parsley** and ¼ cup (1 oz.) grated **cheese.** Sprinkle an additional ¼ cup grated cheese over omelet while it is cooking.

▲ Chicken Liver Omelet

Clean ¼ lb. **chicken livers.** To coat evenly, shake livers in plastic bag containing a mixture of ⅓ cup **flour,** ½ teaspoon **salt** and ¼ teaspoon **paprika.** Brown livers with 2 tablespoons minced **onion** in 3 tablespoons **butter** or **margarine,** turning frequently. Follow ▲ Recipe, enclosing chicken livers in omelet just before serving. (Cut livers into smaller pieces if necessary.)

▲ Jam or Jelly Omelet * 12

Follow ▲ Recipe. Just before folding omelet, spread with ⅓ to ½ cup **jam** or **jelly.**

▲ Sausage Omelet Fold *

Prepare **Panbroiled Link Sausages** (*p.161*), allowing at least two links per serving. Drain on absorbent paper; keep hot. Proceed with ▲ Recipe, enclosing sausages in folded omelet before serving. Serve at once with **Tomato Sauce** (*page 326*).

▲ Sauce-Topped Omelet *

Prepare **Mushroom Sauce** (*p.323*), **Cheese Sauce** (*p.323*) or **Tomato Sauce** (*p.326*). Follow ▲ Recipe. Pour sauce over omelet after it has been placed on serving plate. One cup hot cooked **peas** may be added.

▲ Cantonese Omelet *

Panfry in 2 to 3 tablespoons **butter** or **margarine,** 2 tablespoons finely chopped **onion** and ½ cup sliced **mushrooms** (*page 12*) or drained **bean sprouts.** Mix in 1 cup of a combination of cut-up cooked **shrimp** (see Cooked Shrimp, *p.242*) and chopped, cooked **pork** and ½ teaspoon **soy sauce.**

Continue heating for 2 to 3 min. Add **salt** and **pepper** to taste. Keep hot while proceeding with ▲ Recipe. Enclose vegetable-meat combination in folded omelet before serving.

⚠ Cottage Cheese Omelet * 16

Follow ▲ Recipe, blending with egg mixture
½ to 1 cup **cottage cheese**, 2 tablespoons
finely chopped **pimiento** and 1 tablespoon
minced **chives** before pouring into skillet.

⚠ Sea Food Omelet 17

Rub a mixing bowl with cut side of 1 clove of
garlic (*page 12*; optional). Follow ▲ Recipe,
using garlic-seasoned bowl. Add to egg mixture
1 cup finely chopped or shredded **lobster,
shrimp, crab meat** (bony tissue removed) or
tuna. Serve with **Tomato Sauce** (*page 326*).

Or—Prepare 1½ cups **Medium White Sauce**
(*p.323*), **Mushroom Sauce** (*p.323*) or
Cheese Sauce (*p.323*). Combine the sauce
with sea food. Lift top of folded omelet. Spoon
hot mixture over lower half and fold again.

*These variations may be adapted to **Puffy
Omelet** (*on this page*).

▲ Puffy Omelet

*The perfection of puffy omelet is fragile and
fleeting. Serve at once to prevent falling.*

Set out a heavy 10-in. skillet.

Combine, beat until thick and lemon-colored
and set aside
> **6 egg yolks**
> ⅛ **teaspoon pepper**

Using clean beaters, beat until frothy
> **6 egg whites**

Add to egg whites
> ¼ **cup cold water**
> ¾ **teaspoon salt**

Continue beating the egg-white mixture until
rounded peaks are formed. Set aside.

Puffy Omelet and tomato slices

Heat skillet until just hot enough to sizzle a
drop of water. Heat in the skillet
> **3 tablespoons butter or margarine**

Spread egg-yolk mixture over egg whites and
gently fold (*page 12*) together. Turn omelet
mixture into skillet. Gently level surface. Cook
slowly over low heat until bottom of omelet
is lightly browned when edge is lifted with a
spatula (about 5 min.). Do not stir omelet at
any time.

Place skillet with omelet in 325°F oven 12 to
15 min., until top is dry but not browned, and
a knife inserted in center comes out clean.

To serve, loosen edges with spatula, make a
quick, shallow cut through center and fold
one side over. Gently slip onto a warm serving
platter. Or using two forks, tear omelet gently
into wedges. Invert wedges on serving dish so
browned side is on top. Garnish with sprigs of
parsley or **water cress.** If desired serve with
tomato slices.   *4 to 6 servings*

⚠ Citrus Omelet

Follow ▲ Recipe. Use 2 tablespoons **lemon,
orange** or **grapefruit juice** and 2 tablespoons
water for liquid.

⚠ Sweet Omelet

Follow ⚠ Recipe; add ¼ cup **sugar** to fruit
juices. Bake at 300°F 15 to 20 min.

93

▲ Scrambled Eggs

Set out an 8- to 10-in. skillet.

Put into a bowl
6 eggs
6 tablespoons milk or cream
¾ **teaspoon salt**
⅛ **teaspoon pepper**
For uniform yellow color beat until blended with rotary beater. For streaks of yellow and white beat slightly.

Heat skillet until just hot enough to sizzle a drop of water. Heat in skillet
3 tablespoons butter or margarine
Pour in egg mixture and cook slowly over low heat. With a fork or spatula lift mixture from bottom and sides of pan as it thickens, allowing uncooked part to flow to bottom. Stir only occasionally. Cook until scrambled eggs are thick and creamy throughout but are still moist.

Serve plain on hot buttered **toast** or **English muffin halves**, or in **Toastee Baskets** (*page 65*). Garnish with **parsley** or **water cress**.

4 servings

⚠ Kippered Herring Scramble

Remove contents of 1 can (about 3 oz.) **kippered herring** and drain thoroughly on absorbent paper. Discard skin and bones and cut herring into ½-in. pieces. Follow ▲ Recipe; decrease salt to ¼ teaspoon. When eggs just begin to set, quickly mix in fish pieces.

⚠ Ham or Bacon Scramble

In the top of a double boiler combine the milk of ▲ Recipe with 1 pkg. (3 oz.) **cream cheese** and 2 tablespoons **butter.** Heat over simmering water, stirring occasionally, until cheese is softened and ingredients are blended. Cool slightly. Follow ▲ Recipe; decrease salt to ¼ teaspoon. Add cream cheese mixture gradually to eggs while beating. Add ½ cup diced cooked **ham** or **bacon** to eggs before pouring into skillet. Cream cheese flavor is barely detected but eggs will have an added creaminess.

⚠ Corn and Cheese Scramble

Follow ▲ Recipe. Blend into the slightly beaten egg mixture 1 cup (about one half of contents of No. 2 can) drained whole kernel **corn,** ¼ cup (1 oz.) grated **cheese** and ½ teaspoon **prepared mustard.** Serve at once with **Pan-broiled Link Sausages** (*page 161*).

⚠ Anchovy Scramble

Follow ▲ Recipe. For each serving, stripe a slice of hot, buttered **toast** with 3 **anchovy fillets.** Heap with scrambled eggs. (It's wise to determine saltiness of anchovies before adding salt to eggs.)

⚠ Scrambleburgers

Prepare 8 (about 1 lb. bulk pork sausage) **Pan-broiled Sausage Patties** (*p.161*). Remove from pan; drain on absorbent paper. Keep hot.

In 2 tablespoons of the **sausage fat,** cook 3 tablespoons each of finely chopped **green pepper** and **onion** until onion is transparent. Proceed with ▲ Recipe, pouring egg mixture over vegetables; scramble. Split, butter and toast cut sides of 8 **buns.** Place sausage patties on bun halves. Top patties with scrambled eggs and cover with remaining bun halves.

Or—Cut the cooked sausage patties into smaller pieces. Combine with cooked onion and green pepper before pouring in eggs.

Egg Foo Yung 24

MRS. J. E. BUSENHART, ARNOLD, MO.

Set out a large, heavy skillet.

For Foo Yung Sauce—Prepare and set aside
    1 cup quick chicken broth (*page 13***)**
Melt in a saucepan over low heat
    2 tablespoons butter or margarine
Blend in
    2 tablespoons flour
    1 teaspoon sugar
    ¼ teaspoon salt
Heat until mixture bubbles. Remove from heat. Add gradually, stirring constantly, the broth.

Mix in
    1 teaspoon soy sauce
Cook rapidly, stirring constantly, until sauce thickens. Cook 1 to 2 min. longer. Cover and keep warm over hot water.

For Foo Yung Patties—Drain contents of
    1 No. 2 can bean sprouts (about
        2½ cups, drained)
Clean (*page 12*) and finely chop
    1 medium-size onion (about ½ cup,
        chopped)
Mix together and set aside the bean sprouts, chopped onion and
    ½ cup diced, cooked ham
Combine and beat until thick and piled softly
    6 eggs
    ¾ teaspoon salt
    ¼ teaspoon Accent
Heat skillet until just hot enough to sizzle a drop of water. Heat in skillet
    6 tablespoons shortening or cooking oil
Meanwhile, blend the ham-bean-sprout mixture into the beaten eggs.

Slowly pour about ½ cup of the mixture at a time into the skillet, forming a patty. Cook until bottom of patty is browned. Turn and brown other side. Drain on absorbent paper.

Serve Egg Foo Yung patties hot, with the Foo Yung Sauce. If desired accompany with **Perfection Boiled Rice** (*page 275*). *6 servings*

Egg Loaf

MRS. VIRGIL E. HILLS, WARREN, ME.

Grease an 8½ x 4½ x 2½-in. loaf pan.

Prepare and mix together in a small bowl.
    ½ cup sliced, cooked carrots
    ½ cup chopped, cooked celery
    ½ cup cooked peas
    2 chopped Hard-Cooked Eggs
        (*page 87***)**
    1 tablespoon chopped parsley
    1 teaspoon minced onion
Prepare
    ½ cup Medium White Sauce (one-half
        recipe, *page 323*)
Stirring vigorously, slowly pour white sauce into a mixture of
    4 eggs, beaten
    ½ teaspoon salt
    ⅛ teaspoon pepper
Blend in the vegetable-egg mixture. Turn into the greased loaf pan.

Bake at 350°F 40 min., or until a silver knife comes out clean when inserted halfway between center and edge of baking dish.

Serve immediately. If desired, accompany with **Cheese Sauce** (*page 323*). *About 6 servings*

Eggs on Noodle Casserole

Eggs on Noodle Casserole

Grease a shallow 2-qt. casserole or 8 large ramekins.

Prepare
   5 Hard-Cooked Eggs (*page 87*)
Meanwhile, cook (*page 277*)
   3 cups (8 oz.) noodles
When noodles are tender, drain and put into the casserole.

Prepare (*page 10*) and set aside
   ½ cup (1 to 2 slices) buttered fine, dry bread crumbs
Cut the eggs crosswise into halves. Remove egg yolks to a bowl and mash with a fork or press through ricer or sieve into a bowl. Mix in
   2 tablespoons anchovy paste
   1 tablespoon minced parsley
   1 teaspoon minced onion
Stir in, moistening the egg-yolk mixture to a thick, paste-like consistency, about
   2 tablespoons undiluted evaporated milk
   2 to 3 teaspoons lemon juice
Pile mixture lightly into the egg-white cavities; leave tops roughly rounded. Arrange eggs on the noodles and set aside.

Mix in a saucepan and heat
   1⅔ cups undiluted evaporated milk
   1¼ cups (10½- to 11-oz. can) condensed tomato soup

Place over low heat, stirring occasionally, until heated. Pour sauce over eggs and noodles and top with buttered bread crumbs.

Bake at 350°F 20 to 25 min., or until crumbs are lightly browned.   *8 servings*

Egg Croquettes

Prepare and set aside
   4 Hard-Cooked Eggs (*page 87*)
Prepare in double-boiler top over direct heat
   2 cups Medium White Sauce (double recipe, *page 323*; increase flour to ½ cup and salt to 1 teaspoon)
Vigorously stir about ¼ cup of the hot sauce, 1 tablespoon at a time, into
   3 eggs, slightly beaten
Quickly blend into sauce. Cook over simmering water 3 to 5 min., stirring slowly to keep mixture cooking evenly. Remove sauce from simmering water and cool slightly by setting double-boiler top in bowl of cold water.

Peel and dice the Hard-Cooked Eggs and gently mix them with the sauce. Cool completely; chill mixture in the refrigerator 1 hr. or longer. Before shaping the croquettes, prepare and keep warm
   Mushroom-Wine Sauce (see Deep-Fried Eggs with Mushroom-Wine Sauce, *page 91*)
Set out a deep saucepan or an automatic deep-fryer (*page 13*) and heat fat to 375°F.

Shape cold egg mixture into croquettes (balls or cones), using about ¼ cup of mixture for each. Roll them in
   1½ cups (4 to 5 slices) fine, dry bread crumbs
Then dip them into a mixture of
   1 egg, well beaten
   1 tablespoon milk
Again roll them in bread crumbs. Shake off loose crumbs.

Deep-fry croquettes 3 to 5 min., or until golden brown. Fry only one layer of croquettes at a time; do not crowd. Turn them occasionally to brown evenly. Remove croquettes with slotted spoon; drain over fat for a few seconds before removing to absorbent paper.

Serve with the Mushroom-Wine Sauce.

12 croquettes

Egg Casserole
ISABEL NICHOLSON, HAINES CITY, FLA.

Grease a 1½-qt. casserole.

Prepare
    6 Hard-Cooked Eggs (*page 87*)
While eggs are cooking, grate
    1 oz. Cheddar cheese (¼ cup grated)
Mix with the grated cheese
    1 cup buttered cracker crumbs
        (*page 10*)
Set mixture aside.

Heat in a skillet over low heat
    2 tablespoons butter or margarine
Add and cook over medium heat, occasionally moving and turning mixture with a spoon, until vegetables are tender
    ½ cup chopped celery (*page 12*)
    ¼ cup finely chopped onion
    ¼ cup finely chopped green pepper
        (*page 12*)
Remove from heat and set aside.

Prepare
    ½ cup Medium White Sauce (½ recipe, *page 323*; increase salt to ½ teaspoon, increase pepper to ⅛ teaspoon, and add ¼ teaspoon dry mustard with the seasonings)
Blend into the white sauce
    1¼ cups (10½ to 11-oz. can) condensed tomato soup
    ½ teaspoon Worcestershire sauce
Set over low heat, stirring occasionally until thoroughly heated.

Cut each egg into halves lengthwise. Remove egg yolks to a bowl and mash with a fork.

Chop the egg whites.

Blend into the heated mixture the egg yolks and egg whites, the vegetables and
    ½ cup (4-oz. can, drained) sliced mushrooms
Continue cooking over low heat until mixture is thoroughly heated.

Turn into the greased casserole and sprinkle with the cheese-crumb mixture.

Place casserole in 375°F oven 15 min., or until crumbs are lightly browned and cheese has melted.   *About 6 servings*

Egg Cutlets

Set out a large, heavy skillet.

Prepare and dice
    4 Hard-Cooked Eggs (*page 87*)
Meanwhile, prepare
    1 cup Thick White Sauce (*page 323*; use 3 tablespoons fat and 4 tablespoons flour; blend in 1 teaspoon Worcestershire sauce)
Mix together the diced eggs, sauce and
    ⅓ cup (1 slice) fine, dry bread crumbs
    ¼ cup (1 oz.) grated cheese
Chill in refrigerator for an hour or longer.

Divide mixture and pat into 6 cutlet-shaped patties. Dip into a mixture of
    1 egg, slightly beaten
    1 tablespoon water
Coat well in
    ½ cup (1 to 2 slices) fine, dry bread crumbs
Heat in skillet
    2 to 3 tablespoons fat
Put patties in skillet and cook over medium heat until browned on one side; turn and brown second side. Turn only once. Remove from skillet to warm serving platter.

Serve cutlets hot with **Mushroom Sauce** (*page 323*) or **Tomato Sauce** (*page 326*). *6 servings*

Corn Soufflé

MRS. ROBERT MORTON, CHEROKEE, IOWA

Set out a 2-qt. casserole; do not grease. Heat water for boiling water bath (*page 12*).

Prepare
> **2 cups Thin White Sauce (double recipe, page 323; increase salt to 1 teaspoon, pepper to ⅛ teaspoon and add ⅛ teaspoon dry mustard)**

Remove from heat and mix in
> **1¾ cups (1 12-oz. can, drained) whole kernel corn**
> **¾ cup (2 to 3 slices) fine, dry bread crumbs**
> **1 tablespoon chopped parsley**

Beat until thick and lemon-colored
> **3 egg yolks**

Slowly spoon sauce into egg yolks, while stirring vigorously.

Beat until rounded peaks are formed
> **3 egg whites**

Gently spread sauce over beaten egg whites. Carefully fold (*page 12*) until just blended.

Turn mixture into the casserole.

Bake in boiling water bath at 325°F 1 hr. 10 min., or until a silver knife comes out clean when inserted halfway between center and edge of soufflé.

Serve at once.   *6 servings*

Ham Soufflé

GOLDIE ROSENTHAL, KANSAS CITY, MO.

Set out a 1½-qt. casserole; do not grease. Heat water for boiling water bath (*page 12*).

Grind (*page 107*) enough ham to yield
> **1 cup ground cooked ham**

Set aside.

Prepare
> **1 cup Medium White Sauce (page 323; increase salt to ¾ teaspoon; use ⅛ teaspoon cayenne pepper for pepper)**

Remove white sauce from heat and blend in the ground cooked ham.

Beat until thick and lemon-colored
> **4 egg yolks**

Slowly spoon sauce into egg yolks, while stirring vigorously.

Beat until rounded peaks are formed
> **4 egg whites**

Gently spread sauce over beaten egg whites. Carefully fold (*page 12*) until just blended.

Turn mixture into the casserole.

Bake in boiling water bath at 325°F 50 min. or until a silver knife comes out clean when inserted halfway between the center and edge of soufflé.

Serve at once.   *6 servings*

Cream Cheese Soufflé

WILMA DELLIBAC, KANKAKEE, ILL.

Set out a 1½-qt. casserole; do not grease.

Beat until fluffy
> **6 oz. cream cheese, softened**

Blend in, beating thoroughly
> **1 cup thick sour cream**
> **2 tablespoons white corn sirup**
> **⅛ teaspoon salt**

Blend in
> **3 egg yolks, well beaten**

Beat until rounded peaks are formed
> **3 egg whites**

Gently spread egg-yolk mixture over beaten egg whites. Carefully fold (*page 12*) together until just blended. Turn mixture into the casserole. Insert the tip of a spoon 1 in. deep into mixture in casserole, 1 to 1½ in. from edge; run a line around mixture. (Inner part of the mixture will form a "hat" when baked.)

Bake at 350°F about 30 min., or until a silver knife comes out clean when inserted halfway between center and edge of soufflé.

Serve at once.   *6 servings*

▲ Cheese Soufflé

Set out a 1½-qt. casserole; do not grease. (If necessary, a 1-qt. casserole with straight sides may be used. Fold a 2-ft. piece of waxed paper in half lengthwise; place waxed paper around casserole, cut-side down, overlapping ends of waxed paper. Secure waxed paper around casserole by tying with a string.)

Grate and set aside

6 oz. sharp Cheddar cheese (1½ cups, grated)

Prepare

1 cup Thick White Sauce (page 323; increase flour and butter to ¼ cup each; add ½ teaspoon dry mustard and ⅛ teaspoon paprika with seasonings)

Cool slightly and add grated cheese all at one time. Stir sauce rapidly until cheese is melted.

Beat until thick and lemon-colored

4 egg yolks

Cheese Soufflé: Use folded piece of waxed paper and string to increase capacity of a 1-qt. casserole.

Slowly spoon sauce into egg yolks, while stirring vigorously.

Beat until rounded peaks are formed

4 egg whites

Gently spread egg-yolk mixture over beaten egg whites. Carefully fold (*page 12*) together until just blended. Turn mixture into casserole. Insert the tip of a spoon 1 in. deep in casserole, 1 to 1½ in. from edge; run a line around mixture. (Inner part of the mixture will form a "hat" when baked.)

Bake at 325°F about 50 min., or until a silver knife comes out clean when inserted halfway between center and edge of soufflé.

Serve at once (while top hat is at its height).

6 servings

⚠ Fresh Mushroom Soufflé

Follow ▲ Recipe. Decrease cheese to 1 cup. Clean (*page 12*) and finely chop ½ lb. **mushrooms.** Cook slowly with ¼ cup minced **onion** in 2 tablespoons **butter** or **margarine** until onion is transparent and mushrooms are lightly browned and tender; gently move and turn with fork or spoon. Using slotted spoon, remove vegetables from skillet and blend into sauce just before folding into egg whites.

⚠ Little Soufflés

Follow ▲ Recipe or ⚠; divide soufflé mixture among six 4- to 4½-in. ungreased individual casseroles. Bake 25 to 30 min., or until soufflés test done.

Cheese Fondue

JACK J. NIEBOU, HOLLAND, MICH.

Grease a 1½-qt. casserole. Heat water for boiling water bath (*page 12*).

Scald (*page 13*)
1 cup milk
Grate
4 oz. Cheddar cheese (1 cup, grated)
Set aside.

Combine in a large bowl the grated cheese and
1 cup (about 1 slice) soft bread crumbs
1 tablespoon butter
½ teaspoon salt
¼ teaspoon Accent
⅛ teaspoon pepper
Stir in the scalded milk.

Blend three tablespoons cheese mixture into
3 egg yolks, well beaten
Immediately blend into cheese mixture.

Beat until rounded peaks are formed
3 egg whites
Gently spread beaten egg whites over cheese mixture and fold (*page 12*) together.

Turn mixture into the casserole.

Bake in boiling water bath at 325°F 40 min. or until a silver knife comes out clean when inserted halfway between center and edge of casserole.   *6 servings*

Spanish Egg Cakes

AMELIE M. KINZER, VAN NUYS, CALIF.

In the tradition of the Southwest.

For Filling—Heat in saucepan over low heat
2 tablespoons butter or margarine
Add and cook over medium heat, moving and turning mixture until onion is transparent
¾ cup (about 1½ medium-size)
   chopped onion (*page 12*)
Drain contents of
1 9-oz. can ripe olives
Pit and chop the drained olives.

Grate
6 oz. Cheddar cheese (1½ cups, grated)
Mix together the onions and one half of the cheese and olives; set aside for the filling.

Reserve the remaining chopped olives for the sauce, and the remaining grated cheese for the topping.

For Sauce—Set out a 2-qt. saucepan and a 13x9½x2-in. baking pan.

Heat until very hot
3 cups tomato juice
Dissolve in the hot juice
4 bouillon cubes
Blend together in the saucepan the tomato-bouillon mixture and
1 teaspoon Worcestershire sauce
½ teaspoon chili powder
½ teaspoon salt
¼ teaspoon cumin
¼ teaspoon pepper
Measure
¼ cup cornstarch
Mix in to make a smooth paste
⅔ cup water
Gradually add cornstarch paste to hot mixture, stirring constantly. Bring rapidly to boiling; continue to cook, stirring constantly, about 3 to 5 min., or until mixture thickens.

Remove from heat and stir in reserved olives. Pour into baking pan enough sauce to cover bottom of pan.

For Pancakes—Set a griddle or heavy skillet over low heat.

Sift together and set aside
¾ cup sifted flour
2 teaspoons baking powder
½ teaspoon salt
Beat until thick and piled softly
6 eggs
Blend in
⅓ cup milk
Sift flour mixture over egg mixture. Fold (*page 12*) together.

Test griddle; it is hot enough for baking when drops of water sprinkled on surface dance in small beads.

Lightly grease griddle as manufacturer directs.

Pour the batter from a large spoon into pools about 4½ to 5 in. in diameter, leaving at least 1 in. between. Turn pancakes as they become puffy and filled with bubbles and are lightly browned on one side. Turn only once and brown second side. Remove each pancake to a plate. Place a heaping tablespoon of filling onto each pancake, roll up, and secure with a wooden pick. Place the filled pancake in the baking pan.

Repeat procedure until all pancakes are prepared. Spoon the remaining sauce over the pancakes in the pan and sprinkle with the reserved grated cheese.

Bake at 375°F 15 to 20 min., until cheese is melted and cakes are thoroughly heated.

6 servings

Eggs à la New Orleans
MRS. CHARLES KIESOW, MADISON, WIS.

Set out 4 individual casseroles.

Grate and set aside
   4 oz. Cheddar cheese (1 cup, grated)
Heat in a 1-qt. saucepan
   2 tablespoons butter or margarine

Add and cook over medium heat, occasionally moving and turning mixture with a spoon, until vegetables are tender
   ½ cup chopped celery (*page 12*)
   ¼ cup minced onion
   3 tablespoons finely chopped green pepper
Add
   2½ cups (No. 2 can) tomatoes, cut in pieces
   ½ teaspoon salt
   ¼ teaspoon Accent
   ⅛ teaspoon pepper
   1 bay leaf
Bring mixture to boiling over high heat. Lower heat and simmer 5 min. Remove from heat. Remove bay leaf.

Stir into mixture
   ¾ cup (about ¾ slice) soft bread crumbs
   ½ cup drained canned peas
Pour one half of the mixture into casseroles. Sprinkle with one half of the grated cheese. Pour remaining mixture into casseroles.

Break separately into a saucer or small dish
   4 eggs
Tilting dish toward edge of casserole, quickly slip one egg onto center of mixture in each casserole. Sprinkle remaining cheese over eggs.

Bake at 325°F, uncovered, 12 to 20 min., depending upon firmness desired.   *4 servings*

Rice-Cheese Puffs

Prepare
1¾ cups Perfection Boiled Rice (one-half recipe, page 275)
While the rice is cooking, finely grate and set aside
3 oz. sharp Cheddar cheese (¾ cup, grated)
Melt in a medium-size saucepan over low heat
4 teaspoons butter or margarine
Blend in
4 teaspoons flour
½ teaspoon Accent
¼ teaspoon salt
Few grains pepper
Heat until mixture bubbles. Remove from heat. Add gradually while stirring constantly
⅓ cup milk
Return to heat and bring rapidly to boiling, stirring constantly; cook 1 to 2 min. longer.

Cool sauce slightly and add the grated cheese all at one time. Stir sauce rapidly until cheese is melted. Blend in
½ teaspoon grated onion
¼ teaspoon Worcestershire sauce
¼ teaspoon dry mustard
5 drops tabasco sauce
Few grains cayenne pepper
Mix with the cooked rice and place in refrigerator to chill (about 1 hr.).

Set out a deep saucepan or an automatic deep-fryer (*page 13*) and heat fat to 375°F.

Remove rice mixture from refrigerator. Shape into 2-in. balls, using about 1 tablespoon of the mixture for each ball. Dip balls into a mixture of
1 egg, slightly beaten
1 tablespoon milk
Coat balls by rolling in
½ cup (1 to 2 slices) fine, dry bread crumbs
Deep-fry only as many balls at one time as will float uncrowded one layer deep in the heated fat. Fry 1 to 2 min., or until balls are golden brown. Turn them with a fork as they rise to surface and several times during cooking (do not pierce). Remove balls with a slotted spoon; drain over fat for a few seconds before removing to absorbent paper.

Serve hot with
Tomato Sauce (page 326), or
Quick Tomato Sauce (page 327)
About 1 doz. puffs

Macaroni and Cheese

Thoroughly grease a 2-qt. casserole.

Grate and set aside
½ lb. Cheddar cheese (about 2 cups, grated)
Prepare (*page 10*) and set aside
½ cup (1 to 2 slices) buttered fine, dry bread crumbs
Cook (*page 277*)
2 cups (8-oz. pkg.) macaroni
While macaroni is cooking, prepare
2 cups Thin White Sauce (double recipe, page 323; increase salt to 1 teaspoon and Accent to ¾ teaspoon)
Cool sauce slightly. Stir grated cheese all at one time into the slightly cooled white sauce. Blend the sauce with the cooked and drained macaroni and turn into the casserole. Sprinkle the buttered crumbs around edge of casserole. If desired garnish with chopped **parsley**.

Bake at 350°F about 20 min., or until crumbs are lightly browned. *6 or 7 servings*

Macaroni and Cheese

beaten. Blend into mixture in double boiler top and add the seasonings. Cook 3 to 5 min. longer, stirring constantly.

Vegetable Rabbit 27

ISABELLE N. TARBOUX, ANN ARBOR, MICH.

A hearty variation of an old, honored dish, this tasty rabbit does nicely for lunch or supper.

Grate and set aside

¾ lb. (3 cups) sharp Cheddar cheese
Heat in double-boiler top over low heat

2 tablespoons butter
Add and cook over medium heat, occasionally moving and turning mixture with a spoon, until onion is transparent and pepper is almost tender

1 small onion (*page 12*), chopped
1 green pepper (*page 12*), chopped
½ teaspoon dry mustard
While vegetables are cooking, drain, reserving juice, contents of

1 No. 2 can tomatoes (about 1 cup, drained)
Cut into small pieces and set aside enough tomatoes to yield ½ cup cut tomatoes. Add to the vegetables ½ cup of the reserved tomato juice. (Reserve remaining tomatoes and tomato juice for use in other food preparation.)

Place top of double boiler over simmering water. Add grated cheese, stirring constantly. Continue stirring until cheese is melted and thoroughly blended in. Blend in tomatoes and

1 cup drained whole kernel corn
1 teaspoon Worcestershire sauce
1 teaspoon Accent
¼ teaspoon salt
Few grains cayenne pepper
Heat mixture thoroughly and serve over buttered **Toast Points** (*page 65*) or **crackers.**

8 servings

Welsh Rabbit

▲ Welsh Rabbit 1

Prepare and set aside to keep warm

Toasted, buttered English muffin halves or toast
Heat in a double-boiler top over simmering water until cheese is melted, stirring constantly

4 cups (1 lb.) grated sharp Cheddar cheese
½ cup milk
Stir in

½ teaspoon Worcestershire sauce
¾ teaspoon Accent
½ teaspoon dry mustard
Few grains cayenne pepper
Pour cheese mixture over the muffin halves or toast. Garnish with **parsley.** If desired, top each serving with a tomato slice. Serve immediately.

6 servings

△ Blushing Bunny 26
(Tomato-Cheese Rabbit)

MRS. ELINOR C. BECKWITH
STANFORDVILLE, N. Y.

Follow ▲ Recipe. Decrease cheese to 2 cups (½ lb.). Substitute 1¼ cups (10½- to 11-oz. can) **condensed tomato soup** for milk. Vigorously stir about 3 tablespoons of the hot melted cheese mixture into 1 **egg,** slightly

EGG and CHEESE DISHES in the MICROWAVE OVEN

You have never tasted scrambled eggs and omelets as good as those cooked in the microwave oven! Microwave cooking produces such a smooth, creamy texture and enhances the flavor of scrambled eggs so well you will never want to prepare them again on the stove.

Stirring is very important for that smooth texture in omelets and scrambled eggs; in these recipes we have indicated how often and when to stir each dish.

Our taste is for moist, soft eggs. Cook a little longer for drier, harder eggs. Timing for all the recipes will also vary depending on the number of eggs, the temperature of the eggs and the size of the eggs. We used medium eggs at room temperature and indicate the number of eggs used in each recipe.

Fried and steamed eggs are a little trickier to prepare, since microwaves tend to cook the yolk, which has a high fat content, more quickly than the whites. Our cooked whole eggs had a white which was just set and a yolk still slightly soft.

It is difficult to obtain whole cooked eggs with whites that are very firm and yolks that are runny. For this reason we have omitted the recipies for baked eggs.

The microwave oven is not kind to soufflés. Through the window of the oven they are beautiful to behold, but as soon as the oven door is opened they collapse. We have also omitted the soufflé recipes.

The cheese dishes in this section are excellent, having smooth textures and well-blended flavors. One success, **Blushing Bunny**, is a variation of a basic recipe, **Welsh Rabbit**, with which we did not obtain acceptable results and is, therefore, not included here.

REMINDERS—Do not cook eggs in the shell; they will explode. The yolk membrane of whole eggs must be punctured with a toothpick or similar pointed object or they will explode also.

Remember, eggs with continue to cook after they have been removed from the oven. Therefore, remove them from the oven BEFORE they reach the stage of appropriate doneness.

With eggs, which cook so quickly, this characteristic can make the critical difference between eggs done to perfection and failure.

We emphasize again, many variables enter into cooking eggs in the microwave and personal preference is not the least of them. Some adjustments in timing may be necessary in order to cook the recipes exactly to your taste, but the results are well worth any effort. We have given you the guidelines for preparing these dishes so you will be able to easily recognize when they are done.

The introductory chapter, **Home Cooking in the Microwave Oven**, in the beginning of this book provides additional tips and an easy-to-read chart comparing settings among different brands of microwaves. We suggest that you review this material to also learn how we have adapted these recipes.

Poached Eggs *(page 89)* 1

Use a covered casserole. The timings in this recipe are for the preparation of 4 eggs.

Use enough water to just cover eggs. To boil 2 cups water, COOK about 4 min.

Before eggs are slipped into water, puncture the membrane of each yolk with a toothpick or similar pointed utensil.

COOK, covered, until set (about 1 to 1½ min.). Cover and let stand 3 min.; eggs will continue to cook.

OVERALL COOKING TIME: 5:00

Poached Eggs with Mushroom or Cheese Sauce *(page 89)* 2

Follow 1 Recipe.

Top with **Mushroom Sauce** or **Cheese Sauce** as in ⚠ Recipe.

Poached Eggs and Greens *(page 89)* 3

Follow 1 Recipe for eggs. They will stay hot in the casserole while greens are being prepared. To prepare greens see **Vegetables in the Microwave Oven.**

Assemble individual dishes and add a poached egg to each. Top with cheese. COOK to melt cheese (about 1 min.).

Serve as in ⚠ Recipe.

Eggs Benedict *(page 89)* 4

Follow 1 Recipe for eggs. They will stay hot in the casserole.

Assemble as in ⚠ Recipe and COOK, if necessary, until heated.

Savory Poached Eggs 5 *(page 89)*

Follow 1 Recipe with substitutions as in ⚠ Recipe.

Serve as in ⚠ Recipe.

Fried Eggs *(page 90)* 6

Use a browning skillet. The timings in this recipe are for the preparation of 4 eggs.

COOK 1 tablespoon fat until melted.

Add eggs to browning skillet, being sure to puncture the membrane of each yolk with a toothpick or similar utensil. COOK, rotating the skillet every minute, until eggs are desired firmness (about 4 min. OR 1 min. per egg). Cover and let stand 3 min.

OVERALL COOKING TIME: 4:00

Steamed Eggs *(page 90)*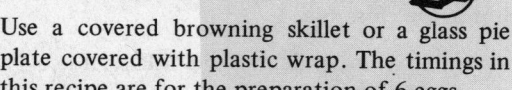

Use a covered browning skillet or a glass pie plate covered with plastic wrap. The timings in this recipe are for the preparation of 2 eggs.

COOK butter until melted.

Add eggs, being sure to puncture the membrane of each yolk with a toothpick or similar utensil. COOK until edges turn white (about 30 sec.).

Add water and COOK to desired firmness (about 1½ to 2 min.).

OVERALL COOKING TIME: 2:00

French Omelet *(page 92)* 8

Use a covered browning skillet or a glass pie plate covered with plastic wrap. The timings in this recipe are for the preparation of 6 eggs.

COOK butter or margarine until foamy.

Add egg mixture, cover and COOK, stirring every minute, until mixture thickens (about 2 min.). Uncover and COOK, stirring every 30 sec., until almost set (about 3 min.). Loosen bottom and edges, fold, cover and let stand 5 min.

OVERALL COOKING TIME: 5:00

Country-Style Omelet 9
(page 92)

Follow 8 Recipe with additions as in ⚠ Recipe.

To brown potatoes COOK (about 3 min.).

Complete as in ▲ Recipe.

Cheese Omelet * *(page 92)* 10

Follow 8 Recipe with additions as in ⚠ Recipe. After eggs have thickened, sprinkle with remaining cheese.

Chicken Liver Omelet
(page 92)

Use a browning skillet for chicken livers and onions.

Follow 8 Recipe for omelet with additions as in ⚠ Recipe.

COOK butter or margarine until melted. Add chicken livers and onions and COOK, turning every 30 sec., until lightly browned (about 2 min.).

Enclose livers and onion in omelet just before folding.

Jam or Jelly Omelet *
(page 92)

Follow 8 Recipe with additions as in ⚠ Recipe.

Sausage Omelet Fold *
(page 92)

Follow 8 Recipe with additions as in ⚠ Recipe.

Complete and serve as in ▲ Recipe.

Sauce-Topped Omelet *
(page 92)

Follow 8 Recipe.

Serve as in ▲ Recipe.

Cantonese Omelet * *(page 92)*

Use a browning skillet for filling mixture.

COOK butter or margarine until melted. Add vegetable mixture and COOK, stirring after 1 minute (about 2 min.).

Add shrimp, pork and soy sauce, COOK 1 min. and stir. Continue to COOK, stirring every 30 sec., until vegetables are wilted (about 1 min.).

Follow △ Recipe. Enclose mixture in folded omelet.

Cottage Cheese Omelet * 16
(page 93)

Follow ⑧ Recipe with additions as in △ Recipe.

COOK, stirring every minute, until thickened (about 4 min.). Continue to COOK, stirring every 30 sec., until almost set (about 5 min.).

Cottage cheese will release water as it cooks; drain skillet, if necessary.

Sea Food Omelet (page 92) 17

Use a covered browning skillet or glass pie plate with plastic wrap. Follow ⑧ Recipe with additions as in △ Recipe.

Cover and COOK 1 min.; stir. Uncover and COOK, stirring every 30 sec., until slightly set (about 5 min.).

Serve as in △ Recipe. With seafood sauce variations fold omelet after filling.

Scrambled Eggs (page 94) 18

Use a covered browning skillet or a glass pie plate covered with plastic wrap.

COOK butter or margarine until melted. Add egg mixture. COOK, uncovered, until slightly thickened (about 1 min.); stir. Remove from oven, cover and let stand 2 min. This produces a soft, creamy texture. For harder eggs, COOK 30 sec. additional before removing from oven.
OVERALL COOKING TIME: 1:00

Kippered Herring Scramble (page 94) 19

Follow 18 Recipe with changes as in △ Recipe.

Add herring just before removing from oven.

Ham or Bacon Scramble 20
(page 94)

Follow 18 Recipe with changes as in △ Recipe.

In a small casserole, combine the milk, cream cheese and butter. COOK, stirring every 30 sec., until cheese is melted and ingredients are blended.

Continue as in △ Recipe.

COOK as in 18 Recipe.

Corn and Cheese Scramble (page 94) 21

Follow 18 Recipe with changes as in △ Recipe.

COOK to melt cheese (about 1 min.); stir. COOK, stirring every 30 sec., until slightly set (about 2½ min.). Remove from oven, stir, cover and let stand 2 min.

Anchovy Scramble (page 94) 22

Follow 18 Recipe and serve as in △ Recipe.

SCRAMBLEBURGERS (page 94) 23

Use a browning skillet. Follow 18 Recipe with changes as in △ Recipe.

COOK fat until melted. Add onion and green pepper and COOK, stirring every minute, until onion is transparent (about 5 min.).

Serve as in ⚠ Recipe.

Egg Foo Yung *(page 95)*

Use a browning skillet and a covered casserole.

*For Foo Yung Sauce—*COOK flour mixture to bubbling (about 1 min.). Remove from oven and add broth and soy sauce. COOK, stirring every 30 sec., until sauce thickens (about 1½ min.).

*For Foo Yung Patties—*Combine ingredients as in Recipe. COOK patties one at a time until set, turn to set other side (about 45 sec. each side). Add oil as needed. Keep cooked patties warm in a covered casserole.

Serve as in Recipe.
OVERALL COOKING TIME: 11:30

Macaroni and Cheese
(page 102)

Use a 3-qt. casserole.

Assemble casserole. COOK until cheese is melted and casserole is thoroughly heated (about 5 min.). (Bread crumbs will not brown.).
OVERALL COOKING TIME: 5:00

Blushing Bunny *(page 103)*

(Tomato-Cheese Rabbit)

Use a 2-qt. casserole.

Follow ▲ Recipe.

COOK cheese-soup mixture stirring every minute, until cheese is melted and mixture is hot (about 3 min.).

Add egg and stir to blend. COOK, stirring every 30 sec., until thickened and smooth (about 2 min.).

OVERALL COOKING TIME: 5:00

Vegetable Rabbit *(page 103)*

Use a 3-qt. casserole.

COOK butter until melted. Add vegetable-mustard mixture and COOK, stirring every 30 sec., until onion is transparent (about 4 min.).

Add the cheese and COOK, stirring every 30 sec., until cheese melts (about 3 min.).

Add remaining ingredients and COOK, stirring every 30 sec., until hot (about 2 min.).

Serve as in Recipe.

OVERALL COOKING TIME: 9:00

EGG and CHEESE DISHES in the SLOW COOKER

Because eggs need to be cooked quickly they are not well-suited to preparation in the slow cooker.

What was very good, however, was the smooth and tasty Welsh Rabbit. We also tried the variation of this recipe included in the main text, **Blushing Bunny**, but found it less successful.

REMINDERS—The introductory chapter, **Home Cooking in the Slow Cooker**, in the beginning of this book contains an easy-to-read chart comparing settings among different brands of slow cookers. Before preparing any of these recipes, we suggest you review this chapter for general hints and to learn how we have adapted these recipes.

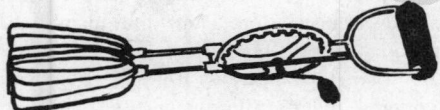

Welsh Rabbit *(page 103)*

Combine all ingredients (except English muffins) in the slow cooker. Cook on LOW for 2 to 3 hrs. This dish can be safely held on LOW for 3 additional hrs.

Prepare English muffins as in ▲ Recipe.

Serve as in Recipe.

What You Should Know About Meat

Meat is king of the American dinner table—the food that holds the center spot in the menu and the hub around which most meals are planned. Preferences vary from region to region: New England and California love lamb, ham is the favorite in the South, in the Midwest pork and beef vie for favor and in the West and Southwest beef is tops.

America is almost unique in the world in the abundance of its meat supplies and the manner in which this abundance is taken for granted. Historically there are good reasons why this came to be. The first colonists found an amazing, almost untouched supply of wild game in the woods and the fields; and as the pioneers pushed westward, they encountered an inexhaustible abundance on the great western plains. Where fruit, grain and vegetables might be scarce, because the land was not yet cultivated and the supplies the pioneers carried with them were exhausted, there was no end to the meat that was theirs for the shooting. And the high meat diet on which the pioneers fed undoubtedly had much to do with the hardiness, toughness and spirit which settled our country.

Meat is an excellent source, perhaps the best, of the complete proteins from which strong bodies are built, with which they are repaired, and which supply those bodies with heat and energy and help them to resist infections. Protein to perform these functions can be obtained from a diet which contains no meat at all, but not so readily and, for most persons, not so palatably. In addition to the high protein content, meat is also rich in the minerals and vitamins which regulate all body functions.

Add to the presence of all these nutrients in meat, which make it such a fine body-building food, the fact that it is extremely palatable and that it has a high satiety value—that is, it satisfies not only when it is eaten but for a longer time thereafter than any other food. All these characteristics add up to good reason why the American diet is built around meat and why the selection and preparation of meat is a vital part of a homemaker's job.

SELECTION—Pioneer homemakers had little choice in the matter of their meat; they cooked what the hunter brought home. The modern homemaker, on the other hand, sees a vast array of meats spread out before her whenever she visits her favorite meat market. Her skill as a cook starts with her ability to select not only the right cut of meat for the method of preparation she means to use, but to select meat of good quality; for the quality of the meat itself determines to a large extent the quality of the cooked food. An experienced family meat buyer learns to recognize the characteristics of meat at a glance; she is aided by a knowledge of meat inspection and grading stamps.

Inspection Stamp—All meats processed by packers who ship their products across state lines must pass Federal inspection. The round purple Federal inspection stamp ("U. S. INSP'D & P'S'D") guarantees that the meat is from healthy animals slaughtered under sanitary conditions and that it is wholesome. Meats handled by packers who market locally must pass city and state inspections. These inspections guarantee wholesomeness, not quality.

Grade Stamp—Quality grading is a separate operation and may be done according to government grade standards or according to packers' own standards, which are usually closely in line with government grades. Grade and brand names are stamped on the meat with a roller stamp which leaves its mark along the full length of the carcass. The purple ink used for both inspection and grade stamps is a harmless vegetable dye which need not be cut away before cooking.

Official U. S. Quality Grades are "Prime," the absolutely top quality found in meat from prize animals, which is seldom seen in the retail market; "Choice," the highest quality usually available for home use; "Good," "Commercial" and "Utility." These grades are applied to beef, veal and (with the exception of the "Commercial" grade) to lamb. Pork is not officially graded, except by the packer. Where grade stamps are in evidence, the homemaker can rely on them as indexes to the quality of the meat. But in many cases, as in selecting pre-cut and pre-packaged meats, her own knowledge of the appearance of quality is a valuable guide.

What To Look For In Beef—Beef of good to prime quality, whatever the cut, is thick-fleshed and compact, implying a plump, stocky animal; in lower grades the flesh is thinner, indicating that the animal was rangy and angular. There is a good covering of fat, which becomes thinner and patchier in lower grades, and a generous marbling or flecking of fat through the lean (almost absent in the lowest grades). Color in all grades varies from light to dark red. Bones of young beef are red and porous; as the animal matures they become harder and white.

What To Look For In Veal—Veal, which always comes from a young animal (calves three months to a year old), is very different in appearance from beef. The lean is a light grayish-pink in color, has no marbling and very little covering fat. The bones are red and porous; in the youngest veal the ends may still be pliable. Veal is fine-grained and less firm than beef of comparable grade; because the animal is young, veal is likely to be tender.

What To Look For In Lamb—Ninety-three per cent of all sheep in this country are marketed as lambs and yearlings; only seven per cent as mutton (lamb more than one year old). The bones, fat and color of lean are all indications of the age of lamb. Young lamb has red bones, which become white as the animal matures. The lean is light to dark pink in lambs, darkening to light red in yearlings and light to dark red in mutton. Lamb fat is rather soft and creamy or pinkish in color; with maturity it becomes white and much harder, even brittle.

What To Look For In Pork—Pork usually comes from animals under a year old and is almost always tender; the quality of American pork is quite uniform, with fewer grades than other meats. The color of young pork is grayish pink, which becomes pinker in older animals. The flesh is firm, fine in grain, well marbled (flecked) with fat and covered with a layer of firm white fat.

Pre-Packaged Meats—In recent years it has become possible to buy meats on a self-service basis in many supermarkets. The meats are cut, weighed, packaged and priced by the meat dealer, and are placed in refrigerated open cases for selection by the homemaker. Because they are wrapped in a transparent material, she can see the exact number of pieces she is buying, judge the quality and quickly compare prices and values.

STORAGE—As soon as possible after purchase, meat should be placed in the home refrigerator. Remove fresh meat from the meat-market wrappings and rewrap it loosely in waxed or parchment paper. For best keeping, put it into the meat-keeping compartment of the refrigerator.

In general, the smaller the proportion of cut surfaces exposed, the longer the meat will keep without deterioration. Ground meat, chops and mechanically tenderized steaks should not be stored more than one to three days. Due to the spicing, fresh pork sausage keeps better than other ground meats, usually up to a week. Beef roasts, legs of lamb and similar large cuts will keep in good condition as long as a week. Variety meats such as hearts, kidneys and liver are highly perishable and should be used within two days. Pre-packaged table-ready sliced meats and frankfurters are exceptions to the loose-wrapping rule; they will keep two or three weeks if left in their original moisture-proof wrappings, or if snugly re-wrapped at home in moisture-proof material.

Longer storage periods are possible in the freezer compartment of the refrigerator, which has a temperature of 25°F or lower. For freezing in this compartment, meats should be closely wrapped in a freezer wrapping material. Even the most perishable meats and ground beef will keep for two or three weeks under these conditions.

Fresh meats can be stored in home freezers at a temperature of 0°F or below for much longer periods. They should first be wrapped in freezer wrapping material which is moisture-vapor-proof. Maximum frozen storage periods recommended are: for ground meat and sausage, 1 to 3 months; fresh pork, 3 to 6 months; veal and lamb, 6 to 9 months; beef 6 to 12 months.

METHODS OF COOKING—Since the first cave-family discovered that meat tasted better when cooked, only two ways of cooking meat have ever been devised: by dry heat and by moist heat. There are several methods of cooking by dry heat: roasting, broiling, panbroiling and frying. There are two methods of cooking by moist heat: braising and cooking in liquid. Most of these methods have been in use for thousands of years, from cave days to the present, but in the comparatively few years since the experimental method was first applied to cooking, more has been learned about the techniques that give cooked meat the best appearance, texture and flavor than in all the millennia that went before.

In general, dry-heat methods are used for the more tender cuts of meat with little connective tissue. Exceptions to this rule are the smaller cuts (steaks, chops and cutlets) of pork and veal, though both are classed as tender meats. Both pork and veal need longer cooking, pork to develop its rich flavor and veal to soften its connective tissue. Long cooking by dry heat tends to dry them out; therefore a moist-heat method, braising, is the method of choice for pork and veal cuts other than roasts.

Roasting—To roast, in modern usage, is to cook in an oven, uncovered and without the addition of any liquid.

Thousands of laboratory tests on all kinds of roasts have revealed many facts about the roasting method which today can be stated as rules. These rules have as their objective the desired degree of doneness combined with maximum palatability and juiciness, the most appetizing appearance and minimum shrinkage.

Rules worth noting:

1. A constant low oven temperature should be maintained.
2. Even though time-weight relationship tables are followed carefully, the only accurate test for doneness is the internal temperature as registered by a roast meat thermometer.
3. Searing (initial high temperature) does not keep in juices but increases their loss.
4. Cooked fat side up, the roast will be self-basting.
5. Covering the roast or adding water produces moist-heat cooking and is not done in roasting.
6. Seasoning may be added before or after cooking; penetration is to a depth of only about ½ inch.
7. A time allowance of 20 to 30 minutes should be added to total roasting time in order that the roast may "set" in advance of carving; this makes carving easier and slices neater.

A low oven temperature throughout roasting cooks the meat more uniformly, with less shrinkage and loss of juices and fat; the covering fat is not charred and the meat is more palatable. A low temperature means less work for the homemaker, too, because there is less spattering of fat, less burning of fat on pans, racks and oven walls, less need for watching and an easier clean-up job.

Even with a constant temperature, it is not possible to predict accurately by means of time-weight tables when any particular piece of meat will be cooked done. The shape of the roast, the proportion of lean to fat, the amount of bone, the aging of the meat—all affect the time that will be required to produce the desired degree of doneness. Time tables are useful in estimating about how much total time will be required, but the only accurate test of actual doneness is the roast meat thermometer which registers the temperature at the center of the roast. When using a roast meat thermometer, the bulb of the thermometer should be inserted as nearly as possible to the center of the largest muscle, but should not come into contact with fat or bone.

Even after the establishment of a low temperature as desirable for roasting, some persons continued to sear meats to "seal in" juices. It has been disproved in test after test that searing results in any saving of juices; rather, it actually increases their loss. It does produce more drippings and a richer brown color in the drippings, which may make a richer brown and a more flavorful gravy.

Broiling—To broil is to cook by direct heat, over hot coals or under a flame or heating element.

As in roasting, a moderately low temperature for broiling produces more uniform cooking, less shrinkage, better appearance, more tender meat, less smoking and spattering of fat and no charring. Broiling temperature is controlled by regulating the distance between the source of heat and the surface of the meat. In broiling too, time tables are only a guide to total broiling time. However, it is quite easy to check on doneness of these comparatively thin pieces of meat without use of a thermometer, by cutting into the meat next to the bone with a sharp knife, and observing the color.

Meat for broiling should not be seasoned until after cooking, because salt tends to draw juices out from the exposed cut surface. Season the first side with a mixture of salt, pepper and Accent just before turning to broil the second side, and season the second side when cooking is complete.

Broiling as a cooking method is reserved for tender steaks and chops of beef and lamb. Veal and pork, although tender meats, are not usually broiled for reasons already explained (*page 106*). Ham steaks, however, are frequently broiled.

Panbroiling—To panbroil is to cook by heat transmitted through the hot metal of a skillet, but without added fat or water.

Panbroiling is used for the same cuts as is broiling. Fat should be poured off as it collects, to insure even cooking; the pan should not be covered. To test for doneness, cut a small gash close to the bone and note the color of the meat at the center.

Frying—To fry is to cook in fat, whether in a large amount (deep-frying) or a small amount (panfrying). Meats most frequently fried are thin steaks and chops and liver. They are usually floured or breaded to produce a brown, flavorful crust. In panfrying the meat is browned in a small amount of fat and then cooked at moderate temperature until done, turning frequently. If the skillet is covered or water is added, the procedure becomes braising rather than true frying.

Braising—To braise meat is to brown it in a small amount of fat; then to simmer it gently either in its own juices (by covering the skillet) or in a small amount of added liquid, which may be water, milk, cream, meat stock, vegetable juice or other liquid. The cooking done after browning may be done either on top of the range or in the oven.

The method is used in cooking pot roasts, veal and pork chops and steaks. These are all either less tender cuts of beef, such as round or flank steak, or small cuts of veal and pork which as previously stated require thorough cooking.

Cooking in Liquid—Stews require that the meat be cooked in liquid. Hams and corned beef are also cooked this way in some cases; veal cuts may be simmered as a preliminary to obtaining diced cooked veal for other recipes. Organs such as heart and tongue, which are much-exercised muscles, are often cooked in liquid.

Meats cooked in liquid should always be simmered rather than boiled; that is to say, cooked at a low temperature, as for meats cooked by dry heat methods.

 **How To Do It**

COAT MEAT PIECES (as for stew) evenly by shaking a few pieces at a time in a plastic bag containing a mixture of flour and seasonings.

GRIND COOKED MEAT—Trim meat from bone; remove any excess fat. Put meat through medium blade of food grinder.

LARD MEAT by laying bacon strips or other fat on top of roast (usually veal); or by inserting fat strips into the lean with a larding needle to increase juiciness and improve flavor.

UNMOLD MEAT LOAVES—With spatula, gently loosen meat from sides of pan. Pour off excess juices; invert onto platter and remove pan. For meat loaves with topping, pour off excess juices and lift loaf onto platter with two wide spatulas.

POUND MEAT—To increase tenderness in less tender cuts of meat, place meat on flat working surface and repeatedly pound it with a meat hammer; turn meat and repeat on other side.

TURN MEAT during broiling, panbroiling or panfrying by inserting fork into the fat rather than the lean portion, thus avoiding loss of juices from lean.

THICKEN COOKING LIQUID—Pour ½ cup cold water into a screw-top jar; sprinkle ¼ cup flour onto the water (or use amounts specified in recipe). Cover jar tightly and shake until well blended. Slowly pour one-half of mixture into cooking liquid, stirring constantly. Bring to boiling. Gradually add only what is needed of remaining mixture for consistency desired. Bring to boiling after each addition. After final addition, cook 3 to 5 min. longer.

▲ Standing Rib Roast of Beef

The prime favorite of all lovers of beef!

Set out a shallow roasting pan.

Wipe with a clean, damp cloth
3-rib (6 to 8 lbs.) standing rib roast of beef
(Have meat dealer loosen chine bone to make carving easier.) Place roast, fat side up, in roasting pan. Season with a mixture of
1½ teaspoons salt
1 teaspoon Accent
⅛ teaspoon pepper
Insert roast meat thermometer in center of thickest part of lean; be sure bulb does not rest on bone or in fat.

Roast at 300°F, allowing 18 to 20 min. per pound for rare; 22 to 25 min. per pound for medium; and 27 to 30 min. per pound for well-done meat. Roast is also done when roast meat thermometer registers 140°F for rare; 160°F for medium; and 170°F for well-done meat.

Meat drippings may be used for **Brown Gravy** (*page 325*), or **Norwegian Wine Gravy** (*page 326*). For a special treat, serve **Yorkshire Pudding** (double recipe, *page 69*) as an accompaniment.   *About 12 servings*

Note: To prepare roast of beef on an outdoor grill see OUTDOOR COOKING (*page 204*).

△ Rolled Rib Roast of Beef

Follow ▲ Recipe. Substitute **rolled beef rib roast** for the standing rib roast. Roast at 300°F, allowing 28 to 32 min. per pound for rare; 34 to 38 min. per pound for medium; and 40 to 45 min. per pound for well-done meat.

Grandma's Beef Pot Roast

MRS. A. L. CHRISTENSEN, METUCHEN, N. J.

Set out a heavy sauce pot having a tight-fitting cover; or use a Dutch oven.

Wipe with a clean damp cloth
3 to 4 lb. rump roast of beef
Set aside.

Heat in the sauce pot over medium heat
2 tablespoons olive oil
Add and cook until onion is transparent, stirring occasionally
1 cup (about 2 medium-size) coarsely chopped onion (page 12)
4 cloves garlic (page 12), minced; or crushed in a garlic press
With a slotted spoon, remove onion to a small dish. Put the meat into the sauce pot, brown on all sides over medium heat.

Meanwhile, dissolve
2 beef bouillon cubes or 1 teaspoon concentrated meat extract
in
1 cup hot tomato juice
When meat is browned, return the onion to the sauce pot. Add the tomato bouillon and
1 cup claret
½ cup chopped celery leaves
2 teaspoons chopped parsley
6 whole cloves
2 bay leaves
and a mixture of
1½ teaspoons salt
1 teaspoon Accent
½ teaspoon paprika
¼ teaspoon pepper
Bring liquid just to boiling, stirring and scrap-

Standing Rib Roast of Beef

ing bottom of pot to loosen all drippings. Reduce heat; cover and simmer (do not boil) 2½ to 3 hrs., or until meat is tender when pierced with a fork. Add hot water or wine if necessary during cooking period.

Remove meat to warm serving platter. If desired, thicken cooking liquid (*p. 107* ; use 1 to 2 tablespoons flour-water mixture.)

6 to 8 servings

Rolled Pot Roast with Sour Cream Gravy

Heat in a Dutch oven over medium heat
3 tablespoons fat
Wipe with a clean, damp cloth
4 lb. rolled pot roast of beef
Add the meat to fat and brown on all sides over medium heat.

Meanwhile, clean (*page 12*), cut into quarters and set aside
1 medium-size onion
Season the browned meat with a mixture of
1 teaspoon salt
1 teaspoon Accent
⅛ teaspoon pepper
Add the onion and
¼ cup water
1 bay leaf
Cover tightly; simmer (do not boil) about 3 hrs. If necessary to add more water during cooking period, add hot water.

About 15 min. before meat is tender, cook and drain (*page 277*)
3 cups (about 4 oz.) noodles

Rolled Pot Roast with Sour Cream Gravy

Using a fork, blend with the noodles
3 tablespoons butter
Serve buttered noodles in warm serving bowl or on platter with the pot roast.

For Gravy—When meat is tender, remove from liquid and keep warm. Strain liquid and return it to Dutch oven. Set over medium heat.

Put into a 1-pt. screw-top jar
½ cup water
Sprinkle onto the liquid
1 tablespoon flour
Cover jar tightly and shake until mixture is well blended. Slowly pour mixture into cooking liquid, stirring constantly. Bring rapidly to boiling, continuing to stir; cook 3 to 5 min.

Remove Dutch oven from heat. Stirring vigorously with a French whip, whisk beater or fork, add to mixture in Dutch oven, in very small amounts, a mixture of
1½ cups thick sour cream
1½ tablespoons lemon juice
1½ teaspoons grated lemon peel
(page 11)
¾ teaspoon sugar
Place over low heat and stir constantly until thoroughly heated (3 to 5 min.); do not boil.

Serve gravy with pot roast and noodles.

About 12 servings

Barbecued Pot Roast ④

MRS. ALFRED VAUGHN, MALVERN, ARK.

Set out a Dutch oven, or use a heavy 3-qt. sauce pot having a tight-fitting cover.

Wipe with a clean, damp cloth
   3 lb. arm or blade pot roast of beef, cut 2 in. thick
Season meat with a mixture of
   2 teaspoons salt
   1 teaspoon Accent
   ¼ teaspoon pepper
Heat in the Dutch oven over medium heat
   3 tablespoons fat
Add the pot roast and brown on both sides over medium heat.

Add to the browned meat
   1 cup (8-oz. can) tomato sauce
   ½ cup water
   3 medium-size onions (page 12), thinly sliced
   2 cloves garlic (page 12), minced; or crushed in a garlic press
Bring liquid rapidly to boiling; reduce heat, cover and simmer (do not boil) 1½ hrs.

Meanwhile, blend together
   ¼ cup ketchup
   ¼ cup vinegar
   ¼ cup lemon juice
   2 tablespoons dark brown sugar
   1 tablespoon Worcestershire sauce
   ½ teaspoon dry mustard
   ¼ teaspoon paprika
Pour mixture over meat and simmer 1 hr. longer, or until meat is tender when pierced with a fork.

Remove meat to warm platter. Skim fat from liquid; pour liquid into serving dish and serve with the meat.   *About 6 servings*

Hungarian Hot Pickled Beef ④ ⑤

A heavy 4-qt. kettle having a tight-fitting cover will be needed. Set out a 3- or 4-qt. bowl.

Wipe with a clean, damp cloth
   3 to 4 lb. pot roast of beef (rump, chuck, blade or round)
Put meat into the bowl and cover with a mixture of equal parts of
   Vinegar
   Water
Add
   1 teaspoon salt
   10 peppercorns
   10 juniper berries
   2 bay leaves
   1 small onion (page 12), coarsely chopped
   1 lemon, rinsed and cut into ¼-in. slices
Cover the bowl tightly and put into refrigerator. Marinate (*page 12*) 2 to 3 days, turning meat once a day.

Set out the kettle and cover.

Remove meat from marinade and drain thoroughly. Strain and reserve marinade.

Heat in the kettle over low heat
   2 tablespoons butter or margarine
Add the pot roast and brown on all sides over medium heat.

Cover meat with a mixture of equal parts of
   Reserved marinade
   Hot water
Bring liquid rapidly to boiling. Reduce heat; cover kettle tightly and simmer (do not boil) about 3 hrs., or until meat is tender when pierced with a fork.

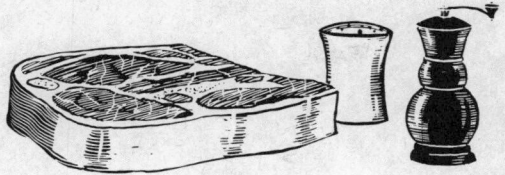

Remove meat to a warm platter; keep meat warm. Pour cooking liquid from kettle and set aside.

For Gravy—Melt in the kettle
¼ cup butter or margarine
Thoroughly blend in
¼ cup flour
Heat until mixture bubbles and is lightly browned, stirring constantly. Remove from heat and add gradually, stirring constantly, 3 cups of the reserved cooking liquid. Return to heat and bring rapidly to boiling, stirring constantly; cook 1 to 2 min. longer. Slice meat and pour the gravy over it.

8 to 10 servings

Sauerbraten

ADELE S. WEILER, DEL NORTE, COLO.

A heavy 4-qt. kettle having a tight-fitting cover or a Dutch oven will be needed. Set out a deep 3- or 4-qt. bowl.

Wipe with a clean, damp cloth
4 to 5 lb. pot roast of beef (rump, chuck, blade or round)
Put the meat into the bowl. Set aside.

Combine in a saucepan and heat just to boiling
2 cups vinegar
2 cups water
1 large onion (page 12), sliced
2 tablespoons sugar
2 teaspoons salt
10 peppercorns
6 whole cloves
2 bay leaves
Remove from heat; cool slightly. Pour mixture over meat in bowl. Add
1 lemon, rinsed and cut into ¼-in. slices

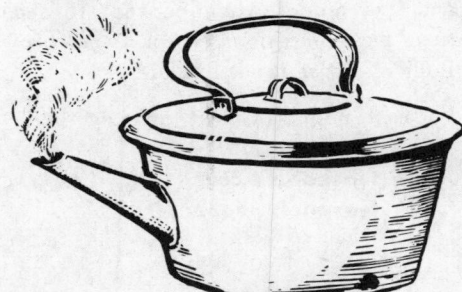

Cool, cover bowl tightly and put into refrigerator. Marinate (*page 12*) for 3 days, turning meat once a day.

Set out the kettle and cover.

Remove meat from marinade and drain thoroughly. Strain and reserve marinade.

Heat in the kettle over low heat
2 to 3 tablespoons butter or margarine
Add the pot roast and brown on all sides over medium heat. Slowly add 2 cups of the reserved marinade (reserve remaining marinade for gravy). Bring liquid rapidly to boiling. Reduce heat; cover kettle tightly and simmer (do not boil) 2½ to 3 hrs., or until meat is tender when pierced with a fork. Add more of the marinade, if necessary.

Remove meat to a warm platter and keep warm. Pour cooking liquid from kettle and set aside for gravy.

For Gravy—Melt in the kettle
¼ cup butter or margarine
Thoroughly blend in
¼ cup flour
Heat until mixture bubbles and is golden brown, stirring constantly. Remove from heat. Add gradually, stirring constantly
3 cups liquid (reserved cooking liquid and enough reserved marinade or hot water to equal 3 cups liquid)
Return to heat. Add, stirring in
8 gingersnaps (about 2 oz.), crumbled
Bring to boiling; cook rapidly, stirring constantly, until gravy thickens. Cook 1 to 2 min. longer.

Serve meat and gravy with **Dumplings** (*p. 69*) **Potato Pancakes** (*page 69*) or **Noodles** (*page 277*).

10 to 12 servings

Broiled Beef Steaks

Broiled Beef Steaks

Wipe with a clean, damp cloth
> **Beef steaks, such as porterhouse, T-bone, sirloin or club, cut about 1 in. thick.**

(Allow ⅓ to ½ lb. meat per serving.)

Set temperature control of range at Broil.

Arrange beef steaks on broiler rack. Place in broiler with tops of steaks 2 in. from heat source; broil 8 to 10 min. (The short cooking time for rare steaks; the longer cooking time for medium-done steaks.)

Meanwhile, for each pound of meat, mix
> **1 teaspoon salt**
> **½ teaspoon Accent**
> **¼ teaspoon pepper**

When steaks are browned on one side, sprinkle with one half of seasoning mixture. Turn and broil second side 8 to 10 min. Test for doneness by cutting a slit along the bone and noting color of meat. Season second side. For 2-in. steaks, broil with top of steaks 3 in. from heat source, allowing 15 to 20 min. on each side. Cut through fat on outside edge of each steak at 1-in. intervals; be careful not to cut through lean.

Serve steaks with
> **Butter-Fried Mushrooms (page 293)**
> **Butter-Fried Onion Slices (page 293)**

Note: To prepare beef steaks on an outdoor grill see Outdoor Cooking (*page 204*).

Panbroiled Beef Steaks

Heat a large, heavy skillet.

Wipe with a clean, damp cloth
> **Beef steaks, such as porterhouse, T-bone, sirloin or club, cut ¾ to 1 in. thick.**

(Allow ⅓ to ½ lb. meat per serving.)

Place steaks in skillet and brown meat slowly over medium heat. Maintain a temperature which allows juices to evaporate rather than collect in pan. With too low heat, the meat will simmer in its own juices and become dry and less tender when cooked. If necessary turn meat occasionally for even browning. Pour off fat as it accumulates.

For each pound of meat, mix together
> **1 teaspoon salt**
> **½ teaspoon Accent**
> **¼ teaspoon pepper**

When steaks are browned on one side, turn and sprinkle one half of seasoning over top. Brown other side and sprinkle with seasoning just before serving. Allow 10 to 20 min. total cooking time, depending on degree of doneness desired. Test for doneness by cutting a slit along the bone and noting color of meat.

Beef Brochettes

Set out six 8-in. skewers.

Wipe with a clean, damp cloth
1½ lbs. beef sirloin
Cut into 12 cubes. Set aside.

Clean (*page 12*), cut into halves lengthwise
6 small (about 1 lb.) onions
Set aside.

Clean (*page 12*, do not slice), remove stems from and set aside
12 large mushrooms
(Mushroom stems may be used in other food preparation.)

Cut into halves
6 slices bacon
Thread onto each skewer in the following order: onion half, bacon, beef, mushroom; repeat. Do not crown pieces on skewer.

Brush meat and vegetables generously with
Melted butter or margarine
Set temperature control of range at Broil.

Arrange skewers on broiler rack. Place in broiler with tops of brochettes about 3 in. from heat source.

Broil about 10 min., frequently turning and brushing brochettes with melted butter or margarine. Test for doneness by cutting a slit in beef cube and noting color of meat.

Sprinkle broiled brochettes with a mixture of
1 teaspoon salt
½ teaspoon Accent
⅛ teaspoon pepper
Serve at once.   *6 servings*

Teriyaki Steak
MRS. JAMES LOTZGESELL
SAN FRANCISCO, CALIF.

Set out a large, shallow dish.

Blend together thoroughly
⅓ cup soy sauce
1 tablespoon wine vinegar
2 tablespoons sugar
1 tablespoon dark brown sugar
1½ teaspoons ginger
1 clove garlic (*page 12*), minced; or or crushed in a garlic press
Wipe with a clean, damp cloth
3 lbs. steak cut at least 1 in. thick (top round steak may be used)
Put steak in the dish; pour marinade (liquid mixture) over meat. Marinate (*page 12*) 30 min., turning meat once or twice.

Set temperature control of range at Broil.

Remove steak from marinade and place it on the broiler rack. Put into broiler with top of steak 3 in. from heat source.

Broil 9 to 12 min. (The shorter cooking time is for rare steak; the longer cooking time is for medium-done steak.) Turn and broil second side 9 to 12 min. If desired, brush steak occasionally with the marinade. Test for doneness by cutting a slit near the bone and noting color of meat. Serve immediately.   *6 servings*

Beef Brochettes

Esterhazy Steak 6 7

Grease an 11x7x1½-in. baking dish; set out aluminum foil and a large, heavy skillet.

Set out
  ½ cup flour
Wipe with a clean, damp cloth and place on a flat working surface
  2 lbs. round steak, cut 1 in. thick
Pound (*page 107*) flour into meat, using about one half for each side. Cut meat into serving-size pieces and coat well with a mixture of
  ¼ cup flour
  2 teaspoons salt
  ¾ teaspoon Accent
  ½ teaspoon pepper
Heat in the skillet over medium heat
  ⅓ cup fat
Add the steak and brown on both sides over medium heat. Put meat in the baking dish; set aside.

Put into the skillet and cook over low heat 10 min., occasionally moving and turning with a fork or spoon
  3 carrots, washed, scraped or pared and thinly sliced
  2 small onions (*page 12*), thinly sliced
  1 stalk celery (*page 12*), chopped
Meanwhile, prepare and set aside
  1 cup quick meat broth (*page 13*)
Spoon the vegetables over the steak. Add
  1 teaspoon capers
Heat in the skillet
  1 tablespoon fat
Blend in a mixture of
  1 tablespoon flour
  ¼ teaspoon salt
  Few grains pepper

Heat until mixture bubbles and is lightly browned, stirring constantly. Remove skillet from heat. Gradually add the cooled meat broth, stirring constantly. Return skillet to heat and bring rapidly to boiling, stirring constantly. Remove from heat. Blend in
  ¼ cup dry white wine
Pour sauce over vegetables and meat in baking dish. Cover dish with aluminum foil.

Bake at 350°F 1¼ hrs. Remove aluminum foil; spread over vegetables a mixture of
  1 cup thick sour cream
  1 teaspoon paprika
Return dish to oven, uncovered, and bake about 15 min. longer, or until meat is tender when pierced with a fork.   *5 or 6 servings*

Tomato-Smothered Steak 7 8

Set out a large, heavy skillet having a tight-fitting cover; or use a Dutch oven.

Wipe with a clean, damp cloth
  1½ lbs. arm or blade steak, cut 1½ in. thick
Coat meat with a mixture of
  ¼ cup flour
  2½ teaspoons salt
  1½ teaspoons chili powder
  1 teaspoon celery salt
  ¼ teaspoon pepper
Heat in the skillet over medium heat
  3 tablespoons fat
Add the steak and brown on both sides over medium heat.

Meanwhile, clean (*page 12*), slice and set aside
  1 large onion

Finely chop enough green pepper to yield

¼ cup chopped green pepper (*page 12*)

When meat is browned, add the onion, green pepper and

2 cups (1-lb. can) tomatoes
3 drops tabasco sauce

Bring liquid rapidly to boiling; reduce heat, cover tightly and cook slowly over low heat or in 300°F oven about 2 hrs., or until meat is tender when pierced with a fork.

Steak may be served with

Perfection Boiled Rice (page 275)

About 4 servings

Tomato-Smothered Steak

Baked Steak with ⁸ Wild Rice Dressing

VIRGINIA SOVELL, MINNEAPOLIS, MINN.

The patiently gathered wild rice of the northern lakes is one of our most delightful native delicacies. Here it furnishes an unusual flavor complement to beef steak.

Set out a Dutch oven or a large, heavy skillet having a tight-fitting cover.

Prepare and set aside

1 cup quick meat broth (page 13; use 2 bouillon cubes or 1 teaspoon concentrated meat extract)

Prepare

Boiled Wild Rice (one-third recipe, page 275)

While rice is cooking, wipe with a clean, damp cloth

1½ lbs. round steak, cut ½ to ¾ in. thick

Coat meat evenly with a mixture of

¼ cup flour
1 teaspoon salt
½ teaspoon Accent
¼ teaspoon pepper

Pound meat (*page 107*). Set aside.

For dressing, melt in the skillet over low heat

2 tablespoons butter or margarine

Blend in

2 teaspoons flour

Heat until mixture bubbles. Remove from heat. Add gradually, stirring in, ½ cup of the meat broth. Stirring constantly, cook until mixture thickens; cook 1 to 2 min. longer. Remove from heat. Stir in the cooked wild rice and

¼ cup (about 2 oz.) drained, sliced mushrooms

and a mixture of

¼ teaspoon thyme
¼ teaspoon salt
¼ teaspoon pepper

Pile dressing on one half of steak and fold other half over it. Fasten with skewers.

Heat in the skillet

3 tablespoons fat

Put steak into the skillet and brown on both sides over medium heat. Pour in the remaining broth. Cover and bake at 325°F about 1 hr., or until meat is tender when pierced with a fork.

About 4 servings

Steak Smothered in Onions 9 9

Set out a large, heavy skillet having a tight-fitting cover.

Wipe with a clean, damp cloth and place on a flat working surface
   1½ lbs. round steak, cut ¾ in. thick
Coat meat with a mixture of
   ⅓ cup flour
   1 teaspoon salt
   ¾ teaspoon Accent
   ⅛ teaspoon pepper
Pound (*page 107*) flour mixture into meat, using about one half for each side.

Cut meat into serving-size pieces and set aside.

Heat in the skillet over medium heat
   2 tablespoons fat
Put meat into skillet and brown on both sides over medium heat.

Meanwhile, clean (*page 12*) and slice
   2 medium-size onions
Put onion slices over the browned steak. Add
   1 cup water
   1 tablespoon vinegar
   1 clove garlic (page 12), cut into halves
   1 bay leaf
   ¼ teaspoon thyme
Bring liquid rapidly to boiling; reduce heat, cover and simmer (do not boil) 1 hr., or until meat is tender when pierced with a fork. Add small amounts of hot water as necessary.

Remove meat to a warm serving plate; arrange onion slices attractively on the meat. Discard garlic and bay leaf. Spoon cooking liquid over meat. *4 to 6 servings*

Swiss Steak 10 10

MRS. V. R. PETERSON, COLUMBUS, OHIO

Set out a Dutch oven, or a large, heavy sauce pot having a tight-fitting cover.

Wipe with a clean, damp cloth
   2 lbs. round, blade or arm steak,
      cut 1 in. thick
Coat evenly with a mixture of
   ¼ cup flour
   1 teaspoon salt
   ¾ teaspoon Accent
   ¼ teaspoon pepper
Pound (*page 107*) flour mixture into meat, using about one half for each side.

Heat in the Dutch oven over medium heat
   2 tablespoons fat
Add steak and brown evenly on both sides over medium heat.

Add to the Dutch oven
   2 cups water
   ¼ cup chopped celery (page 12)
   ¼ cup chopped green pepper (page 12)
   1 tablespoon chopped onion
   1 teaspoon Worcestershire sauce
   ⅛ teaspoon garlic salt
   ⅛ teaspoon cinnamon
Bring liquid in Dutch oven rapidly to boiling; reduce heat, cover and simmer (do not boil) 1½ hrs., or until steak is tender when pierced with a fork.

Remove meat to warm platter. Thicken cooking liquid (*p. 107* ; add flour-water mixture 1 tablespoon at a time).

Serve gravy over the meat. *4 to 6 servings*

Hungarian Beef Roll

Set out a large, heavy skillet having a tight-fitting cover.

Prepare, finely chop and set aside
   2 Hard-Cooked Eggs (page 87)
Wipe with a clean, damp cloth and place on a flat working surface
   1½ lbs. round steak, cut ½ in. thick
Cover with a mixture of the chopped egg and
   3 slices bacon, cut into 1-in. pieces
   1 teaspoon chopped parsley
   ½ teaspoon capers
   ½ teaspoon salt
   ½ teaspoon Accent
   ⅛ teaspoon pepper
Roll up steak lengthwise and tie with a cord or fasten with skewers.

Heat in the skillet over medium heat
   3 tablespoons fat
Add steak and brown on all sides over medium heat. Season with a mixture of
   1 teaspoon paprika
   ¼ teaspoon salt
Slowly pour into the skillet
   1 cup hot water
Bring liquid rapidly to boiling; reduce heat, cover and simmer (do not boil) about 2 hrs., or until steak is tender when pierced with a fork. Remove meat from skillet to serving platter; cover platter and keep steak warm.

Pour drippings from skillet into a bowl, leaving brown residue in skillet. Allow fat to rise to surface of drippings; skim off and reserve fat. Set aside drippings to be used as part of the liquid in gravy; cool to lukewarm.

Measure 3 tablespoons reserved fat into the skillet and heat. Blend in
   3 tablespoons flour
   ¼ teaspoon salt
   ⅛ teaspoon pepper
Heat until mixture bubbles. Remove from heat and add gradually, stirring constantly
   1 cup liquid (drippings or quick meat broth, page 13)
Return skillet to heat and bring rapidly to boiling, stirring constantly. While stirring, scrape bottom and sides of skillet to blend in brown residue. Cook 1 to 2 min. longer.

Remove from heat. Stirring gravy vigorously with a French whip, whisk beater, or fork, add in very small amounts
   1 cup thick sour cream
Heat thoroughly over low heat 3 to 5 min., stirring constantly; do not boil.

Remove cord or skewers from roll. Slice meat and serve with the gravy.   *About 4 servings*

Steak Roll-Ups with Noodles

MRS. RAY GARRISON
BOWLING GREEN, KY.

Set out a Dutch oven; or use a heavy sauce pot having a tight-fitting cover.

Wipe with a clean, damp cloth and place on a flat working surface

1½ lb. flank steak

Pound (*page 107*) or score the meat. Spread one side with

3 tablespoons butter or margarine

Sprinkle with a mixture of

½ teaspoon thyme
¼ teaspoon sage
¼ teaspoon basil

Starting at one of the long sides, roll up meat. Tie with cord.

Heat in the Dutch oven over medium heat

3 tablespoons fat

Add the steak roll and brown on all sides over medium heat. Add

3½ cups (No. 2½ can) tomatoes
¾ cup (6-oz. can) tomato paste
1 cup (about 2 medium size) chopped onion (*page 12*)
1 clove garlic (*page 12*), cut into halves

and a mixture of

2 teaspoons salt
1 teaspoon Accent
1 teaspoon chili powder
¼ teaspoon pepper

Bring liquid rapidly to boiling; reduce heat, cover and simmer (do not boil) 1½ hrs., or until meat is tender when pierced with a fork.

About 20 min. before meat is tender, cook (*page 277*)

4 cups (about 6 oz.) broad noodles

Prepare

¼ cup finely chopped parsley

Add one half of the chopped parsley to the noodles with

2 tablespoons butter or margarine

Toss lightly to blend thoroughly.

Remove garlic from sauce. Remove steak roll. Insert skewers into meat at 1-in. intervals. Remove cord. Slice between skewers.

Place noodles in center of hot platter. Arrange meat around the noodles. Spoon sauce over all. Garnish with remaining parsley.

4 to 6 servings

Flank Steak Roll-Ups with Buttered Cauliflower

Set out a large, heavy skillet having a tight-fitting cover.

Wipe with a clean, damp cloth

1½ to 2-lb. flank steak

Rub both sides of steak with cut side of

1 clove garlic (*page· 12*)

Season meat with a mixture of

1 teaspoon salt
¾ teaspoon Accent
⅛ teaspoon pepper

Starting at one of the long sides, roll up the meat. Fasten meat roll at 1-in. intervals with skewers or wooden picks. Cut meat roll between picks into slices 1 in. thick.

Flank Steak Roll-Ups with Buttered Cauliflower

Heat in the skillet over medium heat

3 tablespoons fat

Add the meat roll-ups and brown on both sides over medium heat. Add

¼ cup water

1 bay leaf

Cover tightly; reduce heat and simmer (do not boil) about 1½ to 2 hrs., or until meat is tender when pierced with a fork. Add small amounts of hot water as needed.

When meat has cooked about 30 min., soak and cook (*page 285*)

1 medium-size head cauliflower

(Do not separate into flowerets.) When cauliflower is tender, drain and place on a large, warm platter. Season with

¼ teaspoon salt

Few grains Accent

Few grains pepper

Paprika

Top with

Butter or margarine

Remove meat from skillet and arrange on platter around the cauliflower.

Spoon liquid remaining in skillet over meat.

4 to 6 servings

Beef "Birds" 14

Grease a 2-qt. casserole having a tight-fitting cover. Set out a large, heavy skillet.

Set out a mixture of

½ cup flour

¾ teaspoon Accent

½ teaspoon salt

⅛ teaspoon pepper

Wipe with a clean, damp cloth

1½ lbs. round steak, cut about ½ in. thick

Pound (*page 107*) flour into meat, using about one half for each side. Cut meat into 6 wedge-shaped pieces; set aside.

Wash, pare or scrape, and cut each lengthwise into 3 pieces

2 small carrots

Beef "Birds" with cauliflower and green beans

Cut into 6 wedges

1 small onion (*page 12*)

Clean (*page 12*) and cut into 6 strips

½ green pepper

Cut into three pieces each

2 slices bacon

Place a piece of bacon, onion, carrot and green pepper on each beef wedge; roll up, starting at tip of meat. Tuck under ends to keep vegetables inside roll. Insert wooden picks through folded ends and through center of each roll.

Heat in the skillet over medium heat

3 tablespoons fat

Add the meat rolls and brown on all sides over medium heat. Remove browned meat rolls to casserole.

Prepare in same skillet

2 cups Thin White Sauce (double recipe, *page 323*)

Stir into completed sauce

½ cup (4-oz. can, drained) mushrooms

1 tablespoon minced parsley

1 teaspoon Worcestershire sauce

Pour sauce over meat.

Cover casserole and bake at 350°F 1 to 1½ hrs., or until meat is tender when pierced with a fork. Remove wooden picks before serving.

6 servings

▲ Beef Stroganoff 15 14
WILLA J. SESSIONS, TAMPA, FLA.

Set out a heavy 10-in. skillet having a tight-fitting cover.

Wipe with a clean, damp cloth
2 lbs. round steak, cut ½ in. thick
Cut into 2x½x½-in. strips. Coat meat evenly
(*page 107*) with a mixture of
⅓ cup flour
1 teaspoon salt
¾ teaspoon Accent
⅛ teaspoon pepper
Heat in the skillet over low heat
⅓ cup butter or margarine
Add the meat strips and
½ cup (1 medium-size) finely chopped onion (*page 12*)
1 small clove garlic (*page 12*), minced; or crushed in a garlic press
Cook over medium heat, frequently moving and turning meat to brown evenly on all sides.

Meanwhile, prepare
1 cup quick meat broth (*page 13*)
When meat is browned, slowly add the broth. Add
1 tablespoon sherry
Bring liquid rapidly to boiling; reduce heat, cover and simmer (do not boil) 20 to 25 min., or until meat is tender.

While meat is cooking, prepare
Butter-Fried Mushrooms (½ recipe, p.293 ; use 3 tablespoons butter)
Blend together
1 cup thick sour cream
1 teaspoon Worcestershire sauce
When meat is tender, remove skillet from heat. Stirring vigorously, add to mixture in

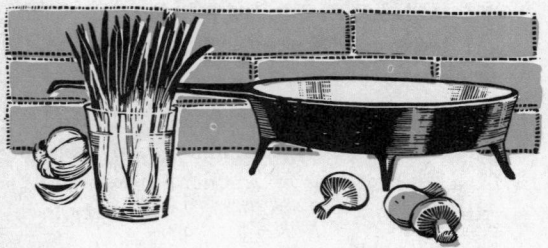

skillet, in very small amounts, the sour-cream mixture. Add the mushrooms. Return to heat. Continue cooking over low heat, keeping mixture moving with a spoon, 3 to 5 min., or until thoroughly heated; do not boil.

Turn the meat mixture into a warm serving dish. Serve immediately. Accompany with
Whipped Potatoes (*page 298*) ,
Noodles (*page 277*) or
Perfection Boiled Rice (*page 275*)
6 servings

△ Beef Stroganoff Par Excellence

Follow ▲ Recipe; substitute **boneless beef**, such as tenderloin, sirloin, or rib for the round steak. Increase quick meat broth to 2 cups. Blend 3 tablespoons **tomato paste** with the sour cream and Worcestershire sauce.

Braised Short Ribs 15 De Luxe
ALICE M. WALCKER, PORTLAND, ORE.

Set out a large heavy kettle, or sauce pot having a tight-fitting cover; or use a Dutch oven.

Wipe with a clean, damp cloth
3 lbs. beef short ribs
Cut into serving-size pieces. Coat meat evenly
(*page 107*) with a mixture of
⅓ cup flour
2 teaspoons salt
1 teaspoon Accent
¼ teaspoon pepper
Heat in the kettle over medium heat
⅓ cup fat
Add the meat and brown on all sides over medium heat.

Meanwhile, clean (*page 12*) and thinly slice
2 medium-size onions, (about 1 cup, sliced)
Prepare
½ cup chopped green pepper (page 12)
Add onion and green pepper to meat with
1 clove garlic (page 12), minced; or crushed in a garlic press
Add to kettle a mixture of
1 cup water
¼ cup ketchup
Bring liquid rapidly to boiling; reduce heat, cover and simmer (do not boil) over low heat until meat is tender when pierced with a fork (about 2 hrs.). Turn meat occasionally. Add small amounts of hot water as needed.

Remove meat to warm serving platter.

Add to the cooking liquid
1½ cups water
Bring rapidly to boiling; reduce heat and simmer gently several minutes. If desired, thicken cooking liquid (*page 107*;  add flour-water mixture one tablespoon at a time).

6 servings

▲ Beef Short Ribs with Vegetables 16 16

Set out a large, heavy kettle or sauce pot having a tight-fitting cover; or use a Dutch oven.

Wipe with a clean, damp cloth
3 lbs. beef short ribs
Cut into serving-size pieces. Coat meat evenly (*page 107*) with a mixture of
⅓ cup flour
2 teaspoons salt
1 teaspoon Accent
⅛ teaspoon pepper
Heat in the kettle over medium heat
⅓ cup fat
Add the meat pieces and brown on all sides over medium heat.

While meat is browning, clean (*page 12*), thinly slice and set aside
1 medium-size onion

When meat is brown, remove kettle from heat and slowly pour in
2 cups hot water
Add the sliced onion. Cover tightly and bring water to boiling over high heat. Reduce heat and simmer (do not boil) about 1½ hrs., or until meat is almost tender (at which time vegetables should be added). Add hot water as necessary.

Before time to add vegetables to ribs, wash and cut off stem ends from
½ lb. green beans
Set beans aside.

Wash, pare, and cut into halves
6 medium-size (about 2 lbs.) potatoes
Add prepared vegetables to kettle with
1 teaspoon salt
¼ teaspoon Accent
⅛ teaspoon pepper
Cover kettle and continue to simmer.

Meanwhile, clean (*page 12*)
12 stalks celery
Cut crosswise into 3-in. pieces and put into kettle. Cover and simmer about 35 min., or until meat and vegetables are tender when pierced with a fork. With a slotted spoon, remove meat and vegetables from kettle to hot serving platter; keep warm. Thicken cooking liquid for gravy (*p.107* ; use ¼ cup water and 2 tablespoons flour).

Serve hot. *6 servings*

△ Spicy Short Ribs and Fruit 17 17

Follow ▲ Recipe; omit vegetables. When ribs have simmered 1 hr., add 1 cup (about 5 oz.) **dried apricots** and 1 cup (about 5 oz.) pitted **prunes**. Remove about 1 cup cooking liquid. Blend into liquid a mixture of ½ cup **sugar**, ½ teaspoon **cinnamon**, ½ teaspoon **allspice** and ¼ teaspoon ground **cloves**. Blend in 3 tablespoons **vinegar**. Pour mixture over ribs. Continue to simmer 30 min. or until meat and fruit are tender. Serve with cooking liquid.

Beef in Lemon Sauce

Give a lift to leftover beef with a lemony sauce that has a transforming touch.

Set out a small saucepan and a 10-in. skillet having a tight-fitting cover.

Cut into ½-in. cubes enough beef to yield
   3 cups cubed cooked beef
Set meat aside.

Prepare and set aside to cool to lukewarm
   ½ cup quick meat broth (page 13)
Dice and put into the cold skillet
   4 slices bacon
Cook slowly, frequently moving and turning pieces with a spoon until bacon is lightly browned. Remove bacon with slotted spoon and set aside. Add the beef to the bacon drippings in the skillet. Cover skillet and cook over low heat 7 to 10 min., or until meat is thoroughly heated.

Meanwhile, heat in the saucepan over low heat
   1 tablespoon fat
Blend in
   1 tablespoon flour
Heat until mixture bubbles, stirring constantly. Remove from heat and gradually add the reserved broth, stirring constantly. Return to heat and bring rapidly to boiling, stirring constantly; cook 1 to 2 min. longer.

Remove saucepan from heat. Stirring vigorously with a French whip, whisk beater or fork, add to contents of saucepan in very small amounts
   1 cup thick sour cream
Blend into sauce
   1 tablespoon lemon juice
   **1 teaspoon grated lemon peel
      (page 11)**
   ½ teaspoon sugar
   ½ teaspoon Accent
Pour sauce over the meat. Return bacon to skillet. Place the mixture over low heat, stirring constantly, until thoroughly heated (about 3 to 5 min.); do not boil. Serve hot.

About 4 servings

Cornish Pasties
ELIZABETH E. STRIKE, MUSKEGON, MICH.

Set out two baking sheets.

Sift together into a large bowl
   6 cups sifted flour
   1½ teaspoons salt
Cut in until pieces are the size of small peas
   **1½ cups lard, hydrogenated vegetable
      shortening or all-purpose
      shortening**
Sprinkle over mixture, a small amount at a time, about
   1 cup water
Mix lightly with a fork after each addition. Add only enough water to hold pastry together. Work quickly; do not overhandle. Divide dough into two portions. Shape each portion into a ball. Set aside.

Combine in a large bowl and mix lightly
   **1½ lbs. flank steak, cut into
      ½-in. pieces**
   **6 cups (about 4 medium-size) ½-in.
      potato cubes**
   1 cup finely chopped onion (page 12)
   ¾ cup finely chopped carrot
Set mixture aside.

Lightly grease the baking sheets.

Flatten one ball of the pastry on a lightly floured surface. Roll from center to edge into a round about ⅛ in. thick. With knife or spatula, loosen pastry from surface whenever

Cornish Pasties: Spoon filling onto rounds. Moisten edges with water to form tight seal.

sticking occurs; lift pastry slightly and sprinkle flour underneath. Cut out 5- to 6-in. rounds, using a saucer or waxed paper pattern as a guide. Repeat with remaining ball of pastry.

Add to the meat and vegetables a mixture of
2 teaspoons salt
1½ teaspoons pepper
1 teaspoon Accent
Spoon an equal amount of filling onto one half of each round. Seal edges (see Little Princess Fried Pies, *page 486*).

Cut a slit in top of each pasty to allow steam to escape during baking. Place pasties on the baking sheets. Brush tops with
Milk or cream
Bake at 350°F about 1 hr., or until pastry is lightly browned. *About 8 pasties*

▲ Caraway Beef Stew Pie

Set out a 3-qt. top-of range casserole having a tight-fitting cover.

Wipe with a clean, damp cloth and cut into 1-in. pieces
1½ lbs. round steak
Coat pieces evenly (*page 107*) with a mixture of
¼ cup flour
1 teaspoon Accent
1 teaspoon salt
¼ teaspoon pepper

Cut a slit in the top of each pasty to allow the steam to escape. Brush with milk or cream.

Heat in the casserole over medium heat
¼ cup fat
Add meat and brown on all sides over medium heat, occasionally moving and turning pieces with fork or spoon. When nearly browned, add
2 medium-size (about ½ lb.) onions (*page 12*), sliced
Finish browning meat. Add
3 cups hot water (added slowly)
1 bay leaf
Cover casserole and simmer (do not boil) 1½ hrs. If necessary, add hot water as meat cooks.

Meanwhile, wash, break off stem ends and cut into julienne strips (*page 11*)
½ lb. (about 1½ cups) green beans
Wash, scrape or pare, and slice
3 or 4 (about ½ lb.) carrots
Add beans and carrots to casserole with
3 large (about 1 lb.) onions, quartered
Cover casserole and simmer 15 to 25 min. longer, or until vegetables are tender when pierced with a fork. Remove bay leaf.

Meanwhile, prepare
Pastry Topping (one-half recipe, *page 443*; stir 2 teaspoons caraway seeds into sifted dry ingredients)
Cut the rolled pastry into strips 1 in. wide. Moisten rim of casserole with cold water. Twist strips and loosely arrange ½-in. apart across top of casserole. Trim strips so ends extend ½ in. beyond edge; turn ends under and press to secure to casserole.

Bake at 425°F 15 to 18 min., or until pastry strips are lightly browned. *8 servings*

△ Beef and Vegetables

Follow ▲ Recipe; omit pastry. Substitute one 12-oz. pkg. frozen **lima beans** for green beans and carrots.

Hungarian Goulash

▲ Hungarian Goulash

Set out a heavy 3-qt. sauce pot having a tight-fitting cover; or use a Dutch oven.

Wipe with a clean, damp cloth, cut into 1½-in. pieces and set aside

1½ lbs. boneless beef (chuck or rump)

Prepare and set aside

2 cups quick meat broth (double recipe, *page 13*)

Dice and put into the sauce pot

4 slices bacon

Cook slowly, moving and turning pieces frequently, until lightly browned. With a slotted spoon, remove bacon to a small bowl; set aside.

Add to the bacon drippings in the sauce pot and cook over medium heat until transparent, occasionally moving pieces with a spoon

1½ cups (about 3 medium-size) chopped onion (*page 12*)

Remove onion with slotted spoon to bowl containing bacon; set aside.

Add meat pieces to the sauce pot and brown

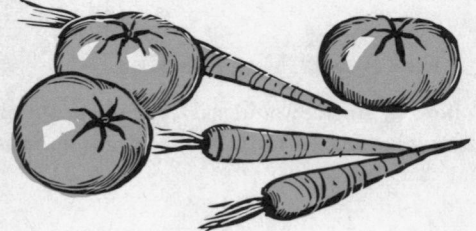

on all sides over medium heat, occasionally moving and turning pieces with fork or spoon.

Sprinkle evenly over the meat a mixture of

1 tablespoon paprika

1½ teaspoons salt

1 teaspoon Accent

¼ teaspoon pepper

⅛ teaspoon marjoram

Add the bacon, onion and

¼ cup (about 1 small) chopped green pepper (*page 12*)

Slowly pour in the reserved meat broth and

¾ cup dry white wine

Bring liquid rapidly to boiling; reduce heat, cover sauce pot and simmer (do not boil) 2 to 2½ hrs., or until meat is tender when pierced with a fork. With slotted spoon remove meat to warm serving dish. If desired, thicken cooking liquid (*page 107*).

Melt

1 tablespoon butter

Blend in, in order

½ teaspoon paprika

1 tablespoon water

Immediately add to liquid in sauce pot, stirring until well blended. Pour this sauce over meat. Serve immediately.   *6 to 8 servings*

⚠ Goulash with Potatoes

Follow ▲ Recipe; use a 4-qt. sauce pot or kettle. About ½ hr. before end of cooking time, add 6 medium-size (2 lbs.) **potatoes,** washed, pared and quartered.

⚠ Goulash with Tomatoes

Follow ▲ Recipe; substitute 1 cup (one half of 1-lb. can) **tomatoes,** sieved, for one half of the quick meat broth.

⚠ Goulash with Carrots

Follow ⚠ Recipe. Substitute 4 medium-size **carrots,** washed, scraped or pared, and cut into ½-in. pieces for the potatoes.

▲ Spicy Brown Beef Stew 23 22

Set out a large heavy kettle having a tight-fitting cover; or use a Dutch oven.

Wipe with a clean, damp cloth
2 lbs. beef for stewing (chuck, round or brisket)
Cut meat into 1½-in. pieces. Coat meat evenly (*page 107*) with a mixture of
⅓ cup flour
2 teaspoons salt
½ teaspoon Accent
⅛ teaspoon pepper
Heat in the kettle over medium heat
3 tablespoons fat
Add meat and brown on all sides over medium heat, occasionally moving and turning pieces. When meat is browned, pour off the excess fat.

While meat is browning, clean (*page 12*), chop and set aside
1 medium-size onion (½ cup, chopped)
Slowly pour into the kettle or Dutch oven
1 qt. hot water
Add to kettle the chopped onion and
1 tablespoon salt
1 teaspoon Worcestershire sauce
1 teaspoon lemon juice
2 bay leaves
½ teaspoon pepper
½ teaspoon Accent
Few grains cloves
Cover and bring liquid rapidly to boiling. Reduce heat and simmer (do not boil) about 1½ hrs., or until meat is almost tender.

About 15 min. before adding vegetables to stew, clean (*page 12*)
12 small onions
Set aside.

Wash, scrape and cut into pieces
8 medium-size carrots
Add prepared vegetables to kettle or Dutch oven. Cover and simmer 30 to 45 min. longer, or until meat and vegetables are tender.

While vegetables are cooking, prepare and set aside to keep warm
Whipped Potatoes (page 298)
Just before removing meat and vegetables from kettle, if desired, dissolve in a small amount of hot water
2 teaspoons concentrated meat extract
With slotted spoon, remove meat and vegetables from stew to hot dish. Stir into the cooking liquid the dissolved concentrated meat extract. Thicken cooking liquid (*p.107*)

Return meat and vegetables to kettle and heat thoroughly. Spoon Whipped Potatoes in a ring onto serving dish. Fill center of and surround potato ring with the stew.   *8 to 10 servings*

△ Individual Pastry-Topped Pies

Follow ▲ Recipe; omit Whipped Potatoes. Grease 5 or 6 small casseroles. Prepare **Pastry for 1-Crust Pie** (*page 442*). Roll pastry into a rectangle about ⅛ in. thick. Cut 5 or 6 strips of pastry 1 in. wide. Cut remaining pastry into strips ½ in. wide. Turn heated stew into casseroles. Moisten rims of casseroles with water. Place one of the 1-in. pastry strips around inside edge of each casserole, pressing strip onto edge. Carefully arrange narrower strips to form lattice pattern (*page 442*), leaving about ¼ in. between the strips. Trim strips so ends extend about ¼ in. beyond edge of casserole. Fold the ends of the strips over the pastry on edge of casseroles; press to seal.

Bake at 425°F 25 to 30 min., or until pastry is lightly browned.

Beef Stew in Casserole 24 23

Always scores a hit with the head of the house.

Set out a 3-qt. top-of-range casserole having a tight-fitting cover.

Wipe with a clean, damp cloth and cut into 1-in. pieces
1½ lbs. round steak
Coat pieces evenly (*page 107*) with a mixture of
¼ cup flour
1 teaspoon Accent
1 teaspoon salt
¼ teaspoon pepper
Heat in the casserole over medium heat
¼ cup fat
Add the meat and brown on all sides over medium heat, occasionally moving and turning with fork or spoon. When meat is nearly browned, add
1 medium-size onion (*page 12*),
   thinly sliced
Finish browning meat. Slowly add
3 cups hot water
1 bay leaf
Bring liquid rapidly to boiling; reduce heat, cover and simmer (do not boil) 1½ hrs. If necessary, add more hot water as meat cooks.

Meanwhile, thaw enough to separate only, contents of
1 12-oz. pkg. frozen peas
Wash, scrape or pare, and cut into thick crosswise slices
4 (about ½ lb.) small carrots
Wash, pare and cut into large cubes
2 medium-size potatoes
Clean (*page 12*) and cut into ½-in. slices
1 large stalk celery
Add the carrots, peas, potatoes and celery to casserole with
½ lb. (about 8) very small whole onions
   (*page 12*)
Cover casserole and simmer 15 to 25 min. longer, or until vegetables are tender when pierced with a fork. Remove bay leaf before serving. *8 servings*

Beef and Kidney Pie

Beef and Kidney Pie

Set out a 2-qt. top-of-range casserole having a tight-fitting cover.

Remove membrane from and split horizontally through center
1 beef kidney
Remove cords and tubes. Rinse thoroughly with cold water. Cut into ¾- to 1-in. pieces and put into a bowl. Pour over pieces
½ cup French Dressing (*page 318*)
Turn each piece of kidney to coat well. Cover bowl and marinate (*page 12*) at least 1 hr., turning pieces occasionally. Drain thoroughly.

Wipe with a clean, damp cloth
1 lb. beef for stewing (chuck, round
   or brisket), cut into 1-in. pieces
Coat kidney and beef pieces evenly (*page 107*) with a mixture of
⅔ cup flour
1½ teaspoons salt
1 teaspoon Accent
¼ teaspoon paprika
¼ teaspoon pepper
Heat in the casserole over medium heat
3 tablespoons fat
Add the meat pieces and
¼ cup chopped onion
Cook over medium heat until meat is browned, occasionally moving and turning mixture with a fork or spoon.

Meanwhile, drain reserving liquid, contents of
1 8-oz. can mushrooms
Combine and pour slowly into casserole the reserved mushroom liquid plus enough hot water to yield 1 cup liquid and
2½ cups (two 10½- to 11-oz. cans) condensed tomato soup
1 tablespoon Worcestershire sauce
(If necessary, add more hot water to allow liquid to just cover meat.) Add
1 bay leaf
¼ teaspoon basil
Cover casserole tightly; simmer (do not boil) 1 to 1½ hrs., or until meat is tender.

Meanwhile, prepare and set aside
Pastry Topping (page 443)
Heat in a saucepan over low heat
3 tablespoons butter or margarine
Add the mushrooms and cook over medium heat about 5 min., turning frequently.

Remove bay leaf. Stir in the mushrooms. If necessary, thicken cooking liquid (*page 107*).

Complete as in Pastry Topping.

Bake at 425°F 15 to 20 min., or until pastry is browned. *6 servings*

Beef and Polenta Pie

Lightly grease a 2-qt. casserole. Set out a double boiler and a large, heavy skillet having a tight-fitting cover.

Wipe with a clean, damp cloth
1½ lbs. beef for stewing (chuck, round or brisket)
Cut into 1-in. pieces. Coat meat evenly (*page 107*) with a mixture of
⅓ cup flour
1 teaspoon salt
1 teaspoon Accent
⅛ teaspoon pepper
Set pieces aside.

Heat in the skillet over medium heat
3 tablespoons fat

Put beef pieces into the skillet with
½ cup (1 medium-size) chopped onion (page 12)
1 clove garlic (page 12), minced; or crushed in a garlic press
Cook over medium heat until meat is browned, occasionally moving and turning mixture with a spoon. Drain off excess fat.

Mix together and pour slowly into the skillet
1¼ cups (10½- to 11-oz. can) condensed tomato soup
1 cup hot water
2 teaspoons chili powder
2 drops tabasco sauce
Cover skillet tightly and bring mixture to boiling over high heat. Reduce heat and simmer (do not boil) 1 to 1½ hrs., or until meat is tender when pierced with a fork.

Meanwhile, mix together
1 cup yellow corn meal
1 teaspoon salt
Mix in thoroughly
1 cup cold milk
Set mixture aside.

Prepare in the top of the double boiler
3 cups quick meat broth (page 13)
Bring rapidly to boiling over direct heat. Reduce heat to medium and add the corn-meal mixture gradually, stirring constantly. Continue cooking, stirring occasionally, until mixture is thickened. Place over simmering water. Cover; continue cooking about 30 min., stirring occasionally. Remove double boiler from heat and set corn-meal mixture aside to cool.

Drain and set aside contents of
1 No. 2 can kidney beans (about 2 cups, drained)
When meat is tender, mix in the kidney beans. Adjust seasonings. If necessary thicken cooking liquid (*page 107*).

Turn corn-meal mixture into casserole and spread evenly over bottom and around sides. Spoon meat mixture into the casserole.

Bake at 350°F 30 min. *6 to 8 servings*

▲ New England Dinner

A typical New England "boiled" dinner.

Set out a large sauce pot or kettle having a tight-fitting cover; or use a Dutch oven.

Wipe with a clean, damp cloth
4 to 6-lb. piece of corned beef
Put the meat into the sauce pot and add
Water to cover
Cover sauce pot tightly and bring water just to boiling over high heat. Reduce heat and simmer (do not boil) 3 to 5 hrs. (allow 40 to 50 min. per pound), or until meat is tender when pierced with a fork.

About an hour before meat is tender, clean (see Sweet-Sour Beets, *page 288*) and cook (*p.285*) 30 to 45 min., or until just tender
6 medium-size (about 1 lb.) beets
While beets are cooking, wash and scrape
6 medium-size (about 1½ lbs.) carrots
Wash and pare (do not cut)
6 medium-size (about 2 lbs.) potatoes
Skim off any excess fat from cooking water in sauce pot. Add the potatoes and carrots. Cover and continue to simmer.

When carrots and potatoes have cooked about 20 min., remove outer wilted leaves and any blemishes from
1 small head cabbage

Hamburgers with Whipped Potatoes (page 298) and red cabbage

Wash thoroughly and cut from top to bottom into wedges. Remove heavy ribs of outer leaves. Put cabbage into the sauce pot about 8 to 12 min. before end of cooking time. Cook, loosely covered, just until tender.

When the beets are tender, peel off and discard skins. Add to beets
2 tablespoons butter or margarine
Keep beets warm while arranging meat platter. When carrots, potatoes, cabbage, and meat are tender, remove meat from cooking liquid and place it on a large, warm platter. Surround with the vegetables. Serve immediately.

6 to 8 servings

△ Corned Beef and Cabbage

Follow ▲ Recipe; omit beets and carrots. Use 1 large head **cabbage**, quartered or cut into wedges. Thicken the cooking liquid (*p.107*) and serve with the meat and vegetables.

New England Dinner

BEEF in the MICROWAVE OVEN

The stews, pot roasts and braised recipes included here are great timesavers for any cook.

Although beef is really not the forte of the microwave oven, nor do these long-cooking dishes take advantage of its finer qualities, we did find several outstanding recipes. The **New England Dinner** is delicious (and a super time-saver) and the pot roasts tasty. The **Beef in Lemon Sauce** is excellent and demonstrates one of the best uses of the microwave oven for beef dishes—turning leftovers into company fare.

Braised meats, such as flank steak and round steak, did not produce as tender a result as conventional cooking. Using a meat tenderizer does help. Also, the flavor of the stock and sauces is more bland than in the long, slow conventional cooking of these recipes.

We do not recommend attempting to broil steaks in the microwave oven. It is difficult to get steak both brown on the outside and rare on the inside and the saving in time over conventional broiling is not sufficient to risk error on an expensive steak.

REMINDERS—Most of the recipes require browning. Use the browning skillet for this step. You will obtain the best results if the skillet is covered while in the oven. It is important to preheat for 3 minutes before melting the fat, butter or margarine and adding the meat. If all the ingredients will fit into the skillet, it can be used to cook the entire recipe. Otherwise, transfer to a casserole or baking dish of the size indicated in each recipe.

Timing of stews and goulashes requires some finesse, since both meat and vegetables must emerge cooked, but not overdone. The times indicated in these recipes produce successful results and are your guides to the point at which to add ingredients which cook in different amounts of time. However, remember that you may need to make adjustments depending on your oven and your taste. In general, add vegetables when the meat is almost tender.

All the dishes must stand, covered, after cooking is completed to permit juices to settle, flavors to blend and to smooth a somewhat rough taste. Use plastic wrap to cover when no other cover is available.

Sauces and gravies made in the microwave are excellent. They must be stirred frequently to achieve that smooth texture. For best results, stir both before and after each addition of ingredients, such as liquid added to flour and butter.

In some recipes, no further cooking is needed after adding sour cream. It is heated sufficiently during the required standing time. This also avoids the possibility of boiling which will ruin the sauce.

For more tips on successful microwave oven cooking and a chart which provides comparisons in settings among different brands of ovens, see **Home Cooking in the Microwave Oven** in the beginning of this book. We suggest you review this chapter to also learn how we have adapted these recipes.

Thicken Cooking Liquid *(page 107)*

Pour half the flour-water mixture into the hot cooking liquid and stir vigorously.

COOK, stirring vigorously every 30 sec., until boiling (about 1 min.).

Continue adding the mixture to the cooking liquid until the desired consistency is reached. When adding the mixture and during the cooking period, be sure to repeat the vigorous stirring every 30 sec. to prevent lumping.

After final addition of flour-water thickening, COOK to blend flavors (about 1 min.).

Grandma's Beef Pot Roast *(page 108)*

Use a browning skillet and a 3-qt. casserole.

Preheat skillet (3 min.). Add olive oil and heat.

Add onions and garlic and COOK, turning pan and stirring every 2 min., until onion is transparent (about 6 min.).

Add meat and COOK, turning meat and rotating pan every 5 min., until brown (about 20 min.). Transfer to casserole.

Add liquids, vegetables and seasonings; cover. (If cover does not fit, use plastic wrap.) COOK, turning and stirring every 3 min., until liquid is boiling (9 min.). SLOWCOOK, turning meat and rotating pan every 10 min., until meat is tender (about 30 min.).

Cover and let stand 20 min. Meanwhile, thicken gravy.

OVERALL COOKING TIME: 68:00

Rolled Pot Roast with Sour Cream Gravy *(page 109)*

Use a browning skillet and a 3-qt. casserole, if necessary.

Preheat skillet to very hot (5 min.). Add fat and melt.

Add meat, cover and COOK, turning meat and rotating pan every 5 min., until brown (about 20 min.). Transfer to casserole, if necessary.

Add onion, seasonings and water; cover. SLOWCOOK until meat is tender (about 35 min.).

Transfer to another dish, cover and let stand (20 min.).

For Gravy—Skim fat from liquid. COOK until simmering (about 1 min.).

Add flour-water mixture one-third at a time; stir and COOK until simmering after each addition (1 min. each). COOK until flavors are well-blended and flour has lost its raw taste (about 2 min.).

Add sour cream mixture and stir. COOK until heated (about 4 min.). Do not boil.

Serve as in Recipe.

OVERALL COOKING TIME: 70:00

Hungarian Hot **4** Pickled Beef *(page 110)*

Use a browning skillet and a 4-qt. covered casserole.

Preheat skillet (3 min.). Add butter and melt.

Add meat, cover and COOK, turning meat and rotating pan every 5 min., until brown (about 20 min.). Transfer to casserole.

Add liquid to cover two-thirds of meat and cover. COOK, stirring and turning pan every 5 min., until simmering (about 10 min.). SLOW-COOK, stirring and turning pan every 10 min., until meat is tender (about 40 min.).

Cover and let stand 20 min.

*For Gravy—*Melt butter in browning skillet. Add flour and COOK until brown (1½ min.).

Add liquid and COOK until simmering (about 3 min.).

Serve as in Recipe.

OVERALL COOKING TIME: 77:30

Sauerbraten *(page 111)* **5**

Use a browning skillet and a 4-qt. covered casserole.

COOK marinade until simmering (about 6 min.). (*Or,* you may prepare this on top of the stove.)

Preheat skillet (3 min.). Add butter and melt.

Add meat, cover and COOK, turning meat and rotating pan every 5 min., until brown, (about 20 min.). Transfer to casserole.

Add liquid to cover two-thirds of meat. COOK until simmering (5 min.). Cover and SLOW-COOK, stirring and rotating pan every 10 min., until meat is tender (about 50 min.).

Cover and let stand 20 min.

*For Gravy—*Melt butter in browning skillet.

Add flour and COOK until mixture bubbles (about 1 min.).

Add liquid one-third at a time; stir and COOK until simmering after each addition (about 1½ min. each).

Add ginger snaps and COOK until simmering (about 1½ min.).

COOK until gravy thickens (1 to 2 min.).

Serve as in Recipe.

OVERALL COOKING TIME: 92:00

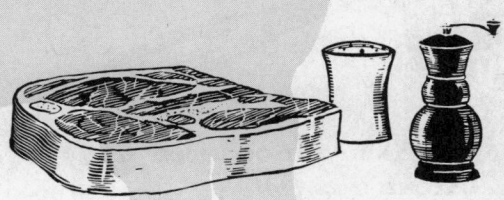

Esterhazy Steak *(page 114)* **6**

Use a browning skillet and a 2-qt. casserole. For the best results, cut meat into ½-in. slices.

Preheat skillet (3 min.). Add fat and melt the 1/3 cup fat.

Add steak and COOK, turning meat and rotating pan every 5 min., until brown (about 15 min.). Transfer meat to casserole.

COOK vegetables in skillet, stirring every 2 min., until onion is transparent (about 6 min.).

Melt the 1 tablespoon fat in skillet. Add flour

mixture and COOK, stirring every 1 min., until bubbling (about 3 min.).

Add meat broth, stir and COOK, stirring every 2 min., until simmering (about 8 min.).

Add wine and stir. Pour sauce over vegetables and meat; cover. SLOWCOOK, stirring and rotating pan every 5 min., until meat is nearly tender (about 20 min.).

Add sour cream mixture. (It will heat during the required standing time.)

Cover and let stand 15 min.

OVERALL COOKING TIME: 55:00

Tomato-Smothered **7** Steak *(page 114)*

Use a browning skillet.

Preheat skillet (3 min.). Add fat and heat until bubbling.

Add steak, cover and COOK, rotating pan when you turn steak, until brown on each side (about 2½ min. each).

Add remaining ingredients and cover. COOK until simmering (about 5 min.). SLOWCOOK, rotating pan every 5 min., until meat is tender (about 15 min.).

Cover and let stand 15 min.

Serve as in Recipe.

OVERALL COOKING TIME: 28:00

Baked Steak with **8** Wild Rice Dressing *(page 115)*

Use a browning skillet.

Preheat skillet (3 min.). Add butter or margarine and melt.

Blend in flour and COOK, stirring every 1 min., until bubbling (about 3 min.).

Add broth and COOK, stirring every 1 min. until mixture thickens (about 2 min.).

Assemble steak, fastening with string or wooden skewers. *Do not use metal.*

Melt fat. Add steak and COOK until brown on both sides (about 3 min. each).

Add broth, cover and SLOWCOOK, stirring and rotating pan every 3 min., until meat is tender (about 9 min.).

Cover and let stand 15 min.

OVERALL COOKING TIME: 23:00

Steak Smothered **9** in Onions *(page 116)*

Use a browning skillet.

Preheat skillet (3 min.). Add fat and melt.

Add steak and COOK until brown on both sides (about 3 min. each).

Add onions, liquid and seasonings, except use ½ bay leaf (instead of 1); cover. COOK until simmering (about 3 min.). SLOWCOOK until meat is tender (about 15 min.).

Cover and let stand 15 min.

OVERALL COOKING TIME: 27:00

Swiss Steak *(page 116)* **10**

Use a browning skillet and a 2-qt. casserole, if necessary.

Preheat skillet (3 min.). Add fat and melt.

Add steak, cover and COOK, turning meat and rotating pan every 3 min., until brown (about 9 min.).

Add liquid, vegetables and seasonings. COOK until simmering (about 5 min.). Cover and SLOWCOOK, stirring and rotating pan after 7½ min., until meat is tender (about 15 min.).

Cover and let stand 15 min.

Serve as in Recipe, slicing across grain.

OVERALL COOKING TIME: 32:00

Hungarian Beef Roll **11**
(page 117)

Use a browning skillet.

When assembling steak roll, use string or wooden skewers. *Do not use metal.*

Preheat skillet (3 min.). Add fat and melt.

Add steak, cover and COOK to brown on both sides (about 3 min. each).

Add paprika, salt and liquid; cover. COOK until simmering. SLOWCOOK, turning meat and rotating pan every 5 min., until meat is tender (about 20 min.). Transfer to another dish.

Heat fat. Add flour mixture and COOK until bubbling (about 1½ min.).

Add liquid and COOK until simmering (about 30 sec.).

Add sour cream and stir with a wire wisk. (It will heat during the required standing time.)

Cover and let stand 15 min.

OVERALL COOKING TIME: 35:00

Steak Roll-Ups **12** with Noodles *(page 118)*

Use a browning skillet.

Preheat skillet (3 min.). Add fat and heat until bubbling.

Add meat, cover and COOK, turning every 1 min., until brown on all sides (about 7 min.).

Add tomato-vegetable mixture and seasonings; cover. COOK, rotating pan once, until simmering (about 5 min.). SLOWCOOK, rotating pan every 5 min., until meat is tender (about 15 min.).

Cover and let stand 15 min.

OVERALL COOKING TIME: 30:00

Flank Steak Roll-Ups **13** with Buttered Cauliflower
(page 118)

Use a browning skillet.

Use string or wooden picks to fasten meat. *Do not use metal.*

Preheat skillet (3 min.). Add fat and melt.

Add meat, cover and COOK, rotating pan when meat is turned, until brown on both sides (about 2½ min. each).

Add water and ½ bay leaf (instead of 1). Cover and COOK until simmering (about 5 min.). SLOWCOOK, rotating pan every 5 min. and turning the meat after 10 min., until meat is tender (about 20 min.).

Cover and let stand 15 min. Meanwhile, prepare cauliflower.

OVERALL COOKING TIME: 33:00

Beef "Birds" *(page 119)* **14**

Use a browning skillet and a 2-qt. covered casserole.

Preheat skillet (3 min.). Add fat and melt.

Add meat, cover and COOK, turning meat and rotating pan every 2 min., until brown (about 6 min.). Remove to casserole.

Combine remaining ingredients; pour over meat; cover. COOK, rotating pan and stirring every 2 min., to heat thoroughly (about 6 min.). SLOW-COOK, stirring and turning every 2 min., until meat is tender (about 12 min.).

Cover and let stand 15 min.
OVERALL COOKING TIME: 27:00

Beef Stroganoff *(page 120)* **15**

Use a browning skillet.

Prepare mushrooms first if you are doing them in the microwave oven.

Preheat skillet (3 min.). Add butter or margarine and melt.

Add meat, onions and garlic and COOK until slightly brown (about 10 min.).

Add broth and sherry, stir and cover. SLOW-COOK until meat is tender (about 20 min.).

Add cooked mushrooms and sour cream mixture and stir thoroughly. COOK, stirring after 1 min., to reheat (about 2 min.). Do not boil.

Serve as in Recipe.

Beef Short Ribs with Vegetables *(page 121)* **16**

Use a browning skillet and a 5-qt. casserole.

Preheat skillet (3 min.). Add oil and heat.

Add meat, cover and COOK, turning meat and rotating pan every 5 min., until brown on all sides (about 15 min.).

Add water and onion; cover. COOK until simmering (about 15 min.).

Add beans, potatoes and seasonings. SLOW-COOK, rotating pan every 10 min., until meat is nearly tender (about 25 min.).

Add celery and SLOWCOOK until celery and meat are completely tender (about 8 min.).

Cover and let stand 15 min.
OVERALL COOKING TIME: 66:00

Spicy Short Ribs and Fruit *(page 121)* **17**

Follow **16** Recipe for browning meat. Transfer to casserole.

Add water, cover and COOK to raise temperature (about 5 min.). SLOWCOOK, turning pan every 5 min., until meat is almost tender (about 20 min.).

Add fruit and liquid-spice mixture. SLOW-COOK, stirring and rotating pan every 3 min., until meat and fruit are tender (about 9 min.).

Cover and let stand 15 min.
OVERALL COOKING TIME: 52:00

Beef in Lemon Sauce *(page 122)*

Use a browning skillet and a 2-qt. casserole.

In the skillet, COOK bacon, turning every 1 min., until lightly brown (about 2 min.). Reserve bacon.

Add meat and COOK until heated (about 3 min.). Return bacon to skillet, cover and set aside.

In the casserole, COOK fat until melted. Add flour and COOK until mixture bubbles (about 2 min.).

Add broth and stir. COOK, stirring every 3 min., until simmering and thickened (about 6 min.).

Combine remaining ingredients with sauce. Pour over meat and bacon. COOK until hot (about 1 min.). Do not boil.

Cover and let stand 5 min.

OVERALL COOKING TIME: 16:00

Hungarian Goulash 19
(page 124)

Use a browning skillet and a 3-qt. casserole. For best results, cut meat into ½-in. slices.

In skillet, COOK bacon, turning every 1 min., until lightly brown (about 2 min.). Reserve.

Add onion and COOK, stirring every 1 min., until transparent (about 3 min.).

Add meat and COOK, turning every 3 min., until brown on all sides (about 9 min.). Transfer to casserole.

Add seasonings, bacon, vegetables and liquids to cover meat by two-thirds. COOK, stirring every 5 min., until simmering (about 12 min.).

SLOWCOOK, stirring every 10 min., until meat is tender (about 20 min.).

Cover and let stand 15 min.

OVERALL COOKING TIME: 46:00

Goulash with 20 Potatoes *(page 124)*

Follow 19 Recipe with additions as in ⚠ Recipe. When meat begins to get tender, add the potatoes. This should be about 12 min. into the 20-min. SLOWCOOK period.

Goulash with 21 Tomatoes *(page 124)*

Follow 19 Recipe with substitutions as in ⚠ Recipe.

Goulash with 22 Carrots *(page 124)*

Follow 19 Recipe with substitutions as in ⚠ Recipe. Add carrots 7 min. into the 20-min. SLOWCOOK period.

Spicy Brown 23 Beef Stew *(page 125)*

Use a browning skillet and a 3-qt. casserole.

Preheat skillet (3 min.). Add fat and melt.

Add meat and COOK, turning every 5 min., until brown (about 15 min.). Transfer to casserole.

Add chopped onion, water and seasonings, except use 1 bay leaf (instead of 2). Cover and COOK, stirring every 5 min., until simmering (about 15 min.). SLOWCOOK, stirring every 5 min., until meat is tender (about 20 min.).

Add carrots and onions and SLOWCOOK until tender (about 10 min.).

Cover and let stand 15 min.

> *OVERALL COOKING TIME: 63:00*

Beef Stew in **24**
Casserole *(page 126)*

Use a browning skillet and a 3-qt. covered casserole.

Preheat skillet (3 min.). Add fat and melt.

Add meat and COOK, turning meat and rotating pan every 5 min., until brown (about 15 min.). Transfer to casserole.

Add liquid and ½ bay leaf (instead of 1) and COOK, stirring every 5 min., until simmering (about 10 min.). SLOWCOOK, stirring every 10 min., until meat is nearly tender (about 40 min.).

Add carrots, potatoes, celery and onions and SLOWCOOK until vegetables are slightly soft (about 10 min.). Add peas and SLOWCOOK until all vegetables and meat are tender (about 5 min.).

Cover and let stand 15 min.

> *OVERALL COOKING TIME: 83:00*

New England **25**
Dinner *(page 128)*

Use a 3-qt. casserole (this will accommodate a 4-lb. corned beef).

Add water to cover two-thirds of corned beef. SLOWCOOK, until almost tender (about 90 minutes).

Add cooked beets, carrots and potatoes. SLOWCOOK until tender (about 20 min.).

Remove meat and vegetables and set aside; keep covered.

Add cabbage to cooking juices and SLOWCOOK until just tender (about 6 min.).

Serve as in Recipe.

> *OVERALL COOKING TIME: 116:00*

Corned Beef and **26**
Cabbage *(page 128)*

Follow **25** Recipe with changes as in △ Recipe.

Serve as in Recipe.

BEEF in the SLOW COOKER

Stews! Pot roasts! Braised beef dishes! The slow cooker can do practically no wrong with these recipes. They are all very, very good—and very easy to prepare. Most of these dishes are equally good for family or guests, expected or unexpected. The **Spicy Short Ribs and Fruit** is outstanding.

These dishes are among those which give the slow cooker its reputation for carefree cooking. In almost every recipe, the ingredients can be added to the slow cooker all at once, the pot turned to LOW, covered and forgotten all day.

One step which can often be omitted is the coating of the meat with flour when the recipe calls for browning. Simply coat the meat with the fat. Do not expect the meat to really brown, but the flavor of the dish will be just as good, if not better, than when it is prepared on top of the stove.

Meat-Vegetable Dishes—Of course, "slow cooking" is characteristic of this appliance. In some cases, we found vegetables still undercooked when the meat was done. Therefore, in some recipes such as **Steak Smothered in Onions**, you will be directed to precook (sauté) vegetables (especially onions) before adding them to the slow cooker.

Liquid—In pot roasts, stews and similar dishes, amounts of liquid may have to be reduced. But there will be no guesswork for you. The recipes in this section specify such adjustments where necessary.

Seasonings as specified in the main text recipes do not need correction, with one exception. True to its nature, the slow cooker extracts more flavor from bay leaf than does cooking on top of the stove. Therefore, we recommend reducing the amount of this seasoning when called for as an ingredient.

Sauces and Gravies can be thickened in the slow cooker with the setting on HIGH. Although this may be more convenient, it may also take a much longer time than thickening on top of the stove; allow at least 30 minutes for this process. We recommend thickening sauces in the slow cooker if the final consistency is rather thin (that is, if only about ¼ cup of thickening mixture is needed). Occasionally, we will suggest finishing sauces on top of the stove, but in most recipes, this is optional.

REMINDERS—Use the 3½-slow cooker for all of these recipes, unless otherwise specified. More tips plus a chart comparing variations in setting among different brands of slow cookers may be found in the introductory chapter, **Home Cooking in the Slow Cooker**, in the beginning of this book. We also suggest that you review this material to learn how we have adapted these recipes.

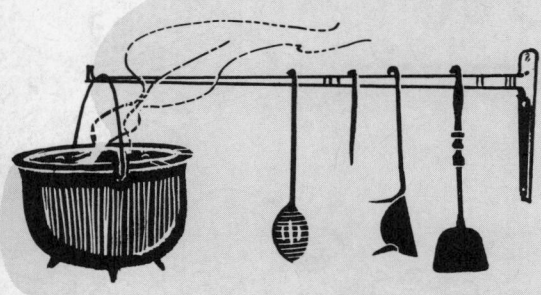

Thicken Cooking Liquid *(page 107)*

It is generally faster to thicken cooking liquid on top of the stove. However, it might be more convenient to do this in the slow cooker. We suggest thickening sauces directly in the slow cooker if the final consistency of the sauce is to be rather thin; that is, if only about ¼ cup of thickening mixture is needed. This process should take about 30 minutes.

Turn the slow cooker setting to HIGH and heat the liquid until simmering.

Prepare the flour-water mixture.

Pour half the flour-water mixture into the hot cooking liquid and stir vigorously. Cover and cook to reheat (about 10 min.).

Add remaining mixture, stir and cover to reheat (about 10 min.).

Reset slow cooker to LOW to keep warm until serving time.

Grandma's Beef Pot Roast *(page 108)*

Heat oil on HIGH. Add meat and turn to coat evenly with oil.

Add all vegetables, seasonings and liquids to cover two-thirds of meat. If more liquid is needed, add wine or tomato juice. Stir to mix.

Cook on LOW for 8 to 9 hrs.

Rolled Pot Roast with Sour Cream Gravy *(page 109)*

Heat fat on HIGH. Add meat and turn to coat evenly with fat.

Add onion and seasonings, except use ½ bay leaf (instead of 1) and water to cover one-half of meat.

Cook on LOW for 8 to 9 hrs.

Remove meat, reset to HIGH. To thicken gravy, use ¼ cup water (instead of ½).

Reset to LOW and add sour cream mixture.

Serve as in Recipe.

Barbecued Pot Roast *(page 110)*

Melt fat on HIGH. Add seasoned meat and turn to coat evenly with fat.

Combine all remaining ingredients and pour over meat. Meat should be two-thirds covered. Add tomato juice if necessary.

Cover and cook on LOW for 8 to 9 hrs.

Serve as in Recipe.

Melt fat on HIGH. Add meat and turn to coat evenly with fat.

Add vegetables, broth, capers, wine, salt and pepper (omit the 1 tablespoon fat); cover.

Cook on LOW for 7 to 8 hrs.

Just before serving, turn off slow cooker, spread the paprika-sour cream mixture over the hot contents of the slow cooker and cover. Contents will be sufficiently hot to heat sour cream.

Hungarian Hot Pickled Beef *(page 110)*

Melt butter or margarine on HIGH. Add marinated meat and turn to coat evenly with fat.

Pour marinade-water mixture over meat to cover by two-thirds; cover.

Cook on LOW for 8 to 9 hrs.

For Gravy—Remove meat and cooking liquid. Melt butter or margarine on HIGH. Blend in flour and cook until bubbling. Add the cooking liquid and cook, stirring constantly, until simmering.

Serve as in Recipe.

Sauerbraten *(page 111)* 6

Melt butter or margarine on HIGH. Add marinated meat and turn to coat evenly with fat.

Add marinade to cover two-thirds of meat; cover.

Cook on LOW for 8½ to 9½ hrs.

For Gravy—Complete on top of stove as in Recipe.

Esterhazy Steak *(page 114)* 7

Prepare meat for cooking as in Recipe, except omit the ¼ cup flour.

Tomato-Smothered Steak *(page 114)* 8

Prepare meat for cooking as in Recipe, except omit the ¼ cup flour.

Melt fat on HIGH. Add meat, turning to coat evenly with fat.

Sauté onions on top of the stove until slightly softened. Add onions and remaining ingredients, except use only enough liquid from the canned tomatoes to cover one-half of the meat; cover.

Cook on LOW for 6 to 8 hrs.

Steak Smothered in Onions *(page 116)* 9

Sauté onions until slightly softened.

Prepare meat for cooking, except omit the 1/3 cup flour.

Melt fat on HIGH. Add meat and turn to coat each piece with fat.

Add remaining ingredients, except use ½ bay leaf (instead of 1); cover.

Cook on LOW for 6 to 8 hrs.

Serve as in Recipe.

Swiss Steak *(page 116)* **10**

Prepare meat for cooking, except omit the ¼ cup flour.

Heat fat on HIGH. Add meat and turn to coat evenly with fat.

Combine remaining ingredients and add to meat; cover.

Cook on LOW for 6 to 8 hrs.

Serve as in Recipe.

Hungarian Beef Roll **11** *(page 117)*

Prepare meat for cooking as in Recipe.

Melt fat on HIGH. Add rolled-up meat and turn to coat evenly with fat.

Add seasonings and water to cover meat by one-half; cover.

Cook on LOW for 6 to 7 hrs.

Complete gravy on top of the stove as in Recipe.

Serve as in Recipe.

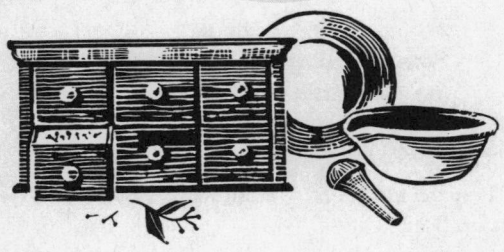

Steak Roll-Ups with Noodles *(page 118)* **12**

Prepare meat for cooking as in Recipe, except use only one-half the amounts of thyme, sage and basil.

Melt fat on HIGH. Add meat and turn in fat to coat evenly.

Combine all ingredients, except use only enough liquid from the canned tomatoes to cover the meat by one-half. Add to slow cooker and cover.

Cook on LOW for 6 to 8 hrs.

Serve as in Recipe.

Flank Steak Roll-Ups **13** with Buttered Cauliflower *(page 118)*

Prepare meat for cooking as in Recipe, except do not cut meat into slices.

Heat fat on HIGH. Add meat and turn to coat evenly in fat.

Add water and ½ bay leaf (instead of 1) and cover.

Cook on LOW for 6 to 8 hrs.

About 1 hr. before serving, prepare cauliflower as in Recipe.

After meat is done, remove and cut into 1-in. slices.

Serve as in Recipe.

Beef Stroganoff *(page 120)* 14

Prepare meat for cooking as in Recipe, except omit the 1/3 cup flour.

Heat butter or margarine on HIGH. Add mushrooms and lightly brown; remove.

Add meat and turn to coat each strip evenly with fat.

Add all remaining ingredients, except sour cream mixture. Return mushrooms to slow cooker; cover.

Cook on LOW for 7 to 8 hrs.

Just before serving, turn off slow cooker and stir sour cream mixture into hot contents.

Serve as in Recipe.

Braised Short Ribs De Luxe *(page 120)* 15

Prepare meat for cooking as in Recipe, except omit the 1/3 cup flour.

Melt fat on HIGH. Add meat and turn to coat evenly with fat.

Add all remaining ingredients, except add just enough water to cover meat by one-half; cover.

Cook on LOW for 8½ to 9½ hrs.

Complete sauce on top of the stove as in Recipe.

Beef Short Ribs with Vegetables *(page 121)* 16

Prepare meat for cooking as in Recipe, except omit the 1/3 cup flour.

Melt fat on HIGH. Add meat and turn to coat evenly with fat.

Add all remaining ingredients; cover.

Cook on LOW for 8½ to 9½ hrs.

Spicy Short Ribs and Fruit *(page 121)* 17

Follow 16 Recipe with changes as in △ Recipe.

Serve as in △ Recipe.

Hungarian Goulash *(page 124)* 18

Prepare bacon and onions as in Recipe.

Transfer bacon drippings to slow cooker set on HIGH and add meat, turning to coat evenly with fat. Sprinkle with seasonings.

Add bacon, onions and remaining ingredients to slow cooker; use enough wine to cover meat by two-thirds; cover.

Cook on LOW for 6 to 7 hrs.

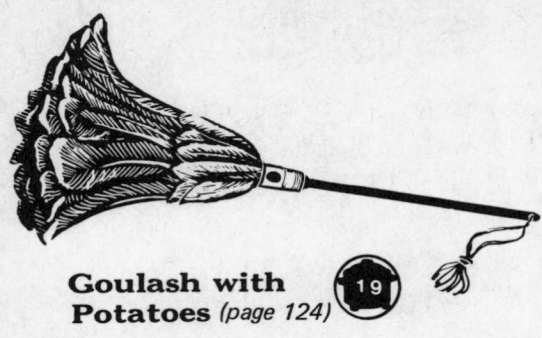

Goulash with Potatoes (page 124) 19

Follow 18 Recipe with changes as in ⚠ Recipe, except add potatoes with other ingredients.

Goulash with Tomatoes (page 124) 20

Follow 18 Recipe with substitution as in ⚠ Recipe.

Goulash with Carrots (page 124) 21

Follow 18 Recipe with changes as in ⚠ Recipe, except add carrots with other ingredients.

Spicy Brown Beef Stew (page 125) 22

Prepare meat for cooking as in Recipe, except omit the 1/3 cup flour.

Melt fat on HIGH. Add meat and turn to coat each piece evenly with fat.

Add all remaining ingredients, except use just enough water to cover contents by two-thirds; cover.

Cook on LOW for 7 to 8 hrs.

Beef Stew in Casserole (page 126) 23

Prepare meat for cooking as in Recipe, except omit the ¼ cup flour.

Melt fat on HIGH. Add meat and turn to coat each piece evenly with fat.

Add all remaining ingredients, except use ½ bay leaf (instead of 1) and add only enough hot water to cover contents by two-thirds; cover.

Cook on LOW for 7 to 8 hrs.

New England Dinner (page 128) 24

Use a 4- to 5-qt. slow cooker.

Place all ingredients, except cabbage, in slow cooker; cover.

Cook on LOW for 9 to 10 hrs.

About 1½ hrs. before dish is done, add cabbage. (If cabbage is cooked longer, it will be too soft.)

Serve as in Recipe.

Corned Beef and Cabbage (page 128) 25

Follow 24 Recipe with changes as in △ Recipe.

Cook on LOW for 9 to 10 hrs.

▲ Hamburgers

Set out a large, heavy skillet.

Mix lightly
1½ lbs. ground beef
with a mixture of
1½ teaspoons salt
¾ teaspoon Accent
¼ teaspoon pepper
Shape into 6 patties about ¾ in. thick or 8 patties about ½ in. thick.

Heat in the skillet over medium heat
1 tablespoon fat
Place patties in skillet and cook until brown on one side. Turn and brown other side. (Allow 10 to 15 min. for cooking thick patties and 6 to 10 min. for cooking thin patties.) Remove from skillet to warm serving platter. Serve hot garnished with **parsley.**

6 to 8 servings

Note: Hamburgers or any of the following variations may be served on toasted, buttered **buns,** if desired.

⚠ Broiler Burgers

Follow ▲ Recipe. Arrange ¾ in.-thick patties on broiler rack. Set temperature control of range at Broil. Brush patties with melted **butter.** Put in broiler with tops of patties about 3 in. from heat source. Broil 6 to 8 min. When patties are browned on one side, turn, brush again with melted butter, and broil second side.

⚠ Cheeseburgers

Follow ▲ Recipe or ⚠. After second sides of patties are browned, cover each patty with 1 thin slice **Cheddar cheese.** Cook 2 min. longer or until cheese is slightly melted.

⚠ Garlic Hamburgers

Follow ▲ Recipe; blend in 1 **egg,** beaten, and 1 clove **garlic** (*page 12*), slivered.

⚠ Barbecued Burgers

Follow ▲ Recipe. Substitute **Bar-B-Q Sauce for Basting** (*page 327*) for butter. When first side is browned, turn and brush patty with sauce, using a pastry brush.

⚠ Surprise Hamburgers

Follow ▲ Recipe. Shape twice as many patties by making them thinner. Place a **Cheddar cheese slice** on each of 6 patties. Top cheese slices with remaining patties. Press edges to seal. Wrap one slice of **bacon** around outside edge of each patty and secure with a wooden pick. Broil as in ⚠ Recipe.

Note: To prepare hamburgers on an outdoor grill see OUTDOOR COOKING (*page 204*).

Spicy Beef Burgers

Set out a large, heavy skillet.

Put into a large bowl
2 lbs. ground beef
Blend together
⅓ cup ketchup
1 tablespoon prepared horse-radish
2 teaspoons Worcestershire sauce
¾ teaspoon Accent
½ teaspoon salt
⅛ teaspoon pepper
2 or 3 drops tabasco sauce
Add seasoning mixture to meat and mix together lightly. Shape into 8 patties about ¾ in. thick.

Heat in the skillet over medium heat
1 to 2 tablespoons fat
Place meat patties in skillet and cook until brown on one side. Turn and brown other side. Allow 10 to 15 min. for cooking patties. Pour off fat as it collects.

Serve with thin slices of onion and
Quick Tomato Sauce (page 327)
6 to 8 servings

Hamburger Steak Dinner

Mix together lightly in a large bowl
2 lbs. ground beef
½ cup milk
1 egg, beaten
4 teaspoons Worcestershire sauce
and a mixture of
2 teaspoons salt
1 teaspoon Accent
¼ teaspoon pepper
Set temperature control of range at Broil.

Shape meat mixture into an oval about 1½ in. thick. Put meat on broiler rack. Place in broiler with top of meat 3 in. from heat source.

Broil about 10 to 12 min. or until browned on one side. Turn and broil second side. Remove to warm serving plate. Serve with
Parsley New Potatoes (page 298)
Butter-Fried Onion Slices (page 293)
8 servings

Triple-Deck Burgers

Grease a 10x6x2-in. baking dish.

Prepare and set aside to keep warm
2 cups Quick Tomato Sauce (page 327; increase water to ¾ cup)

For Stuffing—Heat in a small skillet
¼ cup butter or margarine
Add and cook over medium heat until onion is transparent, stirring gently
¼ cup finely chopped onion
Pour contents of skillet over
1 qt. (4 to 6 slices) soft ½-in. bread cubes
Add to bread cubes and mix gently with a fork
3 tablespoons minced celery leaves
and a mixture of
½ teaspoon salt
⅛ teaspoon pepper
Set bread mixture aside.

Beat together in a small bowl
1 egg, beaten
⅓ cup milk

Hamburger Steak Dinner with parsley new potatoes and butter-fried onion slices

Gently blend egg mixture into bread mixture. Shape stuffing into six patties. Set aside.

For Meat Patties—Prepare
Hamburgers (page 128; add ¼ teaspoon allspice with seasonings)
Shape meat into 12 thin patties. Arrange 6 patties in bottom of baking dish; cover each with a stuffing patty. Top with remaining patties. Pour tomato sauce over patties.

Bake at 350°F 40 to 50 min. Baste occasionally during baking period. *6 servings*

Dinner on a Plank
(See photo on page 299)

Set out a seasoned plank. (To season a new plank, brush a hardwood plank with unsalted fat. Heat in a 250°F oven 1 hr. Cool; store until ready to use.)

Clean *(page 12)*
6 medium-size (about 1½ lbs.) onions
Cook onions whole, uncovered, in boiling, salted water to cover, 20 to 30 min., or just until tender. Drain and set aside to keep warm.

While onions are cooking, prepare
Duchess Potatoes (page 299)
Do not spoon potatoes onto baking sheet to bake; set aside to keep warm.

Mix together lightly

1 lb. ground beef
¼ cup milk or water
2 teaspoons Worcestershire sauce

and a mixture of

1 teaspoon salt
½ teaspoon Accent
¼ teaspoon allspice
⅛ teaspoon pepper

Set temperature control of range at Broil.

Lightly grease the seasoned plank with

Unsalted fat

Heat plank under the broiler pan or in the oven while broiling meat.

Shape meat mixture into an oval about 1½ in. thick. Put meat on broiler rack. Place in broiler with top of meat 3 in. from heat source. Broil about 10 to 12 min., or until meat is browned on one side. (Do not broil other side.)

Meanwhile, rinse, remove stem ends, cut into halves crosswise and set aside

2 large (about 1 lb.) firm tomatoes

When meat is browned on one side, remove from broiler and place browned side down, in center of the heated plank. Surround with the cooked whole onions and tomato halves. Force Duchess Potatoes through a pastry bag and No. 7 star tube to form a border. Cover exposed plank as completely as possible.

Brush onions, tomatoes and potatoes with

Melted butter or margarine

Place plank under broiler with top of meat about 3 in. from source of heat. Broil about 8 min., or until meat is browned and potatoes are lightly browned.

Meanwhile, prepare

3 slices Panbroiled Bacon (page 161)

Remove plank from oven and put on a serving tray. Arrange bacon on top of the meat and serve immediately.   *4 servings*

Note: A **beef steak** (see Broiled Beef Steaks, *page 112;* broil on one side only) may be substituted for the ground meat. (A 2-in. thick steak should be broiled 5 to 10 min. on the second side, before being placed on the plank unless steak is desired very rare.) Garnish with **Butter-Fried Mushrooms** (*page 293*) instead of bacon.

Ground Beef Parmesan

Mix together thoroughly

1½ lbs. ground beef
1 egg, beaten
1 medium-size onion, chopped

and a mixture of

1 teaspoon salt
¾ teaspoon Accent
⅛ teaspoon pepper

Shape meat mixture into a large square about ¾ in. thick. Cut into 6 equal portions.

Set temperature control of range at Broil.

Arrange portions on broiler rack. Place in broiler with top of meat 3 in. from heat source.

Broil 6 to 8 min.; turn and broil second side. Spread with a mixture of

¾ cup (6-oz. can) tomato paste
1 tablespoon grated Parmesan cheese

Top portions with

6 slices (3 oz.) Mozzarella cheese
(1 slice per portion)

Broil until cheese is melted and lightly browned.   *6 servings*

Ground Beef Parmesan
with green salad and hot coffee

Köttbüllar

(Swedish Meat Balls)

MRS. CARL J. A. ERICKSON
LEONARD, MINN.

Set out a large, heavy skillet having a tight-fitting cover.

Mix together in a large bowl
  1 lb. ground round steak
  ½ lb. ground lean pork
  ½ cup whipped potato
  ½ cup fine, dry bread crumbs
  1 egg, beaten
and a mixture of
  ¾ teaspoon salt
  ½ teaspoon brown sugar
  ¼ teaspoon pepper
  ¼ teaspoon allspice
  ¼ teaspoon nutmeg
  ⅛ teaspoon cloves
  ⅛ teaspoon ginger

Form meat mixture into balls about 1 in. in diameter. Coat by rolling in
  ¼ cup flour
Heat in the skillet over low heat
  2 tablespoons butter
Add the meat balls and brown over medium heat. Shake pan frequently to obtain an even browning and to keep balls round. Without removing meat, blend into drippings in pan
  1 tablespoon flour
Pour in slowly, blending in
  1 cup cream
Cover and simmer ½ hr.

Serve the meatballs in the cream gravy.

About 6 servings

Swedish-American Meat Balls

Set out a large, heavy skillet having a tight-fitting cover.

Combine, in order, in a large bowl and set aside
  ⅓ cup (1 slice) fine, dry bread crumbs
  ½ cup water
  ½ cup cream
Heat in the skillet over low heat
  1 tablespoon butter
Add and cook over medium heat until transparent, stirring occasionally
  3 tablespoons finely chopped onion
Add butter and onion to bowl with
  ¾ lb. ground beef
  ¼ lb. ground lean pork
and a mixture of
  1 teaspoon salt
  ¾ teaspoon sugar
  ½ teaspoon Accent
  ¼ teaspoon white pepper
Mix thoroughly and beat until mixture is smooth. Shape meat mixture into balls about ¾ in. in diameter.

Heat in the skillet over low heat
  2 to 3 tablespoons butter
Add meat balls and brown over medium heat.

Shake pan frequently to obtain an even browning and to keep balls round.

Reduce heat, cover skillet, and continue to cook about 10 min., shaking pan occasionally.

Serve meat balls hot or chilled.

About 4 doz. small meat balls

Italian-Style Meat Balls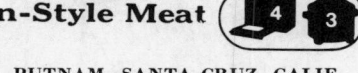

EMMA G. PUTNAM, SANTA CRUZ, CALIF.

Heat in a large, heavy skillet having a cover
   1 teaspoon olive oil
Add and cook until onion is transparent, occasionally moving pieces with a spoon
   ½ cup (1 medium-size) chopped onion (page 12)
   ⅓ cup finely chopped green pepper (page 12)
Add contents of skillet to a bowl containing
   1 lb. ground beef
   1 cup chopped cooked spinach, well drained
   1 egg, beaten
   3 tablespoons grated Parmesan cheese
and a mixture of
   ½ teaspoon Accent
   ¼ teaspoon salt
   ¼ teaspoon pepper
Mix lightly. Form mixture into 1½-in. balls.

Heat in the skillet over medium heat
   2 tablespoons fat
Add meat balls to skillet and brown over medium heat. Turn balls frequently to obtain an even browning and to keep balls round.

Pour over the browned meat balls a mixture of
   2 cups (2 8-oz. cans) tomato sauce
   1 tablespoon grated Parmesan cheese
Cover and simmer 30 to 40 min.

Serve with
   Spaghetti (page 277)

About 4 servings

Norwegian Meat Balls and Gravy

MRS. WILLIAM L. ABLE, PATEROS, WASH.

A delicious reminder of the ground-meat miracles in traditional Scandinavian cookery.

Heat in a large, heavy skillet over low heat
   2 tablespoons butter
Add and cook over medium heat until onion is transparent, stirring occasionally
   ⅓ cup finely chopped onion (page 12)
Mix together lightly the onion and
   1 lb. ground beef
   ¼ lb. ground lean pork
   ½ cup (½ slice) soft bread crumbs
   ½ cup milk
   1 egg, beaten
and a mixture of
   2 teaspoons sugar
   1¼ teaspoons salt
   ¾ teaspoon Accent
   ½ teaspoon nutmeg
   ¼ teaspoon allspice
Shape meat mixture into 1-in. balls.

Heat in the skillet over low heat
   2 tablespoons butter
Add the meat balls and brown over medium heat. Shake pan frequently to obtain an even browning and to keep balls round. Reduce heat, cover skillet and continue to cook about 10 min., shaking pan occasionally. Remove meat balls to warm serving dish; set aside and keep warm.

Blend into the fat in the skillet
   3 tablespoons flour
   1 teaspoon sugar
   ½ teaspoon salt
   ¼ teaspoon pepper
Heat until mixture bubbles and flour is lightly browned. Remove from heat. Add gradually, stirring in, a mixture of
   1 cup water
   ¾ cup cream
Bring rapidly to boiling, stirring constantly; cook 1 to 2 min. longer. Pour gravy over meat balls in dish. Serve at once.   *6 servings*

BEEF

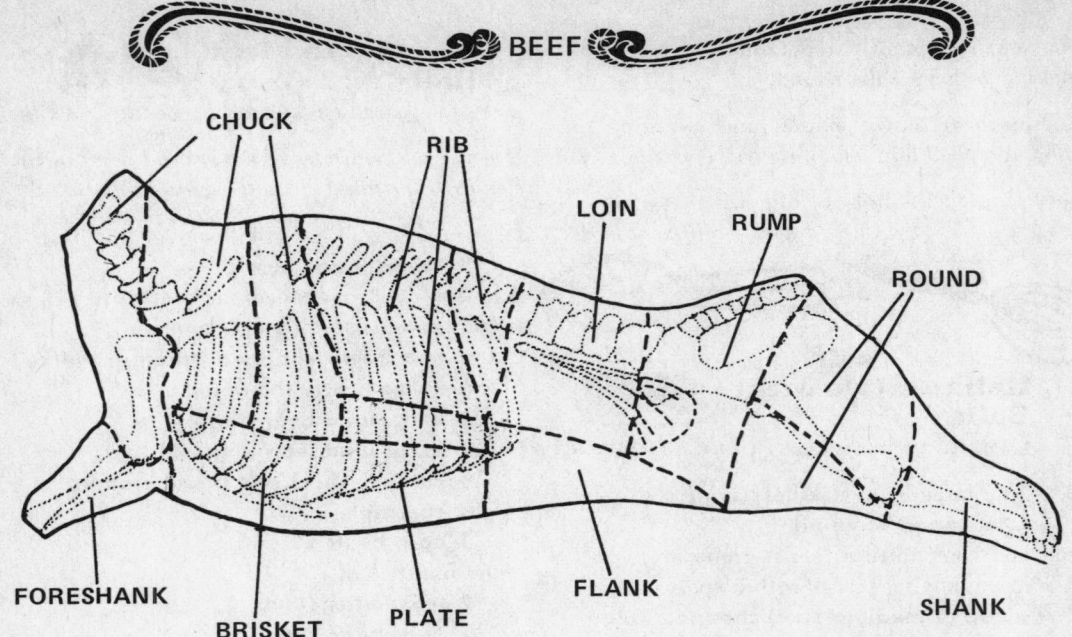

CHUCK

RIB

LOIN

RUMP

ROUND

FORESHANK

BRISKET

PLATE

FLANK

SHANK

VEAL

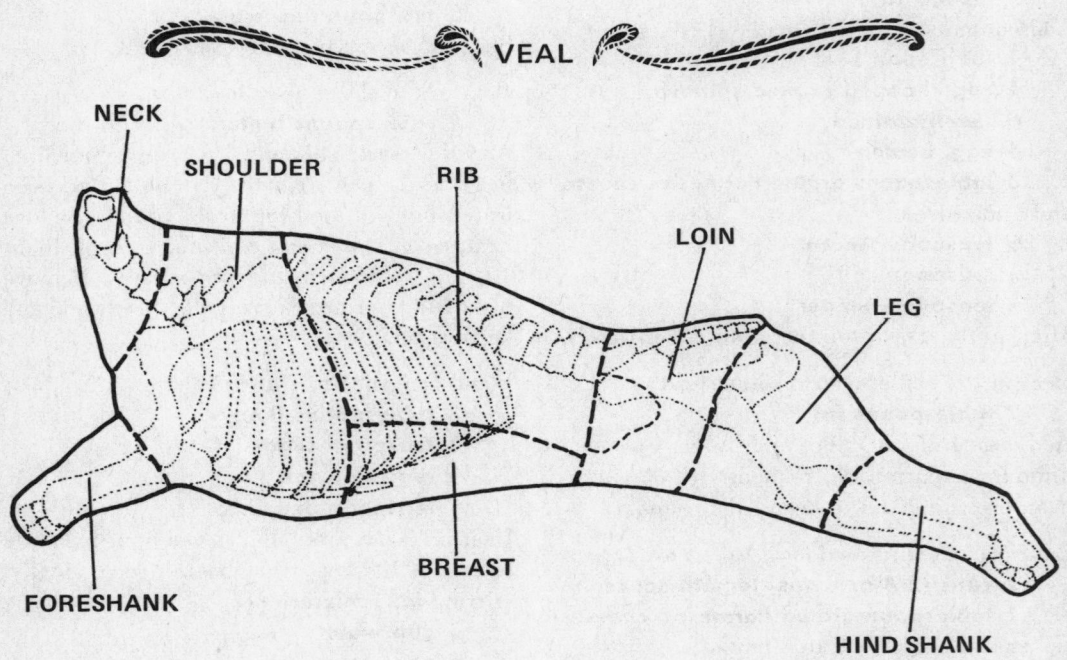

NECK

SHOULDER

RIB

LOIN

LEG

FORESHANK

BREAST

HIND SHANK

PORK

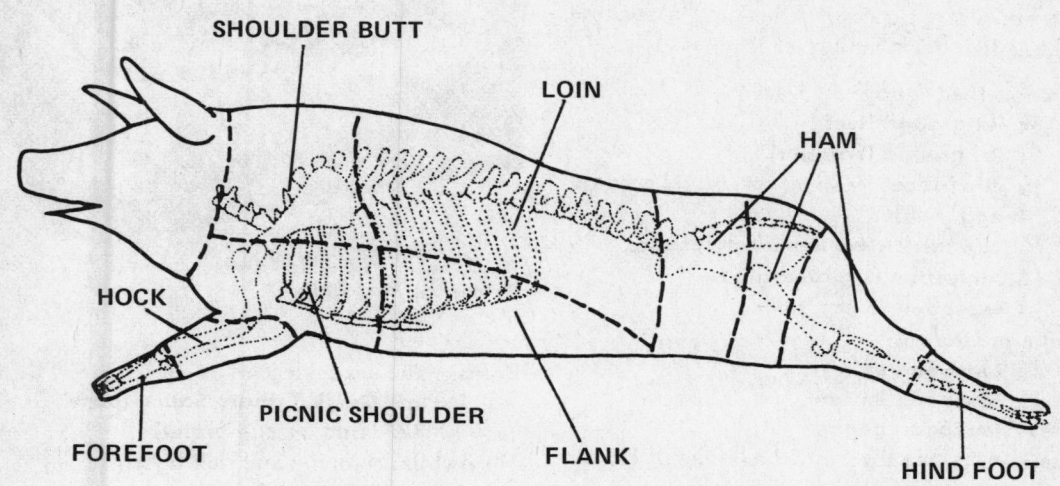

SHOULDER BUTT

LOIN

HAM

HOCK

FOREFOOT

PICNIC SHOULDER

FLANK

HIND FOOT

LAMB

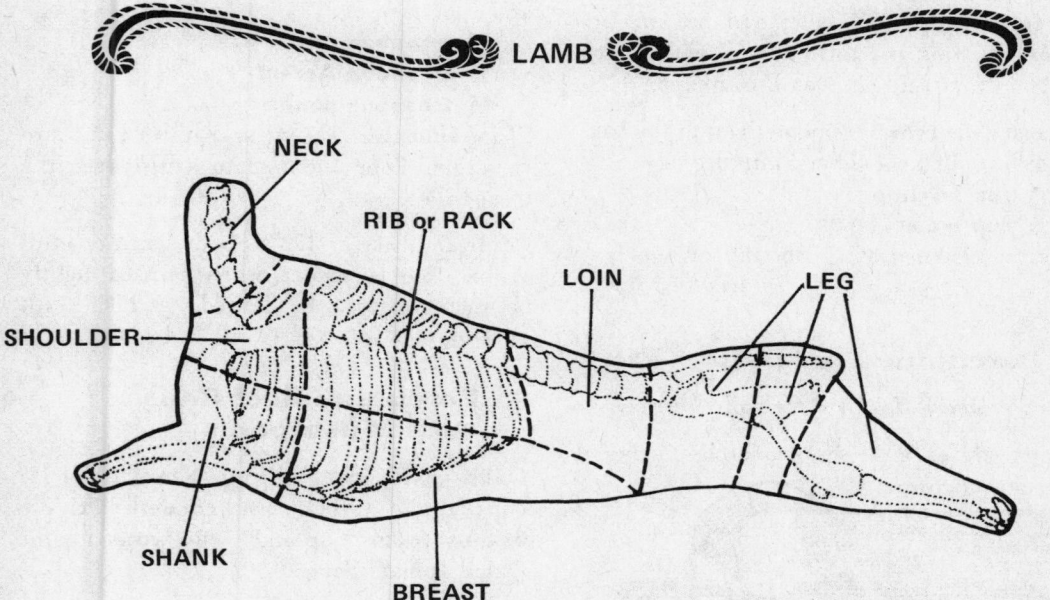

NECK

RIB or RACK

LOIN

LEG

SHOULDER

SHANK

BREAST

Applesauce Meat Balls

MRS. WALTER KALKBRENNER
LITCHFIELD, MINN.

Set out a large, heavy skillet and a shallow baking dish having a cover.

Mix together lightly
- **¾ lb. ground beef**
- **¼ lb. ground lean pork**
- **½ cup (about ½ slice) soft bread crumbs**
- **1 egg, beaten**
- **½ cup thick sweetened applesauce**
- **2 tablespoons grated onion**
- **1 teaspoon lemon juice**

and a mixture of
- **½ teaspoon salt**
- **½ teaspoon Accent**
- **⅛ teaspoon pepper**

Shape meat mixture into balls about 1½ in. in diameter.

Heat in the skillet over medium heat
- **2 tablespoons fat**

Put meat balls into skillet and brown, frequently moving and turning balls with a fork or spoon to obtain an even browning.

As meat balls brown, remove them to the baking dish. Pour over them a mixture of
- **½ cup ketchup**
- **½ cup water**

Cover and bake at 350°F about 1 hr.

About 4 servings

▲ Porcupine Beef Balls

A hearty main dish, fine for buffet service.

Lightly grease a 2½-qt. casserole having a tight-fitting cover.

Porcupine Beef Balls

Prepare and set aside
- **2 cups Quick Tomato Sauce (***page*** 327; add ½ cup water)**

Meanwhile, combine and mix lightly
- **1 lb. ground beef**
- **½ cup uncooked rice**
- **¼ cup minced onion**

and a mixture of
- **1 teaspoon salt**
- **½ teaspoon Accent**
- **⅛ teaspoon pepper**

Shape into balls 1½ in. in diameter; put into casserole. Pour the tomato sauce over the meat balls.

Cover and bake at 350°F about 1 hr., or until visible rice is tender when pressed lightly between fingers. If desired, garnish with **parsley.** *4 to 6 servings*

△ Porcupine Beef Balls with Mushrooms

Follow ▲ Recipe. Substitute a mixture of 1¼ cups (1 10½- to 11-oz. can) **condensed cream of mushroom soup** and 1 cup **water** for the Quick Tomato Sauce.

Spaghetti and Meat Balls

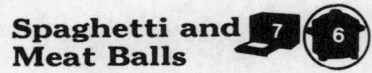

Set out a medium-size saucepan and a large, heavy skillet having a tight-fitting cover.

Heat in the saucepan over low heat

3 tablespoons butter or margarine

Add and cook over medium heat until onion is transparent, occasionally moving pieces with a spoon

½ cup (about 1 medium-size) chopped onion (page 12)

1 clove garlic (page 12), minced; or crushed in a garlic press

Remove from heat and stir in

3½ cups (1 No. 2½ can) tomatoes, sieved

¾ cup (6-oz. can) tomato paste

and a mixture of

1 teaspoon salt

½ teaspoon Accent

⅛ teaspoon pepper

⅛ teaspoon oregano

Simmer 1 hr., stirring occasionally.

Meanwhile, set out

¼ cup (1 oz.) grated Parmesan cheese

Lightly mix the grated cheese with

½ lb. ground beef

½ lb. ground lean pork

1 cup (1 slice) soft bread crumbs

2 tablespoons minced parsley

1 egg, beaten

and a mixture of

¾ teaspoon salt

½ teaspoon Accent

⅛ teaspoon pepper

Shape meat mixture into balls about 1½ in. in diameter. Coat by rolling in

2 tablespoons flour

Heat in the skillet over low heat

2 to 3 tablespoons butter or margarine

Add the meat balls and brown over medium heat. Shake pan frequently to obtain an even browning and to keep balls round. Pour off fat as it collects. Pour sauce over meat balls; cover and cook over low heat 20 min. longer.

Meanwhile, cook (page 277) and drain

8 oz. unbroken spaghetti

Put drained spaghetti in serving dish. Top with the meat balls and sauce.

Serve with grated **Parmesan cheese** and a green salad. *6 to 8 servings*

Note: The appearance of this dish may be varied by serving the meat balls and tomato sauce with **noodles** or other kinds of **pasta**.

Spaghetti and Meat Balls

Best-Ever Stuffed Meat Loaf

Grease a 9½x5¼x2¾-in. loaf pan and set out a large, heavy skillet.

For Wheat-Germ Bread Stuffing—Toast, cut into cubes and set aside

6 slices bread (about 4 cups cubes)

Prepare and set aside

1 cup quick meat broth (*page 13*)

Clean (*page 12*), finely chop and set aside enough celery to yield

1 cup chopped celery (about 2 large stalks)

Heat in the skillet over low heat

¼ cup butter or margarine

Add the toasted-bread cubes. Turn occasionally until they are coated evenly on all sides with butter and are golden brown in color.

Remove skillet from heat source. Add to skillet, mixing lightly with the bread cubes, one half the meat broth (reserve remainder for meat-wheat-germ mixture), the celery and

¼ cup wheat germ
¼ cup finely chopped green pepper (*page 12*)
¼ cup minced onion
1 egg, beaten

and a mixture of

¼ teaspoon salt
¼ teaspoon Accent
⅛ teaspoon pepper

Set stuffing aside.

For Tomato Topping—Put into a bowl

¾ cup (6-oz. can) tomato paste

Blend in

⅓ cup firmly packed brown sugar
1 teaspoon prepared mustard
½ teaspoon Worcestershire sauce

Set topping aside.

Best-Ever Stuffed Meat Loaf

For Meat Loaf—Put into a large bowl

2 lbs. ground beef
½ cup wheat germ
2 tablespoons minced onion

and a mixture of the reserved meat broth and

2 teaspoons salt
½ teaspoon Accent
⅛ teaspoon thyme
⅛ teaspoon pepper

Mix together lightly.

Divide meat mixture into two equal portions. Lightly pack one portion into the loaf pan. Spread Wheat-Germ Bread Stuffing evenly over top of meat layer. Lightly pack remaining meat mixture evenly over stuffing. Spread Tomato Topping evenly over top of loaf.

Bake at 350°F about 1 hour.

Drain off excess liquid. Carefully remove loaf to a warm platter. Garnish as desired.

8 servings

Specialty Macaroni-Beef Loaf

Grease a 9½x5¼x2¾-in. loaf pan, Set out a small skillet.

Cook and drain (*page 277*)

1 cup (4 oz.) macaroni (use tubes broken into 1- to 2-in. pieces)

Meanwhile, prepare and set aside
  ½ cup quick meat broth (*page 13*)
Heat in the skillet over medium heat
  2 tablespoons fat
Add and cook until onion is transparent, stirring occasionally
  ¼ cup finely chopped onion
  **¼ cup finely chopped green pepper
  (*page 12*)**
Meanwhile, mix together lightly
  ¾ lb. ground beef
  ¼ lb. bulk pork sausage
  2 tablespoons minced pimiento
  2 eggs, beaten
and a mixture of
  1½ teaspoons salt
  ¾ teaspoon Accent
  ¼ teaspoon pepper
Add the vegetables, broth and macaroni; mix together lightly, using a fork. Pack mixture lightly into loaf pan.

Bake at 350°F about 1 hour.

Meanwhile, prepare
  Tomato-Cheese Sauce (*page 327*)
Unmold (*page 107*) loaf and serve with sauce.
  6 to 8 servings

▲ Beef and Pork Loaf

Set out a 9½x5¼x2¾-in. loaf pan.

Mix together lightly
  1¼ lbs. ground beef
  ½ lb. ground lean pork
  2 cups (2 slices) soft bread crumbs
  ¼ cup minced onion
  1 cup milk
  1 egg, beaten
and a mixture of
  2 teaspoons salt
  1 teaspoon Accent
  ¼ teaspoon pepper
Pack lightly into loaf pan, rounding top.

Bake at 350°F about 1½ hrs. Unmold (*page 107*) onto warm serving platter. Serve warm.
  About 8 servings

⚠ Ham Loaf 🏠10

Follow ▲ Recipe. Substitute 1¼ lbs. **ground ham** for beef. Reduce salt to ½ teaspoon and pepper to ⅛ teaspoon. Omit onion. Spread top of loaf with a mixture of ¼ cup firmly packed **brown sugar** and 3 tablespoons **prepared mustard** before baking.

⚠ Tangy Beef Loaf

Follow ▲ Recipe. Use ¾ cup **milk**. Add ¼ cup **ketchup** and 1 tablespoon **prepared horse-radish** to the meat mixture.

Beef 'n' Sausage Loaf 🏠12 12

ALTHEA C. SQUIRES, ORANGE, MASS.

Lightly grease an 8½x4½x2½-in. loaf pan.

Mix together lightly in a large bowl
  1 lb. ground beef
  ½ lb. bulk pork sausage
  2 cups (2 slices) soft bread crumbs
  **¾ cup (about 2 stalks) celery
  (*page 12*), finely chopped**
  1 tablespoon prepared horse-radish
  **½ cup (4-oz. can) sliced mushrooms
  and liquid**
  1 egg, beaten
and a mixture of
  ½ teaspoon onion salt
  ¼ teaspoon garlic salt
  ¼ teaspoon pepper
Pack lightly into loaf pan, rounding top.

Bake at 350°F about 1 hr.

Unmold loaf (*page 107*). Serve with **baked potatoes.**
  About 8 servings

   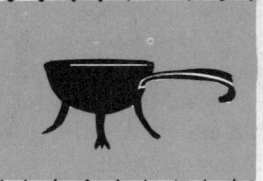

Saucy Burgers

Heat in a large heavy skillet

2 tablespoons fat

Add and cook over medium heat until transparent, stirring occasionally

½ cup (about 1 medium-size) finely chopped onion (page 12)

Add and cook until lightly browned, breaking into small pieces with fork or spoon

1 lb. ground beef

Remove from heat; add and blend in

1 cup chili sauce
1 cup ketchup
¾ cup chopped celery (page 12)
¾ cup chopped green pepper (page 12)

and a mixture of

1 teaspoon salt
½ teaspoon Accent
¼ teaspoon pepper

Simmer, uncovered, about 25 min. Keep mixture moving with fork or spoon.

Serve over

Buttered, toasted hamburger buns

6 servings

▲ Meat Muffins 13

Grease twelve 2½-in. muffin-pan wells.

Combine and mix lightly

1¼ lbs. ground beef
½ lb. ground lean pork
2 cups (2 slices) soft bread crumbs
1 cup milk
1 egg, beaten
1 teaspoon Worcestershire sauce

and a mixture of

2 teaspoons salt
1 teaspoon Accent
½ teaspoon thyme
¼ teaspoon pepper

Divide mixture into 12 equal portions. Pack meat mixture lightly into muffin wells.

Bake at 350°F about 40 min.

Meanwhile, blend together and set aside

⅓ cup firmly packed brown sugar
⅓ cup ketchup

After 20 min. of baking time, spoon about 2 teaspoons ketchup mixture on top of each meat muffin and continue baking. Unmold (page 107). *12 Meat Muffins*

Layered Loaf

Meat Ring

⚠ Layered Loaf 🔟14

Follow ▲ Recipe for meat mixture; increase ground beef to 1¾ lbs., ground pork to 1 lb.; decrease thyme to ¼ teaspoon. Add ¼ cup chopped **onion**, ¼ cup chopped **parsley**, 1 tablespoon **brown sugar** and 1 tablespoon **wine vinegar** to combined ingredients before mixing. Grease a 10x5x3-in. loaf pan.

For Rice Mixture—Bring to boiling in a saucepan 1½ cups **water**. Add 1⅓ cups packaged **precooked rice**, 1 tablespoon chopped **onion**, ½ teaspoon **salt**, ½ teaspoon **Accent**, and a few grains **pepper**. Mix just until rice is moistened. Cover saucepan and remove from heat. Let stand about 13 min. without removing cover to allow rice to steam. Mix in 1 tablespoon chopped **parsley** and 1 slightly beaten **egg**.

Lightly pack one third of meat mixture into pan. Top with one half of rice mixture. Repeat layers and top with remaining meat mixture.

Bake at 350°F about 1½ hrs. Omit brown sugar and ketchup. Unmold onto a serving plate. Garnish with **parsley.**

⚠ Meat Ring

Follow ▲ Recipe. Pack meat mixture lightly into a greased 1½-qt. ring mold instead of muffin-pan wells. Bake about 1½ hrs. Omit ketchup and brown sugar, if desired.

Unmold and fill center of meat ring with cooked and seasoned **potato balls**. Garnish with **parsley.**

⚠ Petite Rings

Follow ▲ Recipe for preparing meat mixture. Omit ketchup and brown sugar. Grease 8 individual ring molds. Divide meat mixture into 8 equal portions and pack lightly into the molds. Bake for 30 to 35 min.

Unmold and place a spoonful of colorful cooked **vegetables** in center of each ring.

Beef and Cheese Pie

Set out a large, heavy skillet.

Prepare (do not bake) and set aside
> **Pastry for 1-Crust Pie (page 442; use 8-in. pie pan)**

Heat in the skillet
> **1 to 2 tablespoons fat**

Add and cook over medium heat until lightly browned, breaking into small pieces with fork or spoon
> **¾ lb. ground beef**

Remove from heat and blend in
> **1 cup (8-oz. can) tomato sauce**
> **½ teaspoon Worcestershire sauce**
> **¼ teaspoon salt**
> **2 drops tabasco sauce**

Simmer for 5 min. Set aside.

Put into a small bowl and beat until softened
> **3 oz. (1 pkg.) cream cheese**

Blend one half of the cream cheese with
> **½ cup (4 oz.) dry cottage cheese**
> **¼ cup thick sour cream**
> **2 tablespoons minced onion**
> **1 tablespoon chopped green pepper**
> **1 tablespoon chopped drained pimiento**
> **½ teaspoon Accent**
> **¼ teaspoon salt**

Carefully spread remaining softened cream cheese over pastry in pie pan. Turn cottage cheese mixture into pie pan over cream cheese layer and spread to edges. Cover with meat mixture.

Bake at 425°F 10 min.; reduce heat to 325°F and bake 30 min. *About 6 servings*

TAVERN

Ranch Shortcake

Set out a baking sheet and a large, heavy skillet having a cover.

Prepare
2 Hard-Cooked Eggs (page 87)
Chop and set aside.

Prepare and bake
Tender-Rich Biscuits (page 62; roll dough 1/3 in. thick and use a 2½-in. cutter)
Heat in the skillet over medium heat
1 to 2 tablespoons fat
Add and cook until transparent, occasionally moving and turning with fork or spoon
1 medium-size onion (page 12), thinly sliced
Remove onion with slotted spoon; set aside.

Add to skillet, breaking into small pieces with fork or spoon
1 lb. ground beef
Cook over medium heat until browned. Mix in the onion and add slowly, stirring in
2 cups (two 8-oz. cans) tomato sauce
1 teaspoon Worcestershire sauce
and a mixture of
1 teaspoon salt
¾ teaspoon Accent
⅛ teaspoon pepper
Cover and simmer about 5 min.

Cook (*page 285*) contents of
1 10-oz. pkg. frozen peas
Drain peas and add to skillet with the chopped eggs. Cook 3 to 5 minutes longer, or until heated thoroughly.

Cut or tear biscuits into halves. Spoon sauce over half of biscuits and top with remaining halves.   *4 to 6 servings*

Lima-Bean Casserole 15 13

Tasty and hearty and made in a hurry.

Set out a large, heavy skillet. Grease a 1½-qt. casserole.

Cook (*page 285*) contents of
1 12-oz. pkg. frozen lima beans
Meanwhile, combine in a large bowl
2½ cups (2½ slices) soft bread crumbs
¼ cup milk
Add and mix lightly
1 lb. ground beef
1 egg, beaten
1 small clove garlic (page 12), minced; or crushed in a garlic press
Blend in a mixture of
1 teaspoon salt
½ teaspoon Accent
¼ teaspoon pepper
Shape into balls about 1 in. in diameter.

Heat in the skillet over medium heat
1 tablespoon fat
Add meat balls and brown, turning occasionally to brown evenly. Pour off fat as it collects. Remove meat balls to casserole. Pour over
¼ cup water
Drain lima beans and season with a mixture of
1½ teaspoons salt
½ teaspoon pepper
¼ teaspoon Accent
Add and mix thoroughly
3 tablespoons butter or margarine
Spoon beans over meat balls in casserole.

Bake, covered, at 350°F about 30 min. Remove from oven and spread with
1 cup thick sour cream
Bake uncovered 5 min. longer.

Serve immediately.   *About 4 servings*

Tamale Perfection 16

A South-of-the-Border inspiration.

Grease a 2-qt. casserole.

Put into a large, heavy, cold skillet
   ¼ lb. bulk pork sausage
Break into small pieces with fork or spoon.
Add
   1½ tablespoons cold water
Cover and cook slowly 8 min. Remove cover
and pour off fat. Mix in with fork or spoon,
breaking meat into pieces
   1 lb. ground beef
Brown meat over medium heat, stirring occasionally. Pour off fat as it collects.

When meat begins to brown, add
   **1 cup (about 2 medium-size) finely
      chopped onion (*page 12*)**
   **½ cup finely chopped celery
      (*page 12*)**
   **⅓ cup finely chopped green pepper
      (*page 12*)**
Cook until meat is well browned and onion is
transparent, stirring occasionally.

Add slowly and mix in
   **2¼ cups (No. 2 can) tomatoes,
      sieved**
   **1¼ cups (12-oz. can, drained) whole
      kernel corn**
Blend in a mixture of
   2 teaspoons chili powder
   1 teaspoon salt
   ½ teaspoon Accent
   ¼ teaspoon pepper
Cover and simmer about 15 min.

Pit and slice enough ripe olives to yield
   1 cup sliced ripe olives
Set aside.

Tamale Perfection

Mix together and add gradually to skillet,
stirring continually
   1 cup cold water
   ½ cup yellow corn meal
Cook over low heat until thickened, stirring
slowly. Stir in the sliced olives. Turn into
casserole.

Bake at 350°F 1 hr.

Remove from oven and sprinkle with
   **¾ cup (3 oz.) grated sharp
      Cheddar cheese**
Return to oven and bake 5 min. longer, or
until cheese is melted.

Garnish with
   Whole ripe olives
   Sprigs of parsley

                              8 servings

GROUND BEEF in the MICROWAVE OVEN

Ground beef is one of the most popular choices for family meals. With the microwave oven, ground beef dishes such as meat loaf are not only economical, but great timesavers. All the meat loaf recipes included here are delicious and light in texture. The **Best-Ever Meat Loaf** is outstanding. The recipes for meat balls are also quite flavorful, although the tomato-based sauces are not as rich as those produced by slower cooking methods.

Unfortunately, that great American favorite, the hamburger, is not ideally suited to microwave oven cooking. An exception is the quite good **Triple-Deck Burgers**, which we have included. For the most part, however, it is almost impossible to produce a rare hamburger in the microwave oven and have it adequately browned. If you like rare hamburgers, stick with the broiler or stove. It should be noted, however, that well-done ground beef from the microwave oven has more flavor and more juice than when cooked under the broiler.

A few more general hints about cooking ground beef in the microwave oven. Much more juice accumulates than in conventional cooking. Recipes which require browning, such as the meat ball recipes, must be drained frequently.

When the cooking is completed, all of these recipes must stand, covered, for the amount of time specified. When the meat emerges from the oven, it has a harsh, "bloody" flavor. However, this quality disappears and the flavor is exactly as it should be after the dish stands for the appropriate amount of time.

MEAT BALLS—All the meat ball recipes call for browning in the covered browning skillet. We used a 10-inch skillet and browned each recipe in batches. We specify the number of batches and the cooking time for a single batch, as well as the *OVERALL COOKING TIME* for the entire recipe. If you use another size skillet or a different number of batches, then cooking times need to be adjusted (more time for more volume; less time for less volume).

Standing Time for meat balls is about 10 minutes, unless specifically noted otherwise.

MEAT LOAVES—All meat loaves are cooked uncovered. We note the appropriate-size pan with each recipe. *Do not grease pans.*

Test for Doneness—Meat loaves prepared in the microwave oven do not have the brown coloring characteristic of doneness with conventional cooking methods. Instead, look for the loaf to pull away slightly from the sides of the pan and for little juice to flow when the loaf is pierced with a fork.

Standing Time for the meat loaves is usually about 15 minutes. Use plastic wrap to cover while standing, if no other cover is available.

REMINDERS—Remember, preparation of ingredients and the manner in which they are assembled are the same as for the recipe given in the main text unless specifically noted otherwise.

The introductory chapter, **Home Cooking in the Microwave Oven**, in the beginning of this book provides additional tips and an easy-to-read chart comparing the settings among different brands of ovens. We also suggest you review this section to learn how we have adapted these recipes.

Triple-Deck Burgers 1
(page 130)

Use a casserole or browning skillet for the stuffing and a covered baking dish for the final dish.

Prepare tomato sauce, except use ½ cup water (instead of ¾).

For Stuffing—Melt butter in casserole. Add onions and COOK until transparent (about 3 min.). Combine with remaining stuffing ingredients.

For Meat Patties—Prepare meat for cooking as in Recipe. Cover and COOK 3 min., then SLOW-COOK, rotating every 3 min., until done (about 12 min.).

Cover and let stand 10 min.

Köttbüllar 2
(Swedish Meat Balls) *(page 132)*

Use a browning skillet. Brown meat balls in two batches.

Preheat skillet (3 min.). Add the 2 tablespoons butter and COOK until melted.

Add half the meat balls to the skillet and COOK until brown (about 5 min.). Brown remaining meat balls (about 5 min.).

Blend in flour and cream as in Recipe. COOK until simmering (about 2 min.).

Cover and let stand 10 min.
OVERALL COOKING TIME: 12:00

Swedish-American 3
Meat Balls *(page 132)*

Use a browning skillet. This recipe must be cooked in batches; the 10-in. skillet accommodates about one-third of the meat balls at a time.

Preheat skillet (3 min.). Add the 1 tablespoon butter and COOK until hot and foam subsides.

Add onions and COOK until transparent (about 1 min. 45 sec.). Combine with remaining meat ball ingredients.

Melt remaining butter. Add as many meat balls as will fit closely together (about one-third of recipe). They will shrink. COOK, turning the meat balls and rotating the pan every 30 sec., until done (about 1½ min. per batch). Drain liquid if necessary. Repeat with remaining meat balls.

Cover and let stand 10 min.
OVERALL COOKING TIME: 6:15

Italian-Style Meat Balls *(page 133)* **4**

Use a browning skillet. Brown meat balls in two batches.

Preheat skillet (3 min.). Heat olive oil. Add pepper and onion and COOK, stirring after 1 min., until onion is transparent (about 2 min.).

Add half the meat balls and COOK, turning meat balls and rotating pan every 2 min., until brown (about 3 to 4 min. each batch).

Return all meat balls to skillet and pour tomato-cheese mixture over all. COOK to complete meat balls and heat thoroughly (about 6 min.).

Cover and let stand 10 min.

Serve as in Recipe.

OVERALL COOKING TIME: 14:00

Norwegian Meat Balls and Gravy *(page 133)* **5**

Use a browning skillet. The browning times in this recipe are for 3 batches of 16 meat balls each.

Preheat skillet (3 min.). Add the 2 tablespoons butter and COOK until melted.

Add onion and COOK, stirring after 1 min., until transparent (about 2 min.). Add onion to meat mixture.

COOK 2 tablespoons butter until melted. Add meat balls to skillet and COOK, tossing to brown evenly and rotating pan every 2 min., until well done (about 6 min. each batch).

COOK flour mixture, stirring every 30 sec., until flour is lightly browned (about 2 min.).

Add water and cream and COOK, stirring every 45 sec., until thickened (about 2 min.).

Pour gravy over meat balls, cover and let stand 10 min.

OVERALL COOKING TIME: 24:00

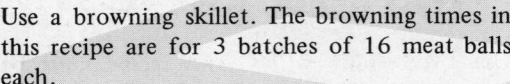

Applesauce Meat Balls *(page 136)* **6**

Use a browning skillet. The times in this recipe are for browning meat balls in two batches.

Preheat skillet (3 min.). Add fat and COOK until melted.

Add meat balls and COOK, turning every 90 sec., until lightly browned (about 5 min. each batch).

Return all meat balls to skillet and add the ketchup-water mixture. COOK, rotating after 4 min., until done (about 8 min.).

Toss to coat with sauce. Cover and let stand 10 min.

OVERALL COOKING TIME: 18:00

Spaghetti and Meat Balls *(page 137)* **7**

Use a casserole and a browning skillet.

In casserole, COOK the 3 tablespoons butter or margarine until melted.

Add onion and garlic and COOK until onion is transparent (about 2 min.).

Add remaining ingredients for tomato sauce and COOK until simmering (about 5 min.), then SLOWCOOK, stirring and rotating pan every 5 min., until sauce thickens (about 10 min.).

Preheat browning skillet (3 min.). Add butter or margarine and COOK until bubbling.

Brown meat balls in two batches. Add meat balls and COOK, turning after 2 min., until lightly browned (about 4 min. each batch).

Pour sauce over meat balls. COOK until simmering (about 20 min.).

Cover and let stand 10 min.

Best-Ever Stuffed Meat 8 Loaf (page 138)

Use a 2-qt. glass loaf pan and a browning skillet. *Do not grease.*

For Wheat-Germ Bread Stuffings—To brown toast cubes, preheat skillet (3 min.). Add the ¼ cup butter or margarine and COOK until melted. Stir in toast cubes and COOK until evenly browned (about 1 min.).

For Meat Loaf—Prepare meat for cooking as in Recipe. COOK 3 min., then SLOWCOOK, rotating pan every 5 min. (about 20 min.).

Cover and let stand 15 min.
OVERALL COOKING TIME: 24:00

Tangy Beef Loaf 11 (page 139)

Follow 10 Recipe with changes as in △ Recipe.

COOK as in 10 Recipe, except SLOWCOOK 24 min.

Specialty 9 Macaroni-Beef Loaf (page 138)

Use a 2-qt. glass loaf pan. *Do not grease.*

COOK fat until melted. Add onions and peppers and COOK, stirring every minute, until onions are transparent (about 2 min.).

Assemble meat loaf as in Recipe and pack into pan, keeping the noodles under a top layer of meat. (If they are not covered they may dry out.)

COOK loaf 3 min., then SLOWCOOK, rotating every 5 min. (about 23 min.).

Cover and let stand 15 min.

Beef 'n' Sausage Loaf 12 (page 139)

Use a 1½-qt. glass loaf pan. *Do not grease.*

Assemble loaf as in Recipe. COOK 3 min., then SLOWCOOK, rotating pan every 4 min. (about 22 min.).

Cover and let stand 15 min.

Unmold and serve as in Recipe.
OVERALL COOKING TIME: 25:00

Beef and Pork Loaf 10 (page 139)

Use a 2-qt. glass loaf pan.

Assemble meat loaf as in Recipe and COOK 3 min., then SLOWCOOK, rotating the pan every 5 min. (about 35 min.).

Cover and let stand 15 min.

Unmold and serve as in ▲ Recipe.
OVERALL COOKING TIME: 38:00

Meat Muffins (page 140) 13

Use 12 small glass custard cups. *Do not grease.*

Prepare meat muffins for cooking as in Recipe.

COOK, 6 cups at a time, 2 min., then SLOWCOOK, rotating every 2 min. (about 4 min. for medium doneness).

Spoon on ketchup-sugar mixture. COOK to heat topping (about 30 sec. each).

Cover and let stand 5 min.
OVERALL COOKING TIME: 13:00

Layered Loaf *(page 141)* `14`

Use a 2-qt. glass baking dish. *Do not grease.*

Follow `13` Recipe for meat mixture with changes as in △ Recipe.

COOK 5 min., then SLOWCOOK, rotating every 5 min. (about 20 min.).

Cover and let stand 15 min.

OVERALL COOKING TIME: 25:00

Lima-Bean Casserole `15`
(page 142)

Use a browning skillet and a 1½-qt. glass casserole. *Do not grease.* Brown meat balls in two batches.

Prepare meat balls for cooking as in Recipe.

Preheat skillet (3 min.). Add fat and COOK until melted.

Add meat balls and COOK, turning meat balls and rotating pan every 5 min. (about 10 min. each batch). Remove meat balls to casserole and repeat with second batch.

Mix water and seasonings, but not lima beans. Pour over meat balls. SLOWCOOK 20 min.

Thoroughly mix drained lima beans with butter or margarine; spoon over meat balls. SLOW-COOK 10 min.

After spreading sour cream, COOK until heated (about 2 min.).

Cover and let stand 15 min.

OVERALL COOKING TIME: 55:00

Tamale Perfection `16`
(page 143)

Use a 2-qt. casserole and a browning skillet. *Do not grease.*

Preheat skillet (3 min.). Add broken-up sausage and COOK until brown (about 5 min.).

Add water and COOK 5 min.

Add beef, COOK until brown (about 15 min.).

Add onion, celery and green pepper; COOK, stirring mixture and rotating pan every 5 min., until onion is transparent (about 15 min.).

Add tomatoes, corn and seasonings and stir; SLOWCOOK 10 min.

Add water and corn meal; SLOWCOOK until thickened (about 10 min.).

Stir in olives. Remove contents of skillet to casserole and COOK 20 min.

Sprinkle with cheese and COOK until melted (about 3 min.).

Cover and let stand 15 min.

Serve as in Recipe.

OVERALL COOKING TIME: 86:00

GROUND BEEF in the SLOW COOKER

Meat loaves and meat balls are delicious when prepared in the slow cooker. Recipes for hamburgers, except the **Triple-Deck Burgers** included here, are obviously unsuitable for slow cooking.

MEAT LOAVES—It is necessary to be more strict with timing than is usual with slow cookers. If the meat loaf cooks too long, it will stick to the pot and fall apart; if it is not cooked long enough, it will simply fall apart. There is only about an hour's leeway beyond the minimum times specified here.

Test for Doneness—Note the color of the juices when pierced with a fork. Ground beef meat loaves will have pink juices. Meat loaves which contain any pork are not fully cooked until the juices run clear. Even when done, the loaf will be soft and without a crust on top. To give it time to firm and for the juices to settle, turn off the cooker and let the loaf stand with the cover off for about 30 minutes. It should then be easy to remove from the pot and ready to serve.

MEAT BALLS—You can hold meat balls in the slow cooker well beyond the recommended cooking times without fear of overcooking. Keep the pot on LOW until you are ready to serve.

To brown meat balls evenly, stir thoroughly halfway through the cooking time. Uneven browning in no way affects the flavor of the meat balls, and variations in color are usually disguised by the sauces.

REMINDERS—Use the smaller, 3½-qt. slow cooker, unless otherwise directed.

Follow the recipes in the main text for preparing ingredients and assembling these dishes unless otherwise directed.

The introductory chapter, **Home Cooking in the Slow Cooker**, in the beginning of this book provides additional tips and an easy-to-read chart comparing settings among different brands of slow cookers. We recommend reviewing this material to also learn how we have adapted these recipes.

Triple-Deck Burgers
(page 130)

Prepare tomato sauce on top of the stove as in Recipe, except do not increase water.

For Stuffing—Prepare on top of the stove as in Recipe.

For Meat Patties—Prepare patties for cooking as in Recipe. When assembling burgers, wrap top layer of meat around stuffing to enclose it.

Place all patties in slow cooker and cover with tomato sauce; cover.

Cook on LOW for 8 to 9 hrs.

Swedish-American Meat Balls *(page 132)*

You may use sautéed or raw onions.

Add onions and the 1 tablespoon butter to the meat mixture.

Place remaining butter in slow cooker and melt on HIGH. Add meat balls and coat with the butter; cover.

Cook on LOW for 3½ to 5½ hrs.

Serve as in Recipe.

Italian-Style Meat Balls *(page 133)*

Sauté onions and green peppers. (To sauté in slow cooker see **Home Cooking in the Slow Cooker** in the beginning of this book.)

Heat fat on HIGH until partially melted.

Add meat balls and coat lightly with fat. To partially brown, cook on HIGH for 15 min.

Pour tomato sauce-cheese mixture over meat balls; cover.

Cook on LOW for 4 to 6 hrs.

Skim fat from sauce and serve as in Recipe.

Norwegian Meat Balls and Gravy *(page 133)*

You may use sautéed or raw onions.

Soften butter in slow cooker set on HIGH. Add meat balls and coat lightly with butter; cover.

Cook on LOW for 3½ to 5½ hrs. Remove meat balls.

Reset slow cooker on HIGH. Blend in flour mixture and cook until flour is browned (about 20 min.). Blend in water and cream and cook on HIGH for 12 min. Gravy will simmer, not boil.

Return meat balls to slow cooker, cover and re-set to LOW to keep warm until serving time.

Applesauce Meat Balls
(page 136)

Melt fat on HIGH. Add meat balls and coat lightly with fat.

Reset slow cooker to LOW and cover meat balls with the ketchup-water mixture; cover.

Cook on LOW for 5 to 6 hrs.

Skim fat before serving.

Spaghetti and Meat Balls *(page 137)*

Preparation of both the meat balls and sauce is a one-step operation in the slow cooker.

Melt 2 tablespoons fat (instead of 3) on HIGH.

Meanwhile, prepare meat balls for cooking, except do not flour.

Add meat balls to slow cooker, shaking and rocking the pot to coat meat balls with the melted fat.

It is not necessary to sauté onions and garlic for the sauce. In a bowl, combine all sauce ingredients; pour over meat balls; cover.

Cook on LOW for 8 to 9 hrs.

Serve as in Recipe.

Beef and Pork Loaf 9
(page 139)

Follow ▲ Recipe.

Cook on LOW for 8 to 9 hrs.

Ham Loaf *(page 139)* 10

Follow 9 Recipe with changes as in ⚠ Recipe.

Cook on LOW for 8 to 9 hrs.

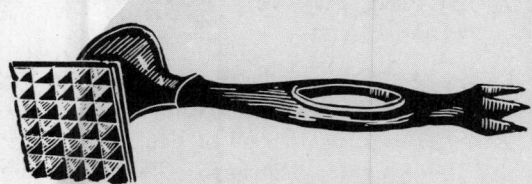

Best-Ever Stuffed Meat Loaf *(page 138)* 7

Do not grease.

For Wheat-Germ Stuffing—Prepare stuffing on top of stove as in Recipe.

For Meat Loaf—When assembling meat loaf, enclose stuffing completely in meat mixture, rather than building layers; this makes the loaf easier to remove from the slow cooker. Cover.

Cook on LOW for 8 to 10 hrs.

Tangy Beef Loaf *(page 139)* 11

Follow 9 Recipe with changes as in ⚠ Recipe.

Cook on LOW for 7 to 8 hrs.

Beef 'n' Sausage Loaf 12
(page 139)

Do not grease.

Cook on LOW for 9 to 10 hrs.

Specialty Macaroni-Beef Loaf *(page 138)* 8

Do not grease.

Sauté onions and peppers. (To sauté in slow cooker see **Home Cooking in the Slow Cooker** in the beginning of this book.

Assemble meat loaf and pack lightly into slow cooker; cover.

Cook on LOW for 9 to 10 hrs.

Serve as in Recipe.

Lima-Bean Casserole 13
(page 142)

Melt fat in slow cooker set on HIGH. Add meat balls and coat lightly with fat. Add water; cover.

Cook on LOW for 8 to 9 hrs.

Add lima beans. (If necessary, cover and reheat on HIGH.)

Top with sour cream, cover and heat on LOW for 5 min. to warm wour cream.

Spring Roast Ham

▲ Spring Roast Ham

Set out a shallow roasting pan with rack.

For Ham—Follow directions on wrapper or wipe with a clean, damp cloth
    10-lb. smoked whole ham
Place ham fat side up on rack. Insert roast meat thermometer in center of thickest part of lean, being sure bulb does not rest on bone or in fat.

Roast uncovered at 300°F.

When ham has roasted about 2 hrs., prepare Pineapple Glaze.

For Pineapple Glaze—Blend together
    ½ cup firmly packed brown sugar
    1½ teaspoons cornstarch
    ½ teaspoon dry mustard
Add and stir in
    1 cup (9-oz. can) crushed pineapple
Bring to boiling and cook until mixture is transparent and slightly thickened, stirring constantly. Keep warm.

To Glaze Ham—Remove ham from oven after it has cooked about 2½ hrs. Remove rind (if any) being careful not to remove fat. Making diagonal cuts, score fat surface of ham to make diamond pattern; or use scalloped cookie cutter to make flower pattern.

Place in center of each pattern
    Whole clove
Spread ham with Pineapple Glaze. Return to oven and continue roasting about 45 min., or until internal temperature reaches 160°F. (Total roasting time is about 3 hrs., allowing 18 to 20 min. per pound.)

Remove ham to warm serving platter; remove roast meat thermometer.   *About 20 servings*

△ Spring Roast Half Ham

Follow ▲ Recipe. Substitute 5 lb. **shank** or **butt half smoked ham** for whole ham. Allow 22 to 25 min. per pound of ham. Substitute the following for Pineapple Glaze. Mix together ½ cup firmly packed **brown sugar**, 2 teaspoons **flour** and ½ teaspoon **dry mustard**. Stir in 1 tablespoon **vinegar**. After ham has roasted about 1½ hrs., remove from oven, trim, score and spread with the glaze. Press into glaze **maraschino cherry halves, pineapple chunks** and whole **cloves** to form an attractive design. Roast until internal temperature reaches 160°F.   *About 10 servings*

Burgundy Roast Ham
MRS. CONRAD MILLER, SPRINGFIELD, ORE.

Set out a shallow roasting pan with rack.

For Ham—Wipe with a clean, damp cloth
    5 lb. shank or butt half fresh ham
Place ham fat side up on rack. Insert roast meat thermometer in center of thickest part of lean, being sure bulb does not rest on bone or in fat.

Roast uncovered at 300°F 2 to 2½ hrs. (Allow 30 to 35 min. per lb. of ham.) About 30 min. before end of roasting time, prepare glaze.

For Glaze—Mix together
    ½ cup brown sugar
    1 tablespoon cornstarch
Blend in, stirring until smooth
    2 to 3 tablespoons Burgundy or claret

To Glaze Ham—Remove ham from oven. Remove rind (if any) being careful not to remove fat. Making diagonal cuts, score fat surface of ham to make diamond pattern; place in center of each diamond

Whole clove

Spread Glaze over the ham. Pour around ham

1 cup Burgundy or claret

Return to oven. Bake 30 min. longer, or until internal temperature is 185°F. Baste frequently with the wine.

Remove ham to a warm serving plate; remove roast meat thermometer. If sauce in pan is too thick, add, blending in, enough wine to achieve desired consistency. Serve sauce hot in a separate dish to be spooned over each serving.

About 10 servings

▲ Pineapple-Glazed Canned Ham

Set out a shallow roasting pan with a rack.

Following directions, remove from can

1 3- to 4-lb. canned ham

Place ham on rack. Score, if desired, by making diagonal cuts on surface of ham to form a diamond pattern. Insert in center of each diamond

1 or 2 whole cloves

Mix thoroughly

1 cup firmly packed brown sugar

1 teaspoon dry mustard

Stir in

1 cup (1 9-oz. can) crushed pineapple

Spoon mixture over ham.

Roast at temperature and for length of time suggested by packer. Baste with pineapple mixture frequently during baking.

Remove from rack to warm serving plate.

About 6 to 8 servings

△ Cranberry-Glazed Canned Ham

Follow ▲ Recipe; for pineapple mixture substitute a mixture of 1 cup whole **cranberry sauce**, ⅛ teaspoon **cloves**, and ⅛ teaspoon **allspice**. Spread over ham before roasting.

▲ Broiled Ham Slice

Wipe with a clean, damp cloth

1 smoked ham slice, cut ¾ to 1 in. thick

Allow ⅓ to ½ lb. meat per serving.

Set temperature control of range at Broil.

Place ham slice (or slices) on broiler rack. Place in broiler with top of slice 2 in. from heat source; broil about 8 to 10 min. Turn and broil second side about 8 to 10 min., or until ham is tender when pierced with a fork. If desired, serve with **Zippy Mustard Sauce** (*page 329*).

△ Broiled Ham with Peaches

Follow ▲ Recipe. About 2 to 3 min. before second side is browned, arrange well-drained **peach halves** around the ham. Garnish the broiled peaches with **water cress** and serve with the ham.

Broiled Ham with Peaches

▲ **Baked Ham Slice** 7

Wipe with a clean, damp cloth and place in an 11¾x7½x1¾-in. baking dish
1 smoked ham slice, cut ½ in. thick
(Allow ⅓ to ½ lb. meat per serving.)

Insert into ham slice at 1-in. intervals
Whole cloves
Sprinkle over ham a mixture of
2 tablespoons brown sugar
2 tablespoons fine, dry bread crumbs
1 teaspoon grated orange peel
(page 11)
½ teaspoon dry mustard
Rinse and cut into ¼-in. slices
1 orange
Arrange slices on ham. Garnish with
Maraschino cherries, cut into rings
Carefully pour over top of ham slice
¾ cup orange juice
Bake at 300°F about 20 min. Remove cloves from ham slice before serving.

⚠ **Pineapple Baked** 8
Ham Slice

Follow ▲ Recipe. Substitute **lemon peel** for orange peel, canned **pineapple juice** for orange juice and 3 canned **pineapple slices** for the orange slices.

⚠ **Ginger Baked Ham Slice** 9

Follow ▲ Recipe. Substitute **lemon peel** for orange peel and **ginger ale** for orange juice. Omit orange and cherry garnish.

⚠ **Plum Baked Ham Slice** 10

Follow ▲ Recipe. Substitute **sirup** drained from 1 No. 2 can of **Italian plums** for orange juice. Arrange plums around ham slice. Omit orange and cherry garnish.

Stuffed Ham Slices

Stuffed Ham Slices 11 5

Set out a 13½x8¾x1¾-in. baking dish.

Wipe with a clean, damp cloth
2 smoked ham slices, cut 1 in. thick
Place one ham slice in the baking dish.

Mix together
4 cups (4 slices) soft bread cubes
½ cup (2½ oz.) seedless raisins
¼ cup firmly packed brown sugar
½ teaspoon dry mustard
Lightly toss with bread mixture
⅓ cup butter or margarine, melted
Spoon stuffing evenly over ham slice in dish. Top stuffing with second ham slice. Insert around edge of top slice of ham
Whole cloves
Drain, reserving sirup
1 No. 2 can sliced pineapple (about 10 slices pineapple)
Place two slices of pineapple in each corner of baking dish. Cut the two remaining pineapple slices into wedges. Brush top ham slice with reserved pineapple sirup. Arrange wedges to resemble flower petals on top of ham.

Bake stuffed ham slices uncovered at 300°F about 1½ hrs. Baste with reserved pineapple sirup several times during baking.

Garnish with **parsley**. *6 to 8 servings*

Ham Balls in Sweet-Sour Sauce

MRS. HARLEY DROZ, FAIRFIELD, IOWA

Set out a shallow 2-qt. casserole.

Combine in a large bowl
- **½ lb. ground cooked ham**
- **½ lb. ground beef**
- **1 cup (3 slices) fine, dry bread crumbs**
- **2 tablespoons minced onion**
- **½ teaspoon Accent**
- **1 egg, beaten**
- **½ cup milk**

Mix together lightly. Form into 1½-in. balls. Put balls into the casserole. Set aside.

Mix together in a saucepan
- **1 cup firmly packed brown sugar**
- **1 teaspoon dry mustard**

Add and stir in
- **½ cup vinegar**
- **½ cup water**

Bring to boiling; pour over the ham balls.

Bake uncovered at 350°F 1 hr., turning once.

Serve hot with sauce spooned over meat balls.

About 5 servings

▲ Pineapple-Glazed Ham Loaf

For Glaze—Mix to form a smooth paste
- **1 cup firmly packed brown sugar**
- **1 cup (9-oz. can) crushed pineapple**
- **1 teaspoon dry mustard**

For Ham Loaf—Grind (*page 107*) enough cooked ham to yield
- **2 cups ground cooked ham**

Combine with ground ham and mix lightly
- **1 lb. ground lean pork**
- **1 cup (3 slices) fine, dry bread crumbs**
- **1 teaspoon Worcestershire sauce**
- **1 cup milk**
- **2 eggs, beaten**

and a mixture of
- **1 teaspoon dry mustard**
- **½ teaspoon Accent**
- **¼ teaspoon salt**
- **¼ teaspoon pepper**

Put meat mixture into a shallow baking pan and shape to resemble a ham. Mark top surface in a diamond pattern. Insert in center of each diamond
- **1 or 2 whole cloves**

Spread glaze over ham loaf.

Bake at 350°F about 1½ hrs. Baste (*page 11*) with glaze frequently during baking.

6 to 8 servings

△ Peach Upside-Down Ham Loaf

Follow ▲ Recipe. Grease a 9½x5¼x2¾-in. loaf pan. Omit glaze. Set out 3 canned **peach halves**. Arrange them cut side down in loaf pan (see photo). Pack ham mixture lightly into pan. After baking, pour off excess liquid and unmold (*page 107*). Fill peach cavities with **jelly**.

Peach Upside-Down Ham Loaf: Arrange the peach halves cut side down in loaf pan.

Pour off excess liquid and unmold the loaf. Garnish the peach halves with any jelly.

HAM in the MICROWAVE OVEN

These ham recipes, when prepared in the microwave oven, are quick, easy and delicious, producing glamorous results with almost no effort.

ROASTS—All the roasts were excellent, with the fresh **Burgundy Roast Ham** especially notable.

All ham roasts should be cooked fat side down, the reverse of the way roasts are started in the conventional oven. They should then be turned halfway through the cooking period.

Test for Doneness—Smoked ham roasts are fully cooked with the internal temperature reaches 160°. If the special microwave meat thermometer is not available, meat may be removed from the oven and a conventional meat thermometer inserted. It will take about two minutes to register. If the meat is not done, it may be returned to the oven without affecting the cooking procedure.

GROUND HAM—The ground ham recipes, which might easily be shrugged off as leftovers, are really elegant and easy-to-prepare dishes.

Cold, the **Pineapple-Glazed Ham Loaf** is impressive picnic fare; the **Ham Balls in Sweet-Sour Sauce** can be used as party appetizers.

OTHER HAM CUTS—The recipe for **Stuffed Ham Slices** included here was acceptable as cooked in the microwave oven, but the stuffing was not quite as flavorful as it is when made in the conventional oven. The **Broiled Ham Slice** tasted rather more like baked, but the flavor and texture were both good.

Test for Doneness—These cuts of ham are fully cooked when the meat is tender.

REMINDERS—All the ham dishes must stand, covered, after cooking to season and permit juices to settle. We have given minimum standing times with each recipe.

The introductory chapter, **Home Cooking in the Microwave Oven**, in the beginning of this book provides additional tips and an easy-to-read chart comparing settings among different brands of ovens. Review this section to also learn how we have adapted these recipes.

Spring Roast Half Ham *(page 144)* 1

Use a large glass baking dish; a rack is optional.

For Ham—COOK (fat side down), turning pan every 3 min., until slightly browned (about 12 min.). Glaze as in Recipe.

SLOWCOOK, turning pan every 3 min., until tender (about 6 min.). (To test temperature, see introduction to this section.)

Cover and let stand 15 min.
OVERALL COOKING TIME: 18:00

Burgundy Roast Ham 2
(page 144)

Use a glass baking dish and a rack.

For Ham—COOK to raise temperature (10 min.). SLOWCOOK, rotating pan every 7 min., until nearly done (about 21 min.). Glaze ham.

COOK to heat (5 min.). SLOWCOOK, basting every 2 min., until done (about 7 min.). Remove from oven when internal termperature reaches 165°. The roast continues to cook while standing and will rise 15° to 20°. (To test temperature see the introduction to this section.)

Cover and let stand 15 min.
OVERALL COOKING TIME: 43:00

Pineapple-Glazed Canned Ham *(page 145)* 3

Use a glass roasting pan; a rack is optional.

Place glazed ham in pan or on rack, fat side down.

SLOWCOOK, rotating pan and basting every 5 min., until heated through (about 20 min.).

Cover and let stand 15 min.
OVERALL COOKING TIME: 20:00

Cranberry-Glazed Canned Ham *(page 145)* 4

Follow 3 Recipe with substitutions as in △ Recipe.

Broiled Ham Slice *(page 145)* 5

Use a browning skillet.

Preheat skillet (3 min.).

COOK ham slice until lightly browned on both sides (about 5 min. each).

Cover and let stand 10 min.

Serve as in Recipe.

Broiled Ham with Peaches *(page 145)* 6

Follow 5 Recipe with additions as in △ Recipe, except add peaches about 3 min. before second side is done.

Serve as in Recipe.

Baked Ham Slice 7
(page 146)

Use a glass baking dish.

SLOWCOOK, rotating pan every 4 min., until ham is tender (about 8 min.).

Cover and let stand 10 min.

OVERALL COOKING TIME: 8:00

Pineapple Baked Ham Slice *(page 146)* 8

Follow 7 Recipe with substitutions as in △ Recipe.

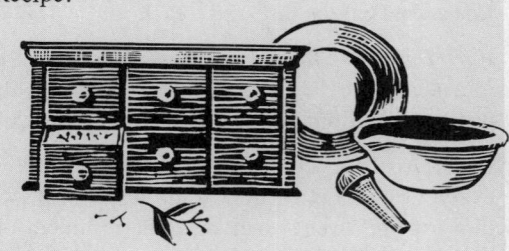

Ginger Baked Ham Slice 9
(page 146)

Follow 7 Recipe with changes as in △ Recipe.

Plum Baked Ham Slice 10
(page 146)

Follow 7 Recipe with changes as in ⚠ Recipe.

Stuffed Ham Slices 11
(page 146)

Use a glass baking dish.

SLOWCOOK, rotating pan and basting every 5 min., until ham is tender (about 20 min.).

Cover and let stand 10 min.

Serve as in Recipe.

OVERALL COOKING TIME: 20:00

Ham Balls
in Sweet-Sour Sauce 12 *(page 147)*

Use a 2-qt. casserole.

COOK sauce, stirring every 3 min., until simmering (about 6 min.). Pour over ham balls.

SLOWCOOK, turning pan and stirring every 5 min., until beef is done (ham balls will be dark pink) (about 20 min.).

Cover and let stand 5 min.

Serve as in Recipe.

OVERALL COOKING TIME: 26:00

Pineapple-Glazed 13
Ham Loaf *(page 147)*

Use a glass baking dish.

SLOWCOOK, rotating pan every 5 min., until pork is well done (about 20 min.). Test pork when the loaf starts to pull away from the sides of the dish; juices should run clear.

OVERALL COOKING TIME: 20:00

Peach Upside-Down 14
Ham Loaf *(page 147)*

Follow 13 Recipe with changes as in △ Recipe.

HAM in the SLOW COOKER

The wonderful characteristic of ham cooked in the slow cooker is that it is just as versatile as ham cooked conventionally, but it does not need any of the careful attention.

The meat is juicy with no hard crust or dry fibers as sometimes happens when prepared in an oven. The hams can be served hot, cold, or sliced and reheated. All of this convenience and flavor emerge from the slow cooker without ever having to baste the meat. The slow cooker does all the work, eliminating any need for basting, even if you use the rack.

ROASTS—There is plenty of leeway in the timing of the larger, smoked ham roasts, if your schedule goes awry.

The glazes are delicious in flavor, but they do tend to be slightly more liquid than when cooked in the conventional oven.

Test for Doneness—Roasts are fully cooked when the meat is tender and the juices run clear.

GROUND HAM—The **Pineapple-Glazed Ham Loaf** and the **Ham Balls in Sweet-Sour Sauce** are excellent, with no hint that they are made

from leftover dishes. Incidentally, the ham loaf is especially good served cold and is ideal for summer picnics or late suppers.

Test for Doneness—The ham balls are fully cooked when the beef ingredient is done; the juices should run clear. The loaf is done when the pork is; the juices should also run clear and the loaf will pull away from the sides of the pot.

OTHER HAM CUTS are equally tasty when prepared in the slow cooker.

Test for Doneness—The length of cooking time for ham slices is not as flexible as for roasts. Ham will overcook if left in the slow cooker an additional hour. When done, a fully cooked ham slice will be tender.

REMINDERS—Use the appropriate size slow cooker as specified in each recipe.

For additional tips on slow cooking, see the introductory chapter, **Home Cooking in the Slow Cooker**, in the beginning of this book which also provides an easy-to-read chart comparing settings among different brands of slow cookers.

Spring Roast Half Ham *(page 144)*

Use a 5-qt. slow cooker.

For the Glaze—Follow ▲ Recipe. Or, substitute one-half recipe for *Pineapple Glaze* of **Spring Roast Ham.**

For Ham—Trim excess fat and score ham before cooking. Place ham in slow cooker and coat with glaze; cover.

Cook on LOW for 7 to 8 hrs.

Burgundy Roast Ham *(page 144)*

Use a 5-qt. slow cooker.

For Ham—Trim, score and insert cloves before cooking. Place glazed ham in slow cooker and add liquid; cover.

Cook on LOW for 10 to 11 hrs.

Pineapple-Glazed Canned Ham *(page 145)*

Use a 3½-qt. slow cooker; rack is optional.

Place ham in slow cooker and spoon on glaze; cover.

Cook on LOW for 7 to 8 hrs.

Cranberry-Glazed Canned Ham *(page 145)*

Follow **3** Recipe with substitutions as in △ Recipe.

Stuffed Ham Slices *(page 146)*

Use a 3½-qt. slow cooker.

Follow Recipe for assembling ham in slow cooker; cover.

Cook on LOW for 4 to 5 hrs.

Ham Balls in Sweet-Sour Sauce *(page 147)*

Use a 3½-qt. slow cooker.

Place ham balls in slow cooker and coat with hot sauce; cover.

Cook on LOW for 7 to 8 hrs.

Pineapple-Glazed Ham Loaf *(page 147)*

Use a 3½-qt. slow cooker.

Cover and cook on LOW for 6 to 7 hrs. (juices should run clear).

Remove by tilting slow cooker and lifting ham loaf with a spatula.

Bar-B-Q'd Pork Steaks

AAGOT HANSON, EAGLE GROVE, IOWA

Set out a large, shallow baking dish or roasting pan.

Wipe with a clean, damp cloth
6 pork steaks, arm or blade, cut ¾ to 1 in. thick
Heat in a heavy skillet over medium heat
1 teaspoon fat
Put steaks into skillet; brown on both sides over medium heat.

While steaks are browning, combine in a saucepan and heat to boiling
1½ cups ketchup
1½ cups water
¼ cup vinegar
¼ cup Worcestershire sauce
2 teaspoons salt
2 teaspoons chili powder
2 teaspoons paprika
1 teaspoon pepper
½ teaspoon Accent
Clean (*page 12*) and thinly slice
2 large (about ⅔ lb.) onions
Season the steaks with a mixture of
1 teaspoon salt
1 teaspoon Accent
¼ teaspoon pepper
Arrange steaks in the baking dish; cover with the onion slices. Pour sauce over all.

Bake at 350°F 50 to 60 min., or until pork is tender and *thoroughly* cooked. (To test for doneness, cut a slit near the bone; no pink color should be visible.) Baste frequently with sauce.

Serve with onion slices and sauce spooned over steaks. *6 servings*

Note: **Pork chops** may be substituted for the pork steaks.

Roast Loin of Pork

Roast Loin of Pork

What flavor surpasses crisp tawny roast pork?

Set out a roast meat thermometer and a shallow roasting pan.

Wipe with a clean, damp cloth
3- to 5-lb. pork loin roast
(Have meat dealer loosen chine bone.) Rub pork with a mixture of
4 teaspoons dry mustard
1 teaspoon salt
1 teaspoon Accent
¼ teaspoon pepper
Place pork, fat side up, in pan. (Bones form a natural rack.) Insert roast meat thermometer in center of thickest part of meat, being sure the bulb does not rest in fat or on bone.

Roast pork uncovered at 350°F 2 to 3 hours. (Allow 35 to 40 min. per pound.) Meat is done when internal temperature of meat reaches 185°F. Remove roast from oven; remove thermometer. Place roast on warm serving platter. Garnish as desired. *6 to 10 servings*

Orange Pork Chops

MRS. NEWMON A. SMITH, STEENS, MISS.

A grand-prize winner, this original recipe with everyday ingredients brings a burst of fresh flavor to an old favorite.

Set out a large, heavy skillet and a large, shallow baking dish or 2-qt. casserole having a tight-fitting cover.

Wipe with a clean, damp cloth
6 pork chops, cut about 1 in. thick
Heat in the skillet over medium heat
1 teaspoon fat
Put chops into skillet; brown on both sides.

Clean (*page 12*) and cut into ¼-in. slices and set aside
2 medium-size (about ½ lb.) onions
Blend together
¾ cup (6-oz. can) frozen orange juice concentrate, thawed
⅔ cup water
1 tablespoon lemon juice
and a mixture of
2 tablespoons brown sugar
1½ teaspoons ginger
1 teaspoon poultry seasoning
1 teaspoon marjoram
½ teaspoon Accent
½ teaspoon salt
Arrange the browned chops in the baking dish. Place onion slices on top of chops. Pour the orange juice mixture over the chops. Cover.

Bake at 350°F 1 hr., or until meat is tender and *thoroughly* cooked. (To test for doneness, cut slit near bone; no pink should be visible.)

6 servings

Pork Chops and Lima Beans

MILDRED HABASEK, BERWYN, ILL.

This dish proves that juicy pork chops and protein-rich limas were made for each other.

Set out a shallow 2-qt. casserole or baking dish and a large, heavy skillet.

Orange Pork Chops

Wipe with a clean, damp cloth
4 pork chops, cut ¾ to 1 in. thick
Heat in the skillet over medium heat
1 teaspoon fat
Put chops into skillet and brown lightly on both sides over medium heat.

While chops are browning, set aside to drain contents of
1 No. 2 can (2¼ cups, drained) lima beans
Drain, reserving liquid for use in other food preparation, contents of
1 No. 2 can tomatoes (about 1 cup, drained)
Sieve the tomatoes; mix in the casserole with the lima beans and
½ cup chopped onion (*page 12*)
1 tablespoon dark molasses
1 teaspoon salt
¼ teaspoon Accent
Season chops with a mixture of
2 teaspoons salt
1 teaspoon Accent
½ teaspoon pepper
Arrange the chops over the lima-bean mixture.

Bake at 350°F 1 hr., or until meat is tender and *thoroughly* cooked. (To test for doneness, cut a slit near the bone; no pink color should be visible.)

4 servings

Pennsylvania Pork Chops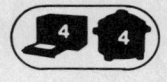

MRS. CAM ISAACSON, NORFOLK, NEBR.

A Pennsylvania Dutch recipe that will be appreciated wherever good cooking is prized.

Set out a large, shallow baking dish or a 2-qt. casserole having a tight-fitting cover.

Wipe with a clean, damp cloth
   4 pork chops, cut about 1 in. thick
Coat chops with a mixture of
   ¼ cup flour
   ½ teaspoon salt
   ½ teaspoon Accent
   ¼ teaspoon pepper
Heat in a large, heavy skillet over medium heat
   1 teaspoon fat
Put chops into skillet and brown on both sides over medium heat. Remove to baking dish.

Insert into each chop, near the bone
   Whole clove
Pour over the chops a mixture of
   ½ cup water
   2 tablespoons vinegar
   1 teaspoon sugar
Add
   1 bay leaf
Cover and bake at 350°F about 1 hr., or until chops are tender and *thoroughly* cooked. (To test for doneness, cut a slit near the bone; no pink color should be visible.) Remove dish from oven. Spread over chops
   ½ cup thick sour cream
Cover and bake about 15 min. longer.

Serve at once.   *4 servings*

Pork Chops 'n' Spaghetti Dinner

Set out a large, shallow baking dish having a tight-fitting cover.

Wipe with a clean, damp cloth
   6 pork chops, cut about ¾ in. thick
Heat in a large, heavy skillet
   1 teaspoon fat

Pork Chops 'n' Spaghetti Dinner

Place chops in skillet; brown on both sides over medium heat.

Meanwhile, cut into six rings
   1 medium-size green pepper (page 12)
Set aside.

Cut into six slices each
   1 large onion (page 12)
   1 lemon, rinsed
Set aside.

Mix together
   2 cups (No. 2 can) tomato juice
   1½ teaspoons salt
   ½ teaspoon Accent
   ¼ teaspoon pepper
Place browned chops in the baking dish. Top each chop with a green pepper ring, an onion slice and a lemon slice. Pour the seasoned tomato juice over the chops.

Cover and bake at 350°F 1 hr. or until meat is tender and *thoroughly* cooked. (To test for doneness, slit near bone; no pink color should be visible.)

Meanwhile, cook and drain (*page 277*)
   2 cups (8-oz. pkg.) spaghetti
Just before serving, remove and discard lemon slices from chops. Arrange chops and spaghetti on serving platter. Spoon part of the sauce over the chops; accompany with remaining sauce.   *6 servings*

Pork Chop Casserole

Grease a shallow, 2-qt. casserole having a tight-fitting cover.

Wipe with a clean, damp cloth
  6 pork chops, cut ¾ in. to 1 in. thick
Coat with a mixture of
  ½ cup flour
  1 teaspoon salt
  ½ teaspoon Accent
  ¼ teaspoon pepper
Heat in a large, heavy skillet over medium heat
  1 teaspoon fat
Place chops in skillet and brown on both sides over medium heat.

While chops brown, mix together and set aside
  ½ cup firmly packed brown sugar
  1 teaspoon salt
Wash, pare and cut crosswise into slices about ⅛ in. thick
  4 medium-size (about 1⅓ lbs.) sweet potatoes
Wash, quarter, core, pare and slice
  3 medium-size (about 1 lb.) tart apples (about 3 cups, sliced)
Arrange browned chops in casserole. Arrange one half of the potato slices in a layer over pork chops. Sprinkle with about 2 tablespoons of the brown sugar mixture. Top with one half the apples and sprinkle again with sugar mixture. Repeat layers.

Pour over layers
  ½ cup apple cider or juice
Cover casserole and bake at 350°F about 1 hr., or until pork is *thoroughly* cooked. Remove cover for last 15 min. of baking. To test for doneness, cut a slit near bone; no pink color should be visible.   *6 servings*

▲ Breaded Pork Chops

Set out a large, heavy skillet having a tight-fitting cover.

Wipe with a clean, damp cloth
  4 pork chops, cut about ¾ to 1 in. thick
Coat chops with a mixture of
  ¼ cup flour
  1 teaspoon salt
  ½ teaspoon Accent
  ¼ teaspoon pepper
Heat in the skillet over medium heat
  2 teaspoons fat
Meanwhile, dip the chops into a mixture of
  1 egg, slightly beaten
  2 tablespoons milk or water
Coat the chops with
  1 cup fine, dry bread or cracker crumbs
Place chops in skillet and brown on both sides over medium heat. Remove from heat and pour off any remaining fat. Slowly add to skillet
  ½ cup tomato juice or water
Cover skillet and cook over low heat 50 to 60 min., or until meat is tender and *thoroughly* cooked. Add small amounts of liquid as needed.

Pork always should be cooked until well done. Test for doneness by cutting a slit near the bone; no pink color should be visible.

4 servings

△ Braised Pork Chops

Follow ▲ Recipe. Omit dipping in egg mixture and coating with crumbs.

Pork Chops with Apple Dressing 6

MRS. VIRGIL E. HILLS, WARREN, ME.

Set out a large, heavy skillet. Lightly grease a 2-qt. casserole having a tight-fitting cover.

Wipe with a clean, damp cloth
   4 pork chops, cut about ¾ in. thick
Heat in the skillet over medium heat
   1 teaspoon fat
Put chops into skillet and brown on both sides.

While chops are browning, prepare dressing.

For Dressing—Heat in a small skillet over low heat
   1 tablespoon butter or margarine
Add and cook over medium heat until transparent, occasionally stirring
   ¼ cup chopped onion
Add the onion to a mixture of
   1 qt. (4 to 5 slices) soft bread cubes
   ¼ cup milk or water
   2 cups (2 large) chopped tart apples
   ¼ cup seedless raisins
   2 tablespoons sugar
   ¾ teaspoon salt
Toss lightly to mix thoroughly. Spoon dressing into the casserole.

Season the chops with a mixture of
   1 teaspoon salt
   1 teaspoon Accent
   ½ teaspoon pepper
Arrange chops on top of dressing.

Cover casserole and bake at 350°F about 1 hr. or until meat is tender and *thoroughly* cooked. (To test for doneness, cut a slit near the bone; no pink color should be visible.)

4 servings

Pork Chops with Dressing and Mushroom Sauce

▲ Pork Chops with Celery Stuffing 9 7

NORMA JEAN HALL, BURNS, TENN.

Set out a large, shallow baking dish and aluminum foil to cover.

Wipe with a clean, damp cloth
   6 rib pork chops cut 1 to 1¼ in. thick
   (have meat dealer cut pockets
   for stuffing)
Combine in a bowl and mix together lightly
   1 cup (1 slice) soft bread crumbs
   ½ cup chopped celery (page 12)
   2½ tablespoons melted butter or
   margarine
   2 tablespoons grated onion
and a mixture of
   ½ teaspoon sage
   ½ teaspoon Accent
   ¼ teaspoon salt
   ⅛ teaspoon pepper
   Few pieces oregano
Fill pocket of each chop with stuffing.

Heat in a large, heavy skillet over medium heat
   1 teaspoon fat
Place chops in skillet and brown on both sides.

Remove chops to baking dish. Add

½ cup hot water

Cover dish and bake at 350°F 1 hr., or until pork is tender and *thoroughly* cooked. (To test for doneness, cut a slit near bone; no pink color should be visible.)   *6 servings*

△ Pork Chops with Dressing and Mushroom Sauce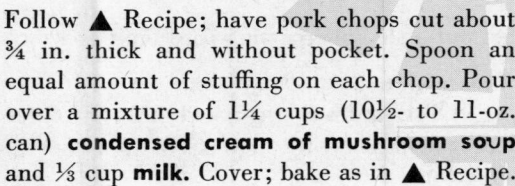

Follow ▲ Recipe; have pork chops cut about ¾ in. thick and without pocket. Spoon an equal amount of stuffing on each chop. Pour over a mixture of 1¼ cups (10½- to 11-oz. can) **condensed cream of mushroom soup** and ⅓ cup **milk.** Cover; bake as in ▲ Recipe.

Glazed Pork Chops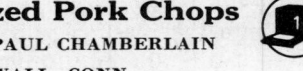

MRS. PAUL CHAMBERLAIN
CORNWALL, CONN.

Set out a large, shallow baking dish and aluminum foil to cover.

Wipe with a clean, damp cloth

6 pork chops, cut about 1 in. thick

Coat chops evenly with a mixture of

¼ cup flour
2 teaspoons salt
½ teaspoon Accent
¼ teaspoon pepper

Heat in a large, heavy skillet over medium heat

1 teaspoon fat

Place chops in skillet and brown lightly on both sides over medium heat. Remove to baking dish. Add

⅔ cup hot water
3 tablespoons minced onion
2 tablespoons minced parsley

Cover and bake at 350°F about 45 min.

While chops bake, mix together

½ cup apple jelly, broken in pieces with a fork
¼ cup hot water
¼ teaspoon cinnamon
¼ teaspoon cloves

Heat over simmering water, stirring occasionally, until jelly is melted.

Uncover baking dish and spread jelly glaze over the chops. Bake uncovered 20 min. longer, or until chops are tender and *thoroughly* cooked. (To test for doneness, cut a slit near the bone; no pink color should be visible.)
        6 servings

▲ Smoked Shoulder Butt

Set out a large, heavy sauce pot or kettle having a tight-fitting cover.

Wipe with a clean, damp cloth

Smoked boneless pork shoulder butt (about 2 lbs.)

Put shoulder butt into the sauce pot and add

Hot water (enough to cover meat)
1 teaspoon Accent
5 or 6 whole cloves
3 or 4 peppercorns
1 clove garlic (page 12)

Bring liquid to boiling; reduce heat, cover and simmer (do not boil) about 1½ hrs., or until meat is tender when pierced with a fork. (Allow 45 min. per lb.) If necessary, add more hot water during cooking period.

To serve, drain off excess liquid and slice.
        About 4 servings

△ Glazed Smoked Shoulder Butt Slices

Follow ▲ Recipe for cooking meat; omit garlic and Accent. Cut meat into slices ½ in. thick. Mix together ½ cup firmly packed **brown sugar,** 2 tablespoons **vinegar,** 1 tablespoon **prepared mustard,** and ⅛ teaspoon **cloves.** Drain one 9-oz. can **pineapple tidbits.** Set temperature control of range at Broil.

Arrange slices on broiler rack. Spread with brown-sugar mixture. Top with the pineapple and **maraschino cherry halves.** Put in broiler with tops 2 to 3 in. from heat source. Broil, basting occasionally with glaze, about 5 to 10 min. Serve hot.

Glazed Smoked Shoulder Butt

Glazed Smoked Shoulder Butt

It's the splash of beer in the glaze that gives such an indefinably wonderful taste to smoked butt prepared in this way. For a special treat serve with a big bowl of hot potato salad.

Set out a large, heavy sauce pot or kettle having a tight-fitting cover.

Wipe with a clean, damp cloth
>   **2 smoked boneless pork shoulder butts, about 1½ lbs. each**

Put shoulder butts into the sauce pot. Add
>   **Hot water (enough to cover meat)**
>   **6 whole cloves**
>   **4 peppercorns**

Bring liquid rapidly to boiling; reduce heat, cover and simmer (do not boil) 45 min. Cool meat in cooking liquid; drain.

Set out a shallow roasting pan with rack.

Place shoulder butts on rack. Stud tops with
>   **Whole cloves**

Blend together thoroughly
>   **1 cup thick applesauce**
>   **⅔ cup firmly packed brown sugar**
>   **½ cup beer**
>   **1 teaspoon cinnamon**
>   **¼ teaspoon nutmeg**

Spread mixture thickly over top and sides of each butt.

Bake at 350°F 1 hr., or until meat is tender when pierced with a fork.

Serve hot or cold with **caraway-seasoned sauerkraut** (1 teaspoon caraway seeds per No. 2½ can sauerkraut).   *About 6 servings*

Barbecued Spareribs 15

MRS. BOYD BENFIELD, NEWTON, N. C.

Set out a shallow roasting pan; omit rack.

Wipe with a clean, damp cloth
>   **4 lbs. spareribs, cracked through center**

Cut into serving-size pieces. Rub pieces with a mixture of
>   **1 tablespoon salt**
>   **1 teaspoon pepper**
>   **1 teaspoon Accent**

Put pieces into the roasting pan, meaty side up. Roast at 350°F 30 min., turning once.

Meanwhile, heat in a saucepan over low heat
>   **¼ cup butter or margarine**

Add
>   **1 cup finely chopped onion** (*page 12*)
>   **1 cup finely chopped celery** (*page 12*)

Cook over medium heat until onion is transparent, stirring occasionally. Add a mixture of
>   **2 cups ketchup**
>   **2 cups water**
>   **⅓ cup Worcestershire sauce**
>   **¼ cup vinegar**
>   **¼ cup firmly packed brown sugar**
>   **¼ teaspoon cayenne pepper**

Heat to boiling. Remove from heat. Stir in
>   **½ cup lemon juice**

Pour sauce over ribs; cover pan. Continue baking, basting frequently with the sauce, until meat is tender (1 to 1½ hrs.). If sauce becomes too thick, add more water. Uncover the last 15 to 20 min.   *6 to 8 servings*

154

Braised Spicy Spareribs

Set out a large, heavy skillet, and a roasting pan having a tight-fitting cover.

For Ribs—Wipe with a clean, damp cloth
    4 lbs. spareribs, cracked through center
Cut into serving-size pieces. Coat meat evenly with a mixture of
    ⅓ cup flour
    1 teaspoon salt
    1 teaspoon Accent
    ¼ teaspoon pepper
Heat in the skillet over medium heat
    3 tablespoons fat
Put ribs into skillet and brown on both sides over medium heat.

While meat is browning, prepare
    1½ cups quick meat broth (page 13)
Mix into the meat broth
    ¼ cup ketchup
    3 tablespoons Worcestershire sauce
    2 tablespoons vinegar
    ½ teaspoon celery salt
    ⅛ teaspoon cayenne pepper
    3 whole cloves
    3 whole allspice
    ½ bay leaf
    ½ clove garlic (page 12), minced; or crushed in a garlic press
Clean (*page 12*), finely chop and set aside
    1 medium-size onion
Put ribs into roasting pan. Pour the broth mixture over them. Add the chopped onion.

Cover and bake at 350°F about 1½ hrs., or until meat is tender.

With a slotted spoon, remove meat from pan to a warm serving platter. Set aside to keep warm while preparing sauce.

For Sauce—If necessary, skim excess fat from cooking liquid. Pour cooking liquid into a small saucepan and thicken (*p.107*; use 2 tablespoons flour and ¼ cup water). Spoon or pour about one half of the hot sauce over spareribs on the platter. Serve remaining sauce in a small bowl or gravy boat.   *6 to 8 servings*

Spareribs and Sauerkraut

MARY RAE STOTTS, SAPULPA, OKLA.

Set out a large, heavy skillet, and a roasting pan having a tight-fitting cover.

Wipe with a clean, damp cloth
    3 lbs. spareribs, cracked through center
Cut into serving-size pieces. Season with a mixture of
    2 teaspoons salt
    ½ teaspoon Accent
    ¼ teaspoon pepper
Heat in the skillet over medium heat
    1 tablespoon fat
Add the ribs and brown well on both sides over medium heat.

Put into the roasting pan contents of
    1 No. 2½ can (about 3½ cups) sauerkraut
Place the browned ribs over the kraut. Add
    ½ cup water
Cover and bake at 350°F 1½ hrs., or until meat is tender and thoroughly cooked.
    3 to 4 servings

Note: Two tablespoons **sugar** and ¾ teaspoon **caraway seed** may be mixed into the kraut.

Braised Spicy Spareribs

Baked Stuffed Spareribs

Baked Stuffed Spareribs 18

Set out a shallow roasting pan with rack.

Prepare
**Apple Stuffing for Spareribs
(page 218)**

Wipe with a clean, damp cloth
2 sections (about 4 lbs.) spareribs
Place one section on rack in roasting pan.

Mix thoroughly
1 teaspoon salt
½ teaspoon Accent
⅛ teaspoon pepper

Sprinkle one half of mixture over spareribs. Spread stuffing on rib section in pan. Cover with second section. Fasten the sections together with skewers. Sprinkle remaining seasoning mixture over top.

Roast at 350°F for 1½ hrs., or until meat is tender when pierced with a fork.

Remove skewers. Cut spareribs into serving-size pieces and serve with stuffing. Garnish as desired. *6 to 8 servings*

Note: To keep top section moist, spread with **applesauce** or cover with **sauerkraut**.

Hawaiian Pork Skillet 19
(Sweet-Sour Pork)
MRS. M. L. KERANEN, PELKIE, MICH.

Set out a large, heavy skillet, or top-of-range casserole, having a tight-fitting cover.

Wipe with a clean, damp cloth
1 lb. boneless pork shoulder
Cut meat into 1-in. pieces. Set aside.

Heat in the skillet over medium heat
1 teaspoon fat
Add the pork and brown lightly on all sides over medium heat. Add
2 tablespoons chopped onion
Continue cooking until onion is transparent, occasionally moving and turning mixture with a spoon.

Pour off excess fat. Add to the skillet
1 cup water
Bring liquid rapidly to boiling. Add
1 cup carrot pieces
¾ teaspoon Accent
Reduce heat; cover and simmer (do not boil) 25 min., or until carrots are almost tender and meat is *thoroughly* cooked. (Test meat for doneness by cutting through largest cube to center; no pink color should be visible.)

Meanwhile, cook and drain (*page 277*)
3 cups (4 oz.) broad noodles
Toss with the cooked noodles
1 tablespoon butter or margarine
Put on warm platter; set aside to keep warm.

Drain, reserving sirup, contents of
**1 14-oz. can pineapple chunks
(about 1⅓ cups, drained)**
Set aside.

Mix together in a small bowl or cup
2 tablespoons cornstarch
2 tablespoons brown sugar
1 teaspoon salt

Add gradually and blend in a mixture of the reserved pineapple sirup and

2 to 4 tablespoons lemon juice
2 teaspoons soy sauce

Gradually add the cornstarch mixture to the meat mixture stirring constantly. Continue cooking until sauce is smooth and thickened (about 5 min.). Blend in the pineapple chunks. Heat thoroughly. Serve over the buttered noodles. *4 servings*

△ **Sweet-Sour Pork**  **in Rice Rings**

Follow ▲ Recipe; cut meat into ½-in. cubes. Substitute 1 cup **green pepper strips,** for the carrots. Omit Noodles. Serve mixture in **Individual Rice Rings** (*page 276*).

Enchiladas

Rinse and cut into quarters

24 fresh hot red peppers

Put peppers into a bowl and cover with

1 qt. warm water

Allow peppers to soak 1 hr. While peppers are soaking, prepare Chorizo (meat filling).

For Chorizo—Mix together lightly

1½ lbs. ground lean pork
3 tablespoons vinegar
3 cloves garlic (*page 12*), minced; or crushed in a garlic press

and a mixture of

1½ tablespoons chili powder
1½ teaspoons salt

Heat in a large, heavy skillet over medium heat

1 tablespoon fat

Add meat mixture and cook until browned, breaking into small pieces with a fork or spoon. Remove contents of skillet to a bowl and set aside.

For Sauce—Transfer peppers and soaking water to a sieve or food mill placed over a bowl. Force peppers through sieve. Blend in

1 tablespoon oregano

Mix thoroughly in a large, heavy skillet the pepper mixture and

½ cup cooking oil

Bring mixture rapidly to boiling, stirring constantly. Reduce heat and simmer gently, stirring occasionally, about 15 min. to allow flavors to blend. Stir in

1 tablespoon salt
⅛ teaspoon cumin seed

Remove from heat.

To Complete Enchiladas—Set out a large, shallow baking pan and

18 tortillas

Grate and set aside

1½ lbs. Cheddar cheese (about 6 cups, grated)

Clean (*page 12*), finely chop and set aside

6 medium-size (about 1½ lbs.) onions

Heat in the skillet in which the meat was browned

1 teaspoon fat

Using a fork or slotted spoon, dip the tortillas into the red pepper sauce, one at a time. Fry tortillas in skillet, 1 or 2 at a time, until lightly browned on both sides. Add more fat as needed.

As the tortillas brown, remove from skillet and place in the baking pan. Generously spoon the Chorizo, the chopped onion, and half the grated cheese over tortillas. Roll up tightly and fasten with wooden picks. Turn so that fastened side is down. Pour remaining sauce over top and sprinkle with remaining cheese.

Bake at 375°F 10 to 15 min., or until cheese is bubbly and lightly browned. Place on a warm serving platter. Serve immediately.

8 to 10 servings

Note: **Canned hot red peppers** may be substituted for fresh peppers. Drain peppers and reserve liquid. Omit soaking. Combine the liquid with enough warm water to make 1 qt.

Pork 'n' Apple Balls

Set out a large, heavy skillet having a tight-fitting cover.

Coarsely grate
   1 medium-size pared apple (about ⅔ cup, grated)
Combine with apple and mix lightly
   1 lb. ground pork
   ½ cup (½ slice) soft bread crumbs
   2 teaspoons minced onion
   1 egg yolk, beaten
and a mixture of
   ½ teaspoon Accent
   ¼ teaspoon mace
   ¼ teaspoon nutmeg
   ⅛ teaspoon salt
   ⅛ teaspoon pepper
Shape into balls about 1½ in. in diameter.

Coat pork balls by rolling in
   ¼ cup flour
Heat in the skillet over medium heat
   2 tablespoons fat
Put pork balls in skillet and brown over medium heat, turning them occasionally to brown on all sides. Remove skillet from heat and add
   ¼ cup hot water
Return to heat, cover and simmer about 30 min., turning meat balls occasionally.

When meat balls are cooked, remove them from skillet with slotted spoon; arrange them in serving dish and set aside to keep warm.

Pour fat from skillet into a cup; return 2 tablespoons of the fat to skillet. Blend in
   3 tablespoons flour
   ½ teaspoon salt
   ⅛ teaspoon pepper
Heat until mixture bubbles. Remove from heat and add gradually, stirring constantly
   2 cups quick meat broth (double recipe, page 13)
Return to heat and bring rapidly to boiling, stirring constantly. Cook 1 to 2 min. longer.

Pour into a warm gravy server. Serve hot.

4 to 6 servings

Frankfurters with Green Pepper and Tomatoes

Set out a large, heavy skillet having a tight-fitting cover.

Heat in the skillet over low heat
   ¼ cup butter
Add and cook over medium heat until onion is transparent, occasionally moving and turning mixture with a spoon
   4 medium-size green peppers (*page 12*), cut in lengthwise strips
   2 medium-size onions (*page 12*), thinly sliced
Meanwhile, rinse, cut out and discard stem ends and cut into slices
   4 large, ripe tomatoes (or use 1½ cups, No. 2 can, drained tomatoes)
Add tomatoes to the skillet. Season the vegetables with a mixture of
   1½ teaspoons salt
   ½ teaspoon Accent
   ¼ teaspoon paprika
   ⅛ teaspoon pepper
Cover skillet and simmer 15 min.

Meanwhile, cut into 1-in. pieces
   8 frankfurters
Add frankfurter pieces to skillet and mix gently with the vegetables; cover skillet and cook about 10 min., or until frankfurters are thoroughly heated.   *6 or 7 servings*

▲ Frilly Frankfurters 23

Set out an 11¾x7½x1¾-in. baking dish.

Prepare
1 cup Whipped Potatoes (one-fourth recipe, page 298)

Add and mix thoroughly
¼ cup finely chopped onion
¼ cup chopped sweet pickle
3 tablespoons chopped pimiento
Set aside.

Make a lengthwise slit almost through
6 frankfurters
Open the slit frankfurters and spread the cut surfaces with
¼ cup prepared mustard
Arrange frankfurters in the baking dish with cut surfaces up; pile potato mixture lightly over top.

Bake at 350°F 20 min., or until lightly browned.

For Broiling—Arrange frankfurters on broiler rack. Pile whipped potato mixture lightly on frankfurters.

Set temperature control of range at Broil.

Place broiler rack in broiler with top of potatoes 4 to 5 in. from source of heat; broil 7 to 8 min., or until lightly browned.   *6 servings*

△ Franks with Cheese Frills 24

Follow ▲ Recipe. Omit chopped ingredients. Blend the Whipped Potatoes with ¾ cup (3 oz.) grated **Cheddar cheese**. Bake or broil as in ▲ Recipe.

Note: To prepare frankfurters on an outdoor grill see OUTDOOR COOKING (*page 204*).

Bacon-Wrapped Frankfurters

Set out a large, shallow baking dish.

Set out
12 slices bacon
Cut almost through lengthwise
12 frankfurters
Mix together
1 cup sweet pickle relish
2 tablespoons prepared mustard
Fill the frankfurters with the relish mixture. Starting at one end, wrap one slice of bacon around each frankfurter; secure ends with wooden picks. Put frankfurters in baking dish.

Bake at 375°F 25 min., or until bacon is crisp.
6 servings

Pigskin Special 25
(Ground "Frank" Meat Loaf)
MRS. W. L. ISBELL, BROOKSTON, IND.

Lightly grease a 9½x5¼x2¾-in. baking pan.

Grind (*page 107*) and put into a bowl
1 lb. frankfurters
Add and mix thoroughly
1 cup (3 slices) fine, dry bread crumbs
2 tablespoons finely chopped onion
2 tablespoons chopped green pepper
½ teaspoon sage
1 cup milk
2 eggs, beaten
Pack mixture lightly into the baking dish.

Bake at 350°F 45 min. Pour off excess liquid and unmold (*page 107*).

Spread over top of loaf
2 tablespoons ketchup or chili sauce
Serve loaf hot or cold.   *About 6 servings*

Glazed Canadian-Style Bacon

Place on a rack in a shallow baking pan
1½ lbs. Canadian-style bacon (one piece)
Insert in upper surface
10 to 12 whole cloves
Spread over surface a mixture of
¼ cup firmly packed brown sugar
1½ tablespoons dry mustard
Roast uncovered at 300°F 30 min.

Pour over meat
½ cup apple cider or juice
Basting occasionally, continue cooking 15 to 25 min. longer, or until meat is tender.

6 servings

▲ Cranberry-Glazed Canadian-Style Bacon

Arrange in an 11¾x7½x1¾-in. baking dish
10 slices (about 1 lb.) Canadian-style bacon, cut about ¼ in. thick
Sprinkle slices with a mixture of
1 tablespoon grated orange peel (page 11)
½ teaspoon sugar
⅛ teaspoon cloves
Few grains nutmeg
Spread over slices
1 cup whole cranberry sauce
Bake uncovered at 350°F about 25 min.

5 servings

Broiled Canadian-Style Bacon with peaches

△ Broiled Canadian-Style Bacon

Follow ▲ Recipe for amount of Canadian-style bacon. Set temperature control of range at Broil. Arrange slices on broiler rack. Place in broiler with top of meat 3 in. from source of heat. Broil about 5 min. on each side, or until browned. Spoon about ½ cup whole **cranberry sauce** into cavities of 5 **canned peach halves** and place on broiler rack after bacon is turned.

Note: Any **jelly** may be used to glaze Canadian-style bacon or to fill cavities of peaches.

Gourmet Canadian-Style Bacon

Lightly grease 4 ramekins.

Clean, separate into flowerets, soak and cook (*page 285*)
1 medium-size head cauliflower
Brush a cold skillet with
Melted fat
Arrange in the skillet
8 slices (about ⅔ lb.) Canadian-style bacon, cut about ¼ in. thick
Cook slowly, browning on each side. Pour off any fat that collects during cooking. Place 2 slices in each ramekin.

Shred and set aside
8 oz. process American cheese (2 cups, shredded)
Prepare
2 cups Medium White Sauce (double recipe, page 323)
Cool sauce slightly. Add three-fourths of the cheese all at one time; stir until blended. Add
1 tablespoon onion juice
½ teaspoon paprika
Divide cauliflower evenly among ramekins. Pour sauce over cauliflower in each ramekin.

Bake at 350°F 10 min.

Sprinkle with the remaining cheese and
½ cup buttered crumbs (page 10)
Return to oven and bake 10 min. longer, or
until cheese is melted and crumbs are lightly
browned. *4 servings*

Panbroiled Bacon 30

(See photo on page 72)

Cooking at one time only as many slices as
will lie flat in skillet, place in a cold skillet
½ lb. bacon slices
Cook slowly over low heat, turning bacon frequently. Pour off fat as it collects. When
bacon is evenly crisped and browned, remove
from skillet and drain on absorbent paper.
Serve hot. *10 to 12 slices bacon*

▲ Little Sausages with Apple Rings 31

Prepare
**24 Panbroiled Link Sausages
(on this page)**
Remove links to absorbent paper. Keep warm.
Drain any remaining fat from skillet and wipe
skillet with absorbent paper.

For Apple Rings—Wash and core
4 medium-size (about 1⅓ lbs.) apples
Cut each apple crosswise into about 5 slices
(½ to ¾ in. thick). Place apple slices flat in
the skillet. Add
⅓ cup pineapple juice
Set over medium heat. Cover and cook about
5 min. on one side. Turn slices and cook about
5 min. longer, or until slices are tender.
Remove from skillet and serve with sausage
links. *6 to 8 servings*

△ Little Sausages with Glazed Apple Rings 32

Follow ▲ Recipe for preparing sausage links.

Little Sausages with Apple Rings

For Glazed Apple Rings—Melt in a small
skillet over low heat ¼ cup **butter** and ¼ cup
firmly packed **brown sugar**. Add **apple rings**
and cook about 5 min. on one side. Carefully
coat slices with sirup and cook until tender.

Panbroiled Sausage Patties 33

Shape into 5 or 6 flat patties and put into a
cold skillet
1 lb. bulk pork sausage
(Or put sausage into skillet and break into
pieces with fork.) Add
3 tablespoons water
Cover and cook slowly 5 min. Remove cover.
Pour off fat. Brown, turning occasionally. Pour
off fat as it collects. Cook 20 to 30 min., or
until browned. Remove to absorbent paper.
5 or 6 sausage patties

Panbroiled Link Sausages 34

Put into a large cold skillet
12 (about ¾ lb.) link sausages
Add
2 tablespoons water
Cover and cook slowly 8 to 10 min. Remove
cover and pour off fat. Brown links over
medium heat, turning as necessary (do not
prick links with a fork). Remove links to
absorbent paper to drain.

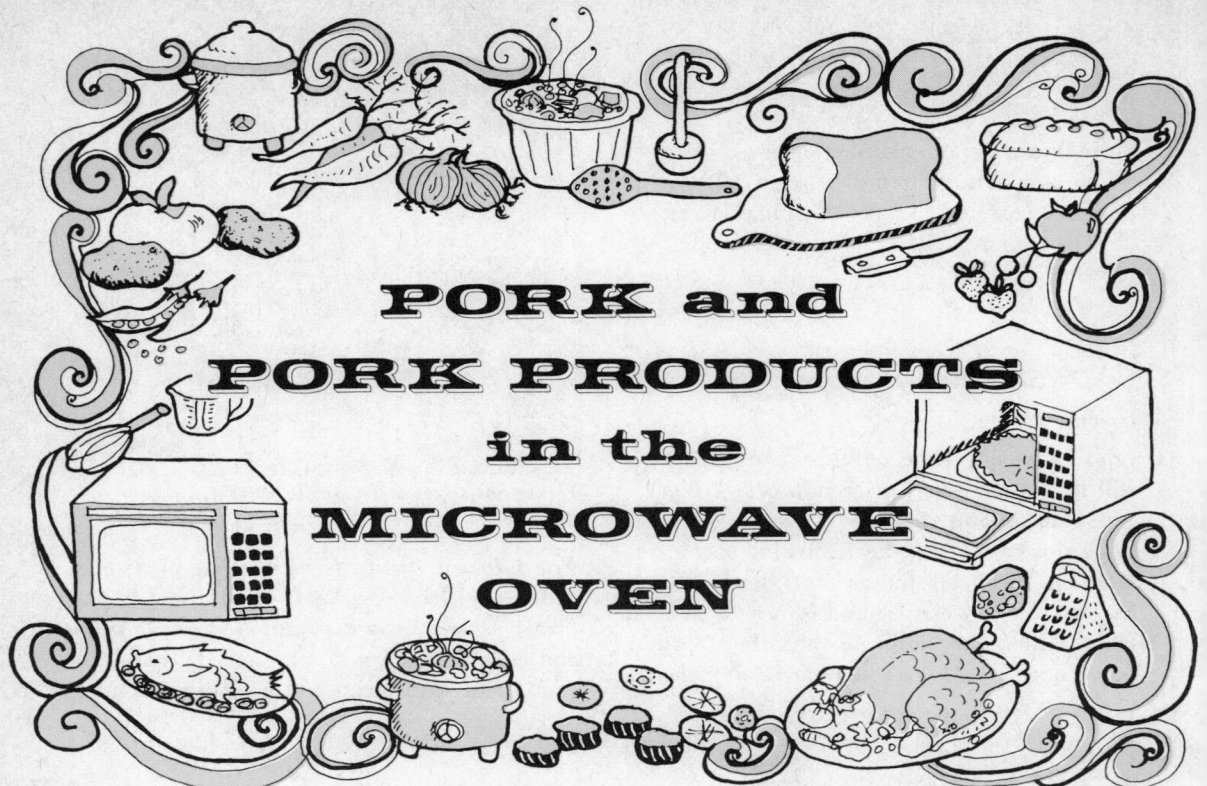

PORK and PORK PRODUCTS in the MICROWAVE OVEN

Pork is generally exceptionally good when prepared in the microwave oven. In fact, when properly timed, it is superior to conventional oven cooking.

Timing does require some finesse and co-ordination. Pork must be well done, but like all meats from the microwave oven, it must stand, covered, for some minutes after being removed from the oven. It will continue cooking while standing and thus runs the risk of becoming overdone. As a general rule, if meat is removed from the oven when it is slightly tender but juices run clear (there should be no pink) it should then become more tender, but not over-done, while standing. Each recipe in this section specifies the amount of standing time necessary.

Browning—Many of the recipes, such as those for chops, require browning. Preheat the browning skillet first (about 3 min.), then add the meat and cover the skillet for most effective browning. Use plastic wrap if no other cover is available. You may have to brown chops in more than one batch.

Roasts—The microwave oven makes the best **Roast Loin of Pork** we have ever tasted!

Roasts should be cooked fat side down, which is the reverse of starting roasts in the conventional oven. Then, turn the roast half-way through the cooking time to insure even cooking. Boneless and bone-in roasts require about the same amount of time, but the bone-less roasts cook more evenly.

Chops, Steaks and Other Cuts—For chops, the exact *OVERALL COOKING TIME* depends on the thickness of the chops. If they are thinner than suggested in the recipe, decrease the SLOWCOOK time and check for doneness every 2 minutes when they are nearly cooked.

The **Braised Spicy Spareribs** are juicy and flavorful, even though it is usually hard to capture a barbecue-type flavor in the microwave oven. The **Barbecued Spareribs** have more of that flavor if marinated overnight. The spareribs, incidentally, can be very successfully reheated without drying.

FRANKFURTERS—The frankfurters are also

flavorful and juicy when cooked in the micro-wave oven, but can overcook easily. Check for doneness each time you rotate the pan or stir.

BACON AND SAUSAGE—Cooking bacon in the microwave oven will turn you into a bacon addict. With paper towelling to absorb the grease and a cooking time of about 1 minute per slice, it seems to be asking too much to also expect a flavor bonus. But the crisp, unshriv-elled texture and flavor of bacon cooked with the microwave method is a revelation to any-one who has not tried it and a continuing joy to those who have.

The flavor of sausages is well-preserved with

microwave oven cooking. But, they do not brown as they do on the stove, so check for doneness by piercing with a fork. Juices should run clear; there should be no pink in the center.

REMINDERS—Cooking times on all recipes will vary slightly depending on your oven and, to some extent, your taste. Just be sure the pork is well done. The standing times indicated with each recipe are minimum times.

The introductory chapter, **Home Cooking in the Microwave Oven**, in the beginning of this book offers additional tips and an easy-to-read chart comparing settings among different brands of microwave ovens.

Roast Loin of Pork **1**
(page 148)

Use a glass roasting pan and a rack. The times in this recipe are for a 4-lb. pork loin roast. (For a roast of a different size, SLOWCOOK approxi-mately 7 min. per lb. before you begin testing for doneness.)

Place meat on rack, fat side down. COOK to heat through (10 min.).

SLOWCOOK, turning after 10 min., until meat thermometer registers 170° (about 30 min.). (Roast may be removed to test temperature and returned to oven without affecting cooking pro-cedure. Cover with aluminum foil while waiting for thermometer to register. If you must return meat to oven, be sure to remove the aluminum foil and the thermometer, if you are not using the special microwave thermometer.) When the roast is done, remove it and cover with alumin-um foil.

Let stand, covered, 20 min.(To insure the meat is thoroughly cooked, recheck the internal tem-perature. It should rise to 185° during the standing time.)
OVERALL COOKING TIME: 40:00

Orange Pork Chops **2**
(page 149)

Use a browning skillet. You may have to brown the chops in batches.

Preheat skillet (3 min.). Add fat and COOK until melted.

Add meat, cover and COOK until brown on both sides (3 min. each side). Repeat with re-maining chops. Return all chops to skillet.

Add onions and orange juice mixture. COOK to heat (5 min.).

SLOWCOOK, rotating pan every 5 min., until meat is *thoroughly* cooked (15 min.).

Cover and let stand 10 min.

Serve as in Recipe.
OVERALL COOKING TIME: 35:00

Pork Chops and Lima Beans **3** *(page 149)*

Use a browning skillet and a 2-qt. casserole. You may have to brown the chops in batches.

Preheat skillet (3 min.). Add fat and COOK until melted.

Add chops, cover and COOK until brown on each side (3 min. each side). Repeat with remaining chops. Transfer all chops to casserole containing remaining ingredients; season.

COOK to heat (5 min.).

SLOWCOOK, rotating pan every 5 min., until meat is *thoroughly* cooked (about 10 min.).

Cover and let stand 10 min.

OVERALL COOKING TIME: 30:00

Pennsylvania Pork **4**
Chops *(page 150)*

Use a browning skillet and a 2-qt. covered casserole. You may have to brown the chops in batches.

Set out sour cream to come to room temperature.

Preheat skillet (3 min.). Add fat and cook until melted.

Add chops, cover and COOK until brown on both sides (about 3 min. each side). Repeat with remaining chops. Transfer all chops to casserole.

Add liquid and seasonings. COOK to heat (5 min.).

SLOWCOOK, rotating pan every 5 min., until *thoroughly* cooked (about 10 min.).

Top with sour cream.

Cover and let stand 10 min. (Sour cream will heat while standing.)

OVERALL COOKING TIME: 30:00

Pork Chops 'n' **5**
Spaghetti Dinner *(page 150)*

Use a browning skillet and a 2-qt. casserole. You may have to brown the chops in batches.

Preheat skillet (3 min.). Add fat and COOK until melted.

Add meat, cover and COOK until brown on both sides (3 min. each side). Repeat with remaining chops.

Arrange all chops, vegetables, lemon and sauce in casserole. COOK until heated (5 min.).

SLOWCOOK, rotating pan every 5 min., until meat is *thoroughly* cooked (about 15 min.).

Cover and let stand 10 min.

Serve as in Recipe.

Pork Chop Casserole **6**
(page 151)

Use a browning skillet and a 2-qt. casserole. You may have to brown the chops in batches.

Preheat skillet (3 min.). Add fat and COOK until melted.

Add coated meat, cover and COOK until brown on both sides (3 min. each side). Repeat with remaining chops.

Assemble casserole. COOK to heat (5 min.).

SLOWCOOK, rotating pan every 5 min., until meat is *thoroughly* cooked (about 20 min.).

Cover and let stand 15 min.

OVERALL COOKING TIME: 40:00

Breaded Pork Chops **7**
(page 151)

Use a browning skillet. You may have to brown the chops in batches.

Preheat skillet (3 min.). Add fat and COOK until melted.

Add breaded chops, cover and COOK to brown on both sides (5 min. each side). Repeat with remaining chops. Return all chops to skillet.

Add liquid and SLOWCOOK, rotating pan every 5 min., until meat is *thoroughly* cooked (about 25 min.).

Cover and let stand 10 min.

OVERALL COOKING TIME: 38:00

Braised Pork Chops **8**
(page 151)

Follow **7** Recipe with changes as in △ Recipe, except to brown, COOK about 3 min. each side. SLOWCOOK about 12 min.

Pork Chops with **9**
Celery Stuffing *(page 152)*

Use a browning skillet and a large glass baking dish. You may have to brown the chops in batches.

Preheat skillet (3 min.). Add fat and COOK until melted.

Add meat, cover and COOK to brown on both sides (3 min. each). Repeat with remaining chops.

Stuff chops, add liquid and COOK to heat (5 min.).

SLOWCOOK, rotating pan every 3 min., until meat is tender and *thoroughly* cooked (about 6 min.).

Cover and let stand 15 min.

OVERALL COOKING TIME: 26:00

Pork Chops with **10**
Dressing and Mushroom
Sauce *(page 153)*

Follow **9** Recipe with changes as in △ Recipe, except SLOWCOOK, rotating every 5 min., until meat is *thoroughly* cooked (about 20 min.).

Glazed Pork Chops **11**
(page 153)

Use a browning skillet and a large glass baking dish. You may have to brown the chops in batches.

Preheat skillet (3 min.). Add fat and COOK until melted.

Add seasoned chops, cover and COOK until brown on both sides (3 min. each side). Repeat with remaining chops. Transfer to baking dish.

Add hot water, onion and parsley. COOK to heat (5 min.).

SLOWCOOK, rotating pan every 5 min., until meat is *thoroughly* cooked (about 15 min.).

Assemble glaze ingredients. COOK to melt jelly. Spread glaze on chops.

COOK, uncovered, until liquid simmers (about 5 min.).

Cover and let stand 10 min.

OVERALL COOKING TIME: 42:00

Smoked Shoulder Butt **12**
(page 153)

Use a covered casserole.

Assemble, cover and COOK until tender (about 15 min.).

Cover and let stand 5 min.

Serve as in ▲ Recipe.

OVERALL COOKING TIME: 15:00

Glazed Smoked Shoulder Butt Slices (page 153)

Use a glass baking dish.

Follow 12 Recipe with changes as in △ Recipe, except only one-half the butt slices will fit into the baking dish.

Arrange slices and fruit in baking dish. COOK, rotating pan and brushing with glaze every 3 min., until browned and hot (about 6 min.).

Cover and let stand 5 min.

OVERALL COOKING TIME: 6:00

Glazed Smoked Shoulder Butt (page 154) 14

Use a covered casserole or a baking dish; rack is optional.

Add meat and spiced liquid to casserole. COOK until heated (8 min.). SLOWCOOK until nearly done (about 12 min.).

Let meat stand until cool (about 15 min.).

Return to baking dish; glaze.

COOK until heated and tender (about 10 min.).

Cover and let stand 5 min.

Serve as in Recipe.

OVERALL COOKING TIME: 30:00

Barbecued Spareribs 15 (page 154)

Use a browning skillet and a glass baking dish.

First, prepare sauce. Preheat skillet (3 min.). Add butter or margarine and COOK until melted.

Add onions and celery, cover and COOK until onions are transparent (about 5 min.). Add remaining ingredients, including lemon juice.

Place seasoned ribs in the baking dish and coat with the sauce; cover.

COOK, rotating pan every 5 min., until meat is tender (about 20 min.).

Cover and let stand 10 min.

OVERALL COOKING TIME: 28:00

Braised Spicy Spareribs 16 (page 155)

Use a browning skillet and a covered glass baking dish. You may have to brown ribs in batches.

Preheat skillet (3 min.). Add fat and COOK until melted.

Add ribs, cover and COOK until browned on both sides (5 min. each side). Repeat with remaining ribs. Transfer all ribs to baking dish.

Add broth mixture and onion. Cover and COOK to heat (5 min.).

SLOWCOOK, rotating pan every 3 min., until tender (about 12 min.).

Cover and let stand 10 min.

OVERALL COOKING TIME: 30:00

Spareribs and Sauerkraut (page 155) 17

Use a browning skillet and a glass baking dish. You may have to brown ribs in batches.

Preheat skillet (3 min.). Add fat and COOK until melted.

Add ribs, cover and COOK until brown on both sides (5 min. each side). Repeat with remaining ribs. Transfer all ribs to baking dish.

Add sauerkraut and water, cover and COOK to heat (5 min.).

SLOWCOOK, rotating pan every 3 min., until tender (about 9 min.).

Cover and let stand 10 min.
OVERALL COOKING TIME: 37:00

Baked Stuffed Spareribs **18**
(page 156)

Use a glass roasting pan with rack.

Fasten spareribs with wooden picks or skewers. *Do not use metal.*

COOK until heated (5 min.). SLOWCOOK, rotating pan every 5 min., until meat is tender (about 20 min.).

Cover and let stand 10 min.
OVERALL COOKING TIME: 25:00

Hawaiian Pork Skillet **19**
(page 156)

Use a browning skillet.

Preheat skillet (3 min.). Add fat and COOK until melted.

Add pork and COOK, turning meat every 1 min., until brown (about 3 min.).

Add onion and COOK until onion is transparent (about 3 min.).

Add water and COOK until simmering (about 5 min.).

Add carrot and Accent and SLOWCOOK, rotating pan every 3 min., until meat is *thoroughly* cooked (about 12 min.).

Blend in cornstarch mixture and COOK, stirring every 1 min., until thickened (about 2½ min.).

Add pineapple and COOK to heat (1½ min.).

Cover and let stand 10 min.
OVERALL COOKING TIME: 30:00

Sweet-Sour Pork in Rice Rings **20** *(page 157)*

Follow **19** Recipe with changes as in △ Recipe.

Pork 'n' Apple Balls **21**
(page 158)

Use a browning skillet. You may have to brown pork balls in batches.

Preheat skillet (3 min.). Add fat and COOK until melted.

Add pork balls and COOK, stirring and turning pan every 2 min., until browned (about 8 min.). Repeat with remaining pork balls. Return all pork balls to skillet.

Add water and COOK, turning every 3 min., until simmering (about 6 min.).

SLOWCOOK, turning pork balls and rotating pan every 3 min. until done (about 9 min.).

For gravy, COOK flour mixture, stirring every 1 min., until simmering (about 3 min.). Stir in broth mixture and SLOWCOOK, stirring every 1 min., until simmering (about 2 min.).

Cover and let stand 10 min.
OVERALL COOKING TIME: 31:00

Frankfurters with Green Pepper and Tomatoes *(page 158)* **22**

Use a browning skillet.

Place butter in skillet and COOK until melted. Add onions and COOK, stirring every 2 min., until onion is transparent (about 4 min.).

Add peppers and COOK until wilted (about 2 min.).

Add tomatoes and seasonings and COOK, stirring every 2 min., until simmering (about 4 min.).

Add frankfurters and COOK, stirring every 3 min., until thoroughly heated (about 6 min.).
OVERALL COOKING TIME: 16.00

Frilly Frankfurters **23**
(page 159)

Use a glass baking dish.

COOK until thoroughly heated (about 8 min.).
OVERALL COOKING TIME: 8:00

Franks with Cheese Frills *(page 159)* **24**

Follow **23** Recipe with changes as in △ Recipe.

Pigskin Special *(page 159)* **25**

Use a glass baking dish. Lightly grease pan with shortening.

SLOWCOOK, rotating pan every 2 min., until set and thoroughly heated.
OVERALL COOKING TIME: 8:00

Glazed Canadian-Style Bacon *(page 160)* **26**

Use a glass baking dish.

Add liquid with sugar mixture.

COOK, basting and rotating pan every 2 min., until tender (about 10 min.).
OVERALL COOKING TIME: 10:00

Cranberry-Glazed Canadian-Style Bacon *(page 160)* **27**

Use a glass baking dish.

COOK, rotating pan every 3 min., until tender (about 6 min.).
OVERALL COOKING TIME: 6:00

Broiled Canadian-Style Bacon *(page 160)* **28**

Use a glass baking dish.

Follow **27** Recipe with changes as in △ Recipe, except use only 8 slices Canadian-style bacon and 4 canned peach halves.

COOK, until slightly brown on both sides (3 min. each side).

Arrange sauce-topped fruit in baking dish and COOK until heated through (about 5 min.).
OVERALL COOKING TIME: 8:00

Gourmet Canadian-Style Bacon (page 160) 29

Use a browning skillet and 4 glass ramekins.

Melt fat. COOK bacon until lightly browned on both sides (3 min. each side).

Assemble ramekins, including crumbs and cheese, and COOK until heated and cheese is melted (about 5 min.).

OVERALL COOKING TIME: 11:00

Panbroiled Bacon 30
(page 161)

Use 1 or 2 layers of paper towelling.

Lay strips of bacon on top of paper towelling. COOK to taste (about 1 min. per strip of bacon). Paper towelling may also be placed on top of the bacon to prevent spattering.

OR,

If bacon drippings are needed for cooking other ingredients, place bacon flat in browning skillet or baking dish. COOK and turn when the bacon starts to shrink (about 1 min. per slice).

Little Sausages with Apple Rings (page 161) 31

Use a browning skillet.

For Apple Rings—Prepare 6 per batch. COOK until lightly browned on each side.

Little Sausages with Glazed Apple Rings (page 161) 32

Use a browning skillet.

For Glazed Apple Rings—Place butter in skillet and COOK until melted. Add brown sugar, stir.

Add apple rings, coat with sirup and COOK, uncovered, until tender (about 5 min.).

Panbroiled Sausage Patties (page 161) 33

Use a browning skillet.

Place sausages and water in skillet. Cover and COOK until simmering (about 5 min.). Pour off fat and water.

COOK, turning patties and rotating pan every 2 min., until lightly browned and juice is clear (about 8 min.).

OVERALL COOKING TIME: 13:00

Panbroiled Link Sausages (page 161) 34

Use a browning skillet.

Place sausages and water in skillet and COOK until simmering (about 5 min.). Pour off fat and water.

COOK, turning links and rotating pan every 3 min., until lightly browned and juice is clear (about 9 min.).

OVERALL COOKING TIME: 14:00

PORK and PORK PRODUCTS in the SLOW COOKER

Pork has always been a meat to cook in a leisurely fashion, but using the slow cooker seems to elicit a rich and satisfying flavor that in the conventional oven only constant attention will produce. The meat is tender, the texture firm. Even pork chops, which so easily dry out when pan frying or baking, remain juicy and tender. However, they do have a potted, stew-like texture, rather than baked or braised.

All the recipes included here are good, but the **Smoked Shoulder Butt** is extraordinary; it tastes as delicious as far more expensive ham.

We emphasize two things. First, meat must be well-trimmed, particularly steaks and chops. Leave no more than 1/8 in. of fat bordering these cuts. Sauces, particularly for dishes using cuts such as pork shoulder where fat cannot be trimmed, should be carefully skimmed.

Browning is called for in some recipes. Meats will not really brown in the slow cooker, but if the meat is well-coated with fat while the slow cooker is set on HIGH, the final results are good.

When a recipe in the main text directs that meat be coated with a flour-spice mixture before browning, omit the flour. The flour will not brown and the slow heat will only turn it into a gluten paste.

FRANKFURTERS, SAUSAGE AND BACON are not foods well-suited to the slow cooker. Frankfurters tend to get mushy. Sausages and bacon give off too much fat. We do include one bacon recipe, the **Glazed Canadian-Style Bacon,** because it more closely resembles ham. It is excellent.

REMINDERS—Each recipe in this section notes the appropriate-size slow cooker.

The introductory chapter, **Home Cooking in the Slow Cooker,** offers additional tips and a handy chart comparing settings among different brands of slow cookers. We suggest you review this chapter to also learn how we have adapted these recipes.

Bar-B-Q'd Pork Steaks
(page 148)

Use a 5-qt. slow cooker. Slice onions very thin.

Place fat in slow cooker and melt on HIGH. Add meat and turn to coat evenly with fat. Season steaks. Add all other ingredients.

Cook on LOW for 8 to 9 hrs.

Orange Pork Chops
(page 149)

Use a 5-qt. slow cooker. Slice onions very thin.

Place fat in slow cooker and melt on HIGH. Add chops and turn to coat evenly with fat.

Place onions on top of the chops.

Combine remaining ingredients and pour over chops.

Cook on LOW for 6 to 7 hrs.

Pork Chops and Lima Beans *(page 149)*

Use a 3½-qt. slow cooker.

Place fat in slow cooker and melt on HIGH. Add seasoned chops and turn to coat evenly with fat.

Add lima beans, tomatoes, onions and all sauce ingredients; cover.

Cook on LOW for 6½ to 7½ hrs.

Pennsylvania Pork Chops *(page 150)*

Use a 3½-qt. slow cooker.

Place fat in slow cooker and melt on HIGH. Season chops, except omit the flour, and turn to coat evenly with fat. Add seasoning and liquid.

Cook on LOW for 7½ to 8½ hrs.

Spread sour cream and turn to HIGH until hot.

Braised Pork Chops
(page 151)

Use a 3½-qt. slow cooker.

Place fat in slow cooker and melt on HIGH. Season chops, except omit the flour, and turn to coat evenly with fat. Add liquid.

Cook on LOW for 6 to 7 hrs.

Pork Chops with Apple Dressing *(page 152)*

Use a 3½-qt. slow cooker.

Place fat in slow cooker and melt on HIGH. Add meat and turn to coat evenly with fat.

Assemble casserole, placing chops on top

Cook on LOW for 7 to 8 hrs.

Pork Chops with Celery Stuffing *(page 152)*

Use a 3½-qt. slow cooker.

Place fat in slow cooker and melt on HIGH. Add seasoned chops and turn to coat evenly with fat. Add water and cover.

Cook on LOW for 8 to 9 hrs.

Smoked Shoulder Butt
(page 153)

Use a 3½-qt. slow cooker.

Add liquid to cover meat by two-thirds; cover.

Cook on LOW for 6 to 7 hrs.

Glazed Canadian-Style Bacon *(page 160)*

Use a 3½-qt. slow cooker.

Place clove-studded bacon in slow cooker. Add sugar-mustard mixture and apple cider; cover.

Cook on LOW for 6 to 7 hrs.

Veal Shoulder Roll Surprise

Stuffed Roast Breast of Veal

MRS. L. A. KING, JACKSONVILLE, FLA.

Set out a shallow roasting pan with rack.

Wipe with a clean, damp cloth
   3 to 4-lb. breast of veal with pocket
(Have meat dealer cut meat away from ribs to form a pocket for stuffing.) Rub roast with a mixture of
   1¼ teaspoons salt
   ¾ teaspoon Accent
Set meat aside.

Clean, cook (*page 285*) and drain
   1 lb. spinach
Mix the cooked spinach with
   3 cups (3 slices) soft bread cubes
   ½ cup (2 oz.) grated Cheddar cheese
   ¼ cup milk
   2 tablespoons butter or margarine
   ½ teaspoon minced parsley
and a mixture of
   ½ teaspoon salt
   ¼ teaspoon Accent
   ⅛ teaspoon pepper
Lightly spoon spinach mixture into pocket. Skewer or sew to keep stuffing in place. Put meat, rib side down, on rack in pan. Place over top of roast
   4 slices bacon
Roast uncovered at 300°F about 2½ hrs., or until meat is tender.   *4 to 6 servings*

Veal Shoulder Roll Surprise

Set out a roast meat thermometer and a shallow roasting pan with rack.

Set out
   1 pt. Blueberry-Lemon Jam (page 574)
Wipe with a clean, damp cloth
   4-lb. veal shoulder roll
Cut one end of the cord tied around the roll; remove and set cord aside.

Carefully unroll veal and spread jelly over it in a layer about ¼ in. thick. Reroll the veal and again tie with cord.

Rub the roll with a mixture of
   2 teaspoons salt
   1 teaspoon Accent
   ¼ teaspoon pepper
Put veal roll on rack in roasting pan. Insert roast meat thermometer at top center of roll, being sure that bulb rests in center of the roll.

Lay over the veal
   4 slices bacon or salt pork
Roast veal uncovered at 300°F. Remove veal from oven after 2 hrs. Remove slices of bacon or salt pork. Spread top of roll with Blueberry-Lemon Jam.

Return veal to oven and continue roasting about ½ hr., or until internal temperature of veal reaches 170°F. (The total roasting time should be about 2½ hrs., allow about 40 min. per pound.)

Remove from oven; remove thermometer and keep veal hot. Remove cord from roll just before carving.

Serve with additional Blueberry-Lemon Jam.
        About 8 servings

Veal Braised in Orange Juice

MRS. LUTHER A. DUNN
FOREST CITY, IOWA

Set out a small saucepan and a large, heavy skillet having a tight-fitting cover.

Wipe with a clean, damp cloth
  1½ lbs. veal shoulder steak, cut 1 in. thick

Cut meat into serving-size pieces. Coat pieces evenly with a mixture of
  ¼ cup flour
  1 teaspoon salt
  ½ teaspoon Accent
  ¼ teaspoon pepper

Heat in the skillet over medium heat
  ¼ cup fat

Put veal into skillet; brown on both sides.

Meanwhile, mix together in the saucepan
  ⅓ cup orange juice
  2 tablespoons white corn sirup
  1 tablespoon grated orange peel (page 11)
  ⅛ teaspoon mace

Heat to boiling. Pour over the meat.

Cover skillet and simmer over low heat until meat is tender when pierced with a fork, (about 1 hr.). Turn meat occasionally.

Remove meat to serving platter. Garnish with
  Orange slices

4 to 6 servings

Schnitzel Holstein
(Veal Cutlets with Fried Eggs)

Set out a large, heavy skillet.

Wipe with a clean, damp cloth
  2 lbs. veal round steak (cutlet), cut ½ in. thick

Pound meat (*page 107*). Cut into 4 serving-size pieces. Coat cutlets with a mixture of
  ¼ cup flour
  1 teaspoon salt
  ¾ teaspoon Accent
  ¼ teaspoon pepper

Dip cutlets into a mixture of
  1 egg, slightly beaten
  1 tablespoon milk

Coat with
  1 cup (about 3 slices) fine, dry bread crumbs

Heat in the skillet over low heat
  4 to 5 tablespoons butter

Add the cutlets; cook over medium heat until browned and tender (about 20 min. on each side). Remove cutlets to warm serving platter; keep warm while preparing
  4 Fried Eggs (page 90)

Place one Fried Egg on top of each cutlet.

4 servings

Braised Veal Chops

Delicate in flavor and fork-tender.

Set out a large, heavy skillet having a tight-fitting cover.

Wipe with a clean, damp cloth
  6 veal chops, rib or loin, cut ¾ in. thick

Coat meat with a mixture of
  ¼ cup flour
  1 teaspoon salt
  ½ teaspoon Accent
  ¼ teaspoon pepper

Heat in the skillet over low heat
  ¼ to ⅓ cup butter or margarine

Add chops and brown slowly on both sides. Pour over the chops
  ¼ cup milk

Cover skillet and simmer 45 to 60 min., or until meat is tender when pierced with a fork. Add small amounts of milk as needed during cooking.

6 servings

Schnitzel Holstein

Breaded Veal Chops

Set out a large, heavy skillet having a tight-fitting cover.

Wipe with a clean, damp cloth
   4 veal chops or small cutlets
Coat chops with a mixture of
   ¼ cup flour
   1 teaspoon salt
   ½ teaspoon Accent
   ¼ teaspoon pepper
Heat in the skillet over medium heat
   2 tablespoons fat
Meanwhile, dip the chops into a mixture of
   1 egg, slightly beaten
   2 tablespoons milk or water
Coat the chops with
   1 cup fine, dry bread or cracker crumbs
Put chops into skillet and brown on both sides over medium heat. Remove from heat and pour off remaining fat. Slowly add to skillet
   ½ cup tomato juice or water
Cover skillet and cook over low heat about 1 hr. or until meat is tender when pierced with a fork. Add small amounts of liquid as needed.

Serve with
   Quick Tomato Sauce (page 327)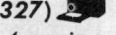
   4 servings

Breaded Veal Chops

Veal Chops Hungarian

A zestful sour cream gravy gives flavor contrast.

Set out a large, heavy skillet having a tight-fitting cover.

Wipe with a clean, damp cloth
   6 veal chops, rib or loin, cut about ¾ in. thick
Coat chops evenly with a mixture of
   ¼ cup flour
   1 teaspoon salt
   ½ teaspoon Accent
   ¼ teaspoon pepper
Heat in the skillet over medium heat
   2 to 3 tablespoons fat
Add the chops and brown evenly on both sides. Spoon over chops
   ½ cup (1 medium-size) chopped onion (page 12)
Sprinkle with
   ½ teaspoon paprika
Add to the skillet
   ½ cup hot water
Cover skillet tightly. Simmer over low heat 45 min., or until chops are tender when pierced with a fork.

Meanwhile, cook and drain *(page 277)*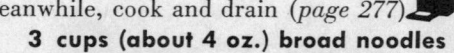
   3 cups (about 4 oz.) broad noodles
Remove chops to hot platter. Remove skillet from heat.

For Gravy—Mix together
   1 cup thick sour cream
   2 tablespoons water
and a mixture of
   1 tablespoon paprika
   ½ teaspoon salt
   ½ teaspoon Accent
   ⅛ teaspoon pepper
Pour into the skillet; set over low heat. Heat thoroughly, stirring constantly. Do not boil.

Toss the drained noodles with
   Butter or margarine
Arrange noodles around chops. Spoon the gravy over the chops. Serve at once.

6 servings

Veal Parmesan 7

Set out an 11x7x1½-in. baking dish and a large, heavy skillet.

Wipe with a clean, damp cloth and pound (*page 107*)
1½ to 2 lbs. veal round steak (cutlet), cut about ½ in. thick
Cut into 6 pieces.

Coat cutlets with a mixture of
**¼ cup flour
1 teaspoon salt
½ teaspoon Accent
¼ teaspoon pepper**
Mix together and set aside
**1⅓ cups (4 slices) fine, dry bread crumbs
⅓ cup grated Parmesan cheese**
Mix together
**3 eggs, beaten
1 teaspoon salt
¾ teaspoon Accent
¼ teaspoon pepper**
Heat in the skillet over medium heat
⅓ cup olive oil
Dip cutlets into egg mixture and then into crumb mixture. Put cutlets into the skillet and slowly brown on both sides. Arrange the browned cutlets in the baking dish. Pour over cutlets
2 cups Tomato Meat Sauce (*page 281*)
Top cutlets with
6 slices (3 oz.) Mozzarella cheese (1 slice per cutlet)
Bake at 350°F 15 to 20 min., or until cheese is melted and lightly browned.   *6 servings*

Veal Creole 8
MRS. GLENN W. JONES, ROGERS, ARK.

Set out a large, heavy skillet and a 2-qt. casserole having a tight-fitting cover.

Prepare and set aside to drain
1 cup Perfection Boiled Rice (one-third recipe, *page 275*)
Wipe with a clean, damp cloth
2 lbs. boneless veal
Cut meat into 1-in. cubes; set aside.

Heat in the skillet over medium heat
2 tablespoons fat
Add the veal and brown well on all sides.

Meanwhile, mix the rice with
**2 cups (1 No. 2 can) cooked tomatoes, cut into pieces
½ cup diced celery (*page 12*)
2 tablespoons chopped green pepper
1 tablespoon chopped onion**
and a mixture of
**1½ teaspoons salt
½ teaspoon Accent
¼ teaspoon pepper**
Transfer the browned veal to the casserole. Spoon the tomato-rice mixture over the meat. Dot with
2 tablespoons butter or margarine
Cover and bake at 300°F 1 hr., or until meat is tender when pierced with a fork.
6 servings

Veal Paprika 9

Put into a large, heavy skillet having a tight-fitting cover

8 slices bacon, diced

**½ cup (about 1 medium-size)
chopped onion (page 12)**

¼ cup chopped green pepper (page 12)

1½ teaspoons paprika

Cook slowly until bacon and onion are lightly browned, occasionally moving and turning mixture with a spoon.

Meanwhile, wipe with a clean, damp cloth and cut into 1-in. cubes

1½ lbs. boneless veal shoulder

Coat meat evenly (page 107) with a mixture of

¼ cup flour

1 teaspoon salt

½ teaspoon Accent

With slotted spoon, remove bacon mixture to small dish, leaving bacon drippings in the skillet. Put meat into skillet and brown on all sides over medium heat.

Return bacon mixture to skillet with

⅓ cup hot water

Cover skillet and simmer, occasionally moving and turning mixture, 45 to 60 min., or until meat is tender when pierced with a fork. Add small amounts of water as needed.

While veal is cooking, prepare and set aside in a warm place

Spätzle (page 280)

Shortly before veal is tender, melt in a small saucepan over low heat

1 tablespoon fat

Blend in

1 tablespoon flour

1½ to 2 teaspoons paprika

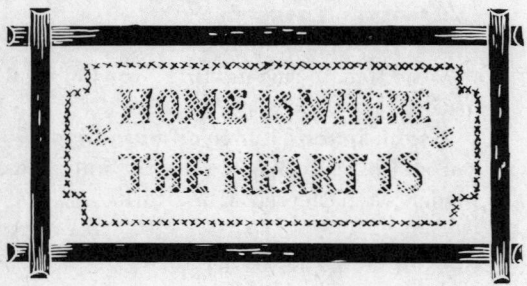

Heat until mixture bubbles, stirring constantly. Remove from heat. Gradually add, stirring in

½ cup milk

Return to heat and bring rapidly to boiling, stirring constantly; cook 1 to 2 min. longer. Remove from heat. Stirring sauce vigorously with a French whip, whisk beater or fork, add in very small amounts

1 cup thick sour cream

When veal is tender, pour sauce into the skillet. Cook mixture over low heat, keeping mixture moving with a spoon, 3 to 5 min., or until thoroughly heated; do not boil.

Serve with the Spätzle.   *4 to 6 servings*

Veal Scaloppine 10

Set out a large, heavy skillet having a tight-fitting cover.

Wipe with a clean, damp cloth and pound (page 107)

**1 lb. veal round steak (cutlet),
cut about ½ in. thick**

Cut veal into 1-in. pieces. Coat pieces evenly (page 107) with a mixture of

½ cup flour

¾ teaspoon Accent

½ teaspoon salt

⅛ teaspoon pepper

Set aside.

Heat in the skillet until garlic is lightly browned

¼ cup olive oil

1 clove garlic (page 12), sliced thin

Put veal into skillet and brown on both sides.

While veal browns, mix together

1¾ cups sieved cooked tomatoes

½ teaspoon salt

¼ teaspoon chopped parsley

¼ teaspoon oregano

⅛ teaspoon pepper

Slowly add tomato mixture to browned veal. Cover skillet and simmer about 25 min., or

Veal Scaloppine

until veal is tender when pierced with a fork. If mixture tends to become too thick, add a small amount of water.   *3 or 4 servings*

△ Veal Scaloppine with Mushrooms and Peppers

Follow ▲ Recipe. Clean 1 **green pepper** (*page 12*) and ½ lb. fresh **mushrooms** (*page 12*). Cook mushrooms and green pepper in 3 tablespoons **butter** or **margarine** until mushrooms are lightly browned, occasionally moving and turning mixture. Add to browned veal with the tomato mixture.

Blanquette of Veal

MRS. GEORGE CASTLEBERRY
JACKSONVILLE, FLA.

Set out a 3-qt. saucepan.

Wipe with a clean, damp cloth and cut into 2-in. pieces
    2 lbs. boneless veal shoulder
Put meat into the saucepan with
    1 onion (*page 12*), cut in half
    4 stalks celery (*page 12*), with leaves
    2 carrots, scraped or pared and sliced
    2 cloves garlic (*page 12*)
    2 sprigs parsley
    1 sprig thyme

Add
    Water (enough to cover meat)
    2 teaspoons salt
    ½ teaspoon Accent
    8 peppercorns
    ½ bay leaf
Bring liquid rapidly to boiling; reduce heat, cover and simmer (do not boil) about 2 hrs.

About ½ hr. before meat is done, clean and slice (*page 12*)
    1 lb. mushrooms
Heat in a large skillet over low heat
    ⅔ cup butter or margarine
Add the mushrooms and
    1 medium-size onion (*page 12*), sliced
Cook over medium heat until onion is transparent and mushrooms are lightly browned, occasionally moving and turning pieces with a spoon. Set aside.

Remove veal from stock (cooking liquid); set aside. Strain stock; reserve.

Melt in the saucepan over low heat
    ¼ cup butter or margarine
Blend in
    ¼ cup flour
Heat until mixture bubbles. Remove from heat. Add gradually and stir in 1½ cups of the reserved stock and
    ½ cup cream
Return to heat and bring rapidly to boiling, stirring constantly; cook 1 to 2 min. longer.

Remove from heat and vigorously stir about 2 tablespoons of the sauce into
    1 egg yolk, slightly beaten
Immediately return the egg mixture to the saucepan and cook over low heat 3 to 5 min., stirring constantly.

Add to the saucepan the cooked onion, mushrooms, and meat; heat thoroughly.

Just before serving, blend in
    1 teaspoon lemon juice
Garnish with
    Chopped parsley
        6 to 8 servings

Veal Casserole 13

MRS. CLARENCE HECKMAN
PEMBERVILLE, OHIO

Lightly butter a 1½-qt. casserole.

Wipe with a clean, damp cloth and cut into 1-in. cubes
1 lb. boneless veal shoulder
Heat in a large, heavy skillet
2 tablespoons butter
Add the veal and brown on all sides over medium heat. Remove meat to casserole.

Meanwhile, cook and drain (*page 277*)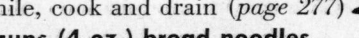
3 cups (4 oz.) broad noodles
Heat in the skillet over low heat
2 tablespoons butter
Add and cook until onion is transparent, occasionally moving and turning mixture with a spoon
½ cup (about 1 medium-size) chopped onion (*page 12*)
½ cup chopped celery (*page 12*)
Add the drained noodles to the meat with the onion, celery and
1¼ cups (10½- to 11-oz. can) condensed cream of mushroom soup
1 cup milk
¼ teaspoon Accent

Lightly but thoroughly mix together. Top with
½ cup buttered bread crumbs (*page 10*)
Bake at 300°F 45 min., or until meat is tender when pierced with a fork.   *4 servings*

Veal with Oysters 14

MRS. W. D. WOOD, CAMP HILL, ALA.

Set out a large, heavy skillet or top-of-range casserole having a tight-fitting cover.

Wipe with a clean, damp cloth
2 lbs. veal round steak (cutlet), cut ¼ in. thick
Cut veal into strips about 2x1 in. Coat pieces evenly (*page 107*) with a mixture of
¼ cup flour
1 teaspoon salt
¾ teaspoon Accent
⅛ teaspoon pepper
Heat in the skillet over medium heat
2 tablespoons fat
Add the veal strips and brown on both sides.

Meanwhile, drain, reserving liquid
1½ pints oysters
Pick over oysters to remove any shell particles. Set oysters aside.

Add liquid from oysters to the browned veal. Cover and simmer over low heat until veal is just tender when pierced with a fork. Add the

oysters. Continue cooking until edges of oysters curl (about 5 min.; do not overcook or oysters will be tough).

Remove veal and oysters to serving dish; keep warm. Blend into cooking liquid in skillet

2 teaspoons Brown Roux (page 325)

Bring rapidly to boiling, stirring constantly; cook 1 to 2 min. Pour over the meat and oysters. Sprinkle with

Paprika

Serve immediately.   *6 to 8 servings*

Note: If desired, add 2 tablespoons **dry white wine** to the veal with the oyster liquid.

Veal and Green Bean Stew with Whipped Potatoes (page 298)

Veal and Green Bean Stew

Set out a Dutch oven; or use a large sauce pot having a tight-fitting cover.

Wipe with a clean, damp cloth

2 lbs. boneless veal shoulder

Cut meat into ¾-in. cubes and set aside.

Heat in the Dutch oven over low heat

2 tablespoons butter or margarine

Add and cook over medium heat until onion is transparent, occasionally moving and turning with a spoon

½ cup (about 1 medium-size) chopped onion (page 12)

With a slotted spoon remove onion to a small dish; set aside.

Put the veal into the Dutch oven and brown on all sides over medium heat. Remove from heat. Slowly pour in

3 cups quick meat broth (page 13)

Return onion to Dutch oven with a mixture of

2 teaspoons Accent
1 teaspoon salt
¼ teaspoon pepper

Bring liquid to boiling; cover, reduce heat and simmer (do not boil) 1 hr.

Meanwhile, wash, remove ends from and cut into 1-in. pieces

1 lb. (about 3 cups) green beans

Add the beans to the Dutch oven. Cover and cook 25 min. longer, or until meat and beans are tender when pierced with a fork. Pour off cooking liquid and reserve.

Melt in a small saucepan

3 tablespoons butter or margarine

Blend in

3 tablespoons flour
1 tablespoon sugar
¼ teaspoon salt
¼ teaspoon pepper

Heat until mixture bubbles and is lightly browned. Remove from heat. Add gradually, stirring constantly, the reserved cooking liquid and

2 tablespoons vinegar

Cook rapidly, stirring constantly, until mixture thickens. Return thickened cooking liquid to Dutch oven. Blend in a mixture of

1 tablespoon chopped parsley
¼ teaspoon savory
Few grains thyme

Cook, uncovered, over low heat 15 min. (If mixture becomes too thick, add enough hot water to achieve desired consistency.)

Serve hot with

Whipped Potatoes (page 298)

6 to 8 servings

▲ Veal Ragout

MARY ELLEN CABLE, CRAIGVILLE, IND.

Set out a heavy 3-qt. saucepan having a tight-fitting cover.

Wipe with a clean, damp cloth and cut into 1-in. cubes

1½ lbs. boneless veal shoulder

Coat veal evenly (*page 107*) with a mixture of

¼ cup flour

½ teaspoon salt

½ teaspoon Accent

⅛ teaspoon pepper

Heat in the saucepan over medium heat

2 tablespoons fat

Add meat and brown on all sides.

Add

1½ cups water

1 cup (8-oz. can) tomato sauce

Bring to boiling; cover and simmer over low heat 40 min., or until meat is almost tender.

Meanwhile, wash, scrape or pare and cut into halves crosswise, then into halves lengthwise

5 medium-size carrots

Add carrots to meat with

10 small whole onions (*page 12*)

Cover and cook 40 min. longer, or until meat and vegetables are tender.

Serve with small, whole **boiled potatoes.**

4 to 6 servings

△ Veal Ragout with Dumplings

Follow ▲ Recipe; increase tomato sauce to two cups. After vegetables have been added to the stew, prepare **Dumplings** (½ recipe, *p.69*). About 20 min. before end of cooking period, uncover stew and bring liquid to boiling. Drop dumpling batter by tablespoonfuls on top of meat and vegetables. (Dumplings should rest on meat and vegetables; if dumplings settle down into liquid, they may be soggy.) Cover tightly and cook over medium heat 20 min. without removing cover. Remove dumplings and stew to hot serving dish.

Veal Rosettes

MARILYN BENADUM, LANCASTER, OHIO

Set out a large, heavy skillet and a 2-qt. casserole having a tight-fitting cover.

Crush (*page 12*) enough crackers to yield

¾ cup cracker crumbs (18 to 20 crackers, crushed)

Set aside.

Wipe with a clean, damp cloth

2 lbs. veal steak, cut 1 in. thick

Cut steak into 2-in. squares. Form rounds, by wrapping around each piece of veal

Bacon slice (about 12 slices will be needed)

Secure bacon with a wooden pick. Season rosettes with a mixture of

2 teaspoons salt
1 teaspoon Accent
½ teaspoon pepper

Dip rosettes, one at a time, into

1 egg, slightly beaten

Coat by rolling in the crumbs.

Heat in the skillet over low heat

¼ cup butter

Add the rosettes and brown on both sides over medium heat.

Remove meat to casserole. Blend into the drippings in the skillet

2 teaspoons flour

Cook until mixture bubbles and is lightly browned, stirring constantly. Remove from heat and add gradually, blending in

¼ cup milk
¼ cup cream

Pour over meat in casserole.

Cover and bake at 300°F 1½ hrs., or until veal is tender when pierced with a fork.

Remove meat to warm serving plate. Blend enough warm milk (⅛ to ½ cup) into gravy in casserole for desired consistency.

Serve Rosettes with the gravy and

Whipped Potatoes (page 298)

6 servings

Swiss Veal Balls
(Chalber Balleli)
VIOLET FISHER, WADENA, MINN.

Set out a large, heavy skillet and a 2-qt. top-of-range casserole having a tight-fitting cover.

Lightly mix together

1¼ lbs. ground veal
¼ lb. ground lean pork
1 cup fine, dry bread crumbs
2 tablespoons finely chopped onion
2 eggs, beaten
½ cup cream
2 tablespoons milk

and a mixture of

½ teaspoon salt
½ teaspoon Accent
¼ teaspoon pepper
⅛ teaspoon nutmeg

Shape meat mixture into balls about 1½ in. in diameter.

Heat in the skillet over low heat

3 tablespoons butter or margarine

Put veal balls into skillet; brown over medium heat, turning occasionally. Turn contents of skillet into the casserole.

Cover and bake at 350°F 30 min. Uncover and bake 10 min. longer. Remove veal balls to warm serving dish. Set aside to keep warm.

Blend into drippings

4 teaspoons flour

Heat until mixture bubbles and is lightly browned. Remove from heat. Add gradually, stirring constantly

1 cup milk

Return to heat. Cook rapidly, stirring constantly, until mixture thickens. Cook 1 to 2 min. longer. Pour gravy over veal balls or serve in a separate bowl.   *About 6 servings*

Veal Balls with Sour Cream

Set out a large, heavy skillet having a tight-fitting cover.

Lightly mix together
    1 lb. ground veal
    **½ cup (about 1½ slices) fine,
        dry bread crumbs**
    **½ cup (about 1 medium-size)
        chopped onion (page 12)**
    2 tablespoons chopped parsley
    ¾ cup milk
    1 egg, beaten
and a mixture of
    1 teaspoon salt
    ½ teaspoon Accent
    ¼ teaspoon pepper

Shape veal mixture into medium (2-in.) or small (1-in.) balls and set aside.

Heat in the skillet over medium heat
    ¼ cup fat
Add balls to skillet; brown over medium heat, turning balls occasionally. Add contents of
    **1 4-oz. can (about ½ cup) sliced
        mushrooms**
Cover skillet and simmer 30 to 45 min., or until veal balls are done, turning balls occasionally and adding small amounts of water as needed.

Meanwhile, cook and drain (page 277)
    4 cups (about 5 oz.) noodles
Prepare
    ½ cup quick meat broth (page 13)
Set broth aside to cool to lukewarm.

When veal balls are done, remove skillet from

heat. Drain off cooking liquid into a cup; set skillet aside.

Put into top of a double boiler
    1 cup thick sour cream
Add gradually to sour cream, stirring constantly, the liquid drained from skillet and the cooled broth. Cook sauce over simmering water, stirring occasionally, until heated thoroughly.

Put noodles into a serving dish. Top with the veal balls and sour cream sauce. Sprinkle with
    Paprika
Serve immediately.   *6 servings*

Veal-Mushroom Timbales

Set out a large, heavy skillet and a double boiler. Grease, or oil with salad or cooking oil (not olive oil), 8 heat-resistant custard cups. Heat water for boiling water bath (page 12). Cut into thin crosswise strips
    1 canned pimiento
Arrange 2 or 3 pimiento strips in bottom of each custard cup. Set aside.

Clean and slice (page 12)
    ½ lb. mushrooms
Heat in the skillet over low heat
    **2 to 3 tablespoons butter or
        margarine**
Add mushrooms to skillet with
    2 tablespoons minced onion
Cook over medium heat, occasionally moving and turning with a spoon or fork, until mushrooms are lightly browned. Set aside.

Grind (*page 107*) and set aside enough cooked veal to yield

2 cups ground cooked veal

Combine in top of the double boiler

1½ cups milk

⅓ cup (1 slice) fine, dry bread crumbs

Place over simmering water until milk is scalded (*page 13*). Remove from simmering water. Blend in veal, onion, mushrooms and

2 tablespoons butter or margarine

and a mixture of

1 teaspoon salt

½ teaspoon Accent

⅛ teaspoon paprika

Add gradually, while vigorously blending mixture into

3 eggs, well beaten

Fill custard cups two-thirds full with mixture.

Bake in boiling water bath at 350°F 20 to 30 min., or until a silver knife comes out clean when inserted in center of timbale. Run a spatula around inside of each cup to loosen timbales. Unmold onto hot serving plates.

Serve with

Tomato-Cheese Sauce (page 327)

4 servings

Jellied Veal Loaf

Set out a 9½x5¼x2¾-in. loaf pan or a 1½-qt. ring mold.

Prepare and chill

1 Hard-Cooked Egg (page 87)

Prepare in a small saucepan

1¾ cups quick meat broth (page 13)

Add to broth

½ cup (about 1 medium-size) chopped onion (page 12)

½ teaspoon celery seed

3 or 4 peppercorns

Simmer over low heat about 8 min.

Meanwhile, empty into a small bowl

1 pkg. lemon-flavored gelatin

Strain broth; pour the hot liquid over gelatin, stirring until gelatin is completely dissolved.

Jellied Veal Loaf

Add and stir in

1 tablespoon prepared horse-radish

1 teaspoon salt

½ teaspoon Accent

Cool; chill (*page 12*) until gelatin is slightly thicker than consistency of thick, unbeaten egg white.

Meanwhile, lightly oil the loaf pan or mold with salad or cooking oil (not olive oil). Set it aside to drain.

Grind (*page 107*) and set aside enough cooked veal to yield

2 cups ground cooked veal

Cut the Hard-Cooked Egg into three slices and arrange in bottom of prepared pan. Spoon a small amount of the slightly thickened gelatin mixture (enough to make a thin layer covering egg slices) in bottom of pan. Chill in refrigerator until slightly set.

Blend into remaining gelatin mixture, the ground veal and

¼ cup finely chopped parsley

When first layer in mold is slightly set, immediately turn veal mixture onto first layer. (Both layers should be of almost same consistency to avoid separation of layers when unmolded.) Chill in refrigerator until firm.

Unmold (*page 12*) as for gelatin. Garnish as desired.

8 servings

VEAL in the MICROWAVE OVEN

The microwave coddles veal, handling it exactly as a tender, young meat should be. All the recipes included are very good prepared in the microwave oven, with the meat even more tender than in conventional cooking. The delicate texture of veal is enhanced; the flavors of the sauces are delicious. Especially memorable are the **Veal Scaloppini** and **Blanquette of Veal.**

Both roasts, **Breast of Veal** and the **Veal Shoulder Roll Surprise**, are outstanding! Very tender and flavorful, these economical cuts of veal produce an impressive main course.

Browning—If a recipe in the main text calls for browning the meat, first preheat the skillet about 3 minutes. A 10-inch skillet will accommodate 2 to 3 steaks or chops. When the recipe calls for more, brown in batches and then return all the meat to the skillet or casserole to complete cooking.

Sauces and Gravies, particularly cream or milk sauces, are, as always, extraordinarily good when prepared in the microwave oven. Frequent stirring is the key to achieving that silky-smooth texture. Sauces should be stirred before and after the addition of each ingredient and stirred about every minute while cooking. More frequent stirring, if called for, is indicated in the individual recipes.

TEST FOR DONENESS—You will know when veal is cooked by checking to see if the meat is slightly tender and the juices are a light pink. As with all meat, veal from the microwave oven must stand, covered, to season for a short time after cooking; cooking will be completed during this standing period.

Minimum Standing Times are given with each recipe. Plastic wrap can be used to cover, if necessary.

The quick-cooking assets of the microwave can make preparing veal chops and steaks a little tricky. If the cut you are using is thin, such as veal cutlet for the **Schnitzel Holstein**, the meat will be almost completely cooked in the browning step and will finish cooking while standing. Great care must be taken to not overcook chops and steaks.

These veal dishes are very satisfactorily

frozen and can be returned to the microwave to defrost and even complete the recipe by the addition of the proper sauce. For example, prepare and freeze the breaded veal cutlets for **Veal Parmesan.** Then, defrost and complete when company arrives.

REMINDERS—The introductory chapter, **Home Cooking in the Microwave Oven,** provides additional tips and an easy-to-read chart comparing settings among different brands of microwave ovens. By reviewing this section, you will also learn how we have adapted these recipes.

Stuffed Roast Breast of Veal *(page 162)*

Use a glass baking dish with rack.

COOK until heated (about 5 min.).

SLOWCOOK, rotating pan every 5 min., until almost done (juices should be slightly pink) (about 20 min.).

Cover with aluminum foil and let stand for 10 to 15 min.

OVERALL COOKING TIME: 25:00

Veal Shoulder Roll Surprise *(page 162)*

Use a glass baking dish with rack.

You may substitute prepared jam (1 part lemon marmalade and 1 part blueberry, raspberry or other jam).

COOK to heat through (about 5 min.).

SLOWCOOK, rotating pan every 5 min., until nearly done (about 15 min.).

Spread top with jam. SLOWCOOK, rotating pan every 5 min., until internal temperature reaches 170° (about 10 min.). (Removing meat to test temperature with conventional thermometer will not interfere with the cooking proc-

ess. Cover meat with aluminum foil while waiting for thermometer to register. Be sure to remove both thermometer and foil if you must return the meat to the microwave oven.)

Cover and let stand 20 min.

OVERALL COOKING TIME: 30:00

Schnitzel Holstein *(page 163)*

Use a browning skillet. The times in this recipe are for cooking 2 cutlets at a time.

Check this dish frequently for tenderness as this delicate cut of meat can easily overcook.

Preheat skillet (3 min.). Add butter and COOK until foamy. Add cutlets and COOK, checking every 30 sec., until brown on both sides (about 1 min. each side). Repeat with remaining cutlets.

If cutlets are thin, no further cooking may be necessary. Otherwise, SLOWCOOK, covered, checking every 30 sec., until slightly pink.

Cover and let stand 5 min.

Braised Veal Chops *(page 163)*

Use a browning skillet.

Preheat skillet (3 min.). Add butter or margarine and COOK until foamy.

Add 2 chops and COOK until brown on both sides (about 2½ min. each side). Brown remaining chops 2 at a time.

Return all browned chops to skillet, add milk, cover and COOK to heat through (about 1min.).

SLOWCOOK, checking and rotating pan after 3 min., until juices are slightly pink (about 5 min.).

Cover and let stand 5 min.

OVERALL COOKING TIME: 24:00

Breaded Veal Chops 5
(page 164)

Use a browning skillet.

Preheat skillet (3 min.). Add fat and COOK until melted.

Add 2 coated chops and COOK until brown on both sides (about 3 min. each side). Repeat with remaining chops. Pour off fat.

Return all chops to skillet, cover and COOK, rotating pan every 2 min., to heat through (4 min.).

SLOWCOOK, rotating pan every 5 min., until juices are slightly pink (about 15 min.).

Cover and let stand 5 min.
OVERALL COOKING TIME: 34:00

Veal Chops Hungarian 6
(page 164)

Use a browning skillet.

Preheat skillet (3 min.). Add fat and COOK until melted.

Add 3 chops and COOK until brown on both sides (about 2½ min. each side). Repeat with remaining chops. Return all chops to skillet.

Add onion, paprika and water to cover. SLOWCOOK, checking after 3 min. and then every 1 min., until nearly tender (about 5 min.). Remove chops to covered serving casserole.

*For Gravy—*Stir gravy ingredients into skillet, mix thoroughly and SLOWCOOK to heat (1 min.). Do not boil. Pour over chops.

Cover and let stand 5 min.
OVERALL COOKING TIME: 16:00

Veal Parmesan *(page 165)* 7

Use a browning skillet and a glass baking dish.

Preheat skillet (3 min.). Add olive oil and COOK until heated.

Add 3 cutlets and COOK, checking every 30 sec. to prevent overcooking, until brown on both sides (about 1 min. each side). Repeat with remaining cutlets. Return all cutlets to baking dish and add sauce and cheese.

COOK, rotating pan every 1 min., until cheese melts and sauce is hot (about 2 min.).

Cover and let stand 5 min.

Veal Creole *(page 165)* 8

Use a browning skillet and a 2-qt. casserole.

Preheat skillet (3 min.). Add fat and COOK until melted.

Add half the veal and COOK, turning meat and rotating pan every 1½ min., until brown on all sides (about 10 min.). Repeat with remaining veal.

Return all meat to casserole. Add rice mixture; cover.

COOK to heat through (5 min.). (If rice mixture is cold, increase COOK time.) Cover.

SLOWCOOK, rotating pan every 3 min., until meat is tender (about 9 min.).

Cover and let stand 15 min.

Veal Paprika *(page 166)* 9

Use a browning skillet and a small casserole for the sauce.

SLOWCOOK half the bacon mixture in the skillet, stirring every 2 min., until slightly brown (about 4 min.). Repeat with remaining bacon mixture. Remove bacon and set aside.

Add meat to bacon drippings and COOK, turn-

ing every 1½ min., until brown on all sides (about 9 min.).

Return bacon mixture to skillet and add hot water to cover contents by two-thirds; cover.

COOK to heat through (about 5 min.).

SLOWCOOK, rotating pan every 3 min., until nearly tender (about 9 min.).

For the sauce, place fat in the casserole and COOK until melted. Add flour and paprika and COOK, stirring every 1½ min., until simmering (about 3 min.).

Add milk and COOK until simmering (about 1 min.). Stir vigorously.

Add sour cream as in Recipe, pour over veal and COOK to heat through (1 min.).

Cover and let stand 10 min.

Veal Scaloppine *(page 166)* 10

Use a browning skillet.

Preheat skillet (3 min.). Add olive oil and garlic and COOK until heated.

Add meat and COOK until brown on both sides (about 1 min. each side).

Add sauce, cover and COOK, rotating pan every 3 min., until juices are slightly pink (about 12 min.).

Cover and let stand 5 min.

OVERALL COOKING TIME: 17:00

Veal Scaloppine with Mushrooms and Peppers
(page 167)
11

Follow 10 Recipe with additions as in △ Recipe, except COOK butter or margarine until melted. Add green pepper and COOK until slightly softened (about 1 min.).

Add mushrooms and COOK until tender (about 3 min.).

Add to veal-tomato mixture as in   Recipe.
OVERALL COOKING TIME: 21:00

Blanquette of Veal 12
(page 167)

Use a 3-qt. covered casserole and a browning skillet.

In casserole, place meat, vegetables, seasonings and enough water to cover contents by two-thirds; cover.

COOK, stirring every 5 min., to heat through (15 min.).

SLOWCOOK, stirring every 5 min., until meat is barely tender (about 20 min.). Cover and set aside while you prepare mushrooms.

Preheat skillet (3 min.). Add butter or margarine and COOK until melted.

Add mushrooms and onion and COOK, stirring every 2 min., until lightly browned (about 7 min.).

For sauce, COOK butter or margarine until melted. Add flour and COOK, stirring every 1 min., until bubbling (about 3 min.).

Blend in stock and cream. COOK, stirring every 30 sec., until thickened and simmering (about 1 to 2 min.).

Add egg yolk. COOK, stirring every 30 sec., until well blended (about 1½ min.).

Add mushrooms, onions and meat and COOK, stirring every 1 min., until heated thoroughly (about 2 min.).

Cover and let stand 15 min.

Complete and serve as in Recipe.
OVERALL COOKING TIME: 52:30

Veal Casserole *(page 168)* 13

Use a browning skillet and a 2-qt. casserole.

Preheat skillet (3 min.). Add butter and COOK until melted.

Add meat and COOK, turning meat every 1½ min., until brown on all sides (about 10 min.). Transfer meat to casserole.

In browning skillet, COOK remaining butter until melted. Add onions and celery and COOK until onion is transparent (about 3 min.).

Combine all ingredients for casserole; mix.

Top with bread crumbs. SLOWCOOK, uncovered, stirring every 5 min., until meat is tender (about 15 min.).

Cover and let stand 15 min.

OVERALL COOKING TIME: 31:00

Veal with Oysters *(page 168)* 14

Use a browning skillet and a covered casserole. The times given in this recipe are for browning the meat in 2 batches.

Prepare **Brown Roux.**

Preheat skillet (3 min.). Add fat and COOK until melted.

Add one-half the coated veal and COOK until lightly browned on both sides (about 2½ min. each side). Repeat with remaining veal.

Add oyster liquid and SLOWCOOK, rotating the skillet every 5 min., until almost tender (about 10 min.).

Be sure to puncture the outer membrane of each oyster with a toothpick.

Add oysters and SLOWCOOK until edges curl (about 7 min.). Remove veal and oysters to covered casserole.

Add brown roux to cooking liquid; mix thoroughly. COOK, stirring every 30 sec., until

boiling (about 3 min.). Pour over veal and oysters.

Cover and let stand 5 min.

Veal and Green Bean Stew *(page 169)* 15

Use a browning skillet.

Preheat skillet (3 min.). COOK butter or margarine until foamy.

Add onion and COOK until transparent (about 3 min.). Remove and set aside.

Add half the meat and COOK, stirring every 1½ min., until brown (about 10 min.) Repeat with remaining meat.

Add broth, onion, and seasonings. Cover and COOK, stirring every 5 min., until heated through (about 10 min.).

SLOWCOOK, covered, stirring every 5 min., until meat is nearly tender (about 35 min.).

Add green beans, cover and SLOWCOOK, stirring every 5 min., until meat and beans are tender (about 10 min.).

Cover and let stand 15 min.

For the sauce, COOK butter or margarine until melted.

Add seasoned flour and COOK, stirring every 1 min., until bubbly (about 3 min.).

Add liquid and vinegar and COOK, stirring every 30 sec., until thickened (about 5 min.).

Blend in seasonings and COOK, stirring every 1½ min., until simmering (about 3 min.).

Serve as in Recipe.

OVERALL COOKING TIME: 92:00

Veal Ragout *(page 170)* 16

Use a browning skillet and a 3-qt. casserole.

Preheat skillet (3 min.). Add fat and COOK until melted.

Add meat and COOK, stirring and turning every 1½ min., until brown (about 10 min.). Transfer to casserole.

Add tomato sauce and enough water to cover contents by two-thirds; cover.

COOK, stirring every 5 min., to heat (10 min.).

Add vegetables; cover. SLOWCOOK, stirring every 5 min., until meat and vegetables are tender (about 30 min.).

Cover and let stand 15 min.

OVERALL COOKING TIME: 53:00

Veal Ragout with Dumplings *(page 170)* 17

Follow 16 Recipe with additions as in ⚠ Recipe, except add dumplings 15 min. after adding vegetables.

Swiss Veal Balls *(page 171)* 18

Use a browning skillet and a 2-qt. casserole.

Preheat skillet (3 min.). Add butter or margarine and COOK until melted.

Add veal balls and COOK, turning every 1 min., until brown on all sides (about 3 min.). Transfer to casserole; cover.

SLOWCOOK, stirring every 5 min., until done (juices should be a very light pink) (about 8 min.).

For the gravy, COOK flour-fat mixture, stirring every 1 min., until bubbly (about 3 min.).

Add milk one-third at a time, stirring before and after each addition; COOK to heat after each addition (about 30 sec.).

COOK, stirring every 1 min., until thickened (about 1 to 2 min.).

Cover and let stand 15 min.

OVERALL COOKING TIME: 19:30

Veal Balls with Sour Cream *(page 172)* 19

Use a browning skillet and a casserole for the sauce.

Preheat skillet (3 min.). Add fat and COOK until melted.

Add veal balls and COOK, turning every 2 min., until brown (about 4 min.).

Add mushrooms, SLOWCOOK, stirring every 5 min., until meat is done (about 10 min.).

For the sauce, skim fat from cooking liquid. Combine with meat broth. Add sour cream in thirds, COOK until heated after each addition (about 1 min.). Do not boil. Stir frequently.

Veal-Mushroom Timbales *(page 172)* 20

Use a browning skillet, a small casserole and 8 6-oz. glass custard cups. Do not grease.

Preheat skillet (3 min.). Add butter or margarine and COOK until melted.

Add mushrooms and onions and COOK, stirring every 1½ min., until mushrooms are lightly brown (about 5 min.).

In small casserole, COOK milk and bread crumbs until milk is scalded (about 3 min.).

Combine all ingredients and assemble custard cups as in Recipe. Cover with plastic wrap.

COOK until an inserted knife emerges clean (about 4 min.).

Cover and let stand 5 min.

OVERALL COOKING TIME: 15:00

VEAL in the SLOW COOKER

All the recipes included in this section are delicious when prepared in the slow cooker. The stewed veal recipes, such as **Veal Ragout,** are tender, with the sauce a delicate blend of flavors.

Blanquette of Veal is particularly good and also an excellent company dish. The **Veal Balls with Sour Cream** not only makes a fine main dish, but may be served as an interesting appetizer, as well. Remember to use the slow cooker set on LOW to keep them warm until ready to serve.

We have eliminated recipes to be cooked with rice and noodles; this type of ingredient tends to overcook as the starches break down.

Recipes which call for steaks and chops are also omitted from this slow cooker section, since they tend to resemble stews more than chops when cooked by this method.

Browning—Some of the recipes call for browning meat first. Our method of browning in the slow cooker eliminates an extra step on the stove while preserving the juiciness and flavor of the meat. First, omit the flour from any coating mixture called for in a recipe from the main text. Next, set the slow cooker on HIGH and melt the fat. Then, add the meat, with or without a coating of spices, and turn it to coat evenly with the fat. It will not brown as thoroughly as in a skillet on top of the stove, but the resulting flavor is as good.

TEST FOR DONENESS—The cooking times given in these recipes will produce tender, but not overdone meat. You will know the veal is ready to serve when the juices run clear and the meat tender when pierced with a fork. You can safely leave these dishes in the slow cooker set on LOW for an extra hour without worrying about overcooking.

Occasionally, the amount of liquid called for in the master recipe must be reduced. If this adjustment is necessary, it is indicated in the directions.

We also suggest which sauces are best finished on top of the stove (usually a much quicker method) or provide directions for completing them in the slow cooker.

REMINDERS—Use the appropriate-size slow cooker as directed in each recipe.

When preparing stews, be sure to arrange the contents of the slow cooker so vegetables are totally covered by the cooking liquid.

The introductory chapter, **Home Cooking in the Slow Cooker**, provides additional tips and an easy-to-read chart comparing settings among different brands of slow cookers.

Blanquette of Veal 1
(page 167)

Use a 3½-qt. slow cooker.

Slice onions very thin.

Place all ingredients in slow cooker, except use only enough liquid to cover contents by two-thirds.

Cook on LOW for 7 to 8 hrs.

Finish sauce on top of the stove.

Veal and Green Bean Stew 2
(page 169)

Use a 3½-qt. slow cooker.

Place fat in slow cooker and melt on HIGH. Add meat and turn to coat evenly with fat.

Add all remaining ingredients, except use only enough broth to cover contents by two-thirds.

Cover and cook on LOW for 7 to 8 hrs.

Finish sauce on top of the stove as in Recipe.

Return sauce to slow cooker and reheat on HIGH for 10 min. Reset to LOW until ready to serve.

Veal Ragout *(page 170)*

Use a 3½-qt. slow cooker.

Quarter carrots.

Place fat in slow cooker and melt on HIGH. Add meat and turn to coat evenly with fat.

Add all remaining ingredients, except use only enough liquid to cover contents by two-thirds.

Cook on LOW for 8 to 9 hrs.

Swiss Veal Balls *(page 171)*

Use a 3½-qt. slow cooker.

Place butter or margarine in slow cooker and melt on HIGH. Add veal balls and turn to coat evenly with fat; cover.

Cook on LOW for 8 to 9 hrs.

Complete sauce on top of the stove as in Recipe.

Veal Balls with Sour Cream *(page 172)* 5

Use a 3½-qt. slow cooker.

Place fat in slow cooker and melt on HIGH. Add veal balls and turn to coat evenly with fat.

Add mushrooms with liquid; cover.

Cook on LOW for 5 to 6 hrs.

Remove meat balls from liquid. Add sour cream and meat broth, if necessary.

Cook on HIGH, stirring frequently, to heat. Do not boil. Return meat balls to sauce and heat thoroughly. Reset to LOW until ready to serve.

Roast Leg of Lamb with spiced peaches and buttered peas

Crown Roast of Lamb

Set out a shallow roasting pan with rack.

Wipe with a clean, damp cloth
   4- to 6-lb. (12 to 16 rib) crown roast of lamb

(Have meat dealer remove backbone to make carving easier.) Rub lamb with a mixture of
   2 teaspoons salt
   1 teaspoon Accent
   ¼ teaspoon pepper
Cover each rib bone with a piece of
   Salt pork or bacon
If desired, insert into meaty portion in center of crown
   2 cloves garlic (page 12), slivered
Place lamb, rib bones up, on rack in pan. Insert roast meat thermometer between ribs into center of thickest part of meat, being sure bulb does not rest in fat.

Roast lamb uncovered at 300°F 3 to 4½ hrs., or until thermometer registers 180°F. (Allow about 45 min. per lb.)

Remove from oven to warm serving plate. Replace bacon with paper frills.

Fill center of crown with cooked small whole **potatoes**, fresh **peas**, tiny **carrots** or **cauliflowerets**. *6 to 8 servings*

Note: Center of roast may be filled before roasting with seasoned, ground **lamb trimmings,** or a **bread** or **sausage stuffing.** Proceed as above, allowing about 1 hr. longer for roasting time.

▲ Roast Leg of Lamb

Set out a shallow roasting pan with rack.

Wipe with a clean, damp cloth
   5- to 6-lb. leg of lamb
Do not remove the fell (thin papery covering).

Rub lamb with a mixture of
   2 teaspoons salt
   1 teaspoon Accent
   ¼ teaspoon pepper
Place lamb skin side down on rack in pan. Insert roast meat thermometer in center of thickest part of meat, being sure that bulb does not rest on bone or in fat.

Roast lamb uncovered at 300°F about 3 hrs., allowing 30 to 35 min. per pound. Meat is medium done when thermometer registers 175°F and well done at 180°F.

Place a paper frill around end of leg bone.

Serve on warm platter. Garnish with **parsley** or **mint leaves.** *About 10 servings*

△ Roast Leg of Lamb, French Style

Follow ▲ Recipe. Before roasting, cut several small slits in surface of meat. Insert into each slit 1 sliver of **garlic.** Melt 3 tablespoons **butter.** Use butter to brush meat frequently during roasting. Remove meat from pan and pour off fat from drippings in pan.

Make gravy by stirring into drippings in pan 1 cup cold **quick meat broth** (*page 13*) or **water.** Bring to boiling over direct heat, stirring constantly. Season with a mixture of ½ teaspoon **salt,** ¼ teaspoon **Accent** and ¼ teaspoon **pepper.**

Roast Shoulder of Lamb  3

A roast that is especially appealing to those who haven't conquered their carving shyness.

Set out a shallow roasting pan with rack.

Wipe with a clean, damp cloth
> **3- to 5-lb. rolled lamb shoulder**

Do not remove fell (thin, papery covering). Rub lamb with cut side of
> **1 clove garlic (*page 12*), cut**
> **lengthwise**

Rub lamb with a mixture of
> **2 teaspoons salt**
> **1 teaspoon Accent**
> **¼ teaspoon pepper**

Place lamb on rack in roasting pan. Insert roast meat thermometer in center of thickest part of meat, being sure that bulb does not rest in fat.

Roast lamb uncovered at 300°F 2 to 3½ hrs., allowing 40 to 45 min. per lb. Meat is medium done when thermometer registers 175°F and well done at 180°F.

Remove from oven to warm serving platter. Garnish as desired.　　　*About 8 servings*

Broiled Lamb Chops

Wipe with a clean, damp cloth
> **Lamb chops, (shoulder, rib or loin)**
> **cut ¾ to 1 in. thick**

Allow about ½ lb. meat per serving.

If desired, rub each chop with cut side of
> **1 clove garlic (*page 12*), cut into halves**

Set temperature control of range at Broil.

Arrange chops on broiler rack. Place in broiler with tops of chops 2 in. from heat source; broil 5 to 6 min.

Meanwhile, for each pound of meat, mix together
> **1 teaspoon salt**
> **½ teaspoon Accent**
> **¼ teaspoon pepper**

When chops are browned on one side, sprinkle with one half of the seasoning mixture. Turn and broil second side 5 to 6 min. Test for doneness by cutting a slit along the bone and noting color of meat. Season second side of meat.

Note: Broil chops cut 2 in. thick 3 in. from source of heat for a total of 20 to 22 min.

Panbroiled Lamb Chops

Panbroiled Lamb Chops

Heat a large, heavy skillet.

Wipe with a clean, damp cloth
  4 lamb chops, cut about ¾ in. thick
Cut through fat on outside edge of each lamb chop at 1-in. intervals; be careful not to cut through the lean. Place chops in skillet and brown meat slowly over medium heat. Maintain a temperature which allows juices to evaporate rather than collect in pan. With too low heat, the meat will simmer in its own juices and become dry and less tender when cooked. If necessary, turn meat occasionally for even browning and pour off fat as it accumulates.

For each pound of meat, mix together
  1 teaspoon salt
  ½ teaspoon Accent
  ¼ teaspoon pepper
When chops are browned on one side, turn and sprinkle one half of the seasoning mixture over top. Sprinkle remaining seasoning over other side of chops just before serving. Allow 10 to 12 min. for complete panbroiling time. Test for doneness by cutting a slit along the bone and noting color of meat.   *4 servings*

Oven-Dinner Lamb Chops
MRS. ALLEN HUGHES, MIDDLEPORT, OHIO

Lemon lends a subtle bouquet to this dish.

Set out a shallow 2-qt. casserole having a tight-fitting cover.

Wipe with a clean, damp cloth
  6 lamb shoulder chops, cut ½ in. thick
Cut through fat on outside edge of each chop at 1-in. intervals; be careful not to cut lean.

Heat in a large skillet over medium heat
  1 tablespoon fat
Add the lamb chops and brown on both sides.

Meanwhile, cut into six rings and set aside
  1 medium-size green pepper
    (page 12)
Cut into six slices each and set aside
  1 large onion (page 12)
  1 lemon, rinsed
Mix together
  2 cups (1 No. 2 can) tomato juice
  1½ teaspoons salt
  ½ teaspoon Accent
  ¼ teaspoon pepper
Arrange browned chops in the casserole. Top each with a green pepper ring, an onion slice and a lemon slice. Pour the seasoned tomato juice over the chops.

Cover and bake at 300°F about 1 hr., or until meat is tender when pierced with a fork.

Just before serving, remove and discard the lemon slices. Spoon sauce over chops.

6 servings

Lamb Chops with Dill Sauce

Set out a large, heavy skillet having a tight-fitting cover.

Heat in the skillet over medium heat
  3 tablespoons fat
Add and cook until transparent, occasionally moving pieces with a spoon
  ½ cup (about 1 medium-size)
    chopped onion (page 12)

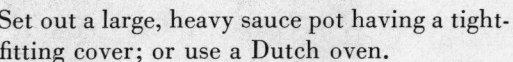

With a slotted spoon, remove onion from skillet to a small dish; set aside.

Wipe with a clean, damp cloth
> **4 lamb shoulder chops, cut ½ in. thick**

Cut through fat on outside edge of each chop at 1-in. intervals, being careful not to cut through lean. Put chops in the skillet; brown both sides over medium heat.

Meanwhile, mix together
> **2 tablespoons water**
> **1 tablespoon vinegar**
> **1 teaspoon salt**
> **½ teaspoon Accent**
> **¼ teaspoon pepper**

Add
> **1 bay leaf**

Slowly add this mixture to the browned lamb chops. Return onion to skillet. Cover skillet and simmer 25 to 30 min., or until lamb is tender when pierced with a fork. Add small amounts of water as necessary as lamb cooks.

For Sauce—When meat is almost tender, prepare and set aside
> **½ cup quick meat broth (page 13)**

Melt in a small skillet over low heat
> **2 tablespoons butter or margarine**

Blend in
> **2 tablespoons flour**
> **¼ teaspoon salt**
> **¼ teaspoon Accent**
> **Few grains pepper**

Heat until mixture bubbles and is lightly browned. Remove skillet from heat.

Add gradually, stirring constantly, a mixture of the reserved broth and
> **1 tablespoon chopped fresh dill**

Bring rapidly to boiling, stirring constantly; cook 1 to 2 min. longer. Remove sauce from heat and add gradually, stirring constantly
> **½ cup dry white wine, such as Chablis or sauterne**
> **2 tablespoons vinegar**

Serve the sauce over the lamb chops.

4 servings

Curried Lamb with Rice

MRS. CHARLES F. GIBSON
HENDERSON, TEXAS

Set out a large, heavy sauce pot having a tight-fitting cover; or use a Dutch oven.

Wipe with a clean, damp cloth
> **2 lbs. boneless lamb shoulder**

Cut into 1-in. cubes. Set aside.

Heat in the sauce pot over medium heat
> **3 tablespoons fat**

Put the meat into the sauce pot and brown on all sides over medium heat. Add
> **2 small onions (page 12), coarsely chopped**

Cook until onion is transparent, occasionally moving and turning mixture. Add
> **1 cup hot water**
> **1 teaspoon chopped parsley**
> **1 bay leaf**
> **6 whole peppercorns**

and a mixture of
> **1 teaspoon curry powder**
> **1 teaspoon salt**
> **½ teaspoon Accent**
> **¼ teaspoon pepper**

Bring liquid rapidly to boiling. Reduce heat to low; cover and simmer (do not boil) about 1½ hrs., or until meat is tender when pierced with a fork. Add small amounts of hot water as needed. Remove meat and set it aside to keep warm.

Remove bay leaf and peppercorns from liquid. Thicken cooking liquid (*p. 107*; add flour-water mixture one tablespoon at a time). Return meat to gravy and heat. Serve with
> **Perfection Boiled Rice (page 275)**

About 6 servings

Shish Kabobs and tossed salad

▲ Lamb Kabobs

For Marinade—Mix together thoroughly
   ¾ cup tarragon vinegar
   ⅓ cup salad oil
   2 teaspoons salt
   ¾ teaspoon Accent
   ½ teaspoon pepper
Add
   1 bay leaf
   ½ clove garlic (page 12)

For Kabobs—Wipe with a clean, damp cloth
   1½ lbs. boneless lamb (shoulder or leg)
Cut into 1½-in. cubes. Cover lamb with marinade and set in refrigerator for at least 24 hrs., turning meat several times.

Set out six 8-in. skewers.

Clean (*page 12*), cut into halves from top to base and set aside
   6 small (about 1 lb.) onions
Clean (*page 12*, do not slice), remove stems from and set aside
   12 large mushrooms
(Mushroom stems may be used in other recipes as desired.)

Rinse and pat dry with absorbent paper
   6 chicken livers

Cut into halves and wrap around livers
   3 slices bacon
Thread onto each skewer in the following order: lamb, onion half, mushroom, liver, lamb, onion half and mushroom. Do not crowd pieces on skewer.

Brush meat and vegetables generously with
   Melted butter or margarine
Arrange skewers on broiler rack.

Set temperature control of range at Broil.

Place in broiler with tops of kabobs about 3 in. from source of heat. Broil 15 to 20 min., turning kabobs several times and brushing with melted butter or margarine. Test for doneness by cutting a slit in lamb cubes and noting color of meat. Season kabobs with a mixture of
   1 teaspoon salt
   ¼ teaspoon Accent
   ⅛ teaspoon pepper
Serve at once.   *6 servings*

△ Shish Kabobs

Follow ▲ Recipe; increase lamb to 2 lbs.; omit mushrooms, chicken livers, and bacon. Clean and cut into quarters 3 small **green peppers.** Beginning with an onion half, thread onto each skewer in the following order: onion half, lamb, green pepper, lamb; repeat.

Lamb with Green Beans

Set out a large, heavy skillet having a tight-fitting cover.

Wipe with a clean, damp cloth
   2 lbs. boneless lamb shoulder
Cut meat into 2-in. cubes and set aside.

Put into the skillet
   4 slices bacon, diced
Cook slowly, moving and turning pieces frequently, until bacon is lightly browned. With slotted spoon, remove bacon to a small dish; set aside.

Add to the bacon drippings in the skillet
   ½ cup (about 1 medium-size)
      chopped onion (page 12)
Cook until onion is transparent, occasionally moving and turning with a spoon. Remove onion with slotted spoon to dish containing the bacon. Set aside.

Add the meat to the bacon drippings and brown on all sides over medium heat. Sprinkle over meat a mixture of
   2 teaspoons salt
   1 teaspoon Accent
   1 teaspoon caraway seeds
   1 teaspoon paprika
Remove skillet from heat and slowly pour in
   2 cups quick meat broth (double
      recipe, page 13)

Return bacon and onion to skillet. Bring liquid rapidly to boiling; reduce heat, cover and simmer (do not boil) 1½ to 2 hrs., or until meat is tender when pierced with a fork. About an hour before meat is tender, wash, remove stem ends, cut into 1-in. pieces and cook (*p. 285*) 15 to 30 min., or until just tender
   1 lb. (about 3 cups) green beans
If necessary, drain beans (reserving any cooking liquid) and set aside. Cool the cooking liquid completely.

For Gravy—Pour into a small screw-top jar
   ½ cup liquid (reserved bean cooking
      liquid plus water)
Sprinkle onto the liquid
   ¼ cup flour
Cover jar tightly and shake until mixture is well blended. Bring contents of skillet to boiling. Slowly pour the flour mixture into skillet while stirring constantly; cook 3 to 5 min. longer. Remove from heat and vigorously stir about ½ cup of the gravy, 1 tablespoon at a time, into
   ½ cup thick sour cream
Pour the mixture gradually into the skillet, stirring constantly. Gently mix in the green beans. Cook ingredients over low heat, moving mixture gently, until heated thoroughly (3 to 5 min.); do not boil. Serve at once.

5 to 7 servings

▲ Irish Stew

Set out a large kettle having a tight-fitting cover; or use a Dutch oven.

Wipe with a clean, damp cloth
2 lbs. boneless lamb for stew
Cut meat into 2-in. pieces. Coat meat evenly (*page 107*) with a mixture of
⅓ cup flour
2 teaspoons salt
½ teaspoon Accent
⅛ teaspoon pepper
Heat in the kettle over medium heat
3 tablespoons fat
Add lamb and brown on all sides over medium heat, moving and turning pieces occasionally. Pour off excess fat. Remove from heat and slowly pour into the kettle
1 qt. hot water
Cover and bring liquid to boiling over high heat. Reduce heat; simmer (do not boil) about 1½ hrs., or until meat is almost tender. Add small amounts of hot water as necessary.

Add vegetables to kettle about 45 min. before end of cooking period. About 15 min. before adding vegetables to stew, clean (*page 12*) and set aside
6 small onions
Clean (*page 12;* do not remove leaves) and cut crosswise into slices ½ in. thick
4 stalks celery, with leaves
Set pieces aside.

Wash, scrape or pare, cut into ½-in. pieces and set aside
4 small carrots
Wash, pare and quarter
6 medium-size (about 2 lbs.)
  potatoes
1 medium-size turnip
Add the prepared vegetables to the stew with
1½ teaspoons salt
½ teaspoon Accent
⅛ teaspoon pepper
Cover and simmer about 45 min., or until meat and vegetables are tender when pierced with a fork. With slotted spoon, remove meat and vegetables from stew to hot dish. Thicken cooking liquid (*page 107*).

Return meat and vegetables to kettle and heat thoroughly. Serve hot.   *8 to 10 servings*

△ Savory Lamb Stew

Follow ▲ Recipe; omit turnip. Add to stew with seasonings ¼ teaspoon **savory**, ¼ teaspoon **basil** and ¼ teaspoon **marjoram**.

△ Irish Stew with Dumplings

Follow ▲ Recipe. After adding vegetables to stew, prepare **Dumplings** (*p. 69*). Bring stew to boiling. Drop dumpling mixture by tablespoonfuls on top of stew. (Dumplings should rest on meat and vegetables; if dumplings settle down into the liquid, they may be soggy.) If necessary, remove some of the liquid temporarily to prevent this. Cover tightly and cook over medium heat 20 min. without removing cover. Remove stew and dumplings to hot serving dish.

△ Lamb Pies

Follow ▲ Recipe; omit celery and turnip. Substitute 2 medium-size **onions**, sliced, for the small whole onions. Cube potatoes and slice the carrots ¼ in. thick. Stir into the finished stew 1 cup (8-oz. can, drained) **peas**.

Set out 8 individual casseroles.

Lamb Pies

After adding vegetables to stew, prepare **Tender-Rich Biscuits** (*page 62*; roll dough ¼ in. thick and cut to fit tops of casseroles; bake as for biscuits). Spoon stew into the casseroles and top each with a baked biscuit.

Spicy Lamb Shanks 9
EVELYN N. REED, WHITE RIVER JUNC., N. H.

Set out a large, heavy skillet and a large, shallow baking dish with aluminum foil to cover.

Wipe with a clean, damp cloth
4 lamb shanks, about 1 lb. each
(Have meat dealer crack shin bone.)

Coat shanks evenly with a mixture of
¼ cup flour
1 teaspoon salt
¾ teaspoon Accent
¼ teaspoon pepper
Heat in the skillet over medium heat
¼ cup fat
Put shanks in the skillet. Brown well on all sides. Remove shanks to baking dish. Add
½ cup water
Cover; bake at 300°F about 1½ hrs., or until meat is almost tender when pierced with fork.

Meanwhile, prepare
1⅔ cups Cooked Apricots (one-third recipe, page 494)
1 cup Stewed Prunes (one-third recipe, page 494)
Drain. Remove and discard pits from prunes. Put fruit into a saucepan. Add
1 cup water
½ cup sugar
3 tablespoons vinegar
½ teaspoon cinnamon
½ teaspoon allspice
¼ teaspoon cloves
¼ teaspoon salt
Bring rapidly to boiling and simmer 5 min.

Drain fat from cooked shanks. Add the cooked fruit mixture. Cover and bake 30 min. longer. Serve hot.   *4 servings*

Barbecued Lamb Shanks
MRS. JOHN SWETKA, RED BLUFF, CALIF.

Set out a large, shallow baking dish having a tight-fitting cover and a large, heavy skillet.

Wipe with a clean, damp cloth
4 lamb shanks, about 1 lb. each
(Have meat dealer crack shin bone.)

Coat shanks evenly with a mixture of
¼ cup flour
1 teaspoon salt
½ teaspoon Accent
¼ teaspoon pepper
Heat in the skillet over medium heat
¼ cup fat
Place shanks in the skillet. Brown well on all sides. Remove shanks to baking dish. Meanwhile, mix together in a saucepan
1 cup ketchup or chili sauce
½ cup water
¼ cup wine vinegar
4 teaspoons Worcestershire sauce
2 teaspoons sugar
2 teaspoons paprika
1 teaspoon dry mustard
1 teaspoon salt
½ teaspoon Accent
½ teaspoon pepper
5 drops tabasco sauce
1 cup (about 2 medium-size) chopped onion (page 12)
2 cloves garlic (page 12), minced; or crushed in garlic press
Heat sauce to boiling. Remove from heat and pour over meat.

Bake, covered, at 300°F 1½ to 2 hrs., or until meat is tender when pierced with a fork. Turn and baste shanks frequently.

Serve with
Perfection Boiled Rice (page 275)
4 servings

*Lamb Burgers with
Horse-radish Sour Cream Sauce*

Lamb Casserole 10

Set out a 2-qt. top-of-range casserole having a tight-fitting cover.

Prepare and set aside
> ½ cup garlic buttered bread crumbs
> (See buttered crumbs, *page 10*; put
> 1 clove garlic, cut into halves,
> into hot melted butter and allow
> to stand until butter has absorbed
> garlic flavor. Remove garlic from
> butter before adding crumbs.)

Wipe with a clean, damp cloth and cut into 1-in. pieces
> 1½ lbs. boneless lamb shoulder

Heat in the casserole over medium heat
> 2 tablespoons fat

Add the lamb and brown pieces on all sides. Add gradually
> 2½ cups water

Add
> 1½ teaspoons salt
> ½ teaspoon curry powder
> ⅛ teaspoon pepper

Cover casserole and simmer 1¼ hrs.

Meanwhile, cut into thin slices
> 1 medium-size bunch (about ½ lb.)
> celery (*page 12*)

Clean, pare or scrape and slice
> 1 lb. carrots (about 2½ cups, sliced)

Prepare and mix with the carrots and celery
> ½ cup (about 1 medium-size)
> chopped onion (*page 12*)
> ¼ cup chopped green pepper
> (*page 12*)

Mix vegetables with meat in the casserole. Cover and cook over medium heat 20 to 25 min., or until vegetables are tender.

Meanwhile, cook and drain (*page 277*)
> 1½ cups (about 2 oz.) noodles

Stir noodles into casserole; simmer 10 min.

Thicken cooking liquid (*page 107*).

Top with the garlic crumbs. Set temperature control of range at Broil. Place casserole under broiler with top of casserole 4 in. from source of heat. Broil until crumbs are lightly browned.   *6 to 8 servings*

▲ Lamb Burgers 11

Combine and mix lightly
> 1½ lbs. ground lamb
> 3 tablespoons minced parsley
> 1 egg, beaten

and a mixture of
> 1 teaspoon salt
> ½ teaspoon Accent
> ¼ teaspoon allspice

Shape mixture into 5 patties about 1 in. thick.

Set temperature control of range at Broil.

Arrange patties on broiler rack. Put in broiler with tops of patties about 3 in. from heat source. Broil about 9 min. When browned on one side, turn and broil second side about 9 min. or until browned.

Meanwhile, toast and butter
> **Hamburger bun halves**

Put the burgers on bun halves. Top with
> **Onion rings**

Serve with
> **Horse-radish Sour Cream Sauce**
> (*page 330*)

5 servings

⚠ **Minted Lamb Burgers**

Follow ▲ Recipe. Set out 2 tablespoons **mint jelly.** When second sides of lamb burgers are browned, put about 1 teaspoon of the jelly on each patty. Broil 2 or 3 min. longer, or until jelly is melted and heated.

⚠ **Apricot Lamb Burgers**

Cut 4 slices of **bacon** into small pieces and cook as in **Panbroiled Bacon** (*p.161*). ▢ Follow ▲ Recipe. Divide the meat mixture into 5 portions. Fill 5 large cooked **apricot halves** with the bacon pieces. Place an apricot half on each meat portion; gently enclose the apricot with the meat, forming a patty. Broil as in ▲ Recipe.

Lamb Patties

Lamb Patties
JOAN BRYAN, PAXTON, ILL.

For an easy-on-the-budget dinner serve these juicy little bundles of ground lamb seasoned with an intriguing hint of sage.

Set out
   6 slices bacon
Mix together lightly
   1 lb. ground lamb
   1½ cups (1½ slices) soft bread crumbs
   ¼ cup finely chopped onion
   1 tablespoon chopped parsley
   1 tablespoon Worcestershire sauce
   ½ cup milk
and a mixture of
   ½ teaspoon salt
   ½ teaspoon Accent
   ⅛ teaspoon pepper
   ⅛ teaspoon sage

Shape mixture into 6 patties about ¾ in. thick. Wrap 1 bacon slice around edge of each patty; secure bacon with wooden picks.

Set temperature control of range at Broil.

Arrange patties on broiler rack. Put in broiler with tops of patties about 3 in. from source of heat. Broil about 8 min. on each side.

Serve immediately. If desired, accompany with **French Fried Onions** (*page 294*). Garnish with **mint leaves.**   *6 servings*

Frosted Lamb Loaf

Ground Lamb Scallop 15

Grease a 2-qt. casserole.

Heat in a large skillet
2 tablespoons fat
Add and cook over medium heat until brown, breaking into small pieces with fork or spoon
2 lbs. ground lamb
When lightly browned, add and continue cooking until onions are transparent
2 tablespoons chopped onion
1 small green pepper (*page 12*), chopped
Meanwhile, mix
1 egg, well beaten
1 cup thick, sour cream
2 tablespoons minced parsley
and a mixture of
1½ teaspoons salt
1 teaspoon Accent
¼ teaspoon pepper
⅛ to ¼ teaspoon marjoram
Pour over browned lamb and mix well. Turn one half of mixture into casserole. Top with
1 cup coarsely grated carrot
Cover with remaining meat mixture.

Cut into thin slices
1 medium-size onion (*page 12*)
Separate into rings. Using a fork, blend with
3 to 4 tablespoons melted butter or margarine
Arrange onion rings over meat (reserving remaining butter).

Bake at 350°F 35 to 45 min. After 15 min. of baking, drizzle remaining butter over onions.

6 servings

Frosted Lamb Loaf 14

Grease a 9½x5¼x2¾-in. loaf pan.

Mix together lightly
1½ lbs. ground lamb
¾ cup uncooked rolled oats
¼ cup minced onion
2 tablespoons minced parsley
½ clove garlic (*page 12*), minced or crushed in a garlic press
1¼ cups (10½ to 11-oz. can) condensed tomato soup
2 eggs, beaten
and a mixture of
1½ teaspoons salt
¾ teaspoon Accent
¼ teaspoon pepper
Pack lightly into loaf pan.

Bake at 350°F about 1½ hrs.

While loaf is baking, prepare
Whipped Potatoes (*page 298*)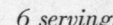
Unmold (*page 107*) loaf onto heat-resistant platter or baking pan. Spread whipped potatoes over top and sides of loaf. Brush with
Melted butter or margarine
Return to oven for 15 to 20 min., or until potato is lightly browned.

Remove loaf from oven and sprinkle over top
2 tablespoons chopped chives
Serve immediately.   *6 to 8 servings*

LAMB in the MICROWAVE OVEN

The microwave oven is a bonanza for the less expensive cuts of lamb, including stew meat, lamb shanks and ground lamb.

The stews, such as **Lamb Stew with Green Beans**, are not only ready to serve in less than 50 minutes, but are tender and flavorful and not too fatty, a drawback not always easy to escape with lamb.

Roasts fare well in the microwave oven, with the meat medium-well done and the fat not crisp, but flavorful and cooked through. Roasts are started fat side down, the reverse of conventional oven cooking.

Chops—We have eliminated the chop recipes from this section. The microwave oven is simply too efficient for them. They tend to get overdone before they are sufficiently browned.

Ground Lamb dishes are juicy and delicious, with the **Frosted Lamb Loaf** a real discovery worthy of party fare. It can be prepared ahead of time, covered with the potato frosting and refrigerated. It can then be reheated and ready to serve in 5 minutes; perfect for a hearty, after-football dinner.

Browning—Use the browning skillet to brown meat where indicated. It is important to preheat the skillet, usually about 3 minutes, to get the most effective results. Cover the meat-filled skillet before browning. Use plastic wrap if necessary.

Standing Time—As with all meats, lamb must stand, covered, after cooking in the microwave oven to permit the flavor to develop and juices to settle. Standing times are indicated with each recipe.

Gravies and Sauces are delicious and silk-smooth in texture with well-blended flavors. Frequent stirring is the key to achieving this delicate smoothness, especially for those sauces and gravies which call for cream or sour cream to be added.

REMINDERS—Cooking times for each recipe will vary somewhat, depending on your oven and, to some extent, your taste. Do not be hesitant about checking frequently as the dish nears the end of the cooking time.

The introductory chapter, **Home Cooking in the Microwave Oven**, offers additional tips and an easy-to-read chart comparing settings among different brands of microwave ovens. Review the entire chapter before preparing any of these recipes.

Roast Leg of Lamb
(page 174)

Use a glass baking dish with rack. The times given in this recipe are for a 4-lb. leg of lamb. (For a different-size roast, allow 5 min. per lb. before testing for doneness.)

Place meat, fat side down, on rack. COOK, rotating pan every 5 min., until it starts to brown (about 10 min.).

For medium doneness, turn roast and COOK, turning pan every 5 min., until juices are a light pink and the internal temperature reaches 150° (about 10 min.). The temperature will continue to rise during the standing time. If you do not have the special microwave thermometer, remove the roast from the oven (this will not interfere with the cooking process), insert thermometer and cover with aluminum foil while waiting for temperature to register. If you must return the roast to the oven, be sure to remove the thermometer and the aluminum foil.

Cover and let stand 20 min.

OVERALL COOKING TIME: 20:00

Roast Leg of Lamb, French Style *(page 174)*

Follow **1** Recipe for roasting times. Follow △ Recipe for seasoning, except omit the butter basting.

To make gravy, COOK liquid to heat (about 1½ min.). Add seasonings, stir and COOK, stirring every 30 sec., until simmering (about 4 min.).

OVERALL COOKING TIME: 25:30

Roast Shoulder of Lamb
(page 175)

Use a glass baking dish with rack. The times given in this recipe are for a 4-lb. roast. (For a different-size roast, allow 5 min. per lb. before testing for doneness.)

Place meat, fat side down, on rack. COOK, rotating pan every 5 min., until it starts to brown (about 12 min.).

For medium doneness, turn roast and COOK, rotating pan every 5 min., until juices are a light pink and the internal temperature reaches 150° (about 12 min.). The temperature will continue to rise during the standing time. If you do not have the special microwave thermometer, remove the roast from the oven (this will not interfere with the cooking process), insert a conventional thermometer and cover with aluminum foil while waiting for temperature to register. If you must return the roast to the oven, be sure to remove both the thermometer and the aluminum foil.

Cover and let stand 20 min.

OVERALL COOKING TIME: 24:00

Curried Lamb with Rice **4**
(page 177)

Use a 2-qt. casserole.

Preheat skillet (3 min.). Place fat in casserole and cook until melted.

Add meat and cover. COOK, rotating pan and stirring every 5 min., until brown (about 10 min.).

Add onion and COOK, stirring every 1½ min., until transparent (about 3 min.).

Add remaining ingredients and cover. COOK until liquid simmers (about 8 min.). SLOW-COOK until meat is tender (about 20 min.).

Use some cooking liquid to make the thickening mixture and add to heated liquid, stirring vigorously with a wire whisk. COOK, stirring after 1 min., to heat and thicken (about 2 min.).

Return meat to gravy and COOK to heat (about 5 min.).

Cover and let stand 15 min.

OVERALL COOKING TIME: 51:00

Lamb with Green Beans **5**
(page 179)

Use a browning skillet and a casserole for the beans.

Prepare beans, cover and set aside.

In skillet, COOK bacon, turning every 1 min., until lightly browned (about 3 min.). Remove bacon and set aside.

Add onion and COOK, stirring every 1 min., until transparent (about 3 min.). Remove onion and set aside.

Add meat and seasonings to bacon drippings and COOK, rotating pan and stirring every 5 min., until brown (about 10 min.).

Return bacon and onion and add hot broth; cover. COOK, rotating pan and stirring every 5 min., until simmering (about 5 min.). SLOW-COOK until meat is tender (about 20 min.).

Add beans and COOK until simmering (about 5 min.).

For Gravy—Use some cooking liquid to make the thickening mixture and add to heated liquid, stirring. COOK until thickened (about 3 min.).

Add sour cream and stir thoroughly; it will heat during the standing time.

Cover and let stand 15 min.

Pour off excess fat, add water, cover and COOK until boiling (about 8 min.). SLOWCOOK, rotating pan and stirring every 5 min., until meat is almost tender (about 20 min.).

Add vegetables and seasonings, cover and SLOWCOOK, rotating pan and stirring every 5 min., until vegetables and meat are tender (about 15 min.).

Cover and let stand 15 min.

OVERALL COOKING TIME: 56:00

Savory Lamb Stew
(page 180)

Follow Recipe with changes as in ⚠ Recipe.

Irish Stew *(page 180)*

Use a browning skillet and a 3-qt. covered casserole.

Preheat skillet (3 min.). Add fat and COOK until melted.

Add meat and COOK, turning meat and rotating pan every 5 min., until brown (about 10 min.).

Irish Stew with Dumplings *(page 180)*

Follow Recipe with addition as in ⚠ Recipe, except add dumplings when vegetables are almost tender.

Add 2 cups water, seasonings and cover. COOK, stirring every 5 min., until meat is almost tender (about 20 min.).

Add vegetables, cover and COOK, stirring every 5 min., until vegetables and meat are tender (about 15 min.).

Add noodles and crumbs. COOK, uncovered, until crumbs and noodles are hot (about 5 min.).

Cover and let stand 15 min.

Spicy Lamb Shanks 9
(page 181)

Use a browning skillet, a covered baking dish and a casserole.

Prepare apricots and prunes.

Preheat skillet to very hot (3 min.). Add fat and COOK until melted.

Add meat to skillet, cover and COOK, turning every 5 min., until brown on both sides (about 10 min.).

Transfer shanks to baking dish. Add water, cover and COOK, turning meat every 15 min., until almost tender (about 30 min.). Remove, cover and set aside.

COOK fruit mix until simmering (about 5 min.). SLOWCOOK until flavors are blended (about 5 min.).

Add fruit mixture to meat, cover and COOK until meat is tender (about 5 min.).

Cover and let stand 15 min.

OVERALL COOKING TIME: 59:00

Lamb Burgers (page 182) 11

Use a browning skillet. The times given in this recipe are for preparing 3 burgers.

Preheat skillet (3 min.). Add burgers and COOK until brown on both sides and done to taste (about 3 min. each side).

Cover and let stand 5 min.

OVERALL COOKING TIME: 6:00

Lamb Casserole (page 182) 10

Use a 2-qt. casserole.

COOK to melt fat and heat casserole (3 min.).

Add meat and COOK, rotating pan and turning meat every 3 min., until brown (about 10 min.).

Minted Lamb Burgers 12
(page 183)

Follow 11 Recipe with addition as in ⚠ Recipe.

Apricot Lamb Burgers
(page 183)

Follow Recipe with changes as in △ Recipe.

Frosted Lamb Loaf 14
(page 184)

Use a 2-qt. loaf pan. Do not grease.

COOK, unfrosted lamb loaf rotating pan every 3 min., to raise temperature (6 min.). SLOW-COOK, rotating pan every 5 min., until juices run clear (about 10 min.).

Frost with potatoes and COOK to heat (about 5 min.).

Cover and let stand 15 min.

Ground Lamb Scallop 15
(page 184)

Use a browning skillet and a 2-qt. casserole.

Preheat skillet (3 min.). Add fat and COOK until melted.

Add meat and COOK, stirring every 1½ min. and rotating pan every 3 min., until browned (about 6 min.).

Add onion and pepper and COOK, turning every 2 min., until onion is transparent (about 4 min.).

Assemble remaining ingredients for casserole as in Recipe; cover. COOK, turning pan every 5 min., until set and heated through (about 20 min.).

Cover and let stand 15 min.

OVERALL COOKING TIME: 23:00

LAMB in the SLOW COOKER

Irish Stew cooked in the slow cooker is exactly what an Irish stew is supposed to be—a really hearty stick-to-your-ribs dish, satisfying to the most demanding appetites. For that matter, the same can be said for all these stew recipes. A bonus for the cook—do not be hesitant to hold these one-dish meals on LOW until you are ready to serve.

Some cuts of lamb are not well-suited to preparation in the slow cooker. We have eliminated these recipes. Roasts and lamb shanks are too fatty to be cooked in this manner without additional browning. Chop recipes are tasty, but emerge with a stew-like character. Because lamb is fatty by nature, we recommend you always work with lean meat or trim as much fat as possible.

Browning—Those meats which are the basis of stews and casseroles can be browned in the slow cooker to seal in flavor and juices. Place the fat in the slow cooker set on HIGH. Coat the meat with seasonings where directed, but always omit any flour from the coating mixture. When the fat has melted, add the meat and turn to coat evenly. Do not expect the meat to really turn brown in color as it would if browned on top of the stove, but the flavor will be enhanced in a similar manner.

Sauces and Gravies—In recipes which call for thickened sauces or gravies we may suggest they be thickened on top of the stove (it's quicker) or give directions for completing them in the slow cooker.

REMINDERS—Use a 3½-qt. slow cooker unless specifically director otherwise.

When preparing stews, be sure to arrange the contents of the slow cooker so vegetables are totally covered by the cooking liquid.

The introductory chapter, **Home Cooking in the Slow Cooker**, in the beginning of this book offers additional tips and a handy chart comparing settings among different brands of slow cookers. We recommend you read this material before preparing any of these recipes.

Curried Lamb with Rice *(page 177)* ①

Place fat in slow cooker and melt on HIGH. Add meat and turn to coat evenly with fat.

Add remaining ingredients, except add just enough water to cover contents by two-thirds.

Cover and cook on LOW for 7 to 8 hrs.

Serve as in Recipe.

Lamb with Green Beans *(page 179)* ②

Line bottom of slow cooker with diced bacon. Add all remaining ingredients, including beans, except use only enough water to cover contents by two-thirds.

Cover and cook on LOW for 7 to 8 hrs.

For Gravy—Strain cooking liquid from slow cooker and skim fat; use ½ cup for thickening mixture (instead of green bean cooking liquid). Complete gravy on top of the stove as in Recipe.

Return to slow cooker set on LOW to reheat.

Irish Stew *(page 180)* ③

Use a 5-qt. slow cooker.

Omit the 1/3 cup flour from coating mixture.

Place fat in slow cooker and melt on HIGH. Add meat and turn to coat evenly with fat.

Add all remaining ingredients, except use only enough water to cover contents by two-thirds (approximately 3 cups). Be sure to arrange the contents of the slow cooker so vegetables are covered with the liquid.

Cover and cook on LOW for 8 to 9 hrs.

Savory Lamb Stew ④ *(page 180)*

Follow ③ Recipe with changes as in ⚠ Recipe.

▲ Smothered Liver with Onions

Grease a 1½-qt. casserole having a cover.

Wipe with a clean, damp cloth and, if necessary, remove tubes and outer membrane from
1 lb. liver (beef, lamb, veal or calf's)
Cut into serving-size pieces. Coat with a mixture of
⅓ cup flour
½ teaspoon salt
½ teaspoon Accent
Few grains pepper
Heat in a large heavy skillet over medium heat
2 tablespoons bacon drippings
Add liver to skillet and brown on both sides over medium heat. Remove liver to casserole. Set aside.

Heat in the same skillet over low heat
¼ cup butter or margarine
Add to skillet and cook until onion is transparent, occasionally moving and turning mixture with a spoon
5 medium-size (about 1 lb.) onions (*page 12*), thinly sliced
⅔ cup (6¾-oz. can, drained) sliced mushrooms
¼ cup chopped green pepper (*page 12*)
Spoon vegetable mixture over liver.

Prepare
1½ cups Thin White Sauce (1½ times recipe, *page 323*; use 2 tablespoons flour, and use tomato juice for liquid. Add 1 teaspoon sugar and ⅛ teaspoon chili powder)

Smothered Liver with Onions

Remove sauce from heat and blend in
1 tablespoon lemon juice
2 teaspoons Worcestershire sauce
Pour over meat and vegetables in casserole.

Cover and bake at 350°F 25 to 30 min.
4 servings

△ Liver and Rice Piquant

Prepare 2 cups **Perfection Boiled Rice** (*page 275*; use ⅔ cup rice). Follow ▲ Recipe. With a fork, blend rice with cooked onion, green pepper and mushrooms. Spoon over liver and top with sauce.

△ Liver and Noodles

MRS. V. H. CLOSE, FORT PIERCE, FLA.

Follow △ Recipe. Substitute 2 cups **Noodles** (*page 277*; use 1 cup raw noodles) for the rice. Cut the browned liver into 1-in. pieces; blend with the noodles and vegetables.

Calf's Liver with Bacon

Calf's Liver with Bacon

Set out a large, heavy skillet.

Prepare, reserving bacon drippings
12 slices Panbroiled Bacon (page 161)
Wipe with a clean, damp cloth and, if necessary, remove tubes and outer membrane from
6 slices (about 1½-lbs.) veal or calf's liver, cut about ½ in. thick
Coat slices evenly with a mixture of
½ cup flour
1 teaspoon Accent
¾ teaspoon salt
¼ teaspoon pepper
Meanwhile, return to skillet and heat 3 tablespoons of the reserved bacon drippings. Put liver slices in skillet and brown on both sides over medium heat; do not overcook. Arrange on warm serving plate with bacon slices. Serve at once. *6 servings*

Liver Loaf

Grease a 9½x5¼x2¾-in. loaf pan. Set out a large skillet having a tight-fitting cover.

Wipe with a clean, damp cloth, and, if necessary, remove tubes and outer membrane from
¾ lb. pork liver

Put liver in skillet with
1 cup hot water
Cover and simmer 5 min. Drain; set liver aside to cool.

Meanwhile, combine and mix lightly
¾ lb. bulk pork sausage
1½ cups cracker crumbs
¼ cup ketchup
2 tablespoons lemon juice
1 tablespoon Worcestershire sauce
2 eggs, beaten
½ cup milk
and a mixture of
1½ teaspoons salt
½ teaspoon chili powder
½ teaspoon Accent
¼ teaspoon pepper
Grind (*page 107*) the liver. Mix lightly with the sausage mixture. Pack lightly into loaf pan.

Bake at 350°F about 1½ hours. Unmold (*page 107*). *6 to 8 servings*

Liver Balls in Onion Gravy

Set out a large skillet and a small skillet, each having a tight-fitting cover.

Wipe with a clean, damp cloth and, if necessary, remove tubes and outer membrane from
½ lb. liver (beef, lamb, pork or veal)
Put liver into the small skillet with
¾ cup hot water
Cover and simmer 5 min. Drain; set liver aside.

Meanwhile, prepare in the large skillet, reserving drippings
4 slices Panbroiled Bacon (p.161)

While bacon is cooking, mix in a large bowl

1 egg, beaten
¼ cup milk
¼ cup chopped onion
3 tablespoons well-drained, chopped
   sweet pickle
⅓ cup (1 slice) fine, dry bread crumbs

and a mixture of

½ teaspoon salt
¼ teaspoon Accent
⅛ teaspoon pepper

Crumble bacon and add to bread-crumb mixture. Grind (*page 107*) the liver. Add to bacon mixture and mix lightly. Shape into 1½-in. balls. Return reserved drippings to skillet and heat. Brown liver balls in skillet over medium heat, turning occasionally to brown evenly.

Meanwhile, prepare and set aside

2 cups quick meat broth (double
   recipe, *page 13*)

With slotted spoon, remove browned liver balls from skillet; set aside to keep warm.

Heat in the skillet over low heat

½ cup butter or margarine

Add and cook until onion is transparent, occasionally moving and turning with a spoon

¼ cup chopped onion
3 tablespoons (about 1 small)
   chopped carrot
1 bay leaf

Blend into mixture in skillet

4½ tablespoons flour

Heat until mixture bubbles, stirring constantly. Remove from heat.

Gradually add broth, stirring constantly. Bring rapidly to boiling, stirring constantly; cook 1 to 2 min. longer. Add liver balls and simmer about 30 min. Remove bay leaf.

Meanwhile, heat in the small skillet

2 tablespoons butter or margarine

Add and cook until transparent, occasionally moving and turning with a fork

1 large onion (*page 12*), sliced thinly

Garnish liver balls and gravy with onion slices.

About 4 servings

Smoked Tongue Platter

Smoked Tongue Platter

Put into a large, heavy sauce pot having a tight-fitting cover

1 smoked beef tongue

Add enough boiling water to cover the tongue. Cover and simmer 3 to 4 hrs. or until tender. (Or cook according to directions on package.) When tongue is cool enough to handle, slit skin on underside of tongue and peel it off. Cut away roots and gristle. If not used immediately, cool tongue in cooking liquid. Drain; store in refrigerator.

Slice tongue and arrange slices in a ring on serving platter. Fill center of ring with

Garden Potato Salad (*page 310*)

Garnish with

Parsley
Sliced Hard Cooked Eggs (*page 87*)

6 to 8 servings

Beef Tongue with Tomato Sauce

A large, heavy skillet having a tight-fitting cover will be needed.

Wash
1 3- to 4-lb. fresh beef tongue
Put tongue into a 4-qt. kettle or sauce pot having a tight-fitting cover. Add
Hot water (enough to cover tongue)
1 tablespoon salt
2 or 3 bay leaves
1 stalk celery with leaves (page 12),
cut in pieces
1 small onion (page 12)
1 teaspoon peppercorns
Cover and simmer about 1 hr. per lb., or until tongue is tender when pierced with a fork.

Place tongue on platter. When cool enough to handle, remove skin; cut away roots, gristle and small bones at thick end. Diagonally cut tongue into ¼-in. slices. Put slices into the skillet and set aside.

Mix together thoroughly
1½ cups (2 6-oz. cans) tomato paste
1¼ cups (10½- to 11-oz. can)
condensed tomato soup
½ to ¾ cup water
¼ to ½ teaspoon thyme
Pour the tomato sauce over tongue slices. Cover and heat thoroughly (about 20 min.).

Meanwhile, cook and drain (*page 277*)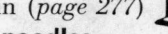
6 cups (8-oz. pkg.) noodles
Serve tongue and sauce with the noodles.
About 12 servings

Tongue and Greens

Set out a large kettle or sauce pot having a tight-fitting cover.

Wash and cook (see Beef Tongue with Tomato Sauce, *on this page*)
1 fresh veal tongue (about 1 lb.)
When tongue is cool enough to handle, slit skin on underside and peel it off. Cut away roots and gristle.

Grease a 1½ qt. casserole. Slice tongue diagonally. Line bottom and sides of casserole with tongue; set aside.

Wash, cook (*page 285*) and chop
2 lbs. greens, such as spinach, chard
or tender beet tops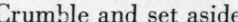
(Or use two 12-oz. pkgs. frozen spinach; cook according to directions on package.)

Meanwhile, prepare, reserving drippings
4 slices Panbroiled Bacon (page 161)
Crumble and set aside.

Return 2 teaspoons of the reserved drippings to skillet. Add
¼ cup finely chopped onion
Cook over medium heat until onion is transparent, stirring occasionally. Using a fork, gently combine the greens, onion, crumbled bacon and
½ cup heavy cream
1 tablespoon prepared horse-radish
Few grains pepper
Lightly pile greens in tongue-lined casserole.

Sprinkle over top a mixture of
½ cup buttered bread crumbs
(page 10)
½ teaspoon grated lemon peel
(page 11)
Bake at 350°F 20 to 25 min., or until crumbs are browned. *6 servings*

Note: **Fresh beef tongue** may also be used. If **smoked tongue** is substituted for fresh tongue, prepare according to directions on wrapper. Leftover tongue should be tightly covered and stored in refrigerator.

Glazed Stuffed Beef Heart 4

Set out a Dutch oven.

Cut arteries, veins and any hard parts from

1 3- to 3½-lb. beef heart

Wash and set aside to drain.

To Prepare Stuffing—Heat in a skillet over low heat

¼ cup butter or margarine

Add and cook over medium heat, until onion is transparent, stirring occasionally

¼ cup finely chopped onion

Add contents of skillet to a large bowl containing a mixture of

1 qt. (4 or 5 slices) soft bread
      crumbs
1 tablespoon minced parsley
1 teaspoon poultry seasoning
¼ teaspoon salt
¼ teaspoon Accent
      Few grains pepper

Glazed Stuffed Beef Heart

Mix lightly until thoroughly blended. Stuff heart with the mixture. Fasten with skewers. Set aside.

To Complete—Heat in the Dutch oven over medium heat

3 tablespoons fat

Add and cook until onion is transparent, stirring occasionally

1 cup (about 2 medium-size) finely
      chopped onion

Remove onion with slotted spoon. Set aside.

Put the beef heart into the Dutch oven and brown lightly on all sides. Add

3 cups hot water
3 cups quick meat broth (page 13)
2 teaspoons salt
1 teaspoon Accent
1 teaspoon celery salt
¼ teaspoon pepper

Return onion to Dutch oven. Bring liquid rapidly to boiling; reduce heat, cover and simmer 2½ to 3 hrs., or until heart is tender.

About 15 min. before end of cooking, add

1 teaspoon marjoram

Heat together over hot water until jelly is melted, stirring occasionally

½ cup red currant jelly, broken
      into small pieces
1 tablespoon water

Remove heart from liquid. Strain and reserve cooking liquid. Brush beef heart with the jelly to glaze. Set heart aside to keep warm.

To Prepare Gravy—Measure 3 cups of the reserved cooking liquid. Heat in the Dutch oven over low heat

⅓ cup butter or margarine

Blend in

⅓ cup flour

Heat until mixture bubbles and flour is lightly browned. Remove from heat and add, stirring in, the reserved cooking liquid and

2 teaspoons lemon juice

Return to heat. Cook rapidly, stirring constantly, until mixture thickens; cook 1 to 2 min. longer. Serve the gravy with the stuffed heart. *About 8 servings*

Heart with Apple-Raisin Dressing

A 2-qt. top-of-range casserole having a tight-fitting cover will be needed.

Cut arteries, veins and any hard parts from
2 lbs. heart (beef, lamb, veal or pork)
Wash heart; drain on absorbent paper. Cut into 1-in. cubes. Coat pieces evenly (*page 107*) with a mixture of
½ cup flour
2 teaspoons salt
1 teaspoon Accent
½ teaspoon pepper
Heat in the casserole over medium heat
3 tablespoons fat or bacon drippings
Add meat and brown on all sides, occasionally moving and turning pieces. Add
1 cup hot water
1 lemon, rinsed and sliced
8 whole cloves
1 bay leaf
Cover casserole. Simmer 1½ to 2½ hrs., or until meat is tender when pierced with a fork. If necessary, add hot water during cooking.

Meanwhile, wash, quarter, core, pare and dice
3 medium-size (1 lb.) tart apples
Heat in a large skillet over medium heat
¼ cup fat or bacon drippings
Add the apples and
½ cup chopped onion (page 12)
½ cup firmly packed brown sugar
½ cup seedless raisins
2 tablespoons water
Cover and simmer 5 min., moving and turning mixture occasionally. Drain meat; discard lemon, cloves and bay leaf. Lightly mix together apple mixture, meat and
1 qt. (4 or 5 slices) bread cubes
½ cup milk
2 tablespoons melted butter or margarine
½ teaspoon salt
Spoon mixture into casserole.

Bake at 350°F 15 to 20 min., or until browned.
6 or 7 servings

Creamed Sweetbreads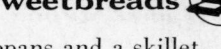

Set out 2 large saucepans and a skillet.

As soon as possible after purchase, rinse with cold water and put into one of the saucepans
1 lb. sweetbreads
Immediately add
1 qt. water
2 teaspoons lemon juice
1 teaspoon salt
Cover saucepan and simmer 20 min. Drain sweetbreads; immediately cover with cold water. Drain sweetbreads again. (Cool and refrigerate now if sweetbreads are not to be used immediately.) Remove tubes and membranes; cut sweetbreads into pieces and set them aside.

While sweetbreads are cooking, cut into pieces and set aside enough cooked chicken to yield
1 cup cooked chicken
Cook (*page 285*)
1 10-oz. pkg. frozen green beans
Break block apart gently with fork or spoon while cooking. When beans are just tender, drain, if necessary, and set aside.

Prepare and set aside
1 cup quick meat broth (page 13)
Clean and slice (*page 12*)
½ lb. mushrooms
Melt in the skillet over low heat
¼ cup butter or margarine
Add the mushrooms and cook for 5 min., until delicately browned, moving and turning with a spoon. Set aside.

Melt in the saucepan over low heat
⅓ cup butter or margarine
Add and cook until onion is transparent, moving and turning with a spoon
1 tablespoon chopped onion

Blend in a mixture of

½ cup flour
1½ teaspoons Accent
¾ teaspoon salt
½ teaspoon savory
½ teaspoon celery salt
Few grains pepper

Heat until mixture bubbles. Remove from heat. Add gradually, while stirring constantly, the meat broth and

2 cups milk
1 cup cream

Return to heat and bring rapidly to boiling, stirring constantly; cook 1 to 2 min. longer. Blend in the sweetbreads, chicken, mushrooms and beans. Reduce heat and occasionally move and turn with a spoon until heated thoroughly.

Remove from heat and stir in

1 small green pepper, cut into julienne strips (page 11)
2 tablespoons chopped pimiento

Serve immediately.   *6 to 8 servings*

Sweetbreads with Mushrooms and Peas

Set out a large, heavy skillet and a 2-qt. saucepan having a tight-fitting cover.

As soon as possible after purchase, rinse with cold water and put into a saucepan

1 lb. sweetbreads

Immediately cover with

1 qt. cold water

Add

1 tablespoon vinegar or lemon juice
1 teaspoon salt
½ teaspoon Accent

Cover saucepan and simmer 20 min. Drain sweetbreads; immediately cover with cold water. Drain sweetbreads again. (Cool and refrigerate now if sweetbreads are not to be used immediately.) Remove tubes and membrane. Separate the sweetbreads into smaller pieces; set aside.

Cook (See FROZEN VEGETABLES, *page 285*) and set aside contents of

1 10- or 12-oz. pkg. frozen peas

Meanwhile, prepare and set aside

2 cups quick meat broth (double recipe, page 13)

Clean and slice (*page 12*)

½ lb. mushrooms

Heat in the skillet over low heat

⅓ cup butter or margarine

Add mushrooms to butter and cook slowly, occasionally moving and turning with a spoon, until lightly browned and tender. With a slotted spoon, remove mushrooms to a small dish. Melt in the skillet over low heat

3 tablespoons butter or margarine

Blend in a mixture of

3 tablespoons flour
½ teaspoon salt
¼ teaspoon Accent
⅛ teaspoon pepper

Heat until mixture bubbles and is lightly browned, stirring constantly. Remove from heat and gradually add reserved broth, stirring constantly. Return to heat and bring rapidly to boiling, stirring constantly. Cook 1 to 2 min. longer.

Vigorously stir about ⅓ cup hot mixture, 1 tablespoon at a time, into

4 egg yolks, slightly beaten

Immediately and thoroughly blend into mixture in skillet, stirring constantly. Cook 2 to 3 min. over low heat, stirring constantly. Mix in the drained peas, sweetbreads and mushrooms. Heat thoroughly, but do not boil. Serve immediately.   *4 to 6 servings*

Savory Sweetbreads

Savory Sweetbreads

Set out a chafing dish or large skillet and a 2-qt. saucepan having a tight-fitting cover.

As soon as possible after purchase, rinse with cold water and put into a saucepan

1½ lbs. sweetbreads

Immediately cover with

Cold water

Add

¼ cup lemon juice
1 teaspoon salt
½ teaspoon Accent

Cover saucepan and simmer 20 min. Drain sweetbreads; cover with cold water. Drain again. (Cool and refrigerate if sweetbreads are not to be used immediately.) Remove tubes and membranes; reserve. Separate sweetbreads into smaller pieces and slice; set aside.

Prepare

1½ cups quick meat broth (*page 13*)

Pour broth into the saucepan. Add the tubes and membranes and

2 stalks celery with leaves, cut into 1-in. pieces (*page 12*)
2 sprigs parsley

and a mixture of

¼ teaspoon savory
¼ teaspoon thyme
⅛ teaspoon allspice
⅛ teaspoon nutmeg

Cover and simmer 30 min.

Strain broth, reserving 1 cup.

Melt in the chafing dish or skillet

⅓ cup butter or margarine

Blend in

2 tablespoons flour
2 teaspoons dry mustard
1 teaspoon Accent
⅛ teaspoon pepper

Add, stirring in, the reserved broth and

1 tablespoon vinegar

Cook, stirring constantly, until thickened. Add the sliced sweetbreads and

¼ cup coarsely chopped parsley

Heat until sweetbreads are thoroughly heated. Serve at once over **Melba toast**.

About 6 servings

▲ Kidney Kabobs

Set out four 8-in. skewers.

Remove the membranes and split lengthwise through center

8 lamb kidneys

Remove cores and tubes. Rinse thoroughly in cold water.

Put kidneys into a bowl and pour in

½ cup French Dressing (*page 318*)

Turn each piece of kidney to coat well. Cover bowl and let kidneys marinate (*page 12*) in refrigerator at least 1 hr.

Clean (*page 12*, do not slice), remove stems from and set aside

12 medium-size mushrooms

(Mushroom stems may be used in other food preparation.)

Cut into halves

8 slices bacon

Wrap each kidney piece in a bacon slice. Insert skewer through bacon end. Then insert skewer through center of a mushroom. Continue in same way, alternately threading four bacon-wrapped kidney pieces and three mushrooms. Do not crowd pieces on skewer.

Brush mushrooms and meat generously with
Melted butter or margarine
Set temperature control of range at Broil.

Arrange skewers on broiler rack. Place in broiler with tops of kabobs about 3 in. from heat source.

Broil 10 to 15 min., or until bacon is crisp and kidneys are tender. Turn to brown evenly.

Sprinkle broiled kabobs with a mixture of
½ **teaspoon salt**
¼ **teaspoon Accent**
⅛ **teaspoon pepper**
Serve at once. If desired, serve with **Perfection Boiled Rice** (*page 275*).   *4 servings*

△ Veal Kidney Kabobs

Follow ▲ Recipe. Substitute 2 **veal kidneys** for 8 lamb kidneys. Clean as directed and cut each kidney into 8 pieces.

Oxtail Ragout

Set out a large, heavy sauce pot having a tight-fitting cover; or use a Dutch oven.

Wipe with a clean, damp cloth
2 oxtails (about 1 lb. each), disjointed
Coat evenly (*page 107*) with a mixture of
¼ **cup flour**
½ **teaspoon salt**
½ **teaspoon Accent**
⅛ **teaspoon pepper**
Heat in the sauce pot over low heat
3 tablespoons butter or margarine

Add and cook over medium heat until onion is transparent, occasionally moving and turning with a spoon
1 cup (about 2 medium-size) chopped onion (*page 12*)
Remove onion from sauce pot with slotted spoon and set aside. Put meat into sauce pot and brown on all sides over medium heat.

Meanwhile, drain, reserving liquid
1 No. 2 can tomatoes (about 1 cup, drained)
Cut tomatoes into pieces and set aside.

Return onion to sauce pot. Slowly add the reserved liquid and
1 cup hot water
Bring liquid rapidly to boiling; reduce heat, cover tightly and simmer 2½ to 3 hrs., or until meat is just tender when pierced with a fork. Add the tomatoes and
4 medium-size (about 1⅓ lbs.) potatoes, pared and cut into large cubes
3 carrots, pared and sliced
2 stalks celery (*page 12*), cut crosswise into ½-in. slices
1 tablespoon paprika
1 teaspoon salt
¼ **teaspoon pepper**
Cover and simmer 30 min. longer, or until vegetables are tender.

Remove meat and vegetables from sauce pot. Thicken cooking liquid (*page 107*; use ¼ cup water and 2 tablespoons flour).

Return meat and vegetables to kettle and heat thoroughly. Serve immediately.
          About 4 servings

VARIETY MEATS in the MICROWAVE OVEN

Can you imagine cooking a whole beef tongue in less than two hours or an oxtail stew in about one hour? That's exactly what the microwave oven can offer for these meats which are as nutritious as they are inexpensive, but often seem too time consuming to prepare on a conventional stove. And, every one of these recipes is excellent.

For such sensitive meats as liver and sweetbreads, the microwave is also ideal. Sweetbreads are beautifully cooked to the point of tender perfection. The **Creamed Sweetbreads** takes advantage of some of the best qualities of microwave oven cooking—combining the delicate handling of the sweetbreads with a smooth and creamy sauce. The **Liver Balls in Onion Gravy** is just simply delicious.

Pan-broiled liver recipes are difficult to adapt to the microwave method. When the flour coating is cooked thoroughly, the liver is overdone; if the liver is removed from the oven when it loses its pink color, the flour is still raw.

Browning—When browning is called for in the master recipe, use the browning skillet. Do not forget to preheat the skillet at least 3 minutes.
Sauces and Gravies—Remember to stir sauces and gravies frequently, particularly cream sauces. Stirring before and after each addition of ingredients will help to insure that unusually smooth texture and integrated taste which the microwave produces and is so highly praised.
Standing Time—As with all meats prepared in the microwave oven, these dishes must stand, covered, after cooking to allow full flavor to develop and, in some cases, to finish cooking. Minimum standing times are given for each recipe.

REMINDERS—Cooking times on all the recipes may vary slightly, depending on your oven and, to some extent, your taste. Check frequently (it will not affect the cooking process) when the cooking period nears its end.

The introductory chapter, **Home Cooking in the Microwave Oven**, in the beginning of this book provides additional tips and an easy-to-read chart comparing settings among different brands of microwave ovens. By reviewing this section, you will also learn more about how we have adapted these recipes.

Liver Loaf *(page 186)* 1

Use a browning skillet and a 2-qt. loaf pan. *Do not grease.*

Add liver and water to skillet. COOK, uncovered, until simmering (about 5 min.).

Assemble loaf as in Recipe. COOK to raise temperature (about 5 min.). SLOWCOOK, rotating pan every 3 min., until done (about 6 min.).

Cover and let stand 15 min.
OVERALL COOKING TIME: 16:00

Liver Balls in Onion  Gravy *(page 186)*

Use a browning skillet and a 1½-qt. casserole.

Prepare bacon in skillet, remove and set aside.

Place liver in water in casserole. Cover and COOK until simmering (about 3 min.).

Assemble liver balls as in Recipe.

To reheat bacon drippings, COOK (about 3 min.). Add liver balls and COOK, turning every 3 min., until evenly brown (about 6 min.). Remove liver balls and set aside.

Place butter or margarine in casserole and COOK until melted. Add vegetables and bay leaf and COOK, stirring every 1½ min., until onion is transparent (about 4 min.).

Add flour and COOK, stirring every 1 min., until mixture bubbles (about 3 min.).

Add broth, stir thoroughly and COOK, stirring every 30 sec., until boiling (about 1 min.).

Add liver balls. COOK to raise temperature (about 5 min.). SLOWCOOK, stirring every 3 min., until thoroughly heated (about 9 min.).

Cover and let stand 10 min.
OVERALL COOKING TIME: 31:00

Smoked Tongue Platter 3
(page 187)

Use a 3½-qt. casserole.

Place tongue in casserole and add enough water to cover by two-thirds. SLOWCOOK, rotating every 20 min., until tender (about 1 hr. 45 min.).

Cover and let stand 10 min.

Serve as in Recipe.
OVERALL COOKING TIME: 105:00

Beef Tongue 4
with Tomato Sauce *(page 188)*

Use a 3-qt. casserole.

In casserole, place tongue, vegetables and seasonings, except use only enough liquid to cover contents by two-thirds. Cover and SLOWCOOK until tender (about 1 hr. 45 min.).

Pour tomato sauce over tongue slices. Cover and COOK to heat through (about 5 min.).

Cover and let stand 10 min.

Tongue and Greens **5**
(page 188)

Use a 3-qt. covered casserole. *Do not grease.*

Prepare bacon.

Add onion and COOK until transparent (about 1 min.).

Prepare greens.

Assemble casserole and COOK until heated through and flavors are blended (about 5 min.).

Cover and let stand 10 min.

Heart with Apple-Raisin Dressing **6** (page 190)

Use a browning skillet and a 2-qt. covered casserole.

Preheat skillet (3 min.). Add fat and COOK until melted.

Add coated meat and COOK, turning meat and rotating pan every 1 min., until brown (about 5 min.).

Transfer to casserole. Add water, lemon, spices. Cover and COOK, to heat (about 5 min.). SLOWCOOK, turning pan every 3 min., until meat is tender (about 9 min.).

For the dressing, heat fat. Add apple-onion mixture, cover and COOK to simmering, until apples are softened (about 5 min.).

Assemble casserole. SLOWCOOK, rotating pan every 5 min., until browned (about 15 min.).

Cover and let stand 20 min.
OVERALL COOKING TIME: 42:00

Creamed Sweetbreads **7**
(page 190)

Use a 2-qt. covered casserole and a browning skillet.

Prepare greens and have the chicken handy.

Preheat skillet (3 min.). Add butter or margarine and COOK until melted. Add mushrooms and COOK, turning every 2 min., until lightly browned (about 4 min.).

COOK sweetbreads in covered casserole until tender (about 10 min.). Remove.

In casserole, place the 1/3 cup butter or margarine and COOK until melted. Add onion and COOK until transparent (about 1 min.).

Blend in flour mixture. COOK, stirring every 1 min., until bubbling (about 4 min.).

Combine milk and cream and add to flour mixture in thirds. Stir before and after each addition and COOK after each addition, stirring every 1 min., until simmering (about 6 min.).

Combine ingredients and COOK, covered, until heated through (about 5 min.).

Cover and let stand 10 min.

Sweetbreads with Mushrooms and Peas *(page 191)* **8**

Use a 2-qt. covered casserole and a browning skillet.

Prepare peas.

Preheat skillet (3 min.). Add butter or margarine and COOK until melted. Add mushrooms and COOK, turning every 2 min., until lightly browned (about 4 min.).

COOK sweetbreads in covered casserole until tender (about 10 min.). Remove.

Add butter and COOK until melted. Blend in flour mixture and COOK, stirring every 1 min., until mixture bubbles (about 3 min.).

Blend in broth and COOK, stirring every 1 min., until hot and smooth (about 5 min.).

Add egg yolks, stirring vigorously. SLOWCOOK, stirring every 15 sec., until heated through (about 1 min.).

Add sweetbreads and vegetables, cover and COOK to heat through (about 5 min.).

Cover and let stand 10 min.

Savory Sweetbreads **9**
(page 192)

Use two 2-qt. casseroles.

COOK sweetbreads until tender (about 10 min.). Remove.

COOK broth mixture until celery is tender and flavors are blended (about 10 min.).

COOK butter or margarine until melted. Blend in flour, seasonings, broth and vinegar and

COOK, stirring every 1½ min. for smooth texture, until thickened (about 5 min.).

Add sweetbreads and parsley and COOK to heat through (about 10 min.).

Cover and let stand 10 min.

Serve as in Recipe.
OVERALL COOKING TIME: 35:00

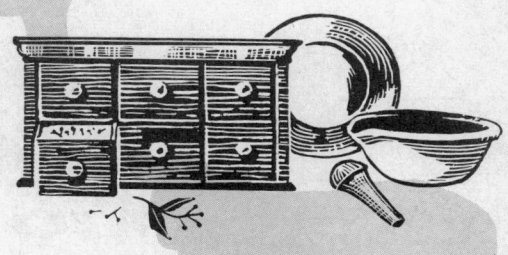

Oxtail Ragout *(page 193)* **10**

Use a browning skillet and a 3-qt. covered casserole.

Preheat skillet (3 min.). Add the butter or margarine and COOK until melted.

Add onions and COOK until onions are transparent (about 3 min.). Remove and set aside.

Add meat to skillet and COOK, turning every 5 min., until brown on all sides (about 10 min.).

Transfer meat to casserole, add onions and hot water; cover. COOK to heat (about 5 min.). SLOWCOOK, rotating pan every 5 min., until meat is just tender (about 20 min.).

Add all vegetables, cover and COOK to heat (about 5 min.). SLOWCOOK, turning pan every 5 min., until vegetables and meat are tender (about 15 min.).

Cover and let stand 15 min.

Meanwhile, thicken cooking liquid. Then return meat and vegetables to casserole and COOK to heat through (about 10 min.).

OVERALL COOKING TIME: 71:00

VARIETY MEATS in the SLOW COOKER

Variety meats are just that; they bring variety to the dinner table and economically, too. Preparing such recipes as **Beef Tongue with Tomato Sauce** and **Oxtail Ragout** in the slow cooker is a real boon for the cook. On the stove, such dishes must be nursed along for hours. In the slow cooker, they must be cooked for hours, but no one has to be nearby to babysit.

All of these meats have little or no fat attached—one reason for their highly touted nutritional value—so there is no need to trim the meat or skim the sauces.

Quick-cooking, delicate meats such as liver and sweetbreads are not, of course, suitable for the slow cooker. Therefore, we have omitted these recipes.

Browning—When recipes call for browning, as in the **Oxtail Ragout**, omit any flour from the coating mixture. Melt fat in the slow cooker set on HIGH. Add the meat and turn to coat evenly with the fat. Then proceed with the recipe.

The dish will be as flavorful as if the meat were browned on the stove.

Sauces and Gravies—We suggest the gravy for the **Glazed Stuffed Beef Heart** be finished on top of the stove. Meanwhile, the heart can be held on LOW in the slow cooker until ready to serve.

REMINDERS—Use the appropriate-size slow cooker as specified in each recipe.

Remember to follow directions as given in the master recipe in the main text, unless specifically otherwise directed.

The introductory chapter, **Home Cooking in the Slow Cooker**, in the beginning of this book contains an easy-to-read chart comparing settings among different brands of slow cookers. We suggest reviewing this entire section for additional tips and to learn how we have adapted these recipes.

Smoked Tongue Platter 1
(page 187)

Use a 5-qt. slow cooker.

Place tongue in slow cooker and add water to cover by two-thirds.

Cook on HIGH for 6 to 7 hrs.

Serve as in Recipe.

Beef Tongue with Tomato Sauce 2 *(page 188)*

Use a 5-qt. slow cooker.

Place tongue in slow cooker and add remaining ingredients, except use only enough water to cover contents by two-thirds.

Cover and cook on HIGH for 6 to 7 hrs.

Complete as in Recipe.

Tongue and Greens 3
(page 188)

Use a 3½-qt. slow cooker.

Place tongue in slow cooker. Add spices and water to cover by two-thirds.

Cover and cook on HIGH for 5 to 6 hrs.

Complete as in Recipe.

Glazed Stuffed Beef Heart 4 *(page 189)*

Use a 3½-qt. slow cooker.

Place fat in slow cooker and melt on HIGH. Add stuffed heart and turn to coat with fat. Sprinkle with chopped onion.

Add seasonings and liquids to cover.

Cook on HIGH until liquid is simmering and meat heated thoroughly (about 1 hr.).

Reset to LOW and cook for 7 to 8 hrs. Remove and brush with glaze as in Recipe.

To Prepare Gravy—Follow Recipe.

Oxtail Ragout *(page 193)* 5

Use a 3½ qt. slow cooker.

Coat meat with seasonings, except omit the flour.

Place butter or margarine in slow cooker and melt on HIGH. Add meat and turn to coat evenly with fat.

Add remaining ingredients, except use only enough liquid to cover contents by two-thirds. Be sure vegetables are completely covered by liquids.

Cover and cook on LOW for 8 to 9 hrs.

POULTRY and Stuffings

Poultry includes all domesticated birds used for food: chicken (including capon), turkey, goose, duckling, guinea and squab. Recently the Rock-Cornish game hen, a delicious hybrid, has been added. Wild duck and pheasant are game birds which are handled like domestic poultry. Rabbit, either domestic or wild, has meat so similar to poultry that it is included here.

CLASSES—Chickens and turkeys are classified according to size, age and sex. Age influences tenderness of the meat and therefore determines the cooking method. Size determines the cooking time.

Chicken—*Broiler*, either sex, 1½ to 2½ lbs. ready-to-cook weight, 10 to 12 weeks old; *fryer*, either sex, 2 to 3 lbs. ready-to-cook weight, 12 to 16 weeks old; *roaster*, either sex, usually over 3½ lbs., usually under 8 months; *capon*, unsexed male, usually under 10 months, 4 lbs. or over, exceptionally good flavor, especially tender, with large proportion of white meat; *stewing chicken*, female, usually more than 10 months, 3 to 5 lbs. ready-to-cook weight.

Turkey—*Fryer-roaster*, either sex, usually under 16 weeks, 4 to 8 lbs. ready-to-cook weight; *young hen or tom*, female or male, usually under 8 months, 8 to 24 lbs. ready-to-cook weight; *mature hen or tom*, over 10 months, less tender and seldom found on the consumer market.

Duck—*Duckling*, either sex, 8 to 9 weeks old, 3½ to 5 lbs. ready-to-cook weight (the only class in which ducks are marketed commercially).

Goose—Classifications less well established, but weights range from 4 to 8 lbs. ready-to-cook weight for young birds, up to 14 lbs. for mature birds.

STYLES—*Dressed poultry* refers to birds which have been bled and feather-dressed but have head, feet and viscera intact. *Ready-to-cook poultry* is fully cleaned inside and out and is ready for cooking; it may or may not be tagged or stamped with official inspection or grade labels. (Since 1953, only ready-to-cook poultry is permitted to carry United States Department of Agriculture grades on individual birds; but the use of official inspection and grading services is entirely voluntary on the part of the packers.) Ready-to-cook poultry is marketed either fresh, ice-chilled or quick-frozen. In many markets, chicken and turkey halves, quarters, pieces and giblets are sold separately, fresh or quick-frozen. These pieces—especially breast, thighs and drumsticks—greatly simplify cooking and serving poultry and facilitate meal-planning. Quick-frozen *stuffed* turkeys must be cooked without thawing. DO NOT FREEZE YOUR OWN STUFFED TURKEYS as the time required to freeze them with stuffing encourages the growth of bacteria.

BUYING GUIDES—Where tags or stamps provide information as to quality established by inspection and grading or both, this is the consumer's most reliable guide in the selection of poultry. The grading and inspection program of the United States Department of Agriculture employs three easily recognizable marks: 1) *inspection mark*, indicating that the bird has been processed under sanitary conditions and is wholesome food; 2) *grade mark*, indicating the quality, class and kind—there are three grades, A, B and C; 3) *grade and inspection mark*. Poultry bearing the combined grade and inspection marks is guaranteed to be of top quality.

When grading and inspection labels are not present, the consumer may be guided by some of the standards used in official grading. Young birds have smooth, soft, thin skin, little fat and flexible-tipped breastbones; as the bird ages, the skin coarsens, more fat is deposited along the backbone and the breastbone becomes more rigid.

Grade A quality requires that a bird be well-formed and full-fleshed, with no defects, tears or bruises in the skin, clean and free from pinfeathers.

STORAGE—Poultry is a perishable food and must be safeguarded against spoilage or deterioration of flavor by proper care. *Quick-frozen* poultry must be kept frozen until ready to use and once thawed must not be refrozen. In thawing frozen poultry before cooking, directions on the label should be followed. *Fresh or ice-chilled* poultry should be purchased only at markets where the birds are kept refrigerated. To store poultry of this style at home, remove it from the meat dealer's wrappings and rewrap it loosely; then store in the coldest part of the refrigerator (about 40°F). Cut-up poultry should be held no more than 24 hours before using; whole birds with the giblets wrapped separately may be stored up to two days.

PREPARATION FOR COOKING—*Ready-to-cook* poultry, whole or in pieces, should be rinsed in cold water, drained immediately and patted dry. It should never be allowed to soak in water, as soaking dissipates flavor. *Dressed* poultry should be drawn immediately, preferably at the market. Remove pinfeathers with a sharp-pointed knife or a strawberry huller. Singe the bird over a flame, turning quickly until all down and hair are burnt off. Then wash as for ready-to-cook poultry.

Before roasting, neck and body cavities of whole birds are rubbed with a mixture of salt and Accent, then usually stuffed (never stuff until ready to roast), trussed and roast-meat thermometer inserted. Poultry pieces generally are coated with a mixture of flour, salt, pepper, Accent and other seasonings if desired, before frying or browning; before broiling, they are seasoned with salt, pepper and Accent.

COAT POULTRY PIECES EVENLY—Put a mixture of flour and seasonings into a bowl or onto a piece of waxed paper. Coat one or a few pieces of poultry at a time. Or shake a few pieces at a time in a plastic or clean paper bag containing the flour mixture.

COOKING POULTRY—Two general principles apply to the cooking of all kinds of poultry: 1) Cook at low to moderate constant heat for a suitable length of time. High temperatures shrink the muscle tissue and make the meat tough, dry and hard. Poultry should always be cooked until well done; the meat should separate easily from the bone and should be tender to the fork. An exception is wild duck, which is traditionally served rare. 2) Suit the method of cooking to the age or class of the bird. Young birds of all kinds may be broiled, fried or roasted in an open pan. Older, less tender birds require cooking by moist heat, either in a covered casserole or Dutch oven, or in water or steam.

STUFFING POULTRY FOR ROASTING—Ingredients for a stuffing should be mixed *just before needed* and the bird should be stuffed *just before roasting*. Never stuff bird a day in advance and store in refrigerator or freezer. These are safety precautions to prevent food poisoning, since stuffing is the perfect medium for disease-producing bacteria. *Immediately* after the meal is served, remove the stuffing from the bird and store, covered, in the refrigerator. Use leftover stuffing within 2 or 3 days and heat thoroughly before serving.

Any extra stuffing which cannot be put into the bird may be put in a greased, covered baking dish or wrapped in aluminum foil and baked in the oven during the last hour of roasting.

TESTS FOR DONENESS OF ROAST POULTRY—A roast-meat thermometer, if used, should register 190°F when bird is done (insert in center of inside thigh muscle). The thickest part of drumstick feels soft when pressed with fingers protected with clean cloth or paper napkin. Or drumstick moves up and down or twists out of joint easily.

STORING COOKED POULTRY—Cooked poultry, gravy and stuffing should not be left at room temperature for longer than it takes to finish the meal. Never store bird with stuffing; remove stuffing and store it covered in refrigerator; cover gravy and refrigerate. If only one side of a roast bird has been carved, wrap remainder of bird in waxed paper, aluminum foil or moisture-vapor-proof material; store in refrigerator. If more than one half of the meat has been used, remove the remaining meat from the bones and wrap tightly before storing. Cooked pieces should be tightly wrapped and refrigerated. Do not keep cooked poultry, however carefully stored, for more than a few days.

CUT-UP COOKED CHICKEN—For recipes in this book that call for *cut-up cooked chicken*, use **Stewed Chicken** (*page 205*) or canned chicken.

*Roast Chicken with Giblet Gravy
(page 325) and buttered carrots*

Roast Chicken  [1]

(*See photo on page 325*)

Set out a shallow roasting pan with rack.

Clean

**1 roasting chicken, 3 to 4 lbs.,
ready-to-cook weight**

Cut off neck at body, leaving on neck skin. (If chicken is frozen, thaw according to directions on package.) Rinse and pat dry with absorbent paper; set aside. Reserve giblets for gravy; or use in other food preparation.

Prepare and cool

**Herb Stuffing (p. 218; see note) or
Apple Stuffing for Poultry (p. 218)**

Rub cavities of chicken with a mixture of

**1 teaspoon Accent
½ to 1 teaspoon salt**

Lightly fill body and neck cavities with stuffing. To close body cavity, sew or skewer and lace with cord. Fasten neck skin to back and wings to body with skewers. Tie drumsticks to tail. Brush skin thoroughly with

Melted fat

Place chicken breast side up or down, as desired, on rack in roasting pan. If roast-meat thermometer is used, place it in center of in-

side thigh muscle. (When chicken is done, roast-meat thermometer will register 190°F.) Place fat-moistened cheesecloth over top and sides of chicken. Keep cloth moist during roasting by brushing occasionally with fat from bottom of pan.

Roast uncovered at 325°F about 3 hrs., or until chicken tests done (*page 195*). If bird was started breast down, turn breast up when about three-quarters done.

When chicken is tender, remove from oven. Remove thermometer and keep bird hot. Allow to stand in pan 15 to 30 min. before serving. This allows chicken to absorb its juices and become easier to carve. This also allows time to prepare gravy and garnishes.

To serve, remove cord and skewers. Place chicken on heated platter. Serve with

**Dumplings (page 69)
Brown Gravy (page 325) or Giblet
Gravy (page 325; use drippings for
part or all of liquid)**

About 6 servings

▲ Broiled Chicken

DORIS WADE, DANVILLE, IND.

Clean, rinse and pat dry with absorbent paper

**2 broiling chickens, 1½ to 2 lbs. each,
ready-to-cook weight**

(Have meat dealer split birds into halves lengthwise and remove backbone, neck and keel bone.) Reserve giblets for use in other food preparation.

Brush pieces with

**Juice of 1 lemon (about
3 tablespoons)**

Set the remaining lemon juice aside. Season chicken pieces with a mixture of

1 tablespoon salt
1 teaspoon Accent
1 teaspoon paprika
¼ teaspoon pepper

Melt

⅓ cup butter or margarine

Brush pieces with some of the melted butter; reserve remainder for basting sauce. Set out

3 tablespoons sugar

Sprinkle one half of the sugar over the chicken pieces; add remainder to reserved butter with the remaining lemon juice.

Set temperature control of range at Broil. Arrange the chicken pieces skin side down in broiler pan (not on rack). Bring wing tips onto backs under the shoulder joint. Press down.

Place pan in broiler so that surface of chicken is 7 to 9 in. from heat source. Broil 10 min. without turning pieces. Continue to broil chicken 30 to 40 min., brushing pieces frequently (about every 10 min.) with the butter mixture; turn chicken occasionally to brown evenly. Chicken is done when browned and when drumstick moves easily.   *4 servings*

△ Wine-Broiled Chicken

BARBARA MALMUTH, LOS ANGELES, CALIF.

Follow ▲ Recipe. Decrease sugar to 1 teaspoon; do not sprinkle over chicken. Add the sugar, ½ teaspoon **garlic salt** and ⅓ cup **sherry** to basting sauce.

Note: To prepare chicken on an outdoor grill see OUTDOOR COOKING (*page 204*).

Golden Crusty Chicken

Set out a deep saucepan or automatic deep-fryer (*page 13*); heat fat to 350°F.

Clean

1 frying chicken, 2 to 3 lbs. ready-to-cook weight

Broiled Chicken, Corn-on-the-Cob and Baked Potatoes cooked on an outdoor grill (page 204)

Disjoint chicken and cut into serving-size pieces. (If chicken is frozen, thaw according to directions on package.) Rinse and pat dry with absorbent paper. Set aside.

Sift together

1 cup sifted flour
2½ teaspoons salt
1 teaspoon Accent
1 teaspoon sugar
½ teaspoon pepper
¼ teaspoon paprika

Blend together and add to flour mixture

1 egg, slightly beaten
1 cup milk

Mix until batter is thoroughly blended. Dip pieces of chicken into batter; coat well. Allow any excess coating to drip off before lowering chicken into the heated fat.

Fry only as many pieces at one time as will lie uncrowded one layer deep in the fat. Fry chicken about 10 to 13 min., or until tender and golden brown. (Liver requires only about 1 min. frying time.) Turn pieces with tongs several times during cooking. Drain over fat a few seconds; remove to absorbent paper.

Serve hot.   *2 to 4 servings*

Fried Chicken: Coat chicken pieces evenly. Place skin side down in skillet. Turn with tongs.

Cook covered 25 to 40 min. Uncover last 10 min. to crisp skin. Garnish with parsley.

▲ Fried Chicken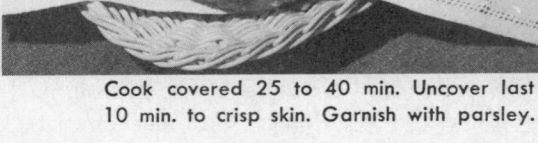

Set out a Dutch oven or a large, heavy skillet having a tight-fitting cover.

Clean

1 frying chicken, 2 to 3 lbs. ready-to-cook weight

Disjoint chicken and cut into serving-size pieces. (If chicken is frozen, thaw according to directions on package.) Rinse and pat dry with absorbent paper.

Coat chicken (*page 195*) with a mixture of

½ cup flour
1 teaspoon paprika
1 teaspoon salt
½ teaspoon Accent
¼ teaspoon pepper

Heat in the skillet over medium heat

Fat (or use cooking oil) to at least ½-in. depth

Starting with meaty pieces of chicken, place them skin side down in skillet. Put in less meaty pieces as others brown. To brown all sides, turn pieces as necessary with tongs or two spoons. When chicken is evenly browned, reduce heat and add

1 to 2 tablespoons water

Immediately cover skillet. Cook slowly 25 to 40 min., or until thickest pieces of chicken are tender when pierced with a fork. Uncover the last 10 min. to crisp skin.

Serve with **Brown Gravy** (Method 1, *p. 325;* use pan drippings and milk for liquid).

2 to 4 servings

△ Maryland-Fried Chicken

Coat chicken pieces with seasoned flour (omit paprika) as in ▲ Recipe. Dip them into a mixture of 2 **eggs** beaten with 3 tablespoons **water**.

Roll pieces in 1½ cups fine dry **bread crumbs, corn meal,** fine **cracker crumbs** or finely crushed **corn flakes.** Let stand 5 to 10 min. to "seal" coating. Cook as in ▲ Recipe.

▲ Oven "Barbecued" Chicken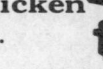

ARLETTA WHALEY, OTWELL, IND.

Set out a shallow baking pan, a large, heavy skillet and a small saucepan.

Clean

1 frying chicken, 2 to 3 lbs. ready-to-cook weight

Disjoint chicken and cut into serving-size pieces. (If chicken is frozen, thaw according to directions on package.) Rinse and pat dry with absorbent paper.

Coat chicken (*page 195*) with a mixture of

- **½ cup flour**
- **1 teaspoon paprika**
- **1 teaspoon salt**
- **½ teaspoon Accent**
- **¼ teaspoon pepper**

Heat in the skillet over medium heat

- **½ cup fat**

Starting with meaty pieces of chicken, place them skin side down in skillet. Put in less meaty pieces as others brown. To brown all sides, turn pieces as necessary with tongs or two spoons. Arrange pieces one layer deep in the baking pan.

While chicken browns, combine in saucepan

- **1⅓ cups (14-oz. bottle) ketchup**
- **1 cup water**
- **½ cup finely chopped onion (*page 12*)**
- **2 tablespoons vinegar**
- **1 tablespoon Worcestershire sauce**
- **1 clove garlic (*page 12*), minced; or crushed in garlic press**
- **1 tablespoon sugar**
- **1 tablespoon paprika**
- **1 teaspoon salt**
- **¼ teaspoon pepper**

Bring sauce to boiling, stirring occasionally. Remove from heat; add

- **¼ cup lemon juice**

Pour sauce over chicken pieces in baking pan.

Turning and basting chicken frequently with the sauce, bake at 325°F about 45 min., or until thickest pieces are tender when pierced with a fork. *About 4 servings*

△ Broiler Barbecued Chicken

Prepare sauce as in ▲ Recipe; set aside. Substitute 2 **broiling chickens**, about 1½ lbs. each, ready-to-cook weight, for the frying chicken. (Have meat dealer split birds into halves lengthwise and remove backbone, neck and keel bone.) Brush chicken halves with ¼ cup melted **butter** or **margarine**. Arrange pieces skin side down in broiler pan (not on rack); brush with the sauce. Set temperature control of range at Broil. Place pan 7 to 9 in. from heat source. Broil 40 to 50 min., turning and basting frequently with the sauce.

Serve immediately.

Oriental Barbecued Chicken

MRS. YOTSUO FUKE, HILO, HAWAII

Do you have a yen for a perked-up chicken dish? Then try this zesty recipe from Hawaii.

Clean

- **1 frying chicken, 2½ to 3 lbs. ready-to-cook weight**

Disjoint and cut into serving-size pieces. (If chicken is frozen, thaw according to directions on package.) Rinse chicken pieces and drain on absorbent paper.

Mix together in a large, shallow dish

- **½ cup soy sauce**
- **¼ cup sugar**
- **3 drops tabasco sauce**
- **1½ teaspoons ginger**
- **½ teaspoon Accent**
- **Few grains paprika**
- **1 clove garlic (*page 12*), minced; or crushed in garlic press**

Turn chicken pieces in the soy-sauce marinade. Cover and set aside in a cool place several hours or overnight, turning pieces occasionally. Remove chicken from marinade. (Reserve marinade for basting.)

Set out

- **8 slices bacon**

Wrap each chicken piece with a bacon slice. Secure slices with wooden picks. Place chicken pieces in a large shallow baking dish.

Frequently turning pieces and basting with reserved marinade, bake at 350°F 1½ hrs., or until thickest pieces of chicken are tender when pierced with a fork.

Serve immediately with

- **Perfection Boiled Rice (*p.275*)**

4 servings

▲ Chicken Cacciatore

Prepare and coat with flour mixture (as for Fried Chicken, *page 198;* omit paprika)

1 frying chicken, 2 to 3 lbs. ready-to-cook weight

Heat in a large, heavy skillet over medium heat until garlic is lightly browned

½ cup olive oil

2 cloves garlic (*page 12*), sliced thin

Starting with meaty pieces of chicken, place them skin side down in the skillet. Add less meaty pieces of chicken as others brown. To brown all sides, turn as necessary with tongs or two spoons.

While chicken browns, mix together

3½ cups (No. 2½ can) tomatoes, sieved

1 tablespoon chopped parsley

1 teaspoon oregano

1¼ teaspoons salt

1 teaspoon Accent

½ teaspoon pepper

Slowly add tomato mixture to the browned chicken. Cover and cook over low heat about 30 min., or until thickest pieces of chicken are tender when pierced with a fork. If mixture becomes too thick, add **water** or **white wine.**

About 4 servings

⚠ Chicken Cacciatore with Mushrooms

Follow ▲ Recipe. Clean (*page 12*) and thinly slice 1 small **onion** and ½ lb. **mushrooms.** Cook in 3 tablespoons **butter** or **margarine** until onion is transparent and mushrooms are lightly browned. Add with tomatoes.

⚠ Chicken Cacciatore with Mushrooms and Peppers

Follow ⚠ Recipe. Substitute 1 cleaned (*page 12*) and diced **green pepper** for the onion. Cook just until green pepper is tender.

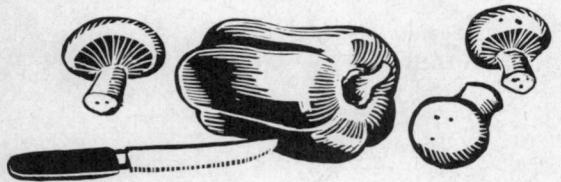

Chicken Cacciatore with Mushrooms

Chicken Vesuvio

Set out a large, heavy skillet and a large, shallow baking dish.

Prepare and coat with flour mixture (as for Fried Chicken, *page 198;* omit paprika)

1 frying chicken, 2 to 3 lbs. ready-to-cook weight

Heat in the skillet over medium heat

½ cup olive oil

Starting with meaty pieces of chicken, place them skin side down in skillet. Add less meaty pieces of chicken as others brown. To brown all sides, turn as necessary with tongs or two spoons. When browned, place chicken one layer deep in baking dish. Set aside.

Heat in skillet until garlic is lightly browned

2 tablespoons olive oil

1 clove garlic (*page 12*), sliced

Stir in

2 tablespoons Marsala wine

½ teaspoon chopped parsley

Pour this mixture over chicken in baking dish.

Bake at 325°F about 45 min., or until thickest pieces of chicken are tender when pierced with a fork. Turn once during baking period. If chicken appears dry, spoon wine over it.

Meanwhile, prepare and keep warm

French-Fried Potatoes (*page 296*)

Place French-Fried Potatoes around rim of baking dish. Pile chicken in center. *4 servings*

Chicken Paprika with Spätzle

Set out a deep, heavy 10-in. skillet having a tight-fitting cover; or use a Dutch oven.

Clean

1 frying chicken, 2 to 3 lbs. ready-to-cook weight

Disjoint and cut into serving-size pieces. (If chicken is frozen, thaw according to directions on package.) Rinse and pat dry with absorbent paper. Cut away and discard tough lining from gizzard. Slit heart; remove blood vessels. Refrigerate chicken and liver.

Cook giblets (*p.205*) 1 hr., or until tender.

Meanwhile, dice and put into the skillet

8 slices bacon

Cook slowly, moving and turning frequently, until bacon is slightly crisp and browned. Add

¼ cup finely chopped onion

Moving and turning occasionally, cook until onion is transparent. With slotted spoon, remove onion and bacon from skillet; set aside. Coat chicken (*page 195*) with a mixture of

½ cup flour
2 teaspoons paprika
1½ teaspoons salt
1 teaspoon Accent

Slightly increase heat under the skillet. Starting with meaty pieces of chicken, place them skin side down in skillet. Put in less meaty pieces as others brown. To brown all sides, turn chicken pieces as necessary with tongs or two spoons. When chicken is lightly and evenly browned, reduce heat.

Add cooked gizzard, heart and neck to the skillet with 1 to 2 tablespoons of the giblet broth. (Strain remainder of broth; reserve 1 cup and cool to lukewarm.) Cover skillet tightly. Add liver to skillet 10 to 15 min. before end of cooking time. Cook chicken *slowly* 25 to 40 min., or until thickest pieces are tender when pierced with a fork.

Meanwhile, heat in a saucepan over low heat

2 tablespoons fat

Blend into the fat

2 tablespoons flour

Heat over medium heat until mixture bubbles, stirring constantly. Remove from heat and add gradually, stirring constantly, the cup of reserved giblet broth. (If giblets are not being used, substitute 1 cup **quick chicken broth,** *page 13*, for giblet broth.) Return saucepan to heat and bring mixture rapidly to boiling, stirring constantly; cook 1 to 2 min. longer. Gradually add to sauce, stirring constantly

⅔ cup milk
1 to 1½ tablespoons paprika

When thoroughly heated, remove saucepan from heat. Stirring vigorously with a French whip, whisk beater, or fork, add to the sauce in very small amounts

1½ cups thick sour cream

Mix in the bacon and onion. Pour the sauce over chicken pieces in the skillet. Stirring sauce and turning chicken frequently, cook over low heat 3 to 5 min., or until thoroughly heated; do not boil. Cover skillet tightly; turn off heat under chicken and let stand about 1 hr. About twice during hour, spoon sauce over chicken. Reheat just before serving.

Serve hot with

Spätzle (page 280)

4 to 6 servings

Chicken Paprika with Spätzle (page 280)

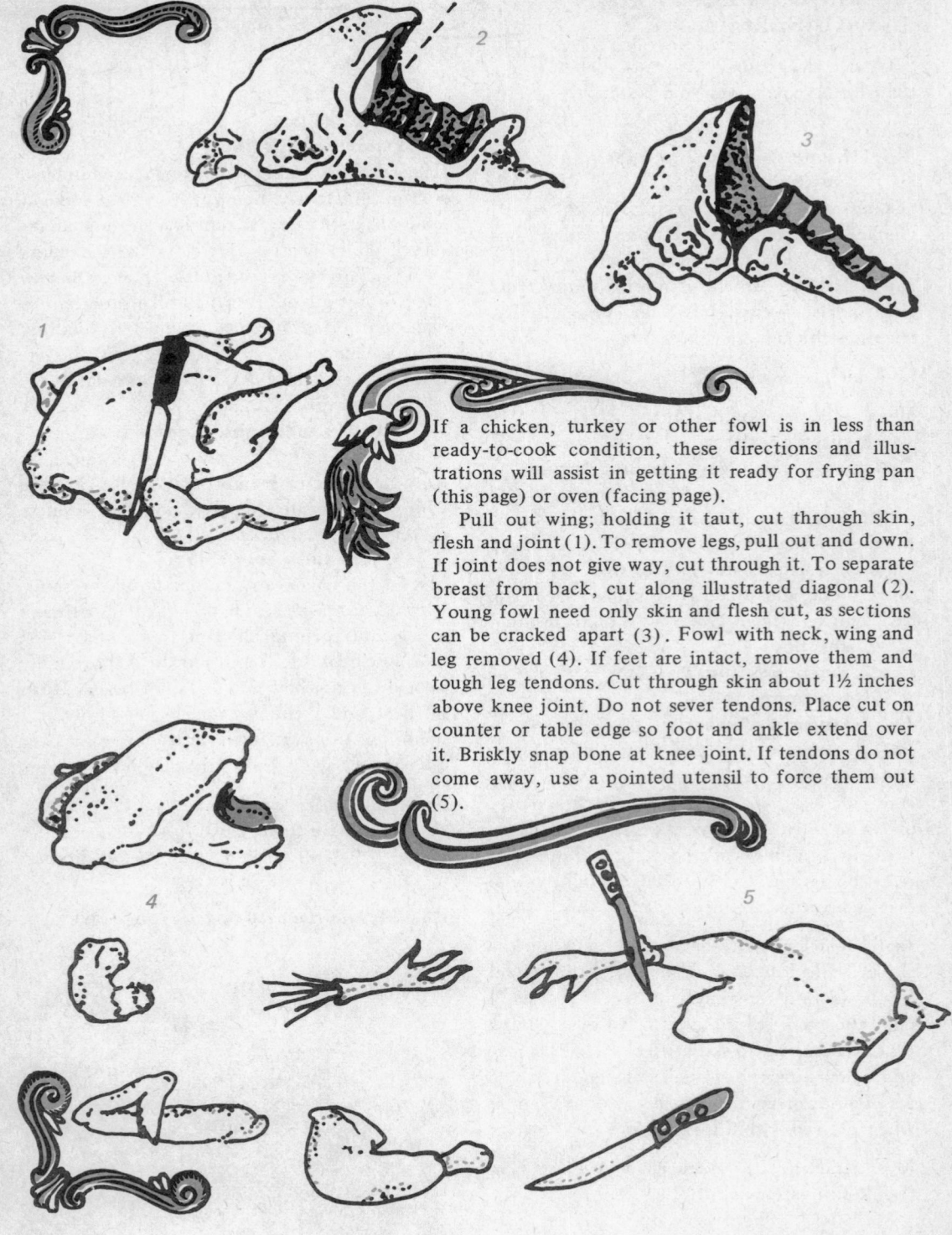

If a chicken, turkey or other fowl is in less than ready-to-cook condition, these directions and illustrations will assist in getting it ready for frying pan (this page) or oven (facing page).

Pull out wing; holding it taut, cut through skin, flesh and joint (1). To remove legs, pull out and down. If joint does not give way, cut through it. To separate breast from back, cut along illustrated diagonal (2). Young fowl need only skin and flesh cut, as sections can be cracked apart (3). Fowl with neck, wing and leg removed (4). If feet are intact, remove them and tough leg tendons. Cut through skin about 1½ inches above knee joint. Do not sever tendons. Place cut on counter or table edge so foot and ankle extend over it. Briskly snap bone at knee joint. If tendons do not come away, use a pointed utensil to force them out (5).

Remove entrails by making a cut, big enough to permit entry of a hand, in the skin just below the breastbone (1). Feel for the firm, round gizzard. Pull it firmly and steadily—it will come out, along with most of the organs. Remove any remaining organs and fat (2). Cut out the oil sac located at the base of tail (3).

For carving, use a large fork and a long, sharp knife. With the fork, keep a firm grip on the leg. Cut through meat to expose ball-and-socket hip joint. While maintaining tension with the fork, give the knife blade a twist, releasing the leg tendons. Cut through joint (4). If large, you may slice some meat from the leg (5). Remove wings by the same method. Thinly slice breast meat across the grain. Begin in the portion closest to the neck and work back. Slice only one side, keeping the other warm and moist for second helpings(6).

Cooking outdoors is one of the most ancient and romantically satisfying ways of cooking; it is an adventure that never palls. All that is needed to become an expert in this increasingly popular kind of cooking is knowledge of a few rules.

EQUIPMENT—Basic equipment is a grill. This may be a small, inexpensive one or a more elaborate one with a motorized rotary spit and other accessories. The hooded grill intensifies the heat, shortens the cooking time and is the most practical grill for spit-roasting. Remember to remove the spit from the grill when preparing the fire and to fasten the meat or poultry securely to the spit.

Additional equipment should include useful items such as: long-handled tools with heat resistant handles (forks, spoons, turners, tongs), asbestos or well-padded mitts, a baster (which doubles as a douser if fat flares in the fire), a wooden cutting board, a sharp knife, a pot for marinades or sauces, a basting brush and paper towels. Skewers, a skillet (with a long handle), a steak broiler and a spit attachment are pieces of equipment that expand outdoor culinary skills

FUEL AND FIRE—Charcoal lumps or briquets or hard woods are fuels preferred by experts. Never use soft woods because they give food a tarry soot coating and do not give a satisfactory bed of coals. Start with a good bed of charcoal, 2 to 3 inches deep or enough to last the entire cooking period. Wait for the coals to burn to a gray color with a ruddy glow underneath (at least 30 minutes). A handful of dampened hickory chips tossed onto a charcoal fire just before grilling will give a superb flavor to anything you grill. The distance from the top of the coals to the foods helps determine the degree of heat. *Timing of cooking period will vary with the size of the firebox, degree of heat, amount and direction of wind and the type of grill used.* Timing and distances suggested are only guides.

GRILLING AND SPIT-ROASTING—Many foods that can be broiled in the kitchen can be grilled outside. Meat and poultry that can be roasted in the kitchen oven will adapt well to spit roasting.

Steak—Sirloin, porterhouse, T-bone or rib, cut 1½ in. thick. Grill 3 in. from coals on greased grill about 6 min. on each side. To test doneness slit meat near bone and note color of meat.

Hamburgers—Grill patties in greased steak broiler or on greased grill 5 in. from coals 4 to 6 min. on each side, depending upon thickness of burger.

Frankfurters—On the grill, in a roaster, in a skillet, in aluminum foil or on a skewer; turn frequently until lightly browned and heated through.

Roast Beef—Boned, rolled rib roast of beef with good layer of fat around outside or an additional layer of suet tied around it. Use motorized rotary spit. Roast 12 in. from coals, allowing 25 min. per pound for medium doneness; brush frequently with barbecue sauce. Test for doneness by cutting slit in meat and noting color of meat.

Chicken—Broiling chicken, about 1½ lbs. ready-to-cook weight, split into halves. Grill, cut side down, on grill 3 in. from coals 10 min. on each side, brushing frequently with Lemon Butter Sauce (page 331) or seasoned melted butter, or until chicken tests done—meat on thickest part of drumstick cuts easily and shows no pink color.

Trout—Small, about 10 oz. each. Wrap in bacon and grill in basket steak broiler 3 in. from coals, turning once, until bacon is very crisp (about 7 min.). Trout will then be cooked.

Rock-Lobster Tails—Thaw and prepare as for Broiled Rock-Lobster Tails, *page 239.* Grill, shell-side down, 4 in. from coals, brushing frequently with Lemon Butter Sauce, 10 min., or until shell is charred. Turn and continue grilling 6 min., or until meat is completely white and opaque.

Vegetables—Wet Spanish or Bermuda *onions* thoroughly and place on grill. Roll onions around occasionally. They are done when black on outside and soft and creamy on inside (about 50 min.).

Loosen husks only enough to remove silk and blemishes from ears of *corn;* dip ears in water. Shake well; rewrap husks around corn. Let ears stand in water until husks are soaked (about 1 hr.). Roast, turning often, on grill until corn is tender (about 15 min.).

Wash, scrub and wipe dry *potatoes;* rub entire surface with fat. Loosely wrap each potato in heavy aluminum foil; seal open ends with double fold. Bake on grill 1 hr., or until potatoes are soft when pressed with fingers (protected from heat by mitt). Turn several times.

▲ Stewed Chicken

Set out a kettle having a tight-fitting cover.

Clean

1 stewing chicken, 4 to 5 lbs., ready-to-cook weight

(If frozen, thaw according to directions on package.) Disjoint and cut into serving-size pieces. Rinse chicken pieces and giblets. Refrigerate the liver. Put chicken, gizzard, heart and neck into the kettle. (Brown chicken pieces first, if desired.) Add

Hot water to barely cover

Add to the water

1 small onion (page 12)
3 sprigs parsley
2 3-in. pieces celery with leaves
1 bay leaf
2 or 3 peppercorns
2 teaspoons salt
1½ teaspoons Accent

Bring water to boiling; remove foam. Cover kettle tightly, reduce heat, and simmer chicken 1 hr., skimming foam from surface as necessary. Continue cooking chicken 1 to 2 hrs. longer, or until thickest pieces are tender when pierced with a fork. During last 15 min. of cooking time, add liver to kettle.

Remove chicken from broth and arrange in a deep serving dish; keep warm. Strain broth and cool slightly; skim fat from surface. Thicken broth (p. 107) for gravy. Pour gravy over chicken pieces.

Serve hot. *About 6 servings*

For Cooked Chicken—To obtain meat for use in other recipes, follow ▲ Recipe; omit browning pieces first. Cook until thickest pieces of chicken are just tender when pierced with a fork. Do not overcook, or meat will separate into small pieces when removed from bone. Remove chicken and giblets from broth.

Cool chicken slightly and remove skin. Remove meat from bones in as large pieces as possible, or cut into pieces as directed in recipes. (One 4- to 5-lb. chicken yields 3 to 3½ cups coarsely chopped chicken meat.)

For Chicken Broth—Strain broth and cool slightly. Remove fat that rises to surface. Refrigerate fat and use in other recipes, such as **Brown Gravy** (p. 325). Use broth (unthickened) for gravy, or use in other food preparation. Unless meat and broth are to be used immediately, cool, cover and refrigerate in separate containers. Use within 3 days.

⚠ Chicken and Dumplings 12

(*See photo on page 69*)

Follow ▲ Recipe. Prepare **Dumplings** (*page 69*) while chicken is cooking. After broth is thickened, return chicken pieces to kettle. Bring liquid to boiling. Drop dumpling batter by tablespoonfuls on top of chicken pieces. Dumplings should rest on meat; if dumplings settle down into liquid they may be soggy. If necessary, pour off excess liquid to prevent this. Cover tightly and cook over medium heat 20 min. without removing cover. Remove dumplings; arrange around edge of serving dish. Put chicken pieces and gravy in center.

⚠ Cooked Giblets 13 4

(Giblets and neck may be cooked separately from poultry.) Follow ▲ Recipe, using only enough water to cover. Decrease salt to ½ teaspoon and Accent to ¼ teaspoon. Simmer until gizzard is tender when pierced with a fork (about 1 hr. for chicken giblets, 2 to 3 hrs. for turkey giblets).

Chicken Fricassee with  Biscuits and Cream Gravy

Set out a Dutch oven or a sauce pot having a tight-fitting cover.

For Chicken—Clean

1 stewing chicken, 4 to 5 lbs., ready-to-cook weight

(If frozen, thaw according to directions on package.) Disjoint and cut into serving-size pieces. Rinse; pat chicken pieces and giblets dry with absorbent paper.

Heat in the sauce pot over low heat

¼ cup butter or margarine

Add the chicken pieces. Brown over medium heat, occasionally moving and turning pieces.

Pour over the browned chicken

3 cups hot water

Add

1 small onion (*page 12*)
3 sprigs parsley
2 3-in. pieces celery with leaves
1 small bay leaf
2 or 3 peppercorns
2 teaspoons Accent
1 teaspoon salt

Cover and simmer 2 to 3 hrs., or until thickest pieces of chicken are tender when pierced with a fork.

While chicken is cooking, prepare

Rolled Baking Powder Biscuits (*page 63*)

Remove chicken to hot serving platter; cover to keep warm while preparing gravy. Strain and reserve the broth for gravy.

Chicken Fricassee, Biscuits and Cream Gravy

For Gravy—Heat in a small saucepan over low heat

¼ cup butter or margarine

Blend in a mixture of

¼ cup flour
¼ teaspoon pepper

Heat until mixture bubbles and flour is lightly browned. Remove from heat. Add gradually, stirring constantly, the reserved chicken broth (about 2 cups) and

½ cup cream

Cook slowly, stirring constantly, until gravy thickens. Cook 1 to 2 min. longer.

To Serve—Split 6 of the biscuits into halves and arrange them around the chicken pieces on the serving platter. (Set remaining biscuits aside to keep warm.) Pour part of the gravy over the chicken and biscuits on the platter. Serve remaining gravy in a small bowl or gravy boat with the remaining biscuits.

6 to 8 servings

Chicken De Luxe

Set out a shallow 2-qt. casserole.

Cut into thick slices enough cooked chicken to yield about
3 cups sliced cooked chicken
Set aside.

Prepare
Pastry for 1-Crust Pie (one- and one-half times recipe, page 442)
Roll dough to shape of casserole and about 2 in. larger than casserole top; fold dough and lay it in casserole. Unfold; gently pat to fit over bottom and up sides of casserole, allowing dough to extend about 1 in. over sides of dish. Fold under; flute (*page 12*) and prick thoroughly on bottom and sides of dough.

Bake at 425°F 15 to 20 min., or until pastry is lightly browned.

Meanwhile, put into a deep saucepan, cover with boiling salted water and cook loosely covered over medium heat about 10 min.
2 medium-size (about ⅓ lb.) onions (page 12), quartered
¾ cup (about 3 stalks) coarsely cut celery (page 12)
½ teaspoon Accent
Add and cook (*page 285*) 10 to 12 min. longer, or until vegetables are tender
1 10-oz. pkg. frozen cut green beans
Meanwhile, prepare
2 cups Medium White Sauce (double recipe, page 323; substitute 1 cup Chicken Broth, page 205, for one half of milk)
Drain vegetables; blend into sauce with chicken. Heat thoroughly. Turn into pastry shell.

Garnish with **pimiento strips.** Serve hot.

6 servings

Chicken-Stuffed Eggplant 15

MRS. WALTER C. DOYSCHER
DES MOINES, IOWA

Set out a 9x9x2-in. baking dish and a medium-size saucepan.

Dice, and set aside, enough chicken to yield
2 cups diced cooked chicken
Wash and cut into halves lengthwise
1 medium-size (about 1 lb.) eggplant
Cook covered in a small amount of boiling salted water about 10 min., or until just tender. Remove eggplant from water; drain.

With a sharp knife, cut down around inside of eggplant about ½ in. from edge, being careful not to pierce shell. With a spoon, scoop out pulp. Set the shells aside. Coarsely chop and set aside the eggplant pulp.

Rinse and dip quickly into boiling water
2 medium-size (about ½ lb.) tomatoes
Peel tomatoes; cut out and discard stem ends. Cut the tomatoes into quarters and discard the seeds. Coarsely chop the tomatoes; mix with the chicken, eggplant pulp and a mixture of
1 teaspoon salt
½ teaspoon Accent
½ teaspoon pepper
Set aside.

Heat in the saucepan over low heat
1 tablespoon butter or margarine
Add and cook over medium heat until golden yellow, stirring occasionally
½ cup (about 1 medium-size) finely chopped onion (page 12)
Add the eggplant mixture and cook over low heat about 10 min. Remove from heat.

Lightly fill shells with the mixture and place in the baking dish. Sprinkle over filling
Grated Parmesan or Cheddar cheese
Bake at 350°F 15 min. *About 4 servings*

Creamed Chicken in Pastry Shells

Creamed Chicken in Pastry Shells

Set out a heavy 2-qt. saucepan.

Prepare, bake and set aside

8 4½-in. pastry shells (one- and one-half times recipe for Pastry for Little Pies and Tarts, (page 443; flute shells, see photo)

Dice and set aside enough chicken to yield

2½ cups diced cooked chicken

Heat in the saucepan over low heat

2 tablespoons butter or margarine

Add

½ cup (4-oz. can, drained) sliced mushrooms

¼ cup finely chopped green pepper (page 12)

2 tablespoons finely chopped onion

Cook until onion is transparent and mushrooms are lightly browned, occasionally moving and turning with a spoon. Add, stirring constantly

2½ cups (2 10½- to 11-oz. cans) condensed cream of chicken soup

½ cup milk

2 tablespoons finely sliced pimiento

¼ teaspoon Accent

Blend in the chicken. Heat, but do not boil.

Spoon the hot mixture into the prepared pastry shells. Serve immediately.   *8 servings*

Chicken à la King 16

Set out a 2-qt. saucepan.

Cut into chunks and set aside enough cooked chicken to yield

3 cups cooked chicken

Prepare and set aside

1½ cups quick chicken broth (page 13; use 2 chicken bouillon cubes)

Cook and set aside (drain if necessary)

1 10-oz. pkg. frozen peas

Meanwhile, clean and slice (page 12)

½ lb. mushrooms

Heat in the saucepan over low heat

⅓ cup butter, margarine, or chicken fat

Add the mushrooms. Cook slowly about 5 min., frequently moving and turning with a spoon. With slotted spoon remove mushrooms, allowing fat to drain back into saucepan; set mushrooms aside.

Blend into butter in saucepan a mixture of

¼ cup flour

1 teaspoon salt

½ teaspoon Accent

Few grains pepper

Heat until mixture bubbles; cook 3 to 5 min. Remove from heat. Add gradually, stirring constantly, the chicken broth and

1½ cups cream

Return mixture to heat; cook until thickened. Add the chicken, peas, mushrooms and

¼ cup (2-oz. can, drained) pimiento strips

Cook mixture slowly until chicken is thoroughly heated. If desired, transfer mixture to a chafing dish.

Serve over **waffles, rusks,** or **Toast Points** (*page 65*), or in **Toast Cups** (*page 65*).

6 servings

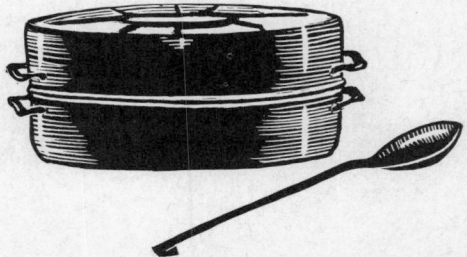

Chicken Livers Orientale 17

Set out a large, heavy skillet.

Drain, reserving sirup, and set aside
**1 No. 2 can pineapple chunks
(about 2 cups, drained)**
Clean thoroughly, rinse with cold water, and
set aside to drain on absorbent paper
2 lbs. chicken livers
Blanch (*page 11*) and set aside
1 cup (5½ oz.) almonds
Mix together in a medium-size saucepan
**¼ cup firmly packed brown sugar
¼ cup sugar
¼ cup cornstarch**
Add gradually, while stirring constantly, a
mixture of the reserved pineapple sirup and
**1½ cups (12-oz. can) pineapple juice
4 to 6 tablespoons vinegar
1 tablespoon soy sauce**
Bring rapidly to boiling, stirring constantly.
Cook 3 min. longer, stirring occasionally. Set
aside and keep hot.

Heat in the skillet over low heat
½ cup butter or margarine
Put livers in skillet. Turning occasionally,
cook about 10 min., or until lightly browned.
Add pineapple chunks, almonds, and sauce.
Moving mixture gently with a spoon, cook a
few min. longer, or until pineapple is heated.

Spoon mixture into chafing dish to keep warm
while serving. Serve over
Perfection Boiled Rice (page 275)
6 to 8 servings

Curried Chicken with Almonds

Cut into strips and set aside enough cooked
chicken to yield
4 cups cooked chicken
Coarsely chop and set aside
**½ cup (about 2¾ oz.) unblanched,
toasted almonds (page 12)**
Clean and slice (*page 12*)
¼ lb. mushrooms

Heat in a chafing pan (or large skillet) over
direct heat
⅓ cup butter or margarine
Add mushrooms to chafing pan with
**¼ cup finely chopped onion
¼ cup finely chopped celery**
Cook over medium heat until onion is transparent and mushrooms are delicately browned,
occasionally moving and turning pieces.

Gently push vegetables to one side of the pan
and blend into butter a mixture of
**½ cup flour
2 teaspoons curry powder
1½ teaspoons Accent
1 teaspoon salt**
Heat until mixture bubbles, stirring constantly. Remove from heat. Add gradually to chafing pan, stirring constantly
**2 cups cream
2 cups Chicken Broth (page 205; or
quick chicken broth, page 13)**
Return to heat and bring rapidly to boiling,
stirring constantly, and carefully mixing in
the vegetables; cook 1 to 2 min. longer. Blend
in the chicken. Cook until chicken is thoroughly heated, occasionally stirring gently.
Sprinkle chopped almonds over top.

Serve with **Perfection Boiled Rice** (*p. 275*)
and curry condiments, such as freshly grated
coconut, golden **raisins**, Indian **chutney** and
Broiled Bananas (*page 305*).   *6 to 8 servings*

*Curried Chicken with Almonds
and Broiled Bananas (page 305)*

Chicken in White Wine Sauce

MRS. A. E. BOYCE, RIVERDALE, N. DAK.

Set out a shallow 2-qt. casserole and a 2-qt. saucepan.

Cook and set aside (drain if necessary)
   1 10-oz. pkg. frozen peas
Cut into cubes and set aside enough cooked chicken to yield
   4 cups cubed cooked chicken
Heat in the saucepan over low heat
   ½ cup butter, margarine or chicken fat
Add, reserving liquid
   ½ cup (4-oz. can, drained) whole mushrooms
Cook until mushrooms are lightly browned, occasionally moving and turning with a spoon. Remove with a slotted spoon and set aside.

Blend into fat in saucepan
   ½ cup flour
Heat until mixture bubbles and flour is lightly browned. Remove from heat. Add gradually, stirring constantly, the mushroom liquid and
   3 cups Chicken Broth (page 205; or quick chicken broth, page 13)
Cook rapidly, stirring constantly, until sauce thickens. Cook 1 to 2 min. longer.

Stir in
   ⅓ cup white wine
   ½ teaspoon salt
   ½ teaspoon Accent
   ¼ teaspoon paprika
   ⅛ teaspoon pepper
Add the chicken, peas and mushrooms; carefully blend with sauce. Turn mixture into casserole.

Bake at 375°F 30 min., or until mixture is hot and bubbly. Remove from oven.

Immediately before serving, border inside of casserole with Almond Toast Points. Sprinkle mixture with
   Paprika

For Almond Toast Points—Finely chop and set aside
   ½ cup blanched almonds (page 11)
Remove crusts from
   5 slices white bread
Combine the chopped almonds with
   ⅓ cup softened butter
Mix until smooth. Spread almond butter over bread slices. Cut slices diagonally, forming four "points" from each slice. Toast in oven until golden brown. Garnish each point with a small strip of **pimiento**.   *About 6 servings*

▲ Roast Rock Cornish Game Hen

Set out a shallow roasting pan with a rack.

Prepare and set aside for stuffing
> **Wild Rice with Mushrooms (one-half recipe, *page 305*; add all mushrooms to rice)**

Clean
> **4 Rock Cornish game hens, about 1 lb. each**

Rinse and pat dry with absorbent paper.

Rub cavities of the four hens with
> **2 teaspoons salt**
> **¼ teaspoon Accent**

Lightly fill body cavities with the stuffing. To close body cavities, sew or skewer and lace with cord. Fasten neck skin to backs and wings to bodies with skewers. Put game hens breast-side up on rack in roasting pan.

Set out
> **¼ cup unsalted butter, melted**

Brush each hen with the butter.

Roast uncovered at 350°F.

Frequently baste hens during roasting period with drippings from roasting pan.

Roast 1 to 1½ hrs., or until hens test done. To test doneness, move leg gently by grasping end bone; drumstick-thigh joint moves easily when hens are done. (Protect fingers from heat with paper napkin.)

Place game hens on a heated platter; keep warm while preparing gravy. Before serving, remove skewers and garnish hens with
> **Sprigs of water cress**

For Gravy—Prepare
> **½ cup quick meat broth (*page 13*)**

Set aside to cool.

Leaving brown residue in roasting pan, pour the drippings into a bowl. Allow fat to rise to surface; skim off fat and reserve. Remaining drippings are meat juices which should be used as part of the liquid in the gravy. Meas-

Roast Rock Cornish Game Hen

ure into roasting pan 1½ tablespoons of the reserved fat. Blend in
> **1½ tablespoons flour**
> **¼ teaspoon Accent**
> **⅛ teaspoon salt**
> **⅛ teaspoon pepper**

Stirring constantly, heat until the mixture bubbles. Remove from heat and add gradually, stirring constantly and vigorously, the broth and ½ cup of the drippings. Return to heat and bring mixture rapidly to boiling, stirring constantly. Cook 1 to 2 min. longer. While stirring, scrape bottom and sides of pan to blend in brown residue. Remove from heat and stir in
> **2 tablespoons Madeira wine**

Pour into a gravy boat and serve hot.

4 servings

△ Roast Squab

Follow ▲ Recipe. Substitute 4 **squabs**, ¾ to 1 lb. each, ready-to-cook weight, for the Rock Cornish game hens.

Roast Ducklings with Orange Rice Stuffing

Roast Ducklings with Orange Rice Stuffing

Set out a shallow roasting pan with rack.

Clean

2 ducklings, 4 lbs. each, ready-to-cook weight

Cut off necks at bodies, leaving on neck skin. (If frozen, thaw according to directions on package.) Rinse and pat ducklings dry with absorbent paper; set aside. Reserve giblets for use in other food preparation.

Prepare and cool

Orange-Rice Stuffing (page 221)

Set out

1 cup orange juice

Rub cavities of ducklings with a mixture of

1 to 2 teaspoons salt

1 to 2 teaspoons Accent

Lightly fill body and neck cavities with the stuffing. To close body cavity, sew or skewer and lace with cord. With skewers, fasten neck skin to back and wings to body. Place ducklings breast side up on rack in roasting pan. Brush with the orange juice.

Roast at 325°F. After 30 min., brush ducklings with juice; brush frequently thereafter. Roast 3 hrs., or until ducklings test done (*page 195*).

Remove skewers and cord. Serve ducklings on heated platter. Garnish with **orange slices.** If desired, accompany with Orange Gravy.

For Orange Gravy—Leaving brown residue in roasting pan, pour into a bowl

Drippings

Allow fat to rise to surface; skim off fat and reserve. Remaining drippings are meat juices and orange juice which should be used as part of the liquid in the gravy.

Measure into the roasting pan 3 tablespoons of the reserved fat. Blend in a mixture of

3 tablespoons flour

¼ teaspoon salt

¼ teaspoon Accent

⅛ teaspoon pepper

Stirring constantly, heat until mixture bubbles. Remove from heat and add slowly, stirring constantly and vigorously

2 cups liquid (cooled drippings plus orange juice)

Return to heat and cook rapidly, stirring constantly, until gravy thickens. Cook 1 to 2 min. longer. While stirring, scrape bottom and sides of pan to blend in brown residue.

About 8 servings

▲ Roast Ducklings with Giblet Gravy

Set out a shallow roasting pan with rack.

Clean

2 ducklings, 4 lbs. each, ready-to-cook weight

Cut off necks at bodies, leaving on neck skin. (If frozen, thaw according to directions on package.) Rinse and pat ducklings dry with absorbent paper; set aside. Refrigerate giblets.

Prepare

Chestnut Stuffing for Roast Duckling (page 220), or Apple Stuffing for Poultry (page 218)

Set aside.

Rub cavities of ducklings with a mixture of

1 to 2 teaspoons salt

1 to 2 teaspoons Accent

Lightly fill body and neck cavities of ducklings with the stuffing. To close body cavities, sew or skewer and lace with cord. With skewers fasten neck skin to back and wings to body. Place breast side up on rack in roasting pan.

Roast uncovered at 325°F about 3 hrs., or until ducklings test done (*page 195*).

To serve, remove skewers and cord. Place ducklings on a heated platter; cover and keep hot. Prepare **Giblet Gravy** (*page 325;* cook giblets during last half of roasting period).

About 8 servings

△ Roast Ducklings
(Unstuffed)

Follow ▲ Recipe; omit stuffing. If desired, place quartered, cored, unpared **apples,** halved **onions,** or ribs of **celery** inside duckling. Roast 2 to 2½ hrs., or until duckling tests done.

▲ Roast Goose with Prune Stuffing

Set out a shallow roasting pan with rack.

For Prune Stuffing—Stew (*page 494*), remove pits and set aside

1 cup (about 7 oz.) large dried prunes

Meanwhile, cook in salted water just to cover, about 30 to 40 min., or until tender

1 lb. lean pork (all visible fat removed), cut in pieces

Drain and put through food chopper. Set aside.

Prepare

½ cup chopped onion (page 12)
¼ cup chopped green olives

Heat in a skillet over medium heat

1 tablespoon fat

Add the onion; cook until transparent, occasionally moving with a spoon. Mix in the pork; season with a mixture of

1 teaspoon salt
1 teaspoon Accent
¼ teaspoon pepper

Remove skillet from heat; stir in

2 egg yolks, slightly beaten

Remove ¼ cup of pork stuffing and combine with the olives. Fill pitted prunes with this mixture and gently mix prunes with remaining stuffing.

To Prepare Goose—Clean, removing any layers of fat from body cavity and opening

1 goose, 10 to 12 lbs. ready-to-cook weight

Cut off neck at body, leaving on neck skin. (If goose is frozen, thaw according to directions on package.) Rinse and pat dry with absorbent paper. (Reserve giblets for use in other food preparation.) Rub cavities of goose with **salt.**

Lightly spoon stuffing into body and neck cavities. To close body cavity, sew or skewer and lace with cord. Fasten neck skin to back with skewer. Loop cord around legs and tighten slightly. Place breast side down on rack in roasting pan.

Roast uncovered at 325°F for 3 hrs. Remove fat from pan several times during this period. Turn goose breast side up. Roast 1 to 2 hrs. longer, or until it tests done (*page 195*). (Total roasting time: about 25 min. per pound.)

To serve, remove skewers and cord. Place goose on heated platter. Garnish as desired.

8 servings

△ Roast Goose with Apple Stuffing

Follow ▲ Recipe; substitute **Apple Stuffing for Poultry** (*page 218*) for the prune stuffing.

Roast Goose with Prune Stuffing

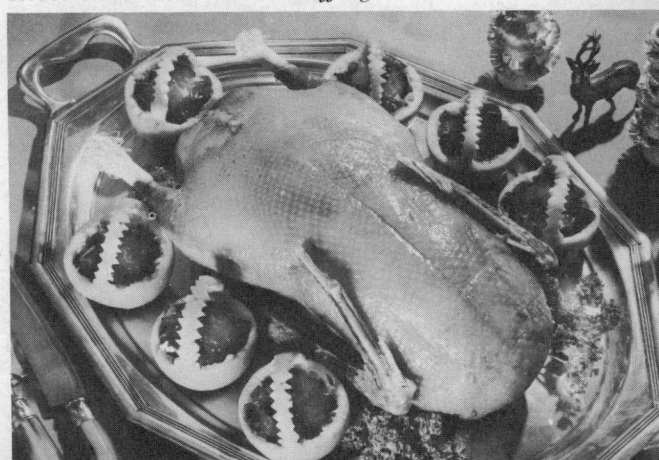

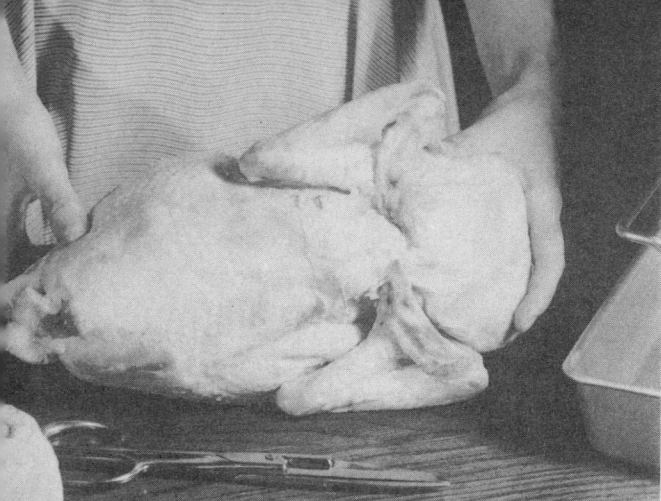

Roast Turkey: Fasten neck skin to back of bird with a skewer. Bring wing tips onto the back.

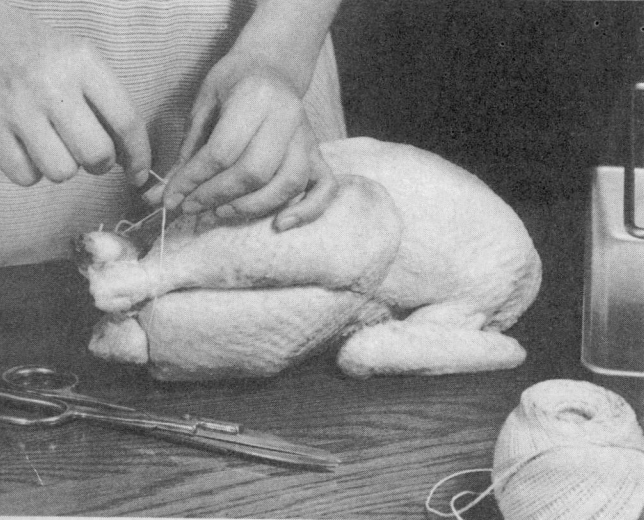

Tie drumsticks of the turkey to the tail with cord. Brush the skin thoroughly with melted fat. Roast.

Test for doneness by pressing thickest part of drumstick with fingers. Meat feels soft to touch.

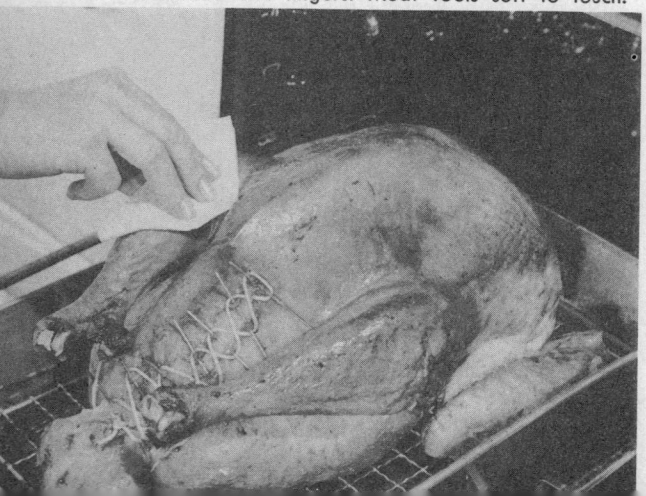

▲ Roast Turkey

Set out a shallow roasting pan with rack.

Clean

1 turkey, 10 to 12 lbs. ready-to-cook weight

Cut off neck at body, leaving on neck skin. (If turkey is frozen, thaw according to directions on package.) Rinse, drain and pat dry with absorbent paper; set aside. Reserve giblets.

Prepare

Herb Stuffing or Oyster Stuffing (*page 218*) or Giblet Stuffing for Roast Turkey (*page 220*)

Rub cavities of turkey with a mixture of

2 teaspoons Accent
1 to 2 teaspoons salt

Lightly fill body and neck cavities with stuffing. To close body cavity, sew or skewer and lace with cord. Fasten neck skin to back with skewer. Tie drumsticks to tail. Bring wing tips onto back. Brush skin thoroughly with

Melted fat

Place breast side up on rack in roasting pan. If roast-meat thermometer is used, place it in center of inside thigh muscle. (When turkey is done, roast-meat thermometer will register 190°F.) Place fat-moistened cheesecloth over top and sides of turkey. Keep cloth moist during roasting by brushing occasionally with fat from bottom of pan.

Roast uncovered at 325°F 4 to 4½ hrs., or until turkey tests done (*page 195*). Remove turkey from oven. Remove roast-meat thermometer and keep turkey hot. Allow to stand 30 to 40 min. before serving. This allows turkey to absorb its juices and become easier to carve. This also allows time to prepare gravy and garnishes. Remove cord and skewers. Serve turkey on hot platter. Garnish with **parsley.** Serve with

Cranberry Sauce (*page 332*)
Brown Gravy or Giblet Gravy (*page 325*)

If desired, put paper frills on drumsticks.

About 16 servings

⚠ **Roast Half Turkey**

Follow ⚠ Recipe; use **half** or **quarter turkey**, 3½ to 5 lbs., ready-to-cook weight. Rub cut side with one-half salt mixture. Skewer skin along cut side to prevent shrinking. Tie leg to tail and wing flat against breast. Place skin-side up on rack. Roast at 325°F 2 hrs.

Meanwhile, prepare **Stuffing for Half Turkey** (*p.218*). Spoon stuffing onto a piece of aluminum foil. Cover stuffing with the half turkey and return turkey and stuffing to rack. Roast 1 to 1½ hrs. longer, or until turkey tests done (*page 195*).   *About 8 servings*

⚠ **Roast Turkey in Aluminum Foil**

Follow ⚠ Recipe for preparing turkey; omit stuffing turkey. (If desired, bake stuffing separately.) Wrap turkey securely in medium weight aluminum foil; close with a drugstore or lock fold to prevent leakage of drippings. Place turkey, breast side up in roasting pan (omit rack).

Roast at 450°F about 3 hrs., or until turkey tests done (*page 195*). About 15 to 20 min. before end of cooking time, remove from oven. Quickly fold foil back away from bird to edges of pan. If using roast-meat thermometer, insert it at this time. Return bird to oven and complete cooking. (Turkey will brown sufficiently in this time.)

Turkey-Rice Dinner

Grease a 2-qt. casserole.

Prepare
     Perfection Boiled Rice (page 275)
Meanwhile, blanch (*page 11*) and sliver
     ½ cup (about 3 oz.) almonds
With fork, toss almonds with
     ½ cup soft bread crumbs
     ¼ cup butter or margarine, melted
Set aside.

Dice and set aside enough turkey to yield
     2 cups diced cooked turkey
Prepare and set aside
     1½ cups Thin White Sauce (1½ times recipe, p.323; if available, use turkey broth for one half of liquid. Add 2 or 3 drops tabasco sauce)
With a fork, gently mix drained rice and
     12 pimiento-stuffed olives, sliced
Mix the diced turkey with
     ½ cup (4-oz. can, drained) sliced mushrooms
     ½ teaspoon Accent
Spoon one third of the rice into casserole. Add one half of the turkey mixture; repeat and top with remaining rice. Pour sauce over all. Sprinkle with crumb-almond mixture.

Bake at 350°F 25 to 30 min., or until top is crusty and golden brown.   *6 to 8 servings*

Note: **Noodles** or **Macaroni** (*p.277*) may be substituted for the rice.

Creamed Turkey and Oysters 22

Cut into chunks enough cooked turkey to yield
     2 to 3 cups cooked turkey
Set in refrigerator until ready to use.

Drain, reserving liquid
     1 pt. oysters
Pick over oysters to remove any shell particles. Set oysters and liquid aside.

Prepare in a chafing dish (or saucepan)
     3 cups Medium White Sauce (three times recipe, p.323) use milk or cream for liquid)
Blend into sauce
     ⅓ cup (2¼-oz. can) deviled ham
     ½ teaspoon Accent
Add the turkey and reserved oysters and liquid, gently blending in. Heat thoroughly.

Meanwhile, prepare **Toast Cups** (*page 65*).

Fill toast cups with the creamed mixture. Serve at once.   *8 servings*

▲ Roast Wild Duck with Wild Rice Stuffing

Set out a shallow roasting pan with rack.

Singe and clean

2 wild ducks, 2 to 3 lbs. each

Cut out oil sac at base of tail; cut off neck at body, leaving on neck skin. Wash ducks in cold, running water; dry with absorbent paper.

Prepare and set aside

**Wild Rice Stuffing (½ recipe,
page 221)**

Set out

4 slices bacon or salt pork

Rub cavities of ducks with a mixture of

1 to 2 teaspoons salt

1 to 2 teaspoons Accent

Lightly fill body and neck cavities of ducks with the stuffing. To close body cavities, sew or skewer and lace with cord. With skewers fasten neck skin to back and wings to body. Put ducks breast side up on rack in roasting pan. Place bacon or salt pork over breasts.

Roast uncovered at 400°F to 450°F 20 to 25 min. for very rare, 30 to 40 min. for medium-rare. (Wild duck is traditionally served rare.) If desired, baste occasionally with

1 cup orange juice, cider or red wine

To serve ducks, remove skewers and cord. Place on heated platter; cover ducks and keep hot while preparing gravy and garnishes.

For Gravy—Scrape pan drippings into a small saucepan. Put into 1-pt. screw-top jar

½ cup water

Sprinkle onto it

1 tablespoon flour

Cover tightly and shake until mixture is well blended. Gradually stir into liquid in pan. Bring rapidly to boiling, stirring constantly until thickened. Cook 3 to 5 min.

About 4 servings

△ Roast Wild Goose

Follow ▲ Recipe; substitute a **wild goose** for ducks. Use full recipe of stuffing. Increase bacon if necessary. Roast at 325°F about 3 hrs. Baste frequently.

Roast Wild Duck

MRS. H. L. BLEVINS, APPALACHIA, VA.

Set out a shallow roasting pan with rack.

Singe and clean

2 wild ducks, 2 to 3 lbs. each

Cut out oil sac at base of tail; cut off neck at body, leaving on neck skin. Wash ducks in cold, running water; dry with absorbent paper.

Set out

3 apples

2 onions (page 12)

1 orange

4 slices bacon

Rub cavities of ducks with a mixture of

1 teaspoon salt

1 teaspoon Accent

¼ teaspoon pepper

⅛ teaspoon ginger

Rub surface of ducks with cut side of

½ lemon

Quarter the apples, onions, and orange. Put pieces inside cavities of ducks. Refrigerate ducks 2 hrs. Discard filling and place ducks breast side up on rack in roasting pan. Lay bacon strips over breasts. Pour over birds

2 cups quick meat broth (page 13)

3 tablespoons melted butter

Roast uncovered at 375°F to 400°F about 30 min. (Wild duck is traditionally served rare.)

Baste occasionally with pan gravy.

About 4 servings

△ Fruit-Filled Wild Duck

Follow ▲ Recipe; do not refrigerate ducks. Close openings of filled ducks with small skewers. Substitute 2 cups **orange juice** or **red wine** for meat broth. Omit butter.

Roast Pheasant

Set out a shallow roasting pan with rack.

Prepare
Wild Rice and Mushrooms (page 305; add all mushrooms to rice)
Set aside for stuffing.

Clean
2 young pheasant, about 2 lbs. each
Cut off necks at bodies, leaving on neck skin. (If frozen, thaw according to directions on package.) Rinse and pat dry with absorbent paper. (Reserve giblets for use in other food preparation.) Rub cavities with a mixture of
1 to 2 teaspoons salt
1 to 2 teaspoons Accent
Lightly fill body and neck cavities with the stuffing. To close body cavities, sew or skewer and lace with cord. With skewers, fasten neck skin to back and wings to body.

Place pheasant breast side up on rack in roasting pan. Brush with
¼ cup unsalted butter, melted
Roast uncovered at 325°F, brushing pheasant frequently during roasting period with drippings from pan. Roast 1½ to 2 hrs., or until pheasant tests done (page 195).

Keep pheasant warm while preparing
Brown Gravy (page 325; add 2 tablespoons red wine)
Before serving, remove skewers and cord.

4 servings.

Rabbit Stew

Set out a large kettle or sauce pot having a tight-fitting cover.

Heat to boiling in a large saucepan
2½ cups water
Meanwhile, sort and wash thoroughly
1 cup (about ½ lb.) dried large lima beans
Add beans gradually to water so boiling will not stop. Simmer 2 min.; remove saucepan from heat. Set beans aside to soak 1 hr.

Meanwhile, clean (page 12), cut into thin slices and set aside
2 medium-size (about ½ lb.) onions
Finely dice, and set aside, enough bacon to yield
½ cup diced bacon
Wipe with a clean, damp cloth and cut into serving-size pieces
1 rabbit, 2½ to 3-lbs., ready-to-cook weight
(If frozen, thaw according to directions on package.) Set aside.

Put diced bacon in kettle and heat over low heat. Add the onion slices and cook over medium heat until onion is transparent and bacon is lightly browned (not crisp). With slotted spoon, remove bacon and onion to a small dish.

Put rabbit pieces into the kettle and cook until lightly browned, turning pieces with tongs or two spoons to brown evenly. Add more fat if necessary.

Add to the browned rabbit
Hot water (enough to half-cover)
Return bacon and onion to kettle. Add
1 tablespoon salt
1 teaspoon Accent
¼ teaspoon pepper
⅛ teaspoon thyme
1 clove garlic (page 12), minced; or crushed in a garlic press
1 bay leaf
Bring liquid rapidly to boiling; reduce heat, cover and simmer (do not boil) 45 min.

Meanwhile, wash, scrape or pare, and slice
1 lb. carrots (about 2½ cups, sliced)
Drain lima beans and add to kettle with sliced carrots. Continue cooking about 45 min., or until rabbit and vegetables are tender. Add more boiling water as needed. During last 15 min. of cooking time, add
2 green peppers (page 12), sliced in rings
If desired, thicken cooking liquid (p. 107). Remove bay leaf. *6 to 8 servings*

STUFFINGS

Apple Stuffing for Spareribs 24

Wash, quarter, core, paré, dice and set aside

1 medium-size apple (1 cup, diced)

Heat in a skillet over medium heat

¼ cup butter or margarine

Add and cook until transparent, occasionally moving and turning with a spoon

½ cup (1 medium-size) chopped onion (page 12)

Meanwhile, toss together the diced apple and

2 cups (about 2 slices) soft bread crumbs or cubes

and a mixture of

1 teaspoon salt
¼ teaspoon Accent
1 teaspoon celery seed
¼ teaspoon marjoram
⅛ teaspoon pepper

Blend with onion and fat. Toss mixture with

¼ cup apple cider (use only enough barely to moisten bread)

About 3½ cups stuffing

▲ Herb Stuffing

Mix together

¾ cup melted butter or margarine
2 teaspoons salt
½ to 1 teaspoon Accent
1 teaspoon sage (or ½ teaspoon each of thyme, rosemary and marjoram)
¼ teaspoon pepper

Lightly toss seasoned butter with a mixture of

2 qts. (about 8 slices) soft bread cubes
¾ cup milk
⅓ cup chopped celery with leaves
⅓ cup chopped onion

Spoon stuffing into neck and body cavities of turkey—do not pack. (See STUFFING POULTRY FOR ROASTING, *page 195*.)

Stuffing for 10-lb. turkey

⚠ Oyster Stuffing 25

Drain 1 pt. **oysters,** reserving liquid. Pick over to remove any shell particles. Simmer oysters in reserved liquid 3 min., or until edges begin to curl. Chop if oysters are large.

Follow ▲ Recipe. Substitute **poultry seasoning** for sage. Add oysters to bread cubes. **Oyster liquid** may be substituted for part of the milk.

⚠ Stuffing for Half Turkey

Follow ▲ Recipe or ⚠ Recipe, allowing ⅔ cup stuffing per serving. Spoon stuffing onto aluminum foil and place under turkey the last 1 to 1½ hrs. of roasting time.

⚠ Apple Stuffing for Poultry

Follow ▲ Recipe; increase onion to ½ cup and substitute ½ teaspoon **marjoram** for sage. Wash, quarter, core, pare, dice and toss with the bread mixture 2 medium-size **apples** (about 2 cups, diced).

For one 10- to 12-lb. goose, prepare one-half recipe Apple Stuffing; for one chicken or two ducklings, prepare one-third recipe.

⚠ Toasted-Bread Stuffing

Follow ▲ Recipe; omit soft bread cubes and milk. Increase onion to 1 cup, celery to ¾ cup. Toast until golden brown and thoroughly dried 11 slices **white bread.** Put bread into a bowl. Pour **milk** or **water** over bread and let stand until slices swell. Squeeze out moisture; pull bread apart. Remove bread to a large bowl. Pour the seasoned butter over the bread. Add the chopped vegetables and 2 **eggs,** well beaten. Mix together lightly with 2 forks.

Note: These stuffings may also be used for chicken, goose or duckling. Allow about 1 cup bread cubes per pound of ready-to-cook weight of bird; if weight is 10 lbs. or less, subtract 1 cup from total; if weight is more than 10 lbs., subtract 2 cups from the total number. Proportionately increase or decrease remaining ingredients in recipe.

Celery-Almond Stuffing

Finely chop and set aside
> **½ cup (about 3 oz.) blanched, toasted almonds (page 11)**

Finely dice enough celery to yield
> **3 cups finely diced celery (page 12)**

Prepare and set aside
> **¾ cup quick chicken broth (page 13)**

Mix together
> **¾ cup butter, melted**
> **2 teaspoons poultry seasoning**
> **1 teaspoon salt**
> **½ teaspoon Accent**
> **¼ teaspoon pepper**

Lightly toss butter mixture with the almonds, celery, chicken broth and
> **2 qts. (about 8 slices) soft bread crumbs**
> **⅓ cup finely chopped onion**

Spoon stuffing into neck and body cavities of turkey—do not pack. (See STUFFING POULTRY FOR ROASTING, *page 195.*)

Stuffing for 10-lb. turkey

Molly's Bread Stuffing 26
(For Poultry and Game)
MRS. BILL SETZER, JOHNSON CITY, TENN.

Molly was a Southern mountain woman who earned her living as a cook for a short time. Innocent of book-learnin' though she was, Molly knew her native mountain cooking lore. Her bread stuffing is especially good with game.

Put in a large cold skillet
> **½ lb. (about 8) sausage links**
> **2 tablespoons water**

Cover and cook slowly 8 to 10 min. Remove cover and pour off fat. With a fork, break links into small pieces. Add
> **1 small onion, finely chopped**

Cook over medium heat, until onion is transparent and sausage is lightly browned, frequently moving and turning with a spoon.

Add
> **½ cup butter**

When butter has melted, stir in a mixture of
> **3 cups (9 slices) fine, dry bread crumbs**
> **1 cup corn-bread crumbs**
> **½ teaspoon sage**
> **½ teaspoon salt**
> **¼ teaspoon Accent**
> **⅛ teaspoon pepper**

Heat, stirring gently and constantly, until crumbs absorb butter. Remove from heat.

Spoon stuffing lightly into small game animals or birds. (See STUFFING POULTRY FOR ROASTING, *page 195.*)

About 3 cups stuffing

▲ Chestnut Stuffing for Roast Duckling

Set out a shallow baking dish.

Wash and make a long slit through shell on both sides of

2 lbs. chestnuts

Put chestnuts into the dish and brush them with

1½ tablespoons cooking oil

Set in 450°F oven for 20 min.

Remove chestnuts from oven, allow to stand until just cool enough to handle, and with a sharp pointed knife remove shells and skins. Put into boiling salted water to cover and boil 20 min., or until tender.

Meanwhile, heat in a skillet over low heat

¼ cup butter

Add to butter and cook over medium heat until onion is transparent, occasionally moving and turning pieces with a spoon

1 small onion (page 12), chopped
½ cup chopped celery (page 12)

Remove skillet from heat; add and mix well

1 cup (about 1 slice) soft bread crumbs
1 tablespoon chopped parsley

and a mixture of

1 teaspoon salt
¼ teaspoon Accent
⅛ teaspoon pepper

When chestnuts are tender, put one half through ricer or food mill. Coarsely chop remaining chestnuts. Combine chestnuts with bread-crumb mixture. Toss lightly with

½ cup cream

Just before roasting, spoon stuffing into neck and body cavities of bird—do not pack. (See STUFFING POULTRY FOR ROASTING, page 195.)

About 3½ cups stuffing
(Enough for two 4-lb. ducklings)

Note: For a 10- to 12-lb. turkey, double recipe; increase bread crumbs to 5 cups.

△ Apple-Chestnut Stuffing

Follow ▲ Recipe; wash, quarter, core and dice 1 medium-size cooking **apple** (about 1 cup, diced). Mix the apple into the stuffing before addition of cream.

Giblet Stuffing for Roast Turkey

Set out a small skillet.

Prepare and cook (See Cooked Giblets, *page 205*; simmer 2 to 2½ hrs.)

Turkey giblets (gizzard, heart, liver) and neck

Remove giblets and neck from broth; allow meat to cool slightly. Remove neck meat from bones and chop with giblets; put into a large mixing bowl. Set aside. Strain and reserve the giblet broth.

Heat in the skillet over medium heat

¾ cup butter or margarine

Add to fat and cook until onion is transparent, occasionally moving and turning with a spoon

½ cup (about 1 medium-size) chopped onion (page 12)

Remove from heat and stir in a mixture of

2 teaspoons salt
½ teaspoon Accent
¼ teaspoon pepper
¼ teaspoon paprika

Set out

2 qts. (about 11 slices) dry bread cubes
2 tablespoons chopped parsley

Add gradually to bread cubes, tossing lightly

¾ cup reserved giblet broth
2 eggs, well beaten

Add the chopped giblets, the onion mixture and the chopped parsley.

Just before roasting turkey, spoon stuffing into neck and body cavities—do not pack. (See STUFFING POULTRY FOR ROASTING, page 195.)

Enough stuffing for a
10- to 12-lb. turkey

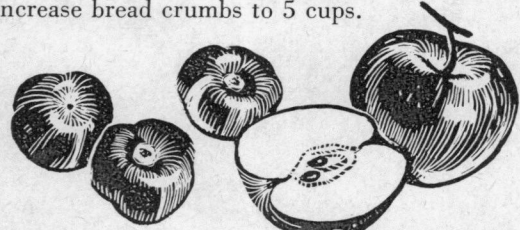

Orange-Rice Stuffing 28

Heat in a heavy 2-qt. saucepan over low heat
3 tablespoons butter or margarine
Add and cook over medium heat until onion is transparent, occasionally moving and turning pieces with a spoon
1 cup diced celery with leaves
(page 12)
2 tablespoons chopped onion
Add to saucepan and bring to rapid boiling
1½ cups water
1 cup orange juice
2 tablespoons grated orange peel
(page 11)
1½ teaspoons salt
½ teaspoon Accent
⅛ teaspoon marjoram
⅛ teaspoon thyme
Add gradually so boiling will not stop
1 cup uncooked rice
Stir to blend thoroughly. Cover saucepan tightly; reduce heat to very low and cook about 25 min. without removing cover. Cool slightly. Spoon stuffing into neck and body cavities of bird—do not pack. (See STUFFING POULTRY FOR ROASTING, *page 195*.)

4 cups stuffing
(Enough for two 4-lb. ducklings or
one 4- to 5-lb. roasting chicken)

To Stuff Poultry: Stuff just before putting in the oven. Lightly fill body and neck cavities with stuffing.

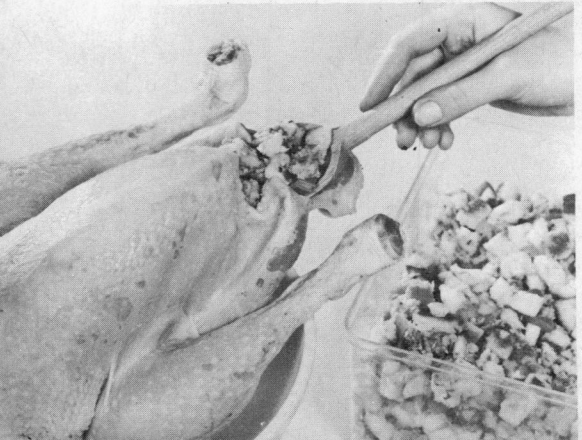

Wild Rice Stuffing 29

MRS. A. E. BOYCE, RIVERDALE, N. DAK.

Set out a 3-qt. saucepan having a tight-fitting cover.

Heat in the saucepan over low heat
⅓ cup butter or margarine
Add, stirring constantly
2 cups wild rice
Cook, stirring frequently, until rice is very hot and tips are lightly browned. Add
1 cup chopped onion (page 12)
1 cup chopped celery (page 12)
Continue cooking until onion is transparent, frequently moving mixture with a spoon. Add, stirring in
4 cups Chicken Broth (page 205; or
quick chicken broth, page 13)
¼ teaspoon Accent
Bring to boiling. Cover tightly and simmer until rice is tender and liquid is absorbed (about 30 min.).

Meanwhile, chop and set aside
1 cup (about 4 oz.) walnuts
Heat in a small skillet over low heat
1 tablespoon butter or margarine
Add
½ cup chopped mushrooms (page 12)
Cook over medium heat until lightly browned, frequently moving and turning pieces with a spoon. Set aside.

Remove rice mixture from heat. Turn into a large mixing bowl. Add the walnuts, mushrooms, and a mixture of
½ teaspoon celery salt
½ teaspoon poultry seasoning
½ teaspoon salt
Dash nutmeg
Blend together lightly but thoroughly. Spoon lightly into cavities of poultry or game. (See STUFFING POULTRY FOR ROASTING, *page 195*.)

About 7 cups stuffing

POULTRY and Stuffings in the MICROWAVE OVEN

Inexpensive, versatile, easy-to-cook poultry is a favorite in most kitchens. Cooking poultry in the microwave oven not only permits you to prepare a wide variety of recipes, but is easier, faster and cleaner than conventional oven cooking. Your **Roast Half Turkey** is done in less than one hour, **Stewed Chicken** in about one-half hour.

Even the classic **Fried Chicken** can be prepared in the microwave oven and, of course, variations on fricassees and casseroles are almost endless. From the main text recipes for game we include the tender **Rabbit Stew.**

These recipes represent a good cross-section, with the **Chicken Cacciatore** and its variations as our personal favorites.

The dishes using precooked (alias leftover) chicken truly demonstrate the magic of microwave cooking. Most of them are out of the oven in less than 20 minutes. The **Chicken-Stuffed Eggplant** is terrific and can be frozen and reheated, as can many of these recipes. The microwave oven is also invaluable for defrosting and reheating; don't forget to take advantage of these timesaving capabilities.

Although the recipes in the following section are all easily cooked in the microwave oven and have tasty results, some poultry does not readily lend itself to this cooking method.

For instance, geese, whole turkey and other birds weighing more than 5 pounds are simply too large to fit in most microwave ovens.

Other birds such as pheasant and squab do not brown sufficiently for most people's taste. After cooking in the microwave oven they can be popped under the conventional broiler for additional browning, but we have avoided such recipes as require this two-appliance cooking process.

COOKING POULTRY—By testing these recipes we have discovered a few cooking tips which will help eliminate experimentation on your part.

With the microwave method, dark meat has the tendency to become drier than white. If you notice the legs getting done before the rest of the bird, help retain moisture by covering them with several layers of damp cheesecloth or plastic wrap.

When arranging chicken which has been cut into pieces in a baking dish, put the smaller, faster cooking parts, such as wings, to the center of the dish. This will insure more even cooking.

Browning—When recipes call for browning, remember to preheat the skillet (usually about 3 min.). For best results, cover the poultry-filled skillet. Of course, you may use plastic wrap.

Test for Doneness—Roast poultry is done when the internal temperature measured on the inside of the thigh reaches a point 15° to 20° less than specified for conventional cooking. The temperature will continue to rise to the appropriate temperature for doneness during the standing time.

If the specially-designed microwave thermometer is not available, the bird may be removed from the oven, covered with aluminum foil to retain heat and tested with a conventional thermometer. This will not interfere with the cooking process. If you must return the bird to the oven, be sure to remove both the thermometer and the foil before doing so.

Other than temperature, look for the juices from the inner thigh to be slightly pink, the leg to pull away easily from the body and for the meat to contain no pink.

The type of stuffing used will not affect the length of cooking time.

Standing Time is very much a part of microwave cooking. All these recipes must stand, covered, after removal from the oven. If sampled immediately, you will notice a rubbery texture and little flavor. However, both texture and flavor develop properly during the standing period. Minimum standing times are given for each recipe.

Sauces and Gravies—Remember to stir, stir and stir the sauce before, during and after cooking to capture the smooth texture and well-blended flavor which microwave cooking does so well.

Stuffings—The recipes included may involve very little cooking, but it is easier, quicker and cleaner to prepare them in the microwave oven.

REMINDERS—We have given you the guidelines for preparing these recipes; but remember, times may vary slightly depending upon your oven and, to some extent, your taste.

To learn more about how we have adapted these recipes and for additional tips, see the introductory chapter, **Home Cooking in the Microwave Oven**, in the beginning of this book. Consult the easy-to-read chart for comparative settings among different brands of ovens.

Roast Chicken *(page 196)* 1

Use a roasting pan with rack. The times given in this recipe are for roasting a 5-lb. chicken. For a chicken of a different size, allow about 5 min. per lb. before testing for doneness.

Prepare chicken for cooking as in Recipe.

Place chicken, breast side up, on rack. COOK, rotating pan and brushing chicken with pan drippings every 5 min., after 20 min. turn chicken breast side down (about 35 min.). Re-

move chicken from oven when juices run slightly pink; temperature tested on the inside of the thigh should register 180°. If not using a microwave thermometer, remove chicken from oven, cover with aluminum foil and insert conventional thermometer. If you must return chicken to oven, be sure to remove both foil and thermometer before doing so. Internal temperature will rise to 190° during the standing time.

Cover and let stand 20 min.

OVERALL ROASTING TIME: 35:00

Fried Chicken *(page 198)*

Use a browning skillet with cover.

Place fat or oil in skillet and COOK until heated (about 4 min.). Add half the chicken and COOK until brown on both sides (about 5 min. each side). Brown remaining chicken.

Add water, return all chicken to skillet. Cover and SLOWCOOK until chicken is tender and juices run clear (about 10 min.).

Cover and let stand 15 min.
OVERALL COOKING TIME: 34:00

Maryland-Fried Chicken *(page 198)*

Use a browning skillet.

Place oil or fat in skillet and COOK until heated (about 4 min.). Add half the chicken and COOK until crisp and browned on all sides (about 5 min. each side). Brown remaining chicken.

Cover and let stand 15 min.
OVERALL COOKING TIME: 24:00

Put fat in browning skillet and COOK until heated (about 4 min.). Add half the chicken and COOK until brown on both sides (about 5 min. each side). Brown remaining chicken.

Transfer all chicken to baking dish, cover with sauce and cover. COOK, basting chicken and rotating pan every 3 min., until chicken is tender and juices run clear (about 6 min.).

Cover and let stand 15 min.
OVERALL COOKING TIME: 40:00

Oriental Barbecued Chicken *(page 199)*

Use a baking dish.

Prepare chicken for cooking as in Recipe.

Cover and COOK, turning pan and basting with marinade every 5 min., until chicken is tender and juices run clear (about 15 min.).

Cover and let stand 15 min.
OVERALL COOKING TIME: 15:00

Oven "Barbecued" Chicken *(page 198)*

Use a browning skillet, a baking dish and a covered casserole.

Assemble sauce ingredients in casserole. COOK, stirring every 3 min., until simmering and flavors are blended (about 10 min.). Set aside.

Chicken Cacciatore *(page 200)*

Use a browning skillet and a covered casserole.

Preheat skillet (3 min.). Add oil and garlic and COOK to heat. Add chicken and COOK until

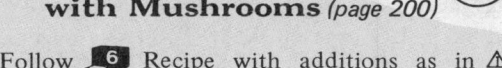

flour loses rawness on both sides (about 5 min. each side). (If flour browns to usual dark color, chicken will overcook in sauce.)

Transfer all chicken to casserole. Top with sauce and cover. COOK to heat through (about 5 min.). SLOWCOOK, rotating pan every 5 min., until chicken is tender (about 20 min.).

Cover and let stand 15 min.

OVERALL COOKING TIME: 49:00

Chicken Cacciatore with Mushrooms *(page 200)* 7

Follow 6 Recipe with additions as in ⚠ Recipe.

In small casserole, COOK butter until melted. Add onions and mushrooms and COOK until onion is transparent and mushrooms browned (about 3 min.).

Complete as in ⚠ Recipe.

OVERALL COOKING TIME: 52:00

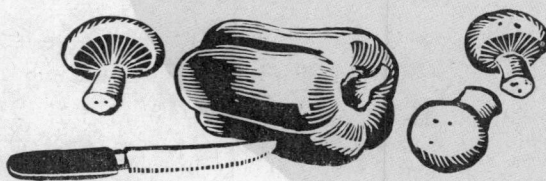

Chicken Cacciatore with Mushrooms and Peppers *(page 200)* 8

Follow 6 Recipe with changes as in ⚠ Recipe.

Chicken Vesuvio *(page 200)* 9

Use a browning skillet and a baking dish.

Put oil in skillet and COOK to heat (about 4 min.). Add half the chicken and COOK to

brown on both sides (about 5 min. each side). Brown remaining chicken.

Transfer all chicken to baking dish.

In skillet, COOK the 2 tablespoons oil and garlic until garlic is browned (about 2 min.). Add wine and parsley; pour over chicken.

Cover and SLOWCOOK, turning after 5 min., until chicken is tender (about 10 min.).

Cover and let stand 15 min.

OVERALL COOKING TIME: 36:00

Chicken Paprika with Spätzle *(page 201)* 10

Use a browning skillet and a small casserole.

Preheat skillet (3 min.). Add half the bacon and COOK until crisp (about 3 min.). COOK remaining bacon.

Add onion and COOK until transparent (about 2 min.). Remove bacon and onion and set aside.

Add half the seasoned chicken and COOK until brown on both sides (about 5 min. each side). Brown remaining chicken.

Return all chicken to skillet. Add giblets and broth, cover and SLOWCOOK, rotating pan every 3 min., until chicken is slightly tender (about 9 min.). Cover and set aside.

To complete the sauce, heat fat in small casserole and blend in flour. COOK, stirring every 1½ min., until bubbling (about 3 min.).

Add broth and stir thoroughly. COOK, stirring every 1 min., to bring to a boil (about 3 min.).

Add milk and paprika, stir thoroughly and COOK until heated (about 2 min.).

Stir in sour cream, bacon and onion and pour over chicken. COOK, stirring every 1 min., until hot (about 2 min.). Do not boil.

Serve as in Recipe.

Stewed Chicken *(page 205)* 11

Use a large covered casserole. Substitute a 4-lb. broiler for the stewing chicken, as the long, slow cooking necessary to tenderize the tougher fowl is not well-suited to microwave oven cooking.

Place chicken and all other ingredients in casserole, except use only enough water to cover chicken by two-thirds. Cover and COOK until boiling (about 10 min.).

SLOWCOOK, turning pan every 5 min. until tender (about 15 min.).

Cover and let stand 20 min.

OVERALL COOKING TIME: 25:00

Chicken and Dumplings 12
(page 205)

Follow 11 Recipe with changes as in ⚠ Recipe. Add dumplings when chicken is tender.

Cooked Giblets *(page 205)* 13

Use a covered casserole.

Place giblets and seasonings in casserole, except use only enough water to cover by two-thirds. SLOWCOOK until gizzard is tender (for chicken giblets, about 5 min.; for turkey giblets, about 11 min.).

Chicken Fricassee with 14 Biscuits and Cream Gravy *(page 206)*

Use a browning skillet, a covered casserole and a small casserole.

Preheat skillet (3 min.). Add butter and COOK until melted. Add half the chicken and COOK, turning every 5 min., until brown on both sides (about 10 min. each side). Brown remaining chicken.

Transfer all chicken to casserole; add vegetables, seasonings and only enough water to cover by two-thirds. Cover and COOK to heat through (about 5 min.). SLOWCOOK, turning pan every 5 min., until chicken is tender (about 20 min.).

For Gravy—In small casserole, COOK butter until melted. Add flour and pepper and COOK until mixture bubles (about 3 min.).

Add broth and cream and COOK, stirring every 30 sec., until gravy thickens (about 3 min.).

Cover and let stand 15 min.

Chicken-Stuffed 15 Eggplant *(page 207)*

Use a baking dish and a casserole.

Put eggplant in casserole, cover with less than 1 in. water and COOK until just tender about 10 min.).

In casserole, COOK butter until melted. Add onion and COOK until golden (about 3 min.).

Add eggplant-tomato-chicken mixture and COOK until tomatoes soften (about 5 min.).

Assemble shells as in Recipe. SLOWCOOK,

rotating pan every 3 min., until cheese is melted and filling is hot (about 9 min.).

Cover and let stand 10 min.

OVERALL COOKING TIME: 27:00

Chicken à la King 16
(page 208)

Use a covered casserole.

COOK butter until melted (about 3 min.). Add mushrooms and COOK, stirring every 2½ min., until lightly browned and tender (about 5 min.). Remove mushroom and set aside.

Add flour mixture. COOK, stirring every 1 min., until bubbly (about 3 min.).

Add broth and cream. COOK, stirring every 1 min., until mixture thickens (about 5 min.).

Add chicken and remaining ingredients. Cover and COOK to heat through (about 5 min.). SLOWCOOK, stirring every 3 min., until thoroughly heated and flavors blended (about 9 min.).

Cover and let stand 10 min.

Serve as in Recipe.

OVERALL COOKING TIME: 30:00

Chicken Livers Orientale 17
(page 209)

Use a browning skillet and a small casserole.

Preheat skillet (3 min.). Add livers and COOK, stirring every 2½ min., until slightly browned (about 5 min.). Set aside.

Combine sauce ingredients, add to casserole and COOK until boiling (about 5 min.). Stir and COOK until blended (about 2 min.).

Add pineapple chunks, almonds and sauce to liver. Cover and COOK, stirring every 2½ min., to heat through (about 5 min.).

Cover and let stand 10 min.

OVERALL COOKING TIME: 20:00

Curried Chicken with Almonds 18 *(page 209)*

Use a covered casserole.

COOK butter until melted. Add mushrooms, onion and celery and COOK, stirring every 1½ min., until onion is transparent (about 3 min.).

Add flour mixture and COOK, stirring every 1½ min., until mixture bubbles (about 3 min.).

Add broth and cream, stirring constantly. COOK, stirring every 30 sec., until boiling (about 5 min.). COOK, stirring every 1 min., to thicken (about 2 min.).

Add chicken, cover and COOK to heat through (about 3 min.).

Cover and let stand 10 min.

OVERALL COOKING TIME: 16:00

Chicken in White Wine Sauce 19 *(page 210)*

Use a covered casserole.

COOK butter until melted. Add mushrooms and COOK until lightly browned (about 3 min.). Remove mushrooms and set aside.

Add flour and COOK, stirring every 2 min., until mixture bubbles (about 5 min.).

Add liquid, stirring constantly. COOK, stirring every 1 min., until mixture thickens (about 4 min.).

Add wine, seasonings, chicken and vegetables. Cover and COOK to heat through (about 5 min.).

Cover and let stand 10 min.

OVERALL COOKING TIME: 17:00

Roast Half Turkey 20
(page 215)

Use a baking dish with rack. The times given in this recipe are for a 4-lb. half turkey. For a different-size quarter or half turkey SLOWCOOK about 10 min. per lb. before testing for doneness.

To Stuff—Prepare stuffing, fill cavity. Secure skin with wooden skewers. *Do not use metal.* Wrap stuffed half turkey in plastic wrap and tie with cord.

Place turkey on rack in baking dish, stuffing side down. COOK to heat (about 5 min.). SLOWCOOK, rotating pan every 10 min., until internal temperature reaches 175° and juices are slightly pink (about 55 min.). To test temperature with a conventional thermometer, remove turkey from oven, cover with aluminum foil and insert thermometer. If you must return the turkey to the oven, be sure to remove both foil and thermometer before doing so. The temperature will continue to rise during standing time and should reach 190°.

Cover and let stand 25 min.

OVERALL COOKING TIME: 60:00

Turkey-Rice Dinner 21
(page 215)

Use a 2-qt. casserole. *Do not grease.*

Assemble casserole as in Recipe. COOK, uncovered, until thoroughly heated (about 15 min.).

Cover and let stand 10 min.

Creamed Turkey and Oysters *(page 215)* 22

Use a 3-qt. casserole.

Assemble as in Recipe, except be sure to puncture the outer membrane of the oysters with a toothpick.

COOK to heat through (about 5 min.).

Cover and let stand 10 min.

Serve as in Recipe.

Rabbit Stew *(page 217)* 23

Use two covered casseroles, 1½-qt. and 2-qt. If frozen, defrost rabbit according to manufacturer's directions for your oven.

In small casserole, COOK water until boiling (about 5 min.). Add lima beans and COOK to soften (about 5 min.). Set aside to soak.

Put diced bacon and onion in larger casserole. COOK until onion is transparent (about 3 min.). Remove bacon and onion and set aside.

Add rabbit to casserole and COOK to brown on all sides, turning every 4 min. (about 8 min.).

Add water and seasonings, except use only ½ bay leaf. COOK to simmer and blend seasonings (about 30 min.).

Add carrots and beans. COOK to return to simmering (about 5 min.). SLOWCOOK, rotating pan every 15 min., until rabbit and vegetables are tender, adding green pepper about 5 min. before rabbit is fully cooked (about 45 min.).

Cover and let stand 15 min.

OVERALL COOKING TIME: 101:00

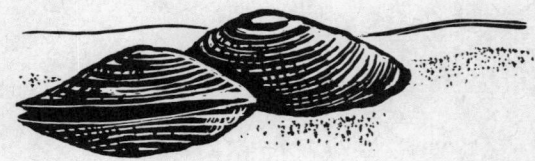

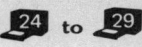

Apple Stuffing for 24
Spareribs *(page 218)*

Use a casserole.

COOK butter or margarine until melted. Add onion and COOK until transparent (about 3 min.).

Combine ingredients as in Recipe.

Oyster Stuffing *(page 218)* 25

Use a small casserole.

Be sure to puncture the outer membrane of each oyster with a toothpick. Cover and SLOW-COOK oysters until edges curl (about 5 min.).

Molly's Bread Stuffing 26
(page 219)

Use a casserole.

Put sausage and water in casserole. Cover and COOK until sausage is done (juices should run clear, (about 5 min.).

Add onion and COOK until onion is transparent and sausage lightly browned (about 3 min.).

Complete as in Recipe.

Giblet Stuffing 27
for Roast Turkey *(page 220)*

Use a casserole.

COOK butter or margarine until melted. Add onion and COOK until transparent (about 3 min.).

Complete as in Recipe.

Orange-Rice Stuffing 28
(page 221)

Use a 2-qt. casserole.

COOK butter or margarine until melted. Add onions and celery and COOK, stirring every 1½ min., until wilted (about 3 min.).

Add remaining ingredients, stir to blend and COOK to bring to a boil (about 5 min.).

Add rice, stir to blend. Cover and COOK until tender (about 8 min.).
OVERALL COOKING TIME: 16:00

Wild Rice Stuffing 29
(page 221)

Use a small casserole or skillet and a 3-qt. casserole.

Put the 1 tablespoon butter or margarine in the small casserole or skillet and COOK until melted. Add mushrooms and COOK, stirring after 30 sec., to brown lightly (about 1 min.). Set aside.

For the rice, use a 3-qt. casserole. Put the ½ cup butter or margarine in casserole and COOK until melted. Stir in rice and COOK, stirring every 1 min., until very lightly browned (about 5 min.).

Add onion and celery and COOK, stirring every 1 min., until wilted (about 3 min.).

Add broth, cover and COOK, stirring every 2 min., to bring to a boil (about 3 min.). SLOW-COOK until rice is tender (about 20 min.).

Complete as in Recipe.
OVERALL COOKING TIME: 27:00

POULTRY and Stuffings in the SLOW COOKER

What a pleasure to turn on a turkey, walk away and leave it without a thought. It needs no basting, the stuffing stays moist and the meat is flavorful and juicy when cooked in the slow cooker. The turkey also turns a pleasant brown color.

The piquant **Oriental Barbecued Chicken** is another dish which practically cooks by itself.

The recipes for roasting chicken, duck and Cornish game hens do not work as well. The birds never acquire an acceptable brown color; the duck is far too fatty. The fat can be skimmed periodically and all the birds can be browned under the conventional broiler before serving, but we have avoided such two-appliance recipes and tried to include only those which really demonstrate the slow cooker's turn-it-on-and-leave-it capacity.

The **Rabbit Stew** and **Stewed Chicken** both take advantage of this virtue very well and taste delicious. And, we were able to omit the browning step in these recipes.

Browning—Several dishes require browning before cooking in a sauce. Most of them have a stew-like flavor and texture if not sautéed on top of the stove. Therefore, with the exception of **Oven Barbecued Chicken,** they are omitted. This recipe can be browned in the slow cooker. Simply omit the flour from the coating mixture, heat the fat on HIGH in the slow cooker, and turn the chicken in the fat to coat it evenly.

REMINDERS—In recipes which call for vegetables, remember they can sometimes take longer to cook than meat. Be sure all vegetables are covered with liquid, layering them under the meat if necessary.

The introductory chapter, **Home Cooking in the Slow Cooker**, in the beginning of this book provides additional tips on using the slow cooker and an easy-to-read chart comparing settings among different brands of slow cookers. We suggest you review this section to also learn how we have adapted these recipes.

Oven "Barbecued" **1** Chicken *(page 198)*

Use a 3½-qt. slow cooker.

Omit flour from coating mixture.

Put fat in slow cooker and melt on HIGH. Add chicken and turn to coat evenly with fat.

Add remaining ingredients, except use only ½ cup water (instead of 1 cup).

Cover and cook on LOW for 6 to 7 hrs.

For chicken giblets, cover and cook on LOW for 6 to 7 hrs.

For turkey giblets, cover and cook on LOW for 7 to 8 hrs.

Oriental Barbecued **2** Chicken *(page 199)*

Use a 3½-qt. slow cooker.

Prepare chicken for cooking as in Recipe.

Put chicken in slow cooker and cover with marinade by two-thirds.

Cover and cook on LOW for 6 to 7 hrs.

Serve as in Recipe.

Roast Half Turkey **5** *(page 215)*

Use a 5-qt. slow cooker with rack.

Cover rack with foil and puncture foil.

Arrange stuffing on foil, lay half turkey over stuffing.

Cover and cook on LOW for 9 to 10 hrs.

Stewed Chicken *(page 205)* **3**

Use a 5-qt. slow cooker.

Omit browning.

Put chicken, vegetables and seasonings in slow cooker and add water to cover by two-thirds.

Cover and cook on LOW for 8 to 9 hrs.

Rabbit Stew *(page 217)* **6**

Use a 3½-qt. slow cooker.

Omit boiling and soaking beans.

Omit browning.

Put all ingredients, except green pepper, in slow cooker.

Cover and cook on LOW for 9 to 10 hrs.

Add green pepper about ½ hr. before stew is done.

Cooked Giblets *(page 205)* **4**

Use a 3½-qt. slow cooker.

Put giblets in slow cooker and add seasonings and water to cover contents by two-thirds.

FISH and SHELLFISH

Fish

AVAILABILITY—**Fresh fish** are best prepared as soon as possible after being caught. When fresh, they have red gills, bright eyes, and bright-colored scales adhering tightly. The flesh is firm and elastic, and practically free from odor. Fresh fish should be packed in ice until purchased; at home, wrap in aluminum foil or moisture-vapor-proof material and store in the refrigerator.

Frozen fish is available the year around in market forms such as steaks, fillets and sticks. It should be solidly frozen and *never refrozen after thawing*; packages should be in perfect condition.

Smoked fish is a delicacy; salmon, whitefish and haddock (finnan haddie) are popular varieties.

Canned fish is easy to store (in a cool, dry place) and convenient to serve. Sardines, tuna, cod, salmon, mackerel and kippered herring are some of the varieties. Fish cakes and balls are also canned.

MARKET FORMS—**Whole or round fish** are just as they come from the water; before cooking they must be scaled and the entrails removed; the head, tail and fins may be removed if desired.

Drawn fish have only the entrails removed; before cooking they must be scaled; the head, tail and fins may be removed if desired.

Dressed fish have been scaled and the entrails, head, tail and fins removed; ready-to-cook.

Fish steaks are cross sections of larger dressed fish; ready-to-cook as purchased.

Fish fillets are the sides of a dressed fish, cut lengthwise away from the backbone; practically boneless.

Fish sticks are uniform pieces of fish dipped in batter, breaded and frozen; they resemble French fried potatoes in appearance and can be purchased uncooked or precooked. Precooked sticks are deep-fried before freezing and need only to be heated.

PURCHASING GUIDE—For *whole or round fish* allow 1 lb. per serving. *Dressed fish* or *fish steaks* allow ½ lb. per serving. Allow ⅓ lb. per serving of *fish fillets* or *frozen fish sticks*.

Shellfish

MARKET FORMS—**Live shellfish** are those which should be alive when purchased, such as crabs, lobsters, clams and oysters (except when purchasing cooked lobsters and crabs in the shell).

Shucked shellfish have been removed from their shells; oysters, clams and scallops come this way.

Headless shellfish are shrimp and rock-lobster tail (spiny lobster) which are marketed in this form.

Cooked meat is the edible portion of the shellfish, cooked and ready to eat; shrimp, crab and lobster meat are marketed this way.

Frozen shellfish now available are shrimp, crab, lobster, rock-lobster tails, scallops and oysters.

OYSTERS—*Oysters in the shell* must have tightly closed shells; this indicates that they are alive and usable. Oysters in the shell, kept in the refrigerator at 40°F, will remain good for several days. They are generally sold by the dozen. *Fresh or frozen shucked oysters* are sold by the pint or quart. They should be plump, with a natural creamy color, free from shell particles and with clear liquid. Fresh shucked oysters packed in cans and labeled "Perishable, Keep Refrigerated" must be refrigerated in the home. Frozen oysters should not be thawed until ready to use and never refrozen.

CLAMS—The market species of the Atlantic coast are the *hard-shelled*, *soft-shelled* and *surf clams*. *Quahog* is the common name for the hard-shelled clam in New England, where "clam" generally refers to the soft-shelled variety. In Middle Atlantic states and southward, "clam" usually means the hard-shelled clam. Dealers' names for smaller sizes of hard-shelled clams are *little necks* and *cherry-stones;* these are served raw on the half shell. The larger sizes, used for soups and chowders, are *chowders. Steamers* are the smaller sizes of soft-shelled clams and *in-shells,* the larger sizes. Common species of the Pacific coast are *pismo, razor, little neck* (different from Atlantic coast hard-shelled clam) and *butter.*

Clams in the shell should be alive when purchased. Hard-shelled clams having gaping shells that do not close when handled are not alive and not usable. There will be some contraction of the siphon or neck of other varieties when the live clam is touched. Shell clams kept in the refrigerator at 40°F will remain alive several days. *Fresh shucked clams,* sold by the pint or quart, should be plump, with clear liquid, and free from shell particles. They are packed in metal or waxed containers and should be refrigerated or packed in ice; they will stay fresh for a week or 10 days if properly handled. *Frozen shucked clams* should not be thawed until ready to use and never refrozen. Clams are canned whole or minced, or as chowder. Clam juice, broth and nectar are also canned.

SCALLOPS—The edible portion is the muscle that opens and closes the scallop shells. There are two kinds, the tiny *bay scallop* and the larger *sea scallop.* Fresh scallops and thawed frozen scallops, should have a sweetish odor.

SHRIMP—*Fresh shrimp* with heads removed are sold by the pound either fresh or frozen. Shrimp are graded according to the number per pound— jumbo (under 25); large (25 to 30); medium (30 to 42); or small (42 and over). *Cooked shrimp* with shells removed are sold by the pound; the meat is pink. *Canned shrimp* are available in several sizes of cans and may be used in place of cooked shrimp.

LOBSTER—Lobster may be purchased *live in the shell, cooked in the shell,* as *lobster meat* or *canned.* Live lobsters are dark bluish-green to brownish-olive in color; they must be alive up to the moment of cooking. The weight may vary from ¾ to 3 lbs. Lobsters cooked in the shell are red in color; they are not generally available in large quantities.

Lobster meat is picked from cooked lobsters and chilled. It is sold by the pound, fresh or frozen. **How to Kill and Clean a Lobster**—Live lobsters may be killed by plunging into boiling water (*page 238*). Or lobsters may be killed by the following method. Place lobster on a cutting board with back or smooth shell up. Hold a towel firmly over head and claws. Quickly insert the point of a sharp heavy knife into center of the small cross on the back of the head. This kills the lobster by severing the spinal cord. Before removing knife, bear down heavily, cutting through entire length of body and tail. Pull halves apart; remove and discard the stomach (a small sac which lies in the head) and the spongy lungs (which lie in upper body cavity between meat and shell). Remove and discard the dark intestinal vein running through center of body. Crack claws with nutcracker.

Lobster may be cooked as directed in **Lobster Thermidor** (*page 240*). Or broil lobster shell side down about 10 min. on preheated broiler pan with top of lobster 3 to 4 in. from source of heat. Brush frequently with melted butter.

ROCK-LOBSTER TAIL—The trade name for crayfish or spiny lobster tail; the meaty tail is the only portion marketed. Usually sold frozen, the meat should be a clear whitish color. Shell color depends on the kind. *Canned rock-lobster meat* is available.

CRABS—Crabs may be purchased *live, cooked in the shell,* as *crab meat* or *canned.* Live crabs are either hard-shelled or soft-shelled. Soft-shelled crabs are blue crabs that have been caught immediately after having shed their old, hard shells. Hard-shelled crabs are sold cooked in the shell. Crab meat comes from cooked crabs and is sold by the pound. It is very perishable and should be refrigerated or packed in ice. Cooked crab meat may be one of the following: *Blue Crab*—Lump meat comes from the large muscles which operate the swimming legs; it is white in color and is sometimes called "special" or "back fin" lump crab meat. Flake meat is the remaining portion of the body meat; it is also white. Claw meat is brownish meat removed from the claws. *Rock Crab*—Meat is brownish in color; there is only one grade. *Dungeness Crab*—Claw and body meat is reddish in color. *King Crab*—Meat from the King Crab of Alaska is removed mostly from the legs, frozen and packed. Entire leg sections, cooked and frozen, are also marketed.

▲ Baked Stuffed Fish

Line a large shallow baking pan with aluminum foil or parchment paper.

For Stuffing—Crush (*page 12*)

½ lb. crackers (or enough to yield 3 cups crumbs)

Turn crumbs into a bowl; set aside.

Heat in a skillet over low heat

⅔ cup butter or margarine

Add, and cook slowly until onion is transparent, occasionally moving with a spoon

¾ cup chopped celery (*page 12*)
¼ cup finely chopped onion

Add to crumbs with a mixture of

2 tablespoons lemon juice
2 teaspoons minced parsley
¼ teaspoon rosemary
½ teaspoon salt
½ teaspoon Accent
¼ teaspoon pepper

Toss lightly with a fork to mix thoroughly. Add

¼ cup hot water

Mix thoroughly and set aside.

For Fish—Rinse body cavity thoroughly with cold water, drain, and pat dry with absorbent paper

4- to 5-lb. dressed fish (such as whitefish, lake trout, shad or bass, with backbone removed)

Rub cavity of fish with

1 tablespoon salt
¾ teaspoon Accent

Lightly pile (do not pack) stuffing into fish. Fasten open edges with skewers or close with wooden picks. Put stuffed fish in baking pan and brush outside surface with

Cooking or salad oil

Bake at 350°F 45 to 50 min., or until fish flakes easily (*page 12*).   *8 servings*

△ Planked Fish Supreme

Follow ▲ Recipe for preparing and baking fish. Set out a seasoned plank. (To season a new plank, see Dinner on a Plank, *page 130*.)

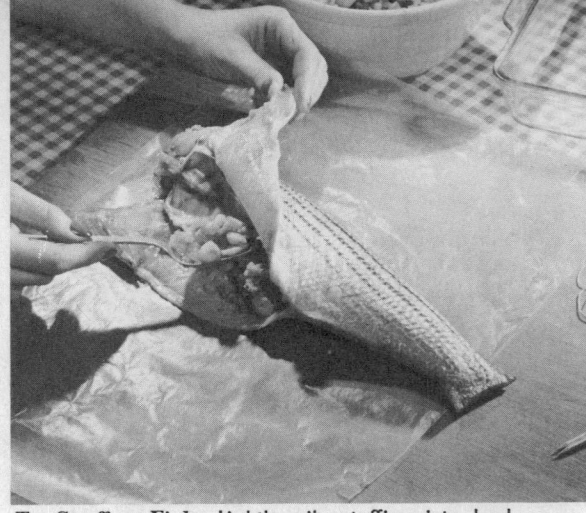

To Stuff a Fish: Lightly pile stuffing into body cavity. Close cavity with skewers or wooden picks.

While fish is baking, prepare **Duchess Potatoes** (*page 299*); do not spoon potatoes onto baking sheet.

Lightly grease the seasoned plank with unsalted fat. Put into oven to heat. When fish is cooked, transfer to the heated plank. Force potatoes through a pastry bag and No. 7 decorating tube into a spiral-shaped border on the plank. Cover exposed plank as completely as possible. Brush potatoes lightly with melted **butter** or **margarine**. Put planked fish and potatoes into a 400°F oven 10 min., or until potatoes are lightly browned.

Arrange on the plank buttered **Brussels sprouts** and **lemon wedges.** Accompany with **Quick Tomato Sauce** (*page 327*).

Planked Fish: Place baked fish on a heated, greased plank. Arrange vegetables. Set in oven.

▲ Baked Fish Steaks 2

Set out a bake-and-serve platter or shallow baking dish.

Wash, coarsely chop and mix (enough to line platter or baking dish) equal quantities of

Parsley
Celery leaves
Onion (*page 12*)

Wipe with a clean, damp cloth

**2 lbs. fish steaks (cod, haddock,
halibut or salmon), 1 in. thick**

(If using frozen steaks, thaw according to directions on package.) Sprinkle both sides of fish steaks with a mixture of

1½ teaspoons curry powder
½ teaspoon salt
½ teaspoon Accent
⅛ teaspoon pepper

Arrange on parsley mixture. Place on steaks

Bacon slices (allow 1 slice per steak)

Bake uncovered at 350°F 25 to 30 min., or until fish flakes easily (*page 12*).

Serve with **Maître d'Hôtel Butter** (*page 331*), or **Lemon Butter Sauce** (*page 331*).

4 servings

△ Baked Fish Fillets 3

Follow ▲ Recipe. Substitute **fish fillets** (such as cod, perch, trout or flounder) for the fish steaks. Substitute **tarragon** for curry powder.

Pompano en Papillote 4

Set out a shallow baking dish and four 12x9-in. pieces of parchment paper.

To Prepare Filling—Set out

½ cup coarsely chopped cooked shrimp
**½ cup coarsely chopped cooked lobster
meat**

Prepare

1 cup Thick White Sauce (page 323 **;
use cream for liquid)**

Stir into the cooked sauce

¼ cup white wine

Mix in the chopped shrimp and lobster meat. Cool mixture and chill in refrigerator.

To Make Papillotes—Fold the pieces of parchment paper into halves crosswise. From other paper make a pattern of a half heart that is as wide and long as the folded parchment paper. Place straight edge of pattern on folded edge of parchment paper, trace and cut out heart shapes. Set papillotes aside.

To Fill Papillotes—Wipe with a clean, damp cloth

4 pompano fillets, about 6 oz. each

Cut each fillet into halves crosswise, keeping halves of the same fillet together. (If frozen, thaw fillets completely.)

Brush inside of each paper heart with **cooking** or **salad oil** (not olive oil). On one half of each paper heart lay a fillet half, skin side down. Sprinkle the four halves with one half of a mixture of

1 teaspoon salt
¾ teaspoon Accent
⅛ teaspoon pepper

Remove filling from refrigerator and divide into fourths. Place one fourth on each fillet half; spread with back of spoon over fish. Place matching fillet half over filling, skin side up. Sprinkle fillets with remaining seasonings. Fold top half of paper heart over fillet. (Top half will not meet edge of bottom half.)

To Seal Papillotes and Complete—Starting at top end of paper heart, fold small portion of bottom edge over top and crease; hold folded portion down with one hand while folding and creasing next portion, overlapping it on folded portion. Repeat, following outline of heart, folding and creasing. At end, twist paper. Repeat with remaining papillotes. Place papillotes in the baking dish.

Bake at 375°F about 30 min., or until papers are puffed and golden brown.

Serve papillotes on warm plates. Cut a cross in top of paper with scissors just before serving.

4 servings

Creole Fish

Combine in a saucepan

2 cups (No. 2 can) sieved cooked tomatoes
¼ cup pitted and chopped green olives
2 tablespoons capers
1 tablespoon chopped parsley
1 teaspoon salt
¾ teaspoon Accent
½ teaspoon pepper
½ teaspoon oregano

Bring to boiling and pour over cod in casserole.

Bake at 350°F 25 to 30 min., or until the fish flakes easily (*page 12*).   *4 servings*

△ Halibut alla Marinara

Follow ▲ Recipe. Substitute **halibut steaks** for the cod.

Fillets of Sole in White Wine

Grease a 2-qt. shallow casserole having a cover.

Wipe with a clean, damp cloth and place in casserole
2 lbs. fillets of sole
Pour over fillets a mixture of
½ cup dry white wine
½ cup (1 medium-size) chopped onion (*page 12*)
3 tablespoons melted butter or margarine
2 bay leaves, crushed
1 teaspoon chopped parsley
½ teaspoon salt
½ teaspoon Accent
¼ teaspoon pepper

Cover casserole and bake at 375°F for 25 min., or until the fish flakes easily (*page 12*).

6 servings

Creole Fish

Set out a large, shallow baking dish.

Heat in a saucepan over low heat
2 tablespoons butter or margarine
Add and cook over medium heat until onion is transparent, stirring occasionally
¼ cup finely chopped onion
¼ cup finely chopped green pepper (*page 12*)
1 small clove garlic (*page 12*), minced; or crushed in a garlic press
Blend in
1¼ cups (10½ to 11-oz. can) condensed tomato soup
1 tablespoon lemon juice or vinegar
and a mixture of
½ teaspoon paprika
¼ teaspoon salt
⅛ teaspoon pepper
⅛ teaspoon oregano
⅛ teaspoon rosemary

▲ Cod alla Marinara

Codfish as it is prepared in Italy.

Grease a 1½-qt. casserole.

Wipe with a clean, damp cloth
2 lbs. cod steaks, about 1 in. thick
Place cod in casserole and set aside.

Cover and simmer gently 15 to 20 min.

Meanwhile, wipe with a clean, damp cloth
1½ lbs. fillets of flounder or whitefish
Cut fillets to yield 6 long pieces. Sprinkle the
pieces with a mixture of
1 teaspoon salt
½ teaspoon Accent
¼ teaspoon pepper
Roll fish, fasten with wooden picks, and put in
baking dish. Pour over them 1 cup of sauce.

Bake uncovered at 375°F about 45 min.

Arrange fillets on platter. Spoon some of the
sauce over them. Serve remaining sauce in
gravy boat.   *4 servings*

Fish Dinner

Fish Dinner

Grease a 2-qt. casserole and set out a small
saucepan.

Blanch (*page 11*), toast (*page 12*) and set aside
½ cup (about 3 oz.) almonds
Grate and set aside
**4 oz. sharp Cheddar cheese (about
1 cup, grated)**
Drain (reserving liquid in a 2-cup measuring
cup) contents of
**1 3-oz. jar (about ½ cup, drained)
pimiento-stuffed olives**
Cut each olive crosswise into about 4 slices.
Set olives and reserved liquid aside.

Clean (*page 12*) and finely chop
1 medium-size onion
Set aside.

Wipe with a clean, damp cloth, remove any
small bones and cut into 1-in. pieces
**2 lbs. fish fillets (such as ocean
perch, haddock or flounder)**
Place one half of the fish in an even layer in
casserole; set remaining fish aside.

Heat in the saucepan over low heat
¼ cup butter or margarine
Add the onion and cook until transparent,
stirring occasionally. Blend in a mixture of
¼ cup flour
½ teaspoon salt
½ to ¾ teaspoon Accent
Few grains pepper
Heat until mixture bubbles. Remove from
heat. Add to olive liquid
**1¼ cups milk (or enough to make
1½ cups liquid)**
Add liquid gradually to the flour mixture,
stirring constantly. Bring to boiling, stirring
constantly; cook 1 to 2 min. longer. Remove
from heat and set aside.

Wash, pare, slice thinly and set aside
**3 to 4 medium-size (about 1½ lbs.)
potatoes**
Sprinkle about one half of the grated cheese
evenly over fish in casserole. Add the toasted
almonds to make a layer. Cover with a layer
of the remaining fish, and then a layer of the
remaining cheese. Top with a layer of the
sliced olives. Pour over about two-thirds of
the sauce. Cover with overlapping layers of the
potato slices and the remaining sauce.

Bake at 375°F about 1 hr., or until potatoes
are tender.   *About 8 servings*

▲ Creamed Finnan Haddie and Cracker Tips en Casserole

Grease 6 individual casseroles or one 2-qt. casserole or baking dish.

In the top of a double boiler or in a covered saucepan, soak for 1 hour

2 lbs. finnan haddie (smoked haddock)
in

Milk to cover

Heat slowly 20 min. Drain, reserving milk for sauce. Set aside.

Prepare, coarsely chop and set aside

2 Hard-Cooked Eggs (page 87)

Melt in top of double boiler over low heat

3 tablespoons butter or margarine

Blend in

3 tablespoons flour

Heat until mixture bubbles. Remove from heat and add gradually, stirring constantly, the milk "stock" from the fish. (If "stock" measures less than 1½ cups liquid, add enough cream to make this amount.) Return to heat. Cook rapidly, stirring constantly, until sauce thickens. Remove from heat and vigorously stir about 3 tablespoons of the sauce into

2 egg yolks, slightly beaten

Immediately return mixture to double boiler.

Cook over simmering water 3 to 5 min. Stir slowly and constantly to keep mixture cooking evenly. Remove from simmering water; cool slightly.

Remove skin and bones from fish. Flake (*page 12*) fish and combine with the sauce. Gently stir in the chopped eggs and

3 tablespoons capers

Pour mixture into the casserole. Insert into mixture on a diagonal

10 to 12 crisp thin crackers, lightly buttered (leave about one half of each cracker exposed)

Bake at 375°F 10 to 12 min. to heat mixture thoroughly and to lightly brown the crackers.

Garnish with **parsley**. Serve at once.

6 servings

Creamed Codfish and Cracker Tips

△ Creamed Codfish and Cracker Tips

Follow ▲ Recipe; substitute **codfish** for finnan haddie. If cod is salted, cover with **water** and heat slowly to boiling. (If dry and/or very salty, drain and again cover with water and bring to boiling.) Drain, cover with **milk** and proceed as in ▲ Recipe.

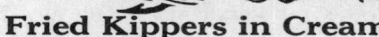

Fried Kippers in Cream

Set out a large, heavy skillet.

Cover with cold water and bring to boiling

4 kippered herring

Drain, dry with absorbent paper and set aside.

Heat in the skillet

3 to 4 tablespoons butter or margarine

Add and cook until transparent, turning occasionally

3 medium-size onions (page 12), cut into ¼-in. slices and separated into rings

Remove onions and keep warm.

Place herring in skillet. Brown over low heat about 5 min. on each side.

Meanwhile, scald (*page 13*)

1¼ cups cream

Slowly pour one half of the cream into skillet with herring and simmer 2 min. Add remaining cream and simmer 3 min. longer.

Serve at once. Garnish with the onion rings.

4 servings

▲ Broiled Fish Steaks

Set temperature control of range at Broil and grease a broiler rack.

Wipe with a clean, damp cloth
**2 lbs. fish steaks, such as cod,
halibut or salmon**
(If using frozen steaks, thaw according to directions on package.) If desired, bring ends of each steak together and fasten with a small skewer to give oval shape. Arrange steaks on the greased broiler rack. Brush tops of steaks with one half of a mixture of
¼ cup butter or margarine, melted
1 tablespoon chopped parsley or chives
Place broiler rack in broiler with top of steaks 2 in. from source of heat; broil 5 to 8 min. (depending upon thickness of steaks). Season steaks with one half of a mixture of

1 teaspoon salt
¾ teaspoon Accent
⅛ teaspoon pepper
Turn steaks carefully and brush second side with remaining butter mixture. Broil 5 to 8 min. longer, or until fish flakes easily (*page 12*).

Sprinkle second side with remaining seasoning

Broiled Fish Fillets

mixture. Remove carefully to warm serving platter. Serve with **lemon wedges** or **Hollandaise Sauce (page 324)**

4 servings

△ Broiled Fish Fillets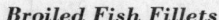

Follow ▲ Recipe. Substitute **fish fillets** for the steaks. Place them skin side down on the greased rack. Broil 10 to 12 min. without turning. Brush fillets with melted **butter** or **margarine** during broiling.

Note: To prepare fish on an outdoor grill see OUTDOOR COOKING (*page 204*).

Broiled Trout

Set temperature control of range at Broil and grease a broiler rack.

Wipe with a clean, damp cloth
**4 small cleaned and scaled trout,
about 10 oz. each**
(If using frozen trout, thaw according to directions on package.) Do not cut off tails or heads; game fish are usually served with the head and tail on. Arrange trout on the greased broiler rack. Brush with one half of a mixture of
¼ cup butter or margarine, melted
1 tablespoon lemon juice
Place broiler rack in broiler with top of trout 2 in. from source of heat; broil 5 to 8 min. (depending upon thickness of trout).

Season trout with one half of a mixture of
2 teaspoons salt
1 teaspoon Accent
½ teaspoon paprika
¼ teaspoon pepper
Turn trout carefully and brush second side with remaining butter mixture. Sprinkle second side with remaining seasoning mixture. Broil 5 to 8 min. longer, or until fish flakes easily (*page 12*).

Remove carefully to a warm serving platter. Garnish with **parsley.** Serve trout with **lemon wedges.** *4 servings*

Perch Kabobs

Perch Kabobs

Set out eight 5-in. skewers and a baking sheet.

While still frozen, cut into 1½-in. chunks
2 lbs. frozen ocean perch fillets
Put into a large bowl and set aside.

Combine in a screw-top jar
¼ cup salad oil
¼ cup lemon juice
2 tablespoons ketchup
1 teaspoon sugar
1 teaspoon Worcestershire sauce
¾ teaspoon Accent
½ teaspoon salt
¼ teaspoon paprika
¼ teaspoon dry mustard
2 drops tabasco sauce
Cover jar and shake until well blended.

Pour marinade (liquid mixture) over fish chunks. Let stand 1½ hrs. at room temperature, turning chunks occasionally with fork.

Drain off marinade and reserve it for basting.

Cut crosswise into fourths
4 slices bacon
Cut crosswise into eighths
2 large whole dill pickles

To Prepare Kabobs—Thread onto each skewer a fish chunk, a piece of bacon, and a piece of pickle.

Repeat threading, ending with a third fish chunk. Place kabobs on baking sheet.

Set temperature control of range at Broil.

Place baking sheet under the broiler with tops of kabobs 2 in. from heat source. Turning frequently and brushing several times with reserved marinade, broil kabobs 12 to 15 min., or until fish flakes easily (*page 12*).

Arrange kabobs on serving platter; garnish with **parsley-dipped lemon wedges** and serve immediately. *4 to 6 servings*

▲ Panfried Fish Fillets 15

Set out a large, heavy skillet.

Wipe with a clean, damp cloth
   **2 lbs. fish fillets, such as perch,
      sole or haddock**
(If fish is frozen, thaw according to directions on package.) Cut into serving-size pieces and set aside.

Mix in a shallow pan and set aside
   **2 cups (about 6 slices) fine, dry
      bread crumbs**
   1 teaspoon salt
   ½ teaspoon Accent
   ¼ teaspoon pepper
Beat slightly in a shallow bowl
   2 eggs
   1 tablespoon milk
Heat in the skillet over low heat
   **¼ cup butter, margarine or bacon
      drippings**
Dip fillets into egg mixture; then coat with crumb mixture. Put into the skillet and brown lightly on both sides, turning only once. Cook only until fish flakes easily (*page 12*). Transfer fish to warm serving platter, scraping loose and removing any bits of fish which may have stuck to the skillet. Cover fish to keep warm.

Heat in the skillet until lightly browned
   ½ cup butter or margarine
Stir in
   ¼ cup lemon juice
   2 tablespoons finely chopped parsley
Heat thoroughly and pour over fish.

5 to 6 servings

△ Panfried Whole Fish 16

Substitute dressed small **whole fish,** such as lake perch, blue gills, sunfish or crappies, for the fish fillets. Proceed as in ▲ Recipe.

Codfish Cakes

A deep saucepan or automatic deep-fryer will be needed.

Set out
   1 lb. salt codfish
Cover with cold water to freshen. Let stand in the cold water at least 4 hrs. Change water 3 or 4 times during that period. (Or follow directions on package.) Drain fish and remove any pieces of bone. Flake (*page 12*) and set fish aside.

About 20 min. before ready to deep-fry, heat fat to 365°F (*page 13*).

Meanwhile, wash, pare and cut into pieces
   **4 to 6 medium-size (about 2 lbs.)
      potatoes**
Combine fish and potatoes in a saucepan. Cook covered in boiling water to cover about 20 min., or until potatoes are tender when pierced with a fork.

Thoroughly drain and mash potatoes and fish. Whip in until mixture is fluffy
   2 tablespoons butter or margarine
and a mixture of
   2 eggs, beaten
   ½ teaspoon paprika
   ¼ teaspoon Accent
   ⅛ teaspoon pepper
Deep-fry by dropping spoonfuls of the mixture into the hot fat. Drop only as many at one time as will float uncrowded one layer deep. Turn cakes as they brown, cooking each 2 to 5 min., or until golden brown. Drain on absorbent paper.

Serve with
   **Tomato Sauce (page 326) or
      Medium White Sauce (page 323)**

6 servings

Poached Fish Veronique: Cut paper to fit. Roll fish fillets and fasten with wooden picks.

Fit greased paper cover over pan. Simmer fish. Hole in paper allows steam to escape.

▲ Poached Fish with Horse-radish Sauce

Set out a large, heavy skillet having a tight-fitting cover.

Wipe with a clean, damp cloth
1½ lbs. fish fillets, such as perch or bass

(If fish is frozen, thaw according to directions on package.) Tie fish loosely in cheesecloth to prevent breaking; place in the skillet. Add, in order

Boiling water (enough to just cover fish)
½ cup dry white wine
1 small onion (*page 12*), chopped
2 tablespoons chopped parsley
1 teaspoon salt
½ teaspoon Accent
⅛ teaspoon pepper

Cover skillet and simmer about 10 min., or until fish flakes easily (*page 12*).

Meanwhile, prepare
Horse-radish Sour Cream Sauce (*page 330*)

Pour sauce into serving dish; set aside.

Drain fish, reserving stock; remove cheesecloth. (Strain stock and use in other food preparation.) Place fish on warm platter. Serve with the sauce. *4 servings*

△ Poached Fish with Butter Sauce

Follow ▲ Recipe; omit Horse-radish Sour Cream Sauce. Pour strained stock into saucepan. Simmer until liquid is reduced to 1 cup. Thicken with 1 tablespoon **Brown Roux** (*page 325*) or 1 **egg yolk**. Add 1 tablespoon **butter**, stirring until well blended. Heat thoroughly. Pour over fish, or serve in a separate dish.

Poached Fish Veronique

Set out a large, heavy skillet having a tight-fitting cover. Cut a circle of white paper to fit skillet; cut a small hole in center to allow steam to escape. Butter one side of the paper.

Wipe with a clean, damp cloth
1½ lbs. fish fillets (such as perch, bass, haddock or sole)

(If frozen, thaw according to directions on package.) Roll fillets; fasten with wooden picks.

Season with a mixture of
1 teaspoon salt
1 teaspoon Accent
¼ teaspoon pepper
Set fillets aside.

Heat in the skillet over low heat
2 tablespoons butter or margarine

Add and cook over medium heat until onion is transparent, stirring constantly

1 tablespoon minced onion

Place the fish in the skillet. Add

½ cup dry white wine

Place paper circle, buttered-side down, on top of the fillets. Bring liquid to boiling; cover and simmer about 10 min., or until fish flakes easily (*page 12*). Carefully remove fish to serving platter. Pour off and reserve the cooking liquid.

Melt in the skillet over low heat

1 tablespoon butter

Blend in

2 teaspoons flour

Heat until mixture bubbles. Remove from heat. Add gradually, stirring constantly, the reserved cooking liquid and

¼ cup cream

Return to heat and cook, stirring constantly, until mixture thickens; cook 1 to 2 min. longer.

Spoon sauce over fish. Garnish with **lemon wedges** and seedless **white grapes**. (If desired, the grapes may be added to the sauce.)

Serve at once.   *4 servings*

Sweet-Sour Salmon Steaks

MRS. C. S. LOBEL, INDIO, CALIF.

Put into a Dutch oven or a deep kettle or sauce pot having a tight-fitting cover

1½ cups water
1 medium-size onion (*page 12*), sliced
1 carrot, sliced
1 lemon, thinly sliced
1 teaspoon Accent
½ teaspoon salt
3 or 4 peppercorns

Bring liquid to boiling.

Meanwhile, wipe with a clean, damp cloth

4 salmon steaks, about ½ lb. each

(If using frozen salmon, thaw according to directions on package.) Arrange the steaks on a large square of cheesecloth. Pull up corners of cheesecloth and tie together. Lower salmon into the kettle. Cover and simmer 10 min.

Melt in a small saucepan over low heat

2 tablespoons butter or margarine

Add, blending in

1 cup firmly packed brown sugar

Continue cooking, stirring frequently until sugar is melted.

Meanwhile, combine

14 gingersnaps, crushed (about 1 cup crumbs)
1 cup vinegar

Remove from heat. Gradually add vinegar mixture, stirring until smooth. Set aside.

Remove kettle from heat. Remove salmon from liquid; carefully remove cloth. Strain the cooking liquid and return it to kettle. Add

¼ cup dark, seedless raisins

Blend in the vinegar mixture. Return to heat and bring liquid to boiling, stirring constantly. Carefully lower salmon steaks into the liquid. (Arrange steaks only one layer deep, if possible.) Cover tightly and simmer gently 5 min., or until salmon flakes easily (*page 12*). Remove kettle from heat; cool salmon in the liquid. Serve warm, or chill in refrigerator. (For a more pronounced sweet-sour flavor, chill overnight.) When ready to serve, carefully remove steaks to serving dish. If desired, accompany with some of the cooking liquid.

4 servings

Sweet-Sour Salmon Steaks

▲ Hot Salmon Loaf

Heat water for boiling water bath (*page 12*). Grease bottom of a 9½x5¼x2¾-in. loaf pan.

Using the fine blade of food chopper, grind enough toasted almonds to yield
1¼ cups (about 7 oz.) ground toasted almonds (page 12)
Finely flake (*page 12*)
2 cups (1-lb. can) salmon
Set almonds and fish aside.

Prepare
1½ cups Medium White Sauce (one and one-half times recipe, page 323)
Vigorously stir about 3 tablespoons of hot sauce into
3 egg yolks, slightly beaten
Immediately return egg-yolk mixture to sauce, stirring vigorously.

Stir into the sauce the salmon, almonds and
1½ cups (1½ slices) soft bread crumbs
¼ cup finely chopped onion
4 drops tabasco sauce
and a mixture of
2 teaspoons salt
½ teaspoon Accent
½ teaspoon pepper
½ teaspoon paprika
Beat until rounded peaks are formed
3 egg whites
Spread beaten egg whites over salmon and fold (*page 12*) together. Turn mixture into pan.

Bake in boiling water bath at 350°F about 1 hr. and 10 min.

Unmold (*page 107*). Garnish with **parsley** and **lemon slices** and serve at once.

About 6 servings

Salmon Loaf with Creamed Peas

△ Salmon Loaf with Creamed Peas

Follow ▲ Recipe for preparing salmon loaf. While loaf is baking, prepare 1 cup **Medium White Sauce** (*p.323*) Stir into sauce 1 cup cooked green **peas;** cook only until peas are heated throughout. Serve over salmon loaf.

Curried Tuna

A Far-Eastern specialty adapted to American tastes. Serve it with an array of traditional condiments and a brew of fine coffee.

Set out a chafing pan or a 2-qt. saucepan.

Prepare and set aside
¾ cup quick chicken broth (page 13)
Wash, quarter and core (do not pare)
1 large, tart red apple
Cut into ½-in. pieces. Sprinkle with
1 to 2 tablespoons lemon juice
Set aside.

Heat in the chafing pan over low heat
¼ cup butter or margarine

Add and cook until onion is transparent, stirring constantly

2 tablespoons grated onion
1 small clove garlic (*page 12*), minced;
or crushed in garlic press

Blend in a mixture of

¼ cup flour
1 to 2 teaspoons curry powder

Heat until mixture bubbles. Remove from heat. Add gradually, stirring in, the chicken broth and

¼ cup dry white wine
1 cup cream

Cook over low heat until thickened, stirring constantly. Add the apple pieces and continue cooking and stirring about 10 min. longer. Add contents of

1 7-oz. can chunk-style tuna, drained
and flaked (*page 12*)

Stir tuna pieces into sauce. Heat until fish is thoroughly heated.

Serve in chafing dish with **curry condiments** (see Fresh Shrimp Curry, *page 243*) and

Perfection Boiled Rice (page 275)

4 servings

Curried Tuna with condiments and coffee

▲ Sea Food Potpourri ㉓

Grease a 2-qt. casserole.

Prepare

3 Hard-cooked Eggs (*page 87*)

Meanwhile, combine gently with a fork

1 cup (7-oz. can, drained) tuna,
coarsely flaked (*page 12*)
1 cup (6- to 7-oz. can, drained) crab
meat, stiff bony tissue removed
⅔ cup (5-oz. can, drained) shrimp,
black veins removed and discarded
(*page 242*) and shrimp cut into halves

Drain, reserving liquid, and set aside

1 cup (8-oz. can) sliced mushrooms

Grate and set aside

4 oz. Cheddar cheese (1 cup, grated)

Prepare

2 cups Thin White Sauce (double recipe,
p.323 ; substitute reserved mush-
room liquid for part of milk)

Cool slightly. Add cheese all at one time. Stir sauce rapidly until cheese is melted. Blend in

3 tablespoons finely chopped chives
10 ripe olives, pitted and sliced

Arrange one half of the sea food in casserole. Slice the eggs and arrange one half of the slices on sea food. Add mushrooms and one half of the sauce. Repeat layers. Cover with remaining sauce and

½ cup coarsely crushed potato chips

Bake at 350°F 20 to 30 min., or until well browned.   *8 servings*

△ Sea Food and Biscuits

Follow ▲ Recipe. Omit potato chips. Prepare dough for **Tender-Rich Biscuits** (one-half recipe, *page 62*; if desired, add 1 tablespoon finely chopped **parsley** to flour-shortening mixture.) Cut 1-in. square biscuits. Arrange casserole layers. Bake at 425°F 10 min. Remove from oven and arrange biscuits in diagonal lines across top of casserole; leave spaces between biscuits. Increase oven temperature to 450°F and bake 10 to 15 min. longer, or until biscuits are lightly browned.

Fried Frog Legs

Fried Frog Legs

Set out a large, heavy skillet.

Soak in salted water (1 tablespoon salt per 2-qt. water) for 15 min.

8 pairs large skinned frog legs

Drain on absorbent paper.

Dip frog legs in

Milk

Coat evenly (*page 107*) with a mixture of

½ cup flour
1 teaspoon salt
1 teaspoon Accent
½ teaspoon pepper

Set aside.

Heat in the skillet over low heat

⅔ cup butter or margarine

Add to the skillet and cook about 5 min. over medium heat

1 clove garlic (*page 12*), cut into halves

Remove garlic from skillet. Add frog legs and

¼ teaspoon savory

Cook frog legs until golden brown (about 20 min.), turning as necessary with tongs or two spoons. Drain on absorbent paper.

Serve with

Lemon Butter Sauce (*page 331*; increase lemon juice to ¼ cup)

4 servings

Smothered Shad Roe

Set out a saucepan and a heavy skillet having a tight-fitting cover.

Wipe with a clean, damp cloth

4 shad roe

Melt in the saucepan over low heat

¾ cup butter

Dip the roe into the warm (not hot) butter to coat completely. Arrange roe in the skillet. Cover and cook over low heat about 12 min., turning roe once.

Remove to warm serving platter. Season with

1 teaspoon salt
¼ to ½ teaspoon Accent
¼ teaspoon pepper
1 tablespoon finely chopped parsley

Serve with the remaining butter and **baked potatoes, panbroiled bacon** and **lemon slices**.

4 servings

Fried Soft-Shell Crabs

Set out a large, heavy skillet.

Kill, by inserting a sharp-pointed, narrow-bladed knife between the eyes

12 soft-shelled crabs

Wash, remove the pointed apron on under-side, cut off face, and remove spongy material beneath points at each end of shell.

Coat crabs evenly (*page 107*) with a mixture of

½ cup flour
½ teaspoon salt
½ teaspoon Accent
¼ teaspoon pepper

Shake off excess flour. Set crabs aside.

Heat in the skillet over low heat

½ cup butter

Fry only as many crabs at one time as will lie flat in the pan. Cook until crabs are delicately browned and crisp on the edges. Serve crabs hot with

Lemon Butter Sauce (*page 331*) or Tartar Sauce (*page 330*)

4 to 6 servings

▲ Crab Meat Ramekins 24

Set out a double boiler. Grease 6 ramekins or individual casseroles.

Drain, remove and discard bony tissue and separate contents of
2 7-oz. cans (1¾ cups) crab meat
Set aside.

Prepare in top of double boiler
1 cup Thin White Sauce (page 323)
Remove from heat and vigorously stir about 3 tablespoons of the sauce into
2 egg yolks, slightly beaten
¼ to ½ teaspoon Accent
Immediately stir mixture into hot sauce in double-boiler top and cook over simmering water 3 to 5 min.; stir slowly to keep mixture cooking evenly.

Remove from heat; add gradually, stirring in
¼ cup minced green pepper (page 12)
1 tablespoon lemon juice
1½ teaspoons onion juice
Add crab meat, gently blending with a spoon.

Turn mixture into ramekins. Top with
¾ cup buttered dry bread crumbs
(page 11)
Bake at 350°F 20 to 25 min., or until crumbs are lightly browned.   *6 servings*

△ Crab Meat and Tomato Ramekins 25

Follow ▲ Recipe. Substitute **Medium White Sauce** (*p. 323* use tomato juice for milk) for Thin White Sauce. Use ½ cup crumbs; combine with ¼ cup grated **Parmesan cheese.**

Crab Meat Ramekins with mixed vegetable salad, potato chips and iced coffee

Crab 'n' Oysters 26

JANE H. BARBER, WATCH HILL, R.I.

Set out a double boiler.

Drain, reserving liquid
2 doz. (about 1 qt.) large oysters
Pick over oysters to remove any shell particles.

Drain, remove and discard bony tissue from
**½ cup (about 2 oz.) fresh lump
crab meat**
Set oysters and crab meat aside.

Melt in top of double boiler
¼ cup butter or margarine
Blend in
1 tablespoon flour
Heat until mixture bubbles. Remove from heat. Add gradually, stirring in, the reserved oyster liquid and
¼ cup ketchup
¼ cup cream
1 teaspoon Worcestershire sauce
½ teaspoon salt
½ teaspoon Accent
Return to heat and bring rapidly to boiling, stirring constantly. Cook 1 to 2 min. longer. Remove from heat. Add all at one time, stirring constantly
2 tablespoons grated Cheddar cheese
Continue stirring until cheese is melted. Stir in the crab meat.

Return to heat and heat to simmering. Add the oysters. Cook until edges of oysters begin to curl; do not overcook or oysters will be tough.

Serve hot over toast. *6 servings*

"Boiled" Lobster

Fill a large deep kettle or sauce pot having a tight-fitting cover about ⅔ full (or enough to cover the lobster) with
**Hot salted water (1 tablespoon salt
per qt. water)**
Bring water rapidly to boiling. Grasp by the back, below the large claws, and plunge head first into the water—one at a time
2 live lobsters, about 1½ lbs. each
Cover, bring water again to a rolling boil. Reduce heat and simmer 15 to 20 min. Drain and cover with cold water to chill. Drain again. Place bottom side up on a cutting board.

Twist off the two large claws, the smaller ones and the tail. With a pair of scissors cut (or with a sharp knife slit) the bony membrane on the underside of tail. Spread tail shell apart and remove meat. Remove and discard the intestinal vein. With a sharp knife slit in one piece underside of body of lobster, cutting completely through entire length of body. Remove and discard the intestinal vein running lengthwise through center of body. Remove and discard stomach (a small sac which lies in the head) and spongy lungs (which lie in upper body cavity between meat and shell).

If present, remove and reserve the tomalley (green liver) and the coral (bright red roe) to be used along with the lobster meat or as a garnish. Remove the small amount of meat present in the body shell. Disjoint the large claws and crack with a nutcracker. A nut pick or cocktail fork may be helpful in removing meat from small joints and claws. Put meat into a bowl or jar, cover and refrigerate until ready to use. *About 2 cups lobster meat*

Note: If lobster is to be served hot, do not plunge into cold water after cooking. Use tongs to remove to cutting board. Leave small claws and tail intact. Slit entire length of body and tail, cutting through meat to shell. Remove and discard the vein, lungs and stomach. Crack large claws with a nutcracker. Serve with melted **butter** and **lemon wedges**.

Broiled Rock-Lobster Tails 27

Thaw according to directions on package

**1 12-oz. frozen rock-lobster tail
for each person**

Prepare and set aside Crumb Topping.

For Crumb Topping—Melt in a saucepan over medium heat

2 tablespoons butter or margarine

Stir in

**½ cup (about 1½ slices) fine, dry
bread crumbs**

Remove saucepan from heat and stir in

**½ teaspoon lemon juice
½ teaspoon onion juice**

and a mixture of

**⅛ teaspoon salt
⅛ teaspoon Accent
Few grains pepper**

Set temperature control of range at Broil and grease a broiler rack.

Melt in a small saucepan over medium heat and set aside to keep warm

½ cup butter

Snip through and remove thin shell on underside of each lobster tail; remove vein. Holding tail in both hands, bend it towards shell side to crack; or insert a skewer lengthwise through meat—this keeps tail flat. (If you buy fresh rock-lobster tails, your dealer may do this.)

Place tails flesh side down on broiler rack. Set rack under broiler with top of lobster tails 4 in. or more from heat source. Broil 6 to 8 min. Turn tails flesh side up with tongs and brush with melted butter. Broil about 4 min.; brush again with melted butter. Sprinkle some of the Crumb Topping over top of each lobster tail. Broil about 2 min. longer, or until meat is completely white and opaque.

Sprinkle with

Paprika

Serve immediately with additional melted butter and **lemon wedges**.

Note: To prepare rock-lobster tails on an outdoor grill see OUTDOOR COOKING (*page 204*).

▲ Lobster Newburg in Pastry Shells

Prepare, bake and set aside to cool

**Pastry for Little Pies or Tarts (*page
443*; use six 3-in. tart pans, or six 3-
in. Vol-au-Vent Shells (*page 444*)**

For Lobster Newburg—Drain, cut into ½-in. pieces and set aside

1½ cups (two 6-oz. cans) lobster meat

Heat in a skillet over low heat

¼ cup butter or margarine

Blend in

**2 cups cream
¾ teaspoon salt
½ teaspoon Accent
⅛ teaspoon pepper
⅛ teaspoon nutmeg**

Bring just to boiling. Stir in the lobster meat and cook over low heat until meat is thoroughly heated. Vigorously stir about 3 tablespoons of this hot mixture into

4 egg yolks, slightly beaten

Immediately blend into hot mixture. Stirring constantly, continue to cook just until mixture thickens. (Do not overcook or allow mixture to boil as sauce will curdle.) Remove immediately from heat. Blend in about

1 tablespoon sherry

Spoon into the pastry shells. Sprinkle with **paprika**.   *6 servings*

△ Crab Meat Newburg

Follow ▲ Recipe; substitute 1½ cups (two 6½-oz. cans) **crab meat** for the lobster. Remove and discard bony tissue from meat.

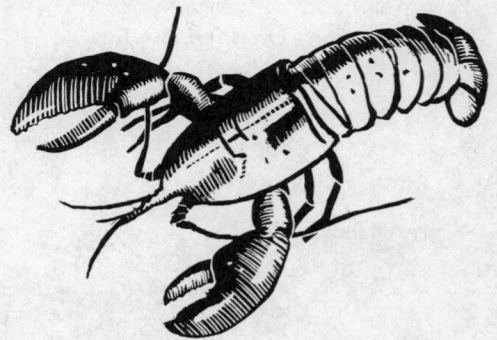

Rock-Lobster Thermidor

▲ **Lobster Thermidor** 28

Kill and clean (*page 223*)
  3 live lobsters, about 1½ lbs. each
(Live lobsters may be killed at the market.)

Heat in a large heavy skillet having a tight-fitting cover
  6 tablespoons butter
Put lobster halves, meat-side down, into the skillet. Place claws on top. Cover; cook slowly 12 to 15 min., or until tender.

Meanwhile, prepare and set aside
  1½ cups Medium White Sauce (one and one-half times recipe, p. 323 ⬛); stir into sauce 3 tablespoons heavy cream after removing from heat)

Heat in a saucepan
  3 tablespoons butter
Add and cook over medium heat until onion is transparent and mushrooms browned
  ⅔ cup chopped mushrooms
  2 tablespoons chopped shallots or onion

Occasionally move and turn mixture. Remove from heat and set aside.

Blend into one half of the white sauce
  3 tablespoons heavy cream
  2 tablespoons white wine
  1 teaspoon finely chopped chervil or parsley
  ½ teaspoon Worcestershire sauce
and a mixture of
  ¾ teaspoon Accent
  ½ teaspoon dry mustard
  ¼ teaspoon salt
  ⅛ teaspoon cayenne pepper
Add to mushroom mixture. Cook over low heat until thoroughly heated, moving and turning mixture gently with a spoon.

Gently pry the cooked lobster meat from shells, starting at tail. Reserve shells. Remove meat from large claws. Cut the lobster meat into 1-in. pieces and blend into the sauce.

Preheat shells, cavity-side up, at 325°F about 7 min. Fill with lobster mixture.

Pour remaining white sauce into the top of a double boiler. Stir over low heat until heated. Vigorously stir about 3 tablespoons sauce into
  1 egg yolk, slightly beaten
Immediately return mixture to top of double boiler. Stirring constantly, cook over simmering water 3 to 5 min. Remove from heat and spoon over lobster mixture in the shells. Sprinkle over the filled shells
  2 tablespoons grated Parmesan cheese (1 teaspoon cheese per shell)
Set temperature control of range at Broil.

Place baking sheet on broiler pan with top of food 2 to 3 in. from heat source. Broil 2 to 3 min., or until lightly browned.   *6 servings*

△ Rock-Lobster Thermidor ° 29

Follow ▲ Recipe. Substitute six 8-oz. **rock-lobster tails** for the whole lobsters. Cook the tails (see Imperial Lobster, *on this page*). Cut through and remove thin shell on underside of each tail. Carefully remove meat. Omit Parmesan cheese and browning in broiler. Reheat filled shells thoroughly in 325° F oven.

Imperial Lobster
(Rock-Lobster Tails)
MRS. WALTER W. HISSEY
CATONSVILLE, MD.

This superb, prize-winning dish, fit for the most imperial taste, was created on the eastern seaboard of the United States where shellfish cookery has been a high art for many years.

Lightly butter 4 ramekins or individual casseroles. If desired, use 6 crab-shaped ramekins.

Set out a baking sheet.

Fill a kettle having a tight-fitting cover about two-thirds full with hot water. Bring salted water (1 teaspoon salt per qt. of water) to a rapid boil. Put into the boiling water
>   **3 medium-size frozen rock-lobster tails**
>   **1 teaspoon Accent**

Cover and bring rapidly just to boiling; reduce heat. Simmer about 11 min. for lobster tails weighing about 10 oz. (or 1 min. longer than individual weight in ounces; add 2 min. if tails are frozen).

Drain lobster tails; rinse under a stream of running cold water until cool enough to handle; drain again. Place on a cutting board, shell side down. Cut through and remove thin shell on underside of each tail. Split lengthwise through the meat. Remove the meat; cut into small pieces and set aside.

While lobster tails are cooking, heat in a small skillet over low heat
>   **1 tablespoon butter**

Add and cook over medium heat until tender, occasionally moving and turning with a spoon
>   **¾ cup (about 1 large) chopped green pepper (page 12)**

Set aside to cool slightly.

Mix thoroughly in a bowl
>   **2 egg yolks, slightly beaten**
>   **⅓ cup mayonnaise**
>   **1 teaspoon Worcestershire sauce**
>   **1 teaspoon prepared mustard**
>   **½ teaspoon dry mustard**
>   **2 or 3 drops tabasco sauce**

Add and mix in the lobster and green pepper.

Set ramekins on the baking sheet and spoon mixture into them. Dot top of each with
>   **Butter (about 1 teaspoon each)**

Bake at 500°F about 15 min., or until mixture is heated thoroughly and lightly browned.

4 to 6 servings

Shrimp Sauté 30
MRS. A. E. BOYCE, RIVERDALE, N. DAK.

Set out a heavy skillet or saucepan.

Remove tiny legs and peel shells from
>   **1½ lbs. fresh shrimp with shells**

Cut a slit to just below surface along back (outer curved surface) of shrimp to expose the black vein. With knife point, remove vein in one piece. Rinse shrimp quickly in cold water. Drain on absorbent paper.

Heat in the skillet
>   **¼ cup butter or margarine**

Add the peeled shrimp and
>   **3 to 4 teaspoons finely chopped parsley**
>   **1 clove garlic (page 12), minced; or crushed in a garlic press**

Cook, stirring frequently, until shrimp turn pink (about 10 min.). Add, stirring constantly
>   **⅓ cup sherry**

and a mixture of
>   **¾ teaspoon salt**
>   **¼ teaspoon Accent**
>   **⅛ teaspoon pepper**

Cook 2 min. longer. Serve hot. Serve some of the cooking liquid as sauce. *About 4 servings*

Cooked Shrimp: Drop shrimp into a boiling mixture of water, lemon juice, salt and Accent.

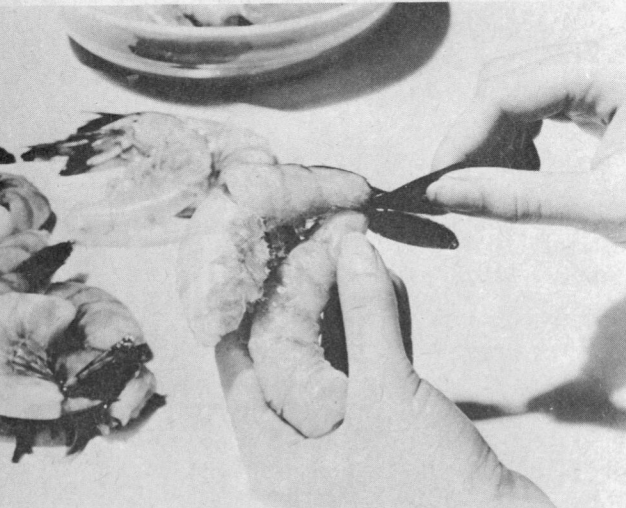

Chill the shrimp in cold water. Drain. Strip away the tiny legs and remove shells from cooked shrimp.

Cut a slit along outer curved surface of shrimp to expose black vein. Remove vein in one piece.

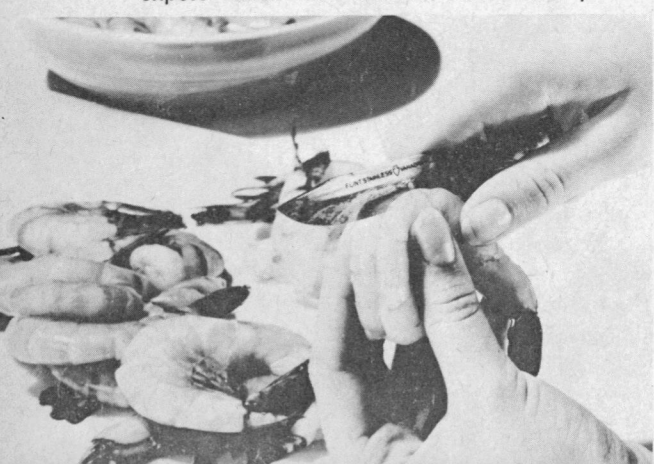

Cooked Shrimp 31

Wash in cold water

    1 lb. fresh shrimp with shells

Drop shrimp into a boiling mixture of

    2 cups water

    3 tablespoons lemon juice

    1 tablespoon salt

    ½ teaspoon Accent

Cover tightly. Simmer 5 min., or only until shrimp are pink and tender. Drain and cover with cold water to chill. Drain shrimp again. Remove tiny legs. Peel shells from shrimp.

Cut a slit to just below surface along back (outer curved surface) of shrimp to expose the black vein. With knife point remove vein in one piece.* Rinse shrimp quickly in cold water. Drain on absorbent paper. Refrigerate. Serve with

    Creamy Sea Food Cocktail Sauce (page 331), or Zippy Cocktail Sauce (page 331), or Shrimp Remoulade Sauce (page 330)

Note: Veins present in canned shrimp are removed in the same way.

Creole-Style Shrimp 32 with Rice

Set out a 2-qt. casserole.

Wash in cold water

    1½ lbs. fresh or frozen large shrimp with shells

Drop shrimp into a boiling mixture of

    3 cups water

    3 tablespoons lemon juice

    1 tablespoon salt

    1 teaspoon Accent

    3 or 4 sprigs parsley

    1 clove garlic, peeled (page 12) and split

    1 bay leaf

    Small piece celery with leaves

Cover tightly. Simmer 5 min., or only until

shrimp are pink and tender. Drain and cover with cold water to chill. Drain, peel and remove vein (see Cooked Shrimp, *page 242*). Put shrimp into casserole and set aside.

Heat in a skillet over low heat
¼ cup butter or margarine
Add and cook slowly until onion is transparent, occasionally moving and turning mixture with a spoon
1 cup (about 4 stalks) diced celery (page 12)
⅔ cup (about 1½ large) chopped onion (page 12)
½ cup (about 1 medium-size) finely chopped green pepper (page 12)
Thoroughly blend in
1 cup water
¾ cup (6-oz. can) tomato paste
1 tablespoon minced parsley
½ teaspoon salt
¼ teaspoon Accent
4 or 5 drops tabasco sauce
Pour mixture into casserole. Mix gently to distribute shrimp evenly.

Heat in oven at 350°F about 30 min.

Meanwhile, prepare
Perfection Boiled Rice (page 275)
Serve shrimp mixture over hot rice.

6 servings

Fresh Shrimp Curry

Cook and clean
2 lbs. fresh shrimp with shells (see Cooked Shrimp, page 242)
Set aside.

Heat in a heavy 3-qt. saucepan
⅓ cup butter or margarine
Add and cook over medium heat until onion is golden yellow, stirring occasionally
3 tablespoons chopped onion
3 tablespoons chopped celery
3 tablespoons chopped green apple
12 peppercorns
1 bay leaf

Fresh Shrimp Curry

Blend in a mixture of
⅓ cup flour
2½ teaspoons curry powder
½ teaspoon Accent
¼ teaspoon sugar
⅛ teaspoon nutmeg
Heat until mixture bubbles. Remove from heat and add gradually, stirring constantly
2½ cups milk
Return to heat and bring rapidly to boiling. Stirring constantly, cook until mixture thickens. Cook 1 to 2 min. longer.

Remove from heat; stir in
2 teaspoons lemon juice
½ teaspoon Worcestershire sauce
Strain mixture through a fine sieve, pressing vegetables against sieve to extract all sauce. Set aside to keep warm.

Heat in a skillet over low heat
½ cup butter or margarine
Add the cooked shrimp and cook over medium heat, moving and turning gently with a spoon, until shrimp are lightly browned. Pour the contents of the skillet into the saucepan and blend thoroughly.

Serve at once with **Perfection Boiled Rice** **(p. 275)** and **curry condiments,** such as freshly grated coconut, golden raisins, preserved kumquats, chutney, and chopped roasted peanuts. *4 servings*

Shrimp Imperial

Cook and clean

1½ lbs. fresh shrimp with shells (see Cooked Shrimp, p. 242 ; use 3 cups water)

Reserve three whole shrimp for garnish; cut remainder into halves. Chill in refrigerator.

Set out a double boiler.

Grate and set aside

3 oz. Cheddar cheese (about ¾ cup, grated)

Prepare (*page 12*) and set aside

¾ cup (about 1 large) chopped green pepper

½ cup (about 1 medium-size) minced onion

Heat in top of double boiler over low heat

¼ cup butter

Add the onion and green pepper and cook until onion is transparent and pepper is tender, occasionally moving mixture with a spoon. Blend in a mixture of

3 tablespoons flour

1 teaspoon salt

½ teaspoon Accent

⅛ teaspoon pepper

Heat until mixture bubbles. Remove from heat. Add gradually, stirring constantly

1 cup undiluted evaporated milk

1 cup water

Return to heat and bring rapidly to boiling, stirring constantly; cook 1 to 2 min. longer.

Vigorously stir about 3 tablespoons of hot mixture into

2 egg yolks, slightly beaten

Immediately blend into mixture in double boiler. Cook over simmering water 3 to 5 min. Stir slowly to keep mixture cooking evenly. Stir in the cooked shrimp and

½ cup (4-oz. can, drained) sliced mushrooms

3 tablespoons chopped pimiento

1 tablespoon finely chopped parsley

1 tablespoon prepared horse-radish

1 teaspoon Worcestershire sauce

Cook, stirring occasionally, until shrimp and mushrooms are thoroughly heated.

Pour into a large serving dish and sprinkle with the grated cheese. Garnish with the reserved shrimp and

Parsley sprigs

Strips of pimiento

Serve in **Toast Cups** (*page 65*), or on buttered **toast.** *6 servings*

Scallops Baked in Shells

Scallops in a sauce with a redolent bouquet.

Butter 6 baking shells or ramekins.

Set out

2 lbs. scallops

(If using frozen scallops, thaw according to directions on package.) Rinse scallops in cold water. Set aside to drain on absorbent paper.

Heat in a saucepan

2 cups dry white wine

Herb bouquet (*page 11*)

Add the scallops to the wine with

½ teaspoon salt

½ teaspoon Accent

Cover and simmer about 10 min., or until scallops are tender. Remove herb bouquet. Drain scallops, reserving the liquid. Cut the scallops into pieces and set aside.

Clean (*page 12*) and chop

½ lb. mushrooms

Put the mushrooms into a saucepan with

6 chopped shallots (or ¼ cup minced onion)

1 tablespoon minced parsley

3 tablespoons butter

2 tablespoons water

1 teaspoon lemon juice

¼ teaspoon Accent

Cover and simmer 5 to 10 min. Add the vegetable mixture to the scallops; set aside.

Melt in the saucepan

¼ cup butter

Scallops Baked in Shells

Blend in

¼ cup flour

Heat until mixture bubbles. Remove from heat. Add gradually, stirring in, the reserved liquid. Return mixture to heat and bring rapidly to boiling, stirring constantly; cook 1 to 2 min. longer. Remove from heat.

Stirring vigorously, gradually add the sauce to a mixture of

2 egg yolks, slightly beaten
¼ cup heavy cream

Stir in the scallop mixture. Fill shells or ramekins, piling high in center. Sprinkle with

⅓ cup (1 slice) buttered dry bread crumbs (page 10)

Set shells on a baking sheet and place in oven at 450°F 8 to 10 min. (or place in broiler 4 in. from source of heat); bake until crumbs are browned.

Serve hot. *6 servings*

▲ Deep-Fried Scallops

Set out a deep saucepan or automatic deep-fryer (*page 13*) and heat fat to 365°F.

Set out

2 lbs. scallops

(If using frozen scallops, thaw according to directions on package.) Rinse scallops in cold water. Set aside to drain on absorbent paper.

245

Put into a shallow pan or dish and set aside

1 cup (about 3 slices) fine, dry bread crumbs

Mix together in a bowl

2 eggs, slightly beaten
2 tablespoons milk
2 tablespoons paprika
1 teaspoon salt
1 teaspoon Accent
¼ teaspoon pepper
⅛ teaspoon cayenne pepper

Dip scallops, one at a time, into egg mixture and then coat by rolling in bread crumbs.

Deep-fry in the heated fat only as many scallops at one time as will lie uncrowded one layer deep in the fat. Fry 2 or 3 min., or until brown. Turn scallops as they rise to surface and several times during cooking. Remove scallops with a slotted spoon; drain over fat for a few seconds before removing them to absorbent paper.

Serve hot with **lemon wedges** and melted **butter** or **Tartar Sauce** (*page 330*).

6 to 8 servings

⚠ Deep-Fried Oysters

Follow ▲ Recipe. Substitute 1 qt. large **oysters** for the scallops. Drain and pick over to remove any shell particles. (Reserve liquid for use in other food preparation.) Coat oysters by rolling in bread crumbs; dip in egg mixture; coat again in bread crumbs. Heat fat to 375°F and deep-fry as in ▲ Recipe.

⚠ Deep-Fried Shrimp

Follow ▲ Recipe. Substitute 2 lbs. fresh **shrimp** with shells for the scallops. Peel and remove vein (see Shrimp Sauté, *page 241*). Heat fat to 350°F. Deep-fry as in ▲ Recipe.

Steamed Clams 36

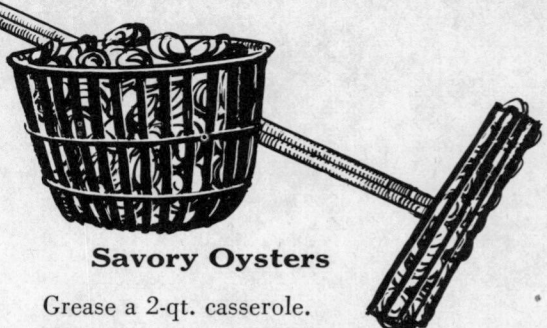

Best clams for steaming are the soft-shelled.

Set out a kettle having a tight-fitting cover.

Wash, scrub and very thoroughly rinse
**24 to 30 clams (allow about 6 to 8
clams per person)**
Put clams into the kettle. Add
1 cup water
Cover tightly and steam over low heat until
shells open. Remove from liquid. (Liquid
may be strained and used for clam juice cocktails or in other food preparation.)

Serve clams from the shell. Accompany with
Melted butter

About 4 servings

Clam Fritters

MRS. MARCUS F. JENSEN
DOUGLAS, ALASKA

If you've never tasted clam fritters, try these.

Set out a deep saucepan or automatic deep-
fryer (*page 13*) and heat fat to 365°F. Set out
a large bowl.

Drain, reserving juice
1 cup shucked clams
Rinse clams and put through food chopper.

Mix together in the bowl the clams and
¼ cup juice from clams
¼ cup milk
1 egg, slightly beaten
3 tablespoons butter, melted
Set mixture aside.

Sift together into a bowl
1 cup sifted flour
2½ teaspoons baking powder
¼ teaspoon salt
⅛ teaspoon pepper
¼ teaspoon paprika
Add clam mixture to the dry ingredients all
at one time. Mix only until well blended. Drop
by teaspoonfuls into hot fat. Fry 2 to 3 min.
Drain on absorbent paper. *6 servings*

Savory Oysters

Grease a 2-qt. casserole.

Prepare coarse crumbs from
6 slices crisp toast (2 cups crumbs)
Set aside.

Heat slowly about 5 min. in a large skillet,
stirring occasionally
½ cup butter or margarine
**⅔ cup (6¾-oz. can, drained) mush-
rooms, finely sliced**
⅓ cup chopped green pepper (*page 12*)
**½ clove garlic (*page 12*; insert wooden
pick for easy removal)**
Remove skillet from heat; discard garlic. Stir
in toast crumbs, blending well. Set aside.

Drain thoroughly, reserving liquid
1 qt. oysters
Pick over oysters to remove any shell particles.
Combine ¼ cup of reserved oyster liquid with
¼ cup cream or rich milk
1 teaspoon Worcestershire sauce
Set aside oysters and liquid.

Mix together
1 teaspoon salt
1 teaspoon paprika
½ teaspoon Accent
⅛ teaspoon mace
Dash of cayenne pepper
Line bottom of casserole with one third of
crumb mixture. Top with layers of one half of
the oysters, one half of the seasonings and
one third of the crumb mixture. Repeat oyster
and seasoning layers. Spoon remaining reserved liquid over oysters before topping with
remaining crumb mixture.

Bake at 375°F 20 to 30 min., or until crumbs
are golden brown. *6 to 8 servings*

▲ Oysters Rockefeller I 37

There is a saying in New Orleans that whoever eats Oysters Rockefeller feels as rich as the famous tycoon. This is one of the most distinguished dishes of a region noted for its imaginative cooking. There are many variations.

Set out a shallow baking dish and fill ¼ in. deep with coarse salt.

Prepare
   2 cups Medium White Sauce (double recipe, page 323)
Remove thickened sauce from heat and vigorously stir about 3 tablespoons hot sauce into
   1 egg, slightly beaten
Immediately return to mixture in saucepan and cook over low heat 1 to 2 min., stirring constantly. Set sauce aside and keep it warm.

Cook (*page 285*) in heavy saucepan contents of
   2 12-oz. pkgs. frozen chopped spinach
Drain thoroughly and set aside.

Meanwhile, place flat side of shell up and carefully open, by inserting the tip of a knife between edges of shell opposite hinges
   2 doz. shell oysters
Loosen the oysters from the top shell and place them in the deep half of the shell. Discard the top shells. Arrange oysters-in-the-shells in the prepared baking dish. (If shell oysters are not available, use 1 pt. shucked oysters and purchased clam shells.)

Set out
   2 tablespoons sherry
Sprinkle ¼ teaspoon wine over each oyster. Set baking dish aside.

Heat in a heavy skillet over low heat
   2 tablespoons butter or margarine
Add and cook over medium heat until onion is transparent, stirring occasionally
   1 tablespoon finely chopped onion

Oysters Rockefeller II

Add to the skillet the drained spinach, 2 tablespoons of the white sauce and
   1 tablespoon minced parsley
   ½ teaspoon Worcestershire sauce
   6 drops tabasco sauce
and a mixture of
   ¼ teaspoon salt
   ¼ teaspoon Accent
   Few grains nutmeg
   Few grains pepper
Mix thoroughly and heat 2 to 3 min. Spoon the spinach mixture over the oysters; then spoon the remaining white sauce over the spinach. Sprinkle over sauce
   Grated Parmesan cheese
Bake at 375°F 15 to 20 min., or until lightly browned.

Serve immediately. *4 to 6 servings*

△ Oysters Rockefeller II 38

Follow ▲ Recipe; omit Medium White Sauce and egg. Blend 2 tablespoons **cream** with the cooked spinach. Top spinach mixture with ¾ cup buttered, fine, dry **bread crumbs** (*page 10*); then sprinkle with the cheese.

FISH and SHELLFISH in the MICROWAVE OVEN

The microwave oven is a master of fish cookery. Because fish has both low cholesterol and low calorie counts it is one of the healthiest foods you can eat. Unfortunately, it is also a food which Americans seem to resist. One of the reasons, perhaps, is that fish must be cooked with great finesse—both rapidly and delicately to just the right degree of doneness. Over-cooked, fish toughens and gets dry; under-cooked, it has a flavor which is disagreeable to many palates.

Cooking fish in the microwave oven will have both fish fanciers and fish haters taking another look. Microwaves cook fish both quickly and gently to perfection. In fact, there is almost no food better suited to the microwave oven. It emerges tender and moist with the natural flavor at its peak. Just taste the **Baked Stuffed Fish** or the **Lobster Thermidor**.

Sauces are outstanding. As usual, the trick is to stir as directed. The seafood casseroles are unusual and delicious. Microwave cooking saves time and assures superb results for such recipes as **Creamed Finnan Haddie and Cracker Tips en**

Casserole and **Fish Dinner**. In other recipes, microwave cooking simplifies preparation by eliminating the need for boiling water baths and double boilers required in such recipes as **Hot Salmon Loaf** and **Crab 'n' Oysters**.

COOKING FISH AND SHELLFISH—Obviously, timing is critical in cooking both fish and shellfish. A minute can make a crucial difference in the perfection of the dish, particularly in such simple recipes as **Baked Fish Steaks** or **Poached Fish Veronique**.

If the fish is not done after the minimum cooking times we give, check every minute until the fish flakes easily when tested with a fork or meets any other test for doneness specified by the recipe.

We have discovered that with these dishes, not only do cooking times vary slightly from oven to oven and cook to cook, but from fish to fish and from cut to cut. For instance, fish steaks cook a little faster than fillets. Cod and flounder cook more quickly than sole and haddock. The amount of fish in the oven (1 lb. vs.

1½ lbs.) and whether the fish has skin or bones can also make a significant difference in cooking times.

For these reasons, when a choice of different types of fish is specified in the master recipe found in the main text, for instance **Fish Dinner**, we have specified the amount and type of fish we used. If there is no description we have followed exactly the master recipe as to the type and amount of fish.

Standing Time—All the dishes must be covered and stand after cooking in the microwave oven. Both texture and taste will develop fully during the standing time. We specify the minimum standing time with each recipe.

Except for those recipes prepared in the browning skillet, such as **Pan Fried Whole Fish**, most fish dishes are cooked covered in the microwave oven to retain moisture. Use a dish with a cover, or substitute plastic wrap.

REMINDERS—For additional tips and an easy-to-read chart comparing settings among different brands of microwave ovens see the introductory chapter **Home Cooking in the Microwave Oven**, in the beginning of this book.

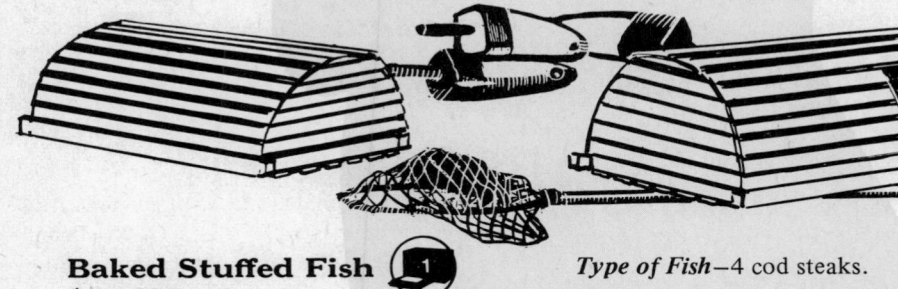

Baked Stuffed Fish **1**
(page 224)

Use a covered baking dish. Line dish with parchment paper. *Do not use aluminum foil.*

Type of Fish—3-lb. (dressed weight) sea bass.

For Stuffing—COOK butter or margarine until melted. Add celery and onion and COOK until onion is transparent (about 5 min.). Combine with remaining stuffing ingredients.

For Fish—Prepare fish for baking as in Recipe, except *do not use metal skewers.* Use wooden picks or sew with cord. Do not use plastic wrap to cover.

COOK stuffed fish until it flakes easily when tested with a fork (about 25 min.).

Cover and let stand 15 min.
                    OVERALL COOKING TIME: 33:00

Baked Fish Steaks *(page 225)*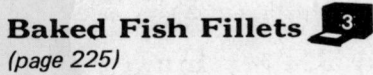

Use a baking dish with cover. You may use plastic wrap.

Type of Fish—4 cod steaks.

Assemble steaks as in Recipe, cover and COOK, checking for doneness every 1 min. after 5 min., until fish flakes easily (about 5 min.).

Cover and let stand 10 min.

Serve as in Recipe.
                    OVERALL COOKING TIME: 5:00

Baked Fish Fillets **3**
(page 225)

Use a baking dish.

Type of Fish—Flounder fillets.

Follow **2** Recipe with substitutions as in △ Recipe. Check for doneness every 1 min. after 10 min.

Pompano en Papillote 4
(page 225)

Use a baking dish.

Prepare papillotes for cooking as in Recipe.

COOK to heat through (about 5 min.). SLOW-COOK until paper puffs (about 7 min.).

Cover and let stand 10 min.

Serve as in Recipe.

Halibut alla Marinara 7
(page 226)

Follow 6 Recipe with substitution as in △ Recipe.

Fillets of Sole in White Wine (page 226) 5

Lightly grease a 2-qt. covered casserole.

Cover assembled casserole and COOK, rotating pan after 3 min., until fish flakes easily (about 6 min.).

Cover and let stand 10 min.

OVERALL COOKING TIME: 6:00

Creole Fish (page 226) 8

Use a baking dish with cover or substitute plastic wrap.

Type of Fish—Flounder fillets.

COOK butter or margarine until melted. Add onion, green pepper and garlic. COOK, stirring every 1 min., until onion is transparent (about 2 min.).

Add sauce mixture. COOK, stirring after 3 min., to simmer and blend flavors (about 5 min.).

Roll fish and add to sauce. Cover and COOK until fish flakes easily (about 6 min.).

Cover and let stand 10 min.

Serve as in Recipe.

OVERALL COOKING TIME: 13:00

Cod alla Marinara 6
(page 226)

Use a 1½-qt. covered casserole. *Do not grease.*

For the sauce, use only 1½ cups tomatoes (instead of 2 cups). COOK sauce to boiling (about 5 min.).

Add sauce to fish in casserole. Cover and COOK to heat through (about 5 min.). SLOWCOOK, rotating pan every 5 min., until fish flakes easily (about 20 min.).

Cover and let stand 15 min.

OVERALL COOKING TIME: 30:00

Fish Dinner (page 227) 9

Use a lightly greased 2-qt. casserole and a small casserole for the sauce.

Type of Fish—Haddock fillets.

In the small casserole, COOK butter or margarine until melted. Add onion and COOK until transparent (about 1 min.).

Add milk mixture in thirds, stirring before and after each addition. After each addition, COOK, stirring every 30 sec., to simmer (about 1 min.). COOK, stirring every 30 sec., until all sauce is thickened (about 1 min.).

Assemble casserole. COOK, rotating pan every 5 min., until potatoes are tender (about 15 min.).

Cover and let stand 20 min.
OVERALL COOKING TIME: 48:00

Creamed Finnan Haddie and Cracker Tips en Casserole *(page 228)* **10**

Use a 2-qt. casserole.

COOK butter or margarine until melted. Blend in flour and COOK to bubbling (about 1 min.).

Add milk "stock" and COOK, stirring every 30 sec., until thickened (about 2 min.).

Add egg yolks and COOK, stirring every 1 min., to heat (about 3 min.).

Assemble casserole, except omit the crackers. COOK to heat through (about 5 min.).

Cover and let stand 20 min.

Add crackers immediately before serving so they will remain crisp. Serve as in Recipe.
OVERALL COOKING TIME: 11:00

Creamed Codfish and Cracker Tips *(page 228)* **11**

Follow **10** Recipe with changes as in △ Recipe.

Broiled Fish Steaks **12** *(page 229)*

Use a browning skillet.

Type of Fish—Cod steaks.

Preheat skillet (3 min.). Grease lightly with butter. Arrange steaks, adding seasonings as in Recipe and COOK until fish flakes easily (about 3 min. each side).

Cover and let stand 10 min.

Serve as in Recipe.
OVERALL COOKING TIME: 9:00

Broiled Fish Fillets **13** *(page 229)*

Follow **12** Recipe with changes as in △ Recipe. COOK until fish flakes easily (about 8 min.).

Serve as in Recipe.
OVERALL COOKING TIME: 8:00

Broiled Trout *(page 229)* 14

Use a browning skillet.

Preheat skillet (3 min.). Grease lightly with butter or margarine. COOK trout, seasoning as in Recipe, until fish flakes easily (about 5 min. per side).

Cover and let stand 10 min.

OVERALL COOKING TIME: 13:00

Panfried Fish Fillets 15
(page 231)

Use a browning skillet.

Type of Fish—Haddock fillets.

Preheat skillet (3 min.). Grease lightly with butter. COOK breaded fillets until fish flakes easily (about 2 min. each side).

Cover and let stand 10 min.

For sauce, COOK to heat (about 1 min.).

Serve as in Recipe.

OVERALL COOKING TIME: 8:00

Panfried Whole Fish 16
(page 231)

Type of Fish—Trout.

Follow 15 Recipe. COOK until fish flakes easily (about 5 min. each side).

OVERALL COOKING TIME: 10:00

Poached Fish with 17
Horse-radish Sauce *(page 232)*

Use a baking dish with cover. You may use plastic wrap.

COOK until fish flakes easily (about 15 min.).

Cover and let stand 10 min.

Serve as in Recipe.

OVERALL COOKING TIME: 15:00

Poached Fish Veronique 18
(page 232)

Use a browning skillet.

Type of Fish—Fillet of sole.

COOK butter or margarine until melted. Add onion and COOK, stirring after 1 min., until transparent (about 1½ min.).

Add seasoned fish and wine and COOK until fish flakes easily (about 6 min.).

For the sauce, COOK butter until melted. Add flour and COOK to bubbling (about 1 min.).

Add half the cream, stir and COOK to heat (about 30 sec.); stir. Add the remaining cream,

stir and COOK, stirring every 30 sec., until mixture thickens (about 1 min.).

Cover and let stand 10 min.

Serve as in Recipe.
OVERALL COOKING TIME: 10:00

Sweet-Sour Salmon Steaks *(page 233)* **19**

Use a 3-qt. covered casserole and a small casserole for the sauce.

COOK vegetable-spice mixture to boiling (about 5 min.). COOK salmon until nearly tender (about 12 min.).

In small casserole, COOK butter or margarine until melted. Add brown sugar and COOK to melt (about 3 min.).

COOK salmon in sweet-sour liquid until it flakes easily (about 5 min.).

Cover and let stand (in liquid) 10 min.
OVERALL COOKING TIME: 25:00

Hot Salmon Loaf **20**
(page 234)

Use a 9x5x3-in. loaf pan. Grease bottom very lightly. The boiling water bath is not necessary.

Assemble loaf. SLOWCOOK uncovered, rotating pan every 4 min., until loaf starts to pull away from sides of pan (about 12 min.).

Cover and let stand 15 min.
OVERALL COOKING TIME: 12:00

Salmon Loaf with Creamed Peas *(page 234)* **21**

Follow **20** Recipe with addition as in △ Recipe.

Curried Tuna *(page 234)* **22**

Use a 2-qt. casserole.

COOK butter or margarine until melted. Add onion and garlic and COOK, stirring every 1 min., until onion is transparent (about 3 min.).

Blend in flour and curry powder and COOK to bubbling (about 30 sec.).

Add broth and COOK, stirring every 30 sec., until smooth (about 1 min.).

Add cream one-third at a time. After each addition, COOK 30 sec., stirring until smooth.

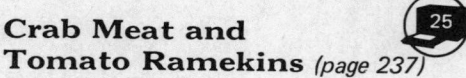

COOK until all sauce is thickened (about 30 sec.).

Add apple and COOK, stirring every 1 min., until apple is nearly tender (about 3 min.).

Add tuna and COOK, stirring every 1 min., until thoroughly heated (about 2 min.).

Cover and let stand 5 min.

Serve as in Recipe.

OVERALL COOKING TIME: 11:30

Sea Food Potpourri 23
(page 235)

Use a lightly greased 2-qt. casserole.

Assemble casserole and COOK, uncovered, to heat through (about 5 min.).

Cover and let stand 10 min.

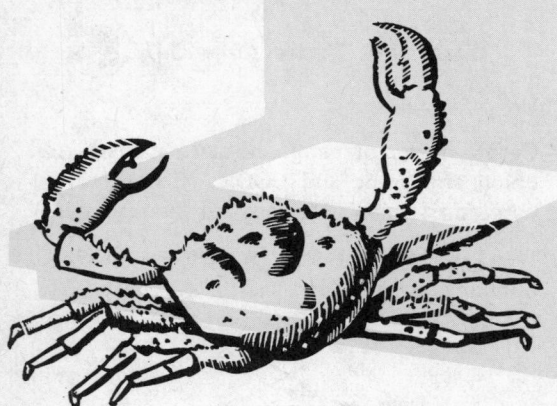

Crab Meat Ramekins 24
(page 237)

Use six 6-oz. custard cups. *Do not grease.*

Add egg yolk to white sauce and COOK, stirring every 30 sec. (about 3 min.).

Assemble ramekins. COOK until heated through (about 3 min.).

Cover and let stand 10 min.

Crab Meat and Tomato Ramekins 25 *(page 237)*

Follow 24 Recipe with changes as in △ Recipe.

Crab 'n' Oysters *(page 238)* 26

Use a 1½-qt. casserole.

Be sure to puncture the outer membrane of each oyster with a toothpick.

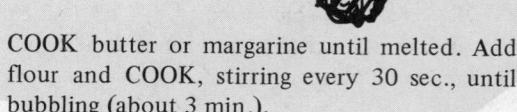

COOK butter or margarine until melted. Add flour and COOK, stirring every 30 sec., until bubbling (about 3 min.).

Add liquids and seasonings and COOK, stirring every 1 min., until thickened (about 5 min.).

Add remaining ingredients. COOK until edges of oysters curl (about 5 min.).

Cover and let stand 10 min.

OVERALL COOKING TIME: 13:00

Broiled Rock-Lobster 27 Tails *(page 239)*

Use a baking dish and a small casserole.

For Crumb Topping—COOK butter or margaring until melted. Add bread crumbs and COOK to coat with butter (about 1 min.). Stir and add juices and seasonings.

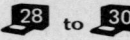

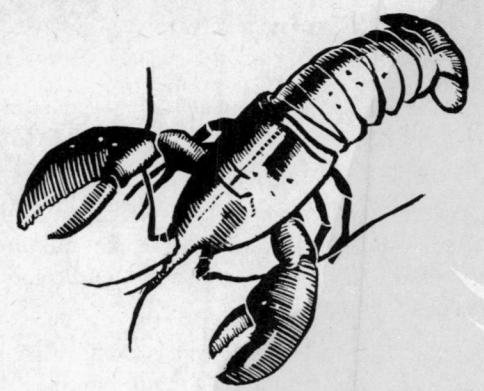

For the Lobster Tails—Cut lengthwise down back through shell. Hold tail in both hands and open flat. Place tails flesh side up in baking dish. Brush with melted butter and cover with plastic wrap. COOK until shell starts to turn pink.

Remove plastic wrap. Rotate dish and brush again with melted butter. Top with crumb mixture. COOK, uncovered, until meat is completely white and opaque.

Cooking time depends on the size and the number of tails. Check for doneness every minute after adding crumb topping.

Approximate total cooking times for 8-oz. tails:
1 tail—2:30
2 tails—4:00
4 tails—7:00

Cover and let stand 5 min.

Lobster Thermidor 28
(page 240)

Use a baking dish and a small casserole.

COOK butter to heat. Add lobsters, meat side down, cover and COOK until tender (about 15 min.).

In small casserole, COOK butter to heat. Add mushrooms and onions and COOK, stirring every 2 min., until onion is transparent (about 5 min.).

Mix white sauce with liquids and spices and add to mushroom mixture. COOK, stirring every 1 min., until thoroughly heated (about 5 min.).

Preheat lobster shells (about 4 min.).

Using a small casserole, add egg yolks to remaining white sauce. COOK egg yolk mixture, stirring every 1 min., until flavors blend (about 3 min.).

Assemble filled lobster tails. COOK until cheese is melted (about 5 min.).

Cover and let stand 5 min.

Rock-Lobster Thermidor (page 241) 29

Follow 28 Recipe, except to cook lobster tails, use only ¼ cup water in baking dish. Put in frozen tails and cover with plastic wrap. COOK until shell is pink and meat starts to pull away from sides (about 14 min.). Continue as in △ Recipe.

Shrimp Sauté (page 241) 30

Use a casserole.

COOK butter or margarine until melted (about 3 min.). Add shrimp, garlic and parsley and COOK until shrimp turn pink (about 5 min.).

Add sherry and spices and cook until flavors are blended (about 3 min.).

Cover and let stand 10 min.
OVERALL COOKING TIME: 11:00

Cooked Shrimp *(page 242)* **31**

Use a 1½-qt. casserole with cover.

COOK water and spices until boiling (about 8 min.). Add shrimp, cover and COOK until pink and tender (about 5 min.).

Cover and let stand 10 min.

OVERALL COOKING TIME: 13:00

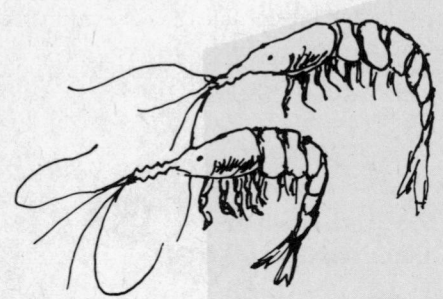

Creole-Style Shrimp with Rice *(page 242)* **32**

Use a 2-qt. covered casserole and a small casserole. You may use plastic wrap.

COOK water and seasonings until boiling (about 12 min.). Add shrimp and COOK until just pink (about 7 min.).

In small casserole, COOK butter or margarine until melted. Add vegetables and COOK until onion is transparent (about 3 min.).

Add remaining ingredients, except use only ½ cup water (instead of 1 cup) for tomato paste mixture.

Assemble casserole, cover and COOK to heat thoroughly (about 10 min.).

Cover and let stand 10 min.

OVERALL COOKING TIME: 32:00

Fresh Shrimp Curry **33**
(page 243)

Use a browning skillet or a 3-qt. covered casserole for the sauce and a browning skillet or 1½-qt. casserole for the shrimp.

COOK the 1/3 cup butter or margarine until melted. Add the onion-celery-apple mixture and COOK, stirring every 1½ min., until onion is golden (about 3 min.).

Blend in flour and spices and COOK, stirring every 2 min., until bubbling (about 5 min.).

Add milk and COOK, stirring every 1 min., to boil (about 3 min.).

COOK the ½ cup butter or margarine until melted (about 3 min.). Add shrimp and COOK until lightly browned (about 5 min.).

Cover and let stand 10 min.

Serve as in Recipe.

OVERALL COOKING TIME: 22:00

Shrimp Imperial *(page 244)* **34**

Use a 3-qt. casserole.

COOK butter until melted. Add onion and green pepper and COOK, stirring every 1½ min., until onion is transparent (about 3 min.).

Add flour mixture and COOK, stirring every 1 min., to bubbling (about 3 min.).

Add milk and water and COOK, stirring every 1 min., to boiling (about 5 min.).

Add egg yolk and COOK, stirring every 30 sec., until flavors are blended (about 3 min.).

Add remaining ingredients and COOK until thoroughly heated (about 3 min.).

Cover and let stand 10 min.

Serve as in Recipe.

OVERALL COOKING TIME: 20:00

Scallops Baked in Shells
(page 244)

Use two casseroles and six 6-oz. custard cups or shells.

COOK to heat wine mixture (about 5 min.). Add scallops and seasonings, cover and COOK until scallops are tender (about 5 min.). Remove and set aside.

In same casserole, COOK mushroom mixture,

stirring every 2 min., until vegetables are nearly tender (about 4 min.). Add scallops and set aside.

In another casserole, COOK butter until melted. Blend in flour and COOK, stirring every 1½ min., until mixture bubbles (about 3 min.).

Add liquid and COOK until thickened (about 3 min.).

Assemble ramekins. COOK until heated through (about 5 min.).

Cover and let stand 10 min.

OVERALL COOKING TIME: 25:00

Steamed Clams *(page 246)*

Use a baking dish. The times given in this recipe are for preparing 12 clams.

Rinse clams and arrange in circle in baking dish. Omit water. Cover with plastic wrap and COOK, rotating the pan every 1½ min., until clams open (about 3 min.). When you rotate the dish, check clams and remove any that have opened. To avoid overcooking, do not cook clams for more than 1½ min. after opening.

Serve as in Recipe.

OVERALL COOKING TIME: 3:00

Oysters Rockefeller I
(page 247)

Use a baking dish and two casseroles.

Thoroughly mix egg yolks and white sauce. COOK, stirring every 30 sec., until flavors are blended (about 1 min.).

In casserole, COOK butter or margarine until melted. Add onion and COOK until transparent (about 1 min.).

COOK spinach mixture, stirring every 1 min., until heated through (about 3 min.). Stir.

Be sure to puncture the outer membrane of each oyster with a toothpick. Assemble oysters and SLOWCOOK until cheese is heated (about 15 min.).

Cover and let stand 10 min.

Oysters Rockefeller II
(page 247)

Follow 37 Recipe with changes as in △ Recipe.

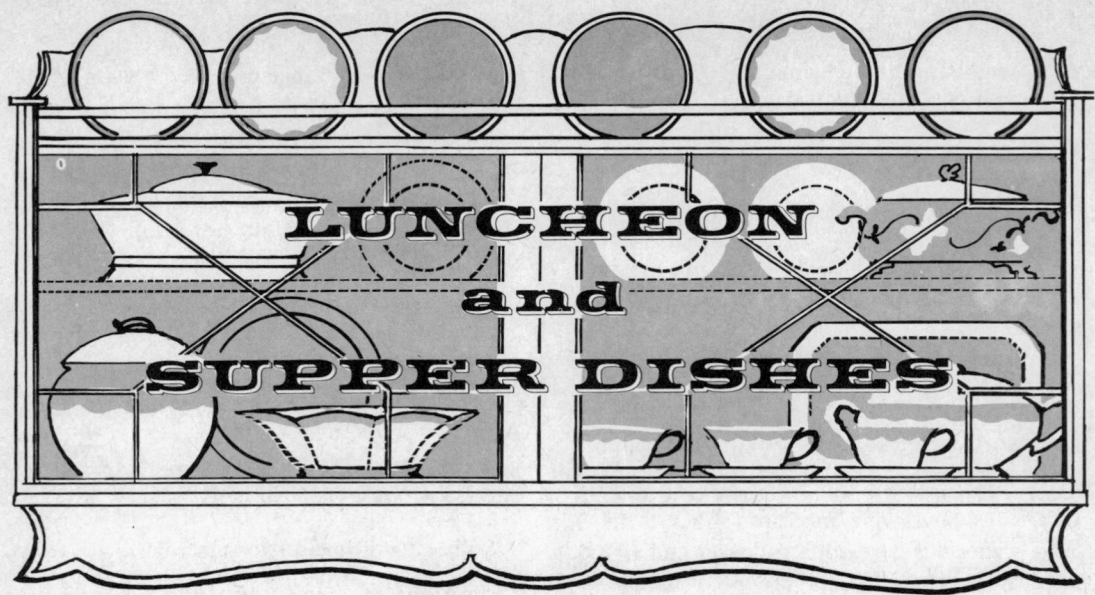

LUNCHEON and SUPPER DISHES

Perhaps the majority of the recipes in this section belong to the class of wonderful family fare. Of course there are a number of exceptions; for example, the **Red 'n' White Salad Mold** (*page 267*) combines cooked chicken with cranberry sauce and pineapple in a manner worthy of your most special luncheon guests. But many others of these recipes are for the hearty, homey type of dish which satisfies the family and saves work for you.

There are old favorites here—**Chili Con Carne** (*page 250*), **Spanish Rice** (*page 276*) and **Flavor-Filled Macaroni and Cheese** (*page 278*). There are delightful new dishes, too—creamed foods, main-dish salads and many oven main dishes, including casseroles, pies and scallops.

TYPES—A true *casserole* mixture contains meat, fish, poultry, eggs or cheese, sometimes more than one of them, combined in a well-flavored sauce, sometimes with rice or some pasta product: all turned into an ovenware dish and baked. A *pie* is a quite similar mixture topped with a crust of pastry, biscuits or mashed potatoes, and baked. A *scallop* has the foods arranged in alternate layers, usually with a well-seasoned white sauce, and it usually has a topping of buttered crumbs, or sometimes crumbs and cheese or simply grated cheese. Many of these oven dishes may be fully prepared ahead of time and stored in the refrigerator or freezer to be cooked when needed.

BAKING—The baking dish in which these mixtures are cooked is generally of heat-resistant glass, pottery or enameled iron ware. It is important to choose a dish of the right size. The mixture, whatever its type, should come to about one-half to two-thirds inch below the rim of the casserole; if the dish is fuller, the mixture may overflow when it bubbles up; if less full, the sides of the dish will interfere with proper heat circulation and may prevent browning of the surface.

Most oven main dishes are cooked uncovered, since a brown surface is usually desired. However, when some ingredient in the mixture requires long cooking, the casserole may be covered during the first part of the cooking time to produce steaming and prevent excessive browning; uncovering for a short time just before taking from the oven browns the surface sufficiently.

INGREDIENTS—**Ground meat** is called for in many recipes in this section. For best flavor in any ground meat dish, always purchase meat that is freshly ground. Many homemakers like to order the cut of beef they favor—round, chuck, brisket or whatever it may be—and have it ground while they wait. A coarse single grind insures juiciness. The same suggestion applies to pork and lamb.

After ground meat is brought home, it should be removed from the meat dealer's wrappings and stored *lightly* covered (not wrapped) in the coldest part of the refrigerator, preferably for not longer than two days. Light handling of ground meat, both in shaping and during cooking, keeps the texture light and juicy. In general, allow about 1 teaspoon salt and ½ teaspoon Accent per pound of meat.

Cheese is another ingredient which appears frequently in casserole cookery. It may be a principal ingredient of the casserole mixture or an important garnish—important because of the rich, tangy flavor imparted by even a light topping of grated cheese, or crumbs and cheese, to almost any food combination. The cheese which is used probably more often than any other in American cookery is Cheddar, mild or sharp as family preference dictates; but dozens of other varieties of cheese, many of them originating in far corners of the world, are now being produced domestically and are therefore available quite generally.

Cheese is of three types: natural, process, and a blend called "cheese food." *Natural cheese*, which is the basis of both other types as well, is made directly from milk—usually cows' milk, though some special cheeses are made from the milk of goats or ewes. The cheese-making process concentrates into the cheese almost all the proteins and most of the fat, minerals and vitamins of the milk; hence all cheese is highly nutritious food. The special character of different varieties of cheese is determined by the manner in which they are aged and "ripened" by bacterial action and molds. Some aging and ripening takes place in all cheeses except cream cheese, cottage cheese and Neufchâtel.

Natural cheese may be soft, semisoft, hard or very hard. *Soft cheeses* include both unripened cream and cottage cheese and some ripened varieties such as Camembert and Brie (both table rather than cooking cheeses). Familiar examples of *semisoft cheeses* are Roquefort and Blue, usually used in spreads and salad dressings, though occasionally in cooked dishes too. The most common cooking cheeses are *hard cheeses*, including Cheddar and Swiss (both Emmentaler and Gruyère). The best-known of the *very hard cheeses* are Parmesan and Romano, which are most frequently used grated as a topping for cooked foods; these are often purchased already grated, though if purchased in the piece and grated as needed, the unused portion will keep almost indefinitely. Many other varieties in these classifications are becoming increasingly recognized and used, including Italian Ricotta and Mozzarella, Norwegian Mysost and Gjetost, Dutch Edam and Gouda, and Swiss Sapsago. Some have cooking uses, others are primarily table cheeses. Most are now produced in this country.

Process cheeses are a development of recent years. They are produced from natural cheeses by methods developed to insure uniformity of flavor, texture, moisture content and cooking quality. They are often blends of more than one variety of cheese; but even when only one variety is used, cheeses selected at different stages of ripeness are blended, thus insuring uniformity.

In processing, the natural cheeses are ground up, mixed together by heating and stirring with an emulsifying agent until melted, and measured into molds lined with a completely moisture-vapor-proof packaging material; the packages are immediately closed and sealed and the cheese is cooled in its air-tight package. This process "fixes" the flavor of the cheese because it destroys the enzymes, bacteria and molds which in natural cheese continue the ripening process until the cheese is used. Process cheeses have good keeping qualities.

Cheese foods are made like process cheeses, but certain dairy products (such as cream, milk or dry mild solids) are added; at least 51 per cent of the weight must be natural cheese. *Process cheese spreads* are made like cheese foods, except that they must be spreadable at room temperature.

Other foods used in luncheon and supper dishes so frequently that they deserve special mention are members of the *pasta* family: macaroni, spaghetti and egg noodles. Pasta comes in many forms other than the three most familiar ones, so much variety in appearance is possible. Shells, bows, little star shapes, elbows, very fine noodles and very wide ones (*lasagne*), slender *vermicelli* and *matassa*, fat *mostaccioli* and *tufoli* are only a few of the available forms. All combine well with meat and cheese, because they absorb and spread flavors rapidly.

Pasta products require careful cooking for maximum palatability. Specific directions on individual packages should be followed; but in general, all pasta should be cooked in a large amount of furiously boiling salted water, for just long enough to make the pasta tender but still firm to the teeth (what the Italians term "al dente"). Use of too little water in cooking produces a sticky texture and a pasty taste; too long cooking makes pasta soft and watery. Cooked pasta should be drained immediately in a colander or sieve, rinsed with hot water to remove loose starch (or with cold water if the product is to be used in a salad), and preferably used at once. Actual cooking time varies from 5 to 20 minutes, depending on the variety.

Chili con Carne

Heat in a large skillet having a tight-fitting cover

2 tablespoons fat

Add and cook until onion is transparent, occasionally moving and turning with a spoon

½ cup (about 1 medium-size) chopped onion (page 12)

Add and cook over medium heat until lightly browned, breaking into small pieces with fork or spoon

1 lb. ground beef

Add slowly, stirring constantly

2 cups (1-lb. can) kidney beans

2 cups (1-lb. can) cooked tomatoes, cut in pieces

and a mixture of

1 tablespoon chili powder

1½ teaspoons salt

¾ teaspoon Accent

⅛ teaspoon pepper

⅛ teaspoon cayenne pepper

Cover and simmer over low heat about 1 hour, stirring occasionally.

Serve hot with rolls or bread sticks and **Southwestern Salad Bowl (page 314)**

4 to 6 servings

Chili con Carne

Beef Pinwheels

Lightly grease a baking sheet.

Heat in a heavy skillet over medium heat

1 tablespoon fat

Add and cook until browned, breaking into small pieces with fork or spoon

½ lb. ground beef

When meat is almost browned, add and cook until onion is transparent

2 tablespoons finely chopped onion

¼ teaspoon salt

¼ teaspoon Accent

Few grains pepper

Remove from heat and moisten with

2 to 3 tablespoons chili sauce

Set meat mixture aside.

Prepare dough for

Tender-Rich Biscuits (page 62)

Roll dough into rectangle ½ in. thick. Spread ground meat mixture over biscuit dough. Beginning with longer side of rectangle, roll tightly, without stretching, into a long roll; pinch ends to seal. Slice into ½-in. pinwheels.

Place on the baking sheet.

Bake at 450°F 10 to 15 min., or until browned.

Serve hot. (If desired, accompany with **Brown Gravy,** page 325.) *About 6 servings*

▲ Ham Pinwheels

Follow ▲ Recipe. Substitute for the ground beef 1½ cups **ground cooked ham;** omit cooking in the fat. Substitute for the chopped onion, salt and chili sauce, ⅓ cup **sweetened condensed milk,** ¼ cup **pickle relish,** 2 tablespoons minced **parsley** and 2 teaspoons **prepared mustard.** Complete pinwheels as in the ▲ Recipe.

▲ Luncheon Meat Pinwheels

Follow ▲ Recipe. Substitute 1½ cups **ground luncheon meat** for ham.

Beef Pinwheels

Shipwreck 2 2

(Beef-Kidney-Bean Casserole)

MRS. HAROLD WHEAT, SAN JOSE, ILL.

A Southern stew that has found a happy home up North and is usually served when Mother is not available for kitchen duty. This recipe is now in its second generation of family service.

Lightly grease a 3-qt. casserole having a tight-fitting cover.

Wipe with a clean, damp cloth
1½ lbs. beef for stewing (chuck, brisket or neck)
Cut meat into ½-in. pieces and set aside.

Thinly slice and place in a layer on bottom of casserole
1 large onion (page 12)
Cover onion with the beef, forming a second layer. Season with a mixture of
1 teaspoon salt
½ teaspoon Accent
¼ teaspoon pepper
Few grains paprika
Sprinkle over the meat layer
½ cup uncooked rice
(The Rice Industry no longer considers it necessary to wash rice before cooking.) Cover rice layer with
1 cup (2 to 3 stalks) diced celery (page 12)

Spread evenly over celery layer
2 cups (No. 2 can, drained) kidney beans
Season with a mixture of
½ teaspoon salt
¼ teaspoon Accent
⅛ teaspoon pepper
Pour over top
3½ cups (1 No. 2½ can) cooked tomatoes, sieved
Cover and bake at 350°F 1½ to 2 hrs.
About 8 servings

Bar-X Sandwiches 3 3

For Bar-X Sauce—Thoroughly mix together
1¼ cups (10½ to 11-oz. can) condensed tomato soup
2 tablespoons lemon juice
2 tablespoons brown sugar
1 teaspoon prepared mustard
1 teaspoon Worcestershire sauce

For Meat Mixture—Heat in a skillet
2 tablespoons fat
Add and cook slowly over medium heat, occasionally moving and turning with a spoon, until transparent
½ cup (about 1 medium-size) chopped onion (page 12)
Add and cook over medium heat, breaking apart with spoon or fork into small pieces
1 lb. ground beef
and a mixture of
½ teaspoon Accent
¼ teaspoon salt
⅛ teaspoon pepper
When meat is browned, blend in the Bar-X Sauce. Simmer about 15 min.

Split into halves and toast
6 hamburger buns
Place two halves on each of six warm plates. Spoon meat mixture over them. If desired, top each serving with
3 or 4 onion rings (thinly sliced, peeled onion, separated into rings)
6 sandwiches

Drumsticks

Drumsticks

Best way to meet the ever-popular demand for drumsticks is to custom-make them at home.

Set out eight 6-in. wooden skewers and a large, heavy skillet.

Mix together lightly
- **2 lbs. ground beef**
- **½ cup (about 1 medium-size) finely chopped onion (page 12)**
- **2 teaspoons prepared mustard**
- **1 teaspoon Worcestershire sauce**
- **2 eggs, beaten**

and a mixture of
- **2 teaspoons salt**
- **1 teaspoon Accent**
- **Few grains pepper**

Divide meat mixture into 8 portions. Shape each portion around a skewer; roll in
- **1 cup (about 3 slices) fine, dry bread crumbs**

Heat in the skillet
- **6 tablespoons fat**

Place drumsticks in the skillet and cook over moderate heat, turning carefully to brown all sides. Reduce heat and continue to cook about 15 min., turning occasionally.

Serve on warm platter or plates. Garnish with **parsley.** *8 servings*

Pillow-shi-key

(Piroshki)

JESSIE J. WENNER, ABERDEEN, MD.

A Japanese version of a Russian recipe, submitted by a Maryland homemaker for the enjoyment of all.

Set out a large, heavy skillet. Two baking sheets will be needed.

Prepare, according to directions on package, dough from
- **1 pkg. prepared hot roll mix**

Set aside to rise while preparing filling.

Heat in the skillet over low heat
- **1 tablespoon butter or margarine**

Add and cook over medium heat until onion is transparent, stirring occasionally
- **½ cup (1 medium-size) finely chopped onion (page 12)**
- **1 clove garlic (page 12), minced; or crushed in garlic press**

Add and cook until meat just loses all pink color (do not brown or turnovers will be dry)
- **1 lb. lean ground round steak**

Blend in a mixture of
- **1 teaspoon salt**
- **½ teaspoon Accent**
- **¼ teaspoon pepper**

Set meat mixture aside.

Lightly grease 2 baking sheets.

Roll out dough ⅛ in. thick. Cut into 10 or 12 five-inch rounds, using a saucer or waxed paper pattern as a guide. Brush each with
- **Melted butter or margarine**

Place an equal amount of the meat mixture onto half of each round. Fold other half over and pinch ends together to seal. Place on greased baking sheet; set aside to rise (1 to 1½ hrs.).

Bake at 400°F about 20 min., or until turnovers are lightly browned.

Serve with **brown gravy** or with heated condensed **cream of mushroom soup** (undiluted) for gravy.   *5 or 6 servings*

Note: For variety, add to the filling mixture a small amount of **ketchup, prepared mustard, tomato sauce, pickle relish, prepared horseradish, brown gravy,** or **mushroom sauce** before shaping turnovers.

Mexican Medley Supper ⑤

MRS. R. C. HOOPER, SACRAMENTO, CALIF.

Set out a large, heavy skillet having a tight-fitting cover.

Mix together lightly

   1 lb. ground beef
   ½ cup quick-cooking rolled oats
   ⅔ cup milk
   1 teaspoon Worcestershire sauce

and a mixture of

   1 teaspoon salt
   ½ teaspoon Accent
   ⅛ teaspoon pepper

Shape meat mixture into 12 balls 1½ to 2 in. in diameter. Coat balls evenly by rolling in a mixture of

   ¼ cup flour
   2 teaspoons paprika

Heat in the skillet over medium heat

   2 tablespoons fat

Add meat balls and brown over medium heat. Shake pan frequently to obtain an even browning and to keep balls round. Add and continue cooking until onion is transparent, stirring occasionally

   ¼ cup finely chopped onion

Add to the skillet

   1 cup (8-oz. can) tomato sauce
   ½ cup water
   ¼ cup chopped green pepper
     (page 12)

Cover; simmer 20 min.

Meanwhile, drain contents of

   1 12-oz. can whole kernel corn

Blend corn into the sauce and cook about 5 min. longer, or until corn is heated thoroughly.

Serve hot.   *4 to 6 servings*

Supperette à la Pizza 6

MRS. NONA BLANK, LAKE WORTH, FLA.

Set out two baking sheets.

Heat in a skillet
1 to 2 tablespoons fat
Add and cook over medium heat until browned,
breaking into pieces with fork or spoon
½ lb. ground beef
Remove from heat and blend in
¾ cup (6-oz. can) tomato paste
and a mixture of
1¼ teaspoons oregano
¼ teaspoon garlic salt
¼ teaspoon salt
¼ teaspoon pepper
¼ teaspoon Accent
Set aside.

Set out
10 thin slices Mozzarella cheese
Ready-to-bake biscuits (1 8-oz.
container)
Pat biscuits into 4-in. rounds and place on
baking sheets. Top each with one slice mozzarella cheese. Top each cheese slice with
3 tablespoons of tomato-paste-meat mixture.

Sprinkle each biscuit generously with
Grated Parmesan cheese
Bake at 450°F 8 to 10 min., or until crust is
browned.   *5 servings*

Stuffed Cabbage Rolls

Stuffed Cabbage Rolls 7 4

Grease a shallow, 2-qt. top-of-range casserole
having a tight-fitting cover.

Remove and discard wilted outer leaves, rinse
and cut about one-half the core from
1 medium-size head (about 2 lbs.)
cabbage
Remove 8 large leaves. Shred enough of the
remaining cabbage to yield 2 cups. Spread
shredded cabbage in casserole. Add
1 bay leaf
1 clove garlic (page 12), uncut; (insert
wooden pick for easy removal)
Set casserole aside.

Pour boiling water into a large saucepan to
1-in. level. Add large cabbage leaves with
½ teaspoon salt
Cover and simmer 2 to 3 min., or until leaves
begin to soften; drain.

Meanwhile, heat in a large heavy skillet
2 to 3 tablespoons butter or margarine
Add and cook over medium heat, occasionally
moving pieces with a spoon, until onion is
transparent
1 cup finely chopped onion (page 12)
Remove from heat and mix in thoroughly
⅔ lb. ground beef (break into small
pieces with fork or spoon)
⅔ cup packaged precooked rice
¼ cup thick sour cream
½ teaspoon Worcestershire sauce
and a mixture of
¾ teaspoon salt
½ teaspoon Accent
⅛ teaspoon pepper
Place ¼ cup of the mixture in center of each
cabbage leaf. Roll each leaf, tucking ends in
toward center. Fasten securely with wooden
picks; place on shredded cabbage in casserole.
Pour over the rolls a mixture of
3½ cups (1 No. 2½ can) tomatoes,
sieved
½ teaspoon salt
¼ teaspoon Accent
Few grains pepper

Cover and simmer over low heat 45 to 60 min., or until tender when pierced with a fork.

About 10 min. before rolls are tender, pile lightly on the rolls

½ cup thick sour cream

Cover casserole and complete cooking.

Place rolls in warm serving dish. Remove bay leaf, garlic and wooden picks. Spoon sauce over rolls and serve with the shredded cabbage.

4 servings

Beef and Potato Scallop

MRS. F. B. JACKSON, ELDRED, PA.

Lightly grease a 2½-qt. casserole.

Grate and set aside

4 oz. Cheddar cheese (about 1 cup, grated)

Wash, pare, cut into cubes and set aside

4 medium-size potatoes (about 4 cups, cubed)

Prepare

2 cups Thin White Sauce (double recipe, page 323)

Cool slightly. Add ¾ cup of the grated cheese to the sauce all at one time, stirring until cheese is melted. Set aside to keep warm.

Mix together the potatoes and

1½ cups (about 4 oz.) dried beef, shredded

1½ tablespoons minced green pepper

1½ teaspoons minced onion

½ teaspoon celery salt

¼ teaspoon Accent

⅛ teaspoon pepper

Add the cheese sauce; blend thoroughly. Turn mixture into casserole and top with remaining grated cheese.

Bake at 350°F 1 hr., or until potatoes are tender when pierced with a fork.   *6 servings*

Meat-Crusted Corn Pie

Set out a 9-in. pie pan.

Heat in a large skillet over low heat

2 tablespoons butter or margarine

Add and cook until transparent, occasionally moving with a spoon

½ cup (about 1 medium-size) chopped onion (page 12)

Drain contents of

1 1-lb. can whole kernel corn (about 1¾ cups, drained)

Add to the skillet, blending with fork or spoon, the corn and

1¼ cups (10½- to 11-oz. can) condensed tomato soup

and a mixture of

1 teaspoon salt

½ teaspoon marjoram

¼ teaspoon chili powder

Simmer uncovered about 10 min., stirring occasionally.

Meanwhile, mix together lightly

¾ lb. ground beef

¼ lb. ground pork

½ cup uncooked brown granular wheat cereal

3 tablespoons minced onion

1 egg, beaten

½ cup milk

1 tablespoon Worcestershire sauce

and a mixture of

1 teaspoon salt

½ teaspoon Accent

⅛ teaspoon pepper

Turn into pie pan. Gently pat mixture to evenly cover bottom, sides and rim of pan. Pour corn mixture into shell.

Bake at 350°F 35 to 45 min.

Garnish with **green pepper rings.**

About 6 servings

Pot o' Dried Beef and Macaroni  10

Grease a shallow 1½-qt. casserole.

Set out
**1½ cups (about 4 oz.) drief beef,
    shredded**

Melt in a large skillet over low heat
2 tablespoons butter

Add 1 cup dried beef (reserve remaining ½ cup for topping) and
**1⅓ cups (two 6¾-oz. cans, drained)
    sliced mushrooms**

Cook over medium heat until edges of beef are curled and mushrooms are lightly browned, frequently moving and turning mixture with fork or spoon. Set skillet aside in a warm place while preparing sauce.

Grate
**6 oz. Cheddar cheese (about 1½ cups,
    grated)**

Prepare
**3 cups Medium White Sauce (3 times
    recipe, p. 323; use 1 cup cream
    for one-third of the liquid; omit salt)**

Cool sauce slightly. Add cheese to sauce all at one time, stirring until cheese is melted.

Cook and drain (*page 277*)
1½ cups shell macaroni

Reserve 1 cup sauce and 1 cup macaroni.

Mix remaining sauce and macaroni together. Turn into casserole. Top with the browned

Pot o' Dried Beef and Macaroni

mushrooms and dried beef. Arrange reserved macaroni over dried beef and pour reserved sauce over all. Tuck reserved dried beef into sauce to form an attractive pattern on top of casserole. Sprinkle with **paprika.**

Bake at 350°F 20 to 30 min., or until heated thoroughly.   *6 to 8 servings*

Dried Beef Wiggle 11
MRS. RUSSELL P. YEATON, VERONA, N. J.

Heat in a 2-qt. saucepan over low heat
¼ cup butter or margarine

Add
**½ cup finely chopped green pepper
    (page 12)**
2 tablespoons minced onion

Cook until onion is transparent, stirring occasionally. Add
**1½ cups (about 4 oz.) dried beef,
    shredded**

Cook over medium heat until edges of beef curl and beef is lightly browned, frequently moving and turning with fork or spoon.

Remove beef and vegetables with a slotted spoon. Set aside.

Using drippings in pan as part of the fat, prepare
**3 cups Medium White Sauce (three
    times recipe, page 323; omit salt)**

Return beef and vegetables to the thickened sauce. Add, stirring in
1 cup drained whole kernel corn
⅛ teaspoon pepper

Heat until corn is thoroughly heated. Serve over **toast,** in **patty shells** or in **Toast Cups** (*page 65*).   *About 6 servings*

Corned Beef Hash and Eggs

Grease a 1½-qt. casserole. Set out a small skillet.

Wash, pare and cook (*page 285*)

    2 large (about ¾ lb.) potatoes, cut into halves

Cook about 20 min., or until potatoes are tender when pierced with a fork. Drain. To dry potatoes, shake pan over low heat.

While potatoes are cooking, finely chop and set aside the contents of

    1 12-oz. can corned beef (about 2 cups, chopped)

Heat in the skillet over low heat

    3 tablespoons butter or margarine

Add and cook until transparent

    ¼ cup finely chopped onion

Meanwhile, finely chop the potatoes. Using a fork, mix the chopped corned beef, potatoes and onion with a mixture of

    ⅓ cup cream
    1 teaspoon salt
    ½ teaspoon Accent
    ¼ teaspoon pepper

Spoon hash into the casserole. Make four depressions in hash with back of spoon.

Break one at a time into a saucer or small dish

    4 eggs

Slip an egg into each depression in the hash. Sprinkle each egg with

    Few grains salt
    Few grains pepper

Bake at 325°F about 25 min., or until eggs are firm.
    4 to 6 servings

Corned Beef Hash with Tomato

Grease a 1½-qt. casserole.

Dice and set aside enough potatoes to yield

    1½ cups diced cooked potatoes

Finely dice or chop enough cooked corned beef to yield

    2½ cups chopped, cooked corned beef

Mix lightly with potatoes and set aside.

Heat in a large skillet over low heat

    3 tablespoons butter or margarine

Add and cook over medium heat until onion is transparent, stirring frequently

    ¼ cup finely chopped onion
    2 tablespoons finely chopped green pepper

Using a fork, stir into potato-corned-beef mixture the onion, green pepper and a mixture of

    ⅓ cup milk
    1 teaspoon salt
    ½ teaspoon Accent
    ¼ teaspoon pepper

Spoon mixture lightly into casserole.

Wash, remove stem ends and cut into ½-in. slices

    2 medium-size (about ½ lb.) tomatoes

Spread one side of each slice with

    Prepared mustard

Arrange slices on top of hash, mustard side down. Sprinkle with

    ½ cup buttered crumbs (*page 10*)
    ¼ teaspoon garlic salt

Bake at 350°F 30 to 35 min., or until crumbs are lightly browned.
    4 or 5 servings

▲ Barbecued Bologna Roll

Score with ½- to 1-in. cuts, 1 in. apart, side of
4 lb. roll of bologna
Secure roll on a shish kabob skewer. Spread with a mixture of
1½ tablespoons prepared mustard
1½ teaspoons brown sugar
1 teaspoon prepared horse-radish
Place directly on grill about 3 in. from coals (see OUTDOOR COOKING, *page 204*).

Baste well with a mixture of
1 cup chili sauce
3 tablespoons vinegar
Turning frequently, grill 15 to 20 min., or until roll is thoroughly heated and browned. Remove skewer and slice.   *16 servings*

Note: For variety, the bologna roll might be roasted on the lowest position of the spit or basted with your favorite **barbecue sauce.**

△ Barbecued Bologna Slices

Follow ▲ Recipe; omit scoring roll. Cut bologna roll into 1-in. slices. Double mustard mixture and spread on slices. Secure slices on shish kabob skewer to reshape roll. Grill.

Baked Luncheon Meat Favorites

Set out an 8x8x2-in. baking dish.

Grind (*page 107*) contents of
1 12-oz. can luncheon meat (1½ to 2 cups, ground)
Combine with meat and mix lightly
½ cup (½ slice) soft bread crumbs
¼ cup (about 1 oz.) finely chopped nuts
1 egg, beaten
and a mixture of
2 teaspoons brown sugar
1 teaspoon dry mustard
¼ teaspoon Accent
¼ teaspoon paprika
Set aside.

Drain, reserving sirup, contents of
1 9-oz. can sliced pineapple (4 slices pineapple)
Lay slices flat in bottom of baking dish.

Shape meat mixture into 4 patties the same size as pineapple slice. Put a patty on each pineapple slice.

Mix reserved pineapple sirup with
2 tablespoons lemon juice
2 tablespoons brown sugar
Spoon sirup mixture over patties.

Bake at 350°F 35 to 45 min. Baste patties with sirup three or four times during cooking.
4 servings

Beans and Franks

Set out a large, heavy skillet having a tight-fitting cover.

Cut into ¼-in. slices and set aside
3 frankfurters
Heat in the skillet over low heat
2 tablespoons butter or margarine
Add and cook until onion is transparent, occasionally moving and turning with a spoon, the sliced frankfurters and
½ cup (about 1 medium-size) chopped onion (page 12)
½ clove garlic (page 12), minced; or crushed in garlic press
Remove from heat and blend in a mixture of
1¼ cups (10½- to 11-oz. can) condensed tomato soup
1 tablespoon sugar
2 teaspoons prepared mustard
Add and stir in
3½ cups (No. 2½ can) lima beans
½ teaspoon Worcestershire sauce
Cover and heat over lowest heat 10 to 12 min., or until flavors are well blended.

Serve warm.   *6 servings*

Note: Two 12-oz. pkgs. **frozen lima beans**, cooked according to directions on package, may be substituted for canned lima beans.

Beans and Franks

Flavor-Rich Baked Beans ⑤

Grease 8 individual casseroles (or 1 bean pot or casserole) having tight-fitting covers.

Heat to boiling in a large, heavy saucepan
1½ qts. water
Meanwhile, sort and wash thoroughly
2⅓ cups (about 1 lb.) pea (navy) beans
Gradually add beans to water so that boiling will not stop. Reduce heat and simmer 2 min.; remove from heat. Set aside to soak 1 hr.

Cut into 1-in. chunks and set aside
½ lb. salt pork (with rind removed)
Add pork chunks to soaked beans with
½ cup chopped celery (*page 12*)
½ cup (about 1 medium-size) chopped onion (*page 12*)
1 teaspoon salt
¾ teaspoon Accent
Cover tightly and bring mixture to boiling over

high heat. Reduce heat and simmer 45 min., stirring once or twice. Drain beans, reserving liquid. Put an equal amount of beans and salt pork chunks into each casserole. Set aside.

Mix together in a saucepan 1 cup of the reserved bean liquid and
¼ cup ketchup
¼ cup molasses
2 tablespoons brown sugar
1 teaspoon dry mustard
½ teaspoon pepper
¼ teaspoon ginger
Bring to boiling. Pour an equal amount of the liquid mixture into each casserole.

Cover casseroles and bake at 300°F about 2½ hrs. If necessary, add more reserved bean liquid to beans during baking. Remove covers and bake ½ hr. longer.

Serve with **Boston Brown Bread.**   *8 servings*

Double-Quick Baked Beans ⑮

Grease 4 individual casseroles or a shallow 1-qt. baking dish.

Mix together
¼ cup ketchup
3 tablespoons minced onion
2 tablespoons molasses
2 tablespoons brown sugar
½ teaspoon salt
¼ teaspoon Accent
2 drops tabasco sauce
Blend thoroughly with
2 cups (1 1-lb. can) baked beans
Turn into the casseroles or baking dish. Cut crosswise into pieces
4 slices bacon (or use salt pork)
Put a few pieces on top of bean mixture in each casserole. (Or leave slices whole and arrange on top of beans in baking dish.)

Bake at 375°F 20 to 30 min., or until heated thoroughly.

Serve with **Boston Brown Bread.**   *4 servings*

Double-Quick Baked Beans

Fresh Vegetable Chow Mein 16

ETHELYN BEORGEON, OCONTO, WIS.

Set out a small skillet and a large, heavy skillet having a tight-fitting cover.

Wipe with a clean, damp cloth and cut into ¾-in. cubes

1¼ lbs. pork steak
1 lb. lean beef

Heat in the large skillet over low heat

2 tablespoons butter

Add the beef and pork and cook over medium heat until well browned, occasionally moving and turning pieces with fork or spoon.

Meanwhile, clean (*page 12*), separate into stalks and cut into thin strips 1-in. long

½ large bunch celery

Clean (*page 12*) and finely chop

3 medium-size onions

Drain contents of

1 8-oz. can bamboo shoots

Add the vegetables to the skillet with enough water to just cover meat and vegetables. Cover and cook over low heat until meat and vegetables are tender (about 40 min.).

Prepare, slice and set aside

2 Hard-Cooked Eggs (page 87)

Meanwhile, blend together until smooth

4 tablespoons soy sauce
2 tablespoons cornstarch
1 teaspoon Accent

Add slowly to cooking liquid while stirring constantly. Bring liquid to boiling; cook over low heat about 15 min. longer.

Spread in a shallow pan, contents of

1 can (about 3¾ oz.) Chinese noodles

Heat in 300°F oven about 10 min.

Drain and set aside contents of

1 8-oz. can water chestnuts

Clean (*page 12*) and cut into small pieces

1 medium-size green pepper

Rinse, remove and discard stem ends, peel and cut into thin slices

2 medium-size tomatoes

Add the chestnuts, green pepper and tomatoes to the hot mixture; cook 2 to 3 min. longer.

Melt in the small skillet over low heat

2 tablespoons butter

Add and cook until lightly browned, occasionally moving and turning pieces with fork or spoon

½ cup (4-oz. can, drained) mushrooms

Rinse and cut into thin slices

1 orange

Cut each slice in half and set aside.

Spread noodles over bottom of large serving platter. Cover with the pork-beef mixture; spoon the mushrooms over meat. Garnish top with the sliced hard-cooked eggs. Place the orange slices around edge of platter.

About 8 servings

China Boy 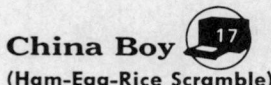 17
(Ham-Egg-Rice Scramble)
MRS. J. A. McCONNELL, PORTLAND, ORE.

Set out a 10-in. skillet and a heavy 2-qt. sauce-pan having a tight-fitting cover.

Bring to boiling in the saucepan
1¼ cups water
¼ teaspoon salt
Add gradually so boiling will not stop
½ cup rice
(The Rice Industry no longer considers it necessary to wash rice before cooking.) Reduce heat to very low. Blend in
1 tablespoon butter
Cover saucepan tightly and cook, without removing cover, about 25 min., or until all the water is absorbed and a rice kernel is entirely soft when pressed between fingers.

Meanwhile, grind enough cooked ham to yield
1½ cups ground cooked ham
Set ham aside.

Heat in the skillet over low heat
2 tablespoons butter
Add
¾ cup (about 1 large) chopped onion
Cook until onion is transparent, occasionally moving and turning with a spoon. Add ham and cook until ham is thoroughly heated, occasionally moving and turning mixture with fork or spoon. Remove from heat. Add all at one time and blend well
3 eggs, slightly beaten
Return skillet to heat. As soon as eggs are cooked (1 to 2 min.), remove mixture from heat. Add the cooked rice, blending in thoroughly.

Serve immediately.   *4 to 6 servings*

Hawaiian Supper  18
MRS. BILLIE L. OWENS, TOPEKA, KANS.

Set out a large, heavy skillet.

Prepare and set aside
2½ cups slivered cooked ham
⅓ cup chopped green pepper (page 12)
Heat in the skillet over medium heat
2 tablespoons fat
Add the ham and the green pepper. Cook until ham is lightly browned, occasionally moving and turning mixture with a spoon.

Meanwhile, drain, reserving sirup, and set aside the contents of
1 9-oz. can pineapple tidbits
Cook according to directions on package
1⅓ cups packaged precooked rice
Add to the water with the rice
⅛ teaspoon cloves
Set aside to keep warm.

Mix together thoroughly
2 tablespoons brown sugar
1½ tablespoons cornstarch
Blend in to form a smooth paste
1½ tablespoons vinegar
Add gradually, stirring to blend, the reserved pineapple sirup and
¾ cup water
1½ teaspoons prepared mustard
⅛ teaspoon pepper
Pour the cornstarch mixture into the skillet. Cook, stirring constantly, until the mixture thickens and is transparent. Stir in the tidbits and cook until heated thoroughly.

Using a fork, blend into the rice
2 tablespoons butter or margarine
Serve the ham mixture over the rice.

4 or 5 servings

Stuffed Peppers

Stuffed Peppers

Set out a shallow 2-qt. baking dish and a medium-size saucepan.

Rinse and cut into halves lengthwise
   4 large green peppers
Remove and discard stems, all white fiber and seeds; rinse cavities. Drop pepper halves into boiling salted water to cover and simmer 5 min. Remove peppers from water and invert. Set aside to drain.

Meanwhile, cook
   **½ cup packaged precooked rice
   (see directions on package)**
While rice is cooking, cut into small pieces and set aside enough cooked ham to yield
   2 cups cooked ham pieces
Cut into 8 slices and set aside
   ¼ lb. Cheddar cheese
Heat in the saucepan
   ½ cup butter or margarine
Add ham and toss lightly with a fork to blend. Blend in the rice and
   **2 tablespoons minced onion
   2 tablespoons finely chopped celery**
Mix together and blend in
   **¼ teaspoon dry mustard
   ¼ teaspoon garlic salt
   ¼ teaspoon Accent
   ⅛ teaspoon pepper**

Lightly fill pepper halves with ham-rice mixture, heaping slightly. Place one slice of cheese on top of each pepper. Place peppers in baking dish. Pour around peppers
   1½ cups tomato juice
Bake at 350°F about 20 min. Increase heat to 400°F and bake 10 min. longer, or until cheese is lightly browned.

Spoon the hot tomato juice over peppers.

4 servings

Crusty Croquettes

A deep saucepan or automatic deep fryer will be needed.

Prepare and set aside
   **2 cups finely chopped or ground
   cooked chicken**
Prepare
   1 cup Thick White Sauce (*page 323*)
Blend in
   **1 tablespoon finely chopped parsley
   1 tablespoon lemon juice
   ½ teaspoon onion juice**
and a mixture of
   **½ teaspoon salt
   ½ teaspoon Accent
   ¼ teaspoon celery salt**
Add the chicken and gently blend in. Chill mixture in refrigerator until firm.

Fill sauce pan with fat; heat to 375°F (*page 13*).

Shape the chilled chicken mixture into balls, cones or cylinders. Roll in
   1 cup (3 slices) fine, dry bread crumbs
Dip into a mixture of
   **1 egg, slightly beaten
   1 tablespoon milk**
Again coat in bread crumbs, shaking off loose crumbs. Deep-fry croquettes, turning often to brown evenly. Drain on absorbent paper.

Serve immediately. *6 servings*

Note: Finely chopped or ground cooked **meat**, or flaked cooked **fish** may be substituted for the chicken.

Chicken and Rice Ring

MRS. DAN CHRISTIE KINGMAN
ALBUQUERQUE, N. MEX.

Thoroughly grease a 2-qt. ring mold. Heat water for boiling water bath (*page 12*).

Prepare and set aside
1 cup Perfection Boiled Rice (one-third recipe, page 275)
Finely chop and set aside enough cooked chicken to yield
2 cups chopped cooked chicken
Prepare
2 cups Medium White Sauce (double recipe, page 323; substitute 1 cup Chicken Broth, page 205 or quick chicken broth, page 13, and 1 cup undiluted evaporated milk for milk)
Vigorously stir about 3 tablespoons of the hot sauce into
3 egg yolks, slightly beaten
Immediately blend into sauce. Mix into the sauce the chicken, rice and
2 tablespoons blanched, slivered almonds (page 11)
1 tablespoon chopped parsley
1 tablespoon lime juice
and a mixture of
½ teaspoon salt
½ teaspoon Accent
½ teaspoon paprika
⅛ teaspoon pepper
Turn mixture into the prepared mold.

Bake in boiling water bath at 350°F 45 to 50 min., or until a silver knife comes out clean when inserted halfway between center and edge of mold.

Remove mold from oven and set aside 5 min. before unmolding. Run tip of knife around top edge of mold and around center ring to loosen. Invert onto warm serving plate. Gently lift off pan. Garnish ring with
Blanched almond halves
Strips of pimiento
Serve hot with **Mushroom Sauce** (*page 323*).
4 to 6 servings

Ham Surprises 20

MRS. MARIE L. WINTON,
HADDONFIELD, N. J.

An interesting new way to use ground ham, and so easy to prepare, Ham Surprises are an ingenious top-of-the-range adaptation of ham loaf with a hidden layer of pineapple. Made in a jiffy, they keep the kitchen (and the cook) cool on days when it's too hot to light the oven.

Set out a large, heavy skillet.

Drain (reserving sirup) contents of
1 9-oz. can sliced pineapple (4 slices)
Meanwhile, grind (*page 107*) enough cooked ham to yield
3 cups ground cooked ham
Set ham aside.

Heat in the skillet over medium heat
2 tablespoons butter
Put pineapple slices into the skillet. Cook until golden brown; turning once. Set aside.

While the pineapple slices are browning, beat together reserved pineapple sirup (¼ to ⅓ cup) and
1 egg
Cut into small pieces and add to egg mixture
3 slices bread
Allow mixture to stand about 5 or 10 min. Lightly mix in the ground ham. Divide the mixture into 8 portions; shape into thin patties slightly larger than the pineapple slices. Lay patties aside on waxed paper.

Thoroughly coat pineapple slices on both sides by dipping them in
Brown sugar
Lay one slice on each of four ham patties and top each with one of the remaining patties. Press patties together, covering pineapple slices completely.

Using the skillet in which the pineapple slices were browned, cook the patties over medium heat until both sides are browned.

Serve on a warm platter and garnish with sprigs of **parsley**. *4 servings*

Pastry-Wrapped Fish Sticks

Lightly grease a baking sheet.

Thaw according to directions on package
> **1 10-oz. pkg. frozen breaded fish
> sticks**

Prepare
> **Cheese Pastry for 1-Crust Pie
> (page 442)**

Roll out pastry on lightly floured surface into
a rectangle approximately 12x9-in. Spread the
pastry with about
> **2½ teaspoons prepared mustard**

Cut pastry into 3-in. squares.

Place a fish stick diagonally on each pastry
square. Bring two points up over fish stick
and overlap on top. Press points firmly together. Arrange on baking sheet. Brush with
> **Melted butter or margarine**

Bake at 450°F 12 min., or until pastry is crisp
and golden brown.

Serve hot with **Zippy Cocktail Sauce** (*page
331*) or **Tartar Sauce** (*page 330*).

4 or 5 servings

Pastry-Wrapped Fish Sticks

Tuna Casserole 21

MRS. D. B. MERRILL, LONG BEACH, CALIF.

Lightly butter a 3-qt. casserole.

Grate and set aside
> **2 oz. Cheddar cheese (about ½ cup,
> grated)**

Cook, drain (*page 277*) and set aside
> **6 cups (about 8 oz.) noodles**

Meanwhile, heat in a small skillet
> **2 tablespoons butter or margarine**

Add and cook until onion is transparent, occasionally moving and turning mixture with a
spoon
> **½ cup (4-oz. can, drained) whole
> mushrooms**
> **¼ cup chopped green pepper (page 12)**
> **¼ cup chopped onion**

Combine in a large mixing bowl the drained
noodles and the cooked vegetables. Add one
half of the grated cheese and
> **½ lb. (about 1 cup) cottage cheese**
> **⅓ cup sherry**
> **¼ cup sliced pimiento**
> **½ teaspoon salt**
> **½ teaspoon Accent**
> **⅛ teaspoon pepper**

Mix together and add to the noodle mixture
> **1¼ cups (10½ to 11-oz. can) condensed
> cream of mushroom soup**
> **⅓ cup water**

Drain and flake (*page 12*) contents of
> **2 7-oz. cans tuna (about 2 cups, flaked)**

Blend into noodle mixture; turn into casserole.
Sprinkle top with remaining grated cheese.

Bake at 350°F about 40 min., or until casserole
is heated thoroughly. *About 8 servings*

Clam Sauce and Macaroni Shells with coffee

Sardine-Stuffed Eggs

Clam Sauce and Macaroni Shells

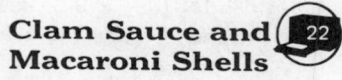

Cook and drain (*page 277*)
2 cups (8-oz. pkg.) macaroni shells
Meanwhile, prepare clam sauce.

Heat in skillet until garlic is lightly browned
¼ cup olive oil
1 clove garlic (*page 12*), sliced thin
Add slowly, stirring in
¼ cup water
Blend in
½ teaspoon chopped parsley
½ teaspoon salt
¼ teaspoon oregano
¼ teaspoon pepper
Add slowly and mix in
1 cup (8-oz. can) whole little neck clams with juice
Cook until clams are heated through. Pour sauce over drained macaroni shells; sprinkle with
1 tablespoon minced parsley
Serve hot.   *4 to 6 servings*

Sardine-Stuffed Eggs

Butter a 2-qt. casserole.

Prepare
6 Hard-Cooked Eggs (*page 87*)
Cut eggs into halves lengthwise; remove yolks. Mash yolks and add, in order, blending in
¼ cup softened butter or margarine
¼ cup mayonnaise
1 teaspoon prepared mustard
and a mixture of
½ teaspoon salt
⅛ teaspoon pepper
Few grains curry powder
Few grains cayenne pepper
Drain, mash and blend in contents of
2 3¼- to 4-oz. cans sardines
Fill egg whites with sardine mixture, rounding tops. Set aside.

Meanwhile, cook and drain (*page 277*)
3 cups (about 4 oz.) noodles
While noodles are cooking, prepare
2 cups Medium White Sauce (double recipe, *page 323*)
Place drained noodles in casserole. Arrange eggs on top of noodles. Pour sauce over all.

Bake at 325°F 15 to 20 min., or until thoroughly heated. Garnish with
Paprika
Serve with **Toast Points** (*page 65*).

6 servings

Tuna Salad Mold

Tuna Salad Mold

Set out a 1-qt. mold (fish-shaped, if desired). Set out a large bowl.

Pour into a small bowl
½ cup cold water
Sprinkle evenly over cold water
2 tablespoons (2 env.) unflavored gelatin
Let stand 5 min. to soften.

Meanwhile, heat until very hot
1 cup quick chicken broth (page 13)
Add softened gelatin, stirring until dissolved.

Grate and set aside
2 oz. Cheddar cheese (about ½ cup, grated)
Put into the large bowl
1 cup Mayonnaise (page 319)
Add gelatin mixture gradually, stirring constantly. Thoroughly blend in the cheese and
2 tablespoons lemon juice
1 tablespoon minced onion
½ teaspoon Worcestershire sauce
½ teaspoon Accent
⅛ teaspoon salt
⅛ teaspoon pepper
Chill (*page 12*) until mixture begins to gel (gets slightly thicker).

Lightly oil the mold with salad or cooking oil (not olive oil). Set aside to drain.

Meanwhile, blanch (*page 11*), sliver, toast (*page 12*) and set aside
½ cup (about 3 oz.) almonds
Slice and set aside enough olives to yield
½ cup sliced stuffed olives
Drain and flake (*page 12*) contents of
1 7-oz. can tuna (about 1 cup, flaked)
Gently fold the slivered almonds, sliced olives and flaked tuna into the thickened gelatin mixture, reserving one slice of olive if using a fish-shaped mold. Turn mixture into mold. Chill in refrigerator until firm.

Unmold (*page 12*) onto a chilled serving plate. If mold is fish-shaped, place reserved olive slice on "head" of fish for the "eye". Garnish with crisp **lettuce leaves**.   *About 8 servings*

Favorite Crab Meat Mold
MRS. WILLIAM HOWLAND
SOUTH DUXBURY, MASS.

Lightly oil a 1-qt. ring mold with salad or cooking oil (not olive oil). Set aside to drain.

Pour into a small cup or custard cup
¼ cup cold water
Sprinkle evenly over cold water
1 tablespoon (1 env.) unflavored gelatin
Let stand about 5 min. to soften.

Meanwhile, drain, remove and discard bony tissue and separate contents of
1 6½-oz. can crab meat (about 1 cup, drained)

Prepare and mix with the drained crab meat

½ cup chopped celery (page 12)
½ cup peeled, chopped cucumber
2 tablespoons minced parsley
2 tablespoons minced stuffed olives

Set crab meat mixture aside.

Put into a bowl

¾ cup Mayonnaise (page 319)

Dissolve gelatin completely by placing over very hot water. Stir the dissolved gelatin and add gradually, stirring constantly, to the Mayonnaise. Thoroughly blend in

1 tablespoon lemon juice

and a mixture of

½ teaspoon salt
½ teaspoon paprika
¼ teaspoon Accent

Blend into crab-meat mixture. Turn into the mold. Chill in refrigerator until firm.

Unmold (*page 12*) onto chilled serving plate. Serve with **mayonnaise.**   *About 8 servings*

Red 'n' White Salad Mold
MRS. W. P. BRILL, WOODSTOCK, VA.

Lightly oil a 3-qt. mold with salad or cooking oil (not olive oil). Set aside to drain.

For Cranberry Layer—Pour into a small cup or custard cup

¼ cup cold water

Sprinkle evenly over cold water

1 tablespoon (1 env.) unflavored gelatin

Let stand about 5 min. to soften.

Blend together in a large bowl

4 cups (2 1-lb. cans) whole cranberry sauce
1 cup (1 9-oz. can) crushed pineapple
½ cup (about 2 oz.) chopped walnuts

Dissolve gelatin completely by placing over very hot water. When gelatin is dissolved, stir it and blend into cranberry mixture. Turn mixture into the prepared mold. Chill (*page 12*) until gelatin mixture is slightly set.

Red 'n' White Salad Mold

For Chicken Layer—Set out

2 cups cubed cooked chicken
1 cup finely chopped celery (page 12)
¼ cup finely chopped parsley

Pour into a small cup or custard cup

¼ cup cold water

Sprinkle evenly over the water

1 tablespoon (1 env.) unflavored gelatin

Let stand about 5 min. to soften.

Blend together until smooth

1 cup Mayonnaise (page 319)
½ cup undiluted evaporated milk
1 teaspoon Accent
½ teaspoon salt
⅛ teaspoon pepper

Dissolve gelatin completely by placing over very hot water. When gelatin is dissolved, stir it and blend into the mayonnaise mixture. Fold in (*page 12*) the chicken, celery and parsley.

When first layer in mold is of proper consistency, immediately turn chicken mixture onto first layer. (Both layers should be of almost same consistency to avoid separation of layers when unmolded.) Place in refrigerator and chill until firm.

Unmold (*page 12*) onto chilled serving plate. If desired, serve with additional **mayonnaise.**
About 12 servings

267

Bewitching Salad

JANE JOHNSON, BRADFORD, PA.

A delightful salad, colorfully flecked with bits of green and sparked with the refreshing tang of ginger ale.

Set out a 1½-qt. mold.

Cut into cubes and set aside enough cooked chicken to yield

2 cups cubed, cooked chicken

Empty into a bowl

1 pkg. lemon-flavored gelatin

Add and stir until gelatin is completely dissolved

1 cup hot water

Blend in

1 cup ginger ale
1 tablespoon lemon juice

Put into a large bowl

1½ cups Mayonnaise (*page 319*)

Add the gelatin mixture gradually, stirring constantly. Chill (*page 12*) until mixture begins to gel (gets slightly thicker).

Meanwhile, lightly oil the mold with salad or cooking oil (not olive oil). Set aside to drain.

Prepare and set aside

½ cup (about 3 oz.) chopped, blanched almonds (*page 11*)
½ cup chopped celery (*page 12*)
½ cup halved and seeded Tokay grapes
¼ cup chopped green pepper (*page 12*)

When gelatin mixture is of desired consistency, blend in the chicken, almonds, celery, grapes and green pepper. Turn mixture into the prepared mold. Set in refrigerator to chill until firm.

Unmold (*page 12*) onto chilled serving plate. Garnish with crisp **salad greens.** Serve with **mayonnaise.** *About 8 servings*

Molded Ham Salad

CAROLYN E. STEPHENSON
WOLFE CITY, TEXAS

Set out a 1½-qt. ring mold.

Pour into a small bowl

½ cup cold water

Sprinkle evenly over cold water

2 tablespoons (2 env.) unflavored gelatin

Let stand about 5 min. to soften.

Put into a bowl and set aside

½ cup Mayonnaise (*page 319*)

Dissolve gelatin completely by placing over very hot water. Stir the dissolved gelatin and thoroughly blend into

1¼ cups (10½- to 11-oz. can) condensed tomato soup

Add gelatin-soup mixture gradually to Mayonnaise, stirring constantly. Chill (*page 12*) until mixture begins to gel (gets slightly thicker).

Meanwhile, prepare

2 Hard-Cooked Eggs (*page 87*)

Dice eggs and set them aside.

Lightly oil the mold with salad or cooking oil (not olive oil). Set aside to drain.

Prepare

2 cups diced cooked ham
½ cup (about 2 oz.) diced process American cheese

Beat together, blending until mixture is of medium consistency

3 oz. (1 pkg.) cream cheese
2 tablespoons lemon juice
1 tablespoon grated onion
2 teaspoons prepared mustard

When the gelatin mixture is about the same consistency as the cheese mixture, stir in several tablespoons of gelatin mixture. Continue to slowly add the gelatin mixture, beating constantly, until mixture is well blended. Mix in the ham, cheese and hard-cooked eggs. Turn into the prepared mold. Chill salad in refrigerator until firm.

Unmold (*page 12*) onto a chilled serving plate. Garnish with

Water cress

If desired, serve with **Cosmopolitan Dressing** (*page 319*).   *About 8 servings*

Swiss Cheese Pie

Flavorful Swiss cheese and bacon bits turn a custard pie into hearty main-dish fare.

Set out a large, heavy skillet and a double boiler.

Prepare (do not bake) and set in refrigerator to chill

Pastry for 1-Crust Pie (page 442; use 8-in. pie pan)

Finely grate and set aside

6 oz. Swiss cheese (about 1½ cups, grated)

Prepare (*page 161*)

8 slices Panbroiled Bacon

Crumble the bacon, toss with the grated cheese, and sprinkle evenly over the bottom of the pastry shell. Set pastry shell aside.

Scald (*page 13*)

1 cup cream
½ cup milk

Meanwhile, beat slightly

3 eggs

Swiss Cheese Pie

Beat into eggs to blend

½ teaspoon Worcestershire sauce
½ teaspoon salt
¼ teaspoon Accent
Few grains pepper
Few grains cayenne pepper

Stirring constantly, gradually add hot milk to egg mixture. Strain mixture into the pastry shell over the bacon and cheese.

Bake at 400°F 10 min. Reduce heat to 300°F and bake about 20 min. longer, or until a silver knife comes out clean when inserted between center and edge of pie.

6 to 8 servings

270

TABLE SETTINGS

Planning and preparing a fine dinner involves considerable time and effort on the part of the cook. The proper table setting not only displays culinary results to the best advantage, but adds to the enjoyment of the meal as well. The following guidelines are for a well-presented dinner table which is attractive and convenient for guests and hostess and/or host.

Evenly Space the place settings around the table, trying to allow 20 to 24 inches for each. **Dinner Napkins** are folded in an oblong, with the open corner at the lower right. Place napkins on the service plate or to the left of the forks. If plates are not on the table when guests are seated, have the napkins positioned in the center of each place setting, between the two sets of silver.

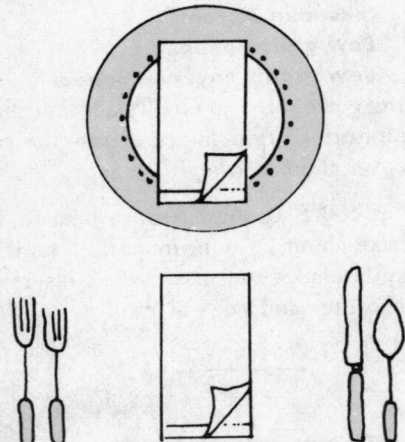

SILVER—Use a maximum of 3 pieces of silver on each side of a plate. Position silver about 1 inch from the table edge and in the order in which they will be used, from the outside in. **Forks**, except cocktail forks, are placed to the left of the plate.

If salad accompanies or follows the main course, place the salad fork to the right of the dinner fork. For informal meals, the dessert fork may be placed to the right of the salad fork.

If salad is the first course, place the dessert fork to the right of the dinner fork. When salad is served with the main course, you may omit a separate salad fork.

The dessert fork may also be placed directly on the plate when dessert is served. For a more formal service, just before serving dessert, place the fork to the right of each plate.

Knives—The dinner knife is placed to the right of the plate, with the cutting edge facing left. If no knife is necessary, you may omit it and place the forks to the right of the plate.

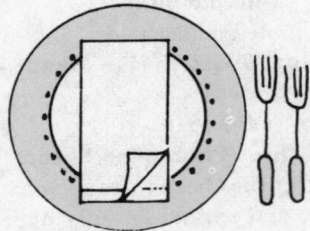

The bread-and-butter knife is positioned horizontally (handle at right) across the top of the bread-and-butter plate, or along its right edge.

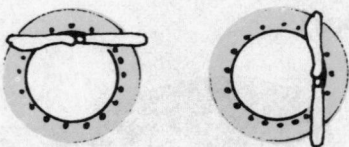

Spoons—Fruit and/or soup spoons are placed to the right of the knife.

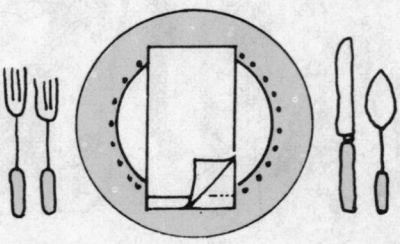

Tea and demitasse spoons should not be on the table during dinner. Instead, place each on a saucer along with the cup when coffee and tea are served. The spoon handle should be horizontal to the cup handle.

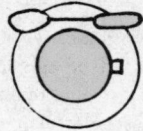

The dessert spoon, for informal settings, is placed to the right of the knife or on the dish when serving dessert. For a formal setting, set the spoon to the right of each place setting just before dessert is served.

CHINA AND GLASSWARE—A service plate (10 inches) is used for formal dining. It should be placed 1 inch from the edge of the table. Appetizer and soup courses are placed on top of the service plate which is then replaced by the dinner plate when the main course is served.
Bread-and-Butter Plate—Place at the tip of the fork. It is not used at formal dinners.
Salad Plate—If salad is served with the main course, it may be placed to either the right or left. If serving coffee with the main course, place the salad plate to the left.

Juice or Fruit—A first course of juice or fruit is set on a small plate and placed on the service plate.
Soup—For a first course of soup, set the soup cup, plate or bowl on a small plate placed on the service plate.
Water Glass or Goblet—Position at the tip of the knife. Fill three-fourths full just before announcing dinner.
Wine Glass—Place the wine glass, if any, to the right of the water glass. If two wines are being served with dinner, you may arrange glasses in a line or triangle, with the water goblet to the left of the wine glasses.

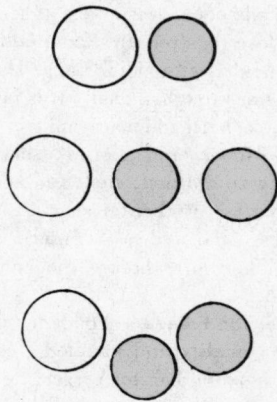

The Know-How of Freezing Casseroles

Add to your leisure hours and your family's enjoyment by making full use of your freezer. On the days when you feel like cooking, cook double or triple your usual amounts—part to be served immediately and the remainder to be frozen and served for future meals.

Freezing changes the texture of some foods. Since some strong flavors become undesirable you may prefer to add some seasonings at serving time. Salt tends to lose its strength. Some fats are likely to become rancid if stored too long. Hard-cooked egg white becomes tough. Usually it is best to omit rice, noodles, spaghetti and macaroni from casserole mixtures—just cook and add at serving time. Vegetables may be omitted; cook and add them to casserole mixtures just before serving. Crisp casserole toppings, such as bread crumbs, should be added 10 to 15 minutes before the end of oven-thawing period.

Preparation for the Freezer—Foods for the freezer must be of top quality and handled carefully but rapidly from shopping bag to freezer. Be sure that fruits and vegetables are carefully sorted and scrupulously cleaned—but never water-soaked. Use clean equipment. Cook meats and vegetables until barely tender to avoid mushy textures. Cool food rapidly by setting the pan containing the food in a larger pan of ice and water (stir occasionally to hasten cooling). When food is completely cooled, package and freeze.

Packaging for the Freezer—Packaging is all-important for proper freezing. Package food in quantities that will be used at a single meal; never refreeze a thawed food. Different shapes and types of foods require different containers and wrappings. Choose moisture-vapor-proof wrapping material and containers of correct size and shape. A tight seal is of utmost importance.

Pack solidly to force out air, leaving space at top of container for expansion of foods—about ½ inch in pint containers and about 1 inch in quarts.

Some mixtures may be layered in containers to hasten removal and thawing; divide layers of about 1 inch with double thicknesses of strong, pliable material.

Food may be frozen in a casserole if freezer space permits and if the kind of casserole used can be subjected to sudden, extreme temperature changes. Put cover over casserole of completely cooled food and tape-seal or wrap; freeze. When frozen, remove casserole from freezer and place over very low heat 1 or 2 minutes, or until contents loosen from casserole; slide onto a large piece or into a bag of moisture-vapor-proof material. Seal, label and freeze. When the vegetable is to be added to the casserole just before serving, package the frozen vegetable and casserole mixture first separately and then together so that the complete casserole dish is in one package.

Labeling for the Freezer—The freezer-storage life of combination or casserole dishes is short; use them within a few days or at the most, in a few weeks. Don't hoard—a rapid turnover of casserole freezer foods is freezer-wisdom and freezer-economy and indicates good freezer management.

Equip yourself with an efficient freezer pen, pencil or crayon. Write plainly on each package its contents, date of freezing and intended use. It is well, too, to keep a handy record near the freezer with the same information. Check off foods as they are used. Store systematically and conveniently.

Serving from the Freezer—Time needed for thawing frozen cooked foods varies with the food, thickness of frozen block and thawing method. Use the method which will least change appearance and texture. Foods to be thawed before heating or serving may be thawed at room temperature or in the food compartment of the refrigerator in their freezer containers. Foods that scorch easily are best when tightly covered and reheated from a frozen state in top of double boiler over simmering water or in the oven, stirring no more than necessary. Set freezer containers in warm water until contents loosen enough to be removed. Unwrap frozen mixtures which were first casserole frozen, and later removed from the casserole for storage. Grease the same top-of-range casserole; return mixture to it. Thaw over direct, low heat or in oven.

Correct freezer-to-table preparation is the last important step to quality freezer casseroles.

Delicious Cheese Dinner Casserole

Set out a 1½-qt. casserole and a baking sheet.

Prepare

Pastry for 1-Crust Pie (double recipe, *page 442*)

Shape two-thirds of the pastry into a ball; flatten and roll as directed. Fit into casserole. Flute (*page 12*). Prick bottom and sides with a fork. Set aside. Shape remaining pastry into a ball; flatten and roll to fit casserole top. Using a pastry wheel, cut evenly into three wedges. Place wedges on baking sheet; prick thoroughly with a fork.

Bake at 450°F about 10 min., or until light golden brown. Cool on cooling rack.

For Filling—While pastry is baking, cook (*page 285*) just until tender

1 cup cauliflower
½ cup sliced carrots
½ cup green beans

Meanwhile, dice and set aside

½ lb. bologna (about 2 cups, diced)

Clean (*page 12*), chop and set aside

1 medium-size onion

Heat in a large skillet over low heat

¼ cup butter or margarine

Add the bologna and onion. Cook over medium heat until onion is transparent, occasionally moving and turning mixture gently with a spoon. With a slotted spoon, lift bologna and onion from skillet to a bowl, allowing butter or margarine to drain back into skillet.

Measure the butter or margarine and add enough to yield ¼ cup melted butter or margarine. Pour into skillet and set over low heat.

Delicious Cheese Dinner Casserole

Blend in a mixture of

¼ cup flour
½ teaspoon salt
⅛ teaspoon pepper

Heat until mixture bubbles. Remove from heat. Add gradually while stirring constantly

2 cups milk
¼ teaspoon Worcestershire sauce

Return to heat and bring rapidly to boiling, stirring constantly; cook 1 to 2 min. longer. Remove from heat; cool slightly.

Meanwhile, grate

6 oz. Cheddar cheese (1½ cups, grated)

Add the cheese all at once to sauce. Stir rapidly until cheese is melted. Gently mix in bologna, onion, and vegetables. Turn into pastry shell; top with wedges.

Bake at 350°F 15 to 20 min., or until heated.

Garnish center with sprigs of **parsley.** Serve immediately.   *6 to 8 servings*

Pizza: Place the dough in the center of the pizza pan. Use fingers to spread dough on the bottom.

Spoon the sieved tomatoes over dough and arrange thin slices of Mozzarella cheese over the tomatoes.

Bake the pizza about 30 minutes or until the crust is golden brown and cheese is melted and bubbly.

▲ Italian Tomato-Cheese Pizza

Lightly grease two 15-in. round pizza pans, two large round griddles or two 15½x12-in. baking sheets.

Soften

    ¼ pkg. (½ teaspoon) active dry yeast

in

    2 tablespoons warm water, 110°F to 115°F (If using compressed yeast, soften ¼ cake in 2 tablespoons lukewarm water, 80°F to 85°F)

Let stand 5 to 10 min.

Meanwhile, pour into a large bowl

    ¾ cup warm water

Blend in

    2 cups sifted flour

Stir softened yeast and add, mixing well.

Measure

    2 to 2¼ cups sifted flour

Add about one-half the flour to yeast mixture and beat until very smooth. Mix in enough flour to make a soft dough. Turn onto a lightly floured surface. Allow to rest 5 to 10 min.

Knead (*page 43*). Form dough into a large ball and place it in a greased, deep bowl just large enough to allow dough to double. Turn dough to bring greased surface to top. Cover with waxed paper and towel and let stand in a warm place (about 80°F) until doubled.

Punch down with fist. Fold edges toward center and turn completely over in bowl. Cover and let rise again until almost doubled.

Again punch down dough. Divide into two equal portions and form into balls. Place one ball in center of each pizza pan. Push dough down in center with hand and spread to ⅛-in. thickness. Shape edge by pressing dough between thumb and forefinger to make ridge.

Set out

    6 oz. Mozzarella cheese, sliced thin

Force through a sieve

    3 cups canned tomatoes

Use one half of sieved tomatoes to cover the

dough on each pizza pan. Then top each with one half of the cheese. Sprinkle over each pizza, in order listed, one half of

- ½ cup olive oil
- ¼ cup grated Parmesan cheese
- 2 teaspoons salt
- ½ teaspoon pepper

Bake at 400°F 25 to 30 min., or until browned.

Cut into wedges. Serve hot.   *6 to 8 servings*

▲ Mushroom Pizza

Follow ▲ Recipe. Place on *each* pizza 1 cup (8-oz. can, drained) **button mushrooms.**

▲ Sausage Pizza

Follow ▲ Recipe. Place on *each* pizza 1 lb. hot **Italian sausage,** cut into ¼-in. pieces.

▲ Anchovy Pizza

Follow ▲ Recipe. Omit Mozzarella cheese and Parmesan cheese. Sprinkle ¼ teaspoon **oregano** over each pizza. Arrange on *each* 8 **anchovy fillets,** cut into ¼-in. pieces.

▲ Miniature Pizzas

Follow ▲ Recipe. Roll dough and cut into 3½-in. rounds with cookie cutter. Shape edges of rounds as in ▲ recipe. Top *each* pizza with 2 tablespoons canned **tomatoes,** sieved, and a slice of **Mozzarella cheese.** Sprinkle over cheese 1 teaspoon **olive oil,** ½ teaspoon grated **Parmesan cheese, salt, pepper** and **oregano.**

Bake at 400°F 15 to 20 min., or until crust is browned.   *About 24 miniature pizzas*

▲ English Muffin Pizza

Split 12 **English muffins** and spread cut sides with **butter** or **margarine.** Toast under the broiler until lightly browned. Top each half as for ▲ Recipe and bake at 400°F 5 to 8 min., or until tomato mixture is bubbling hot.

Perfection Boiled Rice

Bring to boiling in a deep saucepan

- 2 qts. water
- 1 tablespoon salt
- 1 teaspoon Accent

So boiling will not stop, add gradually

- 1 cup rice

(The Rice Industry no longer considers it necessary to wash rice before cooking.) Boil rapidly, uncovered, 15 to 20 min., or until a kernel of rice is entirely soft when pressed between fingers.

Drain rice in colander or sieve and rinse with hot water to remove loose starch. Cover colander and rice with a clean towel and set over hot water until rice kernels are dry and fluffy.   *About 3½ cups cooked rice*

Quick Cooking Rice

Cooked rice prepared from packaged pre-cooked rice may be substituted for Perfection Boiled Rice if directions on the package are followed carefully for amounts and timing.

Boiled Wild Rice

Bring to boiling in a deep saucepan

- 3 cups water
- 1 teaspoon salt

Meanwhile, wash in a colander or sieve

- 1 cup wild rice

Add rice gradually to water so boiling will not stop. Cook covered 30 to 40 min., or until a kernel of rice is tender when pressed between fingers; do not remove cover during this time.

If necessary, drain rice in a colander or sieve. If not used immediately, keep rice hot by placing colander over hot water and covering with a folded towel.   *About 3 cups rice*

Quick Rice Ring: Invert onto platter; lift off mold.

▲ Quick Rice Ring

One of the nicest things about a rice ring is the dressed-up look it gives to your table.

Lightly butter a 1-qt. ring mold.

Prepare
   Perfection Boiled Rice (p. 275)
Turn cooked rice into prepared mold, packing down gently with a spoon. Invert onto a warm serving platter and lift off mold. Sprinkle rice ring with
   Finely chopped parsley
Fill rice ring with buttered and seasoned cooked **vegetables** or any creamed mixture of **meat, fish** or **poultry.**   *A 1-qt. ring mold*

△ Individual Rice Rings

Lightly butter 4 individual ring molds. Divide rice into 4 equal portions and pack down gently into the molds. Proceed as in ▲ Recipe; omit parsley.

▲ Spanish Rice with Bacon 27

Grease a 2-qt. casserole having a cover.

Clean, slice (*page 12*) and set aside
   ½ lb. mushrooms
Dice and put into a heavy skillet
   4 slices bacon
Cook slowly, turning frequently. Pour off fat as it accumulates, and reserve. When bacon is evenly browned, drain on absorbent paper.

Return to skillet ¼ cup of the reserved fat. Add and cook over medium heat, stirring occasionally, the mushrooms and
   1 cup uncooked rice
   ½ cup (about 1 medium-size)
      chopped onion (page 12)
   ½ cup (about 1 medium-size)
      chopped green pepper (page 12)
(The Rice Industry no longer considers it necessary to wash rice before cooking.)

Cook until rice is lightly browned.

Add bacon to rice mixture with
   2½ cups (1 No. 2 can) tomatoes, cut
      in pieces
   1½ cups boiling water
and a mixture of
   1 teaspoon salt
   1 teaspoon paprika
   ½ teaspoon Accent
   ¼ teaspoon pepper
Turn into casserole; cover and bake at 350°F 50 to 60 min., or until rice is tender when a kernel is pressed between fingers. Remove cover for last 10 min. of baking period.
                              6 servings

△ Spanish Rice with Beef 28

Follow ▲ Recipe. Omit bacon. Brown ½ lb. **ground beef** with rice mixture.

Tomatoes Stuffed with Rice and Cheese

Butter an 8x8x2-in. baking dish.

For Filling—Prepare

2 cups Perfection Boiled Rice (two-thirds recipe, page 275)

Meanwhile, grate

2 oz. Cheddar cheese (about ½ cup, grated)

Mix 2 tablespoons grated cheese with

⅓ cup (about ½ slice) soft bread crumbs

2 tablespoons melted butter or margarine

Set prepared crumbs aside.

Heat in skillet

2 tablespoons butter or margarine

Add and cook until lightly browned

½ cup (4-oz. can, drained) sliced mushrooms

Stir remaining grated cheese and mushrooms into rice. Add

1 teaspoon Worcestershire sauce

For Tomatoes—Rinse

6 large, firm tomatoes

Cut a ¼-in. slice from top of each tomato. With a sharp knife, cut down around inside of tomatoes, about ¼ in. from edges, being careful not to cut through bottoms. With a spoon, scoop out center pulp. Sieve pulp and combine with rice mixture. Season each tomato with part of a mixture of

¾ teaspoon salt

½ teaspoon Accent

Lightly fill tomatoes with rice mixture, heaping slightly. Place in baking dish. Top with buttered crumb mixture.

Bake at 375°F 15 to 20 min. *6 servings*

▲ Macaroni

Heat to boiling in a large saucepan

3 qts. water

1 tablespoon salt

Add gradually

2 cups (8-oz. pkg.) uncooked macaroni (elbows, other shapes or tubes broken into 1- to 2-in. pieces)

Boil rapidly, uncovered, 10 to 15 min.

Test tenderness by pressing a piece against side of pan with fork or spoon. Drain macaroni by turning it into a colander or large sieve; rinse with hot water to remove loose starch. *About 4 cups cooked Macaroni*

⚠ Spaghetti

Follow ▲ Recipe. Substitute for the macaroni an equal amount of broken or unbroken **spaghetti**.

⚠ Noodles

Follow ▲ Recipe for the cooking of commercial or **Homemade Noodles** (*page 279*). Substitute 3 cups (about 4 oz.) **noodles** for macaroni. Boil 6 to 10 min., or until tender.

Deviled Ham and Macaroni Ring

Flavor-Filled Macaroni and Cheese

Deviled Ham and Macaroni Ring

Grease a 1½-qt. ring mold. Heat water for boiling water bath (*page 12*).

Cook, drain (*page 277*) and set aside
   2 cups (8 oz.) macaroni (elbows, other small shapes, or tubes broken into 1- to 2-in. pieces)
Meanwhile, grate and set aside
   4 oz. sharp Cheddar cheese (about 1 cup, grated)
Prepare and set aside
   1 cup chopped green pepper (*page 12*)
   ⅔ cup chopped onion (*page 12*)
   3 to 4 tablespoons minced parsley
Beat in a large bowl until well blended
   1 egg, well beaten
   1 cup milk
   ½ teaspoon prepared mustard
   ½ teaspoon salt
   ¼ teaspoon Accent
   ⅛ teaspoon pepper
Add the drained macaroni, grated cheese, green pepper, onion and parsley. Mix lightly until thoroughly blended.

Around bottom and sides of mold, spoon, at intervals, contents of
   2 2¼-oz. cans deviled ham
Turn macaroni mixture into ring mold.

Bake in boiling water bath at 350°F 50 to 60 min., or until mixture is set.

Shortly before macaroni ring is done, prepare
   Quick Tomato Sauce (*page 327*)
Remove ring from oven. Run a spatula around edge of mold and around center ring to loosen. Unmold onto a warm serving platter. Garnish as desired.   *About 6 servings*

▲ Flavor-Filled Macaroni and Cheese 33

Thoroughly grease a shallow, 2-qt. casserole.

Cook, drain (*page 277*) and set aside
   2 cups (8-oz. pkg.) macaroni (use small shapes or break tubes into 2-in. pieces)
Meanwhile, grate and set aside
   6 oz. Cheddar cheese (1½ cups, grated)
Prepare
   2 cups Thin White Sauce (double recipe, p. 323 ; mix ¼ teaspoon dry mustard and a dash of paprika with flour before blending into fat)
Cool sauce slightly.

Add grated cheese to sauce all at one time;

stir rapidly until cheese is melted. Blend in
   ⅓ cup minced onion
   ½ teaspoon Worcestershire sauce
   ¼ teaspoon Accent
Place one half of the macaroni in the casserole and cover with one half of the sauce; repeat.

Set out
   8 slices (½ lb.) Cheddar cheese
Rinse, remove stem ends and cut into slices
   3 medium-size (about 1 lb.) tomatoes
Alternate and overlap cheese and tomato slices in a border around top of macaroni. Lightly brush tomatoes with
   Melted butter or margarine
Bake at 350°F 25 to 30 min., or until cheese slices are softened.   *6 to 8 servings*

△ Bacon Bits Macaroni

Follow ▲ Recipe. Prepare **Panbroiled Bacon** (*page 161*) ; crumble and mix it with sauce.

Mostaccioli and Cheese

Set out an 8x8x2-in. baking dish.

Prepare
         Tomato Sauce (page 326)
Heat to boiling in large saucepan
   3 qts. water
   1 tablespoon salt
Gradually add
   2 cups (8-oz. pkg.) mostaccioli
Boil rapidly, uncovered, 12 to 15 min., or until mostaccioli is tender. Test tenderness by pressing a piece against side of pan with fork or spoon. Drain by turning into a colander or large sieve. Return drained mostaccioli to saucepan and mix with 2 tablespoons Tomato Sauce. Place one half of mostaccioli into baking dish. Add in layers
   1 cup diced Mozzarella cheese
   2 tablespoons grated Parmesan cheese
   ¼ teaspoon pepper
Cover with remaining mostaccioli. Cover with Tomato Sauce.

Bake at 350°F about 15 to 20 min., or until tomato sauce is bubbling.

Serve with remaining hot Tomato Sauce. Sprinkle with
      Grated Parmesan or Romano cheese
                              4 to 6 servings

Homemade Noodles

Sift together into a bowl
   1 cup sifted flour
   ½ teaspoon salt
Make a well in center of flour and add
   1 egg, slightly beaten
While blending ingredients, add gradually
   1 to 2 tablespoons water or milk
Dough should be stiff. Turn dough out onto a lightly floured surface. Shape into a ball and knead (*page 43*). Cover and let rest 5 min.

Roll dough on lightly floured surface ⅛ in. thick. If dough sticks, loosen from surface with knife or spatula; sprinkle flour underneath. Turn dough over and roll until paper thin. Allow dough to partially dry (about 1 hr.)

Cut dough into lengthwise strips, 2½ in. wide, and stack on top of each other. Slice into short strips ⅟₁₆ to ⅛ in. wide. Separate noodles and allow to dry thoroughly. (Noodles can be stored in a tightly covered container.)

To cook, see **Noodles** (*page 277*).
                           About ⅓ lb. noodles

Homemade Noodles: Cut partially dried dough into strips; stack the strips, slice and spread to dry.

Spätzle 35
(Drop Noodles)
(*See photo on page 201*)

Bring to boiling in a 3- or 4-qt. saucepan
> **2 qts. water**
> **2 teaspoons salt**

Meanwhile, sift together and set aside
> **2⅓ cups sifted flour**
> **1 teaspoon salt**

Combine in a bowl and mix together
> **1 egg, slightly beaten**
> **1 cup water**

Gradually add flour mixture to egg mixture, stirring until smooth. (Batter should be very thick and break from spoon instead of pouring in a continuous stream.) Spoon batter into the boiling water by ½ teaspoonfuls, dipping spoon into water each time. Cook only one layer of noodles at one time; do not crowd.

After noodles rise to the surface, boil gently 5 to 8 min., or until tender when pressed against side of pan with spoon. Remove from water with slotted spoon, draining over water for a few seconds, and put into a warm bowl.

Toss noodles lightly with
> **¼ cup butter or margarine, melted**

Serve with **Veal Paprika** (*p.166*) ⬛, **Chicken Paprika** (*p. 201*)⬛, or as a substitute for noodles. *4 to 6 servings*

Cheese-Noodle Dish 36
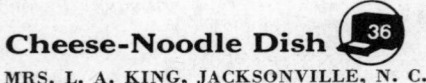
MRS. L. A. KING, JACKSONVILLE, N. C.

Butter a 3-qt. casserole.

Cook and drain (*page 277*)
> **6 cups (8 oz.) fine noodles**

While noodles are cooking, dice and put into a small skillet
> **4 slices bacon**

Cook until browned. With slotted spoon remove bacon bits to a small dish. Add to drippings in the skillet
> **½ cup chopped onion (*page 12*)**

Cook until onion is golden yellow.

Drain, reserving liquid for use in other food preparation, contents of
> **1 No. 2½ can tomatoes**

Sieve tomatoes; mix together the tomatoes, drained noodles, bacon, onion and
> **1 lb. ground cooked pork**

and a mixture of
> **1 teaspoon salt**
> **½ teaspoon Accent**
> **¼ teaspoon pepper**

Turn mixture into casserole. Place over top
> **8 slices (8 oz.) Cheddar cheese**

Bake at 350°F 30 to 40 min., or until casserole is heated through and cheese is melted.
About 8 servings

Noodle Ring
with Crab Meat Sauce
MRS. B. STRYKER, EAST CORINTH, VT.

Butter a 1½-qt. mold.

Cook and drain (*page 277*)
> **4½ cups (about 6 oz.) noodles**

Meanwhile, grate and set aside
> **4 oz. Cheddar cheese (about 1 cup, grated)**

Beat until thick and piled softly
> **4 eggs**

Blend in
> **2 cups milk**

Add and mix in the noodles and cheese. Turn mixture into the mold. Bake at 300°F 50 min., or until mixture is set.

Meanwhile, prepare
> **2 cups Medium White Sauce (double recipe, *page 323*; add ¼ teaspoon dry mustard with the seasonings)**

Add and blend thoroughly
> **1¼ cups (10½ to 11-oz. can) condensed tomato soup**
> **2 tablespoons ketchup or chili sauce**
> **2 teaspoons Worcestershire sauce**

Add and mix in
> **1 cup crab meat (6½-oz. can, drained and bony tissue removed)**

Heat just until crab meat is thoroughly heated.

Remove from heat and stir in

2 tablespoons lemon juice

Run a spatula around edge of mold and around center ring to loosen. Cover with a warm serving plate; invert and remove mold. Fill center of ring with crab meat sauce; accompany with remaining sauce.   *About 8 servings*

Lasagne

Lasagne

Allow about 4½ hrs. for preparing sauce.

For Tomato Meat Sauce—Heat in a large sauce pot having a tight-fitting cover

¼ cup olive oil

Add and cook over medium heat until lightly browned, occasionally moving with spoon

½ cup (about 1 medium-size) chopped onion (page 12)

Wipe with a clean, damp cloth, add and brown, turning occasionally

½ lb. boneless beef (chuck or rump)
½ lb. boneless pork shoulder

Add slowly a mixture of

7 cups (two No. 2½ cans) tomatoes, sieved
1 tablespoon salt
1 bay leaf

Cover sauce pot and simmer about 2½ hrs.

Blend in

¾ cup (6-oz. can) tomato paste

Simmer uncovered over very low heat, stirring occasionally, about 2 hrs., or until thickened. If sauce becomes too thick, add

½ cup hot water

Remove meat and bay leaf from sauce.

For Lasagne—Set out an 8x8x2-in. baking dish and a heavy skillet.

When sauce is partially done, heat to boiling in a large saucepan

6 qts. water
2 tablespoons salt
1 tablespoon olive oil

Gradually add

1 lb. lasagne noodles

Boil rapidly, uncovered, about 15 min., or until tender. Test tenderness by pressing a piece against side of pan with fork or spoon.

Heat in the skillet

3 tablespoons olive oil

Add and cook until browned, breaking into small pieces with fork or spoon

1 lb. ground beef

Meanwhile, prepare

2 Hard Cooked Eggs (page 87)

Drain noodles by turning into a colander or large sieve.

Pour one-half cup of the sauce into the baking dish. Top with a layer of noodles (about one third of the noodles) and one half of

¾ lb. Mozzarella cheese, sliced

Then add one half of the browned ground beef and one hard-cooked egg, sliced. Sprinkle with one half of

¼ cup grated Parmesan cheese
½ teaspoon pepper

Top with one half of

1 cup ricotta cheese

Repeat layering. Top ricotta cheese with ½ cup sauce. Arrange over this remaining lasagne noodles. Top with more sauce.

Bake at 350°F about 30 min., or until mixture is bubbling. Let stand 5 to 10 min. to set.

Cut into 2-in. squares and serve topped with remaining sauce.   *6 to 8 servings*

▲ Ravioli

Prepare (allowing about 4½ hrs.) and set aside
Tomato Meat Sauce (page 281)
Heat in a skillet
2 tablespoons olive oil
Add, and cook until browned, breaking into small pieces with fork or spoon
¾ lb. ground beef
Meanwhile, prepare and cook (*page 285*)
½ lb. spinach
Drain well. Mix spinach and ground beef. Add and mix well
2 eggs, well beaten
and a mixture of
1 tablespoon grated Parmesan cheese
¾ teaspoon salt
½ teaspoon Accent
¼ teaspoon pepper
Set aside.

Sift together into a large bowl
4 cups sifted flour
1½ teaspoons salt
Make a well in center of flour. Add, one at a time, mixing slightly after each addition
4 eggs
Add gradually about
6 tablespoons cold water
Mix well to make a stiff dough. Turn onto a lightly floured surface and knead (*page 43*).

Divide dough into fourths. Lightly roll each fourth into a rectangle ⅛ in. thick. Cut dough lengthwise with pastry cutter into strips 5 in. wide. Place 2 teaspoons filling 1½ in. from narrow end in center of each strip. Continuing along the strip, place 2 teaspoons filling 3½ in. apart. Fold each strip in half lengthwise, covering the mounds of filling. To seal, press the edges together with tines of fork. Press gently between mounds to form rectangles about 3½ in. long. Cut apart with pastry cutter and press out edges of rectangles with tines of fork to seal.

Bring to boiling in a large saucepan
7 qts. water
2 tablespoons salt
Gradually add the ravioli (cook about one half the ravioli at one time). Boil rapidly uncovered about 20 min., or until tender. Test tenderness by pressing a piece against side of pan with fork or spoon. Remove with slotted spoon. To drain, hold spoon on folded paper napkin a few seconds.

Place ravioli on a warm platter and top with the sauce. Sprinkle with
Grated Parmesan or Romano cheese
About 3 doz. Ravioli

△ Ravioli with Ricotta Filling

Follow ▲ Recipe. Substitute 3 cups (about 1½ lbs.) **ricotta cheese** for the ground beef. Omit oil and spinach. Add 1½ tablespoons chopped **parsley.**

American-Style Polenta
MRS. J. W. FOX, MONUMENT, COLO.

Lightly grease two 8½x4½x2½-in. loaf pans.

Bring to boiling in a 2-qt. saucepan
2 cups water
1 teaspoon salt
Add gradually, stirring constantly, a mixture of
1 cup yellow corn meal
1 cup cold water
Continue boiling, stirring constantly, until mixture is thickened. Cover, lower heat, and cook slowly 10 min., or until mushy. Pour into pans. Set aside to cool and become firm.

Prepare
Cheese Sauce (page 323; increase cheese to 2 cups)
Set over simmering water if necessary to melt the cheese. Cover and set aside.

Drain contents of

1 No. 2½ can tomatoes

Reserve liquid for use in other food preparation. Sieve the tomatoes. Mix together with

½ cup chopped celery (*page 12*)
½ cup finely chopped onion (*page 12*)
1 clove garlic (*page 12*)**, minced;
    or crushed in a garlic press**
1 teaspoon Accent
½ teaspoon salt

Set vegetable mixture aside.

Heat in a large, heavy skillet over medium heat

2 tablespoons fat

Add

1 lb. ground beef

Cook over medium heat until meat is grey in color, breaking into pieces with fork or spoon. Pour off any excess fat. Sprinkle over meat.

½ teaspoon Accent

Add the vegetable mixture and continue cooking until meat is lightly browned.

Set out a 3-qt. rectangular casserole.

Cut corn meal into 1-in. squares. Line bottom of casserole with one-half the corn meal. Top with one-half the vegetable-meat mixture, and one-half the Cheese Sauce; repeat.

Bake at 350°F 45 min., or until polenta is heated and Cheese Sauce is lightly browned.

About 8 servings

Vegetable Scrapple

Lightly grease a 9½x5¼x2¾-in. loaf pan.

Prepare and set aside

**½ cup (about 1 medium-size) finely
    chopped onion** (*page 12*)
**⅓ cup (about 1 medium-size) finely
    chopped carrot**
¼ cup finely chopped green pepper
    (*page 12*)

Vegetable Scrapple

Place in top of double boiler

3½ cups boiling water

Add slowly, stirring constantly until thickened, a mixture of

1¼ cups yellow corn meal
1 tablespoon salt
⅛ teaspoon pepper

Cook until thickened, stirring constantly. Add the chopped vegetables and

2 tablespoons finely chopped pimiento
1 teaspoon Accent

Place over simmering water and cook 1 hr.

Meanwhile, chop coarsely

1 cup (about 5 oz.) peanuts

Stir peanuts into cooked corn-meal mixture. Pour into the pan, spreading to edges. Chill in refrigerator 3½ to 4 hrs.

Cut chilled scrapple into slices 1 in. thick.

Heat in a skillet over medium heat

2 tablespoons fat

Arrange slices of vegetable scrapple in skillet. Cook at one time only as many slices as will lie flat in skillet. When lightly browned on one side, turn and brown other side.

Serve warm. *6 to 8 servings*

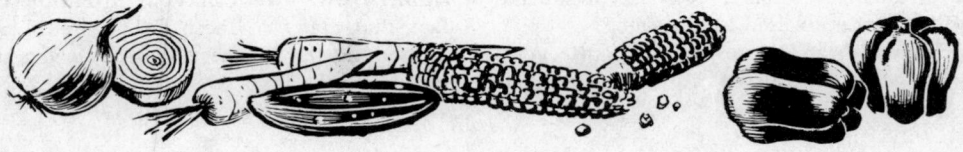

LUNCHEON and SUPPER DISHES in the MICROWAVE OVEN

Using the microwave oven makes this collection of recipes among the most convenient to prepare and the most useful you will have available. The casseroles are quick and easy to assemble, usually in one dish, and some can be cooked in as little as 5 minutes.

That's not all. Most of them can be easily frozen and reheated. (Follow manufacturer's directions for defrosting in your microwave oven.) They are good recipes to make doubles of, earmarking one for a lunch or supper and the other for the freezer.

We have omitted some recipes which we felt did not come up to our standards when cooked in the microwave oven. These include dishes calling for hearty tomato sauces—they simply do not develop the necessary richness.

Pie crusts are also tricky. They really do not brown properly and tend to cook more slowly than the fillings. However, the **Supperette à la Pizza** included here has a good flavor and the colorless crust is covered by the sauce.

Incidentally, an interesting and quite good dish is the **Meat-Crusted Corn Pie.** Also in that category is the recipe for **Drumsticks.** Try them.

Sauces—Particularly gratifying are the casseroles with cream or cheese sauces. They never curdle, separate or burn and the texture is smooth and creamy if directions for stirring are followed. In this group are **Beef and Potato Scallop, Tuna Casserole** and **Pot o' Dried Beef and Macaroni.**

Noodles and Pasta—For recipes which require noodles or pasta, you may find the stove more convenient. However, results from the microwave oven are excellent and we have included instructions for the microwave cooking of these foods. Most of the cooking time goes to boiling the water, so we have reduced the amounts of water to a minimum. We also specify the size of the pasta because cooking times will vary between a thin, linguini-type spaghetti and a thicker variety of spaghetti.

REMINDERS—We call your attention to the fact that many of these dishes should not be greased. Refer to the directions given in the specific recipe.

Remember also that cooking times do vary depending upon the oven and your personal taste. Don't hesitate to check as the dish approaches doneness.

Some casseroles must be covered and stand after cooking in the microwave oven in order to blend the flavors. The necessary times are noted with each recipe where required.

See the introductory chapter, **Home Cooking in the Microwave Oven**, in the beginning of this book for additional tips and an easy-to-read chart comparing settings among different brands of ovens.

Chili con Carne *(page 250)*

Use a 3-qt. covered casserole.

Put fat in casserole and COOK until melted (about 3 min.). Add onion and COOK until onion is transparent (about 5 min.).

Add beef and COOK just enough to break into pieces (about 3 min.).

Add remaining ingredients. Cover and COOK to simmer (about 5 min.). SLOWCOOK, stirring every 5 min., until beef is done and flavors are well blended (about 20 min.).

Cover and let stand 10 min.
OVERALL COOKING TIME: 33:00

Shipwreck *(page 251)*

Use a 3-qt. covered casserole.

Assemble casserole as in Recipe. Cover and COOK to heat through (about 10 min.). SLOWCOOK, rotating pan every 5 min., until meat is tender and flavors blended (about 20 min.).

Cover and let stand 10 min.
OVERALL COOKING TIME: 30:00

Bar-X Sandwiches 3
(page 251)

Use a browning skillet.

Preheat skillet (about 3 min.). Add fat and COOK to heat. Add onion and COOK until transparent (about 3 min.).

Add meat and spices and COOK to brown, stirring after 2½ min. (about 5 min.).

Add sauce, cover and SLOWCOOK, stirring every 5 min., until meat is done and flavors are blended (about 10 min.).

Cover and let stand 10 min.
OVERALL COOKING TIME: 21:00

Drumsticks *(page 252)* 4

Use a browning skillet. The times in this recipe are for cooking 2 batches of 4 drumsticks each.

Place fat in skillet and COOK to heat (about 4 min.). Add 4 drumsticks and COOK to brown on all sides (about 5 min. each side). Brown remaining drumsticks.

Transfer all drumsticks to baking dish, cover and let stand 10 min.
OVERALL COOKING TIME: 24:00

Mexican Medley Supper 5
(page 253)

Use a browning skillet.

Place fat in skillet and COOK to heat (about 3 min.). Add meat balls and COOK, stirring every 1½ min., until brown (about 10 min.).

Add onion and COOK, stirring every 1 min., until transparent (about 1½ min.).

Add sauce ingredients to skillet, except use only ¼ cup water (instead of ½ cup). Cover and

COOK until pepper wilts and mixture is thoroughly heated (about 3 min.).

Add corn. COOK to heat through (about 2 min.).

Cover and let stand 10 min.
OVERALL COOKING TIME: 19:30

Supperette à la Pizza 6
(page 254)

Use a browning skillet.

Put fat in skillet and COOK to heat (about 3 min.). Add meat and COOK, stirring every 2 min., until brown (about 5 min.).

Assemble biscuits, being sure to cover biscuits complete with the topping. COOK, rotating pan every 5 min., until crust is firm and can be lifted with a fork (about 11 min.).

Cover and let stand 5 min.
OVERALL COOKING TIME: 19:00

Stuffed Cabbage Rolls 7
(page 254)

Use a 3-qt. covered casserole. *Do not grease.*

Assemble cabbage rolls as in Recipe, except use only ½ bay leaf (instead of 1 bay leaf).

Cover and COOK to raise temperature (about 10 min.). SLOWCOOK, rotating pan every 5 min., until tender (about 15 min.).

Pile on sour cream, cover and let stand 15 min. Sour cream will heat during standing time.
OVERALL COOKING TIME: 25:00

Beef and Potato Scallop 8
(page 255)

Use a 3-qt. covered casserole. *Do not grease.*

Assemble casserole as in Recipe, cover and COOK to raise temperature (about 5 min.). SLOWCOOK, rotating pan every 5 min., until potatoes are tender (about 25 min.).

Cover and let stand 10 min.
OVERALL COOKING TIME: 30:00

Meat-Crusted Corn Pie 9
(page 255)

Use a browning skillet and a pie plate.

Put butter or margarine in skillet and COOK to heat (about 3 min.). Add onion and COOK, stirring every 1½ min., until transparent (about 3 min.).

Add corn, tomato soup, salt, marjoram and chili powder. COOK, stirring every 5 min., until simmering (about 8 min.).

Assemble pie. COOK to heat through (about 10 min.). SLOWCOOK, rotating pan every 5 min., until "crust" starts to pull away from pan sides (about 15 min.).

Cover and let stand 10 min.
OVERALL COOKING TIME: 39:00

Pot o' Dried Beef and Macaroni 10 *(page 256)*

Use a browning skillet and a 1½-qt. casserole. *Do not grease.*

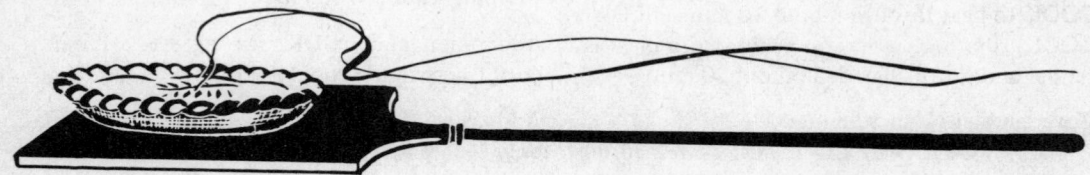

Put butter in skillet and COOK until melted (about 3 min.). Add dried beef and mushrooms and COOK, stirring every 1 min., until beef edges curl and mushrooms are brown (about 5 min.).

Assemble casserole. COOK, rotating pan every 3 min., to heat thoroughly (cheese will bubble) (about 10 min.).

Cover and let stand 10 min.

Dried Beef Wiggle **11**
(page 256)

Use a 2-qt. casserole.

Put butter or margarine in casserole and COOK until melted (about 3 min.). Add onion and pepper and COOK, stirring every 1½ min., until onion is transparent (about 3 min.).

Add dried beef. COOK, stirring every 1 min., until edges curl (about 5 min.).

Assemble mixture as in Recipe. COOK, uncovered, until thoroughly heated and bubbling (about 5 min.).

Cover and let stand 10 min.

Corned Beef Hash **12**
with Tomato *(page 257)*

Use a 1½-qt. casserole. *Do not grease.*

Put butter or margarine in casserole and COOK until melted (about 3 min.). Add onion and pepper and COOK, stirring every 1½ min., until transparent (about 3 min.).

Assemble casserole. COOK uncovered, rotating pan after 3½ min., until heated thoroughly (about 7 min.).

Cover and let stand 10 min.
OVERALL COOKING TIME: 12:00

Baked Luncheon Meat **13**
Favorites *(page 258)*

Use a baking dish.

Assemble patties. COOK, basting and rotating pan every 3 min., until patties are firm (about 15 min.).

Cover and let stand 10 min.
OVERALL COOKING TIME: 15:00

Beans and Franks *(page 258)* **14**

Use a browning skillet with cover.

Put butter or margarine in skillet and COOK until melted (about 3 min.). Add frankfurters, onion, and garlic and COOK, stirring mixture and rotating pan every 2 min., until onions are transparent (about 4 min.).

Add remaining ingredients, cover and SLOW-COOK to heat thoroughly (about 3 min.).

Cover and let stand 10 min.
OVERALL COOKING TIME: 7:00

Double-Quick Baked **15**
Beans *(page 259)*

Use a shallow baking dish. *Do not grease.*

Assemble casserole, cutting bacon into small pieces. COOK until thoroughly heated (about 10 min.).

Cover and let stand 10 min.
OVERALL COOKING TIME: 10:00

Fresh Vegetable Chow Mein *(page 260)* **16**

Use a browning skillet and a covered casserole or baking dish.

Put butter in skillet and COOK to heat (about 3 min.). Add meat and COOK, stirring every 3 min., until brown (about 10 min.).

Add vegetables and water. Cover and COOK until celery is tender and pork is almost done (about 10 min.).

Add soy sauce mixture, stirring well. Continue to COOK, covered, stirring every 1½ min., until simmering (about 5 min.). Check to be sure the pork is thoroughly cooked. Transfer to casserole and cover.

Add water chestnuts, pepper and tomatoes, cover and COOK until pepper is wilted (about 1½ min.).

In skillet, COOK butter or margarine until melted. Add mushrooms and COOK until lightly browned (about 2 min.).

Spread noodles on paper towelling and COOK to heat (about 3 min.). Assemble casserole.

Cover and let stand 10 min.

OVERALL COOKING TIME: 34:30

China Boy *(page 261)* **17**

Use a browning skillet and a 2-qt. covered casserole.

For rice, put water in casserole and COOK until boiling (about 4 min.). Add rice and butter and COOK until rice is soft (about 5 min.). Set aside.

Put butter in skillet and COOK until melted (about 3 min.). Add onion and COOK, stirring every 1½ min, until transparent (about 3 min.).

Add ham and COOK until heated (about 2½ min.).

Add eggs, stirring, and COOK until eggs are set (about 30 sec.). Stir.

Add rice and mix thoroughly.

Cover and let stand 10 min.

OVERALL COOKING TIME: 13:00

Hawaiian Supper *(page 261)*  **18**

Use a browning skillet.

Put fat in skillet and COOK until melted (about 3 min.). Add ham and green pepper and COOK until ham is browned (about 3 min.).

Pour cornstarch mixture into skillet, stirring thoroughly. COOK, stirring every 30 sec., until mixture thickens (about 2 min.).

Add pineapple tidbits and COOK until heated (about 2 min.).

Cover and let stand 10 min.

Serve as in Recipe.

OVERALL COOKING TIME: 7:00

Stuffed Peppers *(page 262)* **19**

Use a baking dish with cover, or you may use plastic wrap.

Assemble peppers. COOK to heat thoroughly (about 5 min.). SLOWCOOK, rotating dish and basting every 3 min., until cheese is melted and filling is set (about 9 min.).

Cover and let stand 10 min.

OVERALL COOKING TIME: 14:00

Ham Surprises *(page 263)* **20**

Use a browning skillet.

COOK butter until melted (about 3 min.). Add pineapple slices and COOK until very lightly browned on both sides (about 3 min. each side).

Assemble patties. COOK until lightly browned on each side (about 3 min. each side).

Cover and let stand 10 min.

Serve as in Recipe.

OVERALL COOKING TIME: 12:00

Tuna Casserole *(page 264)* **21**

Use a lightly greased 3-qt. casserole.

COOK butter in casserole until melted (about 3 min.). Add onion, mushrooms and green pepper. COOK, stirring every 1 min., until onion is transparent (about 3 min.).

Assemble casserole. COOK, uncovered, until thoroughly heated and cheese bubbles (about 10 min.).

Cover and let stand 10 min.

OVERALL COOKING TIME: 10:00

Clam Sauce and Macaroni Shells *(page 265)* **22**

Use a small casserole.

COOK to heat oil and lightly brown garlic (about 3 min.)

Add water, seasonings and clams with juice. COOK until thoroughly heated (about 5 min.).

English Muffin Pizza **23**
(page 2 75)

Use a baking dish.

For muffins, line baking dish with paper towels or place paper towels directly on bottom of oven. Place muffins on paper and COOK until crisp (about 2 min. for 6 halves). Butter muffins.

Add topping and COOK, turning paper after 3 min., until cheese is melted and bubbling (about 4 min.).

Serve immediately.

Perfection Boiled Rice **24**
(page 275)

Use a 3-qt. casserole.

Use 2 cups water for 1 cup rice.

COOK water until boiling (about 8 min.). Add rice, cover and COOK until soft (about 6 min.).

OVERALL COOKING TIME: 16:00

Quick Cooking Rice **25**
(page 275)

Use a 3-qt. casserole.

Use 2½ cups water for 1 cup quick cooking rice.

COOK to boil water (about 4 min. for 1 cup water).

Prepare according to package directions.

Boiled Wild Rice *(page 275)* 26

Use a covered casserole. Follow package directions for preparing rice, except to boil 3 cups water, COOK (about 12 min.). After the water boils, COOK rice approximately 1/3 the amount of time specified for conventional cooking.

Spanish Rice with Bacon *(page 276)* 27

Use a browning skillet and a covered 2-qt. casserole.

Preheat skillet. Add bacon and COOK until brown (about 4 min.).

COOK reserved bacon fat to heat (about 3 min.). Add rice, onion and green pepper and COOK, stirring every 5 min., until rice is lightly browned and begins to soften (about 20 min.).

Add remaining ingredients and transfer to casserole. Cover and COOK until rice is nearly tender (about 15 min.). Uncover and COOK until done (about 10 min.).

Cover and let stand 10 min.

OVERALL COOKING TIME: 52:00

Spanish Rice with Beef 28
(page 276)

Follow 27 Recipe with substitution as in △ Recipe. To brown ground beef, COOK 1 tablespoon butter or margarine until melted. Add ground beef and COOK, stirring every 1 min., until it separates (about 3 min.).

Add rice, onion and green pepper and continue as in 27 Recipe.

Cover and let stand 10 min.

Tomatoes Stuffed with 29
Rice and Cheese *(page 277)*

Use a small skillet and a baking dish.

Put butter or margarine in skillet and COOK until melted (about 3 min.).

Assemble tomatoes, place in baking dish and COOK until cheese melts and tomatoes are slightly softened (about 10 min.).

Cover and let stand 10 min.

Macaroni *(page 277)* 30

Use a 3-qt. casserole.

Put 2 qts. water in casserole and COOK until boiling (about 20 min.). Add macaroni and COOK until tender (about 10 min. for shell macaroni). Exact cooking time depends on size of pasta.

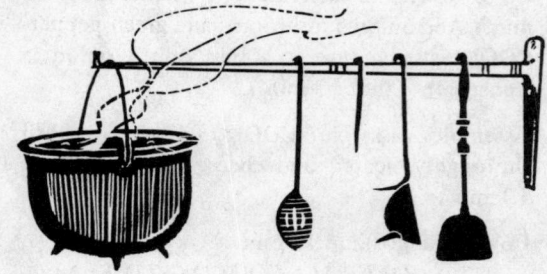

Spaghetti *(page 277)* **31**

Follow **30** Recipe. COOK 1 lb. thin spaghetti (linguini) (about 8 min.).

Noodles *(page 277)* **32**

Follow **30** Recipe, except use 6 cups water for 8 oz. of noodles. To boil water COOK (about 16 min.). For narrow noodles COOK (about 5 min.).

Flavor-Filled **33** Macaroni and Cheese *(page 278)*

Use a 2-qt. casserole. *Do not grease.*

Assemble casserole. COOK uncovered, rotating every 5 min., to heat thoroughly and melt cheese (about 10 min.).

Bacon Bits Macaroni **34** *(page 279)*

Follow **33** Recipe with addition as in △ Recipe.

Spätzle *(page 280)* **35**

Use a 3-qt. casserole.

COOK water until boiling (about 20 min.).

Drop 1/3 noodles. Cover and COOK until they rise to the surface (about 3½ min. for 1/3 the prepared batter). COOK remaining spatzle batter.

Serve as in Recipe.

Cheese-Noodle Dish **36** *(page 280)*

Use a 3-qt. casserole. *Do not butter.*

COOK bacon until browned (about 4 min.).

COOK onion, stirring every 1½ min., until transparent (about 3 min.).

Assemble casserole. COOK uncovered until heated through and cheese is melted (about 10 min.).

Vegetable Scrapple **37** *(page 283)*

Use a 2-qt. casserole, a loaf pan and a browning skillet.

In casserole, COOK water until boiling (about 12 min.). Add corn meal and COOK, stirring every 1 min., until thickened (about 4 min.).

Add vegetables, pimiento and Accent and COOK, rotating every 3 min., until very thick (about 20 min.).

Add peanuts and chill loaf.

To brown scrapple, COOK fat in browning skillet until melted. Add scrapple slices and COOK to brown on both sides (about 5 min. each side).

LUNCHEON and SUPPER DISHES in the SLOW COOKER

Chili afficianados will be happy to know that the **Chili con Carne** prepared in the slow cooker is excellent. Put it on in the morning if it's to be ready for supper; put in on the night before if your chili is on the menu for a football or holiday lunch.

Most of the dishes included here are appropriate for exactly that kind of hot and hearty one-dish meal. They are ready to eat when you are and you can even place the slow cooker directly on the table for family and friends to help themselves. Recipes can be doubled if the party will be a large one. Use the large (5-qt.) slow cooker in that case.

The rice recipes we have included are good and easy, the slow cooker being a real "failsafe" method for cooking rice.

Many of the other recipes in this section call for the use of precooked meats or other ingredients not suitable for the long-cooking methods of the slow cooker.

REMINDERS—It is unnecessary to grease the slow cooker before adding ingredients.

Be sure vegetables are covered with liquid.

The introductory chapter, **Home Cooking in the Slow Cooker**, in the beginning of this book provides additional tips and an easy-to-read chart comparing settings among different brands of slow cookers. By reviewing this section, you will also learn how we have adapted these recipes for your use.

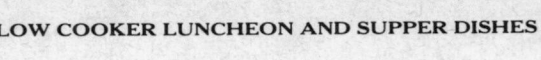

Arrange shredded cabbage base in cooker. Assemble cabbage rolls, except do not sauté onions in butter.

For sauce, use only enough tomatoes to cover by two-thirds.

Cover and cook on LOW for 8 to 9 hrs.

Add sour cream about 10 min. before serving.

Chili con Carne *(page 250)*

Use a 3½-qt. slow cooker.

Omit browning step.

Add all ingredients to slow cooker.

Cover and cook on LOW for 8 to 9 hrs.

Serve as in Recipe.

Shipwreck *(page 251)*

Use a 3½-qt. slow cooker. *Do not grease.*

Layer ingredients in slow cooker as in Recipe.

Cover and cook on LOW for 8 to 9 hrs.

Bar-X Sandwiches
(page 251)

Use a 3½-qt. slow cooker.

Sauté onions. Combine cooked onions with all other ingredients in slow cooker.

Cover and cook on LOW for 3 to 4 hrs.

Serve as in Recipe.

Stuffed Cabbage Rolls
(page 254)

Use a 3½-qt. slow cooker.

Flavor-Rich Baked Beans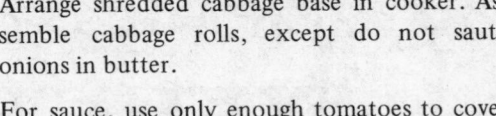
(page 259)

Use a 3¼-qt. slow cooker. *Do not grease.*

Combine soaked beans and all other ingredients in slow cooker. Mix well.

Cover and cook on LOW for 10 to 12 hrs.

Serve as in Recipe.

Perfection Boiled Rice
(page 275)

Use a 3½-qt. slow cooker.

Use 2 cups water to 1 cup uncooked rice.

Put water, rice, seasonings and 1 tablespoon butter or margarine in slow cooker.

Cover and cook on HIGH for 2½ to 3 hrs.

Note: Rice can be left on LOW an additional 2 hrs.

OR, if you are using converted rice, use 2½ cups water for 1 cup rice.

Put rice, water, salt and 1 tablespoon butter or margarine in slow cooker.

Cover and cook on HIGH for 3 to 5 hrs. *OR,* on LOW for 6 to 8 hrs.

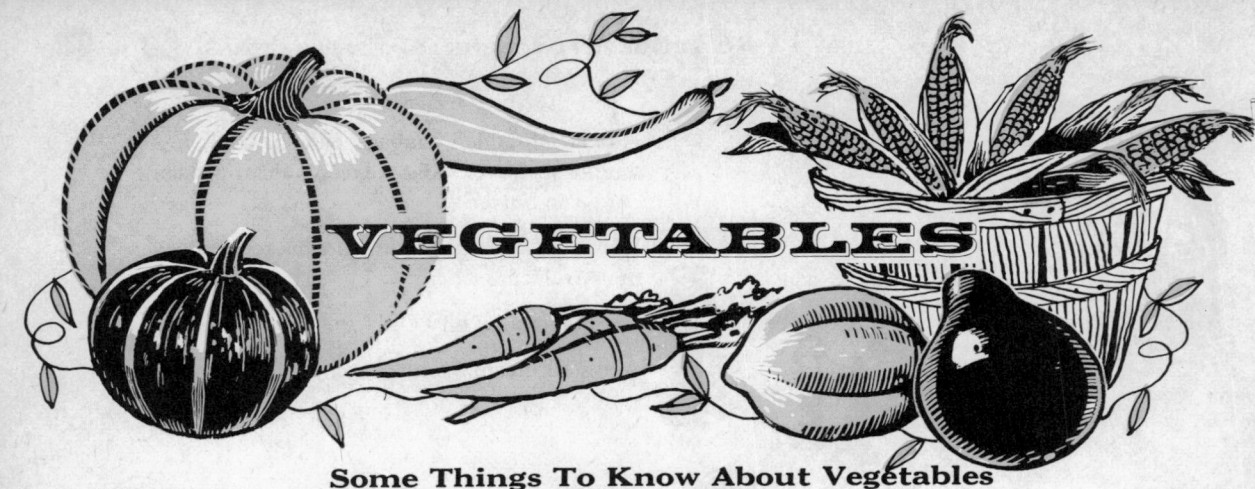

VEGETABLES

Some Things To Know About Vegetables

Nothing bespeaks the bounty of our land and the variety of its climate more dramatically than the handsome vegetables available in all seasons. What a blessing they are to the beauty of our tables and the nutritive value of our menus! Regarded originally as "boiled" drudges, valued chiefly for the seasoning that could be extracted from them, vegetables are enjoyed and prized today for their own special qualities of excellence.

SELECTION—Choose vegetables, whether fresh, frozen or canned, according to the intended use. For example, appearance is of prime importance when selecting vegetables for a vegetable plate while of lesser importance for soup vegetables.

Fresh Vegetables should be firm and blemish-free. Buy from a reliable dealer who practices good methods of handling vegetables and has a quick turnover of the more perishable items.

Vegetables at the peak of their season are usually more flavorful and lower priced than when they are available out of season.

When selecting vegetables at the market refrain from pinching, squeezing or unnecessary touching. Handle gently to prevent bruising.

Garden-Fresh Vegetables should be picked just before using if possible.

Frozen Vegetables should be solidly frozen and never refrozen after thawing. The package should be in perfect condition.

Canned Vegetables, as are all canned foods shipped between states, are subject to the regulations of the Federal Food, Drug and Cosmetic Act.

Can labels must state the net weight or net fluid contents of the can and, in general, carry descriptions of the style of pack, size, maturity, seasoning, amount of food and number of servings.

Dietetic-packed canned foods, including vegetables, are available for those on special diets such as low-sodium, diabetic or weight reduction.

STORAGE—Proper storage facilities are necessary to keep vegetables in good condition.

Fresh Vegetables—Store less perishable vegetables, such as cabbage, potatoes, dry onions, winter squash and rutabagas, in a cool, dry, well-ventilated place without beforehand washing. Keep onions separate from other vegetables. Store potatoes in a dark place and not directly on the floor.

Wash other vegetables such as greens, carrots and radishes before storing; drain thoroughly and gently pat dry with a soft, clean towel or absorbent paper. Place in refrigerator in vegetable drawers or plastic bags, or wrap tightly in waxed paper, moisture-vapor-proof material or aluminum foil to prevent vegetables from wilting unless refrigerator maintains a high humidity. *Never soak vegetables* when washing them. If they are wilted, put them in cold water for a few minutes. Shake off all moisture left from washing or crisping—drain thoroughly and gently pat dry.

Store peas and lima beans in the pod to keep fresh. Pods may be washed before storing; quickly rinse peas and lima beans after shelling.

Frozen Vegetables—Store in home freezer or in freezing compartment of refrigerator until ready to use. If package starts to thaw, use as soon as possible.

Canned Vegetables—Store in a cool, dry place away from heat-producing objects. If either end of can is bulged or swollen, discard the can because this is a sign of spoilage. Rust on a can and dents in a can do not indicate spoilage unless there is evidence of leakage.

PREPARATION—Vegetables are excellent sources of vitamins and minerals. Protect your investment of money and time spent in wise selection and storage by proper and careful preparation. Follow the methods given in How to Cook Vegetables and in recipes.

Leave edible peel on vegetables or use vegetable parer or sharp knife to keep parings thin. Many vitamins and minerals hide just under the peel—do not heedlessly throw them away. Cook whole beets without paring to retain red color.

Since the useable minerals and many vitamins in vegetables readily dissolve in water, DO NOT DISCARD COOKING LIQUID if any remains.

Clean Spinach—Cut off and discard tough stems, roots and bruised or wilted leaves. Wash leaves thoroughly by lifting up and down several times in a large amount of cold water, changing water as necessary. Lift leaves out of water each time before pouring off water. When free from sand and gritty material, transfer to a large, heavy saucepan.

Soak cauliflower, broccoli, artichokes and Brussels sprouts in salted water 20 to 30 min. before they are cooked to remove small insects and dust.

How to Cook Vegetables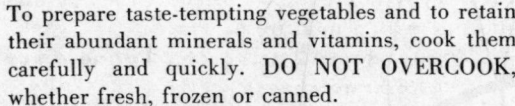

To prepare taste-tempting vegetables and to retain their abundant minerals and vitamins, cook them carefully and quickly. DO NOT OVERCOOK, whether fresh, frozen or canned.

Accent—Add at beginning of cooking period, when vegetables are buttered or sauced and seasoned for service, or sprinkle over raw vegetables and greens.

BAKING—Bake such vegetables as potatoes, tomatoes and squash without removing skins. Pare vegetables for oven dishes; follow directions given with specific recipes.

BOILING—Have water boiling rapidly before adding vegetables. Add salt and Accent at beginning of cooking period (¼ teaspoon of each per cup of water). After adding vegetables, again bring water to boiling as quickly as possible. If more water is needed, add boiling water. Boil at a moderate rate and cook vegetables until just tender.

In general, cook vegetables in a covered pan in the smallest amount of water and in the shortest length of time possible. Exceptions for amounts of water or for covering are:

Potatoes—cooked in water to cover.

Green Vegetables (peas, green or lima beans)—loosely covered.

Spinach—partially covered pan with only the water which clings to leaves after final washing.

Asparagus—arranged in tied bundles with stalks standing in a small, deep pan containing at least 2 in. of boiling water—pan loosely covered.

Broccoli—tied, stalks (over ½ in. thick, split lengthwise) standing in a deep pan containing boiling water up to flowerets—pan loosely covered.

Strong-flavored Vegetables (cauliflower, mature cabbage and Brussels sprouts)—cooked loosely covered in a large amount of water. To restore color of red cabbage, add a small amount of vinegar at the end of the cooking period, just before draining.

A desirable boiled vegetable is free from excess water, retains its original color and is well seasoned. Pieces are uniform in size and attractive.

Canned Vegetables—Heat to boiling point in liquid from can.

Home-Canned Vegetables—Boil 10 min. (not required for tomatoes and sauerkraut).

Dried (dehydrated) Vegetables—Soak and cook as directed for specific recipes.

Frozen Vegetables—Do not thaw before cooking (thaw corn on cob and partially thaw spinach). Break frozen block apart with fork during cooking. Use as little boiling salted water as possible for cooking. Follow directions on package.

BROILING—Follow directions with specific recipes.

FRYING and **DEEP-FRYING**—Follow directions with specific recipes.

PANNING—Finely shred or slice vegetables. Cook slowly until just tender in a small amount of fat, in a covered, heavy pan. Occasionally move pieces with spoon to prevent sticking and burning.

STEAMING—Cooking in a pressure saucepan is a form of steaming. Follow directions given with saucepan as overcooking may occur in seconds.
Note: Some saucepans having tight-fitting covers may lend themselves to steaming vegetables in as little as 1 teaspoon water, no water, or in a small amount of butter, margarine or shortening.

Stuffed Artichokes Sicilian

Set out a 10-in. skillet having a tight-fitting cover.

With a sharp knife, cutting straight across, cut off 1 in. of the tops from

4 medium-size artichokes

Cut off stems about 1 in. from base and remove outside lower leaves. With scissors, clip off tips of leaves and discard. Soak (*page 285*) artichokes.

Meanwhile, mix together and set aside

⅔ cup (2 slices) fine, dry bread crumbs
1 clove garlic (*page 12*), thinly sliced
1 teaspoon grated Parmesan cheese
1 teaspoon chopped parsley
1 teaspoon salt
¾ teaspoon pepper
¼ teaspoon Accent

Rinse artichokes thoroughly in clear water and drain.

Spread leaves apart; place in each artichoke

3 slices garlic

Sprinkle crumb mixture between leaves and over top of artichokes. Sprinkle with

1 tablespoon chopped parsley

Place the artichokes upright in the skillet containing

2 cups water

Sprinkle artichokes with

2 tablespoons olive oil

Cover and cook about 30 min., or until a leaf can be easily pulled from artichoke.

To Eat Artichokes—Pull out leaves, one by one. Eat only the tender part of leaf by drawing it between teeth. Discard less tender tip. Continue with each leaf until choke or fuzzy part in center is reached. Remove choke with knife and fork and discard. Cut heart or base into pieces and eat with a fork.   *4 servings*

▲ Asparagus Parmesan

Butter a 1½-qt. casserole.

Break off and discard lower parts of stalks as far down as they will snap from

1½ lbs. asparagus

Wash remaining portions of stalks thoroughly. If necessary, remove scales to dislodge any sand. Cook (*page 285*) 10 to 20 min., or until asparagus is just tender. (Or cook contents of two 10-oz. pkgs. frozen asparagus, *page 285*).

Melt in small saucepan and add to casserole

½ cup butter or margarine

Place cooked asparagus in the casserole and sprinkle with a mixture of

½ cup (about 2 oz.) grated Parmesan or Romano cheese
1 teaspoon salt
½ teaspoon pepper
½ teaspoon Accent

Bake at 450°F 5 to 10 min., or until cheese is melted.   *6 servings*

△ Asparagus Hollandaise

Follow ▲ Recipe for cooking asparagus. Omit the cheese mixture and baking period. Serve cooked asparagus on a warm platter with **Hollandaise Sauce** (*page 324*).

▲ French-Style Green Beans  in Mustard Sauce

Wash, break off ends and French (cut lengthwise into fine strips)

1½ lbs. (about 5 cups) green beans

Cook (*p. 285*) 15 to 20 min., or until tender. (Or cook contents of two 10-oz. pkgs. frozen French-style green beans, *page 285*).

While beans are cooking, prepare

Creamy Mustard Sauce (*page 329*)

When beans are tender, drain. Put beans into hot serving dish. Pour sauce over beans and serve immediately.   *About 6 servings*

⚠ French-Style Green Beans 19 and Onions

Follow ▲ Recipe, omitting Mustard Sauce. Clean (*page 12*) 8 to 12 small whole **onions**. Cook (*p. 285.*) 15 to 25 min., or until just tender. Drain and combine with cooked green beans. Pour over vegetables a mixture of ¼ cup melted **butter** or **margarine**, ½ teaspoon **salt**, ¼ teaspoon **pepper** and ¼ teaspoon **Accent**. Toss gently. Heat slowly 5 min., or until thoroughly heated.

⚠ French-Style Green Beans 9 with Almonds

Follow ▲ Recipe, omitting Mustard Sauce. Coarsely chop ¼ cup (about 1½ oz.) toasted, blanched **almonds** (*page 11*). Add almonds to cooked green beans with a mixture of 3 tablespoons melted **butter** or **margarine**, ½ teaspoon **salt**, ¼ teaspoon **Accent**, ¼ teaspoon **lemon juice** and ¼ teaspoon **rosemary** or **savory**. Toss gently.

Green Beans Supreme 20

Set out a medium-size saucepan and a shallow 1-qt. baking dish.

Shred and set aside
4 oz. process cheese food (about 1 cup, shredded)
Wash, break off ends and French (cut lengthwise into fine strips)
1 lb. (about 3 cups) green beans
Cook (*p. 285*) 15 to 20 min., or until just tender. (Or cook contents of two 10-oz. pkgs. frozen French-style green beans, *page 285*.)

Heat in the saucepan over low heat
2 tablespoons butter or margarine

Green Beans Supreme

Add and cook over medium heat, occasionally moving and turning with a spoon
2 tablespoons minced onion
Cook until onion is transparent. Remove from heat and blend in a mixture of
1 tablespoon flour
½ teaspoon salt
½ teaspoon paprika
¼ teaspoon dry mustard
¼ teaspoon Accent
and
½ teaspoon Worcestershire sauce
Heat until mixture bubbles. Remove from heat. Add gradually, stirring constantly
1 cup undiluted evaporated milk
Return to heat and bring rapidly to boiling, stirring constantly; cook 1 to 2 min. longer.

When beans are tender, drain if necessary, and add to sauce. Toss mixture gently with a spoon until blended. Spoon into the baking dish. Sprinkle with the shredded cheese food and
2 tablespoons fine, dry bread crumbs
Set temperature control of range at Broil. Place baking dish on broiler rack. Place in broiler with the top of the mixture 2 to 3 in. from source of heat.

Broil 5 min., or until bread crumbs are lightly browned and cheese is melted.

4 to 6 servings

Buttered Lima Beans

Set out a deep saucepan.

Shell, discarding pods, and rinse

2 lbs. green lima beans (about 1⅓ cups or ⅔ lb. shelled)

Cook (*page 285*) 20 to 30 min., or until just tender when pierced with a fork.

When beans are tender, drain, and blend in until melted

3 tablespoons butter or margarine

and a mixture of

½ teaspoon salt
½ teaspoon Accent
⅛ teaspoon pepper

Serve immediately.   *4 or 5 servings*

Buttered Lima Beans, Corn-on-the-Cob and Raw Vegetable Relishes (page 308)

▲ Sweet-Sour Beets
(Harvard Beets)

Set out a 2-qt. saucepan having a tight-fitting cover.

Leaving on 1- to 2-in. stem and the root end (this helps beets retain red color), cut off leaves from

1 lb. (about 5) medium-size beets

Wash and cook (*p.285*) 30 to 45 min., or until just tender.

When beets are tender, drain if necessary and reserve liquid in a measuring cup. Set aside.

Plunge beets into running cold water. Peel off and discard skin, stems and root ends from beets. Dice or slice beets and set aside.

Mix together in the saucepan

2 tablespoons sugar
1 tablespoon cornstarch
½ teaspoon salt
¼ teaspoon Accent

Pour into reserve beet liquid

Cold water (enough to make ¾ cup liquid)

Stirring constantly, gradually add liquid to mixture in saucepan with

3 tablespoons vinegar

Stirring constantly, bring rapidly to boiling and cook 3 min. Add the beets and

2 tablespoons butter or margarine

Keeping mixture moving with a spoon, bring again to boiling; cover and simmer 8 to 10 min.

Serve immediately.   *4 servings*

⚠ Beets in Orange Sauce

Follow ▲ Recipe. Decrease beet-water mixture to ½ cup. Substitute ⅓ cup **orange juice** for vinegar. Add ¼ teaspoon grated **orange peel** (*page 11*). Garnish with **Hard-Cooked Eggs** (*page 87*) chopped.

⚠ Lemon-Buttered Beets 23 3

Follow ▲ Recipe; substitute 1 lb. (about 10) small beets for the medium-size beets. Do not dice cooked beets. Omit cornstarch mixture. Increase butter to 4 tablespoons, melt butter in the saucepan and stir in 2 tablespoons **lemon juice** and a mixture of ¼ teaspoon **salt,** ¼ teaspoon **ginger,** ⅛ teaspoon **Accent,** and few grains **pepper.** Add beets and heat thoroughly, occasionally moving and turning with a spoon.

Broccoli with Horse-radish Cream 24

MRS. W. L. ISBELL, BROOKSTON, IND.

Set out a deep saucepan.

Remove and discard outer leaves and cut off tough ends of stalks from
    2 lbs. broccoli
Wash, soak and cook (*p.285*) 10 to 20 min., or until broccoli is just tender.

Mix together in top of double boiler
    ¾ **cup thick sour cream**
    ½ **teaspoon prepared horse-radish**
    ½ **teaspoon prepared mustard**
    ⅛ **teaspoon salt**
    ⅛ **teaspoon Accent**
Cook over simmering water, stirring constantly, 3 to 5 min., or until thoroughly heated.

Drain broccoli thoroughly, untie bunches and arrange on a serving dish. Pour sauce over broccoli; serve immediately.   *4 to 6 servings*

Broccoli Polonaise 25

Set out a deep saucepan.

Remove and discard outer leaves and cut off tough ends of stalks from
    2 lbs. broccoli
Wash, soak and cook (*p.285*) 10 to 20 min., or until broccoli is just tender.

Meanwhile, prepare Polonaise Topping.

For Polonaise Topping—Prepare
    ½ **cup (1 to 2 slices) fine, soft or dry bread crumbs**
Melt in a small skillet
    2 to 3 tablespoons butter or margarine
Add the bread crumbs and stir over medium heat until they are lightly browned, turning and moving mixture gently with a spoon.

Remove skillet from heat and mix in
    ½ **Hard-Cooked Egg (*page 87*), finely chopped**
    ⅛ **teaspoon salt**
    ⅛ **teaspoon Accent**
    Few grains pepper
When broccoli is tender, drain and place on a warm serving platter. Coat broccoli with a mixture of
    2 tablespoons melted butter or margarine
    ¼ **teaspoon lemon juice**
Spoon Polonaise Topping over broccoli.

Polonaise Topping may also be served over other cooked vegetables, such as asparagus, green beans or cauliflower.   *4 to 6 servings*

Brussels Sprouts with Chestnuts

Grease a 1-qt. casserole.

Wash, soak and cook (*page 285*) about 10 to 20 min., or until just tender
2 cups (about ½ lb.) Brussels sprouts
Meanwhile, wash, make a slit on two sides of each shell and put into a saucepan
½ lb. chestnuts
Cover with boiling water and boil about 20 min. Drain. Peel off shells and skins. Return blanched nuts to saucepan and cover with boiling salted water. Cover and simmer 8 to 20 min., or until chestnuts are tender; drain.

Prepare and set aside
¼ cup buttered bread crumbs (*page 10*)
When Brussels sprouts are tender, drain, reserving liquid.

Measure ½ cup of the hot liquid. Add to liquid
1 beef bouillon cube or ½ teaspoon concentrated meat extract
Set aside.

Turn one half of the chestnuts and Brussels sprouts into casserole. Sprinkle with
    Salt
    Pepper
    Accent
    Nutmeg
Dot generously with
    Butter or margarine
Repeat layering.

Pour the reserved beef broth into casserole. Sprinkle the buttered crumbs over casserole.

Bake at 350°F 15 to 20 min., or until crumbs are lightly browned.   *4 servings*

▲ Candied Carrots 26 4

Butter a shallow baking dish.

Wash, pare or scrape
24 small (about 3 lbs.) carrots
Cook (*p. 285*) whole carrots 15 to 25 min., or until just tender.

Heat in a skillet over low heat
¼ cup butter or margarine
Blend in
1 cup firmly packed brown sugar
½ cup water
Stirring constantly, cook over medium heat until sugar is dissolved and mixture bubbles. Drain carrots and place in the baking dish. Pour sugar mixture over carrots.

Bake at 350°F about 10 min., or until carrots are completely glazed; baste occasionally.

Or, place in skillet over low heat, turning occasionally until carrots are completely glazed.
    8 servings

△ Glazed Carrots 27 5

Follow ▲ Recipe. Leave carrots whole or cut lengthwise into sticks. Omit brown-sugar mixture. Drain cooked carrots and dry thoroughly on absorbent paper. Heat 2 tablespoons **butter** or **margarine** in a skillet over low heat. Stir in ¼ cup **sugar**. Add carrots and turn in mixture until coated.

Glazed Carrots

▲ Deep-Fried Cauliflower with Sour Cream Sauce

A deep saucepan or automatic deep-fryer will be needed.

Remove leaves, cut off all the woody base and trim any blemishes from
>**1 medium-size head cauliflower**

Carefully break into 5 or 6 large flowerets. Soak (*page 285*). Cook (*page 285*) flowerets 8 to 10 min., or until tender but still firm.

Meanwhile, prepare Sour Cream Sauce.

For Sour Cream Sauce—Mix together in top of double boiler
>**2 egg yolks, slightly beaten**
>**1 cup thick sour cream**
>**2 teaspoons lemon juice**
>**½ teaspoon salt**
>**½ teaspoon Accent**
>**¼ teaspoon pepper**
>**¼ teaspoon paprika**

Cook over simmering water, stirring constantly, 3 to 5 min., or until sauce is thoroughly heated. Keep sauce warm by setting it over hot water. Cover tightly.

Fill deep saucepan with fat and heat to 365°F (*page 13*).

When cauliflower is tender, drain and set aside.

Meanwhile, mix and set aside
>**⅔ cup (2 slices) fine, dry bread crumbs**
>**½ teaspoon salt**
>**¼ teaspoon pepper**

Blend together
>**2 eggs, slightly beaten**
>**¼ cup milk**

Dip flowerets into the egg mixture and then into the crumb mixture. Deep-fry only as many flowerets at one time as will float uncrowded one layer deep in fat. Fry them 2 to 4 min., or until golden brown, turning occasionally. Drain flowerets over fat for a few seconds before removing to absorbent paper. Place in a serving dish and top with the sauce.

Serve immediately. *5 to 6 servings*

Festive Corn, French Fried Potatoes, buttered zucchini and baked stuffed tomatoes

△ Batter-Fried Cauliflower

Follow ▲ Recipe; omit egg and bread-crumb mixture. Beat together with rotary beater 1 **egg**, ¾ cup **milk**, ¼ teaspoon **salt** and 1 cup **flour** for a batter coating. Dip cooked cauliflowerets into the batter and deep-fry.

Festive Corn

Heat in a medium-size saucepan having a tight-fitting cover
>**¼ cup butter or margarine**

Add and cook until onion is transparent, occasionally moving and turning with a spoon
>**¼ cup finely chopped onion**
>**¼ cup chopped green pepper (*page 12*)**

Add contents of
>**1 pkg. (10 oz.) frozen corn**

Cook corn, covered, over low heat about 10 min., or until tender. With a fork or spoon gently break block of corn apart while cooking. During last few minutes of cooking, mix in
>**¼ cup diced pimiento**

Season with a mixture of
>**1 teaspoon salt**
>**½ teaspoon Accent**
>**¼ teaspoon pepper**

Toss gently. Garnish with
>**Sweet red pepper slice**

4 servings

Corn-on-the-Cob 7 6

Set out a large saucepan.

Remove husks, corn silk and blemishes from
4 ears corn
If ears are large, cut into halves. Cook covered
in boiling water to cover. (For mature corn,
add ½ teaspoon **sugar** per qt. water.)

Boil corn at a moderate rate about 6 to 12
min., or until just tender.

Remove corn with fork or tongs onto platter.
Serve hot with **salt, pepper, Accent** and lots
of **butter** or **margarine.**   *4 servings*

Note: To prepare corn-on-the-cob on an outdoor grill see OUTDOOR COOKING (*page 204*).

Plantation Corn Pudding 29

Grease a 1½ qt. casserole. Heat water for boiling water bath (*page 12*).

Scald (*page 13*)
1¾ cups milk
Add
1 tablespoon butter or margarine
While milk scalds, beat slightly
4 eggs
Blend eggs with
2 cups (1-lb. can) cream-style corn
2 tablespoons slivered pimiento
2 tablespoons finely chopped
   green pepper (*page 12*)
2 tablespoons grated onion

and a mixture of
1 teaspoon sugar
1 teaspoon salt
½ teaspoon Accent
¼ teaspoon pepper
Stirring vigorously, gradually add the milk to
the corn mixture; pour into the casserole.

Bake in boiling water bath at 300°F 45 to 60
min., or until a silver knife comes out clean
when inserted halfway between center and
edge of casserole.   *6 servings*

▲ Scalloped Corn 30

Butter a 1-qt. casserole

Combine
2½ cups (No. 2 can) cream-style corn
½ cup milk
3 tablespoons melted butter
   or margarine
Thoroughly blend in
1 cup fine, dry bread or cracker crumbs
3 tablespoons finely chopped onion
   (*page 12*)
3 tablespoons finely chopped green
   pepper (*page 12*)
2 tablespoons brown sugar
and a mixture of
1 teaspoon salt
¼ teaspoon Accent
¼ teaspoon pepper
Turn into the casserole. Dot with
2 teaspoons butter or margarine
Bake corn at 350°F 30 min., or until lightly
browned.   *6 servings*

△ Corn-Tomato Scallop 31

Follow ▲ Recipe. Substitute **whole kernel corn** (No. 2 can, drained) for cream-style corn. Substitute 1¾ cups (one-half of No. 2½ can) **tomatoes,** cut in pieces, for milk.

Scalloped Eggplant 32

MRS. JESSIE JACK, MITCHELLVILLE, IOWA

Grease a 1-qt. casserole.

Prepare and set aside
   3 Hard-Cooked Eggs (*page 87*)
Prepare and set aside
   ¾ cup garlic-buttered cracker crumbs (clean 1 clove garlic and cut into halves; add to 2 to 3 tablespoons melted butter or margarine and allow to stand until garlic flavor is absorbed; proceed as for buttered crumbs, *page 10*)
Meanwhile, wash, pare and cut into 1-in. cubes
   1 medium-size (about 1 lb.) eggplant
Cook (*p. 285*) about 7 min., or until just tender. If necessary, drain.

Prepare
   1 cup (about 2 medium-size) coarsely chopped green pepper (*page 12*)
   ½ cup (about 1 medium-size) coarsely chopped onion (*page 12*)
Scald (*page 13*)
   ¾ cup milk
Add to scalded milk
   2 tablespoons butter
Dice the Hard-Cooked Eggs and gently toss them with the chopped green pepper, onion, eggplant, cracker crumbs and a mixture of
   1½ teaspoons salt
   ¼ teaspoon pepper
   ¼ teaspoon Accent
Spoon mixture into the casserole.

Pour scalded milk over mixture. Sprinkle with
   ¼ cup (1 oz.) grated Cheddar cheese
Bake uncovered at 300°F about 55 min.

4 to 6 servings

Butter-Fried Mushrooms 33

Set out a large, heavy skillet.

Clean and slice (*page 12*)
   1 lb. mushrooms
Set mushrooms aside.

Heat in the skillet over low heat
   ⅓ to ½ cup butter
Add the sliced mushrooms.

Cook slowly, carefully turning occasionally, until lightly browned and tender.

Season with
   Salt
   Pepper
   Accent
Serve immediately. *6 servings*

Butter-Fried Onion Slices

Set out a large, heavy skillet.

Clean (*page 12*) and slice ¼ in. thick
   6 medium-size onions
Heat in the skillet over low heat
   ¼ cup butter
Fry onion slices, one layer at a time, in the butter until lightly browned on both sides, turning only once with spatula or pancake turner to keep the slices from separating into rings. Season with
   Salt
   Pepper
   Accent
Serve immediately. *4 to 6 servings*

French Fried Onions

French Fried Onions

Set out a deep saucepan or automatic deep-fryer (*page 13*) and heat fat to 365°F.

Meanwhile, clean (*page 12*) and cut into slices ¼ in. thick
> **3 medium-size (about ½ lb.) onions**

Separate slices into rings and set aside.

Melt and set aside to cool
> **1 tablespoon butter or margarine**

Sift together into a bowl and set aside
> **1¼ cups sifted flour**
> **½ teaspoon salt**
> **½ teaspoon Accent**
> **⅛ teaspoon pepper**

Beat until thick and piled softly
> **2 eggs**

Blend in
> **¾ cup milk**
> **1 teaspoon Worcestershire sauce**

Blend in the butter or margarine. Make a well in center of dry ingredients; add liquid mixture all at once. Blend just until smooth.

Dip onion rings in batter with fork or slotted spoon to coat evenly. Deep-fry only as many at one time as will float uncrowded one layer deep in fat. Fry 2 to 3 min., or until golden brown. Turn onion rings with a fork as they rise to surface and several times during cooking. Drain over fat a few seconds before removing to absorbent paper. *About 6 servings*

▲ Braised Onions 34

Set out a shallow 2-qt. casserole having a cover.

Clean (*page 12*) and cut into crosswise halves
> **8 medium-size (about 1½ lbs.) onions**

Prepare
> **1 cup quick meat broth (*page 13*)**

Pour into the casserole. Place onions in liquid, cut-side down. Sprinkle with a mixture of
> **1 tablespoon sugar**
> **½ teaspoon salt**
> **¼ teaspoon Accent**
> **Few grains pepper**

Dot onions generously with
> **Butter or margarine**

Cover and bake at 350°F 45 to 50 min., or until onions are tender. During baking, baste two or three times with liquid in casserole. Remove casserole from oven and sprinkle onions with a mixture of
> **½ cup (2 oz.) grated Cheddar cheese**
> **⅓ cup fine, dry bread crumbs**
> **½ teaspoon paprika**

Return to oven and bake uncovered 8 to 10 min., or until crumbs are lightly browned.

6 servings

△ Braised Turnips 35

Follow ▲ Recipe. Substitute 2 to 2½ lbs. medium-size **turnips** for onions. Wash, pare and cut into ¼-in. slices. Double the amounts of seasonings. Arrange one half of turnip slices in the bouillon. Sprinkle with one half of seasoning mixture. Dot with **butter** or **margarine.** Repeat layering.

Cover and bake 40 to 45 min., or until turnips are tender. Complete as in ▲ Recipe.

French Peas

This inspired treatment of a popular favorite is a perfect accompaniment for roast chicken.

Set out a 2-qt. saucepan having a tight-fitting cover.

To retain their delicate flavor, rinse and shell just before using, reserving about one third of the pods

3 lbs. fresh peas

Place the reserved pods in a cheesecloth square and tie securely. Set peas and pea pods aside.

Rinse, shake off excess water, and remove outer leaves (leaving heart) from

1 medium-size head lettuce

(Reserve outside leaves for use in other food preparation.)

Tear lettuce heart into bite-size pieces. Place about one half of the lettuce pieces in the saucepan. Set remaining pieces aside.

Cut off roots, trim green tops to 2 to 3 in. and discard any bruised or wilted parts from

4 scallions or green onions

Peel, rinse and chop. Add the chopped scallions, reserved peas and pea pods to the saucepan with

¼ cup butter, cut in pieces
2 teaspoons sugar
1½ teaspoons salt
1 teaspoon Accent
¼ teaspoon pepper
½ bay leaf

Cover with the remaining lettuce pieces. Cover the saucepan and cook over low heat about 20 to 25 min., or until peas are tender but still moist. Remove from heat. Remove and discard bay leaf and pea pods.

Add to saucepan

¼ cup butter
2 tablespoons chopped chives
2 tablespoons finely chopped parsley

Toss lightly to mix thoroughly.

Serve immediately in a warm serving dish.

4 to 6 servings

Baked Filled Potatoes

Wash and scrub with a vegetable brush

6 medium-size (about 2 lbs.) baking potatoes

Dry potatoes with absorbent paper. Rub potatoes well with about

1 tablespoon fat

Place potatoes on oven rack; bake at 425°F 45 to 60 min., or until potatoes are soft when pressed with the fingers (protected by paper napkin).

Remove potatoes from oven. To make each potato more mealy, gently roll potato back and forth on a flat surface. Cut large potatoes into halves lengthwise. Or cut a thin lengthwise slice from tops of smaller potatoes. With spoon, scoop out inside without breaking skin.

Whip and season potatoes as suggested in recipe for **Whipped Potatoes** (*page 298*). Beat in one of the following combinations

⅓ cup (2¼-oz. can) deviled ham (reduce salt in recipe)
3 tablespoons minced parsley

or

⅓ cup (about 1½ oz.) grated Cheddar cheese (2 tablespoons may be reserved for topping)
8 to 10 stuffed olives, finely chopped

Pile mixture lightly into potato skins, leaving surfaces uneven. If desired, top with

⅓ cup crushed buttered corn flakes or crumbs (page 10)

Bake 8 to 10 min. longer, or until potatoes are thoroughly heated and tops are lightly browned. *6 servings*

Note: To prepare baked potatoes on an outdoor grill see OUTDOOR COOKING (*page 204*).

▲ French Fried Potatoes

To keep last-minute dinner flurries down to a manageable size, prepare French Fries by Method 1. It speeds up the job by getting it partially done before serving time.

Method 1—Set out a deep saucepan or automatic deep-fryer (*page 13*) and heat fat to 300°F.

Meanwhile, wash and pare
   6 medium-size (about 2 lbs.) potatoes
Cut potatoes with knife or fancy cutter. Trim off sides and ends to form large blocks. Cut lengthwise into about ⅜-in. slices; stack evenly. Cut lengthwise into sticks about ⅜-in. wide. Pat dry with absorbent paper.

Fry about 1 cup at a time in hot fat until potatoes are transparent but not browned. Remove from fat and drain on absorbent paper.

Just before serving, heat fat to 360°F. Return potatoes to fat, frying 1 cup at a time. Fry until crisp and golden brown.

Drain on absorbent paper.

Sprinkle with
   Salt
   Accent
Serve immediately or keep warm in 300°F oven.   *6 servings*

Method 2—Heat fat to 360°F. Prepare potatoes as in Method 1 and deep-fry until tender and golden brown.

△ Lattice Potatoes

Follow ▲ Recipe, Method 2, for frying. Heat fat to 370°F. Wash and pare potatoes. For lattice effect, cut potatoes with a fancy fluted cutter into thin crosswise slices, turning potato each time to make lattice. Pat slices dry with absorbent paper. Deep-fry until potatoes are crisp and golden brown.

Guatemala Potatoes
AMELIE M. KINZER, VAN NUYS, CALIF.

Grease a shallow 1½-qt. casserole having a tight-fitting cover.

Set aside to drain, reserving liquid in a 2 cup measure, contents of
   1 No. 2 can tomatoes (1 cup, drained)
Break tomatoes into pieces with a spoon.

Wash, pare and thinly slice
   6 medium-size (about 2 lbs.) potatoes
   (about 4 cups, sliced)
Coat potato slices evenly by shaking them in a plastic bag in a mixture of
   3 tablespoons flour
   1½ teaspoons salt
   ½ teaspoon pepper
   ½ teaspoon Accent
Clean (*page 12*) and cut into thin slices
   2 large onions
Carefully place one half of potato slices in even layers in baking dish. Add one half of the onion slices and one half of the tomatoes.

Repeat layers.

Top with
   6 slices bacon
Pour 1½ cups of the reserved tomato liquid over the mixture.

Bake covered at 375°F 30 min. Remove cover and bake 35 min. longer, or until potatoes are tender when pierced with a fork and bacon is cooked.   *6 servings*

▲ Hashed Brown Potatoes

Set out a large, heavy skillet.

Leftover cooked potatoes may be used. Or—
Wash and cook (*page 285*)
   6 or 7 medium-size (about 2 lbs.)
      potatoes
Cook about 25 to 35 min., or until potatoes are tender when pierced with a fork.

Drain potatoes. To dry them, shake pan over

low heat. Peel and dice or chop potatoes and put into a bowl. Add

⅓ cup milk

and a mixture of

1 teaspoon salt
¼ teaspoon Accent
¼ teaspoon paprika

Mix gently.

Heat in the skillet

3 to 4 tablespoons fat

Turn potatoes into the skillet, pressing down to form an even layer. Cook slowly without stirring until crusty and browned on under side. Turn with a pancake turner or spatula, and brown other side. (Add more fat to skillet if necessary.) Quickly turn potatoes onto a warm platter.   *6 servings*

⚠ O'Brien Potatoes

Follow ▲ Recipe for cooking potatoes. Dice or chop. Heat fat in skillet and add ¼ cup chopped **onion**, 2 tablespoons minced **pimiento** and 2 tablespoons minced **green pepper**. Add potatoes, milk and seasonings. Cook, occasionally moving and turning with a spoon, until potatoes are lightly browned.

⚠ Skillet Browned Potatoes

Follow ▲ Recipe; omit milk. Cook 12 small, whole potatoes. Leave whole. Heat fat in skillet. Pan-fry potatoes, turning them in hot fat until lightly browned and crisp. After frying, sprinkle potatoes with seasonings given in ▲ Recipe.

⚠ Fried Sweet Potatoes

Follow ▲ Recipe; use **sweet potatoes**. Peel cooked potatoes and slice evenly into all crosswise or all lengthwise slices. Omit milk and seasonings. Heat fat, add potatoes and season with 1 teaspoon **salt** and 1 tablespoon **brown sugar**. Pan-fry over medium heat, turning pieces frequently and carefully until browned.

Jungle-"Fried" Potatoes 37

MRS. JOE KNOWLES, BELLEVILLE, ILL.

Set out a 10-in. skillet having a tight-fitting cover.

Wash and pare

3 medium-size (about 1 lb.) potatoes

With a sharp knife or vegetable slicer, cut into thin uniform crosswise slices.

Clean (*page 12*) and chop

1 large onion (about ¾ cup, chopped)

Put potato slices and onion in the skillet.

Add

Water (enough to cover potato slices)

Cover skillet and cook over medium heat about 7 min., or until potatoes are just tender when pierced with a fork. Remove cover and add

¼ teaspoon salt
¼ teaspoon pepper
⅛ teaspoon Accent

Cook uncovered over low heat, turning occasionally, about 5 min., or until the water is evaporated.

Serve immediately.   *3 or 4 servings*

Parsley New Potatoes 38 7

(See photo on page 130)

Wash
  24 (about 3 lbs.) small new potatoes
Cook *(p. 285)* about 20 min., or until potatoes are tender when pierced with a fork.

Meanwhile, melt in a small saucepan
  ½ cup butter or margarine
Stir in
  ¼ cup finely chopped parsley
  1 teaspoon salt
  ½ teaspoon Accent
  ¼ teaspoon pepper
Keep mixture warm.

Drain potatoes. To dry potatoes, shake pan over low heat. Peel potatoes immediately.

Place potatoes in warm serving dish. Pour parsley butter over potatoes and turn them to coat well.

Serve immediately.   *6 to 8 servings*

Spud'n-Cheese Puffs

FAY KESSINGER, ROACHDALE, IND.

Lightly butter a baking sheet.

Wash, pare and cook *(page 285)*
  **4 medium-size (about 1⅓ lbs.)
    potatoes**
Cook about 25 to 35 min., or until potatoes are tender when pierced with a fork. Drain.

While potatoes are cooking, grate and set aside
  **4 oz. (about 1 cup) grated sharp
    Cheddar cheese**

To dry potatoes, shake pan over low heat. To heat potato masher, food mill or ricer, and a mixing bowl, scald them with boiling water.

Mash or rice potatoes thoroughly. Whip in until potatoes are fluffy
  ¼ cup butter or margarine
  ½ cup milk or cream (added gradually)
and a mixture of
  2 teaspoons baking powder
  ½ teaspoon salt
  ¼ teaspoon pepper
  ¼ teaspoon Accent
Whip into potatoes the grated cheese and
  1 teaspoon finely chopped onion
Shape mixture into balls or patties, using ¼ cup mixture for each. Carefully roll potato balls or patties in
  1½ cups finely crushed corn flakes
Place on the baking sheet.

Bake at 400°F 20 min., or until heated thoroughly and browned.   *6 servings*

▲ Whipped Potatoes 13

Wash, pare and cook *(page 285)*
  6 medium-size (about 2 lbs.) potatoes
Cook about 25 to 35 min., or until tender when pierced with a fork. Drain.

To dry potatoes, shake pan over low heat. To heat potato masher, food mill or ricer and a mixing bowl, scald them with boiling water.

Mash or rice potatoes thoroughly. Whip in until potatoes are fluffy
  3 tablespoons butter or margarine
  **⅓ to ½ cup hot milk or cream (added
    gradually)**
and a mixture of
  1 teaspoon salt
  ¼ teaspoon Accent
  ⅛ teaspoon white pepper
Whip potatoes until light and fluffy. If necessary, keep potatoes over hot water and cover with folded towel until ready to serve.

About 4 cups Whipped Potatoes

Dinner on a Plank—Duchess Potatoes, broiled ground meat, onions and tomatoes

△ Duchess Potatoes

Follow ▲ Recipe. Beat in 2 **egg yolks** (or 1 whole egg for softer mixture) after addition of hot milk. Spoon potatoes into small mounds on greased baking sheet or force through a pastry bag and a No. 7 star tube into spiral-shaped servings. Brush with melted **butter.** Bake at 450°F about 10 min., or until browned. With spatula, carefully remove potatoes from baking sheet.

Note: Duchess Potatoes are used for planked meals. Force potatoes through pastry bag and No. 7 star tube onto seasoned plank around meat or fish and vegetables forming a spiral-shaped border. Cover exposed plank as completely as possible. Brush with melted butter; bake or broil as directed in recipes until potatoes are lightly browned.

Scalloped Sweet Potatoes 39

WANDA HUFFMAN, EVANS, COLO.

Grease a 1½-qt. casserole having a tight-fitting cover.

Wash

    4 medium-size (about 1⅓ lbs.) sweet potatoes

Cook covered in boiling salted water to cover

for 10 min. Drain. To dry potatoes, shake pan over low heat. Peel. With a sharp knife, cut into crosswise slices ⅛ in. thick. Set aside.

Mix together

    ¼ cup sugar
    2 tablespoons grated orange peel (*page 11*)
    ½ teaspoon salt

Wash, cut away peel and cut into crosswise slices ¼ in. thick

    2 large oranges

Set out

    ¼ cup butter

Arrange one half of the potato slices in an even layer in the casserole. Cover with one half of the orange slices and sprinkle with one half of the sugar mixture. Dot with 2 table-spoons of the butter. Repeat layering.

Pour over casserole

    ⅔ cup orange juice

Bake covered at 375°F about 40 min., or until potatoes are tender when pierced with a fork.

4 or 5 servings

Candied Sweet Potatoes 40

Set out a large, heavy skillet and a large saucepan having a cover.

Wash

    6 medium-size (about 2 lbs.) sweet potatoes or yams

Cook (*p. 285*) 25 to 35 min., or until potatoes are just tender when pierced with a fork. Drain. To dry potatoes, shake pan over low heat. Peel potatoes and set aside.

Heat in the skillet over low heat

    ⅓ cup butter or margarine

Blend in

    ⅓ cup firmly packed brown sugar
    ¼ teaspoon salt

Heat until mixture bubbles. Add potatoes. Cook over medium heat, turning potatoes several times, about 20 min., or until potatoes are well-glazed and thoroughly heated.

4 to 6 servings

Sweet Potato Royal

EDITH R. SPRINGER, MECHANICSBURG, PA.

Butter a 1½-qt. casserole.

Wash
 **4 medium-size (about 1½ lbs.) sweet
  potatoes**
Cook (*page 285*) 25 to 35 min., or until potatoes are tender when pierced with fork. Drain.

To dry potatoes, shake pan over low heat. Peel. To heat potato masher, food mill or ricer and a mixing bowl, scald with boiling water.

Mash or rice potatoes thoroughly. Whip in until potatoes are fluffy
 2 tablespoons butter
 ½ cup hot milk (added gradually)
 **⅓ cup (about 1 oz.) shredded coconut,
  cut**
and a mixture of
 1 teaspoon salt
 ¼ teaspoon pepper
Spoon mixture into the casserole.

Bake at 350°F 20 min.

Meanwhile, cut (*page 12*) into crosswise halves
 8 (2 oz.) marshmallows
Remove casserole from oven and arrange marshmallow halves around top. Return casserole to oven and bake 5 to 10 min. longer, or until marshmallows are lightly browned and partially melted.   *4 servings*

Rutabaga Supreme

SANDRA TETLEY, SAN DIEGO, CALIF.

Grease a 1-qt. casserole.

Wash, pare and cook uncovered in a large amount of boiling salted water
 2½ lbs. rutabaga, cut in cubes or slices
Cook about 25 to 40 min., or until rutabaga is tender when pierced with a fork. Drain.

Rice or thoroughly mash rutabaga.

Whip in until rutabaga is fluffy
 2 tablespoons butter
 1 tablespoon cream or rich milk
and a mixture of
 2 teaspoons salt
 ½ teaspoon Accent
 ½ teaspoon pepper
Spoon rutabaga into casserole. Sprinkle with a mixture of
 1 tablespoon cracker crumbs
 **2 tablespoons grated Romano or
  Parmesan cheese**
Dot with
 2 teaspoons butter
Bake uncovered at 325°F 15 to 20 min., or until lightly browned.   *4 or 5 servings*

Eggs Florentine

Grease 4 ramekins or individual casseroles.

Prepare
 6 Hard-Cooked Eggs (*page 87*)
Prepare and set aside
 ½ cup buttered bread crumbs (*page 10*)
Remove and discard tough stems, roots, and bruised leaves from
 1 lb. spinach
Wash and cook spinach (*page 285*) over medium heat 8 to 10 min.

While spinach is cooking, prepare
 **1½ cups Medium White Sauce (1½ times
  recipe, *page 323*)**
Cool sauce slightly.

Add, all at one time, stirring until thoroughly blended

>**⅓ cup (about 1½ oz.) grated Cheddar or Parmesan cheese**
>
>**1 teaspoon Worcestershire sauce**

Set aside and keep warm.

When spinach is cooked, drain and coarsely chop. Season with a mixture of

>**½ teaspoon salt**
>
>**¼ teaspoon Accent**
>
>**⅛ teaspoon pepper**
>
>**⅛ teaspoon nutmeg or mace**

Divide one half of spinach among the ramekins. Cut 3 of the eggs into crosswise slices and arrange over spinach. Add to each ramekin ¼ cup of the sauce and 1 tablespoon of the buttered crumbs. Cover with remaining spinach. Cut each of remaining eggs into lengthwise quarters. Using 3 of the quarters for a ramekin, form attractive petal arrangements. Spoon remaining sauce into centers where "petals" meet. Sprinkle centers with remaining crumbs and

>**Paprika**

Bake at 350°F 15 to 20 min.   *4 servings*

Spinach in Cream

Remove and discard tough stems, roots and bruised leaves from

>**1 lb. spinach**

Wash and cook spinach (*p. 285*) over medium heat 8 to 10 min.

Drain cooked spinach and chop. Return spinach to saucepan. Blend in

>**¼ cup cream**
>
>**2 tablespoons butter or margarine**
>
>**1 tablespoon minced onion**
>
>**1 teaspoon prepared horse-radish**

and a mixture of

>**½ teaspoon salt**
>
>**¼ teaspoon Accent**
>
>**⅛ teaspoon pepper**

Place over low heat just until thoroughly heated.   *4 servings*

Spinach Timbales

These flavorful molds win friends for spinach.

Grease or oil (with salad or cooking oil—not olive oil) 8 heat-resistant custard cups. Heat water for boiling water bath (*page 12*).

Remove and discard tough stems, roots and bruised leaves from

>**2 lbs. spinach**

Wash and cook spinach (*p. 285*) over medium heat 8 to 10 min.

Drain and finely chop spinach. Combine spinach with a mixture of

>**3 eggs, well beaten**
>
>**1 cup cream or undiluted evaporated milk**
>
>**½ cup (½ slice) soft bread crumbs**
>
>**2 tablespoons melted butter or margarine**
>
>**2 tablespoons minced onion**

and a mixture of

>**1 teaspoon salt**
>
>**¼ teaspoon Accent**
>
>**¼ teaspoon nutmeg**

Mix well. Fill custard cups two-thirds full with mixture.

Bake in boiling water bath at 350°F 30 to 40 min., or until firm.

While timbales bake, prepare

>**Tomato-Cheese Sauce (½ recipe, p. 327) or Cheese Sauce (1½ times recipe, page 323)**

Run a spatula around inside of cups to loosen timbales. Unmold onto hot serving plates.

Serve sauce over unmolded timbales. If desired, garnish each serving with slices of **Hard-Cooked Egg** (*page 87*).   *8 servings*

Squash Supreme  **43**

MRS. STANLEY CARLSON
MARSHALL, MINN.

*An original and very interesting presentation
of one of the hardiest and most delightful
members of the squash family.*

Set out a 13 x 9½ x 2-in. baking dish.

Wash and cut into halves lengthwise

2 medium-size acorn squash

Remove seeds and fibers. Place cut-side down
in baking dish. Pour in boiling water to ¼-in.
depth in baking dish. Bake at 400°F 30 min.

Meanwhile, prepare and set aside

**2 cups (about 8 stalks) finely chopped
celery (page 12)**

**⅔ cup (about 3 small) finely chopped
onion (page 12)**

⅔ cup (about 2½ oz.) grated cheese

Heat in a skillet over low heat

¼ cup butter

Add the chopped onion and celery and cook
over medium heat, occasionally moving and
turning mixture with a spoon. Cook about 10
min., or until onion is transparent and celery
is tender.

Meanwhile, dissolve

2 beef bouillon cubes

in

¼ cup hot water

Add to celery-onion mixture and blend well.
Remove from heat and cool slightly. Add the
grated cheese all at one time. Blend in, with
a mixture of

1 teaspoon dry mustard

1 teaspoon paprika

1 teaspoon salt

½ teaspoon Accent

When squash has baked 30 min., remove baking dish from oven. Reduce temperature to
350°F. Turn squash and fill cavities with
cheese mixture.

Return to oven and bake 25 to 30 min. longer,
or until squash is tender when pierced with
a fork. *4 servings*

Summer Squash with Dill **44**

Set out a 3-qt. heavy saucepan having a tight-
fitting cover.

Wash, trim off ends and cut into thin crosswise slices

2 lbs. summer squash

(Choose young, tender squash; it is not usually necessary to pare them. Pare only if the
outside seems tough.)

Put squash into the saucepan with

½ cup boiling water

**2 teaspoons finely chopped fresh dill
or ¼ teaspoon dill seeds**

½ teaspoon salt

¼ teaspoon Accent

Cover saucepan and cook squash 15 to 20 min.,
or until just tender. Drain if necessary.

Mix together in top of double boiler

1 cup thick sour cream

1 tablespoon lemon juice

2 teaspoons sugar

½ teaspoon paprika

Cook over simmering water, stirring constantly, 3 to 5 min., or until sauce is thoroughly heated. Carefully mix sauce with the squash
and serve immediately. *6 servings*

Zucchini Provençale **45**

Set out a 3-qt. saucepan having a tight-fitting
cover and a 2-qt. casserole.

Wash, trim off ends, cut crosswise into ⅛-in.
slices and set aside

8 to 10 (2½ lbs.) small zucchini squash

Clean and slice (*page 12*)

¼ lb. mushrooms

Coarsely chop enough onion to yield

⅔ cup (about 3 small) coarsely chopped onion (page 12)

Heat in the saucepan

3 tablespoons olive oil

Add zucchini, mushrooms and onion. Cover saucepan and cook zucchini mixture over low heat 10 to 15 min., or until tender, occasionally turning mixture and moving it gently with a spoon.

Meanwhile, set out

⅔ cup (about 3 oz.) grated Parmesan cheese

Remove zucchini mixture from heat; lightly mix in about one half of the grated cheese with a fork. Spoon in a mixture of

1½ cups (2 6-oz. cans) tomato paste
1 clove garlic (page 12), minced; or crushed in a garlic press
1 teaspoon salt
½ teaspoon Accent
⅛ teaspoon pepper

Blend lightly but thoroughly. Turn into the casserole. Sprinkle with the remaining cheese.

Bake at 350°F 20 to 30 min.   *8 servings*

Tomato-Cabbage Scallop

Tomato-Cabbage Scallop 46

Grease 6 ramekins.

Crush finely

3 cups corn flakes

Mix in evenly and set aside

1 cup (4 oz.) grated Cheddar cheese

Remove and discard wilted outer leaves, rinse, cut into quarters (discarding core) and coarsely shred

1 1-lb. head cabbage (about 4 cups, shredded)

Cook (*p. 285*) over medium heat about 7 min., or until cabbage is tender; drain well.

Heat in a large saucepan over low heat

3 tablespoons butter or margarine

Add and cook over medium heat, occasionally moving and turning with a spoon

½ cup (about 1 medium-size) chopped onion (page 12)

Cook until onion is transparent. Blend in a mixture of

3 tablespoons flour
1 teaspoon salt
½ teaspoon Accent
⅛ teaspoon pepper

Heat until mixture bubbles. Remove saucepan from heat.

Add gradually, stirring in

2½ cups (No. 2 can) tomatoes, cut in pieces
⅓ cup chopped green pepper (page 12)

Cook rapidly, stirring constantly, until mixture thickens. Pour one third of tomato mixture into ramekins and add one half of cabbage; repeat. Cover with final one third of tomato mixture. Top with corn-flake mixture.

Bake at 375°F about 25 min.   *6 servings*

Tomato Broil

Mix and set aside

2 tablespoons fine cracker crumbs
1 teaspoon sugar
¼ teaspoon salt
¼ teaspoon Accent
⅛ teaspoon pepper

Rinse, cut away stem ends from and cut into halves crosswise

2 large tomatoes

Brush with

Melted butter or margarine

Sprinkle with the crumb mixture. Arrange tomato halves on broiler rack.

Set temperature control of range at Broil. Place broiler rack under broiler with top of tomatoes about 3 in. from source of heat. Broil 10 min., or until crumbs are lightly browned.   *4 servings*

Scalloped Tomatoes

Grease a 1½-qt. casserole.

Toast until very crisp and cut into cubes

3 slices bread

Meanwhile, clean (*page 12*) and chop

2 medium-size (about ½ lb.) onions
(about 1 cup, chopped)

Drain and break into pieces with a spoon, the contents of

1 No. 2½ can tomatoes (about 2 cups, drained)

Mix in the casserole one half of the chopped onion, the tomatoes and

½ cup cheese-cracker crumbs

and a mixture of

1½ teaspoons sugar
½ teaspoon Accent
½ teaspoon salt

Cover with the remaining chopped onion.

Spoon over mixture

¾ cup thick sour cream

Toss bread cubes over cream.

Lightly brush bread cubes with

Melted butter or margarine

Bake at 325°F 20 min., or until mixture is thoroughly heated.

Serve in sauce dishes.   *6 servings*

Vegetable Medley 47

ESTEL E. COX, JACKSONVILLE, ORE.

Set out a 10-in. skillet having a tight-fitting cover.

Remove and discard wilted outer leaves, rinse, cut into quarters (discarding core) and coarsely shred

1 small head (about ¾ lb.) cabbage
(about 3 cups, shredded)

Set aside.

Clean (*page 12*) and cut crosswise into ¼-in. slices enough celery to yield

1 cup (about 4 stalks) sliced celery

Clean (*page 12*) and coarsely chop enough green pepper to yield

1 cup (about 2 medium-size) chopped green pepper

Clean (*page 12*) and cut into thin slices

1 medium-size onion

Heat in the skillet over medium heat

1 tablespoon shortening

Add the cabbage, celery, green pepper and onion to the melted shortening.

Season with a mixture of

1 teaspoon salt
½ teaspoon Accent
¼ teaspoon pepper

Cover and cook over medium heat. Occasionally moving and turning mixture with a spoon, cook about 7 min. or until vegetables are nearly tender but still slightly crisp.

4 servings

Wild Rice with Mushrooms

Set out a medium-size skillet.

Bring to boiling in a deep saucepan

3 cups water
1 teaspoon salt
½ teaspoon Accent

Meanwhile, wash in a colander or sieve

1 cup wild rice

Add rice gradually to water so that boiling will not stop. Boil rapidly, covered, 30 to 40 min., or until a kernel of rice is entirely tender when pressed between fingers. Drain rice in a colander or sieve.

If necessary to keep rice warm, place colander over hot water and cover with a folded towel.

While rice is cooking, clean and slice

½ lb. mushrooms (page 12)

Heat in the skillet

¼ cup butter

Add mushrooms with

2 tablespoons finely chopped onion

Cook slowly, occasionally turning and moving gently with a spoon, until mushrooms are lightly browned. Remove from heat and re-

Wild Rice with Mushrooms

serve about ¼ cup mushrooms for garnish. Combine remaining mushrooms, onion, wild rice and

⅓ cup butter, melted

Toss gently until mushrooms and butter are evenly distributed throughout rice. Turn hot mixture into a warm serving dish and garnish with reserved mushrooms. *6 to 8 servings*

Broiled Bananas

(*See photo on page 209*)

Bananas are versatile, and today's taste-wise homemakers use them as vegetables.

Peel

6 firm bananas having all-yellow or slightly green-tipped peel

Arrange bananas on broiler rack. Brush generously with

Melted butter or margarine

Sprinkle with

Few grains salt

Set temperature control of range at Broil. Place in broiler with top of bananas 3 in. from source of heat for 5 min., or until bananas are lightly browned and tender when pierced with a fork.

Carefully transfer to a warm serving plate; garnish with sprigs of parsley. *6 servings*

VEGETABLES in the MICROWAVE OVEN

Part of the pleasure of eating is not only in the taste of the food, but in appearance and texture as well. The beautiful, lively colors of vegetables cooked in the microwave oven, particularly the greens of beans, spinach and asparagus, will add appeal to the most prosaic of meals. The flavor and texture of the vegetables are outstanding, too.

Vegetables cooked in the microwave oven are more nutritious than conventionally-cooked vegetables. Quick cooking and smaller amounts of water help preserve vitamins and minerals. Less liquid also decreases the chance of vegetables becoming soggy. The **Braised Onions**, for instance, are perfectly cooked in one-third the time required for conventional cooking methods. In the **Zucchini Provencale**, the sauce is delicious and the squash firm and flavorful.

It it possible to bake potatoes in the microwave oven. However, we found that while the potato cooks through, the skin is simply not crisp and smooth enough as is required for some recipes, such as **Baked Filled Potatoes**, which we have omitted.

COOKING VEGETABLES-The preparation and cooking of vegetables are somewhat different than for conventional cooking. Keep the following procedures in mind when preparing vegetables for microwave oven cooking, instead of those listed on page 285.

Pierce the skin of whole vegetables like squash and eggplant.

Cook both fresh and frozen vegetables covered, unless specified otherwise. Use plastic wrap to cover, if necessary.

Vegetables like broccoli, carrots and asparagus, which vary in size or toughness from one end to the other, should be cooked with the larger or tougher (stalk) end toward the center of the baking dish. This aids in even cooking.

You will note that with some vegetables, for instance eggplant, larger pieces cook faster; this is the reverse of other cooking methods.

Frozen vegetables usually need no water and should be cooked ice side up. We list the number of standard-size packages and the amount of time necessary to cook them.

Because timing is a crucial factor in obtaining maximum flavor and appearance from vegetables, variations in ovens and wattage are important.

Check the vegetables as the end of the recommended minimum cooking time nears. Remove the dish when it is almost done to your taste. Cover and let stand 5 min.; vegetables will continue to cook during this period.

We have prepared an easily-read chart summarizing cooking procedures and times for both fresh and frozen vegetables mentioned in this chapter or referred to elsewhere in this book. For your convenience, the vegetable, quantity, size pan needed, amount of water and the minimum recommended cooking time are all listed. Be sure to note any special instructions.

The recipes included on the chart are for both fresh and frozen plain vegetables. For recipes which call for sauces or glazes or for vegetables to be combined with other ingredients in casseroles or puddings, refer to the vegetable chart for instructions on cooking the basic vegetable. Then, continue with the directions for completing the recipe.

Some dishes using previously cooked vegetables may be served immediately; others must be covered and stand. Where necessary, recipes note the miminum recommended standing time.

If, after cooking the vegetables, no additional cooking is required, as in **Whipped Potatoes**, we simply refer you to the cooking directions for the specific vegetable as given in the chart.

REMINDERS—For more tips and an easy-to read chart comparing settings among different brands of microwave ovens, see the introductory chapter, **Home Cooking in the Microwave Oven**, in the beginning of this book.

MICROWAVE VEGETABLES

HOW TO USE THIS CHART

VEGETABLE—First, look for the name of the vegetable. Then, note the listings for fresh and/or frozen.

QUANTITY—The amounts of vegetable are given in weight (1 (10-oz.) pkg. frozen spinach; 1 lb. fresh green beans, etc.) and/or in numbers (24 small carrots; 4 ears corn; 1 medium eggplant, etc.).

SPECIAL INSTRUCTIONS—Refer to this column for any specific requirements in preparation or cooking.

PAN (covered)—The size of the cooking container is given. Cook vegetables covered, unless otherwise noted.

AMOUNT WATER—Generally, frozen vegetables require no water; exceptions are noted. For fresh vegetables, use amount specified.

MINUTES TO COOK—Minimum recommended cooking times are given. Check vegetables as the end of the cooking period nears and remove them when almost done. Cover and let stand 5 min.

VEGETABLE		QUANTITY	SPECIAL INSTRUCTIONS	PAN (covered)	AMOUNT WATER	MINUTES TO COOK
Asparagus	Fresh	1½ lbs.	None	2-qt.	3 tablespoons	8:00
	Frozen	1 (10-oz) pkg.	Cook icy side up.	1½-qt.	None	8:00
Beets	Fresh	1 lb. (small)	None	1½-qt.	¼ cup	12:00
		1 lb. (medium)	None	1½-qt.	¼ cup	8:00
Broccoli	Fresh	2 lb.	Separate into stalks. Cut an X ¼-in. deep in bottoms. Arrange with stems toward center.	3-qt.	2/3 cup	15:00
	Frozen	2 (10-oz.) pkgs.	Cook icy side up.	2-qt.	None	8:00
Cabbage	Fresh	1 medium	Shred.	3-qt.	½ cup	5:00
Carrots	Fresh	3 lbs. (24 small)	If large, cut.	3-qt.	¾ cup	18:00

VEGETABLE		QUANTITY	SPECIAL INSTRUCTIONS	PAN (covered)	AMOUNT WATER	MINUTES TO COOK
6 Cauliflower	*Fresh*	1 medium	Cook whole.	2-qt.	¼ cup	10:00
	Frozen	1 (10-oz.) pkg.	None	1½-qt.	2 tablespoons	8:00
7 Corn	*Fresh*	4 ears	Remove husks.	baking dish	None	10:00
8 Eggplant	*Fresh*	1 medium	Cut in half.	2-qt.	¼ cup water ½ teaspoon salt	8:00
		1 medium	1-in. cubes.	2-qt.	¼ cup water ½ teaspoon salt	10:00
9 Green Beans	*Fresh*	1 lb.	Crosswise cut or French cut.	1½-qt.	3 oz.	8:00
		1½ lbs.	French cut.	1½-qt.	½ cup	10:00
	Frozen	2 (10-oz.) pkgs.	French cut.	1½-qt.	4 tablespoons	8:00
		1 (10-oz.) pkg.	Crosswise cut.	1½-qt.	None	5:00
10 Lima Beans	*Frozen*	1 (10-oz.) pkg.	None	1½-qt.	¼ cup	7:30
	Baby	1 (10-oz.) pkg.	None	1½-qt.	1/3 cup	8:00
11 Onions	*Fresh*	8-12 small whole	None	1½-qt.	1 tablespoon	8:00
12 Peas	*Frozen*	1 (10-oz.) pkg.	None	1½-qt.	None	8:00
		2 (10-oz.) pkg.	None	1½-qt.	None	10:00
13 Potatoes, White	*Fresh*					
	Boiled	2 lbs.	Quartered.	3-qt.	¼ cup	10:00
	Small new	3 lbs. (24)	None	2-qt.	¾ cup	15:00
	Baked	2 lbs. (6)	Pierce; remove while slightly hard.	Paper plate or dish. Do not cover.	None	4:00-6:00 per potato
14 Potatoes, Sweet	*Fresh*	4 medium (1-1/3	Quartered.	1½-qt.	1/3 cup	12:00

VEGETABLE		QUANTITY	SPECIAL INSTRUCTIONS	PAN (covered)	AMOUNT WATER	MINUTES TO COOK
Potatoes, Sweet (continued)		Boiled to 1½ lbs. 6 medium (2 lbs.)	Quartered.	1½-qt. 2½ lbs.	½ cup	15:00
15 **Spinach**	*Fresh*	1 lb.	None.	3-qt.	¼ cup	8:00
	Frozen	1 (10-oz.) pkg.	None.	1½-qt.	None	8:00
		2 (10-oz.) pkgs.	None.	1½-qt.	None	10:00
16 **Squash, Acorn**	*Fresh*	2 medium	Cut in half. Remove seeds. Cook cut side down.	baking dish	None	12:00
17 **Squash, Summer**	*Fresh*	2 lbs.	¼-in. slices.	1½-qt.	2 tablespoons	10:00
18 **Squash, Zucchini**	*Fresh*		¼-in. slices.	1½-qt.	2 tablespoons	10:00

French-Style Green Beans and Onions **19** *(page 287)*

Use a covered casserole.

Follow **9** Recipe for green beans and **11** Recipe for onions.

Assemble with sauce as in △ Recipe and COOK to heat (about 5 min.).

Green Beans Supreme **20**
(page 287)

Use a 1-qt. casserole or baking dish.

Follow **9** Recipe for green beans.

COOK to melt butter. Add onion and COOK until transparent (about 3 min.).

Add flour mixture and stir thoroughly. COOK, stirring every 1 min., to bubbling (about 2 min.).

Add milk and stir to blend. COOK, stirring every 1 min., to boil (about 3 min.).

Assemble casserole and COOK uncovered until cheese melts and bubbles at edges (about 3 min.).

Sweet-Sour Beets **21**
(page 288)

Use a 1½-qt. covered casserole.

Follow **2** Recipe for beets.

Combine sugar with liquids and COOK, stirring every 30 sec., to boil (about 2 min.).

Add beets and butter, cover and COOK, stirring every 30 sec., to boil (about 3 min.).

Beets in Orange Sauce **22**
(page 288)

Follow **2** Recipe with changes as in △ Recipe.

Lemon-Buttered Beets **23**
(page 289)

Follow **2** Recipe with changes as in Recipe.

COOK beets and sauce, uncovered, tossing every 30 sec., until thoroughly heated (about 3 min.).

Broccoli with Horse-radish Cream **24** *(page 289)*

Follow **3** Recipe for broccoli.

For the sauce, use a small casserole. Add sour cream mixture and COOK, stirring every 30 sec., to heat (about 1 min.); Do not boil.

Broccoli Polonaise **25**
(page 289)

Follow **3** Recipe for broccoli.

For Polonaise Topping— In a small casserole, COOK to melt butter. Add bread crumbs and stir to coat. COOK to heat (about 10 min.).

Candied Carrots 26
(pate 290)

Follow **5** Recipe for carrots.

Use a 3-qt. casserole. COOK to melt butter. Blend in brown sugar and water. COOK, stirring every 30 sec., until sugar dissolves and mixture bubbles (about 3 min.).

Add carrots and COOK uncovered, until heated and glazed (about 3 min.).

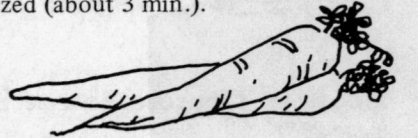

Glazed Carrots *(page 290)* 27

Follow **26** Recipe with changes as in △ Recipe.

Festive Corn *(page 291)* 28

Use a small casserole.

COOK to melt butter. Add onions and pepper and COOK, stirring every 1½ min., until onions are transparent (about 3 min.).

Add corn, cover and COOK, separating and stirring after 2 min., agains after 1 min. more, until corn is tender (about 5 min.).

Mix in pimiento and seasonings. Cover and COOK to heat (about 15 sec.).

OVERALL COOKING TIME: 8:15

Plantation Corn Pudding *(page 292)* 29

Use a 1½-qt. casserole. *Do not grease.*
COOK to scald milk (about 4 min.).

Combine all ingredients and COOK uncovered until a silver knife comes out clean (about 12 min.).

OVERALL COOKING TIME: 16:00

Scalloped Corn *(page 292)* 30

Use a 1-qt. casserole. *Do not butter.*

Assemble casserole. COOK uncovered until mixture bubbles and is heated through (about 10 min.).
OVERALL COOKING TIME: 10:00

Corn-Tomato Scallop 31
(page 293)

Follow **30** Recipe with changes as in △ Recipe.

Scalloped Eggplant 32
(page 293)

Use a 1-qt. casserole. *Do not grease.*

Follow **8** Recipe for eggplant.

COOK to scald milk (about 3 min.). Assemble casserole and COOK uncovered to heat through (about 5 min.). SLOWCOOK uncovered, rotating pan every 5 min., until vegetables are tender and sauce slightly thickened (about 15 min.).

Butter-Fried Mushrooms *(page 293)* 33

Use a browning skillet.

Put mushrooms and butter in skillet and COOK, stirring every 2 min., until tneder and very lightly brown (about 5 min.).

OVERALL COOKING TIME: 5:00

Braised Onions *(page 294)*

Use a 2-qt. covered casserole.

Assemble casserole. COOK to heat through (about 5 min.). SLOWCOOK, rotating pan every 5 min., until onions are tender (about 15 min.).

Uncover, sprinkle with cheese and crumbs. COOK until cheese in melted (about 3 min.).
OVERALL COOKING TIME: 23:00

Braised Turnips *(page 294)*

Follow **34** Recipe with changes as in △ Recipe, except COOK until heated (about 5 min.). SLOWCOOK until tender (about 10 min.).

OVERALL COOKING TIME: 15:00

O'Brien Potatoes
(page 297)

Use a 1½-qt. casserole.

COOK potatoes uncovered using just enough water to cover by one-fourth. Rotate pan every 5 min. (about 15 min.).

Add all ingredients to casserole and COOK uncovered, stirring every 5 min., until lightly browned (about 8 min.). (Potatoes will not crisp.)

Cover and let stand 5 min.
OVERALL COOKING TIME: 23:00

Jungle-"Fried" Potatoes *(page 297)*

Use a 1½-qt. casserole.

Arrange potatoes and onions in casserole, using only enough water to cover bottom of pan by ¼ in. Cover and COOK until potatoes are slightly tender (about 6 min.).

Add seasonings and SLOWCOOK uncovered until water is evaporated (about 5 min.).

Cover and let stand 5 min.
OVERALL COOKING TIME: 11:00

Parsley New Potatoes
(page 298)

Follow **13** Recipe for potatoes.

In a small casserole, COOK to melt butter. Stir in seasonings and serve as in Recipe.

Cover and let stand 5 min.

Scalloped Sweet Potatoes *(page 299)*

Follow **14** Recipe for potatoes. *Do not grease.*

Assemble casserole and cover. COOK until thoroughly heated (about 15 min.).

Cover and let stand 5 min.

Candied Sweet Potatoes 40
(page 299)

Use a 1½-qt. casserole.

Follow 14 Recipe for potatoes.

In a small casserole, COOK to melt butter. Add sugar and slat and COOK, stirring and rotating pan every 1½ minutes., until sugar dissolves and mixture bubbles (about 3 min.).

Add potatoes and COOK, stirring and rotating every 1 min., until heated and glazed (about 5 min.).

Cover and let stand 5 min.

Spinach in Cream 41
(page 301)

Use a 1½-qt. casserole.

Follow 15 Recipe for spinach.

Assemble casserole. COOK uncovered to heat (about 5 min.).

Cover and let stand 5 min.

Spinach Timbales 42
(page 301)

Use 6 (instead of 8) 6-oz. custard cups. *Do not grease.*

Follow 15 Recipe for spinach.

Fill custard cups. COOK uncovered, rotating every 1 min., until firm (about 5 min.). Complete and serve as in Recipe.

Cover and let stand 5 min.

Squash Supreme 43
(page 302)

Use a 1-qt. casserole for stuffing and a baking dish.

Follow 16 Recipe for acorn squash.

COOK to melt butter. Add onion and celery and COOK, stirring every 1 min., until onion is transparent and celery tender (about 5 min.).

Stuff squash and arrange in baking dish. COOK uncovered, rotating pan every 2 min., to heat through (about 10 min.).

Cover and let stand 5 min.

Summer Squash with Dill 44 *(page 302)*

Use a 2-qt. casserole and a small casserole for the sauce.

Follow 17 Recipe for squash, except add dill to water.

Combine sour cream and seasonings in casserole. COOK uncovered stirring every 1 min., to heat (about 3 min.). Do not boil.

Zucchini Provençale 45
(page 302)

Use a 2-qt. casserole.

COOK to heat olive oil (about 3 min.).

Add zucchini, mushrooms, onions and cover. COOK, rotating every 3 min., until vegetables are tender (about 10 min.).

Blend in remaining ingredients and sprinkle with cheese. COOK uncovered until thoroughly heated and cheese melts (about 5 min.).

Cover and let stand 5 min.

Tomato-Cabbage Scallop 46
(page 303)

Use 6 ramekins.

Follow 4 Recipe for cabbage.

COOK to melt butter. Add onions and COOK until transparent (about 2 min.).

Add flour mixture and COOK, stirring every 30 sec., until bubbling.

Add tomatoes and green pepper and COOK, stirring every 1 min., to thicken (about 3 min.).

Assemble ramekins. COOK, rotating every 5 min., to heat through and melt cheese (about 10 min.).

Vegetable Medley 47
(page 304)

Use a 2-qt. casserole.

COOK to melt fat. Add all vegetables and seasonings to casserole. Cover and COOK to heat through (about 5 min.). Stir. SLOWCOOK covered, stirring every 2½ min., until vegetables are nearly tender (about 5 min.).

Wild Rice with 48
Mushrooms *(page 305)*

Use a 2-qt. casserole and a browning skillet.

In browning skillet, COOK to melt butter. Add mushrooms and onions and COOK, stirring every 2½ min., until mushrooms are lightly browned (about 5 min.).

Using the 2-qt. casserole, follow package directions for wild rice. It will cook in about 1/3 the time specified for conventional cooking.

VEGETABLES in the SLOW COOKER

Using the slow cooker for vegetables can be a great boon to the busy cook, even though cooking fresh vegetables on the conventional stove is not usually a time-consuming part of meal preparation.

For example, if you are planning an elaborate meal that will require the use of all stove burners, these recipes can be set to cooking hours ahead of time—some even the night before—with the mess of preparation, such as corn husks or potato peels, all cleared away leaving you free to concentrate on the rest of the menu. If you are planning a quick and easy dinner with a simple meat course such as broiled steaks or chops, the slow cooker can help you to serve a vegetable which has a little extra taste appeal, such as **Glazed Carrots** or **Sweet-Sour Beets.** The vegetables can be cooked well ahead of time, even the day before, and refrigerated. Reheat and add the sauces as mealtime nears.

Most of these dishes will hold on LOW for at least an hour or two until the rest of the meal is ready. That is not usually possible on the stove, where even on the lowest setting, vegetable dishes tend to dry out or scorch.

We have included recipes we consider best suited to the slow cooker—those that won't lose color or texture or get too watery as happens with squash. The **Corn-on-the-Cob** is excellent, although it is usually considered a quick-cooking vegetable. Because it is cooked with no water in the slow cooker, it stays tender and tasty without becoming soggy.

We recommend cooking the vegetables to the right degree of tenderness first, then adding sauces either on the stove or in the slow cooker, whichever is most convenient for you. If the sauce is to be prepared in the slow cooker, the vegetables must usually be removed, the sauce blended, and the vegetables returned to the pot to be mixed with the sauce. We give directions with each recipe for preparing the sauces in the slow cooker.

REMINDERS—The introductory chapter, **Home Cooking in the Slow Cooker,** in the beginning of this book provides additional tips and an easy-to-read chart comparing settings among different brands of slow cookers.

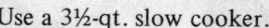

Sweet-Sour Beets *(page 288)*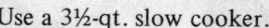

Use a 3½-qt. slow cooker.

Put beets and 1 qt. water in slow cooker. Cove and cook on LOW for 8 to 9 hrs.

Complete sauce on top of the stove.

Beets in Orange Sauce
(page 288)

Follow ① Recipe with changes as ⚠ in Recipe.

Lemon-Buttered Beets
(page 289)

Place small beets and 1 cup water in slow cooker. Cover and cook on LOW for 9 to 10 hrs.

To complete sauce, remove beets. Set slow Cooker on HIGH, add remaining ingredients and cook until butter melts. You may reset to LOW for an additional 1 to 2 hrs.

Candied Carrots *(page 290)*

Use a 3½-qt. slow cooker.

Place carrots in slow cooker. Add water to cover by two-thirds.

Cook on LOW for 12 to 14 hrs. *Or,* on HIGH for 7 to 8 hrs.

Drain carrots and dry. Return to slow cooker and reset to HIGH. Pour sugar mixture over carrots and toss gently to coat.

Cover and cook on HIGH to heat glaze (about 10 min.).

Glazed Carrots *(page 290)*

Follow ④ Recipe with changes as in △ Recipe, except but butter in slow cooker and melt on HIGH. Stir in sugar. Add carrots and toss gently to coat. Heat on HIGH 10 min.

Corn-on-the-Cob *(page 292)*

Use a 3½-qt. slow cooker.

Wrap ears in aluminum foil. Place upright in slow cooker. Do not add water.

Cover and cook on HIGH for 4 to 7 hrs.

Parsley New Potatoes
(page 298)

Use a 3½-qt. slow cooker.

Place potatoes and water to cover by two-thirds in slow cooker.

Cover and cook on LOW for 6 to 8 hrs.

Drain potatoes. Set cooker on HIGH, melt butter and stir in seasonings. Return potatoes and toss gently to coat with butter.

Candied Sweet Potatoes
(page 299)

Use a 3½-qt. slow cooker.

Place sweet potatoes in slow cooker and add water to cover by two-thirds.

Cover and cook on LOW for 8 to 9 hrs.

Drain potatoes. Reset slow cooker to HIGH, melt butter and stir in brown sugar and salt. Cook about 10 min., until heated.

Add potatoes and toss gently to coat with glaze. Cover and cook on HIGH to heat (about 10 min.).

SALADS and Salad Dressings

The Good Salad

Salads bring to the table an ineffable touch of freshness. Composed of fresh or cooked foods, touched to piquancy by the right dressing and usually accompanied by a flash of green, they appeal to eye and taste and satisfy both. Today's salad recipes, conspicuously missing from cookbooks 50 years ago, show a riot of inventiveness in creating new combinations of ingredients for interesting and tantalizing results.

Salads are exciting! Look at the variety—salads made with fruits, vegetables and hearty protein foods; salads tossed, molded or frozen; salads for appetizer, main course, accompaniment or dessert.

Salads are worthwhile eating! Look at the appetite appeal of these health-giving foods—fresh vegetables and fruits chock-full of needed vitamins and minerals; protein-rich meat and fish, poultry, cheese and eggs; salad greens and raw vegetables for bulk, necessary for good digestion.

A salad is only as good as its makings so select the ingredients with care. Greens should be fresh, crisp and dry, vegetables garden-fresh, and fruits firm, fully ripe and free from blemish. When using canned products choose those of good quality and appearance. Meat, poultry, fish, cheese and eggs should be fresh. Use only the appetizing leftovers.

A salad should have a carefree look, not too carefully arranged to look overhandled nor too carelessly prepared to look untidy. A salad should fit the serving dish, not skimpily nor too full.

A salad is complemented by the dressing so suit it to the salad. Dressings should coat the greens, not drown them; they should accompany the salad, not hide it.

GELATIN TECHNIQUES—Recipes will remind you:
Lightly oil molds with a flavorless salad or cooking oil (not olive oil). Invert mold to drain excess oil.
Rinse molds with cold water when shiny coating of oil is not desirable; invert to drain.
Soften gelatin in liquid as specified in recipes.
Dissolve softened gelatin *completely* as recipe directs, over very hot water or in very hot liquid.
Chill gelatin mixtures in the refrigerator, stirring occasionally, or over ice and water, stirring frequently, until of desired consistency. Chill gelatin mixtures until slightly thicker than consistency of thick, unbeaten egg white before adding remainder of ingredients, such as chopped or whole foods which would sink to bottom of mold if the gelatin were not sufficiently thickened. When gelatin mixture is already thick because of ingredients or is not a clear mixture, chill until it begins to gel (gets slightly thicker) before adding chopped or whole foods.
Prevent separation of layered molds by chilling gelatin mixtures until slightly set (each mixture is of same consistency); layers should be of almost same consistency when turning one mixture onto another so that they will be fused when unmolded.
Unmold gelatin by running tip of knife around edge of mold to loosen and to permit air to get into mold. Invert mold onto chilled serving plate. If mold does not loosen because of air lock, wet a clean towel in hot water and wring almost dry. Wrap hot towel around mold for a few seconds only. If mold still does not loosen, repeat.
Beat whipping cream to a medium consistency (piles softly), not soft peaks, when it is to be blended with a gelatin mixture.

SALAD GREENS AND PREPARATION—The many kinds of greens star in the tossed salad and form the background of other salads. Select greens that are fresh, blemish-free and firm. In general, wash before storing, drain thoroughly and gently pat dry with a soft, clean towel or absorbent paper. Place in the refrigerator in vegetable drawers or plastic bags, or wrap tightly in waxed paper, moisture-vapor-proof material or aluminum foil to prevent greens from wilting, unless refrigerator maintains a comparatively high humidity.

Never soak greens when washing them. If necessary, crisp them by placing them for a short time in ice and water. Before using, remove every bit of moisture left from washing or crisping.

Lettuce—Discard bruised and wilted leaves; rinse; drain; dry. *Cups*—Remove core from head lettuce with sharp, pointed knife; let cold water run into core cavity to loosen leaves; drain; gently pull leaves from head; cut off heavy, coarse ends; pat dry. *Head* or *Iceberg*—firm, compact head of medium-green outside leaf, pale green heart. *Butterhead* or *Boston*—soft, lighter head of light green outside leaf, light yellow heart; not as crisp as iceberg. *Romaine* or *Cos*—green elongated head with coarser leaf and stronger flavor than iceberg. *Bibb* or *Limestone*—head similar to Boston in size and shape; deep green leaves with delicate flavor. *Leaf*—many varieties grown commercially and in the home garden; leafy bunches of curly-edged leaves.

Cabbage—Store in cool place without washing. Discard bruised and wilted outside leaves, rinse, cut into quarters and remove core; chop or shred as directed in recipes. *Early* or *new*—pointed heads. *Danish-type*—staple winter cabbage; compact head. *Savoy*—round head of yellowish, crimped leaves. *Celery* or *Chinese*—long, oval-shaped head of pale green to white leaves; characteristics of romaine and cabbage. *Red*—very tight head of purple leaves.

Endive—Discard bruised and wilted leaves; rinse; drain; dry. *Curly endive* (often called chicory)—bunchy head with narrow, ragged-edged curly leaves; dark green outside, pale yellow heart; pleasant bitter taste. *Broad-leaf endive* (often called escarole)—bunchy head of broad leaves that do not curl at tips; dark green outer leaves, pale yellow heart; not as bitter as curly endive. *French endive* (Witloof chicory)—thin, elongated stalk usually bleached white while growing.

Kale—Curly-leafed green of cabbage family; dark green; may have slightly browned edges caused by cold weather in growing season. Trim off tough stems and bruised or wilted leaves; wash; drain; dry.

Parsley—Discard coarse stems and bruised leaves; wash gently but thoroughly in cold water; drain and shake off excess water; pat dry. Store in tightly covered jar or plastic bag in refrigerator.

Spinach—Discard tough stems, roots and bruised or wilted leaves. Wash leaves thoroughly by lifting up and down several times in a large amount of cold water. Lift leaves out of water each time before pouring off water; repeat in clean water until all sand and grit are removed. Drain; pat dry.

Water Cress—See PARSLEY. Water cress also may be stored before it is washed. Stand a tied bunch in a jar or bowl holding enough cold water to reach about halfway up stems. Cover and store in refrigerator. When using, snip off amount needed, rinse, drain and shake off excess water. Or store cleaned water cress in a plastic bag in refrigerator.

Other Greens—*Field salad*—spoon-shaped leaves; *finocchio*—anise-flavored stalk (like celery); *Swiss chard*—use tops only (like beet greens);—*beet, dandelion, mustard, turnip greens*—use tops only.

SALAD DRESSINGS—A twist of the wrist and a turn or two of the imagination—endless variations are possible from the basic French, mayonnaise and cooked dressings. Others are the sweet or sour cream, cream or cottage cheese and yogurt dressings and the bacon-vinegar type for wilted greens.

Mayonnaise has caused many a tear when it has broken or separated because the oil was added too rapidly at the beginning. The problem is to re-form (re-emulsify) the mayonnaise; the solution is to gradually add the mayonnaise, beating constantly, to 1 egg yolk, 1 tablespoon cold water, small quantity of vinegar or small portion of good mayonnaise. Mayonnaise will separate if frozen or kept in the coldest part of the refrigerator.

French dressings need to be shaken before using to mix thoroughly and re-form the emulsion.

Salad dressings should be stored covered in a cool place or in the refrigerator.

Raw Vegetable Relishes

(See photo on page 288)

Use raw vegetables for colorful, easy-to-prepare relishes. Select only those that are in prime condition—crisp, fresh, preferably young and tender. Clean them thoroughly; with a sharp knife trim ends, where necessary, and cut the vegetables into varied shapes as suggested. Chill thoroughly in ice and water or in refrigerator before serving. Sprinkle lightly with Accent.

Carrot Curls—Cut tender cleaned carrots into halves lengthwise. Using a vegetable parer, shave into paper-thin strips. Curl around finger. Fasten with wooden pick and chill in ice and water until curled. Drain and remove pick before serving.

Carrot Sticks—Cut tender cleaned carrots into narrow strips about 3 in. long. Chill in the refrigerator.

Cauliflowerets—Remove outside leaves and stalk from cauliflower head. Separate cauliflower into small flowerets. Let stand in cold salted water 20 to 30 min. to remove any dust or small insects which settle in the cauliflower. Drain and chill in the refrigerator.

Double Celery Curls—Cut tender cleaned celery into 2½- to 3-in. lengths. Slit each into narrow parallel strips from either end almost to center. Chill in ice and water until curled. Drain before serving.

Fluted Cucumber Slices—Draw tines of a fork lengthwise over entire surface of rinsed cucumbers. Cut into thin slices.

Green Pepper Strips—Rinse whole green peppers and cut into halves lengthwise. Carefully remove all white fiber and seeds; slice lengthwise into strips. For rings, slice cleaned whole green peppers crosswise.

Radish Fans—Wash firm red or white radishes. Cut off root ends. Cut thin lengthwise parallel slices almost to end. Chill in ice and water until slices spread apart. Drain.

Radish Roses—Wash firm red radishes. Cut off root ends. On each, leave a bit of stem and a fresh leaf or two for garnish. With a sharp knife, mark petals. Pare each petal thinly from tip almost to stem. Chill in ice and water until petals spread apart. Drain before serving.

Scallions (green onions)—Cut off roots and trim green tops to 2 to 3 in., discarding any wilted or bruised parts. Peel and rinse.

Tomato Wedges—Rinse firm tomatoes and put into boiling water about ½ min., or until skin loosens. Peel, cut out stem ends and chill. Place chilled tomato on flat surface and cut lengthwise into six or eight wedges.

Wilted Lettuce

Rinse, pat dry and separate into leaves
1 large head lettuce

Place in a large bowl and cover. Set aside in refrigerator.

Dice and panbroil *(p.161)*, reserving fat
6 slices bacon

Set bacon aside.

Put into the skillet ¼ cup of the reserved bacon fat and
½ cup vinegar
¼ cup water
3 tablespoons sugar
½ teaspoon salt
¼ teaspoon Accent

Heat mixture to boiling, stirring well. Stir in the bacon. Immediately pour vinegar mixture over the lettuce and toss lightly to thoroughly coat lettuce leaves.

Serve at once.   *About 6 servings*

Caesar Salad

Set out a large salad bowl.

Combine
 ¼ **cup salad or olive oil**
 ¼ **cup lemon juice**
 ¼ **teaspoon Worcestershire sauce**
 1 **clove garlic (page 12), cut in halves**
Chill in refrigerator 1 hr.

Wash, discarding bruised leaves, and thoroughly dry (use as much of each green as desired)
 Curly endive
 Lettuce
 Romaine
 Water cress
Tear enough greens into bite-size pieces to yield about 2 qts. Put into large plastic bag or vegetable freshener. Place in refrigerator to chill at least 1 hr.

When the dressing is chilled, remove from refrigerator and remove and reserve garlic. Return dressing to refrigerator.

Heat over low heat in a large skillet
 2 **tablespoons salad or olive oil**
Add the clove of garlic from the dressing and
 1 **clove garlic, cut in halves**
Meanwhile, stack and, if desired, trim crusts from
 2 **slices toasted bread**
Cut bread into ½-in. cubes. Add to skillet and move gently with a spoon over medium heat until all sides of cubes are well coated and browned. Remove from heat.

Rub the salad bowl with
 1 **clove garlic, cut in halves**
Remove salad greens from refrigerator and put into bowl. Sprinkle over greens a mixture of
 ¾ **cup grated Parmesan cheese**
 ½ **teaspoon dry mustard**
 ½ **teaspoon salt**
 ½ **teaspoon Accent**
 ¼ **teaspoon pepper**
Shake the chilled salad dressing and pour over the greens.

Caesar Salad

Break into a small bowl
 1 **egg**
Add to the seasoned greens. Gently turn and toss salad until greens are well coated with dressing and no trace of egg remains. Add the croutons and toss lightly to mix thoroughly. Top with
 Anchovy fillets (about 12 to 15)
Serve at once.   *6 to 8 servings*

Kidney Bean Salad

Prepare and dice
 4 **Hard-Cooked Eggs (page 87)**
Meanwhile, drain contents of
 1 **No. 2 can kidney beans (about**
 2 **cups, drained)**
Put beans into a bowl. Add the eggs and toss lightly with
 ⅓ **cup coarsely chopped sweet pickle**
 ¼ **cup finely chopped onion**
 3 **tablespoons sweet pickle juice**
 ¼ **teaspoon Accent**
Blend together
 ½ **cup Mayonnaise (page 319)**
 1 **tablespoon sweet pickle liquid**
Turn dressing over salad mixture and toss lightly to coat vegetables. Chill in refrigerator until ready to serve.

Serve in crisp lettuce cups. *About 4 servings*

Hot Potato Salad

△ Garden Potato Salad

Follow ▲ Recipe; increase potatoes to 6. Prepare 2 **Hard-Cooked Eggs** (*page 87*). Dice and add to potatoes. Decrease celery to ½ cup and add ½ cup diced, pared **cucumber** and ¼ cup chopped **onion.** Mix with potatoes and eggs. Add and blend until vegetables are well coated ¼ cup **French Dressing** (*page 318*). Omit shrimp, olives, pickle relish and ketchup. Decrease total amount of Mayonnaise to ¾ cup and blend in with potato mixture shortly before serving. To serve, sprinkle with **paprika.**

▲ Louisiana Potato Salad

MRS. HARVEY SPARKS, KENT, WASH.

Wash and cook (*page 285*) 20 to 30 min.
   4 medium-size (about 1⅓ lbs.)
      potatoes

Drain potatoes. To dry potatoes, shake pan over low heat. Set aside to cool.

Peel potatoes; cut into cubes and toss with
   1 cup chopped celery (*page 12*)
   ¼ cup chopped green pepper (*page 12*)
   ½ cup Mayonnaise (*page 319*)
and a mixture of
   1½ teaspoons salt
   ½ teaspoon Accent
   ⅛ teaspoon pepper
Cover and set aside in refrigerator to chill.

Drain, remove black vein, coarsely chop and chill in refrigerator contents of
   2 5-oz. cans shrimp (about 1½ cups, drained)
(Or prepare 1 lb. fresh shrimp with shells, see Cooked Shrimp, *page 242*.)

Shortly before serving, cut into thin slices
   6 stuffed olives
Mix together
   ½ cup Mayonnaise
   2 tablespoons sweet pickle relish
   2 tablespoons ketchup
Gently blend potato mixture, shrimp, olives and dressing together, tossing lightly to coat vegetables and shrimp.   *4 to 6 servings*

Hot Potato Salad

Wash and cook (*page 285*) 20 to 30 min.
   6 medium-size (about 2 lbs.) potatoes
Drain potatoes. To dry potatoes, shake pan over low heat. Peel potatoes, cut into ¼-in. slices, put in a bowl and toss lightly with
   1 cup (about 2 medium-size) finely chopped onion (*page 12*)
   3 tablespoons finely chopped parsley
and a mixture of
   1½ teaspoons Accent
   1¼ teaspoons salt
   ¼ teaspoon pepper
Set aside.

Combine in a small saucepan and heat to boiling
   ⅔ cup vinegar
   ⅓ cup water
   1½ teaspoons sugar
Beat slightly
   1 egg
Continue beating while gradually adding the vinegar mixture. Add gradually, while beating constantly
   ⅓ cup salad oil
Pour dressing over potato mixture and toss lightly to coat evenly. Turn salad into a large skillet and put over low heat for 10 to 15 min., or until potatoes are heated. Keep mixture moving gently with spoon.   *About 6 servings*

▲ Creamy Cole Slaw

Put a large bowl into refrigerator to chill.

Blend together thoroughly
½ cup Mayonnaise (page 319)
¼ cup thick sour cream
1 tablespoon lemon juice
and a mixture of
2 teaspoons celery seed
1 teaspoon sugar
¼ teaspoon salt
⅛ teaspoon Accent
Few grains pepper
Place in refrigerator to chill.

Wash and finely shred or chop
¾ lb. cabbage (about 3 cups, shredded)
Put cabbage into the bowl, cover and place in refrigerator to chill.

Shortly before serving time, remove cabbage from refrigerator and pour over enough chilled dressing to moisten. Toss lightly to blend.

Wash, quarter, core and thinly slice
3 apples
Gently toss apple slices with the cabbage. Add more dressing if desired.   *About 6 servings*

△ Pineapple Cole Slaw

Follow ▲ Recipe. Omit celery seed. Substitute drained contents of 1 9-oz. can **pineapple tidbits** (about ⅔ cup drained) for apples.

Penny Salad
CLAUDE E. METZ, MORENCI, MICH.

An economy salad with a luxury flavor.

Rinse, shred and put into a large bowl
1 lb. cabbage (about 4 cups, shredded)
Cover and place in refrigerator to chill.

Blend together and set in refrigerator to chill
¾ cup Mayonnaise (page 319)
¼ cup sugar
2 tablespoons vinegar
¼ teaspoon salt
¼ teaspoon Accent
Few grains pepper
Coarsely chop and set aside
1 cup (about 5 oz.) unsalted peanuts, without skins
Shortly before serving, remove cabbage from refrigerator. Pour the chilled dressing over the cabbage. Toss lightly until cabbage is well coated. Mix in the nuts and serve immediately.
About 8 servings

Red Cabbage-Almond Slaw

Wash and finely shred or chop
¾ lb. red cabbage (about 3 cups, shredded)
Put cabbage into a bowl, cover and place in refrigerator to chill.

Prepare and set aside
½ to 1 cup (about 3 to 5 oz.) whole, toasted, blanched almonds (page 11)
Drain thoroughly, reserving sirup, contents of
1 9-oz. can pineapple tidbits (about ⅔ cup, drained)
Blend together 1 to 2 tablespoons of the reserved pineapple sirup and
⅓ to ½ cup Cooked Salad Dressing (page 319)
Place in refrigerator to chill.

Shortly before serving time, remove cabbage from refrigerator and mix lightly with the almonds and drained pineapple tidbits. Pour over cabbage mixture enough chilled dressing to moisten. Toss lightly to blend. Add more dressing if desired.   *About 6 servings*

Fruit Salad Bowl and Pineapple Salad Dressing

Fruit Salad Bowl

A cool and pretty lure for languid appetites.

Thoroughly chill salad ingredients. Place a salad bowl in refrigerator to chill.

Prepare and chill in refrigerator
Pineapple Salad Dressing (page 320)
Wash, discarding bruised leaves, and thoroughly dry (enough to line the salad bowl)
Curly endive, chicory or Bibb lettuce
Line the bowl with the greens.

With a sharp knife, cut away peel and white membrane from
2 grapefruit
Remove sections by cutting on either side of dividing membranes; remove section by section, over a small bowl to save the juice. Set sections aside.

Wash, quarter and core (do not pare)
1 red apple
Cut into slices about ¼ in. thick and add to bowl containing the grapefruit juice. Toss apple slices gently to cover with juice (this helps to prevent discoloring). Arrange apple slices and grapefruit sections on endive along sides of salad bowl (see photo).

Carefully sort and rinse (do not hull)
⅔ cup strawberries
Set aside to drain.

Drain (reserving sirup for use in other food preparation) contents of
1 14-oz. can pineapple chunks (about 1⅓ cups, drained)
Pile pineapple chunks in center of salad bowl. Arrange strawberries around the pineapple. Sprinkle over pineapple
2 tablespoons chopped pecans
Serve immediately with the Pineapple Salad Dressing.   *About 8 servings*

Medley Fruit Salad

Place 5 luncheon plates in the refrigerator to chill. Thoroughly chill salad ingredients.

Drain (reserving sirup for use in other food preparation) contents of
1 No. 2 can pear halves (about 10)
Set aside in refrigerator.

For Frosted Grapes—Beat until frothy
1 egg white
Dip into the beaten egg white
1 bunch Tokay grapes
Shake off excess egg white and dip grapes into
Sugar
Set aside to dry. Chill in refrigerator if desired.

For Cheese-Nut Balls—Set out
3 oz. (1 pkg.) cream cheese
½ oz. Blue cheese
Prepare and set aside
Hazelnuts, chopped
Form into a ball about ½ teaspoon of the Blue cheese. With about 2 teaspoons of the cream cheese form a layer around the Blue cheese ball. Shape into a smooth ball. Roll in chopped hazelnuts. Repeat procedure until 10 balls are formed. Set balls aside.

For Orange Sections—With a sharp knife cut away peel and white membrane from
2 oranges
Remove sections by cutting on either side of dividing membrane; remove sections over a small bowl to save juice. Set the orange sections aside.

To Assemble Salad—Rinse and pat dry
Lettuce or other salad greens
Place lettuce leaves on chilled plates. Arrange two pear halves cut-side up on lettuce on each plate. Place one Cheese-Nut Ball in each pear cavity. Arrange orange sections and frosted grapes on plate (see photo). Garnish with
Water cress
If desired, serve with **Pineapple Salad Dressing** (*page 320*).   *5 servings*

Peachy Salad Plate

Place four luncheon plates in the refrigerator to chill. Thoroughly chill salad ingredients.

Sort, rinse and set aside to drain
2 cups ripe blueberries
Wash and thoroughly dry (enough to line the salad plates)
Lettuce or other salad greens
Place lettuce leaves on chilled plates.

Set out
1 cup cream-style cottage cheese
Spoon about ¼ cup of cottage cheese onto center of each plate. Sprinkle with
Paprika
Rinse and plunge into boiling water to loosen the skins
6 medium-size (about 1½ lbs.) ripe peaches
Plunge peaches into cold water. Gently slip

Peachy Salad Plate

off skins and discard; cut peaches into halves; remove and discard pits. To prevent darkening, brush peach halves with
Lemon, orange or pineapple juice
Place three peach halves onto lettuce on each luncheon plate. Allowing about ½ cup blueberries for each serving, spoon blueberries into the center cavity of each peach half.

Serve immediately with **Fluffy Citrus Salad Dressing** (*page 320*) or **Pineapple Salad Dressing** (*page 320*) and **Iced Tea** (*page 561*).
4 servings

Waldorf Salad

Wash, quarter, core and dice
2 medium-size apples (about 2 cups, diced)
Combine with
1 cup chopped celery (*page 12*)
½ cup (about 2 oz.) chopped walnuts
Lightly toss with
¼ teaspoon salt
¼ teaspoon Accent
¼ cup mayonnaise
Chill in refrigerator until ready to serve.

Serve in crisp lettuce cups. Sprinkle with
Paprika
About 4 servings

Medley Fruit Salad

313

Southwestern Salad Bowl

Creamy avocado slices, juicy grapefruit sections and onion rings—mmmm! A perfect pick-up for days when the mercury soars. The citrus fancier may add slices of orange.

Set out a salad bowl.

Wash, discarding bruised leaves, and thoroughly dry (enough to line the salad bowl)
   Bibb lettuce or leaf lettuce
With a sharp knife, cut away peel and white membrane from
   1 large grapefruit
Remove sections by cutting on either side of dividing membranes; remove section by section, over a bowl to save the juice. Set aside.

Rinse, peel, cut into halves and remove and discard pit from
   1 large avocado
Cut into slices and add to bowl containing the grapefruit juice. Toss avocado slices gently to cover with juice (this helps to prevent discoloring).

Arrange the slices of avocado alternately with grapefruit sections on the lettuce. Cover and place in refrigerator until ready to serve.

Just before serving, arrange over grapefruit and avocado sections
   **7 or 8 thin onion rings (thinly slice
      onion, page 12; separate into rings)**
Serve with
   French Dressing (page 318)
                              4 to 6 servings

Frozen Fruit Salad

Set refrigerator control at coldest operating temperature. Put a bowl and a rotary beater into refrigerator to chill. Set out a 1½-qt. mold, a large refrigerator tray or 3 1-pt. round freezer-type containers.

Coarsely chop and set aside
   **½ cup (about 2½ oz.) salted, toasted,
      blanched almonds (page 11)**
Set aside to drain, reserving sirup, contents of
   **1 No. 2 can crushed pineapple (about
      1½ cups, drained)**
Cut into quarters and set aside to drain
   ½ cup maraschino cherries
(To avoid pink-tinted salad, drain thoroughly.)

Cut (*page 12*) into slivers and set aside
   ½ cup (about 3 oz.) pitted dates
Cut into eighths and set aside
   24 (6 oz.) marshmallows
Combine in a bowl 3 tablespoons of the reserved pineapple sirup and
   8 oz. cream cheese, softened
Beat until smooth and fluffy. Blend in
   ¼ cup mayonnaise
Gently mix in the pineapple, cherries, dates, almonds and marshmallows.

Using chilled bowl and beater, beat until cream is of medium consistency (piles softly)
   1 cup chilled whipping cream
Gently fold (*page 12*) whipped cream into the fruit and cheese mixture. Turn into mold, tray or freezer-type containers and freeze (2 to 4 hrs.).
                              About 8 to 10 servings

▲ Cider Salad

MRS. JOE A. GENGLER, LE MARS, IOWA

Lightly oil with salad or cooking oil (not olive oil) a 1-qt. fancy mold. Set aside to drain.

Pour into a small bowl
½ cup cold water
Sprinkle evenly over cold water
2 tablespoons (2 env.) unflavored gelatin
Let gelatin stand about 5 min. to soften.

Heat until very hot
2 cups apple cider
¼ teaspoon salt
Remove from heat and immediately add softened gelatin, stirring until gelatin is completely dissolved. Spoon a small amount of the gelatin mixture into mold. Chill in refrigerator until partially set. Cool remaining mixture; chill (*page 306*) until slightly thicker than consistency of thick, unbeaten egg white.

Just before gelatin is of desired consistency, prepare
2 cups (about 2 medium-size) diced apple (do not pare)
¼ cup (about 1 oz.) chopped walnuts
1 tablespoon finely chopped parsley
When gelatin is of desired consistency, blend in the apples, walnuts and parsley. Turn into the mold. Chill in refrigerator until firm.

Unmold (*page 306*) onto chilled serving plate. Garnish with
Curly endive

About 6 servings

△ Apple-Jack Salad

Follow ▲ Recipe. Decrease cider to 1¾ cups. Add ¼ cup **apple brandy** to gelatin after it has cooled but before chilling it.

Cider Salad

Sparkling Salad Mold

RUTH GOSERUD, ST. PAUL, MINN.

Set out a 1-qt. fancy mold.

Empty into a bowl contents of
1 pkg. lime-flavored gelatin
Add and stir until the gelatin is completely dissolved
1 cup very hot water
Blend in contents of
1 7-oz. bottle lemon-lime-flavored carbonated beverage
Chill (*page 306*) until slightly thicker than the consistency of thick, unbeaten egg white.

Meanwhile, lightly oil the mold with salad or cooking oil (not olive oil). Set aside to drain.

When gelatin has desired consistency, blend in
1 cup thick, sweetened applesauce
Turn mixture into mold. Chill until firm.

Unmold (*page 306*) onto chilled serving platter. Arrange around sides of mold
Galax leaves
Frosted Grapes (*page 312*)

About 6 servings

315

▲ Tomato Aspic

Lightly oil a 1-qt. ring mold with salad or cooking oil (not olive oil). Set aside to drain.

Pour into a saucepan
4 cups tomato juice
Add to tomato juice
⅓ cup chopped celery leaves
⅓ cup chopped onion
2½ tablespoons sugar
1¼ teaspoons salt
½ teaspoon Accent
½ bay leaf
Simmer, uncovered, 10 min.

Meanwhile, pour into a small bowl
½ cup cold water
Sprinkle evenly over cold water
2 tablespoons (2 env.) unflavored gelatin
Let stand about 5 min. to soften.

Remove tomato-juice mixture from the heat. Strain liquid into a large bowl. Immediately add the gelatin to tomato-juice mixture and stir until gelatin is completely dissolved.

Add and stir well
2½ tablespoons vinegar
Pour tomato-juice mixture into mold. Cool and place in refrigerator to chill until firm.

To serve, unmold (*page 306*) onto a chilled serving plate. *About 8 servings*

▲ Low-Calorie Luncheon Platter

Follow ▲ Recipe. Substitute 6 individual ring molds for the 1-qt. mold. Pour ⅔ cup of the tomato-juice mixture into each mold. Chill in refrigerator until firm. Arrange 7 crisp **lettuce cups** on a large chilled salad platter. Unmold one aspic ring into each cup. Garnish each ring with **parsley**. Spoon **cottage cheese** into the remaining lettuce cup and sprinkle with chopped **chives**. Quarter 3 **Hard-Cooked Eggs** (*page 87*); pile into center of platter.

Tomato Aspic with Tuna Salad

▲ Tomato Aspic with Tuna Salad

Follow ▲ Recipe. Unmold the aspic ring onto a chilled plate. Surround ring with **leaf lettuce**. With a sharp knife, cut away peel and white membrane from 1 chilled **grapefruit**. Remove sections by cutting on either side of dividing membranes; remove section by section, over a small bowl to save the juice. Set sections aside. Rinse, peel, cut into halves and remove and discard pit from 1 chilled **avocado**. Cut avocado halves into crosswise slices. Brush with **grapefruit juice**. Arrange avocado slices and grapefruit sections around the aspic ring (see photo). Pile **Tuna Salad** (*page 317*) into center of ring and serve.

Curried Tuna-Tomato Salad
MRS. HUGH W. GLADDEN, DETROIT, MICH.

Set in refrigerator to chill
4 medium-size (about 1⅓ lbs.) tomatoes (for Tomato Flowers, Shells or slices)
Prepare
Curried Tuna Salad
While salad is chilling, prepare Tomato Flowers or Tomato Shells. Spoon tuna mixture onto center of flowers or fill shells with the tuna mixture. Or spoon tuna salad onto thick tomato slices. Serve on crisp greens.

For Curried Tuna Salad—Drain, flake (*page 12*) and set aside contents of
    1 7-oz. can tuna (about 1 cup, flaked)
Blend together
    ¼ cup mayonnaise
    ½ teaspoon curry powder
    ½ teaspoon Accent
Prepare
    1 cup (about 1 medium-size) chopped apple
    ½ cup diced celery (*page 12*)
Lightly toss the apple and celery with the mayonnaise mixture. Add the tuna. Mix gently and thoroughly. Chill in refrigerator.

For Tomato Flowers—Rinse and cut a slice from tops of the tomatoes. Start at top of tomato and cut through peel and pulp to center. Make 6 equally spaced cuts down to ½ in. from bottom. Pull pieces back to form petals.

For Tomato Shells—Rinse and cut a slice from tops of the chilled tomatoes. Remove pulp from tomatoes with a spoon. Invert the tomato shells and set aside to drain.

4 servings

▲ Salmon-Vegetable Salad

Drain, flake (*page 12*) and turn into a bowl the contents of
    1 7¾-oz. can salmon (about 1 cup, flaked)
Prepare
    ½ cup grated carrot
    ⅓ cup chopped celery
Toss salmon and vegetables lightly with
    ⅔ to 1 cup cooked peas
    ¼ cup chopped sweet pickle
    6 ripe olives, pitted and chopped
and a mixture of
    ½ teaspoon salt
    ¼ teaspoon Accent
    ⅛ teaspoon pepper
Add and toss lightly until vegetables are well coated with a mixture of
    ¼ cup French dressing
    1 tablespoon lemon juice

Set in refrigerator to chill at least 1 hr.

Before serving, add and gently toss with
    ¾ cup Mayonnaise (*page 319*)
Serve on crisp salad greens.

About 6 servings

△ Tuna Salad

Follow ▲ Recipe. Omit carrots and peas. Increase celery to ½ cup.

Shrimp Salad with Herbs
MRS. MARTIN LARSGAARD
DICKINSON, N. DAK.

A touch of herb genius gives you a new recipe for your repertory of exciting shrimp dishes.

Set out a large bowl.

Blend together and set in refrigerator to chill
    ¾ cup Mayonnaise (*page 319*)
    2 tablespoons tarragon vinegar
    2 tablespoons cream
    2 tablespoons finely chopped parsley
    2 tablespoons minced onion
and a mixture of
    ½ teaspoon celery seed
    ½ teaspoon basil
    ½ teaspoon salt
    ½ teaspoon Accent
    ¼ teaspoon pepper
Drain, remove black vein, and coarsely chop contents of
    2 5-oz. cans shrimp (about 1½ cups, drained)
(Or prepare 1 lb. fresh shrimp with shells, see Cooked Shrimp, *page 242*).

Prepare
    2 cups (about ½ lb.) shredded cabbage
    1 cup chopped celery (*page 12*)
Combine the shrimp, cabbage and celery in the bowl. Cover and set in refrigerator to chill.

Shortly before serving, add the dressing to the salad. Toss lightly to mix thoroughly.

Serve at once on lettuce. *About 8 servings*

▲ Chicken Salad

Prepare and put into a large bowl

3 cups cubed cooked chicken (see Stewed Chicken, page 205)

1 cup diced celery (page 12)

Toss lightly and mix in, in order

½ teaspoon salt

½ teaspoon Accent

½ cup Cooked Salad Dressing (page 319)

Chill in refrigerator until ready to serve.

Serve in

Crisp lettuce cups; or spoon into cavities of 3 medium-size chilled avocados, cut into halves and pitted

Garnish with

Capers, olives or water cress

About 6 servings

⚠ Elegant Chicken Salad

Follow ▲ Recipe. Mix with the chicken and celery ½ cup small **seedless grapes** (or halved and seeded green grapes) and ¼ cup moist shredded **coconut**, cut. Just before serving, mix in ½ cup **pecans** or blanched **almonds**, toasted (*page 11*). Whip (*page 13*) ¼ cup chilled **whipping cream**. Blend into dressing.

⚠ Turkey Salad

Follow ▲ Recipe. Substitute 3 cups cubed cooked **turkey** for chicken.

▲ French Dressing

Secret formula for successful salads is the tang and zest of this French Dressing.

Combine in a 1-pt. screw-top jar

¾ cup salad oil

¼ cup lemon juice or vinegar

1 tablespoon sugar

¾ teaspoon salt

½ teaspoon Accent

¼ teaspoon pepper

¼ teaspoon paprika

¼ teaspoon dry mustard

Cover jar tightly and shake vigorously. Store covered in refrigerator.

Shake well before using. *About 1 cup dressing*

⚠ Garlic French Dressing

Follow ▲ Recipe. Cut into halves 1 clove **garlic** (*page 12*); add to completed dressing. To season well, chill dressing about 12 hours before using. Remove garlic before serving.

⚠ Honey French Dressing

Follow ▲ Recipe; use lemon juice. Blend in ½ cup **honey** and ¼ teaspoon grated **lemon peel** (*page 11*). For added flavor, add ½ teaspoon **celery seed**.

⚠ Roquefort French Dressing

Follow ▲ Recipe. Add ½ cup (about 2 oz.) crumbled **Roquefort** or **Blue cheese**.

Cooked Salad Dressing

Mix thoroughly in the top of a double boiler

¼ cup sugar
1 tablespoon flour
½ teaspoon dry mustard
½ teaspoon salt
¼ teaspoon Accent
⅛ teaspoon pepper

Blend in gradually

1 cup water

Place over direct heat. Stirring gently and constantly, bring mixture to boiling. Cook 1 to 2 min. longer. Stir in

¼ cup vinegar

Vigorously stir about 3 tablespoons hot mixture into

4 egg yolks, slightly beaten

Immediately blend egg-yolk mixture into mixture in top of double boiler. Place over simmering water and cook 3 to 5 min. Stir slowly to keep mixture cooking evenly. Remove from heat and stir in

2 tablespoons butter or margarine

Cool. Store salad dressing in tightly covered jar in refrigerator.

Before using, thin to desired consistency with sweet cream, fruit juice or vinegar.

About 1½ cups salad dressing

▲ Mayonnaise

Beat with a rotary beater in a small bowl

2 egg yolks
1 tablespoon lemon juice
1½ teaspoons salt
1 teaspoon sugar
½ teaspoon Accent
½ teaspoon dry mustard
½ teaspoon paprika

Add, 1 teaspoon at a time at first

½ cup salad oil

Beating vigorously after each addition, gradually increase amount of addition. Alternately beat in (in very small amounts)

½ cup salad oil
1 tablespoon lemon juice

(If Mayonnaise separates because oil has been added too rapidly, beat it slowly and thoroughly into 1 egg yolk.)

Store Mayonnaise covered in refrigerator.

About 1½ cups Mayonnaise

Note: Mayonnaise may be thinned with a small amount of **cream** before serving. For a special touch, fold in **whipped cream** (*page 13*).

⚠ Thousand Island Dressing

Follow ▲ Recipe. To ½ cup Mayonnaise add 1 or 2 **Hard-Cooked Eggs** (*page 87*), sieved or finely chopped, 2 tablespoons **chili sauce**, 2 tablespoons finely chopped **scallions** (with tops), 2 tablespoons chopped **sweet pickle**, 1 tablespoon chopped **green olives**, and ½ teaspoon **paprika**.

⚠ Russian Dressing

Follow ▲ Recipe. To ½ cup Mayonnaise add 3 tablespoons **chili sauce**, 1 tablespoon minced **onion** and ½ teaspoon **prepared horse-radish**.

Cosmopolitan Dressing

MRS. H. A. LEWICKI, JR., CONCORD, CALIF.

Blend together until smooth and creamy

5 oz. (1 jar) process cheese spread with Blue cheese
3 oz. (1 pkg.) cream cheese, softened
1 cup thick sour cream
¼ cup sherry
1 tablespoon grated onion
½ teaspoon salt
¼ teaspoon paprika
⅛ teaspoon Accent

Store dressing covered in refrigerator.

About 2 cups dressing

Fluffy Citrus Salad Dressing

This delicate fruit dressing is at its flavorsome best when served with a plate of chilled California orange slices and grapefruit sections.

Put a bowl and rotary beater into refrigerator to chill.

Mix together
3 tablespoons honey
2 to 3 teaspoons lemon, lime or orange juice

Using chilled bowl and beater, whip (*page 13*)
½ cup chilled whipping cream

Beat honey mixture into whipped cream with final few strokes. *1¼ cups salad dressing*

Pineapple Salad Dressing

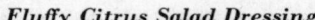

(*See photo on page 312*)

Sift together in the top of a double boiler
½ cup sugar
1 tablespoon cornstarch
⅛ teaspoon salt

Stir in
½ cup unsweetened pineapple juice

Stirring gently and constantly, bring rapidly to boiling over direct heat. Cook 3 min. Place over simmering water.

Vigorously stir about 3 tablespoons hot mixture into
2 egg yolks, slightly beaten

Immediately blend into mixture in double-boiler top, stirring constantly. Cook over simmering water 3 to 5 min. Stir slowly to keep mixture cooking evenly. Remove double boiler from heat.

Beat until frothy
2 egg whites

Add gradually, beating well after each addition
2 tablespoons sugar

Beat until rounded peaks are formed. Gently blend egg whites into pineapple mixture.

Add gradually, stirring constantly
1 cup lukewarm, unsweetened pineapple juice

Cook over simmering water until thick and smooth, stirring constantly (about 10 min.). Remove from heat and blend in
2 tablespoons butter or margarine

Cool and set in refrigerator to chill.

Before serving, whip (*page 13*)
¾ cup chilled whipping cream

Carefully blend whipped cream into pineapple mixture. *About 4 cups dressing*

Peanut Butter Dressing
ETTA DEVINE, FARMINGTON, N. MEX.

Serve this creamy dressing with fresh fruit for a quick and tasty salad.

Cream together until well mixed
½ cup peanut butter
2 tablespoons sugar

Add gradually, mixing well
6 tablespoons cream or undiluted evaporated milk

Beat until smooth and creamy. Store covered in refrigerator. *¾ cup dressing*

Fluffy Citrus Salad Dressing

Melbourne Salad Dressing

A piquant dressing for salad greens.

Combine in a screw-top jar
  ⅔ **cup lemon juice**
  ¼ **cup olive oil**
  ¼ **cup Worcestershire sauce**
  3 **tablespoons plus 1 teaspoon sugar**
Cover jar tightly and shake well. Store covered
in refrigerator. Shake dressing well before
serving. Serve icy cold.

About 1¼ cups dressing

Blue Cheese Salad Dressing

Gourmet's choice for tossed green salad.

Mix in a small bowl
  ½ **cup cream**
  1 **teaspoon prepared mustard**
  ¾ **teaspoon paprika**
  ½ **teaspoon Worcestershire sauce**
  ¼ **teaspoon salt**
  ⅛ **teaspoon coarsely ground pepper**
  2 or 3 **drops tabasco sauce**
Add, about 1 teaspoon at a time, while beating
constantly with a rotary beater
  ¾ **cup salad oil or olive oil**
Continue beating while adding gradually
  2 **tablespoons wine vinegar or**
    cider vinegar
Add to dressing
  1 **cup (about 4 oz.) crumbled**
    Blue cheese
Blend only until mixed. Store dressing in a
screw-top jar in refrigerator. Shake well before
using. *About 2 cups dressing*

Ida's Favorite Dressing
IDA GLESSNER, GROVE CITY, PA.

Put through fine blade of food chopper
  1 **medium-size green pepper** (*page 12*)
  1 **medium-size onion** (*page 12*)
Combine in a 1-pt. screw-top jar with
  6 **tablespoons orange juice**
  ¼ **cup salad oil**
  3 **tablespoons lemon juice**
  2 **tablespoons vinegar**
  2 **tablespoons sugar**
  ½ **teaspoon Accent**
  ½ **teaspoon salt**
  ¼ **teaspoon pepper**
  1 **clove garlic** (*page 12*), **cut in halves**
Cover jar tightly and shake well. Store covered in refrigerator. Shake well before using.

About 1½ cups dressing

Note: The longer garlic remains in salad dressing, the stronger the flavor will be.

Salad Dressing Supreme
MRS. BRYANT PERKINS, HULLS COVE, ME.

A spirited and unusual combination.

Combine in a 1-qt. screw-top jar
  1½ **cups olive oil**
  1¼ **cups (10½- to 11-oz. can)**
    condensed tomato soup
  ½ **cup vinegar**
  5 **tablespoons honey**
  2 **tablespoons tarragon vinegar**
  1 **tablespoon Worcestershire sauce**
  1 **tablespoon dry mustard**
  2 **teaspoons salt**
  1 **teaspoon paprika**
  ¼ **teaspoon Accent**
  1 **clove garlic** (*page 12*), **cut in halves**
  2 or 3 **drops tabasco sauce**
Cover tightly and shake well. Store covered
in refrigerator. Shake well before using.

About 3⅔ cups dressing

Note: The longer garlic remains in salad dressing, the stronger the flavor will be.

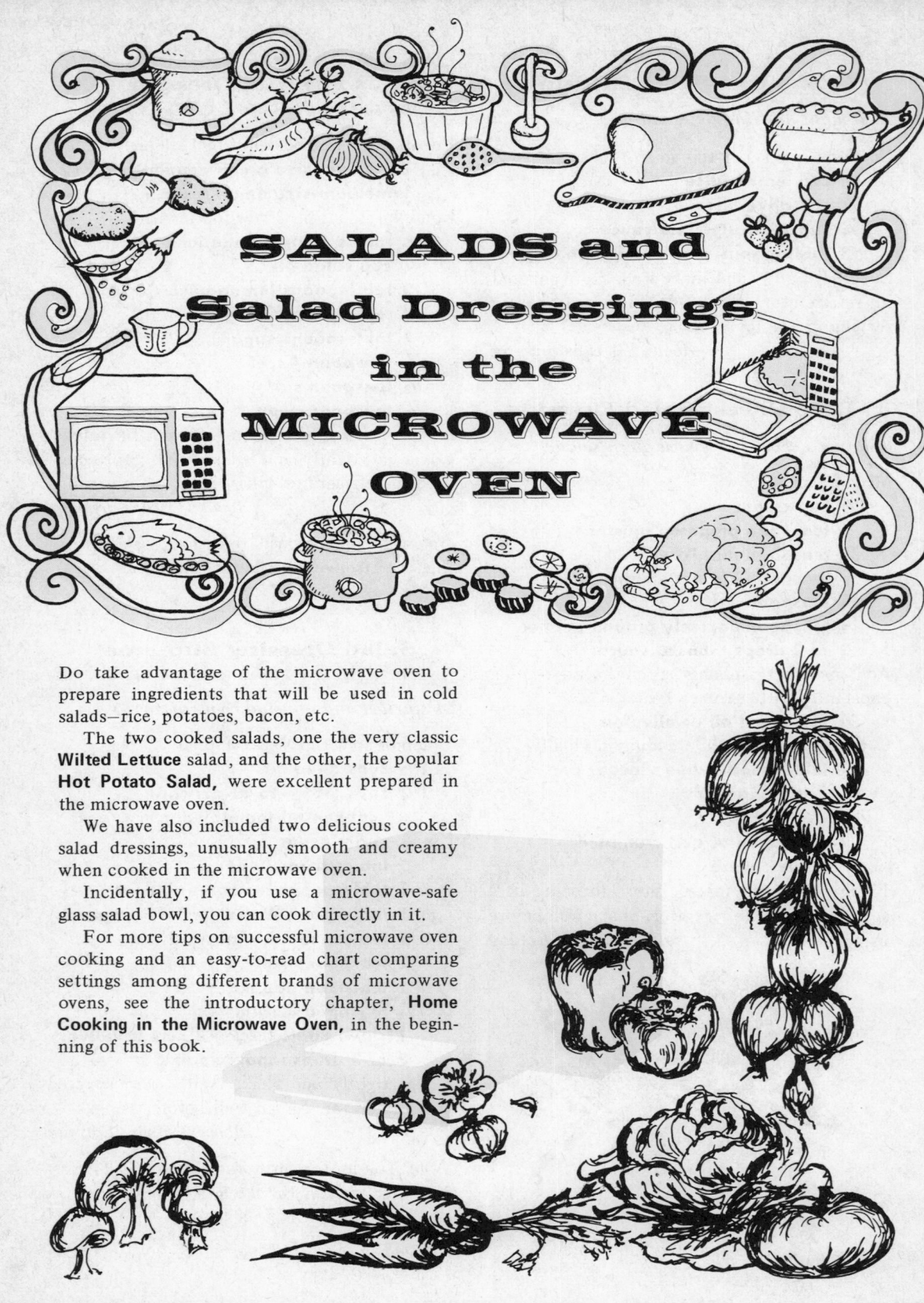

SALADS and Salad Dressings in the MICROWAVE OVEN

Do take advantage of the microwave oven to prepare ingredients that will be used in cold salads—rice, potatoes, bacon, etc.

The two cooked salads, one the very classic **Wilted Lettuce** salad, and the other, the popular **Hot Potato Salad,** were excellent prepared in the microwave oven.

We have also included two delicious cooked salad dressings, unusually smooth and creamy when cooked in the microwave oven.

Incidentally, if you use a microwave-safe glass salad bowl, you can cook directly in it.

For more tips on successful microwave oven cooking and an easy-to-read chart comparing settings among different brands of microwave ovens, see the introductory chapter, **Home Cooking in the Microwave Oven,** in the beginning of this book.

Wilted Lettuce *(page 308)* 1

Use a small casserole.

Prepare bacon.

COOK vinegar mixture to boiling (about 3 min.). Add bacon and stir to blend.

Hot Potato Salad *(page 310)* 2

Use a small casserole for the dressing and a large casserole for the completed salad.

Prepare potato salad mixture.

Combine vinegar, water, sugar and COOK to boiling (about 2 min.).

After dressing salad, COOK uncovered, stirring after 1½ min., to heat (about 3 min.).

Cover and let stand 5 min.

Cooked Salad Dressing 3
(page 319)

Use a small casserole.

COOK sugar-spice mixture, stirring every 30 sec., to boil (about 3 min.). COOK to blend flavors (about 30 sec.).

Add egg yolk mixture. COOK, stirring every 30 sec., to thicken and meld flavors (about 2 min.). Complete as in Recipe.

Pineapple Salad Dressing
(page 320)

Use a small casserole.

COOK pineapple juice mixture, stirring every 30 sec., to boil and thicken (about 5 min.).

Add egg yolk mixture and COOK, stirring every 30 sec., to blend eggs (about 2 min.).

After pineapple juice is added, SLOWCOOK, stirring every 30 sec., until thick and smooth (about 2 min.).

Complete as in Recipe.

OVERALL COOKING TIME: 9:00

SAUCES

The Art of Sauce Making

Sauces enhance the appearance and flavor of food and add to its nutritive value. They should offer pleasing contrasts in color, flavor and consistency to the dishes they accompany. In most cases they should be thin enough to flow but thick enough not to saturate food.

Sauces for Meat, Poultry, Fish and Vegetables— Basic sauces for these are few in number, but their variations are almost limitless. Wherever spices, herbs, seasonings and a few basic ingredients are available, the art of sauce making is open to amateur and professional alike.

Foremost among the basic sauces and keystone of the whole art is white sauce. This is the indispensable base for innumerable sauces and is frequently used in other food preparation as well— in cream soups, casserole dishes, croquettes or soufflés. Four main groups are made from the basic sauce by varying the type of liquid used or by browning the flour. White sauce, as the name implies, is made with milk or cream. Spices, seasonings and condiments add their piquant flavor to many variations of white sauce. A second group is created by the substitution of meat or vegetable stock or water for milk; an example is gravy. When the flour is browned before liquid is added the resulting sauce is a brown sauce. The fourth group of sauces results from the substitution of tomato juice or purée for milk.

For a smooth sauce always blend flour or cornstarch with a cold liquid or with melted fat, or cream the fat thoroughly with the flour before adding hot liquids.

Frequently gravy lumps because hot liquid is added to the fat-flour mixture, causing the starch particles to become sticky and clump together. Therefore only warm or cold liquid rather than hot liquid should be used to avoid lumping.

An easy way to blend flour and liquid for gravy is to put the required amount of cold liquid in a screw-top jar, sprinkle the flour OVER the liquid and shake the mixture to blend. This mixture is also used to thicken liquids for stews. Sauces made with flour or cornstarch must be cooked rapidly and thoroughly to overcome the raw starch taste.

When adding whole eggs or egg yolks to a sauce, always stir a little of the hot sauce into the slightly beaten eggs; immediately blend into the remaining hot sauce. Cook 3 to 5 min., stirring slowly to keep the mixture cooking evenly. Temperature of the mixture should not drop before adding the eggs, to insure an adequately thickened sauce.

Cheese is a protein food and so it is toughened by high heat. Slightly cool a hot sauce before adding grated cheese (add all at one time and stir until blended). If all the cheese does not melt, heat sauce over simmering water and stir.

Dessert Sauces—Create an enticing dessert dish by combining a sweet sauce with any of these: ice cream, sherbet, parfait, mousse, fruit, pudding, pancakes, cookies, cake, or cake bits.

The special-flavor sauces, such as chocolate and butterscotch, and hard sauce do not normally separate and so they can be stored, tightly covered, in the refrigerator for over a month. Harmless mold may form, but it can be skimmed off and the sauce used. The high sugar content of sweet sauces prevents other spoilage organisms from developing.

▲ Medium White Sauce I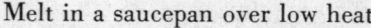

Melt in a saucepan over low heat
>**2 tablespoons butter or margarine**

Blend in a mixture of
>**2 tablespoons flour**
>**¼ teaspoon salt**
>**¼ teaspoon Accent**
>**Few grains pepper**

Heat until mixture bubbles. Remove from heat. Add gradually, stirring in
>**1 cup milk or a mixture of ½ cup**
>**undiluted evaporated milk and**
>**½ cup water**

Cook rapidly, stirring constantly, until sauce thickens. Cook 1 to 2 min. longer.

Use sauce for gravies, scalloped and creamed dishes, for topping cooked vegetables, fish, eggs and meat.   *About 1 cup sauce*

△ Thin White Sauce

Follow ▲ Recipe, using 1 tablespoon flour and 1 tablespoon butter or margarine. Use as base for cream soups.

△ Thick White Sauce

Follow ▲ Recipe, using 3 to 4 tablespoons flour and 3 to 4 tablespoons butter or margarine. Use for preparation of soufflés and croquettes.

△ Mushroom Sauce

Follow ▲ Recipe. Clean and slice (*page 12*) ½ lb. **mushrooms.** Heat in a skillet ¼ cup **butter** or **margarine.** Add mushrooms and 1 tablespoon minced **onion.** Cook slowly, moving and turning with a spoon until mushrooms are tender. Do not brown. Stir into sauce. (Or ½ cup, 4-oz. can, drained mushrooms may be substituted for fresh mushrooms, and mushroom liquid may be used for part of milk.)

△ Cheese Sauce

Follow ▲ Recipe. Blend in ¼ teaspoon **dry mustard** and a few grains **cayenne pepper** with flour and seasonings. Cool sauce slightly. Add all at one time ¼ cup (1 oz.) grated sharp **Cheddar cheese.** Stir sauce rapidly until the cheese is melted and well blended.

△ Mock Hollandaise Sauce

Follow ▲ Recipe, preparing sauce in a double-boiler top and using **chicken stock** (a clear canned chicken soup may be used). When sauce is thickened, vigorously stir about 3 tablespoons of hot mixture into 2 **egg yolks,** slightly beaten. Immediately blend into sauce; cook over simmering water 3 to 5 min. Stir slowly to keep mixture cooking evenly. Stir in 1 tablespoon **lemon juice** and 2 tablespoons **butter** or **margarine.**

Medium White Sauce II

Pour into a saucepan
>**1 cup water**

Sprinkle over top of water, a mixture of
>**⅓ cup instant nonfat dry milk solids**
>**2 tablespoons flour**
>**¼ teaspoon salt**
>**¼ teaspoon Accent**
>**Few grains pepper**

Beat slowly with rotary beater just until blended. Cook over medium heat, stirring constantly. When sauce begins to thicken, stir in
>**2 tablespoons butter or margarine**

Continue cooking, stirring constantly, until sauce thickens. Cook 1 to 2 min. longer.
            About 1 cup sauce

Note: This sauce may be used as the base for any variation of **Medium White Sauce I** (*on this page*).

Hollandaise Sauce: Using a wire whisk, beat egg yolks and cream in the top of a small double boiler.

Hollandaise Sauce 8

In the top of a small double boiler, beat with a wire whisk until thickened and light-colored

2 egg yolks
2 tablespoons cream

Blend in

¼ teaspoon salt
Few grains cayenne pepper

Place top of double boiler over hot (not boiling) water. (Bottom of double-boiler top should not touch the water.) Add gradually, beating constantly

2 tablespoons lemon juice or
tarragon vinegar

Cook over low heat, beating constantly with whisk until sauce is consistency of thick cream. Remove double boiler from heat, leaving top in place.

Add, beating constantly, ½ teaspoon at a time

½ cup butter or margarine

Beat with whisk until butter is thoroughly melted and blended into mixture.

Serve immediately. If necessary, this sauce may be kept warm 15 to 30 min. by setting over hot water. Cover tightly. Stir the sauce occasionally. *1 cup sauce*

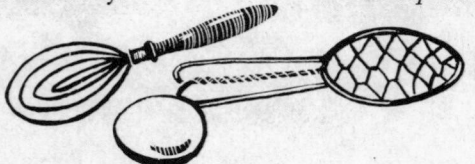

Béarnaise Sauce

JO ELLYN MEADOR, SCOTIA, CALIF.

A sprightly Hollandaise-type sauce.

Set out a small double boiler and a saucepan.

Prepare and set aside

1 tablespoon chopped chives
1 tablespoon chopped parsley
1 tablespoon chopped fresh
tarragon leaves*

Combine in the saucepan

¼ cup white wine vinegar
4 fresh tarragon leaves, minced*
2 sprigs parsley, finely chopped
1 teaspoon chopped chives
3 whole peppercorns, bruised

Boil until only two tablespoons of liquid remain. Set aside.

In the top of the double boiler, beat with a wire whisk until thickened and light-colored

3 egg yolks

Blend in

½ teaspoon salt

Place top of double boiler over hot (not boiling) water. (Bottom of double-boiler top should not touch the water.)

Add, beating constantly with the whisk until butter is melted and blended into mixture

1 tablespoon softened butter

Strain the hot, seasoned vinegar mixture into the egg-yolk mixture, beating constantly. Cook over low heat, beating constantly with whisk until sauce is the consistency of light cream.

Remove double boiler from heat, leaving top in place. Add, beating constantly, one tablespoon at a time

¾ cup softened butter

Beat with whisk until butter is thoroughly melted and blended into mixture. Blend in the chopped fresh herbs.

Serve immediately with broiled fish or with any dark meat. *About 1½ cups sauce*

*If the fresh tarragon leaves are not available, substitute **tarragon vinegar** for wine vinegar.

Brown Roux or Paste

Used for thickening brown sauces, this paste can be made in advance and kept in the refrigerator until needed.

Melt in a heavy saucepan or skillet
1 cup fat or meat drippings
Blend in
1½ cups flour
Place over low heat. Stir constantly to distribute heat evenly. The roux is cooked when the mixture acquires a light brown color.

Cool; store covered in refrigerator.

About 2 cups roux

▲ Brown Gravy

A cook is known by the character of her gravies.

Method 1—Remove roasted meat or poultry from roasting pan. Leaving brown residue in pan, pour into bowl
Drippings
Allow fat to rise to surface; skim off fat and reserve. Remaining drippings are meat juices which should be used as part of liquid in gravy.

Measure into roasting pan
3 tablespoons fat
Blend in until smooth
3 tablespoons reserved flour
½ teaspoon Accent
¼ teaspoon salt
⅛ teaspoon pepper
Stirring constantly, heat until mixture bubbles. Brown slightly if desired. Remove from heat and slowly blend in, stirring constantly and vigorously
2 cups liquid, warm or cool (drippings, water, quick meat broth, page 13, or milk)
Return to heat and cook rapidly, stirring constantly, until sauce thickens. Cook 1 to 2 min. longer. While stirring, scrape bottom and sides of pan to blend in brown residue.

Serve hot with meat or poultry.

6 to 8 servings

Note: Other **fats** may be substituted if pan drippings are not available.

Method 2—Bring to boiling
2 cups chicken or meat broth (from which the fat has been skimmed)
Drippings from roasted meats may be substituted for part of broth; if necessary, add milk or water to drippings to make 2 cups liquid.

Meanwhile, put into a 1-pt. screw-top jar
½ cup water
Sprinkle evenly over water
¼ cup flour
Cover jar tightly; shake until flour and water are well blended. Stirring broth or liquid constantly, slowly pour one half of the flour-water mixture into broth. Bring to boiling. Gradually add only what is needed of remaining flour-water mixture for consistency desired; bring to boiling after each addition.

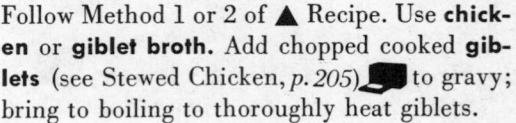

Season with
¼ teaspoon salt
⅛ teaspoon pepper
⅛ teaspoon Accent
Cook gravy 3 to 5 min. longer.

△ Giblet Gravy

Follow Method 1 or 2 of ▲ Recipe. Use **chicken** or **giblet broth**. Add chopped cooked **giblets** (see Stewed Chicken, *p. 205*) to gravy; bring to boiling to thoroughly heat giblets.

Giblet Gravy with Roast Chicken (page 196)

Golden Gravy [12]

Set out a large skillet.

Prepare
**1 cup quick chicken broth (page 13;
use 2 bouillon cubes)**
Stir in
½ teaspoon Worcestershire sauce
½ teaspoon Accent
⅛ teaspoon salt
Set aside to cool slightly.

Heat in the skillet over low heat
3 tablespoons fat
Blend in
3 tablespoons flour
¼ to ½ teaspoon dry mustard
⅛ teaspoon freshly ground pepper
Stirring constantly, heat until mixture bubbles and browns slightly. Remove from heat and slowly add seasoned chicken broth, stirring constantly and vigorously. Thoroughly blend in
1 cup milk
Return to heat and cook rapidly, stirring constantly, until gravy thickens. Cook gravy 1 to 2 min. longer.

Serve with meat, or heat slices of leftover meat or poultry in the gravy.

About 2 cups gravy

Norwegian Wine Gravy [13]
MRS. CARL F. ERICKSON, SPENARD, ALASKA

For a special taste treat try this piquant gravy.

Heat in a small saucepan over low heat
2 tablespoons butter or margarine
Add and cook slowly over medium heat, stirring occasionally
1 small onion (page 12), minced
Cook until onion is transparent.

Blend in
2 tablespoons flour
½ teaspoon dry mustard
⅛ teaspoon pepper
Heat until the mixture bubbles and is lightly browned, stirring constantly.

Remove from the heat; add gradually, stirring constantly
**2 cups meat stock or quick meat broth
(page 13)**
¼ cup sherry
1 anchovy, minced
Simmer 5 min. Strain gravy and serve hot over slices of cold roast beef.

About 2½ cups sauce

Tomato Sauce [14]

Combine in a saucepan and simmer 10 to 12 min., stirring occasionally
2½ cups (No. 2 can) cooked or canned tomatoes
2 tablespoons chopped onion
2 teaspoons sugar
½ teaspoon salt
½ teaspoon Accent
⅛ teaspoon pepper
Force through a sieve to remove tomato seeds and onion pieces. Set aside.

Heat in a skillet
2 tablespoons butter or margarine
Blend in
2 tablespoons flour
Heat until mixture bubbles. Remove from heat and gradually add the tomato mixture, stirring constantly. Blend in
½ teaspoon Worcestershire sauce
Return to heat and cook, stirring gently and constantly, until mixture thickens. Cook 1 to 2 min. longer.

Serve with vegetables, meats, fish or omelets.

About 2 cups sauce

Quick Tomato Sauce 15

Heat in a saucepan over low heat
1 tablespoon butter or margarine
Blend in
1 tablespoon flour
½ teaspoon onion salt
Few grains cayenne pepper
Heat until mixture bubbles. Remove from heat. Add gradually, stirring constantly
1 cup (8-oz. can) tomato sauce
¼ cup hot water
1 teaspoon Worcestershire sauce
Return to heat and bring rapidly to boiling, stirring constantly. Cook 1 to 2 min. longer.

Serve sauce hot. *About 1 cup sauce*

Tomato-Cheese Sauce 16

Set out a large saucepan.

Grate and set aside
2 oz. Cheddar cheese (about ½ cup, grated)
Drain and chop contents of
1 4-oz. can (about ½ cup, drained) mushrooms
Put mushrooms in saucepan with
2½ cups (two 10½- to 11-oz. cans) condensed tomato soup
Simmer about 10 min., or until mixture is bubbling hot, stirring occasionally.

Cool sauce slightly and add the grated cheese all at one time. Stir sauce rapidly until cheese is melted and well blended.

Serve sauce hot. *About 3 cups sauce*

▲ Tangy Bar-B-Q Sauce 1

Prepare, combine, and set aside
1 medium-size onion (*page 12*), finely chopped
3 tablespoons diced green pepper
1 small clove garlic (*page 12*), minced; or crushed in a garlic press
Heat in a saucepan over low heat
2 tablespoons butter or margarine
Add the chopped vegetables. Cook, keeping mixture moving with a spoon, until onion is transparent.

Meanwhile, blend together
1 cup ketchup or chili sauce (or use ½ cup of each)
2 tablespoons brown sugar
1 tablespoon Worcestershire sauce
1 teaspoon prepared horse-radish
1 teaspoon prepared mustard
¼ teaspoon salt
¼ teaspoon pepper
Few drops tabasco sauce
Add ketchup mixture to vegetables in saucepan. Stir to blend well. Simmer 15 to 20 min., stirring frequently.

Remove from heat and blend in
¼ cup lemon juice
Serve hot over any kind of meat.
About 2 cups sauce

△ Bar-B-Q Sauce for Basting 2

Follow ▲ Recipe. Add the lemon juice and 2 tablespoons **vinegar** to the ketchup mixture. Add ½ cup **water**. (Add more water to basting sauce as necessary.) Spoon sauce over meat. Serve basting sauce with meat.

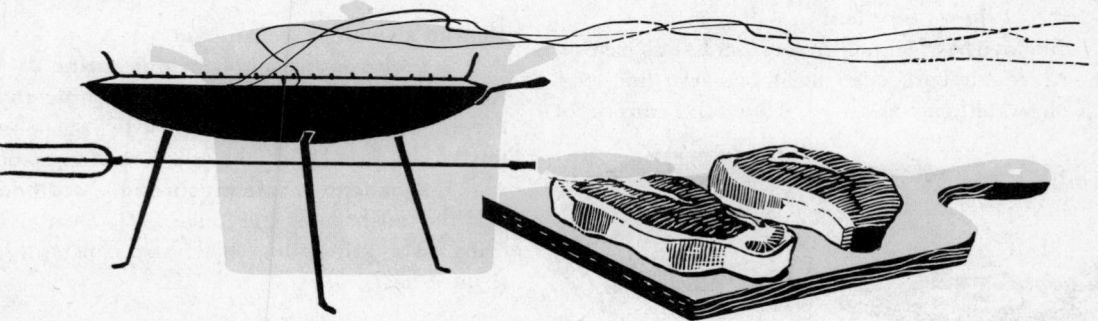

Spaghetti Sauce

Spaghetti Sauce 4

HELEN F. WELLS, SAN JOSE, CALIF.

Set out a large, heavy skillet having a tight-fitting cover.

Finely chop and mix together
   2 large onions (*page 12*)
   1 large green pepper (*page 12*)
Heat in the skillet
   2 tablespoons fat
Add the vegetables and cook, moving mixture with a spoon, until onion is transparent.

Add and cook over medium heat until browned, breaking into small pieces with fork or spoon
   1 lb. ground round steak
Meanwhile, blend together
   2½ cups (No. 2 can) tomatoes
   1¼ cups (12-oz. bottle) chili sauce
   1 cup (8-oz. can) tomato sauce
   ¾ cup (6 oz. can) tomato paste
   2 tablespoons brown sugar
   2 tablespoons Worcestershire sauce
   2 tablespoons vinegar
   1 tablespoon prepared mustard
   2 large cloves garlic (*page 12*)**, minced;
      or crushed in a garlic press**
   1 bay leaf
and a mixture of
   2 tablespoons oregano
   2 teaspoons cumin
   2 teaspoons thyme
   1 teaspoon basil
   1 teaspoon cloves
   1 teaspoon salt
   ½ teaspoon pepper
   ¼ to ½ teaspoon crushed red peppers
Set aside.

Heat in a small saucepan over low heat
   2 tablespoons butter or margarine
Add and cook over medium heat, turning and keeping mushrooms moving with a spoon until they are lightly browned, contents of
   1 8-oz. can whole mushrooms, drained
Add the mushrooms and tomatoes to meat and bring to a full rolling boil; stir constantly. Reduce heat.

Barbecue Sauce Mexicano 3

AMELIE M. KINZER, VAN NUYS, CALIF.

A mild, flavorful barbecue sauce.

Heat in a saucepan over low heat
   ½ cup butter
Add and cook slowly until onion is transparent, keeping mixture moving with a spoon
   1 large onion (*page 12*)**, finely chopped**
   2 cloves garlic (*page 12*)**, minced;
      or crushed in a garlic press**
Blend in, and simmer gently for 5 to 10 min. to heat thoroughly and blend flavors
   **1¼ cups (10½- to 11-oz. can) condensed
      tomato soup**
   ½ cup water
   ½ cup lime juice
   2 teaspoons dry mustard
   2 teaspoons chili powder
   1 teaspoon salt
   ¼ teaspoon crushed cumin seeds
   1 large bay leaf
Remove bay leaf before serving. Use as basting sauce for barbecued meat or serve hot over sliced leftover meat.   *About 3½ cups sauce*

Cover and simmer about 2½ hrs., stirring occasionally to prevent sticking or burning.

Remove cover and simmer at least 1 hr. longer, stirring occasionally. If sauce becomes *too* thick, add
>**Boiling water**

(Sauce should be thick.)

Remove bay leaf before serving. Serve with **Spaghetti** (*page 277*).   *About 8 cups sauce*

Note: If **Spanish red chili sauce** is used, omit crushed red pepper.

Creamy Mustard Sauce 17

A perfect sauce to serve with ham or with cauliflower, asparagus, green beans or broccoli.

Set out
>**1 cup cream or undiluted**
>>**evaporated milk**

Scald (*page 13*) ¾ cup of the cream or evaporated milk in top of double-boiler. Set remaining ¼ cup aside.

Sift together into a small saucepan
>**¼ cup sugar**
>**2 tablespoons dry mustard**
>**2 teaspoons cornstarch**
>**½ teaspoon salt**

Blend in the ¼ cup reserved cream or evaporated milk. Gradually add the scalded cream or milk, stirring constantly.

Stirring gently and constantly, bring cornstarch mixture rapidly to boiling over direct heat and cook for 3 min.

Wash double-boiler top to remove scum.

Pour mixture into double-boiler top and place over simmering water. Cover and cook 10 to 12 min., stirring occasionally.

Remove cover and vigorously stir about 3 tablespoons of this hot mixture into
>**1 egg yolk, slightly beaten**

Immediately blend into mixture in double boiler. Cook over simmering water 3 to 5 min. Stir slowly to keep mixture cooking evenly. Remove from heat. Add gradually, stirring constantly
>**¼ cup vinegar**

Serve hot over vegetables or meat.

>*About 1¼ cups sauce*

Zippy Mustard Sauce 18

MRS. FAROL E. RILEY, ULYSSES, KANS.

A zesty sauce that will add a sharp, tangy flavor to hot or cold ham.

Combine in top of double boiler
>**⅓ cup firmly packed brown sugar**
>**2 teaspoons flour**
>**1 teaspoon prepared mustard**

Blend in
>**⅓ cup vinegar**

Add gradually, stirring constantly
>**⅓ cup water**

Stirring gently and constantly, bring mixture rapidly to boiling over direct heat and cook for 3 min.

Remove from heat and vigorously stir about 3 tablespoons of hot mixture into
>**2 egg yolks, slightly beaten**

Immediately blend into mixture in double boiler. Cook over hot water 3 to 5 min. Stir slowly to keep mixture cooking evenly.

Remove from heat and stir in
>**1 tablespoon butter or margarine**

Serve hot or cold with ham.

>*About 1 cup sauce*

Note: For a milder sauce, use 3 tablespoons vinegar and ½ cup water.

▲ Horse-radish Sour Cream Sauce

The tang of sour cream lends distinction.

Blend together
  1 cup thick sour cream
  ⅓ cup prepared horse-radish
  1 tablespoon grated lemon peel
    (*page 11*)
  ¾ teaspoon salt
  ⅛ teaspoon white pepper
Chill in refrigerator until ready to serve.

Serve with ham or fish. *About 1⅓ cups sauce*

⚠ Sour Cream Cucumber Sauce

Follow ▲ Recipe. Decrease sour cream to ½ cup; blend in ½ cup **Mayonnaise** (*page 319*). Decrease horse-radish to 2 teaspoons. Blend in 1 medium-size **cucumber,** pared and chopped.

Sour Cream Cucumber Sauce with broiled fish

⚠ Apple Sour Cream Sauce

Follow ▲ Recipe. Add to the sauce before chilling 1 medium-size **red apple,** chopped.

Tartar Sauce

Combine in a small bowl
  1 cup Mayonnaise (*page 319*)
  3 tablespoons chopped sweet pickle
  3 tablespoons chopped green olives
  2 tablespoons drained capers
  2 teaspoons minced onion
Stir until well blended. Store in a tightly covered jar in refrigerator and use as needed.

About 1½ cups sauce

Shrimp Remoulade Sauce

MRS. ERIC GUSTAFSON, CLEBURNE, TEXAS

Combine in a large bowl
  3 cups Mayonnaise (*page 319*)
  ⅓ cup minced green onion (*page 12*)
  3 tablespoons drained capers
  3½ teaspoons Worcestershire sauce
  3½ teaspoons prepared horse-radish
  1 tablespoon finely chopped parsley
  1 clove garlic (*page 12*), minced;
    or crushed in a garlic press
  Few drops tabasco sauce
Stir until well blended. Store the sauce in a tightly covered container in refrigerator.

Serve cold. *About 3¾ cups sauce*

Zippy Cocktail Sauce with shrimp

▲ Creamy Sea Food Cocktail Sauce

MRS. NEIL DAMMARELL

MOUNTAIN HOME, IDAHO

Put a small bowl and rotary beater into refrigerator to chill.

Blend thoroughly in a mixing bowl
- **1 cup ketchup or chili sauce**
- **½ cup Mayonnaise (page 319)**
- **1 tablespoon lemon juice**
- **1 tablespoon prepared horse-radish**
- **1 teaspoon minced onion**
- **1 teaspoon Worcestershire sauce**
- **¼ teaspoon Accent**
- **⅛ teaspoon salt**

Beat in the chilled bowl with chilled rotary beater until cream is of medium consistency (piles softly)
- **½ cup chilled whipping cream**

Fold (*page 12*) whipped cream into mayonnaise mixture. Chill at least 1 hr. before serving.

2½ cups sauce

△ Zippy Cocktail Sauce

Follow ▲ Recipe. Omit Mayonnaise and whipping cream. Blend in a few drops of **tabasco sauce.** *About 1¼ cups sauce*

"Dee-lish" Sauce for Fish

BARBARA FORD, DANBURY, N. H.

Brings out the best in food from the sea.

Dice enough cucumber to yield
- **½ cup diced cucumber**

Add to the cucumber
- **1 tablespoon diced pimiento**
- **1 teaspoon minced onion**

Set aside.

Blend together in a bowl
- **½ cup Mayonnaise (page 319)**
- **½ cup thick sour cream**
- **½ cup chopped firm ripe tomato**
- **½ teaspoon salt**
- **¼ teaspoon Accent**

Blend in vegetable mixture. Chill at least 1 hr.

Serve sauce with a salmon loaf or mold or with any fish. *About 2 cups sauce*

Lemon Butter Sauce

Good for basting as well as serving with cooked meat and fish.

Combine in a small saucepan and stir over low heat until butter is melted and ingredients are thoroughly heated
- **1 cup butter**
- **2 tablespoons lemon juice**
- **¼ teaspoon salt**
- **¼ teaspoon paprika**
- **⅛ teaspoon pepper**

About 1 cup sauce

Maître d'Hôtel Butter

Gives a master's touch to sea food or vegetables.

Cream together until thoroughly blended
- **½ cup softened butter**
- **2 tablespoons lemon juice**
- **2 teaspoons chopped parsley**
- **¼ teaspoon salt**
- **⅛ teaspoon pepper**

Serve with fish. *About ½ cup sauce*

Raisin-Cider Sauce over French Toast (page 73)

Raisin-Cider Sauce  20

MRS. C. B. FOSTER, GRINNELL, IOWA

Mix together thoroughly in a saucepan

3 tablespoons brown sugar
1 tablespoon cornstarch
¼ teaspoon salt
¼ teaspoon cloves
⅛ teaspoon cinnamon
   Few grains nutmeg

Stir in

1 cup apple cider
½ cup seedless raisins

Put over high heat and bring rapidly to boiling. Stirring slowly and constantly, cook until mixture is thick and clear (about 3 min.).

Remove from heat and stir in

1 teaspoon lemon juice

Serve hot over ham slices or **French Toast** (*page 73*).   *About 1½ cups sauce*

▲ Spicy Cranberry Sauce 21 5

Combine in a small saucepan and stir over low heat until sugar is dissolved

1 cup sugar
1 cup water
1 3-in. piece stick cinnamon
⅛ teaspoon salt

Bring to boiling; boil uncovered 5 min. Add

2 cups (about ½ lb.) cranberries, washed and sorted

Continue to boil uncovered without stirring, about 5 min., or until skins pop open.

Cool; remove stick cinnamon.

Serve with meat or poultry.

About 2 cups sauce

△ Cranberry Sauce 22 6

Follow ▲ Recipe. Omit stick cinnamon.

Spicy Cherry Sauce 23

Set out two 2-qt. saucepans having tight-fitting covers.

Combine in one of the saucepans

3½ cups (No. 2½ can) pitted red cherries
3 whole cloves
1 stick (2-in.) cinnamon

Cover and cook 5 min. over medium heat.

Remove from heat; discard the cinnamon and cloves. Pour sauce through sieve or food mill placed over the other saucepan. Force cherries through sieve and set aside.

Mix together thoroughly

2 tablespoons cornstarch
2 tablespoons sugar
¼ teaspoon salt

Stir in, in order

2 tablespoons cold water
⅓ cup white corn sirup

Make a smooth paste. Gradually add the cornstarch mixture to the hot sieved cherries, stirring constantly. Bring rapidly to boiling, stirring slowly and constantly. Cook until mixture is thick and clear.

Remove from heat and blend in

2 tablespoons butter or margarine
2 teaspoons lemon juice
¼ teaspoon almond extract
2 or 3 drops of red food coloring

Serve hot with griddlecakes, waffles, omelets, cooked cereals, fritters or **French Toast** (*page 73*).   *About 1½ cups sauce*

▲ Dutch "Honey"
MRS. HARRY WILSON, MOSCOW, KANS.

Combine in a medium-size saucepan
- **1 cup sugar**
- **1 cup cream or undiluted evaporated milk**
- **1 cup dark corn sirup**

Stir over low heat until sugar is dissolved; increase heat and bring to boiling, stirring frequently.

Remove from heat and stir in
- **⅛ teaspoon cream of tartar**
- **½ teaspoon vanilla extract**

Serve warm with pancakes or waffles.

About 3 cups sauce

△ Cinnamon Sauce 25

Follow ▲ Recipe. Add to the sugar-sirup mixture before heating 2¼ teaspoons **cinnamon** and ½ teaspoon **nutmeg.**

Note: These sauces may be stored in covered jars in refrigerator and reheated before using.

▲ Fresh Strawberry Sauce 26

Set out a medium-size saucepan.

Rinse, sort, drain, hull and slice
- **2 cups fresh, ripe strawberries**

Crush ½ cup of the berries; set remaining berries aside.

Put into the saucepan
- **½ cup sugar**
- **¼ cup water**

Place over medium heat and stir constantly until sugar is dissolved. Bring to boiling; stir in the crushed strawberries. Reduce heat and simmer, uncovered, 5 min. Remove from heat. Pour mixture over the sliced strawberries.

Cool and chill thoroughly in refrigerator.

About 2 cups sauce

△ Fresh Raspberry Sauce 27

Follow ▲ Recipe. Substitute 2 cups rinsed, drained whole **raspberries** for the strawberries.

△ Frozen Berry Sauce 28

Follow ▲ Recipe. Substitute 2 16-oz. pkgs. **frozen sweetened berries** (raspberries or sliced strawberries) for the fresh berries; completely thaw according to directions on package. Drain berries, reserving 1 cup sirup. (Use remaining sirup in other food preparation.) Boil reserved sirup until reduced in volume to about ½ cup. Stir in berries. Proceed as in ▲ Recipe.

Strawberry-Rhubarb Sauce

Set out a 2-qt. saucepan having a tight-fitting cover.

Rinse, sort, drain, hull and cut into halves and set aside
- **2 cups fresh, ripe strawberries**

Cut off and discard leaves and stem ends from
- **1 lb. rhubarb**

Rinse and cut into 1-in. pieces (about 3 to 4 cups pieces). Put rhubarb in saucepan and add
- **¾ cup sugar**
- **¼ teaspoon salt**

Stirring occasionally, heat until sugar dissolves and mixture boils. Cover and cook slowly about 10 min., stirring occasionally. Gently mix strawberries with the rhubarb. Cover pan and continue to cook mixture slowly 3 to 5 min., or until rhubarb is tender.

Remove from heat and mix in
- **2 tablespoons butter or margarine**
- **2 teaspoons grated orange peel (page 11)**

Serve sauce warm or chilled over vanilla ice cream, angel-food cake, baked custard, vanilla pudding or blancmange. *About 3 cups sauce*

▲ Strawberry Whip Topping

MRS. HOWARD E. ROSS
PRINCESS ANNE, MD.

Crush and set aside to drain enough strawberries to yield

½ cup drained crushed strawberries

Beat with a rotary beater until frothy

1 egg white
⅛ teaspoon salt

Add gradually, beating well after each addition

¼ cup sugar

Continue beating mixture until rounded peaks are formed and egg whites do not slide when bowl is partially inverted. Set aside.

Mix in a small bowl the *thoroughly drained*, crushed strawberries and

¼ to ½ cup sugar (depending upon sweetness of fruit)

Add sweetened fruit to meringue and beat until stiff peaks are formed.

Serve sauce immediately over puddings, cupcakes, slices of cake, or shortcake. Garnish with whole berries.   *1½ to 2 cups sauce*

△ Pineapple Whip Topping

Follow ▲ Recipe. Substitute ½ cup *thoroughly drained* **crushed pineapple** for the strawberries. (Reserve pineapple sirup for use in other food preparation.)

Eggnog Sauce

MRS. A. E. McNEEL, HILLSBORO, W. VA.

Put a bowl and rotary beater into refrigerator to chill.

Beat until thick and lemon-colored

2 egg yolks

Add alternately, beating until well blended after each addition

¾ cup sifted confectioners' sugar
3 tablespoons brandy

Set aside.

Using the chilled bowl and rotary beater, beat until cream stands in peaks when beater is lifted slowly upright

½ cup chilled whipping cream

Fold (*page 12*) the egg-yolk mixture into the whipped cream.

Serve immediately.   *About 1½ cups sauce*

Note: Sauce may be kept in refrigerator up to ½ hr. without separation. If necessary, beat only to blend mixture before serving.

Rum Sauce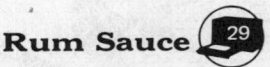

For the peak of elegance serve this creamy sauce over slices of light or dark cake.

Place a bowl and rotary beater in refrigerator to chill. Set out a double boiler.

Set out

1 cup milk

Scald (*page 13*) ¾ cup of the milk; reserve remainder.

Meanwhile, sift together into a saucepan

⅓ cup sugar
2 tablespoons cornstarch

Blend in the reserved ¼ cup milk; add gradually, stirring constantly, the scalded milk.

Bring rapidly to boiling over direct heat, stirring gently and constantly; cook 3 min. Remove from heat.

Wash double-boiler top to remove scum.

Pour mixture into double-boiler top and place over simmering water. Cover and cook about 12 min., stirring three or four times.

Vigorously stir about 3 tablespoons of the hot mixture into

1 egg, slightly beaten

Immediately blend into mixture in double boiler. Cook over simmering water 3 to 5 min., stirring slowly and constantly.

Remove from heat, cover, and cool to lukewarm. Blend in

2 to 3 tablespoons rum

Chill in refrigerator.

Shortly before serving, beat, using the chilled bowl and rotary beater, until cream stands in peaks when beater is lifted slowly upright

1 cup chilled whipping cream

Gently fold (*page 12*) whipped cream into sauce mixture.

Serve cold.   *About 3 cups sauce*

▲ Vanilla Sauce  30

Old stand-by with dozens of uses.

Sift together into a saucepan

1 cup sugar
2 tablespoons cornstarch
¼ teaspoon salt

Add gradually, stirring constantly

2 cups boiling water

Continue to stir; bring to boiling and simmer 5 min.

Remove from heat and blend in

¼ cup butter or margarine
2 teaspoons vanilla extract

Serve sauce hot on **Old-Fashioned English Plum Pudding** (*page 510*).

About 2 cups sauce

⚠ Lemon Sauce 31

Follow ▲ Recipe. Substitute 3 tablespoons **lemon juice** and 2 teaspoons grated **lemon peel** (*page 11*) for vanilla extract.

⚠ Brandy Sauce 32

Follow ⚠ Recipe, decreasing lemon juice to 1 tablespoon. Stir in 3 tablespoons **brandy**.

Creamy Orange Custard Sauce 33

Scald (*page 13*) in top of double boiler

2 cups milk or cream

Meanwhile, beat slightly

4 egg yolks

Blend into egg yolks

⅓ cup sugar
⅛ teaspoon salt

Stirring constantly, add scalded milk gradually to egg-yolk mixture.

Wash double-boiler top to remove scum.

Strain mixture into double-boiler top. Cook over simmering water, stirring constantly and rapidly until mixture coats a silver spoon. Remove from heat and from simmering water at once.

Cool slightly and blend in

¼ cup frozen orange juice concentrate, undiluted but thawed slightly
2 tablespoons butter or margarine
⅛ teaspoon mace

Cover and set sauce aside to cool to lukewarm. Stir, then chill sauce in refrigerator.

Serve sauce with chiffon, sponge or angel-food cake; fruit, fresh or cooked; or puddings.

About 2½ cups sauce

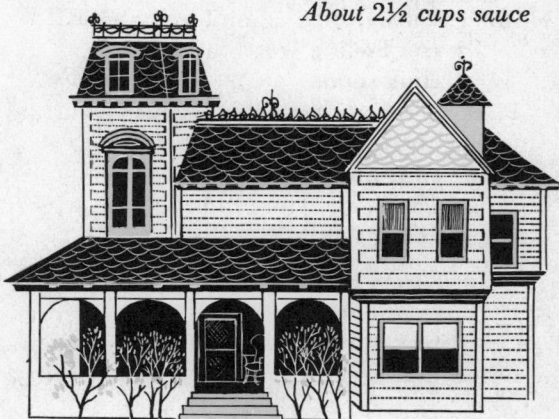

Fudge Sauce Café, Sponge Cake Ring (page 343)

Cocoa Sirup 34

Mix together thoroughly
2 cups sugar
1 cup cocoa
¼ teaspoon salt
Add gradually, stirring to make a paste
½ cup water
Stirring constantly, blend in
2 cups boiling water
Boil, stirring gently, for 6 min.

Remove from heat. Cool. Store in covered jar in refrigerator until needed.

About 4 cups sirup

Chocolate Sirup 35

Melt (*page 12*)
6 sq. (6 oz.) chocolate
Add gradually, stirring until well blended
1 cup boiling water
2 cups sugar
Place over direct heat. Add gradually, stirring constantly
1½ cups boiling water
Bring chocolate mixture to boiling; boil for 6 min., stirring gently.

Remove from heat. Blend in
¼ teaspoon salt
Cool. Store in tightly covered jar in refrigerator until needed. *About 3½ cups sirup*

Fudge Sauce Café 36

Double the mocha pleasure of Fudge Sauce Café by serving with steaming hot coffee.

Mix together in a small, heavy saucepan
½ cup sugar
½ cup double-strength coffee beverage
(page 13)
2 sq. (2 oz.) chocolate, broken in pieces
1 tablespoon cream
⅛ teaspoon salt
Place over low heat. Cook, stirring constantly, until sauce becomes slightly thickened.

Remove from heat and blend in
1 tablespoon butter or margarine
½ teaspoon vanilla extract
Serve sauce warm or cool.

About 1 cup sauce

▲ Chocolate Miracle Sauce 37

Cook in double-boiler top 5 min. or until smooth
5 sq. (5 oz.) chocolate
1½ cups sugar
1½ cups water
¼ teaspoon salt
Add and stir in
1⅓ cups (15-oz. can) sweetened condensed milk
Cook over hot water until mixture coats a silver spoon. *About 3 cups sauce*

△ Miracle Semi-Sweet Sauce 38

Follow ▲ Recipe. Substitute 1 pkg. (6 oz.) **semi-sweet chocolate pieces** for chocolate.

Coconut-Praline Sauce `39`
MRS. RAY GARRISON, BOWLING GREEN, KY.

Heat in a saucepan over low heat
⅓ cup butter or margarine
Add and stir frequently until golden brown
1 cup moist shredded coconut, cut
With slotted spoon, remove coconut to dish.

Add to the butter in the saucepan
½ cup firmly packed brown sugar
2 tablespoons dark corn sirup
⅛ teaspoon salt
Cook over low heat, stirring constantly, until mixture bubbles vigorously. Remove saucepan from heat.

Add gradually, stirring constantly
¾ cup undiluted evaporated milk
Return to heat and stir constantly until thoroughly heated.

Remove from heat. Stir in coconut and
½ teaspoon vanilla extract
Serve warm or cold on ice cream, or on unfrosted white or chocolate cake squares.
About 2 cups sauce

Luscious Butterscotch `40` Sauce

Put in a small, heavy saucepan
1 cup firmly packed light brown sugar
⅓ cup butter
⅓ cup cream
Few grains salt
Stir over low heat until sugar is dissolved and butter is melted. Increase heat to medium and bring mixture to boiling, stirring occasionally. Boil 5 min. without stirring. Remove from heat and beat sauce about 1 min.

Serve warm over ice cream or unfrosted cake squares. *About 1¼ cups sauce*

▲ Vanilla Hard Sauce

Best-of-all sauce for warm, spicy desserts.

Cream together until butter is softened
⅓ cup butter or margarine
1 teaspoon vanilla extract
Add gradually, creaming until fluffy after each addition
1 cup sifted confectioners' sugar
Few grains salt
Beat in about
1 teaspoon cream or undiluted evaporated milk
Pile sauce lightly into serving bowl. Chill until cold but not hard.

Serve with warm pudding or warm gingerbread or spice cake. *About ⅔ cup sauce*

△ Brandy Hard Sauce

Follow ▲ Recipe. Substitute 2 tablespoons **brandy** for vanilla; beat in after adding salt. Omit cream. Increase sugar if necessary.

Orange Hard Sauce
JEWEL GRAHAM, AMES, IOWA

Especially good with spice cake or gingerbread.

Measure
3 cups sifted confectioners' sugar
Set aside.

Set out to thaw slightly contents of
1 6-oz. can (¾ cup) frozen orange juice concentrate
Cream until softened
½ cup butter or margarine
Beating until smooth after each addition, alternately add the sugar in fourths, the liquid in thirds to the creamed butter.

Add gradually, beating until well blended
1½ cups (about 6½ oz.) non-fat dry milk solids
Continue beating until smooth and creamy.
About 3 cups sauce

SAUCES in the MICROWAVE OVEN

The microwave oven is an ideal instrument for producing nearly foolproof sauces and gravies. No longer are sauces the bane of a cook's existence. There is no more burning, curdling or separating.

It's also neater and more efficient, if only because there is no need for a double boiler or a water bath in any of these recipes when prepared in the microwave oven.

As you may have noticed, when we talk about sauces throughout this book, we simply can't rave enough about the microwave product. The cream sauces, the chocolate sauces and the gravies are all delightfully smooth and delicious. Our favorite example is the **Hollandaise Sauce.** We prepared this recipe and reheated it three times over the course of several days—it still did not separate.

These glowing reports are accompanied by an equally strong recommendation to stir, frequently and well. Each recipe indicates when and how often to stir. These directions are not arbitrary. Too much or too little stirring does make a difference in the successful outcome of the sauce.

When a recipe calls for mixing in ingredients outside of the oven, follow the procedures noted in the recipes for conventional cooking. Use the stirring intervals to check if the sauce is done to your liking. Follow the master recipe's directions about whether to cook covered or uncovered.

Absent from this microwave sauces repertoire are the heartier barbecue and spaghetti-type of tomato sauces. The microwave simply does not call forth the rich, full flavor from the ingredients which these sauces demand. The recipes for **Tomato Sauce** and its variations which we do include here are very good, however. They are lighter sauces suggested as accompaniments to fish or omelets.

REMINDERS—See the introductory chapter, **Home Cooking in the Microwave Oven,** in the beginning of this book for additional tips and for an easy-to-read chart comparing settings among different brands of microwave ovens. By reviewing this chapter you will also learn more about how we have adapted these recipes.

Medium White Sauce I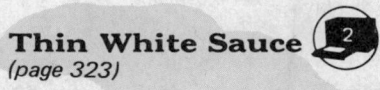
(page 323)

Use a small casserole.

COOK to melt butter. Add flour mixture and COOK, stirring every 30 sec., until mixture bubbles (about 3 min.).

Add milk and COOK, stirring every 15 sec., until sauce thickens (about 2 min.). COOK to meld flavor (about 30 sec.).

OVERALL COOKING TIME: 5:30

Thin White Sauce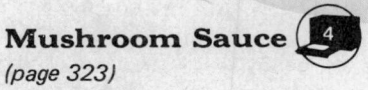
(page 323)

Follow ▤ Recipe with changes as in ⚠ Recipe.

Thick White Sauce ▤
(page 323)

Follow ▤ Recipe with changes as in ⚠ Recipe.

Mushroom Sauce ▤
(page 323)

Follow ▤ Recipe with changes as in ⚠ Recipe, except for mushrooms, COOK to melt butter in a small casserole. Add mushrooms and onions and COOK, stirring every 2 min., until tender (about 5 min.).

Cheese Sauce *(page 323)*

Follow ▤ Recipe with changes as in ⚠ Recipe.

Mock Hollandaise Sauce
(page 323)

Follow ▤ Recipe with changes as in ⚠ Recipe, except stir egg yolk mixture back into sauce and COOK, stirring every 30 sec., until blended (about 3 min.).

Medium White Sauce II ▤
(page 323)

Use a small casserole

COOK, stirring every 30 sec., until mixture starts to thicken (about 3 min.).

Add butter or margarine and COOK, stirring every 30 sec., until thickened (about 1 min.).

OVERALL COOKING TIME: 4:00

Hollandaise Sauce ▤
(page 324)

Use a small casserole.

Place egg yolk, cream seasonings and lemon juice in a small casserole. SLOWCOOK, stirring every 15 sec., until hot and slightly thickened.

Butter should be at room temperature. Add one-third of the butter and stir thoroughly off heat to melt. SLOWCOOK to warm (about 10 sec.). Stir. Add one-third butter and stir thoroughly to melt; SLOWCOOK to warm (about 10 sec.). Stir. Add last one-third butter and stir thoroughly to melt. SLOWCOOK, stirring every 15 sec., until sauce just starts to bubble (about 45 sec.).

OVERALL COOKING TIME: 2:35

Brown Roux or Paste  9
(page 325)

Use a small casserole or browning skillet.

COOK to melt fat. Stir in flour and COOK, stirring every 1 min., until it bubbles and browns (about 5 min.).

OVERALL COOKING TIME: 5:00

Brown Gravy *(page 325)* 10

Method 1—Use the dish in which meat or poultry was prepared. Blend fat, flour and seasonings thoroughly. COOK, stirring every 1 min., until mixture bubbles (about 3 min.).

Blend in liquid. COOK, stirring and scraping bottom every 1½ min., until sauce thickens (about 8 min.).

Method 2—Use a small casserole. COOK to boil stock (about 8 min.).

Stir thoroughly to blend half of flour-water mixture and COOK, stirring every 1 min., to boil (about 3 min.).

Add remaining mixture as in Recipe. COOK to boil after each addition, stirring every 1 min., until desired consistency is reached.

Add spices and COOK until flavors are blended.

Giblet Gravy *(page 325)* 11

Follow 10 Recipe with changes as in △ Recipe.

Golden Gravy *(page 326)* 12

Use a browning skillet or 1-qt. casserole.

COOK to melt fat (about 3 min.). Add flour mixture and COOK, stirring every 1 min., to bubbling and slightly browned (about 3 min.).

Add broth and milk, stirring thoroughly. COOK, stirring every 1 min., until thickened (about 3 min.).

OVERALL COOKING TIME: 9:00

Norwegian Wine Gravy 13
(page 326)

Use a 1-qt. casserole.

COOK to melt butter. Add onion and COOK, stirring every 1½ min., until transparent (about 3 min.).

Blend in flour mixture and COOK, stirring every 1 min., until bubbling (about 3 min.).

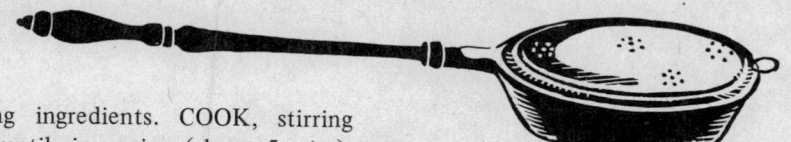

Add remaining ingredients. COOK, stirring every 2 min., until simmering (about 5 min.).
OVERALL COOKING TIME: 11:00

Tomato Sauce *(page 326)* 14

Use a browning skillet and a 1½-qt. casserole.

COOK tomato mixture, stirring every 2½ min., until simmering (about 5 min.).

In skillet, melt butter. Blend in flour and COOK, stirring every 1 min., until bubbling (about 2 min.).

Add tomato mixture and Worcestershire sauce. COOK, stirring every 30 sec., to thicken (about 1 min.).

OVERALL COOKING TIME: 8:00

Quick Tomato Sauce 15
(page 327)

Use a 1-qt. casserole.

Melt butter. Blend in flour mixture and COOK, stirring every 1 min., to bubbling (about 3 min.).

Stir in remaining ingredients thoroughly. COOK, stirring every 30 sec., to boil (about 5 min.).

OVERALL COOKING TIME: 8:00

Tomato-Cheese Sauce 16
(page 327)

Use a 1-qt. casserole.

Combine mushrooms and tomato soup. COOK, stirring every 3 min., to simmer (about 8 min.).
OVERALL COOKING TIME: 8:00

Creamy Mustard Sauce 17
(page 329)

Use a 1-qt. casserole.

COOK to scald milk (about 3 min.).

COOK sugar-milk mixture, stirring every 1 min., to dissolve sugar (about 3 min.).

Add the reserved cream or evaporated milk and continue to COOK, stirring every 30 sec., to bring to a boil (about 2 min.).

Cover and COOK, stirring every 1 min., to thicken (about 5 min.).

Add egg yolk mixture and COOK, stirring every 1 min., to blend (about 2 min.).
OVERALL COOKING TIME: 15:00

Zippy Mustard Sauce 18
(page 329)

Use a small casserole.

Combine sugar mixture, vinegar, water and

COOK, stirring every 30 sec., to boil (about 3 min.).

Add egg yolk mixture and COOK, stirring every 30 sec., to thicken slightly and blend flavors (about 1 min.).

OVERALL COOKING TIME: 4:00

Spicy Cranberry Sauce 21
(page 332)

Use a small casserole.

COOK sugar mixture, stirring every 2 min., until sugar dissolves (about 15 min.). Continue to COOK, stirring every 1 min, until mixture boils (about 3 min.).

Add cranberries and COOK until skins pop (about 3 min.).

OVERALL COOKING TIME: 21:00

Lemon Butter Sauce 19
(page 331)

Use a small casserole. The time in this recipe is for butter at room temperature.

Combine all ingredients and COOK, stirring every 1½ min., to melt butter and heat (about 3 min.).

OVERALL COOKING TIME: 3:00

Cranberry Sauce *(page 332)* 22

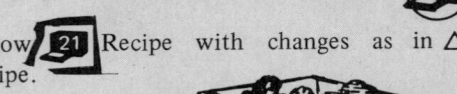

Follow 21 Recipe with changes as in △ Recipe.

Spicy Cherry Sauce 23
(page 332)

Use a 2-qt. casserole.

COOK cherry mixture to boil (about 3 min.). Stir. Continue to COOK to strengthen spice flavor (about 2 min.).

COOK cherry-cornstarch mixture, stirring every 1 min., to boil (about 5 min.). Continue to COOK, stirring every 1 min., until mixture is thick (about 3 min.).

OVERALL COOKING TIME: 13:00

Raisin-Cider Sauce 20
(page 332)

Use a small casserole.

Combine all ingredients, except lemon juice, and COOK, stirring every 1 min., to boil (about 2 min.). COOK, stirring every 30 sec., until mixture thickens (about 1 min.).

OVERALL COOKING TIME: 3:00

Dutch "Honey" *(page 333)* 24

Use a 1-qt. casserole.

SLOWCOOK, stirring every 30 sec., to dissolve sugar and bring to a boil (about 5 min.). COOK, stirring every 30 sec., to thicken (about 2 min.).

OVERALL COOKING TIME: 7:00

Cinnamon Sauce 25
(page 333)

Follow 24 Recipe with changes as in △ Recipe.

Fresh Strawberry Sauce 26
(page 333)

Use a 2-qt. casserole.

COOK sugar-water mixture, stirring every 1 min., to dissolve sugar and bring to a boil (about 5 min.). Continue to COOK until slightly thickened (about 3 min.).

OVERALL COOKING TIME: 8:00

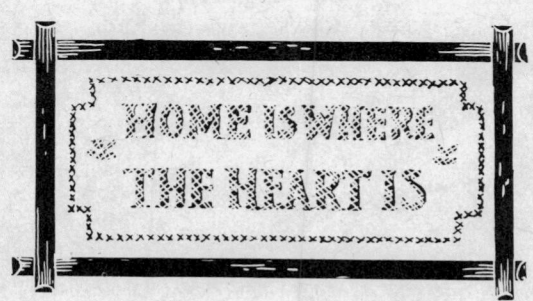

HOME IS WHERE THE HEART IS

Fresh Raspberry Sauce 27
(page 333)

Follow 26 Recipe with substitution as in △ Recipe.

Frozen Berry Sauce 28
(page 333)

Use a small casserole.

COOK sirup to reduce liquid to ½ cup (about 15 min.). Add berries and COOK to heat (about 3 min.).

OVERALL COOKING TIME: 18:00

Rum Sauce *(page 334)* 29

Use a small casserole.

COOK to scald milk (about 4 min.). COOK, stirring every 30 sec., to bring cornstarch mixture to a boil, until slightly thickened (about 3 min.).

SLOWCOOK, stirring every 30 sec., until sauce is thicker and starts to clear (about 1½ min.).

Add egg mixture and COOK, stirring every 30 sec., to heat (about 1 min.).

OVERALL COOKING TIME: 9:30

Vanilla Sauce *(page 335)* 30

Use a small casserole.

COOK to boil water (about 8 min.).

Combine sugar mixture and water and COOK, stirring every 3 sec., to boil (about 3 min.). Continue to COOK, stirring every 30 sec., until sauce thickens (about 3 min.).

OVERALL COOKING TIME: 14:00

Lemon Sauce *(page 335)* 31

Follow 30 Recipe with substitutions as in ⚠ Recipe.

Brandy Sauce *(page 335)* 32

Follow 30 Recipe with changes as in ⚠ Recipe.

Creamy Orange Custard Sauce *(page 335)* 33

Use two 1-qt. casseroles.

COOK to scald milk (about 8 min.). Thoroughly mix milk with egg yolk mixture. Strain into another casserole. SLOWCOOK milk-egg mixture, stirring every 30 sec., until mixture coats a spoon (about 5 min.).

OVERALL COOKING TIME: 10:00

Cocoa Sirup *(page 336)* 34

Use a 1½-qt. casserole.

COOK to boil the 2 cups water (about 8 min.).

COOK the cocoa paste mixture, stirring every 30 sec., until it boils (about 2 min.).

Add boiling water, mixing thoroughly. COOK, stirring every 1 min., to thicken (about 3 min.).

Chocolate Sirup *(page 336)* 35

Use a small casserole.

COOK to melt chocolate, stirring every 1 min. (about 4 min.).

COOK (in glass measuring cup) to boil 1 cup water (about 4 min.). Add water to sugar and chocolate all at once and stir thoroughly.

COOK to dissolve sugar, stirring every 1 min. (about 3 min.).

COOK to boil 1½ cups water (about 4 min.). Add water all at once and stir thoroughly. COOK, stirring every 1 min., to boil and thicken (about 4 min.).

OVERALL COOKING TIME: 19:00

Fudge Sauce Café
(page 336)

Use a small casserole.

COOK sugar-chocolate mixture, stirring every 1 min., until it begins to thicken (about 2 min.). Continue to COOK, stirring every 30 sec., until thick (about 3 min.).

OVERALL COOKING TIME: 5:00

Coconut-Praline Sauce
(page 337)

Use a small casserole.

SLOWCOOK sugar mixture, stirring every 1½ min., until sugar is dissolved and butter melted (about 5 min.).

COOK to boil (about 3 min.).

OVERALL COOKING TIME: 8:00

Chocolate Miracle Sauce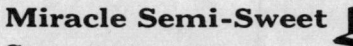
(page 336)

Use a 1½-qt. casserole.

COOK chocolate mixture, stirring every 1 min., until smooth (about 5 min.).

Add milk and COOK, stirring every 30 sec., until mixture coats a spoon (about 5 min.).

OVERALL COOKING TIME: 5:00

Luscious Butterscotch Sauce *(page 337)*

Use a small casserole.

COOK to melt butter (about 3 min.). Add coconut and COOK, stirring every 30 sec., to brown (about 4 min.).

Add brown sugar mixture and COOK, stirring every 30 sec., to bubbling (about 3 min.).

Add milk and COOK, stirring every 30 sec., to heat (about 1 min.). Do not overheat.

OVERALL COOKING TIME: 11:00

Miracle Semi-Sweet Sauce *(page 336)*

Follow 37 Recipe with changes as in Recipe.

SAUCES in the SLOW COOKER

Cooking sauces in the slow cooker can be a great convenience. For instance, if you are preparing an elaborate dinner or trying to accommodate unexpected company you will need both hands, all stove burners and a clear head. Worrying about stirring a sauce can be crossed off your list of concerns when it is cooking in the slow cooker.

Preparation is also cleaner and a space saver, too. The sauce can be brewing in any corner of the house while you're busy with other preparations.

Don't forget that sauces can always be frozen for future meals.

We recommend that onions be sautéed on top of the stove in several recipes which call for this step. This is not only because onions take an inordinately long time to cook in the slow cooker, but because the sauteing mellows the onion flavor.

The flavors of all the sauces included here are good—you will have no complaints. But, they are not as subtely blended as when cooked on the conventional stove. We recommend using the slow cooker for the preparation of sauces largely for its convenience.

REMINDERS—We provide more tips on slow cooking and an easy-to-read chart comparing settings among different brands of slow cookers in the introductory chapter, **Home Cooking in the Slow Cooker**, in the beginning of this book.

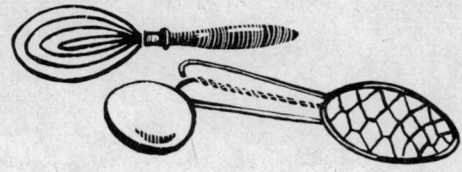

Tangy Bar-B-Q Sauce **1**
(page 327)

Use a 3½-qt. slow cooker.

Cook onions, pepper and garlic on top of the stove.

Transfer vegetables to slow cooker and combine with remaining ingredients, except lemon juice.

Cook on LOW for 2½ to 3½ hrs.

Stir in lemon juice.

Bar-B-Q Sauce for **2**
Basting *(page 327)*

Follow **1** Recipe with changes as in △Recipe, except add vinegar with lemon juice. Do not add additional water.

Barbecue Sauce **3**
Mexicano *(page 328)*

Use a 3½-qt. slow cooker.

Cook onions and garlic on top of the stove.

Transfer onions and garlic to slow cooker and add all remaining ingredients, except use only ½ bay leaf (instead of 1).

Cook on LOW for 2½ to 3½ hrs.

Spaghetti Sauce *(page 328)* **4**

Use a 3½-qt. slow cooker.

Cook onions and pepper on top of the stove.

Transfer onions and pepper to slow cooker and combine with all remaining ingredients, except use only ½ bay leaf (instead of 1) and 1 tablespoon oregano (instead of 2).

Cook on LOW for 8 to 9 hrs.

Spicy Cranberry Sauce **5**
(page 332)

Use a 3½-qt. slow cooker.

Combine all ingredients in slow cooker, except use only ¼ cup water (instead of 1).

Cook on HIGH for 6 to 7 hrs.

Cranberry Sauce *(page 332)* **6**

Follow **5** Recipe with changes as in △Recipe.

The Art of Cakemaking

When a little girl makes her first sally into the kitchen to cook, she does not want to cook an egg, to make French toast, or fry a hamburger. She wants to bake a cake! And though her reach may exceed her grasp, her instincts are leading her in the right direction, for cakemaking is the most womanly of all the household arts. And of all the creations that emanate from the kitchen, none bears a clearer seal of femininity than a cake. All women know that in cakemaking they find expression for many creative impulses, combining form and color and texture to contrast or complement. Women love to bake cakes. And the measure of their devotion and talent may be judged by this collection of some of their masterworks.

TYPES—Basically, cakes are divided into two groups —with and without fat. Actually there are many cakes that are on the borderline of these two main classifications.

Butter-type (shortening) Cakes—These cakes contain a fat (butter, margarine, hydrogenated vegetable shortening, all-purpose shortening or lard) and a chemical leavening agent (baking powder or baking soda). Methods of mixing are: *Conventional* —fat creamed with flavoring extract and then sugar, beaten eggs or egg yolks beaten into creamed mixture and dry and liquid ingredients alternately added and beaten in; egg whites, if used, are beaten and folded in last. *Conventional sponge*—same as conventional except part of sugar beaten with egg whites to make a meringue and folded in last. *Quick-method* (*quick-mix, one-bowl*)—used only when recipe has been developed for the method; dry ingredients and shortening in bowl, eggs and liquid added according to directions; beaten with wooden spoon or electric mixer for specified time.

Chiffon Cakes—These cakes contain a cooking (salad) oil and baking powder. They have the lightness of sponge cake and richness of butter cake.

Sponge-type Cakes—True sponge cakes do not contain any fat, baking powder or baking soda; they are leavened by air and steam. Others may contain a small amount of butter or baking powder. *Angel food cakes* are made with egg whites only and *sponge cakes* with egg yolks or whole eggs.

STORING CAKES—Cakes, except fruitcakes, are at their best when served the same day they are made. But if they are stored properly, most cakes will remain fresh and delicious for a few days.

Plain or frosted cakes—Store in a cake keeper or invert a large, deep bowl over cake on a plate.

Cream filled or whipped cream frosted and filled cakes—Assemble shortly before serving. Always keep frosted cake in refrigerator until ready to serve. Cake may become soggy if kept in refrigerator longer than one hour. Immediately refrigerate any leftover cake.

Fruitcakes—When cake is completely cooled wrap tightly in aluminum foil or moisture-vapor-proof material and store in a cool place to age for several weeks before serving. If desired, once or twice a week, using a pastry brush, paint cake with rum, brandy or other liqueur, or fruit juice; rewrap and store again.

When a Cake Lacks Perfection

A cake may have ...	Because of ... BUTTER-TYPE CAKES	SPONGE-TYPE CAKES
A hard top crust	Temperature too high Overbaking	Temperature too high Overbaking
A sticky top crust	Too much sugar Insufficient baking	Too much sugar Insufficient baking
A humped or cracked top	Too much flour or too little liquid Overmixing Batter not spread evenly in pan Temperature too high	Too much flour or sugar Temperature too high
One side higher	Batter not spread evenly Uneven pan Pan too close to side of oven Oven rack or range not level Uneven oven heat	Uneven pan Oven rack or range not level
A soggy streak or layer at bottom	Too much liquid Underbeaten eggs Shortening too soft Undermixing Insufficient baking	Too many eggs or egg yolks Underbeaten egg yolks Undermixing
Fallen	Too much sugar, liquid, leavening or shortening Too little flour Temperature too low Insufficient baking	Too much sugar Overbeaten egg whites Underbeaten egg yolks Use of greased pan Insufficient baking
Coarse grain	Use of all-purpose flour instead of cake flour Too much leavening Shortening too soft Insufficient creaming Undermixing Temperature too low	Use of all-purpose flour instead of cake flour Omitting cream of tartar (angel food) Undermixing
Tough crumb	Too much flour Too many eggs Too little sugar or shortening Overmixing Temperature too high	Too little sugar Overbeaten egg whites Underbeaten egg yolks Omitting cream of tartar (angel food) Overmixing Temperature too high Overbaking
A heavy, compact quality	Too much liquid or shortening Too many eggs Too little leavening or flour Overmixing Temperature too high	Overbeaten egg whites Underbeaten egg yolks Overmixing
Crumbled or fallen apart	Too much sugar, leavening or shortening Undermixing Improper pan treatment Improper cooling	
Fallen out of pan before completely cooled		Too much sugar Use of greased pan Insufficient baking

A Check List for Successful Cakemaking

(See For These Recipes—What To Use, How To Do It, and Oven Temperatures on *pages 10-13*.)

√ **Read recipe** carefully.

√ **Assemble** all ingredients and utensils.

√ **Have all ingredients** at room temperature unless recipe specifies otherwise.

√ **Select pans** of proper kind and size. Measure inside, from rim to rim.

√ **Use standard measuring** cups and spoons. Use liquid measuring cups (rim above 1-cup line) for liquids. Use nested or dry measuring cups (1-cup line even with top) for dry ingredients.

√ **Check liquid measurements** at eye level.

√ **Level dry measurements** with straight-edged knife or spatula.

√ **Preheat oven** 12 to 20 min. at required temperature. Leave oven door open first 2 min.

√ **Place oven rack** so top of product will be almost at center of oven. Stagger pans so no pan is directly over another and they do not touch each other or walls of oven. Place single pan so that the center of product is as near to the center of the oven as possible.

√ **Prepare pan**—For cakes *with shortening* and for cake rolls, grease bottom of pan only; line with waxed paper cut to fit bottom of pan only; grease waxed paper. For cakes *without shortening* (sponge-type), do not grease or line pan. If recipe directs "Set out pan," do not grease or line pan.

√ **Sift all flour** except whole-grain types before measuring. Spoon lightly into measuring cup; do not jar. Level with straight-edged knife or spatula.

√ **Cream shortening** (alone or with flavorings) by stirring, rubbing or beating with spoon or electric mixer until softened. Add sugar in small amounts; cream after each addition until all graininess disappears and mixture is light and fluffy. Thorough creaming helps to insure a fine-grained cake.

√ **Beat whole eggs** until thick and piled softly when recipe calls for well-beaten eggs.

√ **Beat egg whites** as follows: *Frothy*—entire mass forms bubbles; *Rounded peaks*—peaks turn over slightly when beater is slowly lifted upright; *Stiff peaks*—peaks remain standing when beater is slowly lifted upright.

√ **Beat egg yolks** until thick and lemon-colored when recipe calls for well-beaten yolks.

√ **When dry and liquid ingredients** are added to cake batters, add alternately, beginning and ending with dry. Add dry ingredients in fourths, liquid in thirds. After each addition, beat only until smooth. Finally beat only until batter is smooth (do not overbeat). Scrape spoon or beater and bottom and sides of bowl during mixing.

If using an electric mixer, beat the mixture at a low speed when alternately adding the dry and liquid ingredients.

√ **Fill cake pans** one-half to two-thirds full.

√ **Tap bottom of cake pan** sharply with hand to release air bubbles before placing in oven.

√ **Test cake** when minimum baking time is up. Touch lightly at center; if it springs back, cake is done. Or insert a cake tester or wooden pick in center; if it comes out clean, cake is done.

√ **Cool butter-type cakes** 10 min. in pan on cooling rack after removing from oven.

√ **Remove butter-type cakes** from pan after cooling. Run spatula gently around sides of pan. Cover with cooling rack. Invert and remove pan. Turn cake right side up immediately after peeling off waxed paper. Cool cake completely before frosting.

√ **Cool sponge-type cakes**—After removing tubed cake from oven, immediately invert pan on end of tube and let hang in pan until completely cooled. If cake is higher than tube, invert between two cooling racks so top of cake does not touch any surface. Invert other types of cake pans so opposite edges of pan rest on edges of two cooling racks; let cake hang in pan until completely cooled.

√ **Remove sponge-type cakes** from pan when completely cooled. Cut around tube with paring knife to loosen cake. Loosen sides with spatula and gently remove cake.

√ **Fill layer cakes**—Spread filling or frosting over top of bottom layer. Cover with the second layer. Repeat procedure if more layers are used. If necessary, hold layers in position with wooden picks; remove when filling is set.

√ **Frost filled layer cakes**—Frost sides first, working rapidly. See that frosting touches plate all around bottom, leaving no gaps. Pile remaining frosting on top of cake and spread lightly.

▲ Angel Food Cake

Set out a 10-in. tubed pan.

Measure and pour into a large bowl
1½ cups (about 12) egg whites
Allow to stand at room temperature at least 1 hr. before beating to insure greater volume.

Meanwhile, sift together
1 cup sifted cake flour
½ cup sugar
Set aside.

Add to egg whites
½ teaspoon salt
Beat with wire whisk, hand rotary beater or electric mixer until frothy. Beat in
1½ teaspoons cream of tartar
Continue beating just until rounded peaks are formed and egg whites do not slide when bowl is partially inverted.

Gently sprinkle over surface of egg whites and fold in (*page 12*), 2 tablespoons at a time
¾ cup sugar
Blend in
1 teaspoon vanilla extract
½ teaspoon almond extract
Sift about 4 tablespoons of flour mixture over surface of meringue (egg-white mixture); fold gently together. Repeat until all of the flour mixture is folded in.

Carefully slide batter into pan, turning pan as batter is poured. Cut through batter with knife or spatula to break large air bubbles.

Bake at 350°F about 45 min., or until cake surface springs back when lightly touched.

Immediately invert pan on end of tube; cool and remove from pan as directed for sponge-type cakes (*page 340*).   *One 10-in. tubed cake*

△ Cocoa Angel Food Cake

Follow ▲ Recipe. Decrease cake flour to ⅔ cup. Sift ⅓ cup **cocoa** with cake flour and sugar. Increase vanilla extract to 1½ teaspoons. Omit almond extract.

Mock Angel Food Cake
MRS. ALFRED BRINGE, HOLMEN, WIS.

Set out a 13x9½x2-in. cake pan.

Measure and pour into a large bowl
¾ cup (about 6) egg whites
Allow to stand at room temperature at least 1 hr. before beating to insure greater volume.

Sift together into a bowl
2 cups sifted cake flour
2 cups sugar
1 teaspoon baking powder
Add gradually, stirring in
1 cup boiling water
Stir until well blended (mixture will be a smooth paste). Set aside.

Add to egg whites
½ teaspoon salt
Beat with wire whisk, hand rotary beater or electric mixer until frothy. Beat in
½ teaspoon cream of tartar
Continue beating until rounded peaks are formed and egg whites do not slide when bowl is partially inverted.

Carefully spread beaten egg whites over flour-water mixture and gently fold (*page 12*) together. Fold in with a minimum number of strokes
1 teaspoon vanilla extract
½ teaspoon almond extract
Turn batter into pan.

Bake at 350°F 35 to 40 min. or until cake surface springs back when lightly touched.

Cool and remove from pan as directed for sponge-type cakes (*page 340*).

One 13x9-in. cake

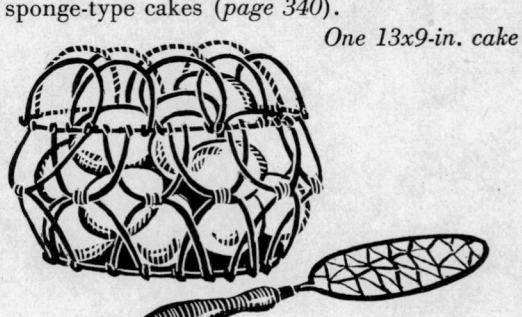

Burnt-Sugar Angel Food Cake

MRS. HENRY K. GAMBER, SCOTTDALE, PA.

Set out a 10-in. tubed pan.

Measure and pour into a large bowl
1½ cups (about 12) egg whites
Allow to stand at room temperature at least 1 hr. before beating to insure greater volume.

Meanwhile, melt in a heavy, light-colored skillet (a black skillet makes it difficult to see the color of the sirup) over low heat
½ cup sugar
With back of wooden spoon, gently keep sugar moving toward center of skillet until sugar is melted. Heat to a rich brown until foam appears. Remove from heat and add gradually, a very small amount at a time
¼ cup boiling water
Cook until bubbles are the size of dimes. Set burnt-sugar sirup aside to cool completely.

Chop finely and set aside
⅓ cup (1¼ oz.) pecans
Sift together and set aside
1½ cups sifted cake flour
1 cup sugar
Add to egg whites
¼ teaspoon salt
Beat with wire whisk, hand rotary beater or electric mixer until frothy. Beat in
1½ teaspoons cream of tartar
Continue beating just until rounded peaks are formed and egg whites do not slide when bowl is partially inverted.

Gently sprinkle over surface of egg whites and fold in (*page 12*), 2 tablespoons at a time
1 cup sugar
Blend in
1 teaspoon vanilla extract
Sift about 4 tablespoons of flour mixture over surface of meringue (egg-white mixture); fold gently together. Repeat until all of the flour mixture is folded in.

Fold in the chopped pecans and 2 tablespoons of the burnt-sugar sirup.

Carefully slide batter into pan, turning pan as batter is poured. Cut through batter with knife or spatula to break large air bubbles.

Bake at 350°F 1 hr., or until cake surface springs back when lightly touched.

Immediately invert pan on end of tube; cool and remove from pan as directed for sponge-type cakes (*page 340*). *One 10-in. tubed cake*

Angel Food Custard Dessert

MRS. HARRIS G. KROES
SANDY SPRINGS, GA.

Put a bowl and a rotary beater in refrigerator to chill.

Cut into 3 layers with a serrated knife
1 10-in. Angel Food Cake (*page 341*) or a purchased angel food cake
Scald (*page 13*) in top of double boiler
1⅓ cups milk
½ cup cream
Meanwhile, pour into a small cup or custard cup
¼ cup cold water
Sprinkle evenly over cold water
1 tablespoon (1 env.) unflavored gelatin
Let gelatin stand about 5 min. to soften. Meanwhile, beat slightly
6 egg yolks

Blend in
 ½ cup sugar
 ⅛ teaspoon salt
Gradually stir scalded milk into eggs.

Wash double-boiler top to remove scum.

Strain mixture and return to double boiler. Cook over simmering water, stirring constantly and rapidly until mixture coats a silver spoon. Remove from heat. Immediately blend in gelatin, stirring until dissolved.

Add and stir until thoroughly blended
 2½ tablespoons lemon juice
 1 teaspoon vanilla extract
Cool mixture; chill (*page 12*) until mixture begins to gel (gets slightly thicker).

Using the chilled bowl and beater, beat until cream is of medium consistency (piles softly)
 1 cup chilled whipping cream
Fold in (*page 12*) whipped cream. Put into refrigerator until of spreading consistency.

When custard is of desired consistency, place bottom layer of the cake on a serving plate. Spread about one fourth of the custard over the cake layer. Cover with the second layer and spread with a second fourth of the custard. Top with remaining cake layer and spread remaining custard over sides and top of cake. Sprinkle with
 3 tablespoons slivered almonds
 About 12 servings

Sponge Cake Ring 1
(*See photo on page 336*)

Set out a 1½-qt. ring mold.

For Sponge Cake Ring—Sift together and set aside
 ½ cup sifted cake flour
 ⅛ teaspoon salt
Beat until very thick and lemon-colored
 3 egg yolks
 ¼ cup sugar
 2 tablespoons water
 1 teaspoon vanilla extract

Gently fold (*page 12*) dry ingredients into egg-yolk mixture until blended. Set aside.

Using clean beater, beat until frothy
 3 egg whites
Add and beat slightly
 ¼ teaspoon cream of tartar
Add gradually, beating well after each addition
 3 tablespoons sugar
Beat until rounded peaks are formed and egg whites do not slide when bowl is partially inverted. Gently spread egg-yolk mixture over egg whites and carefully fold together until blended. Turn batter into mold and spread evenly to edges.

Bake at 325°F about 30 min., or until cake surface springs back when lightly touched.

Invert between two cooling racks (with edges of mold resting on racks) so that top of cake ring does not touch any surface. Allow cake to hang until completely cooled.

When cake ring is completely cooled, run spatula gently around sides and center of mold. Cover with cooling rack. Invert and remove ring mold. When ready to serve, place the cooled cake ring on a serving plate. Prepare and brush over top of cake Coffee Butterscotch Glacé.

For Coffee Butterscotch Glacé—Mix in a small saucepan
 ⅓ cup firmly packed light brown sugar
 ⅓ cup double-strength coffee beverage **(*page 13*)**
Set over medium heat and bring to boiling, stirring constantly. Continue to stir and boil 8 to 10 min., or until slightly thickened. Remove from heat and blend in
 2 tablespoons butter
Cool slightly before brushing on cake.

Fill center of cake ring with scoops of
 Coffee or vanilla ice cream
Drizzle over ice cream
 Fudge Sauce Café (*page 336*)
Pour remaining sauce into a pitcher and serve with the dessert. *6 servings*

▲ Hot-Milk Sponge Cake

Set out two 9-in. round layer cake pans.

Sift together and set aside
1 cup sifted cake flour
1 teaspoon baking powder
¼ teaspoon salt
Beat until very thick and piled softly (about 5 min.)
3 eggs
Add gradually, beating well after each addition
1 cup sugar
2 or 3 teaspoons lemon juice
Put into a small saucepan and set over low heat to heat thoroughly (but do not boil)
6 tablespoons milk
Sift dry ingredients over the egg mixture, about one fourth at a time; gently fold (*page 12*) until just blended after each addition. Add hot milk all at one time and quickly mix just until smooth. Pour batter into pans.

Bake at 375°F about 15 min., or until cake surface springs back when lightly touched.

Cool and remove from pans as directed for sponge-type cakes (*page 340*).
Two 9-in. round cake layers

△ Pineapple Hot-Milk Sponge Cake

Follow ▲ Recipe; decrease lemon juice to 1 teaspoon; add 2 tablespoons **pineapple juice** with lemon juice.

△ Washington Pie

Follow ▲ Recipe. When ready to serve, spread **raspberry jam** or **jelly** over bottom layer; top with second layer. Sift **confectioners' sugar** over top.

Ladyfingers

Dainty, double ladyfingers are intriguing on the tea table or served with a frozen dessert.

Line baking sheets with unglazed paper. To make cardboard patterns, cut 4x1-in. rectangle for large ladyfingers and 2½x¾-in. rectangle for small ones. Round corners of rectangles, and gradually taper at center to ¾-in. width for large and ½-in. width for small fingers. Trace patterns onto unglazed paper.

Sift together and set aside
⅓ cup sifted cake flour
⅛ teaspoon salt
Combine and beat until thick and lemon-colored
2 egg yolks
½ cup sifted confectioners' sugar
Fold (*page 12*) dry ingredients into egg yolk-sugar mixture.

Using clean beater, beat until rounded peaks are formed and egg whites do not slide when bowl is partially inverted
2 egg whites
Fold egg whites into egg-yolk mixture with
½ teaspoon vanilla extract
Force mixture through pastry bag onto prepared baking sheets, using guide lines to shape ladyfingers. Use decorating tube No. 10 for small ladyfingers and pastry bag coupling for large ladyfingers.

Sprinkle lightly with
Confectioners' sugar

Jelly Roll: Spread batter on baking sheet

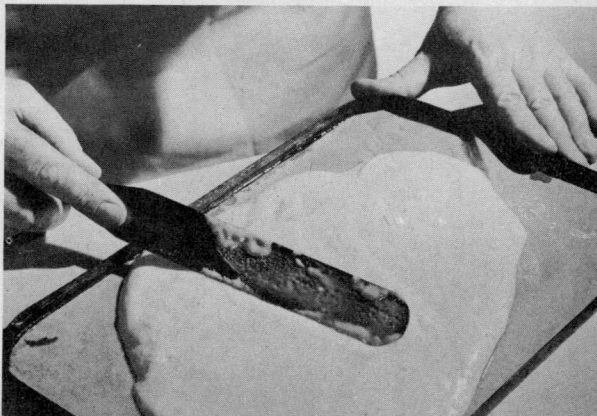

Bake at 325°F for 12 to 18 min., or until delicately browned.

With spatula, remove at once to cooling rack.
2 doz. large or 3 doz. small Ladyfingers

Note: For double ladyfingers, brush bottom sides of baked fingers with slightly beaten **egg white** and press together in pairs.

▲ Cake Roll

Prepare (*page 340*) a 15½x10½x1-in. jelly roll pan.

Sift together and set aside
1 cup sifted cake flour
¼ teaspoon salt
Beat slightly with rotary beater
4 eggs
Add and beat slightly
½ teaspoon cream of tartar
Add gradually, beating well after each addition
1 cup sugar
Beat until thick and piled softly. Beat in
¼ cup water
1½ teaspoons vanilla extract
Add dry ingredients all at one time. Continue beating just until batter is smooth, scraping sides and bottom of bowl once. Turn batter into pan and spread evenly to edges.

Bake at 350°F 15 to 20 min., or until cake surface springs back when lightly touched.

Immediately loosen edges with a sharp knife.

Turn cake onto a clean towel sprinkled with
Sifted confectioners' sugar
Remove paper and cut off any crisp edges of cake. To roll, begin rolling nearest edge of cake. Using towel as a guide, tightly grasp nearest edge of towel and quickly pull it over beyond opposite edge. Cake will roll itself as you pull. Wrap cake roll in towel and set on cooling rack to cool (about ½ hr.).

Meanwhile, prepare
Chocolate Filling (*page 411*) or
Lemon Filling (*page 412*)
When ready to fill, unroll cake. Spread with filling. Carefully reroll. Sift over top
2 to 3 tablespoons confectioners' sugar
One Cake Roll

⚠ Mincemeat Roll

Follow ▲ Recipe for cake roll; substitute 1 teaspoon **lemon extract** for vanilla extract. Substitute 1 to 2 cups **Mincemeat, Home-Style** (*page 458*) for filling. (Or use one 9-oz. pkg. condensed mincemeat; follow directions.)

⚠ Jelly Roll

Follow ▲ Recipe for cake roll. Substitute 1 cup **jelly** or **jam** for filling.

⚠ Chocolate-Chip Roll

Follow ▲ Recipe for cake roll; substitute **Orange Filling** (*page 412*) for filling. Sprinkle with 1 cup **semi-sweet chocolate pieces.**

Peel off paper and cut off any crisp edges.

Unroll the cake. Spread with jelly and reroll.

Ice Cream Cake Roll

▲ Lincoln Log

Prepare (*page 340*) 15½x10½x1-in. jelly roll pan.

Sift together and set aside
¾ cup sifted cake flour
5 tablespoons cocoa
¼ teaspoon salt
Beat until very thick and lemon-colored
4 egg yolks
½ cup sugar
¼ cup water
1½ teaspoons vanilla extract
Sift one fourth of the dry ingredients at a time over egg-yolk mixture; fold (*page 12*) until just blended after each addition. Set aside.

Using clean beater, beat until frothy
4 egg whites
Add and beat slightly
½ teaspoon cream of tartar
Add gradually, beating well after each addition
½ cup sugar
Beat until rounded peaks are formed and egg whites do not slide when bowl is partially inverted. Spread egg-yolk mixture over egg whites and gently fold together. Turn batter into pan and spread evenly to edges.

Bake at 325°F about 30 min., or until cake tests done (*page 340*).

Meanwhile, sift onto a clean towel
Confectioners' sugar
Turn cake onto towel. Remove paper; cut off any crisp edges. Begin rolling nearest edge. Using towel as guide, tightly grasp nearest edge of towel and quickly pull it over beyond opposite edge. Cake will roll itself as you pull. Wrap in towel and set on cooling rack.

Meanwhile, prepare
Pineapple Cream Filling (*page 413;* omit pineapple and increase vanilla extract to 2 teaspoons)
Brown Velvet Frosting (*page 394*)
Carefully unroll cooled cake and spread with filling. Carefully reroll. Trim ends diagonally.

Frost sides, ends and top with Brown Velvet Frosting. Gently draw tines of a fork lengthwise through frosting to make a pattern simulating bark of log.

Chill the cake roll in refrigerator until serving time. (To avoid sogginess, chill roll no longer than 1 hr.)

Garnish top of log with
Maraschino cherries with stems
Or surround base of log with cherries and top each serving with a cherry. With a sharp knife, cut roll into crosswise diagonal slices.
About 8 servings

⚠ Ice Cream Cake Roll

Follow ▲ Recipe. Substitute 1-qt. of **vanilla ice cream** for cream filling. Omit Brown Velvet Frosting. When ready to serve, carefully unroll cooled cake. Spoon ice cream over cake and smooth with spoon. Reroll and sift 2 tablespoons **confectioners' sugar** over top.

⚠ Light Sponge Cake Roll

Follow ▲ Recipe. Increase cake flour to 1 cup. Omit cocoa. Bake at 350°F 20 to 25 min., or until cake tests down (*page 340*). Substitute **Seven-Minute Chocolate Frosting** (one-half recipe, *page 404*) for the Brown Velvet Frosting. Omit marking frosted roll with fork.

⚠ Holiday Roll

Follow ▲ Recipe or ⚠ Recipe; omit filling and frosting. When baked, rolled and cooled, unroll cake and spread with one half of Holiday Filling. Reroll and spread top and sides with filling. Garnish with **maraschino cherry halves** and chopped **candied citron**.

For Holiday Filling—Prepare **Sweetened Whipped Cream** (double recipe, *page 414*). Carefully fold in (*page 12*) ⅔ cup well-drained, chopped **maraschino cherries**, ¼ cup (about 2 oz.) **candied citron**, cut in pieces (*page 12*), and ½ cup (about 2 oz.) chopped, toasted, blanched **almonds** (*page 11*).

Golden Sponge Cake

MRS. DWAYNE BURAK, GLADSTONE, MICH.

Set out a 10-in. tubed pan.

Sift together and set aside
  1¾ cups sifted cake flour
  2 teaspoons baking powder
  ¼ teaspoon salt
Measure and pour into a large bowl
  1 cup (about 12) egg yolks
Add gradually to egg yolks and beat until thick and lemon-colored
  ½ cup orange juice
  ¼ cup hot water
Beat in
  1 tablespoon grated orange peel (*page 11*)
  1 teaspoon orange extract
Add gradually, beating well after each addition
  1¼ cups sugar
Gently fold in (*page 12*) dry ingredients in fourths until just blended.

Carefully turn batter into pan.

Bake at 325°F 60 to 65 min., or until cake surface springs back when lightly touched.

Immediately invert pan on end of tube; cool and remove from pan as directed for sponge-type cakes (*page 340*).   *One 10-in. tubed cake*

▲ Cocoa Sponge Cake

Set out a 9-in. tubed pan.

Sift together and set aside
  ¾ cup sifted cake flour
  ¼ cup cocoa
Combine and beat until very thick and lemon-colored (3 to 4 min. with electric mixer on medium-high speed)
  5 egg yolks
  ½ cup sugar
  2 tablespoons lemon or orange juice
  1 teaspoon grated lemon or orange peel (*page 11*)
  1 teaspoon vanilla extract
Set aside.

Using clean beater, beat until frothy
  5 egg whites
  ½ teaspoon salt
Add gradually, beating well after each addition
  ½ cup sugar
Continue beating until rounded peaks are formed and whites do not slide when bowl is partially inverted. Spread the egg-yolk mixture over beaten egg whites and gently fold (*page 12*) together. Fold in dry ingredients, sifting in about one fourth at a time. Fold after each addition. Turn batter into pan.

Bake at 325°F 60 to 65 min., or until cake surface springs back when lightly touched.

Immediately invert pan on end of tube; cool and remove from pan as directed for sponge-type cakes (*page 340*).   *One 9-in. tubed cake*

△ True Sponge Cake

Follow ▲ Recipe; increase cake flour to 1 cup and omit cocoa.

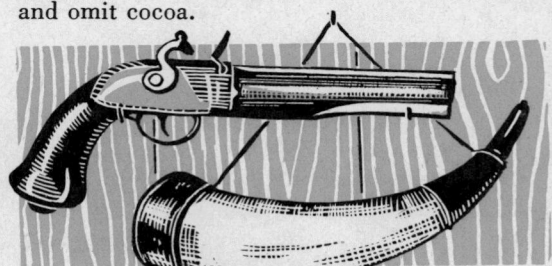

Coffee Sponge Cake

MRS. A. E. SEASTROM, HOPEDALE, MASS.

Set out two 9-in. round layer cake pans.

Sift together and set aside
1½ cups sifted cake flour
1½ teaspoons baking powder
Beat until very thick and lemon-colored
3 egg yolks
Add gradually, beating well after each addition
1 cup plus 2 tablespoons sugar
½ cup cold double-strength coffee
beverage (page 13)
Gently fold (*page 12*) dry ingredients into egg-yolk mixture until blended. Set aside.

Using clean beater, beat until frothy
3 egg whites
Add
¼ teaspoon salt
Beat until rounded peaks are formed and egg whites do not slide when the bowl is partially inverted. Spread egg-yolk mixture over egg whites and carefully fold together until blended. Turn batter into pans.

Bake at 350°F 25 to 30 min., or until cake surface springs back when lightly touched.

Cool and remove from pans as directed for sponge-type cakes (*page 340*).

Prepare
Coffee Whipped Cream (page 414)
Place one layer of cake on a serving platter. Spread cake layer with about 1 cup of the whipped cream. Repeat with second layer.

One 9-in. round layer cake

Spiced Sponge Cake

MRS. AL CASSEZZA, RICHARDTON, N. DAK.

Combines the best of spice and sponge.

Set out a 10-in. tubed pan.

Chop coarsely and set aside
½ cup (about 2 oz.) walnuts
Sift together and set aside
1 cup sifted cake flour
½ teaspoon baking powder
1 teaspoon cinnamon
½ teaspoon cloves
½ teaspoon salt
Beat until very thick and lemon-colored
1 cup (about 12) egg yolks
¼ cup warm water
Add gradually, beating well after each addition
1 cup sugar
Gently fold in (*page 12*) dry ingredients in fourths until just blended. Set aside.

Using clean beater, beat until rounded peaks are formed and egg whites do not slide when bowl is partially inverted
3 egg whites
Spread egg whites over egg-yolk mixture and carefully fold together until blended. Fold in the chopped walnuts and
1 teaspoon almond extract
Turn batter into pan.

Bake at 325°F about 55 min., or until cake surface springs back when lightly touched.

Immediately invert pan on end of tube; cool and remove from pan as directed for sponge-type cakes (*page 340*). *One 10-in. tubed cake*

▲ Genoise Cake ⬡6
(Butter Sponge)

Butter bottom of a 15½x10½x1-in. pan. Line pan bottom with waxed paper cut to fit exactly; butter waxed paper.

Melt over hot water and set aside to cool
   3 tablespoons butter
Put into top of 3-qt. double boiler
   5 eggs
   1 cup less 1 tablespoon sugar
Set over simmering water. Beat constantly until mixture is thick and piles softly (about 10 min. with electric mixer or 20 to 25 min. with hand rotary beater). Remove from simmering water and continue beating until mixture is cold.

Blend in
   ¼ teaspoon vanilla extract
   ⅛ teaspoon almond extract
Divide into four portions
   1¼ cups sifted cake flour
Sift one portion at a time over egg mixture and gently fold in (*page 12*) until just blended. Gradually add melted butter, folding only until blended. Pour batter into pan.

Bake at 325°F 40 to 45 min., or until cake springs back when lightly touched at center.

Loosen edges with a spatula and remove from pan. Carefully peel off paper. Cool on rack, top side up.   *One 15x10-in. cake*

For Three-Layer Cake—Line and butter, as for sheet cake, three 8-in. round layer cake pans. Bake layers at 325°F 30 to 35 min., or until cake springs back when lightly touched at center. Cool and remove from pans as directed for sponge-type cakes (*page 340*).

Assorted Petits Fours

△ Petits Fours

These dainty, decorative little cakes bring charm and beauty to your entertaining.

Follow ▲ Recipe; prepare sheet cake. (Cake will yield about 150 1-in. squares.)

When cool, trim cake edges and cut cake into tiny squares, diamonds, rounds or other fancy shapes. Use the shapes whole or split. Split shapes may be hollowed out and filled or spread with filling. Fill with **Sweetened Whipped Cream** (*page 414*), **Creamy Vanilla Filling** (*page 411*) or **Almond Pastry Cream** (*page 413*). Remove any loose crumbs. Frost as directed in **Fondant Glaze** (*page 409*).

Remove cakes with spatula and trim glaze from bottom edges with sharp knife. Decorate as desired with **chocolate shot,** finely chopped **nuts, coconut** or **candied cherries.** Or force **Decorating Frosting** (*page 398*) through cake decorator or pastry tube to form flowers, leaves and borders.

Banana-Pecan Chiffon Cake

Banana-Pecan Chiffon Cake

Set out a 10-in. tubed pan.

Measure and pour into a large bowl
1 cup (7 to 8) egg whites
Allow to stand at room temperature at least 1 hr. before beating to insure greater volume.

Put into a small bowl
5 egg yolks
Reserve remaining 2 or 3 egg yolks for use in other food preparation.

Chop finely and set aside
1 cup (about 4 oz.) pecans
Peel and force through sieve or food mill enough bananas to yield
1 cup sieved banana (2 to 3 bananas with brown-flecked peel)
Stir in until well blended
1 tablespoon lemon juice
Set aside.

Sift together into a bowl
2¼ cups sifted cake flour
1 cup sugar
1 tablespoon baking powder
¾ teaspoon salt
Make a well in center of dry ingredients and add
½ cup cooking (salad) oil

Add in order the 5 egg yolks and the sieved banana mixture. Beat until smooth. Set aside.

Using clean beater, beat the egg whites until frothy. Beat in
½ teaspoon cream of tartar
Add gradually, beating well after each addition
½ cup sugar
Beat until rounded peaks are formed and meringue (egg-white-sugar mixture) does not slide when bowl is partially inverted.

Slowly pour egg-yolk mixture over entire surface of meringue, then sprinkle pecans over surface of egg-yolk mixture. Gently fold (*page 12*) pecans, egg-yolk mixture, and meringue together until just blended. *Do not stir.* Carefully pour batter into pan, rotating pan as you pour in the batter.

Bake at 325°F 55 min., then at 350°F 10 to 15 min., or until cake surface springs back when lightly touched.

Immediately invert pan on end of tube; cool and remove from pan as directed for sponge-type cakes (*page 340*).   *One 10-in. tubed cake*

Lemon Chiffon Cake 8

MRS. L. A. KING, JACKSONVILLE, N. C.

Frost the cake as suggested in the recipe or split when cold and fill and frost as layer cake.

Set out a 10-in. tubed pan.

Measure and pour into a large bowl
6 (about ¾ cup) egg whites
Allow to stand at room temperature at least 1 hr. before beating to insure greater volume.

350

Put into a small bowl
6 egg yolks
Sift together into a bowl
2¼ cups sifted cake flour
1 cup sugar
1 tablespoon baking powder
1 teaspoon salt
Make a well in center of dry ingredients; add
½ cup cooking (salad) oil
Add in order the 6 egg yolks and
¾ cup water
1 tablespoon lemon juice
1 teaspoon grated lemon peel
(page 11)
Beat until smooth. Set aside.

Using clean beater, beat the egg whites until
frothy. Beat in
½ teaspoon cream of tartar
Add gradually, beating well after each addition
½ cup sugar
Beat until rounded peaks are formed and
meringue (egg-white-sugar mixture) does not
slide when bowl is partially inverted. Slowly
pour egg-yolk mixture over entire surface of
meringue. Gently fold (*page 12*) together until
just blended. *Do not stir.* Carefully pour batter into pan.

Bake at 325°F 55 min., then at 350°F 10 to 15
min., or until cake surface springs back when
lightly touched.

Immediately invert pan on end of tube; cool
and remove from pan as directed for sponge-
type cakes (*page 340*).

Frost sides and top with
Lemon Frosting (page 397)
One 10-in. tubed cake

Sweetheart Cake

Set out three heart-shaped layer cake pans.

Prepare
Lemon Chiffon Cake (*page 350*)
Turn batter into pans.

Bake at 325°F 35 to 40 min., or until cake
surface springs back when lightly touched.

Cool and remove from pans as directed for
sponge-type cakes (*page 340*).

Prepare
Butter Cream Frosting (*page 394*)
When cake is completely cooled, fill the layers
with the frosting.

Prepare
**Sweetened Whipped Cream (double
recipe, *page 414*)**
Reserve 1 cup of the whipped cream for decoration. Spread top and sides of cake with a thin
layer of the remaining cream.

Tint reserved portion a delicate pink with
1 or 2 drops red food coloring
Decorate, using a pastry bag and a No. 27 star
tube (see photo).

Chill well before serving.
One heart-shaped layer cake

Sweetheart Cake

Orange Chiffon Cake 8 9

A cake of exquisite lightness, chock-full of wonderful flavor.

Set out a 9x9x2-in. cake pan or 9½x5¼x2¾-in. loaf pan.

Measure and pour into a large bowl
½ cup (4 to 5) egg whites
Allow to stand at room temperature at least 1 hr. before beating to insure greater volume.

Put into a small bowl
2 egg yolks
Reserve remaining 2 or 3 egg yolks for use in other food preparation.

Sift together into a bowl
**1 cup plus 2 tablespoons sifted
    cake flour**
½ cup sugar
1½ teaspoons baking powder
½ teaspoon salt
Make a well in center of dry ingredients; add
¼ cup cooking (salad) oil
Add in order the 2 egg yolks and
⅓ cup orange juice
**1 tablespoon grated orange peel
    (page 11)**
Beat until smooth. Set aside.

Using clean beater, beat the egg whites until frothy. Beat in
¼ teaspoon cream of tartar
Add gradually, beating well after each addition
¼ cup sugar
Beat until rounded peaks are formed and meringue (egg-white-sugar mixture) does not slide when bowl is partially inverted. Slowly pour egg-yolk mixture over entire surface of meringue. Gently fold (*page 12*) together until just blended. *Do not stir.* Carefully pour batter into pan.

Bake square cake at 350°F 30 to 35 min., loaf cake at 325°F 50 to 55 min., or until cake surface springs back when lightly touched.

Cool and remove from pan as directed for sponge-type cakes (*page 340*).

Orange Chiffon Cake—Peach-Sundae Dessert

For Peach-Sundae Dessert—Cut square cake into 3-in. squares or loaf cake into 1-in. slices. Top with ice cream and peach slices (see photo). *One 9-in. square or 9x5-in. loaf cake*

Marble Chiffon Cake 10

Set out a 10-in. tubed pan.

Measure and pour into a large bowl
1 cup (7 to 8) egg whites
Allow to stand at room temperature at least 1 hr. before beating to insure greater volume.

Put into a small bowl
5 egg yolks
Reserve remaining 2 or 3 egg yolks for use in other food preparation.

Mix together and set aside to cool
⅓ cup cocoa
¼ cup sugar
¼ cup boiling water
⅛ teaspoon red food coloring
Sift together into a bowl
2 cups sifted cake flour
1 cup sugar
1 tablespoon baking powder
¾ teaspoon salt

Make a well in center of dry ingredients; add
½ cup cooking (salad) oil
Add in order the 5 egg yolks and
¾ cup water
2¼ teaspoons vanilla extract
Beat until smooth. Set aside.

Using clean beater, beat the egg whites until
frothy. Beat in
½ teaspoon cream of tartar
Add gradually, beating well after each addition
½ cup sugar
Beat until rounded peaks are formed and
meringue (egg-white-sugar mixture) does not
slide when bowl is partially inverted. Slowly
pour egg-yolk mixture over entire surface of
meringue. Gently fold (*page 12*) together until
just blended. *Do not stir.*

Pour one half of batter into another bowl.
Pour cocoa mixture gradually over it, gently
folding until blended. Immediately pour alternate layers of dark and light batter into pan,
rotating pan as you pour. Cut through batter
with knife or spatula, lifting light batter
through dark batter to break air bubbles and
give a marbled effect.

Bake at 325°F 55 min., then at 350°F 10 to 15
min., or until cake surface springs back when
lightly touched.

Immediately invert pan on end of tube; cool
and remove from pan as directed for sponge-
type cakes (*page 340*). Frost, if desired.
One 10-in. tubed cake

Marble Chiffon Cake

Rum Chiffon Cake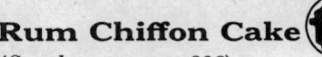
(*See photo on page 398*)

Set out a 10-in. tubed pan.

Measure and pour into a large bowl
1 cup (7 to 8) egg whites
Allow to stand at room temperature at least
1 hr. before beating to insure greater volume.

Put into a small bowl
5 egg yolks
Reserve remaining 2 or 3 egg yolks for use in
other food preparation.

Sift together into a bowl
2¼ cups sifted cake flour
1 cup sugar
1 tablespoon baking powder
¾ teaspoon salt
Make a well in center of dry ingredients; add
½ cup cooking (salad) oil
Add in order the 5 egg yolks and
¾ cup water
4 teaspoons rum extract
Beat until smooth. Set aside.

Using clean beater, beat the egg whites until
frothy. Beat in
½ teaspoon cream of tartar
Add gradually, beating well after each addition
½ cup sugar
Beat until rounded peaks are formed and
meringue (egg-white-sugar mixture) does not
slide when bowl is partially inverted. Slowly
pour egg-yolk mixture over entire surface of
meringue. Gently fold (*page 12*) together until
just blended. *Do not stir.* Pour batter into pan.

Bake at 325°F 55 min., then at 350°F 10 to 15
min., or until cake surface springs back when
lightly touched.

Immediately invert pan on end of tube; cool
and remove from pan as directed for sponge-
type cakes (*page 340*).

Prepare
Raisin-Rum Frosting (page 398)
Frost sides and top of cake.
One 10-in. tubed cake

Pound Cake 9 12

Prepare (*page 340*) a 9½x5¼x2¾-in. loaf pan.

Sift together and set aside
  2½ cups sifted cake flour
  ¾ teaspoon baking powder
  ¼ teaspoon salt
  ¼ teaspoon mace
Cream together until butter is softened
  1 cup butter
  2 teaspoons grated lemon peel
    (*page 11*)
  1½ teaspoons vanilla extract
  ½ teaspoon almond extract
Add gradually, creaming until fluffy after each addition
  1 cup plus 2 tablespoons sugar
Add in thirds, beating well after each addition
  4 eggs, well beaten
Blend in dry ingredients in fourths. After each addition, beat only until smooth. Finally beat only until batter is smooth (do not overbeat).

Turn batter into pan. With spatula, draw batter from center toward edges of pan.

Bake at 325°F 1 hr. 10 min., or until cake tests done (*page 340*).

Cool; remove from pan as directed (*page 340*).
One 9x5-in. loaf cake

Note: Pound cake may be used as a base for Baked Alaska. Bake batter in a deep 9-in. sq. pan about 50 min. When cool, split into two layers. For round Alaska, trim corners.

Spice Cake, Basic Butter Frosting (page 394)

▲ Two-Egg Cake

Prepare (*page 340*) a 9x9x2-in. pan or two 8-in. round layer cake pans.

Sift together and set aside
  1⅔ cups sifted cake flour
  2 teaspoons baking powder
  ½ teaspoon salt
Cream together until shortening is softened
  ½ cup shortening
  1 teaspoon vanilla extract
Add gradually, creaming until fluffy after each addition
  1 cup sugar
Add in thirds, beating well after each addition
  2 eggs, well beaten
Measure
  ½ cup milk
Beating only until smooth after each addition, alternately add dry ingredients in fourths, milk in thirds, to creamed mixture. Finally beat only until smooth (do not overbeat). Turn batter into pans.

Bake square cake at 350°F 35 to 45 min.; bake layers at 375°F 25 to 30 min., or until cake tests done (*page 340*).

Cool; remove from pans as directed (*page 340*).
*Two 8-in. round layers or
one 9-in. square cake*

⚠ Spice Cake

Follow ▲ Recipe. Sift 1 teaspoon **cinnamon**, ¼ teaspoon **cloves** and ¼ teaspoon **nutmeg** with dry ingredients. Bake in square pan, layer or muffin pans. Frost top of cake with **Basic Butter Frosting** (*page 394*). To serve, cut into 2-in. squares.

⚠ Two-Egg Cupcakes
(*See photo on page 380*)

Follow ▲ Recipe; use 12 to 15 muffin-pan wells instead of 9x9x2-in. pan. Line with paper baking cups or grease bottom of wells. Fill each only two-thirds full. Bake at 375°F 20 to 25 min., or until cakes test done (*page 340*). Cool as directed (*page 340*).

⚠ Easy Marble Cake

Follow ▲ Recipe. Divide batter into halves. Blend 1 sq. (1 oz.) **chocolate**, melted (*page 12*) and cooled, into one portion. Spoon batter into prepared pans, alternating light and dark.

Lemon Cake 10

MRS. FOSTER BAILEY
NORTH LEWISBURG, OHIO

Prepare (*page 340*) two 8-in. round layer cake pans.

Sift together and set aside
**1¾ cups sifted flour
2 teaspoons baking powder
⅛ teaspoon salt**
Cream together until butter is softened
**½ cup butter
1 teaspoon lemon extract**
Add gradually, creaming until fluffy after each addition
1 cup sugar
Add in thirds, beating well after each addition
2 egg yolks, well beaten
Measure
¾ cup water
Beating only until smooth after each addition, alternately add dry ingredients in fourths, water in thirds, to creamed mixture. Finally beat only until smooth (do not overbeat).

Beat until rounded peaks are formed and egg whites do not slide when bowl is partially inverted
2 egg whites
Carefully spread egg whites over batter and gently fold (*page 12*). Turn batter into pans.

Bake at 350°F 30 to 35 min., or until cake tests done (*page 340*).

Cool; remove from pans as directed (*page 340*).

When cake is cooled, prepare
Vanilla Fudge Frosting (page 409)
Fill and frost (*page 393*) cake.

One 8-in. round layer cake

Banana Layer Cake 11

MRS. JAMES T. MOORE, SAN ANGELO, TEX.

Prepare (*page 340*) two 9-in. round layer cake pans.

Sift together and set aside
**2¼ cups sifted cake flour
2½ teaspoons baking powder
½ teaspoon baking soda
½ teaspoon salt**
Blend together
**½ cup hydrogenated vegetable shortening or all-purpose shortening
1 teaspoon vanilla extract**
Add gradually, creaming until fluffy after each addition
1 cup sugar
Add in thirds, beating well after each addition
2 eggs, well beaten
Peel and force through sieve or food mill enough bananas to yield
1 cup sieved banana (2 or 3 bananas with brown-flecked peel)
Blend sieved banana with
¼ cup buttermilk or sour milk (page 11)
Beating only until smooth after each addition, alternately add dry ingredients in fourths, banana-buttermilk mixture in thirds, to creamed mixture. Finally beat only until smooth (do not overbeat).

Bake at 375°F 25 to 30 min., or until cake tests done (*page 340*).

Cool; remove from pans as directed (*page 340*).

Meanwhile, prepare
Banana Frosting (page 396)
Fill and frost (*page 393*).

One 9-in. round layer cake

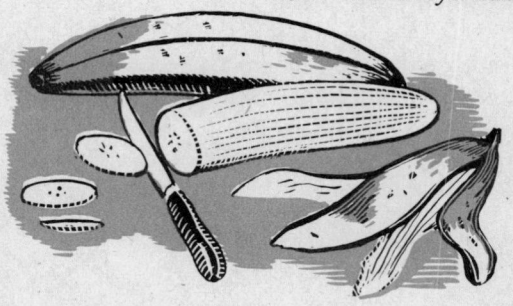

Pistachio Cake with
Butter Cream Frosting (page 394)

Pistachio Cake

Prepare (*page 340*) two 9-in. round layer cake pans.

Chop coarsely and set aside
½ cup (about 2 oz.) pistachio nuts
Sift together and set aside
3 cups sifted cake flour
2½ teaspoons baking powder
¾ teaspoon salt
⅛ teaspoon mace
Blend together
1 cup shortening
¼ teaspoon vanilla extract
¼ teaspoon almond extract
Add gradually, creaming until fluffy after each addition
2 cups sugar
Add in thirds, beating thoroughly after each addition
4 eggs, well beaten
Measure
1 cup milk
Beating only until smooth after each addition, alternately add dry ingredients in fourths, milk in thirds, to creamed mixture. Finally beat only until smooth (do not overbeat). Blend in the chopped pistachio nuts.

Bake at 350°F 35 to 40 min., or until cake tests done (*page 340*).

Cool; remove from pans as directed (*page 340*).

Meanwhile, prepare
Butter Cream Frosting (page 394)
When cake is completely cooled, fill and frost (*page 393*).

Using a shamrock-shaped cookie cutter, press lightly on frosting in center of cake. Fill in pattern with
¼ cup pistachio nuts
One 9-in. round layer cake

Country Cream Cake

MRS. RAYMOND F. MILLER
ROCKFALL, CONN.

Prepare (*page 340*) two 8-in. round layer cake pans.

Sift together and set aside
2 cups sifted cake flour
2 teaspoons baking powder
½ teaspoon salt
Beat until thick and piled softly
2 eggs
Add gradually, beating thoroughly after each addition
1 cup plus 2 tablespoons sugar
Mix together
1 cup cream
1 teaspoon vanilla extract
Beating only until smooth after each addition, alternately add dry ingredients in fourths, liquid in thirds, to egg-sugar mixture. Finally beat only until smooth (do not overbeat). Turn batter into pans.

Bake at 375°F 20 to 25 min., or until cake tests done (*page 340*).

Cool; remove from pans as directed (*page 340*).

Prepare
Sweetened Whipped Cream or any variation (page 414)
Place one layer of cake on a serving platter. Spread cake layer with about 1 cup of the whipped cream. Repeat with second layer.
One 8-in. round layer cake

Coconut Cake Supreme

MRS. EVERETT BLACK, ORANGE, TEXAS

*Generous in size, here is a cake that is tops
for occasions when the best is none too good.*

Prepare (*page 340*) three 9-in. round layer
cake pans.

Sift together and set aside
   3¼ cups sifted cake flour
   4½ teaspoons baking powder
   ½ teaspoon salt
Chop finely and set aside
   ½ cup (2 oz.) moist shredded coconut
Cream together until shortening is softened
   ¾ cup shortening
   1½ teaspoons grated orange peel
      (page 11)
Add gradually, creaming until fluffy after each
addition
   2 cups sugar
Add in thirds, beating well after each addition
   2 egg yolks, well beaten
Combine
   ¾ cup water
   ½ cup orange juice
Beating only until smooth after each addition,
alternately add dry ingredients in fourths,
liquid in thirds, to creamed mixture. Finally
beat only until smooth (do not overbeat).

Blend in the chopped coconut.

Beat until rounded peaks are formed and egg
whites do not slide when bowl is partially
inverted
   4 egg whites
Carefully spread beaten egg whites over batter
and gently fold (*page 12*) together. Turn batter into pans.

Bake at 350°F 30 min., or until cake tests
done (*page 340*).

Cool; remove from pans as directed (*page 340*).

Meanwhile, prepare
   Orange Butter Frosting (page 397)
Fill and frost (*page 393*) cake.
                    One 9-in. round layer cake

Mama's Prize Coconut Cake

MRS. HENRY ANDERSON W. LOS ANGELES, CA.

Prepare (*page 340*) two 9-in. round layer cake
pans.

Chop finely and set aside
   ¾ cup (3 oz.) moist shredded coconut
Sift together and set aside
   2 cups sifted cake flour
   1½ teaspoons baking powder
   ¼ teaspoon salt
Cream together until softened
   ¾ cup butter or margarine
   1 teaspoon vanilla extract
Add gradually, creaming until fluffy after each
addition
   1 cup sugar
Beat together until thick and piled softly
   2 eggs
   2 egg yolks
Add beaten eggs in thirds to creamed mixture,
beating thoroughly after each addition.

Measure
   ½ cup milk
Beating only until smooth after each addition,
alternately add dry ingredients in fourths,
milk in thirds, to creamed mixture. Finally
beat only until smooth (do not overbeat).
Blend in the chopped coconut. Turn batter
into pans.

Bake at 350°F 25 min., or until cake tests
done (*page 340*).

Cool; remove from pans as directed (*page 340*).

When cake is cooled, prepare
   **Marshmallow Coconut Frosting
      (page 405)**
Fill and frost (*page 393*) cake.
                    One 9-in. round layer cake

Golden Honey Cake  14 15

(See photo on page 399)

Prepare *(page 340)* two 8-in. round layer cake pans.

Sift together into a large bowl
2 cups sifted cake flour
⅔ cup sugar
2 teaspoons baking powder
1 teaspoon salt
¼ teaspoon baking soda

Set out
¾ cup buttermilk or sour milk *(page 11)*

Add one half of milk to dry ingredients with
½ cup honey
½ cup hydrogenated vegetable short-ening or all-purpose shortening
1 teaspoon vanilla extract

Stir only enough to moisten dry ingredients. Beat 200 strokes, or 2 min. on electric mixer on medium speed. Scrape sides of bowl several times during beating.

Add remaining milk and
4 egg yolks (about ⅓ cup), unbeaten

Beat 200 strokes, or 2 min. on electric mixer. Scrape sides of bowl several times. Turn into cake pans.

Bake at 350°F about 30 min., or until cake tests done *(page 340)*.

Cool; remove from pans as directed *(page 340)*.

Meanwhile, prepare
Honey-Chocolate Frosting (p.399)

Fill and frost *(page 393)* cake.

One 8-in. round layer cake

Golden Orange Crunch Cake

A golden beauty with its own baked-in topping.

Set out a 9-in. tubed pan.

For Crunch Topping—Chop finely
1½ cups (about 6 oz.) walnuts

Melt in a small saucepan over low heat
⅓ cup butter

Mix thoroughly the nuts, melted butter and
¾ cup fine, dry bread crumbs (about 2 slices bread)
½ cup firmly packed brown sugar
¼ teaspoon cinnamon
¼ teaspoon salt

Using the back of a spoon, press nut mixture very firmly into an even layer on bottom and sides of the tubed pan. Set aside.

For Cake—Sift together and set aside
3 cups sifted flour
1 tablespoon baking powder
½ teaspoon salt

Cream together until butter is softened
¾ cup butter
1 tablespoon grated orange peel (page 11)

Add gradually, creaming until fluffy after each addition
1¼ cups sugar

Add in thirds, beating well after each addition
3 eggs, well beaten

Measure and combine
½ cup undiluted evaporated milk
¼ cup orange juice

Beating only until smooth after each addition, alternately add dry ingredients in fourths, liquid in thirds, to creamed mixture. Finally beat only until smooth (do not overbeat). Turn batter into pan.

Bake at 375°F 55 to 60 min., or until cake tests done *(page 340)*.

Remove cake from oven and place on a cooling rack. Allow cake to cool in pan 30 min. Cover with cake plate, carefully invert and remove pan. Cool thoroughly before cutting.

One 9-in. tubed cake

Banana-Nut Cupcakes 15

(*See photo on page 380*)

CHILTON H. WARREN, POPLAR BLUFF, MO.

You can vary the flavor of these cupcakes by making them with hickory nuts or pecans.

Line with paper baking cups or grease bottoms of 18 2½-in. muffin-pan wells.

Chop coarsely and set aside
   1 cup (about 3½ oz.) walnuts
Sift together and set aside
   2 cups sifted flour
   1 teaspoon baking powder
   1 teaspoon baking soda
   ¼ teaspoon salt
Blend together
   ½ cup hydrogenated vegetable shortening or all-purpose shortening
   1 teaspoon vanilla extract
Add gradually, creaming until fluffy after each addition
   1½ cups sugar
Add in thirds, beating well after each addition
   2 egg yolks, well beaten
Peel and force through sieve or food mill enough bananas to yield
   1 cup sieved banana (2 to 3 bananas with brown-flecked peel)
Blend sieved banana with
   ½ cup buttermilk or sour milk (page 11)
Beating only until smooth after each addition, alternately add dry ingredients in fourths, banana-buttermilk mixture in thirds, to creamed mixture. Finally beat only until smooth (do not overbeat). Stir in the chopped walnuts. Fill cups or muffin wells one-half full.

Bake at 350°F 20 to 25 min., or until cakes test done (*page 340*).

Cool and remove from muffin-pan wells as directed (*page 340*).

Meanwhile, prepare
   Banana Frosting (page 396)
When cupcakes are completely cooled, frost. Garnish with finely chopped walnuts.

1½ doz. cupcakes

Orange Cupcakes 16

(*See photo on page 380*)

MRS. LAWRENCE McGIHERA
MADISON, WIS.

Line with paper baking cups or grease bottoms of 24 2½-in. muffin-pan wells.

Sift together and set aside
   3 cups sifted cake flour
   4 teaspoons baking powder
   ¼ teaspoon salt
Blend together
   ¾ cup hydrogenated vegetable shortening or all-purpose shortening
   2 teaspoons grated orange peel (page 11)
   1 teaspoon orange extract
Add gradually, creaming until fluffy after each addition
   1¼ cups sugar
Add in thirds, beating well after each addition
   3 eggs, well beaten
Measure and combine
   ½ cup orange juice
   ½ cup water
Beating only until smooth after each addition, alternately add dry ingredients in fourths, liquid in thirds, to creamed mixture. Finally beat only until smooth (do not overbeat). Fill cups or muffin-pan wells one-half full.

Bake at 350°F 20 to 25 min., or until cakes test done (*page 340*).

Cool and remove from muffin-pan wells as directed (*page 340*).

Meanwhile, prepare
   Orange Butter Frosting (page 397)
When cupcakes are completely cooled, frost.

2 doz. cupcakes

Peanut Butter Cake 16

MRS. VERLIN L. TEPE, LYNNVILLE, IND.

Prepare (*page 340*) two 8-in. round layer cake pans.

Sift together into a large bowl
2 cups sifted cake flour
1½ cups sugar
1 tablespoon baking powder
1 teaspoon salt
Set out
1 cup milk
Add one half of milk to dry ingredients with
½ cup hydrogenated vegetable short-ening or all-purpose shortening
⅓ cup peanut butter
Stir only enough to moisten dry ingredients. Beat 200 strokes, or 2 min. on electric mixer on medium speed. Scrape sides of bowl several times during beating.

Add remaining milk and
2 eggs, unbeaten
Beat 200 strokes, or 2 min. on electric mixer. Scrape sides of bowl several times. Turn into cake pans.

Bake at 350°F 30 to 35 min., or until cake tests done (*page 340*).

Cool; remove from pans as directed (*page 340*).

Meanwhile, prepare
Peanut Mocha Frosting (page 396)
Fill and frost (*page 393*) cake.

One 8-in. round layer cake

Buttermilk Cake with Butterscotch Sauce 17
(Cottage Pudding)

CLAUDE E. METZ, MORENCI, MICH.

Prepare (*page 340*) an 8x8x2-in. cake pan.

For Cake—Sift together and set aside
2 cups sifted flour
2 teaspoons baking powder
1 teaspoon baking soda
1 teaspoon salt
Blend together
3 tablespoons hydrogenated vegetable shortening or all-purpose shortening
1 teaspoon vanilla extract
Add gradually, creaming until fluffy after each addition
1 cup sugar
Add gradually, beating well after each addition
1 egg, well beaten
Measure
1 cup buttermilk or sour milk (page 11)
Beating only until smooth after each addition, alternately add dry ingredients in fourths, liquid in thirds, to creamed mixture. Finally beat only until smooth (do not overbeat).

Turn batter into pan.

Bake at 375°F 35 to 40 min., or until cake tests done (*page 340*).

Cool; remove from pan as directed (*page 340*).

To serve, cut cooled cake into 2-in. squares. Pour cooled Butterscotch Sauce over each serving. If desired, garnish with chopped **nuts** or **whipped cream.**

For Butterscotch Sauce—Melt over low heat in a saucepan

1 tablespoon butter or margarine

Add, stirring constantly, a mixture of

⅔ cup firmly packed brown sugar
5 tablespoons flour

Cook over low heat, stirring until mixture is thoroughly blended. Remove from heat.

Add gradually, stirring in

2 cups milk

Bring to boiling; boil 1 min., stirring constantly. Remove from heat.

Blend in

1 teaspoon vanilla extract

Cool slightly before serving.   *16 servings*

▲ Pineapple Upside-Down Cake

Lightly grease bottom of an 8x8x2-in. cake pan.

Set out

9 well-drained maraschino cherries
12 (about ⅓ cup) pecan halves

Drain, reserving ¼ cup sirup, contents of

1 No. 2 can sliced pineapple

Set aside 5 pineapple slices. (Reserve remaining slices for use in other food preparation.)

Melt

3 tablespoons butter or margarine

Add pineapple sirup to melted butter with

½ cup firmly packed brown sugar

Blend thoroughly.

Cut 4 pineapple slices into halves. Place whole slice in center of pan. Place a cherry in the center. Arrange half-slices around edge of pan; place a cherry in each. Arrange pecan halves in pan (see photo). Pour brown sugar mixture over pineapple slices. Set aside.

Sift together and set aside

1½ cups sifted cake flour
2 teaspoons baking powder
½ teaspoon salt

Pineapple Upside-Down Cake

Cream together until shortening is softened

½ cup shortening
1 teaspoon vanilla extract

Add gradually, creaming until fluffy after each addition

½ cup sugar

Add gradually, beating well after each addition

1 egg, well beaten

Measure

½ cup milk

Beating only until smooth after each addition, alternately add dry ingredients in fourths, milk in thirds, to creamed mixture. Finally beat only until smooth (do not overbeat). Turn batter over pineapple slices.

Bake at 350°F 40 to 45 min., or until cake tests done (*page 340*).

Using a spatula, loosen cake from sides of pan and invert immediately on serving plate. Let pan rest over cake a few seconds so that sirup will drain on cake. Serve warm.

One 8-in square cake.

△ Apricot Upside-Down Cake

Follow ▲ Recipe. Substitute **Cooked Apricots** (one-half recipe, *p.494*) for pineapple slices, cherries and pecan halves. Substitute ½ cup drained, **crushed pineapple** for pineapple sirup. Arrange apricots in prepared pan. Follow ▲ Recipe for cake batter and baking.

▲ White Cake Squares 20 17

Prepare (*page 340*) a 9x9x2-in. cake pan.

Sift together and set aside
  2 cups sifted cake flour
  1 tablespoon baking powder
  ¾ teaspoon salt
Cream together until shortening is softened
  ⅔ cup shortening
  1 teaspoon vanilla extract
Add gradually, creaming until fluffy after each addition
  ½ cup sugar
Measure
  ⅔ cup milk
Beating only until smooth after each addition, alternately add dry ingredients in fourths, milk in thirds, to creamed mixture. Finally beat only until smooth (do not overbeat).

Beat until frothy
  4 egg whites
Add gradually, beating well after each addition
  ½ cup sugar
Continue beating until rounded peaks are formed. Spread beaten egg whites over batter and gently fold (*page 12*) together. Turn batter into pan.

Bake at 350°F 30 to 35 min., or until cake tests done (*page 340*).

Cool; remove from pan as directed (*page 340*).

Meanwhile, prepare
  Toasted Coconut (page 448)
Prepare
  Chocolate Butter Frosting (page 394)
When cake is completely cooled, frost (*page 393*) sides and top with frosting. Sprinkle top of frosted cake (while frosting is moist) with the Toasted Coconut. To serve, cut cake into 3-in. squares.   *One 9-in. square cake*

⚠ White Cupcakes 21

Follow ▲ Recipe; use 18 to 20 2½-in. muffin-pan wells instead of 9x9x2-in. pan. Line with paper baking cups or grease bottom of wells. Fill each only two-thirds full.

Bake at 350°F about 20 min., or until cakes test done. Cool. If desired, substitute **Lemon Butter Frosting** (*page 394*) for Chocolate Butter Frosting. Omit coconut.

⚠ Nut Loaf Cake 22

Follow ▲ Recipe; prepare 9½x5¼x2¾-in. loaf pan instead of 9x9x2-in. pan. Fold in after egg-white addition, 1 cup (about 4 oz.) finely chopped **nuts** and ¼ cup (about 2 oz.) finely chopped, well-drained **maraschino cherries**.

Bake at 350°F about 50 min., or until cake tests done. Substitute **Lemon Butter Frosting** (*page 394*) for Chocolate Butter Frosting. If desired, sprinkle top of cake with additional finely chopped **nuts** and **maraschino cherries**. Omit the coconut.

Kiss-and-Tell Cake 23 18

Prepare (*page 340*) a 13x9½x2-in. cake pan.

Sift together and set aside
  3 cups sifted cake flour
  1½ tablespoons baking powder
  ¾ teaspoon salt
Cream together until shortening is softened
  ⅔ cup shortening
  2 teaspoons almond extract
Add gradually, creaming until fluffy after each addition
  1⅓ cups sugar
Measure
  1¼ cups milk
Beating only until smooth after each addition, alternately add dry ingredients in fourths, milk in thirds, to creamed mixture. Finally beat only until smooth (do not overbeat).

Beat until frothy
5 egg whites
Add gradually, beating well after each addition
⅓ cup sugar
Beat until rounded peaks are formed.

Spread beaten egg whites over batter and gently fold (*page 12*) together. Pour into pan.

Bake at 375°F 25 to 30 min., or until cake tests done (*page 340*).

Cool; remove from pan as directed (*page 340*).

When cake is cooled, prepare
Seven-Minute Frosting (page 404)
Divide the frosting into two equal portions.

Blend into one portion
1 or more drops green food coloring
Blend into the remaining frosting
1 or more drops yellow food coloring
Reserve about ⅓ cup yellow-tinted frosting for decoration. Frost sides and top of one half of the cake with green-tinted frosting and the other half with yellow-tinted frosting. Mark off 12 squares in the yellow frosting, swirl frosting (see photo) and place a flower, such as a daisy, onto each square. Mark off 12 diagonal sections in green frosting. Spoon a small mound of reserved yellow frosting onto the center of each diagonal piece.

About 24 servings

Marble Cake

Prepare (*page 340*) an 8x8x2-in. cake pan.

Melt (*page 12*) and set aside to cool
1½ sq. (1½ oz.) chocolate
Sift together and set aside
2 cups sifted cake flour
2 teaspoons baking powder
½ teaspoon salt
Cream together until softened
½ cup butter or margarine
2 teaspoons vanilla extract
Add gradually, creaming until fluffy after each addition
1 cup sugar

Kiss-and-Tell Cake

Measure
¾ cup milk
Beating only until smooth after each addition, alternately add dry ingredients in fourths, milk in thirds, to creamed mixture. Finally beat only until smooth (do not overbeat).

Beat until rounded peaks are formed
3 egg whites
Spread beaten egg whites over batter and gently fold (*page 12*) together. Turn one half of batter into cake pan.

Stir into cooled chocolate
1 tablespoon sugar
Immediately stir in a mixture of
2 tablespoons hot water
½ teaspoon baking soda
Stir chocolate mixture into remaining batter. Pour chocolate batter over plain batter. Gently lift white batter through chocolate batter to produce a marbled effect (do not overblend).

Bake at 350°F 30 to 45 min., or until cake tests done (*page 340*).

Cool; remove from pan as directed (*page 340*).

When cake is cooled, prepare
Seven-Minute Beige Frosting
(page 405)
With a spatula, swirl frosting on sides and top of cake. Then decorate the cake with
Toasted pecan halves

One 8-in. square cake

▲ Happy Memories Cake 25 20
WILMA SCHULTZ, STOCKTON, KANS.

Prepare (*page 340*) a 13x9½x2-in. cake pan.

Sift together into a large bowl
2¼ cups sifted cake flour
1½ cups sugar
3½ teaspoons baking powder
¾ teaspoon salt
Set out
1 cup milk
Add one half of milk to dry ingredients with
½ cup hydrogenated vegetable shortening or all-purpose shortening
1½ teaspoons vanilla extract
Stir only enough to moisten dry ingredients.

Beat 200 strokes, or 2 min. on electric mixer. Scrape the sides of bowl several times during beating.

Add remaining milk and
4 egg whites, unbeaten
Beat 200 strokes, or 2 min. on electric mixer. Scrape the sides of bowl several times. Pour batter into pan.

Combine and mix thoroughly
1½ cups firmly packed dark brown sugar
½ cup cream
Pour brown-sugar-cream mixture over batter.

Sprinkle top with
1 cup (4 oz.) moist shredded coconut, cut
Bake at 350°F 30 to 35 min., or until cake tests done (*page 340*).

Using a spatula, loosen cake from sides of pan and invert immediately on serving plate. Let pan rest over cake a few seconds so sirup will drain onto cake. Remove pan, peel off waxed paper and serve warm or cold.

One 13x9-in. cake

△ Upside-Down Cupcakes 26

Line with paper baking cups 18 2½-in. muffin-pan wells.

Follow ▲ Recipe. Fill cups one-half full.

Spoon one tablespoon of the brown-sugar mixture over each and sprinkle with coconut.

Bake at 350°F 20 to 25 min., or until cakes test done (*page 340*). Remove from cups and serve upside down.

Poppy Seed Cake 27 21
MARY REZAC, WILSON, KANS.

Incorporating poppy seeds into cake or pastry is an old European custom. Spread throughout the cake, the tiny seeds impart a delicate nut-like flavor to the snowy layers.

Prepare (*page 340*) two 8-in. round layer cake pans.

Soak for 2 hours
½ cup (about 2½ oz.) poppy seeds
in
¾ cup milk
Sift together and set aside
2¼ cups sifted cake flour
2 teaspoons baking powder
½ teaspoon salt
Cream together until butter is softened
¾ cup butter
1 teaspoon vanilla extract
Add gradually, creaming until fluffy after each addition
1½ cups sugar
Beating only until smooth after each addition, alternately add dry ingredients in fourths, poppy seed-milk mixture in thirds, to creamed mixture. Finally beat only until smooth (do not overbeat).

Beat until rounded peaks are formed and egg whites do not slide when bowl is partially inverted
4 egg whites
Carefully spread beaten egg whites over batter and gently fold (*page 12*) together.

Turn batter into pans.

Bake at 350°F 30 to 35 min., or until cake tests done (*page 340*).

Cool; remove from pans as directed (*page 340*).

When cake is completely cooled, prepare
    White Mountain Frosting (page 406)
Fill and frost (*page 393*) cake.

Sprinkle top of cake with **poppy seeds**.
One 8-in. round layer cake

Carnival Cake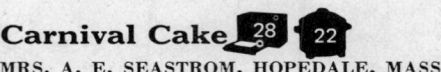
MRS. A. E. SEASTROM, HOPEDALE, MASS.

Prepare (*page 340*) three 8-in. round layer cake pans.

Sift together and set aside
    3 cups sifted cake flour
    2½ teaspoons baking powder
    ¾ teaspoon salt
Blend together
    ¾ cup hydrogenated vegetable short-
        ening or all-purpose shortening
    1 teaspoon lemon extract
Add gradually, creaming until fluffy after each addition
    1½ cups sugar
Measure
    1 cup milk
Beating only until smooth after each addition, alternately add dry ingredients in fourths, milk in thirds, to creamed mixture. Finally beat only until smooth (do not overbeat).

Beat until rounded peaks are formed and egg whites do not slide when bowl is partially inverted
    3 egg whites

Poppy Seed Cake with
White Mountain Frosting (page 406)

Carefully spread beaten egg whites over batter and gently fold (*page 12*) together. Turn batter into pans.

Bake at 375°F 25 to 30 min., or until cake tests done (*page 340*).

Cool; remove from pans as directed (*page 340*).

Drain well, chop finely and set aside
    ¼ cup (about 2 oz.) maraschino
        cherries
Chop finely and set aside
    ¼ cup (about 1½ oz.) blanched almonds
        (page 11)
When cake is cooled, prepare
    Fluffy White Frosting (page 406)
Divide frosting into two equal portions. Reserve one portion for frosting sides and top of cake. Divide remaining portion in half again. Blend the chopped almonds into one portion. Blend the chopped maraschino cherries into the other portion.

Spread almond filling over top of bottom layer. Cover with the second layer. Spread cherry filling over top of second layer. Cover with the third layer. Frost sides and top with reserved frosting.

Garnish with
    Maraschino cherries, well drained
    One 8-in. round layer cake

▲ Valentine Cake

Prepare (*page 340*) two 9-in. heart-shaped or round layer cake pans.

Sift together and set aside
- **3 cups sifted cake flour**
- **1 tablespoon baking powder**
- **½ teaspoon salt**

Cream together until softened
- **1 cup butter or margarine**
- **1 tablespoon vanilla extract**

Add gradually, creaming until fluffy after each addition
- **1 cup sugar**

Set aside.

Beat until frothy
- **6 egg whites**

Add gradually, beating well after each addition
- **¾ cup sugar**

Beat until rounded peaks are formed.

Measure
- **½ cup water**
- **½ cup milk**

Beating only until smooth after each addition, alternately add dry ingredients in fourths, liquid in thirds, to creamed mixture. Finally beat only until smooth (but do not overbeat). Spread beaten egg whites over batter and gently fold (*page 12*) together. Turn into pans.

Bake at 350°F 30 to 35 min., or until cake tests done (*page 340*).

Cool; remove from pans as directed (*page 340*).

Prepare
- **Pineapple Cream Filling (p. 413)**
- **Seven-Minute Frosting (page 404)**
- **White Velvet Frosting (one-third recipe, page 394)**

Place one cake layer on cake plate and spread filling over top. Place other layer over filling. Frost (*page 393*) with Seven-Minute Frosting.

Tint White Velvet Frosting desired color by blending in one or more drops **red food coloring.** Force frosting through pastry bag and No. 3 stem decorating tube to write on cake.

Valentine Cake

To Make Nosegays—Place small red **gumdrops** on wooden picks. Make soft folds in paper doilies from center to edge. Poke wooden picks down through center of doily and tie in place with red ribbon. Place nosegays on plate around cake. Make one nosegay without ribbon and place it on top of cake.

One 9-in. heart-shaped or round layer cake

Note: If round cake layers are used, heart-shaped layers can be made by cutting around a waxed-paper pattern with a knife.

△ Christmas Tree Cake

Prepare three 9-in. round cake layer pans.

Follow ▲ Recipe, making one and one-half times recipe. Do not prepare filling and Seven-Minute Frosting. Prepare **White Velvet Frosting** (double recipe, page *394*). Place one third of frosting in a small bowl and tint by blending in one or more drops **green food coloring.**

Frost (*page 393*) two cake layers with untinted two-thirds of frosting. Cut third layer into a tree-shape by cutting around a tree-shaped waxed-paper pattern with a knife. Frost tree-shaped layer with the tinted frosting and place on top of other two cake layers. Decorate tree with **red cinnamon candies.**

▲ Shower Cake 30

Prepare (*page 340*) two 9-in. round layer cake pans. Set a bowl and a rotary beater in refrigerator to chill.

Prepare and set in refrigerator to chill
   Pineapple Cream Filling (page 413)
Set out
   1½ cups sugar
Sift ½ cup of the sugar with
   2 cups sifted cake flour
   1 tablespoon baking powder
   ½ teaspoon salt
Set mixture aside.

Using chilled bowl and beater, whip (*page 13*)
   1 cup chilled whipping cream
Beat in ¼ cup of the sugar. Set in refrigerator while beating egg whites.

Using clean beater, beat until frothy
   4 egg whites
Add gradually the remaining ¾ cup sugar, beating well after each addition. Beat until rounded peaks are formed. Fold (*page 12*) the whipped cream and the beaten egg whites together with
   ¾ teaspoon almond extract
Measure
   ½ cup water
Folding only until blended after each addition, alternately add dry ingredients in fourths, water in thirds, to whipped cream mixture.

Shower Cake

Finally fold only until blended.

Turn batter into pans.

Bake at 350°F 30 min., or until cake tests done (*page 340*).

Cool and remove from pans as directed (*page 340*). Cool completely and fill with the Pineapple Cream Filling.

Frost sides and top of cake with
   Seven-Minute Frosting (page 404) or
   White Mountain Frosting (page 406)
Reserve ½ cup frosting for decorating.

For Shower Decoration—If necessary, add 1 to 2 tablespoons sifted **confectioners' sugar** to the reserved frosting to give it a decorating-frosting consistency. Blend in **red food coloring,** a drop at a time, until frosting is a delicate pink color. Set frosting aside. To make umbrella, cut a piece of heavy aluminum foil into a wedge shape, 4 in. wide at base and 4 in. long. Curve wedge to form umbrella top (see photo). Using a spatula, spread pink frosting over both sides of umbrella, using lengthwise strokes on the outside to simulate umbrella spokes. Allow frosting to set on umbrella, keeping curved position.

At one side of the frosted cake form the shaft and curved handle of the umbrella by forcing remaining pink frosting through a pastry bag and No. 2 decorating tube. Make the shaft about 4 in. long. Using same decorating tube form small droplets over top of cake (see photo). Set umbrella top in place.

One 9-in. round layer cake

△ Meltaway Whipped Cream Cake 31

(*See photo on page 404*)

Follow ▲ Recipe. Omit Pineapple Cream Filling. Sift the 1½ cups of sugar and 8 tablespoons **cocoa** with the dry ingredients. Do not add sugar to whipped cream and egg whites. Decrease egg whites to 3; substitute 2 teaspoons **vanilla extract** for almond extract and ½ cup **milk** for water.

Bride's Cake with ice cream and assorted nuts

Bride's Cake 32 24

Tradition is dear to weddings, and don't forget to bake into the cake the trinkets that foretell the future—a penny for wealth, a four-leaf clover for luck, a ring for the next bride.

For Cake Layers—Prepare (*page 340*) two 8-in. round layer cake pans, one 12-in. round layer cake pan (2 in. deep) and a 1-lb. coffee can. Grease sides of 12-in. pan and coffee can and line with parchment paper cut ½ in. wider than sides of pans. Lightly grease paper.

Prepare cake batter once for 12-in. layer and again for 8-in. layers and coffee can.

Sift together and set aside
- **3 cups sifted cake flour**
- **1 tablespoon baking powder**
- **½ teaspoon salt**

Cream together until butter is softened
- **¾ cup butter**
- **1 tablespoon vanilla extract**
- **¼ teaspoon almond extract**

Add gradually, creaming until fluffy after each addition
- **1 cup sugar**

Measure and combine
- **½ cup water**
- **½ cup milk**

Beating only until smooth after each addition, alternately add dry ingredients in fourths, liquid in thirds to creamed mixture. Finally beat only until smooth (do not overbeat).

Beat until frothy
- **6 egg whites**

Add gradually, beating well after each addition
- **¾ cup sugar**

Continue to beat until rounded peaks are formed.

Spread beaten egg whites over blended batter and gently, but thoroughly, fold (*page 12*) together. Turn batter into 12-in. pan.

Bake at 350°F 50 to 55 min., or until cake tests done (*page 340*).

Cool; remove from pan as directed (*page 340*).

Repeat recipe for 8-in. layers and coffee-can layer. Fill 8-in. layer pans two-thirds full. Turn remaining batter into coffee can.

Bake at 350°F 30 to 35 min. for 8-in. layers and 40 to 45 min. for coffee-can layer, or until cakes test done.

Cool; remove from pans as directed.

For Bride's Butter Frosting—Cream until butter is softened
- **⅔ cup butter**
- **1½ teaspoons vanilla extract**
- **¼ teaspoon almond extract**

Add gradually, creaming until fluffy after each addition
- **6 cups (about 1¾ lbs.) sifted confectioners' sugar**

Add and continue creaming until smooth
- **1 egg white, unbeaten**

Blend in gradually a tablespoonful at a time, until of spreading consistency
- **3 to 6 tablespoons cream**

To Frost and Decorate Cake—Spread sides and tops of cooled cake layers with a thin coating of frosting. (This coating prevents crumbs from getting in the final frosting and also helps keep the cake moist and fresh.) *Do not put layers together.*

Cover well with waxed paper, tucking paper under cake racks.

The next day, when ready to start decorating, prepare

Bride's Butter Frosting (one and one-half recipe)

Cut 2 rounds of thin cardboard, one about 8 in. and the other 5 in. in diameter. Cover with aluminum foil. (Cardboard merely prevents knife from cutting into lower layer.)

Place 12-in. layer on cake plate. In the center of the layer, spread a thin layer of frosting the size of the larger cardboard round. Press cardboard firmly into the frosting.

Cover with one of the 8-in. layers, frosted surface up. Spread top with frosting; cover with the other 8-in. layer, keeping the frosted surface up.

In the center of the top layer, spread a thin layer of frosting the size of the smaller cardboard. Press cardboard firmly into the frosting. Cover with the top (coffee can) layer, frosted surface up.

Frost sides of all three tiers (layers), completely covering the cake.

To smooth the frosting, dip spatula in hot water and smooth frosting. Frost top of each tier. Decorate cake by forcing frosting through cake decorator or pastry bag and tube using shell, rosette, or star tube. Make a fluting of frosting around edge of base and top of each tier. Tiny icing flowers and other decorations may be used to decorate cake.

Top the cake with a miniature of the bride's or bridesmaid's bouquet. Or the traditional bride and groom dolls may be affixed to the top with frosting.

To Serve a Three-tiered Bride's Cake—Hold knife vertically and cut around outside of middle layer through the bottom layer. Slice bottom layer (part that extends beyond middle layer) into serving-size pieces. Repeat with middle layer, cutting around outside of top layer through middle layer only to top of bottom layer. (See illustrations.)

The top layer may be removed and placed on a small serving plate on the table. The remainder of the cake may be removed to the kitchen and sliced.

Serve on individual plates or from one large plate. It is best to wipe crumbs and frosting from the knife frequently. Dipping the knife in hot water also aids in cutting the cake.

50 to 60 servings

▲ Blender Chocolate Cake

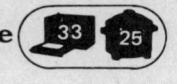

Prepare (*page 340*) two 8-in. round layer cake pans. (Before using electric blender see p. 13).

Melt (*page 12*) and set aside to cool

2 sq. (2 oz.) chocolate

Sift together into a bowl and set aside

2 cups sifted cake flour

1 tablespoon baking powder

½ teaspoon salt

Put into blender container

2 eggs, unbeaten

Cover and blend a few seconds. Turn off motor and add in order

½ cup hydrogenated vegetable shortening or all-purpose shortening

1¼ cups sugar

1½ teaspoons vanilla extract

1 cup milk

Add chocolate, cover and blend 2 min. Scrape sides of container and blend few seconds longer.

Add gradually, stirring after each addition, two-thirds of blended mixture to sifted dry ingredients. Stir until well blended (total strokes, about 100). Add remaining mixture all at one time; mix until smooth. Pour into cake pans.

Bake at 350°F about 25 min., or until cake tests done (*page 340*).

Cool; remove from pans as directed (*page 340*).

Two 8-in. round layers

△ Blender Chocolate Cupcakes

Follow ▲ Recipe; line 18 to 20 2½-in. muffin-pan wells with paper baking cups or grease bottoms of wells. Fill each well one-half full. Bake at 400°F 18 to 20 min., or until cakes tests done (*page 340*).

Prepare **Seven-Minute Frosting** (*page 404*) and frost sides and tops of cooled cupcakes. Pour **melted chocolate** over tops of frosted cupcakes, allowing some to drip slightly down sides. Or sprinkle sides and tops of frosted cupcakes with moist shredded **coconut.**

Nougat Cake

LOIS B. YALE, SEATTLE, WASH.

Use a filling of whipped cream and a seven-minute frosting sprinkled with coconut.

Prepare (*page 340*) two 9-in. round layer cake pans.

Blend together and set aside

6 tablespoons cocoa

5 tablespoons boiling water

Sift together and set aside

1¾ cups sifted cake flour

1½ teaspoons baking powder

½ teaspoon baking soda

Cream together until butter is softened

½ cup butter

1 teaspoon vanilla extract

Add gradually, creaming until fluffy after each addition

1½ cups sugar

Add in thirds, beating well after each addition

4 egg yolks, well beaten

Stir in the cooled cocoa mixture.

Measure

½ cup milk

Beating only until smooth after each addition, alternately add dry ingredients in fourths, milk in thirds, to creamed mixture. Finally beat only until smooth (do not overbeat).

Beat until rounded peaks are formed

4 egg whites

Spread beaten egg whites over batter and gently fold (*page 12*) together. Turn into pans.

Bake at 350°F 25 to 30 min., or until cake tests done (*page 340*).

Cool; remove from pans as directed (*page 340*).

Two 9-in. round layers

Quick Cocoa Cake

Grease bottom of a 2-qt. ring mold or prepare (*page 340*) an 8x8x2-in. cake pan.

Sift together into a large bowl
- **1⅓ cups sifted cake flour**
- **1 cup sugar**
- **½ cup cocoa**
- **1 teaspoon baking powder**
- **½ teaspoon baking soda**
- **¼ teaspoon salt**

Set out
- **¾ cup milk**

Add to sifted dry ingredients
- **6 tablespoons hydrogenated vegetable shortening or all-purpose shortening**

Beat with rotary beater until blended, ¼ cup of the milk and
- **2 eggs, well beaten**
- **1½ teaspoons vanilla extract**

Add to dry ingredients and stir only enough to moisten. Beat 300 strokes or 2 min. on electric mixer on medium speed. Scrape sides of bowl several times during beating.

Add remaining ½ cup milk with
- **2 teaspoons vinegar**

Beat 150 strokes or 1 min. on electric mixer. Scrape sides of bowl several times. Pour batter into mold or pan.

Bake at 350°F about 30 min. for ring and 35 min. for square or until cake tests done (*page 340*).

Quick Cocoa Cake with Mocha Cocoa Frosting (page 396) and ice cream

Cool and remove from cake pan as directed (*page 340*). If using a ring mold, cool cake 10 min. in mold on cooling rack. Invert and remove pan.

When cake is completely cooled, frost with
Mocha Cocoa Frosting (page 396)

One ring-shaped cake or one 8-in. square cake

Grandmother's Sweet Chocolate Cake

Prepare (*page 340*) two 8-in. round layer cake pans.

Combine and set over simmering water
- **3 oz. sweet chocolate**
- **½ cup boiling water**

When chocolate is melted, blend thoroughly. Set aside to cool.

Sift together and set aside
- **2 cups sifted cake flour**
- **1 teaspoon baking soda**
- **½ teaspoon salt**

Cream together until shortening is softened
- **½ cup shortening**
- **1 teaspoon vanilla extract**

Add gradually, creaming until fluffy after each addition
- **1 cup sugar**
- **½ cup firmly packed brown sugar**

Add in thirds, beating well after each addition
- **2 eggs, well beaten**

Stir in chocolate mixture.

Measure
- **⅔ cup buttermilk or sour milk (page 11)**

Beating only until smooth after each addition, alternately add dry ingredients in fourths, buttermilk in thirds, to the creamed mixture. Finally beat only until smooth (do not overbeat). Turn batter into pans.

Bake at 375°F 25 to 30 min., or until cake tests done (*page 340*).

Cool; remove from pans as directed (*page 340*).

Two 8-in. round layers

Toast Cake

MRS. LAVETTE GROVESTEEN
BELLEVILLE, ILL.

Set out a 9-in. tubed pan.

Crush (*page 12*)
**24 zwieback (or enough to yield
2 cups crumbs)**
Blender-grind (*page 13*)
**1 cup (about 5½ oz.) blanched
almonds (page 11)**
Combine with zwieback crumbs and set aside.

Grate (*page 12*) enough chocolate to yield
**1 cup (about 7 oz.) grated sweet
chocolate**
Set aside.

Sift together and set aside
**1 cup sifted flour
1 teaspoon baking powder
1 teaspoon cinnamon
½ teaspoon nutmeg
¼ teaspoon salt**
Cream together until butter is softened
**1 cup butter
½ teaspoon vanilla extract**
Add gradually, creaming until fluffy after each
addition
2 cups sugar
Add in thirds, beating well after each addition
4 eggs, well beaten
Stir in the grated sweet chocolate.

Measure
½ cup milk
Beating only until smooth after each addition,
alternately add dry ingredients in fourths,
milk in thirds, to creamed mixture. Finally
beat only until smooth (do not overbeat). Add
the almond-zwieback-crumb mixture in thirds.
After each addition, blend thoroughly.

Turn batter into pan.

Bake at 300°F 1½ hrs. to 1¾ hrs., or until
cake tests done (*page 340*).

Remove cake from oven and place on cooling rack. Allow cake to cool in pan 15 min.

Cover with cake plate, carefully invert and
remove pan. Cool completely.

Sift over top of cooled cake
2 to 3 tablespoons confectioners' sugar
One 9-in. tubed cake

Yeast-Raised Chocolate Cake

*Mixed today and baked tomorrow, this choco-
late yeast cake will win everyone's approval.*

Have available for tomorrow's baking two
8-in. round layer cake pans.

Melt (*page 12*) and set aside to cool
2 sq. (2 oz.) chocolate
Sift together and set aside
**2 cups sifted cake flour
1 teaspoon salt**
Cream until shortening is softened
½ cup shortening

Add gradually, creaming until fluffy after each addition

1½ cups sugar

Add in thirds, beating well after each addition

2 eggs, well beaten

Set aside.

Soften

1 pkg. active dry yeast

in

¼ cup warm water 110°F to 115°F (Or, if using compressed yeast, soften 1 cake in ¼ cup lukewarm water, 80°F to 85°F.)

Let stand 5 to 10 min. Stir softened yeast and blend into creamed mixture with chocolate.

Measure

⅔ cup milk

Beating only until smooth after each addition, alternately add dry ingredients in fourths, milk in thirds, to creamed mixture. Finally beat only until smooth (do not overbeat). Cover bowl and place batter in refrigerator for at least 6 hours or overnight.

Remove batter from refrigerator and set aside.

Prepare (*page 340*) the two 8-in. round layer cake pans and set aside.

Mix together until baking soda is dissolved

¾ teaspoon baking soda

2 tablespoons warm water

Immediately blend into batter with

1½ teaspoons vanilla extract

Turn batter into pans, spreading to edges.

Bake at 350°F 25 to 35 min., or until cake tests done (*page 340*).

Cool; remove from pans as directed (*page 340*).

Two 8-in. round layers

Caramel Mocha Cake 39

MRS. ELSTON CHITTENDEN
SPRINGFIELD, MO.

Prepare (*page 340*) three 9-in. round layer cake pans.

Sift together and set aside

3 cups sifted cake flour

3 tablespoons cocoa

2½ teaspoons baking powder

½ teaspoon baking soda

¼ teaspoon salt

Cream together until softened

1 cup butter or margarine

2 teaspoons vanilla extract

Add gradually, creaming until fluffy after each addition

2 cups sugar

Add in thirds, beating thoroughly after each addition

5 egg yolks, well beaten

Measure

1 cup buttermilk or sour milk (*page 11*)

5 tablespoons double-strength coffee beverage (*page 13*)

Beating only until smooth after each addition, alternately add dry ingredients in fourths, liquids in thirds, to creamed mixture. Finally beat only until smooth (do not overbeat).

Beat until frothy

5 egg whites

Add gradually, beating well after each addition

½ cup sugar

Beat until rounded peaks are formed and egg whites do not slide when bowl is partially inverted. Carefully spread beaten egg whites over batter and gently fold (*page 12*) together. Turn batter into pans.

Bake at 350°F 30 to 35 min., or until cake tests done (*page 340*).

Cool; remove from pans as directed (*page 340*).

Meanwhile, prepare

Caramel Mocha Frosting (*page 395*)

Fill and frost (*page 393*) cake.

One 9-in. round layer cake

Chocolate Drum Cake

Prepare (*page 340*) two 9-in. round layer cake pans.

Melt (*page 12*) and set aside to cool
3 sq. (3 oz.) chocolate
Sift together and set aside
2½ cups sifted cake flour
1 teaspoon baking soda
¾ teaspoon salt
Cream together until lard is softened
¾ cup lard
2 teaspoons vanilla extract
Add gradually, creaming until fluffy after each addition
2 cups sugar
Add in thirds, beating thoroughly after each addition
5 egg yolks, well beaten
Blend in the cooled chocolate.

Measure
1 cup buttermilk or sour milk (*page 11*)
Beating only until smooth after each addition, alternately add dry ingredients in fourths, buttermilk or sour milk in thirds, to creamed mixture. Finally beat only until smooth (do not overbeat).

Beat until rounded peaks are formed
5 egg whites
Carefully spread egg whites over batter and gently fold (*page 12*) together. Turn batter into pans.

Bake at 375°F 30 to 35 min., or until cake tests done (*page 340*).

Cool; remove from pans as directed (*page 340*).

When cake is cooled, prepare
White Mountain Frosting (p.406)
Fill and frost (*page 393*) cake.

To Decorate as a Drum—Place round peppermint candies around top edge of cake to form rim of "drum". On sides of cake place peppermint candy sticks diagonally, extending sticks from top to bottom of cake.

One 9-in. round layer cake

Chocolate Cake 41

BEULAH RANDALL, PITTSFIELD, MAINE

Prepare (*page 340*) two 8-in. round layer cake pans.

Mix in a saucepan
½ cup sugar
½ cup cocoa
½ cup double-strength coffee beverage (*page 13*)
Bring to boiling. Boil 1 min., stirring constantly. Set aside to cool.

Melt and set aside to cool
½ cup shortening
Sift together and set aside
2 cups sifted flour
1 teaspoon baking soda
½ teaspoon salt
Beat until thick and piled softly
2 eggs
Add gradually, beating well after each addition
1 cup sugar
Stir in the cocoa mixture and the shortening.

Measure
1 cup buttermilk or sour milk (*page 11*)
Beating only until smooth after each addition, alternately add dry ingredients in fourths, buttermilk in thirds, to egg mixture. Finally beat only until smooth (do not overbeat).

Turn batter into pans.

Bake at 350°F 25 to 30 min., or until cake tests done (*page 340*).

Cool; remove from pans as directed (*page 340*).
Two 8-in. round layers

▲ Sour-Cream Chocolate Cake

Prepare (*page 340*) two 8-in. round layer cake pans or one 9x9x2-in. cake pan.

Combine and set over simmering water
3 sq. (3 oz.) chocolate
½ cup double-strength coffee beverage (*page 13*)
When chocolate is melted, blend thoroughly.

Set aside to cool.

Sift together and set aside
2 cups sifted cake flour
1½ teaspoons baking soda
½ teaspoon salt
Combine and beat until well blended
1½ cups sugar
1 cup thick sour cream
2½ teaspoons vanilla extract
Add in thirds, beating well after each addition
2 eggs, well beaten
Beat in the chocolate mixture. Add dry ingredients in thirds, beating only until batter is smooth after each addition. Finally beat only until smooth (do not overbeat). Turn batter into pans.

Bake layers at 350°F 35 min.; bake square cake at 350°F 40 to 45 min., or until cake tests done (page 340).

Cool; remove from pans as directed (page 340).

Meanwhile, prepare
Bittersweet Velvet Frosting (p.395)
Frost (page 393) cake. Garnish (see photo) with

Walnut halves
One 8-in. round layer cake
or one 9-in. square cake

△ **Black Walnut Chocolate Cake** 43

Follow ▲ Recipe. Stir in ⅔ cup (2⅓ oz.) chopped **black walnuts** with final strokes.

Sour-Cream Chocolate Cake with Bittersweet Velvet Frosting (page 395)

Chocolate Potato Cake 44 31

Prepare (*page 340*) two 9-in. round layer cake pans.

Set out
1 cup mashed potato
Melt (*page 12*) and set aside to cool
1 sq. (1 oz.) chocolate
Sift together and set aside
2 cups sifted cake flour
2 teaspoons baking powder
½ teaspoon salt
Blend together
1 cup hydrogenated vegetable shortening or all-purpose shortening
2 teaspoons grated lemon peel (page 11)
Add gradually, creaming until fluffy after each addition
2 cups sugar
Add in thirds, beating well after each addition
4 eggs, well beaten
Stir in the cooled chocolate.

Blend potatoes with
½ cup milk
Beating only until smooth after each addition, alternately add dry ingredients in fourths, potato mixture in thirds, to creamed mixture. Finally beat only until smooth (do not overbeat). Turn batter into pans.

Bake at 350°F 40 to 45 min., or until cake tests done (*page 340*).

Cool; remove from pans as directed (*page 340*).
Two 9-in. round layers

Note: Grated **raw potatoes** may be substituted for the cooked ones; grate them just after adding the eggs to the creamed mixture.

Maple Sirup Cake

Prepare (*page 340*) three 8-in. round layer cake pans.

For Cake—Sift together and set aside

2⅔ cups sifted cake flour
1 tablespoon baking powder
¾ teaspoon salt

Cream until softened

¾ cup shortening

Add gradually, creaming until fluffy after each addition

⅔ cup firmly packed light brown sugar

Set mixture aside.

Add in thirds, beating thoroughly after each addition

7 egg yolks, well beaten

Measure and blend together

⅔ cup milk
⅔ cup maple sirup

Beating only until smooth after each addition, alternately add dry ingredients in fourths, liquid in thirds, to creamed mixture. Finally beat only until smooth (do not overbeat).

Turn batter into pans.

Bake at 350°F 45 to 50 min., or until cake tests done (*page 340*).

Cool; remove from pans as directed (*page 340*).

For Jam Filling—When cake layers are completely cooled, set out

⅔ cup raspberry jam

Spread one half of the jam over top of bottom cake layer. Cover with second cake layer; spread top of second layer with remaining jam. Cover with third layer.

For Frosting—Prepare

Maple Frosting (page 401)

Frost (*page 393*) sides and top of cake.

One 8-in. round layer cake

Burnt Sugar Cake

Prepare (*page 340*) a 9x9x2-in. cake pan.

For Burnt Sugar Sirup—Melt in a heavy, light-colored skillet (a black skillet makes it difficult to see the color of the sirup) over low heat

2 cups sugar

With back of wooden spoon, gently keep sugar moving toward center of skillet until it is melted. Heat to a rich brown, until foam appears. Remove from heat and add gradually, a very small amount at a time

1½ cups boiling water

Cook until bubbles are the size of dimes (about 5 min.). Set aside to cool completely.

Note: Burnt Sugar Sirup may be stored in a tightly covered jar for future use.

For Cake—Sift together
2½ cups sifted cake flour
2½ teaspoons baking powder
½ teaspoon salt
Set aside.

Cream together until shortening is softened
½ cup shortening
1 teaspoon vanilla extract
Add gradually, creaming until fluffy after each addition
½ cup sugar
Add in thirds, beating well after each addition
2 egg yolks, well beaten
Mix together
½ cup water
½ cup Burnt Sugar Sirup (part of remainder to be used for Burnt Sugar Frosting)
Beating only until smooth after each addition, alternately add dry ingredients in fourths, liquid in thirds, to creamed mixture. Finally beat only until smooth (do not overbeat).

Beat until frothy
2 egg whites
Add gradually, beating thoroughly after each addition
¼ cup sugar
Beat until rounded peaks are formed. Spread beaten egg whites over batter and gently fold (*page 12*) together. Turn batter into pan.

Bake at 350°F 35 to 40 min., or until cake tests done (*page 340*).

Cool; remove from pan as directed (*page 340*).

When cake is completely cool, prepare
Burnt Sugar Frosting (page 395)
Frost sides and top of cake. Sprinkle top with
Chopped toasted pecans
One 9-in. square cake

Note: For a square layer cake, double recipe.

Burnt Sugar Cake with
Burnt Sugar Frosting (page 395)

Cocoa Date-Nut Cake
KAY CALHOUN, SITKA, ALASKA

This unusual cake comes from a homestead in Alaska where numerous chores and limited facilities make short cuts in baking important.

Prepare (*page 340*) a 9x9x2-in. cake pan.

Coarsely chop
1 cup (about 7 oz.) pitted dates
½ cup (about 2 oz.) walnuts
Combine the chopped dates and nuts with
1 cup boiling water
Set aside to cool.

Sift together into a large bowl
2 cups sifted flour
1 cup sugar
3 tablespoons cocoa
1 teaspoon baking soda
⅛ teaspoon salt
Make a well in center of dry ingredients and add all at one time, the date-nut mixture and
1 cup mayonnaise
1 teaspoon vanilla extract
Beat only until batter is blended (do not overbeat). Turn batter into pan.

Bake at 375°F 45 min., or until cake tests done (*page 340*).

Cool; remove from pan as directed (*page 340*).
One 9-in. square cake

Cleveland Cake

(Crumb Cake)

MRS. WILL W. COTTINGHAM, ROLLA, MO.

Prepare (*page 340*) a 13x9½x2-in. cake pan.

Coarsely chop and set aside
   1 cup (about 4 oz.) walnuts
Sift together into a large bowl
   3 cups sifted flour
   2 cups sugar
Cut in with pastry blender or two knives until pieces are the size of small peas
   1 cup butter
Measure 1 cup of the crumb mixture and set aside.

To remaining crumb mixture in bowl, stir in until well blended, a mixture of
   2 tablespoons cinnamon
   1 tablespoon cocoa
   1 teaspoon nutmeg
   1 teaspoon baking soda
   ½ teaspoon baking powder
   ¼ teaspoon salt
   ¼ teaspoon cloves
Mix in walnuts and
   1 cup (about 5 oz.) seedless raisins
Make a well in center of dry ingredients and add all at one time
   2 cups buttermilk or sour milk (page 11)
Beat until just blended.

Turn batter into pan and sprinkle top with the reserved crumb mixture.

Bake at 350°F 1 hr., or until cake tests done (*page 340*).

Cool; remove from pan as directed (*page 340*).
   18 to 24 servings

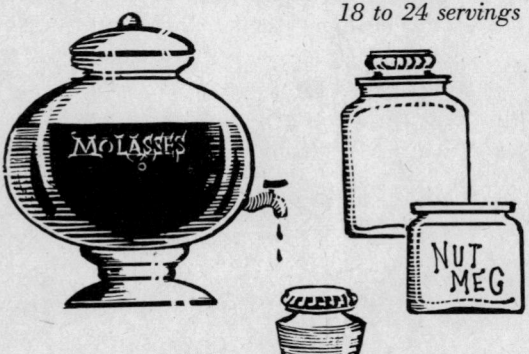

Graham Cracker Cake

MRS. L. E. COX, Jr., GREENEVILLE, TENN.

A truly superior cake, but a bit temperamental. It may choose to dip slightly toward the center on the day you bake it. The flavor, however, is dependable—and thoroughly delicious.

Prepare (*page 340*) a 9x9x2-in. cake pan.

Crush (*page 12*)
   25 graham crackers (or enough to yield 2 cups crumbs)
Turn crumbs into a bowl. Stir in
   2 teaspoons baking powder
Set aside.

Cut into short lengths and set aside
   1 cup (4 oz.) moist shredded coconut
Cream together until butter is softened
   ½ cup butter
   1 teaspoon vanilla extract
Add gradually, creaming until fluffy after each addition
   1 cup sugar
Add in thirds, beating well after each addition
   3 eggs, well beaten
Stir in the graham mixture and the coconut.

Turn batter into pan. With spatula, draw batter from center toward edges of pan.

Bake at 350°F 40 to 45 min., or until cake tests done (*page 340*).

Cool; remove from pan as directed (*page 340*).
   One 9-in. square cake

Honey-Brown Gingerbread 48 35

MRS. M. A. LUDVIGSON
MINNEAPOLIS, MINN.

Prepare (*page 340*) a 9x9x2-in. cake pan.

Sift together and set aside
   2½ cups sifted flour
   1½ teaspoons baking soda
   1 teaspoon cinnamon
   1 teaspoon ginger
   ½ teaspoon salt
   ¼ teaspoon cloves

Combine and set aside
  1 cup boiling water
  ½ cup molasses
  ½ cup honey
Put into a bowl
  **½ cup hydrogenated vegetable short-
    ening or all-purpose shortening**
Add gradually, creaming until fluffy after each
addition
  ½ cup sugar
Add gradually, beating well after each addition
  1 egg, well beaten
Beating only until smooth after each addition,
alternately add dry ingredients in fourths,
liquid in thirds, to creamed mixture. Finally
beat only until smooth (do not overbeat).
Turn batter into pan.

Bake at 350°F 50 to 55 min., or until cake
tests done (*page 340*).

Cool; remove from pan as directed (*page 340*).

To serve, cut gingerbread into 3-in. squares
and top with whipped cream. Or serve with
  Lemon Sauce (*page 335*)

9 servings

Pineapple Gingerbread 49

Butter bottoms of 6 individual casseroles. Put
a bowl and rotary beater in refrigerator to chill.

Drain, reserving sirup, contents of
  **1 No. 2½ can sliced pineapple (8
    slices pineapple)**
Place one slice in each casserole. Cut remaining two slices finely; reserve for topping.

For Pineapple Sauce—Mix in a saucepan
  ⅔ cup water
  1½ tablespoons quick-cooking tapioca
  ⅛ teaspoon salt
Bring quickly to boiling. Boil 1 min., stirring
constantly. Remove from heat and stir in
  ⅓ cup reserved pineapple sirup
Pour sauce over pineapple slices in casseroles.

For Gingerbread—Sift together
  1½ cups sifted flour

Pineapple Gingerbread

and a mixture of
  ½ teaspoon salt
  ½ teaspoon baking powder
  ½ teaspoon baking soda
  ½ teaspoon ginger
  ½ teaspoon cinnamon
  ½ teaspoon nutmeg
  ¼ teaspoon cloves
Prepare
  **½ cup double-strength coffee beverage
    (*page 13*)**
Cream until softened
  ⅓ cup shortening
Add gradually, creaming until light and fluffy
after each addition
  ½ cup firmly packed brown sugar
Add gradually, beating well after each addition
  1 egg, well beaten
Combine with the coffee beverage and blend in
  ½ cup molasses
Add dry ingredients all at one time. Beat until
smooth. Turn batter into casseroles, filling
each two-thirds full.

Bake at 350°F 25 to 30 min., or until cakes
test done (*page 340*).

For Pineapple Topping—Using chilled
bowl and beater, whip (*page 13*)
  ½ cup chilled whipping cream
Fold (*page 12*) the reserved pineapple into
whipped cream.

6 servings

"Mo"-Lasses Cupcakes 50

(See photo on page 394)

Line with paper baking cups or grease bottoms of 24 2½-in. muffin-pan wells.

Sift together and set aside
2½ cups sifted cake flour
2½ teaspoons baking powder
1 teaspoon cinnamon
½ teaspoon salt
Cream until shortening is softened
½ cup shortening
1½ teaspoons vanilla extract
Add gradually, creaming until fluffy after each addition
¾ cup sugar
Add in thirds, beating well after each addition
2 eggs, well beaten
Blend in gradually
½ cup molasses
Measure
¾ cup milk
Beating only until smooth after each addition, alternately add dry ingredients in fourths, milk in thirds, to the molasses mixture. Finally beat only until smooth (do not overbeat). Fill cups or muffin-pan wells one-half full.

Bake at 350°F 25 to 30 min., or until cakes test done *(page 340)*.

Cool and remove from muffin-pan wells as directed *(page 340)*.

Meanwhile, prepare
Lemon Butter Frosting (page 394)
When cupcakes are completely cooled, frost.
2 doz. cupcakes

Assorted Cupcakes

Pumpkin Cupcakes 51

Line with paper baking cups or grease bottoms of 18 2½-in. muffin-pan wells.

Sift together and set aside
2½ cups sifted cake flour
1 tablespoon baking powder
½ teaspoon salt
½ teaspoon cinnamon
¼ teaspoon nutmeg
¼ teaspoon ginger
Cream until softened
½ cup shortening
Add gradually, creaming until fluffy after each addition
¾ cup sugar
¾ cup firmly packed brown sugar
Add in thirds, beating well after each addition
2 eggs, well beaten
Blend in
¾ cup canned pumpkin
Measure
½ cup milk
Beating only until smooth after each addition, alternately add dry ingredients in fourths, milk in thirds, to creamed mixture. Finally beat only until smooth (do not overbeat). Fill cups or muffin-pan wells one-half full.

Bake at 350°F 15 to 20 min., or until cakes test done (*page 340*).

Cool and remove from muffin-pan wells as directed (*page 340*).

Meanwhile, prepare
Burnt Sugar Frosting (page 395)
When cupcakes are completely cooled, frost.
1½ doz. cupcakes

Blackberry Jam Cake

MRS. GARVIE O. BARKER, WICHITA, KANS.

Interesting—has a medley of matched flavors.

Prepare (*page 340*) two 9-in. round layer cake pans.

Sift together and set aside
2 cups sifted flour
1 tablespoon baking powder
½ teaspoon baking soda
½ teaspoon salt
1 teaspoon cinnamon
¼ teaspoon nutmeg
Coarsely chop and set aside
½ cup (about 2 oz.) pecans
Cut into short lengths and set aside
1 cup (4 oz.) moist shredded coconut
Cream together until softened
½ cup butter or margarine
1½ teaspoons vanilla extract
Add gradually, beating well after each addition
2 eggs, well beaten
Combine
1 cup buttermilk or sour milk (page 11)
1 cup blackberry jam
Beating only until smooth after each addition, alternately add dry ingredients in fourths, liquid in thirds, to creamed mixture. Finally beat only until smooth (do not overbeat). Stir in the chopped pecans and coconut. Turn batter into pans.

Bake at 350°F 45 min., or until cake tests done (*page 340*).

Cool; remove from pans as directed (*page 340*).
Two 9-in. round layers

Strawberry-Flavored Cake 36

LEOLA BRODINE, TAYLOR, NEBR.

Prepare (*page 340*) two 9-in. round layer cake pans.

Coarsely chop and set aside
1 cup (about 4 oz.) pecans
Sift together and set aside
3 cups sifted cake flour
2 teaspoons baking powder
½ teaspoon salt
Put into a bowl
¾ cup hydrogenated vegetable short-ening or all-purpose shortening
Add gradually, creaming until fluffy after each addition
2 cups sugar
Measure
1 cup less 2 tablespoons carbonated strawberry beverage
Beating only until smooth after each addition, alternately add dry ingredients in fourths, liquid in thirds. Finally beat only until smooth (do not overbeat). Stir in the pecans.

Beat until rounded peaks are formed and egg whites do not slide when bowl is partially inverted
5 egg whites
Carefully spread beaten egg whites over surface of batter and gently fold (*page 12*) together. Pour batter into pans.

Bake at 350°F 30 to 35 min., or until cake tests done (*page 340*).

Cool; remove from pans as directed (*page 340*).
Two 9-in. round layers

Note: **Grape, cherry** or **orange carbonated beverage** may be substituted for the strawberry beverage for different flavor and color.

Applesauce Cake [52]

Prepare (*page 340*) a 9x9x2-in. cake pan.

For Cake—Set out
   ¾ cup (about 4 oz.) seedless raisins
Sift together and set aside
   2 cups sifted cake flour
   1 teaspoon baking soda
   1 teaspoon cinnamon
   ½ teaspoon cloves
   ½ teaspoon salt
Cream until softened
   ½ cup butter or margarine
Add gradually, creaming until fluffy after each addition
   1 cup firmly packed brown sugar
Add in thirds, beating thoroughly after each addition
   2 eggs, well beaten
Measure and blend together
   1 cup thick, sweetened applesauce
   ⅔ cup undiluted evaporated milk
   2 tablespoons vinegar
Beating only until smooth after each addition, alternately add dry ingredients in fourths, applesauce mixture in thirds, to creamed mixture. Finally beat only until smooth (do not overbeat).

Stir in the raisins. Turn batter into pan.

Bake at 350°F 40 min., or until cake tests done (*page 340*).

Place cake on cooling rack while preparing frosting.

For Brown Sugar Frosting—Coarsely chop and set aside
   ½ cup (about 3 oz.) toasted, blanched almonds (*page 11*)
Cream together until fluffy
   2 tablespoons butter or margarine, softened
   ½ cup firmly packed brown sugar
Add and continue beating
   2 tablespoons undiluted evaporated milk
Stir in the chopped nuts.

Set temperature control of range at Broil.

Spread frosting lightly over the cake. Place cake in broiler with top of cake about 4 in. from source of heat. Broil about 1 min., or until frosting bubbles. Watch closely to avoid scorching.   *One 9-in. square cake*

Apple-Pecan Cupcakes [53]
MRS. L. W. BAUMHEUTER, GREER, S. C.

Line with paper baking cups or grease bottoms of 30 2½-in. muffin-pan wells.

Melt (*page 12*) and set aside to cool
   4 sq. (4 oz.) chocolate
Chop coarsely and set aside
   ¾ cup (about 3 oz.) pecans
Sift together and set aside
   2 cups sifted flour
   1 teaspoon baking powder
   ½ teaspoon baking soda
   ½ teaspoon salt
Blend together
   1 cup hydrogenated vegetable short-ening or all-purpose shortening
   2 teaspoons vanilla extract
Add gradually, creaming until fluffy after each addition
   2 cups sugar
Add in thirds, beating well after each addition
   4 eggs, well beaten
Stir in the cooled chocolate.

Measure
   1½ cups thick, sweetened applesauce
Beating only until smooth after each addition, alternately add dry ingredients in fourths, applesauce in thirds, to creamed mixture. Finally beat only until smooth (do not overbeat). Blend in the chopped pecans.

Fill cups or muffin-pan wells one-half full.

Bake at 350°F 25 to 30 min., or until cakes test done (*page 340*).

Cool and remove from muffin-pan wells as directed (*page 340*).   *2½ doz. cupcakes*

Apple Spice Cake 54 37

CHARLES J. LOVELL, OAK LAWN, ILL.

Prepare (*page 340*) a 9½x5¼x2¾-in. loaf pan.

Coarsely chop and set aside
1 cup (about 7 oz.) pitted dates
1 cup (about 4 oz.) pecans
Wash, quarter, core, pare and grate enough apples to yield
1½ cups grated apple (about 3 medium-size apples)
Combine and pour over grated apple
6 tablespoons water
2 tablespoons lemon juice
Set aside.

Sift together and set aside
2 cups sifted flour
2 tablespoons cocoa
2 teaspoons baking soda
1 teaspoon cinnamon
1 teaspoon nutmeg
Cream together until softened
½ cup butter or margarine
1 teaspoon vanilla extract
Add gradually, creaming until fluffy after each addition
1 cup sugar
Beating only until smooth after each addition, alternately add dry ingredients in fourths, apple mixture in thirds, to creamed mixture. Finally beat only until smooth (do not overbeat). Stir in the chopped dates and pecans. Turn batter into pan.

Bake at 350°F 1 hr. 10 min., or until cake tests done (*page 340*).

Cool; remove from pan as directed (*page 340*).
One 9x5-in. loaf cake

Fresh Apple Cake 55

HELEN V. DYER
CROTON-ON-HUDSON, N. Y.

A recipe that has been in use four generations.

Prepare (*page 340*) an 8x8x2-in. cake pan.

Coarsely chop and set aside
1 cup (about 4 oz.) walnuts
Sift together
1 cup sifted flour
1 teaspoon baking soda
¾ teaspoon cinnamon
½ teaspoon salt
Set aside.

Wash, quarter, core, pare and chop finely enough apples to yield
2 cups chopped apple (2 to 3 medium-size apples)
Set aside.

Put into a bowl
¼ cup hydrogenated vegetable shortening or all-purpose shortening
Add gradually, creaming until fluffy after each addition
1 cup sugar
Add gradually, beating well after each addition
1 egg, well beaten
Stir apples into mixture. Beating only until blended after each addition, add dry ingredients in thirds to creamed mixture. Finally beat only until blended (do not overbeat). Blend in the chopped nuts. Turn into pan.

Bake at 350°F 45 min., or until cake tests done (*page 340*).

Cool; remove from pan as directed (*page 340*).
One 8-in. square cake

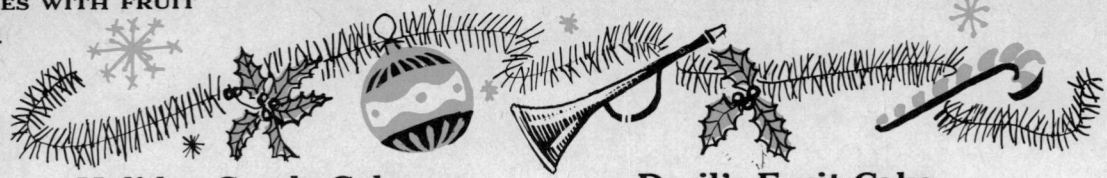

Holiday Candy Cake

MRS. WARREN SPITLER, ELSIE, MICH.

Line bottom and sides of a 10-in. tubed pan with parchment paper cut to fit pan.

Place in a large bowl
2 cups sifted flour
Coarsely chop and combine with flour
4 cups (about 2 lbs.) sugared gumdrops (do not use licorice-flavored)
1½ cups (about 6 oz.) pecans
Add
2 cups (about 10 oz.) seedless raisins
Set aside.

Sift together and set aside
2 cups sifted flour
1 teaspoon baking soda
1 teaspoon cloves
1 teaspoon cinnamon
1 teaspoon allspice
Put into a bowl
1 cup hydrogenated vegetable short-ening or all-purpose shortening
Add gradually, creaming until fluffy after each addition
1 cup sugar
Add in thirds, beating well after each addition
2 eggs, well beaten
Measure
1½ cups thick sweetened applesauce
Beating only until smooth after each addition, alternately add dry ingredients in fourths, applesauce in thirds, to the creamed mixture. Finally beat only until smooth (do not over-beat). Pour batter over candy mixture and mix thoroughly. Turn batter into pan.

Bake at 275°F 2 hrs. 45 min. to 3 hrs., or until cake tests done (*page 340*).

Allow cake to cool in pan 10 min.; remove cake from pan, leaving parchment paper on cake. Cool on cooling rack. Remove paper just before serving.   *One 10-in. tubed cake*

Devil's Fruit Cake

MRS. EARL ENGLES, JR., MIDLAND, MICH.

Prepare (*page 340*) two 9-in. round layer cake pans.

Sift together and set aside
2 cups sifted flour
½ cup cocoa
1¼ teaspoons baking soda
Finely chop and set aside
1 cup (about 4 oz.) walnuts
Wash, quarter, core, pare and grind enough apples to yield
1 cup ground apple (about 3 medium-size apples)
Turn into a fine sieve; stir with a wooden spoon to drain off as much juice as possible. Set aside.

Peel and force through sieve or food mill enough bananas to yield
1 cup sieved banana (2 to 3 bananas with brown-flecked peel)
Set aside.

Cream together until butter is softened
½ cup butter
2 teaspoons vanilla extract
Add gradually, creaming until fluffy after each addition
1¼ cups sugar
Add in thirds, beating thoroughly after each addition
3 egg yolks, well beaten
Combine
½ cup buttermilk or sour milk (*page 11*)
½ cup hot water
Beating only until smooth after each addition, alternately add dry ingredients in fourths, liquid in thirds, to creamed mixture. Finally beat only until smooth (do not overbeat). Fold in (*page 12*) the bananas, nuts and apples.

Beat until frothy
3 egg whites

Add gradually, beating well after each addition

¼ cup sugar

Beat until rounded peaks are formed and egg whites do not slide when bowl is partially inverted. Carefully spread beaten egg whites over batter and fold (*page 12*) together. Turn batter into pans.

Bake at 350°F 35 to 40 min., or until cake tests done (*page 340*).

Cool; remove from pans as directed (*page 340*).

Two 9-in. round layers

Elegant Loaf Cake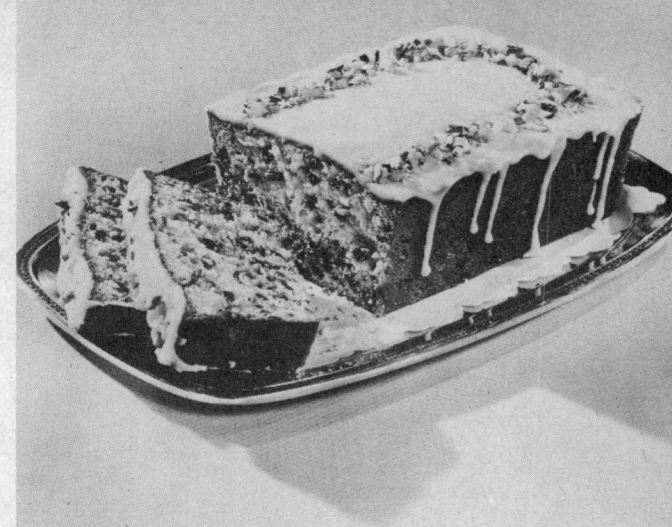

Prepare (*page 340*) a 9½x5¼x2¾-in. loaf pan.

Coarsely chop and set aside

½ cup (about 2 oz.) walnuts

Chop very finely and set aside

1 cup (about 4 oz.) walnuts

¾ cup (about 6 oz.) candied cherries (*page 12*)

2 oz. (about ¼ cup, chopped) candied citron (*page 12*)

Sift together and set aside

2 cups sifted cake flour

2½ teaspoons baking powder

¾ teaspoon salt

Cream together until shortening is softened

⅔ cup shortening

1 teaspoon almond extract

½ teaspoon vanilla extract

Elegant Loaf Cake with Glossy Vanilla Frosting (page 401)

Add gradually, creaming until fluffy after each addition

½ cup sugar

Add in thirds, beating well after each addition

2 egg yolks, well beaten

Measure

⅔ cup milk

Beating only until smooth after each addition, alternately add dry ingredients in fourths, milk in thirds, to creamed mixture. Finally beat only until smooth (do not overbeat). Stir in chopped cherries, citron and the cup of finely chopped nuts.

Beat until frothy

4 egg whites

Add gradually, beating well after each addition

¼ cup sugar

Beat until rounded peaks are formed. Spread beaten egg whites over batter and gently fold (*page 12*) together. Turn batter into pan.

Bake at 350°F 1 hr. 10 min., or until cake tests done (*page 340*).

Cool; remove from pan as directed (*page 340*).

Prepare

Glossy Vanilla Icing (*page 401*)

Top cake with icing and decorate with the coarsely chopped nuts. *One 9x5-in. loaf cake*

Prunella Cake 56

MRS. I. HUGHES, LINN GROVE, IOWA

Prepare (*page 340*) a 9x9x2-in. cake pan.

Rinse and put into a saucepan
¼ lb. (about ⅔ cup) prunes
Cover prunes with
1 cup hot water
Cover pan and allow prunes to soak in pan for 1 hr. Simmer prunes in water in which they have been soaking about 45 to 60 min., or until fruit is plump and tender.

Drain and cool slightly. (Reserve liquid for frosting.) Remove pits (pits are more easily removed when prunes are slightly warm). Finely cut prunes with scissors.

Sift together over the prunes and set aside
1⅓ cups sifted flour
½ teaspoon baking powder
½ teaspoon baking soda
½ teaspoon salt
½ teaspoon cinnamon
½ teaspoon nutmeg
Put into a bowl
½ cup hydrogenated vegetable shortening or all-purpose shortening
Add gradually, creaming until fluffy after each addition
1 cup sugar
Add in thirds, beating well after each addition
2 eggs, well beaten
Measure
⅔ cup buttermilk or sour milk (page 11)
Beating until smooth after each addition, alternately add dry ingredients in fourths, buttermilk in thirds, to creamed mixture. Finally beat only until smooth (do not overbeat).

Turn batter into pan.

Bake at 350°F 35 to 40 min., or until cake tests done (*page 340*).

Cool; remove from pan as directed (*page 340*).

Serve with
Prune Topping (page 410)
One 9-in. square cake

Fruitcake De Luxe 57 39

WANDA W. ALTHAUS, ROSEBURG, ORE.

Prepare (*page 340*) two 9½x5¼x2¾-in. loaf pans.

Bring to boiling
3 cups water
Add, and again bring to boiling
½ lb. (about 1½ cups) seedless raisins
½ lb. (about 1½ cups) currants
Pour off water and drain fruit on absorbent paper. Set aside.

Coarsely chop
½ lb. pitted dates (about 1⅓ cups, chopped)
Combine in a large bowl
½ cup sifted flour
½ lb. (about 1¼ cups) diced, assorted candied fruits
Add the raisins, currants and dates to flour mixture. Set aside.

Grate (*page 11*) and set aside
½ cup (about 2 oz.) pecans
Sift together and set aside
1½ cups sifted flour
1 tablespoon cocoa
1½ teaspoons salt
1½ teaspoons baking powder
1½ teaspoons cinnamon
1½ teaspoons nutmeg
½ teaspoon allspice
½ teaspoon ginger
⅛ teaspoon baking soda
Cream together until softened
½ cup butter
½ cup hydrogenated vegetable shortening or all-purpose shortening
1½ teaspoons vanilla extract
1½ teaspoons rum extract
Add gradually, creaming until fluffy after each addition
1 cup firmly packed brown sugar
Add to creamed mixture, beating well
¼ cup molasses
Add in thirds, beating well after each addition
2 egg yolks, well beaten

Blend in thoroughly
½ cup apple butter
½ cup grape jelly
½ cup thick unsweetened applesauce
Combine
½ cup brandy
⅓ cup water
Beating only until blended after each addition, alternately add dry ingredients in fourths, liquid in thirds, to creamed mixture. Finally beat only until blended (do not overbeat). Pour batter over fruit and mix thoroughly.

Beat until rounded peaks are formed
1 egg white
Carefully spread beaten egg white over batter and gently fold (*page 12*) together.

Place a shallow pan containing 2 cups water on bottom rack of oven during baking time.

Turn batter into pans, spreading to edges.

Bake at 350°F 1½ to 1¾ hrs., or until cake tests done (*page 340*) with cake tester.

Cool completely, remove from pans and store (*page 338*). Once or twice a week, using a pastry brush, paint with brandy and store again.
About 5 lbs. fruitcake

Date and Fig Fruitcake 58 40

MRS. MELVIN McCOMBS, COLUMBUS, OHIO

Prepare (*page 340*) two 9½x5¼x2¾-in. loaf pans.

Bring to boiling
2 cups water
Add, and again bring to boiling
2 cups (about 10 oz.) seedless raisins
Pour off water and drain fruit on absorbent paper. Set aside.

Place in a large bowl
1 cup sifted flour
Chop
1 lb. figs (about 2⅔ cups, chopped)
1 lb. pitted dates (about 2⅔ cups, chopped)
1½ cups (about 6 oz.) walnuts
Combine with flour and add drained raisins. Set aside.

Sift together and set aside
1½ cups sifted flour
1 teaspoon baking soda
½ teaspoon salt
1 teaspoon allspice
1 teaspoon cinnamon
1 teaspoon ginger
1 teaspoon cloves
1 teaspoon nutmeg
Cream until butter is softened
1 cup butter
Add gradually, creaming until fluffy after each addition
1 cup sugar
Add in thirds, beating well after each addition
4 eggs, well beaten
Add, beating well
2 tablespoons molasses
Measure
½ cup brandy, grape juice or coffee beverage
Beating only until smooth after each addition, alternately add dry ingredients in fourths, liquid in thirds, to creamed mixture. Finally beat only until smooth (do not overbeat).

Pour batter over fruit and mix thoroughly.

Place a shallow pan containing 2 cups water on bottom rack of oven during baking time.

Turn batter into pans, spreading to edges.

Bake at 300°F 1 hr. 40 min., or until cake tests done (*page 340*) with cake tester.

Cool completely, remove from pans and store (*page 338*). Once or twice a week, using a pastry brush, paint cake with brandy or grape juice, and store again. *About 4 lbs. fruitcake*

Ambrosia White Fruitcake 41

MRS. E. C. MEREDITH, VICKSBURG, MISS.

Prepare (*page 340*) 10-in. tubed pan.

Put in a large bowl

1 cup sifted flour

Chop and combine with flour

**½ lb. candied pineapple (about
1⅔ cups, chopped)**

**½ lb. candied cherries (about
1⅔ cups, chopped)**

½ lb. pecans (about 2 cups, chopped)

Add and set aside

5 oz. (about 1 cup) golden raisins

**4 oz. (about 1 cup) moist shredded
coconut, cut**

Sift together and set aside

2 cups sifted flour

1 teaspoon baking powder

Cream together until butter is softened

1 cup butter

1 tablespoon vanilla extract

Add gradually, creaming until fluffy after each addition

2 cups sugar

Measure

½ cup unsweetened pineapple juice

Beating only until smooth after each addition, alternately add dry ingredients in fourths, liquid in thirds, to creamed mixture. Finally beat only until smooth (do not overbeat). Pour batter over the fruit-coconut mixture and mix thoroughly.

Beat until rounded peaks are formed and egg whites do not slide when bowl is partially inverted

8 egg whites

Carefully spread beaten egg whites over batter and fold (*page 12*) together.

Place a shallow pan containing 2 cups water on bottom rack of oven during baking time. Turn batter into pan, spreading evenly.

Bake at 275°F about 4 hrs., or until cake tests done (*page 340*) with cake tester.

Cool completely, remove from pan and store (*page 338*). Once or twice a week, using a pastry brush, paint cake with rum and store again.

About 4½ lbs. fruitcake

Christmas Fruitcake 59 42

MRS. CLIFFORD MAREK, BLOOMER, WIS.

Prepare (*page 340*) two 8-in. round layer cake pans.

Combine in a 2-qt. saucepan, bring to boiling and cook over low heat 10 min., stirring occasionally

1 cup (about 7 oz.) pitted dates

1 cup (about 5 oz.) seedless raisins

1 cup plus 2 tablespoons water

1 cup sugar

½ cup hydrogenated vegetable shortening or all-purpose shortening

1 teaspoon cinnamon

1 teaspoon cloves

Remove from heat and set aside to cool.

Meanwhile, mix together in a large bowl and set aside

½ cup sifted flour

4 oz. (about ¾ cup) whole Brazil nuts

2 oz. (about ½ cup) walnut halves

**½ lb. (about 1½ cups) whole
candied cherries**

Sift together

2 cups sifted flour

½ teaspoon baking soda

½ teaspoon salt

Beating only until blended after each addition, add dry ingredients in thirds to cooked fruit mixture. Finally beat only until blended (do not overbeat). Pour batter over nut-cherry mixture and mix thoroughly.

Place a shallow pan containing 2 cups water on bottom rack of oven during baking time.

Turn batter into pans, spreading to edges.

Bake at 325°F 1 hr., or until cake tests done (*page 340*) with cake tester.

Cool completely, remove from pans and store (*page 338*). Once or twice a week, using a pastry brush, paint cakes with brandy or sherry, and store again. *About 3¼ lbs. fruitcake*

Saint Nicholas Cake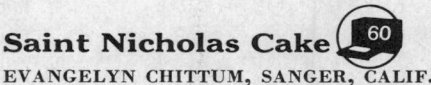
EVANGELYN CHITTUM, SANGER, CALIF.

A grand-prize winner, Saint Nicholas Cake represents originality in one of the oldest of all cakes—the fruitcake. This fine creation offers a bonus of flavor in the unexpected and altogether delightful effect of the semi-sweet chocolate pieces.

Lightly grease bottom of 9½x5¼x2¾-in. loaf pan. Line bottom and sides with parchment paper cut to fit pan. Lightly grease paper.

Coarsely chop and set aside
   2 cups (about 8 oz.) walnuts
Cut (*page 12*) into small pieces and set aside enough dates to yield
   1 cup (about 7 oz.) date pieces
Drain, slice and set aside on absorbent paper
   1 cup (about 8 oz.) maraschino cherries
(A few pats with the paper will absorb the excess moisture.)

Sift together and set aside
   1½ cups sifted flour
   1 teaspoon baking powder
   ½ teaspoon salt
Beat until thick and piled softly
   3 eggs
Add gradually, beating well after each addition
   ¾ cup sugar

Saint Nicholas Cake

Thoroughly blend in fruits, nuts and
   1 pkg. (6 oz.) semi-sweet chocolate pieces
Mixing only until blended after each addition, add dry ingredients in thirds to egg-fruit mixture. Finally mix only until blended.

Place a shallow pan containing 2 cups water on bottom rack of oven during baking period.

Turn batter into pan, spreading to edges.

Bake at 300°F 1 hr. 45 min., or until cake tests done (*page 340*).

Cool cake on cooling rack 10 min. before removing from pan. Run spatula gently around sides of pan. Cover with cooling rack. Invert. Turn right-side up immediately after peeling off parchment paper.

Using a pastry brush, paint cake with brandy or apple cider. Wrap tightly in waxed paper, aluminum foil or moisture-vapor-proof material. Store in cool place to age for 10 days before serving. *About 9x5-in. fruitcake*

Old-Fashioned Fruitcake

MARGIE C. EDIE, BELLMORE, N. Y.

Prepare (*page 340*) two 9½x5¼x2¾-in. loaf pans.

Coarsely chop and combine

  ½ lb. figs (about 1⅓ cups, chopped)
  ½ lb. pitted dates (about 1⅓ cups, chopped)
  ½ lb. (about 2¼ cups) walnuts
  ½ lb. (about 2 cups) pecans
  ½ lb. (about 1½ cups) blanched almonds (page 11)
  ½ lb. (about 1½ cups) Brazil nuts
  ¼ lb. candied citron (about ⅔ cup, chopped)
  ¼ lb. candied cherries (about ⅔ cup, chopped)
  ¼ lb. candied pineapple (about ⅔ cup, chopped)
  1 oz. candied orange peel (about 2½ tablespoons, chopped)
  1 oz. candied lemon peel (about 2½ tablespoons, chopped)

Add and set aside

  ½ lb. (about 1½ cups) seedless raisins
  5 oz. (about 1 cup) currants
  ½ cup (about 2 oz.) moist shredded coconut, cut

Sift together and set aside

  1½ cups sifted flour
  1½ teaspoons cocoa
  1 teaspoon baking powder
  ¼ teaspoon nutmeg
  ¼ teaspoon cinnamon
  ¼ teaspoon mace
  ¼ teaspoon salt

Cream until butter is softened

  ½ cup butter

Add in thirds, beating well after each addition

  3 eggs, well beaten

Blend in

  ½ cup jelly or preserves

Measure

  ¼ cup dry wine or grape juice

Beating only until smooth after each addition, alternately add dry ingredients in fourths, liquid in thirds, to creamed mixture. Finally beat only until smooth (do not overbeat). Pour batter over fruit and nuts and mix thoroughly.

Place a shallow pan containing 2 cups water on bottom rack of oven during baking time.

Turn batter into pans, spreading to edges.

Bake at 300°F 1½ hrs., or until cake tests done (*page 340*) with cake tester.

Cool completely, remove from pans and store (*page 338*). Once or twice a week, using a pastry brush, paint cake with rum and store again.

About 5½ lbs. fruitcake

▲ Light Fruitcake

Prepare (*page 340*) two 8½x4½x2½-in. loaf pans.

Bring to boiling

  2 cups water

Add, and again bring to boiling

  ½ lb. (about 1½ cups) golden raisins
  3 oz. chopped dried apricots (about ½ cup)

Pour off water and drain fruit on absorbent paper. Set aside.

Sliver and set aside

  2 cups (about 11 oz.) blanched, toasted almonds (page 11)

Light Fruitcake

Place in a large bowl
½ cup sifted flour
Chop
    9 oz. candied pineapple (about 1½ cups, chopped)

    6 oz. candied red cherries (about 1 cup, chopped)

    6 oz. candied green cherries (about 1 cup, chopped)

    3 oz. candied citron (about ½ cup, chopped)

    3 oz. candied orange peel (about ½ cup, chopped)

    3 oz. candied lemon peel (about ½ cup, chopped)

    3 oz. pitted dates (about ½ cup, chopped)

    3 oz. dried figs (about ½ cup, chopped)

Combine chopped fruits with flour.

Add drained raisins, apricots, almonds and
    2 cups (8 oz.) finely chopped, moist shredded coconut
Set aside.

Sift together and set aside
    1½ cups sifted flour
    1½ teaspoons baking powder
    1 teaspoon salt
Cream until butter is softened
    1 cup butter
    1 teaspoon lemon juice
Add gradually, creaming until fluffy after each addition
    1 cup sugar
Add in thirds, beating well after each addition
    5 eggs, well beaten
Beat vigorously 150 strokes.

Measure
    ½ cup orange juice
Beating only until smooth after each addition, alternately add dry ingredients in fourths, liquid in thirds, to creamed mixture. Finally beat only until smooth (do not overbeat). Pour batter over fruit and mix thoroughly.

Place a shallow pan containing 2 cups water on bottom rack of oven during baking time.

Turn batter into pans, spreading to edges.

Bake at 275°F 2 to 2½ hrs., or until cake tests done (*page 340*) with cake tester.

Cool completely, remove from pans and store (*page 338*).

Once or twice a week, using a pastry brush, paint cake with rum and store again. Before serving, brush glaze lightly over cakes.

For Glaze—Combine in a saucepan
    ¼ cup white corn sirup
    2 tablespoons water
    1 tablespoon orange juice
Bring to boiling and boil for 1 min.

After brushing glaze over cake, sprinkle with
    Finely ground, toasted almonds
Decorate with candied cherries and candied citron; brush these with glaze. When glaze is dry, slice cake and serve.

About 6 lbs. fruitcake

△ Bite-Size Fruitcakes 63

Follow and prepare one-half △ Recipe. Brush about 6 doz. 1¼-in. paper soufflé cups with cooking (salad) oil or melted shortening. Fill with about 1 tablespoon of batter. Decorate with bits of **red** or **green candied cherries.**

Arrange, with space between cups, on baking sheet on which double thickness of wet paper toweling has been placed.

Bake at 300°F about 30 min., or until cakes test done. Glaze before serving.

△ Miniature Fruitcakes 64

Follow △ Recipe. Brush about 4 doz. 2½-in. paper baking cups with cooking (salad) oil or melted shortening. Put cups in muffin-pan wells. Fill two-thirds full of batter. Decorate tops of cakes with strips of candied cherries, a whole candied cherry, or whole blanched almonds. Set the pan of water in oven.

Bake at 300°F about 45 min., or until cakes test done. Glaze before serving.

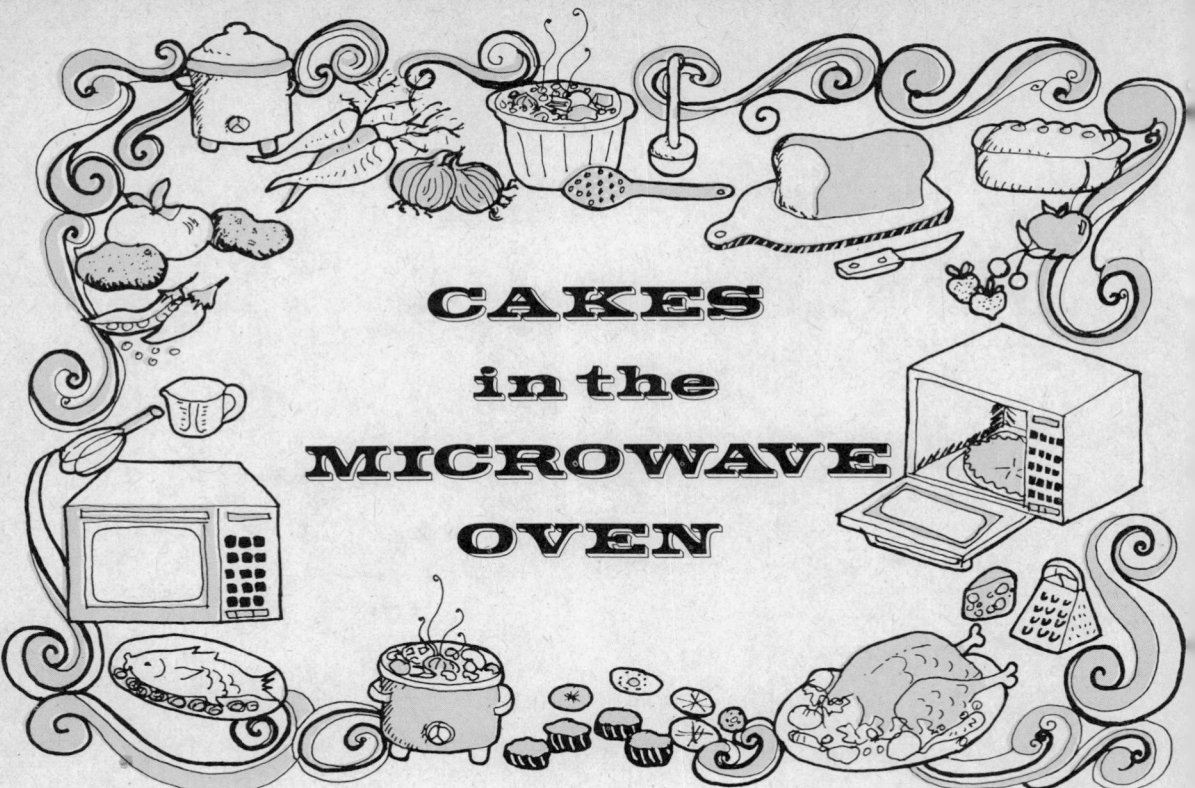

CAKES in the MICROWAVE OVEN

There's an old song that goes something like, "If I knew you were coming, I'd have baked a cake . . ." With the microwave oven, you don't need the excuse of a special occasion or advance notice of friends dropping in to bake a cake. A cake can be ready practically by the time guests' coats are off and the coffee has perked. Included are a recipe for **Maple Sirup Cake** which cooks in 6 minutes and **Pumpkin Cupcakes** which cook in 4 minutes. Most of the cakes can be baked in 10 to 15 minutes. The kitchen and you stay cool and neat, a delicious frosting can be made in the microwave oven while the cake is cooling and you have a dessert or company treat which would usually take hours of preparation and cooking time.

Especially good are the chocolate cakes. All have a rich, tempting flavor and appearance. **Grandmother's Sweet Chocolate Cake** is our favorite. Quick and easy to prepare are the **Quick Cocoa Cake** and the **Blender Chocolate Cake.**

The **Pineapple Upside-Down Cake** is a delightful-tasting cake which cooks in 16 minutes

and needs no additional icing. The **Kiss-and-Tell Cake** is another excellent butter-type cake.

Fruitcakes work particularly well in the microwave oven. Outstanding among these are the **Light Fruitcake** and **Old-Fashioned Fruitcake.**

Angel food cakes and certain types of sponge and chiffon cakes which depend on egg whites for appearance and texture do not work as well. We have eliminated most of these recipes.

Like breads, cakes and cupcakes cooked in the microwave oven do not brown. Taste is good. Texture, if anything, is even lighter than in conventional cooking because cakes rise more quickly. We don't feel the lack of color is a detriment in cakes as it is with certain kinds of breads because cakes are generally iced or decorated (see **Frostings in the Microwave Oven**). Fruitcakes and other types of cakes which do not require icing have ingredients which lend their own color to the cake.

We have arranged the microwave oven recipes in an easy-to-follow chart, which includes

Special Instructions when necessary. However, do read the general hints which follow in order to insure that your microwave cake baking is successful.

RECIPES AND INGREDIENTS—The batters for most of the recipes included in the chart should be prepared exactly as in the master recipe. However, in some recipes, we recommend the amount of baking powder or baking soda be decreased. This promotes more even rising. For recipes which require this adjustment, the exact amounts are noted in the chart under **Special Instructions.**

A NOTE ON PANS—With microwave oven cooking still in relative infancy, it is sometimes difficult to find cooking pans in materials appropriate for the microwave which also duplicate standard sizes of metal pans. In some cases, we substitute a different-size pan for those specified in the master recipe. The pans we used are all microwave-safe glass readily available from both department and hardware stores.

Cooking times given in the chart are for the size pans we describe following. Because the size of a pan does make a difference in cooking time, you may have to make adjustments in timing if you use another size.

Cake Pan—Use an 8-in. round pan. Also called for occasionally is an 8-in. square.

Loaf Pan—The glass loaf pan measures 9x5x3-in. (2-qt.).

Baking Sheet or Baking Dish—Use a baking dish measuring 11¾x7½x1¾-in., the largest size to conveniently fit in a 15-in. microwave oven.

Cupcake Holders—Use pleated paper cupcake or muffin papers placed inside a glass custard cup. A styrofoam or paper cup cut down to the level of the muffin paper is perfectly acceptable. For the **Bite-Size Fruitcakes**, use paper "souffle" cups, contained in a small paper cup. The **Pineapple Gingerbread** may be baked directly in individual glass custard cups.

Preparing Pans—*Do not grease* pans and containers unless specified otherwise under **Special Instructions.** Instead, line the bottom of each pan with ungreased waxed paper.

Pans should be about one-half to two-thirds full. Cakes have a tendency to rise higher in the microwave oven than in the conventional oven,

so beware of overfilling. Before cooking tap the bottom of the pan sharply to release air bubbles which can cause an uneven surface on the cake. Level the batter with a spatula to help keep the surface even.

MICROWAVE BAKING PROCEDURES—Layer cakes should be cooked one layer at a time. The number of cupcakes to be cooked in one batch is indicated with each recipe. If you cook more or less than this number, cooking times must be adjusted.

Cakes should be centered in the oven. Cupcakes should be placed on a paper plate or piece of cardboard or waxed paper to make rotating more convenient. For more even cooking, arrange the cupcakes in a hollow circle.

MICROWAVE COOKING SEQUENCE—Cakes and cupcakes are cooked in two phases—first on SLOWCOOK, then on COOK. The SLOWCOOK cycle permits a slow, gentle rising; the COOK cycle sets and cooks the batter.

Rotating during cooking is crucial to even cooking of cakes and cupcakes. Cakes should be rotated 180 degrees at least once during the SLOWCOOK cycle, again during the COOK cycle. Cupcakes should be rotated even more frequently—90 degrees each rotation. We give rotation times on each cupcake recipe and on some cake recipes where more frequent rotation promotes more even rising.

TEST FOR DONENESS—Cakes and cupcakes can be checked throughout both cycles as frequently as you think necessary, with no need to worry about falling. In a conventional oven, cakes fall when the oven door is opened because of the change in air pressure. Because there is no heat in a microwave oven, there is no difference in air pressure between the outside and the inside of the oven and the cakes do not fall.

Because of the usual variation among brands of ovens and wattage, we suggest you begin checking the cakes for doneness a few minutes before the end of our recommended cooking time.

When Are Cakes and Cupcakes Done—A cake tester is not an accurate indicator of whether a cake cooked in the microwave oven is done.

Instead, look for the following keys to doneness:

They begin to pull away slightly from the sides of the pan. They will continue cooking and pulling away from the pan after being removed from the oven.

They are springy to the touch on the perimeters of the cake and the batter is not sticky. However, the surface of the cake will still be quite moist. It firms and dries during standing.

Crumbs form on the sides and just beneath the moist top layer.

COOLING AND TURNING OUT CAKES— Cakes will continue to cook after they are removed from the oven, so the usual rules about cooling and turning out cakes are not applicable.

All cakes, with exceptions noted for some recipes in the chart under **Special Instructions**, should be cooled in their pans on a rack until the bottom of the pan is just warm to the touch. Then, run a spatula around the sides, invert and turn out. Peel off the waxed paper and turn right side up to complete cooling. Cooling takes longer with a cake cooked in the microwave oven than for cakes cooked conventionally. Don't let cakes cool completely in the pan, however, or the waxed paper may stick and make turning out difficult.

REMINDERS—For other tips on successful microwave oven cooking and an easy-to-read chart of comparative settings among different brands of microwave ovens, read the introductory chapter, **Home Cooking in the Microwave Oven**, in the beginning of this book.

1 *For Butterscotch Sauce—*In a small casserole, COOK to melt butter or margarine. Add the sugar-flour mixture and COOK, stirring every 30 sec., until sugar melts and mixture is blended (about 5 min.).

Add milk, stirring thoroughly. COOK, stirring every 30 sec., to boil (about 8 min.).

2 *To Melt Chocolate—*In a small casserole, COOK chocolate, stirring every 1 min., until melted (about 1 min. per oz.).

3 *For Burnt Sugar Sirup—*Use a browning skillet. COOK sugar, stirring every 30 sec., until it begins to melt (about 2 min.). Continue to COOK, stirring every 1 min., until foam appears (about 3 min.).

Add boiling water gradually, stirring it in completely. COOK until bubbles are dime-size (about 3 min.).

4 *For Pineapple Sauce—*Use a small casserole. COOK water, tapioca and salt, stirring every 1 min., to boil and thicken (about 4 min.).

5 *To Prepare Prunes—*Use a small covered casserole Cover and COOK soaked prunes until plump (about 3 min.).

6 *To Prepare Fruit—*Use a 2-qt. casserole. Combine fruit, shortening, water and spices and COOK, stirring every 2 min., until boiling and blended (about 10 min.).

MICROWAVE CAKES

RECIPE—The recipe title, as well as the page number on which you will find the master recipe, are given. Before preparing batter, note **Special Instructions** for any adjustments in ingredients.

PAN USED—Read the preceding introductory material for detailed descriptions.

MICROWAVE COOKING SEQUENCE—Cakes and cupcakes are cooked in 2 phases: SLOWCOOK and COOK. There is no time given for those which do not require the COOK phase.

SPECIAL INSTRUCTIONS—Carefully read this column for adjustments in recipes and exceptions in rotation and cooling procedures.

Recipe	Pan Used	Microwave Cooking Sequence Minutes to		Special Instructions
		SLOWCOOK	COOK	
SPONGE-TYPE CAKES				
7 Spiced Sponge Cake *(page 348)*	8-in. square	8:00	2:00	Use 3/8 teaspoon baking powder (instead of ½ teaspoon). Let cool until top is dry (about 10 min.) before inverting.
CHIFFON CAKES				
8 Orange Chiffon Cake *(page 352)*	Loaf	9:00	2:00	Let cool until top is dry (about 10 min.) before inverting.
BUTTER-TYPE CAKES • YELLOW				
9 Pound Cake *(page 354)*	Loaf	10:00	2:00	None.
10 Lemon Cake *(page 355)*	8-in. round	6:00	3:00	None.
11 Banana Layer Cake *(page 355)*	8-in. round	8:00	1:00	None.

	Recipe	Pan Used	Microwave Cooking Sequence Minutes to SLOWCOOK	COOK	Special Instructions
12	**Coconut Cake Supreme** (page 357)	8-in. round	6:00	2:30	None.
13	**Mama's Prize Coconut Cake** (page 357)	8-in. round	6:00	2:00	None.
14	**Golden Honey Cake** (page 358)	8-in. round	6:00	1:00	None.
15	**Banana-Nut Cupcakes** (page 359)	8 cupcake holders	8:00	--	None.
16	**Orange Cupcakes** (page 359)	6 cupcake holders	7:00	--	None.
17	**Buttermilk Cake with Butterscotch Sauce** (page 360)	8-in. square	8:00	3:00	*For Butterscotch Sauce,* see 1 .
18	**Pineapple Upside-Down Cake** (page 361)	8-in. square	12:00	4:00	Lightly grease underside of waxed paper before placing in bottom of pan. To remove from pan, let cool about 10 min., then follow Recipe.
19	**Apricot Upside-Down Cake** (page 361)	8-in. square	12:00	4:00	See Pineapple Upside-Down Cake.

BUTTER-TYPE CAKES • WHITE

	Recipe	Pan Used	Microwave Cooking Sequence Minutes to SLOWCOOK	COOK	Special Instructions
20	**White Cake Squares** (page 362)	8-in. square	8:00	3:00	None.
21	**White Cupcakes** (page 362)	6 cupcake holders	3:00	1:00	None.
22	**Nut Loaf Cake** (page 362)	Loaf	12:00	2:00	None.

#	Cake	Container			Notes
23	Kiss-and-Tell Cake *(page 362)*	Sheet	12:00	4:30	None.
24	Marble Cake *(page 363)*	8-in. square	12:00	2:00	Use 1 teaspoon baking powder (instead of 2). *To melt chocolate*, see 2.
25	Happy Memories Cake *(page 364)*	Sheet	20:00	8:00	To remove, let cool (about 10 min.), then follow Recipe.
26	Upside-Down Cupcakes *(page 364)*	6 cupcake holders	14:00	3:00	None.
27	Poppy Seed Cake *(page 364)*	8-in. round	6:00	2:00	None.
28	Carnival Cake *(page 365)*	8-in. round	6:00	2:00	None.
29	Valentine Cake *(page 366)*	8-in. round	6:00	1:30	None.
30	Shower Cake *(page 367)*	8-in. round	6:00	1:30	None.
31	Meltaway Whipped Cream Cake *(page 367)*	8-in. round	8:00	1:00	None.
32	Bride's Cake *(page 368)*	8-in. round	6:00	1:30	Entire recipe will yield 4 layers. For a 2-layer cake, use ½ recipe.

BUTTER-TYPE CAKES • CHOCOLATE

#	Cake	Container			Notes
33	Blender Chocolate Cake *(page 370)*	8-in. round	6:00	2:00	Use 2 teaspoons baking powder (instead of 1 tablespoon). *To melt chocolate*, see 2.
34	Blender Chocolate Cupcakes *(page 370)*	6 cupcake holders	5:00	1:00	Use 2 teaspoons baking powder (instead of 1 tablespoon). Rotate every 1 min. to insure even cooking.
35	Nougat Cake *(page 370)*	8-in. round	6:00	3:00	None.

	Recipe	Pan Used	Microwave Cooking Sequence Minutes to SLOWCOOK	COOK	Special Instructions
36	Quick Cocoa Cake (page 371)	8-in. square	10:00	3:00	Use ½ teaspoon baking powder (instead of 1 teaspoon). Use ¼ teaspoon baking soda (instead of ½ teaspoon).
37	Grandmother's Sweet Chocolate Cake (page 371)	8-in round	8:00	2:00	Use ¾ teaspoon baking soda (instead of 1 teaspoon). To melt chocolate, see [2].
38	Yeast-Raised Chocolate Cake (page 372)	8-in round	12:00	2:00	To melt chocolate, see [2].
39	Caramel Mocha Cake (page 373)	8-in. round	6:00	4:00	To melt chocolate, see [2].
40	Chocolate Drum Cake (page 374)	8-in. round	6:00	4:00	To melt chocolate, see [2].
41	Chocolate Cake (page 374)	8-in. round	6:00	1:30	Use ¾ teaspoon baking soda (instead of 1 teaspoon).
42	Sour-Cream Chocolate Cake (page 374)	8-in. round	6:00	2:00	To melt chocolate, see [2].
43	Black Walnut Chocolate Cake (page 375)	8-in. round	6:00	2:00	To melt chocolate, see [2].
44	Chocolate Potato Cake (page 375)	8-in. round	8:00	2:00	Use grated raw potatoes.

SPECIAL-FLAVORED CAKES

	Recipe	Pan Used	Microwave Cooking Sequence Minutes to SLOWCOOK	COOK	Special Instructions
45	Maple Sirup Cake (page 376)	8-in. round	4:00	2:00	None.

No.	Cake	Pan			Instructions
46	Burnt Sugar Cake *(page 376)*	8-in. square	8:00	4:00	*For Burnt Sugar Sirup,* see 3 .
47	Cocoa Date-Nut Cake *(page 377)*	8-in. square	13:00	5:00	None.
48	Honey-Brown Gingerbread *(page 378)*	8-in. square	8:00	4:30	Rotate 90 degrees every 2 min., as this cake tends to rise unevenly.
49	Pineapple Gingerbread *(page 379)*	6 individual casseroles	12:00	3:30	You may use large glass custard cups lined on the bottom with ungreased waxed paper. Rotate every 1 min. to insure even cooking. To remove, run a spatula around sides, invert, remove waxed paper and serve upside down. *For Pineapple Sauce,* see 4 .
50	"Mo"-Lasses Cupcakes *(page 380)*	6 cupcake holders	9:00	1:30	Rotate every 1 min. to insure even cooking.
51	Pumpkin Cupcakes *(page 380)*	6 cupcake holders	3:00	1:00	Rotate every 1 min. to insure even cooking.

CAKES WITH FRUIT

No.	Cake	Pan			Instructions
52	Applesauce Cake *(page 382)*	8-in. square	12:00	4:00	Use the conventional oven to broil the brown sugar frosting.
53	Apple-Pecan Cupcakes *(page 382)*	6 cupcake holders	5:00	1:00	Rotate every 1 min. to insure even cooking. *To melt chocolate,* see 2 .
54	Apple Spice Cake *(page 383)*	Loaf	14:00	5:00	None.
55	Fresh Apple Cake *(page 383)*	8-in. square	12:00	2:00	None.
56	Prunella Cake *(page 386)*	8-in. square	13:00	4:00	*To Prepare Prunes,* see 5 .

FRUITCAKES

Recipe	Pan Used	Microwave Cooking Sequence Minutes to SLOWCOOK	COOK	Special Instructions
57 **Fruitcake De Luxe** (page 386)	Loaf	19:00	--	*To Prepare Fruit*, see 6.
58 **Date and Fig Fruitcake** (page 387)	Loaf	20:00	--	*To Prepare Fruit*, see 6.
59 **Christmas Fruitcake** (page 388)	8-in. round	16:00	--	*To Prepare Fruit*, see 6.
60 **Saint Nicholas Cake** (page 389)	Loaf	16:00	6:00	Lightly grease underside of parchment with shortening before placing in pan. Rotate every 4 min. to insure even cooking.
61 **Old-Fashioned Fruitcake** (page 390)	Loaf	16:00	--	Rotate every 4 min. to insure even cooking.
62 **Light Fruitcake** (page 390)	Loaf	25:00	--	*To Prepare Fruit*, see 6. Rotate every 5 min. to insure even cooking.
63 **Bite-Size Fruitcakes** (page 391)	12 small cupcake holders	8:00	--	Brush very lightly with oil and wipe bottom of cups to be sure there is no puddle of oil. Fill three-quarters full. Rotate every 2 min. to insure even cooking.
64 **Miniature Fruitcakes** (page 391)	6 cupcake holders	8:00	--	Brush very lightly with oil and wipe bottom of cups to be sure there is no puddle of oil. Fill three-quarters full. Rotate every 2 min. to insure even cooking.

CAKES in the SLOW COOKER

Many types of cakes—sponge, chiffon, "butter," and special-flavored cakes as well as fruitcakes—can be baked successfully in the slow cooker.

We highly recommend all the recipes included here. The fruitcakes are the best—moist and with a full rich flavor. Also particularly good are the sponge cakes, including **Golden Sponge Cake, Cocoa Sponge Cake** and **Genoise Cake.**

The **Orange Chiffon Cake** is delicious and all of the chocolate cakes rich, moist and flavorful, with **Grandmother's Sweet Chocolate Cake** our favorite. The combination of chocolate and apples in the **Apple Spice Cake** is outstanding. It is a cake which could have been invented solely for baking in the slow cooker.

Cakes cooked in the slow cooker are more dense in texture and smaller in size than those cooked in the conventional oven. They do brown on top and can be iced or decorated to your taste. Flavor is often even richer than in conventional cooking.

Since there is little variation from the master recipe in preparing the batters for these cakes, we have arranged the recipes in convenient chart form with a column for **Special Instructions** as necessary. However, do read the general hints which follow in order to assure successful baking in the slow cooker.

RECIPES AND INGREDIENTS—Follow the master recipe for preparing the batter. However, quantities may need to be adjusted, since some of the recipes will produce more than the necessary batter. The standard baking pan or 2-lb. coffee can is usually used instead of a baking tin. Where it is possible, we have suggested cutting the recipe by one-half or one-third to yield about 1-qt. of batter, which is approximately the amount needed to half-fill the tin. Sometimes, it is just not possible to reduce the recipe sensibly. In such cases, the slow cooker baking chart indicates the amount of extra batter; you may have as much as 2 cups of batter left over. Use it to make cupcakes quickly in the oven.

If you use a different-size tin, adjust the amount of batter to fill the tin by no more than one-half.

PREPARATION FOR BAKING—Use the 2-qt. baking tin designed for the slow cooker or a 2-lb. coffee can.

For sponge-type cakes, line the bottom of the baking container with ungreased waxed paper. For all other cakes, grease only the underside of the waxed paper.

Fill Pans—Fill the baking tin only about half-full of batter so there will be planty of room for the cake to rise.

Do not cover the baking tin.

To Absorb Excess Moisture—A great deal of steam forms when a cake is baked in the slow cooker. For successful results, this steam must be prevented from condensing and dripping back onto the cake.

Line the lid of the slow cooker with crumpled paper towels and hold them in place with rubber bands (see illustration pages 66-67).

Place 2 or 3 layers of paper towelling across the top of the slow cooker (not the baking tin) and put the top on. Leave the top slightly ajar to allow moisture to escape.

SLOW COOKER BAKING TIMES — All cakes are baked on the HIGH setting. Cooking time is more critical than other dishes demand in the slow cooker. There is really not much more than 15 minutes variation from our suggested time, so don't abandon the cake for a lengthy appointment.

Cooking times may vary if different-size baking tins are used or the amount of batter is not approximately 1 quart.

TEST FOR DONENESS—Don't test the cake until it is nearly done—definitely not more than one-half hour before the end of the suggested cooking times. Otherwise, the cakes will fall.

The cake is done when it is brown on top, begins to pull away from the sides and your cake tester, inserted in the center, comes out clean.

Cooling and Turning Out Cakes—Turn out the cake as directed in the master recipe, cooling butter-type cakes only about 10 minutes before removing from the tin, sponge-type cakes completely, and so forth.

REMINDERS—Other useful tips and an easy-to-read chart comparing settings among different brands of slow cookers are included in the introductory chapter, **Home Cooking in the Slow Cooker**, in the beginning of this book.

SLOW COOKER CAKES

Read the material in the beginning of this section, **Cakes in the Slow Cooker**, before proceeding with any of these recipes.

RECIPE—For ready reference, the name of each recipe is accompanied by the page number on which you will find the master recipe. Before preparing batter, note any **Special Instructions** to learn if reducing the recipe is necessary.

COOKING TIME—The number of hours to cook approximately 1 qt. of batter are given. Note that all recipes are cooked on the HIGH setting.

SPECIAL INSTRUCTIONS—Check this column for suggestions for reducing a recipe when necessary. You may also be directed to grease the cooking tin for a specific cake which would not normally require this step. For details, read the preceding introductory material.

Recipe	Cooking Time (HIGH setting)	Special Instructions

SPONGE-TYPE CAKES

1 Sponge Cake Ring *(page 343)*	2½ hrs.	None.
2 Golden Sponge Cake *(page 347)*	2¼ hrs.	Use one-half recipe (see **Measurements and Equivalents**).
3 Cocoa Sponge Cake *(page 347)*	2 hrs.	None.
4 True Sponge Cake *(page 347)*	2¼ hrs.	None.
5 Spiced Sponge Cake *(page 348)*	2½ hrs.	Use one-half recipe (see **Measurements and Equivalents**); use 3 tablespoons egg whites.
6 Genoise Cake *(page 349)*	2 hrs.	Butter the bottom of the baking tin before lining with waxed paper.

CHIFFON CAKES

7 Banana-Pecan Chiffon Cake *(page 350)*	2 hrs.	Use one-half recipe (see **Measurements and Equivalents**); use 3 tablespoons plus 1 teaspoon egg yolks.
8 Lemon Chiffon Cake *(page 350)*	2 hrs.	Use two-thirds recipe (see **Measurements and Equivalents**).
9 Orange Chiffon Cake *(page 352)*	2 hrs.	None.
10 Marble Chiffon Cake *(page 352)*	2½ hrs.	Use one-half recipe (see **Measurements and Equivalents**); use 3 tablespoons and 1 teaspoon egg yolks.
11 Rum Chiffon Cake *(page 353)*	2½ hrs.	Use one-half recipe (see **Measurements and Equivalents**); use 3 tablespoons plus 1 teaspoon egg yolks.

BUTTER-TYPE CAKES • YELLOW

12 Pound Cake *(page 354)*	2¼ hrs.	None.

	Recipe	Cooking Time (HIGH setting)	Special Instructions
13	**Coconut Cake Supreme** (page 357)	3 hrs.	Use one-half recipe (see **Measurements and Equivalents**).
14	**Mama's Prize Coconut Cake** (page 357)	2 hrs.	None.
15	**Golden Honey Cake** (page 358)	3 hrs.	None.
16	**Peanut Butter Cake** (page 360)	2½ hrs.	None.

BUTTER-TYPE CAKES • WHITE

	Recipe	Cooking Time (HIGH setting)	Special Instructions
17	**White Cake Squares** (page 362)	2¼ hrs.	None.
18	**Kiss-and-Tell Cake** (page 362)	2½ hrs.	Entire recipe yields 1 qt. plus about 2 cups batter.
19	**Marble Cake** (page 363)	2 hrs.	None.
20	**Happy Memories Cake** (page 364)	2½ hrs.	None.
21	**Poppy Seed Cake** (page 364)	2½ hrs.	None.
22	**Carnival Cake** (page 365)	2¼ hrs.	None.
23	**Valentine Cake** (page 366)	3¼ hrs.	Entire recipe yields 1 qt. plus about 2½ cups batter.
24	**Bride's Cake** (page 368)	2½ hrs.	Use one-half recipe (see **Measurements and Equivalents**).

BUTTER-TYPE CAKES • CHOCOLATE

	Recipe	Cooking Time (HIGH setting)	Special Instructions
25	**Blender Chocolate Cake** (page 370)	2¼ hrs.	None.
26	**Nougat Cake** (page 370)	3 hrs.	Entire recipe yields about 1 qt. plus 1 cup batter.
27	**Quick Cocoa Cake** (page 371)	3 hrs.	None.
28	**Grandmother's Sweet Chocolate Cake** (page 371)	3 hrs.	None.
29	**Yeast-Raised Chocolate Cake** (page 372)	2½ hrs.	Fill a little less than halfway. Entire recipe yields 1 qt. plus about 2 cups batter.

Recipe	Cooking Time (HIGH setting)	Special Instructions
30 **Chocolate Drum Cake** (page 374)	2½ hrs.	Entire recipe yields 1 qt. plus about 2 cups batter.
31 **Chocolate Potato Cake** (page 375)	2¾ hrs.	Entire recipe yields 1 qt. plus about 2 cups batter.

SPECIAL-FLAVORED CAKES

Recipe	Cooking Time (HIGH setting)	Special Instructions
32 **Maple Sirup Cake** (page 376)	2½ hrs.	None.
33 **Burnt Sugar Cake** (page 376)	2¼ hrs.	None.
34 **Cocoa Date-Nut Cake** (page 377)	2½ hrs.	None.
35 **Honey-Brown Gingerbread** (page 378)	3 hrs.	None.
36 **Strawberry-Flavored Cake** (page 381)	2½ hrs.	Use two-thirds recipe (see **Measurements and Equivalents**); use 4 egg whites less 1 tablespoon and 1 teaspoon.

CAKES WITH FRUIT

Recipe	Cooking Time (HIGH setting)	Special Instructions
37 **Apple Spice Cake** (page 383)	2½ hrs.	None.
38 **Elegant Loaf Cake** (page 385)	2½ hrs.	None.

FRUITCAKES

Recipe	Cooking Time (HIGH setting)	Special Instructions
39 **Fruitcake De Luxe** (page 386)	5 hrs.	For one cake, halve recipe.
40 **Date and Fig Fruitcake** (page 387)	4½ hrs.	For one cake, halve recipe.
41 **Ambrosia White Fruitcake** (page 388)	6 hrs.	None.
42 **Christmas Fruitcake** (page 388)	4¼ hrs.	None.
43 **Old-Fashioned Fruitcake** (page 390)	3 hrs.	None.
44 **Light Fruitcake** (page 390)	4½ hrs.	None.

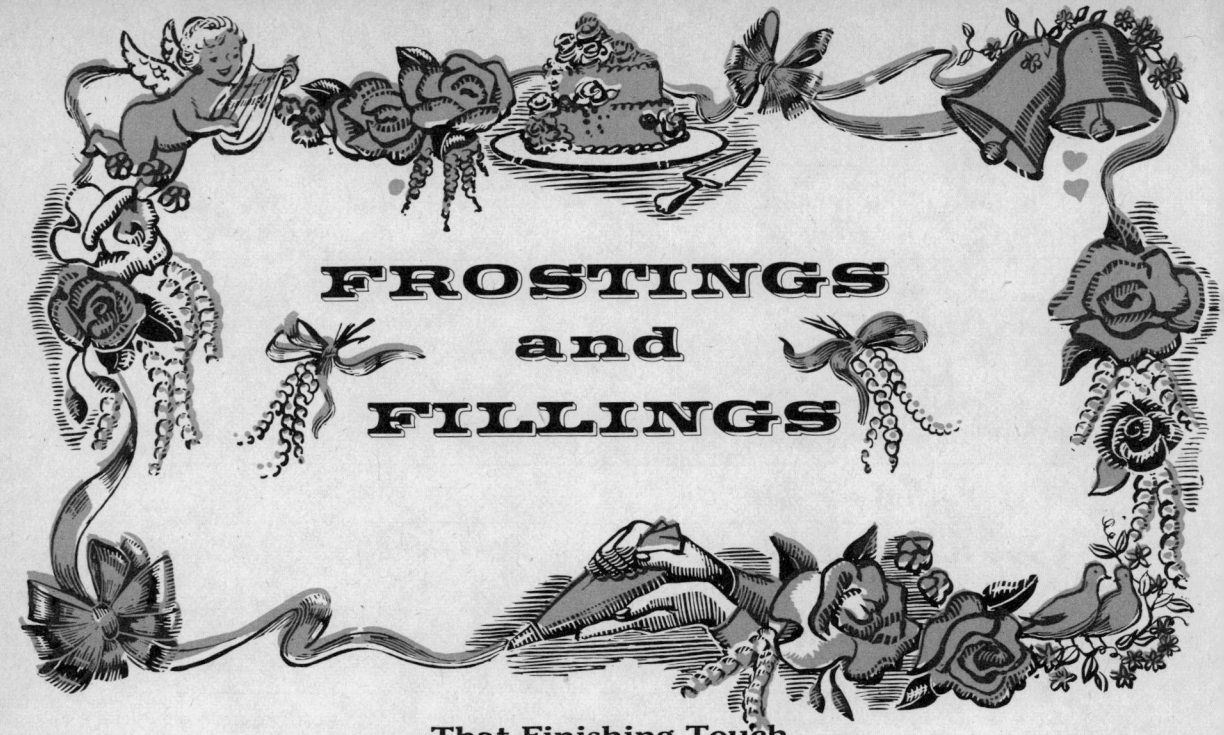

FROSTINGS and FILLINGS

That Finishing Touch

A cake without frosting may be laden with virtues and be a fine creation. Yet somehow, cake seems to come into its glory only when it is decked in a sculptured or swirled coat of sweetness. Frostings may be plain or fancy, chocolate brown or pale as dawn, delicately laced with essence of fruits or flecked with fragments of nuts or candy. They may be prepared in many ways, but they are always designed for delight.

SUGAR, in some form, is the main ingredient in cooked and uncooked frostings. As used in these recipes, *sugar* refers to granulated beet or cane sugar.

Confectioners' or powdered sugar is granulated sugar crushed and screened to a desired fineness. It usually contains a small amount of cornstarch to prevent caking. Generally, confectioners' sugar is finer than powdered sugar although there are no set standard terms in the sugar industry. Uncooked frostings prepared with the finer confectioners' sugar remain softer longer than those prepared with a coarser powdered sugar. The reason—the smaller the particle size the greater the total surface area, thus the greater amount of moisture held.

Brown sugar is a soft sugar that contains three to four per cent moisture. It ranges in color from yellow to dark brown. The intensity of molasses flavor increases as the color deepens. Brown sugar adds color and flavor as well as sweetening to the finished product.

Maple sugar is the solid product that is left after evaporation of maple sap or maple sirup.

Corn sirup, made from cornstarch, is commonly marketed in two forms, white and dark. Dark corn sirup is used in products where the darker color and distinctive flavor are desirable.

Molasses is the sirup remaining when most of the sugar has crystallized from cane sirup.

Maple sirup is made from the sap of the sugar maple tree.

Honey is the nectar of plants gathered, modified and stored in the comb by honey bees. Extracted or strained honey is used in cooking.

COOKED FROSTINGS—Seven-minute, white mountain and fudge frostings are the basic cooked frostings. Special flavorings and other ingredients are added to create any number of frostings.

These frostings are easy to make successfully if certain techniques and rules are followed.

All the sugar crystals must be dissolved before cooking starts to prevent unwanted graininess in the frosting. The steam formed during the first 5 minutes of cooking period, while the saucepan is covered and the mixture boiling, helps to dissolve any crystals that may have formed on the sides of pan. Any crystals that form during cooking may be washed down from sides of pan with a pastry brush dipped in water.

Separate egg whites very carefully from egg yolks. Any trace of egg yolk in the whites will cut down the volume of beaten egg whites and the quality of the frosting. Beat egg whites when they are at room temperature for the greatest volume.

Use a candy thermometer for accurate temperature readings. The cold water tests may be used if a thermometer is not available.

The saucepan used for cooking a sirup or frosting should be large enough to allow contents to boil freely without running over. If a cover is needed, it should be tight-fitting.

The double boiler should be large enough for the amount of frosting to be beaten.

Use clean spoons for each process-stirring, testing and beating. Otherwise undissolved sugar crystals may get into the finished frosting and cause it to become grainy.

When the humidity is high, cook frostings 2 to 4 degrees higher so frosting will hold its shape.

Seven-Minute Frosting—All the ingredients (except flavoring extracts) are combined in the top of a double boiler. As soon as the double-boiler top is set over simmering water the mixture should immediately be beaten. Beating should continue until the frosting holds stiff peaks. Move a rotary beater throughout the mixture while beating for thorough blending. Extract is blended in last.

White Mountain Frosting—A hot sugar sirup is cooked to a given temperature and then poured in a steady fine stream into stiffly beaten egg whites while beating constantly. If using a hand rotary beater, turn it over on its side and beat mixture with one hand while pouring sirup with the other. If the frosting is slow to thicken, let it stand for several minutes; if too firm, blend in hot water, a few drops at a time, until it is of spreading consistency.

Fudge Frosting—The frosting is cooked to a given temperature and beaten, when the mixture has cooled sufficiently (bottom of the pan should feel just comfortably warm), until it becomes creamy and begins to lose its gloss. If it hardens too quickly, beat in about one tablespoon of hot milk or water. It is important to use *clean* spoons each time the frosting is stirred, beaten or tested; this helps to avoid graininess.

UNCOOKED FROSTINGS—Often the uncooked confectioners' sugar frosting is called butter frosting. For a smooth frosting, sift confectioners' sugar before using and add in small amounts to the creamed mixture, beating well after each addition. From a few basic frostings, many variations result with the addition of flavorings, nuts and fruits.

TO FILL AND FROST—Cool cake completely before frosting. Brush loose crumbs off cake. Cover cardboard, cut ½ inch larger than cake, with aluminum foil. Arrange cake or bottom cake layer on covered cardboard. For ease and convenience, put cake on a stand so cake can be turned while frosting. Use a flexible spatula to frost cake.

Tubed, Loaf, Sheet and Square Cake—Place cake on cake plate. Frost sides first, working rapidly. See that frosting touches plate, covering cardboard all around bottom, leaving no gaps. Pile remaining frosting on top of cake and spread lightly.

Layer Cake—Place cake layer, bottom side up, on cake plate. Spread filling or frosting over top of layer. Cover with the second layer, bottom side down, fitting it so that cake is even. (Repeat procedure if more layers are used with top layer, bottom side down.) If necessary, hold layers in position with wooden picks or metal skewers; remove when filling is set. Frost sides of cake first, working rapidly. See that frosting touches plate all around bottom, leaving no gaps. Pile remaining frosting on top of cake and spread lightly.

Decorating—See *page 400* for decorating helps.

WHEN YOU COOK SIRUPS—A candy thermometer is an accurate guide to correct stage of cooking. Hang thermometer on pan so bulb does not touch side or bottom of pan.

Sirup Stages and Temperatures

Thread (230°F to 234°F)—Spins 2-in. thread when allowed to drop from fork or spoon.

Soft Ball (234°F to 240°F)—Forms a soft ball in very cold water; flattens when taken from water.

Firm Ball (244°F to 248°F)—Forms a firm ball in very cold water; does not flatten in fingers.

Hard Ball (250°F to 266°F)—Forms a ball which is pliable but holds its shape in very cold water.

Soft Crack (270°F to 290°F)—Forms threads which are hard but not brittle in very cold water.

Hard Crack (300°F to 310°F)—Forms threads which are hard and brittle in very cold water.

*Lemon Butter Frosting and
"Mo"-Lasses Cupcakes (page 380)*

▲ Basic Butter Frosting

(See photo on page 354)

Cream together until butter is softened
   ¼ cup butter
   1 teaspoon vanilla extract
Add gradually, beating well after each addition
   2 cups sifted confectioners' sugar
Stir in and beat to spreading consistency
   1 tablespoon milk or cream
   *Enough to frost sides and tops of two
   8-in. cake layers or 24 cupcakes*

⚠ Lemon Butter Frosting

Follow ▲ Recipe. Substitute **lemon juice**
for milk. If desired, add a few drops of **yellow
food coloring.**

⚠ Mocha Butter Frosting

Follow ▲ Recipe. Add and beat in 1 teaspoon **concentrated soluble coffee** with the
confectioners' sugar.

⚠ Chocolate Butter Frosting

Follow ▲ Recipe. Melt (*p.12*)  2 sq. (2 oz.)
chocolate. Cool; stir in with milk or cream.

Butter Cream Frosting

(See photo on page 356)

Cream together until softened
   ½ cup butter or margarine
   ½ teaspoon almond extract
Add gradually, beating well after each addition
   5 cups sifted confectioners' sugar
Mix in (enough for spreading consistency)
   4 to 5 tablespoons milk or cream
Tint with **green food coloring if desired.**
   *Enough to generously frost sides and
   tops of three 9-in. round cake layers*

▲ White Velvet Frosting

Cream together until softened
   ¼ cup butter or margarine
   1½ teaspoons vanilla extract
   ⅛ teaspoon salt
Add gradually, beating until smooth after each
addition
   3 cups sifted confectioners' sugar
Blend in
   1 egg yolk
Add slowly to blended mixture
   3 tablespoons milk or cream
Beat until frosting is of spreading consistency.
   *Enough to frost sides and tops of
   two 8- or 9-in. round cake layers*

△ Brown Velvet Frosting

Follow ▲ Recipe. Melt (*p. 12*) and cool 2
sq. (2 oz.) **chocolate;** mix in after addition of
egg yolk.

Bittersweet Velvet Frosting 2

(See photo on page 375)

Melt *(page 12)* together and stir until smooth
- **4 sq. (4 oz.) chocolate**
- **3 tablespoons butter or margarine**

Remove from heat and add, beating well
- **2¼ cups sifted confectioners' sugar**
- **½ cup rich milk or cream**
- **1 teaspoon vanilla extract**

*Enough to frost sides and tops
of two 8-in. round cake layers*

Burnt Sugar Frosting

(See photo on page 377)

Cream together until softened
- **¼ cup butter or margarine**
- **1 teaspoon vanilla extract**

Blend in and beat until thoroughly blended
- **2 cups sifted confectioners' sugar**
- **5 tablespoons Burnt Sugar Sirup
  (page 376)**
- **1½ tablespoons cream**
- **Few grains salt**

*Enough to frost sides and top of
one 9-in. square cake layer*

▲ Cream Cheese-Cocoa Frosting

Blend together
- **3 oz. (1 pkg.) cream cheese, softened**
- **½ teaspoon vanilla extract**

Sift together and add gradually
- **1 cup confectioners' sugar**
- **3 tablespoons cocoa**

Beat well after each addition.

Mix in (enough for spreading consistency)
- **Milk or cream**

*Enough to frost one 8- or
9-in. round cake layer*

△ Cream Cheese-Chocolate Frosting

Follow ▲ Recipe. Melt *(p. 12)* and cool 1
sq. (1 oz.) **chocolate**; mix in after sugar.

Cream Cheese-Lemon Frosting

Blend together
- **3 oz. (1 pkg.) cream cheese, softened**
- **2 teaspoons lemon juice**
- **½ teaspoon grated lemon peel (page 11)**

Add gradually, beating well after each addition
- **2½ cups sifted confectioners' sugar**

If frosting is too stiff to spread, add
- **Several drops milk or cream**

*Enough to frost sides and top of
one 8-in. square cake*

Caramel Mocha Frosting

MRS. ELSTON CHITTENDEN
SPRINGFIELD, MO.

Sift together and set aside
- **3½ cups sifted confectioners' sugar**
- **2 teaspoons cocoa**

Cream together until softened
- **½ cup butter or margarine**
- **1 tablespoon vanilla extract**

Add dry ingredients gradually, beating until
smooth after each addition.

Blend in
- **1 egg yolk**

Add slowly to blended mixture
- **3 tablespoons double-strength coffee
  beverage (page 13)**

Beat until frosting is of spreading consistency.

*Enough to frost sides and tops of
three 9-in. round cake layers*

Peanut Mocha Frosting
LONACE E. GEARHART, SAN DIEGO, CALIF.

Blend thoroughly
  1 tablespoon peanut butter
  ½ teaspoon vanilla extract
Beat in until thoroughly blended
  3 cups sifted confectioners' sugar
  ¼ cup double-strength coffee beverage
  (*page 13*)
> *Enough to frost sides and tops of
> two 8-in. round cake layers or
> one 9-in. square cake layer*

▲ Mocha Cocoa Frosting
(*See photo on page 371*)

Sift together
  3 cups confectioners' sugar
  ½ cup cocoa
Make a well in center.

Add and beat until smooth
  ½ cup butter or margarine, softened
  3 tablespoons double-strength coffee
  beverage (*page 13*)
Add and beat well
  2 egg yolks or 1 whole egg
> *Enough to frost sides and tops
> of two 9-in. cake layers*

⚠ Cocoa Cream Frosting

Follow ▲ Recipe. Substitute for coffee, ¼ cup **cream** or top **milk**.

⚠ Toasted Almond Chip Frosting

Follow ▲ Recipe. Sprinkle 1 cup (about 5½ oz.) sliced, toasted **almonds** (*page 12*) on top and sides of frosted cake.

⚠ Sunshine Chocolate Frosting

Follow ▲ Recipe. Substitute for coffee, 1 or 2 tablespoons **lemon juice** or **orange juice** with 1 teaspoon grated **peel** (*page 11*).

Banana Frosting
MRS. JAMES T. MOORE, SAN ANGELO, TEXAS

Peel and force through a sieve or food mill enough banana to yield
  ½ cup sieved banana (1 banana with
  brown-flecked peel)
Stir in
  ½ teaspoon lemon juice
Cream until softened
  ¼ cup butter
Measure
  3½ cups sifted confectioners' sugar
Add sugar and sieved banana alternately to creamed butter, beating thoroughly after each addition. Finally beat until frosting is of spreading consistency.
> *Enough to frost sides and tops of
> two 9-in. round cake layers*

Honey-Do Frosting
CLAUDE E. METZ, MORENCI, MICH.

Blend together thoroughly
   1 tablespoon butter or margarine
   ¼ cup honey
Blend in thoroughly, in order
   2 cups sifted confectioners' sugar
   ½ cup firmly packed brown sugar
   2 tablespoons sweetened condensed milk
Beat until frosting is of spreading consistency.
   Enough to frost sides and top of
   one 8- or 9-in. square cake

Spiced Honey Topping
CLAUDE E. METZ, MORENCI, MICH.

Combine in a bowl
   ½ cup honey
   1 teaspoon thick, sweetened applesauce
   ⅛ teaspoon ginger
   ⅛ teaspoon cloves
   ⅛ teaspoon salt
   1 egg white, unbeaten
Using hand rotary beater or electric mixer, beat until frosting is of spreading consistency (about 5 min.).
   Enough to frost sides and tops of
   two 8-in. round cake layers

Lemon Frosting

MRS. L. A. KING, JACKSONVILLE, N. C.

Cream together until butter is softened
   ½ cup butter
   2 teaspoons grated lemon peel
   (*page 11*)
Add gradually, beating well after each addition
   4 cups sifted confectioners' sugar
   ⅛ teaspoon salt
Blend in
   3 tablespoons lemon juice
Beat until frosting is of spreading consistency.
   Enough to frost sides and top
   of one 10-in. tubed cake

Orange Butter Frosting
MRS. EVERETT BLACK, ORANGE, TEXAS

Cream until softened
   6 tablespoons butter or margarine
Add gradually, beating well after each addition
   3 cups sifted confectioners' sugar
   ⅛ teaspoon salt
Blend in
   3 tablespoons orange juice
Beat until frosting is of spreading consistency.
   Enough to thinly frost sides and tops
   of three 9-in. round cake layers

Toasted Pecan Frosting

Deliciously crunchy and easy to make.

Stir constantly in a skillet over medium heat until pecans are toasted
   1 cup (about 4 oz.) coarsely chopped pecans
   ¼ cup butter or margarine
Remove from heat. Stir in, in order
   ½ cup cream
   1½ teaspoons vanilla extract
   ⅛ teaspoon salt
   3 cups sifted confectioners' sugar
Blend until smooth enough to spread.
   Enough to frost sides and top of
   one 8- or 9-in. square cake

*Raisin-Rum Frosting on
Rum Chiffon Cake (page 353)*

Raisin-Rum Frosting

Cream together until softened
½ cup butter or margarine
1¼ teaspoons rum
Add gradually, beating well after each addition
4 cups sifted confectioners' sugar
Add slowly and beat to spreading consistency
⅓ cup milk
Fold in (*page 12*)
**¼ cup (about 1½ oz.) chopped golden
raisins**
Tint with
1 drop red food coloring
*Enough to frost sides and top
of one 10-in. tubed cake*

Spice Butter Frosting

MRS. FRED UFTRING, DANA, ILL.

Cream together until butter is softened
¼ cup butter
1 teaspoon vanilla extract
Mix thoroughly and cream with butter
1 teaspoon cocoa
¼ teaspoon cinnamon
⅛ teaspoon cloves
⅛ teaspoon nutmeg
Add gradually, beating well after each addition
4 cups sifted confectioners' sugar
¼ teaspoon salt

Mix in (enough for spreading consistency)
⅓ to ½ cup cream
*Enough to frost sides and top
of one 10-in. tubed cake*

Sour Cream-Chocolate Frosting

Melt (*page 12*) **1** and cool slightly
**2 pkgs. (12 oz.) semi-sweet chocolate
pieces**
Blend melted chocolate into
1 cup thick sour cream
Add and blend in
1 teaspoon vanilla extract
¼ teaspoon almond extract
⅛ teaspoon salt
*Enough to frost sides and tops of
two 8- or 9-in. round cake layers*

Chocolate Bar Frosting

Set out
**5 semi-sweet or milk chocolate bars
(about 2 oz. each)**
Immediately upon removing cake layers from
pans and while cake is warm, place on top of
each layer one half of the chocolate bars.

As chocolate melts, quickly spread around
sides and top of cake layers.
*Enough to frost sides and tops of
two 8-in. round cake layers*

Decorating Frosting

Easy to use for many interesting decorations.

Cream together until softened
2 tablespoons butter or margarine
½ teaspoon vanilla extract
Thoroughly blend in, in order
1½ cups sifted confectioners' sugar
1 tablespoon warm cream
Tint as desired, with about
1 drop food coloring
Use for decorating (see *page 400*) Petits Fours.
About 1½ cups frosting

▲ Confectioners' Sugar Frosting

Combine
1 cup sifted confectioners' sugar
½ teaspoon vanilla extract
Add
Milk or cream
(Use just enough milk or cream to make a frosting that will hold its shape when forced through a pastry bag and tube.)

About 1 cup frosting

Note: Mixture may be tinted by stirring in one or more drops of **food coloring.**

△ Confectioners' Sugar Glaze

Follow ▲ Recipe. Thin frosting to spreading consistency with additional milk or cream (about 2 tablespoons). Or substitute **water** for milk or cream. Drizzle glaze over hot breads, sweet rolls or coffee cake.

Fudge Glaze 4

Perfection for Boston Cream Pie.

Melt (*page 12*) together and set aside
2 sq. (2 oz.) chocolate
3 tablespoons butter or margarine
Heat
¼ cup cream
Mix in
1¼ cups sifted confectioners' sugar
⅛ teaspoon salt
Vigorously stir in the melted chocolate mixture until frosting is smooth.

Enough to glaze top of one 9-in. cake layer

Honey-Chocolate Frosting 5

A frosting with a hint of honey in it to give it an intriguingly "different" flavor.

Combine in top of double boiler and place over simmering water
½ cup sugar
2 sq. (2 oz.) chocolate, cut in pieces
⅓ cup honey
¼ cup cream or rich milk
¼ cup butter or margarine
⅛ teaspoon salt
When chocolate is melted, blend well with rotary beater.

Vigorously stir about 3 tablespoons of the hot mixture into
2 egg yolks, slightly beaten
Immediately blend into the mixture in top of double boiler.

Cook over simmering water, stirring constantly. When slightly thickened (about 2 min.), remove from heat; place pan in bowl of ice and water and beat frosting until of spreading consistency.

Enough to frost sides and tops of two 8-in. round cake layers

Honey-Chocolate Frosting on Golden Honey Cake (page 358)

How to Make
and Use a Pastry Bag

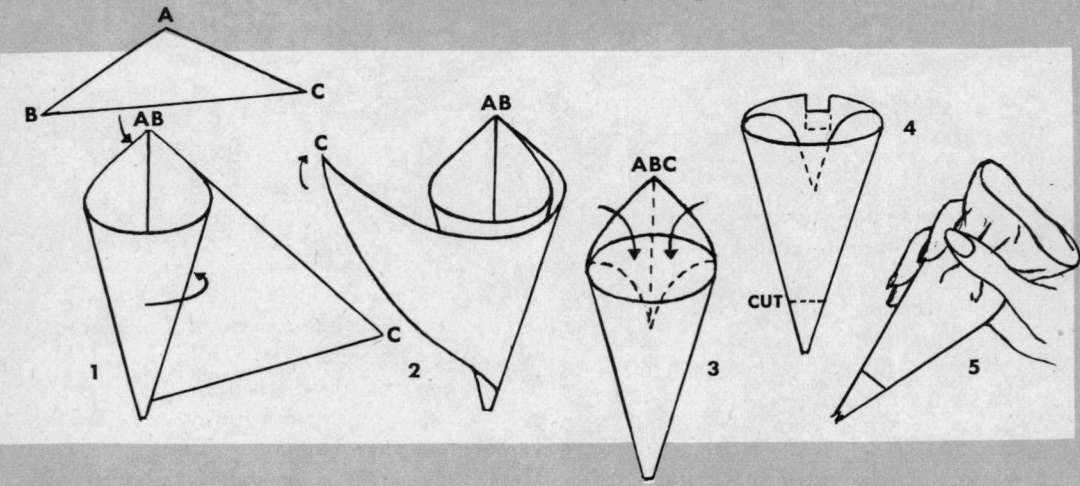

To Make a Pastry Bag: Cut a 24x17x17-inch triangle from parchment paper. Bring points A and B together (1). Bring C around cone so that A, B and C meet (2). Fold point ABC into cone (3) and cut a tab in rim; fold tab outward. Trim ½ to ¾ inch from tip (4). Insert tube indicated in recipe into tip; fill bag half-full; hold bag as in (5) and press. Practice with lard on the back of a cake pan.

STAR TUBE

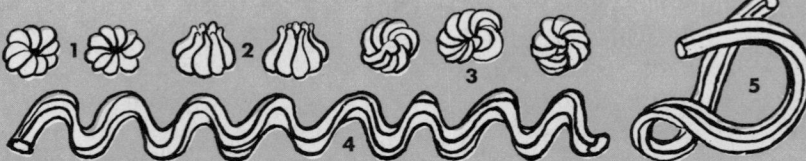

Use star tubes for rosettes (1,2,3), border (4) or writing (5). Use small decorating star tubes (No. 27) for small decorations; plain star tubes (Nos. 1-3) for larger ones.

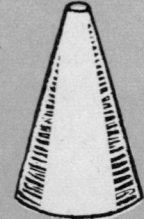

WRITING TUBE

Use decorating tubes Nos. 1, 2 or 3 to form forget-me-nots (1) or lilies-of-the-valley (2) with dots and lines. Or use for writing (3); sketch words first with wooden pick.

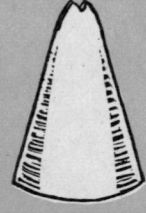

LEAF TUBE

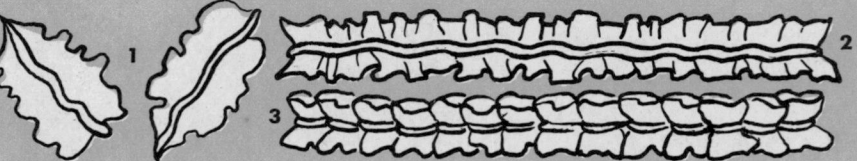

Use leaf tubes such as 65, 66 and 67 to taper leaves (1); vary pressure on bag. For border (2) use steady pressure; hold at angle. For (3) use overlapping motion.

▲ Glossy Vanilla Icing
(See photo on page 385)

Cook in top of double boiler over simmering water, stirring until shortening is melted
¼ cup sugar
¼ cup cream
1½ teaspoons white corn sirup
2 teaspoons butter or margarine
Remove from heat; gradually blend in, in order
1½ cups sifted confectioners' sugar
1¼ teaspoons vanilla extract
If frosting is too stiff to spread, blend in
Several drops cream
With spatula, spread frosting on top of cake, allowing some frosting to trickle down the sides of the cake.   *Enough to frost top of one 9x5-in. loaf cake*

△ Glossy Rum Frosting 7

Follow ▲ Recipe. Substitute ¾ teaspoon **rum extract** for vanilla extract.

Broiler Fudge Frosting

Have ready a hot cake in an 8-in. square pan.

Coarsely chop and set aside
½ cup (about 2 oz.) nuts
Cream until fluffy
2 tablespoons butter or margarine, softened
½ cup firmly packed brown sugar
2 tablespoons cocoa
Blend in until smooth
2 tablespoons cream
Stir in the chopped nuts. Spread lightly over the cake.

Set temperature control of range at Broil.

Place cake in broiler with top of frosting about 4 in. from source of heat. Broil about 1 min. or until frosting bubbles. Watch closely to avoid scorching.   *Enough to frost top of one 8-in. square cake*

Quick Fudge Frosting 8

Heat in double-boiler top over simmering water
1 pkg. (6 oz.) semi-sweet chocolate pieces
⅔ cup (one-half 15-oz. can) sweetened condensed milk
1 tablespoon water
Stir until chocolate is melted and mixture is smooth. Remove from heat; cool in pan of ice and water.   *Enough to frost sides and top of one 8-in. square cake*

Maple Frosting 9

Set out a candy thermometer and a 1-qt. saucepan having a tight-fitting cover.

Combine in the saucepan
¾ cup maple sirup
½ cup sugar
Place over low heat, stirring until sugar is dissolved. Cover saucepan and bring to boiling. Boil 5 min. to help dissolve any crystals that may have formed on sides of pan. Uncover saucepan and put candy thermometer in place (*page 393*). Continue cooking without stirring until mixture reaches 230°F (thread stage, *page 393;* remove from heat while testing).

Using pastry brush dipped in water, wash down crystals from sides of saucepan from time to time during cooking.

Beat until stiff (but not dry) peaks are formed
1 egg white
Few grains salt
Continue beating egg white while pouring the hot sirup over it in a thin steady stream. (Do not scrape sirup from bottom and sides of pan.) After all the sirup is added, continue beating 2 to 3 min., or until frosting is very thick and forms rounded peaks (holds shape). Fold in (*page 12*) with minimum strokes
1 teaspoon vanilla extract
Enough to frost sides and tops of two 8-in. square cake layers or three 8-in. round cake layers

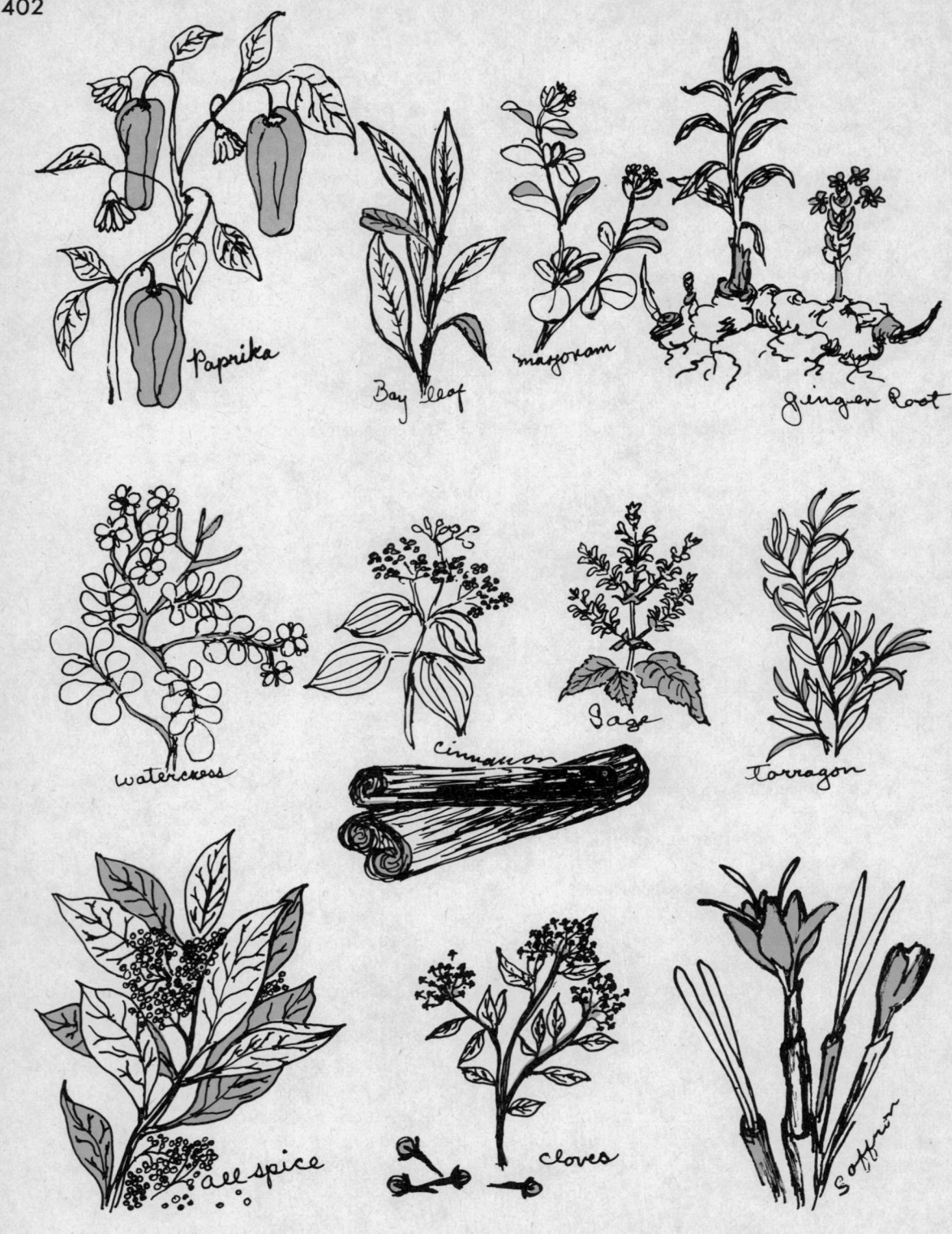

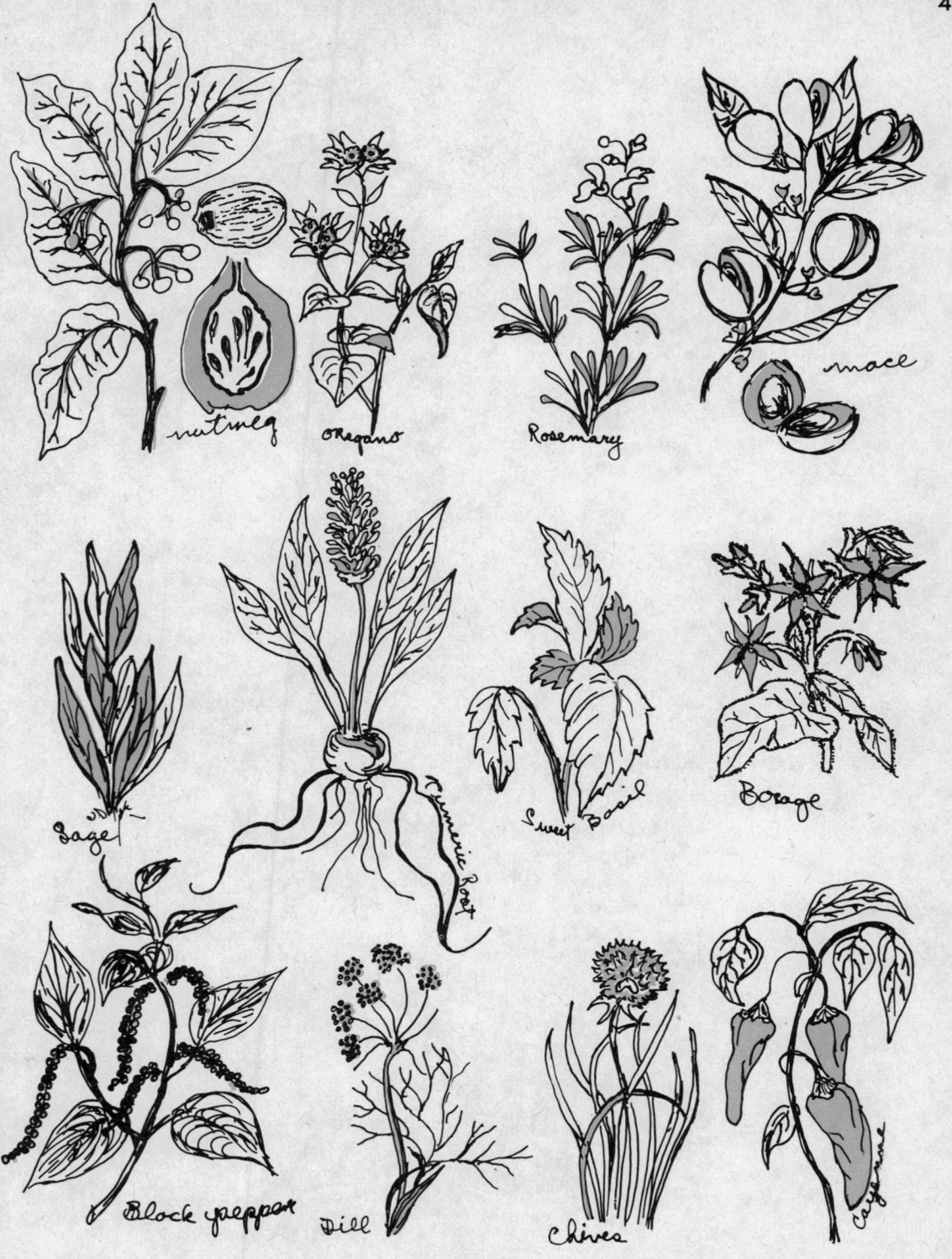

nutmeg

oregano

Rosemary

mace

Sage

Tumeric Root

Sweet Basil

Borage

Black pepper

Dill

Chives

Cayenne

▲ Seven-Minute Frosting

Combine and mix well in top of a double boiler
- **1½ cups sugar**
- **⅓ cup water**
- **1 tablespoon white corn sirup**
- **⅛ teaspoon salt**
- **2 egg whites, unbeaten**

Place over simmering water and immediately beat with rotary beater 7 to 10 min., or until mixture holds stiff peaks.

Remove from heat and blend in
- **1 teaspoon vanilla extract**

Enough to frost sides and tops of two 9-in. cake layers

Note: Mixture may be tinted by gently stirring in one or more drops of **food coloring**.

Seven-Minute Frosting on Meltaway Whipped Cream Cake (page 367)

⚠ Green Valley Frosting

Follow ▲ Recipe; substitute a few drops **peppermint extract** for vanilla extract. Blend in about 2 drops **green food coloring**.

⚠ Seven-Minute Pistachio Frosting

Follow ▲ Recipe; substitute ½ to 1 teaspoon **pistachio extract** for vanilla extract. Blend in 1 or 2 drops **green food coloring**. If desired, sprinkle ½ cup (about 2 oz.) chopped salted **pistachio nuts** evenly over top of frosted cake in any desired pattern.

⚠ Seven-Minute Peppermint Frosting

Follow ▲ Recipe. Fold in (*page 12*) ½ cup finely crushed **peppermint-stick candy** and about 2 drops **red food coloring**.

⚠ Seven-Minute Chocolate Frosting

Melt (*p.12*) █ 1 █ 3 sq. (3 oz.) **chocolate** and set aside to cool. Follow ▲ Recipe. Blend in chocolate when mixture holds stiff peaks.

For Chocolate Swirls—Melt (*page 12*) ½ sq. (½ oz.) **chocolate.** Drop spoonfuls of melted chocolate onto top of frosted cake. Using back of spoon, swirl pools of chocolate. (Especially attractive for chocolate-frosted cake.)

Seven-Minute Beige Frosting

Combine and mix thoroughly in the top of a double boiler

   ½ cup sugar
   ½ cup firmly packed brown sugar
   ¼ cup water
   2 teaspoons white corn sirup
   ⅛ teaspoon salt
   ¼ cup unbeaten egg whites (2 small egg whites)

Place over simmering water and immediately beat with a rotary beater 7 to 10 min. or until mixture holds stiff peaks.

Remove mixture from heat and blend in

   1 teaspoon vanilla extract

Enough to frost sides and top of one 8-in. square cake

Marshmallow-Coconut Frosting

MRS. HENRY ANDERSON
WEST LOS ANGELES, CALIF.

Set out a candy thermometer and a medium-size saucepan having a tight-fitting cover.

Prepare and set aside

   1 cup Toasted Coconut (page 448)

Cut (*page 12*) into quarters and set aside

   10 marshmallows

Combine in the saucepan

   1 cup sugar
   ½ cup boiling water
   ¼ teaspoon vinegar

Place over low heat, stirring until sugar is dissolved. Cover saucepan and bring to boiling. Boil 5 min. to help dissolve any crystals that

may have formed on sides of pan. Uncover saucepan and put candy thermometer in place (*page 393*). Continue cooking, without stirring, until mixture reaches 244°F (firm ball stage, *page 393*; remove from heat while testing). Using a pastry brush dipped in water, wash down crystals from sides of saucepan from time to time during cooking.

Meanwhile, beat until stiff (but not dry) peaks are formed

   2 egg whites

Continue beating egg whites while pouring the hot sirup over them in a steady thin stream. (Do not scrape sirup from bottom and sides of pan.) After all the hot sirup is added, add the marshmallows and continue beating 2 to 3 min., or until marshmallows are melted and frosting is very thick and forms rounded peaks (holds shape).

Frost (*page 393*) cooled cake layers and sprinkle top and sides with the toasted coconut.

Enough to frost sides and tops of two 9-in. round cake layers

Fluffy White Frosting 11

MRS. A. E. SEASTROM, HOPEDALE, MASS.

Set out a candy thermometer and a 1-qt. saucepan having a tight-fitting cover.

Combine in the saucepan
1½ cups sugar
½ cup water
Place over low heat, stirring until sugar is dissolved. Cover saucepan and bring to boiling.

Boil 5 min. to help dissolve any crystals that may have formed on sides of pan. Uncover saucepan and put candy thermometer in place (*page 393*). Continue cooking without stirring until mixture reaches 230°F (thread stage, *page 393;* remove from heat while testing).

Using pastry brush dipped in water, wash down crystals from sides of saucepan from time to time during cooking.

Meanwhile, beat until frothy
2 egg whites
Add
½ teaspoon cream of tartar
Beat until stiff (but not dry) peaks are formed.

Continue beating egg whites while pouring the hot sirup over them in a steady thin stream. (Do not scrape sirup from bottom and sides of pan.) After all the sirup is added, continue beating, 2 to 3 min., or until frosting is very thick and forms rounded peaks (holds shape). Fold in (*page 12*) with minimum number of strokes
½ teaspoon lemon extract
Enough to frost sides and tops of three 8-in. round cake layers

White Mountain Frosting 12

(*See photo on page 365*)

Set out a candy thermometer and a medium-size saucepan having a tight-fitting cover.

Combine in the saucepan
2 cups sugar
¾ cup water
2 tablespoons white corn sirup
⅛ teaspoon salt
Place over low heat, stirring gently until sugar is dissolved. Cover saucepan and bring to boiling. Boil 5 min. to help dissolve any crystals that may have formed on sides of pan.

Uncover saucepan and put candy thermometer in place (*page 393*). Continue cooking, without stirring, until mixture reaches 244°F (firm ball stage, *page 393;* remove from heat while testing). Using pastry brush dipped in water, wash down crystals from sides of saucepan from time to time during cooking.

Beat until stiff (but not dry) peaks are formed
½ cup (about 4) egg whites
Continue beating egg whites while pouring the hot sirup over them in a steady thin stream. (Do not scrape sirup from bottom and sides of pan.) After all the hot sirup is added, continue beating 2 to 3 min., or until frosting is very thick and forms rounded peaks (holds shape). Fold in (*page 12*) with minimum number of strokes
2 teaspoons vanilla extract
½ teaspoon almond extract
Frost (*page 393*) cake immediately.
Enough to frost sides and tops of two 8- or 9-in. round cake layers

Butter Frosting  13

Set out a candy thermometer.

Grate (*page 11*) and set aside
 **½ cup (about 2 oz.) walnuts (about
  ¾ cup, grated)**
Combine in a small saucepan having a tight-fitting cover
 1 cup plus 2 tablespoons sugar
 ⅓ cup water
Bring to boiling over medium heat, stirring gently until sugar is dissolved. Cover saucepan tightly and boil sirup gently 5 min. to help wash down any crystals that might have formed on the sides of saucepan.

Uncover saucepan and put candy thermometer in place (*page 393*). Continue cooking, without stirring, until mixture reaches 230°F (thread stage, *page 393*; remove from heat while testing). Using pastry brush dipped in water, wash down crystals from sides of pan from time to time during cooking. Remove from heat.

Beat until stiff (but not dry) peaks are formed
 2 egg whites
Continue beating egg whites while pouring the hot sirup over them in a steady thin stream. (Do not scrape sirup from bottom and sides of pan.) Continue beating a few minutes until mixture is very thick (piles softly). Cool completely.

Cream together until mixture is light and fluffy
 1½ cups firm unsalted butter
 ½ teaspoon vanilla extract
 ½ teaspoon rum
Add, one at a time, blending in after each addition
 2 egg yolks
Add about 2 tablespoons egg-white mixture at a time to creamed butter, beating until just blended after each addition. (Egg-white mixture and creamed butter should be of same consistency before mixing together.)

Mix in the walnuts. If necessary, chill frosting in refrigerator until firm enough to spread.
*Enough to frost sides and tops of
two 9-in. round cake layers*

French Chocolate  14
Butter Frosting

Set out a candy thermometer.

Put in a heavy saucepan and set over low heat until chocolate melts
 **1 pkg. (6 oz.) semi-sweet chocolate
  pieces**
 **¼ cup double-strength coffee beverage
  (page 13)**
Remove from heat and blend well. Set aside to cool.

Put in a saucepan
 ¾ cup white corn sirup
Put candy thermometer in place (*page 393*). Boil gently until mixture reaches 230°F (thread stage, *page 393*; remove from heat while testing).

Meanwhile, beat until thick and lemon-colored
 4 egg yolks
Continue beating the egg yolks while pouring the hot sirup over them in a steady thin stream. (Do not scrape sirup from bottom and sides of pan.) Beat until mixture is very thick. Cool completely.

Cream together until butter is light and fluffy
 1½ cups firm unsalted butter
 1½ teaspoons vanilla extract
Add about 2 tablespoons egg-yolk mixture at a time to creamed butter until just blended after each addition. (Egg-yolk mixture and creamed butter should be of same consistency before mixing together.) Add gradually, blending in, the chocolate mixture.

If tightly covered, this frosting may be stored for several days in refrigerator.
*Enough to frost sides and tops of
two 8- or 9-in. round cake layers*

Mocha Butter Cream Frosting 15

Set out a candy thermometer and a small sauce-pan having a tight-fitting cover.

Combine in the saucepan
1¾ cups sugar
½ cup water
Bring to boiling over medium heat, stirring gently until sugar is dissolved. Cover saucepan and boil sirup gently 5 min. to help wash down any crystals that might have formed on sides of saucepan. Uncover saucepan and put candy thermometer in place (*page 393*). Continue cooking, without stirring, until mixture reaches 230°F (thread stage, *page 393;* remove from heat while testing). Using a pastry brush dipped in water, wash down crystals from sides of pan from time to time during cooking.

Remove from heat and set aside.

Beat until stiff (but not dry) peaks are formed
3 egg whites
Continue beating egg whites while pouring the hot sirup over them in a steady thin stream. (Do not scrape sirup from bottom and sides of pan.) Continue beating a few minutes until mixture is very thick (piles softly). Cool completely.

Cream until softened and fluffy
2 cups firm unsalted butter
Beat in
1 tablespoon Dutch process cocoa
2 teaspoons concentrated soluble coffee
1 teaspoon vanilla extract
Add, one at a time, blending in after each addition
3 egg yolks
Add about 2 tablespoons egg-white mixture at a time to creamed butter, beating until just blended after each addition. (Egg-white mixture and creamed butter should be of same consistency before mixing together.)

Chill in refrigerator until firm enough to spread.
Enough to frost sides and tops of two 9-in. round cake layers

Brownie Caramel Frosting 16

Set out a candy thermometer and a medium-size saucepan.

Combine in the saucepan
1¼ cups sugar
⅔ cup cream
Stir over low heat until sugar is dissolved. Increase heat and bring mixture to boiling. Put candy thermometer in place (*page 393*). Cook until mixture reaches 234°F (soft ball stage, *page 393;* remove from heat while testing). Using a pastry brush dipped in water, wash down crystals from sides of pan during cooking.

While mixture is cooking, melt (carmelize) in a heavy skillet
¾ cup firmly packed brown sugar
With back of wooden spoon, gently keep sugar moving toward center of skillet until sugar is melted. Stir caramelized brown sugar rapidly into the sirup. Boil again to soft ball stage. Remove from heat.

Set aside to cool to 110°F or until just cool enough to hold pan on palm of hand.

When cooled, blend in
1 teaspoon vanilla extract
Beat until creamy and of spreading consistency. Place frosting over hot water if it becomes too stiff while spreading on cake.
Enough to frost sides and tops of two 8-in. layers or 2 doz. cupcakes

Vanilla Fudge Frosting 17

MRS. FOSTER BAILEY
NORTH LEWISBURG, OHIO

A wonderful frosting for Lemon Cake.

Set out a candy thermometer.

Combine in a 2-qt. saucepan
2¼ cups sugar
¾ cup milk
¼ teaspoon cream of tartar
¼ teaspoon salt
Stir over low heat until sugar is dissolved. Increase heat and bring mixture to boiling.

Put candy thermometer in place (*page 393*).

Cook, stirring occasionally, until mixture reaches 234°F (soft ball stage, *page 393*; remove from heat while testing). Using a pastry brush dipped in water, wash down crystals from sides of saucepan from time to time during cooking.

Remove from heat. Set aside to cool to 110°F or until just cool enough to hold pan on palm of hand. Do not stir.

When cooled, blend in
1½ tablespoons butter
¾ teaspoon vanilla extract
Mix in (enough for spreading consistency)
1 to 2 tablespoons cream
Enough to frost sides and tops of two 8-in. round cake layers

▲ Fondant Glaze
(For Petits Fours)

Prepare (allowing a 24-hr. period for ripening)
Fondant (page 546)
Put ripened fondant in double-boiler top. Place over simmering water. Stirring constantly, melt fondant, heating to 130°F (no higher). Blend in, to taste, any desired
Flavoring or liqueur
To tint, blend in
1 or 2 drops food coloring
If fondant is not thin enough to pour over Petits Fours, gradually add
Hot water
Stir in 1 teaspoonful at a time, until fondant is of pouring consistency. Quickly pour melted fondant over the cake pieces set on a rack over a tray lined with waxed paper. Collect dripped fondant from tray, remelt and use again, repeating process until Petits Fours are completely coated.

△ Chocolate Fondant Glaze

Follow ▲ Recipe; when melting fondant, add 4 sq. (4 oz.) **chocolate**, cut in pieces. When temperature reaches 130°F (no higher temperature), stir in hot **water**, 1 tablespoon at a time (will take about 4 tablespoons), until thin enough to pour.

Glossy Chocolate Frosting

▲ Glossy Chocolate Frosting 18

A frosting with a beckoning gleam. It looks rich, tastes wonderful, keeps well, is easy to make and a pleasure to spread.

Mix thoroughly in a 2-qt. saucepan
   1½ cups sugar
   6 tablespoons cornstarch
Stir in
   1½ cups boiling water
   3 sq. (3 oz.) chocolate, cut in pieces
   ¾ teaspoon salt
Cook over medium heat, stirring frequently, until mixture thickens (about 5 min.). Remove from heat. Beat in
   6 tablespoons butter or margarine
   1 tablespoon vanilla extract
Spread on cake while frosting is hot.

Enough to frost sides and tops of two 8- or 9-in. round cake layers

⚠ Glossy Nut Frosting 19

Follow ▲ Recipe. Sprinkle 1 cup (4 oz.) chopped **nuts** on top and sides of frosted cake.

⚠ Glossy Crunch Frosting 20

Follow ▲ Recipe. Crush ¼ lb. **peanut** or **almond brittle**. Stir into frosting before spreading onto cake.

⚠ Glossy Coconut Frosting 21

Follow ▲ Recipe. Finely chop 1 cup moist shredded **coconut**. Stir into frosting before spreading onto cake.

⚠ Glossy Peppermint Frosting 22

Follow ▲ Recipe. Crush 6 to 8 small sticks **peppermint candy**. Stir into frosting before spreading onto cake.

Prune Topping 23
MRS. ELLSWORTH VAN STEE
EDWARDSVILLE, ILL.

Rich, dark, and wonderful with a spicy cake.

Chop coarsely and set aside
   1 cup (about 4 oz.) pecans
Cut (*page 12*) into small pieces and set aside
   1 cup (about 7 oz.) uncooked prunes
Mix together in top of a double boiler
   1 cup sugar
   1 tablespoon flour
   1 tablespoon cornstarch
Add gradually, stirring in
   ¾ cup prune juice
Stirring gently and constantly, bring rapidly to boiling over direct heat and cook for 3 min. Cover and cook over simmering water 12 min., stirring occasionally.

Vigorously stir about 2 tablespoons hot mixture into
   1 egg, slightly beaten
Immediately blend into mixture in double boiler. Cook over simmering water 3 to 5 min., stirring slowly and constantly.

Remove from heat and blend in the chopped nuts, the prunes and
   2 tablespoons butter
Serve Prune Topping warm.

Enough topping for one 9-in. square cake

▲ Creamy Vanilla Filling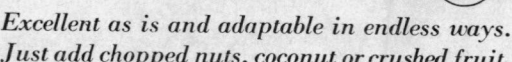

Excellent as is and adaptable in endless ways.
Just add chopped nuts, coconut or crushed fruit.

Set out
1½ cups cream
Scald (*page 13*) in top of double boiler 1 cup of
the cream; reserve remainder.

Meanwhile, sift together into a small saucepan
⅓ to ½ cup sugar
2½ tablespoons flour
¼ teaspoon salt
Blend in the reserved cream; add gradually,
stirring in, the scalded cream. Bring rapidly to
boiling over direct heat, stirring gently and
constantly; cook 3 min. Remove from heat.

Wash the double-boiler top to remove scum;
pour cream mixture into it and place over
simmering water. Cover and cook about 5 to 7
min., stirring three or four times.

Vigorously stir about 3 tablespoons of the
mixture into
3 egg yolks, slightly beaten
Immediately blend into mixture in double
boiler. Cook over simmering water 3 to 5 min.,
stirring slowly and constantly to keep mixture
cooking evenly.

Remove from heat and blend in
1 tablespoon butter or margarine
2 teaspoons vanilla extract
¼ teaspoon almond extract
Cover, cool slightly and chill in refrigerator.
About 1½ cups filling

▲ Creamy Cherry Filling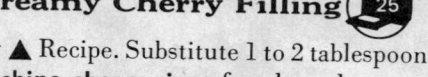

Follow ▲ Recipe. Substitute 1 to 2 tablespoons
maraschino-cherry sirup for almond extract.
Fold ½ cup chopped **maraschino cherries.**

▲ Black-Walnut Cream Filling

Follow ▲ Recipe. Blend in ¾ cup (about 3 oz.)
coarsely chopped **black walnuts.**

Chocolate Filling

Melt (*page 12*) and set aside to cool
2 sq. (2 oz.) chocolate
Bring just to boiling
¾ cup hot water
Sift together into top of a double boiler
1 cup sugar
¼ cup cornstarch
½ teaspoon salt
Stir in and blend well
¼ cup cold water
Gradually add the boiling water. Stirring gently
and constantly bring mixture rapidly to boiling
over direct heat, and cook 3 min. Place over
simmering water; cover and cook 12 min.,
stirring three or four times.

Remove from heat; stir in melted chocolate and
¼ cup butter or margarine
2 teaspoons vanilla extract
Cool filling slightly. *About 1 cup filling*

Marshmallow Chocolate Filling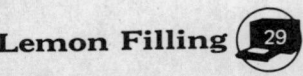

Melt over simmering water
- **32 marshmallows (about ½ lb.), cut in quarters (page 12)**
- **1 sq. (1 oz.) chocolate**

Meanwhile, prepare and set aside
- **¼ cup (about 1 oz.) chopped seedless raisins**
- **¼ cup (about 1 oz.) chopped nuts**
- **½ teaspoon grated orange or lemon peel (page 11)**

Remove melted marshmallows and chocolate from heat and stir in
- **1 tablespoon cream**

Blend in the raisins, nuts and grated peel. Stir until filling is of spreading consistency.

(Omit chocolate if white filling is desired.)

Enough filling for one 8- or 9-in. cake layer

Lemon Filling 29

Combine in double-boiler top and beat slightly with rotary beater
- **3 egg whites**
- **1 cup sugar**
- **3 tablespoons lemon juice**
- **1 teaspoon grated lemon peel (page 11)**

Place over simmering water. Cook about 5 min., or until thickened, stirring constantly.

Vigorously stir about 3 tablespoons of hot mixture into
- **3 egg yolks, slightly beaten**

Immediately blend into mixture in double boiler. Cook over simmering water 10 min.; stir slowly to keep mixture cooking evenly. Remove from heat and cool thoroughly before using. *About 1 cup filling*

Orange Filling

Mix together in top of double boiler
- **½ cup sugar**
- **2½ tablespoons cornstarch**
- **⅛ teaspoon salt**

Add gradually, stirring in
- **½ cup water**
- **½ cup orange juice**

Stirring gently and constantly, bring rapidly to boiling over direct heat and cook for 3 min. Cover and cook over simmering water 12 min., stirring three or four times.

Vigorously stir about 2 tablespoons hot mixture into
- **1 egg yolk, slightly beaten**

Immediately blend into mixture in double boiler. Cook over simmering water 3 to 5 min., stirring slowly and constantly to keep mixture cooking evenly.

Remove from heat and blend in
- **1 tablespoon lemon juice**
- **1 tablespoon grated orange peel (page 11)**
- **2 teaspoons butter or margarine**

Cool filling before spreading on the cake.

About 1 cup filling

Uncooked Orange Filling

Mix together and set aside
- **¾ cup orange juice**
- **½ cup sugar**
- **1 tablespoon grated orange peel (page 11)**

Beat until frothy
- **2 egg whites**

Add gradually, beating thoroughly after each addition
- **¼ cup sugar**

Beat until stiff (but not dry) peaks are formed (peaks remain standing when beater is slowly lifted upright).

Gently fold (*page 12*) orange mixture into beaten egg whites. *About 1 cup filling*

Pineapple Cream Filling 31

Drain contents of
**1 9-oz. can crushed pineapple (about
¾ cup, drained)**
(Reserve sirup for use in other food preparation.)

Set out
1 cup milk
Scald (*page 13*) in top of double boiler ¾ cup of the milk; reserve remainder.

Meanwhile, sift together into a saucepan
¼ cup sugar
1 tablespoon cornstarch
Few grains salt
Blend in the reserved ¼ cup milk. Stirring constantly, gradually add the scalded milk. Bring rapidly to boiling over direct heat, stirring gently and constantly; cook 3 min. Remove from heat.

Wash double-boiler top to remove scum; pour mixture into it and place over simmering water. Cover and cook 10 to 12 min., stirring three or four times. Vigorously stir about 3 tablespoons hot mixture into
1 egg, slightly beaten
Immediately blend into mixture in double boiler. Cook over simmering water 3 to 5 min., stirring slowly and constantly to keep mixture cooking evenly. Remove from heat. Cover the mixture and cool.

Stir in the crushed pineapple and
1 teaspoon vanilla extract
Chill in refrigerator.   *About 1½ cups filling*

Almond Pastry Cream

Finely grind
**⅓ lb. (about 1 cup) blanched almonds
(*page 11*)**
Mix in
½ cup confectioners' sugar, sifted
Set aside.

Cream until softened
3 tablespoons butter
Beat in, one at a time
2 egg yolks
Blend in
1 tablespoon rum or kirsch
Beat until well blended. Blend in almond-sugar mixture until smooth.

1 cup Almond Pastry Cream

▲ Sweetened Whipped Cream

Place a rotary beater and a 1-qt. bowl in refrigerator to chill.

Using the chilled bowl and beater, beat until soft peaks are formed when beater is slowly lifted upright
1 cup chilled whipping cream
Beat into whipped cream with final few strokes until blended
3 tablespoons sifted confectioners' sugar
1 teaspoon vanilla extract
Set in refrigerator if not used immediately.
About 2 cups whipped cream

Note: Mixture may be tinted by gently stirring in one or more drops of **food coloring.**

⚠ Mocha Whipped Cream

Follow ▲ Recipe. Sift 1 teaspoon **concentrated soluble coffee** with the sugar.

⚠ Dutch Cocoa Whipped Cream

Follow ▲ Recipe. Sift 3 tablespoons **Dutch process cocoa** with the sugar.

⚠ Rum Whipped Cream

Follow ▲ Recipe. Substitute 1 to 1½ tablespoons **rum** for vanilla extract.

⚠ Almond Whipped Cream

Blanch (*page 11*), sliver and toast (*page 12*) ½ cup (about 3 oz.) **almonds** and set aside. Follow ▲ Recipe; substitute ¼ teaspoon **almond extract** for vanilla extract.

Fold (*page 12*) the almonds into the whipped cream after blending in the sugar and extract.

Coffee Whipped Cream

Place a rotary beater and a bowl in refrigerator to chill.

Pour into a small cup or custard cup
2 tablespoons cold double- or triple-strength coffee beverage (*page 13*)
Sprinkle evenly over cold coffee
1 teaspoon unflavored gelatin
Let stand about 5 min. to soften. Dissolve gelatin completely by placing over hot water.

Using the chilled bowl and rotary beater, beat only until frothy
1 cup chilled whipping cream
Stir cooled gelatin. *Very* gradually add gelatin to cream and continue to beat after each addition until cream is of medium consistency (piles softly). Work quickly. When all gelatin has been added, beat into whipped cream with final few strokes until blended
⅓ cup sifted confectioners' sugar
Beat until cream stands in peaks when beater is slowly lifted upright.
Filling for 24 Miniature Puffs

Note: The use of gelatin in the whipped cream helps to stabilize the cream or to hold its volume and shape. Therefore, when the stabilized whipped cream is used to decorate molds or used as a filling or frosting, it should hold its shape for hours, if necessary.

Mocha Ginger Cream 32

Coffee and ginger in distinguished partnership.

Set out a candy thermometer.

Combine in a 1-qt. saucepan
1 cup sugar
½ cup double-strength coffee beverage (*page 13*)
Cook slowly over low heat, stirring until sugar is dissolved. Increase heat and bring mixture to boiling. Cover saucepan and boil gently for 5 min. to help dissolve any crystals that may

Mocha Ginger Cream with gingerbread and hot coffee

Vanilla Confectioners' Sugar

Prepare a large quantity of this delicately flavored sugar ahead of time and use it to impart added flavor to cookies, pastries, doughnuts, and other desserts.

Set out a 1- to 2-qt. container having a tight-fitting cover. Fill with

Confectioners' sugar

Remove from air-tight tube, wipe with a clean, damp cloth and dry

1 vanilla bean, about 9 in. long

Cut vanilla bean into quarters lengthwise; cut quarters crosswise into thirds. Poke pieces of vanilla bean down into the sugar at irregular intervals. Cover container tightly and store on pantry shelf.

(The longer sugar stands, the richer the vanilla flavor will be. If tightly covered, sugar may be stored for several months. When necessary, add more sugar to jar. Replace vanilla bean when aroma is gone.)

Note: Flavor **granulated sugar** as directed for confectioners' sugar and store. It, too, has many uses.

have formed on sides of saucepan. Uncover saucepan and put candy thermometer in place (*page 393*). Cook, stirring occasionally, until mixture reaches 234°F (soft ball stage, *page 393;* remove from heat while testing).

Using a pastry brush dipped in water, wash down crystals from sides of saucepan from time to time during cooking.

Place a rotary beater and a bowl in refrigerator to chill.

Beat until thick and lemon-colored

3 egg yolks

Gradually pour sirup over beaten egg yolks, beating constantly. Continue beating until very stiff. Chill mixture in refrigerator.

Chop enough candied ginger to yield

½ cup (about 3 oz.) chopped candied ginger

Set aside.

A few minutes before serving, using the chilled bowl and beater, beat until soft peaks are formed when beater is slowly lifted upright

1 cup chilled whipping cream

Gently fold (*page 12*) the whipped cream into the chilled mixture with the chopped ginger.

Use as a filling or topping for gingerbread or cake squares.   *About 4 cups cream filling*

Colored Sugar

Mix together

3 drops food coloring
3 drops water

Place in a bowl

¼ cup sugar

Pressing and stirring with a teaspoon, work in, one drop at a time, enough of the dissolved food coloring to give sugar desired color.

Put sugar through a fine sieve in order to obtain an even color.   *¼ cup sugar*

FROSTINGS and FILLINGS in the MICROWAVE OVEN

These cake frostings and fillings are absolutely delicious. Smooth and creamy, they spread easily and don't crystallize quickly. The glossy frostings, the chocolates, the mochas, the creamy fillings are all quicker and easier to prepare than in conventional cooking because there is no need for a double boiler or a water bath. They are all so well-suited to the microwave oven that the "most successful" depends upon your personal preference.

The only cooked frostings we found unsatisfactory in the microwave are the 7-minute frostings. We discovered that the egg whites must be cooked and beaten over direct heat or they simply will not blend and cook properly. We have omitted these recipes.

As with sauces, the key to success is in the stirring. Stir thoroughly when adding ingredients and then during cooking as indicated in the recipe.

PREPARATION—When beating is called for, use a mixer to thoroughly blend sugar and other ingredients before cooking.

In some recipes we have been able to combine and shorten the cooking time by bringing the frosting to a boil and thickening it in the same step. In a few recipes, we have added what appears to be an extra step in order to dissolve the sugar thoroughly. The frosting must be stirred every minute after the addition of the sugar until it begins to dissolve. The frequent stirring not only simulates the technique of continuous stirring and beating of the frosting over hot water in conventional cooking, but provides an opportunity for frequent testing. In microwave cooking, stirring and scraping crystals from the casserole sides also differs, since boiling action may not be as violent as in conventional cooking.

In some recipes, the frosting must be cooked covered and then uncovered for the final minute. Follow the directions in the master recipe unless otherwise directed.

TEST FOR DONENESS—Frostings can be tested for doneness either by using a thermometer or by the soft-ball-in-cold-water candy

technique suggested in the beginning of the **Frostings and Fillings** chapter. Unless you have a microwave-safe thermometer, we recommend the soft-ball method of testing. Testing the frosting with a conventional thermometer means removing it from the oven and waiting for the thermometer to register which permits the frosting to cool.

REMINDERS—For other tips on microwave oven cooking and for an easy-to-read chart comparing settings among different brands of microwave ovens, see the introductory chapter, **Home Cooking in the Microwave Oven**, in the beginning of this book.

1 *To Melt Chocolate*—In a small casserole, COOK chocolate, stirring every 1 min., until melted (about 1 min. per oz.).

Bittersweet Velvet Frosting *(page 395)* **2**

Use a small casserole.

Place butter and chocolate in casserole and COOK, stirring every 1 min., until melted (about 5 min.).

OVERALL COOKING TIME: 5:00

Toasted Pecan Frosting **3** *(page 397)*

Use a small casserole.

Place butter and pecans in casserole. COOK until butter melts (about 3 min.). Continue to COOK, stirring every 30 sec., until pecans are lightly browned (about 3 min.).

OVERALL COOKING TIME: 6:00

Fudge Glaze *(page 399)* **4**

Use a small dish for chocolate-butter mixture and a 1-qt. casserole for the cream.

COOK chocolate and butter, stirring every 1 min., to melt (about 3 min.).

COOK to heat cream (about 2 min.).

OVERALL COOKING TIME: 5:00

Honey-Chocolate Frosting *(page 399)* **5**

Use a 1½-qt. casserole.

Combine all ingredients except the egg yolks. COOK, stirring every 1 min., until chocolate is melted (about 5 min.).

After blending in the eggs, COOK, stirring every 30 sec., until slightly thickened (about 2 min.).

OVERALL COOKING TIME: 7:00

Glossy Vanilla Icing **6** *(page 401)*

Use a small casserole.

COOK sugar-cream mixture, stirring every 1 min., until butter is melted (about 3 min.).

OVERALL COOKING TIME: 3:00

Glossy Rum Frosting **7** *(page 401)*

Follow **6** Recipe with substitution as in △ Recipe.

Quick Fudge Frosting 8

(page 401)

Use a small casserole.

COOK mixture, stirring every 30 sec., until chocolate is melted and smooth (about 2 min.).
OVERALL COOKING TIME: 2:00

Maple Frosting *(page 401)*   9

Use a 1-qt. covered casserole.

COOK sirup and sugar, stirring every 1½ min., until sugar dissolves (about 3 min.).

Cover and COOK to boil and dissolve all crystals, scraping the sides and bottom of the casserole every 1½ min. (about 5 min.).

Uncover and COOK, stirring every 1 min., until thread stage or temperature reaches 230° (about 3 min.).

OVERALL COOKING TIME: 11:00

Marshmallow-Coconut Frosting *(page 405)* 10

Use a 1-qt. covered casserole.

COOK sugar mixture, stirring every 1 min., until sugar dissolves (about 5 min.).

Cover and COOK to boil and dissolve all crystals, scraping the sides and bottom of the casserole every 1½ min. (about 3 min.).

Uncover and COOK, stirring every 1½ min., until firm ball stage or temperature reaches 244° (about 5 min.).
OVERALL COOKING TIME: 13:00

Fluffy White Frosting   11

(page 406)

Use a 1-qt. covered casserole.

COOK sugar and water, stirring every 1½ min., until sugar dissolves (about 5 min.).

Cover and COOK to boil and dissolve all crystals, scraping the sides and bottom of the casserole every 1½ min. (about 5 min.).

Uncover and COOK, stirring every 1½ min., until thread stage or temperature reaches 230° (about 4 min.).
OVERALL COOKING TIME: 14:00

White Mountain Frosting *(page 406)* 12

Use a 1-qt. covered casserole.

COOK sugar mixture, stirring every 1½ min., until sugar dissolves (about 5 min.).

Cover and COOK to boil and dissolve all crystals, scraping the sides and bottom of the casserole every 1½ min. (about 5 min.).

Uncover and COOK, stirring every 1½ min., until firm ball stage or temperature reaches 244° (about 3 min.).
OVERALL COOKING TIME: 13:00

Butter Frosting *(page 407)* 13

Use a 1-qt. covered casserole.

COOK sugar-water mixture, stirring every 1½ min., until sugar dissolves (about 5 min.).

Cover and COOK to boil and dissolve all crystals, scraping the sides and bottom of the casserole every 1½ min. (about 5 min.).

Uncover and COOK, stirring every 1½ min., until thread stage or temperature reaches 230° (about 3 min.).

OVERALL COOKING TIME: 13:00

French Chocolate Butter Frosting *(page 407)* 14

Use a 1-qt. casserole.

COOK chocolate, stirring every 1 min., until melted (about 3 min.).

COOK corn sirup, stirring every 1½ min., until thread stage or temperature reaches 230° (about 3 min.).

OVERALL COOKING TIME: 6:00

Mocha Butter Cream Frosting *(page 408)* 15

Use a 1-qt. covered casserole.

COOK sugar and water, stirring every 1½ min., until sugar dissolves (about 5 min.).

Cover and COOK to boil and dissolve all crystals, scraping the sides and bottom of the casserole every 1½ min. (about 5 min.).

Uncover and COOK, stirring every 1½ min., until thread stage or temperature reaches 230° (about 3 min.).

OVERALL COOKING TIME: 13:00

Brownie Caramel Frosting *(page 408)* 16

Use a 1-qt. casserole.

First, COOK brown sugar, stirring every 30 sec., until melted (about 2 min.). Set aside in a pan of warm water.

COOK sugar and cream, stirring every 1½ min., until sugar dissolves (about 3 min.).

Continue to COOK to boil and dissolve all crystals, scraping the sides and bottom of the casserole every 1½ min., until soft ball stage or temperature reaches 234° (about 10 min.).

Add the brown sugar, mixing thoroughly. COOK, stirring every 1½ min., to return to soft ball stage or 234° (about 3 min.).

OVERALL COOKING TIME: 18:00

Vanilla Fudge Frosting 17 *(page 409)*

Use a 1-qt. casserole.

COOK sugar mixture, stirring every 1 min., until dissolved (about 5 min.).

COOK to boil and wash down all crystals, scraping the sides and bottom of the casserole every 30 sec. (about 3 min.).

Continue to COOK, washing down crystals every 1½ min., until the soft ball stage or temperature reaches 234° (about 6 min.).

OVERALL COOKING TIME: 14:00

Glossy Chocolate Frosting *(page 410)* 18

Use a 1½-qt. casserole.

COOK water to boil (about 4 min.).

COOK chocolate mixture, stirring every 1 min., until it thickens (about 3 min.).
OVERALL COOKING TIME: 6:00

Glossy Nut Frosting 19
(page 410)

Follow 18 Recipe with addition as in ⚠ Recipe.

Glossy Crunch Frosting *(page 410)* 20

Follow 18 Recipe with addition as in ⚠ Recipe.

Glossy Coconut Frosting *(page 410)* 21

Follow 18 Recipe with addition as in ⚠ Recipe.

Glossy Peppermint Frosting *(page 410)* 22

Follow 18 Recipe with addition as in ⚠ Recipe.

Prune Topping 23
(page 410)

Use a 1-qt. casserole.

COOK sugar mixture, stirring every 1 min., until sugar dissolves (about 5 min.).

Add prune juice and COOK, stirring every 1 min. to boil (about 2 min.). Cover and COOK, stirring every 1 min., until thickened (about 5 min.).

Add egg mixture and COOK to blend, stirring every 1½ min. (about 3 min.).
OVERALL COOKING TIME: 15:00

Creamy Vanilla Filling 24
(page 411)

Use a 1-qt. casserole.

COOK to scald cream (about 2 min.).

COOK sugar-cream mixture, stirring every 1 min., until it boils (about 3 min.).

Cover and COOK to cook flour (about 3 min.).

Add egg yolk mixture and COOK, stirring every 30 sec., until mixture slightly thickens (about 2 min.).
OVERALL COOKING TIME: 10:00

Creamy Cherry Filling 25
(page 411)

Follow 24 Recipe with changes as in ⚠ Recipe.

Black-Walnut Cream Filling *(page 411)* 26

Follow 24 Recipe with changes as in ⚠ Recipe.

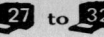

Chocolate Filling 27
(page 411)

Use a 1-qt. and a 1½-qt. casserole.

Sift sugar, cornstarch and salt into the small casserole and blend in cold water.

In the large casserole, COOK to melt chocolate (about 3 min.). Cover and set aside.

In glass measuring cup, COOK to boil water (about 3 min.). Add to the sugar mixture, stirring constantly.

COOK mixture, stirring gently every 1 min., to boil (about 3 min.). Cover and COOK to thicken (about 4 min.).

OVERALL COOKING TIME: 13:00

Marshmallow Chocolate 28
Filling *(page 412)*

Use a 1½-qt. casserole. Substitute plastic wrap for a glass cover, as the marshmallows will rise and may stick to the glass.

Add marshmallows and chocolate to casserole.

Cover with plastic wrap and COOK to melt (about 2 min.).

OVERALL COOKING TIME: 2:00

Lemon Filling *(page 412)* 29

Use a 1-qt. casserole.

COOK egg white mixture, stirring every 30 sec., until thickened (about 3 min.).

Add egg yolk mixture and COOK, stirring every 30 sec., until flavors blend (about 2 min.).

OVERALL COOKING TIME: 5:00

Orange Filling 30
(page 412)

Use a 1-qt. casserole.

COOK sugar-juice mixture, stirring every 1 min., until boiling (about 2 min.). Cover and COOK to dissolve crystals, scraping the sides and bottom of casserole every 1½ min. (about 5 min.).

Add egg yolk mixture and COOK, stirring every 30 sec., to thicken (about 2 min.).

OVERALL COOKING TIME: 9:00

Pineapple Cream 31
Filling *(page 413)*

Use a 1-qt. casserole.

COOK to scald milk (about 3 min.).

COOK milk-sugar mixture, stirring every 30 sec., until boiling (about 3 min.). Cover and continue to COOK, stirring every 1 min., until thickened (about 5 min.).

Add egg mixture and COOK uncovered, stirring every 30 sec., until smooth and flavors are blended (about 1½ min.).

OVERALL COOKING TIME: 12:30

Mocha Ginger Cream 32
(page 414)

Use a 1-qt. covered casserole.

COOK sugar-coffee mixture, stirring every 1½ min., until sugar dissolves (about 3 min.).

Cover and COOK to boil and dissolve all crystals, scraping the sides and bottom of the casserole every 1½ min. (about 5 min.).

Uncover and COOK, stirring every 1½ min., until soft ball stage or temperature reaches 234° (about 3 min.).

OVERALL COOKING TIME: 11:00

The Art of Cookie Making

Surely there is a special place in heaven for the unknown person—probably a grandmother—who created the first cookies! The perfect small treat, cookies are for the eager hands of children and for the child in all of us that never grows up. On these pages are gathered treasured recipes for cookies for all occasions, including the daily, never-ending occasion when some member of the family has a little empty spot and seeks the cookie jar for wherewithal to fill it.

THE PERFECT COOKIE should have good flavor, tender crumb unless the variety is a hard cookie, soft or crisp texture depending upon variety of cookie, uniform color and uniform shape depending upon type of cookie.

TYPES—Cookies are classified in many ways—by the texture of the baked cookie (soft or crisp), the consistency of batter or dough (soft or stiff), the richness of cookie (plain or rich), or by the method used in shaping the cookie.

Bar—Dough is baked in a four-sided pan and cut into bars or squares after baking.

Refrigerator (*icebox*)—Dough is pressed into a cookie mold or shaped into a thick roll or bar, chilled and kept in refrigerator ready to be cut into thin slices with a sharp, thin knife and baked.

Drop—Dough is dropped from a teaspoon onto a lightly greased cookie sheet.

Molded—Dough is shaped by hand.

Pressed—Dough is soft enough to go through a cookie press but stiff enough to hold a shape.

Rolled—Dough is rolled to desired thickness on a lightly floured surface and cut into various shapes with a cookie cutter.

INGREDIENTS—Each ingredient has its own role to play in the cookie batter or dough.

Flour—Generally all-purpose; major ingredient in all batter and dough products; when combined with moisture gives structure to baked products.

Sugar—Contributes sweetness and flavor. As sugar is increased in proportion to flour it tends to increase browning and crispness. Liquid forms of sweetening (honey, sugar sirup, maple sirup and molasses) may supply liquid.

Fat—Increases tenderness, gives flavor and aids in browning.

Liquid—From melted (caramelized) sugar, liquid, sweetenings, melted or liquid fat or eggs is often sufficient. Milk, buttermilk, sweet or sour cream, fruit juices or water are liquids used, but in a small proportion to flour because cookie batters and doughs are meant to be fairly stiff.

Eggs—May or may not be used; increase fineness of texture, add flavor and color, act to bind the ingredients together and sometimes leaven the batter or dough, especially beaten egg whites. Too large a proportion of eggs can make the texture tough; when large number of eggs is used, amount of fat should be increased to counteract toughening effect of eggs.

Leavening Agents—In some cases, no leavening ingredient is needed. Often both baking powder and baking soda are used together. *Air*—may be the only leavening when beaten into egg whites as in ladyfingers and meringue-type cookies. *Baking powder*—may be the sole leavening agent. *Baking soda*—used to neutralize acid foods such as molasses, buttermilk, sour cream, fruit juices and dried fruits. When baking soda is not used to neutralize the acid ingredient in cookies, it nevertheless tends to tenderize the cookies. Some cookies with no baking soda or an insufficient amount tend to have light-colored centers and browned edges.

Other Ingredients—Various flavoring extracts, spices, nuts, fruits in several forms, citrus peels, cereals, chocolate, cocoa, candies, mincemeat and coconut are used alone or in suitable combinations for the various cookies. Wheat germ, when added, increases food value and imparts a pleasing nut-like flavor and crispness. Avoid chunky pieces in the cookie dough when using a cookie press.

A Check List for Successful Cookie Making

(See For These Recipes—What To Use, How To Do It and Oven Temperatures on *pages 10–13*.)

√ **Read** recipe carefully.

√ **Assemble** all ingredients and utensils.

√ **Have all ingredients** at room temperature unless recipe specifies otherwise.

√ **Select pans** of proper kind and size. Measure inside, from rim to rim.

√ **Lightly grease** cookie sheets or pan. If recipe states "set out cookie sheets or pan," do not grease cookie sheets or pan.

√ **Use standard measuring cups and spoons.** Use liquid measuring cups (rim above 1-cup line) for liquids. Use nested or dry measuring cups (1-cup line even with top) for dry ingredients. *Check liquid* measurements at eye level. *Level dry* measurements with straight-edged knife or spatula.

√ **Preheat oven** 12 to 20 min. at required temperature. Leave oven door open first 2 min.

√ **Place oven rack** so top of product will be almost at center of oven. Stagger pans so no pan or cookie sheet is directly over another and they do not touch each other or walls of oven. Place single pan so that center of product is as near center of oven as possible.

√ **Sift all flour** except whole-grain types before measuring. Spoon lightly into measuring cup. Do not jar. Level with straight-edged knife or spatula.

√ **Cream shortening** (alone or with flavorings) by stirring, rubbing or beating with spoon or electric mixer until softened. Add sugar in small amounts; cream after each addition until all graininess disappears and mixture is light and fluffy.

√ **Beat whole eggs** until thick and piled softly when recipe calls for well-beaten eggs.

√ **Beat egg whites** as follows: *Frothy*—entire mass forms bubbles; *Rounded peaks*—peaks turn over slightly when beater is slowly lifted upright; *Stiff peaks*—peaks remain standing when beater is slowly lifted upright.

√ **Beat egg yolks** until thick and lemon-colored when recipe calls for well-beaten yolks.

√ **When dry and liquid ingredients** are added to batters, add alternately, beginning and ending with dry. Add dry ingredients in fourths, liquid in thirds. After each addition, mix only until well blended. Finally mix only until batter is well blended (do not overmix). Scrape spoon or beater and bottom and sides of bowl during mixing. If using an electric mixer, beat at a low speed when alternately adding dry and liquid ingredients.

√ **Apply baking tests** when minimum baking time is up. Thin, crisp cookies are baked to an even, delicate brown. Drop and soft, thicker cookies are done when almost no imprint remains when lightly touched with finger tip. Some bar cookies test done when a wooden pick or cake tester comes out clean when inserted in center.

√ **Remove cookies** from pans as they come from the oven, unless otherwise directed. Set on cooling racks to cool.

√ **Store cookies** when cool in a cookie jar, canister or casserole having a cover.

√ **Pack cookies** for mailing, wrapped (separately if possible) in moisture-vapor-proof material, in sturdy container lined with extra wrapping material. Used crumpled waxed paper, popcorn or shredded packing material to fill extra space.

▲ Marbled Brownies 2

For Cheese Mixture—Cream until softened
  1½ tablespoons butter or margarine
Add gradually, creaming until fluffy after each addition
  3 tablespoons sugar
Blend in, in order
  2 teaspoons cornstarch
  ⅔ cup dry cottage cheese
  1 egg, well beaten
  1 tablespoon milk
  ½ teaspoon vanilla extract
  ⅛ teaspoon salt
Set aside.

For Brownie Dough—Grease and set aside a 9x9x2-in. pan.

Melt (*page 12*) and set aside to cool
  2 sq. (2 oz.) chocolate
Sift together
  1 cup sifted cake flour
  ½ teaspoon baking powder
  ½ teaspoon salt
Set aside.

Chop and mix with dry ingredients
  1 cup (about 4 oz.) nuts
Cream together until softened
  ½ cup butter or margarine
  ½ teaspoon vanilla extract
Add gradually, creaming until fluffy after each addition
  1 cup sugar
Add in thirds, beating thoroughly after each addition
  2 eggs, well beaten
Stir in the chocolate. Blend in dry ingredients in fourths.

Spread one half of dough in pan. Spread cheese mixture over chocolate layer. Spread remaining dough over cheese mixture. Draw spoon through layers until marbled effect is produced.

Bake at 375°F 40 to 45 min., or until wooden pick inserted in center comes out clean. Remove pan to cooling rack; cool in pan and cut into squares.   *16 brownies*

*Fudge Brownies with
Basic Butter Frosting (page 394)*

△ Fudge Brownies 3
(*See photo on page 430*)

Follow ▲ Recipe for dough. Omit cheese mixture. Frost with any **butter-type frosting.**

Double-Decker Brownies
CLAUDE E. METZ, MORENCI, MICH.

An innovation in brownie-making that makes these popular favorites doubly appealing.

Grease and set aside two 9x9x2-in. pans.

Finely chop
  1 cup (about 4 oz.) pecans
Mix with pecans and set aside
  1 pkg. (6 oz.) semi-sweet chocolate pieces
Grind enough dates to yield
  ½ cup (3½ oz.) ground dates
Set aside.

Sift together
  ¾ cup sifted flour
  5 tablespoons cocoa
  ½ teaspoon salt
Set aside.

Cream together

½ cup shortening

1 teaspoon vanilla extract

Add gradually, creaming until fluffy after each addition

1 cup sugar

Add in thirds, beating thoroughly after each addition

3 eggs, well beaten

Mixing until well blended after each addition, add dry ingredients in fourths to creamed mixture. Blend in the ground dates. Turn one half of the batter into each pan, spreading evenly. Sprinkle one half of the pecan mixture over batter. Set aside.

Melt

⅓ cup shortening

Blend into melted shortening

1 cup firmly packed brown sugar

Set sugar mixture aside to cool.

Sift together and set aside

1 cup sifted flour

½ teaspoon baking powder

½ teaspoon baking soda

½ teaspoon salt

Add to sugar mixture, beating thoroughly

1 egg, well beaten

1 teaspoon vanilla extract

Mixing until well blended after each addition, add dry ingredients in fourths. Spread one half of this batter evenly over the batter in each pan.

Bake at 350°F about 30 min., or until wooden pick inserted in center comes out clean. Remove pans to cooling racks. Cut into bars while still warm; cool completely in pan.

4 doz. brownies

Raspberry Squares

MRS. A. E. MARTINSON

DETROIT LAKES, MINN.

Set out an 8x8x2-in. pan.

Chop and set aside

2 cups (about 8 oz.) moist, shredded coconut

Measure and set aside

½ cup raspberry jam

Sift together and set aside

1 cup sifted flour

1 teaspoon baking powder

Cream until softened

½ cup butter or margarine

Add gradually, beating thoroughly after each addition

1 egg, well beaten

Blend in

1 tablespoon milk

Mixing until well blended after each addition, add dry ingredients in fourths to creamed mixture. Spread batter evenly in the pan and cover with the raspberry jam. Set aside.

Melt and set aside to cool

¼ cup butter or margarine

Beat until thick and piled softly

1 egg

1 teaspoon vanilla extract

Add gradually, beating thoroughly after each addition

1 cup sugar

Blend in the cooled butter and chopped coconut. Spread over cookie batter in the pan.

Bake at 350°F 30 min., or until golden brown.

Remove pan to cooling rack. When completely cooled, cut into 2-in. squares.   *16 cookies*

Grandma's Crisscross Cookies

DOROTHY HJORTH, LONG BEACH, CALIF.

Set out a 15½ x 10½ x 1-in. jelly roll pan.

Sift together
3 cups sifted flour
½ cup sugar
Cut in with a pastry blender or two knives until pieces are the size of small peas
1 cup butter
Beat until thick and lemon-colored
3 egg yolks
Blend egg yolks into flour mixture. Mix in
½ cup orange juice
Chill in refrigerator 2 to 3 hrs.

Pat three-fourths of the dough evenly over bottom of pan. Spread evenly over dough about
1 cup strawberry or apricot jam
Roll out remaining dough ¼ in. thick. Cut into strips ½ in. wide and 4 to 5 in. long. With hands, roll and stretch dough into long, pencil-thin strips. Cut to desired lengths. Place strips over jam-covered dough forming a crisscross pattern.

Bake at 300°F 40 min. Remove pan to cooling rack; cool completely. Cut the baked dough into 2½ x 1-in. strips.   *About 5 doz. cookies*

French Nut Sticks

EMILY EWING, EASTON, MD.

Lightly grease a 15½ x 10½ x 1-in. jelly roll pan.

Measure and set aside
3 cups sifted cake flour
Cream together until butter is softened
¾ cup butter
1 teaspoon vanilla extract
Add gradually, beating until fluffy after each addition
1 cup sugar
Add in thirds, beating thoroughly after each addition
2 eggs, well beaten
Mixing until well blended after each addition, add dry ingredients in fourths to creamed mixture. Turn dough into pan, spreading evenly. Spread evenly over dough
1 cup (12-oz. jar) apricot preserves
Bake at 350°F 15 min., or until edges of dough are lightly browned. Set aside on cooling rack; do not remove from pan.

Finely chop
1 cup (about 4 oz.) pecans
Set aside.

Beat until frothy
2 egg whites
⅛ teaspoon salt
Add gradually, beating thoroughly after each addition, a mixture of
1 cup sugar
1 tablespoon flour
Continue beating until rounded peaks are formed and egg whites do not slide when bowl is partially inverted. Fold in (*page 12*) the chopped pecans. Spread meringue evenly over the cooled cookie layer. Chill in refrigerator 2 to 3 hrs.

Remove from refrigerator and cut into strips 2½ x ½-in. Place strips about ½ in. apart onto 2 lightly greased baking sheets.

Bake at 375°F 15 min., or until meringue is delicately browned. Remove bars to cooling racks.   *About 10 doz. cookies*

Crunchy Lemon Squares
ARLETTA WHALEY, OTWELL, IND.

Set out a 13x9x2-in. baking pan.

Finely chop and set aside
½ cup (about 2 oz.) pecans
Measure and set aside
1 cup sifted flour
Cream together
½ cup shortening
2 teaspoons grated lemon peel
(page 11)
Add gradually, creaming until fluffy after each addition
½ cup sifted confectioners' sugar
Add gradually, beating thoroughly after each addition
2 egg yolks, beaten
Mixing until well blended after each addition, add flour in fourths to creamed mixture. Spread batter evenly over bottom of pan.

Bake at 350°F 10 min. Remove to cooling rack.

Meanwhile, beat until frothy
2 egg whites
Add gradually, beating well after each addition
½ cup sugar
Continue beating until rounded peaks are formed and egg whites do not slide when bowl is partially inverted.

Fold in (*page 12*) the chopped pecans and
1 tablespoon lemon juice
Spread evenly over first layer in pan. Return to oven and bake for 25 min. or until meringue is delicately browned.

Cool and cut into 2-in. squares.
About 2 doz. cookies

Spicy Pecan Bars
DORIS H. ESTABROOK, CONCORD, N.H.

Lightly grease an 11x7x1½-in. baking pan.

Coarsely chop and set aside
½ cup (about 2 oz.) pecans
Sift together and set aside
⅔ cup sifted flour
1 teaspoon baking powder
1 teaspoon cinnamon
½ teaspoon cloves
⅛ teaspoon salt
Beat until thick and lemon-colored
3 egg yolks
Add gradually, beating thoroughly after each addition
1 cup firmly packed brown sugar
Blend in
1 teaspoon vanilla extract
Mixing until well blended after each addition, add dry ingredients in fourths to sugar mixture. Stir in the pecans. Set aside.

Beat until rounded peaks are formed
3 egg whites
Spread egg whites over batter and gently fold (*page 12*) together. Turn batter into pan and spread evenly.

Bake at 350°F 30 min., or until wooden pick inserted in center comes out clean. Remove pan to cooling rack and cool slightly. While still warm, cut baked dough into bars. Roll warm bars in a mixture of
⅓ cup sugar
¼ teaspoon cinnamon
¼ teaspoon cloves
Place bars on cooling rack. Cool completely.
About 2 doz. cookies

 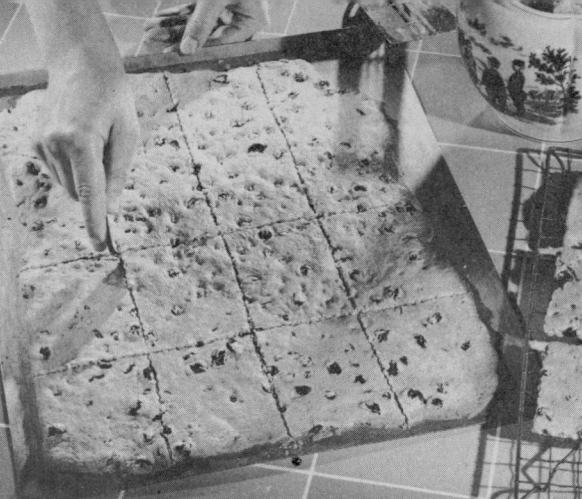

Spicy Raisin Squares: Be sure that dough will be thin by rolling it out on greased sheet.

Cut baked dough with a pastry wheel or a knife and remove immediately to cooling rack.

Spicy Raisin Squares

Coarsely chop and set aside
> **2 cups seedless raisins**

Sift together and set aside
> **2½ cups sifted flour**
> **1 teaspoon salt**
> **½ teaspoon baking soda**
> **1 teaspoon cinnamon**
> **½ teaspoon mace**
> **½ teaspoon nutmeg**

Cream together until softened
> **½ cup butter or margarine**
> **½ teaspoon lemon extract**

Add gradually, creaming until fluffy after each addition
> **1 cup sugar**

Measure
> **½ cup milk**

Mixing until well blended after each addition, alternately add dry ingredients in fourths, liquid in thirds to the creamed mixture. Blend in the raisins. Chill in refrigerator about 1 hr.

Lightly grease 2 cookie sheets.

Divide dough into halves. Place one portion on each cookie sheet and roll out ⅛ in. thick.

Bake at 400°F about 7 min. Cut with a pastry wheel or sharp knife into 2- or 3-in. squares. Remove squares to cooling racks.

About 7 doz. 2-in. cookies

Chip-Filled Wheat-Germ Bars

Lightly grease an 8x8x2-in. pan.

Crush (*page 12*) graham crackers to yield
> **2 cups graham cracker crumbs (26 to 28 crackers, crushed)**

Turn crumbs into a bowl. Add
> **½ cup wheat germ**
> **¼ teaspoon salt**

Mix in and beat until well blended
> **1⅓ cups (15-oz. can) sweetened condensed milk**
> **2 teaspoons vanilla extract**

Stir in contents of
> **1 pkg. (6 oz.) semi-sweet chocolate pieces**

Spread dough into prepared pan.

Bake at 350°F 35 to 40 min. Remove pan to cooling rack; cool in pan. Cut into bars.

About 1 doz. cookies

Almond Sticks

Lightly grease cookie sheets.

Grate (*page 11*) and set aside
> **¾ cup (about ¼ lb.) almonds (about 2 cups, grated)**

Put into bowl and cream until softened
> **½ cup unsalted butter**

Add gradually to the butter, creaming until fluffy after each addition

1 cup sifted confectioners' sugar

Add to bowl, stirring just until ingredients are blended, a mixture of the almonds and

1 cup sifted flour

Gather dough into a ball. Turn out onto lightly floured surface and roll into a rectangle ½ in. thick, keeping edges straight. Cut into strips 2½ x ½-in. Place 1 in. apart on cookie sheets.

Bake at 350°F 20 to 25 min., or until cookies are lightly browned. Immediately remove to cooling racks. When cooled, roll in

½ cup Vanilla Confectioners' Sugar (page 415)

About 3 doz. cookies

▲ Refrigerator Cookies
(Basic Chocolate and Vanilla Doughs)

Melt (*page 12*) and set aside to cool

2 sq. (2 oz.) chocolate

Sift together and set aside

3 cups sifted flour
2 teaspoons baking powder
½ teaspoon salt

Cream together

1 cup shortening
2 teaspoons vanilla extract

Add gradually, creaming until fluffy after each addition

1 cup sugar

Add in thirds, beating thoroughly after each addition

2 eggs, well beaten

Mixing until well blended after each addition, add dry ingredients in fourths to creamed mixture.

Divide dough into halves. Stir into one half of the dough the melted chocolate and

1 tablespoon milk

Wrap each half of dough in waxed paper and chill in refrigerator until easy to handle. Shape each dough into 2 rolls, 1½ in. in diameter. Wrap each roll in waxed paper and chill several hours or overnight.

Set out cookie sheets.

Remove rolls from refrigerator as needed. Cut into ⅛-in. slices. Place them 1½ in. apart on the cookie sheets.

Bake at 400°F 5 to 9 min. Remove to cooling racks.   *10 doz. cookies*

⚠ Pinwheels

Follow ▲ Recipe. After chilling dough enough to handle, divide each dough into three portions. Roll one third of the chocolate and one third of the white dough into rectangles about 8x6x⅛-in. Place rolled chocolate dough on top of white dough and roll up tightly into a roll. Repeat process, forming two more rolls. Wrap each roll in waxed paper and chill in refrigerator several hours or overnight. Proceed as in ▲ Recipe.

⚠ Stripers

Follow ▲ Recipe. After chilling dough enough to handle, divide each dough into six portions. Roll two portions of the chocolate dough into rectangles about 6x2x¼-in. Roll two portions of the white dough to the same size. Line a shallow pan with waxed paper. Stack layers in pan, alternating colors and brushing each layer with slightly beaten **egg white** before putting on the next layer. Repeat process with remaining portions of dough, forming two additional stacks. Wrap waxed paper around each block of dough. Chill several hours or overnight.

Remove blocks from refrigerator as needed. Remove from pan and unwrap. Cut into slices ¼ in. thick and place 1½ in. apart on the cookie sheets. Bake as in ▲ Recipe.

▲ Date Swirls

CLAUDE E. METZ, MORENCI, MICH.

For Filling—Combine in a saucepan and cook over low heat until thickened (about 5 min.)

> **3 cups (about 1¼ lb.) chopped pitted dates**
> **¾ cup sugar**
> **¾ cup water**

Remove from heat. Blend in

> **½ cup (about 2 oz.) chopped nuts**
> **4 teaspoons lemon juice**

Set aside to cool.

For Cookies—Sift together and set aside

> **4 cups sifted flour**
> **1½ teaspoons salt**
> **1 teaspoon baking soda**

Cream together until softened

> **½ cup butter**
> **½ cup shortening**

Add gradually, creaming until fluffy after each addition

> **2 cups firmly packed brown sugar**

Add gradually, beating thoroughly after each addition

> **1 egg, well beaten**

Mixing until well blended after each addition, add dry ingredients in fourths to creamed mixture. After the third addition, blend in

> **2 tablespoons milk**

Chill in refrigerator until easy to handle.

Divide dough into halves. Roll out one portion ¼ in. thick. Spread with one half of the cooled filling. Roll up like a jelly roll. Repeat with second portion of dough. Cut rolls into halves crosswise, forming four short rolls.

Wrap each in waxed paper. Chill in refrigerator several hours or overnight.

Lightly grease cookie sheets.

Remove rolls from refrigerator as needed. Cut into thin slices and place about 2 in. apart on the cookie sheets.

Bake at 400°F 10 to 15 min. Remove to cooling racks.   *About 6 doz. cookies*

△ Butterscotch Refrigerator Cookies

Follow ▲ Recipe; omit date filling. Cream 1½ teaspoons **vanilla extract** and 3 drops **walnut extract** with the shortening. Decrease flour to 3 cups. Add 1 cup chopped **walnuts** to dough before chilling. Form dough into five rolls about 1½ in. in diameter. Bake on *ungreased* cookie sheets at 375°F 10 min.

About 12 doz. cookies

French Pain d'Amande

MRS. GLENA E. WILSON, MADISON, OHIO

A French grandmother taught her grandchild how to make these cookies a half-century ago. They are traditional Christmas cookies in Aniche, France.

Finely chop and set aside

> **½ cup (about 3 oz.) blanched almonds (page 11)**

Sift together and set aside

> **2 cups sifted flour**
> **¼ teaspoon baking soda**
> **¼ teaspoon cinnamon**

Cream until softened

> **½ cup butter**

Add gradually, creaming until fluffy after each addition

> **1 cup plus 2 tablespoons firmly packed brown sugar**

Add gradually, beating thoroughly after each addition

> **1 egg, well beaten**

Mixing until well blended after each addition,

Add gradually, creaming until fluffy after each addition

1 cup sugar

1 cup firmly packed brown sugar

Add in thirds, beating thoroughly after each addition

2 eggs, well beaten

Mixing until well blended after each addition, add dry ingredients in fourths to creamed mixture. Blend in the nuts and

2 cups uncooked rolled oats

½ cup semi-sweet chocolate pieces or raisins

Form into 4 rolls about 2 in. in diameter, chilling dough first if necessary. Wrap each roll in waxed paper. Chill in refrigerator several hours or overnight.

Set out cookie sheets.

Remove rolls from refrigerator as needed. Cut into thin slices and place about 1 in. apart on the cookie sheets.

Bake at 375°F 10 to 12 min. Remove to cooling racks.   *About 8½ doz. cookies*

add dry ingredients in fourths to creamed mixture. Blend in the chopped almonds. Chill dough in refrigerator until easy to handle.

Shape into short rolls about 2 in. in diameter. Wrap each roll in waxed paper. Chill in refrigerator several hours or overnight.

Set out cookie sheets.

Remove rolls from refrigerator as needed. Cut into ⅛-in. slices and place about 1 in. apart on the cookie sheets.

Bake at 375°F 10 min. Remove to cooling racks.   *About 7 doz. cookies*

△ Oatmeal Drops 9

Follow ▲ Recipe. Omit forming rolls and chilling dough. Drop by teaspoonfuls 2 in. apart onto *lightly greased* cookie sheets. Garnish with pieces of **dates** or **nuts**.

Oatmeal Drops

▲ Krispie Oatmeal Cookies 8

MRS. FRANK YOUNG, TOPEKA, KANS.

Coarsely chop and set aside

½ cup (about 2 oz.) nuts

Sift together and set aside

1½ cups sifted flour

1 teaspoon baking soda

1 teaspoon salt

Cream together

1 cup shortening

1 teaspoon vanilla extract

Cherry-Coconut Tea Cookies
MRS. WILL W. COTTINGHAM, ROLLA, MO.

Do not be dismayed by the stickiness of the dough. The cookies are crisp and delicious.

Prepare and set aside
  12 maraschino cherries, coarsely chopped and thoroughly drained
  ½ cup (about 2 oz.) coarsely chopped nuts
  ½ cup (about 2 oz.) moist, shredded coconut, cut
Sift together and set aside
  1½ cups sifted flour
  ¾ teaspoon cream of tartar
  ½ teaspoon baking soda
  ¼ teaspoon salt
Cream until softened
  ½ cup butter
Add gradually, creaming until fluffy after each addition
  ½ cup sugar
  ¼ cup firmly packed brown sugar
Combine and add gradually to creamed mixture, beating thoroughly after each addition
  1 egg, well beaten
  2 teaspoons milk
Mixing until well blended after each addition, add dry ingredients in fourths to creamed mixture. Stir in the fruit and nuts. Chill in refrigerator until firm enough to handle.

Form dough into short rolls 1½ in. in diameter. Wrap each roll in waxed paper. Chill in refrigerator several hours or overnight.

Set out cookie sheets.

Remove rolls from refrigerator as needed. Slice cookies ⅛ in. thick and place 1 in. apart on the cookie sheets.

Bake on top rack of oven at 375°F 10 to 12 min. Remove to cooling racks.

About 3 doz. cookies

Macaroons 10

Line two cookie sheets with unglazed paper.

Measure and force a little at a time through a sieve into a bowl
  ½ lb. almond paste
Add gradually, stirring until smooth after each addition
  ⅓ cup (about 3) egg whites, unbeaten (slightly more or less egg white may be needed, depending upon moistness of almond paste)
Blend in
  ¾ teaspoon vanilla extract
  ¼ teaspoon yellow food coloring
Mix together
  ½ cup sugar
  ½ cup sifted confectioners' sugar
Blend a little at a time into almond-paste mixture. Mix thoroughly. Mixture should be thick enough to hold its shape but not stiff.

Drop by teaspoonfuls onto baking sheets. Flatten top of each macaroon with spatula or back of spoon. Sift over Macaroons
  Confectioners' sugar
Bake at 300°F about 25 min. Using a spatula, remove cookies to cooling racks. If necessary, slightly moisten underside of paper directly under each macaroon to loosen.

About 3 doz. 1½-in. macaroons

▲ Date Kisses
MRS. CARL MOORE, BAYTOWN, TEXAS

Line cookie sheet with unglazed paper.

Mix together and set aside
  1 lb. (about 2½ cups) dates, coarsely chopped
  ½ lb. (about 2 cups) pecans, coarsely chopped
  2 tablespoons flour
Beat until frothy
  3 egg whites
Add and beat slightly
  1 teaspoon vanilla extract
  ¼ teaspoon salt

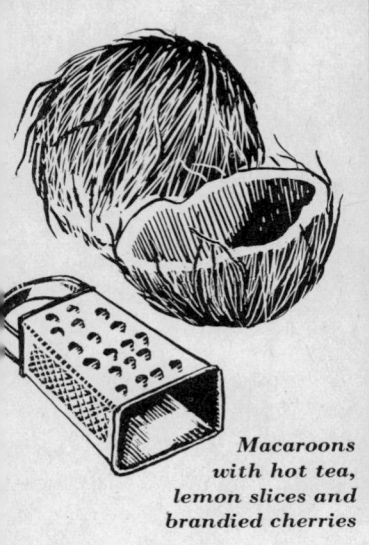

*Macaroons
with hot tea,
lemon slices and
brandied cherries*

Add, one tablespoon at a time, beating well after each addition, finally beating until stiff (but not dry) peaks are formed

1½ cups sugar

Carefully fold (*page 12*) the date-nut mixture into the egg white mixture.

Drop by teaspoonfuls onto unglazed paper. Keep cookies small and uniform.

Bake at 250°F 25 to 30 min. Working quickly and carefully, remove cookies to cooling racks.

If necessary, slightly moisten underside of paper directly under each cookie to loosen.

About 8 doz. small cookies

△ Coconut Kisses

Follow ▲ Recipe. Omit dates, nuts, and flour. Blend into meringue mixture 2 cups moist, shredded **coconut**, cut.

About 3 doz. small kisses

Filbert Cookies
MRS. WILLIAM FAYNE, GEARHART, ORE.

Line cookie sheets with unglazed paper.

Split into halves and set aside for garnish about

36 filberts

Grate (*page 11*) and set aside

2¼ cups (about 11 oz.) filberts (about 4 cups, grated)

For Topping—Beat until frothy

2 egg whites

Add, beating slightly

1 teaspoon vanilla extract

Add gradually, beating well after each addition

1½ cups sifted confectioners' sugar

Continue beating until stiff (but not dry) peaks are formed. Set topping aside.

For Cookies—Beat until frothy

4 egg whites (about ½ cup whites)

Add, beating slightly

1 teaspoon vanilla extract

Add gradually, beating well after each addition

1 cup sugar

Beat until stiff (but not dry) peaks are formed. Fold in (*page 12*) the grated nuts.

Drop by teaspoonfuls about 1½ in. apart on cookie sheets. Top each cookie with about ½ teaspoonful topping and a filbert half.

Bake at 250°F about 25 min., or until just golden tipped. Working quickly and carefully, remove cookies to cooling racks. If necessary, slightly moisten underside of paper under each cookie to loosen. *About 6 doz. cookies*

Date-Nut Cookies 11

EDITH L. SULLIVAN, WASHINGTON, D.C.

Spicy nuggets that recall happy memories of childhood visits to Grandmother's house.

Lightly grease cookie sheets.

Prepare, combine and set aside
- **1¼ cups (about 8 oz.) coarsely chopped dates**
- **½ cup (about 2 oz.) chopped nuts**

Sift together and set aside
- **2 cups sifted flour**
- **1¼ teaspoons baking powder**
- **½ teaspoon baking soda**
- **¼ teaspoon cinnamon**
- **¼ teaspoon cloves**
- **¼ teaspoon nutmeg**
- **⅛ teaspoon salt**

Cream together until shortening is softened
- **¼ cup butter or margarine**
- **¼ cup lard**
- **¼ teaspoon vanilla extract**

Add gradually, creaming until fluffy after each addition
- **½ cup sugar**
- **¼ cup firmly packed brown sugar**

Add gradually, beating thoroughly after each addition
- **1 egg, well beaten**

Mixing until well blended after each addition, add dry ingredients in fourths to creamed mixture. Blend in the nuts and dates, reserving ¼ cup of the mixture for topping. Drop by teaspoonfuls 2 in. apart on cookie sheets. Top each cookie with a piece of **date** or **nut.**

Bake at 350°F 12 min. Remove to cooling racks.

About 6 doz. cookies

French Cookies 12

DOROTHY J. MARCUSSEN, RIVERTON, ILL.

During the Civil War a wounded prisoner in a hospital near Gettysburg tasted cookies brought by a compassionate visitor and he asked for the recipe for his own mother. These cookies became a family favorite.

Lightly grease cookie sheets.

Prepare and set aside to cool
- **1 cup double-strength coffee beverage (page 13)**

Coarsely chop and set aside
- **1 cup (about 4 oz.) nuts**

Measure and set aside
- **2 cups dark seedless raisins**

Sift together and set aside
- **3 cups sifted flour**
- **1 teaspoon baking soda**
- **1 teaspoon allspice**
- **1 teaspoon cinnamon**
- **1 teaspoon nutmeg**

Cream thoroughly
- **⅔ cup shortening**

Add gradually, creaming until fluffy after each addition
- **2 cups firmly packed brown sugar**

Add in thirds, beating thoroughly after each addition
- **2 eggs, well beaten**

Mixing until well blended after each addition, alternately add dry ingredients in fourths, cooled coffee in thirds, to creamed mixture. Stir in the raisins and nuts. Drop by teaspoonfuls about 2 in. apart onto cookie sheets.

Bake at 375°F about 12 min. Remove to cooling racks.

About 6 doz. 2-in. cookies

Frosted Orange Drops

MRS. H. S. NAGLER, ONTARIO, CALIF.

Lightly grease cookie sheets.

Sift together and set aside
1⅓ cups sifted flour
¼ teaspoon baking powder
¼ teaspoon baking soda
⅛ teaspoon salt
Measure and set aside
¼ cup orange juice
Cream together
¼ cup shortening
2 teaspoons grated orange peel
(page 11)
Add gradually, creaming until fluffy after each addition
⅔ cup firmly packed brown sugar
Add gradually, beating thoroughly after each addition
1 egg, well beaten
Mixing until well blended after each addition, alternately add dry ingredients and juice to creamed mixture, beginning and ending with dry. Drop by teaspoonfuls 2 in. apart onto cookie sheet.

Bake at 375°F 12 to 15 min. Remove to cooling racks. When cool, frost with
Confectioners' Sugar Glaze
(page 399)

About 8 doz. small cookies

"Go To School" Cookies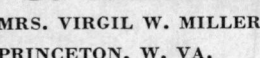

MRS. VIRGIL W. MILLER
PRINCETON, W. VA.

A favorite from kindergarten to college.

Melt (*page 12*) and set aside to cool
2 sq. (2 oz.) chocolate
Coarsely chop and set aside
¾ cup (about 3 oz.) nuts
Sift together and set aside
1½ cups sifted flour
½ teaspoon salt
½ teaspoon baking powder
¼ teaspoon baking soda

Cream together
½ cup shortening
½ teaspoon vanilla extract
Add gradually, creaming until fluffy after each addition
1 cup firmly packed brown sugar
Blend in the melted chocolate. Add gradually, beating thoroughly after each addition
1 egg, well beaten
Measure
½ cup milk
Mixing until well blended after each addition, alternately add dry ingredients in fourths, milk in thirds, to the creamed mixture. Stir in the chopped nuts.

Drop by teaspoonfuls 2 in. apart on cookie sheets.

Bake at 350°F 12 to 15 min. Remove to cooling racks. Frost when cool.

For Frosting—Melt (*p.12*) and set aside to cool
1 sq. (1 oz.) chocolate
Cream together until softened
¼ cup butter or margarine
½ teaspoon vanilla extract
Add alternately, creaming until smooth after each addition
2 cups sifted confectioners' sugar
¼ cup hot water
Put one third of the frosting into another bowl. Add, blending in, the chocolate and
1 tablespoon hot water
Spread cookies with the white frosting. Top each with a small amount of chocolate frosting. Allow frosting to become firm before storing cookies. *About 2 doz. cookies*

Lemon Sugar Wafers, Fudge Brownies, Perky Cookies and strawberry ice cream

Gingersnaps

Lightly grease cookie sheets.

Sift together and set aside
- **2 cups sifted flour**
- **2 teaspoons concentrated soluble coffee**
- **1 teaspoon baking soda**
- **1 teaspoon cinnamon**
- **½ teaspoon ginger**
- **¼ teaspoon cloves**
- **½ teaspoon salt**

Cream
- **¾ cup shortening**

Add gradually, creaming until fluffy after each addition
- **1 cup firmly packed brown sugar**

Add in thirds, beating thoroughly after each addition
- **2 eggs, well beaten**

Blend in
- **¼ cup molasses**

Mixing until well blended after each addition, add dry ingredients in fourths to creamed mixture. Drop by teaspoonfuls about 2 in. apart onto the cookie sheets. (These cookies will puff up, spread, then flatten.)

Bake at 350°F 10 to 12 min. Remove to cooling racks. *About 7 doz. cookies*

Lemon Sugar Wafers

The kind of delicate cookie that is the perfect accompaniment for ice cream, cooling beverages, or a spot of afternoon tea.

Lightly grease cookie sheets.

Set out about
- **¼ cup broken walnut meats**

Sift together and set aside
- **3 cups sifted flour**
- **1½ teaspoons baking powder**
- **1 teaspoon salt**

Cream together until softened
- **1 cup butter or margarine**
- **2 teaspoons grated lemon peel (page 11)**
- **1 teaspoon lemon extract**
- **1 teaspoon vanilla extract**

Add gradually, creaming until fluffy after each addition
- **1½ cups sugar**

Beat together thoroughly
- **1 egg**
- **1 egg yolk**
- **3 tablespoons cream or undiluted evaporated milk**

Add egg mixture in thirds to creamed mixture, beating thoroughly after each addition. Mixing until well blended after each addition, add dry ingredients in fourths to creamed mixture.

Drop by teaspoonfuls 1½ in. apart onto cookie sheets. Flatten slightly with spatula or back of spoon. Top each cookie with a walnut piece.

Bake at 400°F 8 to 10 min., or until cookies are very lightly browned. Remove immediately to cooling racks. *About 5 doz. cookies*

▲ Peanut Butter Honeys 15
MRS. HOBART LELAND, BRICELYN, MINN.

Peanut butter and honey! Ummmm—yummy!

Lightly grease cookie sheets.

Sift together and set aside
2½ cups sifted flour
1 teaspoon baking soda

Cream together thoroughly
1 cup chunk-style peanut butter
½ cup butter
2 teaspoons vanilla extract

Add gradually, creaming until fluffy after each addition
½ cup sugar
1 cup honey

Add in thirds, beating thoroughly after each addition
2 eggs, well beaten

Mixing until well blended after each addition, add dry ingredients in fourths to creamed mixture. Drop by teaspoonfuls onto cookie sheets.

Bake at 375°F 10 to 12 min. Remove to cooling racks. *About 8 doz. cookies*

⚠ Peanut-Butter-Chocolate Honeys 16

Follow ▲ Recipe. Blend in 2 cups **semi-sweet chocolate pieces** before forming cookies.

⚠ Peanut-Butter-Honey Balls

Follow ▲ Recipe. Chill dough at least 1 hr. Form into ¾-in. balls. Roll balls in a mixture of ¼ cup **sugar** and 1 tablespoon **cinnamon**. Place 2 in. apart on cookie sheets.

Pineapple 'n' Chip Cookies
MRS. STANLEY HAMBLIN, KELSO, WASH.

Lightly grease cookie sheets.

Drain, reserving sirup, contents of
1 9-oz. can (about ⅔ cup, drained) crushed pineapple
(Use sirup in other food preparation.)

Coarsely chop and set aside
¼ cup nuts

Sift together
2 cups sifted flour
½ teaspoon baking soda
½ teaspoon cinnamon
½ teaspoon nutmeg
½ teaspoon salt

Set aside.

Cream until softened
¼ cup butter
¼ cup shortening

Add gradually, creaming until fluffy after each addition
1 cup firmly packed brown sugar

Add gradually, beating thoroughly after each addition
1 egg, well beaten

Mixing until well blended after each addition, alternately add dry ingredients in fourths, pineapple in thirds, to creamed mixture.

Stir in the nuts and
1 pkg. (6 oz.) semi-sweet chocolate pieces

Drop by teaspoonfuls about 2 in. apart onto cookie sheets.

Bake at 375°F 12 to 15 min. Remove to cooling racks. *About 9 doz. small cookies*

Perky Cookies

(See photo on page 430)

MRS. FRED H. LARSON, VILLANOVA, PA.

Set out cookie sheets.

Finely chop and set aside
1 cup (about 4 oz.) pecans
Put into a small dish and set aside
½ cup sugar
Sift together and set aside
2¼ cups sifted flour
1 teaspoon cinnamon
1 teaspoon ground cardamom seed
½ teaspoon baking soda
Cream together until softened
1¼ cups butter or margarine
½ teaspoon vanilla extract
Add gradually, beating until fluffy after each addition
1 cup firmly packed brown sugar
Beat until thick and piled softly
1 egg
1 egg yolk
Add in thirds to creamed mixture, beating thoroughly after each addition. Mixing well after each addition, blend in the dry ingredients in fourths. Shape into balls 1 in. in diameter. Set aside.

Beat until frothy
1 egg white
Dip balls into egg white, then in nuts and finally in sugar. Flatten each cookie slightly. Place 1½ in. apart on cookie sheets.

Bake at 350°F 15 to 18 min.

About 5 doz. cookies

Berlinerkranser

MRS. PEARL CARLETON, EMILY, MINN.

Traditional to Christmas, but always a favorite.

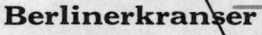

Lightly grease cookie sheets.

Sift together into a large bowl
4 cups sifted flour
½ teaspoon baking soda
Cut in with a pastry blender or two knives until pieces are size of small peas
1 cup butter
Set aside.

Beat until thick and lemon-colored
4 egg yolks
Add gradually, beating well after each addition
1 cup sugar
Blend into the egg mixture
½ cup thick sour cream
1 teaspoon vanilla or almond extract
Blending lightly after each addition, add the liquid mixture in thirds to the flour mixture. Chill dough until firm enough to roll.

Break off small pieces of dough. Roll with hands on a lightly floured surface into rolls about 6 in. long and ¼ in. thick. Form into wreaths or bowknots, or twist into pretzels. Brush top of each cookie with
Egg white, slightly beaten
Dip each cookie in
Crushed loaf sugar
Bake at 350°F until firm and very lightly browned (about 10 min.).

About 8 doz. cookies

Chocolate Snowflake Cookies 17

MRS. W. L. ISBELL, BROOKSTON, IND.

A delightful surprise awaits you when you open the oven door.

Melt (*page 12*) together
   2 sq. (2 oz.) chocolate
   ¼ cup shortening
Add, stirring until sugar is dissolved
   1 cup sugar
Set aside to cool.

Coarsely chop
   1 cup (about 4 oz.) nuts
Set aside.

Sift together
   1 cup sifted flour
   1 teaspoon baking powder
   ¼ teaspoon salt
Set aside.

Add in thirds to the cooled chocolate mixture, beating thoroughly after each addition
   2 eggs, well beaten
   1 teaspoon vanilla extract
Quickly blend in dry ingredients. Stir in the chopped nuts. Chill dough about 3 hrs.

Lightly grease cookie sheets.

Dampen hands slightly and roll small pieces of dough between palms to form balls about 1 in. in diameter. Roll balls in
   Sifted confectioners' sugar
Place 2 in. apart on the cookie sheets.

Bake at 400°F 10 to 12 min. Remove to cooling racks.   *About 4 doz. cookies*

▲ Buttery Nut Cookies

CLAUDE E. METZ, MORENCI, MICH.

From a proud husband comes his wife's Christmas specialty—a cookie "rich as candy."

Set out cookie sheets.

Melt and set aside to cool
   2 cups butter
Finely chop and set aside
   2 cups (about 8 oz.) walnuts
Measure and set aside
   4 cups sifted flour
Mix until well blended, the cooled butter and
   1 cup firmly packed brown sugar
   4 teaspoons vanilla extract
Measure
   ½ cup milk
Mixing until well blended after each addition, alternately add flour in fourths, milk in thirds, to butter mixture. Blend in the walnuts. Place in refrigerator to chill slightly.

Form into balls about 1 in. in diameter; roll in
   ½ cup sugar
Place balls about 2 in. apart on cookie sheets. Using the tines of a fork, flatten each ball, making a crisscross design.

Bake at 400°F 10 to 12 min. Remove to cooling racks.   *About 11 doz. cookies*

△ Pecan Crispies

Follow ▲ Recipe. Substitute 2 cups finely chopped **pecans** for the walnuts.

Mr. Minter's Poconuts

MRS. HARVEY SPARKS, KENT, WASH.

Lightly grease cookie sheets.

For Cookies—Finely chop

1 cup (4 oz.) moist, shredded coconut

Add, mixing thoroughly

1 cup sifted cake flour

Set mixture aside.

Cream together until softened

½ cup butter or margarine

1 teaspoon vanilla extract

Add gradually, creaming until fluffy after each addition

3 tablespoons sugar

Add gradually, blending in, the coconut-flour mixture. Gently shape dough into balls about ¾ in. in diameter. Do not pack or overwork dough. Place balls about 2 in. apart on the cookie sheets.

Bake at 250°F about 40 min.

While cookies are baking, prepare Chocolate-Mint Frosting.

For Chocolate-Mint Frosting—Melt (*page 12*) and set aside to cool

1 sq. (1 oz.) chocolate

Cream together until butter is softened

2 tablespoons butter

4 drops peppermint extract

Thoroughly blend in, in order

1 cup sifted confectioners' sugar

3 tablespoons hot water

Blend in the chocolate.

When cookies are baked, remove from oven. Immediately dip tops into frosting. Place on cooling racks over waxed paper to cool.

About 3 doz. cookies

Pfeffernuesse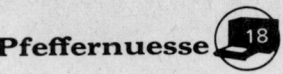

Not as dark or as hard as commercial pfeffernuesse, but crisp and spicy good.

Grate (*page 11*) and set aside

⅓ cup (about 1½ oz.) blanched almonds (*page 11*)

Chop and set aside

⅓ cup candied citron

Sift together and set aside

4 cups sifted flour

2 teaspoons cinnamon

½ teaspoon allspice

½ teaspoon concentrated soluble coffee

¼ teaspoon cloves

¼ teaspoon nutmeg

¼ teaspoon pepper

¼ teaspoon salt

Few grains ground cardamom seed

Beat until thick and piled softly

4 eggs

Add gradually, beating well after each addition

2 cups firmly packed brown sugar

Blend in

1½ teaspoons grated lemon peel (*page 11*)

Mixing until well blended, add dry ingredients in fourths to egg mixture.

Form dough into 1-in. balls. Cover with waxed paper and set aside in a cool, dry place several hours or overnight.

Lightly grease cookie sheets.

Place balls about 2 in. apart on cookie sheets. Bake at 300°F 25 to 30 min. Remove to cooling racks. While cookies are still warm, roll in

Sifted confectioners' sugar

Cool completely and roll again.

About 5 doz. cookies

▲ Swedish Spritz Cookies
ADELINE WEBSTER, BRAINTREE, MASS.

Set out cookie sheets.

Sift together and set aside
5 cups sifted flour
1 teaspoon baking powder
Grate (*page 11*) and set aside
**1 cup (about ⅓ lb.) blanched almonds
(page 11)**
Cream together until butter is softened
2 cups butter
½ teaspoon almond extract
Add gradually, creaming until fluffy after each
addition
1 cup sugar
Add gradually, beating thoroughly after each
addition
1 egg, well beaten
Blend in the nuts. Mixing well after each
addition, blend in dry ingredients in fourths.

Fill a cookie press about two-thirds full with
dough. Following manufacturer's directions,
and using the star-shaped plate, form small
wreaths directly onto cookie sheets.

Bake at 350°F 12 min. (Cookies will be golden
brown; do not brown.) Remove to cooling
racks. *About 10 doz. wreaths*

△ Pressed Butter
or "Spritz" Cookies

Follow ▲ Recipe; omit almonds. Substitute 1
teaspoon **vanilla extract** for the almond
extract. Form cookies of various shapes.
About 12 doz. cookies

▲ Tea-Time Tidbits
MRS. HENRIETTA HOLLOWAY
ALHAMBRA, CALIF.

Lightly grease cookie sheets.

Measure
1 cup sifted cake flour
Set aside.

Finely chop and set aside
1 cup (about 4 oz.) pecans
Cream together until butter is softened
½ cup butter
1 teaspoon vanilla extract
Add gradually, creaming until fluffy after each
addition
2 tablespoons sugar
Mixing until well blended after each addition,
add flour in fourths to creamed mixture. Stir
in the nuts. Chill dough until firm enough to
handle easily (about 1 hr.). Form into balls
about ¾ in. in diameter, and place them 2 in.
apart on cookie sheets.

Bake at 350°F 15 min. or until very lightly
browned. Remove to cooling racks. While
still warm, roll balls in
Sifted confectioners' sugar
Cool completely and roll again so that balls
are well coated with sugar.
About 2 doz. cookies

▲ Christmas Crescents
MRS. VERNON SHEAN, ROCK ISLAND, ILL.

Follow ▲ Recipe. Substitute 2 tablespoons
confectioners' sugar for the granulated sugar.
Mix in 1 tablespoon **water** after the flour. Roll
chilled dough with hands into pencil-thin
(about ¼-in.) strips. Cut strips into 2½-in.
lengths. Form into crescents.

▲ Tea Fingers
MRS. LEWIS HILL, CHERAW, S. C.

Follow ▲ Recipe. Increase vanilla extract to
2 teaspoons. Form chilled dough into "fingers"
2 in. long and ½ in. thick. (Fingers puff up
somewhat in baking.)

▲ Plain and Fancy Sugar Cookies

Sift together and set aside
2 cups sifted flour
1½ teaspoons baking powder
½ teaspoon salt
Cream together until softened
½ cup butter or margarine
1 teaspoon vanilla extract
Add gradually, creaming until fluffy after each addition
¾ cups sugar
Add in thirds, beating thoroughly after each addition
2 eggs, well beaten
Mixing until well blended after each addition, add dry ingredients gradually to the creamed mixture. Chill thoroughly in refrigerator.

Lightly grease cookie sheets.

Roll dough ¼ to ⅛ in. thick on lightly floured surface. Using floured cookie cutter, cut dough into desired shapes. Sprinkle cookies with
Sugar, or Colored Sugar (page 415)
Place cookies on cookie sheets.

Bake at 375°F 10 to 12 min. Immediately remove to cooling racks.   *2 to 3 doz. cookies*

⚠ Ginger Cookies

Follow ▲ Recipe. Reduce baking powder to ½ teaspoon. Sift ¼ teaspoon **baking soda,** 1½ teaspoons **ginger,** ½ teaspoon **cinnamon** and ¼ teaspoon **allspice** with the flour mixture. Decrease sugar to ½ cup and blend 6 tablespoons **molasses** into creamed mixture. Omit vanilla extract.

Plain and Fancy Sugar Cookies

⚠ Chocolate Sugar Cookies

Follow ▲ Recipe. Melt (*page 12*) 2 sq. (2 oz.) **chocolate** and set aside to cool. Blend in after addition of eggs.

Scotch Shortbread
MRS. E. W. SCHENCK, JANESVILLE, WISC.

Set out cookie sheets.

Sift together and set aside
2 cups sifted flour
¼ teaspoon baking powder
¼ teaspoon salt
Cream together until butter is softened
1 cup butter
1 teaspoon vanilla extract
Add gradually, creaming until fluffy
½ cup sifted confectioners' sugar
Mixing until well blended after each addition, add dry ingredients in fourths to creamed mixture. Chill dough until stiff enough to roll easily (at least ½ hr.).

Roll dough ¼ in. thick on a lightly floured surface. Cut into 3-in. rounds; lightly mark each round to indicate 6 wedge-shaped pieces which can be easily broken apart after baking.

Or cut dough into fancy shapes. Place on cookie sheets and prick with a fork.

Bake at 350°F 20 min. or until delicately browned. Remove cookies to cooling racks.
About 2 doz. rounds

For Bars or Squares—Press the chilled dough to a depth of about ¼ in. onto a 14x10-in. cookie sheet with a ½-in. rim on three sides. (Having one side open facilitates removal of bars from sheet.) Prick with a fork. Bake at 350°F 25 min. Remove to cooling rack; do not remove from sheet. Immediately cut into 2-in. squares, or into bars about 2x1-in. Remove cookies from sheet when completely cooled.

Christmas Cookies

MRS. VICTOR PFLIEGER, MENASHA, WIS.

Political differences between a German baker and civil authorities in his country brought this recipe and an old iron nut grater to America four generations ago. The grater is still being used by his descendants.

Lightly grease cookie sheets.

Grate (*page 11*) but do not combine
   **3 cups (about 1 lb.) blanched almonds
      (about 7½ cups, grated)
   3½ cups (about 1 lb.) hazelnuts
      (about 6 cups, grated)**
Set nuts aside.

Beat until thick and piled softly
   4 eggs
Add gradually, beating thoroughly after each addition
   2½ cups sugar
Beat for 15 min., or until very light. Beat in
   **2 teaspoons grated lemon peel
      (page 11)**
Pour one half of the batter into a second bowl and set aside.

Add the almonds to the batter in the first bowl, mixing thoroughly to form a stiff dough.

Lightly sprinkle pastry cloth with
   Sifted confectioners' sugar
Using palm of hand, shape dough, one teaspoonful at a time, into rounds about ¼ in. thick. Bring the opposite sides together and overlap at center. Place on cookie sheets.

To batter in second bowl, add the hazelnuts, mixing thoroughly to form a stiff dough. Using a rolling pin, roll dough about ¼ in. thick on the pastry cloth. Cut dough with diamond-shaped cookie cutter and place on the cookie sheets.

Bake at 350°F 10 to 12 min. Remove to cooling racks.
About 4 doz. cookies

Flaky Nut or Mexican Sugarless Cookies

MRS. DEL LANPHEAR, WOODLAND, WASH.

The flavor of these cookies improves with age. The recipe came to this country through the pen-pal correspondence of two schoolgirls.

Set out cookie sheets.

Finely chop and set aside
   ½ cup (about 2 oz.) nuts
Sift together into a 1-qt. bowl
   **1 cup sifted flour
   1 teaspoon baking powder**
Cut in with pastry blender or two knives until pieces are size of small peas
   **¼ cup butter
   ¼ cup shortening**
Add gradually, mixing well after each addition
   1 egg, well beaten
Blend in the nuts.

Roll dough ⅛ in. thick on lightly floured surface. Cut into desired shapes with floured cookie cutter. Place cookies about 1 in. apart on cookie sheets.

Bake at 375°F 12 to 15 min. Remove to cooling racks and immediately sift over cookies
   Confectioners' sugar
Cool completely.   *About 5 doz. small cookies*

Morning Stars

MRS. BLAZE FORNOFF, PEKIN, ILL.

Lightly grease cookie sheets.

Using fine blade of food chopper, grind and set aside to use in topping

⅔ cup (about 4 oz.) blanched almonds (page 11)

For Cookies—Measure and set aside

2 cups sifted flour

Cream until butter is softened

½ cup butter

½ teaspoon almond extract

Add gradually, creaming until fluffy after each addition

½ cup sifted confectioners' sugar

Add in thirds, beating thoroughly after each addition

3 egg yolks, well beaten

Mixing until well blended after each addition, add dry ingredients in fourths to creamed mixture. Roll dough ⅛ in. thick on a lightly floured surface. Cut with a floured 2-in. star-shaped cookie cutter. Place on cookie sheets.

Prepare topping.

For Topping—Beat until frothy

2 egg whites

Add gradually, beating thoroughly after each addition

¾ cup sifted confectioners' sugar

Continue beating until stiff (but not dry) peaks are formed. Gently fold in (*page 12*) the ground almonds. Place ½ teaspoonful of topping on center of each cookie.

Bake at 375°F 10 to 12 min. Remove cookies to cooling racks.   *About 6 doz. cookies*

Kuchli

MRS. JOHN S. PACH
CLARENDON HILLS, ILL.

Many years ago a young Swiss bride prepared these delicacies for her wedding feast, but they were reduced to crumbs (and she to tears) when two little boys fell into the basket containing them. Now a grandmother, she says of Kuchli, "They taste their best when almost gone."

Set out a deep saucepan or automatic deep-fryer (*page 13*) and heat fat to 360°F.

Sift together

2 cups sifted flour

1 teaspoon sugar

¼ teaspoon salt

Set aside.

Beat until thick and piled softly

2 eggs

Blend in

6 tablespoons heavy cream

Add to dry ingredients all at one time and beat until smooth. Turn dough onto a lightly floured surface and knead (*page 43*). Let stand for ½ hr.

Cut off 1-in. pieces of dough. Roll each piece, as thin as possible, into a round about 5 in. in diameter. Then, using both hands, stretch each piece of dough until paper thin, being careful not to tear dough. Immediately deep-fry in heated fat. Fry only as many at one time as will float uncrowded one layer deep in fat. While deep-frying, using a wooden spoon, gently twist dough in center to give a pin-wheel effect. When Kuchli rise to the surface turn with a slotted pancake turner or slotted spoon (do not pierce). Fry about one min. on one side, or until light golden brown. Turn and fry on second side about one min. or until puffed and golden in color.

Remove with a slotted spoon; drain Kuchli over fat for a second before removing to absorbent paper. Sift over the warm Kuchli

Confectioners' sugar

About 1½ doz. Kuchli

Apple Bandits
MRS. ROSS ANDERSON, TAHLEQUAH, OKLA.

For Dough—Sift together and set aside
  2 cups sifted flour
  ½ teaspoon cinnamon
  ¼ teaspoon baking soda
Cream
  ½ cup shortening
Add gradually, creaming until fluffy after each addition
  1 cup firmly packed brown sugar
Add in thirds, beating thoroughly after each addition
  2 eggs, slightly beaten
Mixing until well blended after each addition, add dry ingredients in fourths to creamed mixture. Chill thoroughly.

Meanwhile, prepare filling.

For Filling—Wash, quarter, core, chop and drain (do not pare) enough red apples to yield
  2 cups chopped apples (2 to 3 medium-size)
Mix together and blend with the apples
  1 cup firmly packed brown sugar
  1 cup bran flakes
  1 tablespoon melted butter or margarine
  ½ teaspoon cinnamon
  ⅛ teaspoon salt
Set mixture aside.

Lightly grease cookie sheets.

Place chilled dough on a lightly floured surface and roll into a 12x7-in. rectangle about ½ in. thick. Spread filling evenly over dough. Starting at wide side, roll dough quickly and carefully. Press edges to seal. Using a sharp, floured knife, cut roll into slices ¼ to ½ in. thick. Place slices on cookie sheets.

Bake at 350°F 30 min., or until lightly browned. *About 2 doz. cookies*

Kipfeln
MRS. CLYDE M. NORTH, BALTIMORE, MD.

A rich butter cookie from Austria-Hungary.

For Pastry—Sift together into a bowl
  2 cups sifted flour
  ½ teaspoon salt
Cut in with pastry blender or two knives until pieces are the size of small peas
  ½ cup butter
Beat until thick and lemon-colored
  2 egg yolks
  1 tablespoon cream
Add gradually to flour-butter mixture, blending ingredients with a fork. Gather dough into a ball. Work with hands, squeezing dough until well blended. Form into balls ¾ in. in diameter. Chill in refrigerator about 1 hr.

Meanwhile, prepare filling.

For Filling—Finely grind and set aside
  1 cup (about 4 oz.) pecans
Beat until frothy
  2 egg whites
  1 teaspoon vanilla extract
  ½ teaspoon salt
Add gradually, beating thoroughly after each addition
  1 cup sifted confectioners' sugar
Continue beating until rounded peaks are formed and egg whites do not slide when bowl is partially inverted. Fold in (*page 12*) the ground pecans and
  1 tablespoon melted butter
Set filling aside.

To Form Kipfeln—Put one ball of dough at a time on a lightly floured surface and roll into a paper-thin round. Place about 1½ teaspoons filling onto center of each round. Fold pastry over filling, overlapping edges at center. Pinch ends to seal and curve cookies into crescents. Place Kipfeln 1 in. apart on the cookie sheets.

Bake at 375°F 15 min., or until lightly browned. Remove to cooling racks.
About 3½ doz. cookies

COOKIES in the MICROWAVE OVEN

When a sweet tooth demands to be placated or the children arrive home from school insisting that they are starving and the refrigerator is empty, the quickest and easiest way to satisfy those demands is with cookies baked in the microwave oven. A batch of cookies can be turned out of the microwave oven in as little as 2½ minutes. They're great for snacks, lunch boxes, picnics and a spectacular timesaver when the holidays roll around. Gift boxes and a plentiful supply of cookies for the home larder can be prepared in one-third the amount of time it takes in the conventional oven.

The best results come with cookie bars. The **Marbled Brownies** and **Raspberry Squares** are outstanding in terms of texture, flavor and appearance. Also good were the chocolate cookies such as **Refrigerator Cookies** and **"Go To School" Cookies.** If you like chewy cookies, try the **Chip-Filled Wheat-Germ Bars.**

Not as successful are cookies which depend heavily on butter for flavor and texture—they tend to be soggy. We have omitted these recipes.

None of the cookies will get really crisp, even after standing. But all the recipes included have good flavor and satisfactory appearance. Like cakes and breads, cookies do not brown in the microwave oven, so we have omitted recipes which are unacceptably white in appearance. However, the light color of some cookies, like the vanilla **Refrigerator Cookies**, can be covered with icing or decorations.

DOUGH PREPARATION—All the cookie doughs are prepared exactly as directed in the master recipes (including refrigeration when called for), so we have assembled the recipes and cooking times in convenient chart form. Following are some general directions on preparing pans and baking cookies in the microwave oven.

PAN PREPARATION—Pans should be lined with ungreased waxed paper.

Cookie Bars—We have substituted pans in sizes more readily available in microwave-safe glass than those suggested with the master recipe. The cooking times given in the chart are based on the size pan specified. If you use a different-

size pan, cooking times may have to be adjusted.
Other Cookies—Use a "cookie sheet" made of cardboard covered with ungreased waxed paper, a baking dish or any other flat, microwave-safe surface which your ingenuity contrives. Remember to always line the bottom with ungreased waxed paper.

Arrange cookies on the sheet in the same size batch recommended in the chart. If you cook more or less cookies at one time, cooking times must be adjusted.

ROTATION is very important for even cooking.
Cookie Bars should be rotated 90 degrees every 2 minutes.
Other Cookies should be rotated 90 degrees every 30 seconds.

TEST FOR DONENESS—Because cookies will not brown as in conventional cooking, use the following guidelines to tell when they should be removed from the oven.
Cookie Bars are done when the dough begins to pull away slightly from the sides of the pan. Cooking will be completed during the standing time and the dough will continue to pull away from the pan sides. Note additional tests for doneness included in the chart. Then follow directions for completing and serving.
Other Cookies are done when the edges thin and the tops are dry and firm, but not hard, to the touch. Other tests for doneness are noted in the chart.

Remove the cookies from the oven and let cool about 3 minutes on the sheet. This standing time completes the cooking and firms the cookies which makes removal easier. Place cookies on a rack and complete the recipe with frosting, a sugar coating, etc., if necessary.

REMINDERS—For more tips on microwave oven cooking and an easy-to-read chart comparing settings among different brands of microwave ovens, see the introductory chapter, **Home Cooking in the Microwave Oven**, in the beginning of this book.

MICROWAVE COOKIES

RECIPE—Check this column for the recipe title as well as the page number on which you will find the master recipe.

PAN USED—Note the type and size pan to be used. Remember, variation in the size of the pan means cooking time must be adjusted.

MINUTES TO COOK—Always use the COOK setting. The given number of minutes to COOK are recommended minimum cooking times. Remember to rotate as frequently as necessary (see preceding introductory material for details).

SPECIAL INSTRUCTIONS—Included here are additional tests for doneness and any variations from the general instructions given in the preceding introduction.

1 *To Melt Chocolate*—Melting chocolate is quick and easy in the microwave oven, with no danger of scorching.

Place the chocolate in a small dish or cup and COOK, stirring every 1 min. until melted (about 1 min. per oz.).

Recipe	Pan Used	Minutes to COOK	Special Instructions
COOKIE BARS			
2 **Marbled Brownies** *(page 418)*	8x8x2-in.	9:30	To melt chocolate, see **1**
3 **Fudge Brownies** *(page 418)*	8x8x2-in.	9:30	None.
4 **Raspberry Squares** *(page 419)*	8x8x2-in.	11:00	Look for bottom to lose "doughy" texture.
5 **Spicy Pecan Bars** *(page 421)*	8x8x2-in.	5:00	None.
6 **Chip-Filled Wheat-Germ Bars** *(page 422)*	8x8x2-in.	8:00	Let cool completely in pan.
REFRIGERATOR COOKIES			
7 **Refrigerator Cookies** *(page 425)* *(12 per batch)*	Sheet	2:30	To melt chocolate, see **1**. Appearance of chocolate cookies is better than vanilla.
8 **Krispie Oatmeal Cookies** *(page 425)* *(12 per batch)*	Sheet	2:30	None.
DROP COOKIES			
9 **Oatmeal Drops** *(page 425)* *(12 per batch)*	Sheet	2:30	None.

	Recipe	Pan Used	Minutes to COOK	Special Instructions
10	**Macaroons** *(page 426)* *(16 per batch)*	Sheet	3:00	None.
11	**Date-Nut Cookies** *(page 428)* *(16 per batch)*	Sheet	3:00	When done, cookies stop spreading and are springy to the touch.
12	**French Cookies** *(page 428)* *(12 per batch)*	Sheet	3:30	None.
13	**"Go To School" Cookies** *(page 429)* *(12 per batch)*	Sheet	4:00	To melt chocolate, see 1
14	**Gingersnaps** *(page 430)* *(12 per batch)*	Sheet	4:00	None.
15	**Peanut Butter Honeys** *(page 431)* *(12 per batch)*	Sheet	3:30	None.
16	**Peanut-Butter-Chocolate Honeys** *(page 431)* *(12 per batch)*	Sheet	3:30	None.

MOLDED COOKIES

	Recipe	Pan Used	Minutes to COOK	Special Instructions
17	**Chocolate Snowflake Cookies** *(page 433)* *(12 per batch)*	Sheet	3:30	For chocolate mixture, COOK chocolate and shortening, stirring every 30 sec., until melted (about 3 min.). Add sugar and COOK, stirring every 1 min. (about 3 min.). When done, check for firmness and dryness on top.
18	**Pfeffernuesse** *(page 434)* *(16 per batch)*	Sheet	3:30	None.

ROLLED COOKIES

	Recipe	Pan Used	Minutes to COOK	Special Instructions
19	**Flaky Nut or Mexican Sugarless Cookies** *(page 437)* *(12 per batch)*	Sheet	4:30	None.

PASTRIES, PIES and TARTS

A Check List for Successful Pie Making

(See FOR THESE RECIPES—WHAT TO USE, HOW TO DO IT and OVEN TEMPERATURES on *pages 10–13*.)

√ **Read** recipe carefully.

√ **Assemble** all ingredients and utensils—*A pastry blender* cuts shortening into flour evenly and quickly; *a pastry canvas and a stockinet-covered rolling pin* prevent sticking and rolling in extra flour.

√ **Select pie pans** of proper size. Measure inside, from rim to rim.

√ **Use standard** measuring cups and spoons. Use liquid measuring cups (rim above 1-cup line) for liquids. Use nested or dry measuring cups (1-cup line even with top) for dry ingredients. Check liquid measurements at eye level. Level dry measurements with straight-edged knife or spatula.

√ **Preheat oven** 12 to 20 min. at required temperature. Leave oven door open first 2 min.

√ **Place oven rack** so top of pie will be almost at center of oven. Stagger pie pans so no pan is directly over another and they do not touch each other or walls of oven. Place single pan so that center of pie is as near center of oven as possible.

FOR PASTRY

√ **Cut** any of the shortenings, such as lard, hydrogenated vegetable shortening, all-purpose shortening and/or butter or margarine, into a mixture of flour and salt with a pastry blender or two knives until the particles are the size of small peas. (Use cooking or salad oil for pastry making only with recipes specifically developed for oil.)

√ **Use cold water** to aid in producing a more tender pastry. (Hot water may be used in making pastry if specific recipe is followed. Usually shortening and hot water are blended together.)

√ **Add only enough water** to hold pastry dough together. An excess tends to cause shrinkage and a less tender pastry. Toss lightly with a fork after each addition of water; work quickly and only until dough holds together. Do not overmix.

√ **Shape pastry dough** (for a 1-crust pie) into a smooth ball and flatten slightly on a lightly floured surface. If preparing double the amount of dough, cut dough into halves and shape one portion at a time. Overhandling dough toughens pastry.

√ **Chill pastry dough** in refrigerator before rolling if the room is warm. This will aid in ensuring a more tender pastry.

√ **Roll pastry dough** from center to edge with fewest number of strokes possible, shaping it round and of same thickness throughout. Test thickness of dough by pressing dough with finger; it should make only a slight dent. Fold into halves or quarters before transferring to pie pan. Gently unfold and fit loosely to pan.

√ **Prevent shrinkage** of pastry by loosely fitting pastry to bottom and sides of pan, being certain not to stretch dough. Be careful not to tear pastry; mend cracks by pressing pastry together or by patching with another piece of pastry. Cracks or tears in bottom crust permit filling to soak through crust and cause pie to stick to pan.

√ **For an attractive edge** on a 1-crust pie allow about ½ in. of pastry to extend beyond edge of pan after trimming excess pastry and just before fluting. Fold this overhanging pastry under, allowing it to rest on pie pan and extend just to edge of pan; flute.

√ **Flute edge of pastry** by pressing index finger on edge of pastry, then pinch pastry with thumb and index finger of other hand. Lift fingers and repeat procedure to flute around entire edge.

√ **Prick pastry shell** *thoroughly* with a fork before baking to prevent buckling and large blisters from forming. If any blisters do appear during the first few minutes of baking, prick them. Omit all pricking if filling is to be baked in shell.

√ **Moisten edge** of bottom crust of 2-crust pie with water after trimming it even with edge of pie pan. Gently press edges of bottom and top crust together for a tight seal. Fold extra pastry of top crust under edge of bottom crust; then flute or press edges together with a fork.

√ **Make enough slits** in top crust of a 2-crust pie to allow steam to escape.

FOR SOFT MERINGUES AND FILLINGS

√ **Add sugar** gradually for soft meringue, beginning in early stage (frothy) of beating egg whites. This lessens the tendency toward formation of sirup beads and meringue's leaking. Beating in the sugar instead of folding it in gives a more stable meringue. Beat meringue until rounded peaks are formed. Generally 2 tablespoons sugar per egg white is the proportion used for soft meringues. Too much sugar tends to produce beading and results in a meringue with sticky crust; too little sugar results in a less tender meringue that is less fluffy in appearance and flat in taste.

√ **Seal meringue** to edge of crust to help prevent meringue from shrinking.

√ **Bake meringue-topped** pie at 350°F 10 to 15 min., or until meringue is delicately browned. A baking temperature that is too high or a baking time that is too long results in a shrunken, tough meringue that sticks to the knife when cut.

√ **Beat whole eggs** until thick and piled softly when recipe calls for well-beaten eggs.

√ **Beat egg whites** as follows: *Frothy*—entire mass forms bubbles; *Rounded peaks*—peaks turn over slightly when beater is slowly lifted upright;

Stiff peaks—peaks remain standing when beater is slowly lifted upright.

√ **Beat egg yolks** until thick and lemon-colored when recipe calls for well-beaten egg yolks.

√ **Prevent soaking of crust** of custard pie by: 1) scalding milk before adding to the other ingredients because this shortens the time for the custard to set during baking; 2) baking pastry shell and custard separately, then slipping custard into shell (see Slipped Custard Pie, *page 476*).

√ **Cook cream filling** by vigorously stirring about 3 tablespoons of hot filling mixture into beaten egg yolks and immediately blending into mixture in top of double boiler. This method blends egg yolks evenly into the hot mixture without lowering the temperature. For maximum thickening power of the egg the temperature of the mixture must not be lowered. *Help prevent the filling from becoming thin and runny* after standing a short time (when it was once of serving consistency) by cooking the mixture 3 to 5 min. over simmering water after the egg yolks have been blended into the mixture.

√ **Fillings** containing a high-acid fruit or fruit juice (such as lemon, lime, or strawberry) usually require more cornstarch or flour than other fillings because of the thinning effect of the acid of the fruit or fruit juice upon starch when subjected to heat. For example, lemon fillings should call for the lemon juice to be blended in after the mixture has been cooked and removed from heat; this ensures a filling which should not thin.

√ **Cool cream filling** by covering cooked filling and cooling slightly, stirring occasionally to prevent film from forming; cool to lukewarm in refrigerator. (Cooling filling before turning into cooled pastry shell helps prevent soaking of crust.) Turn filling into baked and cooled pastry shell and chill in refrigerator until ready to serve.

√ **Thoroughly mix** fruit and sugar-flour mixture for fruit-filled pie to prevent hard sugar lumps in baked pie and produce even thickening.

√ **Baking of fruit pies** at two temperatures helps to prevent soaking of crust; higher temperature sets crust, lower temperature finishes baking pie.

√ **Keep** cooled custard-type, cream, whipped cream topped and filled pies in refrigerator until ready to serve; return any leftover pie to refrigerator. DO NOT ALLOW TO STAND AT ROOM TEMPERATURE because these pies spoil easily and have been known to cause food poisoning if not adequately refrigerated.

▲ Pastry for 1-Crust Pie

Set out an 8- or 9-in. pie pan.

Sift together into a bowl
- **1 cup sifted flour**
- **½ teaspoon salt**

Cut in with pastry blender or two knives until pieces are size of small peas
- **⅓ cup lard, hydrogenated vegetable shortening or all-purpose shortening**

Sprinkle gradually over mixture, a teaspoon at a time, about
- **2½ tablespoons cold water**

Mix lightly with a fork after each addition. Add only enough water to hold pastry together. Work quickly; do not overhandle. Shape into a ball and flatten on a lightly floured surface.

Roll from center to edge into a round about ⅛ in. thick and about 1 in. larger than over-all size of pan. With knife or spatula, loosen pastry from surface whenever sticking occurs; lift pastry and sprinkle flour underneath.

Loosen one half from board with spatula and fold over other half. Loosen remaining part and fold in quarters. Gently lay pastry in pan and unfold it, fitting it to the pan so that it is not stretched.

Trim edge with scissors or sharp knife so pastry extends about ½ in. beyond edge of pie pan. Fold extra pastry under at edge and flute (*page 441*) or press with a fork. Thoroughly prick bottom and sides of pastry shell with a fork. (Omit pricking if filling is to be baked in shell.)

Bake at 450°F 10 to 15 min., or until crust is light golden brown.

Cool on cooling rack.

One 8- or 9-in. pastry shell

⚠ Pastry for 2-Crust Pie

Double ▲ Recipe. Divide pastry into halves and shape each into a ball. Roll each ball as in ▲ Recipe. For top crust, roll out one ball of pastry and cut 1 in. larger than pie pan. Slit pastry with knife in several places to allow steam to escape during baking. Gently fold in half and set aside while rolling bottom crust.

Roll second ball of pastry and gently fit pastry into pie pan; avoid stretching. Trim pastry with scissors or sharp knife around edge of pan. Do not prick.

Fill as directed in specific recipe.

Moisten edge with water for a tight seal. Carefully arrange top crust over filling. Gently press edges to seal. Fold extra top pastry under bottom pastry. Flute (*page 441*) or press edges together with a fork.

Bake as directed in specific recipes.

⚠ Pastry for 1-Crust 10-in. Pie

Follow ▲ Recipe. Increase flour to 1⅓ cups, shortening to ½ cup, salt to ¾ teaspoon, and water to about 3 tablespoons.

⚠ Pastry for Lattice-Top Pie

Prepare pastry as in ⚠ Recipe. Divide pastry into halves and shape into two balls. Follow directions in ▲ Recipe for rolling pastry. Roll one pastry ball for bottom crust; fit gently into pie pan.

Roll the second pastry ball into a rectangle about ⅛ in. thick and at least 10 in. long. Cut pastry with a sharp knife or pastry wheel into strips that are about ½ in. wide.

Fill pastry shell as directed in specific recipe.

To Make a Lattice Top—Cross two strips over the pie at the center. Working out from center to edge of pie, add the remaining strips one at a time, weaving the strips under and over each other in crisscross fashion; leave about 1 in. between the strips. Trim the strips even with the edge of the pastry. Moisten the edge of pastry shell with water for a tight seal. Fold edge of bottom crust over ends of strips. Flute (*page 441*) or press edges together with a fork.

Bake as directed in specific recipe.

⚠ Pastry for Little Pies and Tarts

Prepare ▲ Recipe. Roll pastry ⅛ in. thick and cut about ½ in. larger than over-all size of pans. Carefully fit rounds into pans without stretching. Fold excess pastry under at edge and flute (*page 441*) or press with a fork. Prick bottom and sides of shell with fork. (Omit pricking if filling is to be baked in shell.)

Bake at 450°F 8 to 10 min., or until light golden brown.

Cool on cooling rack. Carefully remove from pans.　　　*Three 6-in. pies, six 3½-in. tarts or nine 1½-in. tarts*

⚠ Pastry for Rose-Petal Tarts

Double ▲ Recipe. Roll pastry ⅛ in. thick. Cut pastry into rounds, using 2½-in. round cutter. Place one pastry round in bottom of each 2¾-in. muffin-pan well. Fit 5 pastry rounds around inside of each well, overlapping edges. Press overlapping edges together. Prick bottom and sides well with fork.

Bake at 450°F 8 to 10 min., or until light golden brown.

Cool on cooling rack. Carefully remove from pans.　　　　　　　　　*Six 2¾-in. tarts*

⚠ Braided-Edge Pastry Shell

Set out a 10-in. pie pan.

Double ▲ Recipe. Shape two-thirds of the pastry into a ball and flatten on a lightly floured surface. Roll and fit into pie pan as in

▲ Recipe. Trim edge with scissors or a sharp knife so that pastry comes just to edge of pie pan. Set aside.

Shape remaining pastry into a ball and flatten on the lightly floured surface. Roll from center into a rectangle about 14 in. long and ⅛ in. thick. Cut into 9 lengthwise strips about ¼ in. wide. With strips on board, carefully braid three strips loosely. Repeat braiding twice for remaining strips.

Brush rim of pastry shell with water and place the three braids on rim. Join by overlapping and pressing ends of braids together.

Bake at 450°F 10 to 15 min., or until crust is light golden brown.

Cool on cooling rack.

⚠ Cheese Pastry for 1-Crust Pie

Follow ▲ Recipe; cut in ½ cup (2 oz.) grated **Cheddar cheese** with the lard or shortening.

⚠ Cheese Pastry for 2-Crust Pie

Follow ⚠ Recipe; cut in 1 cup (4 oz.) grated **Cheddar cheese** with the lard or shortening.

⚠ Pastry Topping

Follow ▲ Recipe for preparing pastry. Roll dough to about ⅛-in. thickness and about 1 in. larger than over-all size of casserole or baking dish top. Cut a simple design near center of pastry to allow steam to escape during baking. Moisten rim of casserole with cold water.

Loosen pastry and place loosely over mixture in casserole; unfold. Trim edge so pastry extends about ¾ in. beyond edge of casserole. Fold extra pastry under at edge and gently press edges to seal to moistened rim of casserole. Flute (*page 441*) or press with a fork.

Bake as directed in specific recipe.

▲ Puff Paste

Not quick and not easy—but incomparable!

Place into a large bowl of cold water and ice cubes or chipped ice

1 cup butter

Work butter with hands. Break it into small portions and squeeze each in water about 20 times, or until butter is pliable and waxy. Remove portions and wipe off excess water. Reserve ¼ cup of this butter. Pat remainder ½ in. thick, divide into five equal portions and wrap each in waxed paper. Chill in refrigerator until firm.

Sift together into a bowl

2 cups sifted flour
½ teaspoon salt

With pastry blender or two knives, cut in the ¼ cup butter until pieces are the size of small peas. Add gradually, mixing in with a fork, about

7 tablespoons iced water

When blended, gather into a ball and knead (*page 43*) on a lightly floured surface. Cover with a bowl and let ripen 30 min.

Roll dough on a lightly floured surface to form a rectangle ¼ in. thick. Keep corners square; gently pull dough into shape where necessary.

Remove one portion of chilled butter and cut into small pieces. Quickly pat butter pieces down center third of dough. Cover butter with right-hand third of dough. Fold left-hand third under butter section. With rolling pin gently press down and seal the open edges. Wrap in waxed paper. Chill in refrigerator about 1 hr.

Remove from refrigerator and place on the board with butter section near top, narrow side toward you. Turn folded dough one-quarter way around, to have under-open edge away from you. Roll to original size. Repeat four times the procedure for folding, sealing and chilling, using second, third, fourth and fifth portions of butter. Each time place dough on floured surface, turn and roll as directed.

With last rolling, fold four sides toward center. Gently press down with rolling pin. Fold in half. Wrap dough in waxed paper. Chill in refrigerator about 2 hrs. before using.

To store for several days, wrap dough in waxed paper and place in refrigerator.

Puff Paste for 1 large or
6 individual Vol-au-Vent Shells

⚠ Individual Vol-au-Vent Shells
(Patty Shells)

Prepare ▲ Recipe. Roll pastry ⅓ in. thick. With a sharp knife or 3-in. cookie cutter, cut out rounds. With a 2-in. cookie cutter cut centers from one half of the 3-in. rounds. (Scalloped-edge cookie cutters may be used.) Remove centers, leaving ½-in. rims. Moisten ½-in. edges of solid 3-in. rounds with cold water. Fit rims on top. Thoroughly prick through rims and bases with fork. Gently and evenly press rims down. Transfer to baking sheet (rinsed in cold water and well drained).

Roll the 2-in. centers ¼-in. thick. These are used as covers and may be cut into shapes such

Vol-au-Vent Shells: Cut bases with 3-in. cutter.

as stars or scalloped rounds. Transfer to baking sheet. Prick well. Chill shells and covers in refrigerator for 30 min.

Bake at 450°F 8 min. Reduce heat to 350°F and bake about 20 min. longer. If browning is too rapid, cover with a sheet of unglazed paper. Remove to rack to cool. Reheat before filling with hot creamed mixture.

△ Large Vol-au-Vent Shell

Prepare ▲ Recipe. Line a baking sheet with three thicknesses of unglazed paper. Divide pastry into two portions. Roll into rounds or ovals of the same size, ⅛ in. thick. Cut out center of one, leaving a rim about ¾ in. wide. Moisten ¾-in. edge of solid round with cold water. Transfer it to one end of the baking sheet. Place rim over round. Thoroughly prick through rim and base with a fork. Gently and evenly press rim down.

Roll remaining center ¼ in. thick. Transfer it to other end of paper-covered baking sheet. Prick well. Chill in refrigerator 30 min.

Bake as in △ Recipe. Reheat before filling with hot creamed mixture. Use center as a cover.

With a 2-in. cutter make rims and tops for the shells.

▲ Butter Pastry

A rich pastry that keeps well in the refrigerator for the repeat performances that are sure to be demanded by devoted fans. Of French derivation, butter pastry is prized by fine pastry cooks and by gourmets for its unique flavor.

Sift together into a bowl
1¾ cups sifted flour
1 tablespoon sugar
¼ teaspoon salt
Cut in with pastry blender or two knives until pieces are size of small peas
½ cup butter
Sprinkle gradually over mixture, about 1 teaspoonful at a time
4 to 6 tablespoons cold water
Mix lightly with a fork after each addition until dough can be gathered easily into a ball. Divide dough into halves. Shape each into a ball. (Part or all may be wrapped in waxed paper, moisture-vapor-proof material or aluminum foil and stored in refrigerator until ready to use.)   *Pastry for about twelve 4-in. tarts, two 9-in. shells or one 2-crust pie*

△ Butter Pastry for 1-Crust Pie

Follow ▲ Recipe. Use one ball of pastry. Follow directions for rolling and fitting pastry as in **Pastry for 1-Crust Pie** (*page 442*). Remaining ball of pastry may be reserved in refrigerator for a second pastry shell.

△ Butter Pastry for 2-Crust Pie

Follow ▲ Recipe. Follow directions for rolling and fitting pastry as in **Pastry for 2-Crust Pie** (*page 442*).

△ Butter Pastry for Little Pies and Tarts

Follow ▲ Recipe. Follow directions for rolling and fitting pastry as in **Pastry for Little Pies and Tarts** (*page 443*).

Perfect Pastry Mix

Sift together into a large bowl

6 cups sifted flour

1 tablespoon salt

Cut in with pastry blender or two knives until pieces are size of small peas

2 cups (1 lb.) lard, hydrogenated vegetable shortening or all-purpose shortening

Store in covered bowl or container in refrigerator and use as needed. This mix will keep at least 1 month. *Six 9-in. or eight 8-in. pie shells*

Graham Cracker Tart Shells: Using a spoon press crumb mixture firmly onto bottoms and sides.

HOW TO USE PERFECT PASTRY MIX

Before measuring for recipe, lighten mix by tossing with fork. Lightly pile mix into measuring cup. Level with spatula.

For 1-Crust Pies—Use 1 cup pastry mix with 2 to 3 tablespoons water for 8-in. pie shells. Use 1¼ cups mix with 2 to 3 tablespoons water for 9-in. pie shells. Proceed as in **Pastry for 1-Crust Pie** (*page 442*).

For 2-Crust Pies—Use 2 cups pastry mix with 3 to 5 tablespoons water for 8-in. 2-crust pie. Use 2¼ cups pastry mix with 3 to 5 tablespoons water for 9-in. 2-crust pie. Proceed as in **Pastry for 2-Crust Pie** (*page 442*).

▲ Graham Cracker Pie Shell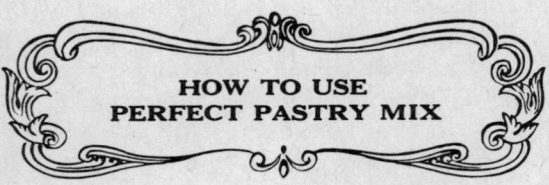

Set out an 8- or 9-in. pie pan.

Crush (*page 12*)

16 to 18 graham crackers (or enough to yield 1⅓ cups crumbs)

Turn crumbs into a medium-size bowl. Stir in

¼ cup sugar

Using a fork or pastry blender, blend in evenly

¼ cup butter or margarine, softened

Using back of spoon, press crumb mixture very firmly into an even layer on bottom and sides of the pie pan. Level edges of pie shell.

Bake at 375°F 8 min. Cool thoroughly before filling. *One 8- or 9-in. pie shell*

⚠ Graham Cracker 10-in. Pie Shell

Follow ▲ Recipe. Increase crumbs to 1⅔ cups, sugar to 5 tablespoons, and butter to 5 tablespoons.

⚠ Graham Cracker Tart Shells

Follow ▲ Recipe. Line 8 2½-in. muffin-pan wells with paper baking cups. Using back of spoon, press crumb mixture firmly into even layers on bottom and sides of the paper cups. Bake. Cool thoroughly on cooling rack; remove paper baking cups.

△ Cookie Crumb Pie Shell 4

Follow ▲ Recipe. Substitute 1⅓ cups **cookie crumbs** (about twenty-four 2⅛-in. cookies such as vanilla or chocolate wafers) for graham cracker crumbs. Omit sugar. Bake at 325°F 10 min.

△ Coffee-Flavored 5 Crumb Pie Shell

Follow △ Recipe. Use either **vanilla** or **chocolate wafers**. Stir into crumbs 2 teaspoons **concentrated soluble coffee**.

△ Zwieback Crumb Pie Shell 6

Follow ▲ Recipe. Substitute 1⅛ cups **zwieback crumbs** (about eighteen 3½x1⅛-in. zwieback) for graham cracker crumbs.

Crispy Crumb Pie Shell 7

MRS. J. W. STEPHENS, PATAGONIA, ARIZ.

A shortage of graham crackers and a knack for experiment led to the discovery of this family-favorite pie crust. The sweetness of the shell makes it a perfect foil for fillings with a tart flavor, such as lemon or lime.

Set out a 9- or 10-in. pie pan.

Crush (*page 12*)
   2⅓ cups pre-sweetened corn flakes (or enough to yield 1 cup, crushed)
   6 graham crackers (or enough to yield ½ cup, crushed)
Mix the crumbs together.

Add gradually, stirring in with a fork.
   ¼ cup butter or margarine, melted
Using back of spoon, press crumb mixture very firmly into an even layer on bottom and sides of pie pan. Level edges of pie shell.

Bake at 375°F 8 min.

Cool thoroughly before filling.
                    One 9- or 10-in. pie shell

Choco-Coconut Pie Shell 8

An intriguingly different kind of pie shell.

Set out an 8- or 9-in. pie pan.

Melt in the top of a double boiler over simmering water
   2 sq. (2 oz.) chocolate
   3 tablespoons butter or margarine
   1 teaspoon vanilla extract
Blend ingredients well and remove from simmering water. Add, stirring constantly
   ¼ cup sweetened condensed milk
Blend in well, in order
   ½ cup sifted confectioners' sugar
   2 cups (8 oz.) moist shredded coconut, cut
Press coconut mixture firmly into an even layer onto bottom and on sides of pie pan. Wrap in waxed paper, aluminum foil or moisture-vapor-proof material. Chill in refrigerator about 1 hr., or until firm.
                    One 8- or 9-in. pie shell

Spice Pastry for 1-Crust Pie

Set out an 8- or 9-in. pie pan.

Sift together
   1 cup sifted flour
   2 tablespoons sugar
   ½ teaspoon salt
   ¼ teaspoon cinnamon
   ⅛ teaspoon ginger
   ⅛ teaspoon cloves
Cut in with pastry blender or two knives until pieces are size of small peas
   ⅓ cup lard, hydrogenated vegetable shortening or all-purpose shortening
Sprinkle gradually over mixture, a teaspoon at a time, about
   2½ tablespoons orange juice
Mix lightly with fork after each addition. Add only enough orange juice to hold pastry together. Work quickly and do not overhandle. Shape into a ball and flatten on a lightly floured surface. Proceed as in **Pastry for 1-Crust Pie** (*page 442*).   *One 8- or 9-in. pastry shell*

Meringue

Meringue Shell

Lightly grease a 9-in. pie pan.

Beat until frothy
4 egg whites
Add and beat slightly
½ teaspoon cream of tartar
Add gradually, beating well after each addition
1 cup sugar
Continue beating until stiff (but not dry) peaks are formed and egg whites do not slide when bowl is partially inverted.

Spread a 1-in. layer of meringue on bottom of pie pan. Pile remaining meringue around edge of pan and swirl with a spatula to form the sides of the shell.

Bake at 250°F about 2¼ hrs., or until meringue is dry. (The door of the oven of some ranges will have to be partially open to maintain low temperature.) To assure even drying of meringue turn pan occasionally. Remove from oven; cool completely on cooling rack. (If the meringue shell is to be stored, keep it in an air-tight container so that the meringue will not absorb moisture and become soft.)

The meringue shell should be crisp and dry and have a very fine texture.

One 9-in. pie shell

▲ Meringue I

Beat until frothy
3 egg whites
⅛ teaspoon salt
Add gradually, beating well after each addition
6 tablespoons sugar
Continue to beat until rounded peaks are formed. Pile meringue lightly over pie filling, sealing meringue to edge of crust.

Bake at 350°F 10 to 15 min., or until meringue is delicately browned. Cool pie on cooling rack.

△ Meringue II

Follow ▲ Recipe. Decrease egg whites to 2 and sugar to ¼ cup.

Toasted Coconut

Set out a large, shallow baking pan.

Cut into short lengths and spread over bottom of the pan
½ cup (2 oz.) moist shredded coconut
Set pan in 350°F oven for 10 to 15 min., or until coconut is lightly toasted.

One-half cup Toasted Coconut

▲ American Glory Apple-Cheese Pie

Prepare and set aside
   **Cheese Pastry for 2-Crust Pie
   (page 443; use 9-in. pie pan)**
Crush (*page 12*) and set aside
   **4 or 5 graham crackers (or enough to
   yield ⅓ cup crumbs)**
Grate and set aside
   **4 oz. Cheddar cheese (about 1 cup,
   grated)**
Wash, quarter, core, pare and thinly slice
   **6 to 8 medium-size apples (about 6
   cups, sliced)**
Sprinkle evenly over apples
   2 teaspoons lemon juice
Toss gently with apples a mixture of
   ¾ cup sugar
   2 tablespoons flour
   ½ teaspoon cinnamon
   ½ teaspoon nutmeg
   ⅛ teaspoon salt
Sprinkle graham cracker crumbs evenly over
bottom of pastry shell. Spoon one third of
apple mixture over bottom of the pastry shell.
Top with one half of the grated cheese. Beginning with apples, repeat layers and end with
apples. Slightly heap the last layer of apples in
the center. Dot with
   2 tablespoons butter or margarine

Complete as in **Pastry for 2-Crust Pie** (*page
442*).

Bake at 450°F 10 min. Reduce heat to 350°F
and bake about 40 min. longer, or until crust
is light golden brown.

Serve warm or cold.   *One 9-in. pie*

△ Favorite-Treat Apple Pie

Follow ▲ Recipe. Substitute **Pastry for 2-
Crust Pie** (*page 442*) for Cheese Pastry. Omit
graham cracker crumbs and cheese from filling. Increase lemon juice to 1 tablespoon and
cinnamon to 1 teaspoon.

Favorite-Treat Apple Pie

Creamy Crumb-Top Apple Pie

Deep-Dish Apple Pie

Butter a 1½-qt. casserole.

Prepare and set aside
>**Cheese Pastry Topping (use Pastry Topping, *page 443*; cut in ½ cup grated Cheddar cheese with lard or shortening)**

Mix thoroughly
>**¾ cup firmly packed brown sugar**
>**3 tablespoons flour**
>**1 teaspoon cinnamon**
>**½ teaspoon salt**
>**¼ teaspoon nutmeg**

Cut in with a pastry blender or two knives until mixture is in coarse crumbs
>**3 tablespoons butter or margarine**
>**1 teaspoon grated orange peel (*page 11*)**

Set aside.

Wash, quarter, core, pare and thinly slice
>**6 to 8 medium-size firm, tart apples (about 6 cups, sliced)**

Put apples into a bowl and sprinkle over them a mixture of
>**¼ cup orange juice**
>**1 tablespoon lemon juice**

Gently turn apples with a fork to coat with juice. Arrange one half of the apple slices in casserole. Sprinkle with one half of sugar mixture; repeat. Complete as in Pastry Topping.

Bake at 450°F 10 min. Reduce heat to 350°F and bake 25 to 30 min. longer, or until apples are tender and crust is slightly browned.

If desired, serve with a pitcher of heavy cream.
One deep-dish pie

Creamy Crumb-Top Apple Pie

Prepare (do not bake) and set aside
>**Pastry for 1-Crust Pie (*page 442*; use 9-in. pie pan)**

Mix together
>**1 cup sugar**
>**4 teaspoons flour**
>**½ teaspoon nutmeg**
>**½ teaspoon cinnamon**
>**⅛ teaspoon salt**

Sprinkle 2 tablespoons of the mixture over bottom of pastry shell. Set remainder aside.

Wash, quarter, core, pare and thinly slice
>**6 large cooking apples (about 6 cups, sliced)**

Turn the sliced apples into the pastry shell; heap the apples slightly at the center. Sprinkle with remaining sugar mixture. Set aside.

Mix together in a bowl
>**¼ cup firmly packed brown sugar**
>**3 tablespoons flour**
>**1 tablespoon sugar**
>**⅛ teaspoon nutmeg**
>**⅛ teaspoon cinnamon**
>**⅛ teaspoon salt**

Cut in with a pastry blender or two knives until mixture is crumbly
>**¼ cup butter**

Sprinkle mixture over apples.

Bake at 450°F 10 min. Reduce heat to 350°F and bake 25 to 30 min. longer, or until apples are tender.

Remove to cooling rack. Pour evenly over pie
>**½ cup heavy cream**

Let stand about 15 min.

Serve warm.
One 9-in. pie

French Apricot Tart

Prepare, bake and set aside to cool
> **Butter Pastry for 1-Crust Pie (page 445; use 9-in. pie or tart pan)**

Drain, reserving sirup, contents of
> **2 No. 2½ cans peeled, whole apricots**

Carefully remove and discard pits, leaving apricots intact.

Combine in a small saucepan 1 tablespoon of the reserved apricot sirup and
> **¼ cup strawberry or other red jelly**
> **2 drops red food coloring**

Heat slowly, stirring occasionally, until jelly is melted and ingredients are well blended. Set glaze aside to cool slightly.

(Remaining apricot sirup may be reserved for use in other food preparation.)

Spread carefully over bottom of pastry shell
> **1 cup apricot preserve**

Place the whole apricots on preserve. Spoon glaze over apricots. Set aside in refrigerator to chill. This allows glaze to thicken slightly before serving. *One 9-in. pie*

Blueberry Pie

Prepare and set aside
> **Pastry for 2-Crust Pie (page 442; use 8-in. pie pan)**

Sort, rinse and drain thoroughly
> **4 cups fresh blueberries**

Sprinkle over the blueberries
> **4 teaspoons lemon juice**

Toss gently with a mixture of
> **¾ cup sugar**
> **¼ cup sifted flour**
> **1 teaspoon grated lemon peel (page 11)**
> **½ teaspoon cinnamon**
> **¼ teaspoon nutmeg**
> **⅛ teaspoon salt**

Turn blueberry mixture into pastry shell, heaping slightly at center. Dot with
> **2 tablespoons butter or margarine**

Complete as in Pastry for 2-Crust Pie.

Bake at 450°F 10 min. Reduce heat to 350°F and bake 30 to 35 min. longer, or until crust is light golden brown.

Cool on cooling rack. *One 8-in. pie*

Luscious Blueberry Pie

Prepare, bake and set aside to cool
> **Pastry for 1-Crust Pie (page 442; use 9-in. pie pan)**

Drain, reserving sirup, contents of
> **2 No. 2 cans blueberries (about 2½ cups, drained)**

Set aside.

Put into a saucepan
> **3 tablespoons cornstarch**

Add gradually and stir in 1 cup of the reserved blueberry sirup. Mix well and bring rapidly to boiling, stirring constantly until mixture is thick and clear. When clear, stir in
> **6 tablespoons sugar**

Remove from heat and mix in
> **2 tablespoons lemon juice**
> **1½ tablespoons butter or margarine**
> **⅛ teaspoon salt**

Gently mix in the blueberries. Cover and set aside to cool.

Spoon filling into pastry shell. If desired, serve with **vanilla ice cream.** *One 9-in. pie*

Blueberry Pie

▲ Cherry Pie

Prepare (do not bake) and set aside
> **Pastry for 1-Crust Pie (page 442; use 9-in. pie pan)**

Sort, rinse, drain, and remove and discard the stems and pits from enough cherries to yield
> **4 cups pitted, fresh, sour red cherries**

Toss gently with a mixture of
> **1½ cups sugar**
> **5 tablespoons flour**
> **⅛ teaspoon salt**

Turn cherry mixture into pastry shell, heaping slightly at center. Sprinkle with
> **¼ teaspoon almond extract**

Dot with
> **2 tablespoons butter or margarine**

Bake at 450°F 10 min. Reduce heat to 375°F and bake about 45 min. longer.

Remove to cooling rack and allow to cool thoroughly.

Prepare
> **Vanilla Hard Sauce (double recipe, page 337; substitute 1 teaspoon almond extract for the 2 teaspoons vanilla extract)**

When pie is cool, force hard sauce through pastry bag and No. 27 star decorating tube, forming a crisscross design over top of pie. At points where lines cross, make small rosettes with same decorating tube.   *One 9-in. pie*

Note: If pie filling is not completely cool when lattice design is formed on it, hard sauce will melt slightly. This alters the appearance but does not affect the flavor.

△ Sweet Cherry Pie

Follow ▲ Recipe. Substitute **dark, sweet cherries** for sour cherries. Decrease sugar to 1 cup. Bake at 450°F 10 min., at 350°F 40 min.

Cranberry Lattice Pie

Lustrous cranberries have been American favorites since the days of early New England.

Prepare and set aside
> **Pastry for Lattice-Top Pie (page 442; use 9-in. pie pan)**

Sort, rinse and drain
> **4 cups (1 lb.) cranberries**

Set aside.

Mix together in a medium-size saucepan
> **2¼ cups sugar**
> **¼ cup orange juice**
> **2 tablespoons water**
> **¼ teaspoon salt**

Stir over medium heat until sugar is dissolved. Increase heat and bring mixture to boiling; add cranberries. Cook slowly 3 to 4 min., or just until skins of cranberries begin to pop.

Mix together
> **2 tablespoons cold water**
> **1 tablespoon cornstarch**

Blend thoroughly to a smooth paste. Gradually add cornstarch mixture to hot cranberries while stirring constantly. Bring rapidly to boiling, stirring constantly; cook 3 min. Remove from heat. Blend in
> **2½ tablespoons butter or margarine**
> **1 teaspoon grated lemon peel (page 11)**
> **1 teaspoon grated orange peel**

Set cranberry filling aside to cool.

When filling is cool, brush pastry shell with
> **Melted butter or margarine**

Pour cooled filling into pastry shell.

Complete as in Pastry for Lattice-Top Pie.

Bake at 450°F 10 min. Reduce heat to 350°F and bake about 20 min. longer, or until pastry is light golden brown.

Serve warm or cold.   *One 9-in. pie*

Grape Arbor Pie

Prepare and set aside

> **Pastry for Lattice-Top Pie (page 442; use 8-in. pie pan)**

Rinse and stem enough grapes to yield

> **3 cups Concord grapes**

Slip skins from grapes. Chop skins; set aside.

Put the pulp in a small saucepan and bring to boiling; reduce heat and simmer 5 min., or until seeds are loosened. Drain pulp, reserving juice. Force the pulp through a fine sieve or food mill to remove the seeds. Discard seeds. Add the chopped grape skins to pulp. Set aside.

Sift together into a medium-size saucepan

> **1 cup sugar**
> **3 tablespoons cornstarch**
> **¼ teaspoon salt**

Gradually add the reserved grape juice, stirring mixture well. Stirring gently and constantly, bring cornstarch mixture rapidly to boiling over direct heat; cook 3 min. Remove from heat. Stir in the pulp and skins with

> **1 tablespoon lemon juice**
> **1 tablespoon orange juice**
> **2 teaspoons grated orange peel (page 11)**

Turn grape filling into pastry shell.

Complete as in Pastry for Lattice-Top Pie.

Bake at 450°F 10 min. Reduce heat to 350°F and bake 20 to 25 min. longer, or until pastry is light golden brown.

Cool on cooling rack. *One 8-in. pie*

Peach Pie

Peach Pie

If you count golden peach pie among life's blessings, you may thank the Spanish colonists who brought the peach tree to the New World.

Prepare and set aside

> **Pastry for 2-Crust Pie (page 442; use 9-in. pie pan)**

Rinse and plunge into boiling water

> **12 medium-size (about 3 lbs.) firm, ripe peaches**

Plunge peaches into cold water. Gently slip off skins. Cut peaches into halves; remove and discard pits. Slice peaches into a bowl and sprinkle with

> **1 teaspoon lemon juice**

Gently toss with slices a mixture of

> **1¼ cups sugar**
> **3 tablespoons quick-cooking tapioca**
> **1 teaspoon grated lemon peel (page 11)**
> **¼ teaspoon salt**

Turn peach mixture into pastry shell, heaping slightly at center. Dot with

> **2 tablespoons butter or margarine**

Complete as in Pastry for 2-Crust Pie.

Bake at 450°F 10 min. Reduce heat to 350°F and bake about 40 min. longer, or until crust is light golden brown.

Serve warm. *One 9-in. pie*

Pineapple Delight Pie

Prepare and set aside

Pastry for Lattice-Top Pie (page 442; use 8-in. pie pan)

Drain (reserving sirup) contents of

1 No. 2½ can crushed pineapple (about 2 cups, drained)

Sift together into top of a double boiler

½ cup sugar
3 tablespoons cornstarch
¼ teaspoon salt

Add the reserved pineapple sirup (about 1½ cups), stirring mixture well. Stirring gently and constantly, bring cornstarch mixture rapidly to boiling over direct heat; cook 3 min. Remove from heat. Blend in the drained pineapple and

3 tablespoons butter or margarine
1 tablespoon lemon juice
1 tablespoon orange juice
2 teaspoons grated lemon peel (page 11)

Turn pineapple filling into pastry shell.

Complete as in Pastry for Lattice-Top Pie.

Bake at 425°F 25 to 30 min., or until pastry is light golden brown.

Cool on cooling rack. *One 8-in. pie*

Pineapple Delight Pie

Delake Prune Pie

MRS. J. C. KERBER, DELAKE, ORE.

Wash and put into a saucepan

¼ lb. (about ⅔ cup) prunes

Cover prunes with

1 cup hot water

Cover pan and allow prunes to soak 1 hr. Simmer in same water 45 to 60 min., or until prunes are plump and tender.

Meanwhile, prepare, bake and set aside to cool

Pastry for 1-Crust Pie (page 442; use 9-in. pie pan)

When prunes are tender, drain well, reserving the liquid. (If necessary, add enough water to make ¾ cup liquid.) Pit the prunes. Force prunes through a sieve or food mill.

Sift together into top of a double boiler

1 cup sugar
⅓ cup cornstarch
½ teaspoon cream of tartar

Add and blend in

1 cup water

Stir in the prune liquid and purée. Stirring gently and constantly, bring mixture rapidly to boiling over direct heat and cook 3 min. Place over simmering water and add

4 marshmallows, cut into quarters (page 12)
1 sq. (1 oz.) chocolate, cut in pieces

Cover and cook 12 min., stirring three or four times. Vigorously stir about 3 tablespoons of hot mixture into

2 egg yolks, slightly beaten

Immediately blend into mixture in double boiler. Cook over simmering water 3 to 5 min. Stir slowly to keep mixture cooking evenly. Remove from heat. Stir in

½ teaspoon lemon extract
½ teaspoon vanilla extract

Cover and cool slightly, stirring occasionally; cool to lukewarm in refrigerator. Turn filling into the cooled pastry shell.

Complete pie with

Meringue I or II (page 448)

Cool on cooling rack. *One 9-in. pie*

Prune 'n' Banana Pie

A few minutes before serving, using the chilled bowl and beater, whip (*page 13*)

½ cup chilled whipping cream

Spread whipped cream over pie and swirl for decorative effect. Peel the reserved banana and draw tines of a fork lengthwise over entire surface. Cut into crosswise slices. Garnish pie (see photo) with banana slices, prunes and

Walnut halves

Serve immediately. *One 8-in. pie*

Prune 'n' Banana Pie

Reveals hidden taste glamour in prunes.

Prepare

Stewed Prunes (page 494)

Meanwhile, prepare, bake and set aside to cool

Pastry for 1-Crust Pie (page 442; use 8-in. pie pan)

Put a small bowl and rotary beater into refrigerator to chill.

When prunes are tender, drain well, reserving the liquid. Pit the prunes; set 6 aside in refrigerator for garnish and chop remaining prunes. Set aside.

Sift together into a medium-size saucepan

⅓ cup sugar

3 tablespoons cornstarch

Blend in 1 cup of the prune liquid. Stirring gently and constantly, bring cornstarch mixture rapidly to boiling over direct heat. Cook about 3 min., or until mixture is transparent. Immediately remove mixture from heat and blend in the chopped prunes. Set aside to cool.

Set out

3 bananas with brown-flecked peel

Reserve one banana for garnish.

Spread one half of the prune mixture over bottom of pastry shell; peel two of the bananas and cut into crosswise slices over the prune mixture. Cover bananas with remaining prune mixture. Set pie in refrigerator to chill.

Rhubarb Pie

Prepare and set aside

Pastry for 2-Crust Pie (page 442; use 9-in. pie pan)

Wash, trim off leaves and ends of stems and cut into 1-in. pieces enough rhubarb to yield

6 cups fresh rhubarb

(Peel stalks only if skin is tough.)

Sift together

1¾ cups sugar

½ cup sifted flour

¼ teaspoon salt

Sprinkle ⅓ of the dry ingredients over the pastry shell. Mix with the remaining dry ingredients

1 teaspoon grated orange peel (page 11)

Turn rhubarb into pastry shell, heaping slightly at center. Sprinkle the remaining dry ingredients over the rhubarb. Dot with

2 tablespoons butter or margarine

Complete as in Pastry for 2-Crust Pie.

Bake at 425°F 10 min. Reduce heat to 350°F and bake 40 to 45 min. longer, or until crust is light golden brown.

Cool on cooling rack. *One 9-in. pie*

Raisin-Rhubarb Meringue Pie

Raisin-Rhubarb Meringue Pie

First-fruit of the garden, delicious tangy rhubarb brings the taste of spring to the table.

Prepare (do not bake) and set aside
  Pastry for 1-Crust Pie (page 442; use 9-in. pie pan)
Wash, trim off leaves and ends of stems and cut into 1-in. pieces enough rhubarb to yield
  4 cups fresh rhubarb
(Peel stalks only if skin is tough.) Put the rhubarb into a saucepan having a cover. Add
  1 cup (about 5 oz.) seedless raisins
  ¾ cup water
Put over medium heat and bring to boiling. Cover and cook until rhubarb is just tender. Remove from heat; remove the raisins and rhubarb with a slotted spoon and set aside.

Pour liquid into a measuring cup.

Sift together into the saucepan
  1½ cups sugar
  ⅓ cup cornstarch
  ¼ teaspoon salt
Add gradually and blend in the reserved liquid. Stirring gently and constantly, bring cornstarch mixture rapidly to boiling over direct heat and cook 3 min. Remove from heat.

Vigorously stir about 3 tablespoons of hot mixture into
  2 egg yolks, slightly beaten
Immediately blend into mixture in saucepan. Add the rhubarb and raisins to the sauce; blend well. Turn into the pastry shell.

Bake at 450°F 10 min. Reduce heat to 350°F and bake 25 to 30 min. longer.

Set aside to cool to lukewarm. Complete with
  Meringue I or II (page 448)
Cool on cooling rack.   *One 9-in. pie*

Strawberry Pie

Prepare and set aside
  Pastry for Lattice-Top Pie (page 442; use 9-in. pie pan)
Sort, rinse, drain, hull and cut into halves
  6 cups fresh, ripe strawberries
Sprinkle over strawberries
  1 tablespoon lemon juice
Gently toss with a mixture of
  1½ cups sugar
  6 tablespoons flour
  ½ teaspoon salt
Turn strawberry mixture into pastry shell, heaping slightly at center. Dot with
  2 tablespoons butter or margarine
Moisten the edge of pastry shell. Arrange 5 pastry strips parallel to each other over top of pie, leaving about 1 in. between the strips. Gently twist each strip several times and press each end to edge of pastry shell. Repeat process with remaining pastry strips, placing them at right angles to the first strips (see color photo). Trim the strips even with the edge of the pastry. Fold edge of bottom crust over ends of strips. Flute (*page 441*) or press edges together with a fork.

Bake at 450°F 10 min. Reduce heat to 350°F and bake 20 to 30 min. longer, or until pastry is light golden brown.

Cool on cooling rack.   *One 9-in. pie*

Strawberry-Sour Cream Pie

MRS. WILL W. COTTINGHAM, ROLLA, MO.

A treasured family recipe that reflects the Pennsylvania-Dutch tradition of imaginative baking.

Prepare (do not bake) and set aside

Pastry for 1-Crust Pie (page 442; use 9-in. pie pan)

Sort, rinse, drain, hull and cut into halves

4 cups fresh, ripe strawberries

Turn strawberries into pastry shell.

Measure into a bowl

1 cup thick sour cream

Sift together and add gradually to sour cream, mixing well

1¼ cups sugar
1 cup sifted flour
¼ teaspoon salt

Pour sour-cream mixture over strawberries. Sprinkle over top of sour-cream mixture

2 tablespoons sugar

Bake at 450°F 10 min. Reduce heat to 350°F and bake 30 min. longer, or until topping is lightly browned.

Cool on cooling rack. *One 9-in. pie*

⚠ Blackberry Sour-Cream Pie

Follow ▲ Recipe. Substitute 4 cups fresh **blackberries** for the strawberries.

⚠ Red or Black Raspberry Sour-Cream Pie

Follow ▲ Recipe. Substitute 4 cups fresh **red** or **black raspberries** for the strawberries.

Tutti Frutti Pie

MARILYN BENADUM, LANCASTER, OHIO

Prepare (do not bake) and set aside

Pastry for 1-Crust Pie (page 442; use 9-in. pie pan)

Set aside to drain contents of

1 No. 2 can pineapple tidbits (about 1½ cups, drained)

(Reserve pineapple sirup for use in other food preparation.)

Prepare and set aside

1 cup (about 4 oz.) chopped pecans
½ cup (2 oz.) moist shredded coconut, cut
¼ cup chopped maraschino cherries, drained

Cut (*page 12*) into small pieces enough pitted dates to yield

1½ cups (about 10 oz.) date pieces

Mix together in a large bowl the pineapple tidbits, pecans, coconut, maraschino cherries, dates and

2 cups corn flakes

Set mixture aside.

Beat until thick and piled softly

3 eggs

Blend in

1 teaspoon vanilla extract

Add gradually, beating constantly

½ cup sugar
½ teaspoon salt

Pour egg mixture over fruit-nut mixture and blend thoroughly. Turn into pastry shell.

Bake at 450°F 10 min. Reduce heat to 350°F and bake 20 to 30 min. longer, or until lightly browned. *One 9-in. pie*

Country-Kitchen Pie

MRS. LEA FILER, LINN, MO.

A homemaker looked into her refrigerator one day, discovered a half-jar each of canned apples and pumpkin. Result? Pie filling with flavor plus!

Prepare (do not bake) and set aside
Pastry for 1-Crust Pie (page 442; use 9-in. pie pan)

For Apple Layer—Mix together
2½ cups (1 No. 2 can) sliced apples
½ cup seedless raisins, chopped
and a mixture of
¾ cup sugar
½ teaspoon cinnamon
Turn into the pastry shell. Set aside.

For Pumpkin Layer—Blend together
2 cups (1 1-lb. can) canned pumpkin
and a mixture of
½ cup sugar
2 teaspoons cornstarch
1 teaspoon cinnamon
½ teaspoon nutmeg
¼ teaspoon cloves
Spread the pumpkin mixture carefully over the apple mixture in the pastry shell. Set aside.

For Topping—Mix together in a small bowl
1 cup sifted flour
½ cup firmly packed brown sugar
Using a pastry blender or two knives, cut in until mixture is crumbly
½ cup butter
Sprinkle mixture evenly over top of pie.

Bake at 450°F 10 min. Reduce heat to 350°F and bake about 25 min. longer.

Serve warm or cool.   *One 9-in. pie*

Mincemeat, Home-Style

Set out a large, heavy skillet.

Grind (*page 107*) enough suet to yield
½ cup (about 4 oz.) ground suet
Grind enough cooked beef to yield
1½ cups ground cooked beef
Set suet and beef aside.

Wash, quarter, core, pare and chop
4 medium-size apples (about 3 cups, chopped)
Put apples and meat in the skillet; add and mix thoroughly
1 cup firmly packed brown sugar
1 cup apple cider
½ cup fruit jelly
½ cup seedless raisins, chopped
½ cup currants
2 tablespoons molasses
and a mixture of
1 teaspoon salt
1 teaspoon cinnamon
½ teaspoon cloves
½ teaspoon nutmeg
¼ teaspoon mace
Stirring occasionally, simmer uncovered about 1 hr., or until most of liquid is absorbed. Add
1 tablespoon grated lemon peel (page 11)
1 tablespoon lemon juice
Blend thoroughly.   *3½ cups Mincemeat*

Note: If mincemeat is not used immediately, pack hot mincemeat into sterilized jars and seal (see How To Do It, *page 571*).

Mincemeat Pie

Prepare (do not bake) and set aside
Pastry for 1-Crust Pie (page 442; use 9-in. pie pan)
Wash, quarter, core, pare and chop
1 large apple (1¼ cups, chopped)
Put apple in saucepan with
3½ cups Mincemeat, Home-Style (on this page)

(Or use packaged condensed mincemeat and follow directions on package.) Add and mix in

1 tablespoon lemon juice
**1 teaspoon grated lemon peel
(page 11)**

Heat mixture thoroughly. Cool slightly. Fill pastry shell with mincemeat mixture.

Bake at 400°F 30 to 35 min.

Set aside to cool.

Prepare

Brandy Hard Sauce (double recipe, page 337)

When pie is cool, force hard sauce through a pastry bag and No. 27 star decorating tube, forming a crisscross design over top of cooled pie. At points where lines cross, make small rosettes with same tube.   *One 9-in. pie*

Note: Hard sauce design will melt slightly if pie filling is not completely cool. This alters the appearance but does not affect the flavor.

Creamy Mincemeat-Pecan Pie

MRS. W. L. ISBELL, BROOKSTON, IND.

Prepare (do not bake) and set aside

Spice Pastry for 1-Crust Pie (page 447; use 9-in. pie pan)

Spread evenly over bottom of pastry shell

**2 cups Mincemeat, Home-Style
(page 458)**

(Or use packaged condensed mincemeat and follow directions on package.)

Mix together

⅓ cup firmly packed brown sugar
2 tablespoons flour

Stir in

1 cup heavy cream

Pour over mincemeat. Arrange over top

⅓ cup pecan halves

Bake at 400°F 45 min., or until pastry is light golden brown.

Cool on cooling rack.   *One 9-in. pie*

Date-Chess Pie

MRS. EULA G. DUNN, WARRENTON, ORE.

Prepare (do not bake) and set aside

Pastry for 1-Crust Pie (page 442; use 9-in. pie pan)

Set out

1 cup (about 4 oz.) chopped pecans

Cut (*page 12*) into small pieces and set aside enough pitted dates to yield

1 cup (about 7 oz.) date pieces

Cream together until butter or margarine is softened

¼ cup butter or margarine
½ teaspoon vanilla extract

Add gradually, creaming until fluffy after each addition

1 cup firmly packed brown sugar

Add gradually, beating well after each addition

2 eggs, well beaten

Blend in

¼ cup cream
1 tablespoon orange juice

Stir in the chopped nuts and dates. Turn into the pastry shell.

Bake at 450°F 10 min. Reduce heat to 350°F and bake 30 min. longer, or until a silver knife comes out clean when inserted halfway between center and edge of filling.

Cool on cooling rack.   *One 9-in. pie*

Mock Apple Pie

MRS. ZANE HOSTBJOR, NOONAN, N. DAK.

There is more than one way to bake an "apple" pie, and this one cleverly does it without apples.

Prepare and set aside
> **Pastry for 2-Crust Pie (page 442;
> use 9-in. pie pan)**

Combine in a saucepan
> **1½ cups water**
> **1½ cups sugar**
> **1 teaspoon cream of tartar**
> **1 teaspoon cinnamon**
> **½ teaspoon nutmeg**

Stir over low heat until sugar is dissolved. Increase heat and bring to boiling; cook rapidly for 5 min. Remove saucepan from heat and set aside to cool.

Break into large pieces
> **16 unsalted soda crackers (about 3 cups, broken)**

Put crackers into pastry shell. Pour cooled sirup evenly over soda-cracker pieces.

Complete as in Pastry for 2-Crust Pie.

Bake at 450°F 10 min. Reduce heat to 350°F and bake about 40 min. longer or until crust is light golden brown.

Cool on cooling rack.   *One 9-in. pie*

Shoofly Pie

MRS. IRA L. HERR, Jr., GLEN ROCK, PA.

One theory as to the origin of this Pennsylvania-Dutch dessert says shoofly is an adaptation of the French word "chou-fleur" (cauliflower), because the crumb topping supposedly resembles a head of cauliflower.

Prepare (do not bake) and set aside
> **Pastry for 1-Crust Pie (page 442;
> use 8-in. pie pan)**

For Crumb Mixture—Mix together
> **1½ cups sifted flour**
> **½ cup firmly packed brown sugar**
> **½ teaspoon cinnamon**
> **¼ teaspoon salt**

Using a pastry blender or two knives, cut in until mixture resembles coarse corn meal
> **¼ cup shortening**

Set aside.

For Molasses Mixture—Blend together
> **⅔ cup molasses**
> **⅔ cup hot water**
> **¼ teaspoon baking soda**

To Complete Pie—Pour about one third of the molasses mixture into the pastry shell.

Sprinkle one third of the crumb mixture evenly over molasses. Repeat layering two more times, ending with crumb mixture.

Bake at 450°F 15 min. Reduce heat to 350°F and bake 10 min. longer, or until crumb topping is browned.

Cool on cooling rack.   *One 8-in. pie*

Lemon Apple Snow Pie

Prepare, bake and set aside to cool
Pastry for 1-Crust 10-in. Pie (page 442)
Pour into a small cup or custard cup
¼ cup cold water
Sprinkle evenly over the cold water
**1 tablespoon (1 env.) unflavored
gelatin**
Let stand about 5 min. to soften.

Heat until very hot
½ cup water
Remove from heat and immediately stir in softened gelatin, stirring until gelatin is completely dissolved. Add and stir until sugar is dissolved
½ cup sugar
2½ tablespoons lemon juice
1 teaspoon grated lemon peel (page 11)
⅛ teaspoon salt
Cool mixture; chill (*page 12*) until mixture is slightly thicker than consistency of thick, unbeaten egg white.

When mixture is of desired consistency, add
1 egg white
Beat until mixture is very thick and piles softly (about 15 min.). Set aside.

Wash, quarter, core, pare and grate enough apples to yield
¾ cup grated apple (about 2 medium-size apples)
Add the grated apple to the gelatin mixture and beat thoroughly. Turn into the pastry shell. Chill in refrigerator until firm.

One 10-in. pie

Blueberry Chiffon Pie

Flavorful blueberries in a foam of sweetness.

Prepare, bake and set aside to cool
**Pastry for 1-Crust Pie (page 442;
use 9-in. pie pan)**
Sort, rinse and drain
2 cups fresh ripe blueberries
Set ¼ cup berries in refrigerator for garnish.

Crush 1 cup of the berries with a fork; combine with remaining ¾ cup whole berries and
¾ cup plus 2 tablespoons sugar
Let stand about 20 min.

Pour into a small cup or custard cup
¼ cup cold water
Sprinkle evenly over cold water
**1 tablespoon (1 env.) unflavored
gelatin**
Let stand about 5 min. to soften.

Meanwhile, heat until very hot
½ cup water
¼ cup orange juice
Remove from heat and immediately add softened gelatin, stirring until gelatin is completely dissolved.

Stir in
1 teaspoon lemon juice
**1 teaspoon grated orange peel
(page 11)**
Add to blueberries and mix well. Cool mixture; chill (*page 12*) until mixture begins to gel (gets slightly thicker).

When gelatin is of desired consistency, beat until rounded peaks are formed
2 egg whites
⅛ teaspoon salt
Spread over gelatin mixture and gently fold (*page 12*) together. Turn into pastry shell. Place in refrigerator to chill.

To serve, prepare
**Sweetened Whipped Cream
(page 414)**
Pile in mounds around top of pie. Garnish with blueberries.

One 9-in. pie

▲ Cocoa Chiffon Pie

Prepare, bake and set aside to cool
> **Pastry for 1-Crust Pie (page 442; use 8-in. pie pan)**

Pour into a small cup or custard cup
> **¼ cup cold water**

Sprinkle evenly over cold water
> **1 tablespoon (1 env.) unflavored gelatin**

Let stand about 5 min. to soften.

Mix thoroughly in top of double boiler
> **⅓ cup sugar**
> **⅓ cup cocoa**
> **¼ teaspoon salt**

Gradually blend in
> **⅔ cup milk**

Stir over medium heat until sugar is dissolved. Bring mixture to boiling. Cook about 3 min. Vigorously stir about 3 tablespoons of hot mixture into
> **4 egg yolks, slightly beaten**

Immediately blend into mixture in double boiler. Stirring constantly, cook over simmering water until mixture is slightly thickened.

Remove from heat and stir in softened gelatin, stirring until gelatin is completely dissolved. Blend in
> **1 teaspoon vanilla extract**

Cool mixture; chill (*page 12*) until mixture begins to gel (gets slightly thicker).

When mixture is of desired consistency, beat until frothy
> **4 egg whites**

Add gradually, beating well after each addition
> **⅓ cup sugar**

Beat until rounded peaks are formed. Spread over gelatin mixture and gently fold (*page 12*) together. Turn into cooled pastry shell. Chill thoroughly in refrigerator.

Spread over top of pie and swirl with a spatula
> **Sweetened Whipped Cream (page 414)**

One 8-in. pie

△ Chocolate Chiffon Pie

Follow ▲ Recipe. Substitute 2 sq. (2 oz.) **chocolate**, grated, for cocoa. Increase each of the sugar measurements to ½ cup.

Coconut Chiffon Pie

Prepare, bake and set aside to cool
> **Pastry for 1-Crust Pie (page 442; use 9-in. pie pan)**

Set out
> **1 cup (4 oz.) moist shredded coconut, cut**

Pour into a small cup or custard cup
> **¼ cup cold water**

Sprinkle evenly over cold water
> **1 tablespoon (1 env.) unflavored gelatin**

Let stand about 5 min. to soften.

Meanwhile, mix together in the top of a double boiler
> **4 egg yolks, slightly beaten**
> **1 cup milk**
> **½ cup sugar**
> **¼ teaspoon salt**

Cook over simmering water, stirring constantly until mixture coats a silver spoon. Remove from simmering water and stir in softened gelatin, stirring until gelatin is completely dissolved. Blend in ¾ cup of the coconut (reserve ¼ cup for garnish) and
> **1½ teaspoons vanilla extract**

Cool mixture; chill (*page 12*) until mixture begins to gel (gets slightly thicker).

Meanwhile, spread evenly in cooled pastry shell and set aside

½ cup jellied cranberry sauce

When gelatin is of desired consistency, beat until frothy

4 egg whites

Add gradually, beating well after each addition

¼ cup sugar

Beat until rounded peaks are formed. Spread over gelatin mixture and gently fold (*page 12*) together. Turn into pastry shell. Sprinkle with the reserved coconut. Chill until firm.

Garnish just before serving with a few stars or other shapes cut from

Jellied cranberry sauce, cut into slices ¼ in. thick

One 9-in. pie

▲ Coffee-Nog Pie

For a double-mocha dessert treat—coffee in the pie and coffee with the pie.

Prepare, bake and set aside to cool

Pastry for 1-Crust 10-in. Pie (page 442)

Put a bowl and rotary beater into refrigerator to chill. Set out a double boiler.

Pour into a small bowl

½ cup cold water

Sprinkle evenly over cold water

2 tablespoons (2 env.) unflavored gelatin

Let stand about 5 min. to soften.

Meanwhile, prepare

2 cups double-strength coffee beverage (page 13)

Pour into top of the double boiler; add

⅔ cup sugar

½ teaspoon nutmeg

Stir over medium heat until sugar is dissolved. Bring mixture to boiling. Vigorously stir about 3 tablespoons hot coffee mixture into

3 egg yolks, slightly beaten

Immediately blend into mixture in double boiler. Stirring constantly, cook over simmering water until mixture is slightly thickened.

Coffee-Nog Pie and hot coffee

Remove from heat and stir in softened gelatin, stirring until gelatin is completely dissolved. Cool mixture; chill (*page 12*) until mixture begins to gel (gets slightly thicker).

When gelatin mixture is of desired consistency, beat, using chilled bowl and beater, until cream is of medium consistency (piles softly)

1 cup chilled whipping cream

Set in refrigerator while beating egg whites.

Using clean beater, beat until rounded peaks are formed

3 egg whites

Spread egg whites and whipped cream over gelatin mixture and gently fold (*page 12*) with

1½ teaspoons vanilla extract

Turn into cooled pastry shell. Chill in refrigerator until firm.

Top with chocolate curls made by pulling across a shredder

½ sq. (½ oz.) chocolate

Place in refrigerator until thoroughly chilled.

One 10-in. pie

△ Coffee-Nog Pie with Almonds

Follow ▲ Recipe. Fold in 1 cup (about 5½ oz.) salted, toasted **almonds** (*page 12*) with the vanilla extract.

Eggnog Chiffon Pie

Prepare, bake and set aside to cool
  Pastry for 1-Crust 10-in. Pie (page 442)
Place a bowl and rotary beater in refrigerator
to chill.

Pour into a small cup or custard cup
  ¼ cup cold water
Sprinkle evenly over cold water
  **1 tablespoon (1 env.) unflavored
   gelatin**
Let stand about 5 min. to soften.

Mix in top of double boiler and heat over simmering water until scalded (*page 13*)
  1½ cups milk
  5 tablespoons sugar
  ½ teaspoon salt
Vigorously stir 3 tablespoons hot mixture into
  4 egg yolks, slightly beaten
Immediately blend into mixture in double
boiler. Stirring constantly, cook over simmering water until mixture coats a silver spoon.
Immediately remove from heat and stir in
softened gelatin, stirring until gelatin is completely dissolved. Cool; chill (*page 12*) until
mixture begins to gel (gets slightly thicker).

When gelatin mixture is of desired consistency, using chilled bowl and beater, beat until
cream is of medium consistency (piles softly)
  1 cup chilled whipping cream
Set in refrigerator while beating egg whites.
Using clean beater, beat until frothy
  2 egg whites
Add gradually, beating well after each addition,
a mixture of
  ¼ cup sugar
  ½ teaspoon nutmeg
Beat until rounded peaks are formed. Spread
egg whites and whipped cream over gelatin
mixture and gently fold (*page 12*) with
  2 tablespoons rum
  2 teaspoons vanilla extract
Turn into pastry shell. Sprinkle over top
  ½ teaspoon nutmeg
Chill in refrigerator until firm.

One 10-in. pie

Tropical Chiffon Pie

Prepare, bake and set aside to cool
  **Pastry for 1-Crust Pie (page 442;
   use 9-in. pie pan)**
Pour into a small cup or custard cup
  2 tablespoons cold water
  2 tablespoons lemon juice
Sprinkle evenly over liquid
  **1 tablespoon (1 env.) unflavored
   gelatin**
Let stand about 5 min. to soften.

Set out
  1¼ cups orange juice
Heat ¾ cup of the orange juice until very hot.
Remove from heat and immediately stir in
gelatin, stirring until gelatin is completely dissolved. Add, stirring until dissolved
  ⅓ cup sugar
  ¼ teaspoon salt
Stir in the reserved ½ cup orange juice and
  **¼ teaspoon grated orange peel
   (page 11)**
Cool mixture; chill (*page 12*) until mixture is
slightly thicker than consistency of thick, unbeaten egg white.

Put a bowl and rotary beater into refrigerator
to chill.

When gelatin is of desired consistency, wash,
cut into halves, remove pit and peel from
  1 large, ripe avocado
Force through sieve or food mill enough to
yield 1 cup of sieved avocado; blend into the
gelatin mixture.

Using the chilled bowl and beater, beat until
cream is of medium consistency (piles softly)
  1 cup chilled whipping cream
Spread over gelatin mixture and fold (*page 12*)
together. Turn mixture into the pastry shell.
Chill in refrigerator until firm. *One 9-in. pie*

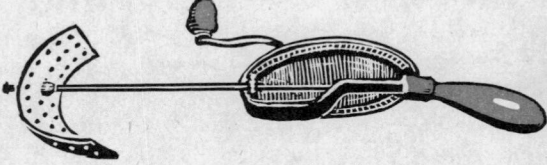

Lemon Cloud Pie

Refreshing as only lemon can be, this light-as-air pie is a welcome dessert at any time.

Prepare, bake and set aside to cool
Pastry for 1-Crust Pie (page 442; use 9-in. pie pan)
Mix together in top of double boiler
½ cup sugar
1 tablespoon (1 env.) unflavored gelatin
¼ teaspoon salt
Set aside.

Mix together
5 egg yolks, slightly beaten
½ cup water
½ cup lemon juice
½ teaspoon vanilla extract
Add gradually to gelatin mixture, stirring constantly, and mix well. Cook over simmering water, stirring constantly, until gelatin is dissolved and mixture is slightly thickened. Remove from simmering water and stir in
1 teaspoon grated lemon peel (*page 11*)
Cool mixture; chill (*page 12*) until mixture begins to gel (gets slightly thicker).

When gelatin mixture is of desired consistency, beat until frothy
5 egg whites
Add gradually, beating well after each addition
½ cup sugar
Beat until rounded peaks are formed. Spread over gelatin mixture and gently fold (*page 12*) together. Turn mixture into the pastry shell. Chill in refrigerator until firm.

If desired, serve with **Sweetened Whipped Cream** (*page 414*).   *One 9-in. pie*

Orange Chiffon Pie

Prepare, bake and set aside to cool
Graham Cracker Pie Shell (*p. 446*), use 9-in. pie pan; reserve 2 to 4 tablespoons of the crumb mixture for topping)
Pour into a small cup or custard cup
2 tablespoons cold water
2 tablespoons lemon juice
Sprinkle evenly over liquid
1 tablespoon (1 env.) unflavored gelatin
Let stand about 5 min. to soften.

Blend together in top of double boiler
4 egg yolks, slightly beaten
⅔ cup sugar
½ cup orange juice
¼ teaspoon salt
Cook over simmering water, stirring constantly until mixture thickens. Remove from heat and stir in softened gelatin and
2 teaspoons grated orange peel (*page 11*)
Stir until gelatin is completely dissolved. Cool mixture; chill (*page 12*) until mixture begins to gel (gets slightly thicker).

When gelatin is of desired consistency, beat until frothy
4 egg whites
Add gradually, beating well after each addition
½ cup sugar
Continue beating until rounded peaks are formed. Spread over gelatin mixture and gently fold (*page 12*) together. Turn into pie shell. Sprinkle the reserved crumbs over filling. Chill in refrigerator until firm.

One 9-in. pie

Elegant Almond Pie

Prepare, bake and set aside to cool
Pastry for 1-Crust Pie (page 442; use 9-in. pie pan)

Blanch and toast (*page 12*)
⅔ cup (about 4 oz.) almonds
Reserve 12 almonds for garnish. Coarsely chop remaining almonds and set aside.

Melt (*page 12*) and set aside to cool
1 sq. (1 oz.) chocolate
Pour into a small cup or custard cup
¼ cup cold water
Sprinkle evenly over cold water
1 tablespoon (1 env.) unflavored gelatin
Let stand about 5 min. to soften.

For Vanilla Filling—Blend together in top of a double boiler
1½ cups milk
¼ cup sugar
⅛ teaspoon salt
Heat over simmering water until milk is scalded (*page 13*).

Vigorously stir about 3 tablespoons of hot mixture into
3 egg yolks, slightly beaten
Immediately blend into mixture in double boiler. Stirring constantly, cook over simmering water until mixture coats a silver spoon.

Remove from heat and stir in softened gelatin, stirring until gelatin is completely dissolved.

Blend in
1 teaspoon vanilla extract
Remove ½ cup cooked mixture from double boiler and set aside to use in chocolate filling. Set remaining mixture aside to cool.

For Chocolate Filling—Stir into the ½ cup of vanilla filling
2 tablespoons sugar
Blend in the melted chocolate. Set aside to cool completely. When cool, pour into pastry shell and spread evenly over bottom.

Chill in refrigerator until firm.

Elegant Almond Pie

To Complete Pie—When chocolate layer is firm, beat until frothy
3 egg whites
Add and beat slightly
¼ teaspoon cream of tartar
⅛ teaspoon salt
Add gradually, beating well after each addition
¼ cup sugar
Continue beating until rounded peaks are formed. Blend chopped almonds into cooled Vanilla Filling. Spread beaten egg whites over cooled filling and gently fold (*page 12*) together. Spoon over chocolate layer in pastry shell. Chill in refrigerator until firm.

Just before serving, prepare
Sweetened Whipped Cream (one-half recipe, page 414)
Top pie with mounds of the whipped cream and garnish (see photo) with the reserved toasted whole almonds. *One 9-in. pie*

▲ Black Bottom Pie I

To be frank about it, there's a bit of making goes into this stunning pie. But the minutes are well-spent, and you'll find your reward in blissful faces and calls for more.

Prepare, bake and set aside to cool
Braided-Edge Pastry Shell (page 443)
Melt (*page 12*) and set aside to cool
1½ sq. (1½ oz.) chocolate

For Custard Filling—Scald (*page 13*) in top of double boiler
1½ cups milk
Meanwhile, pour into a small cup or custard cup
¼ cup cold water
Sprinkle evenly over cold water
1 tablespoon (1 env.) unflavored gelatin
Let stand about 5 min. to soften.

Sift together into a saucepan
½ cup sugar
4 teaspoons cornstarch
Add and blend in well
½ cup cold milk
Stir scalded milk into cornstarch mixture. Bring rapidly to boiling over direct heat, stirring gently and constantly. Cook 3 min.

Wash double-boiler top to remove scum.

Pour cornstarch mixture into double-boiler top. Vigorously stir about 3 tablespoons of hot mixture into
4 egg yolks, slightly beaten
Immediately blend into mixture in double boiler, stirring constantly. Cook, stirring constantly, over simmering water 3 to 5 min., or until mixture thickens and coats a silver spoon. Immediately remove from heat. Remove 1 cup cooked filling from double boiler and set aside to use in Chocolate Filling. Add softened gelatin to mixture in double boiler and stir until gelatin is completely dissolved. Set aside to cool until mixture sets slightly. If it becomes too stiff upon standing, soften mixture over simmering water and cool again.

For Chocolate Filling—Stir melted chocolate into the reserved filling with
2 teaspoons vanilla extract
Cool completely. Pour into pie shell and spread evenly over bottom. Chill in refrigerator until set.

To Complete Pie—Beat until frothy
4 egg whites
¼ teaspoon salt
Add and beat slightly
¼ teaspoon cream of tartar
Add gradually, beating well after each addition
½ cup sugar
Continue beating until rounded peaks are formed. Spread over gelatin mixture and gently fold (*page 12*) together. Blend in
1 tablespoon rum extract
Pour over set Chocolate Filling in pastry shell. Chill in refrigerator until firm.

Put a small bowl and rotary beater in refrigerator to chill.

About 30 min. before serving, using chilled bowl and beater, whip (*page 13*)
1 cup chilled whipping cream
Using a spatula, spread whipped cream over pie and swirl for decorative effect. Top with chocolate curls made by pulling across a shredder
½ sq. (½ oz.) chocolate
Chill in refrigerator until ready to serve.

One 10-in. pie

△ Black Bottom Pie II

Follow ▲ Recipe. Substitute 1 pkg. (6 oz.) **semi-sweet chocolate pieces** for chocolate, reserving about ¼ cup for topping. Omit whipped cream. Arrange reserved semi-sweet chocolate pieces over top of chilled pie.

Banana Cream Pie

▲ De Luxe Cream Pie or Tarts

Prepare, bake and set aside to cool

Pastry for 1-Crust Pie (page 442; use 8-in. pie pan) or Pastry for Little Pies and Tarts (page 443; use 3½-in. tart pans)

Scald (*page 13*) in top of double boiler

1½ cups milk

Meanwhile, sift together into a saucepan

⅔ cup sugar
¼ cup sifted flour
¼ teaspoon salt

Add, stirring well

½ cup cold milk

Add gradually and stir in the scalded milk. Stirring gently and constantly, bring rapidly to boiling over direct heat and cook 3 min.

Wash double-boiler top to remove scum.

Pour mixture into double-boiler top and place over simmering water. Cover and cook about 5 to 7 min., stirring three or four times.

Vigorously stir about 3 tablespoons of hot mixture into

3 egg yolks, slightly beaten

Immediately blend into mixture in double boiler. Cook over simmering water 3 to 5 min. Stir slowly to keep mixture cooking evenly. Remove from simmering water. Blend in

2 tablespoons butter or margarine
2 teaspoons vanilla extract

Cover and cool slightly, stirring occasionally; cool to lukewarm in refrigerator. Turn into the pastry shell or spoon into the tart shells. Chill in refrigerator.   *One 8-in. pie or six 3½-in. tarts*

▲ Banana Cream Pie or Tarts

Follow ▲ Recipe. Set out 3 **bananas** with brown-flecked peel. For pie, peel 2 of the bananas; cut into crosswise slices and arrange over bottom of pastry shell. Turn lukewarm filling over banana slices. Chill in refrigerator. Before serving, peel remaining banana and draw tines of a fork lengthwise over entire surface of banana; cut into crosswise slices. Arrange slices in a ring on top of pie. Garnish with **whipped cream** and a **maraschino cherry**. For tarts, put about 10 slices and about ⅓ cup of filling into each tart shell.

▲ Lemon Cream Pie or Tarts

Follow ▲ Recipe. Increase sugar to ¾ cup and flour to 6 tablespoons. Omit vanilla extract; add ¼ cup **lemon juice** and 2 teaspoons grated **lemon peel** (*page 11*) with the butter. Tint to desired color by blending in 5 or 6 drops **yellow food coloring**.

▲ Lime Cream Pie or Tarts

Follow △ Recipe. Substitute ¾ cup **lime juice** for lemon juice and ½ teaspoon grated **lime peel** for lemon peel. Tint by blending in 3 or 4 drops **green food coloring**.

▲ Butterscotch Cream Pie or Tarts

Follow ▲ Recipe. Decrease sugar to ⅓ cup and add ⅓ cup firmly packed **brown sugar**. Increase butter to 3 tablespoons.

▲ Cocoa Cream Pie

Follow ▲ Recipe. Sift ½ cup **cocoa** with dry ingredients.

▲ Chocolate Cream Pie

Follow ▲ Recipe. Add 2 sq. (2 oz.) **chocolate** to milk; heat until milk is scalded and chocolate is melted.

▲ Mocha Chocolate Cream Pie

Follow ▲ Recipe. Substitute 1 cup **double-strength coffee beverage** (*page 13*) for 1 cup of the milk.

Cream Pie with Gooseberry Glaze

Prepare, bake and set aside to cool
>**Pastry for 1-Crust Pie (page 442; use 9-in. pie pan)**

For Cream Filling—Sift together into top of a double boiler
>¾ **cup sugar**
>¼ **cup cornstarch**
>¼ **teaspoon salt**

Gradually add in order, blending thoroughly after each addition
>¼ **cup cold water**
>1 **cup undiluted evaporated milk**
>¾ **cup very hot water**

Stirring gently and constantly, bring cornstarch mixture rapidly to boiling over direct heat and cook about 1 min., or until mixture begins to thicken. Place over simmering water. Cover and cook about 12 min., stirring three or four times.

Vigorously stir about 3 tablespoons of hot mixture into
>2 **eggs, slightly beaten**

Immediately blend into mixture in double boiler. Cook over simmering water 3 to 5 min. Stir slowly to keep mixture cooking evenly. Remove from simmering water.

Stir in
>1 **teaspoon butter or margarine**
>¾ **teaspoon vanilla extract**

Cover and cool slightly, stirring occasionally;

Cream Pie with Gooseberry Glaze

cool to lukewarm in refrigerator. Turn filling into the pastry shell. Set in refrigerator to chill.

For Gooseberry Glaze—Sort, stem and tail, rinse and drain
>2½ **cups fresh gooseberries**

Put ½ cup of gooseberries in saucepan with
>¾ **cup water**

Cook over medium heat 3 to 5 min., or until tender. Add, stirring constantly, a mixture of
>1 **cup sugar**
>3 **tablespoons cornstarch**

Stir in the remaining 2 cups of gooseberries. Stirring gently and constantly, bring rapidly to boiling and cook for 3 min., or until mixture is thickened. Remove from heat; set aside to cool to lukewarm.

To Complete Pie—Pour the cooled glaze over the cream filling. Chill in refrigerator 2 to 3 hrs. before serving.   *One 9-in. pie*

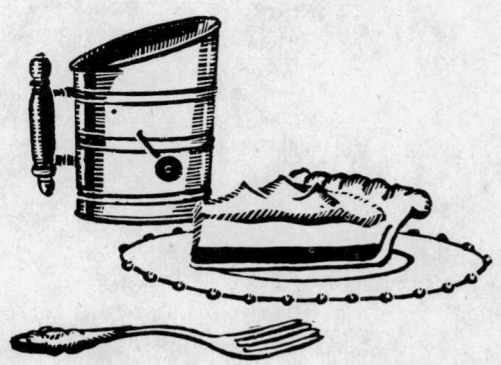

 **DOMESTIC WINES**

CLASSES	TYPES	CHARACTERISTICS	HOW TO SERVE AND WITH WHAT	
Appetizer Wines	**SHERRY**	**SHERRY:** Rich, nutlike flavor, ranging from dry to sweet; pale to dark amber color.	Chilled (2 to 3-oz. glasses)	Hors d'Oeuvres
	VERMOUTH	**VERMOUTH:** Piquant, aromatic flavor. Dry (French type) is pale amber. Sweet (Italian type) is darker amber.		Soup
Red Table Wines	**BURGUNDY** Pinot Noir Red Pinot Gamay Barbera	**BURGUNDY:** Dry, robust; deeper red color than claret. Pinots are especially velvety; have superb bouquet.	At cool or room temperature (except Roses, chilled) (5 to 8-oz. glasses)	Steak Roasts Chops Game Cheeses Spaghetti
	CLARET Zinfandel Cabernet Grignolino	**CLARET:** Dry, tart, zestful, ruby red. Zinfandel is vivaciously fresh, fruity. Cabernet, slightly fuller-bodied.		
	VINO ROSSO	**VINO ROSSOS:** Usually have Italian names; mellow, slightly sweet.		
	ROSE	**ROSES:** Gay pink, fruity, light bodied, good with all food. Some are dry, others slightly sweet.		
	RED CHIANTI	**RED CHIANTI:** Italian flavor; dry, a bit tart, full-bodied.		
White Table Wines	**SAUTERNE** Sauvignon Blanc Semillon	**SAUTERNE:** Golden-hued, full-bodied, fragrant, dry to sweet. Sauvignon Blanc: Usually dry. Haut or Chateau Sauterne is sweet, with delightful aroma. Semillon: Dry or sweet.	Well chilled (5 to 8-oz. glasses)	Seafoods Chicken Omelets Other light dishes
	RHINE WINE Riesling Traminer Sylvaner	**RHINE WINE:** Thoroughly dry, tart with flowery bouquet, light-bodied, pale or green-gold color. Riesling: Delicate in flavor. Traminer: Spicy, fresh.		
	CHABLIS Pinot Blanc Pinot Chardonnay	**CHABLIS:** Soft, dry, fuller-bodied, less tart than Rhine wines.		
Dessert Wines	**PORT** White Port	**PORT:** Deep purple-red and tawny, rich, heavy-bodied, very sweet. White Port:	At room temperature,	Fruits Nuts

Tawny Port		Little less sweet, medium in body, without color.	or chilled (2 to 3-oz. glasses)	Cookies Cheeses
	MUSCATEL	MUSCATEL: Sweet, fruity, full-bodied, pronounced flavor and aroma of Muscat grapes; ranges from gold and dark amber to red.		
	TOKAY	TOKAY: Pinkish amber, nutty or sherry-like flavor; less sweet than port.		
	ANGELICA			
	SWEET	ANGELICA: Light amber, is like a mild		
	SHERRY	cordial.		
Sparkling Wines	CHAMPAGNE Pink Champagne	CHAMPAGNE: Very dry ("brut"), semi-dry ("sec"), or sweet ("doux").	Iced or refrigerated 4 to 6 hrs.	Equally good with all foods
	SPARKLING BURGUNDY	SPARKLING BURGUNDY: Ruby-red, sweet or semi-sweet, fruity, bubbling.		

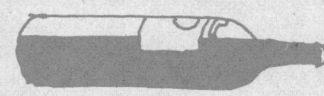

FOR AFTER-DINNER

Anisette: From France. Colorless, mild and sweet. Has an aniseed flavor (also an aperitif when diluted with ice and water).

Apricot Liqueur: Sweetened brandy plus crushed dried apricots.

Aquavit: From Scandinavia, unsweetened grain or potato distillate, caraway flavored (light kummel).

B & B: Brandy and Benedictine, already mixed.

Benedictine: From Normandy, France, from secret formula. Trade-mark ("D.O.M.") comes from the Benedictine Monks' inscription "To God, most good, most great."

Blackberry Liqueur: Blackberries with brandy (sweet).

Brandy: Undisputed after-dinner drink —distillation of fermented juice of a fruit: grape, apples, etc. Finest grape brandy from Cognac, France; is so labeled.

Chartreuse: Yellow and green. (Green, stronger with a more herbal taste, is considered finer.) From secret formula of the monks living in French Alps.

Cherry Liqueur: The best known is made in Denmark, Cherry Heering.

Cointreau: A colorless liqueur with an orange flavor and brandy base made from orange blossoms or peel.

Creme de Cacao: Brown liqueur with chocolate flavor, made from cocoa beans.

Creme de Menthe: Green or white, made from fresh mints and brandy. Very popular.

Curacao: Colorless or burnt orange. Orange flavor from skins of bitter oranges, largely grown in Curacao in West Indies.

Drambuie: A popular cordial made with Scotch whiskey base. (Honey and herbs are added.)

Fior d'Alpe: From Italy. Distinctive blend distilled of herbs (mint, wild marjoram and hyssop). Twig, encrusted with rock sugar crystals, in each bottle.

Grand Marnier: Orange-flavored. A version of Curacao and Cognac.

Kummel: White, strong, sweet. Tastes of coriander and caraway seeds.

Strega: From Italy. Sweet yellow liqueur with an orange flavor, similar to Chartreuse.

Tequila: From Mexico. Made from maguey plant.

Triple Sec: Colorless, like Curacao, but less sweet.

Freezing Baked Products

One of the greatest conveniences of owning a freezer is to have on hand a variety of baked products—ready to be baked or baked.

Remember that freezer space is at a premium, so make efficient use of each inch of storage space. Freezing does not generally improve the quality of a product; therefore, for freezing choose only foods and ingredients of *high quality*.

A rapid turnover of frozen food indicates good management of freezer storage space. Date on label insures proper rotation of food. Keep an up-to-date record of freezer contents.

Thawed frozen foods should not be refrozen.

The best efforts in freezing will be in vain if the food is not protected by proper packaging. And a tight seal is of utmost importance for a successful frozen product.

There are many excellent products on the market—bags, cartons, jars and wrapping materials. In choosing, some important factors to be considered are: proper size, shape and material for the specific food to be frozen, ease of handling and economy of price and space. The packaging material should also be waterproof, moisture-vapor-proof and, when necessary, greaseproof.

The food package should be clearly labeled to indicate contents and date of freezing.

Quick Breads—These may be frozen before or after baking. In general, freezing after baking gives a more desirable product and a longer freezer storage time. Wrap the cooled, baked product in freezer material; seal, label and freeze. If it is to be served hot, place wrapped frozen product in oven until thoroughly heated; if not, thaw in wrapping material at room temperature.

Yeast Breads and Rolls—These may be frozen before or after baking. However, the volume of the product is usually greater if frozen after baking. Cool the baked product on a cooling rack, wrap in freezer material, seal, label and freeze. Place wrapped frozen bread or rolls in oven until thoroughly heated.

Cookies—Most types of cookies freeze satisfactorily whether frozen before or after baking. Meringue-type cookies do not freeze well. Cool baked cookies; then wrap, seal, label and freeze.

Thaw in wrapping material at room temperature. Form cookie dough into rolls; wrap tightly in freezer material, seal, label and freeze. Thaw dough slightly in refrigerator, cut into slices and bake.

Butter-type Cakes—These cakes may be frozen in the batter state or after baking. Pour batter into freezer containers; seal, label and freeze. To bake: Place in refrigerator or at room temperature until just soft; turn into prepared pans and let stand at room temperature 10 to 20 min. longer and bake as directed for the individual cake. Cool baked cakes before freezing; wrap, seal, label and freeze. Thaw in wrapping material at room temperature or in a slow oven.

Angel Food and Sponge Cakes—These cakes are very successful if baked and then frozen. Wrap the cooled cake and seal, being careful not to crush the cake. Place in a sturdy box; label and freeze. Thaw the frozen cake in wrapping material in a slow oven for 20 to 30 min. (if manufacturer advises). Cool to room temperature and serve immediately. Or thaw cake at room temperature.

Pies—Chiffon pies are high on the list of pies suitable for freezing. They keep very well when frozen in baked shells. Cream pies may be frozen in baked shells, but without the meringue. Custard-type pies do not freeze successfully. Freeze chiffon and cream pies before wrapping; place in protective container, seal, label and return to freezer. Serve chiffon pies chilled rather than at room temperature. Pile meringue on frozen cream pies and bake until meringue is lightly browned.

In fruit fillings increase the flour or cornstarch, depending upon juiciness of the fruit. If fruit pies are frozen before baking, the top crusts should not be slit or pricked until after 10 min. of baking time. To freeze a two-crust pie, invert a pie pan of identical size over the prepared pie. Wrap in cellophane; heat-seal by using a warm iron, curling iron or a piece of equipment made especially for this purpose. Wrap in heavy paper to avoid damage to cellophane, label and freeze. Remove wrapping paper, cellophane and the inverted pie pan and bake as directed for specific pie.

Cool baked pie before freezing; place in protective container, seal, label and freeze.

▲ Macaroon Meringue Pie

FRANCES E. MCKNIGHT
CAMPBELLSVILLE, KY.

The kind of pie that acquires legendary fame.

Prepare, bake and set aside to cool
Pastry for 1-Crust Pie (page 442; use 9-in. pie pan)

Arrange on a baking sheet
9 1¾-in. almond-macaroon cookies

Place in 325°F oven for about 15 min., or until cookies are dry. Cool on cooling rack. Crush (*page 12*) enough of the cookies to yield ¾ cup crumbs.

Finely chop and set aside
¼ cup (about 1 oz.) blanched almonds (page 11)

Scald (*page 13*) in top of double boiler
1 cup cream

Meanwhile, sift together into a saucepan
1 cup sugar
2½ tablespoons flour

Add, stirring well
¼ cup cold milk

Add gradually and stir in the scalded cream. Stirring gently and constantly, bring rapidly to boiling over direct heat and cook 3 min.

Wash double-boiler top to remove scum.

Pour mixture into double-boiler top and place over simmering water. Cover and cook about 5 to 7 min., stirring three or four times.

Vigorously stir about 3 tablespoons of hot mixture into
3 egg yolks, slightly beaten

Immediately blend into mixture in double boiler. Cook over simmering water 3 to 5 min. Stir slowly to keep mixture cooking evenly. Remove from simmering water. Blend in
2 tablespoons butter
1 teaspoon almond extract

Stir in the macaroon crumbs. Cover and cool slightly, stirring occasionally; cool to lukewarm in refrigerator. Turn into cooled shell. Complete pie with
Meringue I (page 448; sprinkle the chopped almonds over the meringue before baking)

Cool on cooling rack. *One 9-in. pie*

△ Macaroon Pie

Follow ▲ Recipe. Omit Meringue I. Put the pie into the refrigerator to cool completely. Put a bowl, rotary beater and 1 cup **whipping cream** into refrigerator to chill. To serve, using chilled bowl and beater, whip (*page 13*) the whipping cream. Spread over top of pie and swirl with a spatula. Sprinkle the chopped almonds over top.

▲ Jiffy Lemon Pie

Prepare, bake and set aside to cool
> **Pastry for 1-Crust Pie (page 442; use 8-in. pie pan)**

Blend just until well mixed
> **1⅓ cups (1 15-oz. can) sweetened condensed milk**
> **⅔ cup lemon juice**
> **1½ teaspoons grated lemon peel (page 11)**
> **3 egg yolks, slightly beaten**

Pour into pastry shell. Complete pie with
> **Meringue II (page 448)**

Cool on cooling rack. *One 8-in. pie*

△ Jiffy Lime Pie

Follow ▲ Recipe. Substitute ⅔ cup **lime juice** and 1½ teaspoons grated **lime peel** for lemon juice and peel; tint to desired color by blending in 1 or 2 drops **green food coloring.**

Jiffy Lemon Pie

Lemon Meringue Pie

Prepare, bake and set aside to cool
> **Pastry for 1-Crust Pie (page 442; use 9-in. pie pan)**

Sift together into top of double boiler
> **1½ cups sugar**
> **⅓ cup cornstarch**
> **⅛ teaspoon salt**

Blend in
> **½ cup cold water**

Add gradually and stir in
> **1 cup boiling water**

Stirring gently and constantly, bring cornstarch mixture rapidly to boiling over direct heat and cook 3 min. Place over simmering water. Cover and cook about 12 min., stirring three or four times.

Vigorously stir about 3 tablespoons of hot mixture into
> **3 egg yolks, slightly beaten**

Immediately blend into mixture in double boiler. Cook over simmering water 3 to 5 min. Stir slowly to keep mixture cooking evenly. Remove from simmering water. Blend in
> **2 tablespoons butter or margarine**
> **¼ cup lemon juice**
> **1½ tablespoons grated lemon peel (page 11)**

Cover and cool slightly, stirring occasionally; cool to lukewarm in refrigerater. Turn filling into the cooled pastry shell.

Complete pie with
> **Meringue I (page 448)**

Cool on cooling rack. *One 9-in. pie*

Orange Cream Meringue Pie

BLANCHE E. DUNCAN
JOHNSON CITY, TENN.

Prepare, bake and set aside to cool
**Pastry for 1-Crust Pie (page 442;
use 9-in. pie pan)**
Scald (*page 13*) in top of double boiler
1 cup milk
Meanwhile, sift together into a saucepan
½ cup sugar
¼ cup cornstarch
¼ teaspoon salt
Blend in
1 cup orange juice
Add gradually and stir in the scalded milk.
Stirring gently and constantly, bring cornstarch mixture rapidly to boiling over direct
heat and cook 3 min.

Wash double-boiler top to remove scum.

Pour mixture into double-boiler top and place
over simmering water. Cover and cook 5 to 7
min., stirring three or four times.

Vigorously stir about 3 tablespoons of hot
mixture into
3 egg yolks, slightly beaten
Immediately blend into mixture in double
boiler. Cook over simmering water 3 to 5 min.
Stir slowly to keep mixture cooking evenly.
Remove from simmering water. Blend in
1 tablespoon butter or margarine
1 tablespoon grated orange peel
(page 11)
Cover and cool slightly, stirring occasionally;
cool to lukewarm in refrigerator. Turn filling
into the cooled pastry shell.

Complete pie with
Meringue I (page 448)
Cool on cooling rack. *One 9-in. pie*

Black Raspberry Cream Pie

MRS. T. J. VANDERVELDT, ASTORIA, ORE.

*This is quite literally "like the pies that
Mother used to make"—an old-time favorite.*

Prepare, bake and set aside to cool
**Pastry for 1-Crust Pie (page 442;
use 8-in. pie pan)**
Scald (*page 13*) in top of double boiler
1½ cups milk
Meanwhile, sift together into a saucepan
⅔ cup sugar
¼ cup sifted flour
¼ teaspoon salt
Add, stirring well
¼ cup cold milk
Add gradually and stir in the scalded milk.
Stirring gently and constantly, bring rapidly
to boiling over direct heat and cook 3 min.

Wash double-boiler top to remove scum.

Pour mixture into double-boiler top and place
over simmering water. Cover and cook about
5 to 7 min., stirring three or four times.

Vigorously stir about 3 tablespoons of hot
mixture into
3 egg yolks, slightly beaten
Immediately blend into mixture in double
boiler. Cook over simmering water 3 to 5 min.
Stir slowly to keep mixture cooking evenly.
Remove from simmering water.

Blend in
2 tablespoons butter
1 tablespoon lemon juice
Cover and cool slightly, stirring occasionally;
cool to lukewarm in refrigerator.

Meanwhile, drain thoroughly the contents of
**2 1-lb. cans (about 2 cups, drained)
black raspberries**
(Reserve sirup for use in other food preparation.) Turn well-drained berries into pastry
shell. Turn lukewarm filling over berries.

Complete pie with
Meringue II (page 448)
One 8-in. pie

▲ Custard Pie

Take insurance against the possibility of a soggy crust by using the slipped version.

Prepare (do not bake) and set aside
>**Pastry for 1-Crust Pie (page 442; use 8-in. pie pan)**

To Prepare Custard—Scald (*page 13*)
>**1½ cups milk**
>**¾ cup cream**

Beat slightly
>**4 eggs**

Add and beat just until blended
>**½ cup sugar**
>**½ teaspoon nutmeg**
>**¼ teaspoon salt**

Blend in the scalded milk and cream and
>**1 teaspoon vanilla extract**

Strain mixture into the pastry shell.

To Complete Pie—Bake at 450°F 10 min. Reduce heat to 350°F and bake 15 to 20 min. longer, or until a silver knife comes out clean when inserted halfway between center and edge of filling.

Cool on cooling rack. Place in refrigerator until ready to serve.   *One 8-in. pie*

△ Slipped Custard Pie

Follow ▲ Recipe for amounts of ingredients.

Prepare, bake and set pastry shell aside to cool. Heat water for boiling water bath (*page 12*). Lightly butter a second 8-in. pie pan.

Prepare custard and strain into the buttered pan. Bake in boiling water bath at 325°F 25 to 30 min., or until custard tests done. Set aside to cool.

When custard is cool, run tip of knife around edge of pie pan; hold the pan level and shake gently to loosen custard. Hold pan at a slight angle and slip the custard carefully into the pastry shell. Work quickly to avoid breaking the custard. Set aside for a few minutes to allow custard to settle.

Buttermilk Custard Pie
OPAL A. BLASDEL, LA JUNTA, COLO.

Prepare (do not bake) and set aside
>**Pastry for 1-Crust Pie (page 442; use 9-in. pie pan)**

Melt and set aside to cool
>**3 tablespoons butter**

Beat slightly
>**3 egg yolks**

Blend in a mixture of
>**⅔ cup sugar**
>**2 tablespoons flour**
>**⅛ teaspoon salt**

Stir in the melted butter and
>**1⅔ cups buttermilk**
>**1½ teaspoons vanilla extract**

Beat until rounded peaks are formed
>**3 egg whites**

Spread over buttermilk mixture and fold (*page 12*) together. Turn into pastry shell.

Bake at 450°F 10 min. Reduce heat to 350°F and bake 20 to 25 min. longer, or until a silver knife comes out clean when inserted halfway between center and edge of filling.

Cool on cooling rack.   *One 9-in. pie*

Sweet Potato Pie

NORMA JEAN EASON, LONGVILLE, LA.

For a dessert delight from Mardi-gras land, serve hot coffee and Sweet Potato Pie.

Prepare (do not bake) and set aside
Pastry for 1-Crust 10-in. Pie (page 442)
Set out
1½ cups mashed sweet potatoes or yams
Scald (*page 13*)
1½ cups milk
Combine with the sweet potatoes
2 tablespoons butter
and a mixture of
½ cup firmly packed brown sugar
1 teaspoon cinnamon
½ teaspoon ginger
¼ teaspoon mace
¼ teaspoon salt
Beat well. Add in thirds, beating well after each addition
2 eggs, well beaten
Blend in the scalded milk. Turn into the pastry shell.

Bake at 450°F 10 min. Reduce heat to 350°F and bake 30 to 35 min. longer, or until silver knife comes out clean when inserted halfway between center and edge of filling.

Cool on cooling rack.

To serve, prepare
Sweetened Whipped Cream (one-half recipe, page 414)
Spread over top of pie. Sprinkle with
¼ cup chopped, unblanched almonds

One 10-in. pie

Sweet Potato Pie and hot coffee

Rhubarb-Butterscotch Pie

WANDA HUFFMAN, EVANS, COLO.

A springtime recipe from a farm kitchen, Rhubarb-Butterscotch Pie tastes as if "it contained the new wine of Spring itself."

Prepare (do not bake) and set aside
Pastry for 1-Crust Pie (page 442; use 9-in. pie pan)
Wash, trim off leaves and ends of stems and cut into 1-in. pieces enough rhubarb to yield
4 cups fresh rhubarb
(Peel stalks only if skin is tough.) Turn the rhubarb into pastry shell in an even layer.

Mix together
½ cup firmly packed brown sugar
3 tablespoons flour
⅛ teaspoon salt
Beat together
2 eggs, well beaten
3 tablespoons heavy cream
Pour the egg mixture into the dry ingredients and mix thoroughly. Pour mixture evenly over the rhubarb.

Bake at 450°F 10 min. Reduce heat to 350°F and bake 20 to 25 min. longer.

Cool on cooling rack.

One 9-in. pie

477

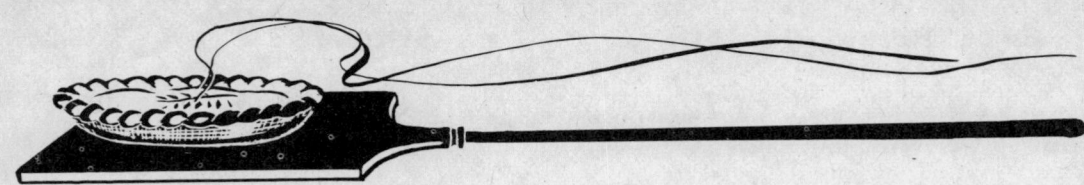

Peanut-Butter Custard Pie

NORMA SCHMID, KIMBERLY, IDAHO

The nut-like sweetness of this unusual pie makes it a delightfully different treat.

Prepare (do not bake) and set aside

Pastry for 1-Crust Pie (page 442; use 9-in. pie pan)

Cream together until blended

1 cup peanut butter
1 teaspoon vanilla extract

Add gradually, creaming until fluffy after each addition

1½ cups sugar
½ teaspoon salt

Add in thirds, beating thoroughly after each addition

2 eggs, well beaten

Blend in

1½ cups milk

Turn into the pastry shell.

Bake at 450°F 10 min. Reduce heat to 350°F and bake 20 to 25 min. longer, or until a silver knife comes out clean when inserted halfway between center and edge of filling.

Cool on cooling rack.   *One 9-in. pie*

▲ Pumpkin Pie

Prepare, bake 10 min. and set aside to cool

Pastry for 1-Crust Pie (page 442; use 9-in. pie pan)

Mix together

2 cups (1 1-lb. can) canned pumpkin

and a mixture of

⅔ cup firmly packed dark brown sugar
1 teaspoon cinnamon
½ teaspoon ginger
½ teaspoon nutmeg
½ teaspoon salt
⅛ teaspoon cloves

Blend together and add, mixing until smooth

2 eggs, slightly beaten
1 cup cream

Pour into the pastry shell.

Bake at 350°F 50 to 60 min., or until a silver knife comes out clean when inserted halfway between center and edge of filling.

Cool on cooling rack.

Serve with

Edam cheese or Sweetened Whipped Cream (page 414)

One 9-in. pie

△ Southern Pumpkin Pecan Pie

MRS. E. E. McKAY, MT. VERNON, ILL.

Follow ▲ Recipe. Blend 1 cup firmly packed **brown sugar** with ¼ cup **butter,** softened. Remove pie from oven and spoon mixture evenly over top. Top with ½ cup (about 2 oz.) **pecans.**

Set temperature control of range at Broil. Set pie on broiler rack and place in broiler with top of pie 3 in. from source of heat. Broil 1 min., or until butter mixture bubbles. Watch closely to avoid scorching.

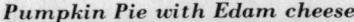

Pumpkin Pie with Edam cheese

▲ Pecan-Topped Pumpkin Tarts

Follow ▲ Recipe; substitute **Pastry for Little Pies and Tarts** (one and one-third recipe, *page 443*; use 8 3½-in. tart pans) for Pastry for 1-Crust Pie. Do not bake. Pour about ½ cup filling into each shell. Bake at 450°F 10 min. Reduce heat to 350°F and bake 10 min. Quickly arrange coated pecan halves over tops. Return to oven; bake at 350°F 10 min. longer, or until a silver knife comes out clean when inserted halfway between center and edge. Remove from oven; cool on cooling rack.

For Coated Pecans—Melt in a small skillet over low heat ¼ cup **butter**. Add 1½ cups (about 6 oz.) **pecan halves;** move and turn pecans gently with a spoon until thoroughly coated with butter. Remove pecans and mix lightly with ¼ cup firmly packed **brown sugar.**

Pecan Pie

Sour Cream-Raisin Pie

Prepare (do not bake) and set aside
   Pastry for 1-Crust Pie (*page 442;* use 9-in. pie pan)
Mix together
   ½ cup sugar
   2 tablespoons flour
   ½ teaspoon cinnamon
   ¼ teaspoon nutmeg
   ¼ teaspoon salt
Blend together
   1 egg, well beaten
   1½ cups thick sour cream
Add dry ingredients to the sour-cream mixture and blend thoroughly. Mix in
   1½ cups (about 7 oz.) seedless raisins
Turn into the pastry shell.

Bake at 450°F 10 min. Reduce heat to 350°F and bake 20 to 25 min. longer, or until a silver knife comes out clean when inserted halfway between center and edge of filling. Place on cooling rack to cool slightly.

Serve slightly warm. *One 9-in. pie*

Pecan Pie
GLENELLEN STEVENSON, BERKELEY, CAL.

A dark rich sweet pie that does honor to the superb flavor of the native American pecan.

Prepare (do not bake) and set aside
   Pastry for 1-Crust Pie (*page 442;* use 9-in. pie pan)
Set out
   ½ cup (about 2 oz.) pecan halves
   ½ cup (about 2 oz.) chopped pecans
Cream together until butter is softened
   3 tablespoons butter
   1 teaspoon vanilla extract
Add gradually, creaming until fluffy after each addition
   ¾ cup sugar
Add in thirds, blending well after each addition
   3 eggs, well beaten
Thoroughly blend in the chopped pecans and
   1 cup dark corn sirup
   ⅛ teaspoon salt
Turn into the pastry shell.

Bake at 450°F 10 min. Arrange pecan halves on top of pie filling. Reduce heat to 350°F and bake 30 to 35 min. longer, or until a silver knife comes out clean when inserted halfway between center and edge of filling.

Cool on cooling rack. *One 9-in. pie*

Sour Cream-Apple Pie [13]

Prepare, bake and set aside to cool

Graham Cracker Pie Shell (page 446; use 9-in. pie pan)

Put into a saucepan contents of

1 No. 2 can (about 2½ cups) sliced apples

Mix gently with

½ cup firmly packed brown sugar

Place over medium heat until mixture bubbles. Reduce heat and cook 5 min., stirring occasionally. Remove from heat and set aside.

Blend together until smooth

1 egg, slightly beaten
2 cups thick sour cream

and a mixture of

3 tablespoons brown sugar
2 tablespoons flour
½ teaspoon cinnamon
⅛ teaspoon nutmeg
⅛ teaspoon mace
⅛ teaspoon salt

Turn about one half of the sour cream mixture into the pie shell; spread evenly. Spoon the apple slices in an even layer over the sour cream mixture; top with the remaining sour cream mixture, spreading evenly.

Bake at 400°F 10 to 12 min., or until sour cream mixture is set.

Remove pie from oven; cool on cooling rack. When cooled, chill pie thoroughly in refrigerator before serving. *One 9-in. pie*

Apricot Delight Pie

MRS. C. C. TAEGER
WEST BURLINGTON, IOWA

Prepare

Cooked Apricots (one-half recipe, page 494)

Meanwhile, prepare (do not bake)

Cookie Crumb Pie Shell (page 447; use chocolate wafers and 9-in. pie pan)

Set pie shell in refrigerator to chill.

When apricots are tender, drain well and force through a sieve or food mill. Measure 1 cup apricot purée; set aside in refrigerator to chill.

Put a bowl and rotary beater into refrigerator to chill.

Cream until softened

½ cup butter

Add gradually, creaming until fluffy after each addition

1 cup sifted confectioners' sugar

Add in thirds, beating well after each addition

2 eggs, well beaten

Turn into pie shell. Spread apricot purée over egg mixture. Chill in refrigerator until firm.

To serve, whip (*page 13*), using chilled bowl and beater

1 cup chilled whipping cream

Spread over top of pie and swirl with spatula.

Serve immediately. *One 9-in. pie*

Almond-Mallow Pie 14

MRS. CLARENCE FARKE, ARMOUR, S. DAK.

Prepare, bake and set aside to cool
Cookie Crumb Pie Shell (page 447;
use vanilla wafers and 8-in. pie pan)
Put a bowl and a rotary beater into refrigerator
to chill.

Coarsely chop
½ cup (about 3 oz.) blanched,
toasted almonds (page 12)
Set aside.

Combine in top of a double boiler
16 (¼ lb.) marshmallows, cut into
quarters (page 12)
4 oz. milk chocolate
½ cup milk
Heat over simmering water, stirring frequently, until marshmallows and chocolate are melted. Remove from heat. Stir in the almonds; let stand until cool but not set. When mixture is cool, using the chilled bowl and beater, beat until cream is of medium consistency (piles softly)
1 cup chilled whipping cream
Blend in with final few strokes
¼ teaspoon almond extract
Spread over cooled chocolate and fold (page 12) together. Turn into pie shell. Chill in refrigerator until firm.   *One 8-in. pie*

Chocolate Dream Pie

MRS. A. E. MARTINSON
DETROIT LAKES, MINN.

Prepare, bake and set aside to cool
Cookie Crumb Pie Shell (page 447;
use vanilla wafers and 9-in.
pie pan)
Put a bowl and a rotary beater into refrigerator to chill.

Chop and set aside
1 cup (about 4 oz.) walnuts
Melt (page 12) and set aside to cool
2 sq. (2 oz.) 9 chocolate

Cream until softened
½ cup butter
Add gradually, creaming until fluffy after each addition
1 cup sifted confectioners' sugar
Add, one at a time, beating well after each addition
3 egg yolks
Blend in the cooled chocolate and the walnuts. Turn mixture into pie shell; chill in refrigerator until firm.

To serve, whip (page 13), using the chilled bowl and beater
1 cup chilled whipping cream
Spread over top of pie and swirl with spatula.

Serve immediately.   *One 9-in. pie*

Chocolate Mint Pie

A flash of mint for perfect taste satisfaction.

Prepare, bake and set aside to cool
Cookie Crumb Pie Shell (page 447;
use vanilla wafers and 9-in.
pie pan)
Melt (page 12) and set aside to cool
1 sq. (1 oz.) 9 chocolate
Cream until softened
½ cup butter or margarine
Add gradually, creaming until fluffy after each addition
¾ cup sugar
Blend in the cooled chocolate and
2 or 3 drops peppermint extract
Add, one at a time, beating about 5 min. after each addition
2 eggs, unbeaten
Turn filling into pie shell. Chill 2 or 3 hrs.

Spread over top of pie and swirl with a spatula
Sweetened Whipped Cream
(page 414)
Top with chocolate curls made by pulling across a shredder
½ sq. (½ oz.) chocolate
Serve at once.   *One 9-in. pie*

Lemon Fluff Pie

MRS. J. W. STEPHENS, PATAGONIA, ARIZ.

Cloud-soft and delicious, this delicate pie will win exuberant acclaim.

Prepare, bake and set aside to cool
Crispy Crumb Pie Shell (page 447; use 10-in. pie pan)
Sift together into top of a double boiler
1 cup sugar
⅓ cup cornstarch
Blend in
½ cup cold water
Add gradually, stirring in
1¼ cups boiling water
Bring cornstarch mixture to boiling over direct heat, stirring gently and constantly, and cook 3 min. Place over simmering water. Cover and cook about 12 min.; stir three or four times.

Vigorously stir about 3 tablespoons of the hot mixture into
4 egg yolks, slightly beaten
Immediately blend into mixture in double boiler. Cook over simmering water 3 to 5 min. Stir slowly to keep mixture cooking evenly. Remove from simmering water. Blend in
½ cup lemon juice
2 tablespoons grated lemon peel (page 11)
2 tablespoons butter or margarine
Set mixture aside.

Beat until frothy
4 egg whites
Add gradually, beating well after each addition
½ cup sugar
Beat until rounded peaks are formed. Spread egg whites over lemon mixture and gently fold (*page 12*) together. Turn into pie shell; put into refrigerator to chill. *One 10-in. pie*

Orange-Marlow Refrigerator Pie

Orange-Marlow Refrigerator Pie

Cool and mellow—a delightful all-occasion pie.

Prepare, bake and set aside to cool
Graham Cracker Pie Shell (p. 446; use 9-in. pie pan; reserve 2 to 4 tablespoons of the crumb mixture for topping)
Put a bowl and rotary beater into refrigerator to chill.

Heat together in the top of a double boiler over simmering water, stirring occasionally, until marshmallows are dissolved
32 (½ lb.) marshmallows
1 cup strained orange juice
1 tablespoon lemon juice
Set aside to cool slightly.

When mixture is slightly cooled, chill in refrigerator until mixture becomes slightly thicker.

When marshmallow mixture is of desired consistency, using the chilled bowl and beater, beat until cream is of medium consistency (piles softly)
½ cup chilled whipping cream
Blend the whipped cream with the marshmallow mixture. Turn into the pie shell. Sprinkle the reserved crumbs over filling. Chill thoroughly in refrigerator. *One 9-in. pie*

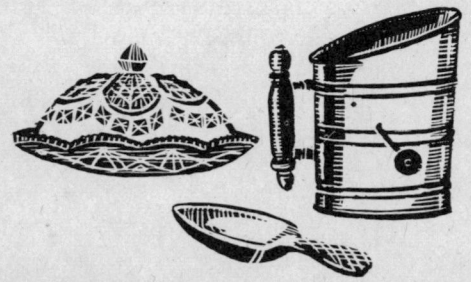

Red Raspberry Mallow Pie 17

JUNE HANSON, BAILEYS HARBOR, WIS.

Prepare, bake and set aside to cool

Cookie Crumb Pie Shell (page 447;
use vanilla wafers and 9-in. pie pan)

Put into refrigerator to chill a bowl, rotary beater and

1½ cups whipping cream

Sort, rinse and drain thoroughly

2 cups fresh red raspberries (or 2 1-lb.
pkgs. frozen red raspberries,
thawed and drained)

Set ¼ cup of the berries aside for topping.

Combine in the top of a double boiler

32 (½ lb.) marshmallows, cut into
quarters (page 12)
½ cup milk

Heat over simmering water, stirring frequently, until marshmallows are melted. Set aside to cool slightly.

When mixture is slightly cooled, chill in refrigerator until mixture becomes thicker.

Using the chilled bowl and beater, beat 1 cup of the chilled whipping cream until cream is of medium consistency (piles softly). Blend in with final few strokes

1 teaspoon vanilla extract
¼ teaspoon salt

Blend the whipped cream and 1¾ cups raspberries into the marshmallow mixture. Turn into pie shell. Chill in refrigerator until firm.

Put a clean bowl and beater into refrigerator.

Just before serving, using the chilled bowl and beater, whip (*page 13*) the ½ cup chilled whipping cream. Fold (*page 12*) the ¼ cup of reserved berries into the whipped cream. Pile in mounds around top of pie.   *One 9-in. pie*

Strawberry Chiffon Pie 18

A wonderful way to use the first strawberries.

Prepare, bake and set aside to cool

Graham Cracker Pie Shell (p.446;
use 9-in. pie pan)

Put a bowl and rotary beater into refrigerator to chill.

Sort, rinse, drain, hull, cut into thin slices and put into a medium-size bowl

2 cups fresh, ripe strawberries

Mix with the strawberries

1 cup sugar

Cover bowl and allow strawberries to stand until sugar has dissolved and sirup formed.

Pour into a small cup or custard cup

¼ cup cold water

Sprinkle evenly over cold water

1 tablespoon (1 env.) unflavored
gelatin

Let stand about 5 min. to soften.

When strawberry sirup has formed, drain strawberries, reserving sirup. If necessary, add to reserved strawberry sirup

Water (enough to make 1 cup liquid)

Heat the sirup until very hot. Remove from heat and immediately add the softened gelatin, stirring until gelatin is completely dissolved. Blend into gelatin mixture

2 tablespoons lemon juice

Cool mixture; chill (*page 12*) until mixture is slightly thicker than consistency of thick, unbeaten egg white.

Meanwhile, pour into the chilled bowl

½ cup icy cold water

Sprinkle evenly over water

½ cup instant nonfat dry milk solids

Using the chilled beater, beat until mixture stands in peaks when beater is slowly lifted upright. When gelatin mixture is of desired consistency, spread the whipped nonfat dry milk solids over the gelatin mixture. Add the drained strawberries and gently fold (*page 12*) together. Turn into prepared pie shell and chill in refrigerator until firm.   *One 9-in. pie*

Butter Tarts

MRS. F. W. BASHAM, RIVERSIDE, CALIF.

Prepare (do not bake) and set aside
  **Pastry for Little Pies and Tarts
  (*page 443*; use 10 2¾-in. muffin-
  pan wells)**
Melt and set aside to cool
  ½ cup butter
Beat slightly
  2 eggs
Add gradually, mixing thoroughly
  2 cups firmly packed brown sugar
Stir in the melted butter and
  1 teaspoon vanilla extract
  1⅓ cups (about 7 oz.) currants
Spoon filling into tarts shells, allowing about
¼ cup for each tart.

Bake at 350°F 35 min., or until filling is
golden brown.

Cool in muffin-pan wells on rack.　　*10 tarts*

Cherry Rose-Petal Tarts

Prepare, bake and set aside to cool
  Pastry for Rose-Petal Tarts (*page 443*)
Drain, reserving sirup, contents of
  **2 No. 2 cans pitted, sour red
  cherries (about 4 cups, drained)**
Put into a saucepan
  3 tablespoons cornstarch
Add gradually and stir in 1 cup of the reserved
cherry sirup. Mix well and bring rapidly to
boiling, stirring constantly; cook until mixture
is thick and clear. When clear, stir in
  ¾ cup sugar

Remove from heat and mix in
  1 teaspoon lemon juice
  ½ teaspoon almond extract
  ¼ teaspoon salt
(For brighter color, stir in a few drops of red
food coloring.) Gently mix in the cherries.
Cover and set aside to cool.

Spoon cooled filling into Rose-Petal Tart
shells.　　*6 tarts*

▲ Lime Chiffon Tarts

*These attractive dainties of pale shimmering
green lend special grace to the tea table or to
the dessert course of a luncheon.*

Prepare, bake and set aside to cool
  **12 Graham Cracker Tart-Shells (one and
  one-half times recipe, *page 446*)**
Pour into a small cup or custard cup
  ¼ cup cold water
Sprinkle evenly over cold water
  **1 tablespoon (1 env.) unflavored
  gelatin**
Let stand about 5 min. to soften.

Meanwhile, mix together in top of a double
boiler
  4 egg yolks, slightly beaten
  ⅔ cup sugar
  ½ cup lime juice
  ¼ teaspoon salt

Cherry Rose-Petal Tarts

Lime Chiffon Tarts

Set over simmering water and cook, stirring constantly, until mixture thickens.

Remove from simmering water and stir in softened gelatin and

2 teaspoons grated lime peel (page 11)

Stir until gelatin is dissolved completely. Tint to desired color by blending in

1 or 2 drops green food coloring

Cool mixture; chill (*page 12*) until mixture begins to gel (gets slightly thicker).

When mixture is of desired consistency, beat until frothy

4 egg whites

Add gradually, beating thoroughly after each addition

½ cup sugar

Beat until rounded peaks are formed. Spread over gelatin mixture and gently fold (*page 12*) together. Spoon into tart shells and chill in refrigerator just until firm.

If desired, serve with

**Sweetened Whipped Cream
(page 414)**

12 tarts

△ **Lemon Chiffon Tarts**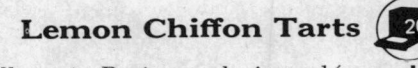

Follow ▲ Recipe; substitute ½ cup **lemon juice** for lime juice and 2 teaspoons grated **lemon peel** for lime peel. Omit food coloring.

Blushing Pear Tarts

Lovely to look at and luscious to taste.

Prepare, bake and set aside to cool

**Pastry for Little Pies and Tarts
(page 443; use 3½-in. tart pans)**

Prepare filling for

**De Luxe Cream Pie or Tarts (one-half
recipe, page 468)**

While cream filling is cooling, drain, reserving sirup, contents of

**1 1-lb. can pear halves (about
6 halves)**

Sift together into top of double boiler

**⅓ cup sugar
1½ tablespoons cornstarch
⅛ teaspoon salt**

Add and blend well

2 tablespoons cold water

Heat 1 cup of the reserved pear sirup until very hot; gradually add to cornstarch mixture, stirring constantly. Stirring gently and constantly, bring mixture rapidly to boiling over direct heat and cook 3 min. Place over simmering water. Cover and cook about 12 min., stirring three or four times. Remove from heat and blend in

**2 teaspoons lemon juice
1½ teaspoons butter or margarine
⅛ teaspoon grated lemon peel (page 11)
2 or 3 drops yellow food coloring
1 or 2 drops red food coloring**

Set glaze aside to cool slightly.

Spoon about 3 tablespoons of the cooled cream filling into each tart shell. Place a pear half, rounded side up, in each tart shell. Put into a small cup or custard cup

Few drops red food coloring

Apply blush to rounded side of pears with a small amount of the food coloring. Spoon the lukewarm glaze evenly over pear halves. Set aside until glaze is completely cool.

While glaze is cooling, prepare

Toasted Coconut (page 448)

Sprinkle the coconut around edge of the tarts.

6 tarts

Individual Pumpkin Pies

Prepare (do not bake)

**Pastry for Little Pies and Tarts (one
and one-half times recipe, page 443;
use 8 4½-in. pie pans)**

Set aside in refrigerator.

Mix together

2 cups (1-lb. can) canned pumpkin

and a mixture of

**⅔ cup firmly packed light brown sugar
1 teaspoon mace
¾ teaspoon ginger
¾ teaspoon nutmeg
½ teaspoon cinnamon
½ teaspoon salt**

Blend together and add, mixing until smooth

**2 eggs, slightly beaten
1 cup cream
1 cup milk**

Pour about ½ cup filling into each pastry
shell. Sprinkle tops with

Nutmeg

Bake at 450°F 10 min. Reduce heat to 350°F
and bake 20 min. longer, or until a silver
knife comes out clean when inserted halfway
between center and edge of filling.

Cool completely on cooling rack.

Using a cookie cutter or waxed-paper pattern
and knife, cut turkeys or other shapes from

Thin slices process American cheese

Garnish pies with cutouts. *8 individual pies*

Individual Pumpkin Pies with cheese cutouts

▲ Little Princess Fried Pies

Prepare and shape into 2 balls (do not roll)

**Cheese Pastry for 2-Crust Pie (page
443; no pie pan will be needed)**

Set aside.

Set out a 2-qt. saucepan, having a tight-fitting
cover, and a heavy 10-in. skillet.

Wash, quarter, core, pare and coarsely dice

**6 medium-size (about 2 lbs.) cooking
apples (about 3 cups diced)**

Put apples into saucepan with

⅓ cup hot water

Cover and simmer, stirring occasionally, 5 to
10 min., or until apples are just tender when
pierced with a fork. Drain thoroughly.

While apples are cooking, mix together

**1 cup (about 4 oz.) grated Cheddar
cheese
¼ to ⅓ cup sugar (depending upon
tartness of apples)
1 teaspoon cinnamon
½ teaspoon nutmeg**

Set aside.

Add to the drained, cooked apples

**2 tablespoons butter
4 teaspoons lemon juice**

Blend in the cheese mixture. Stir only enough
to mix ingredients evenly. Set aside.

Flatten one ball of the pastry on a lightly
floured surface. Follow directions in **Pastry
for 1-Crust Pie** (*page 442*) for rolling pastry.

Cut out 6-in. rounds, using a saucer or waxed-
paper pattern as a guide. Spoon about 2 tablespoons of the apple filling onto one half of
each round. Moisten the edge of one half of
the round with water to help form a tight seal.

Fold the other half of the round over the filling. Press edges together with a fork. Be certain that the seal is tight to avoid leakage of filling. Repeat this process with the remaining ball of pastry. Set pies aside.

Melt in the skillet over medium heat

3 to 4 tablespoons lard, hydrogenated vegetable shortening or all-purpose shortening

Carefully place the pies, as many as will fit uncrowded, into the skillet. Fry pies on one side 8 to 10 min., or until golden brown. Turn and fry until other side is golden brown. Add more shortening to skillet if necessary to keep pies from sticking.

Serve pies warm with slices of sharp **cheese,** a dip of **ice cream** or a mound of **whipped cream;** or sift **confectioners' sugar** over top.

12 to 14 pies

△ Fried Pies à la Roberta

Follow ▲ Recipe. Substitute **Pastry for 2-Crust Pie** (*page 442*) for cheese pastry. Omit cheese in filling.

▲ Deep-Fried Peach Pies

Set out a deep saucepan or automatic deep-fryer (*page 13*) and heat fat to 375°F.

Drain contents of

1 No. 2½ can (about 2½ cups, drained) sliced peaches

Prepare and shape into 2 balls

Pastry for 2-Crust Pie (page 442; no pie pan will be needed)

Flatten one ball of the pastry on a lightly floured surface. Follow directions in **Pastry for 1-Crust Pie** (*page 442*) for rolling pastry.

Using a 3½-in. cookie cutter, cut out pastry rounds. Place 3 peach slices onto each round. Moisten the edge of one half of the round with water to help form a tight seal. Fold the other half of the round over the filling. Press edges together with a fork. Be certain that the seal

Deep-Fried Peach Pies

is tight to avoid leakage of filling. Repeat this process with the remaining ball of pastry.

Lower pies into hot fat. Deep-fry only as many as will float uncrowded one layer deep in fat. Deep-fry about 3 min., or until golden brown. Turn pies as they rise to surface and several times during cooking (do not pierce). Remove with a slotted spoon. Drain over fat for a few seconds before removing to absorbent paper.

Serve warm; sprinkle with

Vanilla Confectioners' Sugar (page 415)

About 15 pies

△ Deep-Fried Apple Pies

Follow ▲ Recipe; omit peaches. Wash, quarter, core, pare and thinly slice 3 to 4 medium-size tart **apples** (about 3 cups, sliced). Put apples into a saucepan having a tight-fitting cover; add ½ cup **water** and 1 teaspoon **lemon juice.** Cook, covered, over low heat about 15 min., or until tender.

Meanwhile, mix together ¼ cup **sugar,** ½ teaspoon **cinnamon** and ⅛ teaspoon **nutmeg.**

Remove apples from heat and drain; add sugar mixture, blending thoroughly. Place about 2 tablespoons apple mixture onto each pastry round. Dot with **butter.** Proceed as in ▲ Recipe.

White Cloud Berry Pie

Prepare, bake and set aside to cool
> **Pastry for 1-Crust Pie (page 442; use 9-in. pie pan)**

Beat until frothy
> **5 egg whites**
> **¼ teaspoon salt**

Add and beat slightly
> **¼ teaspoon cream of tartar**

Add gradually, beating well after each addition
> **⅔ cup sugar**

Continue beating until stiff (but not dry) peaks are formed and egg whites do not slide when bowl is partially inverted.

Pile meringue into pastry shell, swirling the top with a spatula.

Bake at 350°F 15 min., or until meringue is delicately browned. Cool on cooling rack.

Meanwhile, put a bowl and clean beater into refrigerator to chill.

Sort, rinse and drain
> **1 cup fresh, ripe raspberries or hulled strawberries**

White Cloud Berry Pie

(Slice strawberries.) Gently stir in
> **⅔ cup sugar**

Set in refrigerator to chill.

When ready to serve, whip (*page 13*), using the chilled bowl and beater
> **1½ cups chilled whipping cream**

Fold (*page 12*) the sweetened berries into the whipped cream.

Cut pie into serving pieces. Top with the whipped cream mixture.   *One 9-in. pie*

Coconut-Peach Pie

Prepare
> **Choco-Coconut Pie Shell (page 447; use 9-in. pie pan)**

Meanwhile, set aside to drain thoroughly, reserving sirup, contents of
> **1 No. 2½ can peach halves (about 7 large halves)**

Pour into a small cup or custard cup
> **¼ cup cold water**

Sprinkle evenly over cold water
> **1 tablespoon (1 env.) unflavored gelatin**

Let stand about 5 min. to soften.

Combine in a saucepan 1 cup of the reserved peach sirup and
> **½ cup apricot preserve**
> **¼ cup sugar**
> **⅛ teaspoon salt**

Heat, stirring occasionally, until very hot. Remove from heat and stir in softened gelatin, stirring until gelatin is completely dissolved. Cool mixture; blend in
> **¼ cup sherry**

Chill (*page 12*) until mixture is slightly thicker than consistency of thick, unbeaten egg white.

When gelatin mixture is of desired consistency, spoon one half into pie shell. Place drained peach halves onto gelatin mixture, cut side down. Spoon remaining mixture over peach halves. Chill in refrigerator until firm.
One 9-in. pie

Chocolate-Rum Angel Pie

Prepare, bake and set aside to cool
Meringue Shell (page 448)
Put a bowl and a rotary beater into refrigerator
to chill.

Melt (*page 12*) and set aside to cool
4 oz. sweet chocolate
Using the chilled bowl and beater, beat until
cream is of medium consistency (piles softly)
1 cup chilled whipping cream
Blend into the cooled chocolate
3 tablespoons rum
Spread the chocolate mixture over the whipped
cream and gently fold (*page 12*) together.
Turn into cooled meringue shell.

Place in refrigerator until thoroughly chilled.
One 9-in. pie

▲ Lemon Angel Pie

Prepare, bake and set aside to cool
Meringue Shell (page 448)
Spoon into a small cup or custard cup
4 teaspoons cold water
Sprinkle evenly over cold water
1 teaspoon unflavored gelatin
Set aside to soften.

Beat until thick and piled softly
4 egg yolks
2 eggs
Add gradually, beating constantly
1 cup sugar

Mix together
⅓ cup lemon juice
⅓ cup water
2 tablespoons grated lemon peel
(page 11)
Add gradually to egg-yolk mixture, stirring
until well blended. Pour into top of double
boiler and place over simmering water. Cook,
stirring constantly, until thick.

Remove from simmering water. Immediately
stir in softened gelatin, stirring until gelatin
is completely disolved. Cool mixture; chill
(*page 12*) until mixture is partially set.

When mixture is of desired consistency, spoon
into meringue shell. Place in refrigerator to
chill just until mixture is set.

Put a bowl and a rotary beater into refrigerator to chill.

A few minutes before serving, using the chilled
bowl and beater, whip (*page 13*)
1 cup chilled whipping cream
Spread over top and swirl with a spatula.
One 9-in. pie

▲ Orange Angel Pie

Follow ▲ Recipe. Substitute ⅓ cup **orange
juice** and 2 tablespoons grated **orange peel**
for lemon juice and grated lemon peel.

▲ Pineapple Angel Pie

Follow ▲ Recipe. Omit lemon peel and the ⅓
cup water. Reduce lemon juice to 2 tablespoons and mix with ⅔ cup **pineapple juice.**

▲ Raspberry Angel Pie

Follow ▲ Recipe. Omit lemon peel and the ⅓
cup water. Reduce lemon juice to 1 tablespoon and sugar to ½ cup. Drain, reserving
sirup, contents of 1 1-lb. can (about 1¼ cups,
drained) **red raspberries.** Mix ⅔ cup of the
raspberry sirup with the tablespoon of lemon
juice. Fold the raspberries into the whipped
cream before spreading over pie.

Heavenly Pie
AILEEN JONES, PIEDMONT, S. C.

A picture-pretty, luscious pie that promises delight and lives up to its pledge.

For Crust—Prepare (do not bake)
> **Graham Cracker 10-in. Pie Shell**
> **(page 446)**

Set aside.

For Heavenly Meringue Shell—Beat until frothy
> **4 egg whites**

Add and beat slightly
> **½ teaspoon cream of tartar**

Add gradually, beating well after each addition
> **1 cup sugar**

Beat until stiff (but not dry) peaks are formed when beater is slowly lifted upright and egg whites do not slide when bowl is partially inverted. Carefully spread a layer of meringue about 1 in. thick over bottom of the crumb crust. Using a spatula, pile and swirl remaining meringue along sides and edge of pan.

(Work with a small amount of the meringue at one time because the graham cracker crumbs tend to stick to meringue as it is being spread.)

Bake as in **Meringue Shell** (*page 448*). Cool completely on cooling rack.

To Complete Pie—Put into refrigerator to chill a bowl, rotary beater and
> **1 No. 2½ can sliced peaches**
> **1 cup whipping cream**

Prepare
> **Toasted Coconut (page 448)**

Shortly before serving, thoroughly drain the peaches.

To serve, using chilled bowl and beater, whip (*page 13*) the chilled whipping cream. Arrange the peach slices in the shell. Spread the whipped cream over the peaches and swirl with a spatula. Sprinkle the toasted coconut over the top of the pie.

Serve immediately. *One 10-in. pie*

Pineapple Party Pie
AMY S. BOYD, LAKE CHARLES, LA.

One of those ambrosiae creations that transform a meringue shell into an angel pie. It is the kind of wonderful pie that is meant to go to a party and that makes a party of any occasion on which it is served.

Set out a double boiler.

Prepare, bake and set aside to cool
> **Meringue Shell (page 448)**

Drain, reserving sirup, contents of
> **1 9-oz. can crushed pineapple (about**
> **¾ cup, drained)**

Set out
> **1 cup (4 oz.) moist shredded**
> **coconut, cut**

Beat until thick and piled softly
> **4 egg yolks**

Add gradually, beating well after each addition
> **½ cup sugar**
> **⅛ teaspoon salt**

Mix together and add gradually to egg-yolk mixture, stirring until well blended, 2 tablespoons of the pineapple sirup and
> **3 tablespoons lemon juice**

(Remaining pineapple sirup may be used in other food preparation.) Pour into top of the double boiler and place over simmering water.

Cook, stirring constantly, until thick. Remove from simmering water and stir in the drained pineapple and ¼ cup of the coconut. Cover and set aside to cool, stirring occasionally.

When cool, turn into cooled meringue shell and chill in refrigerator for 1 hr.

Meanwhile, toast ½ cup of the coconut (see Toasted Coconut, *page 448*). Set aside.

To serve, prepare
> **Sweetened Whipped Cream (page 414;**
> **fold in the remaining ¼ cup of**
> **coconut)**

Spread over top of pie and swirl with a spatula. Sprinkle the coconut over the whipped cream.

Serve at once. *One 9-in. pie*

Peaches and Cream Pie

Prepare (do not bake) and set aside

**Pastry for 1-Crust Pie (page 442;
use 9-in. pie pan)**

Sift together

**⅓ to ½ cup sugar
¼ cup sifted flour
½ teaspoon cinnamon**

Sprinkle two-thirds of the sugar mixture evenly over bottom of pastry shell; reserve remainder for top of peaches.

Rinse and plunge into boiling water

**4 medium-size (about 1⅓ lbs.) firm,
ripe peaches**

Plunge peaches into cold water. Gently slip off skins. Cut peaches into halves; remove and discard pits. Quickly blot peaches, if necessary, on absorbent paper. Place peach halves in pastry shell, cut side up; do not overlap. Sprinkle with reserved dry ingredients.

Mix together and spread evenly over peaches

**2 cups thick sour cream
½ teaspoon vanilla extract**

Sprinkle over top of pie a mixture of

**2 tablespoons sugar
½ teaspoon cinnamon**

Swirl topping with back of spoon.

Bake at 450°F 10 min.; reduce heat to 350°F and bake about 25 min. longer.

Cool slightly on a cooling rack. Serve slightly warm. *One 9-in. pie*

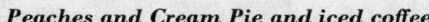

Peaches and Cream Pie and iced coffee

Double Strawberry Parfait Pie

Set refrigerator control at coldest operating temperature.

Prepare, bake in a 9-in. pie pan and set aside

**Pastry for 1-Crust Pie (page 442)
or Graham Cracker Pie Shell
(page 446)**

Empty into a bowl

1 pkg. lemon-flavored gelatin

Add and stir until gelatin is completely dissolved

1¼ cups very hot water

Gradually add by heaping spoonfuls, blending well after each addition

2 cups strawberry ice cream

Finally blend until mixture is smooth. Chill in refrigerator 15 to 20 min., or until mixture mounds when dropped from a spoon.

While gelatin mixture is chilling, sort, rinse, hull and cut into pieces

2 cups fresh, ripe strawberries

When gelatin mixture is of desired consistency, blend in berries. Turn into pie shell.

Chill in refrigerator 45 to 60 min., or until filling is set. *One 9-in. pie*

Note: Many other flavor blends are delightful. We suggest **vanilla ice cream** and any of these tempting combinations: **strawberry-flavored gelatin** and 1 medium-size all-yellow or brown-flecked **banana**, cut into small pieces; **orange-flavored gelatin**, 1 8-oz. can **apricot halves**, drained and chopped, ½ cup (2 oz.) moist shredded **coconut**, cut; or **cherry-flavored gelatin**, 1 cup **cranberries**, finely chopped, and ¼ cup (about 1 oz.) **walnuts**, chopped.

PASTRIES, PIES and TARTS in the MICROWAVE OVEN

A successful pie is the true test of a cook's skill. The pie recipes we have included are all selected to help you pass the test. Each pie can be completely assembled using only the microwave oven and all are not only very good to eat, but appealing to look at.

PIE CRUSTS—Crusts for pies are of two varieties, crumb crusts and pastry crusts.

Crumb Crusts—Recipes for these crusts have been put together in a convenient chart including appropriate cooking times and any special instructions. The recipes are all quickly and easily prepared and bake in the microwave in about 2 minutes.

Pastry Crusts—Although traditional pastry shells can be cooked using the microwave oven, it requires a two-step process, calling for browning in the conventional oven. (Like cakes and breads, pastry dough will not brown in the microwave.) Recipes which call for cooking pastry crust and filling together, as in two-crust pies, will more often than not cook unevenly in the microwave. The top crust or filling will be

done and the bottom crust still sticky. We simply cannot recommend the microwave for this type of pie; it is neither convenient nor consistent in results. We have omitted these recipes.

FILLINGS—The pie fillings cooked in the microwave are tasty, smooth and uncomplicated to prepare. The egg yolks blend and thicken easily as in the **Orange Chiffon Pie**; the marshmallows melt quickly with no mess, as in the **Red Raspberry Mallow Pie**. No double boiler is necessary.

Stirring is important when cooking the fillings to assure a smooth texture. We have indicated how often to stir with each recipe.

Also included is the recipe for cooking **Mincemeat, Home-Style** in the microwave oven. While the completed pie calls for pastry dough and must be cooked in the conventional oven, the mincemeat filling can be prepared in the microwave oven in about half the time it takes on the stove. It can be safely stored if you don't plan on using it immediately.

Instructions for Melting Chocolate are also included with these recipes, to be used with the **Chocolate Dream Pie** and the **Chocolate Mint Pie.** The microwave method is a real asset in melting chocolate because there's no need to worry about scorching or sticking.

Meringues, incidentally, do not succeed at all in the microwave oven. They will rise, but fall as soon as the oven door is opened. They also remain sticky, as the microwaves are unable to produce the fine, dry texture generated by heat.

BAKING THE PIE SHELLS—Follow these simple instructions when baking a pie shell in the microwave oven.

Recipe—Prepare the crusts for cooking as directed in the master recipe, except use microwave-safe pie pans in the size specified.

Cooking—All shells are baked on the COOK setting. Proper rotation is very important for even cooking. All shells should be rotated every 30 seconds.

Test for Doneness—Shells are fully cooked when the bottoms are firm to the touch.

Cooling—Allow shells to cool completely before filling.

REMINDERS—For more tips and an easy-to-read chart comparing settings among different brands of ovens, see the introductory chapter, **Home Cooking in the Microwave Oven**, in the beginning of this book.

MICROWAVE PIE and TART SHELLS

Carefully read the preceding introductory information before preparing any of the recipes in this chart or following.

RECIPE—The recipe title and the page on which you will find the master recipe are noted in this column. Prepare the crust for cooking as directed.

MINUTES TO COOK—Always use the COOK setting. The times given are the total number of minutes needed to fully cook the shell. Rotate every 30 seconds and test for doneness at the end of these minimum suggested cooking times.

SPECIAL INSTRUCTIONS—Read this column carefully to note any additional directions.

	Recipe	Minutes to COOK	Special Instructions
1	**Graham Cracker Pie Shell** *(page 446)*	1:15	None.
2	**Graham Cracker 10-in. Pie Shell** *(page 446)*	1:15	None.
3	**Graham Cracker Tart Shells** *(page 446)*	1:30	Use glass custard cups or paper cups to hold the paper baking cups.
4	**Cookie Crumb Pie Shell** *(page 447)*	1:15	None.
5	**Coffee-Flavored Crumb Pie Shell** *(page 447)*	1:15	None.
6	**Zwieback Crumb Pie Shell** *(page 447)*	2:15	None.
7	**Crispy Crumb Pie Shell** *(page 447)*	2:15	None.

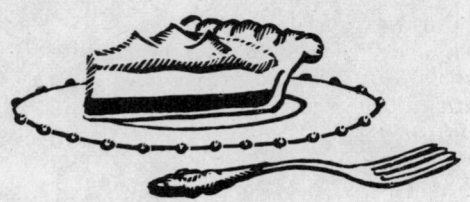

Mincemeat Pie **11**
(page 458)

Use a covered 3-qt. casserole.

Cover and COOK mincemeat mixture, stirring every 1 min. until fat melts, then stirring every 2 min. until all is tender (about 35 min.).

Cover and let stand 10 min.

OVERALL COOKING TIME: 35:00

Choco-Coconut Pie Shell **8**
(page 447)

Use a small casserole.

Combine chocolate, butter and vanilla and COOK, stirring every 1 min., until chocolate is melted (about 3 min.).

OVERALL COOKING TIME: 3:00

9 *To Melt Chocolate*—For the **Chocolate Dream Pie** *(page 481)* and **Chocolate Mint Pie** *(page 481)*.

Use a small casserole.

COOK chocolate in casserole, stirring every 1 min., until melted (about 1 min. per oz.).

Orange Chiffon Pie **12**
(page 465)

Use a 1½-qt. casserole.

COOK egg yolk mixture uncovered, stirring every 1 min., until it thickens (about 5 min.).

Toasted Coconut **10**
(page 448)

Use a large baking dish.

COOK, stirring every 1 min., until lightly browned (about 5 min.).

OVERALL COOKING TIME: 5:00

Sour Cream-Apple Pie **13**
(page 480)

Use a 1½-qt. casserole.

COOK sugar-apple mixture uncovered, stirring every 1 min., until bubbling (about 3 min.). Continue to COOK, stirring every 1½ min., until sirup coats the apples (about 3 min.).

COOK filled pie shell to heat through (about 2 min.).

Almond-Mallow Pie **14**
(page 481)

Use a 1½-qt. casserole.

COOK marshmallow-chocolate mixture uncovered, stirring every 1 min., until melted (about 5 min.).

Lemon Fluff Pie **15**
(page 482)

Use a 1½-qt. covered casserole.

COOK to boil 1½ cups water (about 4 min.).

COOK cornstarch mixture, stirring every 30 sec., until it starts to thicken (about 3 min.). Cover and continue to COOK, stirring every 1 min., to thicken (about 4 min.).

Add egg yolk mixture and COOK uncovered, stirring every 30 sec., to blend eggs (about 3 min.).

Orange-Marlow Refrigerator Pie **16** *(page 482)*

Use a 1½-qt. casserole.

COOK marshmallow mixture, stirring every 1 min., until marshmallows are dissolved (about 5 min.).

Red Raspberry Mallow Pie **17** *(page 483)*

Use a 1½-qt. casserole.

COOK marshmallow mixture, stirring every 30 sec., until marshmallows melt (about 3 min.).

Strawberry Chiffon Pie **18**
(page 483)

Use a 1-qt. casserole.

COOK sirup mixture uncovered, stirring every 1 min., until very hot (about 3 min.).

Lime Chiffon Tarts **19**
(page 484)

Use a 1-qt. casserole.

COOK egg yolk mixture uncovered, stirring every 1 min., until it thickens (about 5 min.).

Lemon Chiffon Tarts **20**
(page 485)

Follow **19** Recipe with changes as in △ Recipe.

DESSERTS

Dessert is the course of the meal that almost everyone enjoys, that children never have to learn to like nor have to be coaxed to eat. But there is more reason than just its popularity for making a practice of ending the meal with dessert. It is often quite important nutritionally, contributing a significant share of the day's food requirements. Furthermore, the course which ends the meal seems to have a definite satiety value, perhaps more psychological than physical; that is, it gives a sense that the meal is now complete.

PIES, CAKES AND COOKIES—These desserts are so important that each has a section elsewhere.

GELATIN DESSERTS—These may range from plain fruit-flavored gelatin through elaborate refrigerator desserts with gelatin; but the techniques are all similar to those described on *page 306.*

FRUIT DESSERTS—Fresh fruits in season, with a dash of liqueur, sugar and cream or a topping, if desired, and unelaborated stewed, frozen or canned fruits, are probably the lightest and easiest to prepare of all desserts. They are also suitable choices to follow an otherwise hearty meal.

PUDDINGS—Baked, steamed or top-of-the-range puddings are usually thickened with flour or cornstarch, or with starchy cereals such as tapioca, rice and corn meal.

Starches and the above-mentioned starchy cereals thicken liquids because the starch granules, as they are heated in the liquid, gradually swell and absorb moisture. The extent of thickening, of course, depends primarily upon the proportion of starch to liquid. Thickening continues as the mixture cools. To make such mixtures smooth, the starch granules should be separated before hot liquid is added: blend until smooth with a little cold liquid after mixing the sugar in the recipe with the starch; help keep granules separated as they thicken by constantly stirring while cooking —this also insures uniform heating. Starch mixtures must be brought to boiling and cooked long enough to destroy the raw starch flavor.

CUSTARDS are mixtures of sweetened and flavored milk and eggs. Custard may be cooked in the oven, without stirring, or with constant stirring on top of the range. Thickening is due to the coagulation of the egg proteins on heating.

Baked Custard—The custard mixture thickens in the form of a "gel" in which the coagulated egg protein encloses and holds the liquid. As in all forms of egg cookery, custards should be baked at a low temperature, because too high a temperature (or too long baking) will cause the protein to toughen and squeeze out liquid, producing "weeping." A useful method of shortening baking time is to scald the milk before stirring it into the slightly beaten eggs. To insure uniform temperature throughout the mixture, custards are usually baked in a boiling water bath. A baked custard is done when a silver knife inserted halfway between the center and edge of custard comes out clean.

Stirred Custard—The custard mixture is cooked over simmering water with constant stirring until it is just thick enough to coat a silver spoon. The custard may not yet appear sufficiently thickened, but it becomes somewhat thicker on cooling. Curdling may occur in a fraction of a second when the mixture is nearing the proper consistency if the cooking is too rapid (that is, if the water under the custard is boiling rather than just simmering) or is continued too long.

SOUFFLÉS—This baked product is made light and fluffy by the addition of beaten egg whites. For maximum volume and easy folding into mixture, beat egg whites until they form rounded peaks and do not slide when bowl is partially inverted.

A baked soufflé may be left in the oven for a short time with the heat turned off if it cannot be served immediately. As a soufflé cools it tends to shrink and fall because the volume of air decreases. An underbaked soufflé will fall rapidly; a soufflé baked until done and cooled slowly will fall slowly upon removal from the oven.

TORTES—These are cake-like desserts, made light with eggs and often rich with nuts; white bread crumbs, cracker crumbs or grated nuts sometimes take the place of flour. Tortes differ in texture from cakes, but are handled in much the same way (See A Check List For Successful Cakemaking, *page 340;* cool tortes 15 min. in pans).

REFRIGERATOR DESSERTS are mixtures that may or may not have gelatin; they must be chilled in refrigerator until firm enough to serve. An example is a rich dessert in a ladyfinger-lined spring-form pan, chilled several hours or overnight.

FROZEN DESSERTS—This term takes in a number of different types of mixtures that can be frozen—in the refrigerator or in an ice-cream freezer. Some frozen desserts should be agitated during freezing to break up large ice crystals while they are forming. The smaller the ice crystals in the frozen dessert, the smoother and creamier-seeming will be the texture of the dessert. Therefore, when the dessert is frozen to a mushy consistency it should be removed from the refrigerator and beaten or stirred until smooth. The whipped cream used in mousses prevents formation of large ice crystals by incorporating air into the mixture. Any substance, such as gelatin, eggs, flour, cornstarch and rennet, which increases the viscosity (resistance to pouring) of the mixture tends to separate the crystals and prevent them from growing.

Stirring (agitation) during freezing process—*American ice cream*—mixture of cream, sugar and flavoring. Cream that can be whipped is highly desirable since the incorporation of air during whipping gives a smooth texture to the ice cream. Whipping also distributes the fat evenly, creating added smoothness as the mixture becomes frozen. Because heavy cream is expensive, recipes have been developed which call for substitution of thin cream, evaporated milk, or milk thickened with gelatin, flour, eggs or marshmallows for part or all of the heavy cream. *French ice cream*—a rich mixture of eggs, cream, sugar and flavorings; virtually a frozen custard. *Philadelphia ice cream*—uncooked mixture of cream, sugar and flavorings; never with gelatin or other binder added. *Frozen custard*—mixture with a custard base; also a frozen product, in the wholesale and retail trade, too low in butterfat content to be legally called ice cream. *Water ices*—fruit juice which is diluted and sweetened with sugar, sirup or honey; has rather coarse texture, melts easily. *Granites*—water ices frozen with little stirring; rough and icy in texture. *Frappé*—water ice frozen to a mushy consistency. *Sherbet*—water ice (the base of which may be fruit juice, fruit pulp or crushed pulp) with beaten egg white or gelatin added—this decreases the size of crystals and gives a smoother product; milk sherbet uses milk as part of liquid in the water ice. *Sorbet*—sherbet made of several kinds of fruit. *Coupe*—frozen cup usually composed of fruit and ice cream and attractively garnished with whipped cream, candied fruits and peels, chopped nuts, mint leaves or fresh fruit; originally served in a special glass similar to the "champagne coupe."

Little or no stirring during freezing process—The following are ice creams made of heavy cream with or without eggs: *Parfait*—made by pouring a hot thick sirup over beaten egg whites or beaten egg yolks, adding flavoring and folding in whipped cream. *Biscuit*—parfait or similar mixture, partially frozen, then packed in small individual paper cases and frozen until firm. *Bombe*—two or more frozen mixtures packed in a melon-shaped or round mold and refrozen. *Mousse*—sweetened and flavored whipped cream; may contain gelatin for firmness.

Creamy Prune Whip

Creamy Prune Whip

Put a bowl and a rotary beater into refrigerator to chill.

Prepare
>   **Stewed Prunes (one-half recipe, on this page)**

When prunes are tender, drain. Pit the prunes. Force prunes through a sieve or food mill placed over a large bowl.

Stir into the sieved prunes
>   **2 tablespoons lemon juice**

Using the chilled bowl and beater, beat until cream is of medium consistency (piles softly)
>   **1 cup chilled whipping cream**

Set whipped cream in refrigerator while beating egg whites.

Using clean beater, beat until frothy
>   **2 egg whites**
>   **⅛ teaspoon salt**

Add gradually, beating well after each addition
>   **½ cup sugar**

Beat until rounded peaks are formed.

Spread beaten egg whites and whipped cream over prune mixture and gently fold (*page 12*) together.

Chill thoroughly before serving.

To serve, spoon into sherbet glasses. Top with
>   **Swirls of whipped cream (Sweetened Whipped Cream; page 414, forced through pastry bag and No. 27 star decorating tube)**
>   **Candied Cherries**

6 servings

▲ Stewed Prunes

Set out a medium-size saucepan having a tight-fitting cover.

Rinse thoroughly and put into the saucepan
>   **1 lb. (about 2½ cups) dried prunes**

Cover prunes with
>   **1 qt. hot water**

Cover pan and allow prunes to soak 1 hr.

Simmer prunes in water in which they have been soaking, 45 to 60 min., or until fruit is plump and tender.

If desired, accompany each serving with a **lemon wedge.**   *About 3½ cups Stewed Prunes*

△ Cooked Apricots

Follow ▲ Recipe. Substitute 1 lb. (about 3 cups) **dried apricots** for dried prunes. Cook 40 min., or until fruit is plump and tender.

Refrigerator Fruit Compote

Set out a large casserole having a cover.

Wash thoroughly contents of
**1 12-oz. pkg. mixed dried fruits,
or use ¾ cup (about 4 oz.) dried
peaches, ¾ cup (about 5 oz.)
dried prunes, and ½ cup
(2 to 3 oz.) dried apricots**
Put into the casserole. Cover with
Boiling water
Add and mix in
**½ cup sugar
3 tablespoons lemon juice
2 teaspoons grated orange or lemon
peel (page 11)
3 3-in. sticks cinnamon, broken**
Cover casserole; allow fruits to cool. Place in
refrigerator for at least 48 hrs. to allow fruits
to soften and flavors to blend.

Add more sugar if you wish the fruit to be
sweeter. *5 or 6 servings*

Cheese and Fruit Tray

*Here's an age-old dessert duo that never fails
to delight the palate.*

Bedeck your favorite tray with an attractive
array of imported and domestic cheeses, soft
and hard, mild 'n' sharp. For instance, at one
end of the tray arrange **grapes** and **apple** and
pear slices (dipped in **lemon juice** to prevent
discoloring). Set an **Edam** or **Gouda cheese**
in the center with slices of **Swiss** or **sharp
Cheddar** beside it. At the other end of the
tray, pose wedges of **Camembert** and **Blue** or
Roquefort cheese.

Or for individual servings, you might arrange
a few shiny leaves, such as grape or galax, on
dessert plates. Add mellow fruit and a few
wedges or slices of cheese for each guest. This
is just the time to use your fruit knives.

And there you have it—a dessert that's the
perfect finale to any meal.

▲ Spiced Applesauce

Wash, quarter and core
8 large (about 4 lbs.) cooking apples
Put into large saucepan with
¾ cup water
Cover and simmer 15 to 20 min., or until
apples are tender when pierced with a fork.
Stir occasionally. Add more water if necessary. Force through a sieve or food mill placed
over a saucepan.

Stir in a mixture of
**½ cup firmly packed brown sugar
1 teaspoon cinnamon
½ teaspoon nutmeg**
and
2 teaspoons lemon juice
Return to low heat and stir until sugar is
dissolved.

Serve hot or cold. *8 to 10 servings*

⚠ Rosy Pink Applesauce

Follow ▲ Recipe. Substitute ½ cup **granulated sugar** for brown sugar. Omit nutmeg
and lemon juice. Add ½ cup (about 4 oz.)
red cinnamon candies; stir until dissolved.

⚠ Fruit Juice Applesauce

Follow ▲ Recipe. Before serving, blend in 2
tablespoons **orange juice** or **pineapple juice.**

Cheese and Fruit Tray

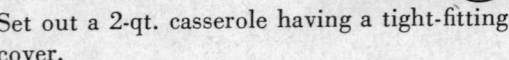
Baked Apples with Meringue

⚠ Variety Baked Apples 8 7

Follow ▲ Recipe for coring and paring apples. In center cavity of each apple, place one of the following mixtures: 2 tablespoons **mincemeat** mixed with 1 teaspoon **orange juice**; 1 tablespoon finely chopped **nuts** mixed with 1 tablespoon **granulated** or **brown sugar**; 2 tablespoons mixed chopped **nuts, raisins,** chopped **dates** or **figs;** or 2 tablespoons thick **cranberry sauce** or **jelly.** Dot with butter or margarine as in ▲ Recipe.

▲ Baked Apples with Meringue

Follow ▲ Recipe; instead of water, use a sirup made by boiling ¾ cup **sugar** and 1 cup **water** for 5 min. Bake apples uncovered 30 to 40 min., or until almost tender, basting frequently with sirup. Remove from oven and cool in sirup. Pile meringue on apples. Bake at 350°F 10 to 15 min., or until meringue is delicately browned.

For Meringue—Beat 2 **egg whites** until frothy; gradually beat in ¼ cup **sugar**; beat until rounded peaks are formed and egg whites do not slide when bowl is partially inverted.

Cherries Jubilee 9

Set out a chafing dish or saucepan. Chill desired number of serving dishes in refrigerator.

Set aside to drain thoroughly, reserving sirup, contents of
1 No. 2 can pitted Bing cherries
(about 2½ cups, drained)

▲ Encore Baked Apples 7 6

Set out a 2-qt. casserole having a tight-fitting cover.

Select and wash
6 medium-size (about 2 lbs.) firm cooking apples
Core by inserting corer in stem end and cutting toward blossom end. Push halfway into apple. Remove corer and insert in opposite end. Make a complete turn with corer in both ends. Remove all the core. Pare upper fourth of each apple. Arrange apples in casserole, pared sides up.

Mix together
¾ cup firmly packed brown sugar
2 teaspoons cinnamon
Fill cavity of each apple with about 2 tablespoons cinnamon-sugar mixture. Allowing ½ teaspoon for each apple, dot tops with
1 tablespoon butter or margarine
Pour into casserole
Water, to a depth of ½ in.
(unsweetened fruit juice may be used as part of liquid)
Cover and bake at 350°F 45 to 50 min., or until apples are tender when gently pierced with a fork. Or bake uncovered and baste frequently with liquid from bottom of casserole.

6 servings

Put the reserved cherry sirup into the chafing dish or saucepan.

Stirring occasionally, bring sirup to boiling over direct heat. Boil about 10 min., or until slightly thicker. Mix in the drained cherries and heat in chafing dish over pan of simmering water (or low heat) until cherries are thoroughly heated. With spoon, gently move cherries in pan occasionally.

When ready to serve, spoon into the chilled serving dishes

1 qt. vanilla ice cream

Heat thoroughly in a small saucepan

⅔ cup brandy

Ignite with match until brandy flames and pour over the cherries. Immediately spoon flaming cherries over ice cream and serve while still flaming.   *6 to 8 servings*

Bananas Guadalcanal

MR. P. PLOWMAN, PAGO PAGO,
TUTUILA, AMERICAN SAMOA

Prize-winning story of a favorite recipe:

"In the year of 1923, I was a young man employed as a plantation overseer in the Solomon Islands, on Guadalcanal.

"Our 'cook' boys were recruited from the labor lines and usually we had to teach them to cook. Our usual fare was tinned beef and baked yams, with green boiled paw-paws as a vegetable. Sweets were many and varied from experiments with local fruits. At week ends when we visited one another we would discuss our recent culinary discoveries.

"One of my discoveries I now like to call 'Bananas Guadalcanal,' flavored with rum. On a business trip to Perth in 1935, I mentioned my discovery to the proprietor of the Hotel Esplande. Six months later I was astounded to find Bananas Guadalcanal on the menu and to learn that the dish was in popular demand. Other flavorings had been substituted for the rum—as in this recipe."

Lightly butter an 8x8x2-in. baking dish.

Mix together and set aside

2 tablespoons water
1 teaspoon vanilla extract
½ teaspoon orange extract
½ teaspoon almond extract

(Two tablespoons rum, claret, cherry brandy or liqueur may be substituted for the above.)

Peel

**4 bananas with all-yellow or
    green-tipped peel**

Measure onto waxed paper

5 tablespoons brown sugar

Roll bananas in brown sugar and place one-half inch apart in baking dish. Sprinkle with the flavoring mixture, rum, or liqueur.

Bake at 350°F 25 min., or until bananas are completely tender. During baking, baste the bananas two or three times with the sirup that has formed.

Serve hot with **cream** or cooled with **Favorite Vanilla Ice Cream** (*page 534*) topped with remaining sirup.   *4 servings*

▲ Banana Fritters

A deep saucepan or automatic deep-fryer for deep-frying will be needed.

Peel, cut into 1½-in. crosswise pieces and put into a bowl

4 firm bananas with all-yellow peel

Gently toss banana pieces with a mixture of

3 tablespoons confectioners' sugar
2 tablespoons lemon juice
1½ tablespoons rum or kirsch

Cover bowl and allow banana pieces to marinate 45 min. to 1 hr., turning occasionally.

Fill deep saucepan with fat and heat to 365°F (*page 13*).

Sift together into a bowl and set aside

1⅓ cups sifted flour
2 tablespoons sugar
1 teaspoon baking powder
½ teaspoon salt

Melt and set aside to cool

1 tablespoon shortening

Drain banana pieces and set aside, reserving liquid for fritter batter.

Beat until thick and lemon-colored

2 egg yolks

Beat in until blended, the melted shortening, the reserved liquid from bananas and

⅔ cup milk
1 teaspoon vanilla extract

Make a well in center of dry ingredients. Pour in liquid mixture all at one time and blend just until batter is smooth.

Beat until rounded peaks are formed

2 egg whites

Spread beaten egg whites over batter and gently fold (*page 12*) together.

Coat banana pieces by rolling in shallow pan containing

¼ cup flour

Using a large fork or slotted spoon, dip banana pieces into batter and coat evenly. Drain excess batter from banana pieces before deep-frying. Deep-fry only as many fritters at one time as will float uncrowded one layer deep in the heated fat. Turn fritters with tongs or a fork as they rise to surface of fat and frequently thereafter (do not pierce). Deep-fry 2 to 3 min., or until golden brown.

Drain fritters over fat for a few seconds before removing to absorbent paper.

Sift over fritters

Vanilla Confectioners' Sugar
(page 415)

Serve immediately.   *About 6 servings*

△ Strawberry Fritters

Follow ▲ Recipe; substitute for bananas 1 qt. large firm **strawberries,** rinsed and hulled. Do not marinate strawberries. Add the rum to the batter; omit lemon juice. Increase the confectioners' sugar to ½ cup and roll the strawberries in it (instead of in flour) before dipping into the batter. Increase flour in batter to 1½ cups.

Peach Melba

Mix in a saucepan

1 cup sugar
1 cup water

Put over medium heat and bring to boiling, stirring constantly. Cover and boil 5 min.

Remove from heat and stir in

1 teaspoon vanilla extract

Rinse, pare, cut into halves and pit

3 large (about 1 lb.) firm, ripe peaches

Quickly blot peaches, if necessary, on absorbent paper.

Set sirup over medium heat. Add peaches, two halves at one time, and simmer 3 min. With a slotted spoon, carefully remove peaches from sirup; allow excess sirup to drain into saucepan. Repeat the above cooking process for the remaining four peach halves. Chill peaches in refrigerator.

Meanwhile, sort, rinse, drain and force through coarse sieve or food mill

2 cups (1 pt.) fresh, ripe, red
raspberries

Stir in

¼ cup sugar

Chill in refrigerator.

When ready to serve, spoon into a large glass serving dish

1 qt. vanilla ice cream

Place chilled peaches on ice cream, cut side down. Top with sauce. Serve immediately.

6 servings

▲ Blushing Pears

Set out a shallow baking dish having a cover.

Wash, cut into halves, core and pare

2 large or 4 small pears

Cut three tiny slits in full part of each rounded side. Insert in each slit

Red cinnamon candy

Place pears in baking dish, cut side down. Pour into dish

¼ cup water
2 tablespoons lemon juice

Cover and bake at 350°F 30 to 50 min. (depending upon size and variety of pears), or until pears are tender when gently pierced with a fork.

Remove pears from oven. Turn pears and fill the center of each half with (in order)

1 tablespoon brown or granulated
sugar
½ teaspoon grated lemon peel (*page 11*)
¼ teaspoon butter or margarine
Sprinkling of cinnamon or nutmeg

Return baking dish to oven uncovered and leave until pears are glazed.

Serve hot or chilled. *4 servings*

Note: For variety, substitute for sugar, butter and spices in each pear center 2 teaspoons colorful tart **jelly** such as currant, mint or cranberry, or orange marmalade.

△ Blushing Peaches

Follow ▲ Recipe. Substitute 2 large or 4 small **peaches** for pears. Bake 15 to 20 min. before turning fruit. In place of the spices, try 1 or 2 drops **almond extract** in each center. Sprinkle each peach half with 1 teaspoon moist, shredded **coconut**. Omit second baking period.

Stewed Rhubarb

Serve refreshingly cold or pleasantly warm.

Set out a 2-qt. saucepan having a tight-fitting cover.

Wash, cut off leaves and ends of stems and cut into 1-in. pieces enough rhubarb to yield
   4 cups (about 1 lb.) fresh rhubarb
(Peel stalks only if skin is tough.)

Put the rhubarb into the saucepan.

Mix together and add to rhubarb
   ¾ cup sugar
   1 teaspoon grated lemon peel (*page 11*)
   ½ teaspoon cinnamon
Drizzle with
   2 teaspoons lemon juice
Put over low heat. Stir until sugar dissolves and a sirup is formed. Cover and cook slowly about 15 min., or until rhubarb is tender.

If deeper pink is desired, carefully stir in
   Few drops red food coloring
Serve hot or cold.   *4 or 5 servings*

Note: If your yen for rhubarb happens to fall on "baking day," this recipe may also be prepared in a casserole in the oven. Prepare the rhubarb the same way, but put it into a casserole instead, cover and bake at 325°F about 25 min., or until rhubarb is tender when pierced with a fork.

Strawberries with Cream Cheese

VIRGINIA H. AUDAS, CANASTOTA, N. Y.

Sort, rinse, drain and hull
   4 cups (1 qt.) fresh, ripe strawberries
Sweeten strawberries with
   ½ cup sifted confectioners' sugar
Spoon into serving dishes.

Put into a small bowl and beat until light and fluffy
   3 oz. (1 pkg.) cream cheese, softened
   ¼ teaspoon salt

Add gradually and beat until well blended
   ⅓ cup milk or cream
Pour over individual servings.   *4 servings*

Note: Two 1-lb. packages **frozen strawberries** may be substituted for the quart of fresh strawberries; omit sugar.

Dressy Peach Dessert 12

MRS. A. E. SEASTROM, HOPEDALE, MASS.

Set refrigerator control at coldest operating temperature.

Drain contents of
   1 No. 2½ can peach halves
Set out 8 of the peach halves. Reserve sirup and remaining peach halves for use in other food preparation. Arrange peach halves in refrigerator tray.

Pour over peaches
   ½ cup muscatel or sherry
Place tray in freezing compartment of refrigerator until peaches are frozen (about 6 hrs.).

Separate frozen peaches and put into individual serving dishes. Pour warm Custard Sauce over peaches and serve immediately.

For Custard Sauce—Scald (*page 13*) in top of double boiler
   1¼ cups milk
Beat slightly
   2 eggs
Add and beat just until blended
   ½ cup sugar
   ⅛ teaspoon salt
Add gradually and blend in the scalded milk.

Wash double-boiler top to remove scum.

Strain mixture into double-boiler top and cook over simmering water, stirring constantly and rapidly until mixture coats a silver spoon. Remove from simmering water at once.

Blend in
   2 tablespoons muscatel or sherry
                                   8 servings

Flan De Piña

(Pineapple Custard)

LUCILE M. BOGUE

STEAMBOAT SPRINGS, COLO.

This recipe for "rich custard of pineapple" (to translate its Spanish name literally) is a souvenir from Nicaragua.

Set out a 1½-qt. casserole. Heat water for boiling water bath (*page 12*).

For Custard—Mix together in a saucepan

    2 cups unsweetened pineapple juice

    2 cups sugar

Stir over medium heat until sugar is dissolved. Remove from heat.

Beat slightly

    4 eggs

    1 egg yolk

    ⅛ teaspoon salt

Stirring constantly, gradually add pineapple mixture to egg mixture. Strain into casserole.

Bake in boiling water bath at 325°F 1½ hrs.

Set aside to cool until lukewarm and immediately chill in refrigerator.

Meanwhile, prepare Caramel Sauce.

For Caramel Sauce—Melt in a heavy light-colored skillet (a black skillet makes it difficult to see the color of the sirup) over low heat

    1 cup sugar

With back of wooden spoon, gently keep sugar moving toward center of skillet until sugar is completely melted and of a golden brown color (lighter than for burnt sugar sirup).

Remove from heat and gradually add, a very small amount at a time

    ½ cup boiling water

(Be careful that steam does not burn hand.) Return to low heat and continue to stir until bubbles are size of dimes. Set aside.

Sift together into a saucepan

    1 cup sugar

    ¼ cup sifted flour

Add gradually, stirring constantly

    2 cups boiling water

Continue to stir; bring to boiling and simmer sauce 5 min.

Remove from heat and blend in

    2 tablespoons butter

Return to low heat. Stirring constantly, blend in the caramel sirup. Cool slightly and serve over Flan De Piña. *6 to 8 servings*

Baked Custard

Caramel-Glazed Custard

▲ Baked Custard

Heat water for boiling water bath (*page 12*). Set out 4 heat-resistant custard cups.

Scald (*page 13*) in top of double boiler
2 cups milk
Beat slightly
3 eggs
Add and beat just until blended
¼ cup sugar
⅛ teaspoon salt
Stirring constantly, gradually add scalded milk to egg mixture. Strain mixture.

Blend in
2 teaspoons vanilla extract
Pour immediately into custard cups and sprinkle each serving with
Nutmeg
Bake in boiling water bath at 325°F 30 to 45 min., or until a silver knife comes out clean when inserted halfway between center and edge of custard.

Serve warm or chilled.   *4 servings*

△ Caramel-Glazed Custard

Set out 5 heat-resistant custard cups.

To Prepare Caramel Glaze—Put ¼ cup **sugar** in a small light-colored heavy skillet. Stir over low heat until sugar is melted and becomes a golden brown sirup. Remove from heat and quickly drizzle on bottom and sides of each custard cup. For a thin, even glaze, twirl custard cup while pouring. Set aside while preparing custard.

Follow ▲ Recipe. Pour custard over sirup in custard cups. Bake in boiling water bath at 325°F 30 to 35 min., or until custard tests done. Remove carefully from boiling water bath. Set on a cooling rack until lukewarm. Chill thoroughly in refrigerator.

When ready to serve, unmold by running a knife around inside edge of custard cups; invert onto chilled serving dishes. The top will be caramel coated and the excess coating will run down the sides to form a sauce at the base of the custard mixture.

Lemon Cake-Top Pudding 13

MRS. VERNON SHEAN, ROCK ISLAND, ILL.

Grease a 2-qt. casserole. Heat water for boiling water bath (*page 12*).

Melt and set aside to cool
2 tablespoons butter
Sift into a large bowl
1 cup sugar
½ cup sifted flour
½ teaspoon baking powder
¼ teaspoon salt
Beat until thick and lemon-colored
3 egg yolks
¼ cup lemon juice
2 teaspoons grated lemon peel
(page 11)
Stir into the egg-yolk mixture the melted butter and
1½ cups milk
Stir mixture into dry ingredients.

Beat until frothy
3 egg whites
Add gradually, beating well after each addition
½ cup sugar
Spread beaten egg whites over batter and gently fold (*page 12*) together. Turn batter into casserole.

Bake in boiling water bath at 350°F 50 min., or until a cake tester or wooden pick inserted in center of casserole comes out clean.

6 to 8 servings

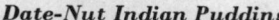

Date-Nut Indian Pudding

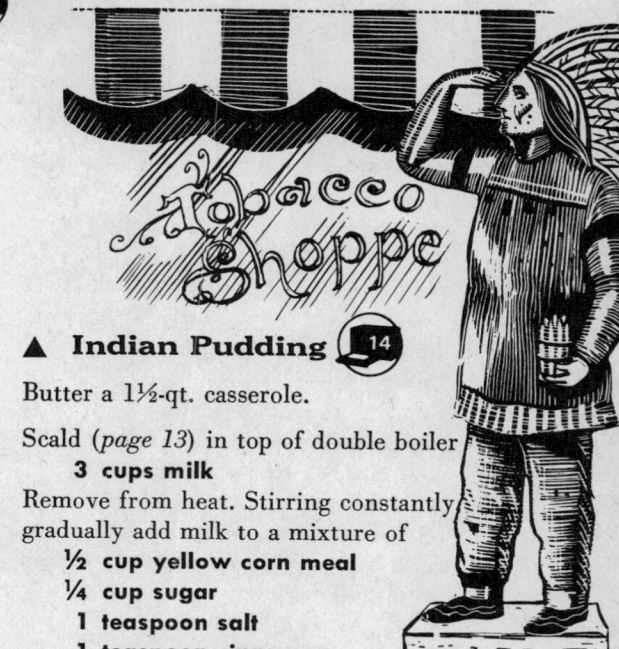

▲ Indian Pudding 14

Butter a 1½-qt. casserole.

Scald (*page 13*) in top of double boiler
3 cups milk
Remove from heat. Stirring constantly, gradually add milk to a mixture of
½ cup yellow corn meal
¼ cup sugar
1 teaspoon salt
1 teaspoon cinnamon
½ teaspoon ginger
Wash double-boiler top to remove scum.

Vigorously stir about 3 tablespoons hot mixture into a mixture of
1 egg, well beaten
½ cup molasses
Immediately blend the molasses mixture into the corn meal mixture. Cook over simmering water about 20 min., or until very thick, stirring constantly. Blend in
2 tablespoons butter or margarine
Turn into casserole. Carefully pour over top
1 cup cold milk
Bake at 300°F 2½ to 3 hrs., or until a silver knife comes out clear when inserted halfway between center and edge of casserole.

Serve warm with **Vanilla Hard Sauce** (*page 337*) or **Sweetened Whipped Cream** (*page 414*) or **vanilla ice cream**. *About 6 servings*

△ Date-Nut Indian Pudding 15

Follow ▲ Recipe. Blend in with the butter ½ cup chopped **nuts** and ¼ cup cut **dates**.

Holiday Bread Pudding 16 10

Butter a shallow 2-qt. casserole.

Scald (*page 13*)
3 cups milk
Meanwhile, toast until very crisp and cut into
½-in. cubes
**5 to 6 slices bread (about 4 cups
toast cubes)**
Put cubes into the casserole. Drizzle over
cubes while turning them lightly with a fork
**3 tablespoons melted butter or
margarine**
Add and mix thoroughly with fork
½ cup (3 oz.) mixed candied fruits
½ cup (about 3 oz.) golden raisins
**½ cup (about 2 oz.) coarsely
chopped black walnuts**
**8 to 10 maraschino cherries, quartered
and well drained**
Set aside.

Blend together
3 eggs, slightly beaten
½ cup sugar
½ teaspoon nutmeg
½ teaspoon cinnamon
½ teaspoon allspice
Add the scalded milk gradually, stirring constantly. Pour over bread cube mixture; turn
with fork to blend well.

Bake at 325°F 35 to 45 min., or until a silver
knife comes out clean when inserted halfway
between center and edge of casserole.

Meanwhile, prepare
**Creamy Orange Custard Sauce
(*page 335*; substitute 2 whole eggs
for the 4 egg yolks)**
Serve pudding warm with warm custard sauce
and sprinkle with
Nutmeg
Serve immediately.   *7 to 8 servings*

Mocha Fudge Pudding 17

MRS. WARREN PURCELL, PETERSBURG, VA.

Grease a 1½-qt. casserole.

Mix together thoroughly and set aside
¾ cup firmly packed brown sugar
¼ cup cocoa
Melt and set aside to cool
2 tablespoons butter or margarine
Coarsely chop and set aside
¾ cup (about 3 oz.) walnuts
Sift together into a large bowl
1 cup sifted cake flour
¾ cup sugar
2 tablespoons cocoa
2 teaspoons baking powder
¼ teaspoon salt
Combine
½ cup milk
1 teaspoon vanilla extract
Add the melted butter or margarine and the
milk mixture all at one time to dry ingredients. Stir until thoroughly blended. Blend in
the chopped nuts.

Turn batter into the casserole. Sprinkle over
batter the brown-sugar-cocoa mixture.

Pour over top of batter
**1¼ cups hot double-strength coffee
beverage (*page 13*)**
Bake at 350°F 40 to 45 min.

Serve warm with **heavy cream, whipped
cream** or **vanilla ice cream.**   *6 to 8 servings*

New England Pumpkin Pudding

New England Pumpkin Pudding ⑱ ⑪

One of America's favorites—fragrant, spicy pumpkin pudding.

Butter a 1½-qt. casserole.

Mix together
    2 cups (1 1-lb. can) canned pumpkin
and a mixture of
    ¾ cup firmly packed brown sugar
    1 teaspoon cinnamon
    ¾ teaspoon salt
    ½ teaspoon nutmeg
    ½ teaspoon ginger
    ¼ teaspoon cloves
Blend together and add, mixing until smooth
    3 eggs, slightly beaten
    1 cup heavy cream
    ¾ cup milk
Pour pumpkin mixture into the casserole.

Bake at 350°F about 1 hr., or until a silver knife comes out clean when inserted halfway between center and edge of casserole.

Cool slightly. Decorate, if desired, with
    Sweetened Whipped Cream (one-half recipe, page 414) or Vanilla Hard Sauce (page 337)
Force through a pastry bag and a No. 27 star tube to form a lattice design on top of pudding.

6 to 8 servings

Blackberry Jam Pudding
MRS. GARLAND ADCOCK,
NASHVILLE, TENN.

Lightly butter a 9x9x2-in. baking pan.

For Pudding—Sift together and set aside
    1 cup sifted flour
    1 teaspoon baking soda
    1 tablespoon cinnamon
    1 tablespoon allspice
    2 teaspoons nutmeg
Cream until softened
    1 cup butter
Add gradually, creaming until fluffy after each addition
    1 cup blackberry jam
Add in thirds, beating well after each addition
    3 eggs, well beaten
Measure
    1 cup buttermilk or sour milk (page 11)
Beating until well blended after each addition, alternately add dry ingredients in fourths, milk in thirds, to creamed mixture. Finally beat only until well blended (do not overbeat). Turn batter into pan.

Bake at 400°F about 45 min.

While pudding is baking, prepare sauce. Cool slightly and cut into 3-in. squares. Serve with the sauce.   *9 servings*

For Whipped Cream Sauce—Put a bowl and a rotary beater into refrigerator to chill.

Cream until softened
    2 tablespoons butter
Add gradually, beating well after each addition
    ½ cup sugar
    ⅛ teaspoon salt
Add, beating thoroughly
    1 egg white
Using chilled bowl and beater, whip (*page 13*)
    1 cup chilled whipping cream
Beat in with final few strokes until blended
    ¼ cup sifted confectioners' sugar
    1 teaspoon vanilla extract
Spread whipped cream over sugar-egg-white mixture and gently fold (*page 12*) together.

Creamy Rice Pudding

Creamy Rice Pudding

Prepare
>**Perfection Boiled Rice (one-fourth recipe, page 275)**

Meanwhile, set out
>**2 cups milk**

Scald (*page 13*) in top of double boiler 1½ cups of the milk; reserve remainder. Sift together into a mixing bowl
>**⅔ cup sugar**
>**1 tablespoon flour**
>**¼ teaspoon salt**

Blend in the reserved milk; gradually add the scalded milk, stirring constantly.

Wash double-boiler top to remove scum.

Pour mixture into double-boiler top and set over direct heat. Stirring gently and constantly, bring rapidly to boiling and cook 2 min. Set over simmering water.

Cover and cook about 5 to 7 min., stirring occasionally. Vigorously stir about 3 tablespoons of the hot mixture into
>**3 egg yolks, slightly beaten**

Immediately blend into mixture in double boiler. Cook over simmering water 3 to 5 min., stirring slowly and constantly to keep mixture cooking evenly.

Fluff rice with a fork and stir into hot mixture. Remove from heat.

Stir in
>**½ cup seedless raisins**
>**2 tablespoons butter or margarine**
>**1 teaspoon vanilla extract**

Cover and set pudding aside to cool slightly, stirring occasionally.

Serve in sherbet glasses. Sprinkle pudding with a mixture of
>**1 teaspoon nutmeg**
>**1 teaspoon cinnamon**

About 6 servings

▲ Soft Custard

Scald (*page 13*) in top of double boiler
>**2 cups milk**

Beat slightly
>**3 eggs**

Add and beat just until blended
>**¼ cup sugar**
>**⅛ teaspoon salt**

Stirring constantly, gradually add scalded milk to the egg mixture.

Wash double-boiler top to remove scum.

Strain mixture into double-boiler top and place over simmering water, stirring constantly and rapidly until mixture coats a silver spoon.

Remove from simmering water at once. Cool to lukewarm over cold water. Blend in
>**2 teaspoons vanilla extract**

Pour into 4 sherbet glasses and immediately chill in refrigerator.

Coarsely chop
>**¼ cup (about 1 oz.) nuts**

Sprinkle 1 tablespoon of the nuts over each serving. *4 servings*

⚠ Fruit Custard 20

Follow ▲ Recipe. Pour custard over **orange sections** or well-drained **fruit**.

⚠ Minty Custard 21

Follow ▲ Recipe. Prepare **Sweetened Whipped Cream** (one-half recipe, *page 414*). Add 1 or 2 drops **peppermint extract** with vanilla extract. Alternate layers of custard and whipped cream in sherbet glasses, ending with whipped cream.

⚠ Floating Island

Double ▲ Recipe. Beat 2 **egg whites** until frothy. Add ⅛ teaspoon **salt** and ¼ teaspoon **vanilla extract**. Add gradually ¼ cup **sugar**, beating well after each addition and continuing to beat until rounded peaks are formed. Drop by tablespoonfuls into 2 cups scalding **milk** (*page 13*). Do not cover. Cook over simmering water about 5 min., or until set. Remove meringues with a slotted spoon and drain on absorbent paper. Float on chilled soft custard. If desired, top each meringue with a **strawberry** and accompany with additional strawberries.

Floating Island

▲ Tapioca Cream 22

Set out a 1-qt. saucepan.

Beat until frothy
   2 egg whites
Add gradually, beating well after each addition
   ¼ cup sugar
Beat until rounded peaks are formed.

Put into the saucepan
   2 egg yolks, slightly beaten
Add gradually, stirring in
   3 cups milk
Add, stirring well
   ⅓ cup quick-cooking tapioca
   ¼ to ⅓ cup sugar
   ¼ teaspoon salt
Set over medium heat and bring mixture to a full boil (about 5 to 8 min.), stirring constantly. Do not overcook.

Remove from heat and stir a small amount of hot tapioca mixture gradually into egg whites. Then quickly blend in remaining tapioca mixture. Blend in
   1½ teaspoons vanilla extract
Cool, stirring once after 15 to 20 min. Spoon into serving dishes.   *8 servings*

⚠ Peach Tapioca Cream 23

Follow ▲ Recipe. Arrange **sliced peaches** in serving dishes. Top with chilled tapioca cream.

⚠ Chocolate Tapioca Cream 24

Follow ▲ Recipe. Add 2 sq. (2 oz.) **chocolate**, cut in pieces, after milk addition.

⚠ Peppermint Tapioca Cream 25

Follow ▲ Recipe. Add ½ cup crushed **peppermint-stick candy** with the vanilla extract.

Lemon Soufflé

MRS. DALE RILEY, CLARKSBURG, W. VA.

Butter bottom of a 2-qt. casserole. Heat water for boiling water bath (*page 12*).

Mix thoroughly in a saucepan
½ cup sugar
4½ teaspoons cornstarch
Add gradually, stirring in
1½ cups milk
Set over direct heat and bring rapidly to boiling, stirring constantly; cook 3 min. longer. Cool slightly.

Beat until thick and lemon-colored
3 egg yolks
2 tablespoons plus 1 teaspoon lemon juice
1 tablespoon grated lemon peel (*page 11*)
Stirring vigorously to blend, pour sauce slowly into egg-yolk mixture. Cool to lukewarm.

Beat until frothy
3 egg whites
Add gradually, beating well after each addition
¼ cup sugar
Beat until rounded peaks are formed.

Spread egg-yolk mixture over beaten egg whites and carefully fold (*page 12*) together.

Bake in boiling water bath at 350°F 1 hr. or until a silver knife, inserted halfway between center and edge, comes out clean.

Serve immediately.   *8 servings*

Chocolate Soufflé

MRS. JAMES C. FAHL, WASHINGTON, D. C.

Butter bottom of a 1½-qt. casserole. Heat water for boiling water bath (*page 12*).

Heat in top of double boiler over simmering water until chocolate is melted and milk is scalded (*page 13*)
½ cup milk
2 sq. (2 oz.) chocolate

Chocolate Soufflé

Blend with rotary beater and set aside.

Mix together
⅓ cup sugar
3 tablespoons flour
Add gradually, stirring in
½ cup cold milk
2 tablespoons water
Add to mixture in double boiler. Cook over simmering water until thickened, stirring constantly. Continue cooking 5 to 7 min., stirring occasionally.

Meanwhile, beat until thick and lemon-colored
4 egg yolks
Remove about 3 tablespoons chocolate mixture and stir vigorously into beaten egg yolks. Immediately blend into mixture in double boiler and cook 3 to 5 min., stirring constantly. Remove from heat and blend in
2 tablespoons butter or margarine
1 teaspoon vanilla extract
Set aside.

Beat until rounded peaks are formed
4 egg whites
Fold (*page 12*) chocolate mixture quickly into beaten egg whites. Turn into casserole.

Bake in boiling water bath at 325°F 1 hr. and 10 min., or until a silver knife, inserted halfway between center and edge, comes out clean.

Serve immediately.   *6 servings*

Casserole Cottage-Cheese Cake

A delicate concoction that can be served warm.

Butter a shallow 1½-qt. casserole.

Crush (*page 12*)
12 vanilla wafers (or enough to yield ½ cup crumbs)
Turn crumbs into a bowl. Add gradually, stirring in with a fork
3 tablespoons butter or margarine, melted
With back of spoon, press crumb mixture very firmly in an even layer on bottom of casserole.

Bake at 325°F 5 min. Remove from oven and set aside to cool.

Sift together and set aside
⅓ cup sugar
3 tablespoons flour
¼ teaspoon salt
Force through a sieve or a food mill into a bowl and set aside
1½ cups cream-style cottage cheese
Beat until thick and lemon-colored
4 egg yolks
Combine egg yolks with the cottage cheese and
½ cup cream or undiluted evaporated milk
1 teaspoon lemon juice
½ teaspoon grated lemon peel (*page 11*)
½ teaspoon vanilla extract
Blend thoroughly. Stir in the dry ingredients.

Beat until rounded peaks are formed
4 egg whites
Spread beaten egg whites over cheese mixture and gently fold (*page 12*) together.

Turn into the casserole and sprinkle with
Nutmeg
Bake at 325°F 1 to 1½ hrs., or until a silver knife inserted halfway between center and edge of casserole comes out clean.

Serve warm. If desired, serve with **Sweetened Whipped Cream** (*page 414*).   *4 to 6 servings*

Luscious Lemon Cheese Cake

Butter the bottom and sides of a 9-in. spring-form pan.

For Crust—Crush (*page 12*)
24 slices (6 oz.) zwieback (or enough to yield 2⅔ cups crumbs)
Turn crumbs into a bowl. Stir in
½ cup sifted confectioners' sugar
1½ teaspoons grated lemon peel (*page 11*)
Using a fork, evenly blend with
½ cup butter or margarine, softened
Turn into spring-form pan, reserving ¾ cup for topping. Using fingers or back of spoon, press crumbs very firmly into an even layer on bottom and sides of pan to rim; set aside.

For Filling—Combine and beat until smooth and fluffy
2½ lbs. cream cheese, softened
1¾ cups sugar (add gradually)
3 tablespoons flour
1½ teaspoons grated lemon peel
½ teaspoon vanilla extract
Add in thirds, beating well after each addition, a mixture of
5 eggs, slightly beaten
2 egg yolks
Blend in
¼ cup heavy cream
Turn into pan. Spread evenly. Sprinkle reserved crumb mixture over top.

Bake at 250°F 1 hr. Turn off heat. Let stand in oven 1 hr. longer. Remove to cooling rack to cool completely (4 to 6 hrs.).

Chill in refrigerator several hours or overnight.   *16 to 20 servings*

*Old-Fashioned
English
Plum Pudding
with Vanilla
Hard Sauce*

Old-Fashioned English Plum Pudding

MRS. R. M. HERKENRATT
NORTHFIELD, MINN.

Prize-winning story of a favorite recipe:

"In our family this pudding has always meant Christmas!

"Each year Father made a special trip to town for nuts and fruit. The family, having procured the other ingredients, would then gather in the kitchen. My brother, sister, and I each held one corner of the sack, Mother took the flour sifter and Father held the key corner to evenly flour the pudding-sack.

"Then we lowered it into the mixing bowl and Mother spooned in the mixture. We each carefully brought in our corners for Father to take, tie and lower the pudding into boiling water. Three hours later Father would gently lift out the pudding with the aid of a clothes stick, letting it drip over a pan. After the dripping stopped Mother would slip a big platter under the pudding, while Father cut the string and peeled the sack. We would all vow it was the best-looking pudding ever."

Here is a streamlined version of the recipe.

Grease a 2-qt. mold or two 1-qt. molds.

Coarsely chop
  1 cup (about 4 oz.) walnuts
  **¾ cup (about 4 oz.) blanched almonds
  (*page 11*)**

Mix the chopped nuts with
  **½ lb. (about 1¼ cups) diced,
    assorted candied fruits**
  2 cups (about 10 oz.) seedless raisins
  2 cups fine, dry bread crumbs (*page 10*)

Set aside.

Break apart, discarding membrane which coats it, finely chop and set aside
  6 oz. suet (about 1½ cups, chopped)

Sift together in a large bowl
  2 cups plus 2 tablespoons sifted flour
  2 tablespoons sugar
  ½ teaspoon baking soda
  ½ teaspoon salt
  1½ teaspoons cinnamon
  1¼ teaspoons nutmeg
  ¾ teaspoon cloves
  Few grains allspice

Blend in
  **½ cup plus 2 tablespoons firmly
    packed brown sugar**

Blend the fruit-nut mixture and the suet into the dry ingredients. Set aside.

Blend together thoroughly
- **4 eggs, slightly beaten**
- **½ cup molasses**
- **½ cup milk**
- **¼ cup double-strength coffee beverage (page 13)**

Add liquid ingredients to dry ingredients, mixing until well blended. Turn batter into mold, filling about two-thirds full.

Cover mold tightly with greased lid or tie on aluminum foil, parchment paper or 2 layers of waxed paper. Place on trivet or rack in steamer or deep kettle with tight-fitting cover. Pour boiling water into bottom of steamer (enough to continue boiling throughout entire steaming period, if possible). If necessary, quickly add more boiling water during cooking period. Tightly cover steamer and steam 3 hrs. Keep water boiling at all times.

Remove pudding from steamer and immediately loosen edges of pudding with spatula. Unmold onto serving plate.

Serve with
Vanilla Hard Sauce (page 337)
About 16 servings

Note: If pudding is to be stored several days, unmold onto cooling rack. Let stand until cold. Wrap in aluminum foil or moisture-vapor-proof material and store in cool place. Steam thoroughly before serving (1 to 2 hrs.).

To Flame a Plum Pudding—Heat **brandy** in a small saucepan. Ignite brandy with match and pour over top of pudding. Serve when flaming stops.

Steamed Chocolate Pudding

Grease a 1½-qt. mold.

Melt (*page 12*) and set aside to cool
- **3 sq. (3 oz.) chocolate**

Sift together and set aside
- **1½ cups sifted flour**
- **1½ teaspoons baking powder**
- **½ teaspoon salt**

Cream together until shortening is softened
- **⅔ cup shortening**
- **1½ teaspoons vanilla extract**

Add gradually, creaming until fluffy after each addition
- **¾ cup sugar**

Add in thirds, beating well after each addition
- **2 eggs, well beaten**

Blend in chocolate.

Measure
- **¾ cup milk**

Beating only until blended after each addition, alternately add dry ingredients in fourths, milk in thirds, to creamed mixture. Finally beat only until blended (do not overbeat). Turn batter into mold.

Cover mold tightly with greased lid or tie on aluminum foil, parchment paper or 2 layers of waxed paper. Place on trivet or rack in steamer or deep kettle with tight-fitting cover. Pour boiling water into bottom of steamer (enough to continue boiling throughout entire steaming period if possible). If necessary, quickly add more boiling water during cooking period. Tightly cover steamer and steam 1½ hrs. Keep water boiling at all times.

Remove pudding from steamer and immediately loosen edges of pudding with a spatula. Unmold onto serving plate.

If desired, garnish pudding with
- **¼ cup (about 1½ oz.) seedless raisins**
- **4 pecan halves**
- **4 candied cherries**

Serve hot with **Sweetened Whipped Cream** (*p. 414*) or **Eggnog Sauce** (*p. 334*). *6 to 8 servings*

Raisin Puff Pudding  with Lemon Sauce

MRS. F. W. PATTISON, BELLEVUE, WASH.

Grease a 1½-qt. mold.

For Pudding—Coarsely chop and set aside
> ½ cup (about 2 oz.) walnuts

Sift together and set aside
> 2 cups sifted flour
> 1 tablespoon baking powder
> ¼ teaspoon salt

Cream until softened
> ½ cup butter or margarine

Add gradually, creaming until fluffy after each addition
> ¾ cup sugar

Add in thirds, beating well after each addition
> 2 eggs, well beaten

Measure
> 1 cup milk

Beating only until blended after each addition, alternately add dry ingredients in fourths, milk in thirds, to creamed mixture. Finally beat only until blended (do not overbeat).

Blend in the chopped nuts and
> 1 cup (about 5 oz.) seedless raisins

Turn batter into mold. Cover mold tightly with greased lid or tie on aluminum foil, parchment paper or 2 layers of waxed paper. Place on trivet or rack in steamer or deep kettle with tight-fitting cover. Pour boiling water into bottom of steamer (enough to continue boiling throughout entire steaming period if possible).

If necessary, quickly add more boiling water during cooking period. Tightly cover steamer; steam 1½ hrs. Keep water boiling at all times.

Remove pudding from steamer and immediately loosen edges of pudding with spatula. Unmold onto serving plate. Serve hot with sauce.

For Lemon Sauce—Sift together into a double-boiler top
> ¾ cup sugar
> 1 tablespoon flour

Add gradually, stirring constantly
> 1 cup boiling water

Bring rapidly to boiling over direct heat, stirring gently and constantly; cook 3 to 5 min. Remove from heat.

Vigorously stir about 3 tablespoons of the hot mixture into
> 2 eggs, slightly beaten

Immediately blend into mixture in double boiler. Cook over simmering water 3 to 5 min., stirring slowly and constantly to keep mixture cooking evenly.

Remove from heat and blend in
> 2 tablespoons butter
> 2½ tablespoons lemon juice
> 1 teaspoon grated lemon peel
> (page 11)

6 to 8 servings

Blitz Torte

MARILYN BENADUM, LANCASTER, OHIO

Prepare (*page 340*) two 9-in. round layer cake pans.

Prepare and place in refrigerator to chill
> Creamy Vanilla Filling (*page 411*)

For Torte—Sift together and set aside
> 1 cup sifted cake flour
> 1 teaspoon baking powder
> ⅛ teaspoon salt

Cream together until shortening is softened
> ½ cup shortening
> 1 teaspoon vanilla extract

Add gradually, creaming until fluffy after each addition
> ½ cup sugar

Add in thirds, beating well after each addition
> 4 egg yolks, well beaten

Measure
> 3 tablespoons milk

Mixing until well blended after each addition, alternately add dry ingredients and milk to creamed mixture, beginning and ending with dry ingredients. Turn batter into pans, spreading to edges.

For Meringue—Set out
   ½ cup (about 3 oz.) slivered almonds
Beat until frothy
   4 egg whites
Add gradually, beating well after each addition
   ¾ cup sugar
Beat until rounded peaks are formed and egg whites do not slide when bowl is partially inverted.

Divide meringue into halves and carefully spread over batter in each pan.

Sprinkle each layer with half of the slivered almonds and half of a mixture of
   1 tablespoon sugar
   ½ teaspoon cinnamon
Bake at 325°F 30 min., or until meringue is golden brown.

Cool layers 15 min. in pans on cooling racks.

After cooling, loosen sides with a spatula. Remove one torte layer from pan, peel off waxed paper and place layer, meringue side up, onto a serving plate. Spread with all of the filling. Repeat with second layer and place, meringue side up, on top of filling.

About 12 servings

▲ Walnut Torte

Grease bottoms of two 9-in. round layer cake pans with removable bottoms or prepare (*page 340*) two 9-in. round layer cake pans.

Sift together and set aside
   ½ cup sifted flour
   ½ teaspoon concentrated soluble coffee
   ½ teaspoon cocoa or Dutch process cocoa
Grate (*page 11*)
   2½ cups (about 10 oz.) walnuts (about 4¼ cups, grated)

Reserve ½ cup grated walnuts for the frosting.

Thoroughly blend the grated walnuts with the flour mixture; divide into four equal portions and set aside.

Combine and beat until very thick and lemon-colored
   6 egg yolks
   ½ cup sugar
Mix gently into egg-yolk mixture
   1 teaspoon grated lemon peel (*page 11*)
   1 teaspoon rum
   ½ teaspoon vanilla extract
Set egg-yolk mixture aside.

Beat until frothy
   6 egg whites
Add gradually to egg whites, beating well after each addition
   ½ cup sugar
Beat until rounded peaks are formed and egg whites do not slide when bowl is partially inverted. Gently spread egg-yolk mixture over beaten egg whites. Spoon one portion of the flour-walnut mixture over egg mixture and gently fold (*page 12*) with a few strokes until batter is only *partially* blended. Repeat with second and then third additions of flour-walnut mixture. Spoon remaining mixture over batter and gently fold *just* until blended. *Do not overmix.* Gently turn batter into pans and spread to edges.

Bake at 350°F 25 to 30 min., or until torte tests done (see cake test, *page 340*).

Cool (*page 493*); remove from pans as directed.

When torte is cooled, prepare
   Butter Frosting (*page 407*; use the reserved walnuts)
Frost (*page 393*) torte and place in refrigerator until ready to serve.   *12 to 16 servings*

△ Hazelnut Torte

Follow ▲ Recipe; substitute 1½ cups (about ½ lb.) **hazelnuts** for walnuts.

Cherry Torte

Set out a deep 9-in. spring-form pan.

Blanch (*page 11*)
1 cup (about ⅓ lb.) almonds
Grate (*page 11*) ⅔ cup of the blanched almonds (about 1⅔ cups, grated); mix with
2 tablespoons fine, dry bread crumbs
Set almond-crumb mixture aside.

Toast (*page 12*) and coarsely chop the remaining almonds; mix with
2 tablespoons sugar
Reserve almond-sugar mixture for topping.

Wash, cut into halves and remove pits from
1 lb. dark sweet cherries (about 2¼ cups, pitted)
Drain cherries and set aside.

Beat until very thick and lemon-colored
6 egg yolks
3 tablespoons sugar
3 tablespoons lemon juice
Set egg-yolk mixture aside.

Beat until frothy
6 egg whites
Add gradually to egg whites, beating well after each addition
3 tablespoons sugar
Beat until rounded peaks are formed and egg whites do not slide when bowl is partially inverted. Gently spread egg-yolk mixture over beaten egg whites. Spoon one fourth of the grated almond-crumb mixture over egg yolks. Gently fold (*page 12*) with a few strokes until batter is only *partially* blended. Repeat with second and then third additions of almond-crumb mixture. Spoon remaining mixture over batter and gently fold *just* until blended. *Do not overmix.* Gently turn batter into pan and spread to edges. Place cherries evenly over top of batter.

Bake at 350°F 30 to 40 min., or until torte tests done (see cake test, *page 340*).

Set torte onto cooling rack. Cool in pan 15 min. Remove the rim from the bottom of the pan and, if desired, cut away torte from pan bottom and return torte to cooling rack. When torte is completely cooled, set on baking sheet.

For Meringue—Beat until frothy
3 egg whites
Add gradually to egg whites, beating well after each addition
6 tablespoons sugar
Beat until rounded peaks are formed.

Completely cover sides and top of torte with the meringue. Sprinkle the reserved almond-sugar mixture evenly over top of the meringue.

Bake at 350°F 10 to 15 min., or until meringue is delicately browned.

Cool torte and transfer to a cake plate. Before cutting each serving of torte, dip knife blade into hot water. When necessary, wipe meringue from knife blade.   *12 to 16 servings*

Orange Date Torte
MRS. ROBERT KANTZ, SPRING GROVE, ILL.

Prepare (*page 340*) a 13x9½x2-in. cake pan.

Grind contents of
1 pkg. (7¼ oz.) pitted dates
Chop finely and set aside
1 cup (about 4 oz.) pecans
Sift together and set aside
2 cups sifted flour
1 teaspoon baking powder
1 teaspoon baking soda
⅛ teaspoon salt
Cream together until shortening is softened
½ cup shortening
1 teaspoon grated orange peel (page 11)
1 teaspoon grated lemon peel
Add gradually, creaming until fluffy after each addition
1½ cups sugar

Add in thirds, beating well after each addition
3 eggs, well beaten
Measure
1 cup buttermilk or sour milk (page 11)
⅓ cup orange juice
Beating only until smooth after each addition, alternately add dry ingredients in fourths, liquids in thirds, to creamed mixture. Finally beat only until smooth (do not overbeat). Blend in the ground dates and chopped nuts.

Turn batter into pan and spread to edges.

Bake at 350°F 50 min., or until torte tests done (see cake test, *page 340*).

Cool (*page 493*); remove from pan as directed. Meanwhile, combine and stir until sugar is dissolved
⅔ cup orange juice
½ cup sugar
Immediately, spoon juice over the torte. If desired, serve torte with **Sweetened Whipped Cream** (*page 414*).   *About 12 servings*

Raspberry Whipped Cream Torte

Set out a 4-qt. double boiler or a 4-qt. heat-resistant bowl and a large kettle. Prepare (*page 340*) two 9-in. round layer cake pans.

Measure and set aside
1⅓ cups sifted flour
Melt over simmering water and set aside
3 tablespoons unsalted butter
Put into top of the double boiler
6 eggs
4 egg yolks
1½ cups sifted confectioners' sugar
Set over simmering water, making sure the bottom of the double-boiler top does not touch water. (Or, use the 4-qt. bowl set over the large kettle containing simmering water, making sure that bottom of bowl does not touch water.) With rotary beater, beat egg mixture constantly for about 5 min., or until mixture is slightly heated.

Remove double-boiler top from simmering water and beat egg mixture until thick, piled softly and completely cooled.

Sift one fourth of the flour over egg mixture; gently fold (*page 12*) with a few strokes until batter is only *partially* blended. Repeat with second and then third additions of flour. Sift remaining flour over batter and gently fold *just* until blended. Gradually add melted butter, folding *just* until blended. *Do not overmix.* Gently turn batter into pans and spread to edges.

Bake at 350°F 25 to 30 min., or until torte tests done (see cake test, *page 340*).

Cool (*page 493*); remove from pans as directed.

While torte layers are cooling, rinse and thoroughly drain
2 cups red raspberries
Select 16 berries for garnish and place in refrigerator.

Cut remaining raspberries and combine with
1 teaspoon rum
Set fruit aside.

Prepare
Sweetened Whipped Cream (double recipe, page 414, beat 1 cup cream at a time)
Put one half of whipped cream in refrigerator. Fold the cut raspberries into the second half and spread the raspberry-whipped cream evenly over one of the torte layers. Top with second layer, and using a spatula, cover sides and top of torte with reserved whipped cream.

Roll reserved berries in about
2 teaspoons sugar
Arrange raspberries in a circle around top edge of torte. Put into refrigerator until ready to serve. To avoid sogginess, chill torte no longer than 1 hr.   *12 to 16 servings*

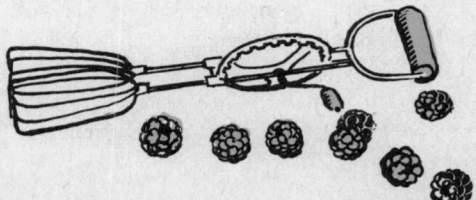

Raspberry Cake Delight

Raspberry Cake Delight

Put a bowl and a rotary beater into refrigerator to chill.

Have ready
  **1 10-in. Angel Food Cake (*page 341*)
    or a purchased angel food cake**
Thaw according to directions on package, contents of
  1 16-oz. pkg. frozen raspberries
Set the thawed raspberries aside to drain.

Reserve ⅓ cup of the sirup for use in frosting. Set aside ½ cup of the raspberries. Gently crush remaining raspberries. Add remaining sirup to the crushed raspberries.

Pour into a small cup or custard cup
  2 tablespoons cold water
Sprinkle evenly over cold water
  1 teaspoon unflavored gelatin
Let stand about 5 min. to soften.

Dissolve gelatin completely by placing bowl over very hot water.

When gelatin is dissolved, stir it and blend into a mixture of the crushed raspberries and
  1½ tablespoons sugar
  1 teaspoon lemon juice
Stir until well blended. Chill (*page 12*) until mixture begins to gel (gets slightly thicker).

Meanwhile, using a knife having a serrated edge, slice a 1-in. layer from top of cake. Lift layer from cake and set aside. Cut about 1 in. inside outer edge, around cake, to within 1 in. of the base. Repeat procedure cutting about 1 in. from inner edge. Using two forks, carefully remove center of cake and tear into small pieces. Set aside for filling. Place cake shell on a serving plate.

When gelatin mixture is of desired consistency, spread over the reserved cake pieces and beat together until smooth and well blended.

Using the chilled bowl and beater, beat until cream is of medium consistency (piles softly)
  ½ cup chilled whipping cream
Spread the remaining ½ cup of raspberries and the whipped cream over gelatin mixture and gently fold (*page 12*) together.

Spoon the filling into cavity of the cake. Carefully replace top of cake. Set in refrigerator to chill until filling is set (about 4 hrs.).

Prepare
  **Seven-Minute Frosting (*page 404*,
    substitute the ⅓ cup reserved raspberry sirup for water)**
Remove cake from refrigerator and quickly frost sides and top of cake. Serve immediately.
  12 to 14 servings

Boston Cream Pie

A famous Yankee sponge-cake dessert.

Prepare
  Hot-Milk Sponge Cake (*page 344*)
Prepare and place in refrigerator to chill thoroughly
  Creamy Vanilla Filling (*page 411*)
Shorty before ready to serve, prepare
  Fudge Glaze (*page 399*)
Place one cake layer onto serving plate. Spread with the filling. Top with second cake layer. Spread Fudge Glaze over top.

If desired, omit glaze and sift **confectioners' sugar** over top layer. *10 to 12 servings*

Meringue Topped Chocolate Cake

MRS. HARRY HAMILTON
EAST AURORA, N. Y.

Prepare (*page 340*) three 8-in. round layer cake pans.

For Cake—Melt (*page 12*) and set aside
  2 sq. (2 oz.) chocolate
Split into halves and set aside
  ⅓ cup (about 2 oz.) blanched almonds (page 11)
Sift together and set aside
  1 cup sifted flour
  2 teaspoons baking powder
  ½ teaspoon salt
Cream together until shortening is softened
  ½ cup shortening
  1 teaspoon vanilla extract
Add gradually, creaming until fluffy after each addition
  ½ cup sugar
Add in thirds, beating well after each addition
  4 egg yolks, well beaten
Stir in the cooled chocolate.

Measure
  6 tablespoons milk
Mixing until well blended after each addition, alternately add dry ingredients and milk to creamed mixture, beginning and ending with dry ingredients.

Turn batter into pans, spreading to edges.

Beat until frothy
  4 egg whites
Add gradually, beating well after each addition
  ¾ cup sugar
Beat until rounded peaks are formed and egg whites do not slide when bowl is partially inverted. Fold in (*page 12*)
  ½ teaspoon almond extract
Spread one third of meringue over batter in each pan. Sprinkle almond halves over only one layer.

Bake at 325°F about 20 min., or until meringue is golden brown.

Cool cake layers in pans on cooling racks.

After cooling, loosen sides with a spatula. Remove one cake layer, without almonds, from pan and peel off waxed paper. Place, meringue side up, onto a serving plate. Spread one half of filling over cake layer. Remove second layer, without almonds, from pan, and place, meringue side up, on top of filling. Spread remaining filling over cake layer. Repeat with third layer and place meringue-almond side up, over filling.

For Filling—Melt (*page 12*) and set aside
  2½ sq. (2½ oz.) chocolate
Mix together in top of double boiler
  1 cup sifted confectioners' sugar
  1 tablespoon cornstarch
  ⅛ teaspoon salt
Stir in and blend well
  ¼ cup milk
Stirring gently and constantly bring mixture rapidly to boiling over direct heat and cook 3 min. Set over simmering water; cover and cook 10 to 12 min., stirring three or four times.

Remove from heat. Stir in the chocolate and
  ½ teaspoon vanilla extract
Cover and cool slightly, stirring occasionally.
About 12 servings

▲ Baked Alaska

Set refrigerator control at coldest operating temperature and chill a 2-qt. mold. Cover a baking sheet with two sheets heavy paper or set out a wooden board.

Line chilled mold with
> **Chocolate Ice Cream (one-third recipe, *page 535*; or use 1 qt. commercial ice cream)**

Pack ice cream firmly against sides of mold.

Fill center of mold, packing firmly, with
> **Strawberry Ice Cream (one-third recipe, *page 538*, or 1 qt. commercial ice cream)**

Place in freezing compartment of refrigerator until very firm.

Meanwhile, prepare and cool
> **Pound Cake (*page 354*; see note for round or square Alaska)**

Split cake into two layers and trim one layer about ½ in. larger than mold. (Remainder of cake may be frosted, sliced and used as dessert.) Place cake slice on baking sheet or wooden board. Set aside.

Prepare meringue by beating until frothy
> **5 egg whites**
> **½ teaspoon vanilla extract**
> **¼ teaspoon salt**

Add gradually, beating well after each addition
> **¾ cup sugar**

Beat until rounded peaks are formed and egg whites do not slide when the bowl is partially inverted.

Quickly but carefully unmold ice cream. To unmold, loosen top edge of mold with a knife. Wet a clean towel in hot water and wring it almost dry. Invert mold onto center of cake. Wrap hot towel around mold for a few seconds only. (If mold does not loosen, repeat.) Working quickly, completely cover ice cream and cake with meringue, spreading evenly and being careful to completely seal bottom edge. With spatula, quickly swirl meringue into an attractive design and if desired garnish with
> **Maraschino cherries**

Place in 450°F oven for 4 to 5 min., or until meringue is lightly browned.

Using two broad spatulas, quickly slide Baked Alaska onto a chilled serving plate. Slice and serve immediately.   *12 to 16 servings*

Note: **Sponge cake** may also be used as a base for Baked Alaska.

△ Baked Alaska Loaf

Follow ▲ Recipe. Substitute a 1-qt. **brick** of **commercial ice cream** for molded ice cream. Prepare **Pound Cake** (loaf, *page 354*) or substitute purchased oblong pound cake. Slice ½-in. layer from bottom of cake and cut layer about ½ in. larger than length and width of brick of ice cream to be used.

Chocolate Funny Cake-Pie

For Pastry—Prepare (do not bake)
> **Pastry for 1-Crust Pie (*page 442*; use 9-in. pie pan)**

Set aside.

For Sauce—Combine in a saucepan
> **½ cup water**
> **1½ sq. (1½ oz.) chocolate**

Put over low heat and stir constantly until chocolate is melted.

Add
⅔ cup sugar
Stirring constantly, bring to boiling; remove from heat and stir in
¼ cup butter or margarine
1½ teaspoons vanilla extract
Set aside.

For Cake—Finely chop and set aside
1 cup (about 4 oz.) walnuts
Sift together into a large bowl
1¼ cups sifted cake flour
¾ cup sugar
1¼ teaspoons baking powder
¼ teaspoon salt
Add to sifted dry ingredients
½ cup milk
¼ cup hydrogenated vegetable short-ening or all-purpose shortening
1½ teaspoons vanilla extract
Beat until dry ingredients are just mixed.

Add
1 egg, unbeaten
Beat 200 strokes, or 2 min. on electric mixer on medium speed. Scrape sides of bowl several times during beating.

Add nuts and beat 100 strokes, or 1 min. on electric mixer. Turn batter into pastry shell. Stir sauce and carefully pour over cake batter. (Sauce will sink to bottom.)

Bake at 350°F 50 to 55 min., or until cake tests done (*page 340*).

Serve warm. Top with **whipped cream.**

6 to 8 servings

△ Apple Butter Funny Cake-Pie
ARLETTA WHALEY, OTWELL, IND.

Follow ▲ Recipe; omit sauce and nuts. Sift ½ teaspoon **cinnamon**, ¼ teaspoon **cloves** and ¼ teaspoon **allspice** with dry ingredients. Spread 1 cup **apple butter** evenly over un-baked pastry shell. Turn cake batter into shell.

Strawberry Shortcakes

For Sweetened Crushed Strawberries—
Sort, rinse, drain and hull
1 qt. fresh ripe strawberries
Reserve ½ cup strawberries for garnish.

Crush remaining berries slightly. Sprinkle with
1 cup sugar
Cover and set in refrigerator to chill thoroughly. Gently mix fruit occasionally.

For Shortcakes—Prepare
Tender-Rich Rolled Shortcakes (*page 62*)

To Serve—Split shortcakes while hot and spoon one half of the crushed berries over the bottom halves. Cover with top halves and spoon remaining berries over top. Top with
Sweetened Whipped Cream (*page 414*)
Serve immediately. *6 servings*

Note: **Raspberries, blackberries** or **blueberries** may be substituted for strawberries.

Cherry Shortbread Dessert

MRS. LESTER H. GRIPP
DODGE CENTER, MINN.

Set out a 9-in. pie pan.

Coarsely chop and set aside
  ¾ cup (about 3 oz.) walnuts
Cut (*page 12*) into small pieces and set aside
  ⅔ cup (about 4 oz.) candied cherries
Cut into short lengths and set aside
  ½ cup (about 2 oz.) moist, shredded
    coconut
Cream until softened
  ½ cup butter
Add and cream until fluffy
  2 tablespoons confectioners' sugar
Add gradually, mixing until well blended (mixture will be crumbly)
  1 cup sifted flour
Turn dough into pan. With hands, carefully press dough into an even layer on bottom and sides of pan.

Bake at 325°F 10 min.

Meanwhile, sift together and set aside
  1 cup sugar
  1 tablespoon flour
  ½ teaspoon baking powder
  ⅛ teaspoon salt
Beat until thick and piled softly
  2 eggs
  1 teaspoon vanilla extract
Add gradually and blend in the dry ingredients. Thoroughly blend in the fruit and nuts. Turn fruit mixture over baked layer and spread evenly.

Bake at 325°F 40 min., or until shortbread is lightly browned.

Cool on cooling rack.

If desired, serve with **whipped cream.**

About 6 servings

▲ Rhubarb Cobbler

Celebrate the return of spring with rhubarb!

Set out a 1½-qt. casserole.

Wash and cut off leaves and ends of stems from
  1 lb. rhubarb
(Peel stalks only if skin is tough.) Cut into 1-in. pieces. Put one half of rhubarb in casserole. Sprinkle with one half of a mixture of
  1 cup sugar
  1 teaspoon grated lemon peel
    (page 11)
  ½ teaspoon cinnamon
Drizzle over rhubarb one half of
  1 tablespoon lemon juice
Dot with
  Butter or margarine
Add remaining rhubarb to casserole and top with remaining sugar mixture, drizzle with remaining lemon juice and dot with butter or margarine.

Bake at 350°F 20 min.

Meanwhile, prepare dough for
  Tender-Rich Drop Biscuit (one-half
    recipe, page 62; sift 1 tablespoon
    sugar with flour mixture)
Remove rhubarb from oven; set temperature control of oven at 450°F. Drop biscuit dough by spoonfuls over top of hot rhubarb. Return casserole to oven. Bake 10 to 15 min. longer, or until biscuits are lightly browned.

Serve warm with **cream.**   *6 servings*

⚠ Blueberry Cobbler

Follow ▲ Recipe; substitute 2 cups fresh **blueberries,** rinsed and drained, for rhubarb. Decrease sugar to ½ cup.

⚠ Cherry Cobbler

Follow ▲ Recipe; substitute 4 cups (two No. 2 cans, drained) **sour red cherries,** for rhubarb. Decrease sugar to ¾ cup and mix in 2 tablespoons **flour.**

Peach Dumplings

JEANNE COLFLASH, DELAWARE, OHIO

Set out a 13x9½x2-in. baking pan.

Prepare (do not roll)
Pastry for Two-Crust Pie (page 442)
Set aside in refrigerator until ready to use.

Coarsely chop and set aside
¼ cup (about 1 oz.) pecans
Mix in a 1-qt. saucepan
1 cup water
¾ cup sugar
½ teaspoon cinnamon
¼ teaspoon nutmeg
Stir over low heat until sugar is dissolved. Increase heat to medium and bring mixture to boiling.

Remove from heat and blend in
3 tablespoons butter
Stir in the chopped pecans. Set sirup aside.

Rinse and plunge into boiling water to help loosen the skins
6 medium-size (about 1½ lbs.) firm, ripe peaches
Plunge peaches into cold water. Gently slip off skins. Cut peaches into halves; remove and discard pits.

Roll pastry into an 18x12 in. rectangle about ⅛ in. thick. With sharp knife or pastry wheel cut into six 6-in. squares. For each dumpling, place a peach half, cut side up, in center of a pastry square. Fill hollow with about 1 tablespoon of a mixture of
6 tablespoons sugar
2 teaspoons cinnamon
½ teaspoon nutmeg
Top with second peach half, cut side down.

Set out
2 tablespoons butter
Top each peach with about 1 teaspoon of the butter.

Carefully draw one corner of pastry up over peach top. Moisten edge with water. Overlap with opposite corner of pastry and press edges together. Repeat for two remaining corners. Place each dumpling in baking pan. Pour sirup around dumplings.

Bake at 375°F 30 min. Remove from oven; brush dumplings lightly with
2 tablespoons cream
Bake 10 min. longer or until lightly browned.

Serve warm with **cream.**　　　　*6 servings*

Grandma's Apple Jack Dessert

MRS. HOWARD J. LEECH
LONGVIEW, WASH.

Prepare and bake
Deep-Dish Apple Pie (page 450, use Pastry Topping; omit orange juice and grated orange peel)
Cut into individual servings and turn into sauce dishes, pastry side down.

Pour warm Nutmeg Sauce over each serving.

For Nutmeg Sauce—Measure
1½ cups milk
Scald (*page 13*) 1 cup of the milk in the top of a double boiler; reserve remainder.

Mix in a saucepan
½ cup sugar
2 tablespoons flour
½ teaspoon nutmeg
Blend in the reserved ½ cup milk; add gradually, stirring constantly, the scalded milk. Bring rapidly to boiling over direct heat, stirring gently and constantly; cook 3 min. Remove from heat.

Wash double-boiler top to remove scum.

Pour mixture into double-boiler top and place over simmering water. Cover and cook about 5 to 7 min., stirring occasionally.

Remove from simmering water and blend in
1½ tablespoons butter or margarine
1 teaspoon vanilla extract
　　　　6 to 8 servings

Pineapple-Orange Fantasies

MRS. VERNON SHEAN, ROCK ISLAND, ILL.

An inspired combination of orange-flavored pastry and a piquant filling, layered into little towers that are topped with a fluff of meringue, make this prize-winner a truly original and distinguished dessert.

For Pineapple-Orange Filling—Cut into short lengths and set aside

¾ cup (3 oz.) moist, shredded coconut

Drain (reserving sirup in a 1-cup measuring cup for liquids) contents of

1 9-oz. can crushed pineapple (about ¾ cup, drained)

Sift together into top of a double boiler

6 tablespoons flour
⅓ cup sugar

Mix with the reserved pineapple sirup

Cold water (enough to make ½ cup liquid)

Add gradually, stirring into flour mixture with

½ cup orange juice
2 teaspoons lemon juice

Bring mixture rapidly to boiling over direct heat, stirring gently and constantly; cook 3 min. Place over simmering water. Cover and cook 5 to 7 min., stirring three or four times.

Vigorously stir about 3 tablespoons hot mixture into

2 egg yolks, slightly beaten

Immediately blend into mixture in double boiler. Cook over simmering water 3 to 5 min., stirring slowly and constantly to keep mixture cooking evenly. Remove from simmering water and blend in the coconut, crushed pineapple and

2 tablespoons butter

Cover and cool slightly, stirring occasionally. Put filling into refrigerator while preparing Orange Pastry.

For Orange Pastry—Set out baking sheets. Sift together into a bowl

1½ cups sifted flour
½ teaspoon salt

Cut in with pastry blender or two knives until pieces are size of small peas

½ cup hydrogenated vegetable shortening or all-purpose shortening

Blend in with a fork

2 teaspoons grated orange peel (page 11)

Sprinkle gradually over mixture, a teaspoon at a time, about

2½ tablespoons cold water

Mix lightly with fork after each addition. Add only enough water to hold pastry together. Work quickly; do not overhandle. Shape into a ball. Divide into halves. Flatten one half at a time on a lightly floured surface. Roll from center to edge into a round about ⅛ in. thick.

With knife or spatula, loosen pastry from surface wherever sticking occurs; lift pastry slightly and sprinkle flour underneath. Cut with lightly floured 2½-in. round cookie cutter. With spatula, gently lift pastry rounds onto baking sheets.

Bake at 400°F 10 min., or until golden brown.

Carefully remove pastry rounds to cooling racks and set aside to cool.

Meanwhile, prepare Meringue.

For Meringue—Beat until frothy

2 egg whites

Add gradually, beating well after each addition

¼ cup sugar

Continue beating until rounded peaks are formed and egg whites do not slide when bowl is partially inverted. Fold in

½ teaspoon lemon juice

To Assemble Fantasies—Using three Orange Pastry rounds for each serving, spread Pineapple-Orange Filling over two rounds. Spread the third round with meringue. Cover one frosted round with the other and top with the meringue-topped round.

Bake at 400°F 3 to 4 min., or until meringue is delicately browned.

Cool and serve.   *About 1 doz. desserts*

Magic Coconut Nests

Butter six 2½-in. muffin-pan wells.

Cook in top of double boiler, stirring frequently, over rapidly boiling water
   ⅔ cup sweetened condensed milk
   1 sq. (1 oz.) chocolate
When mixture is thick (about 10 min.), turn into a large bowl. Stir in
   1 teaspoon vanilla extract
Add and blend well
   2 cups (8 oz.) moist, shredded coconut
Place about ¼ cup of mixture in each muffin well. Pack firmly around bottom and sides, letting mixture extend ½ in. above rim.

Bake at 350°F about 20 min., or until top edges are firm.

Loosen edges and lift carefully from pans. Place on cooling rack to cool.

Just before serving, fill nests with
   Vanilla ice cream

6 servings

Magic Coconut Nests and ice cream

Butter Crunch Rings
MRS. ARTHUR AHMANN, LOUISVILLE, KY.

Set out a candy thermometer and a 1-qt. saucepan. Lightly butter 8 individual ring molds.

Measure into a large bowl and set aside
   5 cups corn flakes
Mix together
   1 cup firmly packed brown sugar
   2 tablespoons flour

Melt in the saucepan over low heat
   ½ cup butter or margarine
Stir in the brown sugar mixture and
   ¼ cup water
Stir over low heat until sugar is dissolved. Increase heat to medium and bring mixture to boiling. Put candy thermometer in place (*page 543*). Cook, stirring constantly, until mixture reached 238°F (soft ball stage, *page 543*; remove from heat while testing). During cooking. wash crystals (*page 543*) from sides of saucepan from time to time. Remove from heat.

Quickly pour sirup over corn flakes and mix lightly but thoroughly to coat corn flakes. Pack lightly in the prepared molds. Set aside.

When cooled, invert and remove mold.

To serve, fill rings with
   Ice cream

8 Butter Crunch Rings

Cream Puffs: Beat mixture with wooden spoon until it leaves sides of saucepan and forms a ball.

Drop dough by tablespoonfuls onto a lightly greased baking sheet. Allow room for expansion.

Fill shells with Mocha Whipped Cream. Frost with Coffee Glaze. Serve with cups of steaming coffee.

▲ Cream Puffs

A coffee duet—cream puffs with a mocha glaze and an elegant coffee-whipped-cream filling.

For Cream Puffs or Choux Paste—Bring to a rolling boil

> **1 cup hot water**
> **½ cup butter**
> **1 tablespoon sugar**
> **½ teaspoon salt**

Add, all at one time

> **1 cup sifted flour**

Beat vigorously with a wooden spoon until mixture leaves sides of pan and forms a smooth ball. Remove from heat. Quickly beat in, one at a time, beating until smooth after each addition

> **4 eggs**

Continue beating until thick and smooth.

Dough may be shaped and baked at once, or wrapped in waxed paper and stored in refrigerator overnight.   *1 doz. large or 4 doz. miniature puffs or éclairs*

For Coffee-Glazed Cream Puffs—Form small puffs. Force dough through a pastry bag or drop by tablespoonfuls 2 in. apart onto lightly greased baking sheet. Bake at 450°F 15 min. Reduce heat to 350°F; bake 5 min. longer, or until golden in color. Remove to racks to cool. To serve, cut off tops and fill shells with **Coffee** or **Mocha Whipped Cream** (*page 414*). Replace tops and frost with Coffee Glaze.

For Coffee Glaze—Measure into a bowl

> **3¾ cups sifted confectioners' sugar**

Add and mix thoroughly

> **¼ cup plus 2 tablespoons warm triple-strength coffee beverage (page 13)**
> **1½ teaspoons rum extract**

For Gourmet Cream Puffs—Form and bake large puffs. Increase baking time at 350°F to 20 to 25 min. Fill shells with **Sweetened Whipped Cream** (three times recipe, *page 414*). Replace tops, pressing down gently until ruffles of whipped cream are formed. Frost with **Chocolate Glaze** (*page 525*).

△ Éclairs

Follow ▲ Recipe for Cream Puffs, forming dough into 4½x1-in. oblongs. When cool, cut small opening at one end and force filling through a pastry bag and a No. 6 decorating tube into éclair. Fill with **Creamy Vanilla Filling** (*page 411*). Frost with Coffee or Chocolate Glaze.

For Chocolate Glaze (*cooked*)—Melt (*page 12*) 2 sq. (2 oz.) **chocolate.** Mix in heavy saucepan with 1½ cups sifted **confectioners' sugar,** 2 teaspoons **dark corn sirup,** 2 tablespoons **cream,** 1 tablespoon plus 1 teaspoon **boiling water** and 2 teaspoons **butter.** Place over low heat and stir constantly until butter melts. Remove from heat and add 1 teaspoon **vanilla extract.** Cool slightly.

For Chocolate Glaze (*uncooked*)—Melt (*page 12*) 3 sq. (3 oz.) **chocolate.** Blend 3 cups **confectioners' sugar** into 2 **egg whites.** Add the chocolate and 1½ teaspoons **vanilla extract.** Mix until smooth.

Savoy Meringues

Heaped with ice cream, fruit or cream filling, these snowy meringues make an elegant dessert.

Line a baking sheet with unglazed paper.

Beat until frothy
2 egg whites
Add and beat slightly
1 teaspoon vanilla extract
½ teaspoon cream of tartar
¼ teaspoon salt
Add gradually, beating well after each addition
½ cup sugar
Beat until stiff (but not dry) peaks are formed and egg whites do not slide when bowl is partially inverted.

Drop 6 large or 18 small mounds from spoon onto baking sheet, allowing 2 in. between mounds. Using back of spoon, form meringue into shells or nests.

Savoy Meringues

Sprinkle over meringue shells
Sifted confectioners' sugar (about ½ teaspoon each for larger shells)
Bake at 250°F about 1 hr., or until meringue is dry to touch. (The oven door of some ranges may have to be propped open partially to maintain low temperature.) With a spatula carefully remove meringues at once and turn upside down onto same paperlined pan. (If meringues are difficult to remove from paper, raise paper from baking sheet. Lightly moisten underside of paper directly under each meringue; carefully remove shells at once with a spatula. Re-line baking sheet with dry paper.)

Return to oven 5 min. to complete drying. Cool completely on cooling rack. Meringues should be crisp, dry, and very fine textured. (Store meringues in an air-tight container so that they will not absorb moisture and soften.)

Prepare filling for
Lemon Cream Pie or Lime Cream Pie (page 468)
Fill meringue shells with the filling. Top with
Fresh, ripe strawberries
About 6 large or 18 small meringue shells

Note: Meringue shells may also be filled with **ice cream, sherbet** or **fruit;** garnish with **fruit, whipped cream,** chopped **nuts** or **fruit** flavored with any one or any combination of **kirsch, curaçao, Cointreau, brandy** or **rum.**

▲ Blancmange

Set out
2 cups milk
Scald (*page 13*) in top of double boiler 1½ cups of the milk; reserve remainder.

Meanwhile, sift together into a saucepan
⅓ cup sugar
3 tablespoons cornstarch
⅛ teaspoon salt
Blend in the reserved milk; gradually add the scalded milk, stirring constantly. Bring rapidly to boiling over direct heat, stirring gently and constantly; cook 3 min. Remove from heat.

Wash double-boiler top to remove scum.

Pour mixture into double-boiler top; set over simmering water. Cover and cook about 12 min., stirring three or four times.

Lightly oil a 1-qt. mold with salad or cooking oil (not olive oil); set aside to drain.

Remove cornstarch mixture from simmering water. Cool slightly.

Beat until rounded peaks are formed
4 egg whites
Blend into cornstarch mixture
1 teaspoon vanilla extract
Spread beaten egg whites over mixture and fold (*page 12*) together. Turn into prepared mold and chill until firm.

When ready to serve, unmold onto chilled serving plate. Serve with
Fresh Strawberry Sauce (page 333)

4 to 6 servings

⚠ Coconut Blancmange

Follow ▲ Recipe. Blend in 1 cup finely chopped, moist shredded **coconut** with vanilla extract.

⚠ Fruit Blancmange

Follow ▲ Recipe. Blend in 1 cup well-drained, canned or sweetened fresh **fruit** with vanilla extract.

Blancmange

Trifle 31

Set out a shallow 2-qt. casserole. Chill a small bowl and rotary beater in refrigerator.

Cut into 1-in. pieces
Day-old pound cake (enough to line bottom of casserole)
Arrange over bottom of casserole. Pour over
½ cup brandy or rum
Cover and set aside.

Pour into a small cup or custard cup
¼ cup cold water
Sprinkle evenly over cold water
1 tablespoon (1 env.) unflavored gelatin
Let stand 5 min. to soften.

Meanwhile, scald (*page 13*) in the top of a double boiler
1½ cups milk
Beat slightly
5 egg yolks
Blend in
¼ cup sugar
Add gradually and blend in the scalded milk.

Wash double-boiler top to remove scum.

Return mixture to double-boiler top. Cook over simmering water, stirring constantly and rapidly until mixture coats a silver spoon.

Remove from heat and immediately stir in softened gelatin until gelatin is completely

dissolved. Cool; chill (*page 12*) until mixture begins to gel (gets slightly thicker).

When gelatin mixture is of desired consistency, prepare whipped cream. Using the chilled bowl and beater, beat until cream is of medium consistency (piles softly)

¼ cup chilled whipping cream

Set in refrigerator while beating egg whites.

Using clean beater, beat until frothy

3 egg whites

Add gradually, beating well after each addition

¼ cup sugar

Beat until rounded peaks are formed.

Spread egg whites and whipped cream over gelatin mixture and gently fold (*page 12*) together. Turn into the casserole. Chill in refrigerator until firm.

When ready to serve, garnish (see photo) with

Candied cherry

Slivered blanched almonds

Pieces of angelica

Prepare

Sweetened Whipped Cream (one-half recipe, page 414)

Force through pastry bag and No. 27 star decorating tube, forming a border around Trifle.   *About 12 servings*

Trifle

Angel's Delight

MRS. FRANK J. CORDERA, BENLD, ILL.

Line bottom and sides of a 9½x5¼x2¾-in. loaf pan with waxed paper.

Melt (*page 12*) and set aside to cool

1 pkg. (6 oz.) semi-sweet chocolate pieces

Coarsely chop and set aside

1 cup (about 4 oz.) walnuts or pecans

Tear into small pieces enough angel food cake to yield

4 cups angel food cake pieces

Beat until thick and lemon-colored

4 egg yolks

6 tablespoons sugar

Stirring vigorously to blend, add melted chocolate to the egg-yolk mixture. Stir in the chopped nuts.

Beat until rounded peaks are formed

4 egg whites

Spread beaten egg whites over chocolate mixture and gently fold (*page 12*) together.

Put about 1 cup of the cake pieces in the loaf pan. Cover with about one fourth of the chocolate mixture. Repeat, ending with chocolate mixture.

Chill in refrigerator until firm (at least 4 hrs.).

When ready to serve, invert onto chilled serving plate; remove waxed paper. If desired, garnish with **whipped cream** and **maraschino cherries.**

Serve immediately.   *8 to 10 servings*

Brown-Edge Wafer Roll

Date-Marshmallow Dessert Roll

▲ Apple-Butter Refrigerator Roll

ELBERT LUNA, AVA, MO.

Put a bowl and a rotary beater into refrigerator to chill.

Set out
27 vanilla wafers
Coarsely chop
½ cup (about 2 oz.) walnuts
Set aside.

Using chilled bowl and beater, whip (*page 13*)
1 cup chilled whipping cream
Gently but thoroughly blend into the cream
⅔ cup apple butter
Spread a thin layer on each wafer.

In a large shallow pan or dish, turn wafers on end and press together to form one long roll made up of alternate layers of wafers and whipped cream mixture. Cover outside of roll with remaining whipped cream mixture. Sprinkle with the chopped nuts.

Chill in refrigerator 3 hours. To serve, cut into diagonal slices about 1 in. thick.

8 to 10 servings

△ Brown-Edge Wafer Roll

Follow ▲ Recipe. Substitute 27 **brown-edge wafers** for vanilla wafers. Substitute **Quick Fudge Frosting** (*p. 401*) 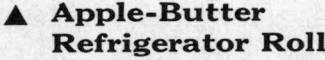 for apple-butter and the whipped cream mixture. Omit nuts, if desired.

▲ Date-Marshmallow Dessert Roll

Chill a bowl and rotary beater in refrigerator.

Crush (*page 12*)
32 graham crackers (or enough to yield 2⅔ cups crumbs)
Turn crumbs into a medium-size bowl, reserving 1 cup crumbs for topping.

Mix in
2 cups (about 14 oz.) pitted dates, cut in pieces (page 12)
32 (½ lb.) marshmallows, cut in pieces
¾ cup (about 3 oz.) finely chopped walnuts
⅓ cup chopped maraschino cherries, well drained
Using chilled bowl and beater, beat until cream is of medium consistency (piles softly)
½ cup chilled whipping cream
Beat in with final few strokes
1 teaspoon vanilla extract
Spread the whipped cream over the fruit mixture and gently fold (*page 12*) together.

Put the reserved graham-cracker crumbs onto a sheet of waxed paper. Shape the date-marshmallow mixture into a roll 14 in. long and about 2½ in. in diameter. Roll in the crumbs, coating it evenly. Wrap in waxed paper and chill in refrigerator until firm (about 12 hrs.).

To serve, cut into ¾-in. slices.

About 15 servings

△ Graham-Cracker Marshmallow Roll
MRS. G. LAMBERT, OKLAHOMA CITY, OKLA.

Follow ▲ Recipe. Do not chill bowl and beater. Reduce dates to ⅓ cup, coarsely chopped. Substitute 1½ cups (about 8 oz.) **seedless raisins** for marshmallows and cherries. Blend in 1 cup (about ½ lb.) **marshmallow cream.** Add the graham-cracker crumbs in thirds to the marshmallow-cream mixture; blend well after each addition. Omit whipping cream and vanilla. Measure ½ cup **cream** and mix in enough to hold mixture together. Do not roll in crumbs.

Chill in refrigerator 1 to 2 days.

Peppermint-Candy Fluff
MRS. CLAUDE A. WELCH, TRIBUNE, KANS.

Set out a 13x9½x2-in. baking pan. Put a bowl and a rotary beater into refrigerator to chill.

Crush (*page 12*)
1 lb. vanilla wafers (or enough to yield 4 cups crumbs)
Turn crumbs into a large bowl. Stir in
½ cup sugar
Add gradually, stirring in with a fork
¾ cup butter or margarine, melted
Using back of spoon, press one half of crumb mixture evenly onto bottom of pan. Set aside.

Crush and set aside
10 small (about 3 oz.) peppermint candy sticks
Coarsely chop and set aside
1 cup (about 4 oz.) walnuts
Cut (*page 12*) into quarters
28 (about 7 oz.) marshmallows
Using the chilled bowl and beater, beat until cream is of medium consistency (piles softly)
3 cups chilled whipping cream (beat one cup at a time)
Fold (*page 12*) the nuts, candy and marshmallows into the whipped cream. Turn into pan. Sprinkle with reserved crumbs. Chill in refrigerator 12 hrs.   *About 18 servings*

Cherry Refrigerator Pudding
MRS. JOHN R. HITTSON
APO, SAN FRANCISCO, CALIF.

Put a bowl and a rotary beater into refrigerator to chill. Lightly butter a 9x9x2-in. pan.

Crush (*page 12*)
¾ lb. vanilla wafers (or enough to yield 3 cups crumbs)
Turn crumbs into a medium-size bowl. Using a fork or pastry blender, evenly blend with the crumbs
½ cup butter or margarine, softened
With back of spoon, firmly press one half of crumbs into an even layer on bottom of pan. Set pan aside. Reserve remaining crumbs for the topping.

Drain and set aside contents of
1 8½-oz. can pitted, sour red cherries (about 1 cup, drained)
Coarsely chop and set aside
1 cup (about 4 oz.) pecans
Cream until softened
½ cup butter
Add gradually, creaming until fluffy after each addition
½ cup sifted confectioners' sugar
Add in thirds, beating thoroughly after each addition
2 eggs, well beaten
Beat until rounded peaks are formed
2 egg whites
Spread beaten egg whites over creamed mixture and gently fold (*page 12*) together.

Turn into pan.

Add to cherries, mixing lightly
½ cup sifted confectioners' sugar
Using chilled bowl and beater, beat until cream is of medium consistency (piles softly)
½ cup chilled whipping cream
Fold cherries and pecans into whipped cream. Spread evenly over mixture in pan. Sprinkle top with reserved crumbs.

Chill thoroughly (about 4½ hrs.).
About 9 servings

Pineapple-Cheese Refrigerator Cake

MRS. L. R. SIDDERS, SHATTUCK, OKLA.

Set out a 7-in. spring-form pan.

For Crust—Crush (*page 12*)
   **16 graham crackers (or enough to
         yield 1½ cups crumbs)**
Turn crumbs into a medium-size bowl. Stir in
   ¼ cup sugar
Add gradually, stirring in with a fork
   ¼ cup butter or margarine, melted
Reserve ⅓ cup crumbs for topping.

Using back of spoon, firmly press remainder of crumb mixture into an even layer on bottom of pan. Set aside.

For Filling—Empty into a medium-size bowl
   1 pkg. lemon-flavored gelatin
Combine in a saucepan and heat until very hot
   ½ cup unsweetened pineapple juice
   ½ cup water
Pour the hot liquid over the gelatin and stir until gelatin is completely dissolved. Stir in
   1 tablespoon lemon juice
Beat until thick and lemon-colored
   3 egg yolks

Beating constantly, gradually pour the gelatin mixture into the egg yolks.

Beat until fluffy
   8 oz. cream cheese, softened
Add, mixing until well blended
   ½ cup drained, crushed pineapple
Add gradually, beating constantly, the gelatin mixture to the cream-cheese mixture.

Chill (*page 12*) until mixture begins to gel (gets slightly thicker).

When gelatin is of desired consistency, beat until frothy
   3 egg whites
   ⅛ teaspoon salt
Add gradually, beating well after each addition
   ¼ cup sugar
Continue beating until rounded peaks are formed. Spread beaten egg whites over thickened gelatin mixture and gently fold (*page 12*) together.

Turn into pan. Sprinkle reserved crumbs over top. Place in refrigerator for 10 to 12 hrs., or until firm.

Carefully run a spatula around inside of pan to loosen cake. Remove sides of pan. Do not remove cake from bottom of pan.

12 to 14 servings

Grape Bavarian Cream

JUNE HANSON, BAILEYS HARBOR, WIS.

A 1-qt. mold will be needed. Put a bowl and a rotary beater into refrigerator to chill.

Set out
   2 cups unsweetened grape juice
Pour into a small bowl ⅓ cup of the juice.

Sprinkle evenly over the juice
   **1 tablespoon plus 1 teaspoon
      (1⅓ env.) unflavored gelatin**
Let stand about 5 min. to soften.

Heat 1⅔ cups of the grape juice until very hot. Stir in softened gelatin, stirring until gelatin is completely dissolved.

Add, stirring until sugar is dissolved

⅔ cup sugar

2 tablespoons plus 2 teaspoons lemon juice

Cool mixture; chill (*page 12*) until mixture is slightly thicker than consistency of thick, unbeaten egg white.

Lightly oil the mold with salad or cooking oil (not olive oil) and set aside to drain.

When gelatin mixture is of desired consistency, using the chilled bowl and beater, beat until cream is of medium consistency (piles softly)

1 cup chilled whipping cream

Fold (*page 12*) whipped cream into slightly thickened grape mixture. Turn into the prepared mold.

Chill in refrigerator until firm (about 3½ hrs.).

When ready to serve, unmold (*page 12*) onto chilled serving plate.　　*6 servings*

Peach Cloud Dessert　32

MRS. ABEL JOHNSON, LYMAN, S. DAK.

Cool and refreshing and stands well overnight.

Set out a 9½x5¼x2¾-in. loaf pan.

Drain (reserving sirup for use in other food preparation) contents of

1 9-oz. can crushed pineapple (about ¾ cup, drained)

Set aside.

Drain, reserving sirup, contents of

1 No. 2½ can peach slices (about 2½ cups, drained)

Sprinkle over ¼ cup of the peach sirup

1 tablespoon (1 env.) unflavored gelatin

Let stand about 5 min. to soften.

Beat until thick and lemon-colored

4 egg yolks

Add gradually, beating constantly

⅓ cup sugar

Blend in ¾ cup of the reserved peach sirup. Pour into top of double boiler and place over simmering water. Cook, stirring constantly, until thick. Remove double-boiler top from simmering water. Immediately stir in softened gelatin until it is completely dissolved.

Cool mixture; chill (*page 12*) until mixture begins to gel (gets slightly thicker).

Lightly oil the loaf pan with salad or cooking oil (not olive oil) and set aside to drain.

When mixture is of desired consistency, stir in the drained crushed pineapple and

½ teaspoon almond extract

Beat until rounded peaks are formed

4 egg whites

⅛ teaspoon salt

Spread beaten egg whites over gelatin mixture and gently fold (*page 12*) together.

Line bottom of loaf pan with about one half of the drained peach slices. Spread over them one half of the gelatin mixture. Arrange remaining peach slices over mixture. Spread remaining gelatin mixture over peach slices.

Chill dessert in refrigerator for several hours or overnight.

Unmold (*page 12*) onto chilled serving plate.

8 to 10 servings

Apricot Snow

CAROLYN E. STEPHENSON
WOLFE CITY, TEXAS

Pour into a small bowl
½ cup cold water
Sprinkle evenly over cold water
1½ tablespoons (1½ env.) unflavored gelatin
Let stand about 5 min. to soften.

Heat until very hot
1 cup water
Remove from heat and immediately stir in softened gelatin, stirring until gelatin is completely dissolved. Add and stir until sugar is dissolved
1 cup sugar
¾ cup apricot nectar
2 tablespoons lemon juice
¼ teaspoon salt
Cool mixture; chill (*page 12*) until mixture is slightly thicker than consistency of thick, unbeaten egg white.

Lightly oil a 2-qt. mold with salad or cooking oil (not olive oil); set aside to drain.

When mixture is of desired consistency, add
3 egg whites
Beat with electric mixer or rotary beater until mixture is very thick and piles softly (about 14 min.). Turn into the prepared mold. Chill in refrigerator until firm (about 4½ hrs.).

When ready to serve, unmold (*page 12*) onto chilled serving plate. *8 to 10 servings*

Frozen Apricot Whip

MRS. A. E. SEASTROM, HOPEDALE, MASS.

Set refrigerator control at coldest operating temperature. Put two bowls and a rotary beater into refrigerator to chill.

Prepare
Cooked Apricots (one-third recipe, page 494)
When apricots are tender, drain well and force through a sieve or food mill. Stir into apricots
1⅓ cups sugar
Let mixture stand about 15 min.

Blend into apricot mixture
1⅓ cups milk
Pour mixture into refrigerator tray; place in freezing compartment of refrigerator until mixture is mush-like in consistency.

Using chilled bowl and beater, beat until cream is of medium consistency (piles softly)
1 cup chilled whipping cream
Set in refrigerator while beating egg whites.

Using a clean beater, beat until rounded peaks are formed
2 egg whites
Turn mushy apricot mixture into chilled bowl and beat until smooth.

Spread whipped cream and beaten egg whites over apricot mixture and gently fold (*page 12*) together.

Return to refrigerator tray and freeze until firm (about 5 hrs.). *About 1½ qts. whip*

Strawberry Mousse
WILLIAM TALBERT, CHICAGO, ILL.

Set refrigerator control at coldest operating temperature. Set out a 1-qt. mold. Put a bowl and a rotary beater into refrigerator to chill.

Sort, rinse, drain and hull enough fresh, ripe strawberries to yield

1 cup sieved strawberries (about 1 pint)

Pour into a small bowl

½ cup cold water

Sprinkle evenly over cold water

1 tablespoon (1 env.) unflavored gelatin

Let stand 5 min. to soften.

Dissolve completely by placing bowl over very hot water. Stir the dissolved gelatin and blend into the sieved strawberries with

1 cup sifted confectioners' sugar

Rinse the mold with cold water and set aside to drain.

Using the chilled bowl and beater, beat until cream is of medium consistency (piles softly)

1 cup chilled whipping cream

Beat into whipped cream with final few strokes until blended

¼ cup sifted confectioners' sugar

¼ teaspoon vanilla extract

Stir softened gelatin and sieved strawberries and gently mix into whipped cream until mixture is thoroughly blended. Spoon into mold.

Place in freezing compartment of refrigerator until firm. *One 1-qt. mold*

▲ Orange Marlow 33
MRS. DALE HARRMANN, OSHKOSH, WIS.

Set refrigerator control at coldest operating temperature. Put a bowl and a rotary beater into refrigerator to chill.

Set over simmering water, stirring mixture occasionally until marshmallows are melted

32 (½ lb.) marshmallows, cut in quarters (page 12)

1 cup orange juice

Remove from heat, cool and put into refrigerator to chill until slightly thickened.

Using the chilled bowl and beater, beat until cream is of medium consistency (piles softly)

1 cup chilled whipping cream

Fold (*page 12*) whipped cream into chilled marshmallow-orange mixture. Pour into 1-qt. refrigerator tray. Place in freezing compartment of refrigerator and freeze until mixture is firm, 4 to 6 hrs.

Serve in chilled sherbet glasses.

6 to 8 servings

▲ Chocolate Marlow 34

Follow ▲ Recipe. Substitute 1 cup **milk** for orange juice. Melt 2 sq. (2 oz.) **chocolate** over simmering water with milk and marshmallows. Increase whipping cream to 2 cups (beat 1 cup at a time).

▲ Raspberry Marlow 35

Set aside to drain, reserving sirup, contents of 1-lb. can (2 cups) **raspberries**. Follow ▲ Recipe. Substitute 1 cup reserved **raspberry sirup** and ¼ cup **lemon juice** for orange juice. Increase whipping cream to 2 cups (beat 1 cup at a time). Blend the drained raspberries into the chilled marshmallow mixture before folding in the whipped cream.

Nesselrode Pudding

AMY S. BOYD, LAKE CHARLES, LA.

American version of a European creation.

Set out a 9½x5¼x2¾-in. loaf pan. Set refrigerator control at coldest operating temperature. Put a medium-size bowl and a rotary beater into refrigerator to chill.

Set out

**1½ doz. ladyfingers (or use sponge
cake cut in 4x1½x1-in. pieces)**

Line sides of the loaf pan with the ladyfingers and set aside.

Put into a large bowl and beat until very thick and lemon-colored

2 egg yolks

Add gradually, beating well after each addition

½ cup sugar

Add gradually, beating constantly

¼ cup (2 oz.) sherry

Set egg-yolk mixture aside.

Beat until rounded peaks are formed

2 egg whites

Spread beaten egg whites over egg-yolk mixture and gently fold (*page 12*) together.

Meanwhile, using chilled bowl and beater, beat until cream is of medium consistency (piles softly)

**1¾ cups chilled whipping cream (beat
only half of this amount at a time)**

Beat into whipping cream, with final few strokes until blended

**¼ cup sifted confectioners' sugar
1 teaspoon vanilla extract**

Gently fold together the whipped cream, the egg-yolk mixture and contents of

**1 10-oz. jar (about 1¼ cups)
Nesselrode mixture**

Turn the mixture into the prepared pan.

Place in freezing compartment of refrigerator until firm (about 12 hrs.).

If desired, garnish with **nuts, maraschino cherries** and **whipped cream.**

8 to 10 servings

▲ Favorite Vanilla Ice Cream

These ice cream recipes may be prepared in a dasher-type freezer or in refrigerator.

If using the dasher-type freezer, wash and scald cover, container and dasher of a 2-qt. ice-cream freezer. Chill before using.

If using a refrigerator, set control at coldest operating temperature, and chill a large bowl and a rotary beater and refrigerator trays.

Scald (*page 13*) in top of double boiler

2 cups milk

Combine and then gradually stir into milk

**1 cup sugar
1 tablespoon sifted flour
¼ teaspoon salt**

Stirring constantly, cook over direct heat 5 min. Remove from heat and vigorously stir about 3 tablespoons of hot mixture into

3 egg yolks, slightly beaten

Immediately stir into hot mixture in top of double boiler. Return to heat and cook over simmering water 10 min., stirring constantly until mixture coats a silver spoon. Remove from heat and cool. Stir in

**2 cups cream
2 teaspoons vanilla extract**

Chill in refrigerator.

For Dasher-Type Freezer—Fill chilled container two-thirds full with ice-cream mixture. Cover tightly. Set into freezer tub. (For electric freezer, follow manufacturer's directions.) Fill tub with alternate layers of

**8 parts crushed ice
1 part rock salt**

Turn handle slowly 5 min. Turn rapidly until handle becomes difficult to turn (about 15 min.), adding ice and salt as necessary. Carefully wipe cover and remove dasher. Pack down ice cream and cover with waxed paper. Replace cover; fill dasher opening with cork.

Repack freezer in ice using

**4 parts crushed ice
1 part rock salt**

Cover with paper or cloth. Let ripen 2 to 3 hrs.

For Mechanical Refrigerator—Pour mixture into refrigerator trays and place in freezing compartment of refrigerator. When mixture becomes mushy, turn into chilled bowl and beat with chilled beater. This helps to form fine crystals and to give a smooth creamy mixture. Return mixture to trays and freeze until firm. *About 1½ qts. ice cream*

French Vanilla Ice Cream Cream

Follow ▲ Recipe. Omit flour and increase egg yolks to 5. Substitute 2 cups **heavy cream** for cream.

Chocolate Ice Cream 38

Follow ▲ Recipe. Add 2 sq. (2 oz.) **chocolate** to milk and heat until milk is scalded and chocolate is melted in top of double boiler.

Chocolate-Chip Ice Cream 39

Follow ▲ Recipe. Just before freezing, blend in 2 oz. **semi-sweet chocolate**, grated.

Butter-Pecan Ice Cream 40

Follow ▲ Recipe. Melt in a skillet 3 tablespoons **butter.** Add 1 cup (about 3¾ oz.) chopped **pecans** and heat to golden brown, occasionally moving and turning. Stir into mixture just before freezing.

Berry Ice Cream 41

Follow ▲ Recipe. Just before freezing, blend in 2 cups crushed **strawberries** or **raspberries,** sweetened.

Peach Ice Cream 42

Follow ▲ Recipe. Substitute 1 teaspoon **almond extract** for vanilla extract. Just before freezing, blend in 1 tablespoon **lemon juice** and 1½ cups crushed fresh **peaches,** sweetened.

Two-Flavored Brick Ice Cream 43

Prepare ▲ Recipe and one-half ▲ Recipe, using refrigerator method. Just before final freezing, form two-flavored ice cream brick by spooning alternate layers of vanilla ice cream and chocolate ice cream into refrigerator trays, starting and ending with vanilla. Return to freezing compartment until firm.

Favorite Vanilla Ice Cream: When mixture is mushlike, turn it into a chilled bowl.

Beat with chilled beater for smooth, creamy texture. Return to refrigerator and freeze.

Caramel Ice Cream

44

MRS. CHARLES HAGUE, GUNTOWN, MISS.

Set refrigerator control at coldest operating temperature. Chill a bowl and a rotary beater and a 1-qt. refrigerator tray in refrigerator.

For Caramel Sirup—Melt in a heavy light-colored skillet (a black skillet makes it difficult to see the color of the sirup) over low heat

¾ cup sugar

With back of wooden spoon, gently keep sugar moving toward center of skillet until sugar is completely melted and of a golden-brown color (lighter than for burnt sugar sirup).

Remove from heat and gradually add (a very small amount at a time)

¾ cup boiling water

(Be careful that steam does not burn hand.)

Return to low heat and continue to stir until bubbles are size of dimes.

Set aside to cool while preparing ice cream.

For Ice Cream—Scald (*page 13*) in top of double boiler

2 cups milk

Remove from heat and stir in a mixture of

¾ cup sugar
2 tablespoons flour
⅛ teaspoon salt

Cook mixture over direct heat 5 min., stirring constantly.

Remove from heat and vigorously stir about 3 tablespoons of hot mixture into

2 egg yolks, slightly beaten

Immediately stir into hot mixture in top of double boiler. Cook over simmering water 10 min., stirring constantly until mixture coats a silver spoon. Remove from simmering water and cool. Stir in the caramel sirup and

1 teaspoon vanilla extract

Set in refrigerator while beating egg whites.

Beat until rounded peaks are formed

2 egg whites

Spread beaten egg whites over egg-yolk mixture and gently fold (*page 12*) together.

Cherry-Nut Ice Cream

Pour mixture into refrigerator tray and place in freezing compartment of refrigerator.

When mixture becomes mushy, turn into chilled bowl and beat with chilled beater until smooth. This helps to form fine crystals and to give a smooth creamy mixture. Return mixture to tray and freeze until firm.

About 1 qt. ice cream

Cherry-Nut Ice Cream

Set refrigerator control at coldest operating temperature. Put a small bowl and a rotary beater and a 1-qt. refrigerator tray into refrigerator to chill. Set out a double boiler.

Coarsely chop and set aside

2 oz. walnuts or pecans (about ½ cup, chopped)

Rinse, drain, and remove stems and pits from

1½ cups fresh, dark sweet cherries

Coarsely chop and set aside enough of the cherries to yield 1 cup chopped cherries. Reserve remaining whole cherries for garnish.

Cut into quarters (*page 12*)

24 (about 6 oz.) marshmallows

Put into top of double boiler over simmering water with

3 tablespoons lemon juice

Stir occasionally until the marshmallows are melted. Remove from simmering water. Stir mixture until smooth. Set aside to cool.

Blend into slightly cooled mixture

**1 cup chilled cream or undiluted
    evaporated milk**

Blend in the chopped cherries, nuts, and

**1 teaspoon grated lemon peel
    (page 11)**

Using the chilled bowl and beater, beat until cream is of medium consistency (piles softly)

1 cup chilled whipping cream

Turn the whipped cream onto the cherry mixture and gently fold (page 12) together. Pour into the chilled refrigerator tray. Place in freezing compartment of refrigerator and freeze until the mixture is mushy.

Meanwhile, chill a large bowl in refrigerator.

Turn mushy ice-cream mixture into the chilled bowl and beat until smooth. Return to refrigerator tray and freeze until firm.

Serve ice cream, garnished with the reserved whole cherries, in chilled sherbet glasses.

About 1 qt. ice cream

▲ Fresh Peach Ice Cream Superbe

Wash and scald cover, container and dasher of a 4-qt. ice-cream freezer. Chill thoroughly before using.

Rinse and plunge into boiling water to help loosen the skins

**12 medium-size (about 3 lbs.) firm,
    ripe peaches**

Fresh Peach Ice Cream Superbe

Plunge peaches into cold water. Gently slip off skins. Cut into halves; remove and discard pits. Force peaches through sieve or food mill into a bowl. Stir into peaches

2¾ cups sugar

1 tablespoon lemon juice

Let peach mixture stand 15 to 20 min.

Blend together

1½ qts. cream, chilled

1 teaspoon vanilla extract

1 teaspoon almond extract

¼ teaspoon salt

Blend into peach mixture.

Fill chilled freezer container two-thirds full with ice-cream mixture. Cover tightly. Set into freezer tub. (For electric freezer, follow manufacturer's directions.) Fill tub with alternate layers of

8 parts crushed ice

1 part rock salt

Turn handle slowly 5 min. Turn rapidly until handle becomes difficult to turn (about 15 min.), adding ice and salt as necessary. Carefully wipe cover and remove dasher. Pack down ice cream and cover with waxed paper. Replace cover; fill dasher opening with cork.

Repack freezer in ice, using

4 parts ice

1 part rock salt

Cover with heavy paper or cloth. Let ripen 2 to 3 hrs. *About 3 qts. ice cream*

△ Apricot Ice Cream Superbe

Follow ▲ Recipe. For peaches substitute 1 lb. (about 3 cups) **dried apricots.** Cook apricots (page 494). Force apricots through a sieve or food mill. Decrease sugar to 1¾ cups. Stir sugar and lemon juice into apricots. Cool. Chill in refrigerator. When chilled, blend into cream mixture. Proceed as in ▲ Recipe.

Strawberry Ice Cream

MRS. ARLAND VOGELER
WEST BROOKLYN, ILL.

A lovely pink and very pretty for a party.

Wash and scald cover, container and dasher of a 2-qt. ice-cream freezer. Chill thoroughly before using.

Thaw, according to directions. Contents of
   **1 16-oz. pkg. frozen strawberries
      (about 1⅔ cups, thawed)**
Set aside.

Empty into a large bowl
   1 pkg. strawberry-flavored gelatin
Add, stirring until the gelatin is completely dissolved
   1 cup very hot water
Add, stirring until sugar is dissolved
   1½ cups sugar
Beat until thick and piled softly
   2 eggs
Blend into the beaten eggs
   **2 cups milk
   1 cup heavy cream
   1 teaspoon vanilla extract**
Add egg mixture to gelatin mixture, and stir until well blended. Stir in the strawberries.

Fill freezer container two-thirds full with ice-cream mixture. Cover tightly. Place in the freezer tub. (For electric freezer, follow manufacturer's directions.) Fill tub with alternate layers of
   **8 parts crushed ice
   1 part rock salt**
Turn handle slowly 5 min. Turn rapidly until handle becomes difficult to turn (about 15 min.), adding ice and salt as necessary. Carefully wipe cover and remove dasher.

Pack down ice cream and cover with waxed paper. Replace cover and fill opening for dasher with cork. Repack freezer, using
   **4 parts ice
   1 part rock salt**
Cover with heavy paper or cloth. Let ripen 2 to 3 hrs.   *About 2 qts. ice cream*

▲ Ice Cream Balls

Set refrigerator control at coldest operating temperature.

Pack into deep refrigerator tray and freeze very hard
   **Favorite Vanilla Ice Cream
      (p.534); or use 1 qt. commercial
      vanilla ice cream)**
Crush (*page 12*)
   **24 chocolate cookies (or enough to
      yield 1 cup crumbs)**
Form ice cream balls with a scoop rinsed each time in hot water. Roll each ball in crumbs until thickly coated. Place balls in shallow refrigerator tray and freeze until serving time.
                           6 to 8 servings

⚠ Floating Snowballs

Follow ▲ Recipe. Substitute 1 cup moist shredded **coconut** for the cookie crumbs. Pour **Chocolate Miracle Sauce** (one-half recipe, *p.336*) into serving dish and float coconut balls in the sauce.

⚠ Peppermint Snowballs

Follow ▲ Recipe. Substitute about 2 cups crushed **peppermint stick candy** for the cookie crumbs. Spoon **Chocolate Miracle Sauce** (one-half recipe, *p.336*) into serving dishes and add a peppermint ball to each.

Peppermint Snowballs

▲ Frozen Lemon Custard 45

Chill until icy cold in refrigerator

1 cup undiluted evaporated milk

Set refrigerator control at coldest operating temperature. Put a bowl and a rotary beater and a 1-qt. refrigerator tray into refrigerator to chill.

Beat slightly in top of double boiler

3 egg yolks

Stir in

½ cup sugar

⅓ cup lemon juice

Cook over simmering water until mixture thickens, stirring constantly. Cool.

Stir in

1 teaspoon grated lemon peel (page 11)

Beat until rounded peaks are formed

3 egg whites

Spread the cooled lemon mixture over the egg whites and gently fold (page 12) together.

Beat chilled milk, using the chilled bowl and beater, until very stiff. Gently fold in egg-white mixture. Pour at once into the refrigerator tray; put tray in freezing compartment of refrigerator. Freeze until firm.

About 1 qt. frozen custard

△ Frozen Coconut Custard 46

Follow ▲ Recipe. Fold ½ cup (2 oz.) moist, shredded **coconut**, chopped, into custard mixture with whipped milk.

Frozen Lemon Custard

Party Delight

JUNE HANSON, BAILEYS HARBOR, WIS.

Prepare

Chocolate Miracle Sauce (p.336)

Making 12 rings, cut into crosswise halves

6 doughnuts (unsugared and unfrosted)

Divide into six equal portions

1 qt. Favorite Vanilla Ice Cream (p.534 ; or use commercial ice cream)

To prepare each serving, put a doughnut half onto a serving dish. Top with one portion of the ice cream and a second doughnut half. Pour desired amount of sauce over dessert.

Serve immediately. *6 servings*

Serve-Yourself Sundaes

Serve-Yourself Sundaes

A cooling and attractive finishing touch to a summer day's meal—smooth, rich, homemade ice cream in the center bowl of a Lazy Susan surrounded by dishes of fruits, nuts and sauces. Everyone can take his choice of topping and make the sundae he desires.

Have these fruits icy cold: canned, sliced cling **peaches** (add ¼ teaspoon **almond extract** for each 2½ cups peaches) and rinsed, hulled, sweetened, fresh **strawberries** or **raspberries.** Slice **bananas** lengthwise into fingers and dip in **pineapple juice.** Don't forget slivered, toasted **almonds** and sauces—**Luscious Butterscotch Sauce** (*p. 337*) or **Fudge Sauce Café** (*page 336*).

Grapefruit Sherbet

MRS. CAM ISAACSON, NORFOLK, NEBR.

Set refrigerator control at coldest operating temperature. Put a bowl, a rotary beater and a refrigerator tray into refrigerator to chill.

Blend together in a large bowl, in order
- 1 cup sugar
- 3 tablespoons lemon juice
- 1 teaspoon grated lemon peel (*page 11*)
- ⅛ teaspoon salt
- 1¼ cups milk

Stir until sugar is dissolved. Add gradually, stirring in
- 1 cup grapefruit juice

Pour sherbet into refrigerator tray and set in freezing compartment of refrigerator. Freeze until mixture is mush-like in consistency.

Turn mixture into chilled bowl and beat with the chilled beater until smooth. Return sherbet to refrigerator tray and put in freezing compartment. Freeze until firm.

About 1½ pts. sherbet

▲ Lemon Sherbet

Set refrigerator control at coldest operating temperature. Put a bowl, a rotary beater and a refrigerator tray into refrigerator to chill.

Blend together in a large bowl, in order
- 1¼ cups sugar
- ⅓ cup lemon juice
- 2 teaspoons grated lemon peel (*page 11*)
- 2 cups cream

Stir until sugar is dissolved. Pour into refrigerator tray and place in freezing compartment of refrigerator. Freeze until mixture is mush-like in consistency.

Turn mixture into chilled bowl and beat with chilled beater. Return sherbet to tray and put in freezing compartment. Freeze until firm.

About 1½ pts. sherbet

Ice Cream Clowns: For a delightful children's treat top unfrosted sugar cookies with large scoops of ice cream. Use raisins for eyes, nose and mouth and top with ice cream cones for clever clown hats.

⚠ Peach Sherbet

Follow ▲ Recipe. Omit lemon peel and decrease lemon juice to 1 tablespoon. Blend in 1 cup crushed **peaches.**

⚠ Orange Sherbet

Follow ▲ Recipe. Use only 2 tablespoons lemon juice. Add ½ cup **orange juice.** Omit lemon peel.

Pineapple-Mint Sherbet
RUTH V. POWELL, CADES, TENN.

Set refrigerator control at coldest operating temperature. Put a bowl and a rotary beater and refrigerator trays into refrigerator to chill.

Rinse, drain and bruise
½ cup fresh mint leaves
Combine in a saucepan
2 cups sugar
2 cups water
Set over low heat and stir until sugar is dissolved. Increase heat and bring to boiling.

Remove from heat. Add bruised mint leaves, cover and set aside for 1 hr.

Meanwhile, drain (reserving sirup for use in other food preparation) contents of
**1 9-oz. can crushed pineapple
(about ⅔ cup, drained)**
Peel and force through a sieve or food mill enough bananas to yield
**⅔ cup sieved banana (about 2
bananas with brown-flecked peel)**
Strain sirup to remove mint leaves. Add and thoroughly blend with sirup, the pineapple, sieved banana and
⅔ cup orange juice
6 tablespoons lemon juice
To tint, stir in, a drop at a time
3 to 4 drops green food coloring
Beat until rounded peaks are formed
2 egg whites
Fold (*page 12*) egg whites into fruit mixture.

Turn sherbet into refrigerator trays. Freeze until mixture is mush-like in consistency.

Turn mixture into chilled bowl and beat thoroughly with chilled beater. Immediately return mixture to refrigerator trays and place in freezing compartment. Freeze until firm.
About 2 qts. sherbet

▲ Lime Ice

Set refrigerator control at coldest operating temperature. Chill a 1-qt. refrigerator tray.

Pour into a small cup or custard cup
¼ cup cold water
Sprinkle evenly over cold water
2 teaspoons unflavored gelatin
Let stand about 5 min. to soften.

Meanwhile, heat until very hot
3 cups water
Remove from heat and immediately stir in softened gelatin until gelatin is completely dissolved. Add, stirring until sugar is dissolved
2 cups sugar
Blend into gelatin mixture
¾ cup lime juice
2 tablespoons lemon juice
**2 teaspoons grated lemon peel
(*page 11*)**
Tint to desired color by mixing in, a drop at a time
Green food coloring (about 4 drops)
Cool. Pour into a refrigerator tray. Place in freezing compartment of refrigerator and freeze until firm (3 to 4 hrs.), stirring 2 or 3 times during freezing.

Serve in chilled sherbet glasses.
About 1 qt. ice

△ Apricot Ice

Follow ▲ Recipe. Decrease hot water to 1½ cups and sugar to 1 cup. Substitute 2 cups **apricot nectar** for lime juice and 2 tablespoons **orange juice** for lemon juice. Omit food coloring.

DESSERTS in the MICROWAVE OVEN

Desserts such as custards, mousse-like puddings and even ice cream are often a challenge to the best of cooks. Cooking in the microwave oven makes many of these recipes virtually failsafe. The texture of the custards and custard bases, puddings and tapiocas are smooth and creamy with no curdling or lumping. The **Mocha Fudge Pudding** is sensational—and chocolate desserts are often the most difficult to prepare successfully.

Ice cream bases are outstanding and even puddings such as **Holiday Bread Pudding** and **Indian Pudding**, which often dry out in conventional cooking, are moist and delicious cooked in the microwave oven. We recommend using the microwave for these recipes not so much for the convenience as for the excellent results.

Some of the recipes, such as those for cooked fruits, take markedly less time to prepare in the microwave oven. Some are also easier, involving fewer steps in preparation or fewer utensils.

We have omitted those recipes which were not so successful when prepared in the micro-wave oven. The tortes use meringue as a key ingredient, and meringues simply will not cook properly. Those recipes which call for pastry do not brown and "sets" of ingredients will often cook unevenly. However, the microwave oven may be used to speed preparation of some of these recipes by melting chocolate, dissolving sugar and so forth, if such steps are called for.

USING WATER BATHS AND STEAMERS—
Some recipes included demand the use of a water bath or a steamer, even in the microwave.
Water Baths—The water bath calls for setting the covered casserole containing the pudding in a larger dish which should then be filled with boiling water to the level of the pudding. The glass sides of the casserole make this easy to observe. Use a 1½-qt. casserole set in an 8-in. round baking dish or in a 3-qt. casserole.
Steamers—This method calls for the same arrangement except the larger dish is also covered, either with plastic wrap or with the appropriate casserole cover.

FREQUENT STIRRING is extremely important to achieve the smooth texture which makes custard-type dishes so good. Each recipe notes when and how often to stir; the directions should be followed closely.

TEST FOR DONENESS—As the baked and steamed puddings near doneness, they will stop bubbling and begin to pull away from the sides. Begin testing then and not before.

Puddings should be tested for doneness by using a cake tester. Insert the tester between the outside edge and the center of the pudding. When the dish is done, the tester will emerge clean.

Some recipes, such as the custards, are done when thick enough to coat a silver spoon.

Each recipe will specify which test to use.

REMINDERS—For other tips and an easy-to-read chart comparing settings among different brands of microwave ovens, see the introductory chapter, **Home Cooking in the Microwave Oven**, in the beginning of this book.

1 *To Melt Chocolate*—In a small casserole, COOK chocolate, stirring every 1 min., until melted (about 1 min. per oz.).

Stewed Prunes *(page 494)*

Use a 1½-qt. covered casserole.

Cover and COOK until tender (about 8 min.).

Cover and let stand 5 min.

OVERALL COOKING TIME: 8:00

Cooked Apricots *(page 494)*

Follow **2** Recipe with substitution as in △ Recipe.

Spiced Applesauce

(page 495)

Use a 1½-qt. and a 3-qt. casserole.

Put apples and water in large casserole. Cover and COOK until tender (about 10 min.).

Put applesauce mixture in small casserole. COOK uncovered, stirring every 1 min., until sugar is dissolved (about 3 min.).

Cover and let stand 5 min.

OVERALL COOKING TIME: 13:00

Rosy Pink Applesauce

(page 495)

Follow **4** Recipe with variations as in △ Recipe.

Fruit Juice Applesauce

(page 495)

Follow **4** Recipe with addition as in △ Recipe.

Encore Baked Apples

(page 496)

Use an 11-in. oblong baking dish.

COOK uncovered, rotating pan every 5 min., until apples are tender (about 15 min.).

Cover and let stand 5 min.

OVERALL COOKING TIME: 15:00

Variety Baked Apples 8
(page 496)

Follow 7 Recipe with changes as in △ Recipe.

Cherries Jubilee *(page 496)* 9

Use a 1½-qt. casserole.

COOK cherry sirup, stirring every 1 min., until boiling and slightly thickened (about 5 min.).

Mix in cherries and COOK, stirring every 2 min., until heated (about 5 min.).
OVERALL COOKING TIME: 10:00

Blushing Pears *(page 499)* 10

Use a baking dish.

COOK pears in water and lemon juice, rotating pan every 5 min., until tender (about 15 min.).

COOK filled pears uncovered until sugar melts to form glaze (about 5 min.).

Cover and let stand 5 min.
OVERALL COOKING TIME: 20:00

Blushing Peaches 11
(page 499)

Follow 10 Recipe with changes as in △ Recipe, except COOK peaches until tender (about 8 min.).

Dressy Peach Dessert 12
(page 500)

Use a 1½-qt. casserole.

For Custard Sauce—COOK to scald milk (about 5 min.). Thoroughly mix in eggs, sugar and salt. Strain into clean casserole.

COOK, stirring every 1 min., until thick enough to coat a silver spoon (about 5 min.).

Lemon Cake-Top 13 Pudding *(page 503)*

Use a 1½-qt. casserole.

Prepare boiling water bath (see preceding introduction).

COOK to melt butter (about 1½ min.).

Pour pudding in small casserole, set into water bath. COOK uncovered until tester comes out clean (about 20 min.).
OVERALL COOKING TIME: 21:30

Indian Pudding *(page 503)* 14

Use a small casserole for the milk and a 1½-qt. casserole. *Do not butter.*

COOK to scald 3 cups milk (about 3 min.).

Stir cornmeal mixture into milk with a wire whisk. Add egg-molasses mixture and COOK uncovered, stirring every 30 sec., until very thick (about 5 min.). Blend in butter and transfer to larger casserole.

Add remaining milk and COOK, rotating pan every 2 min., until knife comes out clean (about 30 min.).
OVERALL COOKING TIME: 43:00

Date-Nut Indian Pudding *(page 503)* 15

Follow 14 Recipe with additions as in △ Recipe.

Holiday Bread Pudding 16
(page 504)

Use a 2-qt. casserole for the pudding, a small casserole for the milk and a baking dish for the bread crumbs. *Do not butter.*

COOK to scald milk (about 3 min.). COOK to crisp bread, tossing every 2 min. (about 5 min.).

COOK assembled pudding covered, rotating pan every 2 min., until a knife comes out clean (about 15 min.).

OVERALL COOKING TIME: 28:00

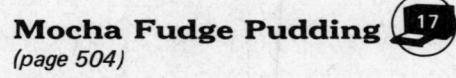

Mocha Fudge Pudding 17
(page 504)

Use a 1½-qt. casserole for the pudding and a small dish to melt butter. *Do not grease.*

COOK to melt butter.

COOK assembled pudding, rotating pan every 1 min., until a knife comes out clean.

OVERALL COOKING TIME: 18:00

New England Pumpkin Pudding *(page 505)* 18

Use a 1½-qt. casserole. *Do not grease.*

COOK assembled pudding, rotating pan every 2 min., until a knife comes out clean (about 20 min.).

OVERALL COOKING TIME: 20:00

Soft Custard *(page 506)* 19

Use a small casserole.

COOK to scald milk (about 5 min.). Blend in eggs, sugar and salt. Strain into a clean casserole.

COOK, stirring every 1 min., until slightly thickened and will coat a silver spoon (about 5 min.).

OVERALL COOKING TIME: 10:00

Fruit Custard *(page 507)* 20

Follow 19 Recipe with addition as in ⚠ Recipe.

Minty Custard *(page 507)* 21

Follow 19 Recipe with changes as in ⚠ Recipe.

Tapioca Cream *(page 507)* 22

Use a 1½-qt. casserole.

COOK tapioca mixture, stirring every 30 sec., until boiling (about 5 min.).

OVERALL COOKING TIME: 5:00

Peach Tapioca Cream 23
(page 507)

Follow 22 Recipe with additions as in △ Recipe.

Chocolate Tapioca Cream 24
(page 507)

Follow 22 Recipe with addition as in △ Recipe.

Peppermint Tapioca 25 Cream *(page 507)*

Follow 22 Recipe with addition as in △ Recipe.

Luscious Lemon Cheese Cake 26 *(Page 509)*

Use an 8-in. round baking pan. *Do not grease.*

Assemble cake and SLOWCOOK uncovered, rotating pan every 2 min., until filling is set (about 20 min.).

Let stand until cool.

OVERALL COOKING TIME: 20:00

Old-Fashioned 27 English Plum Pudding *(page 510)*

Use a 1½-qt. casserole and a 3-qt. casserole as the steamer (see preceding introduction).

Put casserole in steamer, cover and COOK, rotating every 2 min., until bubbling stops and pudding starts to pull away from the pan sides. Test with cake tester; it should come out clean.

OVERALL COOKING TIME: 60:00

Steamed Chocolate Pudding
(page 511) 28

Use a 1½-qt. casserole. *Do not grease.* Use a 3-qt. casserole as the steamer (see preceding introduction).

COOK to melt chocolate (about 3 min.).

Put pudding in casserole and place in steamer. Cover with a greased lid. COOK, rotating every 2 min., until bubbling stops and it starts to pull away from the pan sides (about 10 min.). Then test with a knife or cake tester; it should come out clean.

OVERALL COOKING TIME: 13:00

Raisin Puff Pudding 29 with Lemon Sauce *(page 512)*

Use a 1½-qt. casserole. *Do not grease.* Use a 3-qt. casserole as the steamer (see preceding introduction).

Assemble pudding in casserole. Cover with a greased lid. Put casserole in steamer, cover and COOK, rotating every 2 min., until bubbling stops and it starts to pull away from the pan sides (about 35 min.). Then test for doneness with a cake tester; it should come out clean.

For Lemon Sauce—Use a 1½-qt. casserole.

COOK to boil water (about 4 min.).

Add to sugar mixture and COOK, stirring every 1 min., until boiling (about 3 min.).

Add egg mixture and COOK, stirring every 30 sec., to thicken (about 3 min.).

OVERALL COOKING TIME: 42:00

Magic Coconut Nests 30
(page 523)

Use pleated muffin papers inserted in custard cups and a small casserole.

In small casserole, COOK milk and chocolate, stirring every 30 sec., until thick (about 3 min.).

COOK nests, rotating every 1 min., until top edges are firm (about 8 min.).

Let cool, then peel off muffing papers.
OVERALL COOKING TIME: 11:00

Trifle *(page 526)* 31

Use a 1½-qt. casserole.

COOK to scald milk (about 5 min.).

Blend egg-sugar mixture into milk. Strain into clean casserole.

COOK, stirring every 1 min., to thicken slightly (about 5 min.).
OVERALL COOKING TIME: 10:00

Peach Cloud Dessert 32
(page 531)

Use a 1½-qt. casserole.

Combine egg yolks, sugar and sirup in casserole. COOK, stirring every 1 min., to thicken (about 5 min.).

OVERALL COOKING TIME: 5:00

Orange Marlow *(page 533)* 33

Use a 1½-qt. casserole.

Combine orange juice and marshmallows and COOK, stirring every 1 min., to melt marshmallows (about 5 min.).
OVERALL COOKING TIME: 5:00

Chocolate Marlow 34
(page 533)

Follow 33 Recipe with changes as in ⚠ Recipe.

Raspberry Marlow 35
(page 533)

Follow 33 Recipe with changes as in ⚠ Recipe.

Favorite Vanilla Ice 36
Cream *(page 534)*

Use a 1½-qt. casserole.

COOK to scald milk (about 6 min.).

Add sugar, flour and salt and COOK, stirring every 30 sec., until sugar is dissolved (about 3 min.).

Add egg yolk mixture and COOK, stirring every 30 sec., until slightly thickened and will coat a silver spoon (about 5 min.).
OVERALL COOKING TIME: 16:00

French Vanilla Ice 37
Cream *(page 535)*

Follow 36 Recipe with changes as in ⚠ Recipe.

Chocolate Ice Cream **38**
(page 535)

Follow **36** Recipe with changes as in △ Recipe.

Chocolate-Chip Ice Cream **39** *(page 535)*

Follow **36** Recipe with addition as in △ Recipe.

Butter-Pecan Ice Cream **40** *(page 535)*

Follow **36** Recipe with additions as in △ Recipe, except in browning skillet, COOK to melt butter. Add pecans and COOK, stirring every 1 min., to lightly brown (about 5 min.).

Berry Ice Cream *(page 535)* **41**

Follow **36** Recipe with addition as in △ Recipe.

Peach Ice Cream *(page 535)* **42**

Follow **36** Recipe with changes as in △ Recipe.

Two-Flavored Brick Ice Cream *(page 535)* **43**

Follow **36** Recipe with changes as in △ Recipe.

Caramel Ice Cream **44**
(page 536)

Use a browning skillet for the sirup and a 2-qt. casserole for the ice cream mixture.

For Caramel Sirup—COOK, stirring every 30 sec., to melt sugar (about 5 min.).

Add water and COOK, stirring every 1 min., until bubbling (about 2 min.).

For Ice Cream—COOK to scald milk (about 8 min.). Add sugar, flour, salt and COOK, stirring every 30 sec., until boiling (about 3 min.).

Add egg yolk mixture and COOK, stirring every 1 min., until thick (about 5 min.).

OVERALL COOKING TIME: 23:00

Frozen Lemon Custard **45**
(page 539)

Use a small casserole.

COOK egg yolk-sugar mixture, stirring every 1 min., until thick (about 5 min.).

OVERALL COOKING TIME: 5:00

Frozen Coconut Custard **46**
(page 539)

Follow **45** Recipe with addition as in △ Recipe.

DESSERTS in the SLOW COOKER

The taste of fresh cooked fruits and homemade applesauce are a pleasure which most people enjoy only by remembering Grandmother's kitchen. Today, such dishes are usually considered too time consuming to bother with. If you want to revive a little bit of Grandmother's kitchen in your own home, try these cooked fruit recipes in the slow cooker. They are not only as delicious as you remember them, but they are virtually trouble-free to prepare and nutritious, too. Just arrange the ingredients in the slow cooker and forget them, in some cases as long as overnight. You can even skip the pre-soaking of the dried fruits. The **Encore Baked Apples** are particularly delicious, tender and flavorful, but firm in texture.

The recipes for puddings included are also good, evoking memories of old-fashioned holidays.

The puddings are cooked in the special slow cooker 2-qt. baking tin (a 2-lb. coffee can will do).

Put the pudding mixture in the baking tin, cover the top of the tin securely with plastic wrap and place the tin in the slow cooker. Cover the slow cooker, leaving the top slightly ajar to allow moisture to escape and set on HIGH for the required number of hours.

The **Holiday Bread Pudding** is cooked without a top on the baking tin, but with paper towels lining the top of the slow cooker (hold them in place with rubber bands) and two or three layers of paper towelling laid across the top of the slow cooker. Set on the top on the slow cooker, but again, leave it slightly ajar. It will still hold the paper towel layers in place. The arrangement is similar for the **New England Pumpkin Pudding** except the top of the baking tin is closed.

COOKING TIME—Timing on the puddings is more critical than with most slow cooker recipes. There is not much more than 15 minutes leeway on the timings we recommend, so plan to be near the kitchen towards the end of the cooking time.

TEST FOR DONENESS—The puddings are done when they start to pull away from the sides of the tin and when a cake tester inserted in the center comes out clean. Do not open the slow cooker to test the puddings more than 30 minutes before the end of the specified cooking time, however, or they will fall.

REMINDERS—For other hints on slow cooking and an easy-to-read chart comparing differences in settings among brands of slow cookers, see the introductory chapter, **Home Cooking in the Slow Cooker.**

Stewed Prunes (page 494) **1**

Use a 3½-qt. slow cooker.

Do not pre-soak prunes.

Put prunes in slow cooker and add water to barely cover.

Cook on LOW for 8 to 10 hrs.

Cooked Apricots **2**
(page 494)

Follow **1** Recipe with changes as in △ Recipe.

Spiced Applesauce **3**
(page 495)

Use a 3½-qt. slow cooker.

Assemble all ingredients in slow cooker, except use only ½ cup water (instead of ¾ cup).

Cook on LOW for 8 to 10 hrs.

Rosy Pink Applesauce **4**
(page 495)

Follow **3** Recipe with changes as in △ Recipe.

Fruit Juice Applesauce **5**
(page 495)

Follow **4** Recipe with changes as in △ Recipe.

Encore Baked Apples **6**
(page 496)

Use a 5-qt. slow cooker.

Arrange apples in slow cooker. Add water to a depth of ¼ in. (instead of ½ in.), just to keep apples from sticking to the bottom of the slow cooker.

Cook on LOW for 5 to 6 hrs.

Variety Baked Apples 7
(page 496)

Follow **6** Recipe with changes as in ⚠ Recipe.

Blushing Pears *(page 499)* 8

Use a 3½-qt. slow cooker.

Place all ingredients, including sugar mixture, in slow cooker.

Cover and cook on LOW for 5 to 6 hours.

Blushing Peaches 9
(page 499)

Follow **8** Recipe with changes as in △ Recipe, except cook on LOW for 4 to 5 hrs.

Holiday Bread Pudding 10
(page 504)

Use a 3½-qt. slow cooker with a 2-qt. baking tin.

Line bottom of baking tin with ungreased waxed paper.

Fill baking tin with pudding mixture. Do not cover. Lay paper towels on top of slow cooker. Also line the lid of the slow cooker with paper towelling held in place with rubber bands. Leave cover of slow cooker slightly ajar.

Cook on HIGH for 3 to 3½ hrs.

New England Pumpkin Pudding *(page 505)* 11

Use a 3½-qt. slow cooker with a 2-qt. baking tin.

Line bottom of baking tin with waxed paper. *Do not grease.* Fill tin with pudding mixture and cover. Lay paper towelling on top of slow cooker; also line lid of slow cooker with paper towels held in place with rubber bands. Leave slow cooker lid slightly ajar.

Cook on HIGH for 4 to 4½ hrs.

Steamed Chocolate Pudding 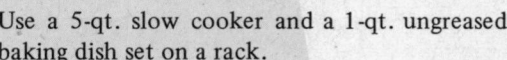 12
(page 511)

Use a 5-qt. slow cooker and a 1-qt. ungreased baking dish set on a rack.

Fill baking dish with pudding mixture and cover with plastic wrap. Cover the slow cooker lid with plastic wrap and place on slow cooker. This insures the appropriate amount of steam.

Cook on HIGH for 4 hrs.

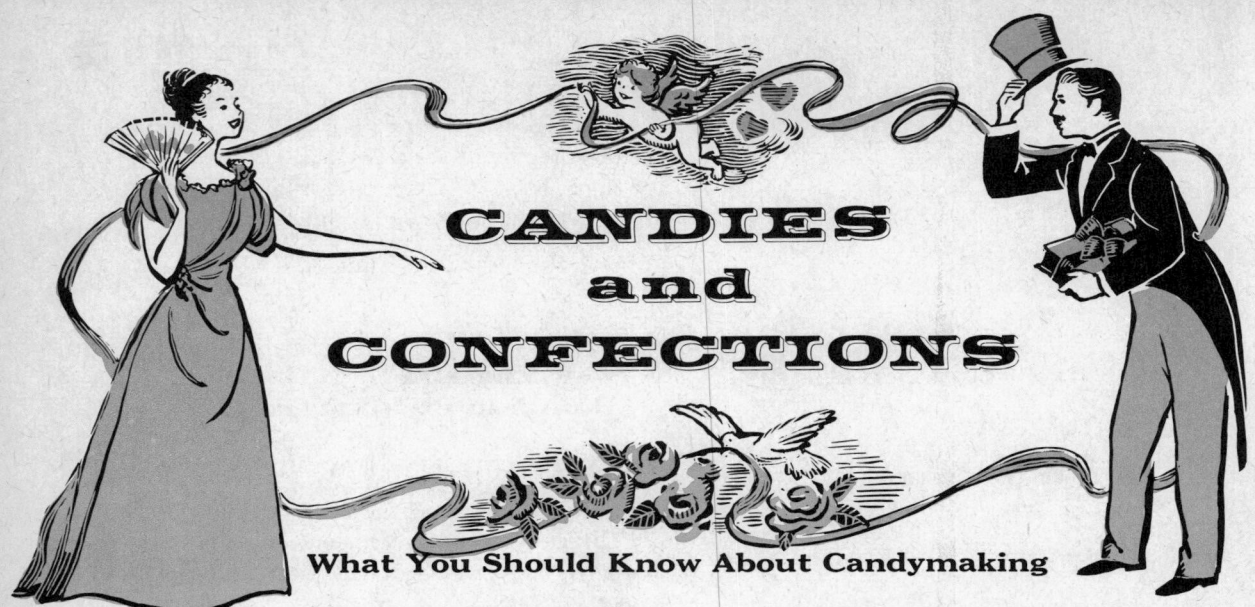

CANDIES and CONFECTIONS

What You Should Know About Candymaking

There is nothing like a box of beautifully made candies for telling some one that you love him— or her. And what promotes good-natured camaraderie more surely than an evening of candymaking in the kitchen? The taffy-pulls and fudgemaking with which young people amused themselves for generations have never wholly passed from our community traditions—and a good thing, too. But candies are more than a casual ministering to the sweet tooth or a means to sociability. At their best they represent a happy blend of art and science, of beauty and delectability that makes candymaking one of the most rewarding of all the household arts.

TYPES—Candies are usually classified as two types —crystalline and noncrystalline.

Crystalline—The outstanding characteristic of standard crystalline candy is that the sugar crystals are so small that the candy at all times feels creamy and velvety to the tongue. Fondant, fudge, panocha, bonbons, pralines, nougat, divinity and kisses are common examples.

To produce great numbers of very tiny crystals and thereby ensure a creamy candy: 1) The sugar must be completely dissolved. 2) The sugar solution must be boiled to a certain temperature and then cooled to a much lower temperature before agitation or beating thereby producing a highly supersaturated solution (a solution holding more dissolved sugar than it ordinarily would at this lower temperature). 3) The sugar crystals in the supersaturated solution must recrystalize in a great number of very tiny crystals. Therefore, when the mixture has cooled to the proper temperature,

it must be extensively agitated or beaten at this temperature so many small crystals may form. 4) Ingredients known as interfering substances help to avoid the formation of large crystals. In fudge, these substances are butter, corn sirup and the starch of chocolate or cocoa; in fondant, corn sirup and an acid such as lemon juice, vinegar or cream of tartar are generally used; in divinity, egg protein is the substance.

Noncrystalline—Toffee, peanut brittle, lollipops, butterscotch and caramels are examples of noncrystalline candies. As in making crystalline candies, completely dissolving the sugar crystals is important. The mixture must be cooked to a high enough temperature to produce a highly viscous (resistance of the solution to pouring) solution which upon cooling quickly immediately becomes thicker (as caramels) or solidifies (as lollipops).

Ingredients which help to produce a viscous mixture in caramels are the large quantities of milk solids and fat. In caramels, the cream with corn sirup, or milk solids are classified as interfering substances and help to prevent the formation of sugar crystals. If the total amount of cream or milk is added at the beginning of cooking period of caramels, the milk or cream may curdle. Therefore, cream or milk should be added in more than one addition to avoid curdling.

During pulling of taffies, air bubbles become incorporated causing taffies to become white or, if made with molasses, become much lighter in color.

Baking soda is frequently added to brittles. It neutralizes the acidity; it also gives a porous texture to the brittle because of gas formation.

When You Make Candy or Cook Sirup

MAKE CANDY on a dry, cool day for best results. If it is necessary to make candy on a day when the humidity is high (an excessive amount of moisture in the air), cook the candy two degrees higher than the temperature given in the recipe; this should help to produce a satisfactory product.

A CANDY THERMOMETER is an accurate guide to correct stages of cooking. Test it for accuracy each time before using as the boiling point of water varies from day to day depending upon atmospheric pressure (barometric reading). Stand thermometer in boiling water (3-in. depth) for 10 minutes. It should read 212°F at sea level; if there is any variation, add or subtract the same number of degrees to or from the temperature required for the candy.

If you do not know at what degree water boils in your community, take the average of several successive daily readings (thermometer standing in 3-in. depth of boiling water for 10 minutes). The boiling point of water drops 1°F for each 500 feet of increased altitude. Correct the temperatures given in the sirup stages in accordance with the altitude in your community.

Hang thermometer on pan so it does not touch side or bottom of pan, being certain that the bulb is covered with mixture, not just foam. Check temperature readings at eye level.

Sirup Stages and Temperatures

Thread (230°F to 234°F)—Spins 2-in. thread when allowed to drop from fork or spoon.
Soft Ball (234°F to 240°F)—Forms a soft ball in very cold water; flattens when taken from water.
Firm Ball (244°F to 248°F)—Forms a firm ball in very cold water; does not flatten in fingers.
Hard Ball (250°F to 266°F)—Forms a ball which is pliable yet hard enough to hold its shape in very cold water.
Soft Crack (270°F to 290°F)—Forms threads which are hard but not brittle in very cold water.
Hard Crack (300°F to 310°F)—Forms threads which are hard and brittle in very cold water.

THE SAUCEPAN used for cooking candy should be large enough to allow contents to boil freely without running over. The cover should be tight-fitting, if cover is needed.

PREVENT GRAININESS in candy by completely dissolving all the sugar crystals; stirring and heating the sugar solution will help. If candy is stirred during cooking, stirring must stop before end of cooking period.

Cover saucepan for the first 5 minutes of boiling time, if recipe so directs. The steam formed helps to wash down any crystals that may have remained on the sides of pan.

Wash down crystals from sides of pan during cooking with a pastry brush dipped in water; move candy thermometer to one side and wash down any crystals that may have formed under thermometer.

Use clean spoons for each process—stirring, testing and beating.

Do not move, jar or stir candy during cooling period because any agitation may cause the formation of large, coarse crystals—the result a grainy, sugary candy.

Pour candy, holding saucepan within an inch or so of cooling pan or surface.

Do not scrape bottom and sides of saucepan.

STIR CANDY gently while cooking without splashing sides of pan, if recipe directs that candy be stirred. Move wooden spoon back and forth across bottom of pan with every few strokes.

AN ELECTRIC MIXER is better for beating divinity than beating it by hand because of the time required to beat divinity and the stiffness of the mass at the end of beating.

A MARBLE SLAB is used by professional candy-makers because it has a smooth cold surface that cools candies quickly. It is easier to work large quantities of fondant and fudge on a marble slab than to beat them.

Chocolate Fudge 1

Butter an 8x8x2-in. pan. Set out a candy thermometer.

Put into a heavy 3-qt. saucepan
1⅓ cups milk
4 sq. (4 oz.) chocolate
Stir over low heat until chocolate is melted. Do not allow mixture to boil. Stir in
4 cups sugar
2 tablespoons white corn sirup
½ teaspoon salt
Stir over low heat until sugar is dissolved. Increase heat and bring mixture to boiling. Put candy thermometer in place. Cook, stirring occasionally to prevent scorching, until mixture reaches 234°F (soft ball stage, *page 543*; remove from heat while testing). During cooking, wash crystals (*page 543*) from sides of pan from time to time. Remove from heat.

Set aside until just cool enough to hold pan on hand. Do not jar pan or stir. When cool, add
¼ cup butter or margarine
4 teaspoons vanilla extract
Beat vigorously until mixture loses its gloss. Quickly turn into the buttered pan without scraping bottom and sides of saucepan and spread evenly. Set aside to cool.

When firm, cut into 1½-in. squares.
About 2 doz. pieces of fudge

⚠ Cocoa Fudge 2

Follow ▲ Recipe. Omit chocolate. Mix ¾ cup **cocoa** with sugar before adding milk.

⚠ Tutti-Frutti Fudge 3

Follow ▲ Recipe. Before turning candy into pan mix in ⅓ cup each: chopped **candied cherries pineapple and raisins.**

⚠ Marshmallow Fudge 4

Follow ▲ Recipe. Add 32 (½ lb.) **marshmallows,** cut in quarters (*page 12*), with the butter or margarine.

Chocolate Fudge and Hawaiian Fudge

⚠ Peanut Butter Fudge

Follow ▲ Recipe. Substitute 6 tablespoons **peanut butter** for butter or margarine.

⚠ Pecan Fudge 5

Follow ▲ Recipe. Mix in 2 cups (about 8 oz.) chopped **pecans.**

Hawaiian Fudge 6

BEATRICE STOCKDALE, GOLDFIELD, IOWA

Butter an 8x8x2-in. pan. Set out a candy thermometer and a heavy 3-qt. saucepan.

Coarsely chop and set aside
1 cup (about 4 oz.) pecans
Drain contents of
1 14-oz. can crushed pineapple
(Reserve pineapple sirup for use in other food preparation.)

Mix in the saucepan the pineapple and
4 cups sugar
1 cup cream
Stir over low heat until sugar is dissolved. Increase heat and bring mixture to boiling. Put candy thermometer in place. Cook, stirring occasionally to prevent scorching, until mixture reaches 234°F (soft ball stage, *page*

543; remove from heat while testing). During cooking, wash crystals (*page 543*) from sides of pan from time to time. Remove from heat.

Set aside until just cool enough to hold pan on hand. Do not jar pan or stir. When cool, add

2 tablespoons butter
2 teaspoons vanilla extract

Beat vigorously until mixture loses its gloss. With a few strokes stir in the chopped pecans. Quickly turn into the buttered pan without scraping bottom and sides of saucepan and spread evenly. Set aside to cool.

When cool, cut into 1½-in. squares.

About 2 doz. pieces of fudge

Note: For extra-smooth, mellow flavor, allow fudge to stand overnight before serving.

Black Walnut-Caramel Fudge

DORA C. BLOSE, ELYSBURG, PA.

The family will love this delectable candy.

Butter an 8x8x2-in. pan. Set out a candy thermometer and a heavy 3-qt. saucepan.

Chop and set aside

2 cups (about 7 oz.) black walnuts

Measure into a large, heavy light-colored skillet (a black skillet makes it difficult to see the color of the sirup)

2 cups sugar

Put the skillet over low heat. With back of wooden spoon, gently keep sugar moving toward center of skillet until it melts. Remove from heat and set aside.

Mix together in the saucepan

4 cups sugar
2 cups milk

Stir over low heat until sugar is dissolved. Increase heat and bring to boiling. Add the melted sugar very slowly, stirring constantly. Put candy thermometer in place. Cook, stirring occasionally to prevent scorching, until mixture reaches 234°F (soft ball stage, *page*

543; remove from heat while testing). During cooking, wash crystals (*page 543*) from sides of pan. Remove from heat.

Set aside until just cool enough to hold pan on hand. Do not jar pan or stir. When cool, add

2 teaspoons vanilla extract

Beat vigorously until mixture loses its gloss. With a few strokes stir in the chopped nuts. Quickly turn into the buttered pan without scraping bottom and sides of saucepan and spread evenly. Set aside to cool.

When cool, cut into 1½-in. squares.

About 2 doz. pieces of fudge

Penuche

(Panocha)

BETHEL OAKLEY, OWENSBORO, KY.

Butter an 8x8x2-in. pan. Set out a candy thermometer.

Coarsely chop and set aside

¾ cup (about 3 oz.) pecans

Mix together in a heavy 2-qt. saucepan

3 cups firmly packed brown sugar
1 cup plus 2 tablespoons milk
¼ teaspoon salt

Stir over low heat until sugar is dissolved. Increase heat and bring mixture to boiling, stirring frequently. Put candy thermometer in place. Cook, stirring occasionally to prevent scorching, until mixture reaches 234°F (soft ball stage, *page 543*; remove from heat while testing). During cooking, wash crystals (*page 543*) from sides of pan. Remove from heat. Set aside until just cool enough to hold pan on hand. Do not jar pan or stir. When cool, add

3 tablespoons butter
1½ teaspoons vanilla extract

Beat vigorously until mixture loses its gloss. With a few strokes stir in the chopped nuts. Quickly turn into the buttered pan without scraping bottom and sides of saucepan and spread evenly. Set aside to cool.

When cool, cut into 1½-in. squares.

About 2 doz. pieces of Penuche

▲ Chocolate Divinity 7

Creamy texture and smooth flavor justify the time required to make this superb candy.

Lightly butter a baking sheet. Set out a candy thermometer.

Melt (*page 12*) and set aside to cool
   2 sq. (2 oz.) chocolate
Mix together in a heavy 2-qt. saucepan having a tight-fitting cover
   2 cups sugar
   ⅔ cup water
   ½ cup white corn sirup
   ¼ teaspoon salt
Stir over low heat until sugar is dissolved. Increase heat and bring mixture to boiling. Cover saucepan and boil mixture gently 5 min. Uncover and put candy thermometer in place. Cook without stirring until mixture reaches 252°F (hard ball stage, *page 543*; remove from heat while testing). During cooking, wash crystals (*page 543*) from sides of pan from time to time.

Meanwhile, beat in a large mixer bowl until stiff (but not dry) peaks are formed
   3 egg whites
When sirup reaches 252°F, immediately remove from heat and remove thermometer. Beating constantly with an electric mixer on high speed, pour the sirup in a steady stream onto the stiffly beaten egg whites (do not pour onto beaters). When mixture begins to lose its gloss, turn off motor and lift beaters. In the early stage, the mass flows down from the beaters in a continuous ribbon. Continue beating until mixture no longer flows but holds its shape (about 35 min.).

At this point, *quickly* blend in the cooled chocolate and
   1 teaspoon vanilla extract
Drop by teaspoonfuls onto the baking sheet. Cool thoroughly.

Wrap in waxed or glassine paper and store in a cool place in a tightly covered container.
   About 4 doz. pieces of divinity

⚠ Divinity 8

Follow ▲ Recipe. Omit chocolate.

⚠ Seafoam Divinity

Follow ▲ Recipe. Omit chocolate. Decrease sugar to ¾ cup and blend in 1¼ cups firmly packed brown sugar. Blend in 1 cup (about 4 oz.) chopped nuts with vanilla extract.

▲ Fondant

Allow this creamy confection to ripen for twenty-four hours before shaping into candies.

Set out a candy thermometer and a large platter or marble slab. (Surface must be smooth and level.)

Mix together in a heavy 3-qt. saucepan having a tight-fitting cover
   3 cups sugar
   1½ cups water
   ¼ teaspoon cream of tartar
Stir over low heat until sugar is dissolved. Increase heat and bring mixture to boiling. Cover saucepan and boil mixture gently 5 min. Uncover and put candy thermometer in place. Continue cooking without stirring. During cooking, wash crystals (*page 543*) from sides of saucepan from time to time. Cook until mixture reaches 238°F (soft ball stage, *page 543*; remove mixture from heat while testing). Remove candy thermometer.

Wipe the platter or slab with damp cloth. Immediately pour sirup onto the platter or slab; do not scrape pan. Without stirring, cool to lukewarm or until just cool enough to hold platter on hand. Pour onto cooled sirup

1 teaspoon vanilla extract

With a wide spatula or wooden spoon, work fondant in circles from edges to center until white and creamy. Pile into a mound, cover with a bowl and allow to rest 20 to 30 min.

With hands, work fondant (in a kneading motion) until soft and smooth.

Ripen at least 24 hrs. in a tightly covered jar. Shape into candies or use in following recipes.

About 1¼ lbs. fondant

⚠ **Bonbons**

Follow ▲ Recipe. Reserve about one third of ripened fondant for dipping. Divide remainder into three or more portions. Work into one portion several drops **pistachio extract** and less than a drop of **green food coloring** (dip tip of a wooden pick into food coloring, then into fondant). In another portion use **vanilla extract** or **almond extract**. Use **rose extract** and **red food coloring** for the remainder. If adding finely chopped **nuts, coconut, candied fruits, dates, figs** or **raisins**, work in with fingers only until blended. (Use alone or in any combination.)

Shape into rolls 1 in. in diameter. Cut into small uniform pieces and shape into balls or ovals, slightly flattened on one side. Keep small; dipping increases size. Allow fondant to stand on racks or trays lined with waxed paper. Dry several hours before dipping.

When ready to dip, place reserved fondant in top of double boiler. Melt over simmering water, stirring constantly. Heat to 130°F (no higher). Add flavoring and coloring. Dip a center to test for proper coating consistency.

Using a fork or candy dipper, lower a center, rounded side down, into fondant and cover completely with fondant. Immediately remove, scraping bonbon on edge of pan to remove excess fondant. Place flattened side down onto waxed paper. Make fancy swirl on top by twirling fork or dipper. (Dipping fondant may be reheated to maintain proper consistency.)

⚠ **Fondant Patties**

Follow ▲ Recipe. Fondant can be used for making patties about 1 hr. after working fondant with hands. Cover a flat surface with waxed paper or aluminum foil.

Stirring constantly, melt fondant over simmering water, heating fondant to 130°F (no higher). Add desired coloring and flavoring. If fondant is not the consistency of thick cream, thin it with **hot water,** stirring in 1 teaspoonful at a time. Pour fondant into rounds (about the size of quarters) from measuring cup or small pan having a sharp lip. (Warm measuring cup or pan with hot water and dry before filling with fondant.)

When patties are firm, arrange on edge, side-by-side, with small squares of waxed paper separating them. *About 5 doz. patties*

⚠ **Peppermint Patties**

Follow ⚠ Recipe. Blend into the melted fondant, a drop at a time, **red food coloring** and **peppermint extract.**

▲ Nougat Fingers

Butter a 10x6x1½-in. pan. Set out a candy thermometer and a heavy 2-qt. saucepan.

Coarsely chop and set aside
½ cup (about 3 oz.) blanched almonds (page 11)
Cut (*page 12*) into halves and set aside
½ cup (about 3 oz.) candied red cherries
(If necessary, pat cherries dry between pieces of absorbent paper.)

Mix together in the saucepan
2½ cups sugar
¾ cup white corn sirup
½ cup water
Stir over low heat until sugar is dissolved. Increase heat and bring mixture to boiling. Cover saucepan and boil mixture gently 5 min. Uncover and put candy thermometer in place. Cook without stirring until mixture reaches 270°F (soft crack stage, *page 543*; remove from heat while testing). During cooking, wash crystals (*page 543*) from sides of saucepan from time to time.

Meanwhile, beat in a large mixer bowl until stiff (but not dry) peaks are formed
⅓ cup egg whites (about 3 egg whites)
⅛ teaspoon salt
When the sirup reaches 270°F, immediately remove from heat and remove thermometer. While bubbles are subsiding, carefully wash down crystals from pouring side of pan.

Beating constantly with an electric mixer on medium speed, pour the sirup in a steady fine stream into center of egg whites (do not pour onto beaters). Do not scrape bottom or sides of saucepan. Stop beating as soon as ingredients are well mixed.

(If a hand rotary beater must be substituted for the electric mixer, turn the beater on its side; beat mixture in spoon fashion while adding the sirup. Then turn beater upright and beat hard to thoroughly mix the sirup and egg whites.)

Stir in the almonds, cherries and
1 teaspoon vanilla extract
½ teaspoon almond extract
Beat with spoon until mixture falls in chunks from the spoon held about 12 in. above the bowl. Turn candy into the prepared pan and press down firmly and evenly with hand. Set aside on cooling rack.

When nougat is completely cool, cover pan tightly. Set aside to ripen at least 24 hrs.

Loosen sides of candy and shake well to remove block of candy from pan to cutting board. Cut with a sharp, long-bladed knife into pieces about 2x1 in. Wrap each piece in waxed or glassine paper.

Store in a tightly covered container in a cool, dry place.   *About 2½ doz. Nougat Fingers*

△ Nougat Centers for Caramel-Pecan Roll

Butter a 15½x10½x1-in. jelly roll pan and set out a 1-qt. saucepan having a tight-fitting cover. Prepare one-half ▲ Recipe. Substitute finely chopped **pecans** for toasted almonds; chop cherries finely. Omit almond extract.

Turn the mixture onto buttered pan and divide into two equal mounds. With buttered hands shape each mound into a roll or block about 15 in. long. Allow nougat to set a few minutes. Wrap each portion tightly in waxed paper; let stand until nougat holds its shape.

See recipe for **Caramel-Pecan Roll** (*on this page*) to complete candy.   *Two Nougat Centers*

Caramel-Pecan Roll

Here's a double chance to use your candy-making skill and to feel the thrill of pride that comes from creating something fine.

Prepare and set aside
Nougat Centers for Caramel-Pecan Roll (on this page)

Butter a 15½x10½x1-in. jelly roll pan. Set out a candy thermometer and a heavy 1½-qt. saucepan. Lay out two sheets of waxed paper about 20 in. long; lay the two sheets side by side and clip lengthwise edges together.

Spread out on the waxed paper over an area the size of the jelly roll pan
2½ cups (about 10 oz.) pecan halves
Set aside.

Set out in a warm place
1 cup cream
¼ cup butter
Mix together in the saucepan
1 cup sugar
1 cup white corn sirup
Few grains salt
Stir over low heat until sugar is dissolved. Increase heat and bring mixture to boiling. Put candy thermometer in place. Cook, without stirring, until mixture reaches 244°F (firm ball stage, *page 543*; remove from heat while testing). During cooking, wash crystals (*page 543*) from sides of saucepan from time to time.

Gently stir mixture and add ¼ cup of the cream so slowly that boiling will not stop. Keeping mixture boiling vigorously, add the remaining cream by tablespoonfuls. Occasionally stir mixture between additions of cream. (The addition of the cream will take about 25 min.) Stir in the butter. Cook mixture to 244°F.

Set pan on cooling rack; cool mixture to 200°F.

Remove candy thermometer. Mix in
1½ teaspoons vanilla extract
Turn into buttered pan without scraping bottom and sides of saucepan. Let stand on a cooling rack a few minutes until caramel is just cool enough to handle quickly with the hands. (If caramel gets too cool, it will not stick to the pecans.)

Loosen the caramel from the sides of the pan; carefully turn sheet of caramel over the pecans. Carefully and gently press the caramel onto nuts.

Lay one Nougat Center at edge of caramel sheet. Roll until the nougat is coated with caramel. Cut caramel where coating meets. Form a second roll.

Wrap each caramel roll tightly in waxed paper. Set aside until firm enough to cut. To store caramel pecan rolls, wrap in waxed or glassine paper and place in a tightly covered container. Store in a cool, dry place.

For serving, slice candy with a sharp knife into pieces about ½ in. thick.
About 5 doz. pieces of candy

Molasses-Pecan Kisses

Butter a 15½x10½x1-in. jelly roll pan. Set out a candy thermometer.

Set out
48 (about 1 cup) pecan halves
Mix together in a heavy 3-qt. saucepan
1 cup firmly packed brown sugar
1 cup cream
½ cup light molasses
2 tablespoons butter
Stir over low heat until sugar is dissolved. Increase heat and bring mixture to boiling. Put candy thermometer in place. Cook, stirring constantly, until mixture reaches 250°F (hard ball stage; *page 543*; remove from heat while testing). During cooking, wash crystals (*page 543*) from sides of pan from time to time.

Remove saucepan from heat and remove thermometer. Stir in
1 teaspoon vanilla extract
Pour into the buttered pan without scraping bottom and sides of saucepan. Set aside until just cool enough to hold pan on palm of hand.

Cut candy into rectangles about 2½x1¼ in. Place a pecan half in center of each rectangle. Keeping pecan in center, roll candy over pecan half, forming a pecan kiss.

Wrap kisses in waxed or glassine paper. Store in a covered container in a cool, dry place.
About 4 doz. kisses

Chocolate Caramels Supreme

Butter an 8x8x2-in. pan. Set out a candy thermometer and a heavy 3-qt. saucepan.

Chop and set aside
⅔ cup (about 3 oz.) nuts
Melt (*page 12*) and set aside to cool
4 sq. (4 oz.) chocolate
Set out
3 cups heavy cream
2 tablespoons butter
Pour 1 cup of the cream into the saucepan and mix in
2 cups sugar
1 cup white corn sirup
¼ teaspoon salt
Stir over low heat until sugar is dissolved. Increase heat and bring mixture to boiling. Put candy thermometer in place. Cook, stirring frequently, until mixture reaches 234°F (soft ball stage, *page 543*; remove from heat while testing). During cooking, wash crystals (*page 543*) from sides of saucepan from time to time. Stirring constantly, gradually add another cup of cream to saucepan, so slowly that boiling will not stop. Continue cooking, stirring frequently, over low heat until mixture reaches 234°F. Stirring constantly, gradually add remaining cream and the butter to mixture so slowly that boiling will not stop.

Stirring frequently, cook to 244°F (firm ball stage, *page 543*; remove from heat while testing). (Consistency of the candy tested in cold water will be the consistency of the caramel. Caramel mixture cooked to 246°F will give a slightly firmer caramel than mixture cooked to 244°F.)

Remove mixture from heat and remove candy thermometer. Immediately add the melted chocolate and nuts to mixture with
1 tablespoon vanilla extract
Stir just until blended. Immediately pour hot mixture into the buttered pan. Do not scrape bottom and sides of saucepan. Set caramel mixture aside on cooling rack in a cool place.

Creamy and Cocoa Taffy

When completely cooled, (several hours or overnight) invert onto a cutting board and remove pan. Working in a cool place, mark candy into 1-in. squares; using a sharp, long-bladed knife, cut candy with a sawing motion. Wrap each caramel tightly in waxed or glassine paper. Store in a covered container in a cool, dry place.   *About 5½ doz. caramels*

Note: For **Vanilla Caramels,** omit chocolate.

▲ Creamy Taffy

Butter a large, shallow pan or platter. Set out a candy thermometer.

Mix together in a heavy 2-qt. saucepan
2¼ cups sugar
1½ cups white corn sirup
4 teaspoons vinegar
¼ teaspoon salt
Stir over low heat until sugar is dissolved. Increase heat and bring to boiling, stirring constantly. Add slowly so boiling does not stop
½ cup undiluted evaporated milk
Put candy thermometer in place. Continue cooking, stirring constantly, until mixture reaches 248°F (firm ball stage, *page 543*; remove from heat while testing). During cooking, wash crystals (*page 543*) from sides of saucepan from time to time. Remove from heat and remove thermometer. Immediately

pour mixture into the buttered pan without scraping bottom and sides of saucepan.

When mixture is just cool enough to handle, butter hands. Work in a cool place. Pull a small portion of the taffy at a time, using only the tips of the fingers, until candy is white in color and no longer sticky to the touch. Twist pulled strip slightly and place on waxed paper or on a board. Cut with scissors into 1-in. pieces. Wrap in waxed or glassine paper.

Store in a tightly covered container in a cool, dry place.   *About 8 doz. pieces of taffy*

⚠ Brown Sugar Taffy

Follow ▲ Recipe. Substitute 2¼ cups firmly packed **brown sugar** for the sugar.

⚠ Cocoa Taffy 10

Follow ▲ Recipe. Mix ⅔ cup **Dutch process cocoa** with the sugar.

Salt Water Taffy
NAOMI CHILDS, TIONESTA, PA.

Butter a large, shallow pan or platter. Set out a candy thermometer.

Mix together in a heavy 2-qt. saucepan
   2 cups sugar
   1¼ cups white corn sirup
   1 cup water

Stir over low heat until sugar is dissolved. Increase heat and bring mixture to boiling. Put candy thermometer in place. Continue cooking, stirring constantly, until mixture reaches 244°F (firm ball stage, *page 543*; remove from heat while testing). During cooking, wash crystals (*page 543*) from sides of saucepan from time to time. Remove from heat and remove thermometer. Immediately blend in
   1 tablespoon butter
   1½ teaspoons salt
Pour mixture into the buttered pan without scraping bottom and sides of saucepan.

When mixture is just cool enough to handle, butter hands. Work in a cool place. Pull a small portion of the taffy at a time, using only the tips of the fingers, until candy is firm and cool and no longer sticky to the touch. While pulling, work in
   Food coloring
   Extract
The amounts of food coloring and flavoring will depend on the amount of taffy being pulled and the color and flavor desired. Twist pulled strip slightly and place on waxed paper or on a board. Cut with scissors into 1-in. pieces. Wrap in waxed or glassine paper.

Store in a tightly covered container in a cool, dry place.   *About 6 doz. pieces of taffy*

Note: Good flavor and color combinations are **peppermint extract** and **red food coloring; wintergreen** and **green; lemon** and **yellow.** Or use **vanilla extract** and omit coloring.

Crackle Peanut Brittle 11

Lightly butter two baking sheets. Set out a candy thermometer.

Mix together in a heavy 3-qt. saucepan having a tight-fitting cover
- **2 cups sugar**
- **1 cup white corn sirup**
- **1 cup water**

Stir over low heat until sugar is dissolved. Increase heat and bring mixture to boiling. Cover saucepan and boil gently 5 min. Uncover and put candy thermometer in place. Continue cooking without stirring until mixture reaches 234°F (soft ball stage, *page 543*; remove from heat while testing). During cooking, wash crystals (*page 543*) from sides of saucepan from time to time. Mix in
- **2 cups (about 11 oz.) raw peanuts**
- **2 teaspoons butter**

Cook over low heat, stirring frequently, until mixture reaches 300°F (hard crack stage, *page 543*; remove from heat while testing). Remove from heat and remove thermometer. Add, mixing well
- **2 teaspoons baking soda**
- **1 teaspoon vanilla extract**

Pour onto the baking sheets, spreading as thinly as possible. As soon as candy is cool enough to handle, wet hands in water and stretch candy as thin as desired. Turn candy over and cool completely.

When cool and firm, break candy into medium-size pieces. Store in tightly covered container.

About 2 lbs. peanut brittle

Butterscotch  12

ESTHER E. BRUCKER, WHEATON, ILL.

A rich butterscotch that "melts in your mouth."

Butter an 8x8x2-in. pan. Set out a candy thermometer.

Mix together in a heavy 2-qt. saucepan
- **1 cup sugar**
- **½ cup butter**
- **¼ cup molasses**
- **2 tablespoons water**

Stir over low heat until sugar is dissolved. Increase heat and bring mixture to boiling.

Put candy thermometer in place. Cook, stirring constantly, until mixture reaches 300°F (hard crack stage, *page 543*; remove from heat while testing). During cooking, wash crystals (*page 543*) from sides of pan from time to time.

Remove from heat and remove thermometer.

Pour sirup into the buttered pan without scraping bottom and sides of saucepan. Mark candy quickly into squares with a sharp knife before it cools. Set aside to cool.

When hard, break candy into pieces. Store in tightly covered container in cool, dry place.

About ¾ lb. Butterscotch

Toffee

JEANNE BARRIE, RAYMOND, S. DAK.

Butter an 8x8x2-in. pan. Set out a candy thermometer.

Chop very finely and set aside
- **1½ cups (about 6 oz.) pecans**

Melt in a heavy 2-qt. saucepan
- **1 cup butter**

Add, stirring constantly until well blended
- **1 cup sugar**
- **3 tablespoons water**

Put candy thermometer in place. Stirring occasionally to prevent scorching, cook until mixture reaches 300°F (hard crack stage, *page 543*; remove from heat while testing). Remove from heat and remove thermometer.

Blend in

1 teaspoon vanilla extract

Quickly turn into the buttered pan and spread to corners. Immediately mark the candy into squares with a sharp knife. Set aside to cool.

Partially melt over simmering water, being careful not to overheat

½ lb. milk chocolate

Remove chocolate from simmering water and stir until completely melted. Set aside to cool.

When candy is cool, spread with one half of the melted chocolate. Sprinkle half of the chopped nuts over the chocolate. Invert pan onto a piece of waxed paper and remove pan. Cover with remaining chocolate and nuts. Set aside on cooling rack in a cool place.

When candy is hard, break into pieces. Store in a tightly covered container between layers of waxed paper, aluminum foil or moisture-vapor-proof material. Texture improves after several days. *About 1½ lbs. Toffee*

Pecan Pralines

Pralines are a Creole candy. French colonists in New Orleans adapted them from an old French recipe, substituting native American pecans for the almonds of France.

Set out a heavy 2-qt. saucepan and a candy thermometer. Line baking sheets with aluminum foil or greased waxed paper.

Measure

2 tablespoons butter
1½ cups (about 6 oz.) pecan halves

Set aside.

Mix together in the saucepan

1 cup firmly packed dark brown sugar
1 cup granulated sugar
½ cup cream

Stir over low heat until sugar is dissolved. Increase heat and bring mixture to boiling. Put candy thermometer in place. Cook without stirring until mixture reaches 230°F

Pecan Pralines

(thread stage, *page 543*; remove from heat while testing). During cooking, wash crystals (*page 543*) from sides of pan from time to time.

Stir in the butter and pecan halves.

Continue cooking, stirring occasionally to prevent scorching, until mixture reaches 234°F (soft ball stage, *page 543*; remove from heat while testing).

Remove from heat and remove thermometer. Cool mixture 2 to 3 min. without stirring. Gently stir mixture for about 2 min., or until it becomes slightly thicker and pecans appear well coated with sugar mixture. Quickly drop by tablespoonfuls onto the aluminum foil or greased waxed paper. The candy will flatten. Allow to stand until cool.

When completely cooled, wrap each praline in waxed or glassine paper. Store in a covered container in a cool, dry place.

About 1½ doz. pralines

⚠ Dark Pecan Pralines

Follow ▲ Recipe. Omit granulated sugar, increase brown sugar to 2 cups.

⚠ Almond Pralines

Follow ▲ Recipe. Omit pecans; add 1½ cups (about 8 oz.) blanched **almonds** (*page 11*).

Anise Lollipops 13

MRS. EDWARD M. LEE, MAPLETON, IOWA

Set out a candy thermometer and 16 to 20 small wooden skewers. Line baking sheets with aluminum foil or greased waxed paper.

Mix together in a heavy 2-qt. saucepan having a tight-fitting cover

> **2 cups sugar**
> **⅔ cup white corn sirup**
> **½ cup water**

Stir over low heat until sugar is dissolved. Increase heat and bring mixture to boiling. Cover saucepan and boil mixture gently 5 min. Uncover and put candy thermometer in place. Continue cooking without stirring. During cooking, wash crystals (*page 543*) from sides of saucepan from time to time. Cook until mixture reaches 300°F (hard crack stage, *page 543*; remove from heat while testing). Remove from heat and remove thermometer.

Add and stir in just to mix

> **¼ teaspoon anise oil**
> **8 to 10 drops red food coloring**

Quickly pour sirup into small rounds on the aluminum foil or waxed paper. The sirup will flatten out. Press a wooden skewer into each lollipop immediately. Allow to cool slightly. Remove from foil or waxed paper before lollipops are completely cooled.

When cool, wrap each lollipop in waxed or glassine paper. Store in covered container in a cool, dry place. *About 1½ doz. 3-in. lollipops*

Candied Orange Peel 14

MRS. WILL W. COTTINGHAM, ROLLA, MO.

Set out a candy thermometer and a heavy 2-qt. saucepan having a tight-fitting cover.

Rinse and carefully remove peel in large pieces from

> **3 large oranges (thick peel is preferred)**

(Set orange pulp aside for other use.)

Put the orange peel in the saucepan and add

> **1½ cups water**

Bring to boiling and cook until peel is almost tender (about 15 min.). Remove from heat and drain well. Add

> **1½ cups water**

Bring to boiling. Drain immediately. Repeat heating and draining process two more times. When finally drained, scrape the white part from the peel. Cut peel into ¼-in. strips.

Mix together in the saucepan

> **1 cup sugar**
> **½ cup water**

Stir over low heat until sugar is dissolved. Increase heat and bring mixture to boiling. Cover saucepan and boil gently 5 min. Uncover and put candy thermometer in place. Continue to cook without stirring. During cooking, wash crystals (*page 543*) from sides of saucepan from time to time. Cook until mixture reaches 230°F (thread stage, *page 543*; remove from heat while testing). Remove thermometer. Add the strips of peel and cook very slowly, stirring frequently, until most of the sirup is absorbed.

Place waxed. paper under cooling racks to catch sirup drippings. Remove peel from saucepan and spread over the racks. When peel has cooled slightly, roll, a few pieces at a time, in

Sugar (about ½ cup)

Cool completely. Store in a tightly covered container. *About 2 cups Candied Orange Peel*

▲ Candied Delights

Lightly butter an 8x8x2-in. pan. Set out a heavy 2-qt. saucepan.

Pour into a small bowl

1 cup cold water

Sprinkle evenly over cold water

4 tablespoons (4 env.) unflavored gelatin

Let stand about 5 min. to soften.

Meanwhile, mix together in the saucepan

3 cups sugar
½ cup hot water

Stir over low heat until sugar is dissolved. Increase heat and bring mixture to boiling. Cook rapidly for 10 min. without stirring. During cooking, wash crystals (*page 543*) from sides of saucepan from time to time.

Stir in softened gelatin, stirring until gelatin is completely dissolved. Simmer the mixture 10 min. longer, stirring occasionally. Remove from heat. Stir in

¾ cup (1 6-oz. can) frozen orange juice concentrate (do not add water)

Pour mixture into prepared pan; cool.

Candied Delights

Chill in refrigerator about 6 hrs.

Cut into 1-in. squares with a sharp knife and roll squares in

Sifted confectioners' sugar

Set in refrigerator until ready to serve.

About 5½ doz. pieces of candy

△ Orange-Pineapple Delights

Follow ▲ Recipe. After orange juice has been added, chill (*page 12*) until gelatin mixture is slightly thicker than consistency of thick, unbeaten egg white. Meanwhile, drain contents of 1 9-oz. can **crushed pineapple** and set aside. When gelatin mixture is of desired consistency, fold in drained pineapple. Turn into the prepared pan.

▲ Coffee Truffle Balls [17]

Set out
1/3 cup butter
10 oz. milk chocolate
Grate (*page 12*) 2 oz. of the chocolate (about 3/4 cup, grated). Mix with the grated chocolate
1½ teaspoons concentrated soluble coffee
Set aside in refrigerator.

Place remaining chocolate in the top of a double boiler with
¼ cup heavy cream
Heat over simmering water, stirring occasionally, until chocolate is melted. Remove from simmering water and cool slightly.

Divide the butter into small pieces and stir into the melted chocolate until butter is melted. Add and mix in thoroughly
½ teaspoon concentrated soluble coffee
Chill thoroughly in freezing compartment of refrigerator about 1 hr., or until firm.

When mixture is chilled, spoon about 1 teaspoonful at a time onto the reserved chocolate-coffee mixture. Quickly work with fingers to form a ball and to coat with the chocolate.
About 1½ doz. truffle balls

⚠ Liqueur Truffle Balls [18]

Follow ▲ Recipe. Omit total amount of concentrated soluble coffee. Blend in with the butter 1½ teaspoons **kirsch** and 1½ teaspoons **curaçao**.

⚠ Rum Truffle Balls [19]

Follow ⚠ Recipe. Substitute 2½ teaspoons **rum** for total amount of liqueurs.

Caramel Popcorn Balls [20]

For Popped Corn—If using an electric popper, follow the manufacturer's directions. Otherwise, for each pan of corn, melt in heavy skillet or saucepan having a tight-fitting cover
1 tablespoon hydrogenated vegetable shortening, all-purpose shortening, lard or cooking oil
Add enough popcorn (about ¼ cup) to just cover bottom of skillet and cover tightly. Shake pan over medium heat until popping stops. Turn corn into a large bowl. Set aside to keep warm. In the same way prepare
3 qts. popped corn

For Sirup—Measure and set aside
1/3 cup undiluted evaporated milk
Mix together in a saucepan
1 cup firmly packed brown sugar
¾ cup white corn sirup
2 teaspoons vinegar
¼ teaspoon salt
Stir over low heat until sugar is dissolved. Increase heat and bring mixture rapidly to boiling without stirring. Put candy thermometer in place. Cook until mixture reaches 280°F, (soft crack stage, *page 543*; remove from heat while testing). During cooking, wash crystals (*page 543*) from sides of pan from time to time.

When temperature has reached 280°F, add the evaporated milk gradually (so that mixture does not stop boiling), while stirring con-

Caramel Popcorn Balls

stantly. Bring caramel mixture to 280°F again, stirring constantly. Remove from heat and remove thermometer. Stir in

1 teaspoon vanilla extract

For Popcorn Balls—Gradually pour hot caramel sirup into center of warm popped corn. With long-handled fork, *quickly* blend to coat corn with sirup. Dot corn with

2 tablespoons butter or margarine

With buttered hands, gather and press into firm balls.   *About 1½ doz. 3-in. popcorn balls*

△ Peanut-Popcorn Balls 21

Follow ▲ Recipe. Mix 1 cup (about 5 oz.) warm, salted, roasted **peanuts** with popped corn before pouring on caramel sirup.

Spiced Nuts 22

Set out a candy thermometer and a double boiler having a cover. Lay out on a flat surface a long piece of waxed paper.

Set out

4 cups (about 1 lb.) nuts (such as walnuts or pecans)

Mix together in a large bowl and set aside

¼ cup sugar
2 tablespoons cinnamon
½ teaspoon cloves
½ teaspoon nutmeg
½ teaspoon ginger

Mix together in the top of the double boiler

1 cup sugar
¼ cup water
2 tablespoons cinnamon
½ teaspoon cloves
½ teaspoon nutmeg
½ teaspoon ginger

Stir over low heat until sugar is dissolved. Increase heat and bring mixture to boiling. Cover and boil mixture gently for 5 min. Uncover and put candy thermometer in place. Continue cooking without stirring until mixture reaches 238°F (soft ball stage, *page 543*;

remove from heat while testing). During cooking, wash crystals (*page 543*) from sides of pan from time to time.

Remove thermometer and place double-boiler top over simmering water. Immediately add the nuts and mix until well coated with the sirup. Turn into the reserved sugar mixture in the bowl. Toss lightly until all nuts are well coated. Turn onto the waxed paper and separate the nuts. Set aside to cool completely.

Store in a tightly covered container in a cool, dry place.   *About 4 cups Spiced Nuts*

▲ Caramel-Nut Mallows

Made in a jiffy and consumed in a flash.

Line a baking sheet with waxed paper.

Put into the top of a double boiler

½ lb. vanilla caramels
3 tablespoons hot water

Heat over simmering water, stirring frequently, until caramels are melted.

Meanwhile, finely chop

¾ cup (about 3 oz.) pecans

Set out

32 (½ lb.) marshmallows

Using a fork, dip each marshmallow into the melted caramel and turn until well coated. Roll in the chopped nuts. Place on the waxed paper. Set in a cool place until caramel is firm.

Store in a covered container in a cool, dry place.   *32 pieces of candy*

△ Coconut-Chocolate Mallows

Follow ▲ Recipe. Substitute 6 oz. **semi-sweet candymaking chocolate for dipping** for the caramels and water. Partially melt chocolate over simmering water, being careful not to overheat. Remove chocolate from heat and stir until completely melted. Blend in ½ teaspoon **vanilla extract**. Substitute **Toasted Coconut** (double recipe, *page 448*) for the nuts.

CANDIES and CONFECTIONS in the MICROWAVE OVEN

Making candy in the microwave oven is not only quicker and cleaner than on the conventional stove, but very nearly a guarantee that the final product will be smooth and professional looking. As a result, these candies make good holiday or house gifts.

If you have friends who are fudge aficionados, the **Chocolate, Pecan** and **Hawaiian** fudges are quite impressive and so is the **Crackle Peanut Brittle.** Children will particularly enjoy the **Anise Lollipops.**

COOKING CANDY—Because liquids do not evaporate as readily with the microwave method as with conventional cooking, some recipes such as the nougat candies, do not adapt successfully. We have omitted them.

In the recipes which are included, we compensate for the lack of evaporation, if necessary, by cooking the candies to a higher temperature than recommended in the master recipe.

Test for Doneness—We do urge the use of a candy thermometer to test these recipes. If you do not have a microwave-safe thermometer, be sure to remove the dish from the oven each time you test the temperature. If no thermometer is available, then use the traditional soft ball and hard ball tests *(page 543).* Remember, sometimes the candy will be cooked to a higher temperature than associated with these tests.

To protect against variations in oven settings and wattage fluctuations, test the candies about every 5 minutes as they near the end of the minimum recommended cooking time.

STIRRING is of prime importance for producing a smooth, firm candy without graininess, but we suggest a gentle hand to accompany the gentle cooking quality of the microwave method.

With each recipe we note the recommended intervals for stirring and washing down crystals from the sides of the pan.

REMINDERS—For additional tips and for an easy-to-read chart comparing settings among different brands of microwave ovens, see the introductory chapter, **Home Cooking in the Microwave Oven**, in the beginning of this book.

Chocolate Fudge *(page 544)* 1

Use a 3-qt. casserole.

COOK milk and chocolate, stirring every 1 min., to melt chocolate (about 5 min.).

Add sugar mixture and SLOWCOOK, stirring and washing down crystals every 2 min., until mixture reaches 260° or soft ball stage (about 25 min.).

OVERALL COOKING TIME: 30:00

Cocoa Fudge *(page 544)* 2

Follow 1 Recipe with changes as in ⚠ Recipe.

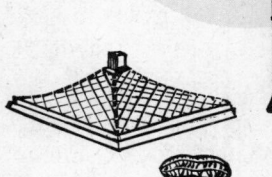

Tutti-Frutti Fudge *(page 544)* 3

Follow 1 Recipe with changes as in ⚠ Recipe.

Marshmallow Fudge 4
(page 544)

Follow 1 Recipe with changes as in ⚠ Recipe.

Pecan Fudge *(page 544)* 5

Follow 1 Recipe with changes as in ⚠ Recipe.

Hawaiian Fudge *(page 544)* 6

Use a 3-qt. casserole.

COOK pineapple-sugar mixture, stirring and washing down crystals every 30 sec., until sugar dissolves (about 15 min.).

SLOWCOOK, stirring every 2 min., until mixture reaches 260° or soft ball stage (about 20 min.).

OVERALL COOKING TIME: 35:00

Chocolate Divinity *(page 546)* 7

Use a 3-qt. covered casserole.

COOK chocolate, stirring every 1 min., until melted (about 3 min.).

COOK sugar mixture, stirring every 1 min., to dissolve sugar (about 15 min.). Continue to COOK, stirring and washing down crystals every 1 min., until boiling (about 5 min.).

Cover and SLOWCOOK until mixture reaches 260° or hard ball stage (about 20 min.).

OVERALL COOKING TIME: 43:00

Divinity *(page 546)* 8

Follow 7 Recipe with changes as in ⚠ Recipe.

Creamy Taffy *(page 550)* 9

Use a 3-qt. casserole.

COOK sugar mixture, stirring and washing down crystals every 30 sec., until sugar is dissolved (about 15 min.).

Add milk and COOK, stirring every 30 sec., until boiling (about 5 min.).

SLOWCOOK, stirring and washing down crystals every 2 min., until mixture reaches 260° or firm ball stage (about 25 min.).

OVERALL COOKING TIME: 54:00

Cocoa Taffy *(page 551)* **10**

Follow **9** Recipe with changes as in ⚠ Recipe.

Crackle Peanut Brittle **11**
(page 552)

Use a 3-qt. casserole.

COOK sugar mixture, stirring every 2 min., until melted and then until boiling (about 5 min.). Cover and continue to COOK, scraping crystals from sides until all are dissolved (about 5 min.).

Uncover and COOK, stirring and washing down crystals every 2 min., until mixture reaches 234° or soft ball stage (about 20 min.).

Add peanuts and butter and COOK, stirring every 2 min., until mixture reaches 300° or forms hard, brittle threads (about 15 min.).

OVERALL COOKING TIME: 45:00

Butterscotch *(page 552)* **12**

Use a 2-qt. casserole.

COOK sugar mixture, stirring every 30 sec., until dissolved (about 10 min.).

SLOWCOOK, stirring and washing down crystals every 2 min., until mixture reaches 310° or forms hard, brittle threads (about 25 min.).

OVERALL COOKING TIME: 35:00

Anise Lollipops *(page 554)* **13**

Use a 3-qt. casserole.

COOK sugar mixture, stirring every 30 sec., to dissolve sugar (about 15 min.). Cover and continue to COOK until boiling (about 3 min.).

Uncover and SLOWCOOK, stirring and washing down crystals every 2 min., until mixture reaches 310° or forms hard, brittle threads (about 25 min.).

OVERALL COOKING TIME: 43:00

Candied Orange Peel **14**
(page 554)

Use a 1½-qt. covered casserole.

COOK until orange peel is almost tender (about 10 min.). Drain, add water and COOK to boil (about 10 min.). Repeat as directed (about 10 min. each time).

COOK sugar and water, stirring every 1 min., until sugar is dissolved (about 5 min.). Continue to COOK until mixture is boiling and forming bubbles about dime-size (about 3 min.).

Cover and SLOWCOOK, stirring and washing down crystals every 2 min., until mixture reaches 250° or thread stage (about 25 min.).

Add orange peel strips off heat.

OVERALL COOKING TIME: 73:00

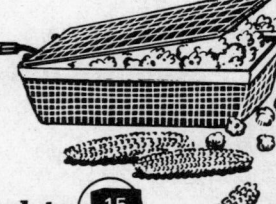

Candied Delights  **15**
(page 555)

Use a 3-qt. casserole.

COOK sugar and water, stirring every 1 min., until boiling and sugar is dissolved (about 15 min.).

Add gelatin and continue to COOK without stirring, until mixture starts to thicken (about 5 min.). SLOWCOOK, stirring every 2 min., until very thick (about 15 min.).

OVERALL COOKING TIME: 35:00

Orange-Pineapple **16** Delights (page 555)

Follow **15** Recipe with changes as in △ Recipe.

Coffee Truffle Balls **17** (page 556)

Use a 1½-qt. casserole.

COOK chocolate and cream, stirring every 30 sec., to melt chocolate (about 6 min.).

OVERALL COOKING TIME: 6:00

Liqueur Truffle Balls **18** (page 556)

Follow **17** Recipe with changes as in △ Recipe.

Rum Truffle Balls **19** (page 556)

Follow **17** Recipe with changes as in △ Recipe.

Caramel Popcorn Balls **20** (page 556)

Use a 1½-qt. casserole.

COOK sugar mixture, stirring and washing down crystals every 1 min., to boil and dissolve sugar (about 10 min.). Continue to COOK until mixture reaches 280° or soft crack stage (about 15 min.).

Add milk as directed and COOK, stirring every 1 min., to return to 280° (about 5 min.).

OVERALL COOKING TIME: 30:00

Peanut-Popcorn Balls **21** (page 557)

Follow **20** Recipe with addition as in △ Recipe.

Spiced Nuts (page 557) **22**

Use a 3-qt. covered casserole.

COOK sugar-water mixture, stirring every 1 min., to boil and dissolve sugar (about 10 min.).

Cover and continue to COOK, scraping crystals from sides and bottom every 1 min., until all crystals are dissolved (about 3 min.).

Uncover and COOK, stirring and scraping every 1 min., until mixture reaches 238° or soft ball stage (about 15 min.).

OVERALL COOKING TIME: 28:00

Hot and Cold

All over the world people have their favorite beverages. Here in the United States, where many different peoples have made their homes, we have no truly national beverage and incline to many favorites—judging the rightness of a drink by the occasion for which it is intended. But there is almost universal agreement among Americans that the day properly starts with coffee.

COFFEE—Each cup of coffee should be clear and sparkling. It should have a rich coffee flavor without bitterness or off-taste.

Use only fresh coffee—To ensure freshness use coffee within 7 to 10 days after opening.

Store unsealed coffee in a cool place or in the refrigerator in a tightly covered container of air-tight material.

Measure coffee and water accurately. (National Coffee Association Standard Measure—2 level measuring tablespoons of coffee to each ¾ standard measuring cup of water.)

Brew coffee at full capacity of coffee maker for best results—never less than three-fourths full.

Use freshly drawn cold water; water preheated or drawn from the hot water faucet may give an undesirable flat taste to the brew.

Serve coffee as soon as possible after brewing; keep coffee hot but do not boil it.

For uniform results, use same timing secured after finding exact time for desired brew.

Never boil coffee beverage; boiling causes complete breakdown of true coffee flavor and aroma.

Thoroughly wash coffee maker and rinse with clear boiling water after each use.

Rinse coffee maker with boiling water before using. **Never re-use coffee grounds.**

Wash cloth filters for vacuum-type coffee makers in clear cold water; keep immersed in cold water.

TEA—The brisk, full flavor and bright, clear color of tea are obtained only from a good quality of fresh tea properly brewed.

Choose a tea that suits your taste: *Black*—rich aroma, mild flavor; *Green*—little aroma, pungent flavor; *Oolong*—aroma of black tea, flavor of green; *Flower* (*such as jasmine*)—scented with flowers.

Teas are graded according to leaf size, such as Pekoe and Orange Pekoe (a smaller leaf) of black teas and Gunpowder, smallest leaf of green teas.

Buy the quantity of tea that fits your needs.

Store tea in an airtight container in a cool, dry place to preserve freshness.

Water for making tea should be freshly drawn and brought just to a brisk boil. Prolonged boiling gives water, thus the tea, a flat taste. Water that is alkaline or high in iron may cloud the beverage.

Brew tea 3 to 5 min. to reach desired flavor peak. Strength of beverage is determined not only by length of brewing time, but also by amount of tea used and freshness of leaves.

Heat tea pot or cups with boiling water.

Tea pots made from glass, china, porcelain or other forms of glazed pottery are desirable because the materials do not affect the flavor of the beverage and they tend to retain the heat.

Wash tea pots and tea holders or tea balls with hot soapy water after each use to keep them free from oily deposits and sediment.

MILK—As soon as received, put milk (whole or skimmed), flavored milk drinks, cream and buttermilk into the coldest area of the refrigerator, about 40°F. Store in the original container and wipe container with a clean, damp cloth. Keep milk out of strong light to retain riboflavin, one of milk's important vitamins.

Always keep milk covered—it quickly absorbs the odors of other foods. Return milk to the refrigerator immediately after using.

Always use pasteurized milk to safeguard the family's health. Use milk within two days, keeping it under proper storage, for best flavor and quality. Buttermilk is best when used the same day.

A package of non-fat dry milk solids kept in a cool, dry place spells convenience to the homemaker, especially the instant milk. Reconstitute the solids and use as fluid milk. Increasing the amount of milk solids used in a beverage gives added nutrients—a good way to get extra protein, calcium and the B vitamins.

CHOCOLATE and COCOA BEVERAGE—Preliminary cooking of the chocolate or cocoa mixture before the addition of milk helps to keep the chocolate or cocoa from settling out.

Beating the beverage with a rotary beater forms a froth and prevents a film from forming.

OTHER BEVERAGE FACTS—Add chilled carbonated beverages to mixtures just before serving and mix only enough to blend to retain carbonation.

Fruits used in beverages should be fully ripe, especially when added to a milk drink.

An electric blender is an invaluable aid to beverage preparation. Add liquid to container, then semisolids while motor is running. Add ice cream or cracked ice last.

Beverage Serving Tips

PARTY POINTERS—Beverages served with a flair and a bit of imagination are conversation starters. Here are a few ideas and helps.

For Decorative Punch Bowl—Trim stems of daisies, sweetheart roses or other small flowers to 1 in. Secure flowers around edge of bowl with pieces of cellulose tape. Secure two flowers to ladle handle and one flower to each punch cup handle.

For Frosted Glasses—Rub the edge of each glass with cut surface of lemon, lime or orange. Or brush rim with citrus juice. Dip the rim of each glass in fine granulated or confectioners' sugar. Place glasses in refrigerator to chill. Carefully pour beverage into glasses without touching frosted edges.

Pink Sugar for Pink-Frosted Glasses—Measure ½ cup sugar into a shallow pan. Tint sugar the desired pink color by thoroughly mixing in, one drop at a time, a mixture of red food coloring and water (equal amounts of each). To obtain a more even-colored sugar, put through a fine sieve.

For Fruit Kabobs—Thread onto each stirrer or skewer, in order, a strawberry, lime slice, maraschino cherry, mint leaves, orange wedge, seedless grape and pineapple chunk. Chill.

For Decorative Ice Cubes—Fill ice-cube tray one-third full with water. Place in freezing compartment of refrigerator; remove ice-cube tray when water is partially frozen. Place well-drained maraschino cherry, mint sprig, pineapple chunk, orange wedge, berry, or small piece of fruit and a mint leaf in each cube section. Fill tray with water and freeze.

For Decorative Ice Blocks—Fill a loaf pan or fancy mold one-third full with water. Place in freezing compartment of refrigerator; remove pan or mold when water is partially frozen. Arrange flowers, such as roses or gardenias, or fruits (small whole, pieces or slices) in interesting designs and combinations suitable for the occasion. Fill pan or mold, covering flowers or fruit, with water and freeze. Boiling water before freezing or stirring water as it freezes helps to make the ice clear.

For Sugar Sirup—Mix together in a saucepan 2 cups sugar and 2 cups water; stir over low heat until sugar is dissolved. Cover, bring to boiling and boil 5 min. Cool and store covered in refrigerator. Use to sweeten beverages.   *About 2½ cups sirup*

BEVERAGE SERVINGS—Average servings for beverages are: *Hot beverages,* such as coffee, tea, chocolate and cocoa—6-oz. cup; *Cold beverages* with large quantity of ice, such as iced coffee and tea—10- to 12-oz. glass; cold beverages with little or no ice, such as lemonade, ginger ale and milk drinks—8-oz. glass; *Fruit and vegetable juices*—4-oz. serving; *Punch*—3- to 4-oz. punch cup; *Milk*—8-oz. glass or mug.

▲ Drip Coffee

Preheat a drip coffee maker by filling it with boiling water. Drain.

For each standard measuring cup of water, using standard measuring spoons, measure
2 tablespoons drip grind coffee
Place in filter section of drip coffee maker. Do not overload coffee compartment.

Bring to boiling
Freshly drawn water
Measure and pour boiling water into upper container. Cover. Allow all of water to drip through the coffee, keeping coffee maker over low heat 5 to 8 min., or as long as coffee is dripping. Do not let coffee boil at any time. Remove coffee compartment; stir and cover the brew. If not served immediately, place coffee maker over low heat. Stir before serving.

⚠ Percolated Coffee

Use regular grind coffee. Follow ▲ Recipe for amount to use. Put into strainer basket of coffee maker. Measure freshly drawn cold water into bottom of percolator. Place basket in coffee maker. Cover.

Place over heat. When percolating begins, reduce heat to low so that percolating will be gentle and slow. Timing varies from 5 to 10 min. after percolation starts. It's wise to experiment to determine exact timing for the amount of coffee generally made in your percolator. Larger amounts of coffee require the longer timing.

Remove coffee basket, cover coffee maker and keep coffee hot over low heat. Do not let coffee boil at any time.

⚠ Steeped Coffee

Use regular grind coffee. Follow ▲ Recipe for amount to use. Put into coffee maker. To clarify coffee, mix in 1 teaspoon slightly beaten **egg** for each 2 tablespoons coffee used. Measure and add freshly drawn cold water.

Bring very slowly to boiling, stirring occasionally. Remove from heat at once. Pour ¼ cup cold water down spout to settle grounds.

Let stand 3 to 5 min. without heat. Strain through a fine strainer into a server which has been preheated with boiling water. If necessary to keep hot, let coffee stand over low heat without boiling.

⚠ Coffee for Twenty (Steeped)

Thoroughly mix ½ lb. **coffee**, regular grind, with 1 **egg** and crushed **egg shell**. Tie loosely in fine cheesecloth or put into a lightweight muslin bag. Put into a large kettle with 1 gal. freshly drawn cold **water**. Cover tightly.

Place over low heat and bring very slowly to boiling. Boil 3 to 5 min. Taste to test strength. Remove bag when coffee is of desired strength. Cover kettle and let stand 10 to 15 min. over low heat without boiling.   *20 servings*

⚠ Vacuum-Drip Coffee

Use drip or vacuum grind coffee. Follow ▲ Recipe for amount to use.

Specific directions for making vary according to the type of coffee maker used. Usually, freshly drawn cold water is measured and poured into the decanter or lower bowl. Coffee is measured into upper bowl. Cover.

Place coffee maker over moderate to low heat. When all but a small amount of water has risen to upper bowl, remove coffee maker from heat. Remove top bowl when the brew has run into decanter. Cover. Serve immediately or keep hot over very low heat. Do not boil at any time.

Demitasse
(After-Dinner Coffee)

Using 1½ to 2 times the amount of coffee, prepare

Drip Coffee (page 560) or any variation

Serve hot in demitasse or after-dinner cups.

Quick Coffee Beverage

For one cup coffee beverage, place 1 teaspoon **concentrated soluble coffee** into a cup. Add boiling **water** and stir until coffee is completely dissolved. Concentrated frozen coffee may be reconstituted with freshly boiling water. Follow directions on container.

Iced Coffee

For stronger flavor pour over coffee ice cubes.

Using double the amount of coffee, prepare

Drip coffee (page 560) or any variation

Do not overload coffee compartment. If there is danger of this, use capacity amount of coffee with one-half as much water as for regular-strength coffee.

Fill tall glasses to brim with

Crushed ice or ice cubes

Pour the hot coffee over the ice. Serve with

Iced Tea and Fruit Kabobs (page 559)

granulated or **confectioners' sugar, sugar sirup, cream,** or **whipped cream** (*page 13*) sprinkled with **cinnamon.**

▲ Tea

Fill teapot with boiling water. When heated thoroughly, pour off water.

Put into pot for each cup of tea to be brewed

1 rounded teaspoon tea or 1 prepared tea bag

Bring to boiling

Freshly drawn water

For each cup of tea, pour into teapot 1 cup of the briskly boiling water. Cover pot and let brew 3 to 5 min.

Remove tea bags or strain tea into a preheated pot or into cups. Serve immediately with any of the following: thin slices or wedges of **lemon, orange** or **lime; lemon, orange** or **lime juice;** whole **cloves;** sprigs of fresh **mint; cream; sugar** or **sugar sirup.**

△ Iced Tea

Prepare tea as in ▲ Recipe. Use 6 tablespoons tea and 6 standard measuring cups of freshly boiling water. Strain and pour hot tea into tall glasses filled with crushed ice or ice cubes. Serve as in ▲ Recipe or serve with **Fruit Kabobs** (page 559).

Iced Coffee with sugar sirup and cream

Dressy Tea

GRACE HAWKINSON, GALLUP, N. MEX.

Combine in a 2-qt. saucepan
1 qt. freshly drawn water
½ cup sugar
4 whole cloves
1 stick cinnamon
Set over medium heat and stir until sugar is dissolved. Increase heat and bring mixture to boiling.

Meanwhile, put into a preheated teapot
2 rounded teaspoons tea or 2 prepared tea bags
Pour the spice mixture into the teapot. Cover and let tea brew 3 to 5 min.

Meanwhile, heat until very hot
1 cup orange juice, strained
After tea has brewed required time strain and return to teapot.

Mix in the hot orange juice. Serve hot in preheated cups and garnish with
Thin lemon or orange slices
About 6 servings

Mint Iced Tea

MRS. A. E. BOYCE, RIVERDALE, N. DAK.

Rinse and shake excess water from
12 sprigs of mint
Put 8 sprigs of mint into refrigerator to chill. Bruise the 4 remaining sprigs and set aside.

Combine in a 2-qt. saucepan
1 qt. freshly drawn water
1⅓ cups sugar
Stir over low heat until sugar is dissolved. Increase heat and bring to boiling. Boil sirup gently for 5 min.

Put into a preheated teapot the bruised sprigs of mint and
5 tablespoons tea
Pour the sugar sirup into the teapot. Cover pot and let mixture brew 3 to 5 min. Strain mixture and return to teapot with the bruised

sprigs of mint. Cover and let stand 10 min. longer. Remove the sprigs of mint. Pour mixture into a pitcher and stir in
1 qt. freshly drawn water
½ cup lemon juice, strained
Sprinkle over the chilled sprigs of mint
Confectioners' sugar
Pour the tea into tall glasses over crushed ice or ice cubes.

Garnish with the sugared sprigs of mint and
Lemon slices
About 8 servings

▲ Hot Cocoa

Mix in a saucepan or top of a double boiler
5 to 6 tablespoons cocoa
5 to 6 tablespoons sugar
¼ teaspoon salt
Blend in slowly
1 cup water
Boil gently 2 min. over direct heat, stirring until slightly thickened.

Reduce heat and stir in
3 cups milk
Heat slowly over direct heat or simmering water until scalding hot; stir occasionally. Remove from heat. Cover and keep hot, if necessary, over hot water.

Just before serving, add
½ teaspoon vanilla extract
Beat with rotary beater until foamy. Serve steaming hot, plain or with **whipped cream** (*page 13*), **marshmallow cream** or **marshmallows.**
6 servings

⚠ Hot Chocolate

Follow ▲ Recipe. Substitute 2 sq. (2 oz.) **chocolate** for cocoa. Break into pieces and combine with sugar, water and salt. Mix and stir constantly over low heat. When chocolate is melted, increase heat and boil 2 min., stirring constantly. Add milk and continue as in ▲ Recipe.

⚠ Spicy Chocolate Mocha

Follow ⚠ Recipe. Reduce chocolate to 1½ sq. (1½ oz.). Heat the water to very hot and pour over the chocolate. Increase sugar to ½ cup and add to chocolate mixture with the salt and ¼ cup **concentrated soluble coffee.** Increase milk to 1 qt. Serve with **whipped cream** (*page 13*), and put a **cinnamon stick** for a stirrer into each mug. If desired, sprinkle each serving with **nutmeg.**

Spicy Chocolate Mocha

Hot Mint Chocolate

FERN E. GREINERT, HORTOMILLE, WIS.

Put in top of a double boiler

20 (about ½ cup) chocolate mint wafers
1 cup milk
⅛ teaspoon salt

Heat over simmering water, stirring constantly until wafers are melted and mixture is well blended. Add, stirring constantly

2 cups milk
1 cup cream

Heat until scalding hot, stirring occasionally. Serve hot, plain or, if desired, with **whipped cream** (*page 13*).   *4 to 6 servings*

Iced Cocoa or Chocolate

Put a bowl and a rotary beater into refrigerator to chill.

Prepare, using 6 tablespoons sugar in either
    Hot Cocoa (page 562) or Hot
    Chocolate (on this page)
Cool and put into refrigerator to chill.

Just before serving, using the chilled bowl and beater, whip (*page 13*)
    ½ cup chilled whipping cream
Stir the chilled beverage and pour over ice in tall glasses. Top each serving with about three tablespoons of the whipped cream.

Sprinkle each serving lightly with
    Cinnamon, nutmeg or ginger
                        6 servings

Tomato Cocktail
(*See photo on page 20*)

Mix together
    3 cups chilled tomato juice
    1½ tablespoons lemon or lime juice
    2 teaspoons sugar
    ¼ teaspoon salt
    ¼ teaspoon Accent
    9 drops tabasco sauce
Pour into chilled glasses; garnish with
    Lemon slices

                        6 servings

Hot Apricot Nip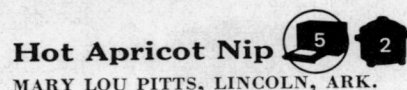

MARY LOU PITTS, LINCOLN, ARK.

Combine in a small saucepan
  1 cup water
  2 tablespoons sugar
  4 whole cloves
  1 3-in. stick cinnamon
Set over low heat and stir until sugar is dissolved. Increase heat and bring to boiling. Boil gently 5 min.

Add the contents of
  1 12-oz. can (1½ cups) apricot nectar
and
  2 tablespoons lemon juice
Continue to heat until very hot. Remove spices and serve immediately.   *4 servings*

Note: Beverage may be cooled, chilled and served over ice cubes.

▲ Hot Spiced Apple Juice ❸

MRS. ELDEN SAMP, FLANDREAU, S. DAK.

Combine in a 2-qt. saucepan
  4 cups apple juice
  1 cup water
  ½ cup firmly packed brown sugar
  ½ cup orange juice
  3 tablespoons lemon juice
  ¼ teaspoon nutmeg
  1 3-in. stick cinnamon
Set over medium heat and stir until sugar is dissolved. Bring to boiling; reduce heat and simmer 15 min.

Strain through a fine sieve into heated serving cups. If desired, garnish with thin **orange** or **lemon slices**.   *About 8 servings*

△ Cold Spiced Apple Juice

Double ▲ Recipe. Cool and chill the strained, spiced juice and serve in a punch bowl. Add Decorative Ice Cubes or Ice Block (*page 559*) garnished with **orange slices** topped with **maraschino cherries**.

Minted Apple Juice Cocktail

Rinse and shake excess water from
  7 sprigs of mint
Chill all but one sprig in refrigerator. Bruise the remaining sprig of mint and set aside.

Mix together
  2 cups apple juice
  1 cup pineapple juice
  2 teaspoons lemon juice
Add the bruised sprig of mint and put into refrigerator to chill.

Remove the bruised sprig of mint before serving. Garnish each serving with one of the chilled sprigs of mint.   *6 servings*

Cherry-Tea Refresher

MRS. ANNA B. HUME, TOLLESON, ARIZ.

Set out a large pitcher.

Mix in a saucepan having a tight-fitting cover
  1 cup water
  ½ cup sugar
Set over low heat and stir until sugar is dissolved. Increase heat, cover and boil mixture gently 5 min. Remove from heat; set aside to cool.

Prepare and cool to room temperature
  1 cup tea (*page 561*; use 2 teaspoons tea or 2 tea bags and 1 cup water)
Drain, reserving sirup in a 1 cup measure
  1 No. 2 can pitted sour cherries packed in extra heavy sirup
Force through a sieve or food mill and add to the sirup enough of the cherries to yield a total of 1 cup cherry purée and sirup. (Reserve remaining cherries for use in other food preparation.)

Put into the pitcher the cherry purée, cooled tea and

1 qt. cold water
¼ cup lemon juice, strained
2 tablespoons pineapple juice

Add the sugar sirup and stir until well blended. Put into refrigerator to chill. Stir beverage just before serving. Add ice and serve in tall glasses.   *About 6 servings*

Note: This beverage may also be served as a punch for small gatherings.

▲ Lemonade

Mix in a saucepan having a tight-fitting cover

1 cup sugar
1 cup water

Set over low heat and stir until sugar is dissolved. Increase heat, cover and boil 5 min. Remove from heat; cool.

Mix together the cooled sirup and

4 cups cold water
¾ cup lemon juice

Pour over chipped ice or ice cubes in tall glasses.   *4 or 5 servings*

⚠ Limeade

Follow ▲ Recipe. Substitute ¾ cup **lime juice** for lemon juice.

⚠ Orangeade

Follow ▲ Recipe. Reduce lemon juice to ¼ cup (or substitute ¼ cup lime juice for lemon juice), and reduce cold water to 1 cup. Mix 3 cups **orange juice** with lemon juice, sirup and water.

Raspberry Shrub

This sirup must stand for two days before completion.

To Prepare Sirup—(*This makes about 4 pts. sirup.*) A large heavy sauce pot or kettle will be needed for cooking the sirup.

The first day, set out a large bowl. Sort, rinse and thoroughly drain

4 qts. ripe red or black raspberries

Put raspberries into the bowl and crush thoroughly. Add, mixing well

1 qt. cider vinegar

Cover and let mixture stand 48 hours in refrigerator or in cool place, stirring to blend well 3 or 4 times.

The third day, set out the sauce pot or kettle. Make a jelly bag (*page 571*). Strain (*page 571*) the raspberries through the jelly bag into the sauce pot. Set over medium heat and add, stirring until sugar is dissolved

6 cups sugar

Increase heat and bring mixture to boiling. Boil mixture uncovered 5 min. Skim to remove any foam. Remove from heat and set aside to cool. Store in covered container in refrigerator. Sirup may also be preserved by following directions in How to Do It (*page 571*). Sterilize four 1-pt. jars and their covers. Immediately after skimming sirup fill the drained jars and seal.

To Complete Shrub—For each measuring cup of beverage desired, mix together

⅔ cup water
⅓ cup Raspberry Shrub Sirup

Serve over ice cubes or crushed ice.

Raspberry-Mint Cooler

MRS. WARREN SLANE, RUDOLPH, OHIO

Rinse and shake excess water from
6 or 7 sprigs of mint
Chill all but one sprig in refrigerator. Bruise
the remaining sprig and set aside.

Sort, rinse and drain thoroughly
½ cup fresh red raspberries
Crush the raspberries in a large bowl, and
add the bruised sprig of mint and
1 qt. Lemonade (page 565)
Stir to blend ingredients. Chill in refrigerator.
Remove mint before serving.

Garnish each serving with one of the chilled
sprigs of mint.   *5 or 6 servings*

Raspberry Shrub Punch

MRS. R. W. DICKINSON, SALINAS, CALIF.

Pour into a punch bowl or a large pitcher
3¾ cups water
**1 cup undiluted Raspberry Shrub Sirup
   (page 565)**
1 cup orange juice
½ cup lemon juice
Add and stir until sugar is dissolved
¾ cup sugar
Add crushed ice or ice cubes to the punch
bowl or pitcher.   *16 servings*

Festive Strawberry Sparkle

MRS. RICHARD VAPPI
CENTER HARBOR, N. H.

Rinse and shake excess water from
10 to 12 sprigs of mint
Put into refrigerator to chill.

Thaw according to directions on package
1 16-oz. pkg. frozen strawberries

Apricoffee Drink with Nibblers (page 21)

Force thawed strawberries through a sieve or
food mill and set them aside.

Pour into a large bowl
1 qt. cold water
Stir in contents of
**2 6-oz. cans (1½ cups) frozen
   orange juice concentrate**
Add the sieved strawberries and their sirup.

Add, just before serving, and blend well
1 qt. carbonated water
Serve immediately over crushed ice in tall
glasses. Garnish with sprigs of mint.
                                   10 to 12 servings

Apricoffee Drink

Mix in a large bowl
1½ cups cold coffee beverage
1 cup apricot nectar, chilled
⅔ cup cold milk
Add to milk mixture and beat until smooth
with a rotary beater
**1 pt. (2 cups) commercial coffee ice
   cream, softened**
Serve immediately in tall glasses, accompanied
with **Nibblers** (page 21).   *4 servings*

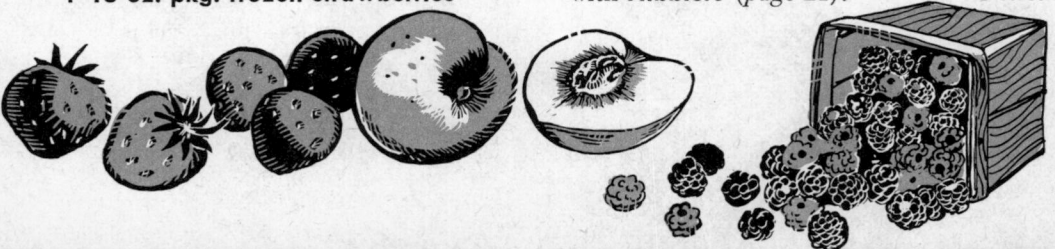

Cranberry-Orange Cooler

LORA MADOUSHEK, OBERLIN, PA.

Six 6-oz. glasses will be needed.

Chill in refrigerator
1 pt. ginger ale
1½ cups cranberry juice cocktail
Spoon into the glasses
¾ cup orange sherbet (about 2 table-spoons per glass)
Pour into each glass ¼ cup of the chilled cranberry juice cocktail. Fill each glass with chilled ginger ale. Mix slightly to blend.

Serve immediately. *6 servings*

Frosty Ginger Pick-Up

Set out 4 tall glasses.

Pour into the glasses
1 qt. chilled pale dry ginger ale
Spoon into the ginger ale
1 pt. fruit sherbet, such as Orange (page 541), Pineapple Mint (page 541), or Lemon (page 540), or any commercial sherbet, slightly softened

4 servings

Frosty Ginger Pick-Up

Black Cow

Put into a tall glass
2 scoops vanilla ice cream
Pour over ice cream
1 cup cold root beer
Mix slightly and serve immediately.

1 serving

▲ Chocolate Soda, Home-Style

Have ready for each serving
2 or 3 scoops softened vanilla or chocolate ice cream
Blend together in a tall glass one scoop of the softened ice cream and
2 tablespoons Chocolate Sirup (page 336)
Pour over the ice cream mixture
½ cup cold milk
½ cup sparkling water or ginger ale
Mix thoroughly, but do not shake. Float the remaining ice cream in the soda and serve.

1 large serving

△ Fruit-Flavored Sodas, Home-Style

Follow ▲ Recipe. Use vanilla or fruit-flavored ice cream. Substitute ⅓ cup crushed sweetened **strawberries, raspberries, peaches, apricots,** or **pineapple** for sirup. Reduce milk to ¼ cup.

Chocolate Malted

Voted first choice by young and old!

Mix together
1 cup cold milk
2 tablespoons malted milk powder
2 tablespoons Chocolate Sirup (page 336)
Beat with rotary beater or mix in shaker until thoroughly blended. Add
1 or 2 scoops softened chocolate or vanilla ice cream
Beat until well blended. Pour into a tall glass.

1 large serving

Eggnog: For a holiday punch bowl, prepare double the recipe for Bobbie's Best Eggnog (*on this page*) or use dairy eggnog. Serve with fruitcake and something small but hearty in the way of party sandwiches.

Bobbie's Best Eggnog

MRS. GEORGE CASTLEBERRY
JACKSONVILLE, FLA.

Set out a small bowl and a large bowl. Put a second small bowl, a rotary beater and 4 glasses into refrigerator to chill.

Put into the large bowl and beat until frothy
 4 egg whites
 ¼ teaspoon salt
Add gradually, beating well after each addition
 ½ cup sugar
Continue beating until rounded peaks are formed and egg whites do not slide when bowl is partially inverted. Set aside.

Put into the small bowl, beat until thick and lemon-colored and set aside
 4 egg yolks
Beat, using chilled bowl and beater, until cream is of medium consistency (piles softly)
 ½ cup chilled whipping cream
With final few strokes beat in
 1½ teaspoons vanilla extract
Gently fold (*page 12*) the whipped cream and beaten egg yolks into the egg whites. Put into refrigerator to chill thoroughly.

Top with a generous sprinkling of **nutmeg.**
About 4 servings

Malted Choco-Milk

MRS. W. L. ISBELL, BROOKSTON, INDIANA

Put a bowl and a rotary beater and 4 tall glasses into refrigerator to chill.

Beat until thick and lemon-colored
 4 egg yolks
Add to egg yolks and beat until well blended
 4 cups cold milk
 ½ cup chocolate malted milk powder
 ¼ teaspoon nutmeg
Using chilled bowl and beater, whip (*page 13*)
 ¼ cup chilled whipping cream
Pour the beverage into the chilled serving glasses and top each serving with about 2 tablespoons of the whipped cream.

Garnish with chocolate curls, made by pulling across a shredder
 Semi-sweet chocolate

4 servings

▲ Eggnog

Put into a largel bowl and beat until thick and piled softly
 3 eggs
Add and beat until well blended
 2 cups milk
 ⅓ cup sugar
 1 tablespoon vanilla extract
 ¼ teaspoon salt
Put into refrigerator to chill thoroughly.

Serve in tall glasses and top with a generous sprinkling of **nutmeg.**
5 to 6 servings

⚠ Lemon Eggnog

Follow ▲ Recipe; increase sugar to ½ cup. Omit vanilla extract. Blend in ¼ cup **lemon juice.** Omit nutmeg.

△ Chocolate Eggnog

Follow ▲ Recipe; decrease sugar to ¼ cup. Blend in ⅓ to ½ cup **Chocolate Sirup** (*page 336*). Omit nutmeg.

Pink Fruit Punch

MRS. L. R. SIDDERS, SHATTUCK, OKLA.

A party favorite from Middle America!

A punch bowl and serving cups will be needed.

Put into refrigerator to chill
1 qt. ginger ale
Put into a large bowl
1 qt. water
4 cups unsweetened pineapple juice
1 cup cranberry juice cocktail
1 cup orange juice
⅔ cup lemon juice
½ cup lime juice
Add and stir until sugar is dissolved
1 cup sugar
Chill fruit-juice mixture in refrigerator.

When ready to serve, pour mixture into the punch bowl. Add the ginger ale and stir to blend. Do not fill punch bowl too full so that a Decorative Ice Block (*page 559*) may be floated in the punch. *About 3½ qts. punch*

Party Punch

Set out two large bowls. A punch bowl and serving cups will be needed.

Put into refrigerator to chill
1½ qts. ginger ale
Bring to full rolling boil
5 cups freshly drawn water
Meanwhile, put into one of the bowls
5 tablespoons tea
As soon as water reaches a full boil, pour it over the tea. Brew for 5 min. Strain into the second large bowl. Set aside to cool at room temperature.

When tea is cool, add to it
2½ cups orange juice
1½ cups unsweetened grapefruit juice
⅔ cup lemon juice
¼ cup lime juice
Add and stir until sugar is dissolved
2¼ cups sugar
Chill fruit-juice mixture in refrigerator.

When ready to serve, pour mixture into a Decorative Punch Bowl (*page 559*). Pour in the chilled ginger ale and stir to blend thoroughly. Do not fill punch bowl too full so that a Decorative Ice Block (*page 559*) may be floated in the punch. Serve in Pink-Frosted Punch Cups (*page 559*). *About 3 qts. punch*

Party Punch with Decorative Ice Block, Pink-Frosted Cups

BEVERAGES in the MICROWAVE OVEN

A hot punch or a generous pot of hot chocolate is certainly a welcome treat on a raw winter day. Particularly delicious are the recipes which, when prepared in the microwave oven, produce smooth and creamy hot chocolates with no worry about scorching or boiling over. The **Hot Apricot Nip** is a refreshing change from hot chocolate and a good energy booster.

If an afternoon of skating or other outdoor activity is planned, use the drink to fill a take-along thermos or try preparing it ahead of time and refrigerating it. Then, when you come home, reheat the drink in individual paper cups or microwave-safe pottery mugs, adding a marshmallow if you wish.

Remember to stir as directed to assure a smooth blend of flavors.

REMINDERS—For more tips and an easy-to-read chart comparing settings among different brands of microwave ovens, see the introductory chapter, **Home Cooking in the Microwave Oven**, in the beginning of this book.

Hot Cocoa *(page 562)*

Use a 1½-qt. casserole.

COOK cocoa, sugar, salt and water, stirring every 1 min., until slightly thickened (about 5 min.).

Blend in milk and COOK, stirring every 30 sec., until hot (about 5 min.).

OVERALL COOKING TIME: 10:00

Hot Chocolate *(page 563)*

Follow Recipe with changes as in ⚠ Recipe, except COOK chocolate, stirring every 1 min., until melted (about 2 min.). Continue to COOK, stirring every 30 sec., until boiling (about 5 min.).

Spicy Chocolate Mocha
(page 563)

Follow Recipe with changes as in ⚠ Recipe.

Hot Mint Chocolate
(page 563)

Use a 1½-qt. casserole.

COOK wafer mixture, stirring every 1 min., to melt wafers (about 5 min.).

Thoroughly blend in milk and cream. COOK, stirring every 30 sec., until hot (about 5 min.).

OVERALL COOKING TIME: 10:00

Hot Apricot Nip *(page 564)*

Use a 1½-qt. casserole.

COOK sugar mixture, stirring every 1 min., until sugar dissolves and mixture boils (about 5 min.). Continue to COOK, stirring every 2 min., until slightly thickened (about 3 min.).

Add remaining juices and COOK to heat (about 3 min.).

OVERALL COOKING TIME: 11:00

BEVERAGES in the SLOW COOKER

Hot drinks prepared in the slow cooker are not only timesavers, but also provide a warm welcome for a crowd coming home from a football game or an afternoon of skating or skiing. It's easy to mix all the ingredients in the slow cooker, turn it to LOW and take off to the day's activity with family or friends. Set out cups or mugs and let each person serve himself right from the slow cooker as the crowd drifts in.

Drinks should not remain too many hours, even on the LOW setting, beyond the recommended cooking times or the flavor may become distorted. Two to three hours is safe, however.

REMINDERS—For more tips and an easy-to-read chart comparing settings among different brands of slow cookers, see the introductory chapter, **Home Cooking in the Slow Cooker**, in the beginning of this book.

Dressy Tea *(page 562)* **1**

Use a 3½-qt. slow cooker.

Pour 1 qt. boiling water over tea bags in slow cooker. Cover and let steep 5 min.

Remove tea bags and stir in remaining ingredients.

Cover and cook on LOW for 2 to 3 hrs.

Remove spices and serve directly from slow cooker.

Hot Apricot Nip *(page 564)*

Use a 3½-qt. slow cooker.

Combine all ingredients in slow cooker, except use ½ cup water (instead of 1 cup).

Cover and cook on LOW for 3 to 5 hrs.

Remove spices and serve directly from slow cooker.

Hot Spiced Apple Juice **3**
(page 564)

Use a 3½-qt. slow cooker.

Combine all ingredients in slow cooker.

Cover and cook on LOW for 3 to 5 hrs.

Remove spices and serve directly from slow cooker.

PRESERVING and PICKLING

What You Should Know

BEFORE YOU START—Before starting to preserve, assemble and check all equipment. Jars must be free of chips and cracks. When using two-piece metal jar caps, new sealing lids must be used. For other types of jar caps, use new rubber rings. Read carefully beforehand the manufacturer's directions for sealing jars. Read the recipe through and plan the work step by step. Work with quantities that can be easily and quickly handled.

Included in the special equipment needed for pickling and preserving are 2 large sauce pots or kettles (one to be used for sterilizing jars or glasses), long-handled tongs, ladle, slotted spoon, wide-mouthed funnel, colander, coarse sieve or food mill, 1-qt. measures, cheesecloth, food chopper, Mason jars and covers, and jelly glasses and covers.

ABOUT PRESERVING—Select firm fruits only, using a mixture of ripe and slightly under-ripe fruits. The under-ripe fruits contain a large amount of pectin (the substance which makes jelly jell). When making jellies and marmalades, cook the fruit with the peel or skin and core because these contain needed pectin substances. Cook the juice-sugar mixture rapidly; do not simmer. Slow cooking destroys the pectin and produces a tough, gummy product.

All types of preserves, with the possible exception of butters, should be cooked in small amounts. No more than 4 to 6 cups of juice should be cooked at one time when making jelly, and no more than 3 to 4 quarts of fruit for other products. **Jellies** are made from the strained fruit juice. A

good jelly is clear, sparkling and transparent. It contains neither sediment nor crystals and has the natural color and flavor of fresh fruit. Jelly is firm but tender and holds its shape when turned from the glass.

Jams are made from whole, cut or crushed fruit. The fruit is cooked with sugar until it is tender and the sirup is thick.

Preserves are made from whole or evenly chopped fruit cooked in a sugar sirup. The fruit is tender and transparent, but retains its shape. The sirup will be thick and clear without causing the fruit to shrink and become tough. Shrinking can be avoided by adding the sugar gradually, or by allowing the fruit to remain in the sirup for several hours or overnight to absorb the sirup.

Marmalades are clear, jelly-like and transparent, with small pieces or thin slices of fruit or peel suspended throughout the sirup. Marmalades can be made of almost any firm fruit.

Conserves are a combination of two or more fruits (a citrus fruit is usually included), nuts and raisins. The mixture is cooked until thick and jamlike. Nuts should be added 5 minutes before removing from heat. Longer cooking destroys their flavor.

Butters are made of fruit that has been cooked and put through a coarse sieve or food mill. The fruit is then cooked with sugar until thick enough to spread.

ABOUT PICKLING—The fruits and vegetables to be pickled should be fresh, firm and slightly under-ripe. Sort them for size, using fruits or vegetables of the same size in any one recipe. Cider vinegar's mellow taste and aroma make it better for general pickling than white vinegar, which has a harsher, less fruit-like flavor. However, cider vinegar has a tendency to color white vegetables—such as onions and cauliflower—a reddish-brown. For these light-colored vegetables, a white vinegar is preferred. High-quality, fresh spices are essential for best results. Whole spices are preferred because ground spices tend to lose their flavor in an opened box on the shelf, and may discolor the pickles. Whole spices, when tied together in a spice bag, can easily be removed at the end of the cooking period.

In all pickling, it is important to preserve the crispness of the fresh vegetables. This may be done in a variety of ways. Vegetables may be soaked in a brine (solution of salt and water) overnight, scalded in hot salted water or chilled in iced salted water. A coarse salt should be used for pickling; table salt contains chemicals (added to prevent lumping) and therefore is unsatisfactory.

How To Do It

Sterilize Jars or Glasses—Put a rack or folded dish towel onto bottom of large sauce pot or kettle. Place clean jars or glasses on the rack or towel. Pour boiling water over them and boil 15 min., keeping jars or glasses covered with water at all times; if more water is needed, add boiling water.

Drain Jars or Glasses—Using long-handled tongs, carefully remove one jar or glass at a time and thoroughly drain. Set right side up on cooling rack away from drafts.

Fill and Seal Jars—Immediately after draining jars, pour or ladle mixture to within ½ in. of top. A wide-mouthed funnel will aid in the pouring process. Using a clean, damp cloth or paper towel, remove any food that may be on inside of jar above the surface of the contents or on the mouth of the jar. Be sure sealing edge is free of food particles. Drain the covers; seal jars at once, following cover manufacturer's directions. Cool jars away from drafts. Label; store in a cool, dry place.

Pack Pickles or Fruit in Jars and Seal—Immediately after draining jars, pack pickles or fruit into the jar. Ladle hot liquid to within ½ in. of top. Insert a knife or narrow spatula along the side of the jar at several places to remove any air bubbles. Add additional liquid if needed. With a clean, damp cloth, or paper towel, remove any of the sirup that may be on mouth of jar. Be sure sealing edge is free of food particles. Drain the covers; seal jars at once, following cover manufacturer's directions. Cool jars away from drafts. Label; store in a cool, dry place.

Fill Glasses and Seal with Paraffin—Immediately after draining glasses, pour the mixture to within ½ in. of top. With a clean, damp cloth or a paper towel, remove any particles of food that may be on the inside of glass above surface of mixture.

Immediately pour enough melted paraffin onto top of mixture to make a layer about ⅛ in. thick on each glass. When paraffin has cooled completely, pour enough melted paraffin over first layer to make another layer about ⅛ in. thick. Carefully tilt glasses to distribute paraffin evenly over the top and seal it to edges of the glass. Cool glasses away from drafts. Label and cover glasses; store in a cool, dry place.

Make a Spice Bag—Cut a double thickness of cheesecloth about 9 in. square. Put measured spices in center of the cheesecloth and tie the ends together. Adjust size of cheesecloth to amounts of spices used.

Make a Jelly Bag—Cut a double thickness of cheesecloth about 36 in. long and fold in half. Dip the cloth into hot water and wring well. Put a large strainer or colander over a bowl and lay the cloth in the strainer or colander.

Strain Juice—Pour the cooked fruit carefully into the cheesecloth. Gather the four corners of the cloth together and tie firmly. Allow the juice to drip through the cheesecloth into a bowl. A commercial jelly bag and frame may be used.

A faster method for extracting juice is to force the juice from the bag by pressing the bag against the side of a colander, using a wooden spoon. Pour this juice through a second jelly bag and allow the juice to drip through. This method does not produce as clear a jelly as the first one.

Make a Jelly Test—Dip spoon into boiling liquid; lift it out and tip it to allow mixture to run over edge. At first, the sirup will run off in a thin stream. When the last two drops in the spoon run together or "sheet", the mixture should be removed from the heat. Always remove the pan from the heat while testing.

Spiced Grape Jelly and Rolled Baking Powder Biscuits (page 63)

▲ Spiced Grape Jelly
ELIZABETH S. RUDE, HAMBURG, N.J.

Make an extra batch of this spicy, shimmering jelly. It is sure to create a demand for more.

Set out a large, heavy sauce pot or kettle having a cover and eight 8-oz. jelly glasses.

Make a jelly bag (*page 571*).

Rinse, discarding stems and imperfect grapes, drain and put into the sauce pot or kettle
   3 lbs. Concord grapes
Crush grapes thoroughly. Blend well and mix thoroughly with crushed grapes
   ½ cup cider vinegar
   2 teaspoons cinnamon
   1 teaspoon cloves
Heat to boiling, reduce heat, cover and simmer for 10 min. Remove mixture from heat and strain through jelly bag.

Meanwhile, wash the sauce pot to use later.

Wash and sterilize (*page 571*) jelly glasses.

When juice has strained through jelly bag, melt over simmering water about
   ½ lb. paraffin
Measure 4 cups of juice into the sauce pot.

Put sauce pot over high heat and heat until very hot. Add, stirring until sugar is dissolved
   7 cups sugar
Rapidly bring the mixture to boiling and immediately stir in
   ½ cup bottled fruit pectin
Boil rapidly 1 min., stirring constantly. Remove from heat and skim off any foam.

Immediately fill the drained jelly glasses and cover with paraffin (*page 571*).
   About eight 8-oz. glasses jelly

⚠ Strawberry Jelly

Follow ▲ Recipe. Substitute 2½ qts. rinsed, hulled **strawberries** for grapes. Omit vinegar mixture. Do not cook the berries. Crush berries and put into jelly bag. Force juice through bag by pressing bag against colander with a wooden spoon. Measure 3¾ cups **strawberry juice**. Add ¼ cup strained **lemon juice**. Follow directions for cooking jelly. Increase sugar to 7½ cups and bottled fruit pectin to 1 cup.

⚠ Red Raspberry Jelly

Follow ⚠ Recipe. Substitute **red raspberries** for strawberries.

▲ Currant Jelly

Set out a large, heavy sauce pot or kettle having a cover, and six 8-oz. jelly glasses. Make a jelly bag (*page 571*).

Rinse, remove leaves (do not remove stems), drain and put into sauce pot or kettle

4 lbs. (about 4 qts.) ripe red currants

Crush currants thoroughly. Add and mix in

1 cup water

Heat to boiling, reduce heat, cover and simmer for 10 min. Remove mixture and strain through jelly bag.

Meanwhile, wash the sauce pot to use later.

Wash and sterilize (*page 571*) jelly glasses.

When juice has strained through jelly bag, melt over simmering water about

¼ lb. paraffin

Measure 4 cups of juice into the sauce pot. Put sauce pot over high heat and heat until very hot. Add

4 cups sugar

Stir until sugar is dissolved. Continue cooking rapidly until sirup responds to jelly test (*page 571*). Remove from heat and skim off any foam.

Immediately fill the drained jelly glasses and cover with paraffin (*page 571*).

About six 8-oz. glasses jelly

△ Grape Jelly

Follow ▲ Recipe. Substitute 3 lbs. **Concord grapes** for currants. Remove stems (do not remove skins); simmer grape-water mixture for 15 min. Use 4 cups grape juice and decrease sugar to 3 cups.

△ Crab Apple Jelly

Follow ▲ Recipe. Omit currants. Rinse, remove stem ends and cut into quarters enough crab apples to yield 3 qts. chopped **crab apples** (do not remove cores or peel). Increase water to 3 cups and cook for 20 min., or until very tender. Decrease sugar to 3 cups.

△ Quince Jelly

Follow ▲ Recipe. Omit currants. Wash well, remove stems and cut into pieces enough to yield 3 qts. diced **quince** (do not remove cores or peel). Increase water to 6 cups and cook for 25 min., or until very tender.

Rosemary Jelly

MRS. HAROLD WHEAT, SAN JOSE, ILL.

Tart Rosemary Jelly is the ideal accompaniment for meat.

Set out a heavy 3-qt. saucepan and four 8-oz. jelly glasses.

Wash and sterilize (*page 571*) jelly glasses.

Measure into a small bowl

2 teaspoons dried rosemary

Pour over the rosemary

1½ cups boiling water

Set aside for 15 min.

Meanwhile, melt over simmering water about

¼ lb. paraffin

Strain rosemary-water mixture into the saucepan and add

3½ cups sugar

2 tablespoons cider vinegar

4 drops red food coloring

Put saucepan over medium heat and stir until sugar is dissolved. Increase heat and bring mixture to boiling. Immediately add

½ cup bottled fruit pectin

Boil rapidly 1 min., stirring constantly. Remove from heat and skim off any foam.

Immediately fill the drained jelly glasses and cover with paraffin (*page 571*).

About four 8-oz. glasses jelly

Blueberry-Lemon Jam

Set out a large, heavy sauce pot or kettle and eight 8-oz. jelly glasses.

Wash and sterilize (*page 571*) jelly glasses.

Melt over simmering water about
> **½ lb. paraffin**

Rinse, drain and put into sauce pot or kettle
> **4 cups firm, fresh blueberries**

Crush berries thoroughly. Add
> **⅔ cup lemon juice**
> **1½ tablespoons grated lemon peel (page 11)**

and a mixture of
> **7 cups sugar**
> **¼ teaspoon salt**
> **¼ teaspoon cloves**

Put the sauce pot over medium heat and stir until sugar is dissolved. Bring mixture to boiling and boil rapidly 1 min. without stirring. Remove mixture from heat and blend in
> **½ cup bottled fruit pectin**

Skim off any foam.

Immediately fill the drained jelly glasses and cover with paraffin (*page 571*).

About eight 8-oz. glasses jam

Red Raspberry Jam

(Uncooked)

Set out four 8-oz. jelly glasses.

Sort, rinse, drain and force through coarse sieve or food mill enough raspberries to yield
> **1½ cups sieved fresh red raspberries**
> **(about 3 cups whole berries)**

In a medium-size bowl mix the sieved raspberries and
> **3 cups sugar**

Set aside for 20 min.

Meanwhile, wash in hot, sudsy water the jelly glasses and their covers. Rinse with boiling water. Cover and set aside.

Mix thoroughly with the raspberry mixture
> **¼ cup bottled fruit pectin**

Fill jelly glasses (*page 571*) to within ½ in. of top. Cover with a jelly-glass cover, aluminum foil or several thicknesses of waxed paper tied over the top of the glass.

Allow jam to stand at room temperature overnight or until jellied.

Jam must be stored in refrigerator or freezer. It cannot be stored at room temperature.

About four 8-oz. glasses jam

Peach Jam

Set out a large, heavy sauce pot or kettle and six 8-oz. jelly glasses.

Wash and sterilize (*page 571*) jelly glasses.

Rinse and plunge into boiling water (to loosen the skins)
> **12 medium-size (about 3 lbs.) firm, ripe peaches**

Plunge peaches into cold water. Gently slip off skins. Cut peaches into halves; remove and discard pits. Finely chop peaches (enough to yield 4 cups chopped peaches). Put peaches into the sauce pot and add
> **3 cups sugar**
> **2 tablespoons lemon juice**

Put sauce pot over medium heat and stir until sugar is dissolved. Increase heat and cook rapidly until clear and thick, stirring frequently to prevent sticking. Length of cooking time will vary with the ripeness and type of peaches. Remove from heat and skim off any foam.

While jam is cooking, melt over simmering water about
> **¼ lb. paraffin**

Immediately fill the drained jelly glasses and cover with paraffin (*page 571*).

About six 8-oz. glasses jam

Pineapple Preserve

MRS. RILEY C. FOSTER, MEMPHIS, TENN.

This preserve must stand overnight before completion.

A large, heavy sauce pot or kettle and three 8-oz. jelly glasses will be needed.

For Preparing Pineapple—Cut off and discard crown (spiny top) and rinse
2 medium-size (about 2 lbs. each) fresh pineapples
Cut into crosswise slices about ½ in. thick. With a sharp knife, cut away and discard the rind and "eyes" from each slice. Cut out the core and cut slices into small wedges.

For Preparing Preserve—Measure 4 cups of the pineapple wedges.

Measure
3 cups sugar
Place one half of the pineapple wedges in a bowl. Cover with one half of the sugar. Add remaining pineapple to make a layer. Cover with the remaining sugar. Cover the bowl and set aside overnight.

The following day, drain the pineapple, reserving the sirup. Bring sirup to boiling and boil 1 min. Remove from heat and add the drained pineapple. Pour the mixture into a shallow heat-resistant dish to cool.

Wash and sterilize (*page 571*) jelly glasses.

Melt over simmering water about
2 oz. paraffin
When preserve has cooled, immediately fill drained jelly glasses and cover with paraffin (*page 571*). *About three 8-oz. glasses preserve*

Tomato Preserve

This preserve must stand overnight before completion.

A large, heavy sauce pot, a candy thermometer and seven 8-oz. jelly glasses will be needed.

Rinse
5 lbs. (about 15 medium-size) ripe tomatoes
Taking a few at a time, dip tomatoes into boiling water for several seconds, peel, cut out and discard stem ends. Cut into thin wedges, discarding seeds. Put into a large bowl and add
8 cups sugar
Mix gently, cover and set aside overnight.

The following day, wash and sterilize (*page 571*) jelly glasses.

Drain the tomatoes, reserving the sirup. Put the sirup into the saucepan and set over high heat. Bring to boiling and put thermometer in place. Cook sirup to 230°F (thread stage, *page 543*; remove from heat while testing).

Shortly before sirup reaches 230°F, rinse, remove ends and thinly slice (discarding seeds)
1 medium-size lemon
Melt over simmering water about
½ lb. paraffin
When the sirup reaches 230°F, remove thermometer and add the tomatoes and lemon. Cook rapidly until sirup is thick, stirring frequently to prevent sticking. Remove from heat and skim off any foam.

Immediately fill the drained jelly glasses and cover with paraffin (*page 571*).

About seven 8-oz. glasses preserve

Strawberry Delight

MRS. CHARLES FOX, DETROIT, MICH.

This preserve must stand overnight before completion.

Set out a large, heavy sauce pot or kettle and a large, shallow heat-resistant dish. Three 8-oz. jelly glasses will be needed.

Sort, rinse, drain and hull
  4 cups (1 qt.) fresh, ripe strawberries
Put berries into a bowl and add
  2 cups boiling water
Set aside for 10 min.

Drain thoroughly; put into sauce pot and add
  1½ cups sugar
Set sauce pot over medium heat and gently stir until sugar is dissolved. Increase heat and cook rapidly for 10 min., stirring frequently to prevent sticking. Remove from heat and add
  1½ cups sugar
Set sauce pot over medium heat and gently stir until sugar is dissolved. Increase heat and cook rapidly for 15 min., stirring frequently to prevent sticking. Remove from heat and skim off any foam. Pour preserve into shallow dish to cool. Cover and set aside overnight.

The following day, wash and sterilize (*page 571*) jelly glasses.

Melt over simmering water about
  ¼ lb. paraffin
Stir preserve and immediately fill the drained jelly glasses. Cover with paraffin (*page 571*).
About three 8-oz. glasses preserve

Holiday Treat

MRS. O. P. KNIGHT, GRANTS PASS, ORE.

Three fruits blend their distinctive flavors in this very sweet but refreshing preserve. An interesting treat for holidays or special days, it is an ideal spread for crackers or bread at any time.

Set out a heavy 3-qt. saucepan having a tight-fitting cover, and five ½-pt. jars and covers.

Wash and sterilize (*page 571*) jars and covers.

Drain, reserving sirup, contents of
  1 14-oz. can pineapple tidbits (about 1 cup, drained)
Wash, sort and set aside
  4 cups (1 lb.) cranberries
Rinse, cut into halves, core, pare and dice enough pears to yield
  2 cups (about 3 small) diced pears
Sprinkle evenly over pears ¼ cup of reserved pineapple sirup. (Reserve remaining sirup for use in other food preparation.)

Measure into the saucepan
  2 cups sugar
  ½ cup water
Put the saucepan over medium heat and stir until sugar is dissolved. Bring mixture to boiling, cover and boil 5 min. Uncover; add the

Homemade jellies and preserves represent an investment of time, money and space. Protect this investment by using quality ingredients and by storing the finished product with care. Use fine granulated sugar and sound,, ripe, blemish-free fruit for superior results. Carefully seal glasses or jars with paraffin and cover. Label and date.

cranberries and cook until cranberry skins pop. Add the diced pears with sirup and the tidbits. Continue cooking until thick, about 20 min. Remove from heat and skim to remove any foam.

Immediately fill drained jars and seal tightly (*page 571*).   *About 2½ pints preserve*

Citrus Marmalade
MARTHA McGEE, McGEE'S MILLS, PA.

This marmalade must stand for 3 days before completion.

A large, heavy sauce pot or kettle, a large, shallow heat-resistant dish and twelve 8-oz. jelly glasses will be needed.

The first day, rinse and remove ends from
1 medium-size grapefruit
1 medium-size orange
1 medium-size lemon
Cut the fruit into quarters, discard seeds, and put fruit through fine blade of a food chopper. Measure the chopped fruit and make a note of the amount for future reference.

For *each* cup of chopped fruit, measure
¾ cup water
Combine the chopped fruit and water in a large bowl. Cover and set aside overnight.

The second day, put the fruit and liquid into the sauce pot or kettle and set over high heat. Bring to boiling and cook rapidly for 10 min., stirring frequently to prevent sticking.

Remove from heat and pour into large dish to cool. Cover and set aside overnight.

The third day, wash and sterilize (*page 571*) jelly glasses.

Melt over simmering water about
½ lb. paraffin
Put the fruit into the sauce pot. For *each* cup of raw chopped fruit (as measured on first day) add
4 cups sugar

Put sauce pot over medium heat and stir until sugar is dissolved. Increase heat and cook rapidly, stirring frequently to prevent sticking, until jelly tests done (*page 571*).

Remove from heat and skim off any foam.

Immediately fill the drained jelly glasses and cover with paraffin (*page 571*).
              About twelve 8-oz. glasses marmalade

Peach Marmalade
MRS. JAMES C. FAHL, WASHINGTON, D. C.

Set out a large, heavy sauce pot or kettle and three 8-oz. jelly glasses.

Wash and sterilize (*page 571*) jelly glasses.

Rinse, cut off ends and thinly slice (discarding seeds)
1 orange
Set aside.

Rinse and plunge into boiling water (to loosen the skins)
12 medium-size (about 3 lbs.) firm, ripe peaches
Plunge peaches into cold water. Gently slip off skins. Cut the peaches into halves; remove and discard the pits. Coarsely chop peaches (enough to yield 4 cups chopped peaches).

Put peaches and orange into sauce pot with
3 cups sugar
Put sauce pot over medium heat and stir until sugar is dissolved. Increase heat and cook rapidly until clear and thick, stirring frequently to prevent sticking. Length of cooking time will vary with the ripeness and type of peaches.

While marmalade is cooking, melt over simmering water about
¼ lb. paraffin
Remove the marmalade from the heat and skim off any foam.

Immediately fill the drained jelly glasses and cover with paraffin (*page 571*).
              About three 8-oz. glasses marmalade

Cranberry Conserve

MRS. ALBERT MAGHAN, DEERWOOD, MINN.

Set out a large, heavy saucepan and four ½-pt. jars and covers.

Wash and sterilize (*page 571*) jars and covers.

Coarsely chop and set aside
   1 cup (about 4 oz.) walnuts
Chop and set aside
   1 cup (about 5 oz.) seedless raisins
Rinse and sort
   4 cups (1 lb.) cranberries
Put cranberries in saucepan and add
   1 cup water
Heat to boiling and cook for 5 min., or until cranberry skins pop.

Force cranberries through a coarse sieve or food mill (enough to yield 2 cups sieved cranberries). Combine the sieved cranberries and chopped raisins in the saucepan and add
   2½ cups sugar
   ⅓ cup orange juice
   1 tablespoon grated orange peel
      (page 11)
Put saucepan over medium heat and stir until sugar is dissolved. Increase heat and cook rapidly for 10 min., stirring frequently to prevent sticking. Remove from heat and add the walnuts, mixing thoroughly. Return to heat and cook 5 min. longer. Remove from heat and skim to remove any foam.

Immediately fill drained jars and seal tightly (*page 571*).   *About 2 pints conserve*

▲ Almond-Plum Conserve

A potpourri of fine flavors, this jewel-bright Almond-Plum Conserve may be served with meat or as a spread at breakfast or tea time.

Set out a large, heavy sauce pot or kettle and six 1-pt. jars and covers.

Wash and sterilize (*page 571*) jars and covers.

Blanch (*page 11*), toast (*page 12*), coarsely chop and set aside
   1 cup (about 5 oz.) almonds
Rinse, drain, pit and cut into pieces enough plums to yield
   8 cups (about 4 lbs.) fresh, firm ripe plums, cut into pieces
Put plums into the sauce pot or kettle and add
   5½ cups sugar
   3 cups (15 oz.) seedless white raisins
   ½ teaspoon salt
Set sauce pot aside.

Rinse and remove ends from
   1 medium-size orange
   1 medium-size lemon
Cut fruit into quarters, discard seeds, and put through the coarse blade of a food chopper. Add to ingredients in the sauce pot and mix together thoroughly.

Put sauce pot over medium heat and stir until sugar is dissolved. Stirring frequently to prevent sticking, continue cooking rapidly about 40 min., or until plums are plump and tender and sirup responds to jelly test (*page 571*).

Remove from heat and add almonds, mixing thoroughly.

Immediately fill drained jars and seal tightly (*page 571*).   *About 6 pints conserve*

△ Pineapple-Plum Conserve

Follow ▲ recipe. Thoroughly drain contents of one 9-oz. can **crushed pineapple** (about ¾ cup, drained). Reserve pineapple sirup for use in other food preparation. Add pineapple to the mixture in sauce pot with citrus fruits.

Apple Spread

PHINA W. NORMAN, PORTLAND, ORE.

Set out two large, shallow heat-resistant baking dishes and five 1-pt. jars and covers.

Wash, core and place in baking dishes
6 lbs. (about 18 medium-size) firm cooking apples
Bake at 350°F 30 to 40 min., or until apples are tender when pierced with a fork. Remove from oven and set aside to cool.

When cool, force apples through coarse sieve or food mill (enough to yield 6 cups sieved apples). Mix the sieved apples with
4½ cups sugar
½ cup cider
¼ cup cider vinegar
Turn the apple mixture into a baking dish. Bake at 300°F about 1 hr. 30 min., or until thick, stirring occasionally.

About 30 min. before apple spread is done, wash and sterilize (*page 571*) jars and covers.

About 15 min. before apple spread is done, add, mixing carefully
½ teaspoon oil of cinnamon
When spread is thick, remove from oven.

Immediately fill drained jars and seal tightly (*page 571*). *About 5 pints spread*

Grape Butter

MRS. HUGH JAMISON, MEDIAPOLIS, IOWA

This is a delightful butter that preserves the rich, harvest tang of vine-ripened grapes.

Set out a large, heavy sauce pot or kettle and five 8-oz. jelly glasses.

Wash and sterilize (*page 571*) jelly glasses.

Rinse (discarding stems and imperfect grapes), drain and put into sauce pot or kettle
2 lbs. Concord grapes
Add and mix thoroughly
4½ cups sugar
Put the sauce pot over medium heat and stir until sugar is dissolved. Increase heat and cook rapidly for 20 min., stirring frequently to prevent sticking.

While grapes are cooking, melt over simmering water about
¼ lb. paraffin
Remove mixture from heat and force through coarse sieve or food mill. Return grape pulp to sauce pot and put over high heat. Heat to boiling, stirring constantly. Boil rapidly 1 min. Remove from heat and skim off any foam.

Immediately fill the drained jelly glasses and cover with paraffin (*page 571*).

About five 8-oz. glasses butter

Bread and Butter Pickles I

MRS. E. H. CARLYON, WILLIMANTIC, CONN.

From old New England—A blue-ribbon contender for bread-and-butter-pickle honors.

A large, heavy sauce pot or kettle and three 1-pt. jars and covers will be needed.

Wash thoroughly, drain and cut into ¼-in. slices enough cucumbers to yield

2 qts. (about 16 4- to 5-in.) sliced cucumbers

Thinly slice

2 medium-size onions (*page 12*)

Put the cucumbers and onions into a large bowl and toss with

½ cup coarse salt

Put into a 1-qt. measure for liquids

Ice cubes

Add, bringing water level to the 1-qt. mark

Cold water

Pour the water and cubes over the vegetables. Cover and set aside for 3 hrs.

Wash and sterilize (*page 571*) jars and covers.

Thoroughly drain the vegetables, discarding liquid. Measure into sauce pot or kettle

2 cups sugar
2 cups cider vinegar
2 tablespoons cassia buds
1 tablespoon mustard seed
½ teaspoon turmeric
¼ teaspoon celery seed

Put the sauce pot over medium heat and stir until sugar is dissolved. Increase heat and heat to boiling. Add the drained onions and cucumbers and simmer for 10 min.

Immediately pack the pickles into drained jars and seal tightly (*page 571*).

About 3 pints pickles

Bread and Butter Pickles II

MRS. HERMAN NEBIKER, SR.
CEDAR RAPIDS, IOWA

Another star for the pickle parade comes from the Middle West and merits rave notices from all true pickle fans.

These pickles must stand overnight before their completion.

A large, heavy sauce pot or kettle and four 1-pt. jars and covers will be needed.

Wash thoroughly, drain and cut into ¼-in. slices enough cucumbers to yield

2 qts. (about 16 4- to 5-in.) sliced cucumbers

Put cucumbers into a large bowl and toss with

½ cup coarse salt

Pour over the cucumbers

1 qt. boiling water

Cover and set aside overnight.

The following day, wash and sterilize (*page 571*) jars and covers.

Rinse and coarsely chop enough to yield

2 cups (about 4 medium-size) chopped onion (*page 12*)
2 cups (about 4 medium-size) chopped green pepper (*page 12*)
¾ cup (about 1 large) chopped red pepper

Set aside.

Thoroughly drain cucumbers, discarding liquid. Measure into the large sauce pot or kettle

2 cups cider vinegar
2 cups sugar
1 teaspoon celery seed
1 teaspoon mustard seed
¾ teaspoon turmeric

Put the sauce pot over medium heat and stir until sugar is dissolved. Increase heat and heat to boiling. Add the chopped vegetables and cucumbers and simmer for 5 min.

Immediately pack the pickles into drained jars and seal tightly (*page 571*).

About 4 pints pickles

Smith's Mustard Pickles

(See photo on page 586)

MRS. PHILENA E. EMPET, HARFORD, PA.

These pickles must stand overnight before completion.

A large, heavy sauce pot or kettle and six 1-pt. jars and covers will be needed.

Remove all leaves from
1 small head cauliflower
Cut off woody base; trim off blemishes. Break into flowerets and soak in cold salted water about 30 min. to remove dust or small insects which settle in the cauliflower.

Wash thoroughly, drain and cut into ¼-in. slices enough cucumbers to yield
6 cups (about 12 4- to 5-in.) sliced cucumbers (If preferred, use 1 qt. sliced cucumbers and 2 cups whole gherkins.)
Put into a large bowl.

Thinly slice and add to cucumbers enough to yield
2 cups (about 4 medium-size) sliced onion (page 12)
2 cups (about 3 medium-size) sliced green tomatoes
3 cups (about 6 medium-size) sliced green pepper (page 12)
Rinse and drain the flowerets (about 3 cups) and add to vegetables.

Mix together until salt is dissolved and pour over the vegetables
2 qts. water
1 cup coarse salt
Cover and set aside overnight.

The following day, wash and sterilize *(page 571)* jars and covers.

Put vegetables and brine into large sauce pot

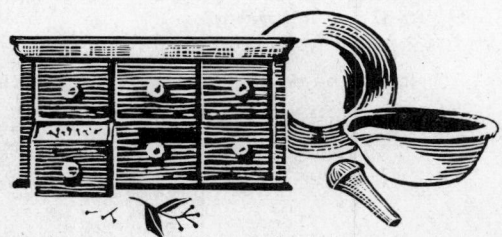

or kettle and heat to boiling. Reduce heat and simmer for 10 min. Remove from heat and turn into a large colander to drain thoroughly.

Sift together into top of double boiler
½ cup sifted flour
3 tablespoons dry mustard
½ teaspoon turmeric
Add and mix together
¾ cup sugar
1½ teaspoons celery seed
Place over simmering water.

Add slowly, stirring constantly
4 cups white vinegar
Cook about 10 min., or until sauce thickens.

Put the drained vegetables in the sauce pot and add the sauce, stirring gently. Simmer for 5 min.

Immediately pack the pickles into drained jars and cover; seal tightly *(page 571)*.

About 6 pints pickles

Dill Beans

MRS. RALPH MUNSON, RIVERSIDE, CALIF.

Wash and sterilize *(page 571)* three 1-pt. jars and their covers.

Rinse and break off ends of
2 lbs. fresh green beans
If necessary, trim beans to fit upright into jars. Set aside.

Heat to boiling
4 cups water
1⅓ cups cider vinegar
3 tablespoons coarse salt
Quickly drain *(page 571)* sterilized jars and place in each jar
Large spray of fresh dill
Clove garlic (page 12)
Pack *(page 571)* green beans upright into jars.

Pour boiling liquid into jars to within ½ in. of top. Seal at once *(page 571)*.

Let Dill Beans stand 3 mos. before opening to allow flavors to blend. *About 3 pints beans*

Sweet Dill Slices
MRS. HUGH D. RANSOM, FREEPORT, KANS.

Set out a large, heavy sauce pot or kettle and four 1-pt. jars and covers.

Wash and sterilize (*page 571*) jars and covers.

Wash thoroughly, drain and cut into ¼-in. slices enough cucumbers to yield

1 gal. (about 32 4- to 5-in.) sliced cucumbers

Measure into the sauce pot or kettle

3 cups cider vinegar
2¼ cups sugar
2 tablespoons dill seed
2 tablespoons mustard seed
2 tablespoons salt

Put the sauce pot over medium heat and stir until sugar is dissolved. Increase heat and heat to boiling. Add the cucumbers and simmer for 20 min.

Immediately pack the pickles into drained jars and seal tightly (*page 571*).

About 4 pints pickles

Sweet Mixed Pickles
EILEEN C. SLEDGE, PLAINVILLE, CONN.

These pickles must stand overnight before completion.

A large, heavy sauce pot or kettle and four 1-pt. jars and covers will be needed.

Remove all leaves from

1 small head cauliflower

Cut off woody base; trim off blemishes. Break into flowerets and soak in cold salted water about 30 min. to remove dust or small insects which settle in the cauliflower.

Wash thoroughly, drain and cut into ¼-in. slices enough cucumbers to yield

1 qt. (about 8 4- to 5-in.) sliced cucumbers (If preferred, use 2 cups sliced cucumbers and 2 cups whole gherkins.)

Put into a large bowl.

Thinly slice and add to cucumbers enough to yield

3 cups (about 6 medium-size) sliced green pepper (*page 12*)
2 cups (about 4 medium-size) sliced onion (*page 12*)
2 cups (about 3 medium-size) sliced green tomato

Rinse and drain the flowerets (about 3 cups) and add to vegetables.

Mix together until salt is dissolved and pour over the vegetables

2 qts. water
1 cup coarse salt

Cover and set aside overnight.

The following day, wash and sterilize (*page 571*) jars and cover.

Put vegetables and brine into large sauce pot or kettle and heat to boiling. Reduce heat and simmer for 15 min. Remove vegetables and brine from heat and turn into a large colander to drain thoroughly.

Combine in large sauce pot

3 cups white vinegar
3 cups sugar
1½ teaspoons mustard seed
1½ teaspoons turmeric

Tie together in a spice bag (*page 571*)

1 teaspoon whole mixed pickling spices
½ teaspoon whole cloves
1 3-in. stick cinnamon, broken

Add the spice bag and put the sauce pot over medium heat. Stir until sugar is dissolved. Bring mixture to boiling. Add the drained vegetables and simmer for 15 min.

Immediately pack the pickles into drained jars and cover; seal tightly (*page 571*).

About 4 pints pickles

Candy Pickles
MRS. ELMER P. LEONHARDT
FRANKFORT, IND.

Set out a large, heavy sauce pot or kettle and three 1-pt. jars and covers.

Wash and sterilize (*page 571*) jars and covers.

Wash thoroughly, drain and cut into ¼-in. slices enough cucumbers to yield
  2 qts. (about 16 4- to 5-in.) sliced cucumbers
Measure into the large sauce pot or kettle
  1½ cups sugar
  1 cup cider vinegar
  2 tablespoons salt
  1 tablespoon mustard seed
  1½ teaspoons celery seed
  ⅛ teaspoon red pepper
Put the sauce pot over medium heat and stir until sugar is dissolved. Increase heat and heat to boiling. Add the cucumbers and simmer for 5 min.

Immediately pack the pickles into drained jars and seal tightly (*page 571*).

About 3 pints pickles

Green Tomato Sweet Pickles
KATE BROOKS, NEW RICHMOND, OHIO

These pickles must stand overnight before completion.

A large, heavy sauce pot or kettle and four 1-pt. jars and covers will be needed.

Rinse, remove stem ends and slice enough green tomatoes to yield
  1 gal. (about 7 lbs.) sliced green tomatoes
Measure
  1 cup coarse salt
Place one half of the tomatoes in a bowl. Cover with one half of the salt. Add the remaining tomatoes to make a layer. Cover with remaining salt. Cover and set aside overnight.

The following day, wash and sterilize (*page 571*) jars and covers.

Drain tomatoes thoroughly, discarding liquid. Heat to boiling in the sauce pot or kettle, stirring until sugar is dissolved
  4 cups cider vinegar
  2 cups sugar
Tie together in a spice bag (*page 571*)
  4 teaspoons whole cloves
  4 teaspoons whole mace
  2 3-in. pieces stick cinnamon, broken
Add spice bag to sauce pot. Add the tomatoes and simmer for 10 min.

Immediately pack the pickles into drained jars and cover; seal tightly (*page 571*).

About 4 pints pickles

Spiced Peaches

(See photo on page 586)

To obtain a spicier version of these piquant favorites stud each peach with several cloves and add a bit of stick cinnamon to the jar.

Set out a large, heavy sauce pot or kettle having a cover, and three 1-qt. jars and covers.

Wash and sterilize *(page 571)* jars and covers.

Set out
> 24 medium-size (about 6 lbs.) firm, ripe peaches

Measure into the sauce pot or kettle
> 8 cups sugar
> 2¾ cups cider vinegar
> 1⅓ cups water

Tie together in a spice bag *(page 571)*
> 4 3-in. sticks cinnamon
> 4 teaspoons whole cloves

Add the spice bag and put the sauce pot over medium heat. Stir until sugar is dissolved. Bring mixture to boiling. Cover and boil 5 min. Uncover; cook 5 min. longer. (Enough sirup for three quarts of spiced peaches.)

Meanwhile, rinse and plunge 7 or 8 of the peaches into boiling water to loosen skins. Plunge peaches into cold water. Gently slip off skins. (If desired, cut peaches into halves and remove pits.)

Set out
> 24 whole cloves

Insert a whole clove into each peach.

Add peaches to hot sirup. Bring to boiling; simmer 10 min., or until peaches are tender.

Quickly drain *(page 571)* one sterilized jar. Pack hot peaches into jar. Cover jar with waxed paper and set aside away from drafts.

Loosen and slip skins from 7 or 8 more peaches and proceed as above. Pack as for first quart. Repeat process for remaining peaches.

Bring sirup to boiling and pour into jars to within ½ in. of top. Seal at once *(page 571)*.

About 3 qts. peaches

Cantaloupe Pickles

MRS. ELDEN SAMP, FLANDREAU, S. DAK.

Not as tart as pickles, nor as sweet as preserves—a delightful hybrid flavor.

These pickles must stand overnight before completion.

A large, heavy saucepan, a large heat-resistant dish and three ½-pt. jars and covers will be needed.

Rinse, pare and cut into halves
> 1 medium-size cantaloupe

Remove and discard seedy center. Cut melon into 1-in. cubes and put into a large bowl.

Mix together until salt is dissolved and pour over the melon cubes
> 1 qt. water
> ¼ cup coarse salt

Cover and set aside for 3 hrs.

Drain the melon cubes (discarding liquid).

Measure into a spice bag *(page 571)*
> 1 tablespoon whole allspice
> 1 tablespoon whole cloves
> 1 teaspoon whole mace
> 1 3-in. piece stick cinnamon, broken

Mix together in saucepan
> 1 qt. water
> 4 cups sugar
> 1 cup white vinegar

Add spice bag to the saucepan and put over medium heat. Stir until sugar is dissolved.

Spiced Peaches: Select only firm, ripe and blemish-free fruit. Wash, handling carefully.

Bring mixture to boiling, reduce heat, cover and boil 10 min. Put cantaloupe in heat-resistant dish. Remove spice bag and pour sirup over the melon. Cool, cover and set aside overnight.

The following day, wash and sterilize (*page 571*) jars and covers.

Drain the melon, reserving the liquid. Put the liquid into the large saucepan and set the pan over high heat. Bring to boiling and cook until sirup is thick. Add the melon and cook rapidly, stirring frequently to prevent sticking, until sirup is thick and melon is clear.

Immediately pack the pickles into drained jars and cover; seal tightly (*page 571*).

About 1½ pints pickles

Watermelon Pickles

(*See photo on page 586*)

MRS. HERMAN NEBIKER, SR.

CEDAR RAPIDS, IOWA

These pickles must stand for 4 days before completion.

Set out a large, heavy sauce pot or kettle and a large, heat-resistant dish. Three 1-pt. jars and covers will be needed.

The first day, set out

1 large, ripe watermelon

Pare and discard outer green rind. Remove pink pulp and set aside for use in other food preparation. Cut enough of the white rind into

1-in. cubes to yield 9 cups watermelon rind. Put rind into sauce pot or kettle and add

6 cups boiling water

Simmer until rind is tender when pierced with a fork. Drain thoroughly and turn into heat-resistant dish.

Combine in a saucepan

4 cups sugar

1 cup white vinegar

¼ teaspoon oil of cinnamon

¼ teaspoon oil of cloves

Put over high heat and bring to boiling, stirring until sugar is dissolved. Pour sirup over rind and set aside to cool. Cover and set aside overnight.

The second day, drain rind, reserving sirup. Heat sirup to boiling. Put rind in the heat-resistant dish and pour sirup over rind. Set aside to cool. Cover and set aside overnight.

The third day, drain rind, reserving sirup. Heat sirup to boiling. Put rind in heat-resistant dish and pour sirup over rind. Set aside to cool. Cover and set aside overnight.

The fourth day, wash and sterilize (*page 571*) jars and covers.

Put rind and sirup in large sauce pot and heat to boiling. If desired, add

1 or 2 drops red or green food coloring

Immediately pack the pickles into drained jars and seal tightly (*page 571*).

About 3 pints pickles

Plunge the peaches first into boiling water and then into cold water to loosen the skins.

Pull loosened peach skins away from the fruit. Pack the peach halves cavity-side down in jars.

Spiced Peaches, Watermelon Pickles,
Smith's Mustard Pickles and Indian Relish

Last of the Garden Relish

MRS. WILLIAM J. DUNN, BUHLER, KANS.

This relish must stand overnight before completion.

A large, heavy sauce pot or kettle and three 1-pt. jars and covers will be needed.

Rinse and coarsely chop enough to yield

1 cup (about 2 medium-size) chopped green tomatoes

1 cup (about 2 medium-size) chopped green pepper (page 12)

1 cup (about 2 medium-size) chopped red pepper (page 12)

1 cup (about 2 medium-size) chopped onion (page 12)

1 cup (about 1 medium-size) chopped peeled cucumber

Combine chopped vegetables in a large bowl. Mix together until salt is dissolved and pour over the vegetables

1 qt. water

½ cup coarse salt

Cover and set aside overnight.

The following day, wash and sterilize (*page 571*) jars and covers.

Wash, scrape or pare, and cut into ¼-in. slices

4 carrots (about 1 cup sliced)

Rinse, break off ends and cut into 1-in. pieces

¼ lb. green beans (about 1 cup sliced)

Clean (*page 12*) and cut into 1-in. pieces

4 stalks celery (about 1 cup sliced)

Cook (*page 285*) sliced vegetables for 15 to 20 min., or until tender. Drain and set aside.

Combine in the large sauce pot or kettle

2 cups cider vinegar

2 cups sugar

2 teaspoons mustard seed

1 teaspoon celery seed

Put the sauce pot over medium heat and stir until sugar is dissolved. Bring the mixture to boiling. Add all the vegetables, mix thoroughly and simmer for 15 min.

Immediately fill drained jars and seal tightly (*page 571*). *About 3 pints relish*

Indian Relish

GLADYS PYLE, HURON, S. DAK.

An easy-to-make relish for those who prefer a mildly flavored accompaniment for meat.

Set out a large, heavy sauce pot or kettle and four 1-pt. jars and covers.

Wash and sterilize (*page 571*) jars and covers.

Rinse, remove and discard stem ends, cut into quarters and put through coarse blade of food chopper enough to yield

3 qts. (about 8 lbs.) chopped green tomatoes

Put through the coarse blade of food chopper enough to yield

2 cups (about 4 medium-size) chopped green pepper (page 12)

1 cup (about 2 medium-size) chopped onion (page 12)

Put the chopped vegetables in the sauce pot or kettle and add

- 1½ cups sugar
- 1¼ cups cider vinegar
- 4 teaspoons salt
- 1 tablespoon dry mustard
- 1 tablespoon mustard seed
- 1½ teaspoons celery seed
- 1 teaspoon turmeric

Put the sauce pot over medium heat and stir until sugar is dissolved. Increase heat and cook rapidly for 25 min., stirring frequently to prevent sticking.

Immediately fill drained jars and seal tightly (*page 571*).   *About 4 pints relish*

Aunt Vinnie's Piccalilli

MARTHA J. CHASTAIN, ST. GEORGE, UTAH

Set out a large, heavy sauce pot or kettle and four 1-pt. jars and covers.

Wash and sterilize (*page 571*) jars and covers.

Remove and discard wilted outer leaves, rinse, cut into quarters (discarding core) and put through coarse blade of food chopper

- 1 head (about 1 lb.) cabbage (enough to yield 4 cups chopped cabbage)

Rinse, remove and discard stem ends, cut into quarters and put through coarse blade of food chopper enough to yield

- 1 qt. (about 8 medium-size) chopped green tomatoes

Put through the coarse blade of food chopper enough to yield

- 1 cup (about 2 medium-size) chopped green pepper (*page 12*)
- 1 cup (about 2 medium-size) chopped onion (*page 12*)
- ½ cup (about 1 medium-size) chopped red pepper

Put the vegetables into the sauce pot and add

- 3 cups cider vinegar
- 1¾ cups sugar
- 1 tablespoon mustard seed
- 1 tablespoon dry mustard
- 1½ teaspoons ginger
- ¼ teaspoon cinnamon
- ¼ teaspoon cloves
- ¼ teaspoon mace

Tie in a spice bag (*page 571*)

- ¼ teaspoon dried hot red peppers

Add spice bag to the sauce pot and set over medium heat. Stir until the sugar is dissolved. Increase the heat and cook rapidly for about 20 min., or until vegetables are tender, stirring frequently to prevent sticking.

Immediately fill drained jars and seal tightly (*page 571*).   *About 4 pints relish*

Chili Sauce

CLARK W. CYPHERS, ELNORA, N. Y.

Spicy and full of zest, this Chili Sauce is hot enough to be served with sea-food cocktails. Try it too for a spot of lusty flavor with a roast or with grilled hamburgers.

Set out a large, heavy sauce pot or kettle and three 1-pt. jars and covers.

Rinse

6 lbs. (about 18 medium-size) ripe tomatoes

Taking a few at a time, dip tomatoes into boiling water for several seconds, peel, cut out and discard stem ends. Cut the tomatoes into quarters, discarding the seeds. Coarsely chop the tomatoes (enough to yield 9 cups).

Put through the coarse blade of food chopper and set aside enough to yield

1½ cups (about 3 medium-size) chopped green pepper (*page 12*)

1½ cups (about 3 medium-size) chopped onion (*page 12*)

Finely mince enough for

1 tablespoon hot red pepper

Measure into the large sauce pot or kettle

1½ cups cider vinegar

¾ cup firmly packed brown sugar

1 tablespoon salt

Tie together in a spice bag (*page 571*)

1 teaspoon whole cloves

1 3-in. piece stick cinnamon

Add the spice bag and put the sauce pot over medium heat. Stir until sugar is dissolved.

Bring mixture to boiling. Add the chopped vegetables and cook rapidly until thick, stirring frequently to prevent sticking. Length of cooking time will vary with ripeness of the tomatoes.

While Chili Sauce is cooking, wash and sterilize (*page 571*) jars and covers.

When sauce is thick, skim to remove foam.

Immediately fill drained jars and seal tightly (*page 571*).　　　*About 3 pints Chili Sauce*

Tomato Ketchup

ESTHER C. McCALLISTER, ROCK PORT, ILL.

Set out a large, heavy sauce pot or kettle and three 1-pt. jars and covers.

Rinse

14 lbs. (about 1 peck) firm, ripe tomatoes

Taking a few at a time, dip tomatoes into boiling water for several seconds, peel, cut out and discard stem ends. Cut the tomatoes into quarters, discarding the seeds, and force through coarse sieve or food mill. Measure 4 qts. sieved tomato into sauce pot or kettle.

Tie together in a piece of cheesecloth

2 cups (about 4 medium-size) chopped onion (*page 12*)

½ cup chopped hot red pepper

Put chopped vegetables into sauce pot and add

2 cups sugar

2 cups cider vinegar

1 tablespoon paprika

2 teaspoons salt

1 teaspoon garlic salt

Tie together in a spice bag (*page 571*)

½ teaspoon whole cloves

1 clove garlic (*page 12*)

1 3-in. piece stick cinnamon, broken

Add the spice bag and put the sauce pot over medium heat. Stir until sugar is dissolved. Bring mixture to boiling and cook rapidly until thick (about 1 hr.). Length of cooking time will vary with ripeness of tomatoes.

While ketchup is cooking, wash and sterilize (*page 571*) jars and covers.

When ketchup is thick, skim to remove foam.

Immediately fill drained jars and seal tightly (*page 571*).　　　*About 3 pints ketchup*

CONVENIENCE FOODS

The heat-it-and-eat-it school of thought has taken hold, and what a boon it is for busy-day meal planning. But the homemaker with flair and imagination finds gratification in expressing her personality in the foods she serves. For her we suggest the use of convenience foods—time-saver items such as canned and frozen products and packaged mixes to which she can add fanciful combinations of seasonings, herbs, sauces, and other ingredients. These recipes include appetizers, soups, breads, vegetables, main dishes, and desserts. The dishes, flavorful and easy to make, should give the homemaker a start toward dreaming up ideas of her own.

Snappy Dunk

Thoroughly mix together in a small bowl
- **1 roll (6 oz.) smoked or garlic pasteurized process cheese food, softened**
- **½ cup thick sour cream**

Sprinkle with
- **Chopped chives**   *About 1 cup dunk*

Creamy Corn Dip

Crusty Vienna- or French-bread cubes make perfect "dippers" for this mixture. Spear cubes with a fork, dunk, and twirl them in the dip.

In the top of a double boiler or chafing-dish blazer over direct heat, melt
- **2 tablespoons butter**

Add and cook until just tender, turning occasionally with a spoon
- **2 tablespoons finely chopped green pepper**

Blend in a mixture of
- **¼ cup flour**
- **¼ teaspoon salt**
- **⅛ teaspoon cayenne pepper**

Heat until mixture bubbles, stirring constantly.

Remove from heat. Stir in gradually
- **1½ cups quick chicken broth (dissolve 1 chicken bouillon cube in 1½ cups hot water)**

Cook rapidly, stirring constantly, until sauce thickens. Remove from heat. Add all at one time, stirring until melted
- **1 cup (about 4 oz.) grated Swiss cheese**

Blend in
- **1 cup (8-oz. can) cream-style corn**
- **4 drops tabasco sauce**

Keep warm over hot water.   *About 6 servings*

Jiffy Deviled Ham-Tomato Dip

Thoroughly mix together in a bowl
- **1 6-oz. can tomato paste**
- **1 2¼-oz. can deviled ham**
- **½ cup chopped celery**
- **¼ cup chopped onion**
- **½ teaspoon salt**
- **⅛ teaspoon cayenne pepper**

Cover and set aside in refrigerator 1 to 2 hrs. to chill and to allow flavors to blend.

About 1 cup dip

589

Good Resolutions Dip

This dip has special appeal for calorie counters.

Pour into a bowl
   3 tablespoons icy cold water
   2 teaspoons lemon juice
Sprinkle evenly over cold water mixture
   3 tablespoons nonfat dry milk
Whip together until stiff.

Fold into beaten mixture
   **½ cup small-curd, cream-style
      cottage cheese**
   1 4½-oz. can deviled ham
   2 tablespoons French dressing
Turn into a serving bowl and garnish with a
1-in. border of
   Finely minced parsley
Serve with crackers.   *About 1¼ cups dip*

Cheese Puff Appetizers

Remove biscuits from
   **1 8-oz. container ready-to-bake
      biscuits**
On a lightly floured surface, roll each into
a round 4 to 5 in. in diameter.

Heat a large heavy skillet until hot; turn heat
very low; arrange flattened biscuits in skillet
and heat until golden brown, about 2 min.
Turn biscuits and brown other side; repeat
procedure, browning remaining biscuits.

Arrange browned biscuits on a broiler rack;
set aside to keep warm.

Blend together
   ¼ cup butter, softened
   ½ teaspoon Worcestershire sauce
   2 drops tabasco sauce
   **1 cup (about 4 oz.) shredded sharp
      Cheddar cheese**
Beat until rounded peaks are formed
   1 egg white
Gently fold the egg white into the cheese-
butter mixture. Spread about 2 tablespoons of
cheese mixture on top of each biscuit.

Place under broiler about 3 in. from source
of heat; broil about 4 min., or until lightly
browned.

Cut each biscuit into six wedge-shaped pieces.
Serve immediately.   *60 appetizers*

Saucy Cocktail Franks

Put into a saucepan and melt over low heat
   1 10-oz. jar currant jelly
Add and heat thoroughly
   ⅓ cup prepared mustard
Meanwhile, cut into 1-in. diagonal pieces
   1 lb. frankfurters
Add frankfurter pieces to hot mixture and
blend to coat each piece. Simmer about 30
min., stirring occasionally.

Serve with wooden picks as hors d'oeuvres.
     About 10 servings

Onion Soup Les Halles

*Canned vegetable juices and consommé are sub-
stituted for the time-consuming soup stock used
in the traditional recipe for onion soup made
famous by Les Halles, famous market in Paris.*

Melt in a saucepan over medium heat
   2 tablespoons butter or margarine
Add and cook until tender, about 5 min.
   2 large onions, coarsely chopped
   1 clove garlic, finely chopped

Stir in and simmer about 10 min.

½ teaspoon salt
⅛ teaspoon black pepper
⅛ teaspoon thyme
1 large sprig parsley, snipped
2 teaspoons tarragon vinegar
1 can condensed beef consommé
1 soup can water
1 12-oz. can (about 1½ cups) cocktail vegetable juices

Serve piping hot, topping each serving with buttered **toast rounds** well coated with shredded **Parmesan cheese.** *4 servings*

Dutch-Style Chowder

Put into a saucepan and cook until crisp

4 slices bacon, diced

Remove bacon from pan to absorbent paper; pour off fat and return one tablespoon fat to pan. Add and cook until tender, occasionally moving and turning with a spoon

⅓ cup chopped onion

Blend in and heat thoroughly, stirring frequently

1 can condensed cream of chicken soup
1 can condensed chicken-vegetable soup
1 soup can milk
1 soup can water
1 cup drained whole kernel corn

Garnish with bacon and **snipped parsley.**

4 to 6 servings

Ginger-Tomato-Rice Soup 4

Combine in a saucepan, cover, and simmer 5 min.

1 can condensed tomato-rice soup
1 soup can water
1 teaspoon finely chopped crystallized ginger
¹⁄₁₆ teaspoon rosemary

Serve with slices of **lemon** or **lime**, sprinkled with finely minced **parsley,** or top with a dollop of **thick sour cream.** *About 4 servings*

Herb-Seasoned Tomato 5 Soup

Blend together in a saucepan and heat just to boiling, stirring occasionally

1 10½- to 11-oz. can condensed tomato soup
1¼ cups milk
1 teaspoon sugar
1 teaspoon parsley flakes
½ teaspoon seasoned salt
¼ teaspoon oregano
¼ teaspoon dill seed

Top each serving with **thick sour cream.**

About 4 servings

Chicken Gumbo-Cream of 6 Vegetable Soup

Combine in a saucepan

1 can condensed chicken gumbo soup
1 can condensed cream of vegetable soup

Blend in

2 soup cans water

and a mixture of

¼ teaspoon fennel
¼ teaspoon crushed sweet basil
Few grains ginger

Simmer, covered, about 10 min.

Meanwhile, blend together thoroughly

½ cup thick sour cream
½ cup mashed ripe avocado
⅛ teaspoon coriander

Serve with the soup. *About 6 servings*

Chilled Blender Pea Soup

Set out a 1½-qt. saucepan.

Put into blender container

1 cup milk
2 tablespoons butter or margarine
2 teaspoons flour
½ teaspoon salt
⅛ teaspoon pepper
½ teaspoon Accent
½ teaspoon nutmeg
¼ teaspoon sugar
1 small onion, quartered

Cover and blend.

Continue to blend while gradually adding one-half of

1 lb. can peas (do not drain)

When thoroughly blended, empty contents of container into saucepan.

Put into the blender container and blend

½ cup milk
Remaining peas

Stir contents of blender into mixture in saucepan.

Place over medium heat and bring to boiling, stirring occasionally. Cool. Chill thoroughly.

4 servings

Borscht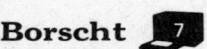

Set out a 1½-qt. saucepan.

Drain, reserving juice in a 1-qt. measuring cup

1 1-lb. can whole beets

Force beets through a food mill (or crush beets in a blender, using ½ cup of the reserved liquid).

Add beet pulp to the beet juice in measuring cup and add water to make 1 qt. Place mixture in saucepan adding

¾ teaspoon salt
¼ cup sugar
5 tablespoons lemon juice

Heat mixture to boiling, stirring occasionally. Remove from heat and add gradually ¾ cup of the hot mixture to

1 egg, well beaten

Stirring constantly, stir egg mixture into beet mixture in saucepan. Return to heat; continue stirring and cook until simmering (do not boil).

Garnish each serving with **thick sour cream.**

About 4 servings

Crab-Meat Bisque

Remove and discard any bony tissue and separate into ½-in. pieces

1 6-oz. pkg. frozen crab meat, thawed

Mix together in top of double boiler

1 10½- to 11-oz. can condensed
   tomato soup
1 10½- to 11-oz. can condensed
   cream of pea soup
½ teaspoon seasoned salt
   Few grains white pepper
¼ teaspoon oregano
3 drops tabasco sauce
2 tablespoons ketchup

Add gradually and blend into the mixture

2 cups cream

Heat over simmering water until mixture is well blended and thoroughly heated; stir occasionally.

Add the crab meat; heat thoroughly. Sprinkle with **paprika.**

About 6 servings

Creamy Brussels Sprouts Soup

Combine in blender container and blend thoroughly

1 10-oz. pkg. frozen Brussels sprouts, thawed and cut in halves
1 cup thick sour cream
½ teaspoon salt
¼ teaspoon black pepper

Blend in

1¾ cups chicken stock or broth

Pour mixture into heavy saucepan and heat thoroughly (do not boil).

Garnish with **parsley** or **water cress**.

About 8 servings

Herbed Soup 10

Put into a saucepan

1 can condensed chicken gumbo soup
1 can condensed cream of celery soup

Blend in

2 soup cans water
⅛ teaspoon fennel seed, crushed
¼ teaspoon basil leaves, crushed
Few grains ginger

Bring to boiling; reduce heat and simmer, covered, about 10 min.

Meanwhile, blend until smooth

½ cup mashed ripe avocado
½ cup thick sour cream
⅛ teaspoon coriander

Top each serving of hot soup with a dollop of avocado mixture. *About 6 servings*

Cheese Finger Rolls 11

Lightly grease baking sheets.

Follow directions on package for preparing rolls, using

1 14½-oz. pkg. hot roll mix

and blending into the dry ingredients

1 cup (about 4 oz.) grated sharp Cheddar cheese

Knead dough and let rise according to package directions. When dough has doubled, punch down and turn onto a lightly floured surface. Divide dough into four portions.

Break off a small portion of dough and shape into an oblong 2½x1 in. and about ½ in. thick. Pinch both ends to points, making roll 3 in. long. Place on baking sheet about 1 in. apart. Repeat, using remaining dough.

Brush tops with a mixture of

1 egg
1 tablespoon water

Cover and let rise again until doubled.

Bake at 375°F about 20 min., or until golden brown. *About 3 doz. rolls*

Cheese-Sausage Rolls 12

Lightly grease a baking sheet.

Prepare according to directions on package

1 14½-oz. pkg. hot roll mix

Mix together in a small bowl

½ lb. Mozzarella cheese, cut in thin strips
¼ lb. cervelat sausage, cut in thin strips
⅛ teaspoon salt
⅛ teaspoon black pepper

Cut off small pieces of dough and pat into rounds about ¼ in. thick and about 3 in. in diameter. Brush with melted **butter**. Spoon about 2 tablespoons of the cheese mixture onto each. Moisten edges, fold in halves and press edges with fork to seal. Place on baking sheet and brush tops with melted **butter**.

Bake at 400°F about 12 min., or until delicately browned. Remove from oven; sprinkle with grated **Romano cheese** and serve hot.

About 1½ doz.

Fig Coffee Braid 13

Lightly grease baking sheets.

Combine in a bowl
- **1 14½-oz. pkg. hot roll mix**
- **2 tablespoons sugar**
- **¼ teaspoon salt**

Soften yeast in
- **1 cup warm water, 110°F to 115°F**

Let stand 5 to 10 min.

Stir yeast into the dry ingredients and add, mixing well
- **½ teaspoon vanilla extract**

Form dough into a ball in the bowl and lightly grease top. Cover with waxed paper and towel and let stand in a warm place (about 80°F) until dough is doubled (about 1 hr.).

Punch down dough and turn onto a lightly floured surface. Knead into the dough a small amount at a time
- **1 lb. fig bars, cut in small pieces**
- **½ cup chopped walnuts**

Divide dough into four equal parts; roll and stretch each portion into a strip about 12 in. long. Twist two strips together and seal ends; repeat. Place each braid on a baking sheet. Cover and let rise again until doubled.

Bake at 375°F about 25 min., or until golden brown.

While warm brush with a glaze of
- **1½ cups sifted confectioners' sugar**
- **3 tablespoons orange juice**
- **¼ teaspoon grated orange peel**

2 coffee cakes

Glazed Honey Pinwheels 14

Put into an 8-in. square pan
- **½ cup honey**
- **2 tablespoons butter or margarine**

Set pan in a 425°F oven to melt butter.

When butter is melted, remove pan from oven. Stir to blend honey and butter. Sprinkle evenly with
- **½ cup coarsely chopped pecans**

Set aside in a warm place.

Put into a bowl
- **2 cups biscuit mix**

Prepare a dough, following the rolled biscuit directions on the package for amount of liquid and mixing instructions.

Turn the dough onto a lightly floured surface and knead gently with fingertips. Roll into a 10x6-in. rectangle, about ¾ in. thick. Spread over surface of dough
- **3 tablespoons honey**

Sprinkle evenly over the honey
- **¼ cup dark seedless raisins**
- **½ teaspoon cinnamon**

Dot with
- **1 tablespoon butter or margarine**

Roll dough jelly-roll fashion, beginning with a long side; pinch edge to seal. Cut roll into 9 slices. Arrange slices in pan.

Bake at 425°F about 20 min., or until top is golden brown.

Remove from oven and let stand 1 min. in pan. Invert immediately on a serving plate and remove pan.

9 rolls

New Moon Yeast Rolls 15

Lightly grease baking sheets.

Soften, using a large bowl
1 pkg. active dry yeast
in
¾ cup warm water, 110°F to 115°F
Add and beat vigorously until well blended
3 cups biscuit mix
2 tablespoons sugar
1 egg
Turn dough onto a lightly floured surface and knead until smooth (about 20 times).

Roll dough into a 10-in. square and spread over one half of dough
2 tablespoons butter, softened
Fold unbuttered half over buttered portion; press edges to seal. Roll dough into a 12-in. circle and distribute evenly over surface
4 oz. (about ½ cup) almond paste, sieved
Cut dough into 16 wedge-shaped pieces. Roll up each wedge beginning at wide end. Place rolls on baking sheets with points underneath. Curve into crescents.

Cover lightly and let stand in a warm place (about 80°F) 1 hr.

Bake at 375°F about 15 min., or until golden brown. If desired, brush with melted butter.

16 rolls

Prune Twists 16

Lightly grease baking sheets.

Mix together in a bowl
2 cups biscuit mix
¼ cup firmly packed brown sugar
¼ teaspoon cinnamon
Cut in with a pastry blender or two knives until mixture resembles coarse corn meal
6 tablespoons butter
Mix in
½ cup finely cut prunes
½ cup grated sharp Cheddar cheese
Make a well in center of dry ingredients; add
½ cup cream

Stir with a fork until dough follows fork. Gently form dough into a ball and place on a lightly floured surface. Roll into a 12x6-in. rectangle. Cut into twelve 6x1-in. strips; roll each strip 8 in. long. Brush with **milk**.

Roll strips in
1 cup chopped walnuts
On greased baking sheets, shape each strip into a "figure 8" overlapping ends at center. Press a **candied cherry** onto center of each; sprinkle with **sugar**.

Bake at 400°F about 10 min. Serve warm.

1 doz. twists

Pan o' Rolls 17

Set out a 9-in. round cake pan.

Heat in a small skillet until melted
¼ cup butter or margarine
1 clove garlic, minced
Mix in and remove from heat
2 tablespoons finely cut parsley
Open
2 8-oz. containers ready-to-bake biscuits
Dip each biscuit into the garlic butter.

Overlap 15 of the biscuits around the outer edge of the cake pan; form inner circle by overlapping remaining biscuits. Drizzle any remaining butter over top of biscuits and sprinkle generously with **Parmesan cheese**.

Bake at 425°F 15 to 20 min., or until golden brown. Serve hot. *20 rolls*

Herbed Biscuit Ring 18

Set out a baking sheet.

Cream
¼ cup butter or margarine
Blend in
½ teaspoon lemon juice
½ teaspoon celery seed
½ teaspoon sage
¼ teaspoon thyme
Few grains salt
Few grains paprika

Cover and set in refrigerator at least 1 hr. to allow flavors to blend thoroughly.

Remove herb butter from refrigerator to soften slightly before using.

Open
1 8-oz. container ready-to-bake biscuits
Spread each biscuit with herb butter.

Place on baking sheet arranging biscuits slightly overlapping to form a ring.

Bake at 400°F 15 min., or until golden brown.

10 biscuits

Quick Doughnuts

Set out a deep saucepan or automatic deep-fryer (*page 13*) and heat fat to 365°F.

Using a small cutter about 1 in. in diameter, cut the centers from biscuits in
1 8-oz. container ready-to-bake biscuits
Deep-fry doughnuts and "holes" in heated fat. Fry only as many doughnuts at one time as will float uncrowded one layer deep in the fat.

Turn doughnuts with a fork as they rise to surface and several times during cooking (do not pierce). Fry 2 to 3 min., or until lightly browned. Drain doughnuts and "holes" over fat for a few seconds before removing to absorbent paper.

Serve plain, or shake 2 or 3 warm doughnuts at a time in a plastic bag containing
¼ cup confectioners' sugar

10 doughnuts plus "holes"

Frankfurter Quick Bread 19

These rolls make an especially good accompaniment for a main-dish salad or soup.

Lightly grease 12 muffin-pan wells; set aside.

Mix in a saucepan
⅓ cup sugar
¼ cup cooking oil
⅓ cup orange juice
1 teaspoon prepared mustard
Bring rapidly to boiling; simmer 2 min. Spoon about 1 tablespoon of the mixture into the bottom of each muffin-pan well.

Put into a bowl
2 cups pancake mix
Stir in
¼ cup cooking oil
1 egg, slightly beaten
½ cup milk
Gently form dough into a ball and turn onto a lightly floured surface; knead gently 10 to 15 times. Roll dough into 16x9-in. rectangle ¼ in. thick.

Place end to end on longer side of rectangle
3 frankfurters
and roll up as for a jelly roll; press edge to seal. Cut roll into 12 slices; place one slice, cut side down, over orange mixture in each muffin-pan well.

Bake at 450°F about 20 min. Invert muffin pan on cooling rack; allow to stand a few minutes before lifting off pan. Serve warm.

1 doz. rolls

Orange-Raisin Muffins

Grease bottoms only of 16 2-in. muffin-pan wells.

Mix together in a bowl
2 cups buttermilk pancake mix
1 tablespoon sugar
¼ teaspoon salt
Mix in
⅔ cup dark or golden raisins
1 teaspoon grated orange peel
Blend together in a small bowl
1 egg, well beaten
¼ cup melted butter
1 cup orange juice
Make a well in the center of dry ingredients and add liquid all at one time. With no more than 25 strokes, stir quickly and lightly until dry ingredients are barely moistened. (Batter will be lumpy and break from spoon.) Cut against side of bowl with spoon to get enough batter at one time to fill each muffin-pan well two-thirds full; push batter off with another spoon or spatula.

Bake at 400°F about 15 min., or until golden brown. *16 muffins*

Skillet Beans with Pineapple

Set out a skillet and heat a serving dish.

Panbroil in the skillet until crisp, pouring off and reserving fat as it collects
6 slices bacon, diced
Remove bacon; set aside and keep warm. Return to skillet
1 teaspoon bacon fat
Stir in
2 tablespoons brown sugar
Few grains cloves
Few grains ginger
Place over low heat, stirring constantly, until sugar is dissolved. Add to skillet and brown lightly on each side
4 pineapple slices, cut in halves

Arrange pineapple around edge of warm serving dish. Heat in skillet about
1 tablespoon reserved bacon fat
Add and cook until transparent
¼ cup chopped onion
Add and mix together
1 1-lb. can pork and beans in tomato sauce
½ teaspoon dry mustard
2 tablespoons dark corn sirup
Heat thoroughly, stirring occasionally. Stir in the reserved bacon pieces and turn mixture onto center of serving dish. *About 4 servings*

Lightning Beef Stew

Set out a skillet with a tight-fitting cover and a bowl.

Empty into the skillet
2 1½-lb. cans beef stew
1 10¾-oz. can beef gravy
Mix in
½ teaspoon onion juice
1 4-oz. can sliced mushrooms, drained
1 8½-oz. can peas, drained
Set over medium heat, stirring occasionally, until mixture bubbles.

Meanwhile, put into the bowl
2 cups prepared biscuit mix
1 tablespoon chopped parsley
¼ teaspoon thyme
¾ cup milk
Mix thoroughly with a fork. Drop by teaspoonfuls over meat and vegetables in simmering stew. Cook for 5 min.; cover, and cook 10 min. longer. *6 servings*

Saucy Ham Omelet 23

Set a large heavy skillet over medium heat.

Add and brown evenly on all sides
1 10-oz. can ham sticks
Add and turn heat to low
2 tablespoons butter or margarine
Combine in a bowl
1 tablespoon flour
⅛ teaspoon salt
2 tablespoons milk
Add and beat until thoroughly blended
4 eggs
Pour mixture into skillet and arrange ham sticks spoke-fashion. Cook until egg mixture is set.

Cut into wedges and serve with warm **Apple Sauce.** *About 4 servings*

For Apple Sauce—Pour into a saucepan and heat until hot
1 12-oz. can (about 1½ cups) apple juice
Stir in a mixture of
2 tablespoons brown sugar
1 tablespoon cornstarch
¼ teaspoon cinnamon
2 tablespoons lemon juice
Bring to boiling, stirring constantly. Simmer about 10 min., or until slightly thickened. Remove from heat and stir in
1 tablespoon butter

About 1¼ cups

Sweet and Speedy 24

Mix together in a large skillet
1 8-oz. can tomato sauce
¼ cup peach sirup, drained from 1-lb. can sliced peaches (use remaining sirup for other food preparation)
¼ cup firmly packed brown sugar
2 tablespoons lemon juice
1 teaspoon dry mustard
½ teaspoon salt
½ teaspoon Worcestershire sauce
Cover; simmer 5 min.

Cut into nine uniform slices almost through to bottom
1 12-oz. can luncheon meat
Slip one drained **peach slice** into each cut in meat.

Place loaf in sauce in skillet. Spoon some of the sauce over meat. Add remaining peach slices to sauce. Cover; simmer 5 min.

4 servings

Pear-Topped Special 25

Set out a large bowl and grease a shallow 1½-qt. baking dish.

Drain and set aside
1 1-lb., 4-oz. can pear halves
Put into bowl
1 12-oz. can luncheon meat, shredded
2 medium-size onions, chopped
⅔ cup diced celery
⅓ cup slivered green pepper
4 medium-size potatoes, cooked and cubed
1 cup quick meat broth (dissolve 1 beef bouillon cube in 1 cup hot water)
and a mixture of
1 teaspoon Accent
½ teaspoon salt
Few grains black pepper
Toss ingredients lightly to mix thoroughly. Turn into baking dish and heat in 400°F oven 30 min.

Remove from oven. Arrange pear halves, cut side down, over top. Brush pears lightly with

Softened butter or margarine

and sprinkle with

¼ cup firmly packed brown sugar

Return to oven and heat 15 min. longer.

About 6 servings

Spinach-Tongue Casserole

Set out a shallow 1-qt. baking dish.

Cook according to directions on package

1 10-oz. pkg. frozen chopped spinach

Meanwhile, mix together

1 10½- to 11-oz. can condensed cream of celery soup

¼ cup cream

1 tablespoon instant minced onion

2 or 3 drops tabasco sauce

Drain cooked spinach thoroughly. Mix in

1 tablespoon butter

⅛ teaspoon black pepper

Arrange spinach in bottom of baking dish.

Arrange over spinach

1 6-oz. can beef tongue slices

Spoon soup mixture over tongue slices; sprinkle with

½ cup grated Parmesan cheese

Put baking dish on broiler rack with top of mixture about 4 in. from source of heat. Broil 8 min., or until thoroughly heated.

About 4 servings

Chili-etti

Turn into a heavy skillet

1 1-lb. can chili with beans

1 15¼-oz. can spaghetti in tomato sauce with cheese

Stir in

1 tablespoon instant minced onion

Cook over low heat 8 to 10 min., stirring occasionally, until thoroughly heated.

When ready to serve, sprinkle with

2 tablespoons grated Parmesan cheese

4 servings

Confetti Macaroni and Cheese Ring Mold

Lightly grease a 1½-qt. ring mold.

Mix together in a bowl

2 15¼-oz. cans macaroni with cheese sauce (about 3½ cups)

1 4-oz. pkg. (1 cup) shredded sharp Cheddar cheese

2 tablespoons chopped pimiento

2 tablespoons chopped parsley

1 teaspoon instant minced onion

Add and mix lightly until well blended

3 eggs, beaten

Turn into the mold.

Bake in boiling water bath (*page 12*) at 350°F about 1 hr., or until mixture is set.

4 to 6 servings

Wiener Mix-Up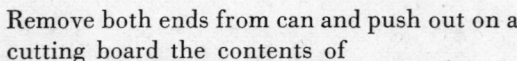

Set out a large bowl and lightly grease a 1½-qt. casserole with cover.

Lightly mix together in bowl
8 frankfurters, sliced
1 4½-oz. can sliced ripe olives, drained
1 1-lb. can whole kernel corn
1 1-lb. can cut green beans
1 cup (about 4 oz.) diced sharp Cheddar cheese
2 cups ketchup
1 tablespoon sugar
½ teaspoon salt
⅛ teaspoon garlic salt
1 small onion, finely chopped
Turn into casserole; cover, and heat in 350°F oven 1 hr. *6 to 8 servings*

Hash Distinctive

Remove both ends from can and push out on a cutting board the contents of
1 1-lb. can corned beef hash
Cut hash into four equal slices and place on broiler rack. Brush with
2 teaspoons melted butter or margarine
Place under broiler with top of meat 3 in. from source of heat. Broil 3 to 5 min., or until browned. Turn and spread slices evenly with
2 teaspoons prepared horse-radish
Place on each hash-round
1 tomato slice

Brush with
2 teaspoons melted butter or margarine
Sprinkle over tomato slices
2 oz. sharp Cheddar cheese, grated
½ teaspoon salt
¼ teaspoon Accent
Few grains pepper
Broil about 5 min. longer. *4 servings*

Chicken-Broccoli Casserole

Set out a saucepan and grease a shallow 1½-qt. baking dish.

In saucepan, cook according to directions on package until almost tender
2 10-oz. pkgs. frozen broccoli spears
Drain. Blend together
1 10½- to 11-oz. can condensed cream of chicken soup, undiluted
½ cup mayonnaise
½ teaspoon lemon juice
Arrange cooked broccoli in baking dish; top with
2 cups sliced cooked chicken
Pour sauce evenly over broccoli and sliced chicken. Sprinkle with a mixture of
½ cup fine dry bread crumbs
2 tablespoons melted butter
Top with
¼ cup grated sharp Cheddar cheese
Heat in a 350°F oven 25 min., or until topping is lightly browned. *About 6 servings*

Note: If desired, add ¼ teaspoon **curry powder** to sauce mixture; blend well.

Quick Company Dinner

Lightly grease an 11x7x1½-in. baking dish; set aside.

Cook according to directions on package
1 2½-lb. pkg. frozen breaded frying chicken
Remove from oven 20 min. before end of cooking time.

Put into the baking dish and spread evenly
2 15¼-oz. cans macaroni with cheese sauce (about 3½ cups)
Arrange the chicken pieces on top of the macaroni in baking dish.

Blend together and pour over chicken
1 10½- to 11-oz. can condensed cream of celery soup
½ cup milk
Sprinkle over top
¼ cup grated Romano cheese
Paprika
Heat in 400°F oven 30 min., or until top is lightly browned. *About 6 servings*

Fish Stick Special  31

Arrange in a shallow baking dish
1 8-oz. pkg. frozen fish sticks
Mix together and spoon over fish
¼ cup chopped toasted almonds
1 cup (about 4 oz.) grated Cheddar cheese
2 tablespoons chopped onion
¼ cup milk
½ cup chopped sweet mixed pickles
Top with
2 tablespoons buttered dry bread crumbs
Heat in a 425°F oven 15 to 20 min.

About 4 servings

Skillet Tuna Supreme 32

Heat in a large heavy skillet
2 tablespoons cooking oil
Add and cook, occasionally moving and turning with a spoon, until the vegetables are just tender
⅔ cup chopped onion
1 green pepper, cut in slivers
Stir in
1 10½- to 11-oz. can condensed tomato soup
2 teaspoons soy sauce
2 tablespoons brown sugar
1 teaspoon grated lemon peel
3 tablespoons lemon juice
Bring to boiling and simmer 5 min.

Mix in, separating into small pieces
2 7-oz. cans tuna, drained
Heat thoroughly.

Serve with fluffy cooked **rice.** Garnish tuna mixture with toasted **sesame seed** and **chow mein noodles.** *About 6 servings*

Scandinavian Supper Dish 33

Heat in saucepan about 5 min., or until butter is melted
1 can frozen condensed cream of shrimp soup, thawed
2 tablespoons butter
¼ cup milk
Add
1 15-oz. can fish balls in bouillon, drained
1 1-lb. can potatoes, drained
Cover and simmer until mixture is thoroughly heated, about 10 min.

Serve garnished with chopped **parsley.**

About 4 servings

Tuna-Chili Chowder 34

Heat in a large saucepan having a tight-fitting cover

¼ cup tuna oil (drained from 3 7-oz. cans tuna)

Add and cook over medium heat, stirring occasionally, until celery is just tender

1 cup sliced celery
1 cup chopped green pepper
1½ teaspoons paprika

Then add

¾ cup instant minced onion
1 10½- to 11-oz. can condensed tomato soup
3 soup cans water (about 1 qt.)
2 tablespoons tomato paste
2 1-lb. cans red kidney beans, drained
2 tablespoons cider vinegar
1 teaspoon salt
¼ teaspoon pepper
1½ teaspoons chili powder

Separate into large pieces and add the

Drained tuna

Cover and cook until thoroughly heated.

About 8 servings

Top of the Range Corn Pudding 35

Grease five 5-oz. custard cups. Set out a bowl and a large skillet, having a tight-fitting cover.

In the bowl, beat well

2 eggs

Gradually stir in

1 6-oz. can evaporated milk
1½ teaspoons instant minced onion
1 tablespoon finely chopped green pepper
¼ teaspoon salt
⅛ teaspoon black pepper
¼ teaspoon nutmeg
1 12-oz. can whole kernel corn, drained
1½ tablespoons butter, melted

Spoon mixture into the custard cups; place the custard cups into the skillet. Pour hot water into skillet to depth of corn mixture in cups. Bring water to boiling, cover, and cook over very low heat about 10 min., or until a silver knife inserted in center of puddings comes out clean.

Remove from skillet at once; place on rack to cool slightly. Unmold onto warm serving plate and garnish each mold with **water cress.**

5 servings

Creamy Green Bean Casserole

Set out a 2-qt. casserole.

Cook according to directions on package and drain, if necessary

2 10-oz. pkgs. frozen green beans

Put into a large mixing bowl

1 8-oz. can water chestnuts, drained and sliced
1 lb., 4-oz. can bean sprouts, drained
1 4-oz. can mushrooms, drained
1 10½- to 11-oz. can condensed cream of mushroom soup
½ teaspoon salt
Few grains black pepper

Add beans; toss lightly. Turn into casserole and top with

> **1 3½-oz. can French fried onion rings**

Heat in 325°F oven about 25 min.

About 8 servings

Green Beans with Mayonnaise Sauce

Cook according to directions on package and drain, if necessary

> **2 10-oz. pkgs. frozen cut green beans**

Toss hot beans with a mixture of

> **½ cup mayonnaise**
> **⅛ to ¼ teaspoon curry powder**
> **1 teaspoon celery seed**
> **2 tablespoons shredded Parmesan cheese**

6 to 8 servings

Broccoli with Lemon-Olive Sauce

Cook according to directions on package and drain

> **2 10-oz. pkgs. frozen broccoli**

Heat in a heavy saucepan about 5 min.

> **½ cup butter or margarine**
> **1 clove garlic, minced**

Add

> **1 4½-oz. can finely chopped ripe olives**
> **½ teaspoon salt**
> **Few grains black pepper**
> **2 to 4 tablespoons lemon juice**

Heat thoroughly; pour over hot broccoli arranged on a heated serving dish.

6 to 8 servings

Cauliflower-Spinach Sensation

Cook according to directions on package

> **1 pkg. frozen cauliflower**

Drain and cool.

Cook according to directions on package

> **1 pkg. frozen chopped spinach**

Stir in, and cook 1 min. longer

> **⅓ cup chopped water cress**
> **2 tablespoons chopped parsley**
> **½ teaspoon tarragon, crushed**

Drain spinach mixture thoroughly and force through a food mill or sieve.

Blend together

> **½ cup mayonnaise**
> **½ cup heavy cream, whipped**

Mix with sieved spinach and cauliflower; chill.

About 4 servings

Limas in Sour Cream 38

Cook according to directions on package; drain
  1 10-oz. pkg. frozen lima beans
Blend into beans
  3 slices bacon, diced and pan-broiled
  1 cup thick sour cream
  3 tablespoons milk
  2 tablespoons tomato paste
  1½ tablespoons instant minced onion
Heat over low heat, stirring constantly, until hot (do not boil). Garnish with sieved hard-cooked **egg yolk** and additional crisp crumbled **bacon**, if desired.   *About 4 servings*

Lima Beans with Water Chestnuts 39

Cook according to directions on package
  1 pkg. frozen baby lima beans
Drain and combine with
  ½ cup sliced water chestnuts
Heat thoroughly in a small saucepan
  ¼ cup butter or margarine
  2 tablespoons wine vinegar
  2 teaspoons dill seed
  ½ teaspoon salt
  ¼ teaspoon black pepper
  ¼ teaspoon Accent
Pour over vegetables; toss lightly to coat.
      About 4 servings

Jiffy Green Pea Relish

Prepare according to directions on package
  1 env. Italian salad dressing mix
Drain and put into a bowl
  1 lb. can peas
Pour ½ cup of the salad dressing over peas. Set in refrigerator to marinate about 1 hr., stirring occasionally. Mix in
  ½ cup coarsely chopped onion
Return to refrigerator until ready to serve.

Before serving, toss lightly with
  ⅓ cup crumbled crisp bacon
      About 8 servings

Quick Wild Rice with Mushrooms

This wild rice combination is not only delicious served with a meat course but it makes a deluxe stuffing for duckling.

Set out a heavy skillet and warm a serving dish.

Heat in skillet
  ¼ cup butter
Add and cook until mushrooms are lightly browned
  ½ lb. sliced mushrooms
  ¼ cup chopped onion
Blend together until dissolved
  2 chicken bouillon cubes
  1 cup hot water
Stir chicken broth into skillet and add
  1 10-oz. can instant wild rice
Simmer, uncovered, until most of liquid is absorbed. Turn into dish and garnish with minced **parsley**.   *About 6 servings*

Note: If used as a stuffing, prepare just before needed; stuff and roast bird immediately. (This recipe yields about 4 cups stuffing.)

Cinnamon-Pecan Yams 40

Melt in a saucepan
  ¼ cup butter or margarine
Add and mix well
  ¼ cup chopped pecans
  ½ teaspoon cinnamon
Add
  1 1-lb. can yams, drained
Cook over low heat; turn occasionally to coat evenly.   *About 4 servings*

Springtime Potatoes 41

Heat and drain thoroughly
1 1-lb. can whole potatoes
Meanwhile, mix together in a saucepan
⅓ cup chopped pared cucumber
2 tablespoons chopped green pepper
2 tablespoons sliced radishes
1½ tablespoons chopped green onion
1 teaspoon salt
Few grains black pepper
½ cup thick sour cream
Cook over very low heat (do not boil), stirring frequently.

Pour sour-cream mixture over hot potatoes; toss lightly to coat evenly. *About 4 servings*

Cheese-Whipped Potatoes

Prepare according to directions on package
Instant mashed potatoes (about 2 cups, cooked)
Whip into the potatoes until light and fluffy
½ cup grated sharp Cheddar cheese
½ teaspoon grated onion
2 drops tabasco sauce
Spoon into a warm serving bowl and garnish with finely chopped **green pepper** and **pimiento**. *About 4 servings*

Water Chestnut-Celery Stuffing

Prepare according to directions on package for moist stuffing
1 8-oz. pkg. stuffing mix
Add
1 cup diced celery
¼ cup finely chopped onion
1 8-oz. can water chestnuts, drained and sliced
2 tablespoons parsley flakes
Lightly toss to mix. Spoon stuffing into body and neck cavities of poultry (do not pack).
About 5½ cups stuffing

Quick Potato Salad

Put into a bowl and toss together lightly
2 1-lb. cans potato salad
⅔ cup thinly sliced radishes
1 medium-size cucumber, rinsed, pared, and diced
6 green onions, cut in ½-in. pieces
Chill thoroughly in refrigerator.

About 8 servings

Potato-Salad Mold

Lightly oil a 5½-cup ring mold with salad oil or cooking oil (not olive oil); drain.

Pour into a small bowl
¾ cup quick chicken broth, cooled (dissolve 2 chicken bouillon cubes in ¾ cup hot water)
Sprinkle evenly over broth
1 tablespoon (1 env.) unflavored gelatin
Let stand 5 min. to soften.

Dissolve gelatin completely over hot water; chill until mixture is slightly thicker than consistency of thick, unbeaten egg white, stirring occasionally.

When gelatin is of desired consistency, blend in a mixture of
2 1-lb. jars mayonnaise-style potato salad
½ cup sliced celery
¼ cup sliced green onions
1 teaspoon garlic salt
Blend in
1 cup thick sour cream
Turn into mold; chill until firm.
About 8 servings

Pineapple-Cucumber Relish

Set out an 8x8x2-in. pan.

Empty into a bowl contents of
1 pkg. pineapple-flavored gelatin
Add and stir until the gelatin is completely dissolved
1 cup very hot water
Blend in
¼ cup cold water
¼ cup cider vinegar
Chill (*page 306*) until mixture is slightly thicker than the consistency of thick, unbeaten egg white.

Drain (reserving sirup for use in other food preparation) contents of
1 1-lb., 4-oz. can crushed pineapple
(1⅔ cups, drained)
Wash, pat dry, and chop cucumber to make
2 cups chopped cucumber
When gelatin is of desired consistency, blend in pineapple and chopped cucumber. Turn into the pan. Chill until firm. Cut into squares and serve as relish with fish.   *9 servings*

Tuna Luncheon Mold

Lightly oil a 1-qt. mold with salad or cooking oil (not olive oil); set aside to drain.

Drain contents of
1 9-oz. can crushed pineapple
Add enough water to sirup to make ½ cup liquid. Empty into a bowl contents of
1 pkg. lime-flavored gelatin
Add and stir until the gelatin is completely dissolved
1 cup very hot water
Blend in the pineapple liquid and
2 tablespoons lemon juice
Stirring constantly, gradually add to
1 cup mayonnaise
Chill (*page 306*) until slightly thicker than consistency of thick, unbeaten egg white.

Mix in drained pineapple and
1 6½-oz. can tuna, drained and flaked
½ cup chopped celery
¼ cup chopped green pepper
Turn into mold. Chill until firm.   *6 servings*

▲ Cucumbers in Creamy Dressing

By drawing tines of fork lengthwise over entire surface, score and slice thinly
2 medium-size cucumbers, rinsed
Put into a bowl.

Blend together
½ cup thick sour cream
2 teaspoons sugar
1 teaspoon French-style salad dressing mix
1 tablespoon cider vinegar
Pour mixture over cucumber slices and toss to coat evenly; chill thoroughly.

4 to 6 servings

△ Cucumbers in Blue-Cheese Dressing

Prepare cucumbers as in ▲ Recipe; omit creamy dressing. Prepare 1 pkg. **Blue-cheese salad dressing mix** according to directions on package. Pour dressing over cucumber slices and toss to coat evenly; chill thoroughly.

Spicy Gelatin Cubes

These cubes make an attractive garnish in a border or in mounds around a cold ham or chicken mousse, or a cold sliced meat platter.

Set out an 8x8x2-in. pan.

Empty into a bowl contents of
1 pkg. cherry-flavored gelatin
Heat until very hot
1 cup spicy peach sirup drained from 1-lb., 13-oz. can spiced peaches (reserve peaches for relish tray or other food preparation)
Add to the gelatin and stir until completely dissolved. Stir in
⅔ cup spicy peach sirup
⅓ cup water
¼ teaspoon almond extract
Pour into pan and chill until firm. When ready to serve, cut gelatin into ½-in. cubes.

Corned Beef Salad Mold

Lightly oil a 1-qt. mold with salad oil or cooking oil (not olive oil); set aside to drain.

Heat in a saucepan until very hot
1 10½- to 11-oz. can condensed beef consommé
Empty into a bowl the contents of
1 pkg. lemon-flavored gelatin
Add the hot consommé, stirring until gelatin is completely dissolved. Blend in
½ cup cold water
Chill (*page 306*) in refrigerator until mixture is slightly thicker than consistency of thick, unbeaten egg white.

Meanwhile, empty into a bowl and shred with two forks
1 12-oz. can corned beef
Mix in
⅓ cup chopped pimiento-stuffed olives
¼ cup chopped celery
1 tablespoon prepared horse-radish
When gelatin mixture is of desired consistency, stir in the corned beef mixture. Turn into the prepared mold and chill until firm.

Unmold (*page 306*) onto chilled serving plate and garnish with thin half-slices of scored **cucumber** pressed gently around bottom of the mold. Pile 3 to 5 small **onion rings** on top of mold and place a sprig of **parsley** in center.

6 servings

Creamy Tomato Mold

Creamy Tomato Mold

Lightly oil a 1-qt. fancy mold with salad or cooking oil (not olive oil). Set aside to drain.

Blend in a small bowl
  1 pkg. lemon-flavored gelatin
  1 tablespoon sugar
Add and stir until gelatin is completely dissolved
  1 cup hot tomato juice
Stir in
  ¼ cup lemon juice
Chill (*page 306*) until slightly thicker than the consistency of thick, unbeaten egg white.

When gelatin is of desired consistency, thoroughly blend in
  ½ cup undiluted evaporated milk
Stir in
  1 cup cream-style cottage cheese
  1 cup chopped celery
  2 tablespoons chopped green pepper
  2 tablespoons minced onion
  ¼ teaspoon celery salt
Turn mixture into mold. Chill until firm.
About 6 servings

Festive Salad

Put a bowl and rotary beater into refrigerator to chill. Lightly oil with salad or cooking oil (not olive oil) a 1½-qt. mold. Set aside to drain.

Drain contents of
  **1 1-lb. 4-oz. can fruit cocktail
    (reserve sirup)**
Heat in a saucepan
  1⅓ cups reserved sirup
Empty into a bowl contents of
  1 pkg. lime-flavored gelatin
When sirup is very hot, pour over gelatin and stir until gelatin is completely dissolved.

Chill (*page 306*) until slightly thicker than the consistency of thick, unbeaten egg white.

Add slightly thickened gelatin, a small amount at a time, to
  1 3-oz. pkg. cream cheese, softened
Stir until well blended after each addition. Mix in the fruit cocktail.

Using chilled bowl and beater, beat until of medium consistency (piles softly)
  1 cup chilled whipping cream
Fold into gelatin mixture until blended.

Turn mixture into mold. Chill until firm.
8 to 10 servings

Cola Salad

Lightly oil with salad or cooking oil (not olive oil) a 1½-qt. mold. Set aside to drain.

Empty into a bowl contents of
  2 pkgs. raspberry-flavored gelatin
Add and stir until the gelatin is completely dissolved
  2 cups very hot water
Blend in
  1⅔ cups cola beverage
Chill (*page 306*) until slightly thicker than the consistency of thick, unbeaten egg white.

Meanwhile, prepare and set aside

1 cup maraschino cherries, drained and cut in eighths
1 cup pecans, coarsely chopped

When gelatin is of desired consistency, blend in the chopped pecans and maraschino cherries.

Turn mixture into mold. Chill until firm.

6 to 8 servings

Sparkling Ginger Molds

Lightly oil six individual molds with salad or cooking oil (not olive oil); set aside to drain.

Pour into a small bowl

½ cup ginger ale

Sprinkle evenly over the ginger ale

1 tablespoon (1 env.) unflavored gelatin

Let stand 5 min. to soften.

Dissolve gelatin completely over very hot water. Stir gelatin into

1½ cups ginger ale

Pour into the molds and chill until firm. Unmold onto chilled salad greens.   *6 servings*

Peach-Chutney Relish Mold

Lightly oil with salad or cooking oil (not olive oil) a 1-qt. mold. Set aside to drain.

Empty into a bowl contents of

1 pkg. lemon-flavored gelatin

Add and stir until the gelatin is completely dissolved

1 cup boiling water

Blend in contents of

1 7-oz. bottle lemon-lime carbonated beverage

Chill (*page 306*) until slightly thicker than the consistency of thick, unbeaten egg white.

Meanwhile, thaw, drain and finely chop

1 12-oz. pkg. frozen peaches (or use 1 cup chopped fresh peaches)

Prepare and set aside

½ cup nuts, coarsely chopped
¾ cup chutney, finely chopped

When gelatin is of desired consistency, blend in peaches, nuts, and chutney. Turn into the mold. Chill until firm.   *6 to 8 servings*

Luncheon-Delight Mold

Lightly oil a 1-qt. mold with salad or cooking oil (not olive oil); set aside to drain.

Drain contents of

1 9-oz. can apricot halves

Add enough water to sirup to make 1 cup liquid; heat until very hot.

Empty into a bowl the contents of

1 pkg. lemon-flavored gelatin

Add and stir until the gelatin is completely dissolved

Hot apricot liquid
2 tablespoons lemon juice

Chill (*page 306*) until slightly thicker than consistency of thick unbeaten egg white.

Mix in

1½ cups cream-style cottage cheese
½ cup diced celery
½ cup chopped pecans

Fold into gelatin mixture

⅔ cup undiluted evaporated milk, whipped until stiff

Arrange apricots in bottom of mold and spoon gelatin mixture over them. Chill until firm.

About 6 servings

Jiffy Curry Sauce

This rich-flavored sauce is a delightful accompaniment for cooked broccoli or asparagus.

Blend thoroughly in top of a double boiler
⅔ cup condensed cream of celery soup
1½ teaspoons instant minced onion
½ teaspoon curry powder
Add gradually, stirring well
¼ cup plus 2 tablespoons milk
Place over simmering water and heat thoroughly, stirring occasionally.

Vigorously stir ¼ cup of the hot mixture into
1 egg, slightly beaten
Return mixture to double boiler; cook over simmering water 3 to 5 min., stirring constantly. Blend in
1½ teaspoons butter or margarine

About 1 cup sauce

Sour Cream Meat Sauce 43

Reheat cooked meat slices or meat balls in this spicy sauce for a delicious quick dish.

Blend together in a saucepan
1 pkg. spaghetti sauce mix
2 cups water
Bring to boiling; reduce heat and simmer 25 min. Remove from heat.

Gradually add, blending well
1 cup thick sour cream
Heat thoroughly; do not boil.

About 3 cups sauce

Piquant Mustard Sauce

A flavorsome accent for a ready-to-serve cold meat platter and for hot meat entrees.

Blend together in a heavy saucepan
½ cup sugar
½ cup prepared mustard
½ cup condensed tomato soup, undiluted
½ cup cider vinegar
3 egg yolks, slightly beaten
Cook over low heat, stirring constantly, until thickened, about 10 min.; cool.

Store in a covered container in refrigerator.

If desired, whipped cream may be folded into chilled sauce before serving.   *1⅔ cups sauce*

Honey-Cream Sauce 45

Here's a quick and easy sauce to serve over hot waffles.

Mix together in a saucepan
1 cup heavy cream
½ cup honey
Cook over low heat about 3 min., stirring constantly until mixture is blended and warm. Remove from heat and stir in
½ cup coarsely chopped walnuts or other nuts
Serve warm over hot waffles. (Use frozen waffles, if desired, heated according to directions on package.)   *About 1½ cups sauce*

Cranberry Upside-Down Cake

Lightly grease bottom of an 8x8x2-in. cake pan.

Melt in a saucepan
  ¼ cup butter or margarine
Add and blend in thoroughly
  ⅔ cup sugar
  1 tablespoon grated orange peel
  ½ teaspoon vanilla extract
Spread mixture over bottom of cake pan.

Mix together thoroughly
  2 cups cranberries, washed and coarsely chopped
  ⅓ cup sugar
Spread over butter mixture in pan. Set aside.

Empty into a bowl contents of
  1 10-oz. pkg. white cake mix
Add
  1½ teaspoons nutmeg
Blend and mix according to directions on package of cake mix. Turn batter over cranberry mixture and spread evenly.

Bake at 350°F 35 to 40 min., or until cake tests done (*page 340*).

Cool 1 to 2 min. in pan on cooling rack.

Using a spatula, loosen cake from sides of pan and invert immediately on serving plate. Let pan rest over cake a few seconds before removing so that sirup will drain over cake. Serve warm or cool.   *One 8-in. square cake*

Quick Applesauce Fruitcake

Grease bottom only of a 9½x5¼x2¾-in. loaf pan.

Put into a large bowl
  ⅓ cup flour
Add and toss lightly with flour
  1 cup (about 4 oz.) pecans, coarsely chopped
  ¾ cup (about 5 oz.) pitted dates, cut in fourths
  ½ cup (about 4 oz.) candied red cherries, cut in fourths
  ¾ cup (about 5 oz.) diced assorted candied fruits
  ¾ cup (about 4 oz.) golden raisins
Empty into a bowl contents of
  1 10-oz. pkg. applesauce cake mix
Put into a 1-cup measuring cup for liquids
  2 eggs
  Water (to make ½ cup)
Add to the cake mix; blend and mix according to directions on package. Pour batter over fruit-nut mixture and mix well. Turn into prepared pan and spread to edges.

Place a shallow pan containing 2 cups hot water on bottom rack of oven during baking time.

Bake at 325°F 1 hr. 10 min., or until cake tests done (*page 340*).

Cool completely; remove from pan and store (*page 338*). Once or twice a week, using a pastry brush, paint cake with **apple cider** or **orange juice**.   *About 2¼ lbs. fruitcake*

Double-Chocolate Fruitcake

Grease a 9-in. tubed pan; line bottom and sides with heavy brown paper; generously grease the paper.

Mix together in a large bowl
2 cups (about 8 oz.) coarsely chopped walnuts
2 cups (about 1 lb.) diced assorted candied fruits
1 cup (6-oz. pkg.) semi-sweet chocolate pieces
Empty into a bowl contents of
2 9-oz. pkgs. chocolate fudge cake mix
Put into a 1-cup measuring cup for liquids
4 eggs
1 tablespoon vanilla extract
Water (to make 1 cup)
Add to the cake mix; blend and mix according to directions on package. Pour batter over nut-fruit-chocolate mixture and blend thoroughly. Turn batter into pan and spread evenly.

Bake at 325°F 1½ hrs., or until cake tests done (*page 340*).

Cool partially; remove from pan and while still warm, peel off paper.

Cool completely and store (*page 338*).

About 3 lbs. fruitcake

Mincemeat Gingerbread

Grease bottom only of an 8x8x2-in. cake pan.

Empty into a bowl contents of
1 pkg. gingerbread mix
Add and mix in
1 to 1⅓ cups moist mincemeat
½ cup coarsely chopped pecans
Proceed according to directions on package of gingerbread mix. Turn batter into pan.

Bake at 350°F 65 to 70 min., or until cake tests done (*page 340*).

Cool in pan; cut into squares and top with **hard sauce** or **sweetened whipped cream**.

About 9 servings

Peach Pudding-Cake 49

Put into 13x9½x2-in. baking pan
½ cup butter
Set pan in a 350°F oven and heat until butter is melted.

Meanwhile, empty into a large bowl contents of
1 pkg. instant vanilla pudding mix
Add and mix in
2 cups white or yellow cake mix
Add and beat with rotary beater until smooth
1 egg
2 cups milk
Stir in until blended
1½ teaspoons almond extract
Add and mix in contents of
1 1-lb., 13-oz. can sliced peaches
When butter in pan is melted, remove from oven and pour batter over it. Distribute butter, which has risen to the top, evenly over batter.

Return to oven and bake about 45 min., or until golden brown.

Serve warm with **whipped cream** sprinkled with **nutmeg**.

8 servings

Choco-Honey Chews

Lightly grease an 8x8x2-in. pan.

Blend together in a bowl
- **1⅓ cups (1 15-oz. can) sweetened condensed milk**
- **2 tablespoons honey**
- **2 tablespoons orange juice**
- **1½ teaspoons grated orange peel**

Stir in
- **1 6-oz. pkg. semi-sweet chocolate pieces**
- **22 honey-flavored graham crackers, crushed (about 1¾ cups crumbs)**
- **½ cup (about 2 oz.) chopped pecans**

Turn mixture into pan and spread evenly to corners.

Bake at 350°F about 30 min., or until wooden pick inserted in the center comes out clean. Remove pan to cooling rack. Cut into bars while still warm. Remove bars to cooling rack. *About 15 cookies*

Firecrackers

Lightly grease cookie sheets.

Prepare according to directions on package for two-crust pie
- **1 pkg. pie crust mix**

Divide dough into two balls.

Sprinkle **red sugar** over a board; using one portion of dough at a time, roll dough into a rectangle 12x6 in. and about ⅛ in. thick.

Mix together
- **¼ cup sugar**
- **1 teaspoon cinnamon**

Brush surface of rolled dough with **melted butter** and sprinkle evenly with one-half of the cinnamon-sugar mixture.

Cut dough in half lengthwise; then cut into 3x1½-in. rectangles.

With longer side nearest you, roll up each section and place on cookie sheet with the open edge down. Insert one **maraschino cherry strip** in the end of each roll for the "fuse."

Bake at 450°F 6 to 8 min. Remove Firecrackers immediately to cooling racks. *32 cookies*

Minted Refrigerator Squares

Butter bottom and sides of 9x9x1¾-in. pan and set aside.

Mix together in a large bowl
- **4 cups graham cracker crumbs**
- **1 cup chopped walnuts**
- **2 cups miniature marshmallows**
- **1 cup confectioners' sugar**

Put into a saucepan over low heat
- **1 12-oz. pkg. semi-sweet chocolate pieces**
- **1 cup undiluted evaporated milk**

Heat, stirring constantly, just until chocolate is melted and mixture is smooth. Remove from heat and stir in
- **¼ teaspoon peppermint extract**

Reserve ½ cup of the chocolate mixture. Pour remaining chocolate into the graham cracker mixture and stir until all crumbs are moistened.

Turn into prepared pan and press into an even layer. Frost with the reserved ½ cup chocolate mixture.

Chill until frosting is firm. Cut into 25 squares. *25 pieces*

Minted Refrigerator Squares

Flaky Macaroons

Ambrosia Cookies 52

Lightly grease two cookie sheets.

Chop and set aside
   1 cup (about 4 oz.) pecans
   3 oz. red candied cherries, chopped
   (about ½ cup)
   3 oz. candied pineapple, chopped
   (about ½ cup)
Bring to boiling
   ¾ cup water
Add and again bring water to boiling
   ½ cup golden raisins
Drain raisins and spread on absorbent paper. Empty into a large bowl
   1 pkg. chocolate chip cookie mix
Stir in nuts, chopped fruit, and raisins. Following directions on package, add and mix in liquid; drop by teaspoonfuls onto cookie sheets and bake.   *3 doz. cookies*

Walnut Brownie Clusters 53

Lightly grease two cookie sheets.

Prepare as label directs for drop cookies
   1 pkg. brownie mix
Stir in
   2 cups broken walnuts
Drop by teaspoonfuls onto cookie sheets; bake at 350°F about 10 min. Frost with **Fudge Glaze** (*page 399*), doubling recipe.
                                   4 doz. cookies

Flaky Macaroons 54

Lightly grease cookie sheets. Set out a large bowl and medium-sized saucepan.

Mix together in the bowl
   4 cups corn flakes
   1⅓ cups (3½-oz. can) flaked coconut
   1 cup chopped nuts
Blend in saucepan
   1 cup sugar
   1 cup light corn sirup
   ½ cup undiluted evaporated milk
   1 tablespoon butter
   Few grains salt
Cook over low heat, stirring constantly until sugar is completely dissolved. Continue cooking to 234°F (soft ball stage, *page 543*).

Remove from heat. Gradually pour over corn-flake mixture, stirring gently to coat corn flakes without crumbling.

Drop by teaspoonfuls onto prepared baking sheets. Lightly shape into mounds with fingers. Allow to set.   *About 40 pieces*

Peppermint Confections 55

Set out cookie sheets.

Crush and set aside enough peppermint candy sticks to yield
   2 tablespoons crushed peppermint
   candy
Put into a bowl
   ¼ cup hydrogenated vegetable shortening or all-purpose shortening
   ½ teaspoon vanilla extract
Add and beat thoroughly
   1 egg yolk
Mix in the crushed candy and contents of
   1 9-oz. pkg. devil's food cake mix
Dough will be crumbly. Work with hands until dough is blended. Press firmly into balls 1 in. in diameter; place 2 in. apart on cookie sheets.

Bake at 350°F 8 min., or until almost no im-

pression remains when cookie is touched lightly. Carefully remove cookies to cooling racks to cool. Sprinkle with
Instant sweet-cocoa mix
About 2 doz. cookies

Raspberry-Lemon Pie

Prepare, bake, and set aside to cool
Graham Cracker Pie Shell (p. 446 **; use a 9-in. pie pan)**
Empty into a bowl contents of
2 pkgs. raspberry-flavored gelatin
Add and mix in
¼ cup sugar
Add and stir until gelatin is dissolved
1½ cups very hot water
Stir in a mixture of
1 6-oz. can frozen lemonade concentrate
1 cup cold water
Chill (*page 12*) until slightly thicker than the consistency of thick, unbeaten egg white.

Fold into gelatin mixture
½ cup whipping cream, whipped
Turn into pastry shell. Chill in refrigerator until firm. *One 9-in. pie*

Torte Pie Temptation

Generously butter a 9-in. pie pan.

Beat until frothy
4 egg whites
Add gradually, beating well after each addition
1 cup sugar
Continue beating until stiff peaks are formed. Blend in
1 teaspoon vanilla extract
Gently fold into the mixture
20 round scalloped crackers, finely crushed
¾ cup (about 3 oz.) chopped pecans
Turn mixture into pie pan and spread evenly. Bake at 325°F 30 min., or until lightly browned.

Serve with **whipped cream.** *About 6 servings*

Pumpkin-Orange Tarts

Prepare, bake, and set aside to cool
Pastry for Little Pies and Tarts (one and one-half recipe, page 443); use 8 4½-in. tart pans
Mix together in a bowl
½ pkg. orange-flavored gelatin
½ cup sugar
Add and stir until gelatin is dissolved
½ cup very hot water
Add gradually, stirring constantly, to a mixture of
1 cup canned pumpkin
¾ teaspoon cinnamon
½ teaspoon ginger
¼ teaspoon nutmeg
½ teaspoon salt
Chill (*page 12*) until slightly thicker than consistency of thick, unbeaten egg white.

Fold into gelatin mixture
½ cup chilled undiluted evaporated milk, whipped until stiff
Spoon into baked tart shells. Chill until firm. Garnish with **salted pecan halves.**
Eight 4½-in. tarts

Mocha Chiffon Pie

Beau-Catcher Pie

Prepare
> **Pastry for a 2-crust 9-in. pie**

Shape pastry into two balls. Prepare a 9-in. pie shell from one ball and an 8-in. pastry round from the other. Bake and cool.

Empty into a heavy saucepan contents of
> **1 pkg. chocolate pudding mix**

Add and blend in
> **½ teaspoon cinnamon**
> **1 teaspoon concentrated soluble coffee**

Add gradually, stirring until thoroughly blended
> **2 cups milk**

Stirring constantly, bring mixture to a full boil. Remove from heat and set aside to cool.

Put into another saucepan contents of
> **1 pkg. butterscotch pudding mix**

Gradually add, stirring until thoroughly blended
> **2 cups milk**

Stirring constantly, bring mixture to a full boil. Cool.

Fold into cooled butterscotch mixture
> **¼ sq. (¼ oz.) unsweetened chocolate, shaved**

Spoon chocolate pudding into pastry shell.

Cover with baked pastry round. Spoon butterscotch pudding over round. Chill.

Serve topped with **whipped cream** and additional shaved chocolate.   *One 9-in. pie*

Mocha Chiffon Pie 56

Split
> **1 doz. ladyfingers**

Cut off one end so ladyfingers are 2- to 2¼-in. long. Arrange upright around inside edge of a 9-in. pie pan. Cover bottom of pie pan with remaining pieces. Set aside.

Mix together in a saucepan
> **½ cup instant sweet-cocoa mix**
> **1 tablespoon (1 env.) unflavored gelatin**
> **1 tablespoon concentrated soluble coffee**
> **Few grains salt**

Blend in
> **2 egg yolks**

Add gradually, blending thoroughly
> **1⅔ cups (14½-oz. can) undiluted evaporated milk**

Set over low heat and cook, stirring constantly, until gelatin is dissolved and mixture is thickened. Cool; chill (*page* 12) until mixture begins to gel (gets slightly thicker).

When gelatin is of desired consistency, beat until frothy

2 egg whites

Add gradually, beating well after each addition

¼ cup sugar

Beat until rounded peaks are formed.

Beat gelatin mixture until foamy, then spread beaten egg whites over it and gently fold (*page* 12) together. Turn into prepared pie pan. Chill in refrigerator until firm.

Garnish (see photo) with **chocolate shot** and **chocolate wafers.**   *One 9-in. pie*

Lime Sherbet De Luxe

Empty into a bowl contents of

1 pkg. lime-flavored gelatin

Add

½ cup sugar

Add and stir until the gelatin is completely dissolved

1 cup very hot water

Stir in

2 cups milk
1 cup heavy cream
2 tablespoons lemon juice

Freeze until mush-like in consistency.

Using a chilled bowl and beater, beat thoroughly. Freeze until firm. Serve in chilled sherbet glasses.   *About 8 servings*

Raspberry Fluff

Set aside to drain

1 1-lb. can raspberries

Whip until cream is of medium consistency (piles softly)

1 cup chilled whipping cream

Beat into whipped cream with final few strokes until blended

3 tablespoons confectioners' sugar
1 teaspoon vanilla extract

Gently fold in drained raspberries and

1 cup miniature marshmallows

Tint to desired color with

5 to 8 drops red food coloring

Cover and chill in refrigerator about 1 hr. Serve with

Finely chopped salted pecans
                              4 to 6 servings

Broiled Butterscotch Pudding

Lightly butter a shallow 3-cup baking dish.

Empty into a saucepan contents of

1 pkg. butterscotch pudding mix

Prepare according to directions on package. Remove from heat and blend in

1 tablespoon butter

Turn into baking dish; sprinkle evenly over top a mixture of

3 tablespoons brown sugar
3 tablespoons moist shredded coconut

Broil about 4 in. from source of heat 2 to 3 min. Serve warm or chilled. *About 4 servings*

Banana Cream Parfait 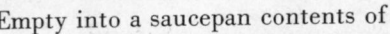 58

Empty into a saucepan contents of
   1 pkg. vanilla pudding mix
Prepare according to directions on package.
Remove from heat and blend in
   1 tablespoon butter
   ¼ teaspoon banana extract
Cool slightly.

Alternate in parfait glasses layers of pudding
and
   **3 tablespoons grated unsweetened
      chocolate**
Chill in refrigerator; top with **chocolate curls.**
About 3 servings

Note: For more banana flavor, alternate
banana slices with the chocolate between the
pudding layers. For a coconut-banana cream
parfait mix ½ cup moist **coconut** into pudding.

▲ Creamy Chocolate Pudding 59

Put a bowl and a rotary beater into refrigerator to chill.

Empty into a saucepan contents of
   1 pkg. chocolate pudding mix
Prepare according to directions on package
using
   1½ cups milk
Using chilled bowl and beater, beat until it
piles softly
   1 cup thick sour cream, chilled
Beat in with final few strokes until blended
   2 tablespoons confectioners' sugar
   ½ teaspoon vanilla extract
Spread whipped sour cream over hot pudding
mixture and gently fold together. Chill in
refrigerator.   *About 4 servings*

△ Festive Chocolate Pudding 60

Follow ▲ Recipe. Gently fold ¼ cup coarsely
chopped **walnuts** and ¼ cup well-drained,
sliced **maraschino cherries** into pudding mixture before chilling.

Cinnamon-Rhubarb Cobbler

Set out a 10x6x1½-in. baking dish.

Wash, cut off stem ends and leaves, and cut
into 1-in. pieces
   1 lb. rhubarb
Put into a saucepan with a mixture of
   ⅔ cup sugar
   2 tablespoons cornstarch
   ⅓ cup red cinnamon candies
Place over low heat; stir frequently until
sugar is dissolved and a sirup is formed. Cover
and cook slowly about 15 min., or until
rhubarb is tender.

Remove from heat and stir in
   2 tablespoons butter
Pour rhubarb mixture into the baking dish.
Arrange on hot rhubarb mixture rolls from
   **1 8-oz. container ready-to-bake
      cinnamon rolls**
Bake at 375°F 20 min. If desired, spread frosting that comes in the package over the hot
rolls. Serve warm with **cream.**   *8 servings*

Peaches a l'Orange 61

Drain, reserving ½ cup sirup
  1 1-lb., 13-oz. can peach halves
Mix together in a saucepan
  ¼ cup firmly packed brown sugar
  1½ teaspoons cornstarch
  1 tablespoon orange peel
  Few grains salt
Add gradually, stirring constantly the reserved sirup and
  ½ cup orange juice
Mix in
  8 whole cloves
  6 whole allspice
Place over medium heat; bring the mixture to boiling, stirring constantly. Reduce heat; add drained peach halves and simmer 5 min., turning carefully several times.

Serve warm or chilled.   *About 6 servings*

Coconut Mallow Salad-Dessert

Drain thoroughly and pat dry contents of
  1 1-lb., 13-oz. can pear halves
  1 1-lb., 14-oz. can pineapple chunks
Cut pear halves into fourths.

Put drained fruit into a bowl and toss lightly to mix thoroughly with
  14 marshmallows, quartered
  1⅓ cups (3½-oz. can) flaked coconut
  2 cups thick sour cream
Cover; chill in refrigerator 12 to 24 hrs.

About 10 servings

Cranberry Sherbet

Chill until icy cold
  1⅔ cups (14½-oz. can) undiluted evaporated milk
Turn chilled evaporated milk into a bowl and add
  1 tablespoon lemon juice
Beat until very stiff. Blend in a mixture of
  1 6-oz. can frozen lemonade concentrate, thawed
  ½ cup sugar
  ¾ cup jellied cranberry sauce
Pour mixture into refrigerator trays. Freeze until firm.   *About 2 qts. sherbet*

Pineapple-Lime Mold

Rinse a 1-qt. fancy mold with cold water; set aside to drain.

Drain contents of
  1 8¾-oz. can crushed pineapple; reserve sirup
Add enough water to sirup to make 1 cup liquid. Heat to boiling; add to
  1 3-oz. pkg. lime-flavored gelatin
Stir until gelatin is dissolved.

Blend in
  2 teaspoons grated lime peel
  ½ cup lime juice
Add by spoonfuls and blend until smooth
  1 pt. vanilla ice cream
Chill until partially thickened. Stir in the pineapple; turn into mold. Chill until firm.

6 servings

CONVENIENCE FOODS in the MICROWAVE OVEN

It does seem rather like gilding the lily to cook so-called "convenience" foods—quick-cooking or instant foods—in the already superfast microwave oven. On the other hand, why not? It's a neater, cleaner, more efficient method, eliminating the need for clumsy arrangements like double boilers, for messy pots and pans and sometimes for any cooking dishes at all, as in some of the bread recipes.

Gentle heating is one of the prime qualities of the microwave oven and that's exactly the kind of cooking that many of these recipes call for: reheating of foods which have already been cooked. However, in these selections, we have concentrated on recipes which require more than merely reheating of prepared foods.

As usual, with sauces, soups and vegetables the microwave oven does a far better job than does the conventional stove. We have circled the microwave references for those recipes which it cooks especially well.

Those recipes which essentially require only reheating, such as most of the soups, are certainly as good, if not better, when prepared in the microwave oven.

This chapter is almost a mini-cookbook in itself, the recipes ranging from appetizers through soups, main dishes, vegetables and desserts. Included here and in the recipes themselves are some of the special hints needed to help make microwave cooking easy and successful. A more thorough discussion is to be found in the chapter introductions relating to the specific foods. Refer to these microwave directions for additional information on utensils, tests for doneness, etc.

SOUPS—To get smooth, well-blended flavors and the elegant texture which the microwave elicits particularly well from the cream soups, remember to stir frequently, as suggested in the recipes. (See also, **Soups in the Microwave Oven.**)

BREAD AND ROLLS—As the microwave oven does not brown breads, color is not a good test for doneness. Most of the bread recipes included are done when they spring back from a light touch on the perimeter, or when crumbs are visible at the edges. Individual recipes specify the proper test for doneness. The **Fig Coffee Braid** is a particularly good bread for baking in the microwave oven because it carries its own color in the ingredients and has an attractive icing. It's also delicious.

Rotating—It's important to rotate the breads during cooking and to let them stand at least 5 minutes after cooking to eliminate any "doughy" taste.

Pans—For those recipes which call for a baking sheet, waxed paper or paper plates will work very well. Muffins can be baked in muffin papers inserted into paper cups or custard cups. (See also, **Breads in the Microwave Oven.**)

MAIN DISHES—All, like the **Lightning Beef Stew**, are lightning-fast and easy to prepare. Our tasters particularly liked the **Fish Stick Special.**

VEGETABLES—Some of the recipes call for the cooking of frozen vegetables. Refer to the chart accompanying the chapter, **Vegetables in the Microwave Oven**, for timings. Canned vegetables need only reheating as directed.

SAUCES—The only word to describe the **Piquant Mustard Sauce** is perfect. All the sauces should be stirred as directed.

CAKES—The cakes included here are all colored by their ingredients. Cake mix batters are even easier to adapt to the microwave method than cakes made from scratch, as rising tends to be more level. Thus, these cakes are baked entirely on the COOK setting.

OTHER SWEETS—Cookies, candies, pies and puddings are all good. Some are ready in as little as 4 minutes, so you can cook them while the table is being cleared.

REMINDERS—See the introductory chapter, **Home Cooking in the Microwave Oven**, in the beginning of this book for more hints plus an easy-to-read chart comparing settings among different brands of microwave ovens.

Saucy Cocktail Franks **1**
(page 590)

Use a 1½-qt. casserole.

To melt jelly, COOK, stirring every 2½ min. (about 5 min.).

Add mustard and COOK to heat (about 1 min.).

Add franks and COOK, stirring every 2½ min., until heated through (about 5 min.).

Cover and let stand 5 min.
OVERALL COOKING TIME: 11:00

Onion Soup Les Halles **2**
(page 590)

Use a 1½-qt. covered casserole.

COOK to melt butter. Add onions and garlic. Cover and COOK, stirring every 1½ min., until onions are tender (about 3 min.).

Add remaining ingredients. COOK until hot and bubbling (about 5 min.).

Cover and let stand 5 min. Add toast rounds.
OVERALL COOKING TIME: 11:00

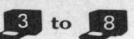

Dutch-Style Chowder 3
(page 591)

Use a 1½-qt. casserole.

COOK bacon to crisp (about 4 min.). Add onion, cover and COOK, stirring every 1½ min., until tender (about 3 min.).

Blend in remaining ingredients. COOK, stirring every 2½ min., to heat through (about 10 min.).

Cover and let stand 5 min. Garnish.
OVERALL COOKING TIME: 17:00

Ginger-Tomato-Rice Soup 4
(page 591)

Use a small covered casserole.

Cover and COOK, stirring every 2½ min., to heat through (about 5 min.).

Cover and let stand 5 min. Complete as in Recipe.
OVERALL COOKING TIME: 5:00

Herb-Seasoned Tomato Soup 5
(page 591)

Use a small covered casserole.

Cover and COOK, stirring every 2½ min., to heat through (about 5 min.).

Cover and let stand 5 min. Top with sour cream.
OVERALL COOKING TIME: 5:00

Chicken Gumbo-Cream of Vegetable Soup 6
(page 591)

Use a small covered casserole.

Cover and COOK, stirring every 2½ min., until heated through (about 8 min.).

Cover and let stand 5 min. Add avocado mixture.
OVERALL COOKING TIME: 8:00

Borscht *(page 592)* 7

Use a 1½-qt. covered casserole.

Cover and COOK beet mixture to boil (about 8 min.).

Add egg mixture and SLOWCOOK to simmer (about 4 min.).

Cover and let stand 5 min. Garnish.
OVERALL COOKING TIME: 12:00

Crab-Meat Bisque *(page 592)* 8

Use a 2-qt. casserole.

COOK soup mixture until it just bubbles (about 5 min.).

Add cream, stirring thoroughly. COOK to heat (about 2 min.).

Cover and let stand 5 min.
OVERALL COOKING TIME: 7:00

Creamy Brussels Sprouts Soup *(page 593)* **9**

Use a 1½-qt. casserole.

COOK soup to heat (about 1 min.). Stir. SLOWCOOK, stirring every 2 min., until hot but not boiling (about 4 min.).

Cover and let stand 5 min. Garnish.
OVERALL COOKING TIME: 5:00

Herbed Soup *(page 593)* **10**

Use a small covered casserole.

Cover and COOK, stirring every 3 min., to simmer (about 10 min.).

Cover and let stand 5 min. Add avocado garnish.
OVERALL COOKING TIME: 10:00

Cheese Finger Rolls **11**
(page 593)

Use a baking dish. *Do not grease.*

COOK rolls, rotating pan every 2 min., until they spring back when touched lightly (about 8 min.).

Cover and let stand 5 min.
OVERALL COOKING TIME: 8:00

Cheese-Sausage Rolls **12**
(page 593)

Use a baking dish or baking sheet. *Do not grease.*

COOK, rotating every 2 min., until they spring back when touched lightly (about 7 min.).

Cover and let stand 5 min.
OVERALL COOKING TIME: 7:00

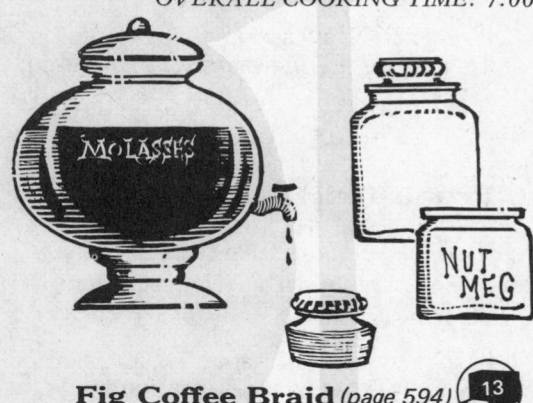

Fig Coffee Braid *(page 594)* **13**

Use a baking dish. *Do not grease.*

Cook cakes, rotating pan every 2 min., until they spring back when touched lightly (about 8½ min.).

Let stand uncovered 5 min.
OVERALL COOKING TIME: 8:30

Glazed Honey Pinwheels **14**
(page 594)

Use an 8-in. square pan.

COOK to melt butter-honey mixture (about 3 min.).

COOK pinwheels, rotating pan every 2 min., until they spring back when touched lightly on the perimeter (about 4 min.).

Let stand uncovered 5 min.
OVERALL COOKING TIME: 7:00

New Moon Yeast Rolls **15**
(page 595)

Use a baking dish or baking sheet. *Do not grease.*

COOK rolls, rotating pan every 2 min., until they spring back when touched lightly on the perimeter (about 6 min.). (These will not brown, but the flavor is good.)

Let stand uncovered 5 min.

OVERALL COOKING TIME: 6:00

Prune Twists *(page 595)* 16

Use a baking dish or baking sheet. *Do not grease.* The times given in this recipe are for cooking 6 rolls per batch.

COOK rolls, rotating pan after 1½ min., until they spring back when touched lightly on the perimeter (about 3 min.).

Let stand uncovered 5 min.

OVERALL COOKING TIME: 6:00

Pan o' Rolls *(page 595)* 17

Use a 1½-qt. casserole and a small casserole.

COOK to melt butter (about 3 min.).

COOK rolls, rotating pan every 3 min., until they spring back when touched lightly on the perimeter and pull away slightly from the sides of the pan (about 10 min.). (They will not brown but flavor is good.)

Let stand uncovered 5 min.

OVERALL COOKING TIME: 13:00

Herbed Biscuit Ring 18
(page 596)

Use a baking dish or waxed paper.

COOK biscuits, rotating pan every 2 min., until they spring back when touched lightly on the perimeter (about 6 min.). (They will not brown, but flavor is good.)

Cover and let stand 5 min.

OVERALL COOKING TIME: 6:00

Frankfurter Quick Bread *(page 596)* 19

Use small ramekins or paper cups. *Do not grease.*

COOK sugar-juice mixture, stirring every 2 min., to boil and thicken slightly (about 5 min.).

COOK rolls until they pull away from the sides of the cup and spring back when touched lightly (about 3 min.).

Let stand uncovered 5 min.

OVERALL COOKING TIME: 6:00

Orange-Raisin Muffins 20
(page 597)

Use muffin papers or a baking dish. *Do not grease.* The times given in this recipe are for baking 8 muffins per batch.

COOK until springy on perimeter and crumbs form around edges (about 8 min.).

Let stand uncovered 5 min.

OVERALL COOKING TIME: 16:00

Skillet Beans with Pineapple *(page 597)* **21**

Use a browning skillet.

COOK bacon, rotating and pouring off fat every 2 min. (about 5 min.).

COOK fat-sugar mixture, stirring every 30 sec., until sugar is dissolved (about 2 min.).

COOK pineapple until heated and softened (about 1 min. each side).

COOK onion, stirring every 30 sec., until transparent (about 1 min.).

Add remaining ingredients and COOK until heated through (about 5 min.).

OVERALL COOKING TIME: 15:00

Lightning Beef Stew **22**
(page 597)

Use a 2-qt. covered casserole.

Cover and COOK stew mixture until heated through (about 3 min.). Stir and SLOWCOOK until boiling (about 5 min.).

Drop dumplings. Cover and COOK until done (about 5 min.).

Cover and let stand 5 min.

OVERALL COOKING TIME: 13:00

Saucy Ham Omelet **23**
(page 598)

Use a browning skillet.

Preheat skillet (about 3 min.). COOK to brown ham sticks, turning them every 1 min. (about 3 min.). Remove and set aside.

Add butter. Pour in egg mixture and arrange ham sticks. COOK until eggs are almost set (about 1 min.).

Cover and let stand while preparing apple sauce.

For Apple Sauce— Use a small casserole. COOK to heat apple juice (about 2 min.).

Stir thoroughly to blend in remaining ingredients. COOK to heat through (about 1 min.). SLOWCOOK until thickened (about 3 min.).

Serve as in Recipe.

OVERALL COOKING TIME: 15:00

Sweet and Speedy **24**
(page 598)

Use a covered baking dish.

Prepare loaf for cooking and set aside.

Cover and COOK sauce, stirring every 1½ min., until simmering (about 3 min.).

Add loaf. Cover and COOK to heat through (about 5 min.).

Cover and let stand 5 min.

OVERALL COOKING TIME: 8:00

Pear-Topped Special **25**
(page 598)

Use a baking dish. *Do not grease.*

COOK luncheon meat mixture, rotating pan

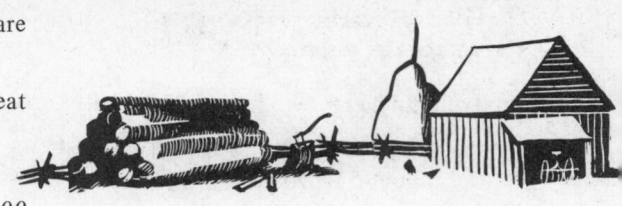

every 5 min., until onions and green peppers are wilted (about 10 min.).

Add pears, butter and sugar. COOK to heat through (about 5 min.).

Cover and let stand 5 min.

OVERALL COOKING TIME: 10:00

Spinach-Tongue Casserole *(page 599)* 26

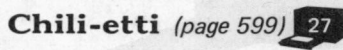

Use a 1-qt. casserole.

Prepare spinach. *(page 285)*

COOK assembled casserole to heat through and melt cheese (about 7 min.).

Cover and let stand 5 min.

Chili-etti *(page 599)* 27

Use a 1½-qt. casserole.

COOK assembled casserole, stirring every 2 min., until heated through (about 5 min.).

Cover and let stand 5 min. Sprinkle with cheese.

OVERALL COOKING TIME: 5:00

Wiener Mix-Up *(page 600)* 28

Use a 1½-qt. covered casserole. *Do not grease.*

Cover and COOK casserole until heated through (about 20 min.).

Cover and let stand 5 min.

OVERALL COOKING TIME: 20:00

Hash Distinctive 29
(page 600)

Use a browning skillet.

Preheat skillet (about 3 min.). Add hash slices and COOK to brown on one side (about 3 min.).

Turn and prepare slices as in Recipe. COOK until tomatoes are soft and cheese is melted (about 3 min.).

Cover and let stand 5 min.

OVERALL COOKING TIME: 9:00

Chicken-Broccoli Casserole *(page 600)* 30

To cook broccoli, use a 2-qt. covered casserole. Place broccoli and ¼ cup water in covered casserole. Arrange spears with toughest parts toward center. COOK until almost tender (about 10 min.).

Assemble casserole. COOK until thoroughly heated and cheese melts (about 10 min.).

Fish Stick Special 31
(page 601)

Use a baking dish.

COOK assembled dish, uncovered, until cheese bubbles slightly and crumbs are crisp (about 8 min.).

Cover and let stand 5 min.

OVERALL COOKING TIME: 8:00

Skillet Tuna Supreme 32
(page 601)

Use a 1½-qt. casserole.

Heat oil. Cover and COOK onion and pepper, stirring every 1½ min., until tender (about 3 min.).

Stir thoroughly to blend soup and seasoning. COOK uncovered, stirring every 3 min., to boil and blend flavors (about 5 min.).

Add tuna and COOK to heat (about 3 min.).

Cover and let stand 5 min. Garnish.
OVERALL COOKING TIME: 11:00

Scandinavian Supper 33
Dish *(page 601)*

Use a 1½-qt. casserole.

To defrost soup, see manufacturer's directions for your oven.

COOK soup mixture, stirring every 1½ min., to melt butter (about 3 min.).

Add remaining ingredients, cover and COOK to heat (about 5 min.).

Cover and let stand 5 min. Garnish.
OVERALL COOKING TIME: 8:00

Tuna-Chili Chowder 34
(page 602)

Use a 2-qt. covered casserole.

COOK to heat oil (about 3 min.). Add celery, green pepper and paprika; COOK covered, until tender (about 3 min.).

Add all remaining ingredients. COOK, stirring every 5 min., to heat (about 15 min.).

Cover and let stand 5 min.
OVERALL COOKING TIME: 21:00

Top of the Range
Corn Pudding *(page 602)* 35

Use custard cups. *Do not grease.*

Cover filled cups with plastic wrap. SLOW-COOK, rotating cups every 5 min., until a knife comes out clean (about 8 min.).

Cover and let stand 5 min. Unmold.
OVERALL COOKING TIME: 8:00

Broccoli with 36 Lemon-Olive Sauce *(page 603)*

Use a 1½-qt. covered casserole.

Prepare broccoli *(page 285)*

COOK butter and garlic until garlic turns dark (about 4 min.).

Add remaining ingredients, cover and COOK to heat through (about 3 min.).

OVERALL COOKING TIME: 7:00

Cauliflower-Spinach 37 Sensation *(page 603)*

Use a 1½-qt. casserole for assembled recipe.

Prepare cauliflower and spinach *(page 285)*

Stir watercress, parsley and tarragon into spinach. COOK until watercress wilts (about 1 min.).

Sieve spinach and assemble as in Recipe.

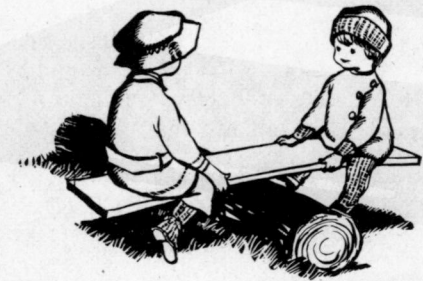

Limas in Sour Cream 38 *(page 604)*

Use a 1½-qt. casserole for assembled recipe.

Prepare lima beans *(page 285)*

COOK bacon (about 2 min.).

Combine ingredients and COOK to raise temperature (about 3 min.). SLOWCOOK, stirring every 30 sec., until heated through (about 3 min.). Do not boil.

Let stand uncovered 5 min. Garnish.

Lima Beans with 39 Water Chestnuts *(page 604)*

Use a 1-qt. casserole.

Prepare lima beans *(page 285)*

Combine all ingredients, cover and COOK, stirring every 2 min., to melt butter and heat through (about 5 min.).

Cinnamon-Pecan Yams 40 *(page 604)*

Use a 1-qt. covered casserole.

COOK to melt butter (about 3 min.).

Add remaining ingredients. COOK, turning yams to coat with butter every 1½ min. (about 5 min.).

OVERALL COOKING TIME: 8:00

Springtime Potatoes 41 *(page 605)*

Use two 1-qt. casseroles.

COOK to heat potatoes (about 3 min.). Cover and set aside.

Combine remaining ingredients. SLOWCOOK, stirring every 30 sec., until heated (about 4 min.).

OVERALL COOKING TIME: 7:00

Jiffy Curry Sauce **42**
(page 610)

Use a 1-qt. casserole.

COOK soup mixture, stirring every 1 min., to blend and heat thoroughly (about 2 min.).

Add milk, stirring well, and COOK to heat (about 1 min.).

Add egg and COOK, stirring every 15 sec., to heat through (about 30 sec.).

Cover and let stand 5 min.

OVERALL COOKING TIME: 3:30

Sour Cream Meat Sauce **43**
(page 610)

Use a 1-qt. casserole.

COOK sauce mixture to boil (about 3 min.). SLOWCOOK to blend flavors (about 10 min.).

Add sour cream, stir thoroughly and COOK to heat (about 2 min.). Do not boil.

Cover and let stand 5 min.

OVERALL COOKING TIME: 13:00

Piquant Mustard Sauce **44**
(page 610)

Use a 1-qt. casserole.

COOK, stirring every 30 sec., until thick and smooth and heated through (about 6 min.).

Cover and let stand 5 min.

OVERALL COOKING TIME: 6:00

Honey-Cream Sauce **45**
(page 610)

Use a small casserole.

COOK honey-cream mixture, stirring every 30 sec., to heat (about 2 min.).

OVERALL COOKING TIME: 2:00

Cranberry Upside-Down Cake *(page 611)* **46**

Use a small casserole and an 8x8x2-in. baking dish. *Do not grease.*

In small casserole, COOK to melt butter. Blend in sugar, orange peel and vanilla.

Mix cake and assemble as directed. COOK until cake pulls away from sides of pan and crumbs form at sides (about 10 min.).

Let cool in pan on rack until top dries (about 5 min.). Invert onto serving plate.

OVERALL COOKING TIME: 13:00

Quick Applesauce Fruitcake *(page 611)* **47**

Use a loaf pan. Line bottom with ungreased waxed paper.

Mix batter as in Recipe.

COOK to set batter (about 5 min.). Continue to COOK, rotating pan every 1½ min., until cake is springy at perimeter, beginning to pull away from sides of pan (about 6 min.).

Let cool in pan on rack until completely cool. Invert and remove waxed paper.

OVERALL COOKING TIME: 11:00

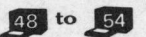

Mincemeat Gingerbread *(page 612)* 48

Use an 8-in. square baking dish. Line bottom with ungreased waxed paper.

COOK, rotating every 3 min., until springy on perimeter and sides just start to pull away from pan (about 9 min.).

OVERALL COOKING TIME: 9:00

Peach Pudding-Cake 49
(page 612)

Use an 11¾x7½x1¾-in. baking dish.

COOK to melt butter (about 3 min.). Mix batter as directed.

COOK to set batter (about 5 min.). Continue to COOK, rotating pan every 1½ min., until cake is firm all over (about 10½ min.).

OVERALL COOKING TIME: 18:30

Choco-Honey Chews 50
(page 613)

Use a baking dish. Line bottom with ungreased waxed paper.

COOK to set batter (about 3 min.). Rotate pan and continue to COOK, rotating every 1¼ min., until mixture begins to pull away from pan sides (about 2½ min.).

OVERALL COOKING TIME: 5:30

Minted Refrigerator Squares *(page 613)* 51

Use a small casserole.

COOK chocolate and milk, stirring every 1 min., until chocolate melts (about 10 min.).

Ambrosia Cookies *(page 614)* 52

Use a baking dish or baking sheet lined with ungreased waxed paper. Times given in this recipe are for baking 18 cookies per batch.

COOK, rotating after 2½ min., until tops are dry, edges are thin and batter no longer spreads (about 5 min.).

When slightly cooled, remove to rack.

OVERALL COOKING TIME: 10:00

Walnut Brownie Clusters 53
(page 614)

Use a baking dish or a cookie sheet lined with ungreased waxed paper. Times given in this recipe are for baking 24 cookies per batch.

COOK, rotating every 2½ min., until dry on top (about 5 min.).

When slightly cooled, remove to rack.

OVERALL COOKING TIME: 10:00

Flaky Macaroons *(page 614)* 54

Use a 1½-qt. casserole and a baking dish or cookie sheet lined with ungreased waxed paper.

In casserole, COOK sugar mixture, stirring every 1 min., until mixture reaches 260° or the soft ball stage (about 6 min.).

OVERALL COOKING TIME: 6:00

Peppermint Confections 55
(page 614)

Use a baking dish or cookie sheet lined with ungreased waxed paper.

COOK, rotating every 2 min., until nearly firm (about 4 min.).

When slightly cool, remove to a rack.

OVERALL COOKING TIME: 4:00

Mocha Chiffon Pie *(page 616)* 56

Use a small casserole.

Combine ingredients for gelatin mixture as in Recipe. SLOWCOOK, stirring every 1½ min., until gelatin is dissolved and thickened (about 5 min.).

Broiled Butterscotch Pudding *(page 617)* 57

Use a small casserole, lightly buttered.

COOK pudding, stirring every 1 min., until thickened (about 3 min.).

Assemble with sugar and coconut. COOK until sugar melts and a film forms on top (about 1 min.).

OVERALL COOKING TIME: 4:00

Banana Cream Parfait 58
(page 618)

Use a 1½-qt. casserole.

Follow package directions for ingredients.

COOK, stirring every 1 min., until mixture thickens (about 3 min.).

Complete as in Recipe.

Creamy Chocolate Pudding *(page 618)* 59

Use a 1½-qt. casserole.

Combine pudding mix and milk. COOK, stirring every 1 min., until mixture thickens (about 3 min.).

Festive Chocolate Pudding 60
(page 618)

Follow 59 Recipe with substitutions as in △ Recipe.

Peaches a l'Orange *(page 619)* 61

Use a small casserole.

Mix sauce ingredients as in Recipe. COOK, stirring every 30 sec., to boil (about 3 min.).

Add peaches. COOK to heat (about 2 min.).

Cover and let stand 5 min.

OVERALL COOKING TIME: 5:00

Index

Measurements and Equivalents

Dash..	Less than ⅛ teaspoon (about 6 drops)
A few grains.....................................	Less than ⅛ teaspoon
60 drops..	1 teaspoon
3 teaspoons......................................	1 tablespoon
¼ cup...	4 tablespoons
⅓ cup...	5 tablespoons plus 1 teaspoon
½ cup...	8 tablespoons
⅔ cup...	10 tablespoons plus 2 teaspoons
¾ cup...	12 tablespoons
1 cup...	16 tablespoons
1 cup...	8 fluid ounces
2 cups..	1 pint
4 cups..	1 quart
4 quarts..	1 gallon
8 quarts..	1 peck
4 pecks...	1 bushel
16 ounces (*dry measure*).......................	1 pound
16 fluid ounces..................................	1 pint
1 fluid ounce....................................	2 tablespoons
1 wine glass.....................................	¼ cup
1 ounce..	28.35 grams
1 pound..	453.59 grams
2 tablespoons butter or margarine...............	1 ounce
½ cup butter or margarine.......................	¼ pound or 1 stick
2 tablespoons sugar or salt.....................	1 ounce
2¼ cups granulated sugar........................	1 pound
2¼ cups firmly packed brown sugar...............	1 pound
3½ cups sifted confectioners' sugar.............	1 pound
4 cups sifted all-purpose flour.................	1 pound
1 cup sifted all-purpose flour..................	1 cup plus 2 tablespoons sifted cake flour
1 cup sifted cake flour.........................	1 cup minus 2 tablespoons sifted all-purpose flour
1 tablespoon cornstarch.........................	2 tablespoons flour
1 square chocolate..............................	1 ounce
1 square chocolate..............................	3 tablespoons cocoa plus 1 tablespoon shortening
1 cup chopped nuts..............................	about ¼ pound
1 pound Cheddar cheese..........................	4 cups, grated
1 pound coffee..................................	40 to 50 servings
Baking powder...................................	1 teaspoon double-action baking powder will leaven 1 cup flour
Baking soda.....................................	½ teaspoon baking soda with 1 cup fully soured milk will neutralize the acid in that amount of milk and leaven 1 cup flour

FAVORITE
RECIPES

FAVORITE
RECIPES

FAVORITE RECIPES

FAVORITE
RECIPES

FAVORITE

RECIPES

FAVORITE
RECIPES

FAVORITE
RECIPES

FAVORITE
RECIPES

FAVORITE
RECIPES

**FAVORITE
RECIPES**

FAVORITE
RECIPES

FAVORITE
RECIPES

FAVORITE
RECIPES

FAVORITE
RECIPES

FAVORITE
RECIPES

FAVORITE
RECIPES

FAVORITE
RECIPES

FAVORITE
RECIPES

FAVORITE
RECIPES

FAVORITE
RECIPES

FAVORITE
RECIPES